Rediscovering the Essentiality of Marketing

Developments in Marketing Science: Proceedings of the Academy of Marketing Science

More information about this series at http://www.springer.com/series/13409

Luca Petruzzellis • Russell S. Winer
Editors

Rediscovering the Essentiality of Marketing

Proceedings of the 2015
Academy of Marketing Science (AMS)
World Marketing Congress

 Springer

Editors
Luca Petruzzellis
Department of Business and Law Studies
University of Bari Aldo Moro
Bari, Italy

Russell S. Winer
Stern School of Business
New York University
New York, NY, USA

ISSN 2363-6165   ISSN 2363-6173   (electronic)
Developments in Marketing Science: Proceedings of the Academy of Marketing Science
ISBN 978-3-319-80676-1   ISBN 978-3-319-29877-1   (eBook)
DOI 10.1007/978-3-319-29877-1

Printed on acid-free paper

This Springer imprint is published by Springer Nature
The registered company is Springer International Publishing AG Switzerland

AMS Officers (2014–2016)

President
Linda Ferrell, Belmont University, USA

Executive Vice President/Director
Harold W. Berkman, University of Miami, USA

President-Elect
Adilson Borges, NEOMA Business School, France

Immediate Past-President
Victoria Crittenden, Babson College, USA

Vice President for Publications
O.C. Ferrell, Belmont University, USA

Vice President for Programs
Julie Guidry Moulard, Louisiana Tech University, USA

Vice President for Membership-North America
Angeline Close, University of Texas at Austin, USA

Vice President for Membership-International
Nicholas Paparoidamis, IESEG School of Management, France

Vice President for Development
Michael Ewing, Deakin University, Australia

Secretary/Treasurer
Lauren Beitelspacher, Portland State University, USA

AMS Board of Governors (2014–2016)

2015 AMS World Marketing Congress—Track Chairs

Conference Co-Chairs
Luca Petruzzellis, University of Bari Aldo Moro, Italy
Russell S. Winer, The Stern School of Business, New York University, USA

Business-to-Business Marketing
Paul Matthyssens, Antwerp University, Belgium
Michele Paulin, Concordia University, Canada

Consumer Behavior
Andrea Bonezzi, New York University, USA
Monika Lisjak, Erasmus University, The Netherlands

Marketing Mix Modeling
Marc Fischer, University of Cologne, Germany
Koen Pauwels, Dartmouth University, USA

Digital and Social Media Marketing
Charles Hofacker, Florida State University, USA
Carlos Flavián, University of Zaragoza, Spain

Entrepreneurship and Small Business
Gaetano Aiello, University of Florence, Italy
Alberto Pezzi, University of Roma Tre, Italy

International Marketing
Saeed Samiee, University of Tulsa, USA
Brian R. Chabowski, University of Tulsa, USA

Cross-Cultural Research
Catherine Demangeot, IESEG, France
Cheryl Nakata, University of Illinois at Chicago, USA

Health and Social Marketing
Debbie Isobel Keeling, Loughborough University, United Kingdom
Ting Yu, University of New South Wales, Australia

Innovation and Creativity
Eitan Muller, New York University, USA
Subin Im, Yonsei University, Korea

Integrated Marketing Communications
Don Schultz, Northwestern University, USA
Gayle Kerr, Queensland University of Technology, Australia

Marketing Research Methods
Tulin Erdem, New York University, USA
Rik Pieters, Tilburg University, The Netherlands

Marketing Strategy
John Roberts, London Business School, United Kingdom
Rajendra K Srivastava, Singapore Management University, Singapore

Product and Branding Strategies
Cleopatra Veloutsou, University of Glasgow, United Kingdom
Francisco Guzman, University of North Texas, USA

Pricing and Price-Related Issues
Gurumurthy Kalyanaram, NMIMS Business School, India
Fabio Ancarani, Alma Mater Studiorum University of Bologna, Italy

Sensory Marketing
Jean-Charles Chebat, HEC Montreal, Canada
Michela Addis, University of Roma Tre, Italy

Relationship Marketing
Dennis B. Arnett, Texas Tech University, USA
Michael Wittmann, University of Southern Mississippi, USA

Retailing
Jonathan Reynolds, Oxford University, United Kingdom
Dirk Morschett, University of Fribourg, Switzerland

Selling and Sales Management
Othman Boujena, NEOMA Business School, France
Michael Ahearne, University of Houston, USA

Services Marketing
Jikyeong Kang, Asian Institute of Management, Philippines
Calvin Wong, The Hong Kong Polytechnic University, China

Advertising Communication
Nancy Spears, University of North Texas, USA
Shintaro Okazaki, Universidad Autónoma de Madrid, Spain

Tourism and Hospitality
Marianna Sigala, University of the Aegean, Greece
Judith Mair, University of Queensland, Australia

Luxury, Fashion and Wine Marketing
Alberto Mattiacci, University of Roma La Sapienza, Italy
Eunju Ko, Yonsei University, Seoul, Korea

Distribution and Supply Chain Management
Walfried Lassar, Florida International University, USA
Dale Rogers, Arizona State University, USA

Doctoral Colloquium Chair
John B. Ford, Old Dominion University, USA

Conference Local-Arrangements Chair
Pierluigi Passaro, University of Bari Aldo Moro, Italy

Preface

The current worldwide business environment is leading marketing scholars and practitioners to reconsider a number of historical and current views of the marketplace and how it functions. Further, determining new marketing theories and practical methods whose effectiveness can be truly measured must be added to the list of current challenges for today and tomorrow. In such a period in marketing history, achieving and managing efficient and effective marketing actions is a necessity. Determining such actions is based on practical experience, solid theory, and appropriate research methodology.

The papers presented at the 18th Academy of Marketing Science World Marketing Congress focused on new research ideas on vibrant topics that could help academics and practitioners get new perspectives and insights for today's marketplace challenges. The range of topics was remarkable. Research track topics ranged from traditional (Marketing Strategy) to contemporary (Digital and Social Media Marketing) to focused (Luxury, Fashion, and Wine Marketing).

The wide range of track topics is reflected in the competitive paper sessions. Again, the session titles ranged from the traditional ("Experimental Methods") to the practical ("Consumer Behavior in Tourism and Hospitality") to the forefront of marketing thought ("Branding in a Digital World"). All in all, there were over 250 papers presented, representing the work of nearly 600 authors.

Bari, Italy　　　　　　　　　　　　　　　　　　　　　　　Luca Petruzzellis
New York, NY　　　　　　　　　　　　　　　　　　　　　　Russell S. Winer

Acknowledgments

We would like to thank all track chairs and reviewers for their tremendous work during the review process and the program creation, the presenters and the session chairs for their active participation in the conference, the AMS Co-Directors of International Programs, Barry Babin and Jay Lindquist, for their help and guidance, and all the program team members.

Contents

Part XIV Pricing and Price-Related Issues

Part XV Product and Branding Strategies

Part I
Advertising Communication

The Role of Anger in the Context of Consumer Reactions to Advertising Incongruity

Silke Bambauer-Sachse and Priska Heinzle

Introduction

Advertisers use incongruent advertising content in order to avoid being ignored due to an overflow of advertising information (Herbig and Kramer 1994) and to bypass processing schemata used by consumers (Brown 2004). The existing literature provides several conceptualizations of incongruity. In our study, we use the degree of how unexpected a stimulus is as main criterion for incongruity (Meyers-Levy and Tybout 1989) and argue that consumers' perceptions of (in)congruity depend on individual characteristics, experiences, and consumer-specific schemata (Fleck and Maille 2010).

Many studies deal with positive effects of incongruent advertising (e.g., Heckler and Childers 1992; Lee and Mason 1999; Smith et al. 2008). Although incongruent advertising can also trigger negative emotions, such negative emotions are less often examined. Anger is one of the negative emotions that occur during the processing of an advertisement (Edell and Burke 1987) and is likely to play an important role in the context of purchase decisions after contact with incongruent advertising because high incongruity can make it difficult to understand the advertising message and thus lead to anger. Therefore, the objective of this chapter is to analyze negative effects of incongruent advertising through anger and positive effects through activation on attitudes toward the ad and the product, and purchase intentions. In addition, we differentiate between goods and services. Although advertising for services faces challenges that do not exist for goods (Stafford et al. 2011), research on advertising incongruity has so far not made such a differentiation.

S. Bambauer-Sachse (✉) • P. Heinzle
University of Fribourg, Fribourg, Switzerland
e-mail: silke.bambauer-sachse@unifr.ch; priska.heinzle@unifr.ch

© Academy of Marketing Science 2016   3
L. Petruzzellis, R.S. Winer (eds.), *Rediscovering the Essentiality of Marketing*,
Developments in Marketing Science: Proceedings of the Academy of Marketing
Science, DOI 10.1007/978-3-319-29877-1_1

Background and Hypotheses

While marketing studies focus on applications of congruity in different contexts (Alden et al. 2000; Lee and Thorson 2008; Walchli 2007), the processes triggered by incongruent advertising are not examined in detail. Previous research dealt extensively with cognitive processing of incongruity in terms of memorability (Forehand and Deshpande 2001; Heckler and Childers 1992) and attitudes toward the ad or brand (Dahlén and Lange 2004), but affective reactions to incongruity received far less attention. We develop a two-path model that examines effects of incongruent advertising in more detail.

Path 1: Effects of Incongruent Advertising Through Perceived Incongruity and Anger on Attitudes Toward the Ad and the Product, and on Purchase Intentions

After contact with incongruent advertising, consumers develop individual perceptions of incongruity (Fleck and Maille 2010), and different types of incongruent ads lead to different perceptions of incongruity (Phillips 2000). While moderately incongruent stimuli can have positive effects (Dahlén et al. 2008), high incongruity can result in intense affects of negative value due to major comprehension problems and irritation, and consequently lead to anger (Mandler 1982). These arguments lead to:

H1: The higher perceived incongruity, the higher is the anger consumers experience subsequent to the contact with incongruent advertising.

Previous research provides the notion that negative emotions such as anger can have considerable negative effects on attitudes toward the ad (Batra and Ray 1986; Burke and Edell 1989). As ad-evoked negative feelings are rather mediated by attitudes toward the ad (Batra and Ray 1986) than being direct, we do not assume a direct effect on attitudes toward the product whereas a study examining a direct effect of negative feelings on purchase intentions suggests a negative correlation (Brown et al. 1998). In addition, the specific negative emotion anger is described as directly influencing action tendencies or even actions (Bougie et al. 2003), and to reduce purchase intentions (Folkes et al. 1987). Therefore, we argue:

H2: The higher the anger consumers experience after contact with incongruent advertising, the more negative are their attitudes toward the ad and the lower are their purchase intentions.

Although effects of attitudes toward the ad on attitudes toward the product, and effects of attitudes toward the product on purchase intentions were already proven in many studies (Brown and Stayman 1992; Shimp 1981; Spears and Singh 2004), we formulate and test the respective hypotheses in the context considered here for reasons of completeness:

H3: The more positive the attitudes toward the ad, the more positive are attitudes toward the product and the higher are purchase intentions.

Path 2: Effects of Incongruent Advertising Through Activation and Anger on Attitudes Toward the Ad and the Product, and on Purchase Intentions

As unexpected elements of incongruent advertising require mental activity, it can be argued that incongruity causes activation (Berlyne 1960; Mandler 1982). In the case of highly incongruent messages, which are in general evaluated negatively (Lee and Mason 1999), such activation leads to negative emotions. Therefore, high activation as a consequence of the exposure to highly incongruent advertising will lead to higher levels of anger. At the same time, several studies report positive effects of activation on cognitions and evaluations (Purcell 1982; Thayer 1978). Research in advertising contexts additionally provides the notion that higher levels of activation are positively related to attitudes toward the ad (Henthorne et al. 1993; LaTour et al. 1990) because activation draws attention to the ad and increases the processing of the information provided by the ad (Heckler and Childers 1992). Research also provides the notion that activation positively affects purchase intentions through a rather subconscious automatic reaction (Batra and Ray 1986; LaTour and Rotfeld 1997). These arguments lead to:

H4: The higher the activation through the contact with incongruent advertising, the higher is the anger that consumers experience, but the more positive are their attitudes toward the ad, and the higher are their purchase intentions.

The hypotheses presented above do not differentiate between services and goods because previous research does not provide a sufficient basis to formulate such hypotheses in the context of incongruent advertising. Such effects will be examined from an exploratory perspective in the study presented below.

Methodology

The sample consisted of 489 respondents (63.4 % women, average age: 30.4 years, mainly students). The study was based on a 2 (type of incongruent advertising: erotic couple vs. baby face)×2 (product type: goods vs. services)×4 (four test products for goods and services, respectively: chocolate bar, shower gel, coffee machine, vacuum cleaner (goods); thermal bath entry ticket, ticket for public transportation, fitness club membership, intercontinental flight (services) between-subjects design. Four different goods and services were tested respectively to cover different product categories. The pictures of an erotic couple and of a baby face were chosen to generate variance in incongruity because the combination of these pictures with the products is considered unexpected and therefore incongruent. The pictures of the erotic couple and the baby face had been pretested with regard to applicability in a real advertising context. Short slogans were added to make the ads more realistic. The respondents were shown the ad and asked to fill in the questionnaire containing the scales described below.

Activation was measured by four slightly adapted items from the general activation measurement scale (Thayer 1967), perceived incongruity by two items closely related to the operationalization described by Lange et al. (2003), and anger by four items proposed by Dillard and Peck (2000). Attitudes toward the ad (A_{ad}) were measured by six items (Machleit and Wilson 1988), attitudes toward the product (A_{prod}) by three items (Goodstein et al. 1990), and purchase intentions (PI) by two items (Park et al. 2007). The high α-values and bivariate correlations ($\alpha_{activation} = .88$; $r_{incongruity} = .87$; $\alpha_{anger} = .94$; $\alpha_{Aad} = .98$; $\alpha_{Aprod} = .91$; $r_{PI} = .87$) show that the items reliably measure the respective variables. The two types of advertising differ with regard to incongruity ($t = -3.79$, $p < .001$), which was measured by directly asking for incongruity (Kamins and Gupta 1994, rating scale: $1 =$ highly incongruent, $7 =$ highly congruent), and they differ from the center value of the scale ($M_{erotic} = 3.25$, $t = -5.67$, $p < .001$; $M_{babyface} = 2.61$, $t = -12.98$, $p < .001$). The respondents also had to indicate whether the respective product is rather a good or a service (rating scale: $1 =$ definitely a good, $7 =$ definitely a service). The respective mean values differ clearly from the center point of the scale ($M_{goods} = 2.12$, $t = -21.87$, $p < .001$; $M_{services} = 5.09$, $t = 9.99$, $p < .001$).

Data Analysis and Results

PLS was used to estimate the path coefficients for the model described above. The model was estimated separately for goods and services (pooled across test products). Advertising incongruity has a negative influence on perceived incongruity in the case of goods ($\beta = -.23$, $t = -3.84$, $p < .001$), which means that the erotic ad leads to lower perceived incongruity than the baby face ad. This effect does not exist for services. Thus, for services, different types of advertising do not necessarily produce different levels of perceived incongruity. Since the literature on advertising for services provides the notion that, due to the intangible character of services, advertising for services needs to provide the consumer with as much information about the service as possible (George and Berry 1981; Pickett et al. 2001; Stafford 1996), solely capturing consumers' attention through combining services with unexpected advertising pictures is generally less appropriate for services, and leads to higher perceived incongruity independently of the type of incongruent advertising. Furthermore, the results show that perceived incongruity positively affects the anger experienced after contact with the ad in case of goods ($\beta = .32$, $t = 4.70$, $p < .001$) and services ($\beta = .25$, $t = 4.04$, $p < .001$). Therefore increasing incongruity leads to more experienced anger (Hypothesis 1). Anger in turn has a negative effect on attitudes toward the ad for both goods ($\beta=-.36$, $t=-8.01$, $p<.001$) and services ($\beta=-.23$, $t=-5.86$, $p<.001$). Thus, the higher the anger experienced, the more negative are the attitudes toward the ad. While anger does not directly affect attitudes toward the product, there is such a direct negative effect of anger on purchase intentions for goods ($\beta=-.15$, $t=-3.42$, $p<.001$). Thus, if consumers are faced with incongruent advertising for goods, an increasing level of anger leads to decreasing purchase intentions. Consequently, Hypothesis 2 is only partly supported. This result can be explained as follows. As purchase intentions for services are highly dependent on verbal tangibility of the service (Stafford 1996), factors such as anger that are independent of aspects related to service tangibility do not have any direct effects on purchase intentions.

The results further show that advertising incongruity has an effect on activation for both goods ($\beta=.45$, $t=8.18$, $p<.001$) and services ($\beta=.38$, $t=7.23$, $p<.001$). The positive sign of the respective path coefficients means that the effect is stronger for the erotic ad than for the baby face ad. However, there is no effect of activation on anger, for neither goods nor services, but activation has a direct positive effect on attitudes toward the ad ($\beta_{good}=.61$, $t_{good}=15.04$, $p<.001$; $\beta_{service}=.64$, $t_{service}=15.70$, $p<.001$) and purchase intentions ($\beta_{good}=.23$, $t_{good}=4.62$, $p<.01$; $\beta_{service}=.30$, $t_{service}=5.62$, $p<.01$). Thus, Hypothesis 4 is only partly supported. Moreover, activation has no direct effect on attitudes toward the product in the case of services but a positive effect in the case of goods ($\beta=.21$, $t=2.61$, $p<.05$), which was not hypothesized. Thus, the higher consumers' activation through the contact with incongruent advertising, the more positive are their attitudes toward the ad and the higher are their purchase intentions. In the case of goods, higher activation also leads to more positive attitudes toward the product. The nonexistent effect in case of services can be explained by the fact consumers need tangible cues in order to evaluate the service and such cues are not provided by incongruent advertising. Finally, as assumed, attitudes toward the ad have positive effects on attitudes toward the product ($\beta_{good}=.47$, $t_{good}=5.58$, $p<.001$; $\beta_{service}=.42$, $t_{service}=4.67$, $p<.001$) which in turn positively affect purchase intentions ($\beta_{good}=.56$, $t_{good}=11.01$, $p<.001$; $\beta_{service}=.55$, $t_{service}=9.25$, $p<.001$). Thus, Hypothesis 3 is supported. The goodness of fit values are for goods: $R^2_{perc.\,incongruity}=.05$, $R^2_{activation}=.20$, $R^2_{anger}=.15$, $R^2_{Aad}=.62$, $R^2_{Aprod}=.42$, $R^2_{PI}=.60$ and for services: $R^2_{activation}=.14$; $R^2_{anger}=.08$; $R^2_{Aad}=.52$; $R^2_{Aprod}=.25$ and $R^2_{PI}=.50$.

Conclusion

Positive effects of incongruent advertising through activation exist for goods and services, but the negative effect through anger has fewer consequences in the case of services. In addition, perceptions of advertising incongruity rather seem to depend on individual differences than on the advertising type in the case of services. While positive effects of incongruent advertising are beneficial, marketers should try to avoid negative effects through anger, which increase with increasing incongruity. In the case of goods, anger has very negative effects on both attitudes toward the ad and purchase intentions, whereas in the case of services, anger only affects attitudes toward the ad. Thus, specifically for goods, marketers should not use highly incongruent ads because such ads could lead to high levels of anger. However, moderate incongruity could be used in advertising because it also triggers high activation, which leads to positive consumer reactions.

Future research could examine other types of incongruent advertising, different product categories, the involvement attached to the advertised product, and the role of consumer-specific variables such as sensation seeking or emotions other than anger (both positive and negative).

References available upon request.

Cross-Language Comparison of the Persuasive Effects of Typeface Shapes: A Conceptual Framework

Yi-Fen Liu, I-Ling Ling, and Jacob Y.H. Jou

Abstract Words constitute a crucial aspect of visual presentation in marketing communication and convey meanings not only through their semantic properties but also through the manner in which they are presented (e.g., typeface and layout). Numerous studies have examined typeface, but few studies have examined Chinese typefaces, particularly the differences between traditional Chinese and simplified Chinese typefaces. In addition, most previous studies have focused on the semantic meaning or affective responses of typefaces; rarely has academic attention been directed toward exploring the persuasive effects of typefaces. The purpose of this research is to propose a conceptual framework showing the influence of typeface shape (circular vs. angular) on the persuasive effects of various types of information (group oriented vs. individual oriented) and to compare the influences of English, traditional Chinese, and simplified Chinese typefaces. We assert that circular (angular) typefaces are more likely to elicit a need to belong (a need to be unique), which in turn positively affects the persuasiveness of group-oriented (individual-oriented) information. In addition, consumers' self-construal (independent/interdependent) and language (traditional Chinese, simplified Chinese, and English) play moderating roles in these relationships. We propose that consumers who engage in interdependent self-construal perceive that group-oriented information presented in circular typefaces is more persuasive than do consumers who engage in independent self-construal, whereas consumers who engage in independent self-construal perceive individual-oriented information presented in angular typefaces as more persuasive than consumers who

Y.-F. Liu (✉)
National Kaohsiung First University of Science and Technology, Kaohsiung, Taiwan
e-mail: yifenliu@nkfust.edu.tw

I.-L. Ling
National Chiayi University, Chiayi, Taiwan
e-mail: yiling@mail.ncyu.edu.tw

J.Y.H. Jou
Kaohsiung Medical University, Kaohsiung, Taiwan
e-mail: jacobjou@cc.kmu.edu.tw

© Academy of Marketing Science 2016
L. Petruzzellis, R.S. Winer (eds.), *Rediscovering the Essentiality of Marketing*, Developments in Marketing Science: Proceedings of the Academy of Marketing Science, DOI 10.1007/978-3-319-29877-1_2

engage in interdependent self-construal do. Furthermore, congruency between typeface shape and information orientation increases processing fluency, thus increasing persuasiveness. We expect that the effects of congruency between typeface shape and information orientation on persuasiveness will be the strongest in traditional Chinese, followed by simplified Chinese, and be the weakest in English.

Testing the Dual Pathway Model of Ad Persuasion Using Celebrity Endorsers

Tanya Drollinger, Schengchen Huang, and Michael Basil

Abstract Marketers frequently employ celebrity spokespersons to promote and build a brand image. Research has shown that ads using celebrities are effective in increasing sales revenues and stock valuations (Elberse and Verleun 2012) as well as raising awareness, gaining higher recall, triggering and maintaining interest, and inducing favorable attitudes. Research has primarily focused on either the information carrier perspective or role model perspective in order to support the compelling reasons that celebrities are effective spokespersons.

In this study the dual pathway of ad persuasion model (Johar and Sirgy 1991) is used to test the effectiveness of celebrity endorsement in print ads. More specifically the aim of the study is to determine whether a celebrity can enhance advertising effectiveness through functional congruity in the event that the celebrity is an expert information carrier in the product category and self-congruity when the celebrity is viewed as a role model who is similar to the viewer. Information regarding celebrities' expertise was manipulated and gender and age were considered when testing similarity of the celebrity and viewer of the ad.

Findings support the dual pathway of ad persuasion model in the celebrity endorsement context and more specifically suggest that highly expert celebrities are most effective when promoting a utilitarian product (insurance) in print ads. Highly similar celebrity endorsers (similar age and gender) were most effective when promoting a value-expressive product (artwork) and ad appeal. Furthermore, this study provides empirical support for the mediating role of functional congruity in the case that the product is utilitarian and self-congruity in thev case that the product is more hedonic on purchase intention. Results suggest that celebrities that are highly expert are more influential when the product is highly utilitarian and celebrities that are more similar to viewers are more influential than less similar

T. Drollinger (✉) • S. Huang • M. Basil
University of Lethbridge, Lethbridge, Canada
e-mail: Tanya.drollinger@uleth.ca; schengchen.huang@uleth.ca; michael.basil@uleth.ca

© Academy of Marketing Science 2016
L. Petruzzellis, R.S. Winer (eds.), *Rediscovering the Essentiality of Marketing*,
Developments in Marketing Science: Proceedings of the Academy of Marketing
Science, DOI 10.1007/978-3-319-29877-1_3

11

others when promoting a value-expressive product. Using the dual pathway model extends the body of research on celebrity endorsement as it disentangles the various theoretical approaches that have been taken in the past and helps unify the literature by clearly noting the type of product, appeal, and the celebrity as an expert or role model.

References available upon request.

Antecedents of Attitude Toward SMS Advertising in the UK

Mehran Darabi, Peter Reeves, and Sunil Sahadev

Abstract A new research report from eMarketer (2014) suggests that firms in the UK were expected to increase their advertising expenditure via mobile phones by 96 %, from £1.03 bn in 2013 to £2.02 bn in 2014. Considering the growth in SMS advertising expenditure in the UK, it is important to understand the underlying factors forming consumers' attitudes toward text marketing. Founded on Fishbein's (1967) expectancy value theory, it is suggested that attitude towards SMS advertising is the result of consumers' beliefs about such practices. Therefore, this research aims to identify beliefs that form consumers' attitude toward SMS advertising in the UK.

A questionnaire research survey was administered. A seven-point Likert survey instrument (ranging from (1) strongly disagree to (7) strongly agree) was developed using validated scales from previous studies in mobile marketing and advertising. Some of the measuring items were reverse coded to prevent biased responses. Data was collected from UK based university students ($N=236$, Females 103, Males 133) in the form of convenience sampling. The sample frame is justified, as students are heavy users of mobile phone technologies and are knowledgeable about SMS advertisements (Muk and Chung 2014).

The results show that five factors directly influence the consumers' attitude toward SMS advertising in the UK. In order of significance (from most important to least important) they are: entertainment, personalisation, irritativeness, credibility and informativeness. Mediation analysis also found that the more knowledgeable the consumers become about mobile communications, the more likely they are to be entertained by SMS advertising messages, and less likely to find text marketing irritating. Furthermore, incentives can increase the credibility of text marketing messages and reduce the level of their irritativeness. It was also concluded that prior permission is fully mediated via irritativeness in terms of its influence on text marketing attitude. Finally, the study shows that both consumer control and privacy concerns influence SMS advertising attitude via mediating variables of credibility and personalisation.

References available upon requests

M. Darabi (✉) • P. Reeves • S. Sahadev
University of Salford, Salford, UK
e-mail: M.Darabi@edu.salford.ac.uk; P.Reeves@salford.ac.uk; S.Sahadev@salford.ac.uk

© Academy of Marketing Science 2016   13
L. Petruzzellis, R.S. Winer (eds.), *Rediscovering the Essentiality of Marketing*,
Developments in Marketing Science: Proceedings of the Academy of Marketing
Science, DOI 10.1007/978-3-319-29877-1_4

What Really Drives Creative Choices in an Advertising Agency?

Douglas West, George Christodoulides, and Jennifer Bonhomme

Introduction

With the increasing concentration of media planning and buying into large media agencies that provide specialist expertise and economies of scale, the role of creativity has become the core function of most advertising agencies. Indeed, the place of creativity in advertising has long been recognized. While the occurrence of eureka moments has been well documented, for the most part creatives are known to come up with multiple ideas for campaign strategies and executions. These are rarely presented directly to clients. Instead advertising executives are tasked with intervening. Aside from motivating and managing their creative teams, advertising executives have to make the final "call" as to what campaign will be presented to the client often with a "plan B" campaign held in reserve just in case Plan A is rejected or is met with resistance. Agency executives can make their reputations on the basis of selecting the work that best fits the clients' brief otherwise the relationship will flounder and the account will eventually be lost. To what extent is the decision eclectic or codified? Do agency executives apply set rules or take each case as it comes? This chapter examines the decision-making employed by a global advertising agency to select creative work. The result provides insights about the nature of

D. West (✉)
King's College, London, UK
e-mail: douglas.west@kcl.ac.uk

G. Christodoulides
Birkbeck, London University, London, UK
e-mail: g.christodoulides@bbk.ac.uk

J. Bonhomme
JWT London, London, UK
e-mail: jennifer.bonhomme@jwt.com

© Academy of Marketing Science 2016
L. Petruzzellis, R.S. Winer (eds.), *Rediscovering the Essentiality of Marketing*,
Developments in Marketing Science: Proceedings of the Academy of Marketing
Science, DOI 10.1007/978-3-319-29877-1_5

and factors that influence decision-making amongst managers when choosing between creative work, decisions that are pivotal to the retention of clients, and the longevity of the relationships.

Background

Advertising creativity has been variously described in terms of thinking, ability, problem-solving, imagination, innovation, and effectiveness (e.g., Bell 1992; Koslow et al. 2003). Advertising practitioners encounter various viewpoints about their work that in turn impacts their views of what constitutes advertising creativity (Crain 2010; Kelley 1992; Smith and Yang 2004). Career advancement in advertising requires that practitioners assimilate cultural codes of professionalism that eventually become instinctive and habitual (Jenkins 2002). Much of this has to do with the correct use of the conventions and norms of the industry rather than any rigid adherence to any creative concept or approaches. An advertising creative needs to appear to be both an artist and concurrently realistic, market oriented and commercially driven (Dahlén et al. 2008; Lehnert et al. 2014). Thus the agency creative "is not a free-floating artist but...is one who works hard [to synthesize and apply] analysis and knowledge" to develop new and novel creative outcomes (Alvesson 1994, p. 547).

The perceptions of what constitutes advertising creativity have been found to differ by role (Hirschman 1989; Runco and Charles 1993; White and Smith 2001). Thus creative talent, or creatives as they are often known, has a tendency to view advertisements as more appropriate if they are artistic, while account executives and account planners are more inclined to view advertisements as more appropriate if they are strategic (Koslow et al. 2003, 2006).

This chapter sets out to examine the nature of decision-making within advertising agencies where "algorithmics" (probability and logic) cannot help with the choice of creative work to show to a client so that heuristics (commonsense) have to be applied. An Account Director or Creative Director cannot simply "punch" numbers into a spreadsheet and find out what creative work to pick. Nevertheless, such decisions have to be made on a regular basis. How do they do it and what guides their choices? Can such decisions be codified to improve practice? Advertising creativity is an execution that surprises and provides insight to its intended audience, with the goal of supporting an intended campaign strategy. Agency executives have to combine the artistic with the strategic to reach appropriate solutions for their clients. Clients are looking to solve problems rather than produce art.

Methodology

A web questionnaire was first developed in liaison with five senior managers at a leading global advertising agency in London. The instrument included items measuring decision-making (Gigerenzer 2008), business practices, market environment, and personal and company demographics. Respondents were prompted to think about a recent project they had worked on and to explain how they picked the one creative solution that they then "pitched" to the client. Responses were measured on 7-point Likert scales. Recipients were directed to pass on the questionnaire link to the most senior marketing person in the company, if not them. The online questionnaire was pre-tested, using a convenience sample of the same five advertising executives at the global agency who had guided the work. The purpose of the pre-test was to ensure the integrity and readability of the questionnaire. Senior managers then sent an e-mail with an explanation inviting responses via the questionnaire out to the European, North American, and Asian offices of the global agency concerned. For example, the Head of Creative in London sent the link to the Head of Creative in New York who then forwarded it to all their staff in the New York agency. Thus the sample consisted of executives working on a range of accounts from a cross-national section of the agency. The database was administered via Qualtrics.com and 144 responses were obtained from executives working across account management, creativity, media, and research. Given the internal nature of the sampling and lack of direct control by researchers, it was not possible to send out a second wave of the questionnaire and many of the standard tests of potential for nonresponse bias were not applicable. However, Armstrong and Overton's (1977) method, where the first 25% of the responses are compared to the last 25% of the responses, was also utilized. No significant differences were found. The primary demographics of the sample were Account Planners 29%, Account Directors (21%) and Digital Specialists (also 21%) with Creative Directors, Art Directors and Copywriters the next largest group (9%). Other roles included (senior) producer, creative technologist, digital strategist, strategic planner, and digital planner. The respondents worked in advertising for an average of 8.6 years (SD=6.9 years), 3.1 of which at the present agency (SD=3.6).

Results

The top two heuristics (take-the-best and tallying) were at the analytical end of the decision-making spectrum, and that all four analytic approaches (including satisficing and algorithmic) were in the top half. Instinct was the top "pure" heuristic coming third in the ranking with majority at fourth. All the other pure heuristics from experience to fluency were in the bottom half. An exploratory factor analysis (EFA) of principal components with a Varimax rotation was performed to examine the underlying structure of the decision-making heuristics used in selecting creative ideas for clients. Given the sample size, factor loadings less than .50 were suppressed from the analysis (Hair et al. 1998). A four-factor solution emerged from the analysis, which accounted for 64.4% of the variance. The factors were labelled: "*Instinct*," "*Recognition*," "*Experience*," and "*Integration of ideas*."

The factor scores were saved as variables and used in a multiple regression analysis to identify the factors of heuristics associated with the greatest level of confidence in the decision-making. Confidence was measured on a 100-point scale. The prediction model was statistically significant $F(4, 57) = 8.32, p < .001$ and accounted for approximately 37% of the variance of confidence. Decisions made on the basis of *Instinct* were found to be associated with higher levels of confidence ($\beta = .584$, $p < .000$), whilst decisions made on the basis of *Recognition*, *Experience*, or *Integration* did not lead to greater confidence.

Discussion and Conclusion

What are the headlines in this exploratory study? Little to nothing is known about how advertising practitioners make decisions in situations where algorithms (i.e., decisions based upon logic and probability) have little or no role to play. The first point to make is that these advertising executives tend to be at the analytic (logical) end of the spectrum of heuristics. They consider their client's needs, choose solutions that have the most favorable points, set benchmarks, and analyze any available data. Sitting amidst these approaches are some pure heuristics—principally "instinct" and "majority." That is, executives combine these analytic heuristics with gut instincts and a majority vote.

There is no "one size fits all" solution and advertising executives are prepared to combine decision-making types to reach a decision. This was demonstrated by a principal components analysis which generated four categories of heuristics employed in the decision-making and revealed the symbiotic nature of logical versus affective heuristics amongst the global agency. Two of the factors (i.e., *Instinct* and *Integration*) comprised both pure (affective) and analytic (logical) heuristics. In terms of outcomes, decisions grounded in *instinct* are associated with greater confidence than any other heuristic type. This result requires further analysis and at this stage it is just conjecture, but perhaps because success was self-reported, managers attributed success to their own experience and insight rather than alternative logical processes. As one practitioner noted on reading the results: "The value of the findings to me, lies in their ability to help executives make swift and meaningful decisions in deciding creative. So often we over-engineer or labor over which creative route is right, when actually instinct and swiftness of our decision is what make the difference."

From a management perspective the study clearly demonstrates that the selection of creative solutions is not made in isolation. A key element in the choice is a good understanding of the needs of the client or sponsor. Despite the contribution of this study, the findings should be interpreted with caution given that the research was undertaken within one agency. Future research could extend this work by investigating the choice of creative work within a range of agencies and also by examining the possible moderating role of culture in this selection process.

Future plans with the study include an investigation of the role of organizational culture in the advertising companies and how this might influence the decision-making processes. Greater generalizability will be attained by collecting data from a wider range of advertising agencies.

References available on request.

Classical Music in Advertising: Brand Supporter or Detractor?

Christina Chung, Gladys Torres-Baumgarten, and Kathryn Woodbury Zeno

Introduction

The purpose of this research is to explore brand image and attitude toward the brand and the relationship to classical music in advertising and perceived music brand congruency. Over the past 30 years, many articles have aimed to study the effect of background music in advertising. Most of these studies though focus on contemporary popular music and omit the use of classical music which is often used in global brand advertisements. Various measures have been used to gauge advertising effectiveness when music is used in advertising, including advertising recall, brand recall, and support of brand benefits for example. Additionally, music in advertising has been assessed in relationship to brand image, identity, attitude toward the brand, and purchase intent.

The extant literature reveals that music in advertising can have varying effects on consumers and that its effects are dependent upon the music's characteristics, such as the tempo (fast paced versus slow paced), vocal versus instrumental, loud versus soft passages, major versus minor keys, harmonious versus discordant music, and consistent rhythmical patterns versus syncopated rhythms. In addition, some research makes the distinction between embodied meaning of music (i.e., "the context-independent hedonic value or favorableness of feelings evoked, due solely to the degree of stimulation afforded by the music's sounds") versus its referential meaning (derived from "the networks of or conceptual associations evoked by prompting of contextual factors such as the place where the music airs, the musician, the instruments used, or other relationships between the music and external world concepts, events, and characters"). In this study, the characteristics and influence of the music

C. Chung (✉) • G. Torres-Baumgarten • K.W. Zeno
Ramapo College of New Jersey, Mahwah, NJ, USA
e-mail: cchung1@ramapo.edu; torresbaumgarten@gmail.com; kzeno@verizon.net

© Academy of Marketing Science 2016   19
L. Petruzzellis, R.S. Winer (eds.), *Rediscovering the Essentiality of Marketing*,
Developments in Marketing Science: Proceedings of the Academy of Marketing
Science, DOI 10.1007/978-3-319-29877-1_6

on the brand image and attitude toward the brand will be explored in relation to the music's historical context. Additionally, this study will extend previous work to better understand the controversy associated with brand incongruent music and music familiarity in relation to brand image.

Background and Hypotheses

As early as 1990, Bruner stated that "music has been treated too generally in most marketing studies." He stated that the characteristics of musical sound can be captured by three basic dimensions: time, pitch, and texture and much of the marketing research has focused on some "variation on this theme." Our research study intends to take Bruner's admonition to heart and build on the work of Zhu and Meyers-Levy by looking at the historical context and the meaning behind the composer's composition. The composer's selected genre or theme may impart a yet unexplored referential meaning to the music in the advertisement for some consumers. When this is the case, the music should be selected in such a way that it is consistent with or at least supports the brand benefits, image, or the overall brand message. Problems can arise when the music and the brand image are incongruent or "misaligned" (An example of "misalignment" would be if an advertisement for a car whose brand image focuses on safety and reliability was to use musical excerpts from Mozart's requiem—a musical setting for a funeral mass—and hardly a piece that embodies safety/reliability.). This example of brand incongruent music may produce a negative effect on the brand image and attitude toward the brand particularly if the consumer has a referential meaning of the music.

On the other hand, consumers—who may be less familiar with the composition's meaning—may simply impart an embodied meaning to the music based on reactions evoked by the music per se, having nothing to do with the composer or the music's historical meaning or context. Thus, those that are familiar with a piece of classical music, its origins and meaning may negatively link the brand incongruent music with the brand image and also have a negative attitude toward the brand. A consumer who is unfamiliar with the music's meaning may react more favorably to an ad with music that is incongruent with the brand's image. The music selection then is a critical decision that can complement a brand's image or can lead to brand confusion on the part of the consumer if it is perceived to be incongruent with the brand's image.

The field of cognitive psychology has recently uncovered a key to understanding the importance of musical selection in brand advertising. Cognitive psychology research maintains that sound is processed first, prior to any processing of visual and verbal message stimuli. The research suggests that listeners have limited processing capability and that there is a processing order. Moreover, it finds that there is a preemptive processing of background sounds—i.e., consumers' first inclination is to focus on the music in an ad, rather than the brand message. This runs counter to previous marketing studies that have assumed that there is a stimuli-processing order in listeners' minds and that the primary focus is on the brand message. The new finding from cognitive psychology implies that music in advertising rather than being "background" music is a critical part of the advertisement and that it will command the listeners' attention more readily than the advertising's text, thus making the "right" musical selection all the more critical. Perceived congruency between music and the brand image then becomes an important factor in shaping attitude toward a brand and argues for careful selection of music in advertising.

Background music is often selected by advertising professionals as a way to capture the listener's attention, evoke certain imagery, or even to communicate brand benefits that might be represented by the music or lyrics. Yet, as we suggest, the music's meaning and historical context might support the brand image or alternatively, it may detract from effective communication of brand image. Equipped with a better understanding of classical music's historical context, brand music congruency, level of consumer's music familiarity, and how each affects consumers' attitude toward the brand, advertisers can be more confident that the music choices they make will be more effective in overall brand communication and more consistent with the brand image.

Based on previous research findings, a model was developed to measure the relationships among several variables including contextual knowledge of music, attitude toward music, perceived brand music congruency, brand image, and attitude toward the brand.

Hypotheses

H1: Brand image is positively related to attitude toward the brand.
H2: Level of brand music congruency is positively related to attitude toward the brand.
H3: Referential meaning of classical music perceived as incongruent to the brand image will have a negative relationship to attitude toward the brand.
H4: An embodied meaning of classical music perceived as congruent to the brand image will have a positive relationship to attitude toward the brand.
H5: The greater the music knowledge the higher the perceived congruency between the music and the brand image.

Methodology

Data will be collected from two groups of respondents: music "expert" (choral members familiar with classical music repertoire) and nonmusic experts using a web survey. Respondents' knowledge of music will be assessed, and then each respondent will be exposed to a television ad containing classical music. After exposure to the treatment, then the attitude toward the music, perceived brand music congruency, and brand image will be examined.

The experimental treatment is a television advertisement for Doritos® corn chips. The 30 s television advertisement uses the same music that was selected for an on-air execution, an excerpt from Giuseppe Verdi's Requiem (the Dies Irae).

Doritos® brand tortilla chips is a market leader in the tortilla chips category and has international distribution. A separate brand image survey was conducted with adults to understand the perceived Dorito's brand image relative to the company's stated brand image. Confirmation of the company's desired brand image was obtained as a majority of respondents reported "bold" as the brand's major characteristic. The Verdi selection is grounded in the historical context of music for a funeral mass and therefore is perceived to be incongruent to the brand image. Additionally, the perceived incongruence could be in reaction to music for a funeral mass coupled with a food item. Administered as a survey, respondent's attitude toward the brand and brand image will be assessed prior to exposure to the advertisements and post exposure in relation to the classical music.

Results and Discussion

Background music is often selected by advertising professionals as a way to capture the consumer's attention, evoke certain imagery, or even to communicate brand benefits that might be represented by the music or lyrics. Given the role of advertising to build awareness and brand image, the selection of music for advertisements plays an integral and complementary role with the other advertising elements in brand building. Yet, as we suggest, knowledge of the music's meaning and historical context may have an effect on brand image or attitude toward the brand. In this study, the classical music's tempo and execution outweigh the perceived brand music incongruence even among consumers who have a referential perspective of the music. This finding supports other research regarding the positive nature of disruptive or incongruent advertising elements that call attention to the advertisement and support the brand image and attitude toward the brand. Alternatively, the music's meaning and historical context may detract from effective communication of brand image if brand music incongruence exists. Equipped with a better understanding of classical music's historical context, brand music congruence, and how each affects consumers' attitude toward the brand, advertisers can be more confident that the background music choices they make will be more effective in overall brand communication and support the brand image.

Part II
Business-to-Business Marketing

Gender and Similarity: Match or Mismatch— When Is B2B Sales Performance Better?

Ozan Peneklioglu and Ayse Banu Elmadag Bas

Introduction

Organizational buying behavior has generally been considered a complex, systematic, and rational behavior, which is not influenced by subjective criteria (Webster and Wind 1972; Sheth 1973). However, more recent research has shown that organizational buying behavior may also be influenced by personal factors (Anderson and Chambers 1985; Ronchetto et al. 1989). Although the decision itself serves organizational goals and may be bound with rational processes, the decision makers are human beings. Therefore, major characteristics of the decision makers or the appraisals they have about their environment in the business to business (B2B) contexts may have a bearing on the decision-making process and the performance of the transactions.

There are two major appraisals salespeople make during sales processes. The first is about the decider and the second is about the sales job itself. Salespeople and the members of the buying center evaluate each other based on certain characteristics. Likewise, the sales job is also appraised by these parties. In this study, salespeople are contacted as evaluators of the sales job, and the decision maker in the buying center.

In many B2B sales situations it is nearly impossible to pinpoint the decision maker (in many cases the decision is made collectively), this study uses the perceptions of the salesperson about the most influential person in the buying center (i.e., the buyer) and explores the personal influences as well as the effects of the characteristics of the sales job on its performance. The effects of gender and perceived similarity of the buyer and seller are considered as individual factors influencing performance of the organizational purchasing (or sales) decisions. Furthermore, since the characteristics of the purchasing (sales) job also influence its performance,

O. Peneklioglu (✉) • A.B.E. Bas
Istanbul Technical University, Istanbul, Turkey
e-mail: ozanpeneklioglu@gmail.com; elmadaga@itu.edu.tr

© Academy of Marketing Science 2016
L. Petruzzellis, R.S. Winer (eds.), *Rediscovering the Essentiality of Marketing*, Developments in Marketing Science: Proceedings of the Academy of Marketing Science, DOI 10.1007/978-3-319-29877-1_7

25

based on the theory of industrial buyer behavior (Sheth 1973) evaluations of the sales job are measured by four variables (risk, time pressure, importance, and complexity). Finally, the effects of both individual factors and perceived evaluations of the sales job on sales performance are assessed.

Background

B2B markets have received great interest both from marketing scholars and practitioners, due to the total volume of sales in B2B markets being more than the consumer markets and the reselling occurs in the channel of distribution in B2B markets (Leblanc 1981; Manaberi and Tina 2005). On the other hand, organizational buying behavior has received significantly less attention compared to consumer behavior, due to being considered more objective and complex. There is a buying center that contains many parties, numerous objectives, and possibly conflicting decision criteria. Therefore the buying decision itself requires a longer period of time, requires more information, and includes many interorganizational relationships (Webster and Wind 1972).

Industrial vendors must understand both industrial and individual decision-making processes to be successful because although B2B sales is an objective task, it is human beings that are making the decisions. Therefore, industrial purchasing decisions are also influenced by the individual factors such as gender, age, income, education, and personality. Research findings prove that both rational and emotional values influence the industrial customers (Manaberi and Tina 2005; Noordewier et al. 1990; Thomas 1980).

In the past few years, the number of women in the job market has radically increased and more than 60 % of married women work outside the home (US Labor Statistics). The increase in the number of women employed in the job market brings a dependable increase in the percentage of women employed in conventionally male-dominated positions, which includes purchasing management. Unfortunately, there are very few studies about the gender differences in B2B purchasing management in scholarly journals. For example, Palmer and Bijou (1995) show that women purchasing managers have the tendency to be more interpersonally oriented than men, so gender has a significant role in the development of buyer/seller relationships. Swift and Gruben (2000) reported that gender differences in supplier selection criteria exist, specifically with regard to dependability and the provision of support. Pullins et al. (2004) conducted a research to find out the behavioral differences about trust, credibility, and customer orientation between male and female buyers in industrial markets.

This study aims to find out the effects of salesperson-buying decision maker gender and perceived similarity on sales performance. Furthermore, the perceived characteristics of the sales job such as complexity, risk, and time pressure are also measured. The mechanisms that are in play when determining sales performance are examined.

Methodology

Different individuals' participation in the decision-making (i.e., the buying center), difficulty of collecting reliable data, and the difference in importance levels of criteria perceived by each individual role are some of the complexities in research design in B2B sales contexts. The *decider* within the buying center has the most important and influential role among others, but it is difficult to determine who the *decider* within the buying organization is. Every individual or group in the buying center states that it has the most important and influential role among others (Webster and Wind 1972; Johnston and Bonoma 1981; Garrido-Samaniego and Gutierrez-Cillan 2004). Considering the difficulties and impossibility to define the *decider* in the buying center, we have used the salespeople's perceptions of who the decider is and the deciders' evaluations. Therefore employing a quantitative approach, salespeople are used as the unit of analysis and the perspective of salespeople is used to measure the perceptions of the decision maker about the sales job.

We designed our measures based on existing scales in the literature and used a convenience sample of B2B salespeople via an online data collection process. We limited the questions in the questionnaire to the latest *new buy* situation the sales person experienced, to make sure that the participants were going through an extensive decision-making process that enabled them to be able to evaluate each other.

Our survey contained measures to find out the individual characteristics and demographics of the seller, the sellers perceptions of the *decider* (*similarity and gender*), the result and duration of process (performance), sellers perceptions of the decider's risk, complexity, time pressure, importance and novelty of the purchasing job, and trust to seller. The measures used are "Similarity between Seller and Decider" (10 items); "Perceived Risk of Buying Task" (12 items); "Perceived Time Pressure for This Buying Task" (3 items); "Perceived Importance of Buying Task" (5 items); and "Perceived Complexity of Purchased Products/Services" (5 items).

A total of 235 usable surveys were obtained after eliminating the unusable responses. The respondents represented 14 different industries. Firstly, the undimensionality, reliability, and validity of the study constructs were examined. The means and standard deviations as well as the reliabilities of the constructs were examined. Cronbach's alpha values were well above the suggested benchmark 7 (Nunnally 1978) in all instances. Secondly, EFAs (exploratory factor analyses) for each construct were conducted and the correlations among these constructs were computed. Finally, the relations among these constructs were studied using three-step hierarchical multiple regression equations. Correlations and relations among these constructs have been examined for three different cases to understand the gender match effect to the constructs: (1) All cases, (2) Same gender cases (M–M or F–F), and (3) Different gender cases (M–F or F–M).

Results and Discussion

We examined the correlations among constructs for three different samples (All Cases, Same Gender Cases, and Different Gender Cases). Two hierarchical multiple regression equations are formed for each subsample. Of these two HMR equations one had the dependent variable S-Performance, a five-point Likert scale, which questioned the comparison of the sales duration versus industrial standards. The second equation, on the other hand, used O-Performance as the dependent variable. O-Performance is measured with a ratio of two scales: (1) Actual duration of the correspondent sales (2) Actual duration of similar sales within the same industry.

In addition to the similarity, perceived risk, importance, complexity, and time pressure, each equation incorporated the four control variables: three at seller level (age, tenure in the profession, tenure in the organization) and one at the decider level (thrust to seller). The least squares technique was used for the control variables entered as a block in step 1, which is followed by the main effects in step 2, and the moderators in step 3.

Step 1 (Control Variables) of hierarchical multiple regression analysis resulted as expected. This step shows *Trust to Seller* has significant associations with both S-Performance and O-Performance. Additionally *Trust to Seller* is affecting the sales performance more significantly in gender mismatch cases comparing to the gender match cases.

Step 2 (Main Effects) of the equation reveals that *similarity* and *perceived risk* are significantly related to S-Performance in gender match cases, whereas they are not significantly related in gender mismatch cases. This can be considered as a proof of gender effect on decision-making. As expected, *similarity* has positive influence on sales performance; on the other hand, *perceived risk* and *perceived importance* have significant negative influence on sales performance for all cases.

In *Step 3* (Interaction Effects) of the hierarchical multiple regression analysis, none of the similarity interactions (Similarity × Perceived Risk, Similarity × Time Pressure, Similarity × Importance, Similarity × Complexity) have significant effects neither to S-Performance nor to O-Performance. Although both similarity and perceived risk have significant direct effects on the sales performance at the Step 2 of the hierarchical multiple regression analysis (Main Effects), as expected, their interaction does not have any effect. These results are showing that the similarity between *seller* and *decider* does not affect the sales performance via evaluated constructs (Perceived Risk, Perceived Time Pressure, Perceived Importance, and Perceived Complexity). In another words, the main constructs of this study are not influenced from the similarity between *seller* and *decider*.

Conclusion and Implications

This study is a preliminary attempt to investigate the influences of gender and similarity between buyer and seller on perceptions of perceived risk, time pressure, perceived importance, and perceived complexity. Results of this study show that there is a relationship between the purchasing decision process and similarity and gender, but the main constructs of this study (Perceived Risk, Perceived Time Pressure, Perceived Importance, and Perceived Complexity) are influenced neither by gender nor by similarity between seller and decider.

The result of this study provides recommendations for sales team managers in assigning the customers to the sales representatives working for them. This study proves that the similarity between seller and decider has significant positive effects on the performance of the sales for gender match cases. On the other hand, the similarity between seller and decider has significant negative effect on gender mismatch cases.

References available upon request.

The Effect of Brands in B2B Purchasing Decisions

"The Feather That Tips the Balance"?

Marc Kuhn and Vanessa Reit

Abstract In the past, brands and brand management in the industrial goods sector have rarely been taken into consideration neither within scientific framework nor in practice. The specifics of industrial goods cast doubt on the realisation of brand-strategy concepts. For some years now, there has been an increase in the significance of brand-policy aspects in industrial goods markets. In many industrial goods companies, greater focus is now being placed on the brand concept. But what role do brands actually play in industrial purchasing processes? In our view, a direct primary evaluation to determine the additional price willingness of brand aspects amongst purchasers of industrial goods providers would not, therefore, be useful. Numerous studies indicate that the direct retrieval of purchasing decision factors amongst industrial purchasers leads to a one-sided emphasis on objective performance factors such as quality and the "price" factor. From a methodical perspective, evaluation processes that confront the purchaser with an overall purchasing situation are more meaningful. In order to evaluate the significance of B2B brands in industrial purchasing processes, we will perform an adaptive choice-based conjoint analysis with 32 industrial purchasers.

Keywords Brand effectiveness • Conjoint analysis • B2B marketing • Industrial purchasing process

M. Kuhn (✉) • V. Reit
Baden-Wuerttemberg Cooperative State University Stuttgart, Stuttgart, Germany
e-mail: marc.kuhn@dhbw-stuttgart.de; vanessa.reit@dhbw-stuttgart.de

© Academy of Marketing Science 2016   31
L. Petruzzellis, R.S. Winer (eds.), *Rediscovering the Essentiality of Marketing*,
Developments in Marketing Science: Proceedings of the Academy of Marketing
Science, DOI 10.1007/978-3-319-29877-1_8

Introduction

Brands and their history are closely intertwined with the consumer goods sector (Low and Fullerton 1994), and it should come as no surprise that consumer goods companies are often referred to as brand manufacturers. Brands have particular relevance in consumer goods markets (Baumgarth 2004), and in many markets and areas, brands serve as the engine for corporate growth. This is reflected not only in the numerous documented success stories of strong consumer goods brands from business practice, but also in a scientific context. However, to date, brand-related research has focussed primarily on products in the consumer goods sector (Webster and Keller 2004). Brands and brand management in the industrial goods sector have rarely been taken into consideration within a scientific framework, and in practice too, brands have always played a lesser role (Baumgarth and Douven 2006). This situation can be attributed to a delayed focus on the marketing of industrial goods as well as the assumed minor significance of industrial goods brands (Köhler 2004). The specifics of industrial goods (including derivative demand, organisational customer, and high rationality in purchasing decisions) cast doubt on the realisation of brand-strategy concepts (Voeth and Rabe 2004). The brand value of consumer goods companies frequently accounts for 50 % of the total company value. In industrial goods companies, this figure is typically less than 20 % of the total company value (Godefroid and Pförtsch 2009). According to Krämer (1993), brands account for just 5 % of all industrial goods marketing activities. To date, sales marketing has focussed primarily on the technical components of an industrial product and less on brands (Voeth and Brinkmann 2004). For some years now, there has been an increase in the significance of brand-policy aspects in industrial goods markets, and in many industrial goods companies, greater focus is now being placed on the brand concept. Specialist literature provides a variety of definitions on the subject of "brand". This study uses a definition of brand name from behavioural science as a basis. Accordingly, "brand" is understood to mean a marketing object, "…that takes on an identification and differentiation function as a concept in the minds of stakeholder groups and that characterises decision-making behaviour" (http://wirtschafts-lexikon.gabler.de/Archiv/57328/marke-v13.html (as at: 17/10/2014)). In the consumer goods sector, the brand is above all attributed a simplification function from the perspective of demand. As the definition above suggests, the brand provides consumers with a familiar image, thus assisting them in the purchasing process. The brand makes it possible for consumers to make their purchase decision more quickly, without the risk of making the wrong purchase.

Other functions of brands include identification (e.g. a certain attitude towards life that is embodied by a brand), prestige (self-expression, demonstrating a certain social status of the consumer) and quality assurance (assuring a certain quality standard) (Scharf et al. 2009; Homburg and Krohmer 2006). From the vendor's perspective, there are two specific benefits of a brand: in the first instance it facilitates a pricing margin that can be enforced based on a customer's emotional connection to a certain brand. Secondly, in the case of comparable prices, brands help to form preferences through artificial differentiation of otherwise similar products (Backhaus and Voeth 2010). In industrial goods marketing, a decision-making process characterised by strict rationality is assumed (Homburg and Krohmer 2006). In a very abstract form, these assumptions can be reduced right down to what is known as the Rational Choice Theory, whereby complex individual and sociological actions are recorded by means of simplified model assumptions (e.g. Becker 1992; Simon 1993). Accordingly, particular institutional customers such as industrial purchasers display objectivity and criteria-orientation in their purchasing behaviour (Kunz 2004).

However, behaviour characterised by strict rationality conflicts to some extent with the functions attributed to brands in the consumer goods sector. For example, the identification function (embodiment of a certain attitude towards life or an emotional influence through artificially produced brand environments) contradicts a more rational, formally organised collective decision that is normally made by a typical industrial buying centre (Meffert et al. 2008). The function of prestige also has no effect on rational procurement behaviour. In spite of this, there is a prevailing opinion within industry that brands do hold a certain function when it comes to purchasing decisions. This is affirmed by a study carried out by Homburg, Jensen and Richter as early as 2007 concerning brand relevance in the industrial goods sector. The authors of this study arrived at the conclusion that while brands do not play a dominant role in industrial purchasing decisions, they do have significance (Homburg et al. 2008). This current study intends to adopt the approach followed by Homburg, Jensen and Richter and use a conjoint analysis to investigate the influence of brands in direct comparison to the selected decision attributes "price" and "product quality" for defined sectors of the industrial goods business. The relevance of B2B brands should be evaluated with specific reference to the purchaser, on whom there is particular relevance owing to his executive role in the purchasing process (Meffert et al. 2008). The issues that must be investigated here are: what drivers influence a purchaser's decisions within his work; and what functions could brands fulfil within this. According to Lynch and de Chernatony, a distinction can be drawn between emotional and functional values in the functioning of brands or the content that is embodied by brands, i.e. in an ideal scenario, brands can respond to and influence the rational or emotional motivation of those involved in purchasing decisions (buying centre) (Lynch and de Chernatony 2007). When it comes to the purchaser, rational motivation is therefore assumed in the first instance: the fundamental assumption is that the purchaser wishes to do a good job in his own interests—to ensure the success of his client (employer) and thus to safeguard his own livelihood. In his role, the purchaser represents the interests of the employer (negotiating favourable offers, working efficiently and economically) while at the same time pursues his own, individual and personal goals (safeguarding his own existence by producing good work). It must therefore be assumed that factors such as the "information function", "uncertainty-reduction function" and "risk-reduction function" that support the purchaser in achieving these aims are perceived by him as positive and positively influence his decisions accordingly.

Industry heterogeneity in the industrial goods sector is taken into account within the study by means of scientific subdivision into four business types (Backhaus and Voeth 2010):

Product business: The product business concerns the marketing of standardised services in anonymous markets. This includes prefabricated products which, without creating a specific relation between the vendor and the buyer, are marketed under standard conditions.

Equipment business: As with the product business, the equipment business is characterised by a self-contained purchasing process. In contrast to the product business, the equipment business concerns more complex service packages that are typically assembled into a single functional unit on the premises of the buyer. These service packages may well be composed of standardised components but are created according to customers' requirements and are therefore highly specific. Moreover, the equipment business usually involves contract manufacturing which is subject to higher costs than the product business, typically associated with specific terms of payment (such as advance payments or instalments).

System business: The system business is characterised by the fact that although the marketed products constitute standardised services designed for an anonymous market, these can only be used in conjunction with other services. In view of this, the system business usually involves a succession of purchasing processes in which all necessary system elements are gradually procured. A fundamental attribute of the system business is therefore the compatibility of the individual system elements.

Supply business: The supply business (also OEM (Original Equipment Manufacturer) business) is characterised in particular by the fact that products and marketing programmes are tailored to and developed for individual customers. In light of the mutual dependency that is established between customer and manufacturer, operations in the supply business have a strong focus on developing long-term business relationships.

Depending on the business type in question, decisions taken by the purchaser can have a variety of consequences. For example, the purchase of a photocopier (product business) is considered much less complex and risky than the purchase of a new production system. If this statement is viewed in relation to the previous statements regarding the function of brands, differences in the significance of brands when making purchasing decisions in alternative business types can be anticipated.

Research Question and Hypotheses

What role do brands actually play in industrial purchasing processes? Do industrial purchasers make decisions in favour of "stronger" industrial goods brands, or do they merely consider quantifiable performance data and price? Are there variations between different industrial business types? Research contributions that tackle this issue are primarily based on compositional approaches in which purchasers are asked directly about the significance of the brand (e.g. Kuhn et al. 2008). Other contributions directly investigate the contribution of B2B brands on risk reduction (e.g. Brown et al. 2011). From our point of view these contributions do not evaluate the extent to which brands have an effect on industrial purchasing decisions. The core research question of this study involves investigating whether or not industrial brands play a part in the purchasing decisions of industrial customers. Do industrial brands merely serve to "tip the balance" when faced with identical pricing, product and quality attributes from the supplier in question? Or are purchasers willing to "buy" themselves "higher quality" brands with price concessions?

Brands are credited with reducing uncertainty (Backhaus and Sabel 2004). Owing to the nature of his function, the purchaser must always bear a certain level of risk depending on the procurement situation with which he is faced. As such, the purchaser's goal is to minimise his personal risk and safeguard his personal success (for example in the form of a secure place of work). A recognised brand simplifies the purchasing decision such that a certain degree of responsibility can be transferred to the brand. This means that if something goes wrong in spite of the decision to purchase a recognised brand, at least the purchaser cannot be reproached for having opted for an unknown and therefore risky vendor. On the basis of this, it can be reasoned that:

H1: Brands significantly influence the purchasing decisions of purchasers in industrial enterprises.

H1 also implies that when faced with comparable services or product features, the brand becomes a criterion for making a purchasing decision. This can be attributed to the fact that the positive characteristics (risk reduction, minimisation of uncertainty) of the brand represent added value to the purchaser (Backhaus and Sabel 2004). As explained above, procurement situations in the B2B sector can be categorised into different business types. Within these different business types (product business, equipment business, system business and supply business) there are both differences with regard to complexity (for example, a simple product compared with a highly complex system) and with regard to company-wide significance (for example, a simple product compared with an individually developed system). Moreover, as part of the different procurement situations and within the individual business types themselves, the purchaser may be faced with situations with heightened uncertainty as well as more trusted situations. Consequently, in addition to differences between the individual business types, there may be a marked difference in the relevance (company-wide significance) of the service being procured within the business types themselves (Backhaus and Sabel 2004). In summary, this leads us to reason that:

H2: The importance of the brand is dependent on the business type.

Experience in purchasing as well as other professional activity is an important factor in knowledge acquisition (availability of information) and the ability to assess risks. The less experienced the purchaser is, and the less knowledge he has been able to acquire within a professional activity, the more important the risk-minimising and informative functions of brands are for him (Backhaus and Sabel 2004). This allows us to reason that:

H3: The influence of the brand on the purchasing decision weakens as the purchaser's professional experience increases.

Research Methodology

In order to verify the hypotheses, the conjoint analysis procedure was used as a multivariate method to evaluate preference and benefit (Baier and Brusch 2009; Teichert et al. 2008; Völckner et al. 2008). The term "conjoint analysis" (synonymous use in specialist literature: "conjoint measurement") refers to a method of illustrating and evaluating a variety of objects by a single person. This means that, in the first instance, conjoint analyses are individual analyses that enable the evaluation behaviour of the test person to be understood. The objects concerned are defined by certain product attributes or features, although an integrated approach is taken to the consideration or evaluation of the individual objects (http://www.saw-toothsoftware.com/-products/acbc/ (as at: 31/08/2012)). This decompositional approach is a specific advantage of the conjoint analysis. Taking this approach allows us to determine the contribution of individual product attributes to the benefit of a product empirically. Benefit is a non-observable construct found in everyday purchasing behaviour.

Combination and further development of the classical conjoint analysis leads to adaptive choice-based conjoint analysis (ACBC). This form of analysis is a new approach that takes the best aspects of choice-based conjoint analysis (CBC) and adaptive conjoint analysis and combines them into a single procedure (http://www.sawtoothsoftware.com/-products/acbc/ (as at: 31/08/2012)). ACBC was launched as marketable software by Sawtooth Software at the beginning of 2009. The basic concept behind the new approach is to improve the efficiency of interviews by allowing the integration of a variety of attributes and considering information relating to the purpose underlying the choice (Pelz 2012). According to data provided by Sawtooth Software, ACBC is currently the most advanced method of its kind. It helps to provide information on how people make decisions concerning complex products and services. ACBC is ideally suited to analyses involving a low number of cases and was therefore chosen in conjunction with this study.

A total of 57 purchasers took part in the conjoint analysis, all of whom came from German industrial enterprises and were recruited through a deliberate selection process. Thirty-two of these purchasers completed the survey. The response rate was 56 %. Amongst participants in the completed data sets, 72 % were male and 28 % were female.

In order to ensure the comparability of the survey results over several industries, the conjoint analysis was interpreted across the four business types—equipment business, product business, supply business and system business (Backhaus and Voeth 2010). A fictitious purchasing scenario was created for each business type. The four purchasing situations, specific to each business type, were presented to each of the purchasers equally. The aim here was for each test person to make an evaluation based on their own general purchasing expertise, irrespective of their actual purchasing activities. The three variables "price", "brand" and "product quality" were defined as attributes to be investigated. All attributes were assigned three characteristic options each—these are provided and explained in more detail in

Table 1 Attribute structure of the conjoint analysis

Attribute/variable	Characteristic	Description
1. Price	Price is above the average (+5 %)	Price corresponds to the industry average +5 %
	Average price	Price corresponds to the industry average
	Price is below the average (−5 %)	Price corresponds to the industry average −5 %
2. Brand	Top brand	A very famous, strong brand with an excellent reputation and high recognisability that evokes very positive associations
	Average brand	A good brand with a good reputation and average recognisability that evokes positive associations
	Weak brand	A little known brand with no noteworthy reputation that evokes no specific associations
3. Perceived, measurable product quality	A quality	A first-class product that satisfies the requirements in full and is above the industry average
	B quality	A good product that satisfies the requirements as is typical for the industry
	C quality	A product that just satisfies the requirements to an acceptable level

Table 1. The variables and their characteristics were adapted to the respective situation for each scenario and business type, and suitable examples and descriptions generated.

The percentage differences in alternative pricing characteristics were transferred equally to all four business-type-specific scenarios in order to ensure optimum comparability. The characteristic differences in the verbal description of the attributes "quality" and "brand" were also distributed as equally as possible amongst the four scenarios.

In order to discover whether certain features and attributes of the individual purchasers are a decisive factor when it comes to market-related purchasing in the industrial sector and whether in principle, the differences in these attributes result in different purchasing behaviour patterns, the following socio-demographic attributes were devised:

- Length of time/duration participant has worked in purchasing
- Previous role in the company, outside of purchasing
- Academic qualifications
- Age
- Gender

As a first step, the data was analysed in Sawtooth using the 32 complete data sets. The individual benefit values and standard deviation of the variables "price", "brand" and "product quality" and their characteristics were analysed. The relative importance of the variables and characteristics across all four business types was also determined. The Hierarchical Bayes Evaluation was used to evaluate the parameters. Intersections with the collected purchaser data were performed in SPSS.

Results

H1: Brands significantly influence the purchasing decisions of purchasers in industrial enterprises.

This hypothesis sets out to determine whether the brand contributes to a reduction in uncertainty, including in the B2B sector. To verify this hypothesis, it was necessary to identify a clear relative importance of the variable "brand". To this end, the relative importance of the three variables over the four scenarios was added up and then divided by four. This produced the relative importance of the variables for each of the four business types. Table 2 provides the calculated values. Across all four business types, the brand accounted for up to 22 % of the decision to purchase the product, constituting a clear brand influence. In the equipment, product and supply business, the relative importance of the brand came second only to the price. H1 can be affirmed. In light of this study design, brands have an important influence on the purchasing decisions of purchasers in the B2B sector.

H2: The importance of the brand is dependent on the business type.

To verify this hypothesis, the results of the relative importance for the variable "brand" were compared across the four business types. Figure 1 shows that the brand

Table 2 Results of the conjoint analysis: significance of attributes and standard deviation ($N=32$)

	Average importance	Standard deviation
Equipment business		
Price	27.02657	12.17196
Brand	25.56914	8.36146
Product quality	47.40430	13.29307
Product business		
Price	30.96930	7.54643
Brand	26.09259	14.58285
Product quality	42.93812	13.06648
Supply business		
Price	22.34672	7.26207
Brand	17.74622	5.97342
Product quality	59.90706	7.49424
System business		
Price	42.46447	13.34532
Brand	17.65740	6.27982
Product quality	39.87812	13.46054

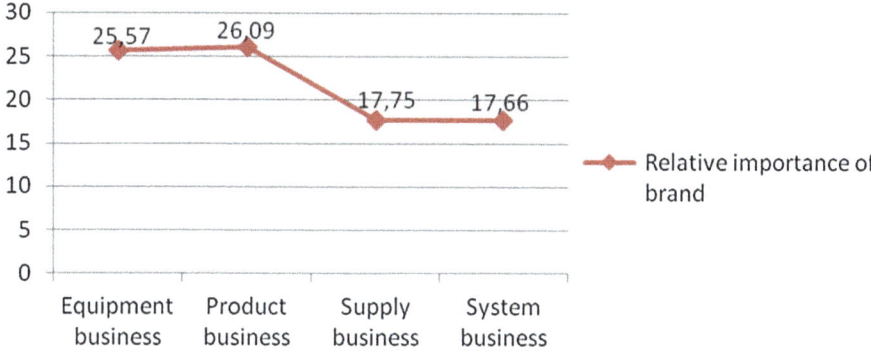

Fig. 1 Comparison of market significance for alternative business types

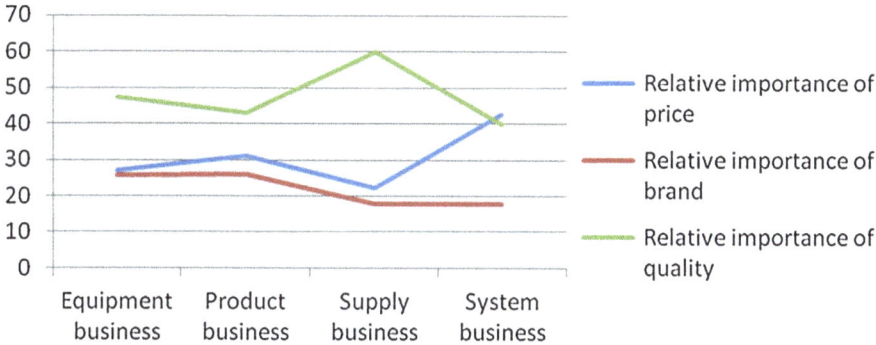

Fig. 2 Relative importance of the variables "price", "brand" and "product quality" across all business types

plays a very significant role in purchasing decisions in the product and equipment business. The values for the supply and system business are considerably lower. The importance of the brand shows clear variation depending on the business type.

Accordingly, there is a dependence between the business type and the importance of the brand when it comes to purchasing decisions. H2 is affirmed. Figure 2 summarises the relative importance of the variables "price", "brand" and "product quality" across all four business types.

H3: The influence of the brand on the purchasing decision weakens as the purchaser's professional experience increases.

To verify this hypothesis, the results of the relative importance of the brand in the individual business types were plotted against "job duration" data, detailing the purchasers' professional experience. Figure 3 shows the results of this. From this descriptive evaluation, it follows that: the influence of the brand rises and falls with employment duration in all business types, with no discernible pattern. H3 is therefore rejected.

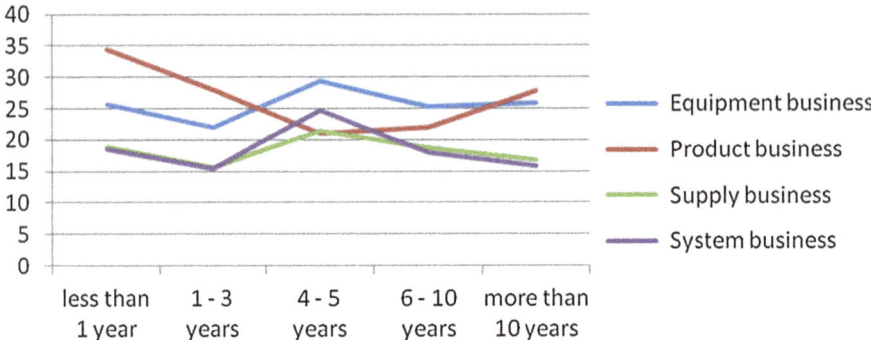

Fig. 3 Relative importance of the brand with regard to professional experience

Conclusion

The three hypotheses were investigated as part of this study. Using the results of the conjoint analysis, it has been possible to confirm that the brand plays a significant role in the B2B sector when it comes to decision-making by industrial purchasers.

Taking all business types into account, the key criterion is product quality and not price, which only occupies second place. Third place is occupied by the brand, which also demonstrated a significant influence on decision-making. In the equipment, product and system business, the relative importance of the brand had a value similar to that of price. There is no relation between the importance of the brand and the professional experience of the purchaser, rather the relevance of the brand is dependent on the business type and the novelty of the purchasing situation.

The study also indicates that a wholly rational decision-making process that is chiefly focussed on price cannot be assumed in the B2B sector.

In this study, we were able to establish a basis for investigating a selected aspect within the purchasing process: the relevance of brands in comparison to the factors "price" and "quality". Reasoning here took a very general or abstract form. For additional investigations, it would, in the first instance, be possible to supplement additional decision attributes in order to considerably expand the scope and complexity of the study. Secondly, it would be conceivable to narrow the considered decision attributes with regard to special procurement objects.

References

Backhaus, K., & Sabel, T. (2004). Markenrelevanz auf Industriegütermärkten. In K. Backhaus & M. Voeth (Eds.), *Handbuch Industriegütermarketing* (pp. 779–798). Wiesbaden, Germany: Gabler.

Backhaus, K., & Voeth, M. (2010). *Industriegütermarketing*. Munich, Germany: Vahlen.

Baier, D., & Brusch, M. (2009). *Conjointanalyse. Methoden, Anwendungen und Praxisbeispiele*. Berlin: Springer.

Baumgarth, C., & Douven, S. (2006). Business-to-business-Markenforschung. Entwicklungsstand und Forschungsausblick. In A. Strebinger, W. Mayerhofer, & H. Kurz (Eds.), *Werbe- und Markenforschung. Meilensteine—State of the Art—Perspektiven* (pp. 138–168). Wiesbaden, Germany: Gabler.

Baumgarth, C. (2004). Markenführung von B-to-B-Marken. In K. Backhaus & M. Voeth (Eds.), *Handbuch Industriegütermarketing* (pp. 799–824). Wiesbaden, Germany: Gabler.

Becker, G. (1992). *The economic way of looking at life*. Chicago: University of Chicago Press.

Brown, B., Zablah, A., Bellenger, D., & Johnston, W. (2011). When do B2B brands influence the decision making of organizational buyers? An examination of the relationship between purchase risk and brand sensitivity. *International Journal of Research in Marketing, 28*(3), 194–204.

Godefroid, P., & Pförtsch, W. (2009). *Business-to-business-marketing*. Herne, Germany: Kiehl.

Homburg, C., Jensen, O., & Richter, M. (2008). Sind Marken im Industriegüterbereich relevant? In H. H. Bauer, F. Huber, & C.-M. Albrecht (Eds.), *Erfolgsfaktoren der Markenführung. Knowhow aus Forschung und Management* (pp. 399–414). Vahlen, Germany: Munich.

Homburg, C., & Krohmer, H. (2006). *Marketingmanagement. Strategie—Instrumente—Umsetzung—Unternehmensführung*. Wiesbaden, Germany: Gabler.

Köhler, R. (2004). Tendenzen des Markenartikels aus der Perspektive der Wissenschaft. In M. Bruhn (Ed.), *Handbuch Markenartikel* (pp. 2061–2089). Stuttgart, Germany: Schäffer-Poeschel.

Krämer, C. (1993). *Marketingstrategien für Produktionsgüter*. Wiesbaden, Germany: DUV.

Kuhn, K. A., Alpert, F., & Pope, N. K. (2008). An application of Keller's brand equity model in a B2B context. *Qualitative Market Research, 11*, 40–58.

Kunz, V. (2004). *Rational choice*. Frankfurt, Germany: Campus.

Low, G., & Fullerton, R. (1994). Brands, brand management, and the brand manager system: A critical-historical evaluation. *Journal of Marketing Research, 31*, 173–190.

Lynch, J., & de Chernatony, L. (2007). Winning hearts and minds. Business-to-business branding and the role of the salesperson. *Journal of Marketing Management, 23*, 123–135.

Meffert, H., Burmann, C., & Kirchgeorg, M. (2008). *Marketing. Grundlagen Marktorientierter Unternehmensführung*. Wiesbaden, Germany: Gabler.

Pelz, J. (2012). *Aussagefähigkeit und Aussagewilligkeit von Probanden bei der Conjoint-Analyse*. Wiesbaden, Germany: Gabler.

Scharf, A., Schubert, B., & Hehn, P. (2009). *Marketing. Einführung in Theorie und Praxis*. Stuttgart, Germany: Schäffer-Poeschel.

Simon, H. (1993). *Homo Rationalis. Die Vernunft im menschlichen Leben*. Frankfurt, Germany: Campus.

Teichert, T., Sattler, H., & Völckner, F. (2008). Traditionelle Verfahren der Conjoint-Analyse. In A. Herrmann, C. Homburg, & M. Klarmann (Eds.), *Handbuch Marktforschung. Methoden—Anwendungen—Praxisbeispiele* (pp. 651–685). Wiesbaden, Germany: Gabler.

Voeth, M., & Brinkmann, J. (2004). Abbildung multipersonaler Kaufentscheidungen. In K. Backhaus & M. Voeth (Eds.), *Handbuch Industriegütermarketing* (pp. 351–368). Wiesbaden, Germany: Gabler.

Voeth, M., & Rabe, C. (2004). Industriegütermarken. In M. Bruhn (Ed.), *Handbuch Markenartikel* (pp. 75–94). Stuttgart, Germany: Schäffer-Poeschel.

Völckner, F., Sattler, H., & Teichert, T. (2008). Wahlbasierte Verfahren der Conjoint-Analyse. In A. Herrmann, C. Homburg, & M. Klarmann (Eds.), *Handbuch Marktforschung. Methoden—Anwendungen—Praxisbeispiele* (pp. 687–711). Wiesbaden, Germany: Gabler.

Webster, F., & Keller, K. (2004). A roadmap for branding in industrial markets. *Brand Management, 11*-5, 388–422.

Factors Determining Channel Selection in the German Trades Sector: An Analysis of Power Tool Purchases

Benjamin Österle and Marc M. Kuhn

Abstract Revenues from E-commerce for businesses in the B2B sector are rising as part of multichannel marketing, the use of different information, communication, and revenue channels. This trend can also be observed in the market for power tools for professional use. The consumer goods sector has already been subject to far-reaching studies regarding the reasons for the choice between online and offline channels, including research in different phases of the purchasing process. In industrial goods marketing, by contrast, the reasons for this choice are less well known. Power tools belong to those product groups in the industrial goods sector that show clear parallels to B2C business.

The present study therefore takes approaches for investigating the determinants of channel selection from the B2C sector and applies them to the B2B sector. The study develops hypotheses on the reasons for the choice of channel based on inherent characteristics of various sales channels, the manifestation of channel-relevant shopping motives among customers and of course the final decision of the B2B customer for a certain channel. These are then tested using a discriminant analysis using customers of the brand Festool as an example.

Keywords Channel selection • Shopping motives • B2B • Wholesale • Power tool industry

B. Österle (✉) • M.M. Kuhn
Baden-Württemberg Cooperative State University Stuttgart, Stuttgart, Germany
e-mail: benjamin.oesterle@dhbw-stuttgart.de; marc.kuhn@dhbw-stuttgart.de

© Academy of Marketing Science 2016
L. Petruzzellis, R.S. Winer (eds.), *Rediscovering the Essentiality of Marketing*,
Developments in Marketing Science: Proceedings of the Academy of Marketing
Science, DOI 10.1007/978-3-319-29877-1_9

Introduction

By their very nature, different sales channels have various characteristics inherent to them (Ehrlich 2011). The channels "in-store retail" and "internet" display opposing inherent characteristics, which can offer the customer clear advantages or disadvantages for choosing such a channel, depending on his/her interests (Vijayasarathy 2002; Schögel 2012). In-store retailers, for example, offer customers the opportunity for direct interaction and communication with staff and other customers, along with a fully multi-sensual product experience. The online channel, by contrast, offers a virtually unlimited product range and is accessible anywhere and at any time.

Shopping motives can generally be defined as the goal-oriented motivation of a customer, which they seek to satisfy through the purchase (Schröder 2005). Shopping motives have been studied as a concept since the 1970s (Tauber 1972). They became well known as a construct in the context of "shopping preference theory" in a study by Sheth on general customer behavior (Sheth 1981). They are considered an important influencing factor and have been analyzed in many studies on online-related customer behavior (Schramm-Klein et al. 2007). It is noticeable that the research has thus far failed to establish a generally accepted catalog of shopping motives. Instead, there exist various systematization approaches that tend to focus on channel-related characteristics or psychographic characteristics of the customer, depending on the background of the approach (Schramm-Klein et al. 2007). However, two recent investigations of shopping motives related to channel selection are particularly relevant for this study: Schroeder and Zaharia (2008) and Schramm-Klein et al. (2007). Both studies investigate different manifestations of shopping motives and their effects on the choice of channel, focusing on multichannel retailers in Germany. The shopping motives relevant for the choice of channel that they identified can be summarized as follows (Ehrlich 2011):

- Convenience

  - Speed or ease of the purchasing process
  - Good accessibility/availability of the channel

- Product risk aversion

  - Personal product experience
  - Personal communication with sellers/other customers
  - Large selection of products

- Transaction risk aversion

  - Risk related to delivery (too late)
  - Risk related to billing/data security

- Price orientation

  - Lowest total price possible
  - High discounts

As society becomes increasingly digital and the internet expands together with channel-related barriers to switching, such as the long-term familiarity of older demographic segments with in-store purchase or their limited familiarity of using computers or the internet (Ehrlich 2011), we can assume that age also plays a role in the choice of purchase channels among tradesmen.

Another potentially relevant characteristic is the size of the trade business. This is due to the fact that the trades sector in particular is overwhelmingly made up of small businesses (Statistisches Bundesamt 2013). As a result, purchasing processes are less formalized, instead subject to the common everyday pattern, i.e., increasing purchases in online channels. The choice of in-store purchase would be more logical for larger trade businesses, due to the higher degree of formalization in the purchasing process and for required services. For this reason, this study also examines whether the size of a business has an influence on the tradesman's choice of channel.

Research Question and Hypotheses

Based on the inherent channel characteristics outline, as well as shopping motives and customer characteristics relevant for channel selection, the central research question is as follows:

"What are the reasons for the selection of purchase channel among tradesmen when purchasing power tools?"

In their investigation of customer migration in a B2B context from in-store purchase to online channels, Cao et al. found significant advantages in favor of online channels for the constructs of "convenience" and "pricing," with in-store retailers being valued higher for "order completion" (Cao et al. 2007). This corresponds with the assumptions drawn from the channel characteristics. The construct of "order completion" includes the duration of delivery, the trust in the receipt of delivery, and the perceived security in payment processing. Therefore, this construct is comparable to that of transaction risk aversion. Due to logical considerations, it is assumed that for the motive product risk aversion, the offline channels have advantages over online channels thanks to the possibility of personal interaction between buyers and sellers, along with the personal product experience.

This results in the following hypotheses that were tested among German customers of the company Festool:

H_1: "A high convenience orientation corresponds with greater use of online channels"

H_2: "A strong desire for achieving the lowest price possible corresponds with greater use of online channels"

H_3: "A strong desire for avoiding product risk corresponds with greater use of offline channels"

H_4: "A strong desire for avoiding transaction risk corresponds with greater use of offline channels"

H_5: *"Low age corresponds with greater use of online channels"*
H_6: *"Small business size corresponds with greater use of online channels"*

Research Methodology

The aforementioned hypotheses on channel selection among tradesmen are tested on the basis of a standardized online survey. The study populations are all tradesmen active in the Federal Republic of Germany. The unit of investigation was selected as a random, conscious partial census, as on the one hand, 1198 Festool customers who purchased a power tool in 2013 and who had not participated in another study group were contacted personally via e-mail and on the other, the survey was shared on Festool's business page on the social networking site Facebook, thus making it accessible to the brand's approx 62,000 "fans." This study is also limited to Festool's target groups in the joining/carpentry, painting/varnishing, and automotive sectors and is as such not representative of the trades sector as a whole.

A total of 492 questionnaires were completed by the test respondents in the survey period from January 17th 2014 to January 22nd 2014. The publication of the survey in social networks also led to private end users participating in the questionnaire. These are not covered in the further considerations in this study.

After being adjusted for non-usable data records, there is a sample of 195 questionnaires answered by tradesmen for further assessment.

All questions relate to the most recent purchase of a power tool, in order to design the questionnaires in the most cognitively simple way for the respondents. In addition to the question on the chosen purchasing channel, the first section of the survey also included general questions on this purchase, such as when it took place, which brand was purchased, and whether the respondent had previously owned a product of this brand, in order to provide an introduction to the topic.

In the second section of the questionnaire, a matrix question surveyed manifestations of the four previously described shopping motives, using a 5-stage Likert scale with the poles "Disagree strongly" and "Agree strongly," with two or three items per motive. This used items from different authors which were deemed by factor analysis to be relevant to the choice of channel. The items were either translated from English where required and the tense adjusted to the question or formulated based on the source itself. The following items, for example, were drawn upon to measure the construct "convenience":

- Minimum effort in the purchase was important for me (e.g., short journey, no detour required) (Böhm 2006)
- It was very important to me that I could purchase at a time that convenient for me (Böhm 2006)
- It was very important to me that the purchases proceeded quickly (Schramm-Klein et al. 2007)

The Likert scale described above for measuring motives and testing the hypotheses H_1–H_4 employs interval scaling (Backhaus et al. 2006). The information provided by the respondents on age is also on the interval scale level and the information on business size for testing hypotheses H_6 is ratio-scaled. Therefore, all independent variables of hypotheses H_1–H_6 achieve the metric scale level, while the dependent variable, i.e., the chosen purchase channel, is nominally scaled.

Analysis

As a structurally testing, multi-variant procedure, discriminant analysis is suitable for this study due to the scale level. It can be used to both analyze the group differences in a sample and use these differences to correspondingly classify elements in a new sample (Backhaus et al. 2006). This analysis is performed using the discriminant analysis function in SPSS. Performing this discriminant analysis requires, however, that seven mathematical conditions are met (Sherry 2006):

1. There must be at least two exclusive groups
2. One group must have at least two elements
3. There may be any number of independent variables, as long as this is lower than the number of elements in the smallest group
4. The independent variables are measured at least on the interval scale level
5. The independent variable is a linear combination of other independent variables
6. The independent variables exhibit a normal distribution for each group
7. The covariance matrices for both groups are approximately identical

Prerequisites 1, 2, and 3 are met, as the study is based on two groups: online and offline purchasers, each group includes more than two elements and the number of independent variables (six, see hypothesis) is lower than the number of elements in the smallest group (50 online purchasers, see Table 1).

Prerequisite 4, the interval scale level of the independent variables is, as already described, assumed for the shopping motives variables measured using Likert scales. The size of the business is measured on a ratio scale level, as well as that for age, measured by year of birth. Prerequisite 4 is therefore also met, as is prerequisite 5, as none of the independent variables represent a linear combination of the others.

Prerequisite 6, the multi-variant normal distribution of the independent variables for each group, was approximately determined with a graphic procedure for determining the single-variant normal distribution using bar charts, box plots, and Q–Q plots. The single-variant normal distribution is an insufficient but necessary condition for the multi-variant normal distribution (Nimon 2012). However, as discriminant analysis represents a robust process against breaching this prerequisite if the breach is more due to lopsidedness than outliers, and a high degree of robustness can be assumed when at least 20 elements are represented in the smallest group with a low number of 5 or fewer independent variables (Tabachnick and Fidell 2013), the author of the present study applies this process for analysis of the multi-variant

Table 1 Mean values and standard deviations of the independent variables in the channels online and offline

Channel	Index	Convenience	Prod. risk aver.	Price orientation	Trans. risk aver.	Year of birth	Business size
Offline	Mean value	3.7310	3.9080	3.6793	4.3345	1974.18	5.70
	N	145	145	145	145	145	145
	Standard deviation	.93648	.84390	1.06829	.79507	11.213	11.029
Online	Mean value	3.8600	2.5867	3.9200	4.2300	1976.46	2.88
	N	50	50	50	50	50	50
	Standard deviation	1.00134	.85332	.92229	.79031	10.286	3.520
Total	Mean value	3.7641	3.5692	3.7410	4.3077	1974.76	4.97
	N	195	195	195	195	195	195
	Standard deviation	.95258	1.02331	1.03588	.79314	11.002	9.743

normal distribution. For the shopping motive, this graphic analysis shows deviation from single-variant normal distribution in transaction risk aversion and particularly clearly in business size. For this reason, a variable transformation was performed for these two variables (Tabachnick and Fidell 2013). Even after the variable transformation, however, the bar charts show clear optical deviations from the normal distribution and a Shapiro-Wilks test indicates significance, which led to both the "transaction risk aversion" and business size variables not being included in the discriminant analysis.

The hypotheses *H4: "A strong desire for avoiding transaction risk corresponds with greater use of offline channels"* and *H6: "Small business size corresponds with greater use of online channels"* and their null hypotheses therefore cannot be examined more closely.

Prerequisite 7 for the performance of a discriminant analysis, the homogeneity of the variance-covariance matrices, can be tested in the discriminant analysis using the Box M test (Sherry 2006). The test, as can be seen in Table 2, is not significant, meaning that prerequisite 7 is also fulfilled.

Complying with these prerequisites for the discriminant analysis, it is possible to use the Wilks' Lambda indicator and the percentage of the correct classification to identify the quality of a discriminant function, as well as use the standardized discriminant coefficients to identify the discriminatory significance of the individual characteristic variables.

When performing the incremental discriminant analysis, those variables that most minimize the quality criterion Wilks' Lambda in the respective step are included one after another in the analysis, as long as the associated significance level (F probability) is smaller than a given F probability (PIN). Conversely, a variable is eliminated if the limit value for the significance level (POUT) is exceeded. The values for PIN and POUT in this case are .05 and .10, respectively.

Table 2 Results of Box-M test

Box-M		1.569
F	Approximate value	.515
	df1	3
	df2	140797.103
	Significance	.672

Table 3 Variables entered in the discriminant analysis

Step		Tolerance	Significance of F-value for exclusion	Wilks' Lambda
1	Prod. risk aver.	1.000	.000	
2	Prod. risk aver.	.918	.000	.990
	Price orientation	.918	.000	.680

Table 4 Variables not entered in the discriminant analysis

Step		Tolerance	Minimum tolerance	Significance of F-value for exclusion	Wilks' Lambda
0	Convenience	1.000	1.000	.410	.996
	Prod. risk aver.	1.000	1.000	.000	.680
	Price orientation	1.000	1.000	.157	.990
	Year of birth	1.000	1.000	.207	.992
1	Convenience	.962	.962	.026	.663
	Price orientation	.918	.918	.000	.638
	Year of birth	1.000	1.000	.331	.677
2	Convenience	.895	.854	.196	.633
	Year of birth	.979	.899	.655	.638

Results

Tables 3 and 4 show which variables were investigated in which step, due to the aforementioned criteria. We can recognize here that among the shopping motives in this study, only product risk aversion and the desire for the lowest possible price contribute to the discrimination of the groups.

The results from Table 5 show that the discriminant function with an error probability of $p < 0.01$ is statistically significant. Wilks' Lambda is a benchmark of quality for the discriminant function, which here has a value of .638. It describes the proportion of the variation explained by the discriminant function (Sherry 2006), which here is 1−.638, i.e., a value of 36.2 % explained variation.

Table 6 shows that 84.6 % of the originally grouped cases were correctly classified by the discriminant function. In a random allocation, this hit ratio would be 74.5 %, due to the uneven size of the two groups. In combination with values for Wilks' Lambda, this data allows us to recognize that although the function separates

Table 5 Discriminant analysis quality criterion Wilks' Lambda

Test of function(s)	Wilks' Lambda	Chi-squared	df	Significance
1	.638	86.168	2	.000

Table 6 Classification results of discriminant function

			Forecast group membership		
		Channel	Offline	Online	Total
Original	Number	Offline	122	23	145
		Online	7	43	50
	%	Offline	84.1	15.9	100.0
		Online	14.0	86.0	100.0

84.6 % of originally grouped cases were correctly classified

Table 7 Group centroids of the discriminant analysis

	Function
Channel	1
Offline	.440
Online	−1.275

the two groups online and offline well, the explained variation of 36.2 % means that, in addition to the price and product risk aversion, other factors must play an important role in the tradesmen's choice of channel.

H_1: *"A high convenience orientation corresponds with greater use of online channels"*

H_5: *"Low age corresponds with greater use of online channels"*

As no discriminatory significance in the choice of channel could be determined in this study for the factors convenience and year of birth, H1 and H5 must be discarded.

H_2: *"A strong desire for achieving the lowest price possible corresponds with greater use of online channels"*

H_3: *"A strong desire for avoiding product risk corresponds with greater use of offline channels"*

Tables 7 and 8 are used to test the hypotheses H_2 and H_3. The group centroids of the online and offline channels are displayed here, along with the standardized canonical discriminant function coefficients for the shopping motives of product risk aversion and price orientation. Using the standardized canonical discriminant function coefficients, we can see that product risk aversion has a greater discriminatory significance than price (see Table 8). Using the positive indicator of the coefficients and the offline channel group centroid, the null hypothesis of H_3 can be discarded with an error probability of $p < 0.01$ and H_3 therefore viewed as confirmed.

Table 8 Standardized canonical discriminant function coefficients		Function
	Motive	1
	Prod. risk aver.	1.034
	Price orientation	−.431

The situation is similar for the null hypothesis of H_2 when the discriminant coefficients for the price motive and the online channel group centroid are considered. The centroid lies at −1.275 (see Table 7), the discriminant coefficient of the price motive is −0.431 (see Table 8). H_2 is therefore also considered confirmed.

Conclusion and Limitations

The aim of the study was to investigate the discriminant factors of channel selection among tradesmen, using the example of a power tool purchase. The study showed that the shopping motive product risk aversion is responsible for the greatest differences between the groups offline and online purchasers. Price orientation represented a further, if less significant discriminatory characteristic. These results correspond with those of investigations in other B2B sectors (Cao et al. 2007) and the retail sector (Schramm-Klein et al. 2007).

Therefore, in an age of multichannel marketing and increasing e-commerce, in-store specialist retailers and other representatives of classic offline channels have an advantage that should not be underestimated, thanks to the possibility of experiencing the product "live" and the personal contact with purchasers. Against the background of a highly competitive market that is changing as the result of online competition, however, these retailers should still examine existing structures and processes. This is because price also plays a role in the choice of purchasing channel alongside product risk aversion and can potentially be the decisive factor if no in-store consultation is required. The task for operators of in-store channels in the power tools market, therefore, is to find the right mixture to ensure that their customers' various shopping motives are satisfied.

The present study is limited first of all by the fact that no sample could be taken that is relevant for the tradesmen population in Germany. Instead, the majority of the respondents came from a joinery or carpentry background. In addition, the sample was selected consciously based on Festool's customer database.

Furthermore, as described above, there are other factors beyond those identified here that have an influence on the tradesmen' choice of purchase channel. The study is also limited to the purchase of power tools. Further studies focusing on other products and with a different sector distribution are required to gain a more comprehensive picture of the determinants of channel selection among tradesmen.

References

Backhaus, K., Erichson, B., Plinke, W., & Weiber, R. (2006). *Multivariate Analysemethoden: Eine anwendungsorientierte Einführung* (11, überarb. Aufl). Berlin [u.a.]: Springer.

Böhm, M. (2006). *Customer channel migration*. Dissertation. Retrieved January 11, 2014, from http://publikationen.ub.uni-frankfurt.de/frontdoor/index/index/docId/2153

Cao, Y., Gruca, T. S., & Klemz, B. R. (2007). An empirical study of B2B migration from traditional stores to the Internet. *Journal of Customer Behaviour, 6*(1), 75–92.

Ehrlich, O. (2011). *Determinanten der Kanalwahl im Multichannel-Kontext: Eine branchenübergreifende Untersuchung. Gabler Research*. Wiesbaden, Germany: Gabler Verlag/Springer Fachmedien Wiesbaden GmbH.

Nimon, K. F. (2012). Statistical assumptions of substantive analyses across the general linear model: A mini-review. *Frontiers in Psychology, 3*, 322.

Schögel, M. (2012). *Distributions management: Das Management der Absatzkanäle. Vahlens Handbücher*. München, Germany: Vahlen.

Schramm-Klein, H., Swoboda, B., & Morschett, D. (2007). Internet vs. brick-and-mortar stores: Analysing the influence of shopping motives on retail channel choice among internet users. *Journal of Customer Behaviour, 6*(1), 19–36.

Schröder, H. (2005). *Multichannel-retailing: Marketing in Mehrkanalsystemen des Einzelhandels* (1st ed.). Berlin: Springer.

Schröder, H., Zaharia, S. (2008). Linking multi-channel customer behavior with shopping motives: an empirical investigation of a German retailer Journal of Retailing and Consumer Services, 15(6) (2008), pp. 452–468.

Sherry, A. (2006). Discriminant analysis in counseling psychology research. *The Counseling Psychologist, 34*(5), 661–683.

Sheth, J. N. (1981). *An integrative theory of patronage preference and behavior. Faculty Working Paper.*

Statistisches Bundesamt. (2013). *Produzierendes Gewerbe: Unternehmen, tätige Personen und Umsatz im Handwerk—Jahresergebnisse*. Retrieved April 10, 2014, from https://www.destatis.de/DE/Publikationen/Thematisch/UnternehmenHandwerk/Handwerkszaehlung/UnternehmenPersonenUmsatz2040720107004.pdf?__blob=publicationFile

Tabachnick, B. G., & Fidell, L. S. (2013). *Using multivariate statistics* (6th ed.). Boston: Pearson Education.

Tauber, E. M. (1972). Why do people shop? *Journal of Marketing, 36*(4), 46–49.

Vijayasarathy, L. R. (2002). Product characteristics and Internet shopping intentions. *Internet Research, 12*(5), 411–426.

Value Co-creation in Project Exchange

Kamran Razmdoost and Hedley J. Smyth

Abstract Contemporary scholars define value creation as the process of extracting value from the use of resources by a customer (Grönroos and Voima 2013). Value co-creation is a unique form of value creation where two or more actors such as a customer and a provider create value in a direct interaction and through a joint process (Grönroos and Voima 2013). Direct interaction refers to the actors' actions that are merged into a collaborative, dialogical process (Grönroos and Gummerus 2014). In these definitions, value refers to value-in-use signifying that value is perceived by the customer in a specific use situation (Vargo and Lusch 2008) through "an interactive, relativistic preference experience" (Holbrook 1996, p. 138).

Existing research on value creation has focused on value in routine service exchanges where the resources are delivered by a provider (or providers) and value is created by the customer in use (Grönroos 2011; Keränen and Jalkala 2013; Salomonson et al. 2012). In this chapter we examine value co-creation in a unique service exchange defined as project exchange, where the resources and processes integrated in use are generated only for that use situation. Project is "a unique endeavour — in the sense of a one-off — undertaken to accomplish a defined objective" (Morris 2002, p. 83). Considering service as the application of resources for the benefit of another party (Vargo and Lusch 2008), we conclude that project is a service with a unique goal and application of resources. In project exchange uniqueness of project inhibits the creation of standardised systems, which prevents any indirect interactions (Grönroos and Gummerus 2014). In fact, indirect interaction is a consequence of routine service exchanges where a standardised resource can be integrated to meet a number of similar objectives. Therefore, in project exchanges (or an exchange of any part of project) value is always co-created through a direct interaction. We define project exchange as the integration of self and others' resources to achieve a unique goal.

A case study method, specifically an inductive approach, was applied (Eisenhardt 1989). In order to represent the complex nature of project exchange, three major international construction contractors and one main infrastructure client were studied via semi-structured interviews. The data collection focused on the interactions between the customer and the provider. The data analysis included identifying the experiential events where an interaction was occurred between the customer and pro-

K. Razmdoost (✉) • H.J. Smyth
University College London, London, UK
e-mail: k.razmdoost@ucl.ac.uk; h.smyth@ucl.ac.uk

© Academy of Marketing Science 2016
L. Petruzzellis, R.S. Winer (eds.), *Rediscovering the Essentiality of Marketing*,
Developments in Marketing Science: Proceedings of the Academy of Marketing
Science, DOI 10.1007/978-3-319-29877-1_10

vider. The analysis was verified through an iterative coding and reflection process conducted by two researchers. The results of this research show that value co-creation begins with the emergence of needs (or problem) awareness by the customer. In the value imagination phase, the customer and provider communicate potential value (i.e., "embedded in the resources offered by a service provider"; Grönroos and Gummerus 2014, p. 209) and value proposition respectively and achieve a value alignment where they agree to integrate a set of resources, processes and outcomes in the value actualization phase. Potential value and value proposition are dynamic and tend to move away from the alignment as a result of each actor's engagement in other service exchanges and contextual changes. Value realignment can facilitate value actualization as the actual events may not be predicted accurately in the value imagination phase. Value co-creation occurs through interrelated joint processes and by different individual actors within the different layers of the customer and provider businesses. Individual actors' continuous or discontinuous direct interactions in the customer–provider joint processes shape B2B direct interaction and B2B relationship quality. We posit that the notion of co-creation is interwoven with the nature of project exchange. Indeed, the uniqueness of a customer's goal leads to the need for integrating unique resources and processes. Development of such resources can only be performed in a joint process between the customer and the provider. In other words, the provider is unable to create those unique resources without an engagement with the customer. Therefore, value co-creation that is defined as an opportunity for value facilitation (Grönroos 2011) is in fact a move from routine service exchanges toward project exchange and unique problem-solving.

References available upon request

Factors Influencing Trust and Commitment in Business to Business Market: A Study on the Distribution Sector of Industrial Supplies

Mariana Regina Silva Linhares, José Marcos Carvalho de Mesquita, Kleinia Anjos Vianna, and Patricia de Cássia Gomes Moreira

Abstract In companies whose main customer is the enterprise, traditional marketing can no longer be applied as before, giving rise to Relationship Marketing, which allows the company to improve its market position and achieve more sustainable relationships with their customers. This study aimed to analyze the determinants of trust and commitment in B2B market of Minas Gerais State, Brazil. The literature review sought to contextualize the relationship model, Key Mediating Variables (KMV), Business to Business characteristics, relationship marketing and constructs: trust, commitment, perceived value, delivery reliability, seller relationship, flexibility, and product quality. It was a descriptive research with quantitative variables, totaling 105 valid interviews, through a self-administered electronic questionnaire. The collected data were analyzed using the Partial Least Squares method, allowing the work with a small sample. The software used was Smart PLS 2.0 with application of factor analysis techniques to estimate a series of interrelated relationships simultaneously and Structural Equation Modeling dependence. Furthermore, it was observed that the product quality has greater weight in the explanation of engagement with the trust relationship. And similarly, this construct is more important than the other (flexibility, perceived value, and delivery reliability) in explaining trust.

Keywords Relationship marketing • B2B marketplace • Trust • Commitment

M.R.S. Linhares (✉) • J.M.C. de Mesquita • K.A. Vianna • P. de C.G.Moreira
Universidade Fumec, Belo Horizonte, Brazil
e-mail: linharesmari@yahoo.com.br; jose.mesquita@fumec.br; kleiniascamilo@hotmail.com; pacgmo@hotmail.com

© Academy of Marketing Science 2016   55
L. Petruzzellis, R.S. Winer (eds.), *Rediscovering the Essentiality of Marketing*,
Developments in Marketing Science: Proceedings of the Academy of Marketing
Science, DOI 10.1007/978-3-319-29877-1_11

Introduction

Time has passed since Berry (1995) proposed the first references concerning relationship marketing concept; however, these ideas remain relevant, especially in a context dominated by increasingly selective consumers making decision about which organizations they will relate. A new competitive period has established rapidly itself in the business environment, and some traditional practices, in the market exchange relations, no longer produce the same results. Hence the demands to reevaluate costs and increase the delivered value to customers have become remarkable (Lovelock and Wright 2001; Zeithaml and Bitner 2000; Bitner 1995). Sheth et al. (2001, p. 658) *point out that for a customer to engage a purchase based on relationship, one needs to rely on the company and then to commit oneself to it.*

In the United States, various researchers have conducted researches addressing some variables considered critical to the development and maintenance of long-term relationships, such as: trust, commitment, cooperation, among others. However the multiplication of these studies in the world has also brought a variety of approaches and techniques for data collection and concept measurement which may be verified in researches of Anderson and Narus (1990), Bucklin and Sengupta (1993), Mohr and Spekman (1994), Morgan and Hunt (1994), Ganesan (1994), Wilson (1995), Boyle and Dwyer (1995), Zaheer and Venkatraman (1995), Mohr et al. (1996), Fontenot and Wilson (1997), Wilson and Vlosky (1997).

In the Brazilian case, the issue has not been studied consistently. There are few studies that seek to evaluate the B2B market in relationship marketing viewpoint. *Therefore, a key challenge for Brazilian researchers emerges, which is to identify and understand how antecedent and mediating variables influence relevant results of the relationship marketing, such as customer's loyalty, trust, and commitment in this specific market.*

So, the central focus of this study is to analyze the determinants of consumers' trust and consumers' commitment in the B2B market in the state of Minas Gerais, Brazil.

Based on this context, it is possible to ensure this research relevance concerning the academic dimension, because even operationalizing concepts already approached in relationship marketing literature, it was conducted in an unprecedented way, enabling an adaptation of antecedent constructs of trust and commitment suggested by Morgan and Hunt's (1994) relationship model, to the characteristics and variables of Brazilian B2B marketplace.

Literature Review

For a long time, it was considered that the key construct to predict consumers' loyal behaviors were satisfaction (Garbarino and Johnson 1999; Henard and Szymanski 2001); then studies on services have included quality (Parasuraman and Grewal 2000) and researches on relationship marketing included commitment and trust as key factors for predicting these behaviors (Morgan and Hunt 1994; Moorman et al. 1993).

The model suggested by Morgan and Hunt (1994), the Key Mediating Variables (KMV), proposes a commitment-trust theory, based on a study conducted among American automobile tire retailers. This model suggests trust and commitment as key variables. It considers as their antecedents, the relationship termination costs, relationship benefits, shared values, communication, and opportunistic behavior, and as their outcomes, acquiescence, propensity to leave, functional conflict, and decision-making uncertainty.

According to Morgan and Hunt (1994), commitment can be summarized as the partners' belief in keeping a valued relationship, guiding their actions to do so. The implicit picture appears with the fact that relationships based on trust are highly valued and actors will desire to engage themselves to a long-term commitment, making it clear that trust is crucial to it, emphasizing positive relationship aspects of both trust and commitment. They propose further that commitment, though it is a recent variable in the context of relationship marketing, it is the central idea in the social exchange literature. Mutual commitments cogitate the dimension of shared goals, incentives, and even contractual commitments.

Santos and Vargas (2002, p. 38) argue that "in an ongoing relationship, trust is associated with qualities such as consistency, competence, honesty, integrity, responsibility, and kindness, and it has a central role in promoting cooperation among the parts."

Kalafatis and Miller (1997) tested Morgan and Hunt's model (1994) in the UK health sector, applying it in a specific market supply of products to treat diabetes, seeking to develop it, adapt it, and propose changes to it.

As a result, these authors confirmed as antecedent concepts of commitment, relationship benefits, and shared values. Relationship termination cost concept, as a commitment antecedent, was not proven. Concerning trust, antecedent concepts of communication and opportunistic behavior were proven but shared value concept was not.

Lancastre and Lages (2006) evaluated also an adaptation of Morgan and Hunt's model (1994) in a relationship between a client and a supplier of the electronic B2B market. Research results indicated that, in the business to business e-market, cooperation is affected positively by relationship termination costs, by relationship practices and policies towards supplier, and by the information exchange and communication. Cooperation is negatively affected by product prices and by opportunistic behavior.

Characteristics Related to Business to Business Trade

Some characteristics related to its dimensions or sales competitive priorities by some authors will be mentioned:

Costs: According to Skinner (1996), low costs could allow low prices, helping the products competitiveness when they are offered in the market.

Quality: Hayes and Wheelwright (1984, p. 23) argue that quality is related to the product and process qualities, involving many factors related to customer satisfaction, such as after-sale services, and products without error, according to the characteristics defined by the project.

Flexibility: According to Moraes (2003), it is the ability to adapt to the changes that could happen on supply, demand, production process, employed technology in the production or other elements that permeate manufacturing environment.

Delivery reliability: Slack (1993) claims that concerning the extent that companies become more dependent on their supply chains to be on time, the assurance that orders will meet the agreed delivery date (delivery reliability) becomes a large value in their choice of suppliers.

Relationship: One of the most important discoveries on sale researches was the recognition that the key to a successful long-term contract is the buyer–seller relationship (Dwyer et al. 1987).

Perceived value: Sirdeshmukh et al. (2002) state that value is defined as the consumers' perception of the benefits minus the costs of maintaining an ongoing relationship with their provider.

Price: Bei and Chiao (2001) define price (from the consumer's point of view) what is renounced or what is sacrificed to obtain a product.

Hypothetical Research Model

Through the literature review, the hypothetical model was created based on Morgan and Hunt's commitment-trust model (1994), but considering as antecedent constructs of trust and relationship commitment, the following factors: perceived value, delivery reliability, relationship with salesperson, flexibility, and product quality, according to Fig. 1, in order to achieve this research purpose.

Sirdeshmukh et al. (2002) argue that customers' trust with providers of service is hypothesized to develop around two distinct aspects: trusting the company's frontline employees and trusting the company's policies and management practices. Therefore it is proposed:

H1: Perceived value positively influences customer's trust
H2: Perceived value positively influences customer's commitment

Lu (2000) conducted a research at a shipping company in China, and he identified a set of service and product aspects and after factorial analysis, those were grouped and called key success factor. Reliability was stressed as key success factor. Therefore there are the following hypotheses:

H3: Delivery reliability positively influences customer's trust
H4: Delivery reliability positively influences customer's commitment

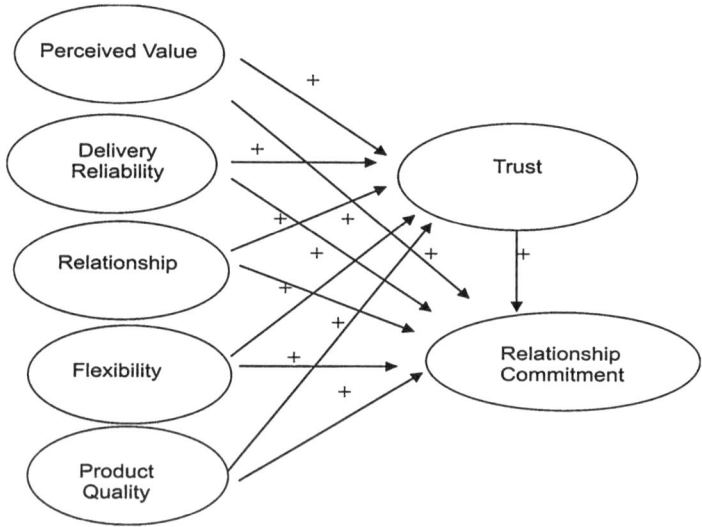

Fig. 1 Theoretical research model

According to Crosby and Stephens (1987), a total consumer satisfaction has three pillars: satisfaction with salesperson (contact person), the service nature, and the organization. Therefore, it is proposed that

H5: Relationship with salesperson positively influences customer's trust
H6: Relationship with salesperson positively influences customer's commitment

The current highly globalized context requires greater flexibility of organizations in order to keep pace with market demands, considering people as their main source of competitive advantage (Oliveira and Simonetti 2010, p. 56). Based on this reasoning, we present the following hypotheses:

H7: Flexibility positively influences customer's trust
H8: Flexibility positively influences customer's commitment

Deming (1990) emphasizes the importance of maintaining the product quality with the purpose of generating customer satisfaction with the product/service. This line of thought emerges as hypotheses.

H9: Product quality positively influences customer's trust
H10: Product quality positively influences customer's commitment

According to Morgan and Hunt (1994), the implicit image arises with the fact that relationships based on trust are so highly valued, that actors will wish to commit to long-term relationship, making it clear that trust is crucial to the relational commitment, emphasizing the positive relationship between trust and commitment. Thus arises the latter hypothesis.

H11: Trust positively influences commitment

Methodology

Considering the objectives and purposes of this study, we decided to conduct a descriptive and quantitative research. Data were collected through online questions sent to industry consumers in the State of Minas Gerais in Brazil. These customers have done business transactions with Nortel Industrial Supplies Company SA. The final questionnaire had 31 questions. Its first part had questions about the respondent's perceived value. The second part asked them about the supplier's delivery reliability. The third one consisted of questions on relationship between buyer and seller. The fourth asked about the company's flexibility construct. The fifth was about the company's product quality. The sixth one asked the respondent's trust concerning the company. Finally, the seventh section examined aspects surrounding the buyer's commitment to the company. An interval five-point scale ranging from "strongly disagree" (1) to "strongly agree" (5) was used and 105 questionnaires were collected.

This research data, the survey type, were treated by statistical procedures through structural equation modeling. For data analysis we used the Partial Least Squares (PLS) method, allowing to work with a small sample. The software used was the Smart PLS 2.0 M3.

Results

In this part we present and analyze the results from the consumers' questionnaire. We also discuss them after the statistical treatment of the research constructs and variables, and demonstrate the model validation and hypothesis evaluations.

The respondents were buyers of medium and large companies, located in Minas Gerais State, Brazil, which perform business transactions with Nortel Supplies Industrial Company SA, for over 7 years. They operate in many economic sectors, such as food, textile, machinery, and equipment. They have a monthly revenue higher than US$ 200,000.00 and more than 100 employees.

To test the theoretical model, we used the PLS method (Smart PLS 2.0), which is indicated in cases of small samples and deviations from normality, as suggested by Henseler and Wang (2009). Two indicators were excluded due to the low factor loading, 1.5 from perceived value and 1.5 from reliability delivery.

The measurement model was evaluated by reliability, convergent and discriminant validity. In the case of reliability, we used the composite reliability and the Cronbach's Alpha. As showed in Table 1, almost all of them showed values exceeding .7, except flexibility, but greater than .6, which is an acceptable value. For convergent validity, we used the average variance extracted (AVE), which should be higher than .5, value achieved for all constructs.

We used the Fornell and Larcker's proposition (1981) for the discriminant validity. In this method, the square roots of AVEs are obtained and their values are compared with the correlations among different constructs. When the AVE is greater

Table 1 Measurement model

	AVE	Composite reliability	Cronbach's alpha
Relationship commitment	.693	.918	.888
Delivery reliability	.557	.827	.710
Trust	.671	.910	.874
Flexibility	.739	.850	.646
Product quality	.537	.820	.704
Relationship	.578	.843	.752
Perceived value	.484	.818	.729

Table 2 Discriminant validity of constructs

	Relationship commitment	Delivery reliability	Trust	Flexibility	Product quality	Relation-ship	Perceived value
Relationship commitment	.832						
Delivery reliability	.393	.746					
Trust	.605	.708	.819				
Flexibility	.487	.646	.719	.860			
Product quality	.625	.607	.813	.606	.733		
Relationship	.454	.344	.570	.564	.615	.760	
Perceived value	.367	.492	.584	.535	.464	.398	.696

than the correlations, it can be stated that there is discriminant validity. This fact is confirmed by Table 2.

In order to assess the statistical significance of the results we used the *Bootstrap* method. This nonparametric method (it does not require a distribution of specific probability) permits to get a *t*-statistic with which we are able to evaluate whether the found coefficients are significantly different from zero. The results of the *t*-statistic to evaluate the significance of the trajectories were also obtained using *bootstrap* method, and they are shown in Table 3.

In this study we used a 1.96 cutoff, which means that the values for *t*-statistic above this level indicate that the respective coefficient is significantly different from zero. Then the model was estimated again, considering only the significant paths.

The second stage of a structural equation model validation, according to Henseler and Wang (2009), is based in evaluating the structural model. In this sense, the determination coefficient (R^2) was obtained for the relationship among delivery reliability, flexibility, product quality, relationship, and perceived value with trust. It was found the value of .782. R^2 coefficient works the same way as in the observed linear regression. That means the indication of explained variability of the dependent variable through independent variables. Thus, these constructs explained 78.2 % of trust variability which could be translated into a high explanatory power. Regarding commitment with relationship construct, the explanatory power of the antecedents, including trust, is 43.1 %.

Table 3 *t*-Statistic for the paths—full version

	Relationship commitment	Trust
Trust	2.01	
Delivery reliability	1.02**	2.60
Flexibility	.78**	2.28
Relationship	.30**	.40**
Perceived value	.15**	2.31
Product quality	2.16	5.43

**Nonsignificant paths at the level of 5 % of significance

Table 4 *t*-Statistic for the paths—final version

	Relationship commitment	Trust
Trust	2.048	–
Delivery reliability	–	3.23
Flexibility	–	3.39
Perceived value	–	2.76
Product quality	2.72	7.58

Based on the results shown in Table 4, we found that:

Hypothesis H1 (Perceived value positively influences consumer's trust) was confirmed, since it had a high explanatory power of the trust construct.

Both hypotheses H9 (Product quality positively influences customer's trust) and H10 (Product quality positively influences customer's commitment) actually proved to be significant enough for the two constructs: relationship commitment and trust. Therefore they have been confirmed.

Hypotheses H3 (Delivery reliability positively influences customer's trust) and H7 (Flexibility positively influences customer's trust) have also shown enough significance in the construct trust, hence their confirmations. Consequently, hypothesis H11 (Trust positively influences commitment) has also been confirmed, since compared to the relationship commitment construct, the explanatory power of these antecedents of trust constructs, plus the trust itself, explains 43.1 % of variability.

In Table 3, it can be verified that the hypotheses H2 (Perceived value positively influences customer's commitment), H4 (Delivery reliability positively influences customer's commitment), and H8 (Flexibility positively influences customer's commitment) were not significant for commitment to the relationship, so they were not accepted.

Hypotheses H5 (Relationship with salesperson positively influences customer's trust) and H6 (Relationship with salesperson positively influences customer's commitment) were also not accepted, since both of them were shown insignificant to commitment and trust constructs.

Final adjusted model is presented in Fig. 2. It is observed that the product quality (coefficient of .395) is more effective and influential in explaining relationship commitment than it is concerning trust. Likewise, that construct has more weight (.496) than the others (flexibility, perceived value, delivery reliability) in explaining trust.

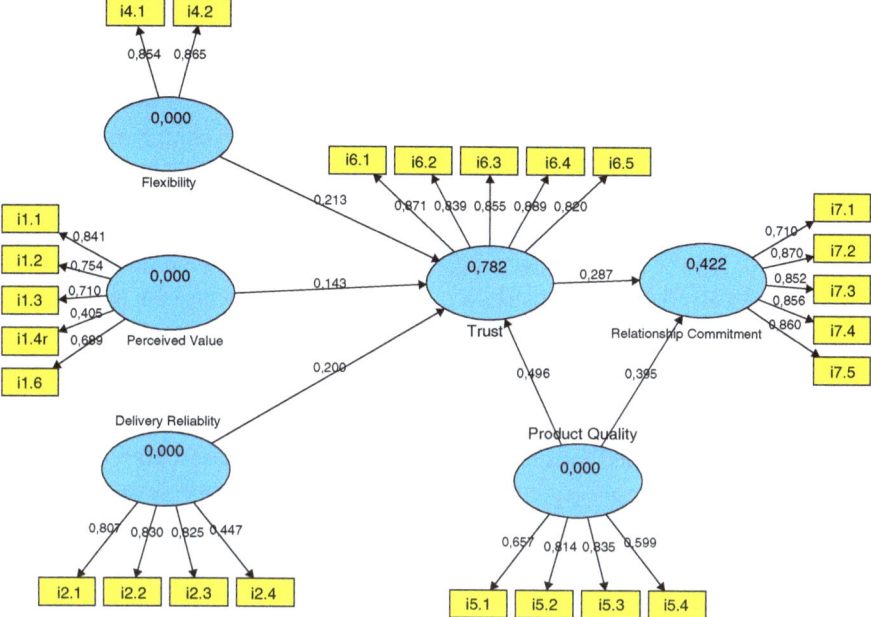

Fig. 2 Adjusted model

Conclusion

In this research we tested an adaptation of Morgan and Hunt's Commitment-Trust Model (1994), considering as antecedent constructs of trust and commitment with relationship: perceived value, delivery reliability, salesperson relationship, flexibility, and product quality.

Considering the research general objective, the hypotheses, H1, H3, H7, H9, H10, and H11, have been confirmed explaining 78.2 % of trust variability. It translates into a high explanatory power. Concerning commitment with relationship construct, the explanatory power of these antecedents constructs of trust, added trust itself, has explained 43.1 % of its variability.

An important result in this study is that through the confirmations of hypotheses H9 (Product quality positively influences consumer's trust) and H10 (Product quality positively influences consumer's commitment), this research has found that the product quality (coefficient equal to .395) has a stronger impact in explaining relationship commitment than trust.

Likewise, that construct has greater weight (.496) than the others (flexibility, perceived value, delivery reliability) in explaining trust. Thus, corroborating with Day (1999), who states that the quality is the most used factor to create value for the customer. This result proved contrary to the research results by the Gonçalves (2012), since it was not what was seen by the customers in 2011/2012, at least for customers at the graphic segment. For them, the quality and technical specification assistance also generate dissatisfaction. They are considered to be minimum required attributes to purchase and therefore they are mandatory.

Instead, H2 (Perceived value positively influences consumer's commitment), H4 (Delivery reliability influences positively consumer's commitment) and H8 (Flexibility positively influences consumer's commitment) have not been confirmed. We believe that this occurred because they have been presented much more significant with trust which precedes commitment, therefore corroborating with Oliveira et al. (2008), who pointed out that, in the B2B market, commitment shows value, and perceived quality, satisfaction, and trust as antecedents concepts and the propensity to loyalty as consequent concept.

Despite Crosby and Stephens (1987) stated that total consumer satisfaction has as its pillars the satisfaction with the salesperson (contact person), and similarly, the results found by Reis et al. (2005) suggest that trusting the company's salesperson influences the choices and intentions concerning future purchases. Hypotheses H5 (Relationship with the salesperson positively influences consumer's trust) and H6 (Relationship with the salesperson positively influences consumer's commitment) were not accepted, because they were not significant according to consumers' responses.

Moreover, this study addresses some relevant issues in the marketing relationship field applied to the industrial supply sector, including: (1) the focus in the context of relational exchanges among companies and (2) operationalization of constructs such as trust, commitment, perceived value, product quality, flexibility, and delivery reliability in the relational context.

Finally, this study sought to contribute to the development of marketing knowledge. It could be considered another step towards offering contributions to future researches on the topics of relationship marketing, commitment, and trust.

As managerial contributions, the results of this study may be valuable for some managers, suggesting how companies can build and sustain competitive advantage in the long run by building relationships with their clients grounded in factors that positively influence the trust and commitment.

One aspect revealed by the research which deserves attention of companies is the importance given by respondents to the product quality, so that it positively influences trust and commitment in the relationship. It should also be noted that the rejection of the majority of the hypotheses that had the factors directly influencing the relationship commitment brings us to the behavioral assumptions of transaction costs, which according to Azevedo (1997) are that economic agents are rational and narrowly opportunistic. The limited rationality prevents the elaboration of complete contracts that cover all possible phenomena during their execution.

One limitation was found in relation to the research universe, which generated a sample of 105 respondents. Furthermore, the questionnaire was limited to a particular market, Minas Gerais State, and treated as an assessment within a single company, making the data and features are specific to a particular local culture. Both limitations compromise the generalization capacity of the model. In face of this limitation, we suggest the reapplication of this work in other business contexts, whether involving products or services, or either for the same sector analyzed in different geographic region.

Research papers that seek longitudinal samples, with data collected using more than one method and the comparison of results among customers of various companies and economic sectors would be very interesting and useful.

Acknowledgment   We would like to acknowledge CAPES (Coordenação de Aperfeiçoamento de Pessoal de Nível Superior) for supporting the participation in the Conference.

References

Anderson, J., & Narus, J. (1990). A model of distributor's perspective of distributor manufacturer working relationships. *Journal of Marketing, 48*, 62–84.

Bei, L., & Chiao, Y. (2001). An integrated model for the effects of perceived product, perceived service quality, and perceived price fairness on consumer satisfaction and loyalty. *Journal of Consumer Satisfaction, Dissatisfaction and Complaining Behavior, 14*, 125–140.

Berry, L. (1995). Relationship marketing 01 services: Growing interest, emerging perspectives. *Journal of the Academy of Marketing Science, 23*, 4.

Bitner, M. (1995). Building service relationship: It's all about promises. *Journal of the Academy of Marketing Science, 23*(4), 246–251.

Boyle, B., & Dwyer, R. (1995). Power, bureaucracy, influence and performance: Their relationships on industrial distribution channels. *Journal of Business Research, 32*, 189–200.

Bucklin, L., & Sengupta, S. (1993). Organizing successful co-marketing alliances. *Journal of Marketing, 57*, 32–46.

Crosby, L., & Stephens, N. (1987). Effects of relationship on satisfaction, retention, and prices & on the life insurance industry. *Journal of Marketing Research, 24*, 404–411.

Day, S. G. (1999). *A dinâmica da estratégia competitiva*. Rio de Janeiro, Brazil: Campus.

Deming, W. E. (1990). *Qualidade: A revolução da administração* (Tradução de Clave Comunicações e Recursos Humanos). Rio de Janeiro, Brazil: Marques-Saraiva.

Dwyer, F., Schurr, P., & Oh, S. (1987). Developing buyer-seller relationships. *Journal of Marketing, 51*(2), 11–27.

Fontenot, R., & Wilson, E. (1997). Relational exchange: A review of selected models for a prediction matrix of relationship activities. *Journal of Business Research, 39*, 5–12.

Fornell, C., & Larcker, D. (1981). Evaluating structural equation models with unobservable variables and measurement error. *Journal of Market Research, 18*, 39–50.

Ganesan, S. (1994). Determinants of long-term orientation in buyer-seller relationship. *Journal of Marketing, 2*(58), 1–19.

Garbarino, E., & Johnson, M. (1999). The different roles of satisfaction, trust, and commitment in customer relationships. *Journal of Marketing, 63*(2), 70–87.

Gonçalves, S. (2012). *Diferenciação como instrumento para obtenção de vantagem competitiva: Um estudo empírico no mercado B2B*. 2012. 113f. Dissertação (Mestrado em Administração)— Faculdade de Ciências Empresariais. Belo Horizonte, Brazil: Universidade Fumec.

Hayes, R., & Wheelwright, S. (1984). *Restoring our competitive edge: Competitive through manufacturing*. New York: Wiley.

Henard, D. H., & Szymanski, D. M. (2001). Why some new products are more successful than others. *Journal of Marketing Research, 38*(3), 362–376.

Henseler, J., & Wang, H. (Ed.). (2009, Springer). *Handbook of partial least squares: Concepts, methods and applications*. Heidelberg, Dordrecht, London, New York. (Springer Handbooks of Computational Statistics Series, v. II).

66 M.R.S. Linhares et al.

Kalafatis, S. P., & Miller, H. (1997). A re-examination of the commitment-trust theory. In H. G. Gemünden, T. Ritter, & A. Walter (Eds.), *Relationships and networks in international markets*. Great Britain: Pergamon.

Lancastre, A., & Lages, L. F. (2006). The relationship between buyer and a B2B emarketplace: Cooperation determinants in an electronic market context. *Industrial Marketing Management, 35*, 774–789.

Lovelock, P., & Wright, L. (2001). *Serviços: Gestão e marketing*. São Paulo, Brazil: Atlas.

Lu, C. S. (2000). Logistics services in Taiwanese maritime firms. *Transportation Research, 36*(Part E), 79–96.

Mohr, J., Fischer, R., & Nevin, J. (1996). Collaborative communication in interfirm relationships: Moderating effects of integrations and control. *Journal of Marketing, 60*, 103–115.

Mohr, J., & Spekman, R. (1994). Characteristics of partnership success: Partnership attributes, communication behavior and conflict resolution techniques. *Strategic Management Journal, 15*, 135–152.

Moraes, E. (2003). *Inovação e competitividade: uma proposta de redefinição da importância e escopo da inovação no modelo de estratégia competitiva baseado em competências cumulativas*. 2003. Dissertação (Mestrado em Administração)—Escola de Administração de Empresas de São Paulo da Fundação Getúlio Vargas, São Paulo.

Morgan, R., & Hunt, S. (1994). The commitment-trust theory of relationship marketing. *Journal of Marketing, 58*, 20–38.

Moorman, C., Deshpande, R., & Zaltman, G. (1993). Factors affecting trust in market research relationships. *Journal of Marketing, 57*, 81–101.

Oliveira, S. R. M., & Simonetti, V. M. M. (2010). Intuição e percepção no processo decisório de microempresa. *Campo Limpo Paulista: Revista da Micro e Pequena Empresa, 3*(3), 52–66.

Parasuraman, A., & Grewal, D. (2000). The impact of technology on the quality-value-loyalty chain: A research agenda. *Journal of the Academy of Marketing Science, 28*(1), 168–174.

Reis, W. O., Botelho, D., & de Almeida, A. R.D. (2005, December). *Confiança como antecedente da escolha de compra na indústria da construção civil*. In: 4th International Meeting of the Iberoamerican Academy of Management, pp. 8–11.

Santos, C., & Vargas, R. C. (2002). *Os Antecedentes da confiança do consumidor em episódios envolvendo reclamações sobre serviços*. In: 26 encontro da associação nacional dos programas de pós-graduação em administração, 2002, Salvador. Anais... Rio de Janeiro, Brazil.

Sheth, J., Mittal, B., & Newman, B. (2001). *Comportamento do cliente: Indo além do comportamento do consumidor*. São Paulo, Brazil: Atlas.

Sirdeshmukh, D., Singh, J., & Sabol, B. (2002). Consumer trust, value, and loyalty in relational exchanges. *Journal of Marketing, 1*(66), 15–37.

Skinner, W. (1996, Spring). Manufacturing strategy on the "s" curve. *Production and Operation Management, 5*(1), 1–14.

Slack, N. (1993). *Vantagem competitiva em manufatura: Atingindo competitividade nas operações industriais*. São Paulo, Brazil: Atlas.

Wilson, D. (1995, Fall). An integrated model of buyer-seller relationships. *Journal of the Academy of Marketing Science, 23*, 335–346.

Wilson, E., & Vlosky, R. (1997). Partnering relationship activities: Building theory from case study research. *Journal of Business Research, 39*, 59–70.

Zaheer, A., & Venkatraman, N. (1995). Relational governance as an interorganizational strategy: An empirical test of the role of trust in economic exchange. *Strategic Management Journal, 16*, 373–393.

Zeithaml, V., & Bitner, M. (2000). *Service marketing: Integrating customer focus across the firm*. Boston: Irwin McGraw-Hill.

Relationship Management Amidst OEM Demands for Supplier Price Cuts: A Cross-Industry Study

R. Mohan Pisharodi, John W. Henke Jr., and Ravi Parameswaran

Abstract Original equipment manufacturers (OEMs) often seek price cuts from their suppliers through an adversarial approach. At the same time, other OEMs have adopted a cooperative approach based on the belief that adversarial tactics will damage the possibility of good supplier–OEM working relationship. While price cuts can obviously improve OEM profitability in certain situations, researchers have also recognized the competitive advantages that can be gained through cooperation with suppliers. This research seeks to find out whether supplier–OEM relationships are adversely affected by OEM demand for price cuts. It seeks to find out whether demands for price concessions can coexist with good supplier–OEM relationships. A research model incorporating relationship constructs as well as a construct representing price pressure and another representing overall relations between the OEM and its supplier is tested using data collected from suppliers in three different industries. Structural equation modeling and analysis lead to the conclusion that price pressure can coexist with good relationships as long as OEMs and their suppliers take the managerial actions required for the maintenance of good working relationships. The general pattern of relationships among the research constructs was found to be substantially similar in the three industries, although cross-industry differences were observed.

R.M. Pisharodi (✉) • J.W. Henke Jr. • R. Parameswaran
Oakland University, Rochester, MI, USA
e-mail: pisharod@oakland.edu; henke@oakland.edu; paramesw@oakland.edu

© Academy of Marketing Science 2016
L. Petruzzellis, R.S. Winer (eds.), *Rediscovering the Essentiality of Marketing*,
Developments in Marketing Science: Proceedings of the Academy of Marketing
Science, DOI 10.1007/978-3-319-29877-1_12

Part III
Consumer Behavior

Conspicuous Consumption of Time: When Busyness and Lack of Leisure Time Become a Status Symbol

Silvia Bellezza, Neeru Paharia, and Anat Keinan

Abstract Movies, magazines, and popular TV shows such as "Lifestyles of the Rich and Famous" often highlight the abundance of money and leisure time among the wealthy. Consistent with this portrayal, Veblen's (1899/2007) theory of the leisure class suggests that the wealthy signal their ability to live idle lives by consuming time unproductively. At the same time though, complaining about being busy and about working all the time is an increasingly widespread phenomenon in modern society. On Twitter, celebrities publicly complain about "having no life" or "being in desperate need for a vacation" (Alford 2012). New York Times social commentator suggests that a common response to the question "How are you?" is "Busy!" (Kreider 2012). An analysis of holiday letters indicates that references to "crazy schedules" have increased since the 1960s (Schulte 2014). Contrary to the prediction that signaling time spent leisurely is associated with high status and wealth, we propose that signaling busyness has also become a status symbol and is regarded as an aspirational lifestyle.

We uncover an alternative kind of conspicuous consumption that operates by shifting the focus from the preciousness and scarcity of goods to the preciousness and scarcity of individuals. Our investigation of the underlying mechanisms reveals that positive status inferences in response to busyness are mediated by the perception that a busy person is in high demand and scarce. Six studies test our conceptual model. In study 1, our aim was to establish that a more-busy individual would be perceived to have more status than a less-busy individual, and to demonstrate a proposed mediating process of being in demand and scarce, while controlling for alternative mechanisms. In studies 2 and 3, we show how the public use of time-saving products (e.g., Bluetooth headset) and services (Peapod delivery) can signal status, regardless of how busy one truly is. In studies 4 and 5, we examine cultural values (the work ethic) and differences among cultures (i.e., North America vs. Europe) to

S. Bellezza (✉) • A. Keinan
Harvard Business School, Boston, MA, USA
e-mail: sbellezza@hbs.edu; akeinan@hbs.edu

N. Paharia
Georgetown University, Washington, DC, USA
e-mail: np412@georgetown.edu

© Academy of Marketing Science 2016
L. Petruzzellis, R.S. Winer (eds.), *Rediscovering the Essentiality of Marketing*,
Developments in Marketing Science: Proceedings of the Academy of Marketing
Science, DOI 10.1007/978-3-319-29877-1_13

demonstrate moderators and boundary conditions of the busyness effect. We find that Americans with values consistent with the protestant work ethic (Mirels and Garrett 1971) are very likely to interpret busyness as a positive signal of status. Moreover, we obtain a reversed effect in Europe, with busyness signaling lower status. Finally, in study 6, rather than measure the inferences an *observer* makes in regard to a busy person, we show that people aspire to be more like a busy individual, especially for status-conscious people, despite the view that busyness is associated with low levels of happiness.

Our work develops a novel and yet unexplored association between time expenditure and status inferences, and contributes to several streams of literature. First, we expand research on the decline of leisure time (Hochschild 1997; Rutherford 2001; Schor 1992) by systematically examining the conditions under which busyness operates as a status symbol. Second, while past research has primarily focused on how the expenditure of *money* has been a vehicle to signal status (Bellezza and Keinan 2014; Berger and Ward 2010; Griskevicius et al. 2007; Han et al. 2010; Rucker and Galinsky 2008; Wang and Griskevicius 2014; Ward and Dahl 2014), we explore how the expenditure of *time* can lead to the same end. Finally, our novel predictions contribute to recent research analyzing more subtle and alternative signals of status (Bellezza et al. 2014; Berger and Ward 2010; Dubois et al. 2012; Han et al. 2010).

References available upon request.

Olympic Games: Does the Host Location Matter?

Anahit Armenakyan, Louise A. Heslop, Irene R.R. Lu, John Nadeau, and Norm O'Reilly

Abstract The Olympic Games (OG) are unique activities that attract a large number of visitors to a country and generate intensive media-coverage and international broadcasting, providing a host country with a powerful tool to communicate desirable country-image messages broadly to the international community. Pairing a mega-event with a destination engenders image transfers between the event and the host, leading countries/regions to compete with each other for the privilege of hosting mega-events with a hope of improving their images, increasing the flow of tourists, and realizing other related benefits. This bilateral transfer of images between a mega-event and a host country can be conceptualized as a co-branding image-transfer exercise with one side being the consolidated image of the country (the people, physical/social aspects of the country, destination) and another side being the image of the mega-event (nature, scale, and uniqueness of the event). The degree to which the images of the mega-event and host country fit together affects the level of effectiveness of the co-branding exercise. Hence, the goal of the current research is to examine and compare the results from the XXII Sochi 2014 Winter Olympic Games (SOG) vs. XXI Vancouver 2010 Winter Olympic Games (VOG) to identify effects of host-country image on the image of the OG.

Study participants ($N_{VOG}=559$; $N_{SOG}=677$) were randomly recruited from the US residents approximately 2 months after each of the 2010 VOG and the 2014 SOG by online market research companies. The study instrument (online questionnaire) contained sections to measure attitudes towards the host-country and people, host-country as a destination, and the OG. Respondents were asked to share their "general impressions" on the measures by selecting the number on a 7-point scale that most closely reflected their opinion on each of the objects of interest. Exploratory

A. Armenakyan (✉) • J. Nadeau
Nipissing University, North Bay, ON, Canada
e-mail: anahita@nipissingu.ca; johnn@nipissingu.ca

L.A. Heslop • I.R.R. Lu
Carleton University, Ottawa, ON, Canada
e-mail: louise_heslop@carleton.ca; irene_lu@carleton.ca

N. O'Reilly
Ohio University, Athens, OH, USA
e-mail: oreillyn@ohio.edu

© Academy of Marketing Science 2016
L. Petruzzellis, R.S. Winer (eds.), *Rediscovering the Essentiality of Marketing*,
Developments in Marketing Science: Proceedings of the Academy of Marketing
Science, DOI 10.1007/978-3-319-29877-1_14

73

factor analysis was used to determine underlying factors as the basis for summary measures development (no substantive concern for collinearity was observed). Summary measures were analyzed using *t*-test means comparison for the independent samples for each OG. Linear regressions were run to examine the relationships among the evaluative summary measures. The current study adds to the stream of studies on OG and host-country co-branding. The results indicate that while the respondents had overall above average positive attitudes towards both host-countries and the OG, there are significant differences in attitudes towards Canada/VOG vs. Russian/SOG. The results indicate that the OG evaluation is significantly influenced by the host country/people and host-country destination evaluations with the latter one mediating the relationships between the evaluations of the country/people image and the OG. This suggests that IOC's communication campaigns while usually strongly focusing on the benefits of the host-country destination should nevertheless be carefully designed to tailor to specific host-country. However, the interpretation of the results needs to be handled with great care as major international conflict involving Russia started to escalate approximately at the time of the data collection.

Does Decision-Making Speed Depend on Non-interactive Others?

Atsuko Inoue and Atsunori Ariga

Abstract As it is experienced in daily life, people are susceptible to others' behaviors, choices, and their mere presence in many ways, even when they are non-interactive. Several studies on consumer behavior have reported this phenomenon. These studies, however, focused on how decision-making outcomes are affected by others, whereas none have examined effects on decision-making speed. Therefore, we investigated the effect of non-interactive others on decision-making speed.

Two laboratory experiments were conducted. In experiment 1, 96 university students were randomly assigned four conditions which include (1) subject by him/herself, with other person performing task with (2) normal/(3) fast/(4) slow speed. In experiment 2, another fast condition added. Under this condition, subjects performed task with fast speed sound. Stimuli were 18 pairs of images, each member of which was derived from the same category. Both experiments were computer based.

The result showed that speed contagion occurred in fast speed condition. But in case of slow it didn't happen. Interestingly, there were no differences of satisfaction for the decision between four conditions. We also found this speed contagion happened only when there is physical presence of other. That means the only fast speed sound cannot make it happen. Because decision-making during a purchase is most frequently made in others' presence, our research would contribute to understanding decision-making under realistic social contexts.

A. Inoue (✉)
Seikei University, Tokyo, Japan
e-mail: ainoue@econ.seikei.ac.jp

A. Ariga
Rissho University, Tokyo, Japan
e-mail: ariga@ris.ac.jp

© Academy of Marketing Science 2016
L. Petruzzellis, R.S. Winer (eds.), *Rediscovering the Essentiality of Marketing*, Developments in Marketing Science: Proceedings of the Academy of Marketing Science, DOI 10.1007/978-3-319-29877-1_15

Compensatory Advice Giving: How Experiencing a Need for Control Makes You Advise More

Alessandro M. Peluso, Andrea Bonezzi, Matteo De Angelis, and Derek D. Rucker

Abstract Consumers often advise other consumers by providing them with explicit recommendations on how to behave with regard to a wide range of purchasing decisions. Although previous literature (e.g., Goldsmith and Fitch 1997; Liu and Gal 2011) typically construes advice giving as a behavior driven by an empathic concern for others, in this research we propose and show across two experiments that advice giving can sometimes serve a compensatory function and thus be driven by a self-serving motive to restore a lost sense of control.

Experiment 1 ($n=82$) shows that individuals who experience a need to restore control are more inclined to give advice than individuals without this need, and that this tendency is stronger for individuals chronically higher in desire for control. We measured respondents' chronic desire for control (Burger and Cooper 1979). Then, we manipulated their sense of control using an episodic recall task (Whitson and Galinsky 2008), in order to either activate or not a transient need to restore it. Finally, respondents recalled a positive consumption experience and wrote a message about it as if they were writing to a friend. Messages were coded based on whether or not they contained an explicit advice or recommendation for the recipient. As predicted, respondents who experienced a need to restore control gave more advice than respondents without this need (55 % vs. 35.7 %), $p=.05$. Moreover, this tendency was stronger for those with a higher chronic desire for control compared to those lower in desire for control (76 % vs. 32.2 %), $p=.008$.

A.M. Peluso (✉)
University of Salento, Lecce, Italy
e-mail: alessandro.peluso@unisalento.it

A. Bonezzi
New York University, New York, NY, USA
e-mail: abonezzi@stern.nyu.edu

M. De Angelis
LUISS University, Rome, Italy
e-mail: mdeangelis@luiss.it

D.D. Rucker
Northwestern University, Evanston, IL, USA
e-mail: d-rucker@kellogg.northwestern.edu

© Academy of Marketing Science 2016
L. Petruzzellis, R.S. Winer (eds.), *Rediscovering the Essentiality of Marketing,*
Developments in Marketing Science: Proceedings of the Academy of Marketing
Science, DOI 10.1007/978-3-319-29877-1_16

Experiment 2 ($n=101$) demonstrates that the presence of an alternative means to restore control attenuates the effect of a need to restore control on advice giving. We orthogonally manipulated sense of control, by using an anticipatory thinking task (Rutjens et al. 2010), and initial opportunity to restore control, by asking participants to engage in a task about brands that either boosted their sense of control or not (Cutright et al. 2013). Finally, participants wrote about a positive experience they had with a product or service and expressed their intention to advise others to buy it. Consistent with our compensatory account, when no initial opportunity to restore control was provided, participants in need to restore control reported a higher intent to advise ($M=8.29$) than participants with no such a need ($M=6.69$), $p=.001$. When an initial opportunity to restore control was provided, intent to advise did not differ as a function of whether or not a need to restore control had previously been activated ($p>.70$).

Our research advances our understanding of the motives that drive advice giving in word-of-mouth conversations by showing that sometimes consumers may offer advice driven by a motive of restoring control. Our research also contributes to personal control literature by showing that, in providing explicit directions as to how others should behave, advice giving may serve a compensatory function as it provides people with a means to reestablish control.

References available upon request.

The Differential Influence of Advice and Opinions on Word-of-Mouth Recipients' Behavior

Matteo De Angelis, Andrea Bonezzi, Derek D. Rucker, and Alessandro M. Peluso

Introduction

When engaging in word-of-mouth (WOM) communications, consumers generally share either opinions, whereby they merely communicate whether they like or dislike a product (e.g., "I like the product I just bought"), or advice, whereby they offer explicit recommendations as to how others should behave (e.g., "buy or do not buy this product"). Past research has not examined whether and when advice and opinions exert similar or differential influence for WOM recipients' behavior. We fill this gap by proposing that advice can be more or less influential than opinions based on how diagnostic consumers assess the information to be (e.g., Ahluwalia 2002; Feldman and Lynch 1988).

M. De Angelis (✉)
LUISS University, Rome, Italy
e-mail: mdeangelis@luiss.it

A. Bonezzi
New York University, New York, NY, USA
e-mail: abonezzi@stern.nyu.edu

D.D. Rucker
Northwestern University, Evanston, IL, USA
e-mail: d-rucker@kellogg.northwestern.edu

A.M. Peluso
University of Salento, Lecce, Italy
e-mail: alessandro.peluso@unisalento.it

© Academy of Marketing Science 2016   79
L. Petruzzellis, R.S. Winer (eds.), *Rediscovering the Essentiality of Marketing*,
Developments in Marketing Science: Proceedings of the Academy of Marketing
Science, DOI 10.1007/978-3-319-29877-1_17

Theoretical Framework

Different factors, such as the expertise of the communicator, the strength of the tie between communicator and recipient, and the recipient's emotional states, have been shown to affect how influential either advice or opinions can be (e.g., Alba and Hutchinson 1987; Duhan et al. 1997; Fitzsimons and Lehmann 2004; Gershoff et al. 2001; Gino and Schweitzer 2008; West and Broniarczyk 1998; Yaniv and Kleinberger 2000). Past studies, however, have only examined the effects of either opinions or advice in isolation, thus leaving the question of whether and when opinions are more persuasive when compared to advice and vice versa unanswered. In this research we put forth a theoretical account based on a common process by which advice and opinions differentially shape decision-making. Building on previous research on the importance of information diagnosticity for persuasion and consumer behavior (e.g., Gershoff et al. 2001; Yaniv et al. 2011), we propose that a key factor that determines whether an opinion or a piece of advice is more likely to influence a recipient's behavior is the degree to which each of these two forms of advocacy leads the recipient to assess the diagnosticity of the information received. A piece of information is defined as diagnostic if it is relevant for the decision maker, helping her reach a clear decision. In contrast, information is defined as nondiagnostic if it does not help an individual reach a decision (Feldman and Lynch 1988; Herr et al. 1991).

Our proposition about the differential likelihood that advice and opinions lead recipients to assess how diagnostic the information is for their own decision-making is based on the fact that advice and opinions differentially implicate the self. Advice directly calls the recipient to action, thus clearly invoking the recipient's self. In contrast, opinions do not invoke a recipient's self, as they are only focused on what the communicator thinks. Past research speaks to the idea that information that directly invokes the self prompts people to more carefully scrutinize its diagnosticity (e.g., Rotliman and Schwarz 1998). Thus, we suggest that advice will be more likely to prompt individuals to consider the diagnosticity of the accompanying information. As a consequence, advice will be more influential than opinions when the accompanying information is assessed to be diagnostic, whereas it be less influential when the accompanying information is assessed to be nondiagnostic. Next, we review two factors leading information to be viewed as diagnostic versus nondiagnostic.

Consumers are more likely to have relatively homogenous preferences in some product categories, but relatively heterogeneous preferences in others. For example, consumers' preferences tend to be very heterogeneous for products such as books, whereas they tend to be less heterogeneous for products such as dental floss. Based on this reasoning, information should be viewed as more diagnostic when it is about products for which preferences tend to be similar among individuals (e.g., Yaniv et al. 2011), as the recipient might conclude that the communicator shares the same preferences. Because advice increases consumers' proclivity to assess the diagnosticity of the information, we hypothesize that advice should be more influential than opinions for categories with homogenous preferences. In contrast, when preferences are heterogeneous among consumers, a recipient of this information might conclude that the communicator has different preferences, and thus infer that the information could well be nondiagnostic. Thus, because advice is more likely to trigger the assessment of how diagnostic the information is, we hypothesize that advice should be less influential than opinions for categories with heterogeneous preferences.

Consumers may receive information from a wide array of communicators. On one extreme, they might receive opinions or advice from people they do not know at all, such as strangers posting online product reviews. On the other extreme, they might receive opinions or advice from people they know very well, such as close friends or family members (Brown and Reingen 1987; Herr et al. 1991). Building on past research suggesting that consumers tend to overestimate how much close friends know their own tastes and preferences (Gershoff and Johar 2006), we propose that when receiving information from a close other, consumers are likely to believe that person has a good knowledge of their own preferences, and thus conclude that the information received is diagnostic. In contrast, when receiving information from a distant other (e.g., an acquaintance), consumers are likely to believe that person does not have a good knowledge of their own preferences, and thus conclude that the information received might not be diagnostic. We hypothesize that if advice leads consumers to assess how diagnostic information is more so than opinions, consumers will be more influenced by advice, rather than opinion, from a close friend; in contrast, we hypothesize that consumers will be less influenced by advice, rather than opinion, from a distant other.

Methodology

In Experiment 1 we examined the influence of opinions vis-à-vis advice in six product categories. Two hundred and ninety-three participants recruited from an online pool of paid respondents were randomly assigned to a 2 (information type: advice vs. opinion) × 6 (product categories: restaurant, movie, book, dental floss, shopping mall, olive oil) between-participants design. Participants were presented with a positive online review framed as coming from yelp.com.

To select the product categories, we first conducted a pretest on a separate sample of 81 respondents drawn from the same population, who were asked to rate on a scale how much they thought consumers' preferences vary in different product categories (1 = most people have the same preferences, 7 = most people have different preferences). Based on the results of the pretest, we selected restaurant ($M = 5.04$, $SD = 1.75$), movies ($M = 4.98$, $SD = 1.82$), and books ($M = 5.19$, $SD = 1.78$) as categories in which preferences among consumers tend to vary more, and dental floss ($M = 3.84$, $SD = 1.48$), shopping malls ($M = 4.27$, $SD = 1.88$), and olive oil ($M = 3.90$, $SD = 1.65$) as categories in which consumers' preferences tend to vary less. For each category, we manipulated information type by crafting the last sentence of the review in such a way that the piece of information became either an opinion (i.e., *I will definitely go back to this restaurant*) or a piece of advice (i.e., *You should definitely try this restaurant*). After reading the review, participants were asked to indicate the likelihood they would try the product discussed in the message on a nine-point scale (1 = very unlikely, 9 = very likely), which served as our dependent measure indicating influence on the receiver.

Based on the results of the pretest, we merged the data from the three "high preference variation" categories and the data from the three "low preference variation" categories, and performed a two-way ANOVA using information type and product category as factors and likelihood to try the product as dependent variable. While no significant effects of information type ($F(1, 289) = .21$, ns) or product category ($F(1, 289) = .22$, ns) emerged, the analysis revealed a significant interaction effect, $F (1, 289) = 40.99$, $p < .001$. Consistent with our hypotheses, for low preference variation categories, respondents indicated they would be more likely to try the product when they read a piece of advice ($M = 7.25$, $SD = 1.46$) rather than an opinion ($M = 5.83$, $SD = 1.83$), $t (289) = 4.48$, $p = .001$. In contrast, for high preference variation categories, respondents indicated they would be more likely to try the product when they read an opinion ($M = 7.25$, $SD = 1.60$) rather than a piece of advice ($M = 6.01$, $SD = 1.94$), $t (289) = 4.66$, $p < .001$.

In Experiment 2 we manipulated relationship closeness by framing the advice or the opinion as coming from either a best friend or an acquaintance of the receiver. One hundred and one participants recruited from an online pool of paid respondents were randomly assigned to a 2 (information type: advice vs. opinion) × 2 (communicator closeness: best friend vs. acquaintance) between-participants design. Participants were asked to read a message about a restaurant and to imagine that it came from either their best friend or an acquaintance. Unlike Experiment 1, Experiment 2 contained negatively valenced messages (*I will definitely not go back to this restaurant* in the case of opinions, *you should definitely try this restaurant* in the case of advice). We employed the same dependent variables as Experiment 1.

Data analyzed with a two-way ANOVA revealed a significant main effect of communicator closeness ($F(1, 97) = 5.49$, $p = .02$), suggesting that respondents were less likely to try the restaurant when the message came from their best friend rather than from an acquaintance, and a significant interaction between information type and communicator closeness, $F(1, 97) = 6.85$, $p = .01$. Consistent with our hypotheses, when the communicator was their best friend, respondents were more influenced by the negative information when it came in the form of a piece of advice ($M = 1.77, SD = .75$) than in the form of an opinion ($M = 2.56, SD = 1.42$), $t(197) = 2.08$, $p = .04$. In contrast, when the communicator was an acquaintance, respondents were more influenced by the negative information when it came in the form of an opinion ($M = 2.48$, $SD = 1.56$) rather than in the form of a piece of advice ($M = 3.21$, $SD = 1.74$), $t(197) = 2.05$, $p = .04$. These results provide convergence for our diagnosticity account of the differential influence of advice versus opinions.

In Experiment 3 we used an unknown communicator (thus, low in closeness to the receiver) but manipulated the salience of information diagnosticity, by varying whether the communicator revealed or not to a listener the underlying reason for her preference. For example, a communicator might say that she likes a new movie, with or without explaining that it is due to the fact that the movie is from a particular genre she likes. We predict that when a communicator reveals the key element on which an opinion or a piece of advice is based she makes the diagnosticity of the information salient for the recipient. If the differences between opinions and advice are due to differences in the likelihood that the recipient assesses how diagnostic the information is, then differences between advice and opinions should be eliminated when information diagnosticity is made salient to everyone. We hypothesize that when a communicator low in closeness does not reveal the rationale for her preferences, opinions will be perceived as more influential than advice, while when she does reveal the rationale for her preferences, the diagnosticity of the information will be made salient, regardless of whether she shares an opinion or a piece of advice. Hence, little difference between opinions and advice should be observed.

One hundred seventy-two participants recruited from an online pool of paid respondents were randomly assigned to a 2 (information type: advice vs. opinion)×2 (information diagnosticity: salient vs. not salient) between-participants design. All read a positive online review about a movie. In the not salient condition, the communicator did not reveal the specific movie genre the message was about, whereas in the salient condition she did. After reading this review, participants were asked to indicate their likelihood to watch the movie on a nine-point scale (1 = very unlikely, 9 = very likely), and whether they like the specific movie genre (i.e., horror). The data were analyzed with a two-way ANOVA, which revealed a significant main effect of information diagnosticity ($F(1, 166)=25.65$, $p<.001$), qualified by a significant interaction between information type and information diagnosticity ($F(1, 166)=3.18$, $p=.04$). Consistent with Experiment 2, when the communicator did not reveal her own preferences, thus information diagnosticity was not salient, respondents were more likely to watch the movie if the message was expressed as an opinion ($M=6.93$, $SD=1.78$) rather than as a piece of advice ($M=5.44$, $SD=2.12$), $t(166)=2.82$, $p<.01$. In contrast, when the communicator revealed her own preferences, and thus the information diagnosticity was salient, we did not observe a differential influence of opinions versus advice either in the salient-consistent ($M_{opinion}=6.78, SD=1.80$ vs. $M_{advice}=6.77, SD=1.50$), $t(166)=.01$, *ns*, or in the salient-inconsistent condition ($M_{opinion}=3.68$, $SD=2.64$ vs. $M_{advice}=4.07$, $SD=2.65$), $t(166)=.57$, *ns*. This supports the idea that when the communicator explicitly stated her preferences, individuals considered the information as diagnostic regardless of whether it was communicated as an opinion or a piece of advice. In the case of salience, the data show that the likelihood to watch the movie was greater when preferences were consistent rather than inconsistent ($t=7.10$, $p<.001$), across both opinions and advice. These results provide additional support for our mechanism, showing that differences between opinions and advice disappear when people are led to consider the diagnosticity of the information received.

General Discussion

This research provides evidence that advice is more likely to lead consumers to assess the diagnosticity of the information received compared to opinions. As a consequence, when information is deemed diagnostic, advice is more influential than opinions; when information is deemed nondiagnostic, advice is less influential than opinions. Our work contributes to extant literature on WOM and social transmission of information in several ways. First, while past research has studied the effect of advice and opinions in isolation, we shed light on when advice is more influential than opinions for consumers' decision-making and when the opposite is true. Second, we investigate the role of information diagnosticity as a theoretical account that explains when advice can be more influential than opinions as well as when opinions can be more influential than advice. Third, this research emphasizes the importance of both heterogeneity within a category and communicator closeness as inputs to assessing the diagnosticity of information. While past research has demonstrated the importance of weak ties in information transmission (e.g., Brown and Reingen 1987), we suggest that whether strong or weak ties bring about a higher impact of the information still depends on the diagnosticity of that information. Fourth, this work should also be of interest to managers, by emphasizing the fact that marketers should not care only about what is said among consumers, but also how it is said. Marketers should leverage consumers' tendency to give positive advice especially when recipients will view the advice as diagnostic. For instance, companies selling products with low variation in preferences among individuals might focus on giving their customers reasons to spread positive advice through personal as well as non-personal channels. In contrast, companies selling products with high variation in preferences might encourage consumers to share more their opinions instead.

References available upon request.

The Impact of Reference Group on Purchase Intention: A Case Study in Distinct Types of Shoppers

Danupol Hoonsopon and Wilert Puriwat

Abstract Past studies explore the effect of purchase intention by reference group in various situations. However, the roles of a reference group (private and public group) on the purchase intention of the distinctive types of shoppers have been over-looked. Drawing from the social influence theory, using experimental research, and analyzing data with *t*-Test and ANOVA, the findings show that utilitarian shoppers tend to have higher purchase intention when a private group is used for information cues. But, a reference group does not have an impact on the purchase intention of hedonic and social shoppers. This research theoretically contributes to social influence theory by revealing that a reference group has a diverse effect on purchase intention in different stimuli.

D. Hoonsopon (✉) • W. Puriwat
Chulalongkorn University, Bangkok, Thailand
e-mail: danupol@cbs.chula.ac.th; wilert@cbs.chula.ac.th

© Academy of Marketing Science 2016
L. Petruzzellis, R.S. Winer (eds.), *Rediscovering the Essentiality of Marketing*,
Developments in Marketing Science: Proceedings of the Academy of Marketing
Science, DOI 10.1007/978-3-319-29877-1_18

An Exploration of Socially Responsible Music Consumption

Todd Green, Gary Sinclair, and Julie Tinson

Introduction

The positive role that music and musicians play in developing awareness and raising funds for a wide variety of social, environmental, and philanthropic causes has been well documented by the popular press and media coverage (Robinson 2012). Consequently, the actions of musicians are under greater levels of scrutiny and fans demand more from musicians than "just" music. For example, live music festivals are expected to address the environmental impact of the events including the availability of recycling, using green power, and offering environmentally friendly merchandise (Laing and Frost 2010). Further, a 2012 survey of over 2000 music festival attendees found that the responsibility to minimize the environmental impact of music festivals generally rests with the organizers and the attendees themselves (A Greener Festival 2012). The question remains regarding how the increasing prominence of such activities by musicians influences music consumers and fans of individual bands and artists. The aim of this study is to explore the role that socially responsible consumption plays in the consumption of music. Specifically we explore the role of social responsibility across a variety of consumption activities including individual decision-making (i.e., downloading music legally, recycling at concerts, avoiding socially irresponsible musicians, and supporting local musicians). In addition we examine the levels of awareness, interest and support for individual musicians, artists, record labels, and live music festivals that engage in socially responsible activities.

T. Green (✉)
Brock University, St. Catharines, ON, Canada
e-mail: tgreen@brocku.ca

G. Sinclair • J. Tinson
University of Stirling, Stirling, UK
e-mail: gary.sinclair@stir.ac.uk; j.s.tinson@stir.ac.uk

© Academy of Marketing Science 2016
L. Petruzzellis, R.S. Winer (eds.), *Rediscovering the Essentiality of Marketing*,
Developments in Marketing Science: Proceedings of the Academy of Marketing
Science, DOI 10.1007/978-3-319-29877-1_19

87

Background

While there appears to be interest and awareness related to environmental issues at live music events and consumer support for charitable donations tied to music sales, previous literature has not explored the role that social and ethical responsibilities have in the consumption of music. In fact, Laing and Frost (2010) note the "paucity of information about the type of person who may be attracted to green events and their motivations for attendance, as well as likely levels of demand for these events in the future (p. 262)." The current research addresses this gap by exploring the role that socially responsible consumption plays in the consumption of music. In order to examine the role that social responsibility plays in the consumption of music, we adopt Mohr and colleagues (2001, p. 47) definition of individual's socially responsible consumption behavior (SRCB) as "a person basing his or her acquisition, usage and disposition of products on a desire to minimize or eliminate any harmful effects and maximize the long-term beneficial impact on society." Further, we seek to explore the influence of socially responsible engagement by individual artists, bands, and organizations in the music industry (i.e., record labels, venue management, ticketing companies) on consumers. Accordingly, we adopt Barnett's (2007, p. 801) definition of CSR as "a discretionary allocation of corporate resources toward improving social welfare that serves as a means of enhancing relationships with key stakeholders." The current research seeks to better understand the types of activities that our participants associate with being a socially responsible music consumer and how these activities influence music consumption decisions.

Method

Since the role of socially responsible consumption in music is relatively unexplored, qualitative depth interviews served as an appropriate methodology (Strauss and Corbin 1990). In addition, the goal of our research is discovery-oriented and we sought to examine a variety of factors that influence socially responsible music consumption. Similar qualitative methods have been used by researchers examining consumer behaviors related to CSR activities and socially responsible consumption behavior (e.g., Carrigan and Attalla 2001). The semi-structured interview guide was developed through the review of the existing socially responsible consumption behavior, CSR and music consumption literatures. Twenty-two interviews, averaging 54 min in length, were recorded and transcribed verbatim. The interview data was sufficient to ensure saturation (Guest et al. 2006). Participants were recruited from multiple cities across the United Kingdom and Ireland and worked across a wide variety of industries including education, social marketing, and leisure. Initial sampling was conducted by asking colleagues for referrals, and subsequent sampling was managed through snowballing.

The coding of the interviews was conducted across four key aspects of socially responsible music consumption. We firstly coded the types of behaviors that consumers identify as examples of individual social responsibility (and irresponsibility) such as downloading music either from legal or illegal sources, and attending local live music events in order to support local emerging talent. Secondly, we coded the types of socially responsible activities that participants identified that individual musicians, bands, and organizations in the music industry (i.e., record labels) engage in. Thirdly, we coded for instances of social responsibility in everyday consumption as a point of comparison with music consumption. Finally, we coded for the purposes of identifying the factors that have the most influence in ultimately determining whether consumers choose to integrate social responsibility information and attributes into their music consumption decisions.

Results and Discussion

Overall, we explored both socially responsible and irresponsible music consumption at the individual consumer level as well as support for socially responsible behavior on the part of musicians, record labels, and music venues through the identification of emerging themes that influence when and why support occurs (or does not). Further, we identified the prevalence of irresponsible behavior in the music industry that often exceeds the importance of positive and responsible behavior. Finally, we compared the importance of social responsibility across music consumption decisions and general consumption decisions.

As the music industry struggles to determine how to respond to the huge shift away from physical purchases of music, the role of illegal downloading has been debated with musicians both advocating and fighting for greater access for consumers to their music (i.e. IFPI 2014). Participants felt that the shift in availability to digital formats represents a significant challenge to the music industry both in terms of the business model but also as a key ethical issue for consumers. In addition, several participants expressed regret at not supporting the music industry to the extent they should (e.g., downloading illegally and copying music from friends). However, while expressing some level of guilt related to downloading free music, participants who downloaded from illegal channels typically offered justifications for their decision to not pay for music such as their personal financial situation and suggesting musicians and labels are not financially impacted by illegal downloads (see Cenite et al. 2009; Kinally et al. 2008).

Du Bhattacharya and Sen (2010) note that consumers have low levels of awareness of CSR-engagement by firms in general. Similarly, a number of our participants evidenced low levels of awareness:

> Well, there's the sort of more obvious examples of those bands that are big enough to use their fame and they get to say when discussions are happening. So we've all heard of Bono and Bob Geldof doing their thing on various world issues. So there's some of the more

screamingly obvious ones that get on the news but beyond that, I don't think I ever, you know, I don't take a music magazine or I don't read up for more background to the music I listen to…I wouldn't really have much connection to it, to be honest. (Male, 37)

While not all participants readily identified specific examples of socially responsible engagement in the music industry, several of our participants discussed a variety of activities that they defined as socially responsible, including musicians raising awareness and money for social and environmental causes, donating money to charitable organizations through charity concerts and albums, supporting local emerging talent, and minimizing the environmental impact of live music events. In addition, while a general lack of awareness of social responsibility in the music industry was cited by a number of our sample, several participants have specific socially responsible consumption aspects that resonate with them. Similar to the findings of Szmigin et al. (2009), we find evidence of flexible socially responsible consumption behavior with priority issues they focus on in the realm of socially responsible consumption. For example:

I can't think of any examples where, you know, musicians have said, "Give to this charity," and I've gone and done it….However, I think, people who create their own record labels to get away from the bigger kind of profit-oriented labels, they're probably in my mind more ethical because their focus would be more on producing the music they want and getting it out to people… (Female, 33)

A number of participants in the study felt that while the general awareness levels are not currently as high as they would hope for, they believed building awareness of socially responsible decisions in the area of music is a worthwhile pursuit. This echoes the findings of Burke and Logsdon (1996) who suggest that firms should recognize and value opportunities that generate positive visibility from their socially responsible activities. For example, the following participant felt acknowledging and promoting "green behavior" on the part of music festivals would be beneficial to the industry as a whole:

Yes, I think all festivals should promote their environmental friendly behavior if that's what they're doing. I think they should make more noise about it. Because the more noise that they make about it than the more, you know, if they can—if that seems to be working for people then they'll potentially have an influence on other festivals, venues, whatever that aren't doing so much, to become more of that themselves. (Female, 34)

In addition, we find several factors influence whether they respond positively or negatively to the socially responsible activities in the industry. These include the perceived authenticity for the engagement in social, ethical, and environmental causes, the size and level of success of the musician as well as the local impact of socially responsible engagement.

Finally, the comparison between more routine, everyday purchases and consumption of music was particularly illuminating. We found that many of the participants identified music consumption spaces as a means of escape from the routine and this included absconding from the pressures of incorporating ethical decisions as a priority in their music consumption decision-making process. For example:

I don't know that a concert is the right place to shove it down people's throats, especially in today's world when there are so many other ways you can communicate that to your fans or your audience. But yeah, it's quite interesting to see what celebrities support. (Female, 43)

Conclusions and Implications for Theory and Practice

The current research explores the role of social responsibility across a variety of consumption activities including individual decision-making (i.e., downloading music legally and supporting local musicians). In addition we examine the levels of awareness, interest, and support for individual musicians, artists, record labels, and live music festivals that engage in socially responsible activities. In doing so, the current research makes a number of contributions to both the socially responsible consumption behavior and music consumption literatures.

Firstly, previous research examining socially responsible consumption behavior has found that consumers respond more positively to hedonic products compared to utilitarian products (i.e., Strahilevitz and Myers 1998). However, we find that counter to previous research, the interest and support for a hedonic product paired with socially responsible attributes is not particularly strong. The participants who expressed less interest and support for the music industry incorporating socially responsible aspects did so for a number of reasons such as wanting music to provide escapism rather than being an ideal platform to discuss social, political, and environmental issues.

Secondly, on a practical level, global ticket sales for live music events totalled a record $4.8 billion with attendance figures growing at 26 % in 2013 (Billboard 2013). Further, charity singles consistently generate millions of dollars for a variety of causes. In addition, the demand from music consumers exists as nearly 50 % of concert attendees surveyed suggested they were willing to pay a premium for environmentally friendly music events (A Greener Festival 2012). Accordingly, practitioners working in the music industry such as executives of record labels and the organizers of live music events have a significant opportunity to develop socially and environmentally responsible products and services for the customers that express the desire to have music and social responsibility be integrated more clearly.

Finally, the current research provides a foundation on which to better understand the role of social responsibility in the consumption of music. Specifically, the consumption of music and the role of ethics and social responsibility on consumption decisions have significant overlap across the themes and motivations examined. For example, music consumption and socially responsible consumption decisions are often driven by the social value afforded to consumers. Specifically, previous research has noted the role of social value provided to consumers via socially responsible consumption behavior such as purchasing environmentally friendly products and donating to charitable organizations (i.e., Basil and Weber 2006). The social value presents itself in a variety of ways including self-presentation concerns (i.e., Green and Peloza 2014; White and Peloza 2010), and the communication of identity to others (Youn and Kim 2008). Similarly, research in music consumption as a context for consumer has included the exploration and development of explanations concerning identity, social groups (see Goulding et al. 2009). Future research can examine the importance of these various sources of social value across general and music consumption.

References available upon request.

Product Failure: Severity and Locus of Causality Effects on Brand Evaluations

Sujin Song, Dan A. Sheinin, and Sukki Yoon

Abstract Although product failures cause marketers and consumers to suffer substantial damages and losses, failures are often beyond control. Building on defensive attribution literature, this study experimentally investigates how locus of causality and outcome severity of product failure interactively shape consumers' brand evaluations. Findings show that following a product failure experience, consumers respond with the lowest brand evaluation for a brand-caused failure, a higher brand evaluation for a natural disaster-caused failure, and the highest brand evaluation for a consumer-caused failure. Outcome severity moderates the effects; however, when the failure causes severe outcomes, positive brand evaluation deteriorates for the consumer-caused failure but not for the brand- and natural disaster-caused failure. In addition, brand-blame attribution mediates the relationships.

S. Song (✉)
Korea University, Seoul, South Korea
e-mail: songsj@korea.ac.kr

D.A. Sheinin
University of Rhode Island, Kingston, RI, USA
e-mail: dsheinin@uri.edu

S. Yoon
Bryant University, Smithfield, RI, USA
e-mail: syoon@bryant.edu

© Academy of Marketing Science 2016
L. Petruzzellis, R.S. Winer (eds.), *Rediscovering the Essentiality of Marketing*, Developments in Marketing Science: Proceedings of the Academy of Marketing Science, DOI 10.1007/978-3-319-29877-1_20

Neuromarketing: The Effect of Attitudes on the Perception of External Business Communication

Kristina Kovac, Marc M. Kuhn, and Natalie de Jong

Abstract For centuries, countless hours of research have been dedicated to explaining human behavior in decision-making situations. As early as the late nineteenth century, John Wannamaker, who opened America's first shopping mall in 1876, said the following: "I know that half of my money spent in advertising is wasted, but I don't know which is such a half". Every year businesses invest billions of euros in communication activities, whose effectiveness cannot be clearly confirmed. This is because classic research efforts could not clearly answer the central question: "What motivates the customer to buy?" For this reason, a new economic discipline known as *neuromarketing* has been trying to find the answer since the 1990s by combining economic and scientific findings. With the help of medical devices used to measure brain activity, the discipline aims to explain mostly unexplored processes and procedures within the human brain's so-called "black box" during economic decision processes. The focus here is on researching processes like perception, attitude, and motivation, which are difficult to record empirically and which can hopefully be used to gain a better understanding of consumers, thus making a contribution to sustainable and efficient use of communication measures.

Despite the new opportunities opened up by neuromarketing, it has yet to receive sufficient attention in classical research. For this reason, this elaboration in an exploratory investigation of a correlation between the central determinants of consumer behavior attitude and perception is based on neuroscientific approaches, thus contributing to the implementation of this new branch of research. Neuromarketing methods are employed here to operationalize the little-researched correlation between an attitude and the perception of business advertising within an industry at neuronal level and then test this with an EEG measurement. The present study design draws upon two industries with different attitudinal connotations: the automotive sector as a generally positively seen branch and the insurance industry, generally seen negatively.

K. Kovac (✉) • M.M. Kuhn • N. de Jong
Baden-Württemberg Cooperative State University Stuttgart, Stuttgart, Germany
e-mail: kristina.kovac@gmx.de; Marc.Kuhn@dhbw-stuttgart.de;
natalie.dejong@dhbw-stuttgart.de

© Academy of Marketing Science 2016
L. Petruzzellis, R.S. Winer (eds.), *Rediscovering the Essentiality of Marketing*,
Developments in Marketing Science: Proceedings of the Academy of Marketing
Science, DOI 10.1007/978-3-319-29877-1_21

In summary, significant differences in the attitudes on the two industries studied were recorded. Despite the fact that a correlation of the two behavioral determinants *attitude* and *perception* could not be proven under the mentioned experiment condition, the achieved results nevertheless show a clear tendency that confirms the assumption that a deeply embedded attitude affects the perception of business advertising.

Exploring Voids and Consumer Addiction

Emily Chung, Michael Beverland, and Francis Farrelly

Introduction

Consumers can form intense relationships with products and brands (Fournier 1998), where some may "fall in love" with and become highly passionate, devoted, and deeply committed to their favorite product/brand (Batra et al. 2012; Lastovicka and Sirianni 2011; Ortiz et al. 2013). These highly devoted consumers voluntarily engage in behaviors that are beneficial to the product/brand such as by remaining loyal to its repeat purchases, spreading positive word-of-mouth and/or being protective of the product/brand and its continued pursuit, sometimes despite criticisms from others (Chung et al. 2008). The existing literature, however, also reveals a dark side to some of these highly intense attachments to products/brands, where some consumers can become obsessed, consumed, or addicted to its continued pursuit and acquisition (e.g., Belk 1995; Holbrook 1987; Hill and Robinson 1991; Lehmann 1987).

Existing literature on addiction has traditionally focused on the area of substance abuse (Brucks et al. 2012), such as in terms of drugs (Bozinoff et al. 1989; DePaulo 1987; Hirschman 1992; Powers 1993), alcohol (Bozinoff et al. 1989; DePaulo 1987), and tobacco (Benowitz 2008; Stolerman and Shoaib 1991). Other commonly explored forms of consumer addiction include gambling and gaming (including to the internet) (Burns et al. 1990; Bartholomew and Mason 2011; Hodis and Bruner II 2009; Peters and Bodkin 2007) and compulsive buying/shopping (d'Astous 1990; Eccles 2002; Elliott 1994; Elliott et al. 1996; Faber and O'Guinn 1989, 1992; Faber et al. 1987; Krych 1989; O'Guinn and Faber 1989). Studies of consumer addiction

E. Chung (✉) • F. Farrelly
RMIT University, Melbourne, Australia
e-mail: emily.chung@rmit.edu.au; francis.farrelly@rmit.edu.au

M. Beverland
University of Bath, Bath, UK
e-mail: mbb26@management.bath.ac.uk

© Academy of Marketing Science 2016
L. Petruzzellis, R.S. Winer (eds.), *Rediscovering the Essentiality of Marketing*,
Developments in Marketing Science: Proceedings of the Academy of Marketing
Science, DOI 10.1007/978-3-319-29877-1_22

outside these contexts are rare. Furthermore, there is a need to better understand "How consumer progresses from normal to maladaptive consumption and addiction" (Brucks et al. 2012, p. 1089). To this end, this study aims to contribute insights by exploring the role of "voids" in the development (and sustenance) of consumer addiction.

Methodology

Data for this study was derived from a larger study that explored intense consumer–product/brand relationships. Screening criteria consisting of 15 items derived from the existing literature on intense consumer attachments to products/brands (such as on brand love, consumer devotion, fanaticism, and addiction) were used to sample informants. In-depth phenomenological and life story interviews were conducted only on those that believed at least eight of the 15 items applied to them. The phenomenological interviews aimed to obtain comprehensive descriptions about the informants' relationships with a their (favorite) product or brand, while the life story interviews aimed to obtain in-depth information about the influences and past experiences that resulted in the development and evolution of the informants' intense attachments to their favorite product/brand. Interviews were also conducted with their significant other(s) such as a partner, family member(s), and/or friend(s), which served to corroborate important information and provide further insights about the informant and the phenomenon of interest. Interviews occurred over multiple meetings and were audio-recorded and transcribed. Data analysis was performed on the transcripts according to the guidelines provided by Strauss and Corbin (1998). Of the 12 informants interviewed, only four appeared to exhibit the characteristic of addiction.

Results and Discussion

An analysis of the interviews revealed that amongst informants that displayed the characteristics of being addicted (e.g., have experienced struggles of self-control such as in curbing consumption, which results in negative consequences), "voids" could be identified in their life stories (where the consumption of that very specific product/brand is used to symbolically represent what is missing in their lives in order to fill these voids). The transition from "normal to maladaptive consumption and addiction" appears to occur as an indirect result of these attempts to fill the void via consumption—which becomes only a temporary distraction from or "bandaid solution" to the void that still remains in the informants' lives. Due to space limitations, we draw upon the comments of one informant (Whitney, Asian female, 27 years old) to illustrate our key findings.

Filling Voids via Consumption

A "void" is a subjective state involving feelings of emptiness within or outside oneself. According to Ashton (2007, p. 14), "as an internal state it may feel like a lack of something definite, a vague incapacity, or the loss of something once had. As an external state it is more related to a feeling of disconnection and lack of protection or containedness or holding." In the interviews, Whitney, a devotee to Louis Vuitton handbags, explained about her family's poor migrant background. She spoke about her "most vivid" memory involving attending a birthday party in her "brand new tracksuit" (something she was rather proud of given most of her clothes were "hand me downs") when she was 6 years old. She explained:

"The look [the birthday girl's] mum gave me... was like, [of] disgust. Like, 'How dare you come to my daughter's party in a tracksuit?' I didn't know a tracksuit wasn't a nice thing. I thought it was nice new clothes! [But] Everyone was wearing dresses and stuff like that. So yeah, I just felt like, 'What have I done wrong?' You know, is what I'm wearing that terrible? I felt like shit. She was like, treating me like a disease or something. She was like, 'Don't touch this. Don't step on that', you know, as if like I was doing everything wrong."

Whitney's ability to provide rich and vivid descriptions of the event (down to the detail of the full names of the girls, as well as the colors of their dresses, shoes, hair, and eyes) attests to the significant impact this one event have had on her. Whitney provided details of two other separate experiences—being rejected (once more) by her group of friends (this time, as a teenager in high school), and also being told by one of her high school teachers that she "would never amount to anything." These incidents appear to have resulted in a void in Whitney, characterized by a "lack of something definite" such as material wealth, and feelings of inadequacy or "incapacity" (Ashton 2007, p. 14), which she tries to overcome through her consumption of Vuitton bags:

"I just need for people to perceive me a certain way I guess because I was perceived a certain way back then... They [i.e., the Vuitton bags] just symbolise so much more than anything I have. It's almost like a sense of achievement that I've gotten to this place in my life, where I've got luxury goods. Not like when I was a kid and wearing tracksuits."

Her comments above show her consumption of Vuitton products as a deliberate strategy used to normalize void states centered around the feelings of being poor or that she is not good enough in the eyes of other people. The consumption of Vuitton helps Whitney feel successful and therefore accepted, ameliorating the negative feelings associated with the rejection she experienced in her past. In particular, the choice of Vuitton is explained by the fact that it symbolizes wealth, achievement, and status, which she lacked in her younger years when she felt rejected and looked down upon by other people.

The Transition from Normal to Maladaptive Consumption

This section explores how "individuals move on a continuum from engaging in seemingly normal consumption behaviors to engaging in potentially addictive behaviors characterized by uncontrolled use and frequency of the behavior" (Brucks et al. 2012, p. 1089). Whitney's comments shed light on this "transition":

> "It just makes me feel better just looking at it. So I will periodically bring it out to look at it and just go, 'It's so beautiful' and 'I love it!', and I'll stroke it... [and] I just want[ed] more [of it]... And more, and more, and more! ... You really do get addicted because once I got [my first] two, I started going onto the websites and learning the names of all the different bags and you just get really obsessed with it, so every time I knew about a new limited edition coming out I would like to go and see it, read up all about it. 'Cause it really does become quite an obsession, it's really bad..."

The above comment shows Whitney clearly deriving positive feelings (such as pleasure and enjoyment from "just looking" at) her Vuitton bags. She explained that once making her first purchases, she became increasingly more interested in the brand and its products, which still appears to fall under the realm of "normal" consumption. However, this eventually turned "bad," developing into an "obsession" and a growing uncontrollable desire for "more." She added:

> "Due to my financial circumstances, I can no longer afford them... I [have] credit card debts like nothing else! ... Unbelievably huge! Ridiculously huge! ... However, I still walk past the store... I'll still go in and look at them and long for them and then get upset that I can't afford it. And then call [my boyfriend] and get upset because I can't afford anything... I think because I can't afford it at the moment it makes me want them more! And then I'm always standing there for ages, going, I wish I could get that. I want that (points finger), I want that (points finger)."

Whitney's descriptions indicate a dark side to her intense attachment to Vuitton as she experiences pain associated with her strong urges to acquire more Vuitton bags and subsequent sadness over her inability to "afford" them. Whitney, however, continues to make more purchases and goes into further debt. Her inability to exert self-control in curbing these purchases and suffering negative consequences as a result fits the descriptions of consumer addiction (see Hirschman 1992), and implies maladaptive consumer behavior.

The analysis of the interviews showed that the experience of pleasure and the experience of pain as a consequence of consumption both work to drive further consumption—for example, informants may continue to consume because it makes him/her "feel good" and therefore desires to repeat it, or they continue to consume because it helps make him/her "feel better" after experiencing "pain." The consumption cycle then appears to be perpetuated both proactively and reactively/compulsively. Similar to other informants of this study that revealed voids in their life stories, ultimately, Whitney's consumption of Vuitton bags appears to only be a temporary solution to her void states. She consumes/uses Vuitton bags in her attempt to portray a wealthier and more successful desired/ideal self/identity, but in reality, has failed to accumulate any significant financial wealth as her very pursuit of these bags prevents her from doing so (and in contrast, has put her into heavy debt), and the void (i.e., a lack of wealth) remains (where further consumption are repeated attempts to fill this void).

Conclusions and Implications for Theory and Practice

The findings suggest that the presence of a void can be used to explain the eventual development of the dark side of intense attachments to products/brands involving obsessive-compulsive and addictive qualities. The exploration of voids as a potential precursor (i.e., antecedent) to the development of consumer addiction contributes to an area where empirical research is limited. This research also contributes to an improved understanding particularly in terms of the development of or conversion to the "darker" forms of consumption, thereby also contributing to recent conversations about "understanding how consumer progresses from normal to maladaptive consumption and addiction" (Brucks et al. 2012, p. 1089). Although the example (e.g., Whitney's case) provided here shows strong resemblance to materialism (Richins et al. 1992; Richins 2014), other informant stories (not reported here due to space limitations) showed that not all intense relationships involving voids that eventually lead to addiction are characterized by materialism (such as in the sports context or involving other forms of behavioral addictions).

We extend existing perspectives and frameworks by introducing voids as a trigger that may eventually result in, as well as a driver that can sustain/perpetuate, addiction. The identification of voids as an antecedent to consumer addiction broadens our understanding of the developmental process to before the "pre-addiction phase" (Brucks et al. 2012). The identification of "voids" as the foundation or "seed" to consumer addiction (and potentially, other "darker" forms of consumption, e.g., materialism, impulsive and compulsive consumption behaviors) differs to existing explanations in the literature, which often suggest psychological weaknesses (e.g., lack of self-control) as the underlying driver of these consumer behaviors. It is argued that a void is different to a psychological weakness in that while psychological weaknesses relate purely to one's internal state, voids can be due to something that is external to the individual (Ashton 2007), which exists in other informant stories not reported here. Voids based on the *feeling* of vague incapacity or loss of something once had (Ashton 2007) as an internal (affective) state, is also different to the inability to exert self-control (i.e., a psychological weakness; a cognitive state). Extending the study of addiction to also explore voids will therefore expand our understanding of the development and drivers of addiction to beyond the limited context of psychological weaknesses.

Existing research on consumer addictions has had a focus on chemical addictions (e.g., to drugs and alcohol) and behavioral addiction in the form of gambling/gaming and compulsive shopping/buying. This paper extends the study of addiction by exploring addictions to other seemingly "harmless" products/brands (at least under "normal" consumption contexts/circumstances) such as to handbags (in

Whitney's case), as well as toys and model cars (not reported here due to space limitations). Future research should further explore "voids" (including teasing out the different types of voids) and their role in the development of consumer addiction and other potentially maladaptive consumer behavior. It may also be worthwhile to study recovered consumer addicts to understand what has helped them break their addictive cycle. This will respond to calls for transformative consumer research that contributes towards consumers' well-being and quality of life (Mick 2006).

References available upon request.

From Ownership to Sharing, Through Barter Communities

Motivations, Behaviors, and Value at zerorelativo.com

Daniele Dalli and Fulvio Fortezza

Introduction

Recent literature, as well as practice, highlights the growing importance assumed by new forms of access to consumption resources, such as renting, sharing, and swapping (Albinsson and Perera 2009, 2012; Bardhi and Eckhart 2012; Belk 2010). Free and upon payment systems grew and are integrating the consolidated buy and own approach: Zipcar, Airbnb, Couchsurfing, Bookcrossing. These forms differ from traditional market transactions in many respects (Humphreys and Giesler 2007). For example, consumers often access goods, services, and information without purchasing or possessing them. The development of the Internet made access based consumption systems viable and attractive.

We are interested in these processes for two main reasons: first of all, in given conditions, consumers are able to access free resources, while in other conditions they are asked to provide some form of compensation and/or to respect norms of reciprocity (Belk 2014a). Second, when accessing these resources the degree of appropriation is largely lower than the traditional buy and own approach. In given cases, consumers simply access resources, while in other cases they can get part time possess or control over these resources.

From the theoretical point of view, the purpose of this chapter is that of reconsidering the role of barter in extant literature about consumer research from a market-based mechanism to a form of collaborative consumption or sharing. Even if it is based on market-like transactions, barter often turns out to be a form of part time

D. Dalli (✉)
University of Pisa, Pisa, Italy
e-mail: dalli@ec.unipi.it

F. Fortezza
University of Ferrara, Ferrara, Italy
e-mail: fulvio.fortezza@unife.it

© Academy of Marketing Science 2016
L. Petruzzellis, R.S. Winer (eds.), *Rediscovering the Essentiality of Marketing*, Developments in Marketing Science: Proceedings of the Academy of Marketing Science, DOI 10.1007/978-3-319-29877-1_23

103

access to consumption goods, especially in a platform like the one studied. In such a condition, personal endowments are exchanged between people several times and they could then be considered as collective endowments to be shared.

The empirical setting in which we gather our data is a *synchronous* swap platform (Zerorelativo.it, or ZR) in which consumers exchange their products with other consumers. The difference between synchronous and asynchronous is that in the former case, participants cannot sell items for money, nor for credit of any kind so that they are forced to actually trade and negotiate the relative value of the items they want to exchange.

This contribution shows some important peculiarities with respect to previous studies about collaborative consumption and bartering:

(a) Unlike some of them (e.g., Albinsson and Perera 2009, 2012; Kozinets 2002), we focus on online platforms for exchanging goods and services.
(b) We focus on bartering and not on generic forms of collaborative consumption (Botsman and Rogers 2010) or other kinds of online platforms.
(c) We consider barter exchanges within a specific platform in given time period: this allows the emergence of dynamic and collective processes that are difficult to identify in discrete events (Albinsson and Perera 2009, 2012).
(d) We study bartering between common people, some of whom present ethical instances. The setting is then different from Burning Man (Kozinets 2002).
(e) Following Albinson and Perera (2012), this chapter addresses the infrastructure level that is necessary to enable individuals to actually exchange, barter, share, etc.
(f) Existing literature about bartering and collaborative consumption does not explain accurately why people get involved in such practices and who they are.
(g) Existing studies about bartering don't state clearly or specifically the nature and the dynamics of the exchanges that take place among barterers.
(h) We argue that studying bartering is an interesting opportunity to understand the growing phenomenon of collaborative consumption, but also interesting instances that emerge from the demand side of the market: sustainability, frugality, and liquidity (Bardhi et al. 2012).
(i) Dealing with individual members that belong to a given community we are able to show how important is the relational dimension of the exchange regime (Kozinets 2002), unlike Belk (2014b) and Arsel (2013) stated.

This chapter aims at answering four research questions about the relationship between bartering and sharing.

First of all we are interested in identifying the objectives that ZR members want to pursue in bartering. We consider economic, ethic, critical, and social motivational factors and the way in which they transform into actual conducts, given rules, and goals to be pursued through bartering.

Second, we are interested in the kind of value which ZR givers and takers seek or consider when dealing with barters.

Third, we believe that communities like ZR are made of people with very different characteristics, values, goals, and motivations. So we want to highlight the importance of different profiles and roles within a communitarian regime of exchange.

Finally, we want to find a way to demonstrate that, in a barter community like ZR, dyadic, quasi-market transactions lead to a distribution regime with properties that are very close to sharing (Belk 2010).

Methodology

Many of the most-known international websites for bartering are hybrid (they mix bartering and selling, e.g., www.swap.com, www.swapz.co.uk) or asynchronous (they use some forms of credits in order to enhance exchanges, e.g., www.swaptreasures.com, www.barterquest.com).

Within this scenario, Zerorelativo.it (ZR) shows very interesting features. ZR is the most popular bartering website in Italy. It was created in 2006 with the aim of recovering secondhand products thanks to non-monetary exchanges between end users. There are now more than 37,000 registered users over this website.

Its main features are the following:

- Synchronous exchanges
- Boards for barterers to discuss in order to accomplish and manage their deals
- Rules and steps for barterers to upload their ads and manage their deals
- A sort of moderation done by the organizers of the website
- The importance of trust among users marked by the organizers of the website

We collected two types of data. First, 25 interviews with ZR members were carried out through Skype. Interviewees have been randomly selected among those who are more active in terms of the number and the frequency of exchanges they have accomplished and the assessments they received over the time. This selection implies that interviewees do not represent the "average" ZR member, but the more committed, active, and fair participants: we are interested in these profiles as they are probably those who more likely live ZR as a community and a source of collective resources.

The second source of data consists in participant observation, where it was possible to collect statements and evaluations through their offers, comments, assessments, and complaints. From June 2012 to January 2014 we have analyzed the following ZR web resources: users' personal notice boards, the website help section, the community blog, and the Facebook fan-page.

Data analysis was carried out by either authors following the standard coding procedures (Romano et al. 2003; Spiggle 1994; Thompson 1997).

Results and Discussion

Motivations and Related Behaviors

The primary (early) objectives for which ZR members enter the community are recycling and disposal of unused items, search for convenience, a more sustainable lifestyle and the willing to use alternative marketing channels (Albinsson and Perera 2012). These factors are primary in the sense that they are related to the very first attempts to use the platform and could be also defined original or elementary. They belong to different motivational factors, such as sustainability or ethics (e.g., recycling and sustainable lifestyle) and convenience or utility (e.g., disposing unused stuff and economizing)

Recycling is one of the most frequent motivations mentioned by ZR members and has a mix of utilitarian and ethical components. Some members initially engage in barter for extracting some value from their items (Brace-Govan and Binay 2010; Epp and Price 2010; Kozinets 2002) while more ethically minded members want to circulate their items, giving them a sort of new life and let other people benefit from the residual value these items still hold (Albinsson and Perera 2009). A second, frequent factor considered when approaching barter is disposal: the need to remove unused objects from the house, freeing room for new ones.

A limited number of respondents explain their first attempts to barter as economizing that is searching for convenient offerings and saving money. Other members, an even smaller number, began to barter on ZR due to their desire to take on a more sustainable consumption lifestyle: they basically want to consume less, to purchase less new goods, and reduce waste.

As long as members attend the community and begin to barter, some rules of conduct emerge. The most important is kindness: this is the discriminant quality that ZR members consider when they have to decide with whom to initiate and manage exchange relationships. Kindness has to do with formal and elementary rules of online and off-line interaction (politeness, welcoming, etc.), but also with more substantial aspects of the economic, human, and technical dimensions of the swap.

A second set of objectives (advanced) emerge after some time of barter practicing and explain a sort of enduring, more mature and reflexive form of participation in the ZR community. Many of our informants refer that they feel the more and more involved in ZR due to their need to get in touch with like-minded people. Bartering and exchange objects are often seen as means for socializing and, at the same time, the focus of attention moves away from the value of the exchanged items and gets closer to friendship and solidarity.

As long as ZR members participate in the barter activity and develop their networks, they often look for (and actually get) products on ZR with the purpose of giving them away as gifts (barter for gifting). Some ZR members barter for exchanging voluptuary goods, things that they would never buy, but that let them feel good (Arsel 2010). Bartering for gifts and exchanging voluptuary goods are closely related to a specific experiential dimension of ZR practice: bartering as a playful pastime (Arsel 2013), like a hobby in which practical activities (disposal, clearing the house, etc.) are managed in a lively way. In so doing, they experience bargaining, negotiation, and business like activities as a kind of game. In some cases, barters say that barter is good per se: like a sort of self-fulfilling activity.

While trying to pursue these (more advanced) objectives, ZR members follow specific behavioral rules. An important one is reciprocity: as long as barters know each other, they develop cooperative and fair relationships that rely upon reliability, trust, and mutual commitment.

The attitude toward bartering is strongly influenced also by the solidarity toward other members, as individuals and a collective. This often implies a reduced attention for strict economic considerations and the willingness to give products and resources for free (time, shipping costs, etc.), both upon request or even as a general act of generosity (Black and Cherrier 2010).

Member Profiles

In ZR there seems to be a sort of evolutionary path from early experiences to more mature and established ones: in an initial phase, some new entrants are so fully involved in bartering that they end up practicing it for its own sake. However, as ZR members increase their experience, their attitudes and behaviors change and assume a more moderate and reflexive stance (Albinsson and Perera 2012).

As in many communities, instead of a homogeneous, average, or even ideal types of members, ZR is made of people that assume different roles (Tandy-Chalmers et al. 2013). According to the process of acculturation and due to personal traits, ZR members can be classified according to different profiles:

- The greedy: they want to experience a further channel (usually not the preferred one) to improve their consumption possibilities through getting the most value out of the products they own. They want to get value out of items they no longer use or are not interested in. Their value driver is mostly the market value of the items they offer, that is its monetary value. Because of this they often seem subject to the endowment effect (Kahneman et al. 1990; Thaler 1980) and have arguments with other users about the fairness of the proposed exchanges. They present shorter memberships if compared with other profiles. Finally, they rely upon ZR if and when they are not able to sell their items on other platforms, such as eBay. In some cases, some of these members try to cheat other users or profit from information asymmetry (Albinsson and Perera 2009).
- The educated: they are the largest and most active group in the community. They practice bartering at first in order to get rid of extra-stuff and free up space in their homes, to get something useful in return and to perform exchanges in a clever way, even ethical and mindful. Some of them may be also looking for some sort of social recognition for performing exchange activities in a clever way. The relational and social dimension of bartering is important and it grows

up time by time. In this process they develop a network of relationships with preferred exchange partners. Therefore, when dealing with their "best friends" on Zerorelativo they tend to act in a completely different way with respect to usual deals. In fact, in such situations they show a really lower—even absent— endowment effect. These users tend to gradually experience a kind of educational path in their daily life over the community (Albinsson and Perera 2012). So they become more acculturated and responsible regarding their consumption and disposition choices.

- The communard: this is the smallest group within the community. They are strongly committed to the emancipatory and transformative dimension of ZR. Bartering for them is part of personal strategy of sustainable consumption. They mainly use bartering as a way to strengthen their relationships over the community with like-minded people. They often offer homemade products (craftwork, food, etc.) and their free-time as well. They frequently practice also gift giving and other forms of solidarity in and outside the community.

Value

According to our informants, there are two major forms of value that are considered when bartering: exchange and use value. ZR members consider exchange value when they explicitly refer to the monetary value of their items: in some cases they speak of the price they paid, while in others they refer to other elements (e.g., brand) as proxies of the items intrinsic value.

Even those who criticize materialistic attitudes and behaviors clearly identify the exchange value as a driver for value assessment, even if in critical terms.

The difference between exchange and use value explicitly emerges from our respondents: some of them recognize the conflict between the two and assess the importance of use value vs. exchange vale.

Identity value has to do with the subjective characteristics of the barterer who offered the item: in given cases objects assume an additional value because they have been given by a specific person. In this sense, we see also a sort of linking value, which can modify the way users estimate what they are giving and receiving (Askegaard and Linnet 2011).

Discussion

As evidenced in the literature review, barter is a quasi-market exchange system in which two parties negotiate the relative value of their offerings and try to get the most out of what they offer (Graeber 2012). In the conditions we found on ZR, some members show that this practice turns out to be something different. Something in which expected selfish and economic or utilitarian attitudes and behaviors assume an altruistic, collaborative, and communal dimension.

First of all, barterers sometimes behave as if they are practicing gift giving, for affective or solidarity reasons.

In other, more limited cases, ZR members seem to live some of their endowments as flowing or circulating within the community.

Conclusion

The Internet makes it easier to boost bartering thanks to many chances of satisfying exchanges for users. Nowadays people have new values, new needs, a new environmental sensitivity and struggle with new challenges from the economic crisis. In such a scenario, online bartering presents several interesting features. Some people see barter exchanges just in the light of market exchanges. So even in the absence of money when evaluating what they offer and what they can get in return they just aim at maximizing the economic value they can get out of the exchange. From this point of view, bartering exchanges look very similar to exchanges that take place in secondhand markets.

But reasons for users to barter vary from one kind of barterer to another as well as the way they assess exchanges and the same concept of value they consider. The community may have a strong influence thanks to the trust and the relationships which occur among like-minded people. Under these conditions bartering may really tend to sharing. In fact, as our findings show, within the community people feel that the boundary between "yours" and "mine" may become less relevant as users are less focused on owning specific items and more oriented at accessing them.

References available upon request.

Brand Addiction: A New Concept for Understanding Consumer Brand Behavior

Mona Mrad and Charles Cui

Abstract This research introduces the concept of "brand addiction" as a new marketing construct. Employing conceptual development, the concept of brand addiction is defined as a psychological state that entails an obsessive relationship between the consumer and a specific brand. To examine the phenomenon of brand addiction, the present research was designed based on partial sequential mixed methods in which a qualitative study was followed by two quantitative studies, a pretest and a main survey. Arguing that research on brand addiction should be built based on an understanding of how consumers experience this phenomenon in reality, the research incorporated a series of four qualitative focus group studies to uncover the possible core features of the brand addiction prototype using discursive psychological perspective.

Survey data were subsequently used to generate the brand addiction measurement scale. Based on the qualitative study and critical review of the extant literature, we developed and tested a measurement scale of brand addiction to gauge the consumer's addictive behavior toward particular brands. As a result from exploratory and confirmatory factor analyses, the brand addiction measurement scale employed 14 items. The results appear to be promising for using this scale for further validation and more complicated research that may involve possible consequences caused by consumers' brand addictive behavior.

Therefore, rather than limiting to the interpersonal-relationship-based and addiction-based theories, this research has gone further in building an understanding of how consumers truly experience brand addiction, thus sheds new lights on this underrepresented phenomenon in the literature.

M. Mrad (✉)
Lebanese American University, Beirut, Lebanon
e-mail: mona.mrad@lau.edu.lb

C. Cui
University of Manchester, Manchester, UK
e-mail: charles.cui@mbs.ac.uk

© Academy of Marketing Science 2016
L. Petruzzellis, R.S. Winer (eds.), *Rediscovering the Essentiality of Marketing*,
Developments in Marketing Science: Proceedings of the Academy of Marketing
Science, DOI 10.1007/978-3-319-29877-1_24

111

Adding New Perspectives to the Zero-Price Effect: The Role of Non-monetary Cost Perceptions

Björn A. Hüttel, Christian J. Wagner, and Jan H. Schumann

Abstract Research shows that free offers lead to positive affective consumer reactions which result in an irrationally high demand (i.e., zero-price effect). Based on the assumption of constant costs prior research argues that consumers attribute extra benefits to free offers. Yet, so far there is no empirical evidence for this claim. In this research we test this assumption but also challenge the assumption of constant costs. In a first study in the context of free e-services we show that consumers perceive not only the benefits of free offers but also their non-monetary costs. Moreover, we show that consumers actually overemphasize the benefits of a free e-service but also less perceive its non-monetary costs (i.e., advertising intrusiveness). Further we show that the lower perception of non-monetary costs does not occur for critical non-monetary costs like personal data. In a second study we show that both the attribution of extra benefits and the lower perception of non-monetary costs disappear when the offer is mainly utilitarian. Consequently under these conditions also the zero-price effect vanishes. This research extends prior marketing theory by adding a new explanatory aspect to and outlining boundary conditions of the zero-price effect. The results are also relevant for marketing practitioners currently offering free services or products or considering switching to a free business model.

B.A. Hüttel (✉) • C.J. Wagner • J.H. Schumann
University of Passau, Passau, Germany
e-mail: Bjoern.Huettel@uni-passau.de; Christian.Wagner@uni-passau.de; Jan.Schumann@uni-passau.de

© Academy of Marketing Science 2016
L. Petruzzellis, R.S. Winer (eds.), *Rediscovering the Essentiality of Marketing*,
Developments in Marketing Science: Proceedings of the Academy of Marketing
Science, DOI 10.1007/978-3-319-29877-1_25

Representing Value Co-creation as a Practice of Consumption: Customers' Perspectives and Actions

Joaquim Silva and Cláudia Simões

Abstract The notion of value co-creation conveys that resource exchange among social and economic actors is the basis for value creation. Service Dominant Logic (S-D logic) develops a holistic view that gives the customer an active role in co-creation, as value is created during the consumption experience (Vargo and Lusch 2008). Theoretical models represent co-creation as a collaborative exchange of resources (service) between the firm and the customer, where the firm is in control (e.g., Lusch and Vargo 2014; Vargo et al. 2008). The firm–customer interactions are at the center of multiple co-creative interactions among different actors, within (eco)systems of value. S-D logic evolved from a dual representation of co-creation to a systemic view, centered on the (eco)systems of value (Vargo et al. 2008), without fully understanding how the customer acts, which resources are exchanged and integrated, and the nature of interactions performed when offers are consumed. Customer's interactions are diverse and service exchange may occur beyond firm's intervention or control. In some cases, co-creation is independent or dissonant from the firm (Hollenbeck and Zinkhan 2010). In this research we propose a representation of co-creation as a practice, focused on the centrality of customer's interactions with the offer and with service (eco)systems. The study integrates theoretical insights from S-D logic (e.g., Vargo and Lusch, 2004, 2008), practice theory (e.g., Schatzki 1996), and a cultural resource-based theory of the customer (Arnould et al. 2006). Theory is applied in an empirical qualitative study, designed to understand customers' perspectives and routine practices of using a tangible offer (kitchen appliance), and interacting with service (eco)systems. Studying an infinite experience and a tangible product is innovative, and is consonant with the materialist view of practice theory that considers objects as elements of the practice (Reckwitz 2002). Data collection entailed 45 in-depth interviews,

J. Silva (✉)
University of Minho, Braga, Portugal
e-mail: josilva@eeg.uminho.pt

C. Simões
Open University Business School, Milton Keynes, UK
e-mail: claudia.simoes@open.ac.uk

© Academy of Marketing Science 2016
L. Petruzzellis, R.S. Winer (eds.), *Rediscovering the Essentiality of Marketing*,
Developments in Marketing Science: Proceedings of the Academy of Marketing Science, DOI 10.1007/978-3-319-29877-1_26

115

two direct observation sessions, and multiple secondary physical and digital data. Findings suggest that customer's practices integrate multiple elements that configure and organize the bodily and mental actions, such as know-how, images, materials, operant resources, and life goals. Customers are practitioners, because they carry social practices when executing sequences of actions in the consumption of an offer, which are structured by the social practice. Customers are also imaginative interpreters, integrators of multiple resources, and autonomous, creating unique value. Due to its technological nature, the offer becomes part of the practice as it runs autonomously, being positioned as an "assistant." Practice is conceived as a co-practice, in the same sense that value creation is a co-creation. Resources are shared in (eco)systems of peers and the firm, in a co-creative process, contributing to reconfiguring the social practice. The firm is one among other service providers, but it is not the main source, or even a direct source for the exchange of service. For the customer, value-in-use represents the true meaning for value. Value includes several functional, hedonic, and procedural aspects, and has a hierarchical, complex, and multifaceted nature. Consumption emerges as a means to reach life goals that are beyond the consumption episodes. Findings contribute to theory, by proposing a renewed representation of co-creation, from the customer's perspective, as a practice of consumption. It positions the interactions customer-offer and customer-(eco)systems at the center of co-creation. The control over co-creation shifts from the firm to the customer, and from the service exchange arena to the customer's life space. This study endures the limitations of a qualitative research. Future studies should deepen the analysis of customer's practices, and systematically classify the most significant elements involved in co-creation.

References available upon request.

Cause I'll Feel Good! The Influence of Anticipated Emotions on Consumer Pro-environmental Behavior

Zeinab Rezvani and Johan Jansson

Abstract Although consumers express environmental attitudes, the pro-environmental behaviors are not dominant. Despite the benefits of sustainable technologies in reducing the environmental impacts of consumption, consumer adoption of these technologies is very slow to take off. We propose an integrated approach for investigating the effect of consumer anticipated emotions and moral norms on consumer adoption of a sustainable technology (electric vehicles). 576 Swedish car drivers participated in an online survey during winter of 2013. Our findings suggest that anticipated emotions directly influence consumer adoption intentions and the effect of moral norms on behavioral intentions is mediated by the anticipated emotions. The findings have implications for policymakers and car producers in promoting the zero emission transportation. We suggest communicating the positive emotions related to driving an electric vehicle and use of emotions in cars' energy labelling.

Keywords Anticipated emotion • Moral norm • Consumer pro-environmental behavior • Ascription of responsibility • Attitude • Sustainable technology

Introduction

Technologies such as Alternative Fuel Vehicles (AFVs) and solar power generators are examples of sustainable technologies which replace fossil fuels with renewable energy in the areas of transportation and energy generation. Marketing of these technologies is an essential part of a transition to a less environmentally harmful economy. An important part of this marketing process is to understand the drivers for consumer adoption of these sustainable technologies. This pro-environmental behavior has been referred to the behavior that "harms the environment as little as possible, or even benefits the environment" (Steg and Vlek 2009, p. 1). However, research shows that consumer adoption and thus use of sustainable technologies is

Z. Rezvani (✉) • J. Jansson
Umeå School of Business and Economics, Umeå, Sweden
e-mail: zeinab.rezvani@umu.se; johan.jansson@umu.se

© Academy of Marketing Science 2016   117
L. Petruzzellis, R.S. Winer (eds.), *Rediscovering the Essentiality of Marketing*,
Developments in Marketing Science: Proceedings of the Academy of Marketing
Science, DOI 10.1007/978-3-319-29877-1_27

very slow to take off. It has been concluded that "consumers' ecological attitudes often fail to materialize into actual purchase of green products like renewable energy" (Claudy et al. 2013, p. 1), or adoption of eco-friendly cars (van Rijnsoever et al. 2009). Thus, further research on determinants and drivers for pro-environmental behaviors is warranted to understand how the attitude-behavior gap can be bridged.

Steg and Vlek's (2009) review and Bamberg and Möser's (2007) meta-analysis of the drivers for pro-environmental behavior indicate the dominance of "weighing costs and benefits" in theorization of drivers, whereas other factors than rational evaluations of costs and benefits also influence behavior. They emphasize the importance of emotions and moral norms and assert that studies on emotional aspects of consumer pro-environmental behaviors have received less attention in previous research (Bamberg and Möser 2007; Steg and Vlek 2009). Only a few studies have explored the influence of emotions on consumer pro-environmental behaviors (i.e., Steg and Vlek 2009; Schuitema et al. 2013; Moons and De Pelsmacker 2012). Most often, these studies focus on the role of negative emotions such as guilt and shame (Onwezen et al. 2013). Studies on positive emotions driving pro-environmental behaviors are even fewer (Corral Verdugo 2012; Onwezen et al. 2013). Thus, it is not well understood how emotions in general, and positive emotions in particular, are related to pro-environmental consumer behavior. Furthermore, while moral norms, defined as "a moral obligation to perform or refrain from specific actions", are shown to be important drivers for consumer pro-environmental behaviors (Jansson et al. 2010), their relations with emotions are investigated in only a few studies (i.e., Bamberg and Möser 2007; Onwezen et al. 2013) with results being inconsistent.

Norm Activation Model (NAM) demonstrates the process in which moral norms are activated and influence consumer pro-environmental intentions. NAM asserts that "one must be aware of the consequences of behaviour before feeling responsible to engage in this behaviour or acknowledging that one's own contribution may be useful. In turn, ascription of responsibility increases feelings of moral obligation to act pro-socially, and these feelings of obligation induce pro-social behavioural intentions" (De Groot and Steg 2009). In the sustainable consumption situation, moral norms are linked to anticipated emotions on the grounds that an individual may anticipate experiencing negative emotions (e.g., shame, guilt) after having broken internalized moral norms. Similarly, that person might anticipate experiencing positive emotions (e.g., pleasure, pride) following committing to the moral norm (Manstead 2000; Rivis et al. 2009). Consequently, both positive and negative anticipated emotions in these cases are drivers to consumer's intentions for pro-environmental behaviors. However, anticipating negative emotions of embarrassment, regret, and nervousness by potential consumers are found to be barriers against adoption of Electric Vehicles (EVs) (Schuitema et al. 2013) and it is not known whether the higher levels of moral norms can influence or lessen anticipating these negative emotions.

This chapter contributes to the literature on consumer pro-environmental behavior, an important part of sustainability marketing management, by extending the NAM and investigating the associations between moral norms and positive and negative emotions in the context of adopting a sustainable technology, namely the EV. In line with previous research showing a direct effect of anticipated emotions (Bagozzi et al. 1999; Rivis et al. 2009; Elgaaied 2012; Onwezen et al. 2013), this study proposes a direct effect of anticipated emotions on intentions to adopt EVs and a mediating role of anticipated emotions on the influence of moral norms on consumer intentions. In line with the NAM, moral norms are activated with environmental awareness and attitudes and ascription of responsibility.

Method

A questionnaire survey was carried out concerning EVs. The target population was Swedish car drivers/owners, since people who own a car likely can relate themselves more to the product and behavior of the current study. Data was collected utilizing an online user-friendly third party survey system. In December 2013, the link to the online survey was sent to the email addresses of 926 car drivers who opted to participate in the survey via a car inspection site (www.bilprovningen.se). Respondents were promised to receive a lottery ticket with the value of 30 SEK (circa 3 Euros) for participating. They received the link to the lottery ticket in electronic format after having completed the survey. After one reminder, 573 answers (response rate of close to 62%) were received and formed the database of this research. The questionnaire survey covered different aspects of cars, EVs, driving, emotions, and background factors. Not all measures in the survey were utilized for this specific study.

Compared to the total population of Swedish car drivers, the sample has a significantly higher representation of males (90%) than females (10%) which usually occurs in studies related to cars (Egbue and Long 2012; Olson 2013). The sociodemographic data of the sample is presented in Table 1. The proportion of AFV car owners in the sample (18%) is also higher compared to the Swedish car driving population (8%). The overall sample is proportionate to car drivers in Sweden in terms of age, education, and miles driven per year. It should be noted that the sample may not necessarily be representative of the general population of Sweden.

Measures

To lessen possible measurement errors, instruments from previous studies were used. Six constructs of environmental awareness, responsibility, moral norms, positive emotions, negative emotions, and intentions to adopt EVs were measured using multiple items selected from literature. The measures and related statistics are presented in Table 2. All items were measured on five-point Likert scale. Environmental awareness was measured with three specific items about the environmental impacts of car driving selected from Jansson et al. (2010). Ascription of responsibility to

Table 1 Sample sociodemographic characteristics

		$n = 573$
		%
Gender	Male	90
	Female	10
Age	18–25	6
	26–35	16
	36–45	23
	46–65	41
	>66	14
Education	High school	5
	Pre-college	32
	2 years of college	18
	4 years of college or higher	45
Annual driving distance (×10 km)	1–500	7
	501–1000	16
	1001–1500	25
	1501–2000	20
	2001–3000	18
	3001–4000	9
	Over 4000	5
Fuel of current car	Gasoline	50
	Diesel	13
	Efficient gasoline	5
	Efficient diesel	10
	Bio and Natural gas	5
	Ethanol	11
	Hybrid electric	3
	Plug-in hybrid electric	1
	Battery electric	2

oneself for environmental problems relating to fossil fuel-based car driving was measured with three items based on Steg et al. (2005) and Jansson et al. (2010). Personal moral norms in relation to fossil fuel-based car driving were measured with four items adapted from Steg et al (2005) and Jansson et al. (2010). To assess respondents anticipated emotions, they read the following text first and then answered questions on emotions: "Imagine that you want to purchase a new car for yourself and you have two options which are equally affordable for you: A battery electric vehicle and a regular fuel based car. You think about the battery electric vehicle as an option. Answer the following questions as you think about the battery electric vehicle." The question on emotions started as: "What emotions do you anticipate to have by owning and driving a battery electric vehicle?" The answers were phrased as: "Compared to a regular fuel based car, I will feel [emotions] from owning and driving an EV. "The specific positive and negative emotions were

Table 2 Measurement items loadings, reliability, and validity

Latent construct	Observed indicators	Factor loadings	Composite reliability (CR)	Average variance extracted (AVE)	Cronbach's alpha
Environmental awareness/beliefs	Driving with fossil fuels contributes to environmental degradation	.97	.95	.87	.89
	Driving with fossil fuels contributes to that other people's health deteriorates	.93			
	Driving with fossil fuels has created a lot of CO_2 emissions and environmental problems	.91			
Responsibility	I feel partly responsible for the increase in the use of fossil fuels such as oil/gasoline/diesel	.81	.91	.77	.91
	I am partly responsible for the problems related to the fossil fuels in the society today	.91			
	I feel partly responsible for global warming	.91			
Moral norms	I would be a better person if I drove using electricity or any other biofuel such as ethanol/bio gas	.83	.85	.74	.88
	Item parcel:	.89			
	• I feel a moral obligation to drive cars which run based on electricity or any other biofuels such as ethanol/bio gas instead of fossil fuels such as oil/gasoline/diesel				
	• If I were to replace my car today I would feel a moral obligation to replace it for a car fuelled by electricity or any other biofuel such as ethanol/bio gas				
	• I feel a moral obligation to conserve fossil fuels no matter what other people do				
	• Compared to a regular fuel based car, I will feel less guilt from driving an EV				
Positive emotions	Proud	.92	.83	.62	.83
	Excited	.64			
	Pleasant	.78			
Negative emotions	Embarrassed	.72	.77	.53	.77
	Nervous	.70			
	Regret	.77			
Intentions to adopt EVs	1 year	.60	.77	.64	.73
	5 years	.97			

adapted from literature" (Schuitema et al. 2013; Steg 2005). Positive emotions included single item measures on pride, pleasure, and excitement. Negative emotions included single item measures on regret, embarrassment, and nervousness. Anticipated guilt was also measured with "Compared to a regular fuel based car, I will feel less guilt from driving an EV." Intention, consumer readiness and willingness to adopt an innovation, is the main predictor of adoption behavior and, is in many studies considered as a proxy variable for adoption behavior (Arts et al. 2011; Schuitema et al. 2013). Thus, intentions to adopt EVs were measured using two items, whether the respondent had intentions to adopt EVs in the next year or in the next 5 years.

Structural Model

The hypothesized model was tested using structural equation modelling. The fit indices for the model were as follows: $\chi^2 = 316.963$, df$= 97$, $\rho = 0.000$, $\chi^2/$df$= 3.268$, NNFI$= 0.951$, IFI$= 0.965$, CFI$= 0.965$, RMSEA$= 0.063$ and indicated good fit. All the proposed relationships in the model were significant as illustrated in Table 3. Figure 1 demonstrates the model and standardized estimates. Moreover, the squared multiple correlations for the structural equation were all significant indicating that the substantial proportion of variance in each construct was explained with the measured items. The explained variance in responsibility, moral norms, positive emotions, negative emotions, and intentions was 41%, 58%, 76%, 17%, and 38%, respectively.

As the results demonstrated in Table 3 and Fig. 1 show, the effect of environmental awareness on ascription of responsibility for reducing the negative environmental impacts of car driving was significant and positive ($\beta = .64$, $\rho < .001$). The relationship between responsibility and moral norms was significant and positive ($\beta = .41$, $\rho < .001$), indicating that the higher the ascription of responsibility for the negative environmental impact of car driving, the higher the moral norms and feelings of obligation for reducing this impact. Moreover, modification indices indicated a relationship between environmental awareness and moral norms which was positive and significant ($\beta = .43$, $\rho < .001$). The relationship between moral norms for

Table 3 Standardized regression weights

Construct		Construct	β
Responsibility	←	Awareness	.636
Moral norms	←	Responsibility	.413
Moral norms	←	Awareness	.428
Positive emotions	←	Moral norms	.872
Negative emotions	←	Moral norms	−.407
Intentions	←	Positive emotions	.577
Intentions	←	Negative emotions	−.089

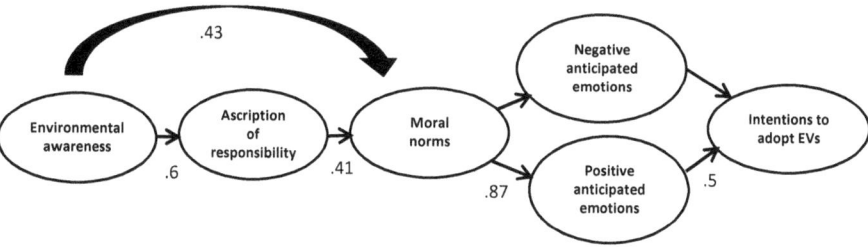

Fig. 1 Standardized path coefficients

reducing the environmental impacts of car driving with fossil fuels was positively correlated with anticipating positive emotions towards owning an EV ($\beta=.87$, $\rho<.001$) and negatively correlated with anticipating negative emotions from owning an EV ($\beta=-.41$, $\rho<.001$). Anticipating positive emotions from owning an EV positively correlated with intentions to adopt an EV ($\beta=.58$, $\rho<.001$) while anticipating negative emotions correlated negatively with intentions to adopt an EV ($\beta=-.09$, $\rho<.05$).

Discussion and Managerial Implications

This study proposes an integrated model of NAM and anticipated positive and negative emotions to explain the normative and emotional drivers for consumer intentions to adopt a sustainable technology. A sample of Swedish car drivers was utilized to empirically evaluate the robustness of the proposed model which investigates the associations between environmental awareness, ascription of responsibility, moral norms, anticipated emotions, and consumer adoption of electric vehicles. The results showed that moral norms regarding car driving and reducing the negative environmental impacts of car driving are activated by the awareness of environmental problems and ascription of responsibility. A stronger personal moral norm about reducing the negative environmental impacts of car driving can thus increase the probability of anticipating positive emotions (pride, pleasure, excitement) from driving an EV which in turn increases the probability of intentions to adopt an EV in the future. Strong personal moral norms also correlate negatively with anticipating negative emotions (regret, embarrassment, nervousness) from driving an EV which has negative effect on intentions to adopt EVs. These results extend the NAM with anticipated emotions and show that the effect of anticipated emotions on intentions to adopt a sustainable technology is a direct effect while the effect of moral norms on intentions is mediated by anticipated emotions. The extended NAM with anticipated emotions challenges the NAM as it asserts that anticipated emotions play an important role in activating pro-environmental intentions while previously, moral norms were supposed to activate the intentions directly. The extended NAM with anticipated emotions is in line with previous research on emotions on pro-environmental behavior (Onwezen et al. 2013) and also on emotions in human behavior which assert that emotions directly influence behavior and are based on evaluation of the situation/stimuli (Baumeister et al. 2007; Lazarus 1991).

As the results of SEM analysis show, the positive influence of anticipated positive emotions is stronger on the intentions than the negative influence of anticipated negative emotions. This finding indicates the importance of positive emotions in promoting the adoption of EVs. As for the car manufacturer and marketing practitioners, this study highlights the important role of consumers' anticipated emotions on AFV adoption intentions. Moreover, the findings show that consumers with higher levels of awareness, responsibility, and moral norms are more prone to anticipate positive emotions and less prone to anticipate negative emotions towards AFVs and thus are more prone to adopt an AFV. Communicating the positive emotions from adopting an AFV could be one way for car manufacturers and marketers of AFVs to improve the market breakthrough. Moreover, marketers and car manufacturers can utilize emotional design in energy labels of cars (with so-called emoticons), in a way that positive emotions would be linked to the zero or close to zero emissions and negative emotions linked to the higher emissions.

As for policymakers and activists, this study discusses some of drivers for and barriers against consumer adoption of environmentally sustainable solutions. Creating awareness and communicating personal responsibilities and moral norms related to the environment and consumption are important drivers for consumer adoption of sustainable solutions. However, one should note that consumer anticipated emotions about sustainable solutions (such as AFVs) have important influences on this behavior as well. Thus consumer anticipated emotions should be considered in designing the education and promotion plans by policymakers. At the time that survival and well-being of all lives on earth is threatened by environmental problems, envisioning feeling good and positive from adopting a less harmful behavior can be an added trigger to the scientific and normative education and promotions that are provided for citizens. This study suggests that policymakers and environmental organizations not only communicate the scientific results of their research on environmental issues and the effect of sustainable solutions by presenting facts and moral arguments, but also use emotional arguments and promote the positive emotions that can be felt with using sustainable solutions. Another implication for policymakers is to encourage car companies to use emotionally laden advertising and marketing for AFVs and EVs to gain a positive outcome in terms of replacing the fossil fuel based cars with AFVs and EVs. Moreover, policymakers can limit the use of emotionally laden advertising for fossil fuel cars or even ask to relate the fossil cars promotions with negative emotions which could act as barriers to adoption of fossil cars. Also, as policymakers try to influence the market breakthrough for AFVs with policies that motivate the use of AFVs (i.e., the Swedish fossil fuel free car fleet by 2030 policy) the use of emotional messages for communicating about policies, and AFVs are recommended.

References

Arts, J. W. C., Frambach, R. T., & Bijmolt, T. H. A. (2011). Generalizations on consumer innovation adoption: A meta-analysis on drivers of intention and behavior. *International Journal of Research in Marketing, 28*(2), 134–144.

Bagozzi, R. P., Gopinath, M., & Nyer, P. U. (1999). The role of emotions in marketing. *Journal of the Academy of Marketing Science, 27*(2), 184–206.

Bamberg, S., & Möser, G. (2007). Twenty years after Hines, Hungerford, and Tomera: A new meta-analysis of psycho-social determinants of pro-environmental behaviour. *Journal of Environmental Psychology, 27*(1), 14–25.

Baumeister, R. F., Vohs, K. D., DeWall, C. N., & Zhang, L. (2007). How emotion shapes behavior: Feedback, anticipation, and reflection, rather than direct causation. *Personality and Social Psychology Review, 11*(2), 167–203.

Claudy, M. C., Peterson, M., & O'Driscoll, A. (2013). Understanding the attitude-behavior gap for renewable energy systems using behavioral reasoning theory. *Journal of Macromarketing, 33*, 273–287.

Corral Verdugo, V. (2012). The positive psychology of sustainability. *Environment, Development and Sustainability, 14*(5), 651–666.

De Groot, J. I. M., & Steg, L. (2009). Morality and prosocial behavior: The role of awareness, responsibility, and norms in the norm activation model. *The Journal of Social Psychology, 149*(4), 425–449.

Egbue, O., & Long, S. (2012). Barriers to widespread adoption of electric vehicles: An analysis of consumer attitudes and perceptions. *Energy Policy, 48*, 717–729.

Elgaaied, L. (2012). Exploring the role of anticipated guilt on pro-environmental behavior—A suggested typology of residents in France based on their recycling patterns. *Journal of Consumer Marketing, 29*(5), 369–377.

Jansson, J., Marell, A., & Nordlund, A. (2010). Green consumer behavior: Determinants of curtailment and eco-innovation adoption. *Journal of Consumer Marketing, 27*(4), 358–370.

Lazarus, R. S. (1991). Progress on a cognitive-motivational-relational theory of emotion. *The American Psychologist, 46*(8), 819–834. Retrieved from http://www.ncbi.nlm.nih.gov/pubmed/1928936

Manstead, A. S. R. (2000). The role of moral norms in the attitude-behavior relations. In D. J. Terry & M. A. Hogg (Eds.), *Attitude, behavior and social context* (pp. 11–30). Mahwah, NJ: Erlbaum.

Moons, I., & De Pelsmacker, P. (2012). Emotions as determinants of electric car usage intention. *Journal of Marketing Management, 28*(3–4), 195–237.

Olson, E. L. (2013). It's not easy being green: The effects of attribute tradeoffs on green product preference and choice. *Journal of the Academy of Marketing Science, 41*(2), 171–184.

Onwezen, M. C., Antonides, G., & Bartels, J. (2013). The norm activation model: An exploration of the functions of anticipated pride and guilt in pro-environmental behaviour. *Journal of Economic Psychology, 39*, 141–153.

Rivis, A., Sheeran, P., & Armitage, C. J. (2009). Expanding the affective and normative components of the theory of planned behavior: A meta-analysis of anticipated affect and moral norms. *Journal of Applied Social Psychology, 39*(12), 2985–3019.

Schuitema, G., Anable, J., Skippon, S., & Kinnear, N. (2013). The role of instrumental, hedonic and symbolic attributes in the intention to adopt electric vehicles. *Transportation Research Part A: Policy and Practice, 48*, 39–49.

Steg, L. (2005). Car use: Lust and must. Instrumental, symbolic and affective motives for car use. *Transportation Research Part A: Policy and Practice, 39*(2–3), 147–162.

Steg, L., Dreijerink, L., & Abrahamse, W. (2005). Factors influencing the acceptability of energy policies: A test of VBN theory. *Journal of Environmental Psychology, 25*(4), 415–425.

Steg, L., & Vlek, C. (2009). Encouraging pro-environmental behaviour: An integrative review and research agenda. *Journal of Environmental Psychology, 29*(3), 309–317.

Van Rijnsoever, F., Farla, J., & Dijst, M. J. (2009). Consumer car preferences and information search channels. *Transportation Research Part D: Transport and Environment, 14*(5), 334–342.

The Devil You Know: Service Failures, Self-Esteem, and Behavioral Loyalty

Irene Consiglio and Stijn M.J. van Osselaer

Abstract We investigate one of the factors that might explain behavioral loyalty in face of service failures. Research suggests that individuals with low self-esteem who experience relational transgressions develop an avoidant attachment style, which impairs their interpersonal functioning and their willingness to take further interpersonal risks (Park and Maner 2009), and in particular to engage in other long-term relationships (Walker 2009). Drawing on this research, we propose that low self-esteem (LSE) consumers who experience service failures become unwilling to commit themselves to alternative brands, even when they have the opportunity to do so, thus—paradoxically—they remain trapped in their current brand relationship. High self-esteem (HSE) consumers, instead, are more likely to switch to other available service providers when they experience service failures, as compared to when they do not experience failures. We also predict that LSE consumers who experience service failures tend to avoid new commitments *in general*, thus favoring transactions relative to long-term contracts, even in consumption domains that are unrelated to the service failure.

In study 1a, participants completed a measure of self-esteem (Rosenberg 1989) and reported the quality of their internet connection. Finally, participants indicated how likely they would be to switch to a competitor of their current Internet provider. As the quality of their internet connection decreased, HSE consumers were more likely to switch. However, frequency of failures did not have an effect on LSE consumers' likelihood to switch. In study 1b, we replicated these findings in an experimental setting: HSE consumers who imagined to use an extremely faulty Internet connection were more likely to switch to an available provider as compared to their counterparts who imagined to use a perfectly functioning Internet connection; LSE consumers did not express different switching intentions between conditions. Since we had hypothesized that the loyalty of LSE consumers in face of service failures is

I. Consiglio (✉)
RSM, Erasmus University, Rotterdam, The Netherlands
e-mail: iconsiglio@rsm.nl

S.M.J. van Osselaer
Cornell University, Ithaca, NY, USA
e-mail: stijn.vanosselaer@cornell.edu

© Academy of Marketing Science 2016
L. Petruzzellis, R.S. Winer (eds.), *Rediscovering the Essentiality of Marketing*,
Developments in Marketing Science: Proceedings of the Academy of Marketing
Science, DOI 10.1007/978-3-319-29877-1_28

driven by their avoidance of new long-term relationships, in study 2 we manipulated the length of the contract offered by an alternative Internet service provider. When an alternative service provider offered a long-term contract (1 year), HSE consumers were more likely to switch to this alternative service provider as the quality of their internet connection worsened, but LSE consumers were not. Instead, when an alternative service provider offered a short-term contract (1 month, renewable), LSE consumers were as likely as HSE consumers to switch to this provider. In study 3, we demonstrate that the fear of new commitments induced by service failures extends to unrelated domains. LSE consumers who imagined to use an extremely faulty Internet connection expressed a greater preference for buying a magazine at the newsstand relative to subscribing to this magazine, as compared to their counterparts who imagined to use a perfectly functioning Internet connection and participants in a negative mood condition. The preferences of HSE consumers, instead, were not affected by service failures.

References available upon request.

Female Self-Gifts Buying Behaviour: Impulse Purchase and Product Involvement

Laurence Kemp, Li-Wei Mai, and Kleopatra Konstantoulaki

Abstract This research examines the effect of product involvement on impulse buying behaviour for self-gifts. An experiment based on a factorial design was conducted among 152 females. Product involvement and self-gift giving context were manipulated by using two scenarios. The dependent variable of impulse buying behaviour was measured with a 6-item impulsivity scale. Results indicate that impulse self-gifting is likely to happen when consumers want to reward themselves after a success. Impulse buying tendency is found to be the best predictor for impulse self-gifting. The higher the level of product involvement is the more impulsive the purchase of a self-gift.

Keywords Self-gifting • Product involvement • Impulse purchase • Experiment design

Introduction

Using consumption as a way to deal with feelings is becoming a way of life (Kalla and Arora 2011). Consumers purchase products when they want to reward themselves, celebrate an accomplishment, relieve stress or cheer ourselves up (Mick and DeMoss 1990a). Such special indulgences have been named as self-gifts in consumer behaviour research. It is most often assumed that self-gifts are premeditated, and consumers might plan in advance to buy themselves something special (Mick and DeMoss 1990b). However, the actual purchase process can be of a highly impulsive nature (Luomala and Laaksonen 1999). The concept of self-gift giving has been linked to impulse buying, even though there is a lack of empirical research on the relationship between the two concepts (Silvera et al. 2008). Product involvement refers to a consumer's long-term attachment to a specific object and has a significant impact on his or her decision-making process (Bauer et al. 2006).

L. Kemp (✉) • L.-W. Mai • K. Konstantoulaki
Westminster Business School, London, UK
e-mail: kemp.laurence@gmail.com; D.L.Mai@wmin.ac.uk; K.Konstantoulaki@wmin.ac.uk

© Academy of Marketing Science 2016   129
L. Petruzzellis, R.S. Winer (eds.), *Rediscovering the Essentiality of Marketing*,
Developments in Marketing Science: Proceedings of the Academy of Marketing
Science, DOI 10.1007/978-3-319-29877-1_29

Academic literature on the topic has been relatively scarce (Ward and Tran 2008; Heath et al. 2011). Mick et al. (1992) called for quantitative research approaches in self-gifting behaviour. Knowing to what extent potential self-gift buyers act impulsively in-store can help practitioners to use meaningful and effective self-gift themes in their communication.

The aim of this research is to examine two different self-gifting behaviour contexts, namely reward and therapy, the levels of product involvement with a specific self-gift scenario and the relation to impulse buying.

Literature Review

Current research on self-gifts is generally pre-theoretical (Mick and Faure 1998). Much of the research is contributed by Mick, DeMoss, Faure, McKeage and Luomala. The link between involvement and impulsive buying of a self-gift has not yet been examined by academic research.

Self-Gift Giving

Self-gifts were first discussed by Mick and DeMoss (1990a) who defined them as personally symbolic self-communication through special indulgences that "tend to be previously planned and highly related to different contexts" (p. 328). They are clearly distinct from ordinary personal acquisitions (Mick and DeMoss 1990a) and can be distinguished by a particular motivation and context (Heath et al. 2011). Self-gifts constitute a hedonic form of consumption rather than a utilitarian one (Mick and DeMoss 1990b). Self-gift giving is fairly common among Western societies (Faure and Mick 1993) with advertising and promotion using self-gift themes such as 'you deserve it' or 'give yourself a treat'. 'Self-love' seems to be a commonly used theme while reward, escape and compensation were found less often in the recent study (Heath et al. 2011).

Women are more likely to buy themselves gifts than men (Ward and Tran 2008). Age and the likelihood of self-gift is negatively related while living alone increases the probability of engaging in self-gift giving (Mick et al. 1992). The common contexts for self-gifting are: 'to reward yourself for an accomplishment', 'to cheer yourself up because you are feeling down', 'when a holiday arrives' and 'because you have some extra money to spend', 'to be nice to oneself', 'to relieve stress' or 'to provide an incentive towards a goal' (Mick and DeMoss 1990a, b; Mick et al 1992); 'when a holiday arrives' was later replaced by 'for your birthday' (Mick et al 1992). The two underlying contexts for a self-gift are: reward: 'a reward for having accomplished personal goal', and therapeutic: a purchase 'to cheer yourself up because you are feeling down' (Mick and DeMoss 1990a; Mick and Faure 1998; Luomala and Laaksonen 1999; Heath et al. 2011).

Reward and Therapeutic Self-Gifts

Reward self-gifts are indulgences following an achievement thanks to an effort and the feeling of deserving a gift and a certain feeling of deservedness is often associated with the end or the completion of a task (Heath et al. 2011). Achievements that trigger a reward self-gift are mostly work-related (Mick and Faure 1998; Tynan et al. 2010). Therapeutic self-gifts on the other hand can serve as a way to temporarily escape negative emotions (Mick and DeMoss 1990a; Heath et al. 2011). Such emotions can be triggered by external events such as a break-up, a dismissal or an accident. Consumers engage in therapeutic self-gift giving if they fail (Mick and Faure 1998). The failure can be of a private or professional nature (Heath et al. 2011). Consumers engage in therapeutic self-gift giving 'to raise their spirits', 'when they feel low or depressed' or 'when they need their self-esteem to be raised' (Sherry et al. 1995). Therapeutic self-gifts are considered as a way to escape problems, to deal with loneliness, abandonment or loss (Sherry et al. 1995; Heath et al. 2011).

Product Involvement

Product involvement can be considered as a type of enduring involvement for which the object of concern is a particular product category. If a consumer is uninvolved with a product, it means that he or she does not care about it and is indifferent towards it (Mittal 1995). High involvement products tend to be relatively expensive, long-lasting goods while low involvement products are mostly cheap and of limited durability (Laurent and Kapferer 1985). Moreover, products of a hedonic, self-expressive, or symbolic nature, such as jewellery or designer clothes, are likely to show higher levels of product involvement than largely functional products (Mittal 1989). Self-gifts can vary in terms of price, ranging from cheap convenience products to expensive, high involvement products (Mick and Faure 1998). They do not necessarily have to be physical products. The reward self-gifts tend to be associated with clothing, restaurant food and travel; in contrast, therapeutic self-gifts are more likely to involve food, music products and personal care (Mick et al. 1992).

Impulse Purchase and Self-Gifts

Impulse buying fulfils a sudden urge to purchase a certain product and entails feelings of pleasure and excitement (Rook 1987; Verplanken et al. 2005). Impulse purchases are made fast and spontaneously without considering or evaluating the possible consequences (Beatty and Ferrell 1998; Rook 1987). Fun plays an important role within impulse buying (Verplanken et al. 2005). Consumers engage in impulse buying to satisfy their wish to indulge (Kalla and Arora 2011). Impulse buying is driven by hedonic, pleasure-seeking goals that cause a consumer to experience the desire for a product (Silvera et al. 2008). Similar to self-gifting, impulse buying behaviour is often motivated by the desire to escape negative feelings or prolong positive ones (Youn and Faber 2000). Some individuals use impulse buying as a self-regulatory mechanism to reduce negative emotions or to repair an unpleasant mood, to 'cheer themselves up' (Verplanken et al. 2005). This behaviour can be seen as a form of escape from negative affective states (Silvera et al. 2008). On the other hand, impulsive purchases are often triggered by positive emotions such as pleasure, carelessness or excitement (Hirschmann 1991). Impulse buying can be considered as a manifestation of a consumer's wish to indulge, to give oneself a treat (Kalla and Arora 2011). Consumers may consciously plan to engage in self-gift giving to reward or console themselves, while the actual purchase may be determined impulsively and extraneously (1993; Luomala and Laaksonen 1999). The link between impulse buying and self-gift giving has been established by academic research, although there is clearly a lack of empirical analysis into how exactly the two concepts are related (Silvera et al. 2008; Kalla and Arora 2011). Previous research provide insufficient explanations on how consumers purchase self-gifts impulsively in various, positively or negatively connoted contexts and this research attempts to fill to this gap.

Impulse Buying Tendency and Materialism

Impulse buying tendency was originally defined as "the degree to which an individual is likely to make unintended, immediate, and unreflective purchases" (Jones et al. 2003, p. 506), a definition which has also been used in more recent studies (Flight et al. 2012). Although consumers with a highly impulsive nature have a tendency to buy items of different product categories on impulse (Jones et al. 2003), the relationship between buying impulsiveness and actual impulse buying behaviour is only significant when consumers believe that the impulse purchase is appropriate (Rook and Fisher 1995). Women tend to be more impulsive in their purchase behaviour than men (Coley and Burgess 2003; Tifferet and Herstein 2012). Women are more likely to engage in hedonic consumption, which is closely linked to impulse buying, and their behaviour is more emotional and psychologically rooted than men's resulting in women being more susceptible to impulse buying (Tifferet and Herstein 2012).

There is a significant association between impulse buying tendency and materialism (Watson 2003; Podoshen and Andrzejewski 2012). Highly materialistic people tend to be impulse buyers. Highly materialistic people have a higher propensity to spend money, and they are likely to view themselves as spenders a desire to show off possessions (Watson 2003). There are three categories of materialism: success, centrality and happiness (Richins and Dawson 1992). Materialists judge their own and other's success by considering the value and quantity of material possessions; they place possessions and their acquisitions at the centre of their lives and they see

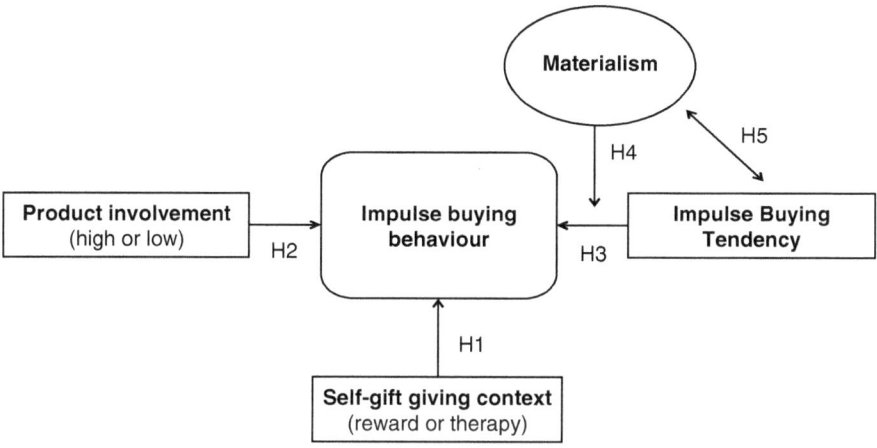

Fig. 1 Research framework

consumption as essential to their satisfaction and well-being (Richins and Dawson 1992). Podoshen and Andrzejewski (2012) suggest the implications of materialism should be considered by researchers.

Research Hypotheses

Research hypotheses were developed after a review of literature. The relationships between the hypotheses' statements are shown in Fig. 1:

H1: Reward self-gifts are associated with higher levels of impulse buying behaviour than therapeutic self-gifts.
H2: Higher levels of product involvement will lead to higher levels of impulse buying behaviour.
H3: Higher levels of impulse buying tendency will lead to higher levels of impulse buying behaviour.
H4: Differences in the level of materialism positively moderates the effect of product involvement on impulse buying behaviour.
H5: Materialistic consumers tend to be impulse buyers.

Data Collection

A factorial experiment design was used to study causal relationships between the independent variables, i.e. self-gifting contexts (Scenario A: Therapeutic: failing an exam or Scenario B: Reward: passing an exam, and level of product involvement:

Between-participant		Low Product Involvement	High Product Involvement
Variables	**Reward**	P1	P1
		P2	P2
	Therapeutic	P3	P3
		P4	P4

Fig. 2 Factorial design: self-gift giving context and level of product involvement, adapted from Christensen et al. (2011), p. 25 (*With-participants variables*)

high or low) (see Fig. 2). A self-administered questionnaire containing one of the two possible self-gifting contexts with stimuli and measures was delivered to participants via email or social media. The final sample comprised of 152 females aged 18–40. The moderating effects of materialism and impulse buying tendency were measured using established scales; 'impulsivity' (Beatty and Ferrell 1998), 'impulse buying tendencies' (Rook and Fishers 1995), 'materialism' (Killbourne and Pickett 2008). Subjects were asked to rate the believability and the level of difficulty in imagining the situation on a 7-point scale (Dholakia 2001; Mick and Faure 1998).

A pretest ($n = 18$) was conducted in order to identify two product categories with a difference in the level of product involvement. Amongst a range of common self-gifting product categories, two products, i.e. a chocolate bar and a pair of shoes, show significant different levels of product involvement. A manipulation of these two products was used to evaluate the effect of product involvement (Mittal 1995).

Data Analysis and Hypotheses Testing

A total of 152 valid responses of female students was collected. There were no significant differences between age groups in terms of level of materialism. A reliability test was used to test the multiple-item scales for internal consistency and reliability, and the items show very good fit and internal consistency ($\alpha > .70$). The manipulation of product involvement was effective. A paired samples t-test revealed a significant difference in the levels of involvement for chocolate and shoes ($p = 0$) (Table 1).

In testing the hypotheses, the significance is set at 1 %: (1) Although the result shows impulse buying behaviour scores are lower for a therapeutic than for a reward self-gift, the difference is not statistically significant. H1 is rejected. (2) Pearson's product–moment correlation coefficient is used to assess the strength of the relationship between product involvement and impulse buying behaviour. The result shows impulse buying behaviour and product involvement are positively correlated within both product categories. The findings suggest that higher levels of product involvement are associated with higher levels of impulse buying behaviour across different product categories. H2 is accepted. (3) Correlation analysis is used to test the relationship between impulse buying tendency and actual impulse buying

Table 1 Realism of the scenarios

Self-gifting context	n	Believability of scenario		Ease of imagining oneself in scenario	
		Chocolate	Shoes	Chocolate	Shoes
Therapeutic	78	5.10	5.26	4.82	5.00
Reward	74	4.93	5.97	4.97	5.96
Total	152	5.02	5.61	4.89	5.47

behaviour. There is a significant positive correlation between impulse buying tendency and actual impulse buying behaviour in both product categories. H3 is accepted and is true for both involvement product categories. (4) A moderated regression was used to test the individual difference variable of materialism. Materialism has no significant moderating effect on both product categories. H4 is therefore rejected. (5) The analysis shows there is a significant positive correlation between impulse buying tendency and materialism ($r=.475$; $p=0$) indicates that highly materialistic people tend to be impulse buyers. H5 is accepted.

Conclusion and Limitations

High realism scores on the experiment scenarios indicate consumers engage in impulse buying behaviour both therapeutically in mood lifting and to reward themselves. The results show reward self-gifts are not associated with higher levels of impulse buying behaviour than therapeutic self-gifts. When purchasing a self-gift, a higher level of product involvement is likely to lead to higher levels of impulse buying behaviour. Higher levels of impulse buying tendency are likely to lead to higher levels of impulse buying behaviour. The personality trait of impulse buying tendency has a positive influence on actual impulse buying behaviour. This study provides support to previous findings showing that the greater the level of buying impulsiveness, the greater the frequency of feeling urges to buy on impulse (Beatty and Ferrell 1998; Verplanken and Herabadi 2001). Finally, in the context of self-gifting, materialism has a positive moderating effect of product involvement on impulse buying behaviour but materialistic consumers cannot be labelled as impulse buyers.

The use of convenience sampling is a limitation of this study. The other limitation is that only two possible contexts for self-gift giving are analysed in this research; there are other possible scenarios that have not been tested in this study, e.g. 'feeling stressed', 'to be nice to oneself' or 'to provide an incentive toward a goal' (Mick and DeMoss 1990b). For future research, the influence of situational factors such as store environment, money availability or sales staff, should be considered. Research can be strengthened by adding the variables with moderating effects and using a good combination of self-gifting scenarios.

References

Bauer, H. H., Sauer, N. E., & Becker, C. (2006). Investigating the relationship between product involvement and consumer decision-making styles. *Journal of Consumer Behaviour, 5*, 342–354.

Beatty, S. E., & Ferrell, E. M. (1998). Impulse buying: Modelling its precursors. *Journal of Retailing, 74*(2), 169–191.

Coley, A., & Burgess, B. (2003). Gender differences in cognitive and affective impulse buying. *Journal of Fashion Marketing and Management, 7*(3), 282–295.

Dholakia, U. M. (2001). A motivational process model of product involvement and consumer risk perception. *European Journal of Marketing, 35*(11/12), 1340–1360.

Faure, C., & Mick, D. G. (1993). Self-gifts through the lens of attribution theory. *Advances in Consumer Research, 20*(1), 553–556.

Flight, R. L., Rountree, M. M., & Beatty, S. E. (2012). Feeling the urge: Affect in impulsive and compulsive buying. *Journal of Marketing Theory and Practice, 20*(4), 453–465.

Heath, M. T., Tynan, C., & Ennew, C. T. (2011). Self-gift giving: Understanding consumers and exploring brand messages. *Journal of Marketing Communications, 17*(2), 127–144.

Hirschmann, E. C. (1991). Secular mortality and the dark side of consumer research. *Advances in Consumer Research, 18*, 1–4.

Jones, M. A., Reynolds, K. E., Weun, S., & Beatty, S. E. (2003). The product-specific nature of impulse buying tendency. *Journal of Business Research, 56*, 505–511.

Kalla, S. M., & Arora, A. P. (2011). Impulse buying: A literature review. *Global Business Review, 12*(1), 145–157.

Killbourne, W., & Pickett, G. (2008). How materialism affects environmental beliefs, concern, and environmentally responsible behavior. *Journal of Business Research, 61*, 885–893.

Laurent, G., & Kapferer, J.-N. (1985). Measuring consumer involvement profiles. *Journal of Marketing Research, 22*, 41–53.

Luomala, H. T., & Laaksonen, M. (1999). A qualitative exploration of mood-regulatory self-gift behaviors. *Journal of Economic Psychology, 20*, 147–182.

Mick, D. G., & DeMoss, M. (1990a). Self-gifts: Phenomenological insights from four contexts. *Journal of Consumer Research, 17*, 322–332.

Mick, D. G., & DeMoss, M. (1990b). To me from me: A descriptive phenomenology of self-gifts. *Advances in Consumer Research, 17*, 677–682.

Mick, D. G., & Faure, C. (1998). Consumer self-gifts in achievement contexts: The role of outcomes, attributions, emotions, and deservingness. *International Journal of Research in Marketing, 15*, 293–307.

Mick, D. G., DeMoss, M., & Faber, R. J. (1992). A projective study of motivations and meanings of self-gifts: Implications for retail management. *Journal of Retailing, 68*(2), 122–144.

Mittal, B. (1995). A comparative analysis of four scales of consumer involvement. *Psychology and Marketing, 12*(7), 663–682.

Podoshen, J. S., & Andrzejewski, S. A. (2012). An examination of the relationships between materialism, conspicuous consumption, impulse buying, and brand loyalty. *Journal of Marketing Theory and Practice, 20*(3), 319–333.

Richins, M. L., & Dawson, S. (1992). A consumer values orientation for materialism and its measurement: Scale development and validation. *Journal of Consumer Research, 19*, 303–316.

Rook, D. W. (1987). The buying impulse. *Journal of Consumer Research, 14*(2), 189–199.

Rook, D. W., & Fisher, R. J. (1995). Normative influences on impulsive buying behavior. *Journal of Consumer Research, 22*(3), 305–313.

Sherry, J. F., Jr., McGrath, M. A., & Levy, S. (1995). Egocentric consumption: Anatomy of gifts given to the self. In J. F. Sherry Jr. (Ed.), *Contemporary marketing and consumer behavior: An anthropological sourcebook*. Thousand Oaks, CA: Sage.

Silvera, D. H., Lavack, A. M., & Kropp, F. (2008). Impulse buying: The role of affect, social influence, and subjective wellbeing. *Journal of Consumer Marketing, 25*(1), 23–33.

Tifferet, S., & Herstein, R. (2012). Gender differences in brand commitment, impulse buying, and hedonic consumption. *Journal of Product & Brand Management, 21*(3), 176–182.

Tynan, C., Heath, M. T., Ennew, C., Wang, F., & Sun, L. (2010). Self-gift giving in China and the UK: Collectivist versus individualist orientations. *Journal of Marketing Management, 26*(11–12), 1112–1128.

Verplanken, B., Herabadi, A. G., Perry, J. A., & Silvera, D. H. (2005). Consumer style and health: The role of impulsive buying in unhealthy eating. *Psychology and Health, 20*(4), 429–441.

Ward, C., & Tran, T. (2008). Consumer gifting behaviors. *Services Marketing Quarterly, 29*(2), 1–17.

Watson, J. J. (2003). The relationship of materialism to spending tendencies, saving, and debt. *Journal of Economic Psychology, 24*(6), 723–739.

Youn, S., & Faber, R. J. (2000). Impulse buying: Its relation to personality traits and cues. *Advances in Consumer Research, 27*, 179–185.

Consumer Experiences of Marketing: Pervasive, Problematic, and in Need of a Caring Perspective

Teresa Heath and Lisa O'Malley

Abstract The "corporate mantra" (Liedtka 1996, p. 179) of marketing calls for the care of customers. Indeed, meeting or serving the needs of customers has long been regarded as a core aspect of the discipline. However, such customer-centrality is at odds with public views. Amongst other criticisms, marketing has been accused of using manipulative, misleading, and outright dishonest techniques (Heath and Heath 2008) and of lacking ethics (Sheth and Sisodia 2005). Such views may have a negative impact on marketing's credibility and effectiveness (see Smith 2006). Despite their importance, little effort has been made to explore the origins of these attitudes in depth or to advance insights to address them. This study offers an attempt to address this void by looking at consumers' criticisms of marketing in the light of the school of moral philosophy known as the ethics of care (Held 2006).

Data were collected from consumers in the UK. This comprised 21 in-depth interviews followed by 71 interviews, in which we used a critical incident technique to explore consumers' lived experiences that have contributed to their perceptions of marketing. Less than one-fifth of our participants were "mostly positive" (16.7 %) about marketing and nearly half were "mostly negative" (46.3 %) while 37 % reported mixed attitudes. Those who held positive views focused on the role of marketing communications as well as technological developments which assist companies to target their offerings in a relevant way to consumers. On the other hand, participants' discontentment arises, to a great extent, from a perception of a collective "onslaught" of powerful and faceless marketing institutions. While this does not necessarily mean that individual marketers are excessive in their marketing efforts, the cumulative impact of marketing's actions on consumers builds their perception of marketing being overly pervasive, invasive, and imposing to the extent of "violence."

T. Heath (✉)
Nottingham University Business School, Nottingham, UK
e-mail: Teresa.Pereiraheath@nottingham.ac.uk

L. O'Malley
University of Limerick, Limerick, Ireland
e-mail: lisa.omalley@ul.ie

© Academy of Marketing Science 2016
L. Petruzzellis, R.S. Winer (eds.), *Rediscovering the Essentiality of Marketing*, Developments in Marketing Science: Proceedings of the Academy of Marketing Science, DOI 10.1007/978-3-319-29877-1_30

The use of technology by contemporary marketers, while seen as a positive development by some, is simultaneously viewed as the reason for an increase in unsolicited and intrusive appeals. Such perceptions are worsened by incidents of marketing being manipulative, deceptive, or exploitative of consumers' vulnerabilities. While participants are generally accepting that this is just the way marketing is, results indicate that they yearn for a less domineering and more caring approach. Drawing on the ethics of care, we propose ways to address consumers' concerns and inform marketing practice. The relational focus of these ethics and their concern for "the needs of particular others for whom we take responsibility" (Held 2006, p. 10) should encourage marketers to move away from a context-independent and instrumental view of customers as "abstract others" who can easily be replaced (Thompson 1995; Liedtka 1996, p. 186). A shift in this direction was a large part of what our participants called for. Equally we claim that these ethics' focus on empathy (Noddings 2002) and its respect for the other's autonomy (e.g. Gilligan 1982) provide useful guidance for augmenting consumers' autonomy and addressing criticisms of manipulation, especially targeted at vulnerable consumers. We argue how, by "humanizing" their customers, companies may become more empathetic and wary of any negative effect they might have on them and more likely to be responsive to their interests (see also Thompson 1995). This, as our participants suggest, would also be in the companies' own interests, as consumers would be less resistant to marketing.

References available upon request.

Between Frenzy and Collection: Towards a Characterization of Female Accumulative Buying Behavior

Othman Boujena, Isabelle Ulrich, Coralie Damay,
and Laetitia Chicheportiche

Abstract Consumer markets are increasingly becoming places where consumers develop specific relationships with products and expectations of psychological benefits. For example, many women seem to treasure large numbers of shoes and bags without necessarily being compulsive. Drawing on consumer behavior theory, this research examines accumulative buying behavior among women so as to better characterize it and understand its dimensions and antecedents from a different perspective. A broad qualitative exploratory study is conducted and combines focus group technique with in-depth semi-structured interviews in order to revisit accumulative buying behavior, identify consumer motivations, and specify the major product categories related to this phenomenon. Results reveal a new approach of accumulative buying distinct from compulsion and collecting behavior.

Keywords Accumulative buying • Impulsive/compulsive buying • Focus group • Semi-structured interviews • Collecting behavior

Introduction

Changes in consumption patterns in economically developed societies (increased competition, abundant supply, etc.) have been accompanied by a shift from an exclusively utilitarian perception of products to a more psychological dimension. Similarly, brand positioning and promises have gradually moved away from the straightforward promotion of a product towards proposals of commercial solutions

O. Boujena (✉) • I. Ulrich • L. Chicheportiche
Neoma Business School, Mont-Saint-Aignan, France
e-mail: othman.boujena@neoma-bs.fr;
isabelle.ulrich@neoma-bs.fr; laetitia.chicheportiche@neoma-bs.fr

C. Damay
ISC Paris Business School, Paris, France
e-mail: coralie@damay.eu

© Academy of Marketing Science 2016
L. Petruzzellis, R.S. Winer (eds.), *Rediscovering the Essentiality of Marketing*,
Developments in Marketing Science: Proceedings of the Academy of Marketing
Science, DOI 10.1007/978-3-319-29877-1_31

141

designed to meet various expectations and solve consumers' problems. Consequently, the scope for marketing strategies has widened to such an extent that consumption has shifted from an objective in itself towards a means of achieving other objectives and benefits of a more psychological nature such as identity transformation, projecting a more socially desirable image, or even attaining positive emotional states. In addition, postmodern evolution of consumption emphasized the symbolic role of products by extending beyond their simple, immediate, and tangible nature to specific conveyed meanings.

In such an environment, consumer behavior—now often described as complex and volatile—reveals certain phenomena that call for a deeper examination or revisiting of our relationship with products and with consumption. The consumer's notion of utility seems to be increasingly extensible, although without systematically falling into the realm of the irrational. How can we explain, for example, the low levels of frugality witnessed among female consumers faced with certain product categories such as shoes, handbags, or fashion items, where they acquire a large number of products? According to a study conducted by TNS Sofres in France in 2008, women own an average of just over nine pairs of shoes compared to six for men. The study also found that 33 % of women who owned more than 20 pairs of shoes consider this to be a "reasonable" figure. Also, the average US women are reported to own 19 pairs of shoes in 2007.[1] In parallel, a recent survey in 2014 reveals that US women possess 11 handbags on average, and 10 % of them have more than 20 bags.[2] How can we explain such consumer behavior? And to what extent can this behavior—often adopted consciously—be seen as reflecting rational buying decisions and constitute a positive consumer experience?

So far, researchers have investigated extreme buying behavior connected mostly with negative feelings and issues of self-control or guilt, like with compulsion (O'Guinn and Faber 1989), fixated buying (Schiffman and Kanuk 2007), or hoarding (Tolin et al. 2010). In parallel, others have explored collecting, a process where the items are passionately acquired by consumers with a displaying purpose and not routinely used (Belk 1995). More recently Bose et al. (2013) propose "acquisitive buying" to qualify consumers—mostly females, but also males—who exhibit an extreme yet controlled acquisition process for items in a product category, enriching their inventory with a logical justification, but not displaying the negative feelings and characteristics of previous behaviors. However their research raises several issues.

In consequence, it appears that the extreme purchasing behavior displayed by women needs further investigation. Therefore the aim to this chapter is to reexamine this phenomenon of accumulative purchasing behavior among female consumers in an effort to understand this process and how it may relate or not to existing concepts

---

[1] Poll of 1057 women led in 2007 by the Consumer Reports National Research Center for shopping magazine Shopsmart.
[2] ThredUP.com survey conducted in November 2014 as an online omnibus study by global research company ORC International.

from the literature—especially compulsion—and be confined to specific product categories. In other words, the objective is to answer the following research questions: (1) How can we characterize accumulative buying behavior among female consumers? (2) What is the importance of compulsion in our understanding of this phenomenon? (3) To what extent can this behavior be linked to certain product categories?

The following section provides an account of the theoretical framework used herein and presents the methodology adopted. This is followed by an outline of the main findings and the implications of this research.

Theoretical Framework

Several studies have focused on the types of purchases made by consumers. The motivations and consequences associated with purchasing behavior have attracted particular attention from a wide range of authors. The tendency among consumers to own a large number of products has therefore already been analyzed from various perspectives.

Accumulative Purchasing Behavior

Accumulative purchasing behavior has essentially been positioned by theorists within the context of unplanned purchases, whereby a certain outcome is sought at the expense of the temporal perspective that is necessary in the decision-making process or the apprehension of utility. Compulsion has therefore been defined as a chronic and repetitive form of purchasing behavior that occurs in response to negative events or feelings and which affects women in particular (O'Guinn and Faber 1989). This means that when individuals consume in a compulsive manner, they purchase excessive quantities of products which they do not need and cannot afford (Hoyer and McInnis 2001). King (1981) identifies three symptoms that characterize compulsive consumption: (1) an obsessive desire and a compulsion to consume; (2) dependence and the loss of personal control; and (3) a tendency to increase the consumption of a product. Other studies have linked accumulation behavior to impulsive buying (Rook 1987), status buying (O'Cass and McEwen 2004), conspicuous buying (Frank 2000), excessive buying (Ridgway et al. 2006; Wu et al. 2006), fixated buying (Schiffman and Kanuk 2007), and hoarding (Tolin et al. 2010). Overall, these studies have mostly investigated accumulative buying behavior connected with negative feelings, issues of self-control or remorse post purchase, and negative consequences such as financial problems.

Similarly but with a more positive perspective, Arnould et al. (2002) focused on the tendency to collect products by way of explaining this phenomenon of accumulation. Collecting has been defined as the process of actively, selectively, and passionately acquiring and possessing things removed from ordinary use

(Belk 1995). More recently, Bose et al. (2013) carried out a study to examine what they describe as acquisitive buying. The authors argue that an acquisitive purchase can be described as an acquisition designed to increase the consumer's inventory of products and for which there is a logical and defensible justification in the consumer's mind. They point out that there are consumers who make regular purchases and build up an above-average set of certain products (shoes, pens, accessories, etc.) which they use, yet do not display the negative characteristics associated previously by the literature to this extreme buying behavior. Their research attempts to uncover this new concept of "acquisitive buying" via a qualitative study conducted mostly among women, followed by a quantitative study focusing on the buyers' personality traits, the buying process (articulated needs, expanding product list, goal-directed search), and outcomes (refined preferences, low brand loyalty, preparedness) of such behavior. However their study raises several issues, calling for further research. First, their definition of acquisitive buying is based on a qualitative research conducted mostly on women, which does not clearly reveal how "acquisitive buying" exactly differs from compulsion in the different steps of the purchasing process. And the focus of their quantitative study does not clarify how "acquisitive buying" really differs from compulsion and other existing extreme buying concepts. Hence, the contours of this notion could be better demarcated from compulsion and other existing concepts from the literature. Second, it seems their research integrates both consumers who acquire a large amount of exactly the same item—like 20 pairs of similar black shoes—and consumers who acquire a large amount of various items in a single product category—like 20 pairs of various shoes—which can be seen as a distinct behavior. Third, their study mentions several product categories where female consumers exhibit this atypical behavior, such as clothes, shoes, pens, accessories, or home decoration, but there is no deep explanation for the choice of these categories by consumers, and no understanding as to whether such behavior is limited to these categories and why.

Motivations Behind Accumulative Purchasing Behavior

The study of the phenomenon of owning many products has included several attempts to identify explanatory factors or motivations underlying this behavior. Some authors have highlighted the considerably different levels of consumers' psychological involvement in the purchase of products with high potential for self-expression and communicating one's identity, compared to those that are strictly functional (Csikszentmihalyi and Rochberg-Halton 1981; Dittmar 1992; Kamptner 1991). Identity is about an individual's conception or subjective representation of him/herself (Vignoles et al. 2006). This suggests that accumulative purchasing behavior is a response to one's identity deficit, the gap between an individual's actual self and ideal self.

As well as identity deficit, an individual's materialist values are among the determining factors of this behavior. Consumer materialism relates to the range of beliefs about the importance of possessions in an individual's life (Richins and Dawson 1992).

Materialist consumers are therefore thought to believe that the acquisition of certain goods is vital, especially those that reflect social status, glory, and image (Dittmar 2008; Kasser and Kanner 2004). Finally, the process of acquiring products is also considered in the literature as an element that can lead to accumulation. More specifically, there is the notion that shopping can have a value that may be functional or hedonic (Basin et al. 1994).

Connection with Product Categories

Beyond the classification of purchases and the motivations that may explain accumulative behavior, some authors have addressed the nature of the product categories most likely to be affected by this phenomenon. There are several such publications in North America, such as *Shoe Addicts Anonymous*, which addresses the consumption of shoes as a potentially addictive practice (Harbison 2008), *The Perfect Fit*: *What your shoes say about you* and *Shoe are you?*, which set out to reveal personalities through shoes (Cleary 2005, 2011).

Finally, Miller and Kanazawa (2006) offer an explanation of the differences between men and women based on evolutionist psychology, according to which "men gamble and women buy shoes." The perceived symbolic power of a product can play an important role in the consumer's predisposition to purchase several units thereof. A study by Belk (2003) sets out to understand the consumption of shoes by revealing their symbolic significance, both as self-expression and as repositories of meaning and memories in the lives of consumers, women in particular. In the same vein, Gillath et al. (2012) show how an individual's shoes are deciphered by others and used to reveal information about the wearer. In short, accumulative purchasing behavior appears to have been studied so far in the context of purchases that are mainly compulsive or associated to negative characteristics, except for Bose et al. (2013) research on acquisitive buying, which raises however several issues. So how can we characterize this behavior, its relation to compulsion, and the concerned product categories? The following methodological approach is designed to answer these questions.

Methodology

In order to better understand the product accumulation phenomenon, an exploratory qualitative approach was adopted. Given the state of art and the nature of the examined issue, the methodological process combined focus group method, followed by in-depth semi-structured interviews. At this stage, the focus group allows for a better identification and understanding of common and shared perceptions and behaviors about accumulation and its context. Indeed focus groups are able to provide insights into the sources of complex behaviors and motivation, because when participants hear about experiences of other group members, they are motivated to expand and refine their own ideas and perceptions on the topic and, as a result, meanings and emotions that might not have been articulated elsewhere surface (Bloor et al. 2001). The second step of individual interviews provides a deeper and more idiosyncratic view of the examined phenomenon, allowing respondents to better share and reveal their thoughts in a one-to-one discussion and uncover potential intimate antecedents to such behavior. Moderation and interview guides were built in accordance with our research objectives.

Since Bose et al. (2013) research on acquisitive buying was conducted mostly with women and compulsion affects mainly women (O'Guinn and Faber 1989), it was decided to focus this research first on females. As far as the focus group is concerned, a convenience sample of eight women aged 23–55 was compiled. Participants were also invited after the focus group to respond to an individual small questionnaire at home, where they were asked to indicate the number of items they owned in each product category, the main brands purchased, and their average purchasing budget. We also asked them to take pictures of the locations in which the products concerned were kept or tidied up.

The semi-structured interviews were conducted among a sample of 23 women aged 20–60. We made sure that interviewees were not hostile to the world of fashion or to consumption. We began by using the "favorite possessions" paradigm to identify the product categories most likely to be concerned by accumulation (Csikszentmihalyi and Rochberg-Halton 1981; Dittmar 1989, 1992, 2008). We then tried to identify and understand the mechanisms and behaviors that contribute to this phenomenon. A thematic content analysis was then operated on all fully transcribed corpuses, using an iterative process (Spiggle 1994) in order to identify categories and themes, which were coded and then compared by the authors to reach agreement.

Main Findings

This section summarizes the main results from the focus group and the individual interviews steps. A first part is dedicated to the characterization of the accumulative purchasing phenomenon while the second one identifies the concerned product categories.

Accumulative Buying Behavior: How Much of It Is Compulsion?

The qualitative results revealed the existence of accumulative purchasing behavior in relation to some specific products but that seems not to be linked to compulsion. In other words, a large majority of the informants displayed this accumulative behavior in one or more product categories, but without expressing the various characteristics associated with compulsive behavior as mentioned in the literature (O'Guinn and Faber 1989).

No Regrets

First, our respondents who said they made accumulative purchases on different product categories did not express strong negative feelings or post-purchase regret. Only two of the informants finally mentioned that they may happen to experience some guilty feeling post-purchase but rarely, on specific occasions connected to the high price of the purchase.

On the contrary, all participants expressed strong feelings of pleasure both during and after the purchase, a sense of overall satisfaction although without sliding towards the kind of frenetic behavior often described in psychological terms as an affective state of exaltation or a paroxysm of mental agitation. This is illustrated in the quote from Clémence, who owns 300 clothing items:

> Clémence: *"After the purchase, I'm so happy! I say to myself: this is cool. It's not like I'm ecstatic about some clothes, but still I feel very happy and satisfied. I'm sort of eager to try out my new clothes at home, I'm this kind of girl who buys something and wears it just after"*

The most common post-purchase reactions expressed with accumulative buying behavior are the desire to try out the new purchased item back at home and use it rapidly, if possible the day after. There is no frenetic urge in doing so: it appears more as a desire to experience the pleasure associated with the object and the desire to show the new item to one's friends or family, as in the quote from Amandine, possessing 200 clothes:

> Amandine: *"Often I try it out the day after, or not long since I purchased it. You know, in order to show it to my mother and friends. Sometimes I try it on at home after the purchase, just to see it once again on me"*.

This desire to show the new item to one's partner, family, or friends is revealed by most of our informants—whatever their age, and is connected with a feeling of post-purchase pride which can lead some of the younger consumers to take photographs which are then shared on social media platforms. Pride appears as the dominant feeling for some respondents like Alexia, who even quotes her total absence of remorse post-purchase. The pride associated with owning an item sometimes stretches to seeing it as a trophy, made all the more precious if it is not owned by many others:

> Alexia: *"Afterwards I head out and have a drink with my friends to show them my new bags. I feel no remorse, generally my friends say: 'oh, nice handbag', 'yeah and I'm the one who has it!' No remorse about that whatsoever"*.

A Planned and Reasoned Process, with a Touch of Impulsion for Affordable Purchases

Beyond the positive post-purchase feelings expressed here, many informants described their purchasing process as planned and reasoned: it is not therefore compulsive. Sophie, for example, who owns 25 pairs of shoes, explained that she takes the time to think before making a purchase, so she can be sure she has made the right choice:

"So sometimes I think: 'okay I want those ones, but it is a big purchase'. And so I allow some time to pass and I tell myself: 'if I still want them in a month's time, then a part of me must really need them!' But I give myself some time. And if in the meantime I spot an ad or something, then I say: 'okay, I really need those ones'. Sometimes you get a little reminder. And sometimes I allow a small amount of time to pass to make sure I go and get them".

Taking the time and having a planned and reasoned process in the accumulative buying decision seems important for items whose price and symbolic charge appear as higher, like bags, shoes, or lingerie, as opposed to small tops or make-up. The respondents also describe a purchasing process in which the search for information and the choice of the "right product" play an important role and, in the vast majority of cases, are considered enjoyable:

Marion: *"I spend a lot of time for my handbags, because first in the stores there is so much choice, so I need time to search. And then when you have made up your choice, well generally you have 2 or 3 options left, so then I consider price and aesthetics, I need to try, to touch.."*

Moreover, several informants reveal that their accumulative purchasing behavior proceeds by considering their existing inventory at home and justifying the new item because it enriches this inventory appropriately. There is a logical justification in acquiring new products that complement the inventory which one has in mind, mostly in terms of colors or shapes:

Brigitte: *"I always take into account the handbags I have at home when I purchase a new one. I'd never buy two identical bags because it's not worth it: you never carry two handbags at the same time! So before I go shopping for handbags I usually have a look in my cupboard at my current range of bags."*

Because some purchases may be made on a whim and be considered impulsive, whereby they do not correspond to a real need, these women put in place carefully considered strategies to remain reasonable and assume responsibility for the financial consequences of their behavior. Price features in their responses as a key variable that is taken into account when deciding whether or not to purchase, as explains Cindy who owns 20 handbags:

Cindy: *"When I enter the store, I first have a quick look around, then I watch carefully the selected handbag to see if I like it, and I look at its price. If it's too expensive, I will reason myself. Either I will wait to buy it later, or I will try to find a way to get someone to offer it to me".*

Many respondents exercise self-control in terms of their budget when buying the items they tend to accumulate, as says Lucie, owning 50 pairs of shoes:

Lucie: *"The last time I wanted to buy two pairs of shoes, so I thought: 'this isn't reasonable, do I really need them? Just take the ones you need more [...]'. I buy shoes too often, so I hold back!"*

However, for affordable items, most informants explains they buy on impulse, some of them having in mind a price limit under which they authorize themselves not to resist. This is expressed by Cindy and many others:

> Cindy: « *As soon as I see some clothes, like small tops, I need them right away. It's an impulse purchase. That's because it's affordable, so… It's the financial side which would hinder me from purchasing*."

Compensation or No Compensation?

Finally, the last characteristic of compulsive behavior is that it is supposed to occur in response to negative events or feelings (O'Guinn and Faber 1989). Yet when these women talk about what they do to compensate for feeling low or for a recent disappointment, some of them do not refer in the first place to shopping in the product categories where they display accumulative behavior. Instead some informants cite services and activities that give them a sense of well-being: going to the hairdresser or for a massage, or giving in to an indulgent treat. In response to the question "which products do you buy if you are feeling low?", some respondents began by spontaneously referring to wellness services and products, others quoting first tasting treats:

> Alexia: "*A face mask, go for a facial. Body treatment products. When you're feeling down and you go to the hairdresser's, you know you're going to see your hairdresser because you usually have your own hairdresser, and you get pampered*".

> Haba: "*If I'm feeling down, I'll go to the hairdresser's and change my head, have a new hair color to change my spirits*".

In parallel, several informants made it clear that feeling down does not encourage them to make purchases, indeed on the contrary it refrains them from shopping. Major disappointments would also lead to a natural disengagement from normal accumulation buying activities:

> Blandine: "*It actually depends on the kind of disappointment.* […] *I lost someone close to me and in that case no, no I don't want to talk about anything, spending is so futile*".

Yet half of our respondents explained that one option for them, perhaps to compensate, is to go shopping for the products they tend to accumulate. Lucie, for example, who accumulates shoes, clothes, and make-up, either gets some exercise or goes clothes shopping:

> Lucie: "*First it depends on when it happens, you know I might go to H&M for example, otherwise I do some sport. I'd say clothes, my first choice is to go and buy some clothes, I'd do some browsing and look at the window displays to clear my head*".

Overall, compensation does appear as one dimension of the accumulative buying behavior for some respondents. But this dimension is absent for many others, as they do not specifically purchase things in their favorite accumulated product categories when feeling a disappointment.

Accumulative Buying Behavior, Distinct from Collecting

In order to explore how much of their accumulative purchasing behavior could be connected to collecting, we specifically asked women about their potential collections, their understanding of and relations to collecting. Literature has defined collecting as the process of actively, selectively, and passionately acquiring and possessing things removed from ordinary use (Belk 1995). It differs from other types of buying in terms of the passion invested in the behavior and the lack of ordinary use associated with the collected objects (Belk 1995, 2003). First, none of our informants declare they are collecting the products which they tend to amass at home with accumulative buying: they do not perceive themselves as collectors for these products. They accumulate shoes, bags, clothes, jewels, or the like with extreme buying, but it is not meant to be a collection. Second, the process of accumulative purchasing really differs from collection, since all items are acquired by these women to be used and consumed, not to be kept and displayed at home. This is evident in the following report of Géraldine:

> *"I possess 30 bags. I have used all of them at least once! Most of the time, I do not change my bag in the morning, because I'm late and run out of time. But I like to vary the colors of my bags, have it match my clothing of the day."*

Indeed for all informants, the purchased items are acquired with an objective of using them in the future, for a specific occasion or for an anticipated match with whatever element of their wardrobe. Some respondents even insist that they make a point in using their whole inventory on different product categories, like Emilie:

> Emilie: *"I've got 40 pair of shoes which I consider a reasonable amount. And I have around 20 lingerie sets. I use them all. Because my mother always told me that if you purchase something, it's meant to be used, not to decorate"*

Third, accumulative buying behavior cannot be assimilated to collecting, as some respondents explain they regularly get rid of part of their inventory, as a strategy to avoid too much stockpiling at home. This is illustrated by Brigitte's words:

> *"I try to sort out my clothes regularly. Twice a year, I change my clothing items for winter and summer seasons and then I eliminate those things I have not worn for several years. It's the same for my handbags: I empty my cupboard regularly and I give them away to others."*

Fourth, several informants who accumulate products have in parallel a rather negative image of collections, reject this hobby and could not see themselves behaving like that. Collecting seems for them to be associated to time in a problematic way, since it's a pastime which is repetitive and where things are stuck in time and in the past, as explained Clémence:

> Clémence: *"I couldn't do a collection for 20 years on the same things you see. I have many different teas at home, but I use them, I taste them. Collecting objects like that, no!"*

Finally, very few informants declared collecting other objects, after having explained their accumulative buying behavior on specific product categories. Hence, accumulative purchasing behavior is not necessarily linked with a consumer profile of collector. In our sample, only three informants are collecting things (cherubs and small hears, or vases). And their extreme buying of products is different from a collection, since their products are acquired to be used, not to be displayed.

Accumulative Buying Behavior and Product Categories

The products that all of these women spontaneously say they tend to buy when they go shopping are clothing. Going shopping is synonymous first with clothes for all respondents, followed by quotations of shoes, then handbags, lingerie, make-up, jewels, and skin care at a lesser extent. It seems that younger informants tend to cite make-up more than older women, which is linked to its more affordable price. When asked again about the products they most like to buy, a majority of participants cited handbags and shoes for the aesthetic pleasure and positive image associated with them. Several respondents, both young and not so young, then spoke in length about lingerie, which carries a strong hedonic charge as well as an intimate, secret—even forbidden—aspect which tends to make them accumulate many purchases in this category also.

Next, in which product categories do these women admit to accumulating items via extreme buying? The shoe category and the clothing category feature strongly, cited by a majority of respondents and also emphasized in the study by Bose et al. (2013). In the clothing category, the most quoted items were small tops, dresses, jeans, and then coats. The youngest respondents cited make-up often after clothing, with the need for variety using new colors and the need to match items causing them to make accumulative purchases. The handbag category also drives many women to make accumulative purchases, and to a lesser extent other product categories emerged such as lingerie, then jewels, body creams, and scarves. The product categories identified above confirm results from previous studies and reveal additional categories, such as handbags, lingerie, and make-up.

Discussion

The aim of this research was to examine accumulative purchasing behavior and explore the nature of possible connections with certain product categories. The approaches adopted in previous studies identified in the literature, as well as the observations made in various market studies, encouraged us to focus more on female consumers. The conducted qualitative study confirmed some of the theoretical observations already made, while at the same time providing new perspectives to revisit and better understand the phenomenon of accumulation.

First, as indicated by our findings, accumulative behavior does not appear to be systematically grounded in compulsion as defined by the literature (King 1981; O'Guinn and Faber 1989). The products affected by this behavior may also be purchased in a way that is homeostatic, in order to satisfy needs previously identified by consumers and without the presence of negative emotional states. Similarly, in contrast to certain studies, the temporal dimension does not appear to be particularly contracted or limited, but rather occupies a central place within the decision-making process. Indeed, the expressive and communicative functions associated with the product categories concerned cause consumers to initiate a very real and dynamic cognitive process prior to purchase.

Although removed from the functional dimension of the products concerned, this aspirational and identity-transforming function paradoxically serves to significantly increase the rational nature of both the purchasing process and possession itself. First, possession of these products as a vector of image and status encourages in-depth reflection in terms of brand and design choice, whereby subjective norms (family, colleagues, friends, partners, etc.) have been considered. Second, it would appear that the egocentric and identity-related dimension of these products often makes price considerations central to the decision-making process, thus tending to limit the extent to which the consumer's behavior is impulsive or compulsive. The role of price concerns in accumulative purchasing, as revealed in this study, had never before been addressed by the literature. Finally, the information-processing phase is affected by the use of certain functions now available on technological devices such as mobile telephones, the Internet and social media, both during the pre- and post-purchase stages, indicative of what is at stake in the eyes of the consumers when making this type of purchase.

Second, this research provides some evidence that accumulative purchasing behavior differs from collecting as defined by the literature (Belk 1995, 2003). It reveals that the acquired products are accumulated not to be displayed at home as in a collection, but to be used and consumed by the buyer. None of the informants acquire these items with an objective of collecting, but with an objective of wearing and using them, at least once for a specific occasion. Moreover, accumulative shoppers elaborate strategies to get rid of their exceeding inventory, scrutinizing their pile of things to eliminate the items they feel they will not continue to use and to give them away if need be. This behavior indeed differs strongly from collecting, where people keep their possessions with passion. The study also reveals that being an accumulative buyer on one product category is not linked to being a collector of other types of objects. On the contrary, several accumulative buyers have a negative image of collections and would not consider beginning one. All this adds to previous literature, and specifically to Bose et al. (2013), who did not show in which way accumulative buying behavior—defined and called "acquisitive buying behavior" in their research—could be different from collecting.

Third, in terms of the product categories concerned, the findings of this qualitative study have not only confirmed the preponderance of products such as shoes, but have also revealed other categories such as handbags, certain clothing items, make-up, lingerie, and accessories. This makes it clear that the common denominator across these categories is the dimension of gender expression for female consumers. For many of the respondents, it would appear that femininity is essentially reflected by wearing certain products with a highly sexualized charge. This perspective can be traced back to the historical changes that have marked society, as well as a certain number of mental representations that are largely shared, and even conditioned or learned, based on the communication strategies and codes used by the concerned brands.

Nonetheless, this instrumental function found across these product categories does not appear to accord them the same exact role and status in the eyes of consumers. Whereas many respondents feel that shoes have the power to transform their figure or generate self-confidence due to added height, handbags possess a more integral function in that they are described as belonging to or as an extension of the body, or even as the focal point of intimacy or as a secret garden for some women. Richard et al. (2011) revealed the dimension associated with handbags by a sample of young consumers in a post-modernist context. In the same vein, according to the results of our focus group, the lingerie category can be seen to be characteristic of the relationship between the body and the outside world. In contrast to the approach adopted by Bose et al. (2013) in defining acquisitive buying, lingerie's hidden and mysterious dimension clearly raises the issue of expanding the product categories most likely to be affected by accumulative purchases. Indeed, accumulation would appear to affect products considered to be dedicated to "strictly personal consumption" every bit as much as products with strong social visibility.

This symbolic power of the various product categories identified as part of our qualitative study has an impact on the purchasing process, the reference groups considered, and the shopping experience, which may change in accordance with the nature of the products in question. Similarly, the semiotic nature of these products appears to evolve in sync with the life-cycle of their consumers. Certain categories such as make-up and accessories were cited in particular by the youngest respondents. The diversity of the product categories potentially affected by accumulative behavior makes it clear that beyond product values related to usage and combination with other wearable items, terminal values related to "being" independently of "appearing" are also covered.

This research constitutes an initial attempt to understand accumulative purchasing behavior and its analytical framework. The exploratory study provides a fresh look at this phenomenon and an exploration of the spectrum of product categories potentially affected. In terms of theory, this chapter invites researchers to rethink the concept of accumulation by adopting a broader view of what makes it intelligible. Similarly, it raises clear questions about the extent to which compulsion can be used to explain this phenomenon. In addition, this study contributes to better conceptual delimitation by clearly distinguishing accumulative purchase from collecting behavior. Finally, the findings of the qualitative study reveals new product categories linked with the type of behavior examined. With regard to managerial implications, this research provides a different and more comprehensive framework to enable marketing managers to better understand the behavior of female consumers who make accumulative purchases and thereby rethink their proposition value. By identifying the contingency factors related to accumulation as well as the consumption values associated with the products concerned, managers can better anticipate and sharpen segmentation practices (including emotional segmentation), brand and product development, storytelling and brand content, as well as store design and experience.

This research has some limitations. First, a deeper examination of motivations related to accumulative buying could allow a better comprehension of the phenomenon. Second, the importance and scope of the qualitative findings should be followed by a quantitative survey, designed to empirically specify the dimensions of accumulative buying. Third, the study focused on women only; however the exploration of the phenomenon and its relevance within the male target would be of valuable contribution, especially to settle the gender variable status.

References

Arnould, E., Price, L., & Zinkhan, G. M. (2002). *Consumers*. New York: McGraw-Hill.

Basin, B. J., Darden, W. R., & Griffin, M. (1994). Work and/or fun: Measuring hedonic and utilitarian shopping value. *Journal of Consumer Research, 20*, 644–656.

Belk, R. W. (1995). Collecting as luxury consumption: Effects of individuals and households. *Journal of Economic Psychology, 16*, 477–491.

Belk, R. W. (2003). Shoes and self. In P. A. Keller & D. W. Rook (Eds.), *Advances in consumer research* (pp. 27–33). Valdosta, GA: Association for Consumer Research.

Bloor, M., Frankland, J., Thomas, M., & Robson, K. (2001). *Focus groups in social research*. London: Sage.

Bose, M., Burns, A. C., & Garretson Folse, J. A. (2013). My fifty shoes are all different! Exploring, defining, and characterizing acquisitive buying. *Psychology & Marketing, 30*, 614–631.

Cleary, M. (2005). *The perfect fit: What your shoes say about you*. San Francisco: Chronicle books.

Cleary, M. (2011). *Shoe are you?* Miss Meghan Media, Inc.

Csikszentmihalyi, M., & Rochberg-Halton, E. (1981). *The meaning of things: Symbols and the self*. Cambridge, England: Cambridge University Press.

Dittmar, H. (1989). Gender identity-related meanings of personal possessions. *British Journal of Social Psychology, 28*, 159–171.

Dittmar, H. (1992). *The social psychology of material possessions: To have is to be*. Hemel Hempstead/New York: Harvester Wheatsheaf/St. Martin's Press.

Dittmar, H. (2008). Consumer culture, identity, and well-being: The search for the 'good life' and 'body perfect'. In R. Brown (Ed.), *European monographs in social psychology*. London: Psychology Press.

Frank, R. (2000). *Luxury fever: Money and happiness in the era of excess*. Princeton, NJ: Princeton University Press.

Gillath, O., Bahns, A. J., Ge, F., & Crandall, C. S. (2012). Shoes as a source of first impressions. *Journal of Research in Personality, 46*, 423–430.

Harbison, B. (2008). *Shoe addicts*. Pocket.

Hoyer, W., & McInnis, D. (2001). *Consumer behavior*. Belmont, CA: Wadsworth.

Kamptner, N. L. (1991). Personal possessions and their meanings: A life-span perspective. *Journal of Social Behavior & Personality, 6*, 209–228.

Kasser, T. E., & Kanner, A. D. (2004). *Psychology and consumer culture: The struggle for a good life in a materialistic world*. Washington, DC: American Psychological Association.

King, A. (1981). In K. Bernhardt et al. (Eds.), *Beyond propensities: Toward a theory of addictive consumption, the changing marketing environment new theories* (pp. 438–440). Chicago: American Marketing Association.

Miller, A. S., & Kanazawa, S. (2006). *Why men gamble and women buy shoes*. Oxford, England: Oxford University Press.

O'Cass, A., & McEwen, H. (2004). Exploring consumer status and conspicuous consumption. *Journal of Consumer Behavior, 4*, 25–39.

O'Guinn, T. C., & Faber, R. J. (1989). Compulsive buying: A phenomenological exploration. *Journal of Consumer Research, 16*(2), 147–157.

Richard, E., Wong, K. Y., & Liu, W.-S. (2011). Dump it out! A study on the handbag. In Z. Yi, J. J. Xiao, J. Cotte, & L. Price (Eds.), *Asia-Pacific advances in consumer research, 9*. Duluth, MN: Association for Consumer Research.

Richins, M. L., & Dawson, S. (1992). A consumer values orientation for materialism and its measurement: Scale development and validation. *Journal of Consumer Research, 19*, 303–316.

Ridgway, N. M., Kukar-Kinney, M., & Monroe, K. B. (2006). The development and validation of a scale to measure excessive buying. *Advances in Consumer Research, 33*, 132.

Rook, D. W. (1987). The buying impulse. *Journal of Consumer Research, 14*, 189–199.

Schiffman, L. G., & Kanuk, L. L. (2007). *Consumer behavior* (9th ed.). New York: Prentice-Hall.

Spiggle, S. (1994). Analysis and interpretation of qualitative research in consumer research. *Journal of Consumer Research, 21*, 491–503.

Tolin, D. F., Frost, R. O., & Steketee, G. (2010). A brief interview for assessing compulsive hoarding: The Hoarding Rating Scale-Interview. *Psychiatry Research, 178*, 147–152.

Vignoles, V. L., Jen, G., Regalia, C., Manzi, C., & Scabini, E. (2006). Beyond self-esteem: Influence of multiple motives on identity construction. *Journal of Personality & Social Psychology, 90*, 308–333.

Wu, L., Malhotra, N. K., & Van Ittersum, K. (2006). Excessive buying: Conceptual typology and scale development. *Advances in Consumer Research, 33*, 401–402.

Complexity of Dyadic Gift-Giving Forms: A New Framework

Ines Branco-Illodo, Teresa Heath, and Caroline Tynan

Abstract This chapter illuminates the complexity of dyadic gift-giving by identifying new forms of dyadic gift-giving and their links to givers' relationship-maintenance goals. For this, we employ Attachment Theory which addresses humans' need to be close to significant others (Bowlby 1969). Gift-giving is often identified as a mechanism to manage important but insecure relationships (Caplow 1982), which occurs within significant interpersonal relationships (Ruth 1996). Considering this, and that the UK gift market is worth £40 billion (Mintel 2013), it is important to understand how relationships operate as antecedents to gift-giving. Traditionally gift-giving has been assumed to be an aggregate of dyadic exchange rituals, thus leaving many dimensions of gift-giving unexplored (Giesler 2006). Recent research (e.g. Weinberger and Wallendorf 2012) has acknowledged the need to analyse gift-giving structures other than the giver–receiver dyad. The inherent assumption concerning dyadic gifts is that givers give only to maintain their relationship with the receiver, which neglects the link between the dyad and their networks (Parks et al. 1983). This limits the understanding of dyadic gift-giving forms and the relationship-maintenance goals of givers through gift-giving.

We collected 28 online diaries, reporting 158 gift-giving experiences, from 28 informants in the UK with diverse gender, age, income and marital status to examine a variety of gift-giving behaviours. Twenty-seven follow-up interviews were conducted to obtain a fuller description from diarists of their experiences. We combined a quantitative content analysis (Kassarjian 1977; Neuendorf 2002) with a subsequent interpretive analysis approach to enable new themes to emerge as used by Ruth et al. (1999).

Our findings revealed three dyadic gift-giving forms: direct, mediated and indirect. First, direct dyadic gift-giving acts as a mechanism to maintain the relationship with the receiver, thus supporting the traditional definition of dyadic gifts (Weinberger and Wallendorf 2012). This definition is extended by showing that direct dyadic gifts can help to maintain relationships with the goals of: (1) keeping

I. Branco-Illodo (✉) • T. Heath • C. Tynan
University of Nottingham, Nottingham, UK
e-mail: lixib5@nottingham.ac.uk; teresa.pereiraheath@nottingham.ac.uk; caroline.tynan@nottingham.ac.uk

© Academy of Marketing Science 2016
L. Petruzzellis, R.S. Winer (eds.), *Rediscovering the Essentiality of Marketing*, Developments in Marketing Science: Proceedings of the Academy of Marketing Science, DOI 10.1007/978-3-319-29877-1_32

157

the receiver's support as a manifestation of attachment and (2) taking care of the receiver in response to the receiver's attachment. Second, in mediated dyadic gift-giving, the giver's aim is to keep close to someone with whom he/she shares an important relationship (mediator) through giving a gift to a receiver who is close to the mediator but not close to him(her)self, thus extending the classic notion of dyadic gifts. Our data demonstrates that the giver's goals are in this case both to: (1) acknowledge the importance of the receiver to the mediator and (2) maintain the receiver's support to the mediator. Third, indirect dyadic gift-giving involves giving a gift to a receiver on behalf of another person (a proxy figure) who acts as the giver in the eyes of the receiver. In this case the goals of the giver are to: (1) enhance a receiver's experience by involving a fictional character (e.g. Santa Claus); (2) allevi-ate tension between the giver and the receiver by giving gifts through a significant other (e.g. a baby); and (3) to socialise the giving figure by giving a gift to be regifted to another person (e.g. getting a gift for one's child to give to his/her teacher). This investigation contributes to gift-giving research by proposing a new conceptualization of dyadic gift-giving beyond the traditional definition and sug-gesting important implications for practitioners. By understanding different gift-giving structures indicating how givers, receivers, mediators and proxy figures interact and how this affects givers' goals, marketers can design more effective targeting strategies responsive to the relationships in which people are involved.

References available upon request.

Price Framing and Choice Order Effects in Bundle Customization Decisions

Johannes C. Bauer and Tim M. Böttger

Abstract One-to-one marketing has become increasingly popular in the consumer product and service industry. Customization emerged as a marketing trend and allows consumers to proactively participate in the configuration or production process by choosing one or more elements of the marketing mix (Arora et al. 2008). Today, consumers can customize a wide variety of products and services. For example, Dell Computers allows customers to choose the hardware components (e.g., processor, RAM, hard drive) which best fits their needs when buying a new laptop. By offering consumers the opportunity to tailor products and services to their individual preferences, needs, and budgets, firms aim to differentiate themselves from competitors, increase customer satisfaction, and generate loyalty (Arora et al. 2008). During the customization process of a service bundle (e.g., smartphone plan), consumers typically have to make a series of choices, one for each bundle component (e.g., a choice for minutes, SMS, and data). In this research, we will provide evidence that consumers' satisfaction with the final bundle configuration, bundle price perceptions, and overall spending amounts are determined by (1) whether the choice options for the bundle components are presented all at the same time and decision are made simultaneously versus sequentially (i.e., only the options of one bundle component are presented and choices for each component are made step-by-step) and (2) the price framing used in the configuration process (aggregate bundle price as a running total vs. aggregate bundle price together with the detailed option prices). The results of two online experiments show that consumers are more satisfied with the outcome of the customization process and less price sensitive if only the aggregate bundle price (i.e., the running total) is advertised in simultaneous (vs. sequential) customization processes. In contrast, when decisions for each bundle component were made step-by-step, consumers are more satisfied and less

J.C. Bauer (✉) • T.M. Böttger
University of St. Gallen, St. Gallen, Switzerland
e-mail: johannes.bauer@unisg.ch; tim.boettger@unisg.ch

© Academy of Marketing Science 2016   159
L. Petruzzellis, R.S. Winer (eds.), *Rediscovering the Essentiality of Marketing*,
Developments in Marketing Science: Proceedings of the Academy of Marketing
Science, DOI 10.1007/978-3-319-29877-1_33

price sensitive if detailed option prices are provided in addition to the aggregate bundle price. Our two studies also shed some light into the psychological process that underlies consumers' different reactions. Besides contributing to consumer decision-making and behavioral pricing research, our findings have important implications for service providers on how to design a bundle configuration process that increases both customer satisfaction and spending at the same time.

References available upon request.

The Dark Side of Giving Monetary Gifts

Yaniv Shani, Shai Danziger, and Marcel Zeelenberg

Abstract Social events such as weddings, christenings, and bar mitzvahs are very important to many people. They commemorate noteworthy occasions and enable hosts and guests to rejoice with and honor each other. Recently, a shift has occurred whereby hosts ask guests for money, instead of presents, as gifts at such social events (particularly weddings). Interestingly, hosts report feeling uncomfortable for making this request. In the present research, we ask whether these feelings are justified. We ask whether giving money at social events troubles guests; we explore their cognitions, emotions, and behavior; and if giving money troubles them, we investigate whether these thoughts can somehow be lessened.

The present research represents the first study to explore the psychological outcomes of giving a substantial amount of money as a gift in the context of an ongoing social relationship. We believe that the study of monetary gifts is both timely and important. It is timely because monetary gifts are becoming the norm in many societies. It is important because it teaches us new things about the psychological outcomes of mixing money and friendship. Our research extends past findings in several important ways. First, we show that monetary gifts induce a mindset associated with a constellation of self-serving, utility-driven thoughts and behaviors, and a desire to get (consume) what one paid for (what we term an economic motive). Second, we demonstrate that adopting a monetary mindset when giving troubles close friends of the recipient but not acquaintances. Last, utilizing a manipulation that reduces the saliency of the monetary gift, we provide a means to lessen the negative impact of adopting a money-market mindset in the context of an otherwise social market relationship.

Y. Shani (✉) • S. Danziger
Tel Aviv University, Tel Aviv, Israel
e-mail: shanivya@tau.ac.il; shaid@post.tau.ac.il

M. Zeelenberg
Tilburg University, Tilburg, The Netherlands
e-mail: M.Zeelenberg@uvt.nl

© Academy of Marketing Science 2016
L. Petruzzellis, R.S. Winer (eds.), *Rediscovering the Essentiality of Marketing*,
Developments in Marketing Science: Proceedings of the Academy of Marketing
Science, DOI 10.1007/978-3-319-29877-1_34

161

Part IV
Cross-Cultural Research

Anxiety About Cultural Dilution and Adoption of a Global Lifestyle

Amro A. Maher

Abstract The main purpose of this study is to examine how Kuwaitis, as a minority, react to the influx of expatriates living in Kuwait and how such a reaction affects their consumption behavior. We build upon findings from the social psychology literature to build our theoretical model. Research supports that local populations feel threatened by immigrant populations (Stephan et al. 2002). When the local population is threatened, then locals might express concern about the future existence of the group. This concern is referred to as collective angst in the social psychology literature (Whole et al. 2010). We seek to examine how concern about the future affects Kuwaitis' lifestyle in the present. Data was collected from Kuwait where foreign migrants represent around 60 % of the total population. The results reveal several interesting findings. First, we find that when expatriates are perceived by Kuwaitis as a source of symbolic threat then Kuwaitis are more likely to be concerned about the existence of Kuwaiti culture in the future (i.e., collective angst). Second, we find that this high level of collective angst leads to the preference for a global consumer lifestyle versus a local lifestyle. Finally we find that individualism strengthens the indirect effect of symbolic threat on the preference for a global lifestyle through collective angst. Thus our results are not consistent with previous literature in suggesting that the experience of collective angst results in behaviors that would seek to eliminate the source of threat.

References available upon request.

A.A. Maher (✉)
Qatar University, Doha, Qatar
e-mail: amaher@qu.edu.qa

© Academy of Marketing Science 2016
L. Petruzzellis, R.S. Winer (eds.), *Rediscovering the Essentiality of Marketing*,
Developments in Marketing Science: Proceedings of the Academy of Marketing
Science, DOI 10.1007/978-3-319-29877-1_35

National Homophily in Multicultural Newcomer Networks

Kishore Gopalakrishna Pillai, Constantinos N. Leonidou, and Xuemei Bian

Abstract Understanding the relational and network dynamics among newcomer networks is important to devising appropriate strategies that will maximize the productivity of the incoming workforce. Nevertheless, there are limited empirical contributions on newcomer networks with a handful of studies examining newcomer networks in international environments. In this study, we focus on national homophily defined as the "tendency for people to associate with others similar to them in terms of attributes (e.g., race, gender) and values" (Mollica et al. 2003, p. 123). Studies have not examined ethnic or national homophily in newcomer networks. Understanding this issue is important as global companies recruit significant numbers of postgraduate students from countries such as China, India, and Brazil and spend a lot of money in trying to enhance interpersonal relationships among employees to boost effectiveness and efficiency. To better understand national homophily, we use a multicultural student sample drawn from newly formed networks, to examine how identity salience, academic self-efficacy, individualism, and ethnocentrism are associated with the occurrence of national homophily in newcomer networks. A questionnaire was devised based on prior research and distributed to students enrolled in postgraduate management programs in two British universities. The final sample comprises of 182 usable responses which were analyzed using Smart PLS 2.0 (Ringle et al. 2005). The study results show that in a multicultural newcomer context individuals who have strong identity salience tend to forge close ties with others of the same national identity and this manifests in national homophily. The study also shows that individuals high in academic self-efficacy are likely to form ties with individuals from other cultures and show

K.G. Pillai (✉)
University of Bradford, Bradford, UK
e-mail: K.GopalakrishnaPillai1@bradford.ac.uk

C.N. Leonidou
University of Leeds, Leeds, UK
e-mail: C.Leonidou@leeds.ac.uk

X. Bian
University of Kent, Canterbury, UK
e-mail: X.M.Bian@kent.ac.uk

© Academy of Marketing Science 2016
L. Petruzzellis, R.S. Winer (eds.), *Rediscovering the Essentiality of Marketing*,
Developments in Marketing Science: Proceedings of the Academy of Marketing
Science, DOI 10.1007/978-3-319-29877-1_36

167

less national homophilic tendencies, compared to those who are low in academic self-efficacy. The findings also reveal that individualism is not conducive to the formation of homophily, while ethnocentrism was found to be significantly but negatively related to homophily. This study provides an incremental contribution in understanding how homophily emerges in newcomer networks. Managers interested in promoting greater collaboration between group members in their companies will need to pay particular attention on individual characteristics (e.g., self-efficacy, identify salience) when forming teams, organizing groups, and allocating projects in the workplace. In this way, the full potential of multicultural relationships could be effectively unfolded. Future researchers can broaden and deepen knowledge on national homophily by investigating other variables as factors influencing homophily (e.g., personality, demographic characteristics), or even explore the consequences of homophily in terms of individual and group performance.

References available upon request.

A Cross-Cultural Approach to Annual Report Through Impression Management

Salvatore Romanazzi, Luca Petruzzellis, and Roberto Aguiari

Introduction

The bunch of information a company sends to its market and stakeholders has to meet their expectations in terms of accuracy, credibility and understandability in order to face the increasing complexity of national and international economic environments. Both literature (e.g. Rogers and Brown 1999) and non-academic journals/press (e.g. Forbes 1996, p. 192) have widely concluded that the annual report is a marketing tool to attract new investors. Firms target various stakeholders not only with financial information but also with messages regarding the corporate image, corporate social responsibility and other communication objectives, providing varied images and encoded messages for their targets. So far research has shown that managers use annual report to provide a self-interested view of the corporate performance. Recently, attention has shifted from the management of the accounting numbers or earnings management (Schipper 1989) to presentation management (Aerts 1994) and/or the presentational format with which the information is displayed (Graves et al. 1996).

This chapter discusses the elements that make up an annual report and models the relative importance of the items as determined by users. The selection of disclosure items is based on a review of the current literature and on expert evaluations.

S. Romanazzi (✉)
Italian Ministry of Economy and Finance, Rome, Italy
e-mail: salvatore.romanazzi@gmail.com

L. Petruzzellis
University of Bari Aldo Moro, Bari, Italy
e-mail: luca.petruzzellis@uniba.it

R. Aguiari
University of Roma Tre, Rome, Italy
e-mail: roberto.aguiari@uniroma3.it

© Academy of Marketing Science 2016
L. Petruzzellis, R.S. Winer (eds.), *Rediscovering the Essentiality of Marketing*,
Developments in Marketing Science: Proceedings of the Academy of Marketing
Science, DOI 10.1007/978-3-319-29877-1_37

It will then focus on the international role of the annual report in a marketing perspective, thus proposing the research questions. Methods of data collection and analysis are explained. Finally, it offers discussion, conclusion and practical implications.

Background and Research Questions

The importance of the annual report has been well documented in academic literature. Generally speaking, disclosures are mainly made because they are useful to decision makers; the information and their presentation have a varied value according to the objectives and the decision maker. Readers place high credibility in corporate annual reports especially in assessing whether to buy, keep or sell stock in the company (Bouwman et al. 1987; Hooks and Moon 1993; Collins et al. 1993; Day 1986). Disclosure management also deals with the interpretation and presentation of data by shading sensitive data or highlighting good news (Gibbins et al. 1990). Although each stakeholder has their own strategic reason for reading annual reports (Scholes and Clutterbuck 1998), only one document is published which ought to be varied and meet all their requirements.

The report's communication task is immediately evident through the concept of visual rhetoric, in the wide notion of both images and language (Kenney and Scott 2003). Visual rhetoric is a true marketing concept, like the use of images in advertising or the packaging itself. Through the use of an image, word or colour, companies (the sender) try to persuade the stakeholders (the receiver); both visual and verbal elements convey the meanings and effects of the messages. Pictorial and graphical representations are remembered more easily and more accurately than numbers (Leivian 1980). Graphs are very effective at communicating financial information. Patterns, trends, relationships and anomalies become more apparent, facilitating comparisons and projections. For the unsophisticated reader in particular, they may facilitate the understanding of the traditional financial statements. Especially in an international context, graphs also constitute a readily understood, largely language-independent, communication tool. In particular, they represent an alternative method to the traditional alphanumeric table and continuous narrative text formats of presenting financial information (Lewandowsky and Spence 1989), since, by their very nature, they attract the reader's attention. Therefore, it has been hypothesised:

H1: The extent to which text (narrative) and visual cues are used or not vary between countries in terms of any financial or non-financial variable.

Previous studies have extensively analysed the different accounting environments at national level (Nobes 1983; Gray 1988; Salter and Doupnik 1992; Doupnik and Salter 1993, 1995; Salter and Niswander 1995). In particular, Nobes (1983) classified national accounting environments into two broad hierarchical categories: micro-Anglo Saxon practices (e.g. USA, UK and the Netherlands) and macro-continental accounting practices (e.g. France, Italy and Germany known as 'code law countries' [Mueller et al. 1991]). The former are generally characterised by comparatively weak government influence, relatively strong accounting professions and comparatively active equity markets. The focus is on measuring the company net worth and earnings for the benefit of the external stakeholders. On the other hand, macro accounting practices are generally characterised by comparatively strong government influence, relatively weak accounting professions and comparatively inactive equity markets. Accounting practices are legalistic and tax-based tending to be uniform and inflexible. More specifically, annual reports are prepared on the needs of 'outsiders' rather than 'insiders' (Nobes 1998), especially in micro based countries where the needs of outsider stockholders are primarily considered. In macro based countries insider lenders dominate since they are less likely to demand extensive levels of financial information. In micro based countries accounting is also likely to be geared towards the needs of stockholders while in macro based countries the needs of other external users (such as banks and creditors) are likely to dominate. These other external users have more alternative channels of financial communication and not just the corporate annual report. Such a classification is reflected in the format and structure of corporate annual report with a relative increase in non-financial, presentational and voluntary disclosures and a relative decrease in financial and compulsory disclosures.

Even though the IAS/IFRS international principles tend to standardise the content and the presentational format of the annual reports, each national legislation and each cultural approach differentiate the way the information is presented. The international standards specify the information to be shown but do not norm the way companies have to display them. Annual reporting practices have evolved in each country based on the nature of its capital market, the level of economic development, tax regulations, legal systems, the regulatory enforcement regime, the level of inflation, political and economic ties and the status of the accounting profession (Saudagaran 2004). The information level dynamically depends on the combination of two factors: the corporate culture and the country regulations. Thus, it has been hypothesised that:

H2: The cultural approach to public disclosures directly impacts its marketing function.

Methodology

This chapter aims to analyse the elements of the annual report that are more marketing oriented. From the review of the accounting and finance literature (Beattie and Jones 1992, 1997, 2000a, b; Aguiari and Nurra 1996; Mather et al. 2000; Beattie et al. 2008) the disclosure items, that result as being the most widely accepted and investigated, have been considered, such as cover, internal pages, graphs, images, and contents.

A panel of experts from consultancy firms and chartered accountants has been selected to participate in the study; they were asked to rank their opinion on the annual report in its function of communicating and relationship building, which measures the marketing impact. Then, they were asked to rank the three dimensions for each of the above-mentioned items using a seven point Likert scale, which ranges from 1 (not important) to 7 (very important).

Annual reports from the United States, the United Kingdom and Italy were considered. These countries are representatives of the two major international taxonomical groups: macro (Italy) and micro (UK and USA). Further, UK and USA are believed to strongly influence reporting practices internationally (Nobes and Parker 2004); however, even though they are similar in many respects such as the legal system, the capital market and the strong investor protection (La Porta et al. 1999, 2000), they show some diversity of practice. Companies were asked to supply a copy of both their last report published for domestic users and the relative English translation for the Italian ones, where appropriate and available.

One hundred and thirteen annual reports were collected from a sample of 385 firms from the three above-mentioned countries (Italy, 44 companies; United States, 56; and United Kingdom, 13), thus representing a response rate of 29.3 %. They were retrieved from the CERVED database for Italy, the Bureau van Dijck for UK and USA. The sample has been divided into two subgroups: 'Financial' (45 companies: Italy, 25; UK, 4; USA, 16) and 'Industrial' (68 companies: Italy, 19; UK, 9; USA, 40), due to their homogeneity in reporting practices related both to the industry and the country. Obviously, the two macro groups have different communication needs and strategies with respect to their main stakeholder targets. The 'financial' group is more interested to target 'technicians' since its companies mostly communicate performance data to enable stockholders to fully assess the financial performances. On the other hand, the 'industrial' group is more interested in establishing a strong relationship with the consumer market and thus uses more marketing tools, being more likely to communicate non-financial data (social, employee and environmental) which are of less interest to stockholders.

Findings

MANOVA was carried out in order to investigate the correlation among the items and, respectively, the two groups, namely countries and industries. The high variability in relation to the country ($p < .000$) has been highlighted, while the industry is significant only for increased level of p values ($<.071$). Companies in micro based countries are also likely to be keener than those in macro based countries to communicate performance data that will enable stockholders to better assess the financial performance of the company. In addition, external financial reporting in micro based countries is particularly focused on the external investor and upon the needs of the equity market.

The difference between the countries proves to be significant for all the elements of the annual report, except for the graphs. The Italian annual reports are character-ised by less creativity and more technical aspects compared to the Anglo-Saxon ones. This is probably due first to the marketing culture, which traditionally is part of the Anglo-Saxon one (especially USA), and secondly to the economic system in which these firms operate. While in Anglo-Saxon countries capitalism is based on equity market and collecting investments from external sources, in Latin ones (espe-cially Italy) the huge presence of family businesses reduces the recourse to external sources, whether financial or organisational; in fact, the management of most of Italian firms usually includes family members in order to directly control the family legacy. In addition, since the primary objective of the annual report is to transpar-ently communicate performance information or to instrumentally influence stake-holders to act in the interests of the company, its communicative actions need to be comprehensible, truthful, sincere and legitimate (Habermas 1984, 1987). These dif-ferences have been confirmed by the results of the factor analysis (KMO$=.853$; Variance explained: 87%). Two components have been highlighted: (1) the com-municability, or better the PR oriented variable, the interpretive language, that iden-tifies the elements of the annual report that contribute to attracting and convincing the reader; and (2) the technicality, the reportese language, which describes the technical information, basically the financial data. Both the dimensions recall the different cues that the readers can use to easily access the content of the annual report and to quickly find all the information they are looking for. In particular, the interpretive language dimension is similar to extrinsic cues that can help in clearly identify the identity of the company, its strategies and relational aspects (not only communication). On the other hand, the reportese language dimension is similar to the intrinsic cues and needs that both the stakeholders and the company 'speak the same language' in order to better understand all the messages.

In order to understand how each element of the annual report contributes to the marketing perception of the company data, a regression model has been carried out (Adjusted R-squared: 0.7384). As dependent variable the first impact the experts have in evaluating the annual report has been used, while the independent variables are represented by the two dimensions of the factor that measure the cultural variable and the elements of the annual report.

The regression model highlights graphs ($b=-.65$), contents ($b=-.75$) and inter-pretive language (2.52) as significant key information processing variables. The form of display organisation and the salience of visual cues clearly affect the way in which decision makers acquire and attend to information (Jarvenpaa 1990). Given the variety of readers and the difficulty in finding a common language, the effective-ness of the communication role is mostly linked to the presentation format. It is through the proper combination of images and contents that firms communicate to their public both the annual performance and the prospects for the following year. As users of annual reports and investors may spend only 15 min looking at a report during their decision-making (David 2001), the three significant elements guide the reader through the pages of the annual report highlighting the meaningful informa-tion. For example, investors look only at either the annual report or the narrative section (Fisher and Hu 1989) or the financial graphs when making their decision. Indeed, the annual report is used to transparently communicate performance information or to instrumentally influence stakeholders to act in the interest of the company.

The findings highlight the communication power of the annual report. On the one hand, the 'Contents' variable confirms the basic marketing concept of the source credibility and in general of satisfaction; while the 'Graphs' and the 'Interpretive language' variables underline the necessity of various instruments to communicate in order to make technical issues more attractive and understandable. This confirms the marketing function of an annual report.

Conclusion

The chapter, by analysing annual reports from three different countries, concurs with the wide international accounting research that focuses on cross-national similarities and differences (Gernon and Wallace 1995). It shows how attitudes and perceptions of users of annual reports ought to be investigated in order to determine the extent to which general purpose information satisfies the different needs of different user-groups, since the primary objective of the annual report is to provide a wide variety of stakeholders with the information that will be useful for decision-making process. The study is significant in that it compares more than one country, but certainly has some limitations in the sample size and composition, the broad homogeneity of the industries and the expert evaluations. Future research should focus on a better understanding and appreciation of different managerial cultures across countries. The difference between what has been disclosed and what should be disclosed is paradoxical. Since managers control the sources of information and the amount of disclosures, they control the level and type of information the reader receives. The latter may not know how reliable and complete the information is (Tennyson et al. 1990).

References available upon request

How an Individual's Self-Construals, Cosmopolitan and Local Orientation Affect the Impact of the Four Self-Congruity Types on Brand Attitude

Hector Gonzalez-Jimenez, Fernando Fastoso, and Kyoko Fukukawa

Abstract Recent research questions the universality of the self-congruity effect on brand perceptions and highlights the need for further clarifying the boundary conditions of self-congruity theory. Current evidence suggests that it is individual characteristics that determine the superiority of branding strategies focused on appealing to a consumers' actual versus ideal self-congruity. This study extends that research by modelling how four individual characteristics of value for cross-cultural market segmentation purposes (an individual's level of independence, interdependence, and their cosmopolitan and local orientations) affect which of the four self-congruity types (actual, ideal, social, and social ideal) has the strongest impact on brand perceptions. Empirically, the validity of the conceptual framework is tested using survey data from non-student samples in the USA and India. Findings show that an individual's level of independence and interdependence, cosmopolitan and local orientation determine which self-congruity type has the strongest effect on brand attitude. Specifically, the results show that for locals and interdependents, actual self-congruity has the strongest effect on brand attitude. In contrast, for cosmopolitans and independents, ideal self-congruity has the strongest effect on brand attitude. Interestingly, overall actual and ideal self-congruity types have the strongest effect on brand attitude for the consumer types tested. Moreover, the findings are partially validated in both countries and suggest that other factors pertaining to the USA and India may influence the self-congruity effect. The study offers practitioners with insights on which self-concept type they should try to match in their brand communications to elicit most positive brand attitude among consumers depending on their individual characteristics.

H. Gonzalez-Jimenez (✉) • F. Fastoso
University of York, Heslington, UK
e-mail: hgj503@york.ac.uk; fernando.fastoso@york.ac.uk

K. Fukukawa
Bradford University, Bradford, UK
e-mail: K.Fukukawa@bradford.ac.uk

© Academy of Marketing Science 2016
L. Petruzzellis, R.S. Winer (eds.), *Rediscovering the Essentiality of Marketing*,
Developments in Marketing Science: Proceedings of the Academy of Marketing
Science, DOI 10.1007/978-3-319-29877-1_38

The Moderating Role of Language in the Relationship Between Perceived Risk, Perceived Usability, and Satisfaction Online

Juan Miguel Alcántara-Pilar, Salvador Del Barrio-García, Lucia Porcu, and Esmeralda Crespo-Almendros

Introduction

The Internet can be considered one of the greatest contributors to the globalization of markets (Constatinides et al. 2010). Within this context, it is vital to take into account the cultural differences that exist between different markets (Rey et al. 2013), as well as the particular language that is most advisable for each context. There are currently 7106 living languages in the world, spoken by 6200 million people, with the most widely spoken as first languages (L1) being Chinese (1197 million users), Spanish (414 million users), and English (335 million users) (Lewis et al. 2014). On the Internet, these three languages are also the most widely used but English is in top position with 800 million users, followed by Chinese (649 million), and Spanish (222 million) (Internet World Stats 2014). Some 80 % of those who browse in English use it as their second language (L2) (Internet World Stats 2014). These data are of particular interest to firms operating in international markets as, depending on the language in which users process information, consumer behavior may vary. Language conveys cultural references that shape cognitive processing (Luna et al. 2008).

The aim of the present work is to analyze the extent to which the language in which a user processes online information moderates the relationship between perceived risk, perceived usability, and user satisfaction while browsing the website of a fictitious tourist destination. To achieve this analysis, two experimental studies were carried out on two samples (Spanish and British). In both cases the independent variable was the language in which the subject processed the online information—that is, their mother tongue (L1) versus their second language (L2).

J.M. Alcántara-Pilar (✉) • S. Del Barrio-García • L. Porcu • E. Crespo-Almendros
University of Granada, Granada, Spain
e-mail: jmap@ugr.es; dbarrio@ugr.es; luciapor@ugr.es; ecrespo@ugr.es

© Academy of Marketing Science 2016
L. Petruzzellis, R.S. Winer (eds.), *Rediscovering the Essentiality of Marketing*,
Developments in Marketing Science: Proceedings of the Academy of Marketing
Science, DOI 10.1007/978-3-319-29877-1_39

177

Background

From the perspective of the communicator, the language used by the bilingual person influences their cognitive processing style (Marian and Kaushanskaya 2004). Recent research has demonstrated that because language is associated with cultural frameworks, communicating in a given language can increase a person's cognitive access to values associated with that language (Luna et al. 2008; Unsworth et al. 2005).

Having established the relevance of language as a vehicle for cultural frameworks, it is worth referring to a particular research model designed to differentiate between cultures. Of all the many theoretical frameworks looking at the differences between national cultures, that of Hofstede (2001) enjoys the greatest acceptance among academics in the field of business administration and marketing (Engelen and Brettel 2011; Taras et al. 2011). The five dimensions he uses to classify cultures are as follows: power distance (PD); uncertainty avoidance (UA); individualism (IND); masculinity (MAS); and long-term orientation (LTO).

Applying this framework to the tourism sector, Sabiote et al. (2012) demonstrated how UA moderated the negative relationship between perceived risk (RISK), hotel quality, and overall perceived value among British and Spanish users. In light of this finding, it is logical to assume a relationship—in the same direction—between RISK and perceived usability (USAB), the latter being understood as the quality of the website design.

Taking language as a moderating factor and conveyor of cultural values, it is widely accepted that the words used in each language activate a series of conceptual frameworks (Li et al. 2009). In this regard, those users belonging to a culture with a high value in UA (such as Spain, with a UA score of 86) who browse in a second language (L2)—such as English, which pertains to a culture with a lower value in this particular cultural dimension (UK, with a UA score of 35)—will register a lower perceived risk score than in the case of those same users browsing in their own mother tongue (L1) (Spanish users browsing in Spanish). The same can be said, albeit in the opposite direction, for British users browsing in English (L1) (lower perceived risk) or in Spanish (L2) (higher perceived risk) (Alcántara-Pilar et al. 2013). On this premise, the following hypothesis is proposed:

H_1: *There is a negative relationship between perceived risk and perceived usability which will be moderated by the level of uncertainty avoidance (UA) associated with the language used during browsing.*

$H_{1.1}$: *The negative relationship between perceived risk and perceived usability will be greater among users from cultures with a high level of UA who are browsing in L1 (Spanish sample browsing in Spanish), compared to users from the same culture who are browsing in a language from a culture with low UA (L2) (Spanish sample browsing in English).*

$H_{1.2}$: *The negative relationship between perceived risk and perceived usability will be lesser among users from cultures with a low level of UA who are browsing in L1 (British sample browsing in English), compared to users from the same culture who are browsing in a language from a culture with high UA (L2) (British sample browsing in Spanish).*

A further important element of the user's online information-processing is the degree of satisfaction they experience during the process (Sabiote et al. 2013). Casaló et al. (2008) demonstrated that there is a direct and positive relationship between USAB and satisfaction online (SAT). Elsewhere, Sabiote et al. (2012) undertook a cross-cultural study among Spanish and British subjects and demonstrated the existence of a direct and positive relationship between perceived effectiveness and satisfaction online, moderated in this case by the IND cultural dimension. In view of these findings, and switching the moderating effect of culture onto that of the language as a cultural framework, the following hypothesis is proposed:

H_2: *There is a positive relationship between perceived usability and satisfaction online which will be moderated by the level of individualism (IND) associated with the language used during browsing.*

> $H_{2.1}$: *The positive relationship between perceived usability and satisfaction will be lesser amongst users from cultures with a low level of IND who are browsing in L1 (Spanish sample browsing in Spanish), compared to users from that same culture who are browsing in a language from a culture with high level of IND (L2) (Spanish sample browsing in English).*
>
> $H_{2.2}$: *The positive relationship between perceived usability and satisfaction will be greater amongst users from cultures with a high level of IND who are browsing in L1 (British sample browsing in English), compared to users from that same culture who are browsing in a language from a culture with low IND (L2) (British sample browsing in Spanish).*

A between-subjects experimental design was deemed to fit best with the research objectives. The language used to process the website information was the independent variable: processing in Spanish versus processing in English. The rationale for selecting these two languages was that they belong to two very different cultures, according to the dimensions proposed by Hofstede (2001) (Spain IND: 51; UA: 86 / UK IND: 89; UA: 35). The values of Spain were taken to represent the cultural references of the Spanish language (ES) and the values of the UK taken to represent those of the English language (EN).

Research Methods

The experiment itself required a professional website to be purpose-built, with its own domain name, providing information on the fictitious tourist destination (www.buyuada.org). The fact that the site had its own domain meant that natural browsing conditions could be simulated for subjects. Two versions of the site were created—one written in Spanish and the other in English. The subjects were selected by an external company commissioned to establish an online survey panel for the experiment. The planned sample size was 480 individuals—120 for each of the four treatments: T1 (Spanish browsing in Spanish); T2 (Spanish browsing in English); T3 (British browsing in English); and T4 (British browsing in Spanish). The final sample comprised 491 Internet users, of whom 47% were Spanish (227) and 53% British (264). The final sample was distributed according to treatment, as follows: T1, 118 subjects; T2, 109 subjects; T3, 196 subjects; and T4, 68 subjects. To ensure that users came from Spain and the UK, Google Analytics was used during the data collection. The external company made e-mail contact with each panel member and asked them to complete a filter questionnaire to establish their level of competence in their second language. Before beginning the experiment they were informed as follows: "The site you will now be asked to browse will be in Spanish or English."

The online risk perceived by the individual when processing the information on the experimental website was measured using the scale proposed by Wakefield and Whitten (2006). Perceived usability of the site was measured from the user's perspective by applying the scale adapted by Flavián et al. (2006). To measure satisfaction online during browsing, the scale developed by Szymanski and Hise (2001) was used. The study also measured variables of a sociodemographic nature such as gender and age, together with the cultural dimensions using the VSM94 scale developed by Hofstede (2001).[1]

Results and Discussion

Before testing the hypotheses, the method proposed by Cheung and Resvold (2000) was used to test for the existence of cultural response bias. The results having revealed that this bias was indeed present, the "method of standardization among cultures" (Fischer 2004) was then applied. The values calculated for the samples were also checked, in the IND and UA dimensions. The cultural scores obtained for the Spanish sample were 88.37 (IND) and 80.62 (UA). The British sample obtained 89 (IND) and 35 (UA). The works of García et al. (2008) also found high values in the IND dimension of a sample comprising Spaniards.

Testing the proposed hypotheses required the proposed causal model to be estimated by means of a multigroup SEM analysis (L1 vs. L2) for each sample (Spanish vs. British). The measurement models were found to be satisfactory, with all the items presenting individual reliability (R^2) above .50, and composite reliability and average variance extracted values for the three scales being above recommended values (.7 and .50, respectively). The overall goodness-of-fit indices revealed that the estimated multigroup models were quite acceptable (Hair et al. 2010).

The main effects proposed in H_1 and H_2—that is, the negative relationship between RISK and USAB, and the positive relationship between USAB and SAT—are confirmed for both samples (Spanish vs. British). Elsewhere, the moderating effect of language on the relationship between RISK and USAB is also confirmed in the proposed direction ($\beta_{H1.1.\_Spanish-Spanish}$: $-.70 > \beta_{H1.1.\_Spanish-English}$: $-.33$ and $p < .01$;

---

[1] *The complete questionnaire (VSM94) can be found on Professor Hofstede's website, together with the formulas for calculating cultural scores (www.geerthofstede.nl/research*DOUBLEHYPH EN*vsm).*

$\beta_{H1.2._{British-English}}$: $-.25 < \beta_{H1.2._{British-Spanish}}$: $-.48$ and $p < .05$). By contrast, the moderating effect of language on the relationship between USAB and SAT could not be confirmed as it proved to be non-significant ($\beta_{H2.1._{Spanish-Spanish}}$: $.64 > \beta_{H2.1._{Spanish-English}}$: $.61$ and $p > .10$; $\beta_{H2.2._{British-English}}$: $.82 < \beta_{H2.2._{British-Spanish}}$: $.88$ and $p > .10$).

The results demonstrate the existence of a direct and negative relationship between risk and perceived usability, and a direct and positive relationship between perceived usability and satisfaction during browsing. With regard to the moderating effect of language, significant differences were only found to exist for the relationship between perceived risk and perceived usability in both samples. Therefore, in the case of users browsing in a L2 (second language) representative of a culture with a lower level of UA than that of L1 (mother tongue), this will reduce the negative effect of perceived risk on perceived usability. By contrast, in the case of those users browsing in a L2 associated with a higher level of UA than that of L1, the perceived risk will be greater. Meanwhile, the moderating effect of language as a conveyor of cultural values could not be confirmed in the relationships between usability and satisfaction for either of the two samples. One possible explanation for this may be the scant differences found in the IND dimension for the Spanish sample.

These findings will be of help to marketers in their decision-making regarding the design of corporate websites and how to translate or adapt them to other languages, particularly in the context of the tourism sector. The web content should be offered in the language that provides the best fit with the cultural values that need to be conveyed to the target user.

Looking to the future, further studies could focus on confirming this relationship for other cultures, or measuring the psycholinguistic effect with other languages.

Acknowledgements The authors appreciate the financial help provided via a research project of group ADEMAR (University of Granada) under the auspices of the Andalusian Program for R&D, number P12-SEJ2592, and Research Program from the Faculty of Education, Economy and Technology of Ceuta.

References available upon request.

The Myth of Self-Centeredness in Materialism: Reconciling Collectivism and Materialism in Asia

Sandra Awanis, Bodo B. Schlegelmilch, and Charles C. Cui

Abstract Materialism, which is the importance placed on the acquisition and possessions of material objects, is often depicted as a self-prioritizing trait rooted in an individualistic value (Belk 1985; Richins and Dawson 1992). Materialistic consumers are seen as self-centered individuals who prefer to build meaningful relationships with possessions rather than people (Burroughs and Rindfleisch 2002; Kasser and Ryan 1993). However, this theory is incongruent with the reality, as cultural studies routinely find that materialistic consumption manifests strongly among collectivistic Asian consumers (Cleveland and Chang 2009; Ger and Belk 1996). Such contradiction points to an inconsistency between the theories developed primarily in the United States and the realities surrounding non-Western consumers' attitudes and behavior (Sharma 2010). The present research thus aims to reconcile theory and practice by reassessing the pertinence of self-centeredness as the central domain of materialism among Asian consumers.

Extant literatures rarely recognize that individuals may dexterously commit to materialistic and collectivistic values. Rather, materialism is often depicted as opposite of collective values, such as religious commitment, moderation, and self-sacrifice (Bauer et al. 2012; Burroughs and Rindfleisch 2002). Hence, individuals who hold materialistic and collectivistic ideals experience *value-conflict*, defined as psychological tensions resulting from incongruent values that lead to diminished life satisfaction and reduced psychological welfare (Burroughs and Rindfleisch 2002; Kasser and Ryan 1993). However, cultural studies maintain that collectivist societies are more successful than their individualist counterparts in balancing personal goals and collective interests (Wong and Ahuvia 1998; Ahuvia 2002). Contrary to extant research's prediction, materialism does not appear to have an adverse effect on

S. Awanis (✉)
Lancaster University Management School, Lancaster, UK
e-mail: S.awanis@lancaster.ac.uk

B.B. Schlegelmilch
WU Vienna, Vienna, Austria
e-mail: Bodo.schlegelmilch@wu.ac.uk

C.C. Cui
Manchester Business School, Manchester, UK
e-mail: Charles.cui@manchester.ac.uk

© Academy of Marketing Science 2016   183
L. Petruzzellis, R.S. Winer (eds.), *Rediscovering the Essentiality of Marketing*,
Developments in Marketing Science: Proceedings of the Academy of Marketing
Science, DOI 10.1007/978-3-319-29877-1_40

well-being among Asian consumers. Instead, these consumers are catching up to those in advanced economies in terms of life satisfaction, which is fuelled largely by their satisfaction towards material well-being (Pew Research 2014). Therefore, consumers from non-Western and less developed countries may not simply emulate the principles of Western-based materialism (de Mooij and Hofstede 2002). As such, our research aims to address the following questions:

1. To what extent do consumers from collectivistic cultures experience personal conflict between material and collective values?
2. What impacts do the interaction between materialism and collective-oriented values have on Asian consumers' consumption evaluation?

We draw from optimal distinctiveness theory (Brewer 1991) to inform how Asian consumers use material consumption to fulfill social goals. This perspective provides an additional vantage point to the dominant collectivist cultural perspective that confounds Asian consumers' prosocial attitudes towards consumption. Further, we explain how consumers with incongruent values evaluate the attractiveness of material goods to achieve socially desired goals. Our international research draws from a sample of Asian consumers from China, India, Brunei, Indonesia, Malaysia, Singapore, and Thailand. The research design is twofold. First, we utilized Schwartz's (1992) circumflex model of human values to examine the perceptual distances between materialism and the larger value system amongst collectivistic Asian consumers. Second, we studied the interaction effect between material and collective-oriented values on Asian consumers' prepurchase evaluation. Our findings suggest that collectivist Asian consumers are able to balance materialistic and social pressures and as a result, evaluate the social cost of goods more favorably than other competing conspicuous attributes, such as brand and price information.

References available upon request.

Psychological Distance in Cause-Related Product Buying Decisions

Tao Xue, Sarah Hong Xiao, and Gopalkrishnan R. Iyer

Abstract Cause-related marketing (CRM) is now increasingly gaining prominence as a global form of promotion to support an organisation's corporate social responsibility aims and to increase market share (Barone et al. 2007). While prior research has focused on charitable donations and other methods of helping causes and constituents, less attention has been directed to the perceived distance/closeness of a social cause in driving consumers' cause-related product (CRP) buying decisions. For example, even though research has often called attention to personal relevance and presentation of cause-related cues in CRM promotion (Pracejus and Olsen 2004), psychological distance has not obtained the attention it deserves. It cannot be denied that psychological distance is a key antecedent to pro-social and intertemporal decision-making among consumers. Moreover, perceptions of psychological distance may vary widely in different cultural contexts. We contribute to the emerging literature on cause-related shopping by empirically demonstrating the impacts of various psychological distance constructs on cause-related shopping among samples of consumers in the UK ($n = 220$) and China ($n = 225$).

References available upon request.

T. Xue (✉)
Sheffield Hallam University, Sheffield, UK
e-mail: m.tao-xue@shu.ac.uk

S.H. Xiao
Durham University, Durham, UK
e-mail: hong.xiao@durham.ac.uk

G.R. Iyer
Florida Atlantic University, Boca Raton, FL, USA
e-mail: giyer@fau.edu

© Academy of Marketing Science 2016
L. Petruzzellis, R.S. Winer (eds.), *Rediscovering the Essentiality of Marketing*,
Developments in Marketing Science: Proceedings of the Academy of Marketing
Science, DOI 10.1007/978-3-319-29877-1_41

Part V
Digital and Social Media Marketing

Consumer Ethical Judgement and Controversial Advertising Avoidance on Social Media

Caroline Moraes, Carlos Ferreira, Nina Michaelidou, and Michelle McGrath

Introduction

Controversial advertising can be defined as advertising that offends or shocks viewers (Dahl et al. 2003). While some research on the ethical issues linked to controversial advertising offline can be found (Drumwright and Murphy 2009; Fam and Waller 2003), more research is needed on controversial advertising online and whether it may lead to ad avoidance on specific platforms, such as social media. This topic is important for marketers and researchers, given that the proliferation of social media advertising is driving brands to produce adverts which attempt to cut through the ad clutter with the use of controversial appeals (Dahl et al. 2003; Drumwright and Murphy 2009; Fam and Waller 2003; Waller 2005). Thus, this study aims to address this research gap and its objective is to examine the impact of controversial ad perception and consumer ethical judgment on ad avoidance, in the specific context of social media.

C. Moraes (✉) • C. Ferreira
Coventry University, Coventry, UK
e-mail: caroline.moraes@coventry.ac.uk; carlos.ferreira@coventry.ac.uk

N. Michaelidou
Loughborough University, Loughborough, UK
e-mail: n.michaelidou@lboro.ac.uk

M. McGrath
University of Winchester, Winchester, UK
e-mail: michelle.mcgrath@winchester.ac.uk

© Academy of Marketing Science 2016   189
L. Petruzzellis, R.S. Winer (eds.), *Rediscovering the Essentiality of Marketing*,
Developments in Marketing Science: Proceedings of the Academy of Marketing
Science, DOI 10.1007/978-3-319-29877-1_42

Theoretical Background

Advertising avoidance refers to audiences' actions which aim to reduce their exposure to ad content (Speck and Elliott 1997). The concept has been researched in traditional media contexts with research classifying avoidance as cognitive and behavioural in type (e.g., Speck and Elliott 1997; Abernethy 1991; Rojas-Méndez et al. 2009). In contrast, limited research has been devoted to examining ad avoidance in online contexts (Cho and Cheon 2004; Kelly et al. 2010). However, ad avoidance has become prominent given the increase in consumer exposure to high numbers of adverts through both traditional (e.g., television, newspapers) and online media (Gritten 2007; Schutz 2006a). Recent exploratory research shows that consumers try and avoid advertising on social media such as Facebook and YouTube (Kelly et al. 2010; Michaelidou and Moraes 2013).

A number of factors have been identified as antecedents of ad avoidance. Consumers often process and use the ads they view online to accomplish specific goals (Rodgers and Thorson 2000). However, such ads may also impede consumers' non-commercial goals, so they may avoid such ads due to perceptions of goal impediment (Cho and Cheon 2004). Additionally, according to Cho and Cheon (2004) audiences tend to avoid online ads if they perceive them as clutter, or if they have previously had a negative interaction or experience with online ads. In such instances, audiences are expected to dislike ads and intentionally ignore them through cognitive avoidance. On this basis, we hypothesise that:

H1 Consumers' antecedents (i.e. goal impediment, ad clutter and prior negative experience) will be positively related to avoidance of social media ads.

Further, ad avoidance is argued to be affected by audiences' perceptions of ads. Such perceptions are concerned with the execution style and creative appeals used in the ad, and can be positive or negative (Hampel et al. 2012; Chan et al. 2007). Previous research shows that ads can be perceived as controversial due to either the nature of the product or the advertising appeal used (e.g., fear, sexual, anxiety, violence), leading to ad avoidance (Dens et al. 2008). On this basis, we hypothesise that:

H2 Consumers' perceptions of social media ads as controversial will be positively related to avoidance of social media ads.

Perceptions of ads as controversial are grounded on contextual factors such as where and when the ad is shown, and who is exposed to the ad (Fam et al. 2003; Fam and Waller 2003; Phau and Prendergast 2001; Prendergast et al. 2002; Waller 1999). On this basis, the media platform on which the ad is shown can impact the extent to which the ad is perceived as controversial. Previous research has shown that audiences present more tolerance, and perceive less offense, for online ads relative to other media (Prendergast et al. 2002; Prendergast and Hwa 2003; Christy and Haley 2008). However, this means that such ads may be perceived as more intrusive (Ha and McCann 2008). Hence, the extent to which audiences perceive social media ads as goal impeding, cluttering and negatively experienced will relate to perceptions of ads as controversial. Thus, we hypothesise that:

H3 Consumers' antecedents (i.e. goal impediment, ad clutter and prior negative experience) will be positively related to perceptions of social media ads as controversial.

Moreover, ethical judgment of ads has been found to impact audiences' responses and behaviour (Beltramini 2006). For example, Simpson et al. (1998) have examined the impact of consumers' ethical judgement of deceptive advertising on responses toward ads, suggesting that the extent to which such advertising is perceived as unethical impacts attitude towards the ad, attitude toward the brand and purchase intention (Beltramini 2006). According to this stream of research we argue that, in the context of social media, ads that are perceived as less unethical will suffer less avoidance. Therefore, we hypothesise that:

H4 Consumers' ethical judgment of social media ads will be negatively related to avoidance of social media ads.

Simultaneously, we expect that the more ethical the ads are judged to be, the less they will be perceived as controversial. Thus:

H5 Consumers' ethical judgment of social media ads will be negatively related to perceptions of social media ads as controversial.

Additionally, we expect ethical judgment to moderate the relationship between controversial ad perceptions and ad avoidance on social media. On this basis, we hypothesise that:

H6 Consumers' ethical judgment of social media ads will moderate the relationship between consumers' controversial ad perceptions and ad avoidance on social media.

Methodology

A three-phase research design was used in this study. First the researchers conducted four focus groups with UK consumers to establish if consumers avoided social media ads and what led them to do so. This was followed by the development and refinement of hypotheses, in line with previous research (Cho and Cheon 2004; Kelly et al. 2010). A conceptual model was also developed and a quantitative pilot survey sought to test the appropriateness of exiting scales to measure the impact of consumer ad perception (Chan et al. 2007), ethical judgment of ads (Vitell and Muncy 2005) and ad avoidance antecedents (Cho and Cheon 2004) on social media ad avoidance.

Once the pilot survey was concluded, the main survey collected data through an online quota sample of 270 UK consumers. Thirty-eight percent of respondents were male and 62 % were female. Age distribution was appropriate for the study, with 8 % of the total sample between 18 and 25 years old, 38 % between the ages of 26 and 35, 21 % in the 36–45 range, 25 % in the 46–55 bracket and 8 % in the 56–65 age range. Educational achievement was also varied, with 18 % of the sample having completed GCSEs, 35 % possessing further education (A-level or equivalent), 30 % with undergraduate degrees and 15 % with postgraduate qualifications.

Results and Analysis

Measures were adapted from existing survey instruments. Social media ad avoidance antecedents and ad avoidance measures were derived from Cho and Cheon's (2004) work. Ethical judgment was measured using the multidimensional ethics scale (Nguyen and Biderman 2008), and controversial ad perception measures were based on Chan et al. (2007). All scales showed Cronbach's Alpha above .7, and Average Variable Extracted (AVE) scores above the required level of .5, in line with Fornell and Larcker (1981).

Further, confirmatory factor analysis (CFA) was used to assess the psychometric properties of the variables. CFA revealed satisfactory model fit ($\chi2 = 114.914$ (65), $p = .000$; $\chi2/df = 1.768$; RMSEA $= .053$; NFI $= .974$; CFI $= .989$; GFI $= .943$).

The hypotheses were then tested using structural equation modelling (SEM). The model and moderation analysis were estimated following the unconstrained method described by Steinmetz et al. (2011). The analysis generated the fit indices for the structural model ($\chi2 = 547.78$ (228), $p = .000$; $\chi2/df = 2.39$; RMSEA $= .071$; NFI $= .963$; CFI $= .978$; GFI $= .875$; Standard RMR $= .049$), and the hypotheses' tests for the SEM (*Direct effects*: H1: Antecedents $\rightarrow$ Ad Avoidance $= .49**$; H2: Controversial Ad Perception $\rightarrow$ Ad Avoidance $= .13**$; H3: Antecedents $\rightarrow$ Controversial Ad Perception $= .55**$; H4: Ethical Judgment $\rightarrow$ Ad Avoidance $= -.18**$; H5: Ethical Judgment $\rightarrow$ Controversial Ad Perception $= -.14*$; *Interaction*: Controversial X Ethical Judgment $\rightarrow$ Ad Avoidance $= .08**$; ** $p < .01$, * $p < .05$, one-tailed regression tests. Numbers are rounded to two decimal points).

Data analysis confirmed that the model presents a generally good fit. All the relationships are significant, and the moderation effect of ethical judgment on the impact of controversial ad perception on ad avoidance is also demonstrated.

Discussion and Conclusion

This research contributes to theory by conceptualising additional antecedents of ad avoidance, namely ethical judgment of social media ads and consumer perception of social media ads as controversial. Furthermore, it shows that ethical judgment serves as a moderator of the relationship between the perception of an ad as controversial and its avoidance.

The unexpected direction of the direct effect of ethical judgment on ad avoidance, as well as its moderation of the effect of negative ad perception on ad avoidance, indicate that the effect of ethical judgment over ad avoidance is more complex than previously hypothesised. This may be due to the effect of source factors and message appeals in controversial ads. For example, social marketing campaigns on social media may cause discomfort in viewers, but may not lead to social media ad avoidance due to their resonance with consumers' ethical judgments and moral values. This suggests consumers may find certain social media ad appeals uncomfortable, but may judge them acceptable if they are used for a good cause (e.g. for the communication of non-profit, social causes).

This study is original in that it empirically investigates the link between consumer avoidance of social media ads, controversial ad perception and consumer ethical judgment of social media ads. Thus, this work extends previous research in this area by advancing knowledge in the domain of advertising avoidance in a social media context, and by examining consumers in the UK. This research is also relevant to marketing practitioners, as it highlights the importance of evaluating consumer ethical judgment before running social media campaigns (Simpson et al. 1998), given that social media ad avoidance impacts social media ad effectiveness (Bellman et al. 2010; Pashkevich et al. 2012; Zufryden et al. 1993).

References available upon request.

Experiencing Brand on Mobile Augmented Reality

Shing-Wan Chang and Yuri Heikal Siregar

Abstract Mobile augmented reality (MAR) has emerged as a prominent and innovative app (Alkhamisi and Monowar 2013; Juniper Research 2013). MAR is a system within mobile app that superimposed virtual graphics on the real environment (Azuma 1997; Langlotz et al. 2014). The consumers nowadays expect beyond the brand and would like to be actively involved (Cascalo et al. 2007; Argyriou and Melewar 2011). It is believed that MAR, with its strong visual graphic, is able to convey rich information in an innovative way and could evoke unconventional experience (Huang and Liu 2014). Thus, MAR could be utilised to convey brand experience (Fogg 2003; Brakus et al. 2009) that may impact on attitude and attachment of the consumers towards brands (Mikulincer and Shaver 2003). Drawing with uses and gratifications theory and media richness theory, this study attempts to find out the impact of MAR on brand experience, brand attitude and brand attachment. Moreover, we propose four dimensions for the purpose of measuring MAR characteristics; integration, object registration, interactivity and narrative.

Structural Equation Modeling was performed to test the hypotheses. MAR was confirmed to positively impact on brand experience as well as attitude. However, there was no significant effect of MAR on attachment and brand experience did not positively affect attitude. As predicted, brand experience appeared to positively influence attachment and attitude positively impacted on attachment. Moreover, it was found that MAR gave positive effect on attachment indirectly, through brand experience and attitude. In this regard, despite that the relationship between MAR and attachment appeared to be insignificant, the effect of MAR on attachment was significantly mediated by brand experience and attitude. Additionally, the findings corroborated that media richness theory and uses and gratifications theory can be applied to explain MAR. Consequently, MAR implementation should focus more on strong brand-related visual graphics that are associated with brand experience. Good combination of virtual graphics and real environment should be also considered into the design of MAR. Similarly, more attention should be paid to the relevance with current situation and moment while creating the content for MAR (e.g. the relevance of McDonalds Gol! app with world cup 2014).

S.-W. Chang (✉) • Y.H. Siregar
Middlesex University, London, UK
e-mail: s.chang@mdx.ac.uk; yuriheikalsiregar@gmail.com

© Academy of Marketing Science 2016
L. Petruzzellis, R.S. Winer (eds.), *Rediscovering the Essentiality of Marketing*,
Developments in Marketing Science: Proceedings of the Academy of Marketing
Science, DOI 10.1007/978-3-319-29877-1_43

195

   The results of this study improve the current understanding of experiencing the brand on MAR. Subsequently, this study made a significant contribution to the mobile marketing field, by providing evidence of the effectiveness of MAR, and it shed light on the growing importance of augmented reality (AR) research for consumers' experience. Due to the small sample size and only one stimulus (MAR application) adopted in the study, the finding of this study may not be generalised.

References available upon request.

Assessing Social Media e-Visibility: A Framework to Compare Goods vs. Service Firms

Iris Vilnai-Yavetz, Olga Levina, and Nataliia Medzhybovska

Introduction

In this interdisciplinary work we develop the Social Media e-Visibility (SMEV) framework and use it to assess the potential of a set of firms to engage the customer in the global e-business market through the usage of Social Media. The Internet opened a new procurement channel for firms that allows them reaching customers all over the world. The growth of Social Media (SoM) in recent years accelerated this development by enabling fast and even real-time interaction between customers and firms. The usage of SoM for marketing purposes has been an active topic in research and practice in recent years (Hollenbeck and Kaikati 2012; Papasolomou and Melanthiou 2012). SoM allows the company and the customer communicating with each other, but also allows customers communicating with each other about the company and creating an electronic word of mouth (Hennig-Thurau et al. 2004). For the firms, well-managed SoM provides a potential tool to gain insight about customers' attitudes, as well as an opportunity to spread commercial information using the customer as an information channel (Parka et al. 2011). Firms in various countries and industries have chosen to use SoM for their customer and product communication (Coelho et al. 2014). For example, Parka et al. (2011) documented

I. Vilnai-Yavetz (✉)
Ruppin Academic Center, Emek Hefer Area, Israel
e-mail: yavetzir@ruppin.ac.il

O. Levina
Technische Universität Berlin, Berlin, Germany
e-mail: olga.levina.1@tu-berlin.de

N. Medzhybovska
Odessa National Economic University, Odessa, Ukraine
e-mail: nmedzh@oneu.edu.ua

© Academy of Marketing Science 2016
L. Petruzzellis, R.S. Winer (eds.), *Rediscovering the Essentiality of Marketing*,
Developments in Marketing Science: Proceedings of the Academy of Marketing
Science, DOI 10.1007/978-3-319-29877-1_44

197

how health organizations employ their Facebook accounts for communicating with their customers and for health advertising and promotions. SoM enables people to effortlessly access information, providing increased visibility (Boyd 2010) and therefore potential for further engagement in the e-market.

SoM is defined as an internet-based application that requires user interaction (Bryant 2006). Rafaeli and Sudweeks (1997) defined interactivity as "a condition of communication in which simultaneous and continuous exchanges occur, and these exchanges carry a social, binding force." This definition implies that interactivity can be shown to lead to more cooperation and socialization. Based on this definition as well as on the social presence theory (Gefen and Straub 2004), the current work explores the degree of the involvement of firms and industries in a mutual customer–firm interaction. Building on Capriotti's (2009) definition of corporate visibility, we define SMEV as the firm's potential to interact with its customers and involve them in the e-market through the currently available means of communication, namely SoM. The SMEV framework is based on the assumption of Kaplan and Haenlein (2010) that SoM allow firms to engage in timely and direct end-consumer contact at lower cost and higher levels of efficiency than can be achieved with more traditional communication tools.

Based on the literature review and building on Levina and Vilnai-Yavetz's (2013) e-visibility maturity model, we propose that SMEV score of a firm or set of firms in the e-market should take into account three main elements: Interactivity (to what extent the firm applies the opportunities for interaction provided by the e-market), Sociability (to what extent the firm tries to achieve social presence (Gefen and Straub 2004) and social impact (Latané 1981)), and Globalization (to what extent the firm tries to achieve these goals at a global, as opposed to local, level).

Differences between service and goods firms in general, and between specific goods and service industries were tested. Based on the differences between goods and service industries (Anderson et al. 1997) that are reflected in the differences between the product marketing mix (the four P's) and the services marketing mix (the seven P's), we predicted that service firms would be more sociable and interactive and would thus achieve a higher SMEV scores in general and in the Sociability and Interactivity components in particular.

Methodology

To assess the specific SMEV score of a set of firms, we translated the three dimensions—Interactivity, Sociability, and Globalization—into evaluation criteria (e.g., interaction intensity is one of the criteria for evaluation of the Interactivity dimension). Each criterion is further assigned to its indicators (e.g., the intensity of dynamic interaction is the sum of usage of dynamic communication means). The indicators were selected based on the principles of the social impact theory (Latané 1981), and the score values were based on the social presence theory (Gefen and Straub 2004) as well as on the definition of interactivity (Rafaeli and Sudweeks 1997).

Data Collection

We conducted a cross-sectional-cross-country survey of 890 firm websites of various sizes from 21 different industries, chosen randomly from the lists of firms in each of three countries: Germany, Israel, and Ukraine. The countries were chosen from among partners in an e-commerce-related European Union project (http://www.ecommis.eu) with the aim of representing advanced and developing nations with regard to e-business. Two of the countries—Germany and Israel—are considered fully developed economies as defined by Lefebvre and Lefebvre (2002), while the third—Ukraine—can be considered transition economy, on its way from centrally planned to market economy. A transition economy is characterized by a tremendous amount of environmental turbulence and unfamiliar organizational forms, and as such the development of e-commerce in such states is still in its initial stages (Lefebvre and Lefebvre 2002). To produce a pool of firms in each country, we used comprehensive lists of active firms maintained by established organizations (e.g., WeltOnline, Germany; Dun & Bradstreet, Israel; Mercury. odessa.ua, Ukraine) from which we sampled the required quota. The surveyed firms were all B2C only (in contrast to business-to-business firms) and included private and public companies of various sizes, among them producers, marketers, and service providers. The industry categorization (e.g., higher education and real estate) was adapted from the Israel Central Bureau of Statistics (ISCBS 2011) to the context of European countries. The initial data included 1068 firms from 27 industries. Since the aim of this analysis was to compare service firms with goods firms, we sorted the industries into merely goods (producers and marketers, e.g., drug producers), merely services (e.g., higher education), and goods-services mix (e.g., cellular phones). The 6 "mixed" categories were omitted from the analyses, leaving 6 goods industry categories and 15 service categories.

Scoring tool, sampling rules, and coding guidelines were developed to be used for the quantitative online content analysis based on the e-visibility maturity model (Levina and Vilnai-Yavetz 2013). The SMEV score of a firm is calculated using only the relationship-oriented aspects of the e-visibility maturity model. For the current work the more technical aspects of e-business (e.g., security) were omitted. First, we examined each firm's presence in the internet and recorded the percentage of firms having a website. Then, for firms represented by a homepage, we examined the homepage further for indicators related to the defined dimensions (e.g., the amount and intensity of SoM usage by the firm), transactions (e.g., means for order and payments), customer relations (e.g., means for online communications), and globalization (e.g., local vs. global language, local vs. global SoM). We then calculated the SMEV scores of set of firms, using the following equation: SMEV = W* (Interactivity + Sociability + Globalization), where W stands for the percentage of firms having a webpage in the set of firms (operating a webpage was defined as the initial step toward the achievement of e-visibility), and the three elements are calculated using the full set of criteria and indicators. For more extensive description of the variables and score definition please refer to Levina and Vilnai-Yavetz (2013).

Results

Based on the above framework, in this section we compare SMEV of service industries and of goods industries as well as SMEV of specific service industries with SMEV of specific goods industries. All comparisons were analyzed across the three countries. Using the SMEV Framework we found minor differences in the level of Interactivity, Sociability, and Globalization employed by service firms in comparison to goods firms in general. However, substantial differences in the level of Interactivity, Sociability, and Globalization were found between the specific service and goods industries compared. Specifically, our analyses reveal that, supporting our prediction, the service industries show a higher level of SMEV (.77*(9 + 6 + 6) = 16.2), while goods industries show a lower level (.718*(9 + 6 + 7) = 15.8). For the comparison between specific industries, Financial and Healthcare services (FS and HCS, respectively) show a higher level of SMEV in general (FS:.89*(9 + 7 + 6) = 19.6; HCS: .80*(8 + 7 + 8) = 18.4), while the Fashion (Fsn) and Food (Fd) industries show a much lower level (Fsn:.54*(9 + 6 + 8) = 12.4; Fd: .66*(8 + 7 + 8) = 15.2).

In addition, presenting the results along two dimensions—the Interactivity and Sociability and the Globalization (Interactivity and Sociability are summed together and the scores are weighted by W)—the Financial services and Healthcare industries lead in terms of Interactivity and Sociability over the goods industries, as predicted (FS:13.4; HCS:12.8 compared to Fsn:9.7 and Fd:10.6). They also lead in Globalization for which we did not have a prediction (FS: 6.2; HCS:5.8 compared to Fsn: 3.2 and Fd:4.6). The SMEV elements create four possible groups of industries based on their alignment along the two dimensions. We titled them: "beginners" (low in both axes), "globals" (high in Globalization and low in Interactivity and Sociability), "sociables" (high in Interactivity and Sociability and low in Globalization), and "celebrities" (high in both axes).

Discussion

The SMEV framework provides a tool for measurable and comparable description of the social visibility of a firm on the e-market. The data show that, as predicted, the service industries are more interactive and sociable than the goods firms. This finding fits the more relationship-based nature of service firms (Parasuraman et al. 1991). However, a closer look shows that the main cause for these differences is the variance in firm's presence in the internet (or the percentage of firms having a website) and to a lesser degree the internal mix of SoM elements. Future research should test the SMEV of additional industries to allow the discussion about whether and what would goods industries benefit from higher sociability. It can also focus on countries from other geographical areas or with different development stages of technology (e.g., North and South America) or on categories of firms with unique characteristics (e.g., born-global firms; see Efrat and Shoham 2011).

Implications for Theory and Practice

Measuring the usage of SoM by the firms is a unique way to evaluate the industry's adaptation to the challenges of the e-market. The SMEV framework, and the division into four groups suggested in, can be used by policy makers for instance for identifying strengths and weaknesses of a firm in the context of e-commerce as well as the threats posed by firms in the same industry. Thus, the scores can be used to provide an overview for strategy developers, while marketing managers can use them for benchmarking among competitors as well as for tracking progress in the SoM usage, since the framework provides insights on the potentials and hints of how to achieve a higher e-market presence.

References available upon request.

Are Operating Systems of Smart Phones Relevant in Behavioral Intention to Use Mobile Internet?

F. Javier Rondán-Cataluña, Jorge Arenas-Gaitán, Patricio E. Ramírez-Correa, and Antonio Navarro-García

Introduction

Mobile Internet (MI) usage intensity has grown substantially over the past years. The number of mobile subscriptions set to surpass seven billion and reach the whole world population in 2014. The explosion of MI business comes together with the development from the old mobile phones into the current smart phones. This is a combination of personal device assistants and mobile phones that use advanced operating systems and permit users to install new applications, be constantly connected to the Internet, and provide multifarious functionalities of both (Norazah Mohd 2013). According to a report from the specialized consultant Analysis Mason, there are 1700 million of smart phones around the world in 2014, which means an annual growth of 32 %. Furthermore, the number of Smartphone connections is set to grow by 136 % in the next 5 years to reach 3.9 billion connections worldwide in 2018 (de Renesse 2014). However, nowadays a small minority of users generates a disproportionate share of the total data volume. These are some of the reasons that justify the huge importance of studying factors, which influence consumer behavior of mobile Internet users (Gerpott and Thomas 2014).

The aim of this research is to analyze the moderator effect of the operating system of smart phones on the relationships between self-image and price value on behavioral intention of MI use. Preceding literature has revealed a solid relationship between self-image congruence and satisfaction (He and Mukherjee 2007), but a straight influence between self-image and behavioral intention in mobile internet is

F.J. Rondán-Cataluña (✉) • J. Arenas-Gaitán • A. Navarro-García
University of Seville, Seville, Spain
e-mail: rondan@us.es; jarenas@us.es; anavarro@us.es

P.E. Ramírez-Correa
Catholic University of the North, Antofagasta, Chile
e-mail: patricio.ramirez@ucn.cl

© Academy of Marketing Science 2016
L. Petruzzellis, R.S. Winer (eds.), *Rediscovering the Essentiality of Marketing*,
Developments in Marketing Science: Proceedings of the Academy of Marketing
Science, DOI 10.1007/978-3-319-29877-1_45

203

an original proposition. Price value is particularly essential when customers have to pay for the tools they use, as in the case of the greater part of the people of our sample; this is why including this variable in this study is required.

OS has been controlled in this research, but not Smartphone device. Some studies found slight differences in the perceptions of operating system-related characteristics, such as complexity and comfortableness. The Apple system was perceived better and more user-friendly than Android (Gafni and Geri 2013).

Conceptual Framework

Since its beginning, iPhone devices have been designed to include a range of software and applications, which require the MI connection for its full operation. According to market shares in Chile, the two main operating systems of smart phones are Android and IOS (IPhone); this is the reason why we choose these OSs. Currently, this is not a distinctive feature of Apple products; however, there is a wide variety between the Android devices, many of them targeting user segments less interested in these advanced uses. In this sense, the great amount of Smartphone users who utilize only basic tools, i.e., calls and SMS messages may be surprising. Based on the above argument, we formulate the first hypothesis:

H1: Operating system (OS) of the Smart phone is related to the intention to use Mobile Internet (MI)

MI usage may be considered as social because normally, the majority of people use mobile phones near to others. Consumption of some products or services is a way of self-expression, and people usually buy goods perceptually reliable with their particular self-concept. Especially, the match between consumers' self-concept and brand image is relevant in consumer behavior (Hosany and Martin 2012). Previous literature has shown a strong relationship between self-image congruence and satisfaction (He and Mukherjee 2007), but a direct effect between self-image and behavioral intention is an innovative hypothesis. Although Wang et al. (2013) already investigates a comparable hypothesis by observing at the behavioral intention of using Mobile Apps. Summarizing, this is our second research hypothesis:

H2: Self-Image is positively related to behavioral intention of MI usage.

Price value or monetary value is one dimension of perceived value. The other dimensions are: emotional value, social value, and performance/quality value (Hsiao 2013). The concept of price value is defined as "consumers' cognitive trade-off between the perceived benefits of the applications and the monetary cost for using them" (Dodds et al. 1991; Venkatesh et al. 2012). The price value is positive when the advantages of using MI are perceived to be higher than the financial cost, and such variable has a favorable influence on behavioral intention. This variable is especially important when users have to pay for the technology they use, as in the case of the majority of our respondents who have to give over the costs of using mobile internet. This technology requires from clients two payments: (1) the device that enables people to connect to the mobile network, (2) the fee they have to pay to the service provider company (Cheong and Park 2005). In this research, we measured the price value of the second cost. Obviously, price value is one of the major determinants of behavioral intention of MI usage; according to this idea hypothesis three is the following:

H3: Price value is positively related to behavioral intention of MI usage.

In general, iPhone users expend more money in their mobile phones than other customers using devices based on Android operating system. Therefore, these iPhone users tend to be people that are willing to pay more for their cellular, and they are likely to be more matured and wealthier than the other group of clients. As a consequence, different consumer behaviors are expected between both types of users. Hypotheses 4a and 4b are based on these ideas:

H4a: There is a moderating effect of the use of iPhone OS on the importance of self-image as a determinant of behavioral intention of MI usage.

H4b: There is a moderating effect of the use of iPhone OS on the importance of price value as a determinant of behavioral intention of MI usage.

Methodology

Empirical research was based on a non-random sampling method. Quota sampling was used to select participants based on age range and gender. Quotas were selected according to the profile of Chilean Internet users (IPSOS 2012). We chose this method because one advantage of quota sampling is that it provides sufficient statistical power to detect group differences. Data were collected in Chile in two major cities in November 2012 by personal interviews. The exclusion of invalid questionnaires provided a final sample size of 331 Chilean mobile Internet users (237 using Android and 94 using IOS).

The measurement scales used were similar to those proposed by Venkatesh et al. (2012). All items were measured using a seven-point Likert scale. Operating System (OS) was codified to 0 (Android) and 1 (iPhone). The partial least square approach was applied to test the research model (Chin 1998). Specifically, WarpPLS 4.0 software (Kock 2014) was used for model analysis.

Results

A partial least square path model is described by two models: (1) a measurement model and (2) a structural model. To assess the constructs, we conducted a confirmatory factor analysis (CFA) using PLS. Based on the CFA results, we analyzed

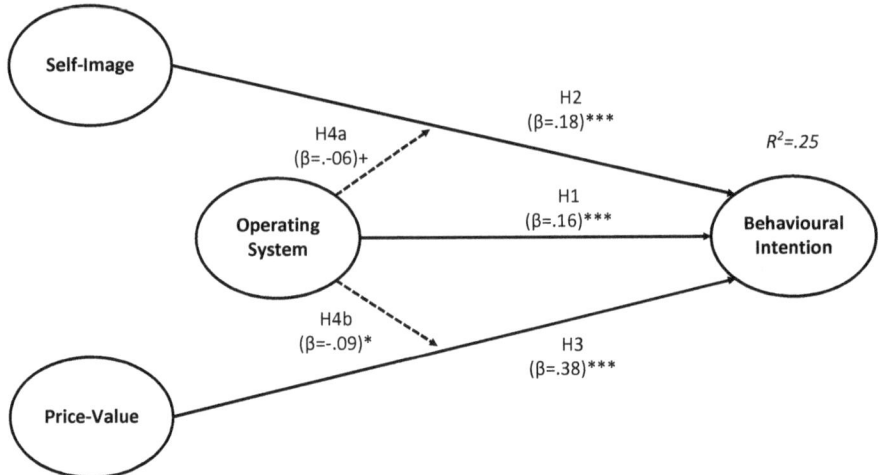

Fig. 1 Results of the structural model

Table 1 Path coefficients, p values, and effect size

Path	Beta	p value	Effect size
IMG → BI	.176	***	.044
PV → BI	.381	***	.166
OS → BI	.160	***	.029
OS × IMG	−.059	n.s.	.003
OS × PV	−.091	n.s.	.010

$***p<.001; **p<.01; *p<.05; +p<.1$

convergent validity, discriminant validity, and the reliability of all the multiple-item scales, following the guidelines from previous literature (e.g., Fornell and Larcker 1981; Gefen and Straub 1997). All the measures and tests have scores that confirm the goodness of the measurement model.

The results of the structural model are reflected in Fig. 1 and Table 1.

Discussion

The OS has a weak effect on behavioral intention. This is to say; IOS users (OS of Apple) have a large behavioral intention of MI. These results are related to the idea that Apple targets to consumer segments of greater purchasing power and Internet consumption.

OS of smart phones does not have a moderating role in the relationship between self-image and intention to use MI. This is to say, self-image possessed by the respondents of using MI affects the intention to keep using it, regardless of the OS that individuals have in their devices. The results do not exhibit sufficient impact (beta) nor a significant effect (size effect). These results can be explained by the diversity of Android devices on the market. The Apple devices are targeted to a very specific segment of the market, and their products present high homogeneity. However, the Android OS is installed in a large number of devices by a wide variety of brands and directed to practically every market segment. There are Android devices that directly compete in the same segment against Apple, but there are also many other devices targeted to other types of users. The heterogeneity between Android users may provoke that the moderation does not appear in hypothesis H4a.

The direct relationship between OS and intention to use MI is interesting. The results suggest that iPhone users have an increased intention to use MI than the Android ones. These results can be explained because iPhone devices have been designed to integrate MI in their use since their beginning. However, although there are Android gadgets including these characteristics, there are other more basic devices that are mainly used as a simple mobile phone, not as a Smartphone. These results are in line with those obtained by recent literature (Gerpott et al. 2013; Sell et al. 2014). This work has relevant implications in the field of Information Systems, and especially on models of acceptance of technology. Up to now researchers have been using as moderating variables characteristics of users such as age, gender, or experience using the technology. This work explores with relative success to include other variables relating to the characteristics of the technology used as moderators. Since they are variables related to the application of technologies, they may be able to offer a much richer explanation about their acceptance by users (Sarker and Wells 2003). In many cases, behind these variables different situations, motivations, and life styles are included.

References available upon request.

The Effect of Brand Intimacy on Consumer Responses: An Application on a Social Media Context

Renato Barcelos, Danilo Dantas, Sylvain Sénécal, and Carlos Rossi

Introduction

The increased popularity of such social media as Facebook and Twitter among consumers has opened up opportunities for the development of new business models of online branding and social commerce (Zhou et al. 2013). In particular, consumers look increasingly to social media to form opinions about unfamiliar brands (Newman 2011). However, while social media has been becoming an important tool for branding and customer marketing, there remain many questions concerning the best ways for brands to represent themselves or address their customers in this highly interactive and personal environment of conversation. This important gap in knowledge may be due to the lack of adequate social relationship constructs in many traditional models of electronic commerce (Choi et al. 2011; Liang et al. 2011; Pöyry et al. 2013). New social relationship constructs could improve understanding of the consumer responses to marketing stimuli in the social media environment. The present research-in-progress aims to address this issue by analyzing the influence of a yet under explored construct—*brand intimacy*—on social media. The question that then emerges is: how and when can brand intimacy improve consumer responses on social media?

In the context of this study, we define brand intimacy as the degree to which the brand interacts in a psychologically close way to its customers. In the literature of

R. Barcelos (✉) • C. Rossi
Federal University of Rio Grande do Sul, Porto Alegre, Brazil
e-mail: renato.barcelos@ufrgs.br; cavrossi@ea.ufrgs.br

D. Dantas • S. Sénécal
HEC Montréal, Montreal, QC, Canada
e-mail: danilo.dantas@hec.ca; sylvain.senecal@hec.ca

© Academy of Marketing Science 2016
L. Petruzzellis, R.S. Winer (eds.), *Rediscovering the Essentiality of Marketing*,
Developments in Marketing Science: Proceedings of the Academy of Marketing
Science, DOI 10.1007/978-3-319-29877-1_46

209

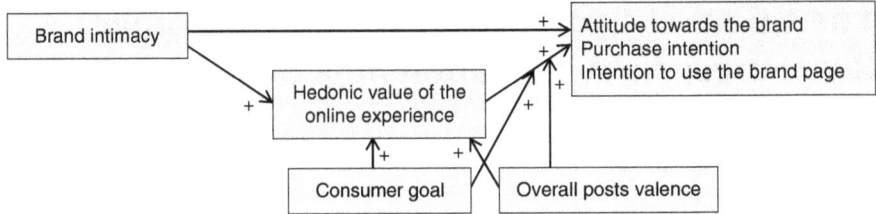

Fig. 1 Research model for the effect of brand intimacy on consumer responses

online marketing and information systems, intimacy, in a more general sense, usually refers to how close individuals feel to similar users in online communication
and has been related to the level of social presence available on different media
(Kumar and Benbasat 2002; Wang et al. 2007). Brand intimacy, however, refers
more specifically to the form of self-presentation of the brand within social media
(for example, as either an impersonalized entity or a named employee responsible
for addressing customers) and to its language (more formal and distant vs. more
informal and affectionate). The importance of the level of intimacy the brand
decides to use in its communication resides in the probability of influencing customer perceptions about the brand, and therefore their attitudes and purchase
intentions.

In this study, we argue that a high (vs. low) brand intimacy level should contribute to a more (vs. less) pleasurable online consumer experience. Using different
Facebook brand pages as the context for an experiment, we test a model of influence
of brand intimacy in which the hedonic value of consumers' experience on social
media mediates consumers' responses. We also test some boundary conditions to
this influence, in particular, the type of consumer goal and the overall valence of
other customers' posts on the media. Thus, the results of this study not only contribute to the literature on online marketing and social commerce, but are useful also in
informing brand managers about how and when they should expect to obtain better
responses in addressing customers in a more (or less) intimate way.

Model

In the context of social media, we argue that increased brand intimacy may lead to
a more pleasurable online experience with the brand page. Hence, satisfied users are
more likely to engage in more favorable behaviors towards the brand, such as attitude towards the brand and purchase intention. Another expected response to this,
in the specific case of Facebook brand pages, is a continued intention to use the
brand page, an outcome that is relevant in promoting customer engagement with the
company (Zhou et al. 2013) (Fig. 1).

Some studies have already shown that feelings of human contact and personal connection with a company's website may influence the attitudes of online shoppers by increasing interest and trust (Choi et al. 2011; Gefen and Straub 2003). Brand intimacy is expected to improve these feelings, as well as the flow associated to the experience on social media (Huang 2006). As a consequence, and based on previous work that has linked increased feelings of sociability in the online experience to the hedonic value and to patronage intentions of websites (Wang et al. 2007), we also expect this hedonic value to be a mediator of the effect of brand intimacy on consumer responses.

H1:   The brand intimacy on social media positively influences the consumer's responses, such as his/her attitude towards the brand, his/her purchase intention and his/her intention to continue using the brand page.

H2:   The influence of brand intimacy on the consumer's responses is mediated by the hedonic value of the consumer's experience on the social media.

Moreover, we expect the type of consumer goal in the community to moderate this effect. Several studies indicate there is congruence between hedonic and utilitarian factors in an online consumption experience and the type of dominant motivation among consumers (Cai and Xu 2011; Childers et al. 2001). For example, it has been shown that shoppers seeking products of hedonic nature are more sensitive to the website's social presence compared to those seeking utilitarian products (Choi et al. 2011). Accordingly, we expect that brand intimacy on social media might have a stronger effect when the customer enters the online community with a hedonic goal (like enjoyment) rather than a utilitarian one (such as finding the solution to a problem), because of the consistency between the type of goal and the hedonic value provided by the online experience.

H3:   The influence of brand intimacy on the consumer's responses is moderated by the type of consumer goal, so that this influence is stronger when the customer seeks a hedonic goal rather than a utilitarian one.

On the other hand, we also expect the effect of brand intimacy to be conditioned to the valence of communication on social media. As argued, increased flow and feelings of human connection with the brand should imbue the online experience with a greater hedonic value. However, intimacy and social presence should also increase the transmission of emotions in the online communication (McKenna et al. 2002). These emotions are not always positive on social media, especially when several unsatisfied customers post complaints or negative remarks about the brand or the product. In this situation, we expect the influence of brand intimacy to be hindered by existent negative opinions and to be non-beneficial to the brand when there are too many negative posts on social media.

H4:   The influence of brand intimacy on the consumer's responses is moderated by the valence of other consumers' posts on the social media, so that this influence is reduced when posts are negative (rather than positive) overall.

Research Methods

We tested the research hypotheses through two studies. In Study 1, hypotheses H1, H2, and H3 were tested using a 2 (brand intimacy: low vs. high)×2 (consumer goal: utilitarian vs. hedonic) between-subjects experimental design. The experimental setting was the Facebook brand page for a fictitious hotel in New York, presented online to a sample of 200 qualified participants on Amazon MTurk. Two brand pages were built: in the high intimacy condition, the brand profile was represented by an employee who addressed customers by their first names and used personal language; in the low intimacy condition, the brand profile was represented by the hotel logo, which addressed customers by their last names and used impersonal language. The contents of the page were based on real posts and comments from actual hotel pages on Facebook, but names and pictures were changed and adapted to the study's objectives. Except for the manner in which the brand profile presented itself and addressed customers, everything else in the two pages was identical—such as number of likes, main contents of posts, customers' replies, and page cover. The consumption goal was manipulated by directing participants to imagine themselves either searching a hotel for a vacation (hedonic goal) or a business trip (utilitarian goal).

Study 2 was also a 2×2 between-subjects experimental design ($n = 200$), similar in design to Study 1, manipulating two levels each of brand intimacy and consumer goal. However, this time we included many more negative posts on the Facebook page in order to create a more unfavorable overall feeling about the brand (60% of posts were complaints, compared to just 20% in Study 1). Therefore, H4 could be tested comparing results from Studies 1 and 2. All stimuli were pretested. The questionnaires included seven-point scales adapted from the literature. For interested readers, standard statistical descriptions of these measures can be obtained by contacting the authors.

Results and Discussion

We analyzed the results from the two studies using MANCOVA tests and mediation analyses using PROCESS (Hayes 2012). Participants who failed the attention question filter or looked at the brand page for fewer than 15 s were removed prior to the analyses (mean visualization time of valid answers = 117 s). Our final sample population consisted of 174 participants for Study 1 and 167 for Study 2. Summarizing both samples, 48% of participants were male and 52% were female; 54% had degrees of bachelor or higher; 82% were at least 25 years old.

Manipulations in Study 1 were checked with T-tests, confirming the difference between levels of brand intimacy ($M_{low} = 4.98$, $M_{high} = 6.30$; $p < .01$) and consumer goal ($M_{business} = 3.46$, $M_{vacation} = 4.80$; $p < .01$) between scenarios. To test H1, a

MANCOVA ($n=174$) using gender, age, education, involvement with hotels and Facebook usage as covariables was used to analyze the effect of the manipulations over the proposed dependent variables. As predicted, the results demonstrated the positive effect of brand intimacy on the consumer's attitude towards the brand ($M_{low}=5.30, M_{high}=6.12; p<.01$), his/her purchase intention ($M_{low}=4.87, M_{high}=5.83$; $p<.01$), and his/her continued intention to use the brand page ($M_{low}=4.08$, $M_{high}=5.22; p<.01$), supporting H1.

Results from the MANCOVA also demonstrate a significant interaction between brand intimacy and consumer goal for the consumer's attitude towards the brand ($F(1164)=4.15; p<.05$), his/her purchase intention ($F(1164)=4.15; p<.05$), and his/her continued intention to use the brand page ($F(1164)=6.9; p<.01$). This interaction is such that the positive effect of brand intimacy is more pronounced when the consumer has an enjoyment goal when accessing the page rather than a utilitarian one (for example, consumer's attitude towards the brand: $M_{low,business}=5.24$, $M_{high,business}=5.83$; $M_{low,vacation}=5.36$, $M_{high,vacation}=6.38$), therefore supporting H3. Among the tested covariables, involvement and Facebook usage were identified as significant, in the sense that high users of Facebook and those less involved with the service's category showed responses more favorable towards the brand than others.

Moving to the test of hedonic value as a mediator in the effect of brand intimacy on consumers' responses (H2), we tested a moderated mediation model using the PROCESS SPSS application provided by Hayes (2012). We estimated the conditional process model using a bootstrapping procedure (5000 bootstrap samples) in order to address potential concerns with nonnormality of the distribution of the indirect effect (MacKinnon et al. 2004). Results showed that the hedonic value of the online experience partially mediated the effect of brand intimacy on the consumer's attitude towards the brand (indirect effect$=.10$; SE$=.04$; 95% CI$=.04$ to .19) and his/her purchase intention (indirect effect$=.14$; SE$=.42$; 95% CI$=.07$ to .23), while fully mediating the effect on his/her continued intention to use the page (indirect effect$=.30$; SE$=.06$; 95% CI$=.18$ to .45). H2 was therefore supported.

Finally, H4 was tested by analyzing the results of Study 2. As before, manipulation checks confirmed the difference between levels of brand intimacy ($M_{low}=4.85$, $M_{high}=5.46$; $p<.01$) and consumer goal ($M_{business}=3.51$, $M_{vacation}=4.68$; $p<.01$) between scenarios. MANCOVA results showed that even though there was a small significant increase in the measure of hedonic value of the online experience associated with brand intimacy ($M_{low}=3.73$, $M_{high}=4.15$; $p<.05$), general consumer responses were consistently lower than in the previous study and, more importantly, mean differences between scenarios of low and high brand intimacy were not significant (for consumer's attitude towards the brand: $M_{low}=3.56, M_{high}=3.71; p=.59$; for purchase intention: $M_{low}=3.35, M_{high}=3.44; p=.74$; for continued intention to use the brand page; $M_{low}=3.53, M_{high}=3.53; p=.99$). Therefore, the overall negative valence of the posts in the brand page greatly reduced the influence of brand intimacy, confirming the hypothesis of moderation (H4) (Fig. 2).

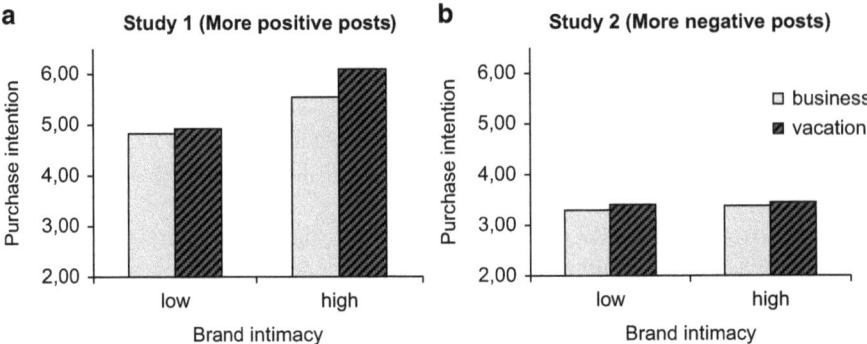

Fig. 2 Purchase intention as a function of brand intimacy and consumer goal

References available upon request.

Developing and Validating the Measurement Scale of e-Marketing Orientation

Yue-Yang Chen and Hui-Ling Huang

Abstract Nowadays, firms have realized the importance of using electronic facilities for supporting services to their customers and suppliers. For achieving a higher value about operating activities, firms must emphasis on R&D and technological development to integrate customer needs and develop the capabilities for searching and acquiring information via e-Business tools. Furthermore, managers and decision makers may use marketing 4P mix to plan their marketing activities in order to enter into a new market. Thus, it's the most important thing for firms to know how to acquire market information to satisfy customers' needs. In this vein, electronic marketing is regarded as a strategic weapon for firms. Given the important issue for electronic marketing orientation (EMO), we try to develop an assessment instrument of EMO according to the empirical data collected from top-ranked companies of manufacturing and service industries in Taiwan. Confirmation Factor Analysis (CFA) is employed to analyze and examine the items. A pool contains 14 items for measuring EMO is generated. The measurement scale contains of three constructs, namely cultural philosophical, initiation, and system development and integration. Finally, meaningful implications and future directions for this topic are also proposed.

Keywords EMO • Cultural philosophical • Initiation • System development and integration

Introduction

Nowadays, many enterprises start to realize that they should integrate supply and demand of service providers and users by information technology (IT) and develop different types of applications in facing of the dynamic situations. For operational

Y.-Y. Chen (✉)
I-Shou University, Kaohsiung, Taiwan
e-mail: ray@isu.edu.tw

H.-L. Huang
Chang Jung Christian University, Tainan, Taiwan
e-mail: ling@mail.cjcu.edu.tw

© Academy of Marketing Science 2016
L. Petruzzellis, R.S. Winer (eds.), *Rediscovering the Essentiality of Marketing*,
Developments in Marketing Science: Proceedings of the Academy of Marketing
Science, DOI 10.1007/978-3-319-29877-1_47

activities with higher value, future business model should be based on electronic business (e-Business) process to reinforce corporate R&D and rapidly integrate market with customer demand. When enterprises initiate e-Business systems, they tend to encounter inconsistent data and process between new and old systems and inferior information quality. Therefore, how to effectively integrate various information systems (IS) and processes to be as an e-business in order to increase operational value is the key issue for traditional enterprises (Nakata and Zhu 2006).

e-Marketing (electronic marketing) is the extension of online marketing. It is not simply the marketing activities by the Internet (Asikhia 2009). It effectively adopts related information technology and technique to support business demand and marketing of products or services (El-Gohary 2010). Therefore, it is not simply one-way marketing on the Internet; it also includes preference analysis on customer information in database as two-way interaction and communication model and construction of effective community (Strauss et al. 2006). Therefore, customer relation management, promotion, customer service, marketing research, and planning are in the scope (Brady et al. 2002). Generally speaking, advantages of e-Marketing are the following. It lowers cost by automation and e-media, it immediately responds to marketing personnel related information, it enhances data collection and analysis capacity, develops new market by customization and increases interaction with customers. Regarding corporate operation, value of e-Marketing for organizations is below. First, with e-Marketing, customers are closely connected with operational process in enterprises and directly acquire corporate resources (Trainor et al. 2011), such as Extranet, B2C, and B2B. Since customers and product life cycle of enterprises are closely associated, customer demand and opinions can immediately become criteria for enterprises' product manufacturing, improvement and R&D to avoid the limitation. Effective use and sharing of customer information and opinions are the important sources to develop and maintain positive customer relationship (Jayachandran et al. 2005). In addition, in enterprises with a positive e-Marketing capacity, the employees develop consistent activities and information and treat customers as priority to develop organizational innovation value (Trainor et al. 2011). The valuable information are integrated in current customer database for marketing managers' effective use, analysis, and simulation in order to approach customers' expressive and potential needs (Slater and Narver 1999). With the enhancement of e-Marketing capacity, productivity and organizational efficiency can be increased (Kim and Jae 2007).

In order to respond to dynamic and technology-oriented business environment, e-Marketing Orientation (EMO), market competition behavior of organizations upon e-Marketing, is developed. Based on related research (Shaltoni and West 2010; Tsiotsou and Vlachopoulou 2009, 2011), this study defines EMO and the underlying meanings as:

> *e-Marketing Orientation can be treated as a kind of organizational culture. It focuses on use of new technology (Internet related technology) to construct strategic marketing and decision making to increase customer value and acquire continuous competitive advantages. Upon the cultural background, e-Marketing is not simply the responsibility of marketing department. It is the principle adopted and followed by employees in organization and it guides all corporate activities to lead to positive marketing behavior.*

Thus, when academia explains organizational "orientation," it suggests that strategy orientation is the organizational principle and it directly guides business activities and develops behavioral intention to guarantee organizational sustainability and performance (Gatignon and Xuereb 1997). It is similar to the concept of market orientation. EMO should include behavioral and cultural descriptions and views (Kohli and Jaworski 1990; Narver and Slater 1990). Product-oriented marketing in the past can no longer respond to current service-based marketing demand. Innovation and marketing are two essential capacities of organization. Corporate performance is based on marketing strategic behavior and innovation (Oakey 1991; Olson et al. 2005). The Internet and information electronic industry make progress, including computer communication, mobile network, and digital information. From past traditional marketing to modern e-Marketing, how to acquire advantages in severely competitive market and increase organizational performance for corporate profits is currently the key of e-Business marketing (Trainor et al. 2011). Thus, content and key points of EMO should be the focus for e-Business. Accordingly, according to the arguments aforementioned, the purposes of this present study tries to develop and construct the e-Marketing oriented dimensions and items to form the measurement scale of EMO.

Literature Review

e-Marketing Orientation

Based on different concerns, marketing orientation is defined differently. However, most of researchers suggested that core concept of marketing orientation is to confirm customers' needs and expectation and based on customer-centered thought of "belief and value sharing" (Deshpandé and Webster 1989). Avlonitis and Gounaris (1997) suggested that enterprises should establish ranking of marketing orientation activities: capacity to satisfy special customers' needs and products, marketing as main culture of enterprise and capacity to adjust products to respond to changed customers' needs and satisfy customers by innovation. Thus, marketing orientation can be treated as the enterprises' basic attitude toward marketing activities and it is criterion of corporate behavior (Avlonitis and Gounaris 1999). Deshpandé and Webster (1989) and Dixon (1990) indicated that marketing orientation should be regarded as philosophy and cultural content of enterprises and the rule. Deshpandé et al. (1993) proposed the concept "customer orientation" and they suggested that in comparison to stakeholders, customers' profit should be the priority of enterprises and it is the most essential and important corporate culture followed by corporate members. In addition, from perspective of behavior, Elliot (1987) explained marketing orientation and indicated that although it is important to treat satisfaction with customers' needs as cultural philosophy of enterprises, it is still insufficient. Hence, enterprises should establish strategies regarding marketing orientation and strengthen corporate capacity to satisfy customers.

In development of marketing orientation, with the interaction between external competitive environment and internal performance stress, organizations encounter significant challenge in corporate operation. Internal drive influences employee relationship in the organizations and customers of marketing activities (Kotler 2000). Therefore, combination among internal, external, and interactive marketing considerably influences operational performance of enterprises. Service Triangle proposed by Gronroos (2001) demonstrates the importance of interaction among enterprises, marketing personnel, and customers. In current environment, without marketing direction, enterprises will not be able to survive and grow in profit. Implementation of marketing orientation is the highest level of organizational development and critical factor of successful operation. The process is from management operation (marketing management), preparation and coordination (marketing planning) and execution (Becherer et al. 2001). With clear definition of marketing orientation, enterprises can effectively design the action to collect information of customers and competitors. The information is exchanged among departments to create customer value (Kobylanski and Szulc 2011).

Based on the previous literature review, understanding the effects of marketing orientation on enterprises are important. However, it lacks the common consensus on the dimensions EMO. In general, related studies suggested that it may include the factors of philosophical and behavioral for marketing orientation (e.g., Avlonitis and Gounaris 1997, 1999; Kobylanski and Szulc 2011), they are still at the stage of conceptual development, as well as lacks the definition and measurement items from the perspectives of strategic orientation and Internet-based technology, and there can be result in the misunderstandings for research findings (Levenburg 2005).

Dimensions of e-Marketing Orientation

Drawing on previous related studies, this study proposes a conceptual model of EMO and its measurement items for each aspect. Specifically, this study suggests that EMO should include the following three dimensions.

Cultural philosophy. It is the most essential background of corporate culture, including organizational members' values and corporate regulation and behavioral model followed by the members. It emphasizes the basic assumption to treat corporate culture as philosophical level to be the guideline to solve corporate problems (Barley 1991). Corporate culture helps enterprises to accomplish their goals, guides employees to work for the objectives and cultivates new employees' expected behavioral model. Corporate culture indicates organizational characteristics to guide the members' attitude and behavior (Ebert and Griffin 2000). e-Marketing oriented cultural philosophy is based on regulation and value formed in organizations and encourages the members to be consistent with EMO (Shaltoni 2006).

Initiation. EMO is a new paradigm for modern business. Nowadays, selling of goods and services are provided from the Internet and other electronic devices. The goals of marketing are accomplished by digital technology (Smith and Chaffey

2005). In other words, enterprises plan and execute marketing activities by electronic data and applications and change the concepts of sales and pricing in order to satisfy individual and organizational goals. They must concern about all types of products in electronic market and treat e-marketing as the main goal to create interaction and satisfy individual's needs. Therefore, the key at this stage is to collect e-Marketing related information (market intelligence) by information and communication technology and diffuse them to different departments in order to effectively evaluate and plan different marketing programs.

System development and integration. Through implementation of information and communication technology and seamlessly integrate with marketing strategy, enterprises will achieve the goal of EMO. Because integration mechanism is the management tool to coordinate different units in the organization (Martinez and Jarillo 1989), therefore, information system integration means to combine independent and subordinate information systems and support overall organizational goals (Plouffe 1990). Information system integration allows enterprises with e-Marketing to consistently deal with orders and guarantees consistency of different systems in order to reduce time of product development cycle and inventory cost. By integration, enterprises can coordinate information system with different functions in individual department for seamless connection of whole enterprise information and process. This so-called e-Business capacity, then, can be reinforced to strengthen competitiveness of value chain or supply chain members (Basu and Muylle, 2007).

One of the main functions of e-Business is to establish and reinforce interaction and communication between business owners, suppliers, and customers through application of information technology and information system. Thus, system integration and connection between enterprises and the partners is the key of e-business (Horst and Andreas 2008). For instance, in terms of introduction of business resource planning system, it is not only related to business process reconstruction, but also associated with integration between new and old systems, transfer of data model and integration of different locations and systems (Motwani et al. 2005). Kalakota and Robinson (2001) studied CRM and suggested that CRM is the strategic action of enterprises developed by coordinated marketing, sales, and after-sale service through IT. The purpose is to discover customers' needs by integration between IT and business related process. In addition, collaborative cooperation and information sharing between enterprises, upstream and downstream suppliers and retailers are critical in supply chain. Network systems (e.g., Intranet and Extranet) constructed by information and communication devices and Internet can not only integrate related business process, but also result in more efficient communication and connection among supply chain partners. Corporate internal application integration, such as e-mails, work process systems and community software and inter-business integration, such as e-conference tools, collaborative management tool, EDI, SCM and B2B, can be adopted to execute internal and external information transfer and communication service, program communication and transaction in enterprises (O'Brien and Marakas 2009). Therefore, with the complete system integration, enterprises can effectively reinforce e-Marketing oriented practice and application.

Research Methodology

Measurement Items

From the foregoing discussions, this study classifies the dimensions of EMO into cultural philosophy, initiation, and system development and integration which including 3 factors and 14 items. By the three factors, this present research tries to specifically measure e-Marketing oriented measures for enterprises. The measurement items are listed in Table 1.

Sampling and Data Collection

We use primary data survey research and cross-sectional as our research strategy. For collecting the empirical data though mailed survey research in a time frame. Mailing lists are excerpted from "Common Wealth Magazine" database, including top-ranked companies of manufacturing and service industries in Taiwan. The questionnaires were distributed to companies being selected using a simple random sampling method. Two weeks later, each recipient was sent a reminder postcard. Four weeks after the initial mailing, a follow-up letter and a second questionnaire were sent to all eligible subjects who had not yet returned the questionnaire. Finally, a total of 162 surveys had been returned, of which 5 were incomplete, yielding 157 valid samples. As a result, the gross response rate was about 23.79 %.

Data Analysis and Results

Sample Characteristics

With respect to the characteristics of the sample, the largest number of respondents is from the manufacturing industry, representing 75.4 % of the responding companies. Most of the companies have 100–500 employees (36.5 %). The respondents hold various job titles, such as top managers, middle managers, first-line managers, and others. Approximately 41 % of the respondents have experiences more than 10 years in their companies. It indicates that the respondents have enough experience and knowledge to answer the questionnaire. The largest category (47.1 %) of educational level is undergraduate degree. The second largest category is master degree (29.9 %). The age of the participants ranged from 21 to 51 or above, with a largest percentage (36.9 %) in 31–40 category. Furthermore, about 77.1 % of the respondents are male, whereas 22.9 % of the respondents are female.

Table 1 Items for measuring e-Marketing orientation

Dimension	Item	Source
Cultural philosophical	(phi1) In our organization, we believe that it is a strategic necessity to be involved in e-marketing	Srinivasan et al. (2002)
	(phi2) In our organization, we tell employees that success depends on the adoption of advanced e-marketing resources	Shaltoni and West (2010)
	(phi3) We encourage the development of e-marketing initiatives in our organization	
	(phi4) We feel that that our organization should be highly involved in e-marketing	
Initiation	(ini1) In our organization, we follow the developments in e-marketing using several secondary sources (e.g., industry magazines, government statistics)	Jaworski and Kohli (1993)
	(ini2) In our organization, we monitor competitors' adoption of e-marketing	Shaltoni and West (2010)
	(ini3) We do in-house research about e-marketing	
	(ini4) Several meetings are held yearly in our organization to prepare e-marketing plans	
System development and integration	(sdi1) The latest e-marketing technologies (e.g., web applications) are installed in our organization	Jaworski and Kohli (1993)
	(sdi2) In our organization, there is adequate technical support for e-marketing implementation	Shaltoni and West (2010)
	(sdi3) In our organization, the implementation of e-marketing is done by employees who have e-marketing knowledge	
	(sdi4) The activities of the different departments which are responsible for e-marketing implementation are well coordinated	
	(sdi5) To make the company's systems easily transmit, our organization integrate and process data from suppliers, customers, and employees	
	(sdi6) In our organization, allow the company's systems continuous monitoring of order status at various stages in the process	

Measurement Model and Analysis of Reliability and Validity

Structural Equation Modeling with LISREL software was used to examine the measurement model. The validity of the research constructs was assessed from an estimation and respecification of the measurement model by confirmation factor analysis (CFA). The important step in scale validation is to assess the strength of measurement between the items and associated constructs. In the estimated model, items that demonstrate cross load, poor loadings, and reliability are dropped and the model is re-estimated. This is done to ensure that data is good fit to the measurement. We used the value of .5 as the threshold for factor loading assessment (Hair et al. 2006).

Table 2 Scale properties for the measurement model

Construct indicator	Standardized loading[a]	T value	IIR[b]	CR[c]	AVE[d]
Cultural philosophical				.92	.74
phi1	.82	–	.67		
phi2	.85	13.63	.72		
phi3	.87	14.24	.76		
phi4	.89	16.23	.79		
Initiation				.90	.70
ini1	.80	–	.64		
ini2	.81	11.81	.66		
ini3	.87	12.99	.76		
ini4	.86	12.78	.74		
System development and integration				.96	.80
sdi1	.80	–	.64		
sdi2	.96	19.22	.92		
sdi3	.96	19.29	.92		
sdi4	.90	14.59	.81		
sdi5	.82	12.03	.67		
sdi6	.91	15.69	.83		

Note:
[a]All item loadings (λ) are significant at $p < .05$ level
[b]Individual item reliability (IIR) = (Standardized loadings)^2
[c]Composite reliability (CR) = $(\Sigma L_i)^2/((\Sigma L_i)^2 + \Sigma \mathrm{Var}(E_i))$
[d]Average variance extracted (AVE) = $\Sigma L_i^2/(\Sigma L_i^2 + \Sigma \mathrm{Var}(E_i))$

Consequently, the parameter estimates, fit indices imply that the dimensions demonstrate a good fit for the observed covariances among their item measures. Furthermore, the composite reliability (ρ value) of each construct (shown in Table 2) is also greater than the recommended value of .6 (Fornell and Larcker 1981). Furthermore, in accordance with previous literature, the most commonly used fit indices and guidelines for SEM were: (1) $\chi^2/\mathrm{d.f.}$ (<5 is preferred), (2) adjusted goodness-of-fit index (AGFI, greater than .80 is desirable), (3) comparative fit index (CFI, greater than .90 is desirable), (4) normed fit index (NFI, greater than .90 is desirable), (5) non-normed fit index (NNFI, greater than .90 is desirable), and (6) standardized root mean square residual (SRMSR, less than .08 is desirable) (Bagozzi and Yi 1988). Consequently, the parameter estimates and fit indices imply that the dimensions of the KM strategy are a good fit for the observed covariances among the item measures ($\chi^2/\mathrm{d.f.} = 3.86$, $p < .001$; AGFI = .86; CFI = .95; NFI = .94; NNFI = .93; SRMSR = .041).

AVE can calculate the explanatory power of the average variance of various observed variables of one potential variable for the given potential variable, and the results could be used to determine the validity of potential variables. The validity could be divided into convergent validity and discriminant validity, whereby the higher the AVE of convergent validity to the potential variable was, the higher the convergent validity was. The AVE standard value must be greater than .5 (Fornell and Larcker 1981). The results showed that the all of the AVE values were greater than .5 for all constructs. Therefore, the items for each construct showed a good convergent validity. Discriminant validity was compared and determined using AVE and the squared values of the correlation coefficients of pairwise variables. The criterion was that the AVE value should be greater than the squared values of the correlation coefficients (Fornell and Larcker 1981). The results showed that the AVE value for each construct was greater than all of the square value of the correlation coefficient between itself and other constructs. Therefore, it suggested that the scale used in this study had good convergent and discriminant validity.

Implications

Researchers have conducted a number of studies investigating the relationship between marketing orientation and business performance in academic settings. Currently, with introduction and application of the Internet and information technology in enterprises, some scholars start the research on e-Marketing. However, they mostly emphasized the definition on EMO (Asgharizadeh et al. 2010; Chaffey et al. 2006; Richardson 2001) and few of them explored specific concept of EMO (Shama 2001) and developed the related indicators (Shaltoni and West 2010; Tsiotsou and Vlachopoulou 2009). Currently, related research topics include the cause and effect of e-Marketing (Asikhia 2009; Chailom 2012; Trainor et al. 2011; Tsiotsou and Vlachopoulou 2011) and empirical research on success of marketing management or e-commerce (Chailom 2012; El-Gohary 2012; Eid and El-Gohary 2012). Therefore, research on strategy of EMO is still limited. At present, marketing is an important activity for organization. For academic research or business operations, it is necessary to find how to apply new electronic technologies to organizational marketing practices and strategic planning.

For organizations, when analyzing and planning market oriented measures and activities, they should consider and use resources to enhance and effectively execute marketing management (e.g., information technology and Internet application) as well as to strengthen marketing activity and information quality (Capon and Glazer 1987) and employee satisfaction. Therefore, it is necessary to integrate market oriented measure with strategic application of information technology to form e-Marketing oriented organizations and recognize the effect on business performance. In other words, in e-Marketing oriented corporate culture, all organizational members are committed to create excellent value for customers and stakeholders and effectively provide information related to marketing organization development and market by e-technology. Intranet marketing, extranet marketing, short message service, e-mail marketing, Internet marketing, Mobile marketing, e-CRM, e-SCM, B2B, and B2C are useful tools (El-Gohary 2012). Enterprises should deal with the complicated and diverse market change and customer preference, corporate customers and consumers continue increasing online activities. e-Marketing can specifically control the figures. In this vein, most of enterprises turn marketing activity into e-Marketing and invest in e-Marketing by capital (Eid and El-Gohary 2012). Therefore, for effectively and efficiently deploy Internet-based technologies to marketing activities, firms must have the e-Marketing regulations and value formed and proliferated to all of the members in organization. In addition, the concept of business e-Marketing must be transformed into formal project for the managers, including collection of e-Marketing information by different sources, evaluation of the projects, and construction of actions.

To sum up, this present study aims to develop a scale to measure EMO. Related dimensions and items are validated and examined by empirical data to show their reliability and validity. Thus, it can clearly recognize the characteristics of electronic orientation in enterprises. Future research can take this instrument as a theoretical basis for measuring EMO in the context of e-Business. With rapid development of Internet and information and community devices, it is necessary for enterprises to regard EMO practices as organizational culture to form a strong basis with e-Business. Therefore, by scale development on EMO from this study, it can be recognized and identified the preparation for a firm to be an e-Business. EMO is introduced in business environment. According to scale development model suggested, this study developed the criteria of measurement and conducts investigation by empirical data to consolidate the analysis of the optimal measurement model for EMO. We hope this measurement scale is helpful in holding a better position to develop strategies and tactics to yield high performance.

Acknowledgement This study was funded by the Taiwan Ministry of Science and Technology under project number MOST 102-2410-H-214-013 and MOST 103-2410-H-214-006.

References

Asgharizadeh, E., Ekhlassi, A., & Toloei, P. (2010). Evaluation of the relationship between electronic-marketing and market-driven companies. *Proceedings of 2010 International Conference on e-Education, e-Business, e-Management and e-Learning*, 168–172.

Asikhia, O. U. (2009). The moderating role of e-Marketing on the consequences of market orientation in Nigerian firms. *International Journal of Business and Information, 4*(2), 243–270.

Avlonitis, G. J., & Gounaris, S. P. (1997). Marketing orientation and company performance: Industrial vs. consumer goods companies. *Industrial Marketing Management, 26*, 385–402.

Avlonitis, G. J., & Gounaris, S. P. (1999). Marketing orientation and its determinants: An empirical analysis. *European Journal of Marketing, 33*(11/12), 1003–1037.

Bagozzi, R. P., & Yi, Y. (1988). On the evaluation of structural equation model. *Journal of the Academy of Marketing Science, 16*(1), 74–94.

Barley, S. R. (1991). Contextualizing conflict: Notes on the anthropology of disputes and negotiations. *Research on Negotiation in Organizations, 3*, 165–199.

Becherer, R. C., Halstead, D., & Haynes, P. (2001). Marketing orientation in SMEs: Effects of the internal environment. *Journal of Research in Marketing and Entrepreneurship, 3*(1), 1–17.

Brady, M., Saren, M., & Tzokas, N. (2002). Integrating information technology into marketing practice—The IT reality of contemporary marketing practice. *Journal of Marketing Management, 18*(5/6), 555–577.

Capon, N., & Glazer, R. (1987). Marketing and technology: A strategic coalignment. *Journal of Marketing, 51*(3), 1–14.

Chaffey, D., Ellis-Chadwick, F., Johnso, K., & Mayer, R. (2006). *Internet marketing: Strategy, implementation and practice.* Harlow, England: Pearson Education.

Chailom, P. (2012). Antecedents and consequences of e-Marking strategy: Evidence from e-Commerce business in Thailand. *International Journal of Business Strategy, 12*(2), 75–87.

Deshpandé, R., Farley, J. U., & Webster, F. E. (1993). Corporate culture, customer orientation and innovativeness in Japanese firms: A quadrant analyses. *Journal of Marketing, 57*(1), 23–37.

Deshpandé, R., & Webster, F. (1989). Organizational culture and marketing: Defining the research. *Journal of Marketing, 53*(1), 3–17.

Ebert, R. J., & Griffin, R. W. (2000). *Business essentials.* Upper Saddle River, NJ: Prentice-Hell.

Eid, R., & El-Gohary, H. (2012). The impact of e-Marketing use on small business enterprises' marketing success. *Service Industries Journal, 33*(1), 34–50.

El-Gohary, H. (2010). E-Marketing—A literature review from a small businesses perspective. *International Journal of Business and Social Science, 1*(1), 214–244.

El-Gohary, H. (2012). Factors affecting e-Marketing adoption and implementation in tourism firms: An empirical investigation of Egyptian small tourism organisation. *Tourism Management, 33*(5), 1256–1269.

Elliot, G. (1987). The marketing concept: Necessary but sufficient? *European Journal of Marketing, 21*(2), 20–30.

Fornell, C., & Larcker, D. E. (1981). Evaluating structural equation models with unobservable and measurement error. *Journal of Marketing Research, 18*(1), 39–50.

Gatignon, H., & Xuereb, J. M. (1997). Strategic orientation of the firm and new product performance. *Journal of Marketing Research, 34*, 77–90.

Grönroos, C. (2001). *Service management and marketing: A customer relationship management approach* (2nd ed.). New York: Wiley.

Hair, J. F., Black, W. C., Babin, B. J., Anderson, R. E., & Tatham, R. L. (2006). *Multivariate data analysis.* Upper Saddle River, NJ: Pearson Education.

Horst, T., & Andreas, S. (2008). The effect of e-Commerce on the integration of IT structure and brand architecture. *Information Systems Journal, 18*(5), 479–498.

Jaworski, B. J., & Kohli, A. K. (1993). Market orientation: Antecedents and consequences. *Journal of Marketing, 57*(3), 53–70.

Jayachandran, S., Sharma, S., Kaufman, P., & Raman, P. (2005). The role of relational information processes and technology use in customer relationship management. *Journal of Marketing, 69*(4), 177–192.

Kalakota, R., & Robinson, M. (2001). *E-Business 2.0: Roadmap for success.* Reading, MA: Addison-Wesley.

Kim, N., & Jae, H. P. (2007). Utilization of new technologies: Organizational adaption to business environment. *Journal of the Academy of Marketing Science, 35*(2), 259–269.

Kobylanski, A., & Szulc, R. (2011). Development of marketing orientation in small and medium-sized enterprises evidence from Eastern Europe. *International Journal of Management and Marketing Research, 4*(1), 49–59.

Kohli, A. K., & Jaworski, B. J. (1990). Market orientation: The construct, research propositions, and managerial implications. *Journal of Marketing, 54*(2), 1–18.

Kotler, P. (2000). *Marketing management-analysis, planning implementation and control* (10th ed.). Englewood Cliffs, NJ: Prentice-Hall.

Levenburg, N. M. (2005). Delivering customer value online: An analysis of practices, applications, and performance. *Journal of Retailing and Customer Services, 12*(5), 319–331.

Martinez, J. I., & Jarillo, J. C. (1989). The evolution of research on coordination mechanisms in multinational corporations. *Journal of International Business Studies, 20*(3), 489–514.

Motwani, J., Subramanian, R., & Gopalakrishna, P. (2005). Critical factors for successful ERP implementation: Exploratory findings from four case studies. *Computers in Industry, 56*(6), 529–544.

Nakata, C., & Zhu, Z. (2006). Information technology and customer orientation: A study of direct, mediated, and interactive linkages. *Journal of Marketing Management, 22*(3–4), 319–354.

Narver, J. C., & Slater, S. F. (1990). The effect of a market orientation on business profitability. *Journal of Marketing, 54*(4), 20–35.

O'Brien, J. A., & Marakas, G. M. (2009). *Management information systems* (9th ed.). New York: McGraw-Hill Irwin.

Oakey, R. (1991). Innovation and the management of marketing in high technology firms. *Journal of Marketing Management, 7*(4), 343–356.

Olson, E. M., Slater, S. F., & Hult, T. M. (2005). The performance implications of fit among business strategy, marketing organization structure, and strategic behavior. *Journal of Marketing, 69*(1), 49–65.

Plouffe, R. L. (1990). System integration: An integrator's perspective. *Information Executive, 3*(3), 25–27.

Richardson, P. (2001). *Internet marketing*. Boston: McGraw-Hill Irwin.

Shaltoni, A. M. (2006). E-marking adoption in organization. In C. Gray & S. Zappala (Eds.), *Impact of e-Commerce and small firms* (pp. 129–138). London: Sage.

Shaltoni, A., & West, D. (2010). The measurement of e-Marketing orientation (EMO) in business-to-business markets. *Industrial Marketing Management, 39*, 1097–1102.

Shama, A. (2001). E-Coms and their marketing strategies. *Business Horizons, 44*(5), 14–20.

Slater, S. F., & Narver, J. C. (1999). Market-oriented is more than being customer-led. *Strategic Management Journal, 20*(12), 1165–1168.

Smith, P. R., & Chaffey, D. (2005). *E-Marketing excellence: At the heart of e-Business* (2nd ed.). Oxford, England: Butterworth Heinemann.

Srinivasan, R., Lilien, G., & Rangaswamy, A. (2002). Technological opportunism and radical technology adoption: An application to e-Business. *Journal of Marketing, 66*(3), 47–60.

Strauss, J., El-ansary, A., & Frost, R. (2006). *E-Marketing*. Upper Saddle River, NJ: Prentice Hall.

Trainor, K. J., Rapp, A., Beitelspacher, L. S., & Schillewaert, N. (2011). Integrating information technology and marketing: An examination of the drivers and outcomes of e-Marketing capability. *Industrial Marketing Management, 40*, 162–174.

Tsiotsou, R., & Vlachopoulou, M. (2009). E-marking orientation: Conceptualization and scale development. *Proceedings of 2nd Biennial International Conference on Services Marketing*, Thessaloniki, Greece, 580–590.

Tsiotsou, R. H., & Vlachopoulou, M. (2011). Understanding the effects of market orientation and e-Marketing on service performance. *Marketing Intelligence & Planning, 29*(2), 141–155.

Influence of Different Types of Online Interaction on Brand Attitudes: A Cross-Cultural Analysis

Agnieszka Zablocki, Bodo Schlegelmilch, and Michael Houston

Abstract The online purchasing process usually follows the same pattern: Search the web; read recommendations and reviews; decide. Thus, reviews and recommendations are central to the online purchasing process, since they contain information about the functionality of the brand and the experiences other consumers made. Consequently, some researchers postulate a development from manager-ruled to customer-ruled brands and an empowerment of consumers.

Our research focuses on the impact of consumer-to-consumer interactions in the online environment. Specifically, we use a cross-cultural setting to analyze the influence of different types of online interactions (public vs. private, and active vs. passive) on brand attitudes (cognitive and affective). We also propose that the relationship between these two key constructs is partially mediated by different levels of brand commitment (high vs. low), mainly in interplay with active and passive online interaction. In addition, we expect a number of different contextual factors to moderate this relationship, such as the type of brand (functional vs. emotional), the valence of online interaction (positive vs. negative), and the self-construal (independent self vs. interdependent self).

Hypotheses are developed and tested in a 2 (online interaction: public vs. private)×2 (online interaction: passive vs. active)×2 (valence: positive vs. negative)×2 (brand type: functional vs. emotional) between-subjects design. Experiments are conducted with respondents from collectivistic cultures with predominantly interdependent self-construal, and respondents from individualistic cultures with predominantly independent self-construal.

Based on the above research framework, we address the following questions: (1) Do different types of online interaction—depending on their content and intensity—vary in their influence on brand attitudes? (2) And does the influence of different

A. Zablocki (✉) • B. Schlegelmilch
WU Vienna University of Economics and Business, Vienna, Austria
e-mail: agnieszka.zablocki@wu.ac.at; bodo.schlegelmilch@wu.ac.at

M. Houston
Carlson School of Management, Minneapolis, MN, USA
e-mail: mhouston@umn.edu

© Academy of Marketing Science 2016
L. Petruzzellis, R.S. Winer (eds.), *Rediscovering the Essentiality of Marketing*,
Developments in Marketing Science: Proceedings of the Academy of Marketing
Science, DOI 10.1007/978-3-319-29877-1_48

227

types of online interaction differ over brand categories and cultures with an independent and interdependent self-construal?

Our research offers a number of insights to marketing managers, such as how to position brands differently in an online environment according to the ratio of emotional and rational content consumers might share in their interaction about brands, and whether to adapt online positioning based on cultural settings.

The Relationship Between Viral Marketing, Purchase Intention, and Brand Visibility: Study with Brazilian Customers

Kleinia Anjos Vianna, José Marcos Carvalho de Mesquita, Mariana Regina Silva Linhares, and Patricia de Cássia Gomes Moreira

Abstract The present study aimed to evaluate the influence of viral marketing such as advertising communication strategy in purchase intent and brand visibility from the perspective of the online consumer. The literature review sought to contextualize the internet marketing; aspects of digital marketing, viral marketing and advertising communication strategy, social media in relationships between organizations and consumers, brand awareness, purchase intent, plus an overview of scientific literature on the viral marketing and constructs: consumer perception on advertising campaigns posted on the network, viral marketing, brand awareness and purchase intent. We sought to examine the positive relationship between consumer perception of advertising campaigns posted on the network, viral marketing, brand awareness, and purchase intent. In a descriptive research with quantitative variables, totaling 321 respondents through an electronic survey with the adoption of a structured questionnaire with responses in a Likert scale. The collected data were analyzed using the Partial Least Squares method, allowing the work with a small sample. We found statistically positive values for the relationship between consumer perception of social media advertising, viral marketing, brand awareness, and purchase intent. Statistical data served as the basis for the validation of the model proposed in this work.

Keywords Viral marketing • Brand visibility • Purchase intent • Social media

Introduction

In the face of multiplying information channels and consumers, who have become more demanding and participative, the efficiency of advertising on mass media has been widely discussed by marketing and publicity professionals. According to

K.A. Vianna (✉) • J.M.C. de Mesquita • M.R.S. Linhares • Patricia de Cássia Gomes Moreira
Universidade Fumec, Belo Horizonte, Brazil
e-mail: kleiniascamilo@hotmail.com; jose.mesquita@fumec.br; linharesmari@yahoo.com.br; pacgmo@hotmail.com

© Academy of Marketing Science 2016
L. Petruzzellis, R.S. Winer (eds.), *Rediscovering the Essentiality of Marketing*, Developments in Marketing Science: Proceedings of the Academy of Marketing Science, DOI 10.1007/978-3-319-29877-1_49

Salzman et al. (2003), the problem of traditional advertising consists on assuming a certain naivety level that no longer exists among consumers. The informed, active and demanding client is not a just supporting character anymore in the relationship with a company. Consumers assume a new profile arguing, researching and been aware of their power in an enlarged social and cultural context, as purchasers and citizens (Canclini 2008). "A series of technological innovations have been giving important contributions to the capacity of the consumers to become the lead conductors of interactive marketing by controlling the amount and the type of information they receive" (Boone and Kurtz 2009, p.25).

The downfall of audience, high costs of production and distribution and growth of the internet-connected consumers have motivated organizations to search for new alternatives to diffuse their products and services in an innovating and more efficient manner (Bentivegna 2002). Several tendencies are rising and causing a change in the way companies see both publicity and marketing.

The marketing professionals suggest, as substitute strategy, the use of alternative medias. According to Sissors and Bumba (2001), alternative medias are those that exclude traditional ones: television, radio, magazines, and newspapers.

One of the means of communication used as alternative media to propagate products and services is the Internet. It is opportune to highlight that Internet has been transforming the way the whole society thinks and acts, providing the creation of new strategies to increase market share and virtual clients, improving the efficiency of managing processes and increasing in efficacy, in which goals are achieved (Drucker 2000). Without geographic limitations, Internet has made possible a faster and uncomplicated communication.

Considering viral marketing in the context of social media, an effective alternative emerges to business by using consumers in the propagation of messages on the Internet. Videos, photos, audio files, and links to websites are received and passed on to the social media contacts forming a viral marketing. This mode of conveying an advertising campaign can bring interesting results (Silveira and Mattos 2009).

Social networks are regarded as the set of actors who are connected through social relationships (Burt 2000). According to this concept, we conclude that social media is recognized as a social structure consisting of individuals or organizations tied by one or more ways of interdependence, which is manifested in an interaction mediated by the internet (Sangwan et al. 2009). We can mention as examples of social media: Blogs; Orkut (extinct in 2014); Facebook; Twitter; YouTube; Instagram; and LinkedIn.

According to Recuero (2009), in social media, individuals are judged and perceived by their words. To get even closer to face-to-face interaction, people post pictures and information that are capable of generating empathy and individuality. The interactions among users, established through creation of virtual communities, cause an even greater interaction among network members. Therefore, this interactivity is the main attraction in these communities (Dalmoro et al. 2010).

According Mizruchi (2009), social networks can explain the structural influence of groups in economic activity, since they are prominent in the relationships among people, organizations, and market position.

In this sense, the multiple social media used by consumers and organizations can become an important tool with relatively low cost in monitoring consumption habits and clients. "Customers create shared experiences that can lead the brand in a direction that it might be interesting for the company" (Schmitt 2000, p. 195).

Due to the need an individual has to share and generate word-of-mouth in spontaneous networks, viral marketing can be an alternative in the advertising communication among consumers on social media process. It relies on the available digital resources, having the intention of providing consumers with spontaneous content sharing, while boosting a brand (Barichello and Oliveira 2010).

Sterne and Priore (2000) said that viral marketing covers planning and performing actions that have the main purpose to stimulate the word-of-mouth marketing of a company on the Internet, taking advantage of social networks.

Originated in Biology, the name viral expresses the potential of a message to be rapidly reproduced in geometric progressions, proliferating from one host to another, like a virus. Using the Internet resources, viral marketing rescues the principles of word-of-mouth communication, in an online way. The used resource leans in the belief that trust is bigger in people than in companies, even due to loss of credibility in the means of communication: "7 of every 10 people that receive a message through the computer pass that ahead to other friends" (Salzman et al. 2003, p.149).

In this context, the strategy to use a viral action as a publicity and advertising act offers significant advantages. The low cost of a viral marketing advertising is one of the reasons that makes a company invest in this kind of strategy, since e-mailing reduces costs, and users do most of the work. Immediacy is also considered a relevant factor of this kind of campaign. The speed in which Internet makes propagation of information available, through e-mail, online communities and chat rooms provides instant communication, even when users are very distant.

According to Barichello and Oliveira (2010), the free access to the Internet and the information universe turned the Internet user into a consumer who cannot be understood only as a message receiver. Aware of that, publicity communication has come up with new strategies expecting to catch these new consumers' attention. Viral marketing is one of those.

Starting from that point, this is the research question: what is the influence of viral marketing, as a publicity communication strategy, in the purchase intention and brand visibility from the perspective of online consumers?

In this way, the objective of this study is to evaluate the influence of viral marketing, as a publicity communication strategy, in the purchase intention and brand visibility from the online consumer's viewpoint.

In this study, viral marketing will be approached as a strategic phenomenon of publicity communication, and not as a phenomenon that occurs spontaneously. Knowing that consumers have never been so connected, it is relevant to understand how these viral actions can interfere with the search for new markets, considering, also, aspects such as purchase intention and brand visibility.

Literature Review

The development of the Internet and the creation of virtual communities allowed the phenomenon of word-of-mouth communication to reach areas free of geographic limitations (De Bruyn and Lilien 2008) and clients to create resistance to traditional publicity communication (Leskovec et al. 2007).

Viral marketing is a way to multiply a word-of-mouth message through the Internet. There are different ways to transmit these messages, such as e-mail, video, audio, games, websites, social networks, photography, or documents. Compared to traditional word-of-mouth communication, the strategies of viral marketing are more effective due to its capacity to rapidly expand and the fact that it does not involve social pressure such as face-to-face communication.

Viral marketing phenomenon is directly related to word-of-mouth communication; however, it occurs exclusively in virtual environments. De Bruyn and Lilien (2008) highlight three characteristics that separate viral marketing from traditional word-of-mouth communication: viral marketing does not involve face-to-face contact and assumes the propagation exclusively of electronic contents; the messages can be ignored, since they were not requested; and contents sent from close referrals have more chance of being accepted.

According to Almeida et al. (2011), the terminology "viral marketing" received several contributions over the last years, but it does not have a consensual definition. Even in the face of many definitions, it is impossible to deny that the key concept on the approach of viral marketing concerns about how the developer of marketing strategies can perform actions capable of, after an initial effort, reaching comparable scales to the disseminating power of publicity communication with the use of mass medias, having lower costs and at the same time, using the consumer as the positive message disseminator (Andrade et al. 2006).

Silva (2008) comments that viral marketing has a strong influence on the individuals in their social environment, since they stand between the interruption marketing and the permission marketing. Interruption marketing presents to the target audience numerous advertising stimuli and deals with the intention of making the consumer crumble to the specific offer; on the other hand, in permission marketing, the organizations offer their clients the opportunity to accept, voluntarily, what is presented (Godin 2000).

Silva (2008) also claims that this reality opens up space for the consumers of an organization to act like coauthors and participants in the process of communication, and not only receivers.

Those who build a viral marketing strategy must have a concern about making a good impression to the individual in the face of the provocative content of the message. Thus, the receiver is stimulated to pass along the message to its contact network. To do so, the content must be, somehow, extraordinary, with emotionally rich messages, or messages funny enough to generate dissemination (Porter and Golan 2006).

This situation corroborates to the honest communication inside the contact network of the consumer. The prominent aspect is of people who generally are not message disseminators, which possess an important impact in the process, customizing and selecting the audience (Phelps et al. 2004). From that, it can be assumed:

H1: Consumer's perception on social media advertising influences positive and significantly viral marketing.

Viral marketing strategies are based on the fact that people's attitudes and actions are influenced socially by other people's behaviors. According to Delre et al. (2007), in cases where part of a social group of one person possess a product, it is quite likely that this person will buy it, even without actual need.

Dalmoro et al. (2010) complement this thought and point out the capacity of users to influence the buying decisions of the others through tweets and posts. These influences are the result of a social network formed, since, according to these authors, users receive messages from people with whom they maintain some bond, whether it is of friendship or admiring. These opinions shared on the network can influence the buying decisions of others, especially if the tweet or post was written by someone with credibility, considered an opinion former.

For De Bruyn and Lilien (2008), word-of-mouth communication plays a fundamental role in the flow of available information and it can influence each stage of the consumer's decision-making process. The authors also highlight that this kind of communication captures not only the consumer's attention, but it also stimulates interest and it can result in the adoption of products and the increasing of sales.

Patrocínio et al. (2013) found positive relation between electronic word-of-mouth and purchase behavior, and Rapp et al. (2013) say that social media usage positively affects consumer retailer loyalty.

Other authors have researched the relation between electronic word-of-mouth and consumption decisions (Senecal and Nantel 2004; Godes and Mayzlin 2004; Hung and Li 2007; Cheung et al. 2008; Hong and Cho 2011; Yoo and Lee 2012). From what has been exposed, it is proposed:

H2: Consumer's perception on social media advertising influences positive and significantly purchase intention.

H3: Viral marketing influences purchase intention.

Goldsmith and Horowitz (2006) comment that electronic word-of-mouth plays a fundamental role in electronic markets. Companies are more interested in the power of this type of interpersonal influence to value their brands. The available online resources offer opportunities for companies to implement electronic word-of-mouth in their communication strategies, setting and managing the relationship with their consumers (Dellarocas 2003).

Considering viral marketing inside the social media context, another effective alternative rises for the business activity to use its consumers to propagate the Internet messages. Videos, photos, audio files, and website links are received and forwarded to contacts of the relationship network, forming viral marketing. This vehicle for publicity campaigns can have interesting outcomes (Silveira and Mattos 2009).

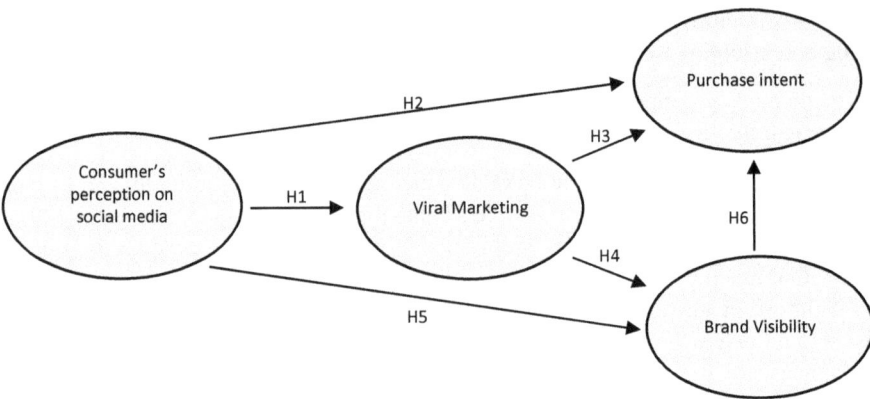

Fig. 1 Theoretical model

Gitomer (2006) points out the importance of brand reinforcing. Following shared opinions among the consumers creates opportunity for companies to act assertively, guarantying the maintenance of their images with already conquered markets and the brand's attractiveness to potential clients. Therefore, it is proposed:

H4: Viral marketing influences brand visibility.
H5: Consumer's perception on social media advertising influences positive and significantly brand visibility.

The brand represents a clear difference between products. Researchers prove that a brand in which the consumer trusts has lower risk and diminishes cognitive dissonance (Doyle 1990).

Trust results in loyalty, and a brand that can reach this level of compromise puts the client in a buying and repeating process (Chaudhuri and Holbrook 2001).

In this study, the constructs of brand visibility and purchase intention will be evaluated in order to understand the link between them. Based on that, the following hypothesis can be drawn:

H6: Brand visibility influences positive and significantly purchase intention.

Based on the theoretical foundation and the constructed hypothesis the model that summarizes these assumptions is presented, as in Fig. 1.

Method

To achieve the objectives of this study, the research was descriptive and quantitative. According to Malhotra (2001, p. 155), "quantitative researches pursuits to quantify the data and somehow apply a statistical analysis." Besides, it is frequently used in descriptive studies (Demo 2000), and according to Vergara (2007), it shows the characteristics of a specific population or phenomenon. Yet, still according to Vergara, the descriptive research helps establishing correlations among variables indicating its nature.

The data were collected by survey, with applications of online questionnaire to people with profiles on social networks. According to Cervo and Bervian (1996), every questionnaire must be impersonal, ensuring the uniformity in the evaluation of a fact or a situation.

The data were collected from the users of social network and the questionnaire was sent via web (Google Docs). It is highlighted that it was at hand of the online respondents, been filled by them and charted by the own system.

The research's universe or the population sample is comprehended as the social network's users. The choice of the sample, according to Vergara's classification (2004), was non-probabilistic and by accessibility. Therefore, the research reached the number of 321 valid respondents.

Final data collection instrument presented 23 questions distributed among consumer's perception constructs on social media advertising (five items), viral marketing (five items), brand visibility (four items), purchase intention (five items), and socio-demographic information (four items). An interval scale of seven points was used, which varied from totally disagree (1) to totally agree (7). Given the specificity of the subject, all scales were developed by the authors, based on cited authors' propositions, and validated by an expert committee.

The data concerning the survey research were treated by means of structural equation modeling. To data analysis, we used Partial Least Squares (PLS) method, enabling study from a reduced sample. The software used was Smart PLS 2.0 M3.

Results

Regarding the respondent's profile, we found 48.3% of male respondents and 51.7% of female. As for the age group, it was observed that most of the sample is composed by individuals above 35 years old.

When considering the educational level, the sample is mostly composed by individuals who have a high school degree, and 80% of the sample is composed by people who have a higher education degree and a monthly income greater than R$5000 (US$2000).

The model was validated through the structural equations modeling. For that matter, the PLS method was used, which does not require multivariate normality of the variables and it can function with a reduced sample size, besides suiting better to exploratory studies than the method used by LISREL (Chin 1998). The software used was Smart PLS 2.0 M3.

The measurement model is the element of the general model that carries the latent variables. In the present study, the latent variables are: consumers' perception on social media advertising, viral marketing, brand visibility, and purchase intention. As a result, all items presented high factor loadings (values above 0.5), with

Table 1 Description of adjusted model 2

	AVE	Composed reliability	R square	Cronbach's alpha
Purchase intention	.561	.863	.543	.801
Viral marketing	.727	.914	.453	.874
Perception on social media advertising	.564	.866		.806
Brand visibility	.638	.876	.315	.811

the exception of q2.5, which was excluded of the model, evidencing the relevant relation between the latent variables and the set of indicators and attesting the measurement model.

Following, there was the evaluation of the model regarding convergent validity. This evaluation is executed based on Average Variance Extracted (AVE). The values, according to Chin (1998), must have minimum of .5. This baseline can be proved by Table 1.

Concerning the construct's reliability, Chin (1998) indicates that this should be evaluated primarily according to the composite reliability and its value should be above .7. In accordance with what was presented in Table 1, all constructs complied with the standard.

On the other hand, the convergent validity is related with the loads' magnitude regarding the respective construct. All items hold high loads in its respective constructs (above .5—Fig. 2).

Fornell and Lacker (1981) indicate a form of evaluation of the discriminant validity to the latent variables. In this method, the square roots of the AVEs are obtained and its values are compared with correlations between the various constructs. When the AVE is superior to the correlations it can be affirmed that exists the discriminant validity. By matters of intelligibility, the results obtained of the square roots of the AVEs were put in the main diagonal of the correlation matrices (distinguished in bold). The verification to be completed next is between the AVE and the correlations in the same row and in the same column. The results of Table 2 attest the existence of discriminant validity to all the constructs.

In order to verify if the found coefficients are significant to the level of 5% of significance we used the bootstrap method. The values showed in the model refer to the "t" statistic of the test to evaluate the significance of the coefficients found. "t" Values above 1.96 indicate that the coefficients are significant at the level of 5%. All the coefficients presented values superior to 1.96, including the coefficient concerning the relation between viral marketing and purchase intention (1.993).

It was also verified in the structural model a strong impact ($R^2 = .543$) of the latent variables consumers' perception, viral marketing and brand visibility on purchase intention and a smaller impact ($R^2 = .315$) of the latent variables consumers' perception and viral marketing on brand visibility. It was noticed, likewise, a significant impact of the latent variable consumers' perception on viral marketing ($R^2 = .453$), demonstrating the strong relation between these variables.

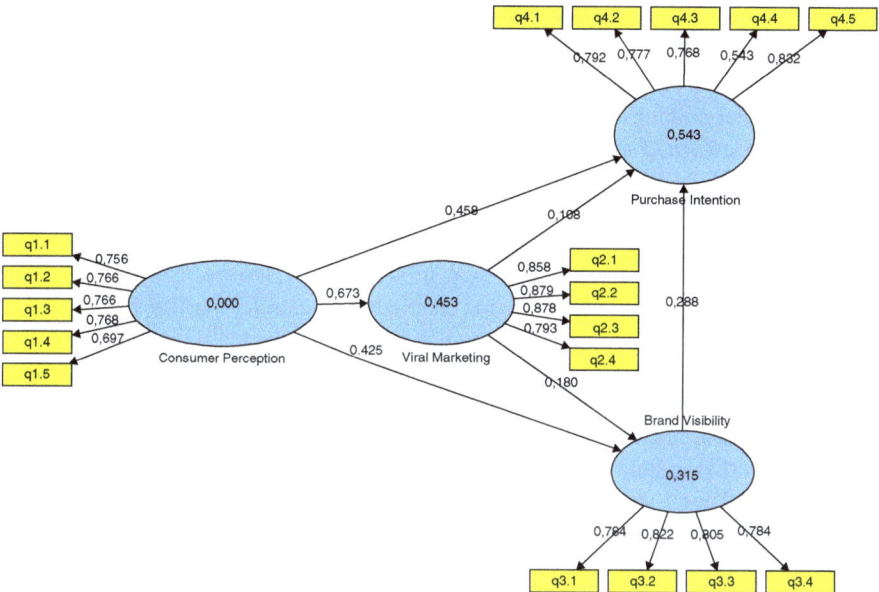

Fig. 2 The model results

Table 2 Crossed loads of the latent variables

	Purchase intention	Viral marketing	Consumers' perception on social media ad.	Brand visibility
Purchase intention	**.749**			
Viral marketing	.549	**.853**		
Perception on social media advertising	.687	.673	**.751**	
Brand visibility	.588	.465	.546	**.799**

Conclusion

The strength of viral marketing is in the consumer-to-consumer communication, disseminating information about brands, products, and services, and influencing consumers consumption (Krishnamurthy 2001). Generally speaking, none of the hypothesis labored in this study was rejected: it is observed that the viral marketing, as a strategy of advertising communication, grants the consumer knowledge that can influence other consumers to consume or not a product or a service. This phenomenon also influences a brand's visibility.

The emergence of the Internet brought out countless transformations that exceeded the virtual environment and extended to various sectors of society, changing the habits of individuals and organizations. Consumer, that used to function passively, became the leading figure of marketing's strategic context. Aware of this scenario, the advertising communication begins to change its strategies to get closer to the consumer again (Gabriel 2010). Viral marketing is considered a strategy of digital marketing encouraging individuals to disseminate network messages (Cavallini 2008). The decrease of audience in traditional medias evidences consumers' saturation to thousands of advertisements in the day-to-day routine.

H1 confirmed that consumers' perception on social media advertising influences positively viral marketing, evidencing that the new consumer is open to publicity campaigns that uses the Internet as propagation means. Leskovec et al. (2007) affirm that, against the Internet emergence that enabled the creation of virtual communities and larger access to information, consumers have created a resistance to traditional advertising communication. They have being more induced to search information about products and services in the virtual environment. Bentivegna (2002), complementing the idea, highlights the importance of viral marketing as an alternative so that the advertising communication reaches the consumer. The author concluded that successful viral strategies can influence positively the consumers' perception on publicity campaigns with network dissemination.

H2 demonstrated that consumer perception of the social media advertising influences positively in the purchase intention. According to Dalmoro et al. (2010), networked consumers influence purchase decisions of other users through network messages. It is observed that individuals are alert to network campaigns and still consult their contacts about brands, products, and services. This aspect was also confirmed in **H5**, which demonstrates the positive influence of consumer's perception in relation to brand visibility. According to Schmitt (2000), consumers create experience with network campaigns and share it with their contacts, resulting in visibility to a certain brand.

Henning-Thurau et al. (2004) comment that the Internet has raised the available options to customers when searching information about products and services. Countless consumers search for other consumers' opinions and are interested in sharing their own perceptions through electronic word-of-mouth communication or viral marketing.

H3 confirms the influence of viral marketing in consumers' purchase intention. It is observed that the consumer relates the product or service to the network available information about it, when having a purchase intention. Consumers have demonstrated preoccupation with other consumers towards influencing their decisions, avoiding that others have negative experiences and buy low quality products or services. A well-elaborated viral marketing campaign stimulates the customer to spread positive information about products and services, influencing his or her purchase intention.

H4 is complementary to the idea and demonstrates that viral marketing also influence brand visibility. Viral marketing occupies a fundamental role in electronic commerce and it is also an important tool concerning brand valuation (Goldsmith and Horowitz 2006). Silveira and Mattos (2009) affirm that it is important to emphasize that both multinational companies and small companies can use viral marketing actions to propagate their brands. De Bruyn and Lilien (2008) point out that this kind of action not only reaches the consumer's attention, but it also triggers interest and it can result in brands adoption and in sales. It is observed that the intended effect of viral actions is to widen the comments that create evidences to the marketing practitioner, aiming the dissemination of positive messages that increase brand valuation.

One of the viral campaigns goals is to create larger visibility to a certain brand, comprehending that this action may result in sales (Bentivegna 2002). Rangel Netto (2012) sums affirming that purchase intention may vary according to wider knowledge of the brand.

H6 confirmed the concept demonstrating that brand visibility influences positively purchase intention.

Next, we highlight the research's limitations. The first one refers to the methodological approach used, which does not allow extrapolations concerning the reasons that lead the viral marketing, as an advertising communication strategy, to influence purchase intention and brand visibility. The study exploratory feature, although it approaching a theoretical range, leaves some theoretical conceptions useful in the understanding of the consumer's perception of publicity campaigns and the reasons that incite the users to share theirs experiences on social networks.

Another feature that affected the analysis was the researched universe, which created a convenience sample of 321 respondents of the online survey questionnaire, restricting the ability to generalize.

Regarding suggestions for future researches, in this study, viral marketing was approached as a phenomenon caused by the advertising communication. It would be interesting to approach the phenomenon under a spontaneous perspective, which would indicate the reasons that induced the consumer to share network messages.

Furthermore, it was also approached the positive relation between the constructs consumer's perception on network publicity campaigns, viral marketing, brand visibility, and purchase intention. It would also be important to study the negative relations, aiming to demonstrate the negative impact between the variables.

Acknowledgement We would like to acknowledge CAPES (Coordenação de Aperfeiçoamento de Pessoal de Nível Superior) for supporting the participation in the Conference.

References

Almeida, M., Coelho, R. L., & Tete, M. F. (2011). Perspectiva evolutiva do Marketing Viral: um Ensaio sobre sua fundamentação teórica e alternativas para futuros trabalhos. *XXXV Encontro da ANPAD*.

Andrade, J., Mazzon, J. A., & Katz, S. (2006). Boca-a-Boca Eletrônico: explorando e integrando conceitos de marketing viral, buzz marketing e word-of-mouth. *II Encontro de Marketing da ANPAD*.

Barichello, E. M., & Oliveira, C. (2010). O marketing viral como estratégia publicitária nas novas ambiências midiáticas. *Em Questão, 16*(1), 29–44.

Bentivegna, F. J. (2002). Fatores de impacto no sucesso do marketing boca a boca on-line. *RAE – eletrônica, 42*(1).

Boone, L. E., & Kurtz, D. L. (2009). *Marketing contemporâneo. Tradução de Roberta Schneider* (p. 832). São Paulo, Brazil: Cengage Learning.

Burt, R. S. (2000). Structural holes versus network closure as social capital. In L. Nan, K. S. Cook, & R. S. Burt (Org.), *Social capital: Theory and research* (p. 233). Chicago: Aldine de Gruyter.

Canclini, N. G. (2008). *Consumidores e Cidadãos: conflitos multiculturais da globalização* (7th ed.). Rio de Janeiro, Brazil: Ed. UFRJ.

Cavallini, R. (2008). *O marketing depois de amanhã: explorando novas tecnologias para revolucionar a comunicação* (2nd ed.). São Paulo, Brazil: Ed. do Autor.

Cervo, A. L., & Bervian, P. A. (1996). *Metodologia científica para uso de estudantes universitários.* São Paulo, Brazil: McGraw-Hill do Brasil.

Chaudhuri, A., & Holbrook, M. B. (2001). The chain of effects from brand trust and brand affect to brand performance: The role of brand loyalty. *Journal of Marketing, 65*(1), 81–93.

Cheung, C. M. K., Lee, M. K. O., & Rabjonh, N. (2008). The impact of electronic word of mouth: The adoption of online opinions in online customer communities. *Internet Research, 18*(3), 229–247.

Chin, W. W. (1998). The partial least squares approach to structural equation modeling. In G. A. Marcoulides (Ed.), *Modern methods for business research* (pp. 295–336). Mahwah, NJ: Lawrence Erlbaum Associates.

Dalmoro, M., Fleck, J. P., Venturini, J. C., Lazzari, F., Leite, R. C., & Rossi, C. A. V. (2010). Twitter: Uma Análise do Consumo, Interação e Compartilhamento na Web 2.0. *XXXIV Encontro da ANPAD.*

De Bruyn, A., & Lilien, G. (2008). A multi-stage model of word-of-mouth influence through viral marketing. *International Journal of Research in Marketing, 25*(3), 151–163.

Dellarocas, C. N. (2003). The digitization of word-of-mouth: Promise and challenges of online feedback mechanisms. *Management Science, 49*(10).

Delre, S., Jager, W., & Janssen, M. (2007). Diffusion dynamics in small-world networks with heterogeneous consumer. *Computational and Mathematical Organization Theory, 13*(2), 185–202.

Demo, P. (2000). *Metodologia do Conhecimento Científico.* São Paulo, Brazil: Atlas.

Doyle, P. (1990). Building successful brands: The strategic options. *Journal of Consumer Marketing, 7*(5), 5–20.

Drucker, P. (2000). Além da revolução da informação. *HSM Management, 18*, 48–55.

Fornell, C. & Larcker, D. (1981) Structural equation models with unobservable variables and measurement error, *Journal of Marketing Research, 18*(1), 39–50.

Gabriel, M. (2010). *Marketing na era digital.* São Paulo, Brazil: Novatec.

Gitomer, J. (2006). *It's not 'What's your brand? It's 'Where's your brand?'* New Orleans: New Orleans City Business, *27*(13).

Godes, D., & Mayzlin, D. (2004). Using online conversations to study word-of mouth communication. *Marketing Science, 23*(4), 545–560.

Godin, S. (2000). *Marketing de permissão: transformando desconhecidos em amigos e amigos em clientes.* Rio de Janeiro, Brazil: Campus.

Goldsmith, R. E., & Horowitz, D. (2006). Measuring motivations for online opinion seeking. *Journal of Interactive Advertising, 6*(2), 2–14.

Henning-Thurau, T., Gwinner, K. P., Walsh, G., & Gremler, D. D. (2004). Electronic word of mouth via consumer opinion plataforms: What motivates consumer to articulate themselves on the Internet? *Journal of Interactive Marketing, 18*(1), 38–52.

Hong, I. B., & Cho, H. (2011). The impact of consumer trust on attitudinal loyalty and purchase intentions in B2C e-marketplaces: Intermediary trust vs. seller trust. *International Journal of Information Management, 31*(5), 469–479.

Hung, K. H., & Li, S. Y. (2007). The influence of e-WOM on virtual consumer communities: Social capital, consumer learning, and behavioral outcomes. *Journal of Advertising Research, 47*(4), 485–495.

Krishnamurthy, S. (2001). Understanding online message dissemination: Analyzing Send a message to a friend data. *First Monday, 6*(5).

Leskovec, J., Adamic, L., & Huberman, B. (2007). The dynamics of viral marketing. *ACM Transactions on the Web, 1*(1), 1–39.

Malhotra, N. K. (2001). *Pesquisa de marketing: uma orientação aplicada* (3rd ed., p. 768). Porto Alegre, Brazil: Bookman.

Mizruchi, M. S. (2009). Análise de redes sociais: avanços recentes e controvérsias atuais. In A. C. B. Martes (Org.), *Redes e sociologia econômica* (pp. 131–159). São Carlos: ed UFSCAR.

Patrocínio, R. F., Mesquita, J. M. C., & Dornas, K. B. H. (2013). Word of mouth communication and its effect on the affective commitment. *Academy of Marketing Annual Conference*, Monterey.

Phelps, J. E., Lewis, R., Mobilio, L., Perry, D., & Rama, N. (2004). Viral marketing or electronic word of mouth advertising: Examining consumer responses and motivations to pass along email. *Journal of Advertising Research, 44*(4), 333–348.

Porter, L., & Golan, G. (2006). From subservient chickens to brawny men: A comparison of viral advertising to television advertising. *Journal of Interactive Advertising, 6*(2), 26–33.

Rangel Netto, N. S. (2012). *Redes Sociais na Internet: A Influência da Recomendação Online na Intenção de Consumo.* Dissertação (Mestrado em Administração de Empresas) – Programa de Pós-Graduação em Administração, Centro de Ciências Jurídicas e Econômicas da Universidade Federal do Espírito Santo, Vitória.

Rapp, A., Beitelspacher, L. S., Grewal, D., & Hughes, D. E. (2013). Understanding social media effects across seller, retailer, and consumer interactions. *Journal of the Academy of Marketing Science, 41*(5), 547–566.

Recuero, R. (2009). *Redes Sociais na Internet.* Porto Alegre, Brazil: Sulina.

Salzman, M., Matathia, I., & Oreilly, A. (2003). *Buzz: A era do Marketing Viral.* São Paulo, Brazil: Cultrix.

Sangwan, S., Guan, C. G., & Siguaw, J. A. (2009). Virtual social networks: Toward a research agenda. *International Journal of Virtual Communities and Social Networking, 1*(1), 2198–2210.

Schmitt, B. H. (2000). *Marketing experimental.* São Paulo, Brazil: Nobel.

Senecal, S., & Nantel, J. (2004). The influence of online product recommendations on consumers' online choices. *Journal of Retailing, 80*(2), 159–169.

Silva, N. (2008). *Marketing viral: quando os internautas são a melhor propaganda.* Dissertação (Mestrado em Comunicação) – Faculdade de Comunicação, Universidade de Brasília, Brasília.

Silveira, R. B., & Mattos, L. (2009). Este é Engraçado! Você Ainda Não Viu? Análise do Efeito do Marketing Viral no Youtube. *Encontro da XXXIII ANPAD.*

Sissors, J., & Bumba, L. (2001). *Planejamento de Mídia.* São Paulo, Brazil: Nobel.

Sterne, J., & Priore, A. (2000). *E-mail marketing.* New York: Wiley.

Vergara, S. C. (2004). *Projetos e relatórios de pesquisa em administração* (5th ed.). São Paulo, Brazil: Atlas.

Vergara, S. C. (2007). *Projetos e relatórios de pesquisa em administração* (9th ed.). São Paulo, Brazil: Atlas.

Yoo, B., & Lee, S. H. (2012). Asymmetrical effects of past experiences with genuine fashion luxury brands and their counterfeits on purchase intention of each. *Journal of Business Research, 65*(10), 1507–1515.

How to Impress Social Media Friends: The Social Motivations for Sharing Viral Content

Elsamari Botha, Michael Karam, Erinma Ogbonna, Kelly Payne, and Beate Stiehler

Introduction

In recent years, online advertising has become one of the most influential means of marketing communication. This stems from the rise of the Internet, which has quickly evolved into the fastest growing advertising medium of the decade (Ha 2008). Social media has come to the forefront of the marketing world as a result of this Internet boom and has been identified as a key online area for marketers to target, as it allows consumers and marketers alike to create content, share it, bookmark it and network at a prodigious rate (Asur and Huberman 2010). This allows marketers to create online advertising content and marketing messages which can subsequently be spread by the consumers themselves (Ha 2008). This translates into the message gaining greater credibility, as consumers trust other consumers more than the companies themselves (Brown et al. 2007; Cheung et al. 2007).

While online marketing is a leader in marketing trends, the majority of marketers still fail to understand which factors lead to the spread of online content. Existing research has looked at various intrapersonal influences such as the consumers' emotional response to the content (Guadagno et al. 2013). Previous studies have also analysed the effects of various social factors on the spread of online content (Khan and Vong 2012; Ho and Dempsey 2008; Chu 2011). However, these social motivations do not appear to have been studied as thoroughly, both in terms of empirical studies and theory development, as the role of emotion in viral marketing. Therefore,

E. Botha (✉) • M. Karam • E. Ogbonna • K. Payne
University of Cape Town, Cape Town, South Africa
e-mail: elsamari.botha@uct.ac.za; KRMMIC006@myuct.ac.za; OGBERI001@myuct.ac.za; PYNKEL001@myuct.ac.za

B. Stiehler
University of Johannesburg, Johannesburg, South Africa
e-mail: b.stiehler@uj.ac.za

© Academy of Marketing Science 2016
L. Petruzzellis, R.S. Winer (eds.), *Rediscovering the Essentiality of Marketing*, Developments in Marketing Science: Proceedings of the Academy of Marketing Science, DOI 10.1007/978-3-319-29877-1_50

243

this study tested the influence of two social motivations for the spread of viral marketing content.

The first of these factors was *altruism*, which has been defined as selfless acts based on affection for others (Ho and Dempsey 2008) as well as a willingness to benefit others through forwarding online content (Fan et al. 2013). The second was *the expression of identity*; an individual's sense of self which they attempt to express to others (Taylor et al. 2012).

The aim of this study was to assist marketers with insights into whether these social motivations affect the spread of online video advertisements, and if so, what the effect is and which of these factors has the greatest influence. This will help marketers to create more successful future viral marketing campaigns. This study was therefore guided by the following research question: *How do altruism and the expression of identity influence the sharing of online video advertisements by young adults?* To achieve this, the study had the following primary objectives:

1. To determine whether altruism influences the sharing of online video advertisements by young adults.
2. To determine whether the expression of identity influences the sharing of online video advertisements by young adults.
3. To determine whether the expression of identity has an effect on how altruism influences the sharing of online video advertisements by young adults.
4. To determine which of these social motivations (altruism and identity) has the most greatest influence on the sharing of online video advertisements by young adults.

The structure of this chapter is as follows: The relevant literature is discussed first followed by the methodology and findings. Thereafter, the conclusions and recommendations are provided. Lastly, the limitations of this study and suggestions for future research are presented.

Motivations for the Sharing of Online

The sharing of online content can be defined as forwarding content to friends, other Internet users, or connections on social media or other online platforms (Ho and Dempsey 2008). More online content than ever before is being shared as a result of a large percentage of consumers, and particularly young adults, spending more time online (Camarero and San Jose 2011; Hargittai and Hinnant 2008). However, not all online content is shared, and previous research shows that it is increasingly difficult to predict viral success.

After a consumer views online content, one of the factors that influences whether or not the consumer will share that content is the emotional reaction which the online message evokes in him/her (Berger and Milkman 2009, 2011). Both these studies found that the valence and level of activation which characterises an emotion affect whether the message which elicited that emotion will be forwarded. Messages which evoked positive emotions were found to be shared more than those which evoked negative emotions (Berger and Milkman 2009, 2011). Messages which evoked emotions with a high activation level, such as anger, were found to be shared more than those which evoked emotions with a low activation level, such as sadness (Berger and Milkman 2009, 2011).

Emotion is an intrapersonal factor; however, the forwarding of online content from one individual to another is a social action, and so it seems intuitive that it would be influenced by social motivations. Schutz's (1966) framework of social motivations, as used by Ho and Dempsey (2008), provides a good foundation for studying these factors. The social motivations tested by Ho and Dempsey (2008) were inclusion, affection and control. Inclusion was defined as the need to belong to a group as well as the need to be seen as an individual within that group. Affection was defined as the need to be altruistic and show concern for others. Control was defined as the need to display personal growth and achievement. Affection and the need to be seen as an individual within a group were found to have a significant positive effect on the sharing of online content, whereas control proved to be significant but did not have a positive effect on sharing. The need to belong to a group was not found to be significant (Ho and Dempsey 2008).

The study conducted by Stonedahl et al. (2010) produced different results. They found that both the need to be seen as an individual and the need to be part of a group were significant predictors of online sharing. Furthermore, Chan and Li (2010) found that individuals who belong to 'virtual communities' share online messages with other members of their communities as a sort of exchange. Thus, belonging to such communities causes individuals to share messages which they believe have value, either because they provide entertainment or information. Camarero and San Jose (2011) also found that belonging to groups influenced sharing. In their study, they found that the degree of closeness in one's online relationships had a positive effect on the incidence of opening and forwarding viral messages (Camarero and San Jose 2011). The sharing of useful information with online contacts, apart from being used as a means of exchange, has also been suggested as a way of expressing affection (Berger and Milkman 2009).

This study focussed on the effect that social motivations have on the sharing of online content (specifically, online video advertisements). From the review of relevant literature, it appears that social motivations are an area of less consensus among researchers than the role that emotion plays in this context, when it comes to their effect on the sharing of online content. Also, as stated by Ho and Dempsey (2008) and Stonedahl et al. (2010), these factors have the potential to be a more powerful marketing tool than the intrapersonal motivators which are more difficult to control.

The next section provides a review of literature pertaining to the social motivations which were tested in this study.

The Social Motivations for Sharing Online Content

Based on the above literature review, this study focused on the effect altruism and identity had on the forwarding of viral content. The review of past research done by Berger and Milkman (2009) and Ho and Dempsey (2008) led to the belief that these constructs may not function entirely separately from each other, and that it would be beneficial to test the relationship between the factors; specifically, whether identity has an effect on altruism.

The Influence of Altruism on the Sharing of Online Video Advertisements

Altruism has often been cited as a key factor which affects online content forwarding (Berger and Milkman 2009, 2011; Fan et al. 2013; Ho and Dempsey 2008). Ho and Dempsey (2008) define altruism as the commission of selfless acts based on affection for others. The definition according to Fan et al. (2013) is more closely related to online altruism; they define it as being willing to benefit others providing them with useful information. These different definitions for altruism led the researchers to conclude that altruism should not be measured directly, but should instead be measured using two sub-constructs.

The first sub-construct under altruism was the desire to show affection for others, based on the study done by Ho and Dempsey (2008). Their research states that affection is the main reason for altruistic acts. This suggests that the desire to show affection for others has a positive effect on the sharing of online advertisements. Consequently, the following hypothesis was formulated:

H1: The desire to show affection for others positively influences the sharing of online video advertisements by young adults.

The second sub-construct under altruism was the desire to provide others with useful information. Fan et al. (2013) mention in their research that altruistic individuals engage in certain behaviours with the intention of benefiting others. The behaviour which they mention is providing information to others. This suggests that the desire to provide useful information to others also has a positive effect on the sharing of online advertisements. Consequently, the following hypothesis was formulated:

H2: The desire to provide others with useful information positively influences the sharing of online video advertisements by young adults.

The Influence of Identity on the Sharing of Online Video Advertisements

It is common knowledge among marketers that consumers purchase products and services not only just for their utilitarian benefits, but also for their symbolic value (Taylor et al. 2012). It could therefore be said that consumers are more likely to share advertising that is consistent with how they see themselves (Taylor et al.

2012). Not much research has been done on identity as a motivating factor for the spread of online content, and therefore this study hoped to shine some more light in this area.

Consumers share online content and advertisements to express their sense of identity, and their online social interactions (in this study, the sharing of online video advertisements) are shaped by their sense of self (Taylor et al. 2012). This suggests that the need to express an identity has a positive effect on the sharing of online content. The researchers therefore posited that:

H3: *The expression of identity positively influences the sharing of online video advertisements by young adults.*

However, as is discussed by Berger and Milkman (2009) and Ho and Dempsey (2008), there is also an interaction between these factors.

The Effect of Identity on Altruism in the Sharing of Online Video Advertisements

Although altruistic acts are committed to benefit others, there might be a conscious or unconscious motivation to perform these acts in order to improve how one sees oneself or how one is seen by others. Berger and Milkman (2009) stated that through sharing useful information over the Internet, an individual is being altruistic by benefiting others, but at the same time that individual is made to appear knowledgeable, thereby improving his/her image. For example, an individual may share an online advertisement with their friends which describes the latest sale at a particular clothing store. This individual may share this advertisement in order to give their friends useful information (altruistic motivations). However, they may also be motivated to share this video with their friends for status reasons, wanting their status to improve as a result of them forwarding this information (identity reasons). Identity may therefore have a mediating effect on altruism as it relates to the sharing of online video advertisements.

As this study used two sub-constructs to measure altruism (the desire to show affection and to provide others with useful information), the following hypotheses were created to test the above theory:

H4: *The expression of identity affects the influence of the desire to show affection for others on the sharing of online video advertisements by young adults.*
H5: *The expression of identity affects the influence of the desire to provide others with useful information on the sharing of online video advertisements by young adults.*

At the same time, one can posit over which of these social motivations has the greatest influence on the sharing of viral content. Ho and Dempsey (2008) found that some of the social motivations they tested had a more significant effect than others. This is an important result as it would allow the individuals who design online advertising videos to focus on the most significant interpersonal factors. This led to the formulation of the final hypothesis:

H6: One of the social motivations (altruism or identity) has a more significant influence on the sharing of online video advertisements by young adults than the other.

Methodology

Two online video advertisements were used to test the hypotheses in this study, and the results of these hypotheses tests are stated separately for each video. Each hypothesis will therefore be listed twice, that is hypothesis 1a–6a for video 1 and 1b–6b for video 2. To discuss this in greater depth, the following section first addresses the research design and method used, thereafter the target population and sampling method is discussed, and finally the measurement instrument.

Research Design and Method

Similar to Guadagno et al. (2013), a causal research design was used to conduct an experiment where two viral videos were used as treatment. The effect of the two social motivations (altruism and identity) on the test units' willingness to share online video advertisements was measured. A pre-experimental design was used to conduct the research, because randomised probability sampling was not used (Malhotra 2010). The specific pre-experimental design used was a post-test only method. The test units were shown two online video advertisements which were deemed by the researchers to have gone viral.

Target Population and Sampling Method

The target population for this study was young adults, defined by Ho and Dempsey (2008) as being aged between 18 and 29. Young adults were well suited to this study based on the fact that a reported 88 % of them are actively involved in online activities including social media, and that they are the 'most connected age group' (Ho and Dempsey 2008).

Non-probability sampling (convenience sampling) was used, as the questionnaire was distributed on Facebook and various other social media networks in an attempt to better access the target market. The fact that the sample was non-representative is a disadvantage of this method, but the data gathered from this sample can nonetheless be used to draw valid conclusions (Malhotra 2010). Sampling in this study was undertaken without replacement, and consisted of 90 test units, all of whom were presented with the same online questionnaire through Qualtrics.

Measurement Instruments

The two sub-constructs used to measure altruism were the desire to show affection for others and the desire to provide others with useful information. Both of these sub-constructs were measured using scales adapted from the research paper by Price et al. (1995).

The desire to show affection for others was measured using an adaptation of the 'Altruism' scale that was used by Price et al. (1995). This scale was also used by Ho and Dempsey (2008) in their research paper. It was found to have a Cronbach's alpha of .84 when used by Price et al. (1995) and .90 when used by Ho and Dempsey (2008). The scale was a seven-point Likert scale which asked respondents to state how important certain actions were to them, with 1 being not at all important and 7 being very important. The statements included 'to help other people' and 'to share what you have'.

The desire to provide useful information to others was measured using an adaptation of the 'Information Provided' scale that was used by Price et al. (1995). It was found to have a Cronbach's alpha of .85. The scale originally asked respondents how often they had engaged in certain behaviours over the last 3 months. The statements include 'offered facts about products or services to others' and 'started a conversation with someone about a product you think they could use'.

The 'Identity' scale (Escalas and Bettman 2005) is a seven-point Likert scale that was slightly adapted in order to be used in this study, with 1 being very strongly disagree and 7 being very strongly agree. The questions were reworded to relate to the online video advertisements instead of 'self-brand connections'.

Finally, the sharing of online video advertisements was the dependent variable for this study and was measured using an 'Intent to forward' scale, a seven-point Likert scale used by Eckler and Bolls (2011).

Selection of Treatments: Viral Video Advertisements

The online video advertisements used in this study were selected using three main criteria. First, the advertisement had to be relevant to young adults. Second, in order to ensure that the questionnaire did not become too lengthy, the advertisement needed to have a duration of less than 3 min. Third, the video needed to have 'gone viral'. Online viral success has been defined as how many views a video received on YouTube (Guadagno et al. 2013). The term 'going viral' is a subjective one, so for the purposes of this study the researchers have defined it as an international advertisement which has more than 20 million views.

The first of the two videos used in this study was the 'Bells's The Reader' video advertisement. The duration of this advertisement is 2:01 min. It had a count of 2,172,839 views on YouTube as of August 20th 2014. The second video used was 'Phonebloks', an advertisement for the concept of recycling and reusing various components of cell phones. The advertisement lasts for 2:47 min and had a view count of 20,638,134 on YouTube as of August 20th 2014.

Results

In this section the results of this study is discussed. The reliability of the scales used are discussed first, followed by descriptive (see Table 1) and then inferential statistics.

Scale Reliability

For video 1, the reliability of the sub-constructs Affection, Information and Identity were measured, as well as the reliability of the summated dependent variable (Likelihood to share the video). The Cronbach's alpha for Affection was .89. For Information, the alpha value was .90 and for Identity, the alpha value was .950. Cronbach's alpha for the dependent variable was also exceptionally high with a value of .917. Each of the alpha statistics for the first video were greater than .6 and therefore were considered to be reliable.

For video 2, the Cronbach's alpha for Affection was .89. For Information, the alpha value was .91 and for Identity, the alpha value was .95. Cronbach's alpha for the dependent variable was again a high value of .94. Each of the alpha statistics for the second video were also greater than .6 and considered reliable. In each scale, if any item had been deleted, the value of the Cronbach's alpha would have decreased. This indicates that overall, all scales were found to be very reliable. Each item measures some aspect of the underlying construct and they are consistent in what they indicate about the construct.

Descriptive Statistics

Video 1 was selected in order to try measure the first sub-construct, the *desire to show affection to others*, which is a sub-construct of *altruism*. While *Affection* did yield slightly positive results, indicating that, on average, respondents answered that they agreed that they would share the video to show affection to others, this score

Table 1 Descriptive statistics

		Mean	SD
Video 1	Altruism_Affection_1	4.12	1.42
	Altruism_Information_1	3.63	1.30
	Identity_1	4.31	1.47
	Likelihood to Share_1	4.95	1.81
Video 2	Altruism_Affection_2	4.49	1.34
	Altruism_Information_2	5.21	1.20
	Identity_2	3.97	1.42
	Likelihood to Share_2	5.47	1.56

was only slightly above a 'neutral' score and definitive conclusions cannot be made. The *desire to provide useful information to others* provided the lowest mean score and on average respondents indicated that they would not share the video to provide others with useful information. The *expression of identity* construct showed the highest mean score of the three. On average, responses ranged from 'slightly disagree' to 'agree' indicating that people shared video 1 in order to express their identity. This provides interesting information to the researches as it shows that when sharing an advert such as video 1, where there is a strong emotional connection created and an inspiring story is told, young adults would share this video to express their own identity, rather than to show affection and provide information to others. Overall, respondents indicated that, on average, they were more likely to share the advert, with 68% of responses ranging from 'somewhat unlikely' to 'likely' to share the video which indicates an overall positive likeliness for them to share the advert.

Video 2 was selected in order to test the sub-construct *providing useful information to others*. As hypothesised, this construct provided the highest mean scores out of all three constructs as the majority of the respondents indicated that they would share the advert in order to provide others with useful information. Intuitively, this makes sense as the advert was an interesting, product–concept advert which was certainly informative, and one would want to share this with others to tell them about this interesting idea and provide them with information about this concept. The *altruism* construct also provided a positive mean score which shows respondents would also share this video to show affection to others—possibly leading on from the advert's message of minimising waste in the world which many would want to share with their friends to show affection to encourage them to live in a healthier, waste-free world. The *identity* construct was equally centred on the 'neutral' score, meaning respondents responses varied.

Overall, 47% of the respondents were male, while 51.8% were female.

Inferential Statistics

In the following sections, each objective stated in the introduction is discussed in turn. Table 2 summarises the findings with regard to each objective (and consequent hypothesis).

The findings with regard to each objective is discussed in greater depth below.

Summary of Findings for Objective 1

Objective 1 aimed to determine whether altruism influences the sharing of online video advertisements by young adults. Altruism was measured by two dimensions: The desire to show affection (a) and the desire to provide others with useful

Table 2 Summary of hypothesis tests for objectives 1 and 2

Objective	Hypothesis	Test statistic	p-value
1	H1a	.21	.03
	H1b	.46	.00
	H2a	.44	.00
	H2b	.57	.00
2	H3a	.66	.00
	H3b	.42	.00

information (b). These two dimensions make up the (a) and (b) parts of the tested hypotheses. Thereafter, the hypotheses tested this statement for each video (1 and 2), therefore resulting in four hypotheses in total.

For H1a, the desire to show affection for others had a positive influence on the sharing of online video advertisements by young adults (measured using video 1). For H1b, the desire to show affection for others has a positive influence on the sharing of online video advertisements by young adults. In H2a, the desire to provide others with useful information has a positive influence on the sharing of online video advertisements by young adults (measured using video 1). Finally, for H2b, the desire to provide others with useful information has a positive influence on the sharing of online video advertisements by young adults (measured using video 2).

Summary of Findings for Objective 2

Similar to Objective 1, this objective was tested for each video (resulting in H3a and H3b). For H3a, the null hypothesis was rejected at a 5 % significance level, with a Pearson Correlation Coefficient of .66 and a p value of .00. The researchers therefore rejected the null hypothesis and concluded that the desire to provide others with useful information has a positive influence on the sharing of online video advertisements by young (measured using video 1). For H3b, the null hypothesis was rejected at a 5 % significance level, with a Spearman's rho Correlation Coefficient of .42 and a p value of .00. The researchers thus concluded that the expression of identity has a positive influence on the sharing of online video advertisements by young adults (measured using video 2).

Summary of Findings for Objective 3

From past research, it appeared that part of the effect of altruism might be channelled through the expression of identity (Berger and Milkman 2009). The researchers thus tested whether identity acted as a mediator on altruism. The process used to test for mediation is described in some detail below. Each of the four tests (one for each pair of hypotheses) for mediation was conducted in the same manner. For the sake of brevity, the process is described only once, in the context of testing H_{4a} against its respective null hypothesis.

We found that in a model to predict the sharing of online video advertisements (using video 1), including the expression of identity reduces the importance of the desire to show affection for others. Therefore, the expression of identity acted as a mediator on the desire to show affection for others in the case of video 1. The fact that β_4 is still significant (with a p value of .022) shows that the mediation effect is only partial. Therefore, the expression of identity acts as a partial mediator on the desire to show affection for others, the researchers rejected the null hypothesis for H_{4a}.

With regard to the hypothesis that the expression of identity acts as a partial mediator on the desire to provide others with useful information, the researchers rejected the null hypothesis for H_{5a}. The expression of identity had an effect on how the desire to provide others with useful information influences the sharing of online video advertisements by young adults (measured using video 1). The expression of identity also acts as a partial mediator on the desire to provide others with useful information, the researchers rejected the null hypothesis for H_{5b}. The expression of identity has an effect on how the desire to provide others with useful information influences the sharing of online video advertisements by young adults (measured using video 2).

Summary of Findings for Objective 4

To test this hypothesis, the following regression model was fitted:

$$Y = .620 + .20X_1 + .24X_2 + .62X_3$$

The regression model was significant with an adjusted R^2 value of .47, therefore able to explain 47.2 % of the variation in the dependent variable. This makes the model a moderately strong predictor of the dependent variable. The expression of identity had a greater level of significance in the model than both of the sub-constructs of altruism. Identity therefore has a greater influence than altruism on the sharing of online video advertisements by young adults (measured using video 1). For the second video, however, the desire to provide information to others had the greatest influence on the sharing of online video advertisements by young adults. This can be seen in the second model tested to test H6b (F-value significant, R-square $= .48$):

$$Y = .605 + .071X_1 + .616X_2 + .335X_3$$

Findings, Conclusions and Recommendations

The hypotheses were supported by nearly all the findings, and the main findings are as follows:

1. The desire to show affection for others had a positive influence on the sharing of viral videos.
2. The desire to provide others with useful information had a positive influence on the sharing of viral videos.
3. The expression of identity had a positive influence on the sharing of viral videos.
4. The expression of identity partially mediates the relationship between the desire to show affection for others and the sharing of viral videos.
5. The expression of identity also partially mediates the relationship between the desire to provide others with useful information and the sharing of viral videos.
6. The expression of identity had the greatest influence on the sharing of video 1, that was geared towards getting an emotional reaction out of viewers.
7. The desire to provide others with useful information had the greatest influence on the sharing of video 2, that was about a new phone coming out.

These findings presented a number of managerial implications. First, the findings concur with Ho and Dempsey (2008), in showing that the desire to show affection for others, does indeed have a positive influence on the sharing of online content, and in this study's case, the sharing of online video advertisements. This was proven for both videos, showing that young adults will share inspirational, emotional videos, as well as informative, concept videos in order to show others affection.

Marketing managers need to be aware of this as they develop their viral marketing campaigns. They need to ensure that the content of their advertisements—be it an informative or inspirational advertisement—has some degree of emotional, affectionate appeal cemented in the video. In video 1, the advertisement has strong emphasis on continually building an emotional connection with the consumer: a story of growth and achievement is told. Therefore, marketing managers creating an inspirational, uplifting advertisement should consider creating a developing storyline in their advertisement where the consumer becomes bound to the advertisement's characters which grow and develop throughout.

On the other hand in the Phonebloks advertisement, which is an information and technology-centred advertisement of a product, promoted that their phone will result in a heavy reduction of waste and contribute to a healthier world for all to live in. Therefore, an area for companies to target, especially technology firms, can be centred on cause-related ideas, for example recycling and promoting a healthier and 'greener' world. For example, an area for many technology firms to capitalise on would be to promote their product as a 'green' product as consumer-to-consumer affection could be enhanced by creating advertisements which promote a healthier world as consumers would be driven to show affection to others based on such environmentally focussed brands and products.

Fan et al. (2013) cited the desire to provide others with useful information as a key component in the online sharing habits of individuals. The findings produced validate this research for both video advertisement types. This shows that young adults share online video advertisements as a way of providing others information regarding a particular brand or product. Furthermore, the desire to provide others with useful information proved the greatest influence for video 2. This shows that when a video advertisement is about an interesting and informative concept, people will share this video with the point to provide their connections with useful information about a new and interesting idea or concept.

Therefore, marketing managers need to ensure that their video advertisements have relevant, useful information and content for their consumers to watch. If they do, the advertisement will become popular to watch due to the interest it will cause, as well as increase sharing of the video as people will look to provide their friends and connections with useful information about a brand or product. This may be as a result of people not wanting to spam their friends with unhelpful advertisements which will not benefit them in any way at all, and instead look to empower them with an informative and helpful advertisement which is of interest. This is especially relevant for advertisements about a product which needs explaining in the advertisement, such as for a new concept or idea, as seen in video 2. Marketing managers need to ensure they balance their advertisements by provide useful and helpful information about the product, while also presenting it all in a clever, eye-catching manner. Simply standing in front of a screen and reading out statistics and facts about a product will not be successful. But providing relevant information about a product in a clever, imaginative and 'fun' manner will achieve greater success for the advertisement.

While limited research has been conducted on the effects of expression of identity on the sharing of online advertisements, Taylor et al. (2012) recognised identity as a strong motivator for why consumers share online content. The findings of this study certainly agree with Taylor et al. (2012), particularly as expression of identity was a partial mediator for both desire to show affection as well as information. This proves that even though people share online video advertisements to benefit others with useful information and show others affection, ultimately, they are doing it for themselves to express their own personal identity. Inspirational advertisements (video 2) are a particular area where one will share the video advertisements to express their identity, and not for others (affection and information constructs), as the regression for video 2 proved.

Therefore, marketing managers need to ensure that they completely understand their target consumer and understand their needs, desires and personalities. They need to ensure that they are able to provide their consumer with an advertisement which appeals to their personality and personal identities in order for the consumer to share and send the advertisement to their friends and connections. A balance between showing emotive and informative scenes in the advertisement and also creating an advertisement which appeals to the generalised personality type of their typical consumer, or community at large is necessary. Therefore, more detailed and more accurate consumer profiling should be conducted by marketing managers to understand their consumer. Bells, in video 1, understood that South Africans are attracted to a story of success. They also understood that their whisky drinkers want to be related to that successful, hard-working but still classy individual—in the form of either the old man, or his son who has just published a book. The Phoneblok (video 2) advertisement understands the need of people who use smartphones, as well as those concerned with the environment. Marketers need to centre the consumers' needs at the heart of their advertisement messages, to appeal to their personality and identity, which we have seen is the main driver as to why people share online video advertisements.

Limitations of the Study

The main limitation of this study was the sample of test units from which data was collected. The first problem was that non-probability sampling was used. It was not feasible for the researchers to create a sampling framework due to time and budget constraints. As non-probability sampling was used, the sample cannot be said to be representative of the target population (Malhotra 2010).

The scales and videos used in this study also created a possible limitation. The videos were chosen to measure the social motivations based on the researchers' judgement and might not have been the best videos for this purpose. Due to time constraints, the researchers were unable to test different videos beforehand to find which ones would be best for measuring these social motivations. The scales used to measure the social motivations were the best that could be found in past research papers, but they contained items which were not well suited to this study. For instance, the last item in the 'Information Provided' scale was 'Explain to someone how I go about shopping for this product', which did not fit well with the content of the videos being used in this study.

Avenues for Future Research

This study measured the effects of just two social motivations; altruism and identity. Research could be done on other social motivations in order to form a more complete picture of how they affect the sharing of online video advertisements.

In trying to find answers to the question of what causes the spread of online advertising content, this study focussed on one specific type of content: online video advertisements. Further research could be done in this area by focussing on, for example online print advertisements.

This study used young adults (between 18 and 29) residing and/or studying as its target population. Similar research could be done using this same age group in other countries or other regions of the world. This would help to determine whether the results from this study are universal. Research could also be done using other age groups as a target population. Young adults share online content more than any other age group (Ho and Dempsey 2008), but this does not mean that other age groups are unimportant in online marketing, especially for products which target these age groups. Future research using the same target population as this study could look into the possible effect of gender on an individual's willingness to share online advertising videos (or other forms of online advertising content).

Two videos which were deemed to have gone 'viral' were used as the treatments for this study. More insight could perhaps be gained by comparing a 'viral' video to one that has not gone 'viral', in order to clearly show the differences between them.

References

Asur, S., & Huberman, B. A. (2010, August). Predicting the future with social media. *Proceedings of the International Conference in Web Intelligence and Intelligent Agent Technology (WI-IAT)* (pp. 492–499). Chicago: IEEE.

Berger, J., & Milkman, K. (2009). Social transmission, emotion, and the virality of online content. *Wharton Research Paper*.

Berger, J., & Milkman, K. L. (2011). What makes online content viral? *Journal of Marketing Research, 49*(2), 192–205.

Brown, J., Broderick, A. J., & Lee, N. (2007). Word of mouth communication with in online communities: Conceptualizing the online social network. *Journal of Interactive Marketing, 21*(3), 2–20.

Camarero, C., & San Jose, R. (2011). Social and attitudinal determinants of viral marketing dynamics. *Computers in Human Behaviour, 27*, 2292–2300.

Chan, K. W., & Li, S. Y. (2010). Understanding consumer-to-consumer interactions in virtual communities: The salience of reciprocity. *Journal of Business Research, 63*(9), 1033–1040.

Cheung, M. S., Anitsal, M. M., & Anitsal, I. (2007). Revisiting word-of-mouth communications: A cross-national exploration. *Journal of Marketing Theory and Practice, 15*(3), 235–249.

Chu, S. C. (2011). Viral advertising in social media: Participation in facebook groups and responses among college-aged users. *Journal of Interactive Marketing, 12*, 30–43.

Eckler, P., & Bolls, P. (2011). Spreading the virus: Emotional tone of viral advertising and its effect on forwarding intentions and attitudes. *Journal of Interactive Advertising, 11*(2), 1–11.

Escalas, J. E., & Bettman, J. R. (2005). Self-construal, reference groups, and brand meaning. *Journal of Consumer Research, 32*(3), 378–385.

Fan, Y. W., Fang, Y. H., & Wang, S. H. (2013). Factors affecting online content forwarding intention in social network. *Electronic Commerce Studies, 11*(3), 331–355.

Guadagno, R. E. Rempala, D. M., Murphy, S., & Okdie, B. M. (2013). Why do internet videos go viral? A social influence analysis. *National Science Foundation*.

Ha, L. (2008). Online advertising research in advertising journals: A review. *Journal of Current Issues and Research in Advertising, 30*, 31–48.

Hargittai, E., & Hinnant, A. (2008). Digital inequality: Differences in young adults' use of the internet. *Communication Research, 35*(5), 602–621.

Ho, J. Y. C., & Dempsey, M. (2008). Viral marketing: Motivations to forward online content. *Journal of Business Research, 63*, 1000–1006.

Khan, G., & Vong, S. (2012). Virality over Youtube: An empirical analysis. *Internet Research Journal*, 1–28.

Malhotra, N. K. (2010). *Marketing research: An applied orientation* (6th ed.). Upper Saddle River, NJ: Pearson.

Price, L. L., Feick, L. F., & Guskey, A. (1995). Everyday market helping behaviour. *Journal of Public Policy & Marketing, 14*(2), 255–266.

Schutz, W. C. (1966). *FIRO: A three dimensional theory of interpersonal behaviour*. Oxford, England: Rinehart.

Stonedahl, F., Rand, W., & Wilensky, U. (2010, July). Evolving viral marketing strategies. *Proceedings of the 12th Annual Conference on Genetic and Evolutionary Computation*, 1195–1202.

Taylor, D., Strutton, D., & Thompson, K. (2012). Self-enhancement as a motivation for sharing online advertising. *Journal of Interactive Advertising, 12*(2), 13–28.

Corporate Brand Representations in B2B Companies' Websites

Cláudia Simões, Marcelo G. Perin, and Jaywant Singh

Abstract In the business-to-business (B2B) domain, the corporate website is an effective platform for communicating to stakeholders the corporate brand (CB) features, such as personality and values. Despite the growing importance of websites as a primary means for corporate communication, research on the dimensions that companies ought to use relevant for online corporate branding is limited. This study examines the representations of CBs on the websites of B2B companies in two emerging markets—Brazil and India. The study provides insights into how B2B companies operating in these markets are managing their corporate branding. In particular the research establishes dimensions used for the representation of the CB in the company's website (e.g., CB personality, CB values). In addition, the study investigates whether the representations of CB have an impact on the company's financial performance.

We analyzed Brazilian and Indian B2B companies' websites, focusing on the pages containing corporate information and/or information about the parent company. The data collection and analysis were developed in 2 stages, entailing a pilot study and a main study. The pilot study aimed at developing and refining the description of the ways companies used for representing their CB in the websites. It further allowed for the testing of the coding procedure. The main study incorporated the final description of the CB dimensions and performance measures based on the stock index data from Bloomberg. The analysis included websites from 158 Indian and 158 Brazilian B2B companies. Findings allow the specification of relevant elements that should be used to express the CB in an online setting. The study proposes that the following dimensions should be considered to express the CB: CB values; CB

C. Simões (✉)
Open University Business School, Milton Keynes, UK
e-mail: claudia.simoes@open.ac.uk

M.G. Perin
Pontifícia Universidade Católica do Rio Grande do Sul, Porto Alegre, Brazil
e-mail: mperin@pucrs.br

J. Singh
Kingston University, Kingston upon Thames, UK
e-mail: j.singh@kingston.ac.uk

© Academy of Marketing Science 2016
L. Petruzzellis, R.S. Winer (eds.), *Rediscovering the Essentiality of Marketing*,
Developments in Marketing Science: Proceedings of the Academy of Marketing
Science, DOI 10.1007/978-3-319-29877-1_51

personality; CB heritage, and company demographics. The study's context of two emerging economies showed the stability of the dimensions when applied to companies from two different emerging countries. The study further showed a positive impact of the level of CB online expressions on business performance. The research allows drawing managerial recommendations and avenues for future research.

CEOs Who Tweet: Metaphors and Gendered Communication

William H. Locander, Daniel M. Ladik, and William B. Locander

Abstract In the nanosecond culture of today's business world, CEOs have been switching from top-down communication platforms to adopting more speedy bottom-up options prevalent in social media. While e-mail is effective for internal stakeholders and press releases sufficient for external ones, these communication channels tend to be slower, as well as, requiring multiple platforms to reach each stakeholder group. Recently, microblogs such as Twitter have become a strategic tool for CEOs to communicate with various stakeholder groups such as employees, the press, investors, and suppliers (Dunn 2010). Because tweets are limited to 140 characters, both their nature and content are important in that they not only deliver information to differing targets but also create cognitive and attitudinal effects in the audience (Hwang 2012). Moreover, these short messages are mostly accessed via our smartphones, which increases the speed to which the message is examined and consumed.

The purpose of the present research is to extend theory on what is known about how CEOs communicate with their stakeholders using Twitter. Interestingly, there has been little or no analysis for what those 140 characters tweets contain, their purpose, and the intended audience. More specifically, there are two rich literature streams, metaphoric language and gendered communication, that provide fertile ground to extend what we know about CEO's use of microblogs.

From the list "The Top 50 Chief Executive Officers (CEOs) on Twitter" (Huffington Post), ten tweet lists were drawn (five from male CEOs and five from female CEOs). For each CEO to be included, 800 tweet lines had to be available. Each sample of 800 tweets was coded so as to answer the six research questions. A total of 8000 tweets were read and metaphors identified and classified. The coding

W.H. Locander (✉)
University of Texas Pan American, Edinburg, TX, USA
e-mail: whlocander@broncs.utpa.edu

D.M. Ladik
Seton Hall University, South Orange, NJ, USA
e-mail: daniel.ladik@shu.edu

W.B. Locander
Loyola University of New Orleans, New Orleans, LA, USA
e-mail: locander@loyno.edu

© Academy of Marketing Science 2016
L. Petruzzellis, R.S. Winer (eds.), *Rediscovering the Essentiality of Marketing*,
Developments in Marketing Science: Proceedings of the Academy of Marketing
Science, DOI 10.1007/978-3-319-29877-1_52

of tweets included: (a) Sex: male, female, (b) Frequency of metaphor usage in each of nine categories, (c) Internal, External Stakeholders, (d) Managerial effectiveness, and (e) Gendered Communication Style—male or female.

The findings of this study suggest that the type of metaphoric language used by CEOs has been consistent with a previously published study predating social media (Coffman and Eblen 1987). That is, metaphors concerning physical activities (e.g., climb the organization) and anatomical references (e.g., giving an arm and a leg) are the most frequently used categories of language. Unique to this study, we found gender differences in the use of metaphoric categories with men using more "game" metaphors than females, but females used more "mechanical" and "other" metaphors than men. What is interesting is that for the top three most frequently used metaphors (physical, anatomical, and architectural), featured no differences between male and female CEOs. Another finding is that both male and female executives equally used male gendered communications while males are less apt to use female gendered communication styles. This study supports the notion that the use of metaphors by CEOs is an important element in communicating through social media channels and that male and female CEOs display some differences in their use of metaphoric language.

References available upon request.

The Effects of Quality Signals Through Website Context Based on Trust in the Internet Service

Flávio Régio Brambilla and Ciro Eduardo Gusatti

Abstract Buyers and sellers involved in a transaction have access to different amounts of information related to the quality of a product or service (Spence 1973). This phenomenon is recognized as "asymmetric information". The uncertainties arising from asymmetric information about a product potentialize the problem recognized as "adverse selection". To avoid adverse selection organizations must invest in quality signals. Wells, Valacich and Hess (2011) suggest that quality signals to the buyer in internet could be presented through the site conditions on the organization's website. This research follows a descriptive and causal approach, to establish through an experiment the cause–effect relations between investment in organization's website and confidence about the service on the internet. Wells, Valacich and Hess (2011) suggest that a potentially credible signal of quality to the buyer on the Internet could provide a very good condition to the consumer believe in the organization's website content. Schlosser, White and Lloyd (2006) argue that investment in the website of an organization could influence the perceptions of online buyers.

H1: The investment of a service organization in the development of website can be recognized by consumers on the internet.

Trust is a multidimensional construct. Cummings and Bromiley (1996) define trust in three dimensions: (1) cognitive; (2) affective; and (3) connotative. Gronroos (2000) introduced the idea of trust as an expectation of one party (buyer) to another (seller), to behave in a predictable way. Online business trust becomes even more important.

H2: The investment on the website positively influences consumer confidence about the internet service.

This study adopted an experimental design 1×3: (1) offering a service on the internet and (2) referring to three levels of perceived investment in a website (high, medium and low). Three distinct websites were created for a fictitious company and service provider. The websites were differentiated by their characteristics and volume of investment that was employed in its development. Characterization of service and

F.R. Brambilla (✉) • C.E. Gusatti
Universidade de Santa Cruz do Sul (UNISC), Santa Cruz do Sul, Brazil
e-mail: flaviobrambilla@terra.com.br; cirogusatti@gmail.com

© Academy of Marketing Science 2016   263
L. Petruzzellis, R.S. Winer (eds.), *Rediscovering the Essentiality of Marketing*,
Developments in Marketing Science: Proceedings of the Academy of Marketing
Science, DOI 10.1007/978-3-319-29877-1_53

brand were created by the authors of this study with the aim of achieving greater control of effects on the prior knowledge by the consumer. We adopted metrics of multi-item scales of semantic differential type of nine points. We include confidence about the service based on Harris and Goode (2004, 2010) and investment signal by Wells, Valacich and Hess (2011). The sample of this study is composed of 56 (43.70 %) males and 79 (56.30 %) females. All the participants are young: 122 individuals (90.37 %) 18–25 years, and the others (9.63 %) between 26 and 30. Considering Hair et al. (2005), the number of 30 observations is enough. We have had 45 records in each treatment. That is, 45 individuals (33.3 %) exposed to high, medium and low investment websites. We perform descriptive statistics and ANOVA. To test hypotheses, we accepted a significance level ($p < .05$), as considered acceptable for applied social sciences (Hair et al. 2005). The result shows significant differences between the three types of websites regarding the consumer's perception of the service organization's investment in the website. Perception of investment on the website F (219,117; $p < .0010$. The results confirm the findings from Wells, Valacich and Hess (2011) and the propositions by Schlosser, White and Lloyd (2006), Mavlanova and Koufaris Benbunan-Fich (2012). The investment in the website can be perceived by consumers on the internet. We found significant differences between the three types of websites, concerning the confidence of the consumer about service. Trust in service F (203,119; $p < .0010$. So, we confirm also the hypothesis H2. This study represents a first step to better understand the relationship between investment in quality signals and trust in websites.

References available upon request.

Brand Contamination in Social Media: Consumers' Negative Influence on Luxury Brand Perceptions—A Structured Abstract

Lorena Blasco-Arcas, Jonas Holmqvist, and Alexandra Vignolles

Introduction

The development of social media on the Internet poses a challenge for luxury brands, as managers need to walk a fine line to keep the balance between ubiquity and exclusivity in social media (Hennigs et al. 2012). Luxury brands are increasingly using social media to raise brand awareness and build relationships with their customer base and try to enhance brand experiences online (Kim and Ko 2010; Phan et al. 2011). The emergence of Web 2.0 (the development of interactive web pages) and social media thus challenges luxury brands' marketing strategies on the Internet, if these brands need to embrace mass marketing media and try to highlight the exclusivity dimension of their products at the same time (Kaplan and Haenlein 2010; Okonkwo 2009).

The luxury brands' presence on social media could risk posing a problem for their image of exclusivity as an aura of exclusivity is crucial to luxury (Bastien and Kapferer 2009). This is a delicate situation and the topic of how other consumers' influence on social media may affect consumer perceptions of luxury brands remains an unexplored area of research (Chu et al. 2013). This is especially relevant as the literature has recently highlighted that there are different luxury consumer segments based on individual motivations' variability (Han et al. 2010; Kastanakis and

L. Blasco-Arcas (✉)
University of Zaragoza, Zaragoza, Spain
e-mail: lorena@unizar.es

J. Holmqvist
KEDGE Business School, Talence, France
e-mail: jonas.holmqvist@kedgebs.com

A. Vignolles
INSEEC Business School, Paris, France
e-mail: avignolles@inseec.com

© Academy of Marketing Science 2016
L. Petruzzellis, R.S. Winer (eds.), *Rediscovering the Essentiality of Marketing*,
Developments in Marketing Science: Proceedings of the Academy of Marketing
Science, DOI 10.1007/978-3-319-29877-1_54

Balabanis 2012), but in social media they interact in the same virtual space and they are likely to influence each other. Consequently, this chapter suggests that marketers need to take into account how differences between current and aspirational customers influence brand perceptions on social media.

This chapter aims to contribute to existing marketing research on social media and luxury brands by analyzing how interacting with noncustomers may exert a negative influence on the actual luxury customers' brand perceptions. We build on the consumer contagion theory, suggesting that consumer heterogeneity in luxury brands' social media sites could lead to what we call *Brand Contamination*. Brand contamination refers to lower brand evaluations regarding the exclusivity and prestige of the luxury brand, as social media allows a large number of nonconsumers to appropriate the brand, possibly diluting its image among its actual customers.

Background

Social Media and the rise of consumer influence

The role of other customers in the focal customer behavior has attracted an increased attention in marketing research due to the emergence of social media (Blazevic et al. 2013; Labrecque et al. 2013). Web 2.0 and social media have exponentially increased consumers' possibilities to interact and communicate between them, so interpersonal influence on social media and how this influence may affect brand perceptions and product evaluations become critical in understanding online consumer behavior.

Research on interpersonal influence or C2C interactions in social media has focused on the direct interactions between consumers to explain consumer influence, but has not fully explored the role of indirect interactions (i.e., mere virtual presence) (Libai et al. 2010; Naylor et al. 2012).

Current social media sites such as Facebook, Instagram, and Twitter are profile-based media, where users create their identity through the available tools. Extant consumer research shows that profile elements on social media are a key element for customer-to-customer interactions as they act as sources of information regarding the members that interact (Lampe et al. 2007). Self-presentation online is thus an important cue to others in order to form impressions and to decide to interact (Ellison et al. 2006). Mere virtual presence of customers reflects how consumers self-presentations in social media influence other customers' brand perceptions (Naylor et al. 2012), consequently being a critical aspect to understand consumer brand evaluations in social media. Accordingly, we propose that the mere social presence of different segments of luxury customers on social media may influence brand perceptions through a process of negative contagion (i.e., brand contamination).

Contagion and consumer behavior

The law of contagion proposes that objects or persons can influence each other merely by touching directly or indirectly (Frazer 1959; Rozin and Nemeroff 1990). Research in the fields of anthropology and consumer behavior has demonstrated that this influence can be either positive (i.e., positive contagion, Argo et al. 2008) or negative (i.e., negative contagion or contamination, Rozin et al. 1986; Morales and Fitzsimmons 2007).

Recently, the field of branding has begun to focus on aspects of contagion. Newman and Dahr (2014) analyze the role of country of origin and brand perceptions, and corroborate that products manufactured in the original manufacturing location are believed to contain the essence of the brand, providing first insights about the influence of contagion in brand perceptions. This is in line with luxury research holding that a luxury brand can never outsource or move country, as part of its inherent value is connected to its traditions and its place of origin (Bastien and Kapferer 2014).

Nemeroff and Rozin (1994) suggest that there are two underlying processes of contagion: physical contagion and nonphysical contagion (i.e., interpersonal moral contagion). Physical contagion refers to the real contact of the recipient to a source of potential contagion. This contact is perceived as a transmission of specific residues (e.g., body heat, germs, or odors) or the "essence" of the source of contagion being left behind after contact. Nonphysical contagion refers to the interpersonal symbols attached to a person that evokes the contagion. Thus, the contagious object/ person acts as a reminder or an association to pleasant or unpleasant aspects. Importantly, the negative contagion or contamination has been shown to be the outcome primarily of a residue model that results from physical contact. Conversely, positive contagion has been found to be the result strictly of a symbolic interaction model that is based on interpersonal/moral factors (Nemeroff and Rozin 1994).

Brand Contamination in Social Media: The Influence of Consumers' Heterogeneity

Building on the contagion theory, we define brand contamination as the process in which either direct or indirect contacts between consumers in social media lead to lower brand perceptions. Consequently, we consider that brand contamination in social media is the result of a symbolic interaction process mainly based on interpersonal factors such as consumer posts and comments on social media and the profile information displayed.

We specifically focus on the influence of indirect contacts (i.e., mere presence through profile cues) between actual customers and aspirational customers in social media as a source of brand contamination that is potentially relevant to managing luxury brands online.

In order to understand how brand contamination for luxury brands operates in social media, we suggest social distance as an underlying mechanism. Within the broader field of psychological distance, the concept of social distance refers to the distance people perceive between themselves and others (Stephan et al. 2010). This distance that people perceive between themselves and others automatically activates even when not related to the task at hand (Bar-Anan et al. 2007). Adapting the concept of social distance to a luxury context, this chapter emphasizes how perceptions of differences between actors go beyond the demographic aspects such as age, gender, or ethnicity, but that other, subtler, indicators of social distance emerge through interactions, including social status differences (Stephan et al. 2010).

Drawing upon on this understanding of social distance as well as contagion theory, we propose that customers in search of reaching a higher social status to which they aspire will subconsciously but automatically react to perceived differences in social distance between themselves and other customers with whom they interact. Furthermore, we posit that customers who want to differentiate themselves from what they perceive as a lower social status will also subconsciously or consciously react to the differences in social status between their own status and the status of noncustomers interested in the brand. This chapter thus concurs with Fuchs et al. (2013) who say that luxury brands *"stimulate vertical comparisons, create social distance, and facilitate downward comparison accompanied by a boost in agentic feelings (e.g. feeling superior to others)"* (p. 78).

We further build on Argo et al. (2006) to identify main cues of contamination for luxury brands in social media. These authors introduce three main cues that influence consumer-product contamination: the proximity of the source of contamination, the time elapsed since the contact occurred, and the number of contact sources. Taking these cues as the starting point, we build on social distance and mere social presence to explain brand contamination in social media, suggesting the following propositions (Table 1).

Discussion

Is social media on the verge of changing the management of luxury perceptions? Previous marketing research recognizes that the prestige that luxury products can bring is an important part of luxury brand's appeal (Han et al. 2010; Roper et al. 2013), but that these same products cease to be luxurious once they become common and no longer serve as a social signifier, or its significance is diminished due to brand contamination effects (Kapferer and Bastien 2009). This chapter argues that the emergence of social media adds a layer of complexity to this situation, and that the effects of social media on luxury remain poorly understood.

Marketing research could ask whether luxury brands should even be present on social media. This chapter holds that the intent of the question is relevant, but also something of a non sequitur, as the nature of social media leaves luxury brands with no choice concerning presence or absence. Even if the brand is not present in the

Table 1 Theoretical propositions

Propositions	Supporting literature
Proposition 1a: Extensive consumer display of using a product/service on social media leads to brand contamination as it decreases the exclusivity of the luxury brand	Brand logo display (brand prominence) may lead to brand contamination (Han et al. 2010)
	User-designed products have a negative influence on luxury brand perceptions (Fuchs et al. 2013)
Proposition 1b: The negative effects of brand contamination via social media are particularly important when aspiring customers display their use of counterfeit brands	Brand logo display (brand prominence) may lead to brand contamination (Han et al. 2010)
	User-designed products have a negative influence on luxury brand perceptions (Fuchs et al. 2013)
Proposition 2: Brand contamination on social media is influenced by the proximity of contacts or sources of contamination	Associative vs. dissociative behavior of luxury consumers may influence brand contamination (Han et al. 2010)
	Perceived social distance between subjects may increase brand contamination (Stephan et al. 2010)
Proposition 3a: The number of potential contact sources of contagion on social media (e.g., composition of customer base on the brand social media site) influences brand contamination	Perceived differences between consumers foster associative and dissociative behavior (Han et al. 2010)
Proposition 3b: The number of aspirational customers in the luxury brand social media site is a source of brand contamination for actual customers	The degree of heterogeneity of the customer base in social media influences brand perceptions (Naylor, Lamberton and West 2012)
	Dissimilar customers foster inferences of low commonality and may lead to brand contamination perceptions (Aaker et al. 2000; Berger and Heat 2008)

form of an official brand page, fan pages for famous luxury brands are omnipresent and the absence of an official page will not discourage aspirational customers from associating with the brand. For this reason, the chapter suggests that an official presence on social media is likely beneficial for the brand, but proposes that the purpose of this presence may be as much aimed at containing association with brand as spreading brand awareness. A low key and tasteful official brand page on social media that retains an aura of distance may be more beneficial to the brand image than being absent and allow dedicated fan pages to set the tone of the brand on social media. A better understanding about what are the main influencing factors and how to avoid brand contamination is a critical aspect of managing a social media strategy for luxury brands.

References available upon request.

Disagreement in Online Ratings: The Effects of Standard Deviation and Skewness of Customer Rating Distributions on Product Quality Perceptions

Sarah Küsgen, Sören Köcher, and Stefanie Paluch

Abstract The way people buy things has fundamentally changed. For instance, due to the internet's growing popularity users can easily interact with each other and share their opinions and experiences about products and services on review websites such as TripAdvisor and Yelp. As a consequence, when making purchase decisions people increasingly rely on online product ratings provided by consumers who previously purchased products as information sources to infer the quality of the available purchase options (e.g., Hu et al. 2008; Li and Hitt 2008; Simonson and Rosen 2014). In addition, consumers' confidence in these reviews is stunningly growing. In 2012, 70 % of participants in a Nielsen (2012) study indicated that they trusted online reviews, which represents an increase of 15 % within a 4 years period. Accordingly, consumers' reliance in these reviews posted by unknown consumers seems to outperform their trust in traditional media (Cheung and Thadani 2012).

Given the great popularity of online reviews, it is hardly surprising that a broad body of literature has been devoted to acquire insights into the effects of this type of electronic word-of-mouth (see Cheung and Thadani 2012 for an extensive review). Most of this research concentrates on the effect of review valence revealing that average ratings are positively related to sales (e.g., Chevalier and Mayzlin 2006; Dellarocas et al. 2007; Godes and Mayzlin 2004; Li and Hitt 2008; Liu 2006; Luca 2011). However, these studies implicitly assume that customers solely focus on the scales of review scores (Hu et al. 2008), neglecting other distribution characteristics. Although the simple average might be the most salient distribution attribute, customers may also pay attention to other distribution characteristics reflecting the degree of disagreement between reviewers' evaluations. Therefore, several researchers focused on the standard deviation of rating distributions which provides a measure for said heterogeneity in customer opinions. However, findings on this

S. Küsgen (✉) • S. Paluch
RWTH Aachen University, Aachen, Germany
e-mail: kuesgen@time.rwth-aachen.de; paluch@time.rwth-aachen.de

S. Köcher
TU Dortmund University, Dortmund, Germany
e-mail: soeren.koecher@tu-dortmund.de

© Academy of Marketing Science 2016
L. Petruzzellis, R.S. Winer (eds.), *Rediscovering the Essentiality of Marketing*,
Developments in Marketing Science: Proceedings of the Academy of Marketing
Science, DOI 10.1007/978-3-319-29877-1_55

distribution characteristic are notably ambiguous, ranging from positive (Clemons et al. 2006; Lu et al. 2014) over non-significant (Chen et al. 2011; Chintagunta et al. 2010) to negative effects (Bao and Chang 2014; Hu et al. 2010; Zhu and Zhang 2010) on sales and related performance figures.

Hence, the purpose of this research is to generate a better understanding of the impact of standard deviation in online ratings on customers' inferences about the product under consideration. Therefore, we incorporate a previously disregarded distribution attribute—namely, skewness—and investigate the extent to which the effects of standard deviation on perceived product quality depend on this distribution characteristic.

The findings of three empirical studies ($N_1 = 197$, $N_2 = 214$, $N_3 = 141$) reveal a positive effect of standard deviation on quality perceptions when the distribution of ratings is left skewed which reverts for right skewed distributions.

References available upon request.

Factors Affecting Online Review Helpfulness: Review and Reviewer Components

Sahar Karimi and Fang Wang

Abstract Today's consumers rely heavily on the opinion of other consumers when making purchase decisions. Understanding the degree to which a review contributes to a purchase decision, its "helpfulness", is important to online businesses. Despite the growing number of studies on online reviews, the impact of visual cues on consumer's evaluation of review helpfulness has remained underexplored. This chapter examines the effect of reviewer image, along with previously examined review attributes, such as review depth, valence, and equivocality, on review helpfulness. With a sample of 1400 reviews from mobile gaming applications, we report that reviewer image can significantly enhance consumers' evaluation of review helpfulness. We did not find significant differential effects of image types (i.e. self, family, or random images) on review helpfulness. The results call for further research on the impact of visual cues as well as reviewer attributes on review helpfulness.

S. Karimi (✉)
Edge Hill University, Ormskirk, UK
e-mail: karimis@edgehill.ac.uk

F. Wang
Wilfrid Laurier University, Waterloo, ON, Canada
e-mail: fwang@wlu.ca

© Academy of Marketing Science 2016
L. Petruzzellis, R.S. Winer (eds.), *Rediscovering the Essentiality of Marketing*,
Developments in Marketing Science: Proceedings of the Academy of Marketing
Science, DOI 10.1007/978-3-319-29877-1_56

Social Media Mix in the University Communication Plan: A Bridge Towards Public Engagement: Structured Abstract

Vittoria Marino and Letizia Lo Presti

Introduction

The role of Higher Education in the social context has been always object of debate within the academic community and not only. Universities have always been responsible for the traditional functions of education and knowledge transfer but, across all the European countries, a "Third Mission" imposes to universities to be also a "partner" that collaborates at the community's growth. In this sense, social networks can be a tool to create an effective bridge between research, teaching, and public services by means of the possibility of sharing information, opinions, and ideas in real time and in a multimedia way. This research investigates which forms of social media communication are mainly used by the European Universities to engage their own stakeholders by performing a comparative analysis of the posts in Twitter and Facebook. Furthermore, this research deals with the problem of gauging the engagement rate in the University by means of social network advancing the current state-of-the-art about the analysis of the social media use within public engagement strategies.

Background

In the academic literature, the concept of engagement has been considered an important component for the survival of higher Education institutions and therefore it is believed that the "engaged campus" in the University activity plans allows the University to reach the tripartite mission: research, teaching, and public service (Furco 2010). Relatively little research captures the notion of engagement starting

V. Marino (✉) • L.L. Presti
University of Salerno, Fisciano, Italy
e-mail: vmarino@unisa.it; llopresti@unisa.it

© Academy of Marketing Science 2016
L. Petruzzellis, R.S. Winer (eds.), *Rediscovering the Essentiality of Marketing*,
Developments in Marketing Science: Proceedings of the Academy of Marketing
Science, DOI 10.1007/978-3-319-29877-1_57

from an empirical point of view, even if some contributions, limited to restricted case studies, already exist in this sense (Cavallo and Romenti 2012). Social media can be considered effective tools to establish constructive relationships among people. In particular, Twitter and Facebook seem to be more likely to stimulate public dialogue. Due to the peculiar features of these social media, previous works explored the effect that social networks have on the college student engagement (Junco et al. 2010; Junco 2011) whereas relatively little research captures the effect on the community engagement even if a preliminary study on Twitter was conducted by Linvill et al. (2012). For this reason, a study on public engagement in the social network environment can better shine a light on this new direction. All the above-described works are missing of a comparative analysis of the different social network use; such analysis might highlight which forms of communication are mainly used by the Universities to communicate with the stakeholders, and what is the probability of raising their engagement. Currently there is not a study about the social network use in the European Universities. The proposed research wants to contribute to the understanding of the importance and the role of social networks inside the strategic community engagement providing, at the same time, an overview of the current level of public engagement within European Universities.

Methodology

A systematic sample of European Universities was drawn from the comprehensive list of universities found in the online edition of "*Ranking web universities 2013–2014.*" Every ninth University listed in the European University rankings was chosen for inclusion in the study. This procedure resulted in a sample composed by 345 European Universities (10 % of population of 3.379 universities). On this sample, an exploratory analysis was conducted to verify the presence on the main social network platforms: Twitter, Facebook, and Linkedin.

The universities that were found in all of the three social networks or that were found at least in Facebook and in Twitter were included in the sample, while the others were discarded. The final sample was composed by 201 Universities (58.2 % of the systematic sample). For each of these institutions, 10 tweets and 10 Facebook posts published by October 14, 2014 were sampled for inclusion in the study for a total of 4020 posts to analyze.

The results presented in this chapter have been obtained on a pilot sample composed by 1000 posts (500 tweets and 500 posts) drawn on the first 50 universities (about 25 % of the final sample). Three different analyses have been carried on these posts. A functional analysis has permitted to study the posts based on five categories adapted from the categories defined in (Hambrick et al. 2010): (1) *Information Sharing*: messages with the intent to inform followers or friends; (2) *Content*: messages with images or videos; (3) *Fanship*: exhortations, exclamations stimulating public and/or internal Community "support," and creating "sense of community"; (4) *Interactivity*: messages for stimulating the interaction with followers and friends; (5)

Promotional: messages that promote an event or activity involving the Community. A target analysis has permitted to identify the stakeholder whom the message was addressed to: Staff, Student, People (external Community including citizens, institutions, profit/nonprofit organizations etc. that could have an interest in the university activities) and University Community (community within the university campus). Finally, a further analysis was designed to gauge the tweetability and likeability rate of the posts. To get a more objective classification of the posts, two coders were asked to assign the posts to the designed categories and identify the targeted stakeholders based on their own judgment, while discussing the eventual divergence. A reliability test was performed for the category and stakeholder classification by means of the Cohen's kappa, providing score of .87 and .83 respectively.

Results and Discussion

The exploratory analysis provides with an initial overview of the current social network use in the European Universities. Figure 1 shows that, considering the main social networks Twitter, Facebook, and Linkedin, the 50% of 345 European Universities (that is 173 Universities) have an account on all of the three social networks, while only the 6% is not present in at least one of them. Facebook seems to be the most used social network among the European Universities. None of the 345 analyzed Universities chose to use only Twitter to communicate with their own stakeholders, while only the 3% of the sample decided to use only Linkedin. As concern the posts analysis, the type of content and the targeted stakeholder of 1000 posts published on the Twitter's and the Facebook's official pages were evaluated.

Fig. 1 Percentage of universities using the main social networks

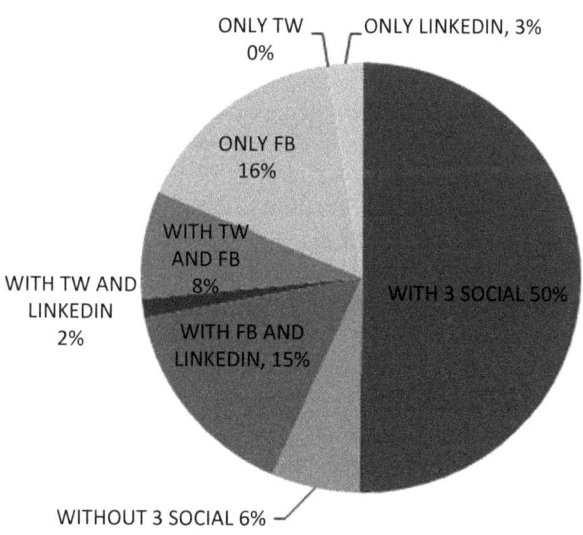

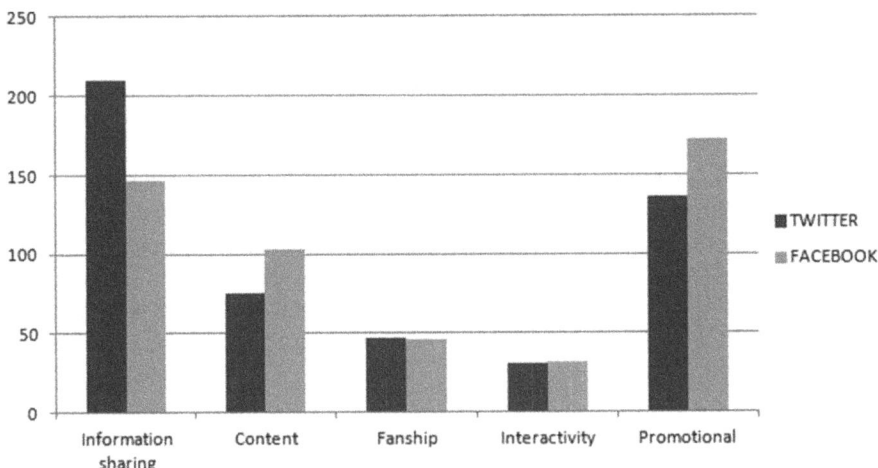

Fig. 2 Distribution of Twitter and Facebook on the 5 communication categories

As shown in Fig. 2, Twitter and Facebook seem to be mostly used to transfer information and promotional content offering a "word-of-mouth" service for the whole "Community" (both for the external and university Community). In contrast to Twitter, Facebook is mainly used for posts belonging to the category "Content." This suggests that the Universities use Facebook to supply "University storytelling" through multimedia posts.

Figure 3 shows that "University Community" and "Student" seem to be the most prominent stakeholders whom the posts in each category are addressed to, even if the distribution changes across the social networks. The category "Fanship" has a similar frequency in the two social networks but the targeted stakeholder distributions change considerably in Twitter and Facebook. In Facebook (see Table 1), the categories "Promotional," "Information Sharing," and "Interactivity" seem to address more the students than the other stakeholders (59%, 44%, and 56% in each category, respectively) while the categories "Content" and "Fanship" seem to address mainly the University Community. In Twitter, instead, the categories "Interactivity" and "Promotional" seem to address more the Student, Staff, and University Community, while all other categories seem to address mostly the University Community.

This result suggests that European Universities try to create an "engaged campus" using both the social networks. To evaluate the ability of a social network to be a valuable tool for involving the community, an analysis of the retweet and the "I Like" was conducted. This analysis made it possible to measure the effectiveness of communication in increasing the public engagement. Therefore by this analysis it is possible to evaluate if the European Universities are oriented towards public engagement, and which social network seems to be more effective.

To estimate the engagement, the retweetability rate was calculated as described in Suh et al. (2010). In analogy with the retweetability rate, a likeability rate has been defined. These rates gauge the probability that a post in a certain category can be

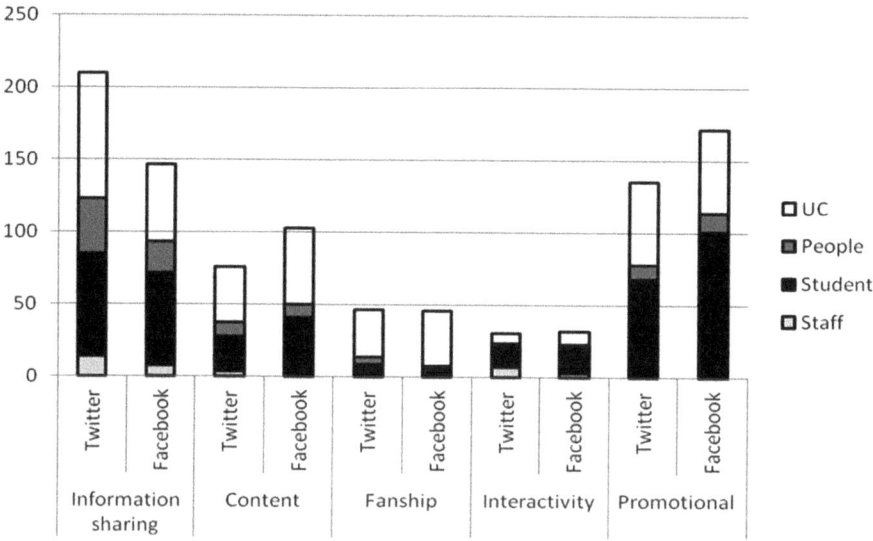

Fig. 3 Distribution of communication categories per stakeholder in Twitter and Fb

Table 1 Distribution of communication categories per stakeholder in Twitter and Fb

		Staff (%)	Student (%)	People (%)	UC (%)
Information sharing	Twitter	7	34	18	41
	Facebook	5	44	14	37
Content	Twitter	5	32	13	50
	Facebook	1	39	9	51
Fanship	Twitter	0	19	11	70
	Facebook	0	13	4	83
Interactivity	Twitter	23	48	6	23
	Facebook	9	56	6	28
Promotional	Twitter	1	49	7	43
	Facebook	0	59	8	34

liked or retweeted. Table 2 reports the p-value of the Fisher's exact test, the retweetability rate, and the likeability rate. There are significant relations between the number of tweet/post and the number of their retweet/"I Like" in all the categories both in Twitter and Facebook with the only exception for the Content and Promotional categories on Twitter. The highest retweetability and likeability rates resulted in the "Content" and "Fanship" categories (retweetability: 1.2 and 1.99; likeability: 1.14 and 2.71, respectively). These categories usually collect contents related to emotion and experience, both essential components of the engagement construct. The category "Promotional" seems to have little chance to engage followers/fans especially in Facebook (retweetability: .75, likeability: .41). Low probability of engagement is

Table 2 Retweetability and likeability rates for communication categories and stakeholders

	Tweets	%	Retweets	%	P (Fisher's exact test)	Retweetability rate	Post	%	I Like	%	P (Fisher's exact test)	Likeability rate
Information sharing	210	42	552	41	.000**	.97	147	29	3895	34	.043**	1.14
Content	76	15	209	15	.190	1.02	103	21	2722	23	.072*	1.14
Fanship	47	9	253	19	.000**	1.99	46	9	2894	25	.023**	2.71
Interactivity	31	6	63	5	.001**	.75	32	6	457	4	.000**	.62
Promo	136	27	277	20	.148	.75	172	34	1631	14	.010**	.41
Staff	27	5	75	6	.000**	1.03	12	2	84	1	.000**	.30
Student	185	37	572	42	.009**	1.14	229	46	3902	34	.000**	.73
People	65	13	164	12	.007**	.93	47	9	630	5	.000**	.58
University Community	223	45	543	40	.004**	.90	212	42	6983	60	.251	1.42

**p<0.01 *p<0.05

also noticeable in the category "Interactivity" (retweetability: .75; likeability: .62). The category "Information sharing" seems to be more engaging in Facebook (1.14) than in Twitter (.97), even if it is the most retweeted category. Finally, looking at the stakeholder to whom the communication seems to have been addressed, in Twitter, the content addressed to the Staff and Students is more likely to be retweeted than in Facebook, while in Facebook the likelihood that a content can receive an "I Like" is higher for messages addressed to the entire University Community. In conclusion, more than the 50% of the analyzed Universities have their own social presence on Twitter and Facebook. The two social networks, albeit with some differences, are used as tools to disseminate information, multimedia content, and promotion; the target of the communication seems to be mostly the University Community and Students. The European Universities are oriented towards the "Engaged Campus" (Furco 2010) and the engagement is fully verified in the categories "Information sharing," "Content," and "Fanship." Yet, few posts are addressed to "People" and to Staff. Comparing the two social networks (Twitter and Facebook), the most effective tool to involve the University Community seems to be Facebook, especially when the messages are related to "word-of-mouth" information, multimedia content or are related to the "University brand" concept; Twitter seems to be more engaging when the messages are of interest to Students and Staff, especially if related to the "Content" or "Fanship" categories.

References

Cavallo, T., & Romenti, S. (2012). Università italiane e territorio: Analisi di statuti e siti internet in ottica di community relations e civic engagement. *In Conference Proceedings—Sinergie XXIV Annual Conference*, October 18–19, Lecce, Italy.

Furco, A. (2010). The engaged campus: Toward a comprehensive approach to public engagement. *British Journal of Educational Studies, 58*(4), 375–390.

Hambrick, M. E., Simmons, J. M., Greenhalgh, G. P., & Greenwell, T. C. (2010). Understanding professional Athletes'. Use of Twitter: A content analysis of athlete tweets. *International Journal of Sport Communication, 3*(4), 454–471.

Junco, R. (2011). The relationship frequency of Facebook use, participation in Facebook activities, and student engagement. *Computers & Education, 58*, 162–171.

Junco, R., Heiberger, G., & Loken, E. (2010). The effect of Twitter on college student engagement and grades. *Journal of Computer Assisted Learning, 27*(2), 119–132.

Linvill, D. L., McGee, S. E., & Hicks, L. K. (2012). Colleges' and universities' use of Twitter: A content analysis. *Public Relations Review, 38*(4), 636–638.

Suh, B., Hong, L., Pirolli, P., & Chi, E. H. (2010). Want to be retweeted? Large scale analytics on factors impacting retweet in Twitter network. *In Social computing (socialcom), 2010 IEEE second international conference on, August 20–22* (pp. 177–184). Minneapolis, MN.

How People Evaluate a Product in an Online Environment: The Role of Uncertainty and Liking Feeling

Francesca Checchinato, Isabella Procidano, and Marta Pisani

Introduction

Although it is well known that travellers look at other travellers' opinions and recommendations to plan their trips, and the number of people reviewing touristic attractions is increasing, little is known about how people judge them. Numerous studies have examined user behaviour in creating contents and participating in the online community using various methods, but research that investigates how consumers express opinions about hotel attributes is still lacking. In particular, since expressed preferences as well as ratings could be the result of both the uncertainty of consumers in evaluating an item and the liking feeling about the item (D'Elia and Piccolo 2005), the aim of this chapter is to understand the role of these components in the evaluating process, in order to segment the market and to define different users' profile.

Background

Previous research about user generated contents (hereafter, UGC) and the rating sites can be divided into two main topics: (1) research related to the use of UGC as a source of information for other consumers and (2) research aimed at understanding contributors, in order to explain their behaviour and characteristics. In this research we focus on the latter point.

In order to understand reviewers' behaviour, it is important to analyse "why", "how" and "what" users evaluate in travel websites such as TripAdvisor. The three

F. Checchinato (✉) • I. Procidano • M. Pisani
Ca' Foscari University of Venice, Venice, Italy
e-mail: f.checchinato@unive.it; Isabella.procidano@unive.it; marta.pisani89@gmail.com

© Academy of Marketing Science 2016
L. Petruzzellis, R.S. Winer (eds.), *Rediscovering the Essentiality of Marketing*,
Developments in Marketing Science: Proceedings of the Academy of Marketing
Science, DOI 10.1007/978-3-319-29877-1_58

questions could be related to each other, since the reasons why users evaluate an object could affect the way a review is written.

Most of the previous studies attempt to understand why people are willing to share their information and contribute their knowledge for free, as it happens in the rating sites such as TripAdvisor and Expedia. McLure, Wasko and Faraj (2000) analysed why people provide knowledge in communities of practice. Some results might be helpful for rating sites as they state that people believe that sharing information is "the right thing to do". Yang and Lai (2011) showed that internal self-concept-based motivation significantly influences the knowledge-sharing intention of Wikipedia contributors. Park et al. (2011) demonstrated that ego-involvement is highly associated with both the attitude toward uploading video content online and the intention to upload. So motivations are related both to social and personal reasons. Other scholars analyse barriers faced in the online content creation (so, the "why not"), finding that some users prefer to participate in communities asking questions rather than adding contents because they need to know more before creating their own contents (Preece et al. 2004). One of the main reasons not to create contents is related to the fact that users are not sure if their knowledge is important, accurate or relevant to specific topics, so their feelings of incompetency become a barrier to share opinions. In the travel sector time constrictions seem to be the main reason for not contributing, but also a lack of experience has been mentioned (Gretzel et al. 2007).

An important factor that affects evaluation process is the consumer uncertainty: usually analysed in the buying process, it is related to the difficulty of comparing options and choosing the right product (Broniarczyk and Griffin 2014). Recently, consumer uncertainty has been analysed in the evaluation and expression of preferences through ratings context; some research (D'Elia and Piccolo 2005; Piccolo and D'Elia 2008) shows that consumer uncertainty adds up to the basic feeling about an item. It was also found that splitting the consumer evaluation into two components—uncertainty and liking feeling—can be helpful in explaining how users evaluate an object, such as a hotel. This model was adopted to explain users' responses during survey, but since users express (ordinal) preferences also voluntarily, providing reviews and rates in travel website such as TripAdvisor, we test the model in this new context in order to verify the theoretical assumptions.

In the rating sites, consumers share their opinions in the form of (1) qualitative descriptions of experiences and (2) ratings. The latter one could be considered the numerical expression of customer satisfaction, a post-purchase evaluative judgment. Therefore considering how the evaluation process might affect the ratings, we test if in voluntary contexts—where consumers decide to judge an item and at the same time he/she can read how previous consumers have judged it—the uncertainty components still exist. In particular we assume:

Hypothesis 1: *In UGC context, in addition to the liking feeling, the evaluations expressed by users also depend on consumer uncertainty.*

Moreover, from the previously mentioned research about motivations and contributors' characteristics in the UGC, we posit that the level of user experience could affect the evaluation process, since high levels of experience reduce barriers to adding reviews and, at the same time, they improve user competences in judging items. The same assumptions are drawn from the classical theory of consumer behaviour that points out that customer satisfaction is influenced by the customers' background (Broniarczyk and Griffin 2014), among the others. So we test:

Hypothesis 2: *The more is the experience in evaluating and rating touristic attractions, the more the liking feeling influences the final review, since the uncertainty component becomes lower.*

We also would verify whether Tripadvisors contributors can be clustered in distinct profiles based on the uncertainty and liking feeling components and on their main travel purpose: leisure or business. The latter has been proven to be a factor that affect consumer expectations and so the satisfaction. As suggested by Yavas and Babakus (2005), hoteliers should conduct guests satisfaction for the two clusters.

Research Method

The more useful statistical tool for analysing preference/evaluation is the mixture model proposed by D'Elia and Piccolo (2008), known as CUB, i.e. Covariate Uniform Binomial, a generalization of MUB, Mixture Uniform Binomial (D'Elia and Piccolo 2005). This model is characterized by a significant flexibility because the covariates of raters are used in order to define and estimate heterogeneity in the evaluation of the perceived quality due to the same covariates. Regarding CUB (0,0) (the MUB model) liking/feeling and uncertainty are represented by a linear combination, Y, of two different random variables: a shifted Binomial and a Uniform; so, Y describes the process that leads a respondent to express the final rating:

$$P(\gamma = y) = \pi \binom{m-1}{y-1}(1-\xi)^{y-1}\xi^{m-y} + (1-\pi)\frac{1}{m}$$

where $y=1,2,...,m$, $m>3$ is a discrete set of values of an hedonic scale; $\xi c[0,1]$ and $\pi c[0,1]$ are the parameters characterizing the shape of the probability distribution of the mixture model. The model postulates the existence of two subgroups of raters, whose evaluation is characterized by a different weight assigned, respectively, to the component of liking/feeling and uncertainty: the informed/thoughtful subgroup and the uninformed/instinctive one. In such a way, the coefficients π and $(1-\pi)$ can be interpreted, respectively, as a measure of their proportion in the population. In the evaluation process $(1-\pi)$ represents a measure of uncertainty (1 maximum uncertainty, 0 no uncertainty), while $(1-\xi)$ measures the liking/feeling (0 disliking, 1 maximum rating).

To test our hypotheses, we focused our research on hotel reviews on TripAdvisor, a leader website in the travel industry. Since hotel ratings also depend on the destination (Bulchand-Gidumal et al. 2013), we analyse hotel reviews in a single destination,

Table 1 CUB (0,0) model summary

$1-\pi$	$1-\xi$	$(1-\pi)/m$	AIC	ICON	DISS
.133	.867	.027	1316.041	.28	.02
(.026)	(.009)	(.005)			

Standard error is reported within brackets

Venice, that is an important touristic destination of the world. Moreover, we restricted our analysis to four-star hotels in order to have a (presumably) standard quality about the rated items. For each hotel, the first ten reviews (the first page of the hotel page) were considered. For each review, we collected the rating (from 1 to 5) for the considered hotel, the trip-purpose (family, couple, friends, business or solo) and the user profile descriptors—number of reviews, number of hotel reviews, number of cities for which reviews are made, and number of helpful votes provided by other TripAdvisor members for the written reviews.

Results and Discussion

A total of 731 reviews were collected and used for our analysis. The average rate is high (4.273) as expected from four-star hotels. In Table 1 the estimated parameters for a CUB (0,0) are reported and the values of AIC and ICON (Information Content) are showed in order to evaluate the goodness of fit. Moreover the normalized dissimilarity index (Diss) is reported: only 2 % of units should be moved among the categories in order to get a perfect fit.

Then a CUB(1,1) model with covariate (reviews' number for each reviewer) was estimated in order to investigate if this variable, as a proxy of users' experience, impacts on the respondents' ratings.

On the basis of the results we can argue that CUB (1,1) performs better than the model without covariates (lower AIC (1308.07) and higher ICON (.29)). The estimated parameters from CUB (1,1) are statistically significant and are used in order to calculate the uncertainty and the liking/feeling for each respondent. So we can state that the uncertainty plays a role in consumers' evaluation process and can be added up to the basic liking feeling. Therefore hypothesis 1 is supported.

The Fig. 1 represents, respectively, uncertainty and liking/feeling versus the number of reviews carried out by raters. The higher is the number of reviews, the lower is the level of uncertainty in the evaluation. At the same time, the influence of the liking/disliking feeling becomes higher since the ranking gets lower, it means that after evaluating and "consuming" a high number of touristic attractions, consumers become more critical. Therefore, also hypothesis 2 is supported postulating a relevant role played by experience in customer evaluations.

Moreover, in order to identify users with similar expectations (related to the purpose trip) we performed a cluster analysis using uncertainty and liking/feeling estimated by the CUB(1,1) as clustering variables.

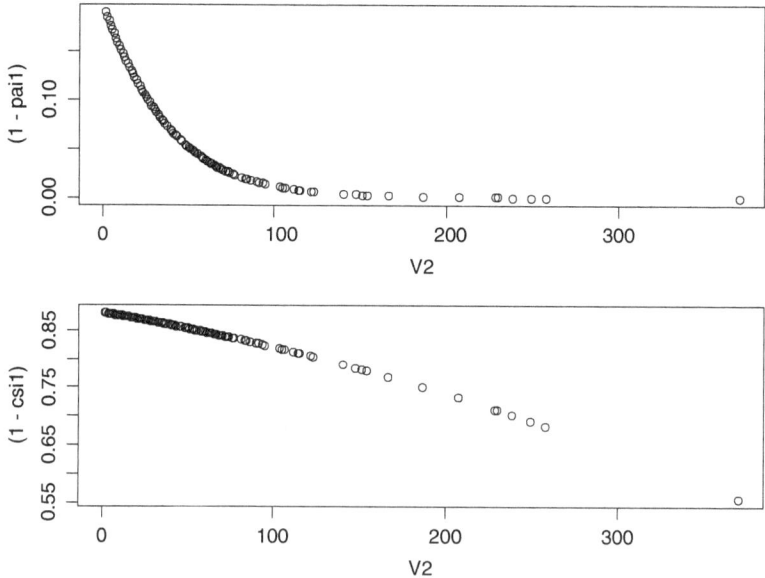

Fig. 1 Uncertainty and liking/feelings vs. number of reviews

Table 2 Clustering and profiling variables: average and relative frequency

	C1	C2	C3	C4	Whole sample
Rate	4.234	4.178	4.298	4.320	4.273
Number of reviews	13.010	100.397	30.742	3.214	24.345
Business	.088	.164	.097	.060	.089
Friends	.075	.123	.056	.102	.087
Couple	.723	.548	.621	.651	.651
Family	.100	.137	.202	.163	.150
Solo	.012	.027	.024	.023	.021
1-pai1	.141	.022	.089	.18	.129
1-csi1	.874	.817	.865	.879	.867
Size (number of statistical units)	159	73	124	215	571

The Euclidean distance and K-means method were used. Four groups are obtained on the basis of higher silhouette index (equal to .5). In the Table 2 the average of all variables for each group (C1,C2,C3,C4) and for the whole sample are reported. The variable for profiling the clusters regarding the trip-purpose declared by reviewer. In TripAdvisor, reviewers get different types of star badges based on the number of reviews they have posted, our cluster analysis supports this division, adding components related how reviewers evaluate a touristic attraction. Users with low experience (C1 and C4 in our analysis, from white to green star badges in TripAdvisor clusters) have the higher level of uncertainty and liking/feeling. It is interesting to point out that in C1 cluster 72.3 % of the reviews are about couple travel. Cluster C2 might be associated to TripAdvisor super contributors (gold star badge): they have the lower level of uncertainty and liking/feeling, in this group we can find the higher percentage of reviews of people who travel for business and with friends. Cluster C3 has the higher percentage of rates about travel with family experiences.

Even if the trip-purpose does not explain the uncertainty and liking feeling, it helps to understand the clusters and which hotels' travellers are more used to write a review.

In this research we demonstrate that also in a voluntary context, rates depend also by uncertainty and the experience plays a role in reducing it. Segmentation helps hoteliers to define different strategy to cope with the different guests profile. Our findings suggest that affecting experienced customers' opinions is more difficult for hotel managers because they are not uncertain. Experienced evaluators tend to be more critical about the hotel service, maybe because they better know what they want, so hoteliers should find the way to know their opinion during their stay in order to drive the right expectations and to find solutions for unsatisfactory situations. Moreover our findings show that "how" reviewers evaluate touristic attractions might be helpful in order to define clusters, contributing to enhance our knowledge about Internet users' behaviour and patterns. Understanding the level of liking/feeling and uncertainty of customers—and not only which attributes they value—can help hotel managers to better know their customers and adopt incentives to stimulate reviews when they face travellers that stay in their hotel in couple and not for business reasons. By understanding the users' concerns and the related level of uncertainty, managers can ultimately define effective strategies and enhance their impact. Online and offline promotions might be developed in order to reach the different groups.

This is the first step of a wide research that aims at analysing how people create online content. Adding more destinations, hotels and touristic attractions' categories, and rating websites it will be possible to enhance our comprehension of how users evaluate items. Moreover adding information about what reviewers evaluate might contribute to the understanding of their behaviour.

References available upon request.

Facebook Fascination of School Children: Some Demographic Insights

Madhupa Bakshi

Introduction

If I am on an island I would not bother even if there is no one as long as there is Facebook is a common sentiment among the school age children using Facebook in India. They are between the age of 13 and 18 years and 40 % of them are online every other day and 53 % are involved in social networking (Economic Times 2013). India ranks number three in Facebook usage in the entire world and Facebook penetration is as high as 73.3 % among online people. Add to this the fact that 75 % of people in this group are below the age of 35 (Times of India 2012). Communication scholars have extensively used the uses and gratification theory to explain internet and social media usage (Charney and Greenberg 2001; LaRose and Eastin 2004; Sheldon 2008; Tewksbury and Althaus 2000). In the Indian context, there are similar researches (Gadekar et al. 2011; Maniar and Deesawala 2011), but none assess the Facebook usage of school going children particularly the impact of brands on them. This particular cohort is important because they would determine the patterns of social media usage in the future.

Literature Review

The most oft used definition of social media is that of Kaplan and Heinlein by which they have categorized Facebook as a social networking site. It has been said that Facebook has brought about a change as far reaching as industrial revolution. The users have found advantages in maintaining, resurrecting and creating new relationships,

M. Bakshi (✉)
NSHM Group of Institutions, Kolkata, West Bengal, India
e-mail: madhupa.bakshi@gmail.com

© Academy of Marketing Science 2016
L. Petruzzellis, R.S. Winer (eds.), *Rediscovering the Essentiality of Marketing*,
Developments in Marketing Science: Proceedings of the Academy of Marketing
Science, DOI 10.1007/978-3-319-29877-1_59

289

reaching out to distant places, organizing social and political movements, using it for sting journalism or expose, marketing of products and branding, aiding in governance. The humble beginning of the college dorm project with a purpose to "share information with people you know, see what's going on with your friends, and look up people around you" (Sheldon 2008) matured "to give people the power to share and make the world more open and connected" (Gadekar et al. 2011) has now evolved to make the world more open and connected (Facebook.com 2013). Connected it certainly has, as more than one billion people worldwide express themselves on Facebook and a new generation has grown up thinking Facebook as the platform for social interaction rather than face-to-face interaction. Not only has it changed social behaviors but also has far reaching implications for the brands.

Brands and Social Media

In April 2011, Facebook launched a new portal for marketers and creative agencies to help them develop brand promotions on Facebook. News and media outlets such as the Washington Post, Financial Times and ABC News have used aggregated Facebook fan data to create various info graphics and charts to accompany their articles. Facebook has now a plethora of brands targeting youngsters and these brands realize that Facebook can be a happy hunting ground for future buyers and their various updates can turn them into loyal buyers influencing the peer group to follow them. In India, cosmetic brands, cars, travel portals, and games portals all try to create subscribers and fan bases so that they can reap the advantage in the marketplace.

Usage of any media has been studied mostly from the theoretical platform of Uses and Gratification (U&G) theory. Broadly speaking, the theory relates psychological needs to media use (or use of a specific medium) and posits that audiences consciously use a particular medium to seek certain gratifications in order to satisfy their psychological needs (Blumler 1979; Cantril 1942; Cha 2010; Rayburn 1996; Ruggiero 2000). Traditional media like television, radio, and newspaper usage has been studied based on this research. Newhagen and Rafaeli (1996) suggested that uses and gratification (U&G) theory might well be suited to study the Internet. Mc-Quail et al. (1972) categorized the needs and gratifications people are looking for into the following categories: diversion (escape from problems; emotional release), personal relationship (social utility of information in conversation; substitute of the media for companionship), personal identity (value reinforcement, self-understanding), and surveillance. However, studies after this period have added some more categories. In fact people who studied the usage of Internet have pointed out the difference of Internet as a media from traditional forms and thus the nature of the usage also.

While Coley (2006) asserted that most students use Facebook for fun, to organize parties, and to find dates, Sheldon (2008) found relationship maintenance, time pass, coolness, and companionship as reasons for Facebook usage. Recent studies that investigated the gratifications sought from Facebook usage found that people use it to maintain relationships with their facebook friends (Alam et al. 2011; Clark et al. 2007; Urista et al. 2009), entertainment (Sheldon 2008; Park et al. 2009), and pass time (Sheldon and Gevorgyan 2008; Foregger 2009). Some other gratification factors include convenience (Clark et al. 2007), social interaction (Park et al. 2009; Joinson 2008), self-expression (Hanson et al. 2010; Hou 2010), virtual community (Sheldon 2008; Sheldon and Honeycutt 2009), popularity (Urista et al. 2009), companionship (Sheldon and Gevorgyan 2008), social information, utilities and upkeep, channel use, market place, maintain/establish old ties, social comparison, sexual attraction, and interconnectedness (Foregger 2009). In the Indian context, Gadekar et al. (2011) found almost the same reasons for Facebook usage; however, they had an additional finding that the user-friendly nature of the platform is also a reason for using Facebook. However, media usage has also been characterized by differences in demographic factors. Most of the studies on new media have used demographic factors to differentiate the usage patterns (Katz and Rice 2003; LaRose and Eastin 2004; Urista et al. 2009; Gadkar et al. 2011). While Herring (2003) established that women are less responsive during online interactions, Maldonado et al. (2001) concluded that women use less online services as compared to men. Acar (2008) concluded that women seem to have larger online social networks as compared to men. He found that gender and extroversion were the major predictors of both online social network size and time spent online for social networking requests is high among them. This study is different from the previous ones because it considers a cohort of 13–18 years olds precisely the teenagers and not the college students as in previous studies.

Research Questions

The first question focused on the reasons for teenager usage of Facebook. The second research question focused on finding out whether there were demographic (gender, age, and income) differences in this usage. The third research question addressed to what extent attitudes about Facebook use were a reflection of the demographic differences and the gratifications sought.

Method

The students of a Mass Communication class were given as a project to survey teenagers between 13 and 18 year olds who used Facebook. In doing so they collected 170 data from four different regions of the city, and out of this 151 were usable. For convenience the age groups were divided into classes they attended. There were 61 boys in the sample and the rest 60 % were girls. 62 % of them spent less than 2 h on Facebook, and 28 % less than 4 h while almost 8 % spent more than 4 h on Facebook. Of the sample surveyed, 96 of them spent less than 2 h on net and 41 of them spent less than 4 h, and 10 spent beyond 4 h on Facebook.

Measures

A battery of thirty five questions was asked to the respondents to assess their usage of Facebook. These constructs were taken from previous studies (Sheldon 2008; Gadekar et al. 2011). Only the constructs on brand viewing were framed as they were not present in any of the previous studies. In the questionnaire the respondents were asked to record their scores in a five point Likert scale with 1 being most important and 5 being least important. To extract the factors Principal Axis Factoring with Varimax rotation was used as this is part of exploratory factor analysis. Once the factors were analyzed T test and regression was done to analyze the demographic differences on the gratifications sought.

Results

The objective was to find out the reasons for Facebook usage of the School goers and how this differed on the demographic variables. The exploratory Factor Analysis which involved Principal Axis Factoring with Varimax rotation yielded six factors with Eigen values of more than 1. However, since one factor had only one item it was dropped. The first factor of Companionship explained 21 % of the variance and was dependent on three items of Feeling less lonely, no one to talk to and so that I won't be alone. This factor was named following Sheldon's (2008) study. The second factor that emerged was that of to Maintain Friendships where the two most important items were communication, having fun and staying in touch with friends yielded one item with Cronbach Alpha of .84. The third factor that the school goers thought important was labeled as Brand Involvement and covered their visits of brand sites, discussing them, buying from advertisements, and liking the Brand sites. This factor the author did not find in any previous studies. Factor 4 Photo viewing contained three items photo viewing, tagging, and being tagged explained 4.2 % of the variance and had a Cronbach Alpha of .71. The fifth factor consisted of two items sending of messages and posting of messages on a friend's wall and was labeled as Messaging; this was similar to Gadekar et al.'s (2011) Social Interaction Factor and explained 4 % of the variance. Finally the school goers were visiting other people's profile and trying to have new experience as items like finding more interesting people and reading other people's profile.

Effect of Demography

To assess the influence of age, gender, and income on the motives of usage of Facebook T test and ANOVA was undertaken. The t test with Gender as the grouping variable revealed that none of the factors explaining usage was significantly influenced by the differences in sexes. However, ANOVA test revealed that there was significant grade level difference in usage of Facebook. It had significant influence on New Experience Gaining Behavior, Companionship and Brand Involvement $F_{(2.148)} = 4.435$, $p < .05$ for New Experience gaining behavior, $F_{(2.147)} = 5.8$, $p < .05$ and $F_{(2.147)} = 4.1$, $p < .05$. Income had a significant role in photo viewing $F_{(3.146)} = 4.20$, $p < .05$ and the post hoc tests revealed that there was considerable difference between children of families earning less than a lakh ($M = 2.28$, S.D = 1.0) and children of families earning less than 5 lakhs ($M = 2.96$, S.D = 1.0) yearly.

Conclusions and Implications for Theory and Practice

In the Indian context there is hardly any research that throws light on school going children's motives for using Facebook. As pointed out earlier this group has immense power to decide the marketing expense therefore necessitating it to understand their social media usage. The reasons for school student's usage of Facebook were Companionship, Messaging, Photo viewing, Brand visits, and New experience gaining. Apart from the Brand visit and New experience gaining factors, all the others had been found as reasons for Facebook usage by previous studies (Clark et al. 2007; Sheldon and Gevorgyan 2008; Urista et al. 2009; Alam et al. 2011). It was surprising to see that Brand Visit was being considered important by the 17- and 18-year group than the other groups. However, this is probably natural in the context of the fact that this group's impending adulthood made them more open to making their own brand choices. Visiting other profiles or looking for new friends has been found to be reasons for Facebook usage, but what is notable here is the age to which respondents belonged, they were mostly from class eight and in the age group of 13–15 year old. This was consistent with the study of Withall (2005) who found that students also search for new people who have recently joined the Facebook and whom they might know or want to meet. Being lonely is one of the problems of the teenager phase therefore it was not surprising that Companionship emerged important for the 17- and 18-year-olds, typically an age where they seek independence. Income had significant impact on photoviewing; this demographic impact was unique as it had not been found in previous studies. School goers belonging to lesser income group viewed more photos than children from higher income groups.

Conclusion

The reasons for Facebook usage were similar for the school goers as with the other youth groups. The contribution of this study is that students visiting brand pages were also indulging in gaining new experiences through new friends. However, in this sphere the study could have done better had they been questioned on whether Facebook usage was influencing their habit of playing computer games or watching cartoons. One of the weaknesses of the study was that the sample was a convenient sample and in such cases the results cannot be generalized. Future studies can look into the differences in School goers who use Facebook and those who do not. Also in relation to demography since there is a demographic divide in Internet usage it would be interesting to see the difference in usage pattern of those who have limited access to those who have unlimited access.

References available on request.

The Impact of Recommendations on the Cross-Channel Shopping Behavior

Carlos Flavián, Raquel Gurrea, and Carlos Orús

Introduction

Consumers can easily combine different channels to search for information and make purchases. Yet, the physical store is the preferred purchase channel. The cross-channel purchase process (i.e., in-store purchase influenced by online research) is the most extended behavior among online users (eMarketer 2014; Forrester Research 2014). The influence of online information on off-line purchases is expected to be especially significant due to the development of mobile technologies (Van Bruggen et al. 2010). In this way, one of the most beneficial innovations that new technologies have incorporated into the consumer's shopping process is the access to other consumers' opinions and evaluations anytime and anywhere (Hennig-Thurau et al. 2010). Despite the great body of research analyzing the effects of traditional word of mouth in conventional shopping environments, and of electronic word of mouth (e-wom) in e-commerce, there is a lack of research on how e-wom influences the consumer's purchase behavior at the physical outlet. This research examines how external recommendations, coming from online users or the company, influence the cross-channel search experience and decision. Specifically, this research analyzes: (1) how online users' recommendations help the consumer to improve their cross-channel shopping experience and (2) how consumer versus seller recommendations received during the physical interaction affect the initial impression of the product.

C. Flavián (✉) • R. Gurrea • C. Orús
University of Zaragoza, Zaragoza, Spain
e-mail: cflavian@unizar.es; gurrea@unizar.es; corus@unizar.es

© Academy of Marketing Science 2016
L. Petruzzellis, R.S. Winer (eds.), *Rediscovering the Essentiality of Marketing*,
Developments in Marketing Science: Proceedings of the Academy of Marketing
Science, DOI 10.1007/978-3-319-29877-1_60

Background

The demarcation of the multichannel behavior is in line with recent definitions developed by the marketing literature, which state that the combination of the online and off-line channels allows consumers to reduce the uncertainty associated with the purchase and to make the decision with a high degree of confidence (e.g., Neslin et al. 2006; Orus 2011). Confidence is a mental state of certainty with which a product, brand, or purchase situation is evaluated (Tormala et al. 2008). For this research, achieving confidence is approaching goal that motivates the multichannel shopping behavior. According to theories of information processing and uncertainty reduction (Greenleaf and Lehmann 1995; Lee 2001; Stafford and Grimes 2012), feeling uncertain has a powerful motivational effect. Consumers strive to reduce such uncertainty and feel confident. Cross-channel consumers combine channels according to their informational needs, creating individuated information that increases their perceived control over the process and that lead them to believe that they are making the right choice (Schul and Mayo 2003).

Dholakia et al.'s (2010) framework to study multichannel shopping behavior proposes that consumers *bring* several particularities with them that affect their interaction with the physical store. In this channel, consumers *encounter* new elements that influence their final evaluations and decision (Dholakia et al. 2010). In this research, consumers bring an initial impression of a product (target hereinafter) formed in a previous online interaction. Moreover, they encounter a new alternative (rival hereinafter) which can be also considered for the purchase. Past research on prior experience effects shows that repeated exposure to a target product can increase awareness and recognition of the product, which ultimately results in a higher preference (Lee 2001; Stafford and Grimes 2012). Consumers repeatedly exposed to a stimulus become familiar with it, which leads to a higher confidence in their judgment and ultimately determines their preference (Lee 2001). Also, if the consumers combine the online and off-line channels to reinforce the idea that the product considered is the best alternative, the likelihood of choosing this product, and the level of confidence with which this product is chosen, is expected to be higher compared to a rival product.

In addition, the influence of external recommendations, coming from other consumers or the company, is examined. On the one hand, consumer recommendations are referred to any recommendation, evaluation, opinion, or advice regarding a product in which the communication content is not created or sponsored by the product manufacturer or related marketing organization (e.g., other consumers, customers, friends, relatives). With the advent of new technologies, the ways consumers gather and exchange information about products have changed dramatically (Hennig-Thurau et al. 2010). In decisions involving uncertainty, consumers may seek for reassurance in their judgments by relying on other consumers' opinions and recommendations (Brown and Reingen 1987). Taking into account that cross-channel shopping processes are carried out to increase the degree of confidence in the decision, the presence of positive recommendations coming from other consumers is expected to reinforce the consumer's impression and confidence in the product's adequacy.

On the other hand, this research examines the effects of a salesman recommendation which does not support but goes against the initial impression of the consumer. If the combination of different media empowers consumers to generate a stable impression of the product, it seems interesting to examine how persuasive attempts consumers encounter at the physical store affect this stability. When consumers have established preferences toward a product, the reception of a recommendation against it may result in a rejection of the recommendation. If the consumer arrives at the physical store with an impression of the product confidently held, rather than adjusting their decision or simply ignoring the recommendation, a backlash may occur such that an increase in the choice and confidence of the option that is recommended against can be observed (Fitzsimons and Lehmann 2004). Therefore, the reception of a salesman recommendation against the target product may result in a reinforcement of the preference, choice, and confidence in this alternative.

Methodology

Two experimental studies were carried out. Both studies followed the same general procedure. They were developed in two parts. In the first part (T1), participants had an online interaction with the target product. In the second part (T2), all the participants interacted physically with the target product and with a new alternative (rival) with similar characteristics. Variables prior to the consumer's choice (purchase intentions), purchase decision, and choice confidence were considered for the analysis. Choice confidence is viewed as an important outcome of the cross-channel shopping process.

Study 1 analyzes how the presence of a positive review coming from an online customer influences the subsequent physical interaction. At the physical store, the differences with respect to the rival alternative and the effects of a salesman recommendation against the target product were examined. The design of the experiment was full factorial, with 2 (online review: yes vs. no)×2 (salesman recommendation: yes vs. no) between-subjects factors. Participants ($n=97$; 43 % male, between 18 and 35 years old; recruited from a multichannel retailer's website) were randomly assigned to one of the four conditions. The context of the study was the purchase of a Smartphone. During the online interaction (T1), the manipulation of the online review was introduced. After interacting with the product presentation for a few minutes, the participants indicated the likelihood of buying the product. Their level of confidence in the product as the most suitable for the purchase was also measured (4 items adapted from Petty et al. 2002). In the second part (T2), participants interacted physically with both the target and the rival products. At this point, participants in the "recommendation" condition received the salesman recommendation. The recommendation was not intended to discredit the target but to persuade the participants that the rival was the best for them. After the physical interaction, the participants indicated their purchase intentions. Then they were told that the products would be raffled at the end of the study. The participant was asked to choose which one he or she would take in case of being a winner. They also indicated their degree of confidence in their choice (4 items adapted from Petty et al. 2002).

The Study 2 implemented two modifications in order to extend and clarify the results of Study 1: first, the consumer recommendation was received at the physical encounter. The development of mobile technologies allows companies to enhance their service delivery through the access to online information at the physical store (Van Bruggen et al. 2010). Consumers can reach (and be reached by) other consumers when shopping in a retail store through mobile devices. Second, the tie strength of the consumer recommendation is manipulated by including a strong-tie source: friend recommendation. In this way, the design of Study 2 consisted of one between-subjects factor with four levels (recommendation: no, customer, friend, salesman). Participants ($n=92$; 53 % male; between 18 and 35 years old) were potential customers recruited from a multichannel retailer. They were instructed to imagine that they had to buy a gift (i.e., strap bag) for a person important to them. The procedure was similar as in study 1. This time, the manipulation of the recommendation was introduced at the physical encounter with the products. Participants in the "customer recommendation" group were directed to the "customer reviews" option of mobile application created by the company and read a positive review of the target. Participants in the "friend recommendation" accessed the chat functionality where they saw a simulated conversation with his or her "best friend." In this conversation, the participant read that his or her best friend recommended the target product. Finally, the salesman recommendation against the target product was developed in the same terms as in Study 1.

Results

Regarding the results of Study 1, the repeated-measures ANOVA showed that purchase intention toward the target increased significantly after having a physical interaction ($\Delta_M=.53$; $F_{(1, 93)}=12.782$, $p<.01$), but it was not significantly different from purchase intention toward the rival (*mean diff.*$=.11$). Furthermore, the target was chosen by more participants (53.6 %) than the rival, although the difference was not statistically significant. Participants who chose the target also held their choice with a higher degree of confidence ($M=6.16$, SD$=.77$) than those who chose the rival ($M=6.02$, SD$=.95$; $p=.24$). However, external recommendations affected these results. On the one hand, the presence of an online customer review did not affect off-line purchase intentions and choice. However, the online review had a significant influence on participants' choice confidence (review: $M=6.32$, SD$=.73$; no review: $M=5.85$, SD$=.93$ $F_{(1, 96)}=10.167$, $p<.01$).

On the other hand, the salesman recommendation did not produce the expected effects but the contrary: it negatively affected purchase intentions ($F_{(1, 93)}=4.499$, $p<.05$). Moreover, the results of a three-way loglinear analysis with choice, review, and recommendation as factors revealed a significant two-way interaction between choice and the salesman recommendation ($\chi^2_{(1)}=4.551$, $p<.05$). The choice of the target product was higher in the absence of recommendation (64.6 %) than with recommendation (42.8 %). Finally, the interaction between the salesman recommendation and the product chosen was significant ($F_{(1, 96)} = 3.391$, $p < .05$). Without recommendation, confidence in the choice of the target ($M = 6.19$, SD $= .76$) was significantly higher than in the choice of the rival ($M = 5.60$, SD $= 1.21$; $F_{(1, 47)} = 5.186$, $p < .05$). The opposite occurred in the presence of the recommendation ($p = .38$).

The participants' level of confidence acquired in the online interaction was measured in order to control for the stability of their preference before having the physical encounter. In fact, confidence in T1 was significantly higher for participants who read the online review ($M = 5.73$, SD $= .96$) than for those who did not ($M = 5.18$, SD $= 1.13$; $t_{(95)} = 2.596$, $p < .05$). The dependent variables were then submitted to a series of regression models with the online review, the salesman recommendation, confidence in T1, and their interactions as independent variables. Confidence in T1 had a significant positive effect on the increase in purchase intentions ($b = .91$, SE $= .11$; $t_{(89)} = 8.298$, $p < .01$), the difference in purchase intentions between products ($b = .73$, SE $= .14$; $t_{(89)} = 5.118$, $p < .01$), the likelihood of choosing the target product ($b = 1.91$, SE $= .67$; $z = 2.831$, $p < .01$), and choice confidence ($b = .41$, SE $= .07$, $t_{(89)} = 5.736$, $p < .01$). Interestingly, the negative effects of the salesman recommendation disappeared for participants with moderate-to-high levels of confidence in T1. Finally, when participants read the review, only confidence in T1 affected choice confidence.

Therefore, although the online customer review did not directly affect the offline purchase intentions and decision, an indirect effect through confidence in T1 was found. The salesman recommendation did not reinforce the preferences toward the target product. Indeed the reverse occurred, given the negative impact on purchase intentions, participants' choice of the target product, and choice confidence. However, when confidence in T1 was relatively high, which was facilitated by the presence of an online customer review, the salesman recommendation no longer affected the dependent variables.

The lack of direct effects of the online customer review may be due to the fact that consumers discounted its value at the physical store. Alternatively, the weak tie between the person making the recommendation and the person receiving it may also explain these results (Brown and Reingen 1987). Thus, in Study 2 participants received the recommendation during the physical interaction, and the tie strength of the consumer recommendation was manipulated by including a strong-tie source: friend recommendation.

The analysis of Study 2 revealed that, consistent with the results of Study 1, purchase intention toward the target in T2 was higher than in T1 ($\Delta_M = .53$; $F_{(1, 91)} = 3.945$, $p < .05$) and toward the rival (*mean diff.* $= .85$; $F_{(2, 91)} = 9.378$, $p < .001$). Also, the results of a binomial test showed that the choice of the target (65.2 %) was significantly higher than that of the rival ($p = .005$). Finally, choice confidence for participants who chose the target ($M = 6.36$, SD $= .61$) was higher than for those who preferred the rival ($M = 5.69$, SD $= .84$; $t_{(90)} = 4.358$, $p < .001$).

Parallel to the analyses of Study 1, several regression models were conducted to examine the effects of the external recommendations on the dependent variables.

The level of confidence in T1 was included as a control variable. Since the experimental treatment contained four levels, the number of models considered was substantial. For the sake of simplicity and to offer a parsimonious test of our hypotheses, only the results of comparison between each recommendation and the control condition are reported. The customer recommendation had a positive impact on purchase intention toward the target, but only for participants with a low level of confidence in T1 (significant interaction between the recommendation and the level of confidence in T1: $b = -1.05$, SE $= .42$; $t_{(89)} = -2.494$, $p < .05$). As in Study 1, the customer recommendation had a significant impact on choice confidence ($b = .29$, SE $= .12$; $t_{(89)} = 2.443$, $p < .05$).

The friend recommendation had a strong and consistent influence on all the dependent variables, irrespective of the level of confidence in T1 (effect on the increase in purchase intentions: $b = .89$, SE $= .29$; $t_{(89)} = 3.043$, $p < .01$; effect on the difference in purchase intentions: $b = 1.85$, SE $= .51$; $t_{(89)} = 3.651$, $p < .001$; effect on choice: $b = 1.70$, SE $= .86$; $z = 1.976$, $p < .05$; effect on choice confidence: $b = .71$, SE $= .19$; $t_{(89)} = 3.666$, $p < .001$). Regarding the salesman recommendation, the results generally replicated the previous study. Only when the participants did not have a stable impression of the target, the salesman recommendation had a negative effect on the preferences toward it. The expected "reactance-style" response was not found (Fitzsimons and Lehmann 2004), but an "ignorace-style" response was revealed for participants who previously acquired a high level of confidence.

Conclusion

Summarizing, this research shows that the preference for a product may be favored when consumers combine the online and off-line channels for searching for information and buying the product. Consumers form an initial impression of the product online and bring it to the physical store. This prior experience gives them a certain degree of confidence in the product's adequacy. At the physical store, consumers may confirm the information to improve their preferences and the likelihood of choosing this product increases. Moreover, if this product is eventually chosen, the choice is made with a high degree of confidence. However, recommendations influence cross-channel behavior. Consumer recommendations, received either at a prior stage in the online channel or at the physical store, may help consumers to reinforce their preferences and their degree of confidence. Even though consumers may not carry with them customer recommendations received on the Internet, these recommendations may serve to obtain confidence to face the off-line purchase decision with enhanced power. In addition, when consumers arrive at the store with low-to-moderate levels of confidence, a customer recommendation can improve the preferences toward this alternative. Recommendations from a strong-tie source, such as a friend, help consumers to reinforce their preferences regardless of the existence of a previous online interaction. Finally, although consumers may take the advantage of new technologies and the ubiquitous access to e-wom information, salesman recommendations may have strong influences on their behavior. This is especially true when the consumer arrives at the store with low and moderate levels of confidence. If consumers are confident enough about the suitability of the product, sales force attempts to convince them otherwise may be futile.

References available upon request.

Impact of Firm-Created Content on User-Generated Content: Using a New Social Media Monitoring Tool to Explore Twitter

Manuel Ceballos, Ángel García Crespo, and Nora Lado Cousté

Introduction

Considering the source of social media conversation, we can distinguish content from consumers (user-generated content, i.e., UGC) and firm (firm-created content, i.e., FCC): both have an impact on brand image and purchase expenditures (Goh et al. 2013; Bruhn et al. 2012). Firm-created social media communication can stimulate user-generated content, as Godes and Mayzlin (2009) have demonstrated. In fact, firms can actively start UGCs about their brands by "leaving indelible impressions on consumers' minds" (Mangold and Faulds 2009).

Companies can create word of mouth, which in turn impacts on awareness. According to Bruhn et al. (2012), FCC and UGC have different effects on the dimensions of brand attitude and brand perception. They perform a deep analysis of social media communications, accomplished by segregating firm-created social media communication from user-generated social media content. By analyzing survey-collected data, they found a different effect for firm-created, compared to user-generated, social media content on several brand image dimensions. In particular, their results reveal that FCC has a significant impact on functional brand image aspects, whereas UGC positively impacts on hedonic brand image dimensions.

Godes and Mayzlin (2009) and Goh et al. (2013) also demonstrate that FCC eventually drives customer purchases and firm market share. Goh et al. (2013) have analyzed the differentiating roles of UGC and FCC on social media, and provide a measure of the direct and relative effectiveness and the economic value of both. Consumers are risk averse, but they often face incomplete product information. In general, customers find themselves in the situation of having to adopt purchase decisions and choices despite being uncertain. On the basis of the economics of

M. Ceballos (✉) • Á. G. Crespo • N.L. Cousté
Universidad Carlos III de Madrid, Getafe, Spain
e-mail: mceballo@emp.uc3m.es; acrespo@ia.uc3m.es; nora@emp.uc3m.es

© Academy of Marketing Science 2016
L. Petruzzellis, R.S. Winer (eds.), *Rediscovering the Essentiality of Marketing*,
Developments in Marketing Science: Proceedings of the Academy of Marketing
Science, DOI 10.1007/978-3-319-29877-1_61

information theory, they posit that the comparative impact of UGC and FCC (in terms of the informative effect) should be different and they expected the FCC information richness to be more influential than UGC information richness. For them, the number of concepts included in the FCC can indicate the richness of information.

A firm can concentrate its FCC on one main topic, directed at the target audience which is interested in it; or, try to address different topics in order to provide richer and more diverse FCC. However, the importance of concentration or, on the contrary, variety within the topics addressed by FCC has not previously been studied. A brand can develop and implement different marketing strategies in terms of positioning. Some brands follow a niche strategy, trying to be the experts in satisfying the needs and interests of a specific market target. On the other hand, other brands can choose a more general and nonspecific positioning, in order to be able to respond to the interests and preferences of several market segments. The communication strategy must be coherent with the positioning strategy of the brand. In that sense, the variety or concentration within topics addressed by the FCC is an important element for a successful brand positioning implementation.

A crucial question, however, that has hitherto not been addressed comprehensively, is which are the more relevant characteristics of FCC? We can consider the effort or amount of FCC, in terms of volume or activity intensity. In addition, we can analyze the content quality of the firm effort in FCC. Most past research has focused on the volume of FCC, with the exceptions reported previously. One of the difficulties in investigating other characteristics is the operationalization of more qualitative concepts and their measurement. For these reasons, a large stream of research has focused on measuring the impact of the volume of activity of FCC. In this chapter, we focus our attention on proposing a measure of FCC richness in terms of variety of themes or topics, included in the firm-created content.

The main objective of this chapter is to measure the impact of FCC about a given brand on the UGC related to the same brand. To address this issue, we use a unique dataset with data of the popular microblogging platform Twitter. We choose Twitter because it is a potentially rich source of data to explore brand related aspects (Zhang et al. 2011). As Jansen et al. (2009) research on word-of-mouth communication on Twitter pointed out, about one fifth of all tweets contain the mention of a brand, product, or service. Among these tweets, about one fifth expresses some sentiment, perception, or association related to the brand, with a linguistic structure of tweets that is comparable to the linguistic patterns of natural language. In addition, the degree of brand centrality defined as the degree to which a brand is the main focus of the content, rather than peripheral, is greater in Twitter than in other SSMM. Because of its technical design (Twitter's 140-character limit), and bigger cultural emphasis on sharing news, information, and opinions, Twitter hosts a superior proportion of brand-central posts (more than 70 %) than Facebook or YouTube (Smith et al. 2012).

The topic analysis of our data has being performed by using a new social media monitoring tool: Twittiment. To perform the analysis we propose new metrics that are useful to summarize and interpret the impact of FCC on UGC. We used panel data analysis to examine more than one million of tweets in Spanish with regard to six brands (Audi, Nissan, Peugeot, Renault, Seat, and Volkswagen) during a 5 months study period (from 1st April, 2014 to 31st August, 2014). We present evidence about the impact of corporate effort on Twitter and also showed how is the effect of differences between content strategies in terms of topic variety in FCC. This result reflects different approaches to the implementation of the brand positioning strategy by different carmakers.

Methodology

In this research, we have used data collected directly from Twitter, using Twitter's application programming interface (API). Crawling was performed using each entity's canonical name and other related words such as query (see appendix for details).

For the text mining analysis, we used the social media monitoring tool called Twittiment; this tool allows us to process and classify a large number of tweets. The classification was carried out by a two-step procedure. By applying a double deductive and inductive process, a human expert was able to assign them into different criterions, or topics. The classification is based on word frequency, the type of users who wrote the tweets, or by hashtags contained. Secondly, the system analyzes the total population of tweets, providing a set of reports on the volume of tweets for each criterion and crosses criteria automatically. We performed several tests in order to check the coverage and accuracy of classification strategy.

The dataset includes information about six automobile firms (Audi, Nissan, Peugeot, Renault, Seat, and Volkswagen) between 1st April, 2014 and 31st August, 2014 for tweets in Spanish. In total we captured about one million "branded tweets." We took into account that they have different communication strategies (the amount of investment in marketing communication, utilization of different channels, the diverse approaches to social media branding, and so on).

For UGC, we define "*popularity*" as the total number of branded tweets generated by noncorporate twitter accounts (total number of branded tweets referring to any user from our set of corporate users group (@carmaker)), "*medium engagement*" is the total number of mentions received to any user corporate-account, and "*high engagement*" count the *number of retweets received by firm* (total number of retweets referring to any corporate users)—they will be dependent variables. For FCC, we identified all the corporate accounts corresponding to each firm and calculated the following independent variables: "*corporate* effort" is the number of corporate tweets per day, "*corporate reach*" is the number of daily corporate tweets multiplied by their followers, "*corporate topic diversity*" (refers to the variety of contents included in the FCC based on topic analysis), "corporate followers" is the daily evolution of number of corporate followers, and finally "*corporate followings*" is the daily evolution of corporate followings. Topic diversity refers to the variety of contents included in the FCC. We propose using the Herfindahl index (HHI) as a topic concentration measurement, and then estimating topic variety as

1-HHI. All the data were processed at daily level since Twitter is intrinsically an immediate communication platform and almost all interactions generated by a corporate action are expected to happen in the same day.

Results and Discussion

We conducted OLS regressions. We estimate using fixed-effect panel data estimation technique to control for any firm idiosyncratic factors that could influence dependent variables. Thus, we include company fixed effects in the model by adding company-specific dummy variables. The company-specific fixed effects capture the idiosyncratic and time-constant unobserved characteristics associated with each company in our data.

The results shows that the different independent variables have always significant coefficient with each different level of engagement (it is possible to think that the variable "popularity" is a proxy of low engagement).

We found empirical evidence of the impact of FCC on UGC. The volume of tweets generated by the firm referring to different topics as product attributes, product launches, communications campaigns, sponsorships etc. creates engagement and enhances the volume of UGC. More specifically, the volume of FCC—in terms of tweets and the number of followers—determining the reach impacts on user engagement with the brand in Twitter. These results suggest that when a firm increases their effort in communicating by Twitter, posting more tweets, including more variety in tweets contents or reaching a more large audience, the user engagement with the brand increases. In addition, the effect of FCC reach increases from low to high levels of involvement. Reach has a higher impact on high engagement metrics. As a result, we can say the quality of engagement increases when the firm effort is higher. The noncorporate tweeters seem to appreciate the effort of the carmaker firms in term of Twitter activity or presence, both, in terms of volume and quality.

We also found evidence of the impact of variety of content or topic diversity of the FCC. This last aspect need to be more investigated in future research. In brief, the company effort on twitter creating contents can stimulate user-generated content. Our dataset also allows us to analyze the relative efficacy of the different social media strategies implemented by diverse brands. Our research has important implications in terms of understanding of corporate strategy in social media communication channel.

References available upon request.

Influence of Customer Orientation and Competitor Orientation on the Intention to Use Social Network Sites as a Communication Tool in Microenterprises

Ángel Herrero-Crespo, Jesús Collado-Agudo, and Héctor San Martín-Gutiérrez

Introduction

The emergence of Web 2.0 has revolutionized the use of the Internet as a communication channel. The term "Web 2.0" includes a wide range of electronic applications, also called "social media" (e.g., social network sites, recommendation websites, blogs, and photo and video sharing platforms), that facilitate interactions among individuals as well as among users and companies. The impact of social media has been especially important in the industries of tourism and hospitality (Leung et al. 2013). In particular, according to a report by Fundetec (2013), in Spain the social network sites (SNS) are used for marketing activities by 48.0 % of small- and medium-sized hotels 63.0 % of large hotels).

However, despite the increasing use of SNS among users and firms in tourism, according to Leung et al. (2013), more research is needed so that scholars and practitioners better understand how to manage these media. Specifically, most studies on this topic have focused on consumers' use of SNS or its adoption by bigger companies, but much less research has been done regarding the adoption of this communication tool by small firms. In order to fill this gap in the literature, this chapter examines the determinants of the SNS acceptance by tourism microenterprises, with special attention to the effect exerted by the manager's market orientation. This approach is especially relevant because, despite the importance of small-sized firms, most research focuses on bigger companies, so the knowledge about decision-making in microenterprises is very limited. In particular, in this type of firms, organizational structure is minimum and is the owner or manager who makes decisions (Lee and Runge 2001) on innovation and marketing activities, among others. Therefore, taking the UTAUT as basis, we propose and test empirically a research

Á. Herrero-Crespo (✉) • J. Collado-Agudo • H.S. Martín-Gutiérrez
Universidad de Cantabria, Santander, Spain
e-mail: herreroa@unican.es; colladoj@unican.es; smartinh@unican.es

© Academy of Marketing Science 2016
L. Petruzzellis, R.S. Winer (eds.), *Rediscovering the Essentiality of Marketing*,
Developments in Marketing Science: Proceedings of the Academy of Marketing
Science, DOI 10.1007/978-3-319-29877-1_62

model that examines the effect of consumer orientation and competitor orientation on the acceptance of SNS as a communication tool in tourism microenterprises.

Literature Review

Unified Theory of Acceptance and Use of Technology and SNS Acceptance

Given that the use of SNS as a communication tool is an innovative behavior that implies the use of technology, the Unified Theory of Acceptance and Use of Technology (UTAUT) (Venkatesh et al. 2003) is used as a reference framework in this research. The UTAUT identifies four key drivers of the adoption of information systems: performance expectancy, effort expectancy, social influence, and facilitating conditions. Venkatesh et al. (2003) define performance expectancy as the degree to which an individual believes that using the system will help him or her improve the performance of a task or work. In turn, the effort expectancy is conceived as the degree of ease associated with the use of the system. The social influence is defined as the degree to which an individual perceives that important people believe he or she should use the system. Finally, the facilitating conditions factor is defined as the degree to which an individual believes that an organizational and technical infrastructure exists to support the use of the system.

In accordance with the UTAUT's formulation proposed by San Martin and Herrero (2012) and supported by Escobar-Rodríguez and Carvajal-Trujillo (2014), we suggest the following hypotheses regarding the online purchase intentions of rural tourists:

H1. The performance expectancy perceived in the use of SNS as a communication tool positively affects intention to use it.
H2. The effort expectancy perceived in the use of SNS as a communication tool positively affects intention to use it.
H3. The social influence regarding the use of SNS as a communication tool positively affects intention to use it.
H4. The facilitating conditions perceived in the use of SNS as a communication tool positively affects intention to use it.

Market Orientation, Customer Orientation, and Competitor Orientation in Microenterprises

Market orientation has been one of the key theoretical concepts in Marketing during the last two decades. Specifically, in this research we take as a basis the conceptualization of market orientation proposed by Narver and Slater (1990), who adopt a cultural perspective and define market orientation as "the organization culture that most effectively and efficiently creates the necessary behaviors for the creation of superior value for buyers and, thus, continuous superior performance for the business." Narver and Slater (1990) propose three different market orientation dimensions: customer orientation, competitor orientation, and interfunctional coordination. This conceptualization of market orientation has been developed for medium-sized and big companies, with a departmental organizational structure that requires "interfunctional coordination." However, this approach is not applicable to microenterprises, in which management is mainly individual and there are not functional departments to be coordinated (Verhees and Meulenberg 2004). Accordingly, this research only takes into consideration the two dimensions applicable to microenterprises: customer orientation and competitor orientation (Chen and Myagmarsuren 2013).

Different authors have suggested that market orientation is an antecedent of innovative behavior in an organization because it implies doing something new or different in response to market conditions (Han et al. 1998; Hult et al. 2004). Herrero et al. (2013) find out that in the case of small retailing firms, the manager's market orientation indirectly influences the adoption of management technologies through the effect on personal innovativeness. Similarly, according to Nguyen (2007), the level market orientation in a firm positively influences the use of specific technologies (e.g., Internet). Given that consumers extensively use SNS in their purchasing process, the manager's intention to use SNS as a communication tool will be higher if he/she has a high market orientation. Therefore, and in order to isolate the effects of customer orientation and competitor orientation, we propose following research hypotheses:

H5. Customer orientation of a microenterprise's manager has a positive influence on the intention to use SNS as a communication tool.

H6. Competitor orientation of a microenterprise's manager has a positive influence on the intention to use SNS as a communication tool.

Nguyen (2007) also found empirical evidence that supports that the level of market orientation in a firm positively influences the usefulness perceived in specific technologies (e.g., Internet), a variable equivalent to performance expectancy according to Venkatesh et al. (2003). This result suggests that managers will perceive a higher performance expectancy on the use of SNS as a communication tool if they have a high market orientation, as they are more aware of the importance of these applications on consumer behavior. Accordingly, we propose following research hypotheses for the separate effects of customer orientation and competitor orientation:

H7. Customer orientation of a microenterprise's manager has a positive influence on the performance expectancy perceived in the use of SNS as a communication tool.

H8. Competitor orientation of a microenterprise's manager has a positive influence on the performance expectancy perceived in the use of SNS as a communication tool.

On the other hand, market orientation reflects a sensibility to act according to customers' needs and competitors' strategies (Narver and Slater 1990). Accordingly, market orientation will enhance the managers' awareness regarding the opinions of customers and competitors with respect to the use of a technology (Bartl et al. 2012), which would lead to a higher subjective norm (D'Ambra et al. 1998), a variable equivalent to social influence (Venkatesh et al. 2003). In this sense, given the widespread use of SNS by consumers and firms, these collectives would exert a positive social influence with regard to the use of SNS as a communication tool, which will be more intense in case of a higher manager's market orientation. Accordingly, we propose following research hypotheses:

H9. Customer orientation of a microenterprise's manager positively influences on the social influence regarding the use of SNS as a communication tool.

H10. Competitor orientation of a microenterprise's manager positively influences on the social influence regarding the use of SNS as a communication tool.

Methodology

In order to test the research hypotheses, we developed a quantitative research based on a survey to owners and managers of tourism microenterprises (accommodations), defined as firms with less than ten employees and an income below two million euros (European Commission 2003). Data was collected using a personal questionnaire that included questions about socio-demographic characteristics of the firm and manager and about the research variables. The variables of the model were all measured using multi-attributes instruments (ten-point Likert scales) adapted from previous works, in order to assure content validity. The original work of Venkatesh et al. (2003) and the proposal by San Martin and Herrero (2012) in the specific field of tourism served to develop the measurement scales of intention to use SNS and the main explanatory factors included in the UTAUT. Customer orientation and competitor orientation were measured using the instruments developed by Chen and Myagmarsuren (2013).

The survey questionnaire was sent by e-mail to 1306 tourism accommodations in the region of Cantabria (Spain) that were listed in the census kept by the Regional Government (there were no reliable data about number of employees and total income). Enterprises that did not fill in the survey were contacted by telephone to obtain a response. The response rate was of 18.57%, obtaining a total of 216 valid responses. However, 16 of them came from enterprises with 10 or more employees and were discarded, which led to a final valid sample of 200 microenterprises (accommodations).

Results

The reliability and the convergent and discriminate validity of the measurement scales are validated using Confirmatory Factorial Analysis (maximum-likelihood robust estimation method with the statistical program EQS 6.1). The *reliability* of the seven factors is highly acceptable, as the Cronbach's Alpha and the composite reliability coefficients in all cases offer values appreciably higher than the recommended value of .7 (Bagozzi and Yi 1988). With respect to the *convergent validity*, all of the items are significant (t-value greater than 1.96) and its standardized coefficients greater than .5 (Steenkamp and Van trijp 1991). Additionally, *discriminant validity* is confirmed following the procedure proposed by Anderson and Gerbing (1988). Finally, the goodness-of-fit values of the confirmatory factor analysis are indicative of a good fit for the model.

The results obtained for the causal model support in the first place the significant effect of most of the explanatory variables included in the UTAUT. Thus, performance expectancy (stand. Lambda = .25, $p < .01$), effort expectancy (stand. Lambda = .47, $p < .01$), and social influence (stand. Lambda = .31, $p < .01$) have a significant influence on the intention to use SNS as communication tool, confirming the correct assertion of H1, H2, and H3. On the other hand, facilitating conditions does not significantly influence on intention to use, so H4 is not supported. With regard to customer orientation, it is observed that it exerts a positive and significant effect on performance expectancy (.17, $p < .01$) and social influence (.30, $p < .01$), but it does not significantly influence on intention to use SNS as communication tool. These results support H5 and H6, but lead to reject H7. In addition, competitor orientation does not significantly influence on performance expectancy, social influence, and the intention to use SNS as communication tool, thus rejecting H8, H9, and H10. Furthermore, Lagrange Multiplier Test suggests a direct effect between effort expectancy and performance expectancy (.39, $p < .01$). This result is consistent with the Technology Acceptance Model that establishes a causal effect from perceived ease of use and perceived usefulness, two variables equivalent to effort expectancy and performance expectancy (Venkatesh et al., 2003). Finally, the goodness-of-fit indices support the correct definition of the theoretical model presented (Normed $\chi^2 = 2.25$; BBNFI = .92; BBNNFI = .95; CFI = .95; RMSEA = .08), and that the research model explains reasonably the variance of the dependant variable ($R^2 = .49$).

Conclusion

This research provides a relevant contribution to the literature on technology adoption for marketing purposes in the case of microenterprises. In this sense, our results support that the intention to use SNS as a communication tool is determined by the performance expectancy, effort expectancy, and social influence perceived by the owner or manager. With regard to the effect of market orientation, through separately analyzing customer orientation and competitor orientation, we found that the adoption of technologies for marketing management is indirectly influenced by the customer orientation but not by competitor orientation. Specifically, our results show that the performance expectancy and social influence with regard to the use of SNS as a communication tool are determined by customer orientation but not by competitor orientation. This would mean that managers' beliefs about a technology are affected by what they perceive that customers demand, but not by the strategy or behavior of competitors about the technology. Accordingly, customer orientation would be the more relevant dimension of market orientation in microenterprises to explain the acceptance of new technologies for marketing management, at least in the tourism (accommodation) sector.

Acknowledgments This research has been funded by the Dirección General de Turismo del Gobierno de Cantabria (Spain).

References available upon request.

Part VI
Distribution and Supply Chain Management

Does Third-Party Logistics Create a Synergy Effect on Firm Performance

Kenneth K. Kwong

Introduction

A firm with strong strategic orientations tends to perform better in the market. However, recent research findings suggested differently. Interfirm collaboration is conceived to be one of the intervening variables, which operate between strategic orientations and firm's market performance. A firm working closely with third parties is likely to achieve a better result because of the synergy effect. Based on this proposition, this study aims to test this synergy effect arising from interfirm collaboration on firm performance in the context of outsourcing the distribution function to third-party logistics (3PLs) providers in Southern China.

Background

Strategic orientations are specific approach adopted by a firm in gathering information on competitors' activities and customers' needs (Narver and Slater 1990). It directs the firm's resource to fight against the competitors and to satisfy the customers. As such, competitor and customer orientations are the two components that constitute strategic orientations in this study. Any positive effect arising from outsourcing a firm's distribution function to the third party is collectively known as 3PLs synergies. The third-party logistics provider shares part or all of the tasks for client firms on sourcing, capacity planning, conversion, and distribution of finished goods. Because of its specialization, the third-party logistics provider is able to help client firms in achieving a better result (Yeung et al. 2006). In this study, 3PLs

K.K. Kwong (✉)
Hang Seng Management College, Hong Kong, China
e-mail: kennethkwong@hsmc.edu.hk

© Academy of Marketing Science 2016
L. Petruzzellis, R.S. Winer (eds.), *Rediscovering the Essentiality of Marketing*,
Developments in Marketing Science: Proceedings of the Academy of Marketing
Science, DOI 10.1007/978-3-319-29877-1_63

synergies are operationalized by a multi-item scale that reflects the degrees of integration and flexibility underlying this interfirm collaboration. The former denotes the closeness between the 3PLs provider and the client firm in sharing information and risk. The latter is the extent of openness among the two parties in accepting the difference of others (Sinkovics and Roath 2004; Slack 2005). Logistics performance indicates the improvement and saving of the client firm due to the outsourcing of distribution function to 3PL providers. Market performance suggests the firm's overall competitiveness in the market that is a proxy of firm performance (Narver and Slater 1990; Yeung et al. 2006). Both logistics and market performance are empirically assessed to ascertain the direct and indirect effects of these orientations and synergies.

Three hypotheses are proposed to test the casual relationship of these research variables. H1 suggests that the positive effect of strategic orientations on firm's market performance is mediated by 3PLs synergies. H2 is to argue that logistics performance is contingent on 3PLs synergies. H3 is about the positive effect between logistics performance and market performance.

Methodology

To empirically test these hypotheses, a survey was conducted in Southern China targeting to firms with an experience of using 3PLs services in distribution. A sample consisting of 200 firms was eventually obtained from a mail survey. It was a quite diversified sample that covered firms from various industries. All have been teamed up for at least 3-year times. Responses were made from senior staff members of sampled companies with a key responsibility in managing the distribution function but they are also knowledgeable on firm performance. They were requested to answer a set of Likert scale-typed questions on firm's strategic orientations, logistics and market performance, and the relationships with 3PLs providers. All questions were modified from the existing measures with references to the local context (Narver and Slater 1990; Sinkovics and Roath 2004).

Results and Discussion

Data was analyzed by using structural equation modeling (SEM). All reported fit indices met the conventional thresholds ($\chi^2/df = 1.677$, CFI $= .920$, TLI $= .902$, RMR $= .055$). The model exhibited a good fit. Based on the results of path analysis, all hypotheses were supported by the data. First, the relationship between strategic orientations and market performance is mediated by 3PLs synergies. Strategic orientations were found to have an indirect effect on firm's market performance via 3PLs synergies ($\beta = .283$, $p < .05$). The standardized total effect was .495 ($p < .001$). Meanwhile, the chance of creating synergies with 3PLs providers is good for firms that are serious about competitor's activities and customer's needs ($\beta = .567$, $p < .001$). Second, 3PLs synergies are important to firms because of the positive effect on logistics performance ($\beta = .458$, $p < .001$) and market performance ($\beta = .267$, $p < .05$). A closer collaboration between the firm and the 3PLs provider can render not only a high efficiency in distribution but also enhance the firm's competitiveness in the market. Last, market performance is also driven by logistic performance ($\beta = .510$, $p < .001$). A strong performance in logistics may translate into a profit by increasing the firm's competitiveness.

Conclusions and Implications

As a terminal variable, market performance was predicted by strategic orientations, 3PLs synergies, and logistics performance in this study. Hence, several implications for theory and practice are drawn from these research findings. On the theory side, a new construct known as 3PLs synergies is successfully created that mediates the relationship between strategic orientations and firm's market performance. As a mediator, 3PLs synergies are promoted by strategic orientations and act as a predictor of firm's market performance. It offers a new path to fully access the total effects of strategic orientations on firm's market performance via the synergy of interfirm collaboration. Market performance is not solely determined by strategic orientations but is also contingent on 3PLs synergies and logistic performance.

Outsourcing the distribution function to third parties for a better result is probably the key implication to practice. It allows the firm to concentrate its resources on the core business. This interfirm collaboration may possibly pave way for creating synergies that leads to a good performance. The firm is advised to work closeness and openness with third parties in searching of these synergy effects. To conclude, this study represents an attempt to link a marketing concept with an idea that is popular in operations management. Results of this study revealed that even though a firm directs all its attentions on the competitor and customer, it may not end up with high performance. Indeed, it lies at the synergy of interfirm collaboration.

References

Narver, J. C., & Slater, S. F. (1990). The effect of a market orientation of business profitability. *Journal of Marketing, 54*(4), 20–35.

Sinkovics, R. R., & Roath, A. S. (2004). Strategic orientation, capabilities, and performance in manufacturer—3PL relationships. *Journal of Business Logistics, 25*(2), 43–64.

Slack, N. (2005). The changing nature of operations flexibility. *International Journal of Operations & Production Management, 25*(12), 1201–1210.

Yeung, J. H. Y., Selen, W., Sum, C., & Huo, B. (2006). Linking financial performance to strategic orientation and operational priorities: An empirical study of third-party logistics providers. *International Journal of Physical Distribution & Logistics Management, 36*(3), 210–230.

Moving Sustainable Consumption from Hype to Reality Through the Value Chain

Gopalkrishnan R. Iyer and Sandra Rothenberger

Abstract With apparently increasing demand from consumers for environmentally sustainable products, several firms have adopted a green positioning strategy and have attempted to develop green products, along with a distinct marketing emphasis to attract "green consumers." Researchers have long emphasized that environmentally sustainable objectives not only contribute to profits, but also strengthen the firm's competitive position (Lovins et al. 1999; Menon and Menon 1997; Porter and van der Linde 1995; Schmidheiny 1992). Thus, received wisdom now appears to suggest that it is very much possible for firms to pursue the trifecta of environmental sustainability, profits, and competitive advantage. And, in recent times, the goals of sustainability are stated to be an imperative that organizations simply cannot ignore; as Nidumolu et al. (2009) argue, sustainability is "a mother lode of organizational and technological innovations" that would redefine the competitive landscape with new business models and new practices (p. 57). However, despite scholarly consensus and confidence on the profitability of environmentally sustainable strategies, green marketing practices are still not widely accepted or embraced in all industries. In this chapter, we develop a framework for the examination of the vital role of the supply chain, especially the retail sector, in implementing the sustainability objectives of companies. We argue that environmental sustainability in the value chain, especially through the three tenets of reduce, recycle, and reuse, is quite feasible and economical.

References available upon request.

G.R. Iyer (✉)
Florida Atlantic University, Boca Raton, FL, USA
e-mail: giyer@fau.edu

S. Rothenberger
Solvay Brussels School of Economics & Management, Brussels, Belgium
e-mail: Sandra.rothenberger@ulb.ac.be

© Academy of Marketing Science 2016
L. Petruzzellis, R.S. Winer (eds.), *Rediscovering the Essentiality of Marketing*,
Developments in Marketing Science: Proceedings of the Academy of Marketing
Science, DOI 10.1007/978-3-319-29877-1_64

Modeling Antecedents in Trust–Commitment Vendor Relationships

Janice M. Payan, Joe Hair, Göran Svensson, Svante Andersson, and Gabriel Awuah

Abstract The primary purpose of this study is to examine the importance of selected antecedents (i.e., cooperation, coordination, and relationship investments) in a commitment–trust vendor relationship model. Collaboration in organizations often is not effective in relationships between purchasers and vendors because cooperation, coordination, and relationship investment are lacking. Research on these constructs is very limited in interorganizational research, so this study is unique, therefore, in examining antecedents in a trust–commitment relationship model. Following examination of both first- and second-order modeling approaches, findings show the influence of these antecedents on trust and commitment, and ultimately vendor relationship satisfaction. All three antecedents are positively related to the higher order management factors construct, and in turn to both trust and commitment, with the stronger relationship being to commitment. Commitment and trust are both positively related to relationship satisfaction. The direct relationship from trust to satisfaction is the strongest, but there is evidence of partial mediation through the indirect relationship from trust to commitment and then to satisfaction.

J.M. Payan (✉)
University of Northern Colorado, Greeley, CO, USA
e-mail: janice.payan@unco.edu

J. Hair
Kennesaw State University, Kennesaw, GA, USA
e-mail: joehair3@kennesaw.edu

G. Svensson
Oslo School of Management, Oslo, Norway
e-mail: gosv@hh.se

S. Andersson • G. Awuah
Halmstad University, Halmstad, Sweden
e-mail: svan@hh.se; Gabriel.Awuah@hh.se

© Academy of Marketing Science 2016   321
L. Petruzzellis, R.S. Winer (eds.), *Rediscovering the Essentiality of Marketing*,
Developments in Marketing Science: Proceedings of the Academy of Marketing
Science, DOI 10.1007/978-3-319-29877-1_65

Dealer Satisfaction in Automotive Channel Relationships: Antecedents and Consequences

Lucrezia Maria De Cosmo and Ada Palumbo

Abstract Drawing from studies on relational capital value and the importance accorded to the satisfaction, we analyzed the relationship between industrial and commercial customers. A gap in literature is due to the major focus on business-to-consumer relationship and a consequent less importance reserved to the business-to-business sector. The effects of variables related to the supplier's product offering, marketing actions, and aftersales assistance in determining dealer satisfaction and trust have been relatively neglected.

We applied industrial consumer satisfaction model to the context of automotive sector and integrated it with other strategic variables as trust and reputation. We argue that supply chain success is also due to dealer satisfaction and propose causal linkages in which dealer satisfaction is recognized as an antecedent of trust and reputation. Empirical results confirm the importance of dealer satisfaction in the process of building a lasting relationship between buyers and sellers.

Keywords Automotive • Dealer satisfaction • Manufacturer reputation • Channel relationships

Introduction

The relationship between companies and their customers has been widely investigated, especially with reference to the role that it has in improving firms' competitive performance in the market (e.g., De Wulf et al. 2001; Palmatier et al. 2006). The two main streams of research, that is, customer satisfaction and relational marketing, focus on the analysis of the dyadic relationship between the customer and the firm as a result of a repeated purchasing behavior. In particular, the relational approach adopts as survey unit social relationships resulting from exchange processes repeated over time, that encourage cooperative behavior and true partnership

L.M. De Cosmo (✉) • A. Palumbo
University of Bari Aldo Moro, Bari, Italy
e-mail: lucreziamaria.decosmo@uniba.it; palumboada@yahoo.it

© Academy of Marketing Science 2016
L. Petruzzellis, R.S. Winer (eds.), *Rediscovering the Essentiality of Marketing*,
Developments in Marketing Science: Proceedings of the Academy of Marketing
Science, DOI 10.1007/978-3-319-29877-1_66

323

between buyers and sellers, especially in business to business markets (Anderson and Narus 1984; Morgan and Hunt 1994). In addition, many studies have confirmed that repeated experiences of satisfaction over time generate a perception of reliability that influence repurchase decision and therefore loyalty, or emphasize the causal relationship between satisfaction, trust, and loyalty (Bitner 1995; Busacca and Castaldo 1996).

Despite satisfaction contributes to the creation of an effective relationship between buyer and supplier, most of the research on it has been conducted within the context BtoC rather than BtoB (Abdul-Muhmin 2002). It is also interesting to note that previous studies on satisfaction in relationships are focused on supplier/buyer (Abdul-Muhmin 2002, 2005; Jap and Ganesan 2000; Sahadev and Jayachandran 2004; Scheer et al. 2003; Smith and Barclay 1997), whereas few studies have focused on the relationship between car manufacturer and dealer (Azila et al. 2011). Geyskens et al. (1999) suggest that further studies of channel relationship in different BtoB contexts are needed, as the results of the relationship can be different. Moreover, few studies focus on the relationship between satisfaction and the performance of distributors (Lai 2007) and on the economic benefits that derive from the relationship (Heide and John 1988; Noordewier et al. 1990).

This chapter aims to fill this gap by analyzing the antecedents and consequences of dealer satisfaction, maintaining that, if the quality of the relationship between a company and its distribution has a positive effect on the distributor satisfaction, it is likely to have an impact on the supplier reputation. This is evident in the automobile sector where relationships between car manufacturers and dealer networks have undergone a major transformation from a "seller's market" to a "market of the buyer" with significant effects in the structure of the distribution system (Volpato and Buzzavo 2003). The starting point is the market orientation of the supplier that determines value creation in the activities and behavior of the distributor. As a result, the relational value perceived by the distributor increases its commitment, collaboration, and satisfaction (Simpson et al. 2001).

Theoretical Background

A relationship between manufacturers and dealers has a direct impact on the dealer's level of dependence through the value of exchanged resources and of the available alternative resources (Cook and Emerson 1984). The use of coercive strategies in channel relationships increases conflict (Brown and Frazier 1978; Brown et al. 1983) and reduces the negative impact on relationship satisfaction (Venkatesh et al. 1995).

Supplier's support to a distributor reinforces the value and mutual dependence within the relationship by helping to satisfy the dealer (Gassenheimer and Ramsey 1994). In particular, in the automotive industry the highest level of vendor support is associated with higher level of satisfaction in the channel (Azila et al. 2011). This means that the coordination of the parties as a result of a greater balance of power and an increase of the level of complexity of the relational context requires mechanisms for integration based on partnership or trust through a mutual understanding and a focus on common goals (Kumar et al. 1992; Webster 1992). Scholars noted that the satisfaction of a member of the channel increases the long-term orientation (Bolton 1998; Selnes 1998) and this leads to relationship building more narrow and integrate between suppliers and intermediaries (Corsten and Kumar 2005; Leonidou et al. 2006).

In this perspective, an important role is attributed to dealers' satisfaction, which has been recognized as an antecedent of trust, as a dependent variable or as a final result of the process of building a long-lasting relationship between buyers and sellers. In particular, Anderson and Narus (1990) have proposed an interpretative model of partnership establishing that, when the actual result of the trade relationship is higher than the expectations of one of the participants, the result is an increased level of satisfaction, trust, and a higher predisposition to collaboration. Satisfaction in the relationship between suppliers and customers has become an important factor in relationship and channel marketing studies (Abdul-Muhmin 2005; Ganesan 1994; Gassenheimer and Ramsey 1994; Ramaseshan et al. 2006; Rodriguez et al. 2006). In particular, satisfaction in business relationships contributes to reducing transaction costs and promoting economic value for both resellers and their final customers (Geyskens and Steenkamp 2000; Ping 2003).

In the automotive sector, in particular, the relationship between car manufacturers and dealers are positively influenced by trust and negatively by power and conflict. As a natural consequence, if automakers want to collaborate with distributors, they should invest in noncoercive behavior in order to enhance their trust (Nadin 2008).

Geyskens et al. (1998, 1999) through a meta-analysis of 71 different studies conducted between 1970 and 1996 built a model that aims to assess mainly the sequential cause–effect relation between antecedents, trust, and its consequences. In particular, the study shows that the economic and noneconomic satisfaction experienced by a distribution partner is different from the trust and commitment, although connected to them. In fact, economic satisfaction stimulates the relaxation afforded to noneconomic, which in turn exerts a positive impact on trust that ultimately influences positively the commitment of the distributor toward the supplier (Morgan and Hunt 1994). Other studies confirm that the distributor satisfaction is positively related to its performance, and that noneconomic satisfaction is more important than the economic one (Lai 2007).

The quality of the relationship between the company and the distribution has a positive effect on the distributor satisfaction, which depends on solidarity, mutuality, flexibility, role of the integrity, and trust (Bandyopadhyay and Robicheaux 1997). Moreover, the quality of e-services contributes to improving the quality of the relationship between suppliers and dealers with a positive effect on retailer satisfaction (Chang et al. 2012).

Since the expectations and the response of a buyer to an offer depend on the manufacturer reputation and the effectiveness of the communication program of the producer (Yoon et al. 1993), the customer relationship can be used to build the supplier reputation in the industrial markets. In fact, reputation is formed through communication between customers and other interested parties (Yoon et al. 1993;

Herbig and Milewicz 1995). Moreover, by choosing appropriately the reference customers, the supplier may motivate them to act as positive word of mouth (Huntley 2006). The baseline report is therefore an effective means for reputation management of SMEs (Helm 2007; Helm and Salminen 2010; Salminen and Möller 2006) to improve the reputation of the client, and in particular the seller (Ou et al. 2006).

Moreover, the manufacturer reputation plays an important role in consumer evaluation of product quality (Purohit and Srivastava 2001).

Research Hypotheses

Dealer satisfaction is due to a series of transactions more than one single purchase. These transactions form a long-term relationship that involves different moments of manufacturer–dealer interactions, such as product purchase, order handling over time, technical assistance, part availability, and staff interactions. A holistic approach considers all these facets as determinants of dealer satisfaction.

Communication quality and transparency in all interaction stages are fundamental to create and develop satisfying and long-lasting channel relationships. Moreover, producer involvement in marketing actions which covers all selling and postselling process could be perceived as a way the provider sustains the dealer in the chain subsequent stages. In order handling process, the provider has to meet dealer's expectations in order fulfillment, as it could also have an impact on dealer order managing with final customers.

In the automotive sector due to the complexity of the products sold, technical service such as maintenance, fitting, repairing but also user training are key dimension of satisfaction in terms of speed of availability, quality, and price/value ratio. Also postselling care, as complaints managing, responses to disappointed customers are key issue in determining dealer satisfaction, as consequences that could derive are very dangerous for the supplier image. Finally, the implementation of integrated engineering project is a way of involving the dealer in value production process.

In summary, we argue that overall dealer satisfaction is a long-term relationship outcome, describing how well the supplier meets dealer's expectations and involves his channel customer in the following areas: communication, marketing actions, order handling, technical services, postselling assistance, and involvement in Research and development.

H1: Communication, Commitment in Marketing Actions, Order Handling, Technical Services, Postselling Assistance, and Involvement in R&D positively affect of Overall Dealer Satisfaction.

Satisfaction and trust are important in developing strong relationships between manufacturers and suppliers (Barry et al. 2008; Rauyruen and Miller 2007; Skarmeas et al. 2008). They are mental constructs that summarize knowledge and experiences with a particular firm (Garbarino and Johnson 1999).

As Overall Satisfaction is a cumulative construct, which sums satisfaction with the total purchase and consumption experience, relational marketing literature suggests to include trust to explain channel relationship quality (Morgan and Hunt 1994). Trust implies a feeling that takes into account all the experiences with the supplier (Moliner et al. 2007) and is built gradually: the longer the period of exposure to a satisfactory partner, the greater the level of trust (Michell et al. 1998).

Trust in the manufacturer encompasses objective values and corporate-culture sharing, manufacturer reliability, and confidence toward the supplier. Moreover, a feeling of trust implies the perception of a supportive climate and therefore the desire to maintain long-lasting relationship. Dealers' trust in the manufacturer implies willingness to rely on the exchange partner. Trust encompasses commitment, as in a trustworthy relationship a partner is more likely to make a long-term commitment (Morgan and Hunt 1994). Trust has a central role for thriving long-lasting channel relationship (Duarte and Davies 2004).

We therefore argue that channel satisfaction promotes a climate of trust, in particular the greater the satisfaction toward the manufacturer, the more trust generated in the dealer. Satisfaction is a leading factor in determining trust.

H2: The higher the Overall Dealer Satisfaction, the stronger the trust in the manufacturer.

Manufacturer's reputation is the cognitive evaluation of what the dealer think and say about the manufacture based on their direct relationship. Reputation can be based on direct experience, named first-order reputation, or it can be based on what other say about the organization, named second-order reputation. However, second-order reputation is more superficial than first-order one (Yang and Grunig 2005). Experiential relationships, which are based on what dealers directly experience, know, and understand (Yang and Grunig 2005), give rise to the deeper manufacturer's reputation. Accumulated impression that dealers derive from the interactions with the firm, its reliability and honesty, create manufacturer's reputation. Trust can be an evaluative criterion for first-order reputation, as trust and reputation are not coincidental (Bennett and Gabriel 2001). Reputation can be a measure of trust, especially when there is no direct experience with the partner.

According to the view that a reputation is a proxy of trust (Bennett and Gabriel 2001), we argue that manufacturer's reputation is determined by trust in the manufacturer. Automotive manufacturer's efforts in improving trustworthy relationships with the dealers enhance its reputation.

H3: The stronger trust in manufacturer–dealer relationship, the better Manufacturer's Reputation.

Methodology

Qualitative interviews were used to generate items and identify possible dimensions in our model of overall dealer satisfaction. Hundred purchasing managers of automakers were interviewed and interviews took approximately 30 min. A questionnaire was administered to 100 independent multibrand dealers, which sold a

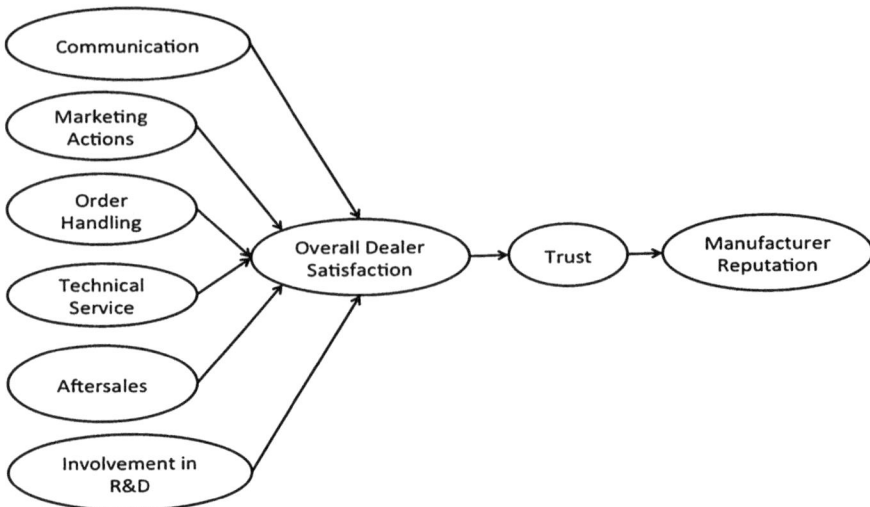

Fig. 1 Conceptual model

particular model produced by an Italian automotive company. The questionnaire was formed by seven 5-point Likert scales. Some existing scales were drawn from the literature: the Communication scale was adapted from Product-related information scale (Homburg and Rudolph 2001) to make it suitable for automotive sector; Satisfaction with Order Handling scale and Satisfaction with technical services were drawn from Homburg and Rudolph (2001). Instead, the scales Marketing Actions, Involvement in R&D, Aftersales, Overall Dealer Satisfaction, Trust in the manufacturer, and Manufacturer's reputation were all drawn from qualitative interviews.

The analysis of the manufacturer's performance with dealers will help determine the antecedents of dealer satisfaction and the consequences on manufacturer's reputation (Fig. 1).

As the scales used in the survey were both adapted from existing scales and completely drawn from qualitative interviews, scales reliability was measured (see Table 1). All Cronbach alphas exceed the threshold suggested in literature (Nunnally et al. 1967).

Results

Data were analyzed through multiple and multivariate regression analysis to estimate causal path for the latent variables. Results indicate that both measurement and causal paths are significant.

The most intense effect is Order Handling Efficacy on Overall Dealer Satisfaction ($\beta = 0.44$, $p < .000$). Dealers put major importance in manufacturer's order managing

Table 1 Items

	Factor loading	Alpha
Communication of product-related information		
Information provided in supplier's technical documentation	.855	.878
Availability of technical documentation	.919	
Communication about orders, parts, and warranties	.775	
Manufacturer's support (e.g., help desk, training, etc.)	.781	
Internet-based communication	.550	
Producer's commitment marketing actions		
Marketing actions on new vehicles	.962	.923
Marketing actions on assistance and parts	.980	
National communication campaigns supporting the products	.825	
Cooperation on dealer marketing actions	.635	
Dealer satisfaction monitoring	.524	
Involvement in dealer marketing actions	.743	
Order handling		
Time taken in returning order confirmation	.985	.951
Reliability of order processing	.918	
Delivery time as given in the order confirmation	.892	
Technical services		
Speed of availability of technical service	.910	.817
Technical quality of the service provided	.884	
Price/value ratio of the technical service provided	.573	
Aftersales		
Immediate part availability	.846	.816
Price/quality parts	.739	
Complaints and dissatisfaction management/handling	.739	
Involvement in R&D		
Involvement in R&D projects	.917	.842
Involvement in production operation enhancement	.796	
Overall dealer satisfaction		
Manufacturer willingness to cooperate	.800	.888
Benefits derived from the economical relationship with the manufacturer	.852	
Overall satisfaction	.803	
Trust		
Desire of long-lasting relationship with the manufacturer	.627	.742
Manufacturer's dealer orientation	.575	
Objectives, values, and culture sharing	.365	
Manufacturer's reputation		
Expertise and skills	.832	.879
Reliability	.824	
Nonopportunistic behavior	.852	
Honesty, truthfulness, congeniality	.670	

efficacy. It is a long process consisting in accepting and issuing dealers' orders, tracking the progress, and updating the dealer, as notifying the dealer when the order is complete. Order handling can include changes, cancellations modifications, for example, in payment methods; therefore, the ability of supporting changes, keeping the dealer informed, managing on time completions is fundamental for dealer satisfaction. From the manufacturer's order, fulfillment could depend the final customer order, so the great importance dealers put in order handling efficacy may have effect on the dealer–final customer relationship, and consequently on the final customer satisfaction with the dealer. The second determinant of Overall Dealer Satisfaction is Aftersales assistance ($\beta = .31$, $p < .05$), in terms of part availability, parts operational excellence, direct shipments, returns, multiple deliveries per day, and complaint management. Aftersales is critical for automotive dealers as final consumers put off new purchases and hold on to their cars longer. Demand is largely based on replacement. Therefore, parts availability, original equipment to replace the damaged parts, and reaction on complaints could determine not only dealer satisfaction but also final customer loyalty. Manufacturer's commitment in marketing actions is appreciated by dealers and it is another cause of their satisfaction ($\beta = .28$, $p < .05$). Marketing activities help dealers selling the products to the final customer, reducing the costs associated to new product launch, communication campaigns, direct marketing, and so on. Another determinant factor of dealer satisfaction is Involvement in R&D ($\beta = .27$, $p < .05$). Dealers positively perceive the involvement in the R&D process, which does not necessary means vertical integration as it is risky and costly, but a coordination and collaboration in the development of new products and in the enhancement of existing ones. Sharing needs, mission, and obtaining participation are crucial for satisfaction. Communication transparency and velocity determine dealer's satisfaction ($\beta = .24$, $p < .05$). Vehicles' production and selling rely on a considerable exchange of business documents between the manufacturer and dealers. Quick communication with the manufacturer, quality in the product-related information, speed in answering question about vehicles, orders, and guarantees result in greater dealer satisfaction. Real-time information about technical characteristics of the products, manuals clarity, and transactions improve dealer satisfaction. Finally, Technical Service is fundamental in automotive industry to guarantee dealer satisfaction ($\beta = .21$, $p < .10$). Due to the complexity of the business, automotive manufacturers have to comply with a continuously increasing demand for technical service to assist both dealers and final customers.

Results show that a dealer is satisfied when the manufacturer is efficient and has high-quality order handling, technical services, and aftersales. This calls for involvement in the producer's R&D process, manufacturer's commitment in marketing actions to support the selling and postselling process with the final customer, clarity, and speed in information exchange. H1 is verified.

The strongest causal relation in the model involves the effect of Overall Dealer Satisfaction on Trust in the manufacturer ($\beta = .815$, $p < .000$). Satisfaction with the manufacturer from whom the vehicles were acquired contributes to create a climate of trust in trade channel. Supplier's technical and human ability to fulfill obligations and, the positive experiences provided, create trust. Trust includes the supplier's concern for its customers' well-being and problems, and the support and assistance

Table 2 Model's causal relationships

	Standardized estimates	SE	p-value
H1: Communication → ODS	.241	.097	.032
H1: Marketing actions → ODS	.276	.073	.011
H1: Order handling → ODS	.435	.078	.000
H1: Technical service → ODS	.211	.097	.063
H1: Postselling → ODS	.311	.083	.011
H1: Involvement in R&D → ODS	.273	.114	.042
H2: ODS → trust in the manufacturer	.815	.154	.000
H3: Trust → manufacturer's reputation	.800	.236	.000

that it gives them (benevolence), and the desire of stay in a long-term relationship (commitment). H2 is verified.

The effect of Trust in the manufacturer is a determinant of its Reputation ($\beta = .80$, $p < .000$); the higher the trust the better the manufacturer's reputation. The great intensity of the relation is due to the direct experience that gives rise to reputation. Dealers had the possibility to directly experience manufacturer performance, which contributed to enhancing trust. Dealers would not do business with suppliers they do not trust and trust is a driver in building manufacturer's reputation. Manufacturers that conduct their affairs with integrity and honesty are trusted and trusted organizations enjoy a good reputation. H3 is verified (Table 2).

Limitations and Future Research

This study analyzes the relationships between one manufacturer and its major dealers, intercepted in one single moment. As causal relationship require longitudinal data, extending the study to other manufacturers–dealers and in different time period, could help results generalizability. Monitoring manufacturer performance with its dealers allowed us to take a picture of the current condition of the relationship, according to relevant antecedent of dealer satisfaction. Anyway future monitoring of the relationship will be helpful for analyzing the dynamic evolution of manufacturer–dealer satisfaction in the automotive sector.

Our model of ODS (Overall Dealer Satisfaction) taps only the positive variables related to the concept, while it does not include dissatisfaction antecedents. Further research should analyze causes of dissatisfaction or conflicts between manufacturer and dealers as an additional facet of the construct. This approach could help developing of strategies and actions for unsatisfied dealer's recovery, such as open discussions and cooperation in problem solving.

Future research could include economic performance indicators in the model, such as cost reduction, gross profits, margins, product performance, as well as explore other consequences of the model, or marketing-related constructs, such as, dealer loyalty and dealer intention to recommend to the final customer manufacturer's products.

Conclusion

The present study contributes to conceptualizing the dealer satisfaction and the flow of antecedents and consequences of channel satisfaction, organized along a structure–conduct–performance framework. We found that in the automotive sector, a manufacturer has to satisfy dealer's expectations in terms of communication effectiveness, commitment in marketing policies, effectiveness in order handling, technical support, postsales service, and dealer's involvement in R&D.

The relationship between the manufacturer and dealers is mutual, as their profitability and competitiveness depends on each other. The dealer is an active part in channel relationships. Dealer satisfaction has an important role in maintaining profitable relations all over the channel. Long-term relationship lowers the costs associated to the research of a new produces, just like it happens in business-to-customers relationship, where retention costs are certainty lower than new customer acquisition. As satisfied channel members are less prone to exit the channel, it is a determinant of long-term channel viability (Geyskens et al. 1999). Satisfaction is necessary for dealers to rebuy. Satisfaction creates the right working atmosphere, in which one member is not perceived as preventing the other from achieving economic and financial goals.

Automakers have to face a number of challenges, including the reduction of technological differentiation between competitor products, decline of product margins, and rising cost of the additional service, whereas at the same time customer expectations for quality and service are increasing. One key to obtain dealer satisfaction is cooperation. Establishing, developing, and maintaining successful relationships between manufacturers and dealers require commitment in different stages, encompasses working partnerships, comarketing alliances, fast and clear communication, interrelationships in recovery of dissatisfaction, coordinated development of research and development processes, efficacy in order handling, and high performance on aftersales. Effective cooperation is required for dealer satisfaction and channel success. Suppliers and manufacturers should focus on establishing connections on the various units of a company and on promoting networks to foster nonhierarchic information sharing between them. As car manufacturing is characterized by long and numerous interactions, producers' responsibility should be expanded to the whole supply chain.

Satisfaction has direct influence in trust-building process, and in its related construct such as commitment and benevolence. Trust is the core of good chain relationships, has a central role between satisfaction and reputation. The continuity of a relationship is based on satisfaction, trust of both partners in the exchange. The automotive sector is noneffective for dealers to frequently rotate supplier partners (Dyer and Chu 2011); long-standing relationship with regular trading partners, characterized by Trust environment and comfortable interaction with the counterpart, is more effective in a win–win perspective.

Satisfied dealers trust their suppliers, this builds a strong reputation. On the one hand, referrals from satisfied dealers strengthens manufacturer's reputation; on the other hand when trust breaks down, the dissatisfied dealer will generate a negative word of mouth with a detrimental effect on the manufacturer reputation. As people can evaluate their relationships with an organization based solely on what they have read or heard from others (Yang and Grunig 2005), final customers, potential buyers, and competitors can form their manufacturer reputation based on "second-hand" (indirect) experiences, which can have an impact on their behavior. Reputation could be used as a signaling cue for other dealers who did not had a direct experience with the supplier. Reputation has been shown to be a determinant in consumer's purchase decision making, as it serves as quality signal and reduces uncertainty prior to the purchase, and it is a determinant in positive word of mouth (Anderson and Srinivasan 2003; Carmeli and Tishler 2005). A favorable reputation adds value to overall effectiveness of an organization giving it a distinct competitive advantage. Likewise, a bad or unfavorable reputation could diminish corporation's value.

A managerial implication derives from the positive relationship between dealer satisfaction and manufacturer's reputation. Manufacturer reputation is even more relevant in the case of products like vehicles that are complex and characterized by uncertainty for the high levels of consumer uncertainty. A dealer, who has a strong opinion of its partner, will feel more confident and exclude potential alternative supplier from consideration. Building a strong reputation leads to more loyal dealers and reduces opportunistic behaviors.

References

Abdul-Muhmin, A. G. (2002). Effects of suppliers' marketing program variables on industrial buyers' relationship satisfaction and commitment. *Journal of Business & Industrial Marketing, 17*(7), 637–649.

Abdul-Muhmin, A. G. (2005). Instrumental and interpersonal determinants of relationship satisfaction and commitment in industrial markets. *Journal of Business Research, 58*, 619–628.

Anderson, J. C., & Narus, J. A. (1984). A model of the distributor's perspective of distributor-manufacturer working relationships. *Journal of Marketing, 48*(4), 62–74.

Anderson, J. C., & Narus, J. A. (1990). A model of distributor firm and manufacturer firm working partnerships. *Journal of Marketing, 54*(1), 42–58.

Anderson, R. E., & Srinivasan, S. S. (2003). E-satisfaction and e-loyalty: A contingency framework. *Psychology & Marketing, 20*(2), 123–138.

Azila, M. N., Selvan, P., & Zolkafli, H. (2011) Globalization in the automobile industry: How Supplier dealer relationship could be effectively managed? In *Annual Conference on Innovations in Business & Management*. London, England.

Bandyopadhyay, S., & Robicheaux, R. A. (1997). Dealer satisfaction through relationship marketing across cultures. *Journal of Marketing Channels, 6*(2), 35–55.

Barry, J. M., Dion, P., & Johnson, W. (2008). A cross-cultural examination of relationship strength in B2B services. *Journal of Services Marketing, 22*(2), 114–135.

Bennett, R., & Gabriel, H. (2001). Reputation, trust and supplier commitment: The case of shipping company/seaport relations. *Journal of Business & Industrial Marketing, 16*(6), 424–438.

Bitner, M. J. (1995). Building service relationships: it's all about promises. *Journal of the Academy of Marketing Science, 23*(4), 246–251.

Bolton, R. N. (1998). A dynamic model of the duration of the customer's relationship with a continuos service provider: The role of satisfaction. *Marketing Science, 17*(1), 45–65.

Brown, J. R., & Frazier, G. L. (1978). The application of channel power: Its effects and connotations. *AMA Summer Educatior's Conference Proceedings* (pp. 266–270) Chicago, IL: American Marketing Association.

Brown, J. R., Lush, R. F., & Muehling, D. D. (1983). Conflict and power dependence relations in relations in retailer–supplier channels. *Journal of Retailing, 59*(4), 53–80.

Busacca, B., & Castaldo, S. (1996). *Il potenziale competitivo della fedeltà alla marca e all'insegna commerciale: una metodologia di misurazione congiunta.* Milano, Italy: Egea.

Carmeli, A., & Tishler, A. (2005). Perceived organizational reputation and organizational performance: An empirical investigation of industrial enterprises. *Corporate Reputation Review, 8*(1), 13–30.

Chang, H. H., Lee, C. H., & Lai, C. Y. (2012). E-service quality and relationship quality on dealer satisfaction: Channel power as a moderator. *Total Quality Management & Business Excellence, 23*(7–8), 855–873.

Cook, K. S., & Emerson, R. M. (1984). Exchange networks and the analysis of complex organizations. *Research in the Sociology of Organizations, 3*(4), 1–30.

Corsten, D., & Kumar, N. (2005). Do suppliers benefit from collaborative relationships with large retailers? An empirical investigation of efficient consumer response action. *Journal of Marketing, 69*, 80–94.

De Wulf, K., Odekerken-Schröder, G., & Iacobucci, D. (2001). Investments in consumer relationships: A cross-country and cross-industry exploration. *Journal of Marketing, 65*(4), 33–50.

Duarte, M., & Davies, G. (2004). Trust as a mediator of channel power. *Journal of Marketing Channels, 11*(2–3), 77–102.

Dyer, J., & Chu, W. (2011). The determinants of trust in supplier–automaker relations in the US, Japan, and Korea: A retrospective. *Journal of International Business Studies, 42*(1), 28–34.

Ganesan, S. (1994). Determinants of long-term orientation in buyer-seller relationships. *Journal of Marketing, 58*(2), 1–19.

Garbarino, E., & Johnson, M. S. (1999). The different roles of satisfaction, trust, and commitment in customer relationships. *Journal of Marketing, 63*(2), 70–87.

Gassenheimer, J. B., & Ramsey, R. (1994). The impact of dependence on dealer satisfaction: A comparison of reseller-supplier relationships. *Journal of Retailing, 70*(3), 253–266.

Geyskens, I., & Steenkamp, J. E. M. (2000). Economic and social satisfaction: Measurement and relevance to marketing channel relationship. *Journal of Retailing, 76*(1), 11–32.

Geyskens, I., Steenkamp, J. B. E., & Kumar, N. (1998). Generalizations about trust in marketing channel relationships using meta-analysis. *International Journal of Research in Marketing, 15*(3), 223–248.

Geyskens, I., Steenkamp, J. B. E., & Kumar, N. (1999). A meta-analysis of satisfaction in marketing channel relationships. *Journal of Marketing Research, 36*(2), 223–238.

Heide, J. B., & John, G. (1988). The role of dependence balancing in safeguarding transaction-specific assets in conventional channels. *Journal of Marketing, 52*, 20–35.

Helm, S. (2007). One reputation or many? Comparing stakeholders' perceptions of corporate reputation. *Corporate Communications, 12*(3), 238–254.

Helm, S., & Salminen, R. (2010). Basking in reflected glory: Using customer reference relationships to build reputation in industrial markets. *Industrial Marketing Management, 38*(5), 737–743.

Herbig, P., & Milewicz, J. (1995). The relationship of reputation and credibility to brand success. *Journal of Consumer Marketing, 12*(4), 5–10.

Homburg, C., & Rudolph, B. (2001). Customer satisfaction in industrial markets: Dimensional and multiple role issues. *Journal of Business Research, 52*(1), 15–33.

Huntley, J. K. (2006). Conceptualization and measurement of relationship quality: Linking relationship quality to actual sales and recommendation intention. *Industrial Marketing Management, 35*(6), 703–714.

Jap, S. D., & Ganesan, S. (2000). Control mechanisms and the relationship life cycle: Implications for safeguarding specific investments and developing commitment. *Journal of Marketing Research, 8*, 227–245.

Kumar, N., Stern, L. W., & Achrol, R. S. (1992). Assessing reseller performance from the perspective of the supplier. *Journal of Marketing Research, 29*(2), 238–253.

Lai, C. S. (2007). The effects of influence strategies on dealer satisfaction and performance in Taiwan's motor industry. *Industrial Marketing Management, 36*(4), 518–527.

Leonidou, L. C., Palihawadana, D., & Theodosiou, M. (2006). An integrated model of the behavioural dimensions of industrial buyer-seller relationships. *European Journal of Marketing, 40*(1/2), 145–173.

Michell, P., Reast, J., & Lynch, J. (1998). Exploring the foundations of trust. *Journal of Marketing Management, 14*(1–3), 159–172.

Moliner, M. A., Sánchez, J., Rodríguez, R. M., & Callarisa, L. (2007). Perceived relationship quality and post-purchase perceived value: An integrative framework. *European Journal of Marketing, 41*(11/12), 1392–1422.

Morgan, R. M., & Hunt, S. D. (1994). The commitment-trust theory of relationship marketing. *Journal of Marketing, 58*(3), 20–38.

Nadin, G. (2008). Dealer-carmaker relationship: The theories of the duality of trust and of power-dependence. *International Journal of Automotive Technology and Management, 8*(1), 71–89.

Noordewier, T. C., John, G., & Nevin, J. R. (1990). Performance outcomes of purchasing arrangements in industrial buyer–vendor relationships. *Journal of Marketing, 54*, 80–93.

Nunnally, J. C., Bernstein, I. H., & Berge, J. M. T. (1967). *Psychometric theory* (Vol. 226). New York: McGraw-Hill.

Ou, W. M., Abratt, R., & Dion, P. (2006). The influence of retailer reputation on store patronage. *Journal of Retailing and Consumer Services, 13*, 221–230.

Palmatier, R. W., Dant, R. P., Grewal, D., & Evans, K. R. (2006). Factors influencing the effectiveness of relationship marketing: A meta-analysis. *Journal of Marketing, 70*(4), 136–153.

Ping, R. A., Jr. (2003). Antecedents of satisfaction in a marketing channel. *Journal of Retailing, 79*, 237–248.

Purohit, D., & Srivastava, J. (2001). Effect of manufacturer reputation, retailer reputation, and product warranty on consumer judgments of product quality: A cue diagnosticity framework. *Journal of Consumer Psychology, 10*(3), 123–134.

Ramaseshan, B., Yip, L. S. C., & Pae, J. H. (2006). Power, satisfaction, and relationship commitment in Chinese store-tenant relationship and their impact on performance. *Journal of Retailing, 82*(1), 63–70.

Rauyruen, P., & Miller, K. E. (2007). Relationship quality as a predictor of B2B customer loyalty. *Journal of Business Research, 60*(1), 21–31.

Rodriguez, I. R., Agudo, J. C., & Gutierrez, H. S. M. (2006). Determinants of economic and social satisfaction in manufacturer-distributor relationships. *Industrial Marketing Management, 35*, 666–675.

Sahadev, S., & Jayachandran, C. (2004). Managing the distribution channels for high-technology products. *European Journal of Marketing, 38*(1/2), 121–149.

Salminen, R. T., & Möller, K. (2006). Role of references in business marketing—Towards a normative theory of referencing. *Journal of Business-to-Business Marketing, 13*(1), 1–51.

Scheer, L. K., Kumar, N., & Steenkamp, J. E. M. (2003). Reactions to perceived inequity in U.S and Dutch inter-organizational relationships. *Academy of Management Journal, 46*(3), 303–316.

Selnes, F. (1998). Antecedents and consequences of trust and satisfaction in buyer-seller relationships. *European Journal of Marketing, 32*(3/4), 305–322.

Simpson, P. M., Siguaw, J. A., & Baker, T. (2001). A model of value creation: Supplier behaviors and their impact on reseller-perceived value. *Industrial Marketing Management, 30*(2), 119–134.

Skarmeas, D., Katsikeas, C. S., Spyropoulou, S., & Salehi-Sangari, E. (2008). Market and supplier characteristics driving distributor relationship quality in international marketing channels of industrial products. *Industrial Marketing Management, 37*(1), 23–36.

Smith, J. B., & Barclay, D. W. (1997). The effects of organizational differences and trust on the effectiveness of selling partner relationships. *Journal of Marketing, 61*, 3–21.

Venkatesh, R., Kohli, A. K., & Zaltman, G. (1995). Influence strategies in buying centers. *Journal of Marketing, 59*, 71–82.

Volpato, G., & Buzzavo, L. (2003). European Automotive distribution; the battle for selectivity and exclusivity is not over in Freyssenet, Shimizu and Volpato. *Globalisation or Regionalisation of the European car industry*.

Webster, J. E. (1992). The changing role of marketing in the corporation. *Journal of Marketing, 56*(4), 1–17.

Yang, S. U., & Grunig, J. E. (2005). Decomposing organisational reputation: The effects of organisation–public relationship outcomes on cognitive representations of organisations and evaluations of organisational performance. *Journal of Communication Management, 9*(4), 305–325.

Yoon, E., Guffey, H. J., & Kijewski, V. (1993). The effects of information and company reputation on intentions to buy a business service. *Journal of Business Research, 27*(3), 215–228.

Part VII
Entrepreneurship and Small Business

What Drives Female Entrepreneurship in Japan?

Ayumi Inaba and Shing-Wan Chang

Abstract Although the number of female entrepreneurs has grown worldwide (Brush and Cooper 2012; Kelley et al. 2013), female self-employment rate in Japan is quite low and there is still a significant gap of entrepreneurship participation between men and women (Welsh et al. 2014). One of the possible reasons why Japanese women are not willing to get self-employed is a Japanese cultural norm, which regards business as the masculine activity and housework as the women's responsibility (Kimoto 2000; Kondo 2001). This strong gender-role perception still affects females' behaviours. For instance, they tend to keep a distance from social capital/relationships and prefer kinship (Brush et al. 2009; Marlow 1997).

The purpose of this study is to examine factors affecting Japanese female entrepreneurship, specifically to find out the impacts of gender stereotypical perception and online social capital obtained via social media on entrepreneurial intention in Japan. The analysis was based on 426 Japanese entrepreneurs consisting of 243 business owners and 183 nascent entrepreneurs. To test the hypotheses and moderating effects of gender and age on entrepreneurial intention, Structural Equation Modelling and Independent Samples t-test were conducted. Results show that gender stereotypes, which referred to business as males' activity and housework as females' responsibility, would still exist in Japan and it decreased women's intention to start their own business. However, the effectiveness of social media to increase females' access to online social capital was also identified. Moreover, gender and age were found to be significant moderators for all hypothesized relationships. These findings can help policymakers understand women entrepreneurial intentions in Japan and take measures to extend their business opportunities. Lastly, this study provides the theoretical implications and extends the entrepreneurship literature.

References available upon request.

A. Inaba (✉) • S.-W. Chang
Middlesex University, London, UK
e-mail: ayumi19860130@gmail.com; s.chang@mdx.ac.uk

© Academy of Marketing Science 2016
L. Petruzzellis, R.S. Winer (eds.), *Rediscovering the Essentiality of Marketing*,
Developments in Marketing Science: Proceedings of the Academy of Marketing
Science, DOI 10.1007/978-3-319-29877-1_67

What Comes After the Honeymoon: Assessing the Process of Franchisee Adjustment

Markus Blut, Christof Backhaus, David Woisetschläger,
and Heiner Evanschitzky

Abstract The decision to enter a franchise system and to become a franchisee represents an important change in an individual's work environment (Kaufmann and Stanworth 1995). Once having signed a franchise contract, franchisees usually give up their current jobs and have to learn how to successfully establish and operate a franchise business. The initial phase of an individual's engagement as a franchisee is often accompanied by entrepreneurial euphoria, resulting from the fascination and excitement of beginning a new phase in their working life (Frazer 2001). However, recent research on relationship formation between franchisees and franchisors indicates that after some time, this initial fascination decreases due to sobering experiences with the franchise system (Blut et al. 2011). The first phase of "honeymoon" (Black and Mendenhall 1991) is followed by a phase of "disillusionment," in which franchisees are confronted with the realities of day-to-day business, leading to a decline in franchisee job satisfaction, trust in the franchisor, and commitment towards the franchise system. Blut and colleagues (2011) argue that this typical downturn of relationship properties may lead to a number of negative consequences such as increased opportunism of the franchisees, reduced investments, and lowered operational input (Oxenfeldt and Kelly 1968). In order to reduce the negative effects of the expected and almost inevitable downturn in relationship properties from "honeymoon" to "disillusionment," we have to investigate the process of what we term "franchisee adjustment." Therefore, our study examines factors associated with the adjustment after entering a franchise system. Based on expatriate adjustment models and social learning theory, we develop a conceptual model of franchisee adjustment focusing on franchisor support variables. This model is tested against a sample consisting of over a thousand franchisees nested within 32 franchise

M. Blut (✉) • C. Backhaus
Newcastle University Business School, Newcastle upon Tyne, UK
e-mail: markus.blut@ncl.ac.uk; christof.backhaus@ncl.ac.uk

D. Woisetschläger
TU Braunschweig, Braunschweig, Germany
e-mail: d.woisetschlaeger@tu-braunschweig.de

H. Evanschitzky
Aston Business School, Birmingham, UK
e-mail: h.evanschitzky@aston.ac.uk

© Academy of Marketing Science 2016
L. Petruzzellis, R.S. Winer (eds.), *Rediscovering the Essentiality of Marketing*,
Developments in Marketing Science: Proceedings of the Academy of Marketing
Science, DOI 10.1007/978-3-319-29877-1_68

systems. Results using hierarchical linear modelling (HLM) indicate that franchisors can facilitate franchisee adjustment through measures in the area of job design (autonomy, participation), knowledge management (knowledge transfer, prior self-employment), and attractiveness of the franchise (initial investments, royalty rate, reputation of the system).

References available upon request.

Networking Entrepreneurship in Non-Technology Sectors. The Case of Olive Oil

Antonia R. Gurrieri and Sabrina Spallini

Introduction

Networking entrepreneurs stimulate the growth of the group through the reinforcement of the relations among the firms involved. The opportunity to work in clusters is particularly necessary for SMEs, which always have a low power, especially for those who work in a low technological sector. Italy is characterized for a massive presence of small and medium enterprises, organized in districts or networks. Despite the economic crisis, some of these groups are able to survive and score positive performances both locally and abroad.

In this work, we investigate the olive-oil biological sector, which is able to tow the Apulian economy based on its vocation. This sector shows a trend in network formation. Moreover, from an entrepreneurial point of view, such a strategy brings advantages both for the single unit and the group. We believe that biological entrepreneurs prefer to form a consortium. The common factors are entrepreneurial culture and social contacts of the team.

A.R. Gurrieri (✉)
University of Foggia, Foggia, Italy
e-mail: antoniarosa.gurrieri@unifg.it

S. Spallini
University of Bari Aldo Moro, Bari, Italy
e-mail: sabrina.spallini@uniba.it

© Academy of Marketing Science 2016
L. Petruzzellis, R.S. Winer (eds.), *Rediscovering the Essentiality of Marketing*,
Developments in Marketing Science: Proceedings of the Academy of Marketing
Science, DOI 10.1007/978-3-319-29877-1_69

Background

Management innovations require open innovation, in which coexist both technology acquisition and technology exploitation (Gassmann 2006; Lichtenthaler 2008). van de Vrande et al. (2009) believe that the first one concerns all the activities that help firms in capturing external knowledge and technology. For example, external networks are able to use outside knowledge for a specific need of internal network enterprises, without passing for the internal vertical integration. On the other hand, technology exploitation is strictly linked either to the presence of spin off and spin out processes of internal knowledge, through the start up of new forms of organizations (i.e. venturing), or to the possibility of capitalize knowledge of involved employees.

In this work, we analyse a group of small firms active in a traditional sector, the agricultural one (Gurrieri and Petruzzellis 2008). In theory, the consideration on open innovation are not in line with the simplicity of this sector, but all the considerations that refer to the presence of a network could also be applied in traditional sectors such as the olive oil one (Gurrieri 2008). The *fil rouge* is the quality of entrepreneurship (Gurrieri 2013); the more the level and characteristics of the entrepreneurial team, the more the level of performances reached.

Each unit involved in the network could benefit from peculiar factors, social elements, and knowledge that coexist among network firms. Moreover, the possibility of measuring the structural intensity of a net represents the opportunity of verifying the dimension of social and knowledge entrepreneurial links and the intensiveness and importance of geographical connections.

Methods

This study aims at investigating the effect of the network on firm performances, considering the identity of the network and its social interactions. We believe that entrepreneurs' ability to innovate and the locational advantages in supporting network necessity are relevant factors for a network identity.

The process of social interaction is stressed on cultural and social links and network structure (Ridgeway and Smith-Lovin 1999). Therefore, culture is a crucial variable, especially in the agricultural sector (Capo-Vicedo et al. 2008). The choice of Apulia and the olive oil sector derives from the agricultural and international vocation of the region. Moreover, the presence of different forms of cooperation helps the small dimension of the firms to achieve successful results. In 2013, the organic Italian area was about 1317.77 ha, more than the previous year, and the olive-organic cultivation was about 129.574 ha, the third cultivation in extension. Among Italian regions, Apulia registered in the same year the best result in the olive production (Ismea 2013), thus confirming the biological vocation of the territory (Table 1).

From the data, we can highlight that, although the demand for organic olive oil or other certified quality products such as DOP and IGT increases, the production scores only a slight increase, which is even less for processors and distributors (Table 2).

Table 1 Areas and crops: regional distribution (hectares)

	Total crops 2013	Var. %'13–'12	Olive trees
Total	1317.177	12.8	175.946
Sicily	280.448	45.0	24.470
Puglia	191.791	12.1	55.715
Sardinia	142.250	7.6	3.815
Calabria	138.312	15.5	51.385
Tuscany	102.443	–4.7	12.110
Lazio	101.680	10.6	6.088
Emilia Romagna	80.924	–0.7	623
Marche	56.899	7.5	1.810
Basilicata	49.233	8.7	2.776
Piedmont	28.876	–1.5	8
Campania	28.673	15.3	8.965
Umbria	28.513	–6.5	4.428
Abruzzo	26.778	–3.2	2.449
Lombardy	20.685	8.9	156
Veneto	15.205	–11.0	347
Adige/Sudtirol	10.965	–2.4	58
Molise	5.266	9.2	498
Friuli	3.730	4.6	55
Liguria	3.090	2.2	190
Aosta Valley	2.417	46.3	0

Source: ISMEA 2013

Table 2 Apulian organic actors

	Producers	Processors	Importers	Producers/processors
2012	5.377	462	10	262
2013	5.289	513	8	444

Source: ISMEA

The vertical integration of the supply chain through a spontaneous network of companies seems to be the best option to overcome the competitive gap determined by the small dimension of the firms the initial and intermediate levels of the chain.

We therefore choose a group of firms, which form a production and marketing consortium. It places on the market only PDO and organic olive oil through its own brand. It purchases from firms that are part of the consortium both the raw material and the finished product. The consortium facilitates the creation of the network and promoting its brand on the market, improves the performance of individual firms, as well as transfers the added value created to the territory. The choice of selecting a single consortium derives from the successful performances scored by this consortium in the last 5 years. It is mostly composed of small firms but large firms also are part of it. In particular, some of these large companies are created by integration of small firms.

This highlights the propensity of Apulian companies to networking and thus strengthens the basic idea of the study represented by the importance of the cultural attitude to cooperate.

The model aims to analyse the antecedents of a network, namely Alliance competence and alliance resources (Lambe et al. 2002).

In order to analyse this reality, we construct a semi-structured questionnaire aiming to obtain information both qualitative and quantitative. We try to verify the real existence of an entrepreneurial network using the level of human linkages among the involved entrepreneurs.

From the qualitative answers emerge entrepreneurs' inclination of acting in an individualistic and opportunistic behaviour. So each entrepreneur is a potential rival not only for the involved firms in the Consortium, but also for the external ones. This behaviour in theory is in contrast with all the networking theory and all our prevision. However, we could read this feature as a stimulus for reinforcing the group because through the opportunistic behaviour of each entrepreneur emerges either the network's propensity and will to close the boundaries of the group, or a choice of the consortium entrepreneurs to work in a high-tension way for achieving best results.

Moreover, because all the firms involved in the olive-oil production have a long historical tradition and a high level of territorial competence, it is possible to suppose that there exists a high level of trust among entrepreneurs and some relative absorptive capacity, measured as the differences in absorptive capacity among the linked firms of the consortium.

The expected results of the analysis put in evidence the real existence of the Apulian entrepreneurial network of organic olive-oil production.

References available upon request.

Determinants of SMEs Growth: The Balance Between Innovation and Tradition as Key Factor for Italian Small Business Development

Gaetano Aiello, Raffaele Donvito, Diletta Acuti, Valentina Mazzoli, and Laura Grazzini

Introduction

The growth of many industrialized developed countries relies on small and medium enterprises (SMEs) that are the basis of a solid industrial sector and contribute to the development of the main macroeconomic variables (Calabrese et al. 2002).

For this reason, academicians and practitioners have analyzed SMEs since decades to study different entrepreneurial set of problems as internal firms' structure, market relationship, performance, competitiveness, and growth. In our perspective, we mean growth not only in a mono-dimensional way: indeed, there are a lot of conceptual frameworks which have tried to identify the multidimensional aspects of small and medium business growth (Laursen et al. 1999; Cohendet et al. 2010; Lee 2010).

Some firms can be assumed to grow in a "traditional" way, by simultaneously increasing the sales and employment of the original business entity. Other firms, however, may increase sales while actually reducing employment. Therefore, a number of scholars recommend the use of multiple growth measures in the study of firm growth (Delmar et al. 2003; Johnsen and McMahon 2005). As for the growth measurement, there is no single theory which can adequately explain the cause of small business growth (Gibb and Davies 1990). According to Smallbone et al. (1995), this is firstly because of the heterogeneity that exists in the various types of SMEs; secondly because of the set of factors that can affect growth, which may interact with each other in different ways in dissimilar circumstances. In recent years, considerable empirical researches on the determinants of small business growth have been developed too. Dobbs and Hamilton (2007) summarized 34 studies published since

G. Aiello (✉) • R. Donvito • D. Acuti • V. Mazzoli • L. Grazzini
University of Florence, Florence, Italy
e-mail: gaetano.aiello@unifi.it; raffaele.donvito@unifi.it; diletta.acuti@unifi.it; valentina.mazzoli@unifi.it; laura.grazzini@unifi.it

© Academy of Marketing Science 2016
L. Petruzzellis, R.S. Winer (eds.), *Rediscovering the Essentiality of Marketing*, Developments in Marketing Science: Proceedings of the Academy of Marketing Science, DOI 10.1007/978-3-319-29877-1_70

347

the mid 1990s which have involved over 30 independent variables. These variables could be classified into four categories as identified by Smallbone and Wyer (2000): firm-specific characteristics, peculiarities of the entrepreneur, environmental/industry-specific factors, and management strategies. Although this work mainly focuses on the variables related to the management strategies, it considers also the other three categories. Regarding the management strategies particular relevance is connected to innovation, diversification, internationalization, and branding patterns.

Innovation. Innovation represents one of the main drivers for firm growth (Cerrato 1999; D'Angelo 2010; Giovannetti et al. 2009; Nassimbeni 2001), and it is widely agreed that the establishment and development of SMEs are based on innovations because the ownership of innovative resources and capabilities contributes to build firm-specific advantages that enable SMEs to compete versus bigger companies both abroad and in the domestic market (Teece et al. 1997). According to Zucchella and Siano (2014), there is a strong tie between innovation and internationalization: the development of innovations opens new market opportunities and/or strengthens the existing ones, and international players benefit from access to wider and more diversified sources of knowledge, thus nurturing innovation.

Diversification. As known one important determinant of small business growth is the diversification of products; anyway this strategic path has driven SMEs not always to an efficient process of development, producing in some case unstable firm configurations. Gort (1962) was one of the first to examine the profitability of diversified firms. Chandler (1962) and following studies by Rumelt (1982), Christensen and Montgomery (1981) in the strategic management literature report a systematic relationship between a firm diversification strategy and economic performance. Recently, Liu and Hsu (2011) argue that dynamic capabilities would enable firms to expand and also act as important antecedents of corporate diversification. On the other hand, a company's degree of corporate diversification has significant impact on the firm performance.

Internationalization. The diversification concerns not only the product but also the markets; according to this point of view internationalization can be considered among the diversification strategies. As widely known, the entrance in new geographical areas can follow two strategic patterns: the development of the market that exploits the same product for new markets, and the diversification that uses new products for the entry in new markets (De Leersnyder 1982; Ferrero 2013). Studies of Kyläheiko et al. (2011) underline how the way to internationalize a firm has a direct connection with the growth of the enterprise. Furthermore, there are many variables that influence the path driving enterprises to internationalize: innovation, human resource management, localization in industrial districts, previous experience of the firm, pro-activity of the entrepreneur, and turbulence of the sector (D'Angelo et al. 2013).

Branding and COO. Literature confers to brand a fundamental role for the growth and the development of a firm (Aaker 1995; Coda Spuetta 1994; Keller 1998); sometimes, the brand equity is intensified by the association with Country-of-Origin (COO) in a coherent way (Haubl and Helrod 1999). In this sense, the COO is considered an important clue for the consumer's perception and the evaluation of a product because it influences the opinion about quality, the perception of risk and the value, and the propensity to purchase. Koschate-Fischer and Diamantopoulos (2012) demonstrate that the COO influence consumer's willing to pay for the purchase of a product, considering both the consumer's participation during the purchase and the familiarity with the brand.

Methodology

This research is structured on a single-case analysis, carried out on the methodological approaches developed by Yin (1994, 2003), Eisenhardt (1989, 2007), and Woodside (2003, 2010).

The phases of the research process are the following ones:

– Analysis of the most representative industrial sectors of Italian territory in terms of tight link with the cultural heritage, development path (from an artisanal laboratory to a structured international and diversified firm). For these reasons, the research has been focused on a specific artisanal production ("goldbeater") because of its cultural heritage and its development pattern.
– Selection of the firm analyzed. This firm (called "Alfa") has been chosen because of its importance in the Italian craftsmanship arena and its particular production of gold leaf; furthermore, nowadays this firm could be considered as one of the leaders in the international gold leaf market.
– Collection of secondary data about Alfa (website, corporate profile, firm brochures, articles on specialized magazines).
– Development of a not structured survey protocol for interviewing the firm managers.
– In-depth interview of the President and the Marketing Manager of Alfa.
– Triangulation of data collected, analysis, and interpretation of principal empirical results gathered.

The authors provide a phenomenal exposition of the results, as exposed in the following paragraph.

Results and Discussion

The case analyses about Alfa points out different drivers of the firm growth, in terms of dimension, turn over and market share: (a) Firm-specific characteristics, (b) Peculiarities of the entrepreneur, (c) Environmental/industry-specific factors, (d) Management strategies.

(a) *Firm-Specific Characteristics*

Tradition and craftsmanship are identity basis of Alfa pursuing the history of the enterprise for 15 generations. The business of the firm Alfa started in sixteenth century and was founded by a Florentine family of decorators, gilders, and goldsmiths. It was a time when Florence was in a great political, economic, and artistic turmoil: most of the major works of art were commissioned and done in this Renaissance period. In nineteenth century, the artisan production shifted in an industrial production one, maintaining a link with traditional processes and artisan passion; in that period the brand was registered becoming an icon of excellent quality in the field of goldbeaters over the years. According to its centenary history, Alfa has based its mission on four values, namely tradition, quality, ethics, and innovation.

(b) *Peculiarities of the Entrepreneur*

The know-how has been transmitted and improved through the modernization and the innovation of the processes. Since origins, the ancestors worked in the gold sector, distinguishing for their peculiar ability to handle gold. The Renaissance period supported the spreading of the craftsmen' reputation of Alfa, focused on the production of thin sheets of gold or other precious metals for gilding or silvering. The technique of production has been shared from fathers to sons throughout years and 15 generations has succeeded in the managing of the firm (six generations since Alfa has become a brand). Each generation of entrepreneur has improved processes, contributing to build the firm-specific advantage on which the value of the brand is based. Therefore, the authors convey that the success and the growth of Alfa mainly rely on skills of succeeding entrepreneurs which have been able to respect so far the balance between tradition and innovation as the main strength of their business, transmitting to customers this strong bond.

(c) *Environmental/Industry-Specific Factors*

Regarding firm development, environmental factors played a crucial role at the beginning of the business, when the Renaissance period and its turmoil strongly support production growth. The main development of the firm took place during that period thanks to the artistic ferment existing in this phase. However, the history of the firm shows that it was able to exploit environmental factors to succeed in its business. In particular, the management took advantage of opportunities displayed in other markets, such as Ex-URSS countries or South Arabia, where the environmental and economic situation was favorable for Alfa's business.

(d)*Management Strategies*

According to the prospective adopted by the authors, the chapter focuses on four kinds of managerial strategic courses, namely innovation, diversification, internationalization, and branding patterns.

Innovation. As reminded in this chapter, innovation is one of the main drivers that lead the firm along the growth path. The peculiar Alfa interpretation of innovation includes the respect of the balance between technology innovation and traditional processes, which still remain the same during years. It means that there are still several steps which can only be done by hand and are accomplished with the same hand tools and methods as were done generations ago. Throughout the Alfa history, the synergy between manual labor and mechanization has allowed for the development of a high-quality production process that follows ancient traditions and methods, but uses some of the most advanced infrastructures and technologies in the world, such as the laser cutting or nanotechnologies. Furthermore, the innovation has led so far the path growth along the drivers of internationalization and diversification.

Diversification. Innovation and continuous investments in research and development have driven the firm to the diversification of the production through new application of gold leaf. Gold leaf, originally used for the decoration of monuments and works of art, is now exploited for different purposes: the production of edible gold and silver, the coating of terracotta tiles (other typical Florentine product) and other uses in the design sector, the creation of a cosmetics line, the collaboration with partners in order to develop new applications of gold leaf. The growth of the enterprise is due not only to the entrance in new fields but also to the continuous improvement of the core business of the firm Alfa.

Internationalization. One of the first drivers of the development of the business is the internationalization in new markets. The firm Alfa began to sell abroad at the beginning of the twentieth century, when it reached other European markets for the first time in its history. The process of internationalization has carried on and now the foreign market share represents the 75% of the firm turnover. The company serves 75 countries all over the world and has founded two subsidiaries in East Europe and Spain. The success of the brand Alfa reached in international markets is mainly due to the strong link with Made in Italy production that represents a guarantee of quality and reliability worldwide.

Branding patterns. The brand Alfa is tightly linked to the main values tied to Made in Italy production, that is to say excellent quality of the product and processes, tradition of the processes, innovation. Alfa has been able to exploit these values to spread its reputation worldwide becoming an icon of Made in Italy; conscious of this strength Alfa continue to invest in Made in Italy, maintaining its production and branding strongly linked to its country of origin.

Conclusion and Implications for Theory and Practice

This chapter shows how the factors analyzed (firm-specific characteristics, peculiarities of the entrepreneur, environmental/industry-specific factors, and management strategies) have driven Alfa to a growth path that still continues. In terms of managerial implications, this work confirms that the aware mix of development variables could lead SMEs to a successful growth both in domestic market and abroad. Obviously, the main limitation of the research relies on the research approach employed that considers a single-case analysis. For this reason, the authors wish for new researches including multiple case analyses on growth patterns.

References available upon request.

The Context and Outcomes of Entrepreneurial Marketing as a Decision-Making Process Under Uncertainty

Elisabete Sampaio de Sá, Minoo Farhangmehr, and José Carlos Pinho

Abstract Previous studies on the marketing/entrepreneurship interface have attempted to identify the core elements that constitute the entrepreneurial marketing construct mainly by describing how new ventures implement marketing activities (e.g., Stokes 2000; Coviello et al. 2000; O'Dwyer et al. 2009). Despite the advances the area has known over the last 30 years, Hills et al. (2008) emphasize the fact that there are still few studies of what characterizes entrepreneurial marketing and of its differences when compared to traditional marketing. This chapter proposes developing the understanding of the concept by focusing on the entrepreneur's marketing decision-making process. Assuming a cognitive perspective, the study is established on the individual level, since how entrepreneurs get, process, and use information affects how they cope with external factors. Bridging entrepreneurial marketing theory and the cognitive approach to entrepreneurship, we suggest a conceptualization of entrepreneurial marketing as a decision-making process shaped by some circumstances, generally characterized by uncertainty.

In order to understand the circumstances under which an entrepreneurial or managerial marketing decision-making is more appropriate, 51 entrepreneurs were interviewed in two research phases. The first involved nine in-depth exploratory interviews and the second consisted in 42 interviews using Critical Incident Technique (CIT). CIT interviews resulted in 146 usable marketing decision-making related incidents that were analyzed both qualitatively and quantitatively regarding: (1) the level of uncertainty involved, measured by the information available to found a given decision and the level of marketing competency, as a proxy of processing capacity, referring to the bounded rationality theory (Simon 1991, 1979); (2) the resulting marketing actions, classified either as entrepreneurial or managerial; and (3) their outcomes, categorized in four types: potential creation; growth; marketing effects; and negative or lower than expected results.

E.S. de Sá (✉) • M. Farhangmehr • J.C. Pinho
University of Minho, Braga, Portugal
e-mail: elisampaio@eeg.uminho.pt; minoo@eeg.uminho.pt; jcpinho@eeg.uminho.pt

© Academy of Marketing Science 2016
L. Petruzzellis, R.S. Winer (eds.), *Rediscovering the Essentiality of Marketing*,
Developments in Marketing Science: Proceedings of the Academy of Marketing
Science, DOI 10.1007/978-3-319-29877-1_71

353

The study concludes that entrepreneurial marketing, is more suitable for highly uncertain environments, characterized by low levels of information and when the decision maker has little marketing competency. On the contrary, in the context of abundant information to found marketing decisions and when the decision maker holds marketing competency, managerial marketing practices are more appropriate since they promote expansion; growth; and efficiency gains. New venture's managers should, therefore, adapt their marketing practices to different contexts in order to maximize marketing decision outputs. The results also show that entrepreneurs with higher marketing competency have a natural tendency to implement managerial marketing even when information is scarce. This is a riskier decision-making style, however, since more resources are committed when managerial marketing is implemented. On the other hand, less proficient decision makers can produce more effective and efficient outputs from their marketing if they acquire marketing competencies to decide in more stable situations, which can occur in different stages of the company development.

References available upon request.

Part VIII
Health and Social Marketing

Exploring the Dual Effects of Waiting on Satisfaction with Health Service

Yi-Fen Liu, Jacob Y.H. Jou, and I-Ling Ling

Abstract Waiting is a major course of service dissatisfaction in most health literature. However, are the effects of waiting all negative? This research aims to explore the dual effects (i.e., both the positive and negative effects) of waiting on health service satisfaction. We expect the relationship between waiting time and satisfaction is "inversed U-shape" and to find that under certain circumstances waiting can positively correlate to satisfaction. We also want to understand the moderating roles of service attributes and patient characteristics. We conduct a survey with 334 patients in three large hospitals and in-depth interviews with 20 participants. The results reveal that the relationship between waiting and satisfaction is "U-shape," the left arm curve which shows the negative correlation between waiting and satisfaction indicating that the longer the waiting, the lower the satisfaction. However, the decrease rate of satisfaction slows with the increase of waiting and satisfaction reaches the lowest point at 2.6 h waiting. After this point, satisfaction positively correlates with waiting. Sociability plays a moderating role as that waiting has stronger effects on satisfaction among high-sociability patients. Furthermore, waiting has positive contribution to satisfaction through social interaction and signaling service quality, but these effects may occur in the later stage of waiting.

Y.-F. Liu (✉)
National Kaohsiung First University of Science and Technology, Kaohsiung, Taiwan
e-mail: yifenliu@nkfust.edu.tw

J.Y.H. Jou
Kaohsiung Medical University, Kaohsiung, Taiwan
e-mail: jacobjou@cc.kmu.edu.tw

I.-L. Ling
National Chiayi University, Chiayi, Taiwan
e-mail: yiling@mail.ncyu.edu.tw

© Academy of Marketing Science 2016
L. Petruzzellis, R.S. Winer (eds.), *Rediscovering the Essentiality of Marketing*,
Developments in Marketing Science: Proceedings of the Academy of Marketing
Science, DOI 10.1007/978-3-319-29877-1_72

Promoting Renewable Energy Adoption: Environmental Knowledge vs. Fear Appeals

Patrick Hartmann, Vanessa Apaolaza, Clare D'Souza, Jose M. Barrutia, and Carmen Echebarria

Abstract This study addresses the effects of knowledge and fear arousal related to climate change issues on intention to switch to green electricity. Participants of an experimental online study were exposed to a fear appeal based on climate change threats. Fear arousal and knowledge concerning energy generation and climate change were assessed with an online questionnaire. Findings confirmed the hypothesized positive influence of fear arousal on the intention to choose residential green electricity. The effect of knowledge was non-significant, however. Findings contribute to reassessing the relevance of cognitive elaboration and have implications for marketers of green electricity products.

Keywords Renewable energy • Environmental behaviour • Fear appeals • Knowledge

Introduction

Since the further development of renewable energy will depend to an important extent on consumer's voluntary switching to green electricity products (Diaz-Rainey and Ashton 2008; Esteban et al. 2012; Ito et al. 2010; Prasad and Munch 2012; Wiser et al. 2001; Wiser et al. 1998), consumer's motives concerning green electricity adoption are being approached by a stream of research. An effective branding and marketing communications strategy may hold the key to the success of consumer oriented green electricity products (Truffer et al. 2001). In this context, previous research has particularly addressed the interplay of environmental

P. Hartmann (✉) • V. Apaolaza • J.M. Barrutia • C. Echebarria
University of the Basque Country UPV/EHU, Leioa, Spain
e-mail: patrick.hartmann@ehu.es; vanessa.apaolaza@ehu.es; josemaria.barrutia@ehu.es; carmen.etxebarria@ehu.es

C. D'Souza
La Trobe University, Melbourne, VIC, Australia
e-mail: cdsouza@latrobe.edu.au

© Academy of Marketing Science 2016
L. Petruzzellis, R.S. Winer (eds.), *Rediscovering the Essentiality of Marketing*,
Developments in Marketing Science: Proceedings of the Academy of Marketing
Science, DOI 10.1007/978-3-319-29877-1_73

359

values and attitudes (Ertör-Akyazi et al. 2012; Faiers et al. 2007; Hartmann and Apaolaza 2012; Hartmann et al. 2013; Paladino and Pandit 2012; Wüstenhagen et al. 2007). However, although research on unspecific environmental behaviour has previously addressed the role of cognitive factors such as environmental knowledge, behavioural effects of specific renewable energy related knowledge have scarcely been attended. Furthermore, the possible influences of particular emotional influences, such as climate change related fears, have also not been attended by previous research. Several studies support fear response as a principal behavioural antecedent (e.g. Arthur and Quester 2004; Dillard and Anderson 2004; Henthorne et al. 1993). While Truelove (2012) dual-process model of energy support analyses both emotions and beliefs about different energy sources including renewable energy, rather than addressing individual influences of fear arousal, the model is based on aggregated affect dimensions. The present study aims to address these gaps in the literature in the scope of an experimental study of the effect of climate change related fear arousal and knowledge of renewable energy and climate change topics on consumers' intention to switch to a premium priced green electricity product.

Theoretical Background

A number of studies have shown that consumers of green electricity aim to contribute to mitigating climate change by supporting electricity generation from renewable sources (Wüstenhagen and Bilharz 2006). An important share of consumers indeed perceives that green electricity adoption would prevent or decelerate climate change and global warming, increase air quality, and decrease energy dependency (Roe et al. 2001). In addition, Clark et al. (2003) found among actual clients of green electricity the prevailing belief that reducing air pollution from electricity production would improve the health of natural ecosystems. Overall, a series of cultural, social, and psychological motives of green electricity choice have been suggested (Faiers et al. 2007; Yamamoto et al. 2008). Directly related to consumer's personality traits are values and environmental concern as principal determinants of general environmentally sound consumption behaviour (Balderjahn 1988; Diamantopoulos et al. 2003). Several studies have identified altruistic values (Rowlands et al. 2003; Wiser et al. 2001) and environmental concern (Clark et al. 2003) as significant drivers of green electricity adoption. Awareness of consequences of energy related environmental problems for humans and for the biosphere has been shown to improve attitudes and intentions concerning green electricity choice (Hansla et al. 2008; Ek 2005). A cognitive perspective of this process suggests that individuals consciously evaluate the consequences of environmental problems (Fransson and Garling 1999) and subsequently develop behavioural responses such as concern about the state of the environment (Bamberg 2003).

Effects of Environmental Knowledge

To experience a significant motivation to adopt green electricity, in line with the above-mentioned cognitive perspective of behavioural influences of awareness of consequences beliefs, the individual must hold a certain level of knowledge regarding the environmental consequences of conventional as well as renewable energy generation. Research has indeed revealed a close relationship between environmental concern and awareness of climate-change issues, clean energy, alternative energy sources, and energy conservation (Zimmer et al. 1994). For general environmental behaviour, the level of knowledge on the environmental impact of products has been shown to be significantly related to the consumer's willingness of paying a price premium for environmentally sound products (Roberts 1996; Scholder-Ellen 1994; Scholder-Ellen et al. 1991). And also for the particular case of green electricity demand, increasing knowledge by exposure to information about energy resource issues led to consumer's being more willing to purchase premium priced electricity from renewable sources (Zarnikau 2003). Cognitive beliefs about renewable energy relate positively to the intention to pay a price premium for green electricity (Bang et al. 2000). Accordingly, Salmela and Varho (2006) argue that residential adoption of green electricity can be enhanced by providing consumers with information about the implications of different forms of electricity generation, in particular with regard to their respective environmental impact. Purchasing decisions may depend even on whether the individual had been previously provided with information only about the supply source of a particular electricity product or, in addition, about the specific emission levels of different energy sources (Johnson and Frank 2006). Thus, Truffer et al. (2001) suggest that information currently provided by green power labelling schemes may be insufficient to inform choice of green electricity products. To direct consumer's motivation toward green electricity, it may be necessary to build clients' knowledge with more accurate and detailed information than provided by green power labelling schemes and marketing communications.

In line with Bang et al. (2000), the effect of cognitive belief based knowledge on intention to switch to green electricity can be addressed in the framework of the theory of reasoned action (Fishbein and Ajzen 1975). Consumer's motivation to adopt green electricity should, to some extent, depend on the individual's level of knowledge regarding the environmental consequences of different energy sources, derived from the deliberate cognitive elaboration of information received previously:

H1: The individual's level of knowledge regarding environmental consequences of different energy sources has a positive influence on intention to switch to green electricity.

Emotional Responses to Environmental Threats

Awareness of environmental threats has been shown to induce coping behaviour aimed at mitigating these threats. Individuals who perceive environmental problems to pose a more serious threat to their health and well-being are more likely to engage in environmental sound behaviour (Baldassare and Katz 1992). The perception of environmental threats was found to lead to a stronger behavioural commitment in terms of donating money or time to an environmental organization and signing a petition (Hine and Gifford 1991). Specifically for energy related environmental threats, increments in the perceived noxiousness, magnitude or severity of the 1970s energy crisis increased willingness to reduce energy consumption (Hass et al. 1975). In the context of energy saving, Obermiller (1995) showed that communications emphasizing the severity of energy related environmental threats lead to individuals' increased perception of importance and severity of the problem.

Apart from cognitive processing of cognitive beliefs concerning environmental threats, individuals also develop significant emotional responses to the awareness of the threat, since appraisal of environmental threats may induce fear or anxiousness. Thus, exposure to environmental risks leads to emotional reactions including fear, hopelessness and worry (Böhm 2003). For instance, mass media information on threats related to genetically modified food contributes to consumer's fears of these food types (Laros and Steenkamp 2004). Comparing behavioural responses to different options of energy generation, Truelove (2012) analysed aggregated energy-related emotions on bipolar emotional adjective pairs happy—dread, optimism—anger, secure—fear. Truelove's composed emotional measure explained a significant amount of variance in attitude towards different energy sources. Although with respect to emotional responses to energy and climate change related environmental threats, fear arousal seems particularly relevant, Truelove did not address the effect of such individual emotional reactions.

The effects of fear arousal have been prominently modelled by Janis 1967 Fear Drive Theory, which postulates that fear motivates behavioural responses. Overall, a stream of research supports direct behavioural effects of fear aroused as a consequence of threat awareness (Dillard 1994) for such diverse behaviours as purchasing a self-defensive device (LaTour and Rotfeld 1997), HIV/AIDS prevention (Manchandra et al. 2003), influenza vaccination (Dillard and Anderson 2004), or supporting victim's rights programmes (Henthorne et al. 1993).

Specific research in fear arousal from appraisal of environmental threats is scarce, however. Previous studies have confirmed the effect of fear arousal on behavioural intentions for environmental threats deriving from naturally occurring radioactive radon gas contamination (LaTour and Tanner 2003) and nuclear power facilities (Peters and Slovic 2007; Roser and Thompson 1995). Overall, it seems reasonable to suggest a positive relationship between fear arousal and behavioural intentions for the case of environmental threats related to climate change.

H2: Fear arousal as a consequence of exposure to an environmental threat appeal related to climate change has a positive influence on intention to switch to green electricity.

Research Method

To test the hypothesized effects, a sample of 200 individuals was drawn from a representative online-panel recruited by a commercial online-panel provider and randomly divided into two groups. One group were exposed to a threat appeal

Table 1 Principal component factor analysis of fear response indicator variables, scale reliability

Indicators	Factor loadings
Afraid	.95
Scared	.93
Fearful	.95
Concerned	.85
Worried	.92
Eigenvalue	4.23
Variance explained	84.59
Cronbach's alpha	.96

presentation consisting of nine slides featuring screen-filling pictures of air pollution and severe impacts of climate change in terms of floods, storms, droughts and wildfires. Subsequently participants had to respond to a questionnaire. Participants in the control condition were directly presented with the questionnaire without previous stimuli exposure.

Knowledge regarding energy and climate change issues was assessed with seven items with the options "correct" and "incorrect". Items referred to the relationship between fossil fuels and CO_2 emissions, the degree of scientific agreement on manmade climate change, the proportion of electricity generated from fossil and renewable energy sources, among similar facts. Participants' knowledge was relatively high with a mean score of 4.7 from a maximum of seven points. 21.3 % scored seven points, while 2.5 % failed in all items.

Fear response was measured prompting climate change and rating on 5 point unipolar scales the extent to which participants experienced each of the emotions afraid, scared, fearful and concerned. Emotion measurement was based on previous scales by Arthur and Quester (2004), Batra and Holbrook (1990), Russell (1980) Watson et al.'s (1988) Positive Affect and Negative Affect Schedule (PANAS), and Edell and Burke's (1987) emotional responses to advertising. The dimensionality of the scale was analysed with principal component factor analysis (Table 1). One single factor was extracted with eigenvalue 4.23, 84.59 % of explained variance and factor loadings ranging from .85 to .95. Scale reliability was high (Cronbach's alpha = .96).

Intention to switch to green electricity was measured with two items. First, participants were asked to choose between two alternative electricity contracts, one standard electricity plan offering electricity generated from non-renewable energy sources and one greenpower plan, providing their home with certified green electricity from renewable energy sources like wind, solar and hydro-energy. Pricing information was derived by averaging real marketplace online offers of different electricity providers for an average level of electricity consumption. The greenpower plan had a 20 % price premium. The second item rated the participant's likelihood of their choosing the certified Greenpower plan, if they had to decide about a new electricity contract for their home.

Table 2 Manipulation check: dependent variable mean values, anova analysis of mean value differences

Dependent variable	Experimental factor	Mean	Std. deviation	Std. error	F	p
Fear arousal	Control	2.21	1.05	.11	20.78	$p < .001$
	Threat appeal	2.92	1.10	.11		

Table 3 Variable correlations

	Knowledge	Fear arousal
Fear response	.45	
Purchase intention	.29	.51

Note: All correlations significant at $p < .001$

Results and Discussion

The manipulation check of the experimental treatment confirms a successful manipulation as a result of threat appeal exposures (Table 2). Anova analysis shows that participants' fear response to awareness of climate change threats increased significantly ($p < .001$). The correlation analysis of variables knowledge, fear response and purchase intention confirms significant positive correlations between all analysed variables (Tables 3 and 4). Thus, fear response and knowledge seem to be also related. The correlation between knowledge and purchase intention is significant, albeit rather low.

Binary logistic regression analysis of the effects of the two independent variables on the choice between the two electricity contracts (Nagelkerke R-square=.26, $p < .001$) confirms a significant positive effect of fear arousal (Exp(B)=2.33; $p < .001$), supporting H2. However, the effect of climate and energy related knowledge on green choice is not significant ($p = .24$), disconfirming H1. Multiple regression analysis (R-square=.27, $p < .001$) of the relationships of both variables with intention to switch to green electricity reveals an identical pattern (Table 5). Fear arousal has a significant positive influence on purchase intention (beta=.48, $p < .001$), whereas the effect of knowledge is non-significant.

The contribution of this study is twofold. On the one hand, in line with previous research on environmental fear appeals (LaTour and Tanner 2003; Peters and Slovic 2007; Roser and Thompson 1995), findings support the hypothesized effect of climate change related fears on some consumers' intention to switch to green electricity. On the other hand, results do not support a significant relationship of the individual's knowledge on energy and climate issues with the voluntary adoption of renewable energy. In this particular case, the effect of cognitive factors as suggested in the literature (e.g. Roberts 1996; Scholder-Ellen 1994; Scholder-Ellen et al. 1991; Zimmer et al. 1994) was significantly less relevant than the emotional impact of perceived environmental threats.

Table 4 Binary logistic regression analysis: effects of fear arousal and knowledge on green electricity choice

Dependent variable	Independent variables	B	S.E.	Wald	p	Exp (B)
Purchase intention	Fear arousal	.85	.18	22.29	$p<.001$	2.33
	Knowledge	.12	.10	1.40	.24	1.13
	(Constant)	−3.36	.60	31.64	$p<.001$	.04
Cox & Snell R-square	.19					
Nagelkerke R-square	.26					
Omnibus tests of model coefficients	$p<.001$					

Table 5 Regression analysis: effects of fear arousal and knowledge on intentions to switch to green electricity

Dependent variable	Independent variables	B	Std. error	Beta	t	p
Purchase intention	Fear arousal	.51	.07	.48	6.73	$p<.001$
	Knowledge	.05	.04	.08	1.16	.25
	(Constant)	.99	.22		4.49	$p<.001$
R-square	.27					$p<.001$

For marketers of green electricity products and institutional supporters of renewable energy adoption, findings of this study imply that the use of environmental threat appeals in marketing communications may be more effective than delivering detailed information to recipients, as often recommended in the literature. Future research should further address the relevance of emotional vs. cognitive factors in consumers' green electricity adoption, for instance comparing actual green electricity clients with clients of conventional electricity contracts.

References

Arthur, D., & Quester, P. (2004). Who's afraid of that Ad? Applying segmentation to the protection motivation model. *Psychology and Marketing, 21*(11), 671–696.

Baldassare, M., & Katz, C. (1992). The personal threat of environmental problems as predictor of environmental practices. *Environment and Behavior, 24*(5), 602–615.

Balderjahn, I. (1988). Personality variables and environmental attitudes as predictors of ecologically-responsible consumption patterns. *Journal of Business Research, 17*, 51–56.

Bamberg, S. (2003). How does environmental concern influence specific environmentally related behaviors? A new answer to an old question. *Journal of Environmental Psychology, 23*, 21–32.

Bang, H. K., Ellinger, A. E., Hadjimarcou, J., & Traichal, P. A. (2000). Consumers concern, knowledge, belief, and attitude toward renewable energy: An application of the reasoned action theory. *Psychology and Marketing, 17*(6), 449–468.

Batra, R., & Holbrook, M. B. (1990). Developing a typology of affective responses to advertising. *Psychology and Marketing, 7*(1), 11–25.

Böhm, G. (2003). Emotional reactions to environmental risks: Consequentialist versus ethical evaluation. *Journal of Environmental Psychology, 23*, 199–212.

Clark, C. F., Kotchen, M. J., & Moore, M. R. (2003). Internal and external influences on pro-environmental behavior: Participation in a green electricity program. *Journal of Environmental Psychology, 23*, 237–246.

Diamantopoulos, A., Schlegelmilch, B. B., Sinkovics, R. R., & Bohlen, G. M. (2003). Can socio-demographics still play a role in profiling green consumers? A review of the evidence and an empirical investigation. *Journal of Business Research, 56*(6), 465–480.

Diaz-Rainey, I., & Ashton, J. K. (2008). Stuck between a ROC and a hard place? Barriers to the take up of green energy in the UK. *Energy Policy, 36*, 3053–3061.

Dillard, J. P. (1994). Rethinking the study of fear appeals: An emotional perspective. *Commun Theory, 4*(4), 295–323.

Dillard, J. P., & Anderson, J. W. (2004). The role of fear in persuasion. *Psychology & Marketing, 21*(11), 909–926.

Edell, J. A., & Burke, M. C. (1987). The power of feelings in understanding advertising effects. *Journal of Consumer Research, 14*(3), 421–433.

Ek, K. (2005). Public and private attitudes towards "green" electricity: The case of Swedish wind power. *Energy Policy, 33*, 1677–1689.

Ertör-Akyazi, P., Adaman, F., Özkaynak, B., & Zenginobuz, U. (2012). Citizens' preferences on nuclear and renewable energy sources: Evidence from Turkey. *Energy Policy, 47*, 309–320.

Esteban, M., Zhang, Q., & Longarte-Galnares, G. (2012). Cost-benefit analysis of a green electricity system in Japan considering the indirect economic impacts of tropical cyclones. *Energy Policy, 43*, 49–57.

Faiers, A., Cook, M., & Neame, C. (2007). Towards a contemporary approach for understanding consumer behaviour in the context of domestic energy use. *Energy Policy, 35*(8), 4381–4390.

Fishbein, M., & Ajzen, I. (1975). *Belief, attitude, intention, and behavior: An introduction to theory and research*. Reading, MA: Addison-Wesley.

Fransson, N., & Garling, T. (1999). Environmental concern: Conceptual definitions, measurement methods, and research findings. *Journal of Environmental Psychology, 19*, 369–382.

Hansla, A., Gamble, A., Juliusson, A., & Gärling, T. (2008). The relationships between awareness of consequences, environmental concern, and value orientations. *Journal of Environmental Psychology, 28*, 1–9.

Hartmann, P., & Apaolaza, V. (2012). Consumer attitude and purchase intention toward green energy brands: The roles of psychological benefits and environmental concern. *Journal of Business Research, 65*, 1254–1263.

Hartmann, P., Apaolaza, V., & Alija, P. (2013). Nature imagery in advertising: Attention restoration and memory effects. *International Journal of Advertising, 32*(2), 183–210.

Hass, J. W., Bagley, G. S., & Rogers, R. W. (1975). Coping with the energy crisis: Effects of fear appeals upon attitudes toward energy consumption. *Journal of Applied Psychology, 60*(6), 754–756.

Henthorne, T. L., LaTour, M. S., & Nataraajan, R. (1993). Fear appeals in print advertising: An analysis of arousal and Ad response. *Journal of Advertising, 22*(2), 59–68.

Hine, D. W., & Gifford, R. (1991). Fear appeals, individual differences, and environmental concern. *Journal of Environmental Education, 23*(1), 36–41.

Ito, N., Takeuchi, K., Tsuge, T., & Kishimoto, A. (2010). Applying threshold models to donations to a green electricity fund. *Energy Policy, 38*, 1819–1825.

Janis, I. L. (1967). Effects of fear arousal on attitude change: Recent developments in theory and experimental research. In L. Berkowitz (Ed.), *Advances in experimental social psychology 3* (pp. 166–255). New York: Academic.

Johnson, B. B., & Frank, P. G. (2006). Public understanding of environmental impacts of electricity deregulation. *Energy Policy, 34*(12), 1332–1343.

Laros, F. J. M., & Steenkamp, J.-B. E. M. (2004). Importance of fear in the case of genetically modified food. *Psychology & Marketing, 21*(11), 889–908.

LaTour, M. S., & Rotfeld, H. J. (1997). There are threats and (maybe) fear-caused arousal: Theory and confusions of fear appeals to fear and fear arousal itself. *Journal of Advertising, 26*(3), 45–59.

LaTour, M. S., & Tanner, J. F., Jr. (2003). Radon: Appealing to our fears. *Psychology & Marketing, 20*(5), 377–394.

Manchandra, R. V., Frankenberger, K. D., & Dahl, D. W. (2003). Does it pay to shock? Reactions to shocking and nonshocking advertising content among university students. *Journal of Advertising Research, 43*(3), 268–280.

Obermiller, C. (1995). The baby is sick/the baby is well: A test of environmental communication appeals. *Journal of Advertising, 24*(2), 55–70.

Paladino, A., & Pandit, A. P. (2012). Competing on service and branding in the renewable electricity sector. *Energy Policy, 45*, 378–388.

Peters, E., & Slovic, P. (2007). Affective asynchrony and the measurement of the affective attitude component. *Cognition and Emotion, 21*, 300–329.

Prasad, M., & Munch, S. (2012). State-level renewable electricity policies and reductions in carbon emissions. *Energy Policy, 45*, 237–242.

Roberts, J. A. (1996). Green consumers in the 1990s: Profile and implications for advertising. *Journal of Business Research, 36*(July), 217–231.

Roe, B., Teislb, M. F., Levyc, A., & Russell, M. (2001). US consumers' willingness to pay for green electricity. *Energy Policy, 29*, 917–925.

Roser, C., & Thompson, M. (1995). Fear appeals and the formation of active publics. *Journal of Communication, 45*, 103–122.

Rowlands, I. H., Parker, P., & Scott, D. (2003). Consumers and green electricity: Profiling potential purchasers. *Business Strategy and the Environment, 12*(1), 36–48.

Russell, J. A. (1980). A circumplex model of affect. *J Pers Soc Psychol, 39*(6), 1161–1178.

Salmela, S., & Varho, V. (2006). Consumers in the green electricity market in Finland. *Energy Policy, 34*, 3669–3683.

Scholder-Ellen, P. (1994). Do we know what we need to know? Objective and subjective knowledge effects on pro-ecological behaviors. *Journal of Business Research, 30*(1), 43–52.

Scholder-Ellen, P., Wiener, J. L., & Cobb-Walgren, C. (1991). The role of perceived consumer effectiveness in motivating environmentally conscious behaviors. *Journal of Public Policy and Marketing, 10*, 102–117.

Truelove, H. B. (2012). Energy source perceptions and policy support: Image associations, emotional evaluations, and cognitive beliefs. *Energy Policy, 45*, 478–489.

Truffer, B., Markard, J., & Wüstenhagen, R. (2001). Eco-labeling of electricity—Strategies and tradeoffs in the definition of environmental standards. *Energy Policy, 29*(11), 885–897.

Watson, D., Clark, L. A., & Tellegen, A. (1988). Development and validation of brief measures of positive and negative affect: The PANAS scales. *J Pers Soc Psychol, 54*(6), 1063–1070.

Wiser, R. H., Fowlie, M., & Holt, E. A. (2001). Public goods and private interests: Understanding non-residential demand for green power. *Energy Policy, 29*, 1085–1097.

Wiser, R. H., Pickle, S., & Goldman, C. (1998). Renewable energy policy and electricity restructuring: A California case study. *Energy Policy, 26*, 465–475.

Wüstenhagen, R., & Bilharz, M. (2006). Green energy market development in Germany: Effective public policy and emerging customer demand. *Energy Policy, 34*, 1681–1696.

Wüstenhagen, R., Wolsink, M., & Bürer, M. J. (2007). Social acceptance of renewable energy innovation: An introduction to the concept. *Energy Policy, 35*, 2683–2691.

Yamamoto, Y., Suzuki, A., Fuwa, Y., & Sato, T. (2008). Decision-making in appliance use in the home. *Energy Policy, 36*, 1679–1686.

Zarnikau, J. (2003). Consumer demand for 'green power' and energy efficiency. *Energy Policy, 31*, 1661–1672.

Zimmer, M. R., Stafford, T. F., & Stafford, M. R. (1994). Green issues: Dimensions of environmental concern. *Journal of Business Research, 30*(1), 63–74.

Predictors of HIV/AIDS-Related Behaviours Within the Population of Kinshasa: The Impact of Socio-Demographic and Environmental Factors

Lutete C. Ayikwa and Johan W. De Jager

Abstract This study investigated the impact of socio-demographic factors, HIV/ AIDS level of knowledge, exposure to HIV/AIDS information, ease of obtaining condoms, and types of outlets offering condoms, whether to abstain from sex or not abstain from sex, being faithful or not being faithful, using condoms or not using condoms, discussing the use of condoms with partner(s) or not discussing the use of condoms with partner(s) and taking an HIV test or not taking an HIV test. Data were obtained by means of a face-to-face questionnaire. Data analysis made use of binary logistic regression procedure. Age, gender, marital status and ease of obtaining condoms were predictors of abstinence while gender, occupation, level of knowledge about the modes of HIV transmission and prevention methods contributed to being faithful. By contrast, only gender was predictive of condom use. Occupation and knowledge about the meaning of HIV/AIDS were predictors of partners' discussions on condom use. Lastly, age, level of education and level of knowledge about the meaning of HIV/AIDS and modes of HIV transmission predicted a decision to take an HIV test. The research ground should be conducted prior to the design of interventions. Consideration of the combined effects of predicting factors would be valuable.

Keywords Abstinence • Sexual behaviour • Condom use • Faithfulness • HIV/ AIDS • HIV knowledge • HIV testing • Kinshasa • Social marketing

Introduction

Social marketing campaigns addressing HIV/AIDS issue are accounted for in numbers. They all work to change people's behaviour in order to stop the spread of the virus and eradicate the epidemic (Noble and Camit 2005:1). In their quest for

L.C. Ayikwa (✉) • J.W. De Jager
Tshwane University of Technology, Pretoria, South Africa
e-mail: chrisayikw@yahoo.fr; DejagerJW@tut.ac.za

© Academy of Marketing Science 2016
L. Petruzzellis, R.S. Winer (eds.), *Rediscovering the Essentiality of Marketing*,
Developments in Marketing Science: Proceedings of the Academy of Marketing
Science, DOI 10.1007/978-3-319-29877-1_74

369

effectiveness, social marketers design campaigns devoted to a large range of behaviours that people should take to win the battle against HIV/AIDS. The pioneer HIV/AIDS intervention campaign, known as the 'ABC' campaign, promotes abstinence, faithfulness and condom use (Ganle et al. 2012:94–96). In recent years, numerous HIV/AIDS programmes promoting different types of behaviour have emerged. Thus, the male circumcision campaign has been launched to reduce the propensity for acquiring the virus for men (Riess 2014), while testing for HIV intends to reduce both contamination through blood transfusion and mother-to-child transmission for pregnant women (Eastlund and Strong 2004; Maputle and Jali 2008:45), as well as encouraging wise behaviour of people according to their sero-status (Liu et al. 2011:129). Other HIV/AIDS campaigns encourage peers, couples and sexual partners to engage in discussion about Sexually-Transmitted Infections (STIs) and Sexually-Transmitted Diseases (STDs), in order to enhance girls' and women's points of view on the appropriate behaviour to adopt within their couple (Corrêa et al. 2008). Therefore, it is pertinent to identify the HIV/AIDS predictive factors/variables that significantly influence a specific behaviour, in order to implement more efficient programmes.

Literature Review

It is a secret of *polichinelle* that human behaviour is influenced by psychological, sociocultural, cultural and environmental factors (Kurtz and Boone 2010:134). Thus, any organisation whose ultimate goal is the behaviour change of a large number of people should understand all the components therein. However, not all factors that can potentially predict a human behaviour are effectively predictive of a specific one. Hence, for social marketers, tailoring programmes to their audience involves research factors that are significantly predictive of the expected behaviour in order to design and implement successful campaigns (Ebert et al. 2012).

Amongst the challenges that face social marketing campaigns are social injustice and inequities (Lefebvre 2011:64). Indeed, girls and women have been identified for a long time as the most vulnerable people that are disproportionately hit by the epidemic in several African communities (Ayikwa et al. 2013:107). A similar observation has been made for young people compared to their adult counterparts, as researchers and HIV/AIDS professionals claim that they are the most at risk of contracting the virus (Ayikwa et al. 2013:107). This clearly highlights why HIV/AIDS is labelled an age-gender related disease. Likewise, there are studies suggesting that the level of educational attainment sharply increases the extent of knowledge about HIV/AIDS and STIs (Singh and Jain 2009:59). Evidence from a study conducted at Wuhan in China demonstrated that education at school has succeeded in reversing the prevailing negative attitude about HIV/AIDS, misconceptions about basic medical knowledge and non-transmission modes of the virus among students (Gao et al. 2012).

An individual's professional status is a strategic key in empowering financially-and economically vulnerable people who engage in risky sexual behaviour because of lack of money. It is not only a concern directed at sex workers, but also at young girls and boys who engage in sexual relationships with much older partners called 'sugar daddies' or 'sugar mommies' (Oyediran et al. 2011). Thus, researchers in the field of HIV/AIDS have noticed that the epidemic is associated with people's socio-economic situation, as the virus flourishes in a context of poverty (Mabala 2006:407). Similarly, marital status has been identified by Mondal et al. (2012:73) as a factor affecting significantly the HIV/AIDS level of awareness. Indeed, this is very crucial when considering that the main strategy pursued by social marketing in addressing the epidemic is to provide people with adequate skills through education campaigns that aim to increase HIV/AIDS knowledge and erase HIV/AIDS-related misconceptions, as well as to improve perceptions towards infected people.

The designed HIV/AIDS education programme, though tailored to the audience, must be accompanied by appropriate communication and distribution strategies. Indeed, it has often been a criticism of HIV/AIDS programmes that they are pro-rich in that they are more likely to reach wealthier than poorer, in terms of both information and condoms (Price 2001). Therefore, the unavailability of information and condoms drives the spread of the epidemic among those who are not reached by HIV/AIDS campaigns.

There are numerous factors that can predict human behaviour, as stated earlier, but the present study emphasised the factors picked up on with regard to the literature review above: namely, age, area of residence (suburb), gender, level of education, occupation, marital status, socio-economic status, level of knowledge about the meaning of HIV/AIDS, knowledge about the modes of HIV transmission, knowledge about HIV prevention methods, exposure to HIV/AIDS information, ease of obtaining condoms and types of outlets offering condoms. The main question it intends to answer is which of these HIV/AIDS explanatory variables are predictive of the following responses: abstain from sex or not abstain from sex, being faithful or not being faithful, using condoms or not using condoms, discussing the use of condoms with partner(s) or not discussing the use of condoms with partner(s) and taking an HIV test or not taking an HIV test?

Methodology

Data Collection

Data have been collected by means of face-to-face questionnaires. For 360 inhabitants of Kinshasa, the capital city of the DR Congo, these data record whether or not a particular individual abstains from sex, is faithful to his/her partner, uses condoms, discusses the use of condoms with partner(s) and took an HIV test. Data on people's behaviour towards HIV/AIDS issues came with information related to the socio-demographic characteristics: age, area of residence (suburb), gender, level of education, occupation, marital status, and socio-economic status. Furthermore, the questionnaire also gathered information on the level of knowledge about the meaning of HIV/AIDS, knowledge about the modes of HIV transmission, knowledge about HIV prevention methods, exposure to HIV/AIDS information, ease of obtaining condoms and types of outlets offering condoms. In order to avoid any misunderstanding of the questionnaire by respondents, an assistance-oriented approach was preferred.

Data Analysis

Given the specific nature of the main question of interest, the present study intends to answer it using a *binary logistic regression*. Indeed, that alternative approach to multiple regression is more appropriate in this case, for two reasons:

- The response variable in this case is binary rather than continuous.
- The assumption that, given the values of the explanatory variables, the response variable has a normal distribution with constant variance is not acceptable for a binary response.

Sample Size

Often, sample size has been an issue with regard to reliable equation. In order to address that issue, the present study observed that each predictor has at least 15 participants, as recommended for a social science research by Stevens (Protogerou and Turner-Cobb 2011:96). In addition, the formula for calculating sample size requirements, taking into account the number of independent variables given by Tabachnick and Fidell, has been applied (Roberts-Lombard et al. 2014:32). It suggests that sample size (n) must be bigger than fifty plus eight times the number of independent variables used, in the case of this study at least 154 [50+(8×13)]. However, the present study gathered 360 respondents chosen randomly from all the four districts of Kinshasa. Table 1 (Descriptive statistics of participants) shows the frequency and percentage of people who made up the sample, with regard to the demographic characteristics retained for the study's purpose.

Survey Instrument

The survey questionnaire was made up of existing questionnaires assessing people's level of knowledge about the meaning of HIV/AIDS, different modes of acquiring the virus and the methods for the prevention of getting infected. It also asks respondents to identify channels that provide them with HIV/AIDS information, in order to determine their level of exposure to HIV/AIDS information. Furthermore, the

Table 1 Descriptive statistics of participants

	Frequency (n)	Percent (%)		Frequency (n)	Percent (%)
Gender			*Age*		
Male	199	55.3	≥18–20 year old	88	24.4
Female	161	44.7	21–30 year old	188	52.2
Total	360	100.0	31–40 year old	67	18.6
Level of education			41–50 year old	17	4.7
Not schooled	11	3.1	Total	360	100.0
Primary	6	1.7	*Marital status*		
Secondary	95	26.4	Single	267	74.2
High school	247	68.6	Married	64	17.8
Higher education	1	.3	Living together	24	6.7
Total	360	100.0	Divorced/Widow(er)	5	1.4
Occupation			Total	360	100.0
Unemployed	79	21.9	*Socio-economic status*		
Employed (Public sector)	20	5.6	Impoverished	171	47.5
Employed (Private sector)	64	17.8	Almost impoverished	50	13.9
Self-employed	64	17.8	Medium	34	9.4
Student	133	36.9	Almost wealthy	67	18.6
Total	360	100.0	Wealthy	38	10.6
			Total	360	100.0

questionnaire invites the respondents to enumerate different types of outlets offering condoms in their area, as well as the ease with which they could obtain condoms.

Most importantly, respondents had to reply straightforwardly if they abstain from sex or not, are faithful to their partner or not, use condoms or not, discuss condom use with partner(s) or not and take an HIV test or not. Besides, the questionnaire gathered socio-demographic information from respondents in an anonymous manner (they did not have to give their names and exact address) and was given an assurance of confidentiality regarding all information provided for the study purpose. Furthermore, ethical approval was granted by the Tshwane University of Technology's research ethics committee.

Findings

The Cronbach Alpha technique was applied to assess the reliability of the six measurement scales that were used in the study. Given the results indicated in Table 2, all the instrument sets are reliable, as they ranged above the minimum value (.6) regarded as a satisfactory level of internal consistency reliability set by Hair et al. (2010).

Table 2 Reliability and descriptive statistics of constructs measured

	Number of items	Cronbach's alpha	Mean	Std. deviation
Level of knowledge about the meaning of HIV/AIDS	6	.723	13.72	1.84
Level of knowledge about the modes of HIV transmission	13	.722	33.34	3.67
Level of knowledge about the HIV prevention methods	9	.716	14.76	1.76
Exposure to HIV/AIDS information	15	.770	24.37	3.32
Types of outlets offering condoms	6	.763	8.11	1.20
Ease of obtaining condoms	2	.784	4.91	1.29

Results in Table 2 demonstrate that people are reasonably knowledgeable regarding HIV/AIDS with a mean score of 13.72(1.84), and highly knowledgeable about modes of HIV transmission with a mean score of 33.34(3.67). This implies that respondents are able to count HIV/AIDS among STDs; they are aware that it is not a curse or curable disease but a preventable and manageable one; they acknowledge that HIV can be contracted during unprotected sexual intercourses, untested blood transfusion, sharing of sharp objects such as needles or razors, while it cannot be transferred through sharing foods or clothes, shaking hands, kissing, hugging an HIV infected person or insect bites; they display a good knowledge about the Mother-to-Child transmission. However, they lack knowledge about all the precautions for avoiding contamination, with a mean score of 14.76(1.76). This suggests that people identify condom use as a mean to protect themselves from getting HIV infected, and they do not emphasise on its consistent use. Also, they are ignorant of the importance of being faithful to one partner or abstaining from sex, while they fail to describe prostitutes as high risk partners. In terms of exposure to information, it is indicated that people have a poor exposure to information promoting HIV/AIDS prevention messages, with a mean score of 24.37(3.32). This is due to the combination of insufficient use of traditional media with the absence of community based interventions relying in churches, schools, public and private offices, community leaders, to spread HIV/AIDS preventive information. Despite the lack of diversified types of outlets offering condoms with a score of 8.11(1.20), people estimate that condoms are easy to obtain with a mean score of 4.91(1.29). Indeed, socially marketed condoms are sold and offered mainly in pharmacies and some hotels.

The outcome of a binary logistic regression analysis conducted to determine which, if any, of the HIV/AIDS explanatory variables are predictive of abstinence—being faithful, condom use, partners' discussions on condom use and testing sero-status—is presented in Table 3. The Wald criterion demonstrated that age, gender, marital status and ease of obtaining condoms made a significant contribution to prediction of abstinence ($p = .000$; .005; .008; .020) with 82.2 % accuracy. The full model against a constant-only model was statistically significant, indicating that the predictors as a set reliably distinguished between abstainers and non-abstainers (chi square $= 17.730$, $p < .000$ with df $= 4$). Nagelkerke's R^2 of .281 indicated a moderately weak relationship between prediction and grouping. Odds Ratio values indicate that age, gender, marital status and the possibility of obtaining condoms are likely to influence abstinence, respectively, by 2.917, .431, 2.710 and 1.300. Results suggest that the proportion of abstinence increases gradually with older age groups; it is lower for male than female, while it is higher for single than ever married or people living together, and it increases gradually with an improvement of the possibility to obtaining condoms.

On the other hand, the Wald criterion in Table 3 showed that gender, occupation, knowledge about the modes of HIV transmission and knowledge about HIV prevention methods predicted significantly being faithful ($p = .000$; .027; .000; .030) with 68.3% accuracy. The full model against a constant-only model was statistically significant, indicating that the predictors as a set reliably distinguished between faithful partners and unfaithful partners (chi square = 41.462, $p < .000$ with df = 4). Nagelkerke's R^2 of .151 indicated a moderately weak relationship between prediction and grouping. Odds Ratio values indicate that gender, occupation, knowledge about the modes of HIV transmission and knowledge about HIV prevention methods are likely to influence being faithful respectively by .341, .840, .877 and .930. Results show that the propensity to being faithful is lower for male than female, while it decreases with an occupational activity, and it decreases gradually with the drop of knowledge about the modes of HIV transmission and knowledge about HIV prevention methods.

By contrast, only gender made a significant contribution towards the prediction of condom use ($p = .002$), explaining correctly the phenomenon at 59.7%. The full model against a constant-only model was statistically significant, indicating that gender as a set reliably distinguished between condom users and non-users (chi square = 9.362, $p < .002$ with df = 1). Nagelkerke's R^2 of .035 indicated a weak relationship between prediction and grouping. Odds Ratio value indicates that gender is likely to influence condom use by .515. Results suggest that condom use is lower for male than female. Hence, the needs for women and girls empowerment in order to make their points of view count within their couples.

Occupation and knowledge about the meaning of HIV/AIDS were significant in predicting partners' discussion on condom use ($p = .001$, .017) with 62.2% accuracy. The full model against a constant-only model was statistically significant, indicating that predictors as a set reliably distinguished between partners who discuss condom use and partners that do not discuss condom use (chi square = 17.730, $p < .000$ with df = 2). Nagelkerke's R^2 of .065 indicated a weak relationship between prediction and grouping. Odds Ratio values indicate that occupation and knowledge about the meaning of HIV/AIDS are likely to influence partners to discuss condom use, respectively, by 1.254 and 1.152. Results indicate that discussion on condom use between partners increases with occupational activity, while it increases gradually with an improvement of knowledge about the meaning of HIV/AIDS.

Lastly, the Wald criterion demonstrated that age, education, knowledge about the meaning of HIV/AIDS and knowledge about the modes of HIV transmission made a significant contribution to predict correctly at 63.9% taking up an HIV test ($p = .019$; 017; .050; .005). The full model against a constant-only model was statistically

Table 3 Binary logistic regression

	*B(SE)	Wald	Sig	95 % CI for odds ratio	Odds ratio	
				Lower	Odds ratio	Upper
Abstinence (y₁)						
Constant	−1.679(.881)					
Age (x₂)	1.071(.249)	.249	.000	1.790	2.917	4.754
Gender (x₃)	−.842(.298)	.298	.005	.240	.431	.773
Marital status(x₁)	.997(.377)	.377	.008	1.295	2.710	5.668
Ease of obtaining condoms (x₄)	.262(.113)	.113	.020	1.042	1.300	1.621

$R^2 = .281$ (Nagelkerke); $\chi^2_{(4)} = 71.546$, $p < .01$; Prediction success overall (%): 79.2–82.2

	*B(SE)	Wald	Sig	95 % CI for odds ratio	Odds ratio	
				Lower	Odds ratio	Upper
Being faithful (y₂)						
Constant	7.047(1.425)					
Gender (x₁)	−1.075(.255)	17.750	.000	.207	.341	.563
Occupation (x₂)	−.174(.079)	4.894	.027	.720	.840	.980
Knowledge about HIV modes of transmission (x₃)	−.131(.034)	14.753	.000	.821	.877	.938
Knowledge about HIV prevention methods (x₄)	−.072(.033)	4.687	.030	.872	.930	.993

$R^2 = .151$ (Nagelkerke); $\chi^2_{(4)} = 41.462$, $p < .01$; Prediction success overall (%): 66.4–68.3

	*B(SE)	Wald	Sig	95 % CI for odds ratio	Odds ratio	
				Lower	Odds ratio	Upper
Condom use (y₃)						
Constant	1.364(.340)					
Gender (x₁)	−.663(.218)	9.261	.002	.336	.515	.790

$R^2 = .035$ (Nagelkerke); $\chi^2_{(1)} = 9.362$, $p<.01$; Prediction success overall (%): 59.7–61.2

Discussion with partner(s) on condom use (y_4)						
Constant	−2.349(.846)					
Occupation (x_1)	.236(.071)	10.250	.001	1.092	1.254	1.440
Knowledge about the meaning of HIV/AIDS (x_2)	.141(.059)	5.676	.017	1.025	1.152	1.294

$R^2 = .065$ (Nagelkerke); $\chi^2_{(2)} = 17.730$, $p<.01$; Prediction success overall (%): 59.2–62.2

Testing sero-status (y_5)						
Constant	−6.909(1.371)					
Age (x_1)	.343(.145)	5.544	.019	1.059	1.409	1.873
Education (x_2)	.427(.179)	5.704	.017	1.080	1.532	2.174
Knowledge about the meaning of HIV/AIDS (x_3)	.121(.062)	3.855	.050	1.000	1.129	1.273
Knowledge about HIV modes of transmission (x_4)	.093(.033)	7.849	.005	1.028	1.098	1.172

$R^2 = .124$ (Nagelkerke); $\chi^2_{(4)} = 35.007$, $p<.01$;
Prediction success overall (%): 53.9–63.9

Note: *B are the logistic coefficients that can be used to create a predictive equation (similar to the b values in linear regression)—SE are standard errors
The table considered only significant variables in predicting the respective dependent variables in a later step

significant, indicating that predictors as a set reliably distinguished between taking up an HIV test and not taking up an HIV test (chi square=35.077, $p<.000$ with df=4). Nagelkerke's R^2 of .124 indicated a moderately weak relationship between prediction and grouping. Odds Ratio values indicate that age, education, knowledge about the meaning of HIV/AIDS and knowledge about the modes of HIV transmission are likely to influence the taking up of an HIV test, respectively, by 1.409, 1.532, 1.129 and 1.172. Results suggest that the chance of taking up an HIV test increases gradually with older group age, higher level of education and an improvement of both knowledge about the meaning of HIV/AIDS and knowledge about the modes of HIV transmission.

Conclusion

This study investigated the impact of socio-demographic and environmental factors on HIV/AIDS related behaviour within the population of Kinshasa. A logistic regression analysis was conducted to predict abstinence, faithfulness, condom use, discussion with partner on condom use and testing sero-status using age, gender, level of education, occupation, socio-economic status and marital status, HIV/AIDS level of knowledge, exposure to HIV/AIDS information, ease of obtaining condoms and types of outlets offering condoms as predictors. The analysis of data collected for the purpose of this study revealed that age, gender, marital status and the possibility of obtaining condoms are predictive of abstinence while gender, occupation, knowledge about the modes of HIV transmission and knowledge about HIV prevention methods have statistically significant effects with faithfulness to one partner. By contrast, results showed that only gender has been proved to be statistically significant in predicting condom use while occupation and knowledge about the meaning of HIV/AIDS are found to be predictive of partners' discussions about condom use. Lastly, results indicated that age, level of education, knowledge about the meaning of HIV/AIDS and knowledge about the modes of HIV transmission are predictors for HIV testing.

In line with these results, it is advisable to HIV/AIDS programmes covering Kinshasa to duplicate efforts to improve people's knowledge of the preventive methods to avoid the epidemic while strengthening their knowledge about the meaning and modes of transmission of HIV/AIDS through the sufficient use of traditional channels and application of community based strategies to spread information. They should also consider focusing energies in groups that have been identified as engaging less in safe sexual behaviours such as younger people, male, ever married, people living together and people with an occupational activity when considering respectively age, gender, marital status and occupation. No less important, HIV/AIDS social marketers should work in women and girls' empowerment as results demonstrated that consistent condom use within a couple is driven by female.

Although the study believes that its findings are reliable, it is important to caution that they are representative of the current situation in Kinshasa. Indeed, variables that have not been found to be predictive of one or other behaviour are not necessarily inutile. For example, a study conducted in China demonstrated that, in addition to motivation, consistent condom use was significantly predicted by HIV/AIDS information and behavioural skills which relate to the increased level of knowledge (Cai et al. 2013:1). Also, the assumption that HIV/AIDS is a 'disease of poverty' emanates from the conclusion that the impact of the virus and its related mortality, and perhaps unsafe sexual behaviour, are lower in higher socio-economic groups (Ayikwa et al. 2014:182). Similarly, the marital situation has been found predictive of extramarital sex (unfaithfulness), although mediated by peers' influence (Coma 2013:872).

Obviously, according to Ayikwa et al. (2013:113), the best way to deal with dilemmas surrounded the determination of the significance of variables predicting HIV/AIDS-related behaviours for social marketers is to conduct the research ground prior to the design of the programmes, in order to be efficient. In addition, the necessity of investigating the combined effect of variables considered in the study would be valuable when designing HIV/AIDS programmes.

Acknowledgement I would like to thank the National Research Foundation (NRF) in South Africa for their financial assistance to attend the 2015 AMS conference.

References

Ayikwa, L. C., De Jager, J. W., & Van Rensburg, D. B. J. (2013). Reconsidering the gender and age-based HIV/AIDS prevention strategies for a successful outcome in Kinshasa—Democratic Republic of Congo. *Mitteilungen Klosterneuburg Journal, 63*(12), 106–116.

Ayikwa, L. C., De Jager, J. W., & Van Rensburg, D. B. J. (2014). Scrutiny of the association between the socio-economic status and magnitude of HIV/AIDS in the general population of Kinshasa. *Journal of Economics and Behavioural Studies, 6*(3), 181–187.

Coma, J. C. (2013). When the group encourages extramarital sex: Difficulties in HIV/AIDS prevention in rural Malawi. *Demographic Research, 28*(30), 849–880.

Corrêa, S., Petchesky, R., & Parker, R. (2008). *Sexuality, health and human rights*. London, England: Routledge/Taylor & Francis Group.

Eastlund, T., & Strong, D. M. (2004). Infectious disease transmission through tissue transplantation. *Advances in Tissue Banking, 7*, 51–131.

Ebert, J. E. J., Southwell, B. G., Slater, J. S., & Nelson, C. L. (2012). Campaigns in context: Promotion, seasonal variation, and resource factors predict mammography program participation. *Health Systems, 1*, 118–128.

Ganle, J. K., Tagoe-Darko, E., & Mensah, C. M. (2012). Youth, HIV/AIDS risks and sexuality in contemporary Ghana: Examining the gap between awareness and behaviour change. *International Journal of Humanities and Social Science, 2*(21), 88–99.

Gao, X., Wu, Y., Zhang, Y., Zhang, N., Tang, J., et al. (2012). Effectiveness of school-based education on HIV/AIDS knowledge, attitude, and behavior among secondary school students in Wuhan, China. *PLoS One, 7*(9), e44881.

Hair, J. F., Black, W. C., Babin, B. J., & Anderson, R. E. (2010). *Multivariate data analysis* (7th ed.). Englewood Cliffs, NJ: Prentice Hall.

Kurtz, D. L., & Boone, G. (2010). *Principles of contemporary marketing* (14th ed.). New York: South-Western Cengage Learning.

Lefebvre, R. C. (2011). An integrative model for HIV. *Journal of Social Marketing, 1*(1), 54–72.

Liu, Y., Canada, K., Shi, K., & Corrigan, P. (2011). HIV-related stigma acting as predictors of unemployment of people living with HIV/AIDS. *AIDS Care, 24*(1), 129–135.

Mabala, R. (2006). From HIV prevention to HIV protection: Addressing the vulnerability of girls and young women in urban areas. Environment & Urbanization. *International Institute for Environment and Development (IIED), 18*(2), 407–432.

Maputle, M. S., & Jali, M. N. (2008). Pregnant women's knowledge about mother-to-child transmission through breast feeding. *Curatonis, 31*(1), 45–51.

Mondal, N. I., Rahman, M., Obaidur Rahman, O., & Akter, N. (2012). Level of awareness about HIV/AIDS among ever married women in bangladesh. *Food and Public Health, 2*(3), 73–78.

Noble, G., & Camit, M. (2005). Social marketing communication in a multicultural environment: Practical issues and theoretical contributions from cross-cultural marketing. *Prism, 3*(2). Retrieved from http://praxis.massey.ac.nz

Oyediran, K. A., Odutolu, O., & Atobatele, A. O. (2011). Intergenerational sexual relationships in Nigeria: Implications for negotiating safe sexual practices. *Social and Psychological Aspects of HIV/AIDS and Their Ramifications*, 49–72.

Price, N. (2001). The performance of social marketing in reaching the poor and vulnerable in AIDS control programmes. *Health Policy and Planning, 16*(3), 231–239.

Protogerou, C., & Turner-Cobb, J. (2011). Predictors of non-condom use intention by university students in Britain and Greece: The impact of attitudes, time perspective, relationship status, and habit. *Journal of Child & Adolescent Mental Health, 23*(2), 91–106.

Riess, T. H. (2014). *Exploring the relationship between male circumcision and sexual risk compensation in Kisumu, Kenya*. Unpublished Thesis. University of Illinois, Chicago.

Roberts-Lombard, M., Van Tonder, E., Pelser, T. G., & Prinsloo, J. J. (2014). The relationship between key variables and customer loyalty within the independent financial advisor environment. *The Retail and Marketing Review, 10*(1), 25–42.

Singh, A., & Jain, S. (2009). Awareness of HIV/AIDS among school adolescents in Banaskantha district of Gujarat. *Health and Population; Perspectives and Issues, 32*(2), 59–65.

Early Findings on Alcohol Consumption: A Licensed Premise Observation Study

Nuray Buyucek and Sharyn Rundle-Thiele

Introduction

According to estimates, about two billion people consume alcohol annually (WHO 2007). Worldwide pure alcohol consumption per person is estimated to be 6.1 L for people aged 15 years and older (WHO 2011a). The highest overall consumption of alcohol is in Europe and high income countries (WHO 2011a) including Australia. For example, in Australia 81 % of people aged 14 years and over in 2011 consumed alcohol according to the Foundation for Alcohol Research and Education (FARE 2012) at least once.

Various methods have been employed to measure alcohol consumption. Commonly used methods include surveys (Deshpande and Rundle-Thiele 2011; Mattern 2004; WHO 2000), depth interviews (Deshpande and Rundle-Thiele 2011), focus groups (Kubacki et al. 2011), national government data including sales (WHO 2000), production and/or taxation on alcohol (WHO 2000) or crops used to produce alcohol (WHO 2000) and observations (Rundle-Thiele 2009).

Data gathered from sales, production and taxation data may not be reflecting the real picture in regard to alcohol consumption for several reasons. First of all, there are many forms of home-made alcohol production that are not recorded which might be the biggest source of most of alcohol consumption (WHO 2000, 2007, 2011b). In fact, more than a quarter of alcohol consumption (28.6 %) was estimated to be unrecorded (WHO 2011a). Secondly, duty-free purchases, imported alcohol, and smuggling are not usually included in those data (WHO 2000). Thirdly, although all alcohol sold included in a particular year's data may be recorded, it may not be consumed in that year. For example, wines and beverages may be cellared and aged

N. Buyucek (✉) • S. Rundle-Thiele
Griffith University, Nathan, QLD, Australia
e-mail: n.buyucek@griffith.edu.au; s.rundle-thiele@griffith.edu.au

© Academy of Marketing Science 2016
L. Petruzzellis, R.S. Winer (eds.), *Rediscovering the Essentiality of Marketing*,
Developments in Marketing Science: Proceedings of the Academy of Marketing
Science, DOI 10.1007/978-3-319-29877-1_75

381

making consumption estimates difficult in the absence of such data (WHO 2000). Furthermore, some products might be sold but never consumed (e.g. wine may oxidise) and bottles get smashed during or after the delivery process. Lastly, serving sizes may vary between countries and even between licensed premises in the same street or entertainment district making volume estimates difficult (WHO 2000).

Surveys are another source of data that may give different insights and understanding of alcohol consumption. Details that have been collected in survey research include abstention (AIHW 2014), different categories of average volume of alcohol consumption (Gomberg 2001; Mattern 2004), different drinking patterns and their correlations with different demographics variables such as gender, income and education level; these are not explained by retail sales and government data (WHO 2007). However, different measures of drinking make it difficult to generalise findings worldwide (WHO 2007). On top of that, self-reported alcohol consumption surveys may be 40–60 % lower than supply-based estimates (WHO 2011a; Rundle-Thiele 2009) which indicates that people may underestimate the quantity of alcohol consumption (Rundle-Thiele 2009). Additionally, due to the nature of drinking behaviour it might be hard to recall the amount of alcohol consumed in any given day, after the drinking episode is concluded. Despite the existing weaknesses, self-reported surveys are one of the most common methods used by researchers to estimate alcohol drinking (AIHW 2014; Banwell et al. 1999; Murphy et al. 2012).

All in all, currently used alcohol consumption research methods are far from drawing the real picture, as surveys and other sources of data used by national and international agencies may be systemically underestimating levels of alcohol consumption. As alluded to above (Hall and Rist 1999; Rundle-Thiele 2009) discrepancies between actual and claimed behaviour exist (Boote and Mathews 1999). A further factor contributing to the discrepancy arises from low knowledge relating to alcohol units (e.g. standard drinks) (Rundle-Thiele 2009).

Observations can be used to understand alcohol consumption in natural environments where the action/particular behaviour occurs (Rundle-Thiele 2009). Observation studies are recommended as a research method to compensate for self-report methods (Hall and Rist 1999) where socially desirable responding occurs (Mick 1996). Observations allow researchers to consider the accuracy of claimed behaviour by observing respondents in their natural environment (Rundle-Thiele 2009). Therefore use of observations can assist to remove self-reporting biases such as over- or understating alcohol intake owing to insufficient knowledge of alcohol units of measurement and memory bias which may occur in surveys. Moreover, interaction with the drinking environment can be observed and captured via observations in natural settings which may provide additional insights into drinking patterns or behaviours thus further extending our knowledge of drinking.

The current study includes early findings of an observational study that sought to understand actual drinking behaviour in licensed premises. Although the majority of drinking occurs in domestic premises (AIHW 2008), licensed premises are the second most popular place to drink among 18–29 age groups (AIHW 2011). Public access to licensed premises gives quick access to researchers to observe drinking behaviour.

Methodology

Observation methods were preferred for the current study. Data obtained for the current study was collected in one venue in a college (university) setting. Ethical approval was received to observe a public behaviour in a public place. An observation manual was developed based on an earlier study (Rundle-Thiele 2009). Variables in the observation manual included duration of drinking, observation time, type and brand of the drink, activity, food consumption, and indicators of driving activity (Rundle-Thiele 2009), group characteristics such as occasional or celebratory drinking, group type (family, friends, informal, formal), consumption pattern; buying individually or buying in rounds, conclusion of the drinking episode, signs of intoxication, observed mood and risky behaviour were added in the observation form.

Four observers were employed in the current study. Three observation sessions were conducted. Two of the nights were weekday nights where alcohol was served cheaper than other places. One jug of mid-strength beer was advertised at a cost of $9 AUD. One session was conducted during an event where alcohol was served at no cost; it was an event hosted by the Postgraduate student association and alcohol was served at no cost to the patron. Before the event, normal trading practices were observed for an hour in the premise. Average observation time was 145 min across three days of observation. Observers chose a location where patrons were easily observed. Sessions commenced with observers seeking to familiarise themselves with serving types and sizes of beverages.

Observation of a particular person was stopped when the observation was distracted by a person or an obstacle emerged between the observer and the subject or when the person was not in the observer's view. Episodes were mainly partly recorded which assists under stating of alcohol drinking (Rundle-Thiele 2009). Data was recorded quantitatively in units according to Australian Government National Health and Medical Research Council (NHRMC, 2009) to prevent any bias caused by researchers (Jones and Somekh, 2005). For example, a glass of a beer was counted as a unit when poured into a glass from a jug.

Results and Discussion

Drinking behaviour observed was reported. Total duration of observation across three occasions was 6 h 45 min and 144 drinkers were observed, 11 of them (6 males, 5 females) being abstainers. More than half (58.3 %) of observed subjects were males while 41.7 % were females. Episodes for individual patrons varied from 4 min to 100 min and the average episode length was 38.50 min. The quantity of drinks varied from 0 to 8 drink units.

Beer and cider is served on tap and can also be served in bottles. Although all beer and cider served was full-strength (5 % AlcVol) with one mid-strength (3.5 % AlcVol) exception which was, in order to avoid over-statement, all beer/cider served was counted as mid-strength. Pre-mixed spirits such as vodka and whiskey were served either in a glass or in a bottle, each of them was counted as one unit (40 % AlcVol).

Time between drinks or drinking duration was analysed. Differences based on gender may be observed although independent samples t-testing did not indicate a significant difference which may be a result of the small sample size. Results may suggest that females drink slower than their male counterparts, ($M = 24.1$ min and $M = 18.4$ min), respectively. However, despite the fact that there is not any significant difference, it was observed that, as females drink more, duration of drinking for each unit decreased while duration of drinking for each unit increased for males. In other words, females drink faster over a drinking session.

Beer and cider category emerged as the most popular category drink categories followed by spirits for males and wine for females. However, as the quantity of drinks increased, there is a tendency observed towards spirits for males. For instance, spirits were preferred by 20.3 % of males for the first drink, whereas, the percentage of spirits preferred by the males increased up to 29.5 % for the third drink with a slight decrease to 21.4 at the fourth drink.

Approximately one in five of people drink more than recommended drinking levels. Further, 80.6 % of risky drinkers are males and 19.4 % are females. This result is higher than the amount of alcohol that people claimed to have consumed which was 18.2 % according to Australian Institute of Health and Welfare (AIHW 2014).

Conclusion and Implications for Theory and Practice

The results are consistent with previous research reported by Rundle-Thiele (2009). The results of the current study provide further evidence that self-reporting behaviour may underestimate the actual drinking behaviour.

The current research has some limitations. The observation study was conducted only in one venue in Eastern Australia, therefore results cannot be generalised. Furthermore, the venue was located in a University campus, thus, findings of the current research may not reflect customers who consume alcohol in licensed premises' outside of college (university settings). Conducting observation studies in commercial settings is recommended. In addition, sample size of the current study has some limitations may not represent the whole phenomena. A larger sample is recommended to capture more observations for the 4–6th drinker range in order to permit full statistical testing to occur. Further, findings of this study are restricted to days and times observed and also time of year. Additional research is suggested to capture full trading/opening times and to collect data across the year to gain a more comprehensive understanding. Lastly, the way of counting drinks is another limitation which leads underestimation of drinking amounts. It is recommended for further research to develop strategies to overcome underestimation of alcohol consumption.

References available upon request.

Key Success Factors for Brand Orientation in Dutch Hospitals

Gerrita van der Veen and Judith Tielen

Introduction

The reorientation of the public sector along market lines has led to the paradigm of New Public Management (NPM): the assumption that the public sector can be improved by management principles and techniques traditionally associated with the private sector. However, market orientation has also become associated with a number of problems, particularly in the public sector. Recent literature suggests that brand orientation can serve as an alternative to market orientation. Our chapter reviews the concept of brand orientation in the healthcare sector, the extent to which Dutch hospitals are currently managed as brands and the key issues in implementing brand management principles in Dutch hospitals.

Background

Brand Orientation as an Alternative to Market Orientation

In 2006, Dutch governmental regulations started directing organizations in the healthcare sector to integrate market orientation into their management. These regulations were based on the paradigm of NPM, which relies heavily on orientation towards the market as a management principle. This entails a strong emphasis on "products" and "customers" and their needs (Cardogan 1995). Since then the

G. van der Veen (✉) • J. Tielen
Hogeschool Utrecht, Utrecht, The Netherlands
e-mail: gerrita.vanderveen@hu.nl; judith.tielen@hu.nl

© Academy of Marketing Science 2016   385
L. Petruzzellis, R.S. Winer (eds.), *Rediscovering the Essentiality of Marketing*,
Developments in Marketing Science: Proceedings of the Academy of Marketing
Science, DOI 10.1007/978-3-319-29877-1_76

healthcare sector has been considered an economic market in which competition and customer focus are essential. For both the private and public sectors, the concept of market orientation is associated with a number of problems. When it comes to the public sector, the number of problems is even larger. A market orientation implies that economic values are dominant, threatening other core values such as trust, legitimacy, justice, rule of law, equality, security, safety and continuity, crucial factors in the public sector that strengthen democracy (Pollitt 2007; Gromark and Melin 2013). Recent marketing literature suggests brand orientation as an alternative concept for the public sector, which is believed to address the shortcomings of market orientation. Although the interest in brand orientation in the public sector is growing, thorough theoretical and empirical research is lacking (Gromark and Melin 2013). Based on literature and field research, our study addresses three key questions:

1. What is the value of the concept of brand orientation for healthcare, specifically?
2. To what extent are Dutch hospitals brand oriented? Are hospitals managed as a brand?
3. What are the key issues to be handled when managing hospitals as a brand?

Framework

The Concept of Brand Orientation in the Health Sector

The concept of "brand orientation" was introduced at the beginning of the 1990s by Swedish researchers such as Urde (1994). The concept reflects the evolution of brands from the mere products and margin carrier to branding as the strategic hub of organizations. Following the work of authors such as Hamel and Prahalad (1990), companies started to consider their brands as identity, a way of summarizing the mission, vision, and core competences of an organization (Van Alsem and Kostelijk 2008). This perspective has proven relevant for the commercial sector, but also for the public sector (Baumgarth 2013) and specifically in healthcare with its explicit public and ethical function. The holistic perspective that focuses on mission and vision is therefore key.

There are several definitions of brand orientation, all of which capture a similar set of elements. Ewing and Napoli (2005) were among the first to research brand orientation in the public sector. They define brand orientation for nonprofit organizations as the "organization-wide process of generating and sustaining a shared sense of *brand meaning* that provides superior value to stakeholders and superior performance to the organization" (p. 842). Their research yielded three process-related factors that determine the degree of brand orientation in the nonprofit sector:

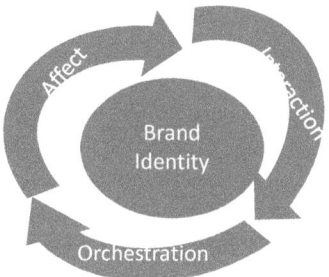

- *Interaction*: The extent to which the organization establishes a dialogue with key stakeholders and responds to changes in the environment
- *Orchestration*: The degree to which the brand portfolio and related marketing activities are structured and effectively communicated to both internal and external stakeholders
- *Affect*: The degree to which an organization understands the extent to which they are liked/disliked by key stakeholders

Interaction in a Complex Stakeholder Network

Interaction as a key factor in brand orientation has been defined as a core process at different levels, bringing both internal and external perspectives into the brand process, rather than an unconditional response to the wants and needs of the customer (Urde 1999; Gromark and Melin 2010; Urde and Merrilees 2013). Mertz et al. (2009) also criticized the customer-centricity of current marketing practices as being too limited. In healthcare, this criticism is even more relevant, since the customer, the patient, does not pay for healthcare services directly. Financial transactions are carried out via a collective system that in many Western European countries is built on notions of democracy and solidarity and operated by the government and insurance companies. This emphasizes the role of other stakeholders, such as the general public, insurance companies, the government, and so on. As an alternative to customer-centricity, Mertz et al. (2009) suggest a focus on branding from a stakeholder perspective.

Orchestration as a Challenge in Healthcare Organizations

In general, formulating a brand identity and its strategy on the one hand and implementing it on the other are two distinct elements. Implementation is important, because developing strong and long-term stable relationships with an organization's different stakeholders is directly correlated with the engagement of employees acting as good brand ambassadors. This is called orchestration. Organizations should "live the brand" (Ind 2007, Gummeson 2008). In healthcare, this internal branding process is a specific challenge, since the healthcare environment requires 'a greater understanding and management of factors that humanize the branding process, which stem from the direct implications of the word care. (Gapp and Merrilees 2006: 63). In addition, Dutch healthcare is organized in a complex way with medical specialists owning a specific part of the hospital organization as entrepreneurs and with no clear connection between the professionals involved in the primary process and between the professionals and auxiliary staff.

Affect of Economic and Emotional Value

Affect, or stakeholder likeability, is the salient antecedent to nonprofit brand performance (Ewing 2005). It is related to, but not equal to, performance. Recent approaches that follow the work of authors such as Sheth et al. (1991) are including the dimensions of emotional and social value in the concept of performance and value. For example Molinos (2006) identified emotional and social indicators of perceived value among hospital patients, using this latter multidimensional concept. Although the conceptualization of perceived value among other stakeholders is not researched, it is reasonable to assume that "likeability" or satisfaction for other stakeholders than patients includes a variety of factors that are related to performance. This means that hospitals have to deal with and match different value concepts.

Methodology

Measuring Brand Orientation in Dutch Hospitals

We used the Nonprofit Brand Orientation scale (NBO) as developed by Ewing and Napoli (2005), which captures the nuances of branding practices and concepts in the public sector. The NBO scale has been developed to compare brand management practices against other organizations and guide internal and external brand management activities. The 12 key questions of the NBO scale were used in a survey among CEOs of hospitals in the Netherlands. All 98 (out of 113) hospitals, which are members of the National Association of Hospitals (NVZ), were approached. 30 % responded ($n = 29$). The survey was supplemented by a series of 6 in-depth qualitative semi-structured interviews with CEOs of hospitals (Interviews 2014).

Results

Brand Orientations Confirmed

The results, presented only in the form of average scores due to the small sample size. show that hospitals score positively on one or more of the brand orientation elements. Differences among the hospitals arise with regard to the orchestration-dimension, resulting in two groups: an orchestrating group and a non-orchestrating group.

Interaction: All hospitals scored positively on the questions that entail the factor of interaction. This positive tendency towards interaction was confirmed in all interviews. It was indicated that intense research had been done and was still being done regarding the reputation and the improvement of opportunities for feedback by external stakeholders, mainly patients. Hospitals are actively looking for positive and critical patient feedback and consider that to be a key element in the overall rating when asked for their most important stakeholder or customer, hospital managers mention different key stakeholders. GPs and health insurance companies are named more often than patients. Also, interaction and feedback processes related to specific stakeholder groups such as GPs were more or less absent among the interviewed hospitals. Clearer specification of stakeholders is needed to better understand the reported level of interaction in hospitals.

Orchestration: Differences among the hospitals were found in the reporting of orchestration. Orchestration questions were rated less positively in general. Ten hospitals answered negative on two or more of the orchestration questions, indicating that they find it hard to make the step from knowing what is needed from a stakeholder perspective to meeting those needs structurally and manage internally. This was confirmed by the interviews in which managers stated that they believe managers and staff within the hospital are not aware of the mission, vision, and strategic choices of the hospital and how these are translated into marketing programs and activities. Two of the interviewed managers indicate they have created internal commitment for brand and strategic choices in a small and specified group of employees. Generating internal commitment seems not to be the general way of working according to the qualitative research.

Affect: Affect is the subjective outcome of the brand management process: in this research it includes the stakeholder likeability. The orchestrating group shows higher scores on this dimension than the non-orchestrating group. However, respondents have not indicated for which of the stakeholders likeability is known.

In order to better understand whether likeability is indeed the antecedent for performance (Ewing and Napoli 2005), additional factual criteria were collected and compared for the two groups. Patient satisfaction and employee satisfaction data were derived from research done by the Dutch patient association board NPCF (Nvz 2014). Customer satisfaction is high in both the orchestrating and the non-orchestrating groups (score 8.3 on a 10-point scale). Interestingly, the level of employee satisfaction differs between the two groups. The orchestrating hospitals score 7.5 on average. The non-orchestrating hospitals score 7.2. Although no statistical significance can be calculated, this is an interesting finding, especially since the non-orchestrating hospitals scored negative on the questions about brand awareness among managers and staff.

This seems to point to a relationship between brand orchestration and employee satisfaction and needs further research. The satisfaction data relating to stakeholders other than patients and employees, such as GPs or insurance companies, are not available. Hospital managers fed back in the qualitative research that they don't collect nor research data of other stakeholder groups than patients and employees. Interestingly, the Dutch law prescribes patient and employee satisfaction research for hospitals.

Conclusion

Positioning brand orientation as an alternative to market orientation in the public sector could have potential benefits due to the nature of the sector: *stakeholder focus, holistic perspective, interactive approach, dynamic approach, and democratic values (instead of economic values)*. Based on the NBO-scale of Ewing and Napoli (2005), we report on a mixed method study in the Dutch healthcare sector, with the aim of exploring the role of branding in the marketing practices of hospitals. Our quantitative and qualitative findings show firstly that brand orientation as a concept is seen as relevant. Hospitals report that they use brand orientation in their management. However, when analyzing the reported data qualitatively, it becomes clear that brand orientation is not always being implemented effectively. Hospitals have different stakeholder rankings, with patients and employees as the only structurally researched stakeholders. Secondly, the implementation (or orchestration) of brand orientation is limited. Only a small number of managers within the hospital organizations are involved in or aware of the brand strategy. The internal stakeholder is not generally seen as an important stakeholder group to bring the brand to live. This may be due to the fact that the internal stakeholder group is very heterogeneous with doctors in significant different positions than other managers and employees. Additionally, strategic choices in hospitals are focused on functional offerings and on which medical areas will be offered. Thirdly, there are hardly any adequate performance measures other than patient and employee satisfaction data. Hospitals are aware of this but are not in the process of generating more. They focus strategic efforts rather on government-initiated financial, quality, and volume measurements than on likeability and perception research among the complexity of stakeholders.

These findings suggest that the Dutch hospitals are in fact still strongly pursuing a market orientation approach with the patient as key customer and strategic choices focused on functional offerings. The advantage of a brand orientation is that it can overcome current strategic limitations. The stakeholder perspective is broader than that of customers, and also a broader spectrum of objectives. Furthermore, brand orientation is about finding a balance between the internal and the external worlds, starting by defining a clear brand identity, i.e., the mission and vision and strategic choices of the hospital. Our study provides first insights into the key issues that limit the potential success of brand orientation in the health sector. The three questions identified as being of particular significance are (1) how to rank and manage stakeholder complexity (2) how to structure and implement brand-related activities within the complexity of the hospital organizations, and (3) how to capture a complete and structural brand performance measurement system. Providing the answers to these key questions constitutes the agenda for future research.

References available upon request.

What Are We Fighting for? The Influence of Perceptions of Risk, Values, Benefits and Enjoyment in Martial Arts Club Membership

Foula Z. Kopanidis and Michael J. Shaw

Introduction

In the 70s the proliferation of popular movies led to increased enrolments into suburban karate schools with their primary stated motive being self-defence. Unstated desires to emulate their screen heroes may have also driven martial arts memberships. Despite being a minority sport in its country of origin, Karate is more popular outside of Japan. In subsequent years with an ageing demographic, self-defence, fitness and well-being have increasingly become major reasons why people sign up for martial arts classes in countries like Australia, Singapore and New Zealand. The purpose of this study is to understand the motives driving membership in Karate through exploring the values, perceptions of risk, participation patterns and specifics of enjoyment of current participants. Results from this exploratory phase will be used to inform the development of an in-depth study of martial arts membership. Preliminary insights into health and social marketing implications are also identified.

Background

People do martial arts for all sorts of reasons and while research in the area of sports marketing is primarily focused on spectatorship rather than participation, comparatively little research has been done in understanding the drivers of membership of martial arts clubs, for example, motives (Ko et al. 2010). This particularly holds true with respect to martial arts clubs which operate primarily at the local level. Even when clubs are members of larger associations, gathering data is usually limited to

F.Z. Kopanidis (✉) • M.J. Shaw
RMIT University, Melbourne, VIC, Australia
e-mail: foula.kopanidis@rmit.edu.au; michael.shaw@rmit.edu.au

© Academy of Marketing Science 2016
L. Petruzzellis, R.S. Winer (eds.), *Rediscovering the Essentiality of Marketing*,
Developments in Marketing Science: Proceedings of the Academy of Marketing
Science, DOI 10.1007/978-3-319-29877-1_77

questionnaires administered face to face, club by club. In contrast spectatorship with pay per view and ticket sales generates easy metrics and demographics for analysis (Nelson 2013). Moreover despite the increasing popularity of the practice of martial arts, studies of the benefits of martial arts remain scarce (Theenoom et al. 2009).

While the fields of growth of martial arts (Kim et al. 2009), participation in martial arts (Nelson 2013), motivations (Frederick-Recsscino and Shuster-Smith 2003), benefits (Lakes and Hoyt 2004) and risk taking (Lim et al. 2010), have been researched, this chapter addresses multiple influences on Karate membership adding to the existing body of literature by understanding the impact of these drivers of participation. It is important to understand because psychological constructs are significant determinants of sport participation (McDonald et al. 2002). This integrative study uses theoretically derived frameworks from the research fields of motivation, personal values, perceptions of risk, personal benefits, enjoyment of specific activates, needs and demographics. It will be of benefit to the emerging discourse of sports marketing and in an era of ageing demographics, will inform social marketing and health campaigns in developing targeted strategies for increasing participation.

Methodology

The data for this study was obtained through written responses distributed to four dojos in Northern and Central Melbourne. Eighty-three questionnaires were distributed with 52 returned representing a 63% response rate. Measures included items based on the instructor's role (Nelson 2013), demographic descriptors (Biernat et al. 2013), items on personal values (Kopanidis and Shaw 2014), perception of risk (Weber Blais and Betz 2002), personal benefits (Kim et al. 2009) and enjoyment of specific activities (Ryan et al. 1997). Analysis is based on descriptive statistics aimed at interpreting and exploring factors influencing membership patterns. This is a unique field which has necessitated the development of an approach which balances perceptions of risk, motivations, values and benefits. This model can be extended to research in other fields including sports participation.

Results and Discussion

Gender imbalance typically found in dojos is reflected in the demographic data with males representing 80% of the sample. The average male participant is aged 35–45 years (44%), is married, holds a qualification from vocational education and a black belt (33%), trains twice per week and engages in an additional 4–6 h of other training. He has trained for durations of more than 10 years. The male participant tends to live in close proximity to the club. The female participant is on average 10 years younger (35%), has a bachelor degree (50%), holds a brown belt (40%) and also trains twice a week and engages in an extra 1–2 h training, a week. She has trained for a duration of 5–10 years. The female participant travels a greater distance to and from their chosen club.

Choice of which martial arts club to train with was influenced predominately by *personal recommendation* (34 %), *followed by location* (27 %), *coaching and instruction* (19 %) and *adverting in the local area* (12 %). Forty three per cent of males trained in martial arts to maintain their *weight and fitness*, followed by *to learn technique and form* (26 %) and *to be able to defend myself* (12 %) with the least important goal being *to compete and or get a place in tournaments* at 4 %. Similarly, 80 % of females gave the same reason as the males of *maintaining weight and fitness* as their primary goal followed by *to be able to defend myself* (20 %). The role of the instructor and other students in the club was measured by seven items ($\alpha = .858$). The instructor's *depth of knowledge* ($M = 6.4$, SD $= 1.1$) and *ability* ($M = 6.3$, SD $= 1.1$) were deemed very important. For the male participants the instructor's *depth of knowledge* is paramount ($M = 6.5$, SD $= .94$) while for female participants the instructor's *ability as a teacher* rated as the most important ($M = 6.2$, SD $= 1.8$).

Personal Values: Personal Values Importance Scale measured nine personal values ($\alpha = .918$) comprising 45 items (Kopanidis and Shaw 2014). The values of *fun and enjoyment* ($M = 5.35$, SD $= 1.8$), *self respect* ($M = 5.16$, SD $= 1.2$) and *sense of accomplishment* were identified as the most important of the value statements. These values are classified as internal values and do not require the judgments or opinions of others. Individuals who rate internal values highly are predominantly internally motivated, believing that they can influence or control outcomes (Kropp et al. 2005). This was followed by *security* ($M = 4.9$, SD $= 2.7$), *sense of fulfilment* ($M = 4.8$, SD $= .7$), *sense of belonging* ($M = 4.7$, SD $= 2.2$), *warm relationships with others* ($M = 4.6$, SD $= 1.0$) and *excitement* that scored the lowest average ($M = 4.4$, SD $= .8$).

Engaging in activities perceived risky: Risk-taking across two domains (Health/ Safety and Recreational) was assessed by 20 items ($\alpha = .794$). The domain of recreational where the participant considered the activities of *travelling on a commercial airplane* ($M = 5.5$, SD $= 1.6$), *going camping in the wild* ($M = 5.1$, SD $= 1.7$), followed by *going on a safari in Kenya* ($M = 4.5$, SD $= 2.0$) were considered as the most likely activities participants were willing to engage with. Participants generally showed a decreased likelihood of engaging in activities that are perceived as high risk that fell in the health/safety domain as *frequent binge drinking* ($M = 2.7$, SD $= 2.1$), *never wearing a seat belt* ($M = 1.8$, SD $= 1.7$), *riding without a helmet* ($M = 2.0$, SD $= 1.4$), *smoking* ($M = 1.8$, SD $= 1.6$) and *engaging in unprotected sex* ($M = 2.7$, SD $= 2.9$). Both genders perceived activities within the health domain as the most risky, for males *smoking a packet* of *cigarettes per day* ($M = 2.0$, SD $= 1.88$) and for females, *never wearing a seat belt* ($M = 1.8$, SD $= 1.8$). This is in contrast to previous findings (Weber Blais and Betz 2002) which suggested a very strong gender component influencing risky choices with males more likely to take risks. What emerges from this research is that male and female karate participants are more or less equally risk averse.

Personal benefits. Personal benefits were measured with 14 questions ($\alpha = .794$). The motivational outcomes driving participation in martial arts centred on primary on developing *one's potential* ($M = 6.3$, SD $= 877$), aligning participation with *having a positive attitude in life* (M=6.15, SD=.957), *developing self-discipline* (M=6.11, SD=.983), *maintaining a good physique* (M=5.9, SD=.737) and *taking pride in what I do* (M=5.9, SD=1.1). Competing to win (M=4.0, SD=1.0) and *competing outside of the club* (M=3.4, SD=2.1) were not considered as persuasive reasons to participate. Similar to prior research findings, participants stressed the importance of physical fitness and spiritual discipline as personal benefits of participating in Karate training (Kim et al. 2009).

Enjoyment of activities. Enjoyment of activities (Ryan et al. 1997) was measured with a 20-item scale (α=.871). Participant's responses affirmed the appeal to Karate as a traditional "stand up" style training agreeing performing *kata and forms* (M=6.0, SD=1.0), *cardio fitness training* (M=5.7, SD=1.3), *strength training* (M=5.7, SD=1.1) and *being taught by other senior students* (M=5.6, SD=1.1) as the most enjoyable activated in training. The least enjoyed activity was *competing outside the club* (M=3.3, SD=2.1).

Conclusion

The findings of this research provide an initial platform from which to build a more in-depth study from a substantive sample size. Given this limitation, these results indicate the goals of maintaining weight and fitness and learning skills and techniques as critical reasons for Karate club membership. Upholding the personal values of fun and enjoyment, self-respect and sense of accomplishment, this cohort considers a positive attitude in life, self-discipline, maintaining a good physique and experiencing pride as the most important benefits they expect to receive from Karate club membership. Participants strongly agreed with the relevance of the instructor's depth of knowledge and ability in both Karate and in teaching in choosing a club. Exhibiting a propensity to avoid participating in risk adverse activities, the participants prioritised the health/safety domain by reporting activities, which fell under this domain as the least likely both genders would engage in. This result is consistent with the desired perceived benefits of physical fitness and a sense of personal well-being, which was also expressed through the enjoyment of the specific activities of kata and forms, cardio fitness training and strength training. The adult participants showed a lifelong path of dedication and commitment through their years of investment in Karate training. This martial art was not perceived as an interim engagement, nor perceived as a forum for competition. Such an insight is useful in guiding communication strategies to promote particular benefits and to position Karate membership as a lifestyle commitment through meeting the specific goals of its members.

To advance social marketing and health policy agendas, it is suggested that communication strategies need to strengthen the positive association between lifetime membership and a state of personal well-being. The personal values that participants uphold can be leveraged as part of this communication message. At a community level promoting a *sense of accomplishment* by appealing to the consequences of good health can also work towards integrating this value as part of lifestyle culture.

Achieving fun and enjoyment and recognition of self-respect can be emphasised for individual goal attainment. The associations between membership, fitness and goal fulfilment should be the focus of any marketing campaign aimed at shifting lifestyle choices towards promoting lifetime participation and membership in Karate clubs. In terms of future research, a qualitative phase is proposed that will focus on senior students to explore the narrative of their training journeys, in particular the original reasons for starting training and the main reasons for continuation.

References available upon request.

Does Authenticity Matter in Corporate Social Responsibility Acts?

Sarah Alhouti, Catherine M. Johnson, and Betsy Bugg Holloway

Abstract The study examines the role of authenticity in corporate social responsibility (CSR) acts through a qualitative and quantitative study. Three hundred and ninety qualitative commentaries are content analyzed to determine antecedents to CSR authenticity. The study finds that impact, perceived motive, reparation, and fit are vital in creating the perception of authentic CSR acts. Impact refers to the amount of resources allocated to assisting a cause and the company's impact on a cause. Perceived motive is the reason why CSR acts are being implemented. Reparation refers to the degree to which a CSR initiative is perceived to be an attempt to compensate for a misdeed. Fit is defined as the CSR initiatives alignment with the firm's offering, brand concept, or target market needs. The quantitative study proves that CSR authenticity mediates the influence on consumer outcome. The structural equation model also shows a significant effect of impact, reparation, and fit on CSR authenticity.

S. Alhouti (✉)
Providence College, Providence, RI, USA
e-mail: salhouti@providence.edu

C.M. Johnson
University of Toledo, Toledo, OH, USA
e-mail: smjohnson8@cba.ua.edu

B.B. Holloway
Samford University, Birmingham, AL, USA
e-mail: bbhollow@samford.edu

© Academy of Marketing Science 2016
L. Petruzzellis, R.S. Winer (eds.), *Rediscovering the Essentiality of Marketing*,
Developments in Marketing Science: Proceedings of the Academy of Marketing
Science, DOI 10.1007/978-3-319-29877-1_78

Make It More Authentic: The Drivers of Positive Ad Evaluations in Co-created Health Communications

Davide C. Orazi, Max N. Theilacker, Liliana L. Bove, and Jing Lei

Introduction

The reported lack of research on consumer-to-health department interactions (Andersen et al. 2012) and the audience's perceptions that many health campaigns greatly exaggerate health risks (Cancer Vic 2012) suggest that increased consumer involvement in the design of health messages and increased message authenticity may enhance the persuasiveness of many, limitedly successful public health campaigns (e.g., Darrow and Biersterker 2008; de Gruchy and Coppel 2008; Kerr et al. 2013). Source effects literature (Wilson and Sherrell 1993) suggests that positive message evaluations may be strengthened when the audience develops a sense of identification with the message source. Similar, audience evaluations may benefit from messages that are perceived to be more authentic, since message authenticity enables self-referencing to the scenarios depicted in the health message (Ertimur and Gilly 2012).

One potential avenue to address the needs for identification and authenticity is to involve consumers in the generation of health messages. The current research combines recent findings on consumer-generated advertising (CGA) in the private sector (Berthon et al. 2008; Ertimur and Gilly 2012; Thompson and Malaviya 2013; Lawrence et al. 2013) and established literature on attribution theory (Kelley 1967; Ohanian 1990; Wilson and Sherrell 1993) to examine the influence of source effects on health messages effectiveness. In particular, we aim at understanding (1) the differential persuasiveness of disclosing that a health message is co-created vs. solely consumer-generated vs. solely health-department created, (2) which factors drive the positive evaluations of co-created health messages, and (3) the role of perceived advertising authenticity in predicting ad evaluations.

D.C. Orazi (✉) • M.N. Theilacker • L.L. Bove • J. Lei
The University of Melbourne, Melbourne, VIC, Australia
e-mail: davide.orazi@unimelb.edu.au; maxnt@unimelb.edu.au; lbove@unimelb.edu.au; leij@unimelb.edu.au

© Academy of Marketing Science 2016   401
L. Petruzzellis, R.S. Winer (eds.), *Rediscovering the Essentiality of Marketing*,
Developments in Marketing Science: Proceedings of the Academy of Marketing
Science, DOI 10.1007/978-3-319-29877-1_79

Theoretical Framework

Our first contention is that the disclosure of a collaborative approach in the creation of health messages leads to more positive ad evaluations in comparison to solely health department created or solely consumer-generated health messages. Our arguments for the superior persuasiveness of co-created health messages follow the PACT (acronym for *personalization, authorization, capabilization,* and *transformation*) routine outlined by Giesler and Veresiu (2014). The PACT routine suggests that issues relevant to the common good must be tackled starting from an empowered, responsible consumer who becomes the central problem-solver (*personalization*). Institutional and informational support complements personalization, ensuring that consumer's contributions are perceived as legitimate (*authorization*), both at an executional and informational levels. Then, through the creation of platforms and programs that enable this collaboration (*capabilization*), it is possible to achieve the positive social change auspicated (*transformation*). Following this, we investigate a structural model of source effects for co-created health messages. We draw from attribution theory and from the idea that the audience draws inferences on the message source on the basis of perceived credibility and perceived attractiveness (Kelman 1961; Ohanian 1990; Wilson and Sherrell 1993). Source credibility is defined by expertise—the audience's expectation that the message source possesses extensive knowledge about the topic (Clark et al. 2012) and trustworthiness—the expectation that the source is telling the truth (Wilson and Sherrell 1993). Source attractiveness, on the other hand, is defined by physical attractiveness and ideological similarity—perceptions of shared interests, opinions, experiences, and beliefs (Wilson and Sherrell 1993). We complement our theoretical framework drawing from literature on perceived motives and consumer identity to assess the influence of perceived egoistic and altruistic motives of the ad creator on credibility and similarity (Vignoles et al. 2006; Fisher et al. 2008; White and Peloza 2009; Berthon et al. 2008; Cohen and Sherman 2014). Finally, we draw from qualitative findings on brand communities' reactions to consumer-generated messages to investigate if the audience's awareness of consumer participation in message creation influences the perceived authenticity of the message (Ertimur and Gilly 2012).

Prior to the presentation of our methods and results, a clarification is warranted with regard to the construct of advertising authenticity. In general terms, authenticity is defined as the "illusion of the reality of ordinary life in reference to a [...] situation" (Stern 1994, p. 388). Most studies investigating the concept of authenticity in advertising attribute authenticity to the advertised brand or product (e.g., Beverland et al. 2008). The few studies that consider authenticity in reference to the advertisement itself rather than the advertised object tend to use "constructs like authenticity and credibility almost interchangeably" (Ertimur and Gilly 2012, p. 126). In a co-creative context, the distinction between the two concepts is relevant as the credibility of the message source is evaluated separately from the outcome of the collaboration (i.e., the message). We contend that, when evaluating a health message, the audience first makes inferences regarding the message source (i.e., credibility and similarity), and then uses these inferences to inform their evaluation of message authenticity. Inferring that a source is credible is thus likely to increase the audience's perception that the message conveys an accurate and faithful representation of a realistic scenario. In addition, assessments of advertising authenticity are influenced by the extent to which the audience can self-reference to the presented scenario (Ertimur and Gilly 2012). Perceiving the message source as similar may thus assist this self-referencing process.

Pilot Study

Prior to conducting an investigation of the key determinants of persuasiveness in co-created health messages, we conducted a pilot study to ensure that co-created health messages are better received than solely health department-created and solely consumer-generated messages. One-hundred-and-two adults residing in the United States ($M_{age}=34.63$ (SD=10.72), 44.1 % male) were randomly assigned to one of three experimental conditions (Creative mode disclosure: Solely health department-created vs. solely consumer-generated vs. Co-created) in a between-subjects design. An analysis of variance (ANOVA) on ad evaluations indicated a significant effect of creative mode disclosure ($F(2, 99)=5.14$, $p<.01$). Planned contrasts analyses with Bonferroni test revealed that consumers evaluate more positively health messages disclosed to be co-created ($M_{co\text{-}created}=4.24$), in comparison to consumer-generated ($M_{CG}=3.87$, $p<.05$) and health department-created ads ($M_{HD\text{-}created}=3.73$, $p<.05$). Given the space constraints, we omit further details and present the results on the driver of effectiveness of co-created health messages.

Main Study

A total of 525 adults residing in the United States ($M_{age}=36.18$ (SD=12.03), 57.5 % male) were recruited from an AMTurk (for an empirical assessment of AMTurk reliability and validity in experimental research, see Paolacci et al. 2010) to complete an online survey on their evaluations regarding a health message disclosed to be co-created between a health department and an affected consumer. Eight latent constructs where measured in this study employing established measures: egoistic and altruistic motives (Cnann and Goldberg-Glen 1991; Daugherty et al. 2008), source credibility as a second-order factor composed of trustworthiness and expertise (Ohanian 1990), source similarity (Lawrence et al. 2013), message authenticity (Kovács et al. 2013), ad evaluations (Thompson and Malaviya 2013), health beliefs regarding fast-food consumption (Dave et al. 2009). In addition, we included socio-demographic (gender, age, and education) and context-specific control factors (height and weight).

Table 1 Summary of results

Predictor	Sign	Criterion	β	Significance
Credibility	(+)	Ad evaluations	.38	$p<.001$
Egoistic motives	(−)	Credibility	.05	$p=.206$
Altruistic motives	(+)	Credibility	.59	$p<.001$
Similarity	(+)	Ad evaluations	.28	$p<.001$
Egoistic motives	(−)	Similarity	.06	$p=.284$
Altruistic motives	(+)	Similarity	.49	$p<.001$
Credibility	(+)	Authenticity	.73	$p<.001$
Similarity	(+)	Authenticity	.08	$p=.068$
Authenticity	(+)	Ad evaluations	.34	$p<.001$
Similarity	(+)	Credibility	.34	$p<.001$
Ad evaluations	(+)	Health beliefs	.46	$p<.001$

Results

Measurement model. Each item loaded over .70 on their respective factor, with the average variance extracted (AVE) of each factor greater than .50. This provided evidence of convergent validity (Bagozzi and Phillips 1991). The average variance extracted (AVE) of each construct was greater than its shared variance with any other construct, providing evidence of discriminant validity (Fornell and Larcker 1981). Credibility was treated as a second-order factor composed by expertise and trustworthiness. The measurement model fit was good (χ^2/df$=863.50/411=2.10$; AGFI$=.88$; CFI$=.97$; RMSEA$=.046$; PNFI$=.83$).

Structural model. The structural model fit was good (χ^2/df$=914/420=2.17$; AGFI$=.88$; CFI$=.97$; RMSEA$=.047$; PNFI$=.81$). Table 1 summarizes the results. Tests for indirect effects using bootstrapping with 5000 repetitions show (1) a strong positive indirect effect of perceived altruistic motives on ad evaluations ($\beta=.63$, $p<.001$), and (2) the indirect effect of similarity on authenticity, mediated by credibility, is highly significant ($\beta=.25$, $p<.001$). Overall, the model explains a considerable amount of variance for ad evaluations ($R^2=.78$) and a reasonable amount of variance for health beliefs ($R^2=.21$).

Discussion

Our results indicate strong support for the proposed model. The downstream effect of disclosing that a health message is co-created is evident not only in the significance of the paths linking credibility, similarity, and authenticity with ad evaluations, but also in the positive relationship between altruistic motives and source effects (i.e., credibility and similarity). Supporting our prior assertion, the audience's attributions regarding the source of the message—credibility and similarity—contribute positively to the assessment of message authenticity. The lack of support for the negative influence of egoistic motives may be explained by the nature of both the creative mode and the health context. As the health message is the expression of a collaborative effort and thus cannot be solely attributed to the consumer, the audience may be less likely to perceive that the consumer–creator is motivated by means of self-promotion.

Our study provides a new perspective on the meanings associated with authenticity in advertising (Chalmers 2007; Ertimur and Gilly 2012). Deviating from prior research considering authenticity and credibility as aspects reflective of the same construct (e.g., Lawrence et al. 2013), we distinguish between the source effects level, pertaining to attributions of source credibility and similarity, and the message content level, pertaining to assessments of message authenticity. Our work also offers some noteworthy implications for public policy, providing insights that might ease the called for shift from a centralized, top-down to a more distributed structure of public policy where consumers are actively involved in the process of responsibilization (Giesler and Veresiu 2014). In addition, social marketers and health communicators should strongly articulate the narrative of authenticity, highlighting how genuine insights and authentic experiences provided by consumers–creators have been used during message development.

Some limitations must be acknowledged for the present study. Our findings relate to a single health issue—obesity. To assess their generalizability, future research should investigate if the proposed model holds for different health contexts. For example, campaigns promoting preventative actions (e.g., breast screenings) and corrective campaigns targeting compulsive consumption behaviors such as smoking may significantly differ in terms of perceived costs for compliance (Fishbein and Cappella 2006). As our study does not employ a longitudinal design it was not possible to test our predictions on actual behavior, but only on proxies of advertising effectiveness such as ad evaluations (MacKenzie et al. 1986; Metha 2000; Thompson and Malaviya 2013). Future research should employ longitudinal designs to assess if and how collaboratively created health messages determine behavioral change. This research only scratches the surface of co-created health messages as an advertising strategy to increase effectiveness. Part of our investigation is limited to the evaluative variation conditional to disclosing that the same message has been created by different sources (i.e., the mere disclosure effect). Yet, the process of collaborative creation and shared responsibility should be investigated on a broader scale. Future research should complement this study by assessing the actual contribution to message effectiveness stemming from active consumer involvement and the consequential provision of authentic experiences, genuine insights, and narratives of success (i.e., the real effect).

References available upon request.

Designing Mobile Applications for Healthcare Professional Use: A Service Marketing Perspective

Athanasia Daskalopoulou, Kathy Keeling, Nikolay Mehandjiev, and Rowan Pritchard Jones

Abstract The investigation of health services is a major area of interest within the field of marketing (e.g. Berry and Bendapudi 2007; Crié and Chebat 2013). Research in the area is heterogeneous, covering the range from healthy individuals, people suffering from chronic diseases along with healthcare professionals. In previous studies, there is inherently an assumption that medical applications have the potential to improve the efficiency of healthcare service delivery and thereby deliver value to consumers, hence generate uptake. However, thousands of consumer-oriented applications have close to zero downloads (Campaign 2014), and the acceptance of medical applications is relatively low by professionals in the hospital context (Wu et al. 2011). This suggests a need to inform the service design cycle for medical applications with insights from technology and design disciplines in order to deliver relevant mobile services. In the contemporary 'electronic' marketplace, encompassing all aspects of service delivery in design appears daunting. Yet, it is crucial to identify those factors that drive positive service experiences in order to maximize consumer value (Sandström et al. 2008). A large and growing body of services research investigates the role of consumer perceptions of value creation as a driver for acceptance, use and/or purchase. S-D logic suggests that *'value is defined by and co-created with the consumer rather than embedded in output'* (Vargo and Lusch 2004). When value is perceived as value in use, functional and economic benefits as well as emotional, social, ethical and environmental dimensions are of significance for consumers (Grönroos and Voima 2013). As a result, if the full potential of mobile services is to be realised in medical care, it is necessary to understand the interplay between technology issues, such as usability and the human side of assessments of experience in the creation of value for the user. We posit that optimal mobile service design could

A. Daskalopoulou (✉) • K. Keeling • N. Mehandjiev
Manchester Business School, Manchester, UK
e-mail: a.daskalopoulou@mbs.ac.uk; kathy.keeling@manchester.ac.uk; n.mehandjiev@manchester.ac.uk

R.P. Jones
St. Helens and Knowsley NHS Trust, Liverpool University, Liverpool, UK
e-mail: Rowan.PritchardJones@sthk.nhs.uk

© Academy of Marketing Science 2016
L. Petruzzellis, R.S. Winer (eds.), *Rediscovering the Essentiality of Marketing*,
Developments in Marketing Science: Proceedings of the Academy of Marketing
Science, DOI 10.1007/978-3-319-29877-1_80

407

be achieved by using human–computer interaction design principles in conjunction with service design theories. The purpose of this chapter is to extend existing studies by investigating consumers' perception of value in using mobile services in context and explore how medical service design and delivery can be optimised for mobile applications. To address these objectives, we follow an inductive approach aligned with grounded theory techniques and procedures (Glaser and Strauss 1967; Strauss and Corbin 1998), and we initially employ an exemplar case study. We report on data concerning a medical mobile application (*Mersey Micro*) for healthcare professionals intended for use inside the hospital. Data are gathered from in-context, in-depth, interviews with representative users, usability studies as well as an exploratory survey aiming at identifying clinicians' interaction with the mobile application. The literature suggests that design of effective and efficient healthcare systems would benefit greatly from integrated models and frameworks that combine consumers' emotions and technical features of service platforms (Ostrom et al. 2010). As a result, this chapter might be seen as an initial attempt towards this direction. Our initial findings are pointing the direction of (medical) mobile service design as a combination of technology issues, such as usability and the human side of assessments of experience in the creation of value for the user.

References available upon request.

A Conceptual Model of Service Providers' Psychological Resilience at the Workplace

Sandy Ng

Abstract This project answers a recent call from the Transformative Service Research (TSR) movement (Anderson et al. 2013) to address a lack of research in understanding the well-being of service providers. In addition, this research also addresses a pressing issue to counteract management problems such as increase turnover rate (Bardoel et al. 2014), which is prevalent in certain service industries such as the hospitality and the retail sectors. Service providers, being boundary spanners, often experience emotional stressors due to conflicting job roles and demands from both internal (within the organisation) and external (e.g., customers) environments (e.g., Lings et al. 2010). This leads to burnout, which creates a psychological strain on service providers that can have serious detrimental consequences for the psychological well-being of employees. Positive psychology literature found that positive emotions serve as markers of flourishing, or optimal well-being (Fredrickson 2001). In an ideal scenario, management would want service employees to be happy and well at all times. However, this is unrealistic. To this end, this research proposes a conceptual model that studies the role of psychological resilience in buffering and regulating service employee's well-being.

Psychological resilience is defined as "the capacity for recovery and maintained adaptive behaviour that may follow initial retreat or incapacity upon initiating a stressful event" (Garmezy 1991, p. 459). The Resilience Framework Model (Kumpfer 2011) is used as the theoretical underpinning in identifying individuals' internal self-resiliency characteristics. Specifically, work locus of control, general health, self-efficacy, emotional regulation, and job competence are proposed as drivers of service employees' resilience at work. Next, the model investigates the links between psychological resilience of service employees and well-being, and work-related outcomes such as retention, job satisfaction, and engagement. As an extension of this study, moderating

S. Ng (✉)
RMIT University, Melbourne, Australia
e-mail: sandy.ng@rmit.edu.au

© Academy of Marketing Science 2016
L. Petruzzellis, R.S. Winer (eds.), *Rediscovering the Essentiality of Marketing*,
Developments in Marketing Science: Proceedings of the Academy of Marketing
Science, DOI 10.1007/978-3-319-29877-1_81

409

effects such as gender and work duration are studied. To the best of knowledge, prior research has not proposed a model of service employees' psychological resilience. This research is timely as it answers a gap in the TSR and Management/Human Resource literature. It can also provide useful insights to service organisations, to develop strategies to improve staff well-being, retention, and also for recruitment purposes.

References available upon request.

An Examination of Food Waste as a Corporate Social Responsibility of the Retail and Wholesale Sector

Verena Gruber, Christina Holweg, and Christoph Teller

Abstract Food waste is a major problem in industrialized nations. In order to develop efficient mechanisms for minimization, a better understanding of the complexities involved in food waste is necessary. This chapter takes a marketing system perspective to provide a holistic exploration of the edible food waste phenomenon on a retail and wholesale store level. By means of 32 in-depth interviews with store managers, we gain insights into the relevance of food waste occurrence, avoidance, and redistribution. The data reveals various factors influencing the occurrence of food waste along formal, informal, and philosophical antecedent classes. We find that managing edible food waste is closely connected to the triple bottom line: reducing its occurrence and enabling processes to redistribute edible food waste can create economic, ecological, and social benefits. Against this background, we propose a dormant sustainability potential in the management of food waste and advance recommendations for realizing these benefits. We suggest that food waste is a key priority area in the realm of corporate social responsibility for retail and wholesale organization. The chapter draws on a framework for public policy change and provides a discussion about how different processes can help reduce edible food waste among various market actors.

V. Gruber (✉) • C. Holweg
WU Vienna, Vienna, Austria
e-mail: verena.gruber@wu.ac.at; christina.holweg@wu.ac.at

C. Teller
University of Surrey, Guildford, UK
e-mail: c.teller@surrey.ac.uk

© Academy of Marketing Science 2016
L. Petruzzellis, R.S. Winer (eds.), *Rediscovering the Essentiality of Marketing*,
Developments in Marketing Science: Proceedings of the Academy of Marketing
Science, DOI 10.1007/978-3-319-29877-1_82

Segmenting Australian High School Students Utilising a Two-Step Cluster Analysis: Differential Effects Following the Game on Know Alcohol Program

Timo Dietrich, Sharyn Rundle-Thiele, Lisa Schuster, Judy Drennan, Rebekah Russell-Bennett, Cheryl Leo, and Jason Connor

Abstract The majority of alcohol education programs in school settings follow a one-size-fits-all approach meaning that they are using the identical program (universal programs) for all participants (Botvin and Griffin 2007; Foxcroft and Tsertsvadze 2012). However, a one-size-fits-all approach may limit program effectiveness as large numbers of the audience may be left dissatisfied, uninterested, or unchallenged (Snyder et al. 2004). This study is part of a larger cluster randomised control design research project that is implementing and evaluating an alcohol social marketing education program named Game On: Know Alcohol (GOKA) that is currently in field.

TwoStep cluster analysis was conducted to segment 2114 Year 10 high school students using data from three segmentation bases; demographic, behaviour and psychographic. Three segments were identified: (1) Abstainers, (2) Bingers and (3) Moderate Drinkers. Next differential effects post-GOKA delivery were analysed using a (2) $\times 2 \times 3$ repeated measures ANCOVA design. Changes in knowledge, attitudes, behavioural intentions, social norms, expectancies and self-efficacy were investigated post-program delivery.

T. Dietrich (✉) • S. Rundle-Thiele
Griffith University, Nathan, Australia
e-mail: t.dietrich@griffith.edu.au; s.rundle-thiele@griffith.edu.au

L. Schuster • J. Drennan • R. Russell-Bennett
QUT Business School, Brisbane, Australia
e-mail: lisa.schuster@qut.edu.au; j.drennan@qut.edu.au; rebekah.bennett@qut.edu.au

C. Leo
Murdoch University, Perth, Australia
e-mail: c.leo@murdoch.edu.au

J. Connor
University of Queensland, Brisbane, Australia
e-mail: jason.connor@uq.edu.au

© Academy of Marketing Science 2016
L. Petruzzellis, R.S. Winer (eds.), *Rediscovering the Essentiality of Marketing*,
Developments in Marketing Science: Proceedings of the Academy of Marketing
Science, DOI 10.1007/978-3-319-29877-1_83

413

414 T. Dietrich et al.

Strongest change effects for GOKA were achieved for the Bingers segment while the Moderate Drinkers and Abstainers had mixed results across the outcome measures. These findings warrant future development of more targeted and differentially delivered programs that meet the needs and wants of each of the identified segments.

References available upon request.

What is the Lived Experience of Trafficked Persons in Nigeria?

Abi Badejo, Sharyn Rundle-Thiele, and Krzysztof Kubacki

Abstract This study aims to understand the lived experiences of individuals who have been trafficked both within and outside of Nigeria for the purpose of sexual exploitation and domestic labour. Interview questions were guided by cultural norms discussed in human trafficking literature. Results of the study reject the notion that women trafficked abroad for sex work are victims who are often exploited by their traffickers. While evident in some cases and certainly the view propagated by the media and activist groups, this chapter reveals exploitation is minimal. However, in the case of individuals being trafficked within the country, exploitation is prevalent and individuals are at the mercy of relatives and *madams* who exploit them for their own gain. Further, contrary to widely held beliefs that individuals trafficked are kidnapped by strangers against their will, this chapter identifies that the trafficked are introduced to the trafficker by someone within their sphere of influence including friends and close relatives. These results can inform future social marketing interventions targeting both individuals at risk and the important others who surround them (midstream) in order to reduce the prevalence of human trafficking. Limitations and future research directions are outlined.

A. Badejo (✉) • S. Rundle-Thiele • K. Kubacki
Griffith University, Nathan, Australia
e-mail: abi.badejo@griffithuni.edu.au; s.rundle-thiele@griffith.edu.au;
k.kubacki@griffith.edu.au

© Academy of Marketing Science 2016
L. Petruzzellis, R.S. Winer (eds.), *Rediscovering the Essentiality of Marketing*,
Developments in Marketing Science: Proceedings of the Academy of Marketing
Science, DOI 10.1007/978-3-319-29877-1_84

Re-examining Value Co-creation in the Age of Interactive Service Robots

Willy Barnett, Adrienne Foos, Thorsten Gruber, Debbie Isobel Keeling, Kathleen Keeling, and Linda Nasr

Introduction

With robots increasingly considered as viable service agents, marketers must explore the nature of value co-creation during service interactions and the consequences for the wider nature of relationships between service providers and customers. This study investigates the nature of the direct interaction between humans and robots and the implications for value co-creation. The aim is to reveal the underlying structures that influence user opinions of robot roles and value-in-use, and so inform the debate on social implications of robot service. Such insights will create awareness for the changing nature of service encounters and help marketers promote positive interactions.

Edvardsson et al. (2011) expanded our understanding of service dominant logic by pointing out that value co-creation follows social structures and occurs within social systems in which both customers and employees adopt certain roles during their interaction. In the context of this research, interaction involves service encounters between customers and interactive service robots (ISRs). The role of companies and organizations is to help customers in their value creation by providing them with necessary resources and processes (e.g., information, goods, and service activities). Value creation, facilitated by companies and organizations, is regarded as a process through which customers should be/feel better off than before (Grönroos 2008, 2011). According to Grönroos (2011), value co-creation can solely occur

W. Barnett (✉) • A. Foos • K. Keeling • L. Nasr
University of Manchester, Manchester, UK
e-mail: willy.barnett@postgrad.mbs.ac.uk; adrienne.foos@postgrad.mbs.ac.uk;
kathy.keeling@manchester.ac.uk; linda.nasr@mbs.ac.uk

T. Gruber • D.I. Keeling
Loughborough University, Loughborough, UK
e-mail: t.gruber@lboro.ac.uk; D.I.Keeling@lboro.ac.uk

© Academy of Marketing Science 2016
L. Petruzzellis, R.S. Winer (eds.), *Rediscovering the Essentiality of Marketing*,
Developments in Marketing Science: Proceedings of the Academy of Marketing
Science, DOI 10.1007/978-3-319-29877-1_85

when frontline employees and customers are interacting directly (rather than organizations being limited to only making value propositions; Vargo and Lusch 2004). Different outcomes are possible depending on how the interaction progresses (Grönroos 2012); therefore, frontline employees interacting with customers play an important role as they influence their customers' value creation process either positively (value creation) or negatively (value destruction) (Grönroos 2011; Echeverri and Skalen 2011).

More recently, interest has shifted away from investigating face-to-face service encounters and moved more towards other service relationships. Due to the rapid advancement of robotic technology, we may soon witness a "comeback" of traditional service encounter research, this time focusing on interactions between customers and ISRs. Thus, technological changes in the macro-environment have a significant impact on how the roles of both customers and employees change in service environments. Already deployed in defense, manufacturing, and warehousing, the integration of robots into service environments is closer than ever (Alonso-Martin and Salichs 2011). A new generation of social robots (i.e., ISRs) capable of working within service environments and interacting with customers through various service encounters (e.g., healthcare and education) is evolving. Although these technological developments may quell some emerging societal problems, such as a shortage of care workers for an increasingly elderly population, the interactive nature of the service encounter also brings with it new challenges. Bartneck and Forlizzi (2004) define a social robot as "an autonomous or semi-autonomous robot that interacts and communicates with humans by following the behavioral norms expected by the people with whom the robot is intended to interact" (p. 593). This definition assumes that humans are assigning roles to the robot in the interaction. However, the nature of those roles and the consequences for service outcomes, perceived value, and relationships with providers of customer–robot service interactions can potentially be destructive. For example, Torrey et al. (2008) find negative social and psychological effects for users stemming from accepting help from service assistive robots. They link negative outcomes to the nature and content of the interaction, providing the counterintuitive recommendation that ISRs might mitigate negative social outcomes resulting from accepting help through emphasizing their "machine like" qualities.

These studies speak to wider consequences, as they strongly suggest that other social changes around the nature of relationships between service providers and service customers could arise from misunderstandings of value sought and user perceptions of robots' place in society. If ISRs are to play a positive role in delivering service, marketers need to understand the interplay between roles assigned to ISRs and value co-creation. Applying the work of Grönroos (2011) and Edvardsson et al. (2011) to this new situation suggests that successful integration of social robots into service environments presumes effective interaction between robots and customers; which in turn is impacted by customers' perceptions of the role status of robots. Robotics research has focused particularly on developing socially interactive robots, e.g., realistic movements, personalities, emotions, social interaction, and communication (e.g., Fong et al. 2003; Mori 1970), with an assumption that this technology will deliver value in the service exchange. Our study questions this assumption, arguing that to offer a viable route for service delivery we must comprehensively understand customers' feelings about robots in specific service contexts: healthcare, education, and retailing.

Method

We utilize the Zaltman Metaphor Elicitation Technique (ZMET), which integrates the visual projection technique, in-depth personal laddering interview, and qualitative data-processing techniques (Lee et al. 2003). According to the method, a purposive sample collects images around a subject chosen by the researcher. We conducted three ZMET studies for three service contexts (retailing, healthcare, or education), asking up to 20 respondents (Reynolds et al. 2001) for each study to bring images related to interacting with a robot in that service context. Some information was provided about each type of use so all participants had a minimum shared knowledge. One-to-one guided conversations followed, initially on what the service interaction means to them at present, then, around a repertory grid framework (Kelly 1955, 1963) for the relative meaning of the images; followed by a short laddering interview. Narrative analysis of the stories in the first part of the interview builds conceptualization of the main thematic categories. The laddering interviews show how attributes of the robot and interaction are ultimately linked to the values or beliefs that are strengthened or satisfied by the consequences of use (Reynolds and Gutman 1988). The complete ZMET technique allows for the discovery of positive and negative connotations that users associate with interactions with ISRs and draws out the underlying structures that influence user opinions of robot roles and value-in-use.

Findings

Laddering: The researchers coded the sequences of A-C-Vs (ladders) using Schwartz's Universal Values for end value categories (Schwartz 2004). A total of 267 ladders were entered into the decision-support software LADDERMAP® to produce a Hierarchical Value Map (HVM), displaying the links between Attributes, Consequences and underpinning Values.

The two most important values were "self-direction ($n=19$)" and "security ($n=18$)." These two values were the most mentioned and possessed the majority of the strongest consequences links. "Self-direction" represented participants' need for independence. For example, in a retail setting many participants felt that service robots would positively impact their ability to make decisions and make better use of their time. Several respondents mentioned that the less time they spent in a retail store, the more time they would have to deal with more important affairs. In order for participants to perceive self-direction, it was important for robots to not violate machine-like expectations, such as returning the correct amount of change at check out. "Security" represented feelings of trust and sincerity. The majority of participants felt that robots were unbiased and nonjudgmental, and therefore felt the robot would not try to upsell them or segment them into stereotypical shopping categories. Paradoxically, although robots were perceived as trustworthy in a retail setting, many participants felt that robots were incapable of being sincere. For example, one participant noted that if a robot asks how his day was, he would be immediately put off because he would know that the robot really did not care.

The attribute-to-consequence link of "personality ($n = 15$)"-to-"human interaction ($n = 18$)" displayed the strongest connections to "security" and "self-direction." Participants related a robot's personality to that of a service employee. Humanlike service behaviors such as friendliness and empathy were examples of perceptions of personality. The consequence of "human interaction" was viewed as the extent in which a participant would want to interact with the robot. This consequence was also viewed in a paradoxical nature. For example, most participants felt that the personality of the robot would directly determine whether or not there would be interaction; however, some participants felt that a robot with a limited personality (i.e., less talkative, less personable) would actually be preferable to a human service employee due to the robot's inability to have bad moods. In contrast, other participants mentioned that they would be more willing to interact with a robot that displayed social norms such as politeness embedded into their personality. It is interesting to note that these same participants expressed reluctance in reciprocating the same norms.

The consequence of "service experience ($n = 15$)" additionally had strong linkages to the values of "security" and "self-direction." "Service experience" was also the direct consequence of "faster service ($n = 19$)" (described as the robot's ability to expedite service transactions) and "service failure ($n = 19$)" (described as robot malfunctions). The majority of participants agreed that a speedy, error-free robot interaction would result in a positive experience. A paradoxical characteristic also existed with the consequence of "service experience." We found that many participants felt that while service experience is enhanced by functional attributes such as "precision" and "speed," it is also degraded by personality characteristics such as empathy and remorse—contradicting the typical expectations of a human-to-human retail interaction.

Visual Metaphors: Several central metaphorical themes emerged to enhance our understanding of perceived value from robot interaction.

Metaphor: "*We've barely scratched the surface.*" The metaphor of an iceberg relates not only to the idea of an icy coldness but also that the visible area of an iceberg that is seen above water is a fraction of the entire iceberg. Many participants perceived robots to be void of personality or a soul. The terms "cold" and "empty" often described the perceived interaction with a robot in a retail scenario. The ability to feel a "connection" during a service interaction was viewed as highly important to most participants. Therefore, the robot's perceived lack of personable traits would negatively impact participants' service experience.

Metaphor: "*You make me want to pull my hair out.*" The metaphor relates to the idea that some people may become so frustrated that they would pull their hair as a means of releasing stress. With regard to robots in a retail setting, majority of the participants felt that interactions with a robot might lead to frustration. The reasons mentioned were the inability to understand human speech and service failures, such as making mistakes at check out. Participants felt that there would be a trade-off for level of frustration and time saved, e.g., they were willing to deal with frustration if the robot presented a faster option for service.

Metaphor: *"Our lives will resemble the Planet of the Apes."* The metaphor relates to the 2011 movie, Rise of the Planet of the Apes, and represents the transition from a world of human control to one of primate control. In this view, many participants felt that introduction of robots in a retail setting would render human shoppers as simple components of a larger system. The participants felt that robots would remove the social characteristic from a service experience and humans would act in a standard mechanized manner, with little individuality.

Metaphor: *"The life struggle begins."* The metaphor relates to the perception of internal and external conflicts that individuals face when they have no means of supporting themselves financially. A large number of participants expressed concern for service workers who may lose their jobs due to the implementation of service robots. In this view, participants' felt that sustainability of the service industries, the economy, and ultimately society, would be threatened if viable robot employees were implemented.

Service Tasks: Several participants mentioned tasks they could envision a robot conducting in a service setting. For example, we compiled a list of the most mentioned retail tasks, agreeing as a group on three main categories: physical assistance, emotional support, and information source. Physical assistance consisted of utilizing the robot to perform tasks on behalf of a customer. In most cases, the customer did not have to be physically present. Examples include carrying heavy items to the car, retrieving items from high shelving, and collecting items while the customer spent time with friends and family. Emotional support consisted of the robot performing tasks in co-operation with the customer. These tasks could be classified as a partnership, where the robot alleviates some of the emotional burden from the customer. Examples included reducing stress by allowing the robot to retrieve shopping items, assisting the customer with planning meals, and allowing the customer to focus on shopping while the robot entertains their child. The final category, information source, consisted of robots providing factual information to the customer. In these examples, the robot would explain the technical features of products, advertise and promote products, and perform complex calculations such as determining the optimal products to fit within a budget.

Conclusion

Taken together, the results of the laddering and metaphor analysis highlight the conflicting meanings consumers derive from robot interaction and the various service tasks that these meanings can be applied to. The most frequent conflict is between the values of self-direction and security. With self-direction, participants expressed the desire to assert their independence and individualism. Participants wanted to be in control of their choices and be treated as individuals. With security, participants worried that through interacting with robots they would lose a sense of belonging and feel lonely. The tension between these values is related to the overarching conflict between openness to change and conservation. The implications of this paradox are that participants expected a robot to behave both machine-like in terms of speed and precision, while also maintaining human attributes, such as empathy (without other human attributes, such as mood swings, mistakes, and biases). Participants expected robots to conform to social norms towards them while not reciprocating politeness themselves. In interacting with consumers, robots are expected to be superhuman.

Another conflict arises between the overarching values of self-enhancement (including power and achievement) and self-transcendence (including benevolence and universalism). Participants desired to be treated with respect and importance during interactions with robots. However, they were also skeptical of the sincerity of and motives of robots. Participants revealed that interacting with robots represented progress, improvement, and modernity while also feeling concerned about a future with robots. They feared the potential loss of jobs and the natural environment. These tensions highlight the moral hazard of robot interaction. The underlying concern is whether the robot is working as an agent on behalf of the organization rather than the customer. In being programed to rigidly follow the organization's best interest, the interaction itself loses meaning and authenticity for the customer. This is linked to the concern for the quality of mercy, or the humanness of the tasks themselves. If the interaction is devoid of humanity, the fear of human replacement and concern for social welfare is emphasized.

References are available on request.

Commercial Programs: Improving Eating and Exercising Behaviour to Reduce Weight Through Increased Self-Efficacy

Joy Parkinson

Abstract The global obesity epidemic has been increasing for four decades, yet sustained prevention efforts have scarcely begun (Finucane et al. 2011). The rates of overweight and obesity amongst adults have doubled over the past two decades with Australia now being ranked as one of the fattest developed nations (ABS 2006). Obesity is a complex problem, with both poor nutrition and low rates of physical activity contributing to its prevalence. The Michelle Bridges 12 Week Body Transformation (12WBT) program seeks to increase participant's self-efficacy for healthy eating and regular exercising to reduce or maintain their weight by providing a holistic approach using a range of online support tools. Self-efficacy comprises two parts: outcome expectancy which is the belief that a particular behaviour will lead to a certain outcome and self-efficacy expectancy which is the personal conviction that one is able to successfully perform those behaviours to produce the desired outcome (Bandura 1977). In order to test the differences between the 12WBT program participants and a control group who currently had a weight management goal, a sample of 820 Australian participants, of which 516 were currently participating in the 12WBT, completed an online survey at three time points, week 1 (T1), week 12 (T2) and follow-up (T3), 12 weeks after program ceased. Previously validated items were adapted: self-efficacy (Bandura 1977), and eating and exercising behaviour (East et al. 2005). Data were analysed using SPSS software. The mean age for the entire sample ($n = 820$) was 36.32 (10.35), with the mean age for 12WBT participants ($n = 516$), 38.30 (10.71) and control participants ($n = 304$), 32.95 (8.75). The results reveal significant differences between the 12WBT participants and the control participants in terms of self-efficacy and actual behaviour for healthy eating and exercise behaviour across the three time points. Importantly, the results show a significant difference in weight loss across time, with 12WBT participants maintaining their weight loss 3 months after program

J. Parkinson (✉)
Menzies Health Institute Griffith University, Nathan, QLD, Australia
e-mail: j.parkinson@griffith.edu.au

© Academy of Marketing Science 2016
L. Petruzzellis, R.S. Winer (eds.), *Rediscovering the Essentiality of Marketing*,
Developments in Marketing Science: Proceedings of the Academy of Marketing
Science, DOI 10.1007/978-3-319-29877-1_86

423

completion. The results of this research demonstrate using a holistic weight management program, such as 12WBT has the potential to increase participants' self-efficacy, which in turn increases healthy eating and exercising behaviour. Higher levels of healthy eating and exercise behaviour were associated with higher levels of weight change outcomes during the program and beyond program participation. The findings from this study contribute new empirical evidence to the literature and are consistent with the argument a persons' self-efficacy is influenced by the support they receive.

References available upon request.

Part IX
Integrated Marketing Communication

Synergy and Integration of Multiple Media to Enhance Exposure and Impact of Out-of-Home Advertising

Thérèse Roux and De la Rey van der Waldt

Abstract For media planners to combine multiple media across platforms to maximize synergy is a critical challenge within integrated marketing communication. For this study, in-depth interviews were conducted with experienced media specialists in leading agencies to explore how they integrate different out-of-home advertising media platforms in IMC strategies. The feedback of these experts was then used to propose a model of strategies to enhance synergy within out-of-home advertising campaigns. This model is a first of its kind for planning out-of-home advertising media across platforms and bridges a gap in the existing literature on media synergy and out-of-home advertising media strategy.

T. Roux (✉)
Tshwane University of Technology, Pretoria, South Africa
e-mail: rouxat@gmail.com

D.l.R. van der Waldt
North-West University, Mahikeng, South Africa
e-mail: Delarey.VanDerWaldt@nwu.ac.za

© Academy of Marketing Science 2016   427
L. Petruzzellis, R.S. Winer (eds.), *Rediscovering the Essentiality of Marketing*,
Developments in Marketing Science: Proceedings of the Academy of Marketing
Science, DOI 10.1007/978-3-319-29877-1_87

Assessing the Impact of Internal Marketing Orientation on an Organization's Performance

Mujahid Mohiuddin Babu and Jikyeong Kang

Abstract In extant literature, although there are a few studies that have investigated impact of internal marketing orientation (IMO) on nonfinancial performance, most IMO studies have focused on how IMO relates to financial performance. Furthermore, even when customer-based performance (e.g., service quality, customer retention, customer satisfaction, customer loyalty) are included in the model, they are generally grouped together with other constructs such as employee competency and willingness to learn and organizational effectiveness and operationalized as an overall nonfinancial performance measure, rather than as a separate customer-based performance measure. Therefore, in order to fill this gap and to understand the impact of IMO on the firm's customer-based performance as well as financial performance, we developed and empirically tested an integrated model of IMO by comprising not only the financial performance variable but also a customer-based performance variable (customer acquisition and retention, customer loyalty, perceived service quality, customer satisfaction, improving products and services based on customers' comments, implementing new ideas, and developing new products and services).

The inclusion of a customer-based performance variable in an IMO model is significant because a direct effect of IMO on a firm's financial performance is rather difficult to demonstrate. This is because the impact of a firm's IMO adoption is generally reflected in the firm's customer-based performance through enhancing employees' behavioral outcomes. The key objective of implementing IMO is to ensure positive employee-related outcomes, rather than to directly affect a firm's financial performance indicators. The firm's IMO focus enhances the employees' customer-focused behavior which results in improved customer-based performance. Moreover, the financial consequence of customer-based performance has been recognized by both academia and practitioners in extant literature. Therefore, we argue that the impact of a firm's IMO focus on its performance should be investigated

M.M. Babu (✉)
Manchester Business School, Manchester, UK
e-mail: mujahid.mohiuddin@mbs.ac.uk

J. Kang
Manchester Business School, Manchester, UK

Asian Institute of Management, Makati, Philippines
e-mail: j.kang@mbs.ac.uk

© Academy of Marketing Science 2016
L. Petruzzellis, R.S. Winer (eds.), *Rediscovering the Essentiality of Marketing*,
Developments in Marketing Science: Proceedings of the Academy of Marketing
Science, DOI 10.1007/978-3-319-29877-1_88

429

through an indirect path comprising customer orientation, employee commitment, employee performance, and customer-based performance rather than a direct path between IMO and performance.

In this study, to empirically test the integrated model, data were collected from middle to top managers from selected service industries in the UK, and the data were analyzed using partial least squares structural equation modelling (PLS-SEM). Results provide statistically significant support for the argument that IMO impacts the firm's customer-based performance through both employee commitment and customer orientation. The study also supported a strong relationship between the firm's customer-based performance and financial performance. As predicted, the relationship between IMO and employee commitment is partially mediated by customer orientation, whereas both employee commitment and employee performance partially mediate the relationship between customer orientation and customer performance. Employee performance also partially mediates the relationship between employee commitment and customer-based performance.

The Effect of Congruence on the Attention and Sponsorship Processing: An Application of Neuromarketing by Electroencephalogram

M. Alonso Dos Santos and S. Baeza

Abstract Academics, professionals, and business strategist agree on the importance of consistency in the act of sponsorship to measure their effectiveness
(Woisetschläger and Michaelis 2012). The congruence measures the relationship fit
between sponsor–sponsee as perceived by the consumer. Previous studies have
linked the ability of neuroimaging to predict the acceptance of advertisements
(Vecchiato Kong and Wei 2012). The objective of the research is to measure the
effect of congruence on the effectiveness of sponsorship and processing information
from a neuroscientific point of view.

To measure the variable of attention, the electroencephalogram (EEG) system
evaluates the change in the signal of the human brain. In such cases, the effectiveness of various marketing strategies may be evaluated by monitoring brain activity.
Neurosky, Inc., develops the device used in this research and comparisons of these
instruments by medical professionals have found significant similarity in results
(Ekandem et al. 2012). The development of the control variables in the experiment
was developed through focus groups and surveys, where four sponsorship messages
were created.

Consumers were utilized in order to obtain results in the degree of attention,
time, and processing method of advertising. Statistical tests confirm a significant
difference between levels of attention in messages. The two models, consistent and
inconsistent messages indicated that only two had similar results accuracy and
attention whereas processing time was significantly higher in inconsistent messages. The degree of attention is showed that it was incremental and less successful
to individuals who are exposed to inconsistent message and could produce an emotional rejection of sponsorship. Thus in turn, would then suggest then that a higher
level of attention combined with higher negative rejection implies the need for more
effective communication campaigns (Tribou 2011). The perception of the viewer in
a meaningful incongruence scenario can lead to a rejection of the brand in which the
viewer would not assimilate the sponsorship (Lindstrom 2008) which would infer in
an opposite result from which it was intended.

M.A.D. Santos (✉) • S. Baeza
Universidad Católica de la Santísima Concepción, Concepción, Chile
e-mail: malonso@ucsc.cl; sbaeza@ucsc.cl

© Academy of Marketing Science 2016   431
L. Petruzzellis, R.S. Winer (eds.), *Rediscovering the Essentiality of Marketing*,
Developments in Marketing Science: Proceedings of the Academy of Marketing
Science, DOI 10.1007/978-3-319-29877-1_89

The importance of the research indicates that it is imperative for companies to know the perception of their messages enabling them to develop more efficient messages, not to mention, the amount of sponsors which are associated to events and sports teams due to the transmission of image and attitude towards brand attributes of the brand sponsored and the sponsoring brand (Gwinner 1997).

References available upon request.

The Mediating Role of Integrated Corporate Communication on the Relationship Between Organizational Culture and Market Performance

Lucia Porcu, Salvador del Barrio-García, Juan Miguel Alcántara-Pilar, and Esmeralda Crespo-Almendros

Introduction

Since the appearance of its first definition as Integrated Marketing Communication (IMC) in the early 1990s, the concept of integration has been increasingly attracting the attention of both academics and professionals (Hackley 2010; Laurie and Mortimer 2011; Kliatchko and Schultz 2014). However, the theoretical background still appears to be fairly disjointed and confused, mainly due to the lack of scholarly consensus over the definition and, especially in the last decade, the terminology to be used to name the concept (Christensen et al. 2008; Smith 2013). This conceptual confusion has hindered the development of valid and reliable measurement scales, preventing scholars from conducting robust empirical research. Based on an extensive literature review, this chapter develops a theoretical framework for "Integrated Corporate Communication" (ICC), opting for a terminology that enables us to explicitly embrace a more holistic approach which holds that the *locus* of integration is the whole organization. The authors of this chapter define ICC as the stakeholder-centered interactive process of cross-functional planning and alignment of organizational, analytical, and communication processes that allows for the possibility of continuous dialogue by conveying consistent and transparent messages via all media in order to foster long-term profitable relationships that create value. Tactical consistency, interactivity, stakeholder-centered strategic focus, and organizational alignment are identified in the present research as the ICC dimensions. Several driving factors and effects of integrated communication have been examined in previous studies, mostly taking a conceptual approach, while empirical research is still fairly scant. In fact, many scholars (Taylor 2010; Laurie and Mortimer 2011; Kliatchko and Schultz 2014) have called

L. Porcu (✉) • S. del Barrio-García • J.M. Alcántara-Pilar • E. Crespo-Almendros
University of Granada, Granada, Spain
e-mail: luciapor@ugr.es; dbarrio@ugr.es; jmap@ugr.es; ecrespo@ugr.es

© Academy of Marketing Science 2016   433
L. Petruzzellis, R.S. Winer (eds.), *Rediscovering the Essentiality of Marketing*,
Developments in Marketing Science: Proceedings of the Academy of Marketing
Science, DOI 10.1007/978-3-319-29877-1_90

for further and more robust empirical efforts to reveal the factors that foster or hinder integration and to demonstrate the positive effects that can be obtained via ICC in terms of market performance. Thus, the chapter aims to empirically analyze the influence of organizational culture on ICC to determine whether ICC fully mediates the relationship between organizational culture–market performance and to prove the beneficial effects derived from ICC in terms of economic–financial results, brand-related outcomes, and customer satisfaction.

Background

The literature review suggests that organizational variables play a key role in promoting/hindering ICC, with the role of different aspects of organizational culture (such as the leadership style) being identified as an important research gap. The extant literature indicates that organizations characterized by flexibility, reciprocal trust, mutual commitment, and horizontal and vertical cooperation are more likely to implement ICC than those presenting a high level of internal competitiveness and a results-driven approach. These descriptions respond (respectively) to the clan and market cultures defined as two diametrically opposed profiles by Cameron and Quinn (1999) in their Competing Values Framework. Based on this rationale, we posit that:

H1: The adoption of a clan culture facilitates the implementation of Integrated Corporate Communication (ICC) to a greater extent than does the adoption of a market culture.

The positive relationship between the implementation of ICC and the achievement of favorable effects on organizational performance has been supported by many authors; however, there is a dearth of empirical research and a clear need "*to measure the positive returns it can provide*" (Taylor 2010). More specifically, the beneficial influence exerted by ICC on financial–economic results (primarily ROI), brand-related outcomes (such as brand equity and awareness) and the organization–stakeholder relationship (especially on customer satisfaction) has received the greatest consensus among authors (Duncan and Moriarty 1998; Low 2000; Reid 2003, 2005; Einwiller and Boenigk 2012). On these premises, we formulated the following hypothesis:

H2: The implementation of Integrated Corporate Communication (ICC) relates positively to market performance.

The extant research has identified that organizational culture is a source of sustained competitive advantage and a key factor for enhancing business performance. However, its influence is not direct but rather exerted by shaping the behavior of the organization's members (Zheng et al. 2010). In this study, we consider that ICC mechanisms and processes enable the translation of cultural values into value for the organization. Thus, we hypothesized that:

H3: Integrated Corporate Communication (ICC) fully mediates the relationship between organizational culture and market performance.

Methodology

In this study, we adopted a single-industry strategy, which is designed to remove potentially confounding interindustry effects on organizational culture, ICC, and market performance. Thus, we deliberately focused on the Spanish tourism industry given its relevance at both national and international level. Spain is one of the world's top tourism destinations in terms of income and tourist arrivals, according to the World Tourism Organization (WTO 2014). Due to the heterogeneity of the tourism industry, we decided to focus our research on the most relevant business activity within this industry, namely accommodation services. On this basis, data were collected via a self-administered online survey conducted between April and July 2013 to Spanish businesses providing accommodation services with at least 40 employees. As a sample frame, a commercial listing of 969 businesses was drawn from the Bureau van Dijk SABI database containing relevant information on over 1.2 million Spanish businesses, the data being based on both national (e.g., CNAE) and international (e.g., Standard Industrial Classification/SIC) classification systems. The key informant method (Seidler 1974) was used, with senior managers being targeted as key informants. A multi-item questionnaire was developed and hosted on the Qualtrics Web platform (www.qualtrics.com). Organizational culture was measured using the Organizational Culture Assessment Instrument (OCAI), developed by Cameron and Quinn (1999) within the Competing Values Framework. This scale has been widely validated in previous research (Richard et al. 2009; Cameron and Quinn 1999) and used in almost 10,000 organizations worldwide (Shih and Huang 2010). In this study, we used the clan (6) and market culture (6) items, scored on a 7-point Likert type scale ranging from "1 = strongly agree" to "7 = strongly disagree." Market performance measures were drawn from the research on IMC and its impact on performance conducted by Reid (2005). This scale was slightly modified resulting in a 10-item scale covering five perceptual items related to economic–financial results in terms of sales and profitability (refi), three related to brand outcomes (rema) and two related to customer satisfaction (sat). All items were measured using a 7-point Likert type scale from "1 = much less compared to the closest competitor" to "7 = much more compared to the closest competitor." To assess ICC, a new scale was developed. First, an extensive literature review enabled us to identify the theoretical domain of the ICC construct (definition and dimensions) and to design an initial set of 59 items. Second, a two-round Delphi study was carried out using an international expert panel for content evaluation of both the ICC theoretical framework and the items proposed. These procedures enabled us to refine the content and reduce duplication, resulting in a Likert-type scale comprising 25 items scored from "1 = strongly disagree" to "7 = strongly agree" (four items for "tactical consistency"; seven for "interactivity"; seven for "stakeholder-centered strategic focus"; and seven for "organizational alignment"). As a preliminary step, the proposed ICC scale was purified via a pretest among a sample of 180 businesses randomly extracted from the aforementioned commercial listing, resulting in a total of 39 valid responses (21.6 % response rate) and enabling us to test basic psychometric properties. The *modus operandi* of the empirical study consisted of two steps. First, a telemarketing firm was contracted to contact the sample (930 managers, after removing the 39 contacts used for the pretest) by telephone to ask for their availability to participate in this study and collect their e-mail addresses (not included in the database due to legal issues relating to privacy protection). Second, a customized link to the online questionnaire was emailed to the 524 managers who agreed to participate. Following an initial e-mailing, a follow-up e-mail was sent to encourage responses. A total of 180 fully completed valid responses were received for an effective response rate of 18.6 % of the total population of 969 managers (34.4 % of the 524 managers who agreed to participate).

Results and Discussion

First, the proposed ICC scale has been validated. To determine the dimensionality, we conducted a Confirmatory Factor Analysis (CFA) using LISREL 8.8. Software and the RML estimation method. We adopted a competing models strategy by estimating two alternative models: M1 (via a first-order CFA) based on ICC as a unidimensional construct and 25 items being loaded onto one factor; and M2 (via a second-order CFA) based on ICC as a multidimensional construct and the 25 items being loaded onto four factors (following the conceptual framework). The results indicate that M2 (S-B $\chi^2 = 470.81$, df $= 271$, p-value $= .00$; Normed $\chi^2 = 1.73$; RMSEA $= .06$; CFI $= .99$; NNFI $= .99$) achieved an acceptable overall fit, while M1 (S-B $\chi^2 = 1301.7$ df $= 275$ p-value $= .00$; Normed $\chi^2 = 4.73$; RMSEA $= .14$; CFI $= .94$; TLI $= .93$) is not acceptable, confirming the dimensionality of ICC measures. The results of the second-order CFA indicate that all standardized coefficients are statistically significant (p-value $< .01$) and above .7, providing evidence of the convergent validity of the ICC scale. Based on these findings, AVE and CR were calculated, and the results show that both exceeded the recommended cut-offs of .5 and .7, respectively, providing evidence of an adequate reliability of the scale, while the criteria proposed by Fornell and Larcker (1981) were applied to test the discriminant validity. Likewise, we applied CFA to examine the psychometric properties of the remaining measures used in this study, the results confirming the reliability and construct validity of the scales. Once the measures had been validated, we conducted a Path Analysis using LISREL 8.8 software, adopting a competing models approach. As a preliminary step, following the recommendations of Hair et al. (2010) we generated the summary variables for each first-order construct (clan and market culture and the dimensions of the ICC and market performance constructs) using the latent factor scores of the original variables. Next, two alternative models were estimated: Model 1, in which ICC fully mediates the relationship between organizational culture and market performance; and Model 2, where ICC partially mediates this relationship and all paths relating to the constructs were to be estimated. Based on the findings, the two models were compared. The results demonstrate that the hypothesized model shows a better overall goodness-of-fit than the saturated model, since the S-B Chi-square and the Normed Chi-square in the latter

(38.48 and 1.673, respectively) are slightly greater than those of the former (38.39 and 1.535, respectively), indicating that Model 1 fits the data better than Model 2. The findings indicate that the adoption of a clan culture is strongly, positively, and significantly ($\beta_{clan \to icc} = .75$; $t = 12.28$; $p < .01$) related to the implementation of ICC, while the positive effect of market culture on ICC has been found to be not significant ($\beta_{merc \to icc} = .11$; $t = 1.66$; $p > .05$). The results of the S-B scaled Chi-square difference test showed that the difference between the more constrained model (where $\beta_{clan \to icc}$ is equal to $\beta_{merc \to icc}$) and the less constrained model is statistically significant (Δ S-B $\chi^2 = 23.26$, $p = 0.00$). As hypothesis H1 predicted, the results suggest that a clan culture facilitates the implementation of ICC to a greater extent than does the adoption of a market culture, thus providing statistical support to H1. Moreover, the results suggest that there is a strong, positive, and statistically significant ($\beta_{icc \to mp} = .64$; $t = 7.17$; $p < .01$) relationship between ICC and market performance, providing empirical evidence to back H2 and confirming that ICC is crucial for organizations to achieve better economic–financial results, brand-related outcomes and customer satisfaction. In addition, this finding enables us to determine the nomological validity of the proposed ICC scale. Finally, H3 predicted that ICC fully mediates the relationship between organizational culture and market performance. The condition for total mediation was supported by the fact that in Model 2 the direct paths between clan culture and market performance ($\beta_{clan \to mp} = .04$; $t = .32$; $p > .05$) and between market culture and market performance ($\beta_{merc \to mp} = .08$; $t = 1.06$; $p > .05$) were close to zero and not significant when ICC was modeled as the mediator. Thus, the findings supported H3.

Conclusions and Implications for Theory and Practice

This study endeavors to respond to the many calls for further empirical research on integrated communication (Schultz et al. 2014; Taylor 2010) as this research area "continues to stir debate, discussion and, in some cases, confusion" (Kliatchko and Schultz 2014). One major contribution of the work lies in the development and validation of a new ICC measurement tool, providing academics and practitioners with the most theoretically consistent, reliable, and valid scale to date for assessing integration from a corporate and organizational perspective. In addition, the findings reveal that the role of organizational culture is crucial for ICC, underlining that a clan culture, characterized by a strong focus on collaborative behaviors among the employees and departments of the organization and supportive leadership, facilitates the building of a more ICC-friendly environment to a greater extent than does a market culture, where internal competitiveness is promoted and leaders adopt a results-focused approach. These findings provide a valuable and unique contribution to the literature as they represent the very first empirical evidence of how organizational culture influences the level of ICC achieved by an organization, highlighting the inadequacy of examining solely the direct linkage between organizational culture and market performance. In fact, ICC was found to fully mediate the effect of organizational culture on market performance, suggesting that how well communication is integrated at a corporate and organizational level is associated with how well cultural values are translated into value to the organization. Moreover, this study empirically demonstrates that the implementation of ICC is likely to lead to superior financial–economic results, better brand-related outcomes and a higher level of customer satisfaction. These contributions are highly relevant for both academics and practitioners as they enable us to progress toward building a strong body of ICC knowledge. They also help achieve a better understanding of how ICC works, shedding light on the role of organizational factors in promoting integration and the beneficial effects deriving from the implementation of ICC in terms of market performance. As with any study, the findings should be interpreted in light of its limitations. A major limitation is the relatively limited generalizability of the results, due to the specific national and sectorial contexts analyzed in the empirical study. In this regard, we suggest future research should replicate the study in other sectors/countries to improve the external validity and broaden the generalizability of the results. Another limitation derives from the use of self-reported data to assess market performance. Future research could use objective measures of performance to demonstrate the relationship between ICC and the "actual" market performance achieved by the organization.

References available upon request.

Beyond Negative Liberties: The Role of the Brand as Value Facilitator

Silvia Biraghi, Rossella C. Gambetti, Guendalina Graffigna, and Don E. Schultz

Abstract Brands are being increasingly recognized as one of the most valuable assets of a company (Simon and Sullivan 1993; Madden et al. 2006; Merz et al. 2009). As such appreciating their value represents a vital priority for all market actors. Traditionally, brands have been conceptualized as a firm-provided property of goods. However, the recent advent of the Service-Dominant Logic perspective (Vargo and Lusch 2004) encouraged scholars to view brands in terms of collaborative, value co-creation activities of stakeholders and firms (Merz et al. 2009). This shift in the conceptualization of brands advocates for a new understanding of their value. So far value co-creation literature has been devoting much of its attention to explore and frame the primary role of customers as ultimate value co-creators, neglecting to adequately acknowledge the new role of the firm as value enabler. The latest supremacy of customers as empirical focus leaves then open the following question: what is the role of the firm in value co-creation (Grönroos 2008)? In the current society, the role of the firm seems to be regulated mainly by "negative liberties" (Berlin 1969) that represent nonaction imperatives or imposed impediments to do something: "do not control, do not take over, do not over-speak, do not show off, do not intrude, do not annoy," just to mention some. We argue that in order to better understand the role of the brand in value co-creation, positive actions need to be uncovered beyond negative liberties to recognize the potential of the firm as value facilitator (Veloutsou 2009). More concretely, we contend that the actions performed by the brand in order to enable value co-creation by customers need to be empirically explored and identified in order to advance our understanding of value co-creation process in an actionable way (Grönroos 2011).

This chapter interpretively investigates how brand decision-makers conceive and represent through the narratives of their branding practices the role of the brand in facilitating the encounter and the interaction with customers to encourage the process

S. Biraghi (✉) • R.C. Gambetti • G. Graffigna
Università Cattolica del Sacro Cuore, Milan, Italy
e-mail: silvia.biraghi@unicatt.it; rossella.gambetti@unicatt.it; guendalina.graffigna@unicatt.it

D.E. Schultz
Northwestern University, Evanston, IL, USA
e-mail: dschultz@northwestern.edu

© Academy of Marketing Science 2016
L. Petruzzellis, R.S. Winer (eds.), *Rediscovering the Essentiality of Marketing*,
Developments in Marketing Science: Proceedings of the Academy of Marketing
Science, DOI 10.1007/978-3-319-29877-1_91

of value co-creation. Our evidence shows that the brand can ultimately act as a silent inspiring promoter of value co-creation by developing empathetic reciprocity with customers as individuals and displaying sociocultural mindfulness and liveliness at the community level. Our findings have detected some seeds that, although requiring further depth investigation, seem to highlight the humanistic approach of the brand, portrayed in its capability to permanently and meaningfully dwell in the life and action sphere of the customer, as the pivotal dimension of its value facilitator role.

References available upon request.

Is IMC "Marketing Oriented"?

Philip J. Kitchen

Abstract The question may seem odd, perhaps facile, but it does need address. Business, everywhere, is challenged in and by the changing market spaces and marketplaces of the twenty-first century. Competitive forces have heightened and accelerated. Customers are demanding and discerning of businesses and brands. Consumers are sophisticated and critical of business practice. Pressure groups scrutinize and criticize corporations online. The tempo of technology has opened horizons for innovation and communication. Social media has gained ground and challenges traditional media. News is transmitted within seconds to different parts of the world. And, the shifting tectonic plates of communication necessitate integration of on/off-line communications. There are no invisible companies. What happens in one geographic market is instantly transmitted via global media to receptive consumer VDU's—computer, television, and cell phone screens, or is almost immediately accessible. The world of information accessibility and the demise of corporate invisibility is today's (not tomorrow's) world.

Today, as is well argued just about everywhere now, businesses need integrated communications, not just locally or nationally, but also from a global perspective. Given the speed, span, and reach of electronic communication, there are no purely local or national firms, only global ones. This situation creates and underpins the need for communications which not only needs to be based on a sound and deep understanding of specific marketplace/space needs, but also adopts an integrated approach.

The corporation or firm is branded (e.g., P&G, Unilever, Coca Cola, Microsoft, Mars, McDonald's). Thus, communication decisions are not just about traditional product branding directed by mid-level managers but corporate and organizational brands and communications as well which are under the aegis of senior corporate managers. The important point to note is that both areas of communication are conceptually and practically interactive, synergistic, and generally global.

In this context and despite IMC's inherent attractiveness, its adoption by companies of all types, by agencies that service their needs, in a world constituting a multiplying kaleidoscope of media options, and despite its ready acceptance by marketing and communication academics, in its initial formulations it was not led, spearheaded,

P.J. Kitchen (✉)
ESC Rennes School of Business, Rennes, France
e-mail: philip.kitchen@esc-rennes.com

© Academy of Marketing Science 2016
L. Petruzzellis, R.S. Winer (eds.), *Rediscovering the Essentiality of Marketing*,
Developments in Marketing Science: Proceedings of the Academy of Marketing
Science, DOI 10.1007/978-3-319-29877-1_92

441

or perhaps not even considered by the marketing discipline itself. Thus, the question arises: Is (or was) IMC marketing orientated? To answer or at least explore the question, the origins and development of both disciplines will be evaluated.

Marketing itself is checkered by change and adaptation. As environmental conditions changed, marketing underwent a series of orientations—or managerial ways of looking at and responding to changing market circumstances. Earlier orientations were—apparently—replaced by newer more "user friendly" versions. The same is true of IMC. In its first appearance on the academic scene, it was not initially marketing oriented at all. Instead, it was concerned with ensuring communication modalities (i.e., advertising, sales promotion, MPR) spoke with one voice via integrated messages.

Thus, via a challenging paper, the antecedents, history, development, and current status of Marketing and IMC will be evaluated. The benefits, interactions, and weaknesses of both will be illustrated. However, and evidently, both must walk hand-in-hand in today's uncertain and ever-changing markets.

Part X
Innovation and Creativity

Predictable Patterns of Prescribing Innovation

Philip Stern, Malcolm Wright, Margaret Faulkner, and Roman Konopka

Abstract Who are the innovative customers for new products? Despite considerable research in this area, a striking characteristic of innovators was identified over 35 years ago. In work since often overlooked, Taylor found innovators tended to be heavy buyers of the parent category. This controversial result has major implications for both theory and practice yet has not, to our knowledge, been replicated. We therefore examine the extent to which heavy buyers dominate the innovator segment, adopting a research design that overcomes some of the limitations of Taylor's original study, and we also extend Taylor's work by examining heavy buyers in general rather than in a 'category specific way'. Using a unique database, we examine the behaviour of British General Practitioners in prescribing radically new drugs and me-too later entrants over an 18-year period. We find regular replicable patterns of innovation among heavy category buyers.

Keywords Segmentation • Innovator • New product launch • New product adoption • Panel data

P. Stern (✉)
University of Exeter, Devon, UK

Ehrenberg Bass Institute, Adelaide, Australia
e-mail: p.stern@exeter.ac.uk

M. Wright
Ehrenberg Bass Institute, Adelaide, Australia

Massey University, Auckland, New Zealand
e-mail: m.j.wright@massey.ac.nz

M. Faulkner
Ehrenberg Bass Institute, Adelaide, Australia

University of South Australia, Adelaide, Australia
e-mail: Margaret.Faulkner@unisa.edu.au

R. Konopka
Massey University, Auckland, New Zealand
e-mail: R.konopka@massey.ac.nz

© Academy of Marketing Science 2016
L. Petruzzellis, R.S. Winer (eds.), *Rediscovering the Essentiality of Marketing*,
Developments in Marketing Science: Proceedings of the Academy of Marketing
Science, DOI 10.1007/978-3-319-29877-1_93

445

Introduction

There has been a great deal of research attempting to identify characteristics of consumers that correlate with innovative behaviour. Such work has long been criticised for simplistic conceptualisations and the lack of clear empirical evidence (Midgley and Dowling 1978) yet the practice continues. For example, an application of using self-reported scale measures to derive innovativeness in the fashion industry is found in Goldsmith and Flynn (1992). More recently, Im et al. (2003) carried out an extensive empirical study of the consumer electronics category and found that innate innovativeness, as measured using a self-completion inventory, was less effective at predicting innovative behaviour than simple measures of age and income. There are many other examples, and a useful review of the problems of defining innovativeness and measuring the construct can be found in Roehrich (2004).

In most empirical studies, relatively complex modelling approaches are adopted (e.g., Im et al. 2003) and in some cases the approach is extended to predicting new product launch performance. A noteworthy example here is found in Ding and Eliashberg (1992) who develop a model based on Markov processes and further refined using random utilities and dyadic decision-making. While these complex models are important in extending academic understanding of the issues, their application by managers to help inform decisions surrounding new product launches are not documented and so their practical applicability seem less significant than their academic contribution.

A major review of Research on Innovation by Hauser et al. (2006) derives five key areas of research: Consumer Response to Innovation, Organizations and Innovation, Strategic Market Entry, Prescriptions for Product Development and Outcomes from Innovation. They review each of these five areas and sub-categorise them according to the key research themes identified from the literature. Consumer innovativeness is one of these 16 sub-categories and Hauser and his co-authors conclude that 'researchers have not yet agreed on a single definition of innovativeness'.

They go on to review the research that tries to link innovativeness to other constructs such as demographics and note the conflicting results of prior work. They conclude 'It is important to understand what drives consumers' propensity to adopt new products'. They conclude by listing a set of research challenges including the development of parsimonious scales for consumer innovativeness and how this varies across product categories.

In considering these issues, we found one study that addressed some of the concerns of Hauser et al. and that also has implications for the applicability of the 'innovator segment' concept. Taylor (1977) found a clear and simple relationship between product class usage and innovative behaviour, but this has not impacted significantly on research on innovation in terms of those who reference the work.

Taylor measured fast moving product class usage for a year (in 11 categories), compared early adopters with later adopters, and found a general tendency for early adopters to be heavy users of the category. The structure of his research did not permit the exclusion of the new product launch as a cause of increased usage, and he did not report the average purchase frequencies of the early and late adopters. We therefore replicate and extend this work to investigate its generalisability and application to determining innovative buyers and potential segment membership.

Methodology

We aim to see whether heavy buyers are predictably those who will innovate, and we do this by examining their choice behaviour before the launch of a new product. In this initial research, we adopt the simplest possible approach by measuring the mean rate of total purchasing in the 12 months before the launch of a new product and compare this to the mean purchase rate of those who subsequently innovate. We define an innovator as someone who makes at least one purchase of a new brand during its first year on the market. We then repeat these analyses for subsequent new launches and also across categories. The specific area we examine (doctor's prescriptions) enables us to research the adoption of real innovations and then subsequent 'me-too' launches to see if the general patterns we seek persist. We therefore test the following proposition:

Heavy buyers/prescribers of each category in the year before a product launch are more likely to buy/prescribe the new product/drug in its first year on the market than are light buyers/prescribers.

Data

Our data comes from a panel of UK General Practitioners who report all new and changes of prescription they write for their patients. The data collection specifically excludes the filling of repeat prescriptions where the patient returns for more of the same medicine and so focuses on real prescription decisions. Either the patient is presenting symptoms that are being treated by the doctor for the first time, or the patient is receiving a different medication to improve results. In this research, we extract a sample of doctors who reported at least one new or switch prescription (for any drug at all) in each of the 2 years which cover the 12 months before and after the launch of a new drug. We do this for a total of 38 new drug launches and report the results.

Results

Our proposition is explored using the data in Table 1 that show the key findings. By way of example, the first row of Table 1 is explained in detail. The first column indicates the order of entry of the new drug in the category—thus 5c means that drug Lumi (Lumiracoxib—branded as Prexige) was the fifth entrant into category c (Cox-2 inhibitors). Innovators (GPs) who prescribed Prexige at least once in the first

Table 1

ID	Drug	W(i)	W	W(i)/W	ID	Drug	W(i)	W	W(i)/W
5c	Lumi	475	318	1.49	2a	Prav	463	374	1.24
6a	Rosu	367	260	1.41	3d	Paro	472	386	1.22
5e	Vard	429	315	1.36	3f	Ralo	483	395	1.22
4a	Ator	454	334	1.36	2f	Etid	456	374	1.22
2d	Sert	520	386	1.35	2b	Vals	480	395	1.22
3e	Apom	448	335	1.34	4b	Cand	477	394	1.21
4c	Vald	438	332	1.32	1d	F103	464	385	1.20
5b	Telm	449	346	1.30	4e	Tada	379	315	1.20
7d	Esci	407	318	1.28	1e	Sild	442	374	1.18
5a	Ceri	470	373	1.26	1a	Sim	424	359	1.18
6b	Epr0	429	341	1.26	1b	Losa	469	399	1.17
8b	Alis	368	293	1.26	6d	Cita	484	413	1.17
6f	Iban	435	346	1.26	5d	Nefa	474	404	1.17
5f	Stro	420	335	1.25	1f	Alen	463	411	1.13
7b	Olme	412	329	1.25	4d	Veni	451	408	1.11
3b	Irbe	483	388	1.25	1c	Rofe	381	346	1.10
8d	Dulo	415	333	1.24	2c	Celx	373	339	1.10
3a	Fluv	449	361	1.24	4f	Rise	365	333	1.10
3c	Etox	410	330	1.24	2e	Alpr	343	346	.99
Ave.		436	341	1.23					

year on the market wrote an average of 475 new or switch prescriptions for any drug in the previous 12 months versus the overall average rate of prescribing of 318 and so the last column in the table indicates that on average the innovative doctors of Prexige prescribed 49 % than the mean rate.

The table is organised in descending value of this innovator ratio ($W(i)/W$), and the results continue in the right-hand section of Table 1 and there are some interesting patterns which emerge. First, as proposed, innovators tend to be heavier prescribers with the innovator ratio averaging 1.23. Second, the range of the innovator ratio is not that large—from about 1 to about 1.5 across 38 new drug launches. Third, there is little variation in the innovator ratio between categories (the left-hand part of Table 2 shows a narrow range of the innovator ratio from 1.20 to 1.28 across six different drug classes). Fourth, the innovator ratio is lower for new to the world drugs as shown in the right-hand section of Table 2 (i.e., the entries with 1 in column 1 of Table 1), and this ratio tends to rise with each subsequent new launch into the category.

Discussion

In this analysis, we confirm Taylor's findings in fast moving consumer goods markets with several extensions. The application in a pharmaceutical setting is useful as it not only replicates prior work but extends the findings to a different country and a

Table 2

Category	$W(i)/W$	Entry order	$W(i)/W$
a (Statins)	1.28	New to world	1.16
b (ARBs)	1.24	Me-too 1	1.19
c (COX-2)	1.25	Me-too 2	1.25
d (SSRi)	1.22	Me-too 3+	1.26
e (ED)	1.22		
f (Osteo)	1.20		

radically different situation—prescribing ethical pharmaceuticals is clearly different from buying snack foods and yet a similar pattern regarding innovators is found. We also extend previous work by relaxing the constraint of heavy category buying to heavy buying per se and by looking at the propensity of previous heavy users (before radically new products are introduced) to innovate. These results provide a strikingly clear basis for segmentation for those wishing to speed up adoption of a new product—that is, target the heavy buyers.

Why should Taylor's result have been so neglected? We offer a speculation. Researchers in marketing are equipped with sensitive statistical techniques and strong interest in the effect of social and personality variables on behaviour. Consequently, smaller effects in these areas are detected and reported as a matter of interest, more so than possibly larger effects that do not involve social or psychological variables. Availability bias leads subsequent researchers to think that, as social and psychological effects are the most discussed, they are also the most important. Yet this does not follow.

This speculation is illustrated by examination one of the most famous early studies in the diffusion innovation literature, concerning network influences on physicians' first prescription of a new drug. Coleman et al. (1957) is a key publication in this area and has been used by Rogers (1962) and other authors to promote diffusion as the study of ideas moving through social networks. Coleman et al. (1957) found new drugs were first prescribed 2.8 months earlier by profession-oriented compared to patient-oriented physicians. Similarly, they measured three aspects of social integration and found that those who scored highly made their first prescription 3.1–4.3 months before those with low scores on the social integration questions. These findings have been highly influential, and imply that social integration is one of the most important variables associated with the innovator segment. Yet, buried in footnote five on the sixth page of their article, and long forgotten in the literature, one more variable is mentioned. This variable discriminated more than any other, with a difference of 5.0 months in the timing of the first prescription of the new drug. What is this briefly mentioned and long forgotten variable? It is total category prescription volume. Those most likely to be early prescribers of a new drug are simply those who are already heavy prescribers of other drugs in the same category.

Further Work

We intend to develop this work in several ways and will report at the conference: First, we will extend the analysis to consider the proportion of sales in the first year arising from previously heavy prescribers. Second, we will examine the extent to which innovation is category specific or a more general process. If it is a more general process, we will use demographics to which we have access to profile innovators. Finally, we will use a completely different market (packaged goods in New Zealand) as an additional control.

References

Coleman, J., Katz, E., & Menzel, H. (1957). The diffusion of an innovation among physicians. *Sociometry, 20*(4), 253–270.

Ding, M., & Eliashberg, J. (1992). Assessing user-agent adoption of sequentially launched new products. *Working Paper*. Philadelphia: Marketing Department, The Wharton School.

Goldsmith, R., & Flynn, L. R. (1992). Identifying innovators in consumer product markets. *European Journal of Marketing, 26*(12), 42–55.

Hauser, J., Tellis, G. J., & Griffin, A. (2006). Research on innovation: A review and agenda for marketing science. *Marketing Science, 25*, 687–717.

Im, S., Bayus, B. L., & Mason, C. H. (2003). An empirical study of innate consumer innovativeness, personal characteristics, and new-product adoption behaviour. *Journal of the Academy of Marketing Science, 31*, 61–73.

Midgley, D. F., & Dowling, G. R. (1978). Innovativeness: The concept and its measurement. *Journal of Consumer Research, 4*(4), 229–242.

Roehrich, G. (2004). Consumer innovativeness: Concepts and measurements. *Journal of Business Research, 57*, 671–677.

Rogers, E. M. (1962). *Diffusion of innovations* (1st ed.). New York: The Free Press.

Taylor, J. W. (1977). A striking characteristic of innovators. *Journal of Marketing Research XIV, 14*, 104–107.

Customer Interaction as a Source for Innovation? Evidence from Hybrid Offerings

Mario Schaarschmidt and Gianfranco Walsh

Abstract The link between customer interaction and innovation has been investigated intensely in relation to different customer–firm interactions (Bartl et al. 2012; Lau et al. 2010), various degrees of innovation (e.g., incremental and radical; Coviello and Joseph 2012), distinct organizational practices and capabilities (Foss et al. 2011), and new services or products (Carbonell et al. 2009; Chen et al. 2011). However, little research addresses customer interactions and their implications for hybrid offerings. Hybrid offerings combine physical products, or goods, and services into innovative solutions, such that they differ from both pure services (e.g., financial, health) and pure manufacturing offerings (e.g., machinery; Gebauer et al. 2011). Hybrid offerings allow goods-oriented firms to capture additional value from the knowledge they possess; understanding the process that leads to innovation in either goods or service components of a hybrid offering thus can help managers recognize when they should stimulate customer interactions. Because extant research has focused on goods or service innovation, not the impact of customer interactions for goods and related service innovations simultaneously, an isolated view has emerged. Yet a firm's integrated ability to offer hybrid offerings often represents a competitive advantage (Ulaga and Reinartz 2011). Therefore, we seek to clarify (1) whether paths that exist in isolation between customer interaction and goods innovation and customer interaction and services innovation remain stable for hybrid offerings and (2) if customer interaction affects one type of innovation, to the detriment of the other. We use primary data from 146 firms and find that customer interaction both benefits goods and service innovation performance in hybrid offerings.

References available upon request.

M. Schaarschmidt (✉)
University of Koblenz-Landau, Mainz, Germany
e-mail: mario.schaarschmidt@uni-koblenz.de

G. Walsh
Friedrich-Schiller-University of Jena, Jena, Germany
e-mail: walsh@uni-jena.de

© Academy of Marketing Science 2016
L. Petruzzellis, R.S. Winer (eds.), *Rediscovering the Essentiality of Marketing*,
Developments in Marketing Science: Proceedings of the Academy of Marketing
Science, DOI 10.1007/978-3-319-29877-1_94

451

Using fMRI Analysis to Unpack a Portion of Prospect Theory for Advertising/Marketing Understanding

Vijay Viswanathan, Don Schultz, Martin Block, Anne J. Blood, Hans C. Breiter, Bobby Calder, Laura Chamberlain, Nick Lee, Sherri Livengood, Frank J. Mulhern, Kalyan Raman, Daniel B. Stern, and Fengqing (Zoe) Zhang

Abstract One of the key elements being used today to support/reject/enhance marketing/advertising theory is Kahneman and Tversky's prospect theory (1979). Interest has been growing on how that concept might support/explain how advertising "works" based on Kahneman's later concepts as found in his text "Thinking Fast and Slow" (2011). All have spawned and supported the field of behavioral economics (Kahneman, American Economic Review, 93: 1449–1475, 2003). Literally thousands of discussions, speculations, hypotheses, and applications of these concepts can now be found in the advertising literature. Yet, in spite of its broad industry and practitioner acceptance, the basic fundamentals of prospect theory, as Kahneman and Tversky outlined them in their original paper, "Prospect Theory: An Analysis of Decision Under Risk" (1979), and their follow-on book, "Choices, Values and Frames" (2000) still rely mostly on support from small scale, academic, laboratory experiments based on questionnaires and researcher interpretations. We employ the new tools of fMRI in an age-related experiment. Loss Aversion has a long history in marketing and communication theory and the ability to connect or refute that concept to aging in marketing theory would seem a major aid to marketers going forward.

Keywords Loss aversion • Aging • Nucleus accumbens • Reward • fMRI • Neurocompensation

V. Viswanathan (✉) • D. Schultz • M. Block • A.J. Blood • H.C. Breiter • B. Calder • L. Chamberlain • N. Lee • S. Livengood • F.J. Mulhern • K. Raman • D.B. Stern • F.(. Zhang
Northwestern University, Evanston, IL, USA
e-mail: Vijay-Viswanathan@northwestern.edu; dschultz@northwestern.edu; Mp-block@northwestern.edu

© Academy of Marketing Science 2016
L. Petruzzellis, R.S. Winer (eds.), *Rediscovering the Essentiality of Marketing*, Developments in Marketing Science: Proceedings of the Academy of Marketing Science, DOI 10.1007/978-3-319-29877-1_95

453

Introduction

Age is among the most commonly used variables in marketing and consumer research. While age is a deceptively simple variable, the underlying construct of biological age and how it relates to behavior is not always as clear. One age effect, supported by a number of social psychology studies, is that older adults put more weight on avoiding potential negative outcomes, as evidenced by their aversion to change (Botwinick 1978) and nostalgia from their earlier life experiences (Schindler and Holbrook 2003). Aging research (e.g., Heckhausen 1997) suggests that older individuals generally try to avoid losses to a greater extent than do younger individuals. A fundamental way to quantify this perspective is with the concept of "loss aversion" (LA), in which negative stimuli have a disproportionate psychological impact relative to positive ones (Kahneman and Tversky 1979). That can be defined mathematically by the ratio of avoidance to approach measures (Tversky and Kahneman 1991; Abdellaoui et al. 2007).

LA has become an important variable in consumer research (Ariely et al. 2005; Paraschiv and L'Haridon 2008) and is consistent with the observation that older individuals are more focused on goals pertaining to maintenance and regulation of loss (Ebner et al. 2006). Cole et al. (2008) suggest, based on "regulatory focus theory" (Avnet and Higgins 2006), that is, older individuals would be more prevention focused, i.e., avoid losses, than promotion focused, i.e., pursuit of gains. While speculations about the age effects of LA persist, there remains a disparity between behavioral findings and neurological differences between age groups. For example, no behavioral differences were found in LA measures when comparing young adults to old adults (Lei et al. 2013) and adolescents and young adults (Barkley-Levenson et al. 2013). However, differences between adolescents and adults neural processing of LA were found in the larger decision-making networks.

Similarly, neuroscience studies have examined the biological basis for age-related changes in cognitive function (Hedden and Gabrieli 2004), which might affect biases in decision-making such as LA. For instance, Raz (2000) found a steady decline in the prefrontal cortex (PFC) structures starting from the age of 20 along with a decline in the striatal volume over the lifespan of an individual. In many studies, the biology of age-related changes in the brain goes in the same direction as behavior (Good et al. 2002). For example, in the domain of episodic memory, older adults have demonstrated decreased activation of various sites in the left and right prefrontal cortices correlating with decreased performance on the task relative to their younger counterparts (Reuter-Lorenz 2002; Grady and Craik 2000; Grady et al. 1995, 1999; Cabeza et al. 1997; Madden et al. 1999; Stebbins et al. 2002). Although not as common, an alternate outcome is also possible, wherein alterations in brain activity are not associated with an alteration of behavior, or increasing amounts of activation are needed to produce the same behavior (e.g., neurocompensation; Daselaar et al. 2015; Cabeza et al. 2002; Park and Reuter-Lorenz 2009). The validation of any of these hypotheses and their relationship to marketing/advertising would seem quite valuable to the marketing and communication planner, i.e., should more frequency of message distribution be used rather than less.

These neuroimaging and behavioral studies thus suggest two potential hypotheses regarding LA and its underlying neural substrate: (1) LA behavior may parallel changes in behavior, specifically, LA behavior may increase with age along with increased activation in tissue required to process it, or (2) LA behavior may increase more slowly than the compensatory activity in tissue processing it (i.e., there may be small differences in LA behavior with age, and strong brain activity differences during its processing). This latter possibility also finds additional support from an early functional MRI (fMRI) study that reported decreases in either performance or IQ were associated with increased brain activation during cognitive function (Seidman et al. 1998), and the observation of potentially compensatory activity in older individuals (Meunier et al. 2014).

In the current study, we test these hypotheses by using a validated measure of LA behavior (Kim et al. 2010) and measuring the neural response within the ventral striatum/nucleus accumbens (VS/NAc). The VS/NAc has been previously shown to reflect LA processing independent of other types of rewards processing, such as reward magnitude, anticipation or receipt (Canessa et al. 2013; Tom et al. 2007). The current study aimed to measure the effects of age on LA and determine if changes in VS/NAc could underlie the reported association of age with making less risky decisions (Johnson and Busemeyer 2010). In other words, marketing and communication activities have less and less influence as the receiver ages.

To examine the underlying physiological effects of age on LA, we used whole brain fMRI to monitor activity within the VS/NAc, using a passive viewing paradigm with affective faces known to evoke positive and negative valuations (Ekman and Friesen 1976), given the VS/NAc is a central region for reward/aversion processing (Hayes and Northoff 2012; Breiter et al. 1997; Breiter and Rosen 1999; Blood et al. 1999), and has been shown to activate to both positive and negative stimuli (Hayes and Northoff 2012; Kober et al. 2008; Aharon et al. 2001; Breiter et al. 2001; Becerra et al. 2001) and to track LA (Tom et al. 2007). For a behavioral LA index, using the same affective faces (Ekman and Friesen 1976) we used a keypress task that allowed an individual multiple potential decisions: (a) to do nothing about the default viewing time of a picture, (b) to view the picture for longer (approach) or (c) to view the picture for shorter (avoidance) time. The keypress data was analyzed to produce a value function (Breiter and Kim 2008; Kim et al. 2010) for each subject that is analogous to a prospect theory value function or utility curve (Kahneman and Tversky 1979). While not directly tied to specific marketing variables, it seems likely that if the function is similar, the relationship between the experimental variable and marketing and communication impact might also be similar.

Unlike any other reward/aversion construct our test actually uses an entropy variable representing information (Shannon and Weaver 1949). The slopes of the negative and positive portions of this curve could be readily sampled to yield a measure of LA. We specifically evaluated if the relative activation of the VS/NAc to negative (avoidance) stimuli vs. positive (approach) stimuli (i.e., the neural differential sensitivity (NDS) of avoidance vs. approach) would increase with age, and whether or not it would parallel any relationship of LA to age.

Methods

Subjects

Seventeen healthy control subjects were studied as part of a larger ongoing phenotype genotype project in addiction and mood disorder (PGP; http://pgp.mgh.harvard.edu; Kim et al. 2010; Gasic et al. 2009; Roy et al. 2008; Makris et al. 2008; Strauss et al. 2005; Makris et al. 2004). Subjects were part of past and ongoing studies and were found by psychiatrist-based SCID for DSM-IV diagnoses, medical review of systems, and physical evaluation to be free of any psychiatric, neurological, or medical issues. Subjects were selected from the PGP project based on the order of acquisition for valid data for the imaging and behavioral paradigm, while also meeting a gender-matched age distribution requirement for this study. Subjects were 17 adults (10 males, 7 females; 5 African Americans and 12 Caucasians) between the ages of 20 and 55 with a mean (±SE) age of 35.8±2.7 years, with no significant difference between men and women ($F(1, 15)$ 1.81, p .20). They had a mean educational history of 15.4±1.9 years, with no significant difference between men and women ($F(1, 15)$ 2.78, p .12). Fifteen of subjects were right handed.

Experimental Paradigm and Offline Behavioral Testing

In Scanner: Two fMRI scans were acquired (8 min 40 s each), each consisting of 20-s blocks of the following seven experimental conditions: angry, fearful, happy, sad, neutral expressions (Ekman and Friesen 1976), along with phase-scrambled stimuli and fixation (Fig. 1). During each scan, the seven conditions (blocks) were presented in a counterbalanced order such that no condition followed or preceded another more than once. This produced a sequence of 25 blocks for the first run, and 24 plus one blocks for the second run, with the extra block in the second run being equivalent to the last block in the first run, placed at the beginning to maintain counterbalancing across all conditions. Each facial expression block included standardized images of faces of eight individuals (four males) in a pseudorandom order (Breiter et al. 1996; Strauss et al. 2005). Each face was displayed for 200 ms with a 300 ms interstimulus interval during which a fixation cross was displayed, with five repetitions of each face stimulus per block (40 faces total per block). Face stimuli (Ekman and Friesen 1976) were previously normalized at the MIT Media Lab (Breiter et al. 1996). The face stimuli were projected via a Sharp XG-2000 V color LCD projector through a collimating lens onto a hemicircular tangent screen and viewed by the subject via a mirror affixed to the head coil. Subjects were instructed to simply look at the faces, keeping their eyes focused on the center of the picture at the location of the cross-hair. After completion of scanning, subjects performed a memory task in which they were asked to identify faces and facial expressions they had seen during the scanning session.

Paradigm Used During fMRI Data Acquisition

Ekman/Friesen Facial Expression stimuli:

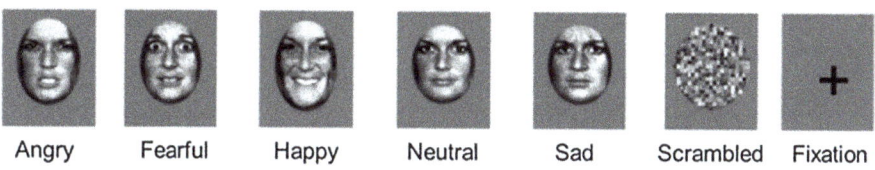

| Angry | Fearful | Happy | Neutral | Sad | Scrambled | Fixation |

Example of a fMRI scan trial stimuli presentation

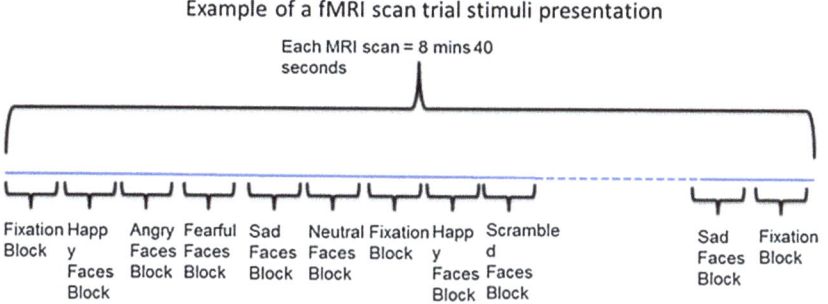

- 8 Facial stimuli, same emotional valence/block (4 males & 4 females) with five repetitions of each face stimulus/block (40 faces total/block).
- Each block of stimuli is presented for 20 seconds in pseudorandom order.

Fig. 1 Schema for experimental paradigm used with fMRI. At *top*, the categories of facial expressions used are shown along with baselines (scrambled faces and fixation). A schema of how these stimuli were presented as blocks is shown at *bottom*, along with details relating to number of stimuli used per block. See Methods for further detail

Offline Behavioral Testing: This experiment utilized a keypress task to determine each subject's relative preference toward the ensemble of faces (Aharon et al. 2001; Strauss et al. 2005; Elman et al. 2005; Levy et al. 2008; Perlis 2008; Makris et al. 2008; Gasic et al. 2009; Yamamoto et al. 2009; Kim et al. 2010), which had been used for passive viewing during scanning. The separation of passive viewing and keypress response allowed the fMRI component to be free of motoric elements, which would otherwise confound interpretation of the fMRI results. The keypress procedure was implemented with MatLab software on a PC (i.e., a personal computer). This task captured the reward valuation attributed to each observed face, and quantified positive and negative preferences involving (i) decision-making regarding the valence of behavior, and (ii) judgments that determine the magnitude of approach and avoidance (Breiter et al. 2006; Perlis 2008) (Fig. 2). The objective was to determine how much effort each subject was willing to trade for viewing each facial expression compared to a default viewing time. We argue that this methodology closely replicates Kahneman's assumptions about how the brain processes external stimuli as discussed in his System 1 process (Kahneman 2011).

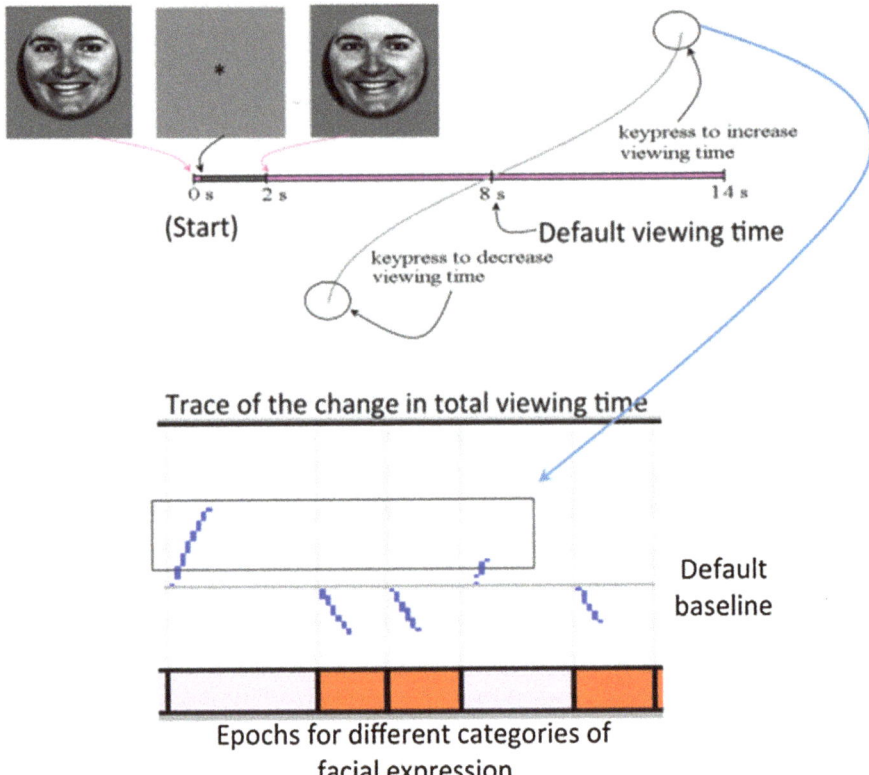

Fig. 2 Keypress paradigm. The behavioral task done outside the MRI to minimize motor confounds to activation is schematized above, with an example raster plot below

Subjects were told that they would be exposed to a series of pictures that would
change every 8 s (the default valuation of 6 s + 2 s decision block; Fig. 2) if they
pressed no keys. If they wanted a picture to disappear faster, they could alternate
pressing one set of keys (#3 and #4 on the button box), whereas if they wanted a
picture to stay longer on the screen, they could alternate pressing another set of keys
(#1 and #2 on the button box). Subjects had a choice to do nothing (default condition), increase viewing time, decrease viewing time, or a combination of the two
responses (Fig. 2). A "slider" was displayed to the left of each picture to indicate
total viewing time. Subjects were informed that the task would last approximately
20 min, and that this length was independent of their behavior, as was their overall
payment. The dependent measure of interest was the amount of work, in number of
keypresses, which subjects traded for face viewtime.

Magnetic Resonance Imaging

All fMRI imaging was performed on a Siemens Trio 3 T MRI system using an eight-channel phased-array receive-only RF coil. Subjects were positioned in the MRI scanner and their heads stabilized using foam pads and adjustable paddles fixed to the RF coil assembly. Blood oxygenation level-dependent (BOLD) functional images were acquired using gradient-echo EPI (TR/TE/a 1⁄4 2.5 s/30 ms/90°, 3.125 mm×3.125 mm×3 mm resolution), with slices situated parallel to the AC–PC line, and parallel to the inside curve of the FOC to minimize signal distortion in this region (Deichmann et al. 2003). Structural images were acquired using a high-resolution T1-weighted MPRAGE sequence (192 sagittal slices over the full head volume, matrix = 224×256, FOV = 224×256 mm^2, thickness = 1 mm, no gap) before functional scanning. Details of the imaging parameters and protocol have been reported previously (Perlis 2008; Gasic et al. 2009).

Data Analysis

Behavioral Data: Keypress data were checked by a relative preference theory analysis of each subject, using previously validated procedures (Breiter and Kim 2008; Kim et al. 2010) (Fig. 3). These procedures produce a valuation graph with variables K and H that encode mean keypress number and Shannon entropy (i.e., information) (Shannon and Weaver 1949). This valuation graph has been interpreted to relate "wanting" of stimuli (Aharon et al. 2001) to the uncertainty associated with making a choice (Kim et al. 2010). This method closely resembles what marketers are attempting to accomplish using other research methods. That is, what is the impact of exposure to product persuasive communication messages using various forms of media.

Using a local definition of LA (Abdellaoui et al. 2007), we computed the slope of the negative value/utility function ($s-$) and the slope of the positive value/utility function ($s+$) to produce $s-/s+$ (Fig. 4). Specifically, $s-$ and $s+$ were computed by the integral of the curve-fit slope over the 10 % of the curve closest to the inflection point or origin (Fig. 4). An absolute value of $s-/s+$ was then computed for each subject. With the full dataset of these subjects, we then assessed the association of LA (i.e., $|s-/s+|$) with age using linear regression. Given it was one test, no correction for multiple comparisons were imposed.

Imaging Data: fMRI data were analyzed using the FSL platform (FMRIB's Software Library, v4.1.9; http://www.fmrib.ox.ac.uk.fsl) and followed signal processing and statistical analysis procedures detailed elsewhere (Perlis 2008; Gasic et al. 2009). Stimuli were grouped based upon emotional valence into negative stimuli (Angry, Fearful, and Sad faces) and positive stimuli (Happy faces). These two stimuli classes were contrasted in order to determine brain areas that responded more highly to negative than to positive stimuli [i.e., the β slope for the negative

Similarities between Prospect Theory & Relative Preference Theory (RPT)

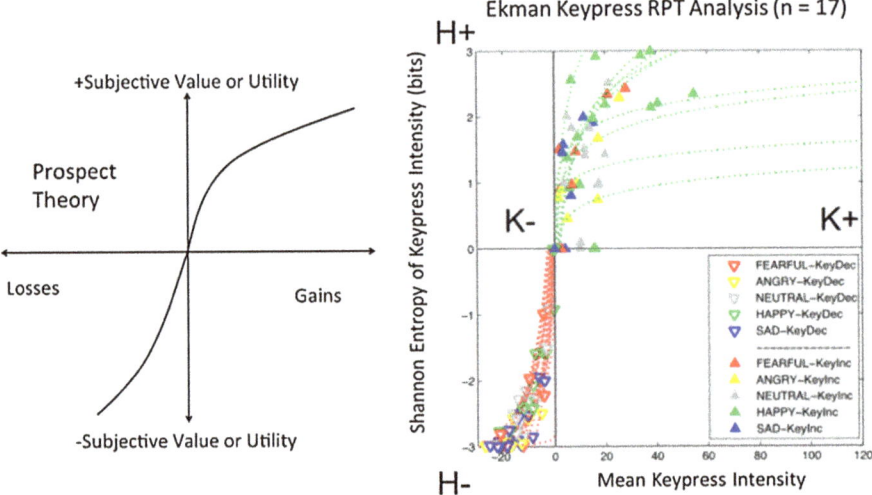

Fig. 3 Relative preference graphs. The output of the keypress paradigm is shown for 17 subjects on the *right*. The variable K stands for the mean number of keypresses made for category of picture viewed (mean viewtime per category can also substituted to produce comparable results). K can be interpreted as the effort expended to approach (+ keypresses) or avoid (– keypresses) stimuli, and approximates wanting. The variable H stands for the Shannon entropy (information or uncertainty related to making a choice) for each category of picture. It can be interpreted as representing memory about the uncertainty related to making choices over this stimulus set. On the *left* is shown a schema for prospect theory (Kahneman and Tversky 1979) to emphasize the similarity, despite different variables, between the two theoretical frameworks of prospect theory and relative preference theory (Breiter and Kim 2008; Kim et al. 2010). Both show an increased slope for negative or avoidance responses relative to positive or approach responses

activation (or PE for the −COPE) was greater than the β slope of the positive activation (or PE for the +COPE)]. Statistical maps of NDS to losses relative to gains (−>+) were constructed as a group map, and voxels selected above a whole brain correction for z-stat=2.3 that overlapped the VS/NAc segmentation volumes from the ICBM152 T1 template (Perlis 2008; Gasic et al. 2009) (Fig. 5). VS/NAc segmentation followed previously published parameters for its boundaries (Breiter et al. 1997), using processes that have been well validated (see Makris et al. 2004; Breiter et al. 1994). For a control analysis, we assessed the correlation of NDS [−(Angry, Fearful, and Sad>Happy)] in the VS/NAc to LA, as described by Tom et al. (2007), using a subset of the 17 subjects who were not statistical outliers (Fig. 6). With the full dataset of these subjects, we then assessed the regression of LA with NDS (Fig. 6) and NDS with age (Fig. 7). Given two independent assessments, significant effects had to meet $p<0.05$.

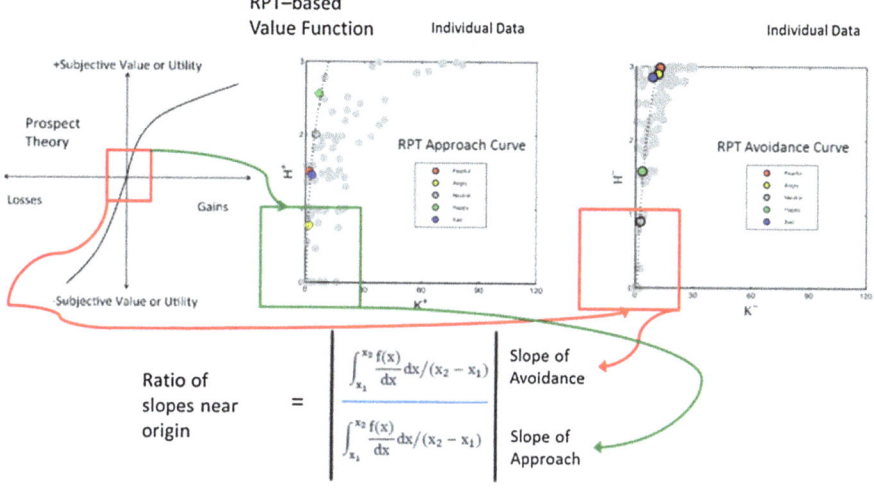

Local (as opposed to Global) Definition of Loss Aversion

Local Loss Aversion with RPT   ~ 2.06 (Range of 0.5 – 4.4)

Fig. 4 Local loss aversion computation. This study used a local rather than a global assessment of loss aversion, meaning that the ratio was computed using the slopes around the inflection point for each graph, rather than the entire graph (Abdellaoui et al. 2007). In this figure, the same cartoon for prospect theory used in Fig. 3 is shown on the *left*, with a box around the inflection point between the positive and negative graphs that meet at the origin. The approach *KH* graphs (variables defined in Fig. 3 legend) and avoidance *KH* graphs for the 17 subjects are shown as unfitted points in *gray* to the right. One example subject is shown with points as defined in each graph with a fitted curve. The lowest 10 % of these curves was then used for assessing the slopes as shown in the mathematics at *bottom*. Of interest, the LA value for these subjects approximates that reported by Tversky and Kahneman (1992)

Results

Behavioral Data

All 17 subjects produced keypress data with value function graphs consistent with relative preference theory (Breiter and Kim 2008; Kim et al. 2010) (Figs. 3 and 4). All graphs produced LA computations (Fig. 3), although five subjects had $s-/s+$ ratios that were >2 standard deviations above or below the cohort mean, and thus were considered outliers. The LA estimate for remaining subjects was $2.06 + .36$ (mean + SE) (Fig. 4), and the confidence interval of this group overlapped the LA mean of 2.25, published by Tversky and Kahneman (1992). The regression of LA to age showed a nonsignificant relationship ($p > .1$).

fMRI signal in NAc that activates more for negative stimuli than positive stimuli

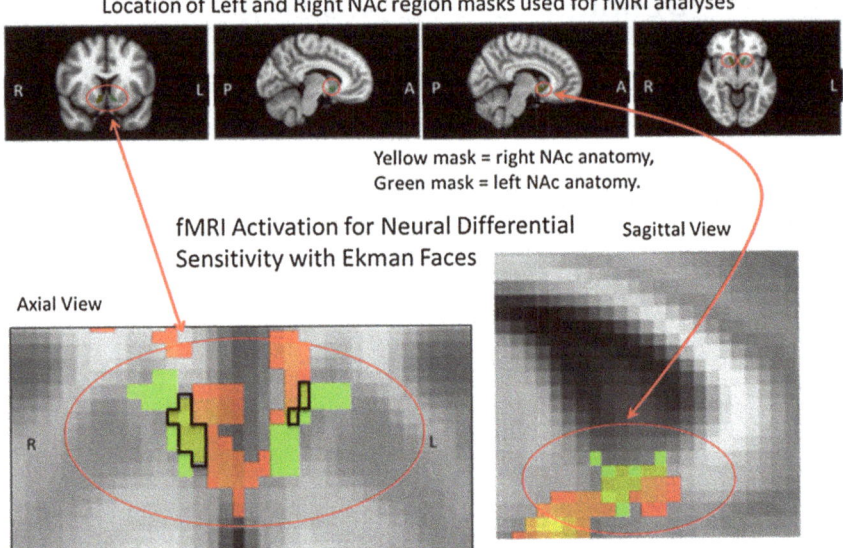

Location of Left and Right NAc region masks used for fMRI analyses

Yellow mask = right NAc anatomy,
Green mask = left NAc anatomy.

fMRI Activation for Neural Differential   Sagittal View
Sensitivity with Ekman Faces

Axial View

Green voxels are segmentation of NAc; Orange-red voxels are statistical map;
Overlap is in yellow with black outline

Fig. 5 fMRI masks and activation for neural differential sensitivity (NDS). The region of interest mask used for the VS/NAc is shown above in color with *circles*, with the statistics for the subtraction of negative stimuli versus positive stimuli in pseudocolor shown below. The segmented VS/NAc is shown in the images below, superimposed on the *gray-tone* ICBM152 T1 template. The light segmentations are overlaid with the statistical map for NDS. Overlap of segmented anatomy and statistical activation map is outlined inside the closed line

Neuroimaging Data

fMRI data showed significant motion artifacts in two subjects. In the remaining subjects, significant fMRI activation was observed in the ventral striatum/nucleus accumbens (VS/NAc) bilaterally in the majority of subjects (see segmentation-based masks of the VS/NAc and group statistical map in Fig. 5). In individuals, voxels of activation with $p < .05$, $z = 1.96$ that overlapped segmentation of the VS/NAc were used to sample BOLD signal representing NDS to losses relative to gains. Across subjects, we found that activation to negative stimuli in left and right NAc was significantly greater than activation to positive stimuli (Fig. 5). This signal was used for a control analysis of the correlation of NDS relative to behavioral LA ($r(2, 11)$ 0.64, $p < .04$). Without outliers (>2 SD from mean NDS), we found the same relationship (Fig. 6) reported by others (Tom et al. 2007). When we assessed the relationship of NDS in the VS/NAc to age, we observed a significant positive correlation ($F(2, 16)$ 9.01, $p < .009$) (Fig. 7).

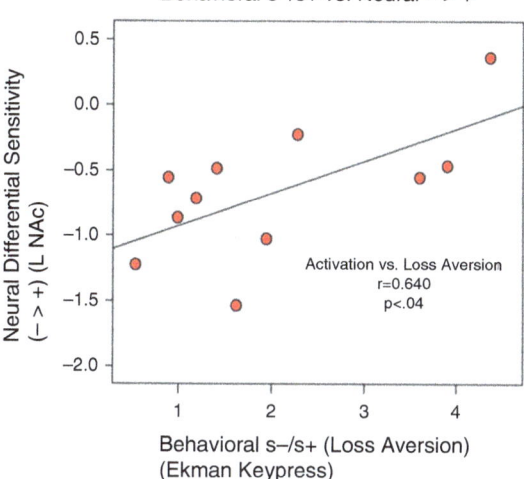

Fig. 6 Association between LA and NDS from BOLD signal collected by fMRI. NDS represents the difference between BOLD signal in the *left* VS/NAc for negative stimuli (Angry, Fearful, and Sad faces) minus positive stimuli (Happy faces). LA is represented as the absolute value of $s-/s+$ from the relative preference graphs of each subject as shown in Fig. 3. The line of best fit is shown from this association

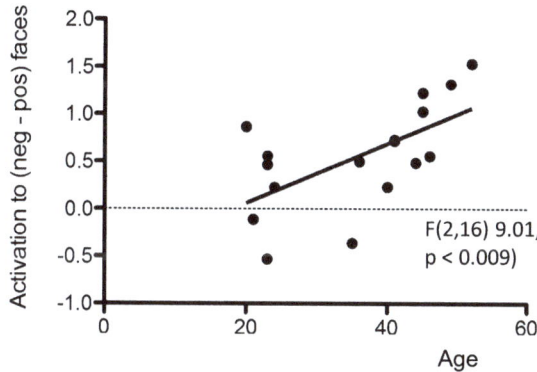

Fig. 7 Association of NDS from BOLD signal collected by fMRI with age. The line of best fit is shown from this association

Discussion

Synopsis

This study showed that a validated keypress paradigm that allowed subjects to trade effort for view-time of emotional faces (Ekman and Friesen 1976), produced a relationship between the mean (K, Fig. 3) and pattern of keypressing (H, Fig. 3) consistent with previous reports using a beauty stimulus set, the International Affective Picture Set, and food stimuli (Breiter and Kim 2008; Kim et al. 2010). This relationship produced a ratio between the slope of the avoidance value function ($s-$) and slope of the approach value function ($s+$) that produced an LA measure similar to that reported by Tversky and Kahneman (1992), which also correlated with a measure of NDS from the VS/NAc, as has been reported by others (Tom et al. 2007). Correlation of LA with age was nonsignificant, whereas correlation of NDS with age showed a significant positive relationship, meaning that as individuals age their NDS also increases but their behavioral index of LA did not. These same results, if found in commercial situations, could have a major impact on traditional marketing theory and the assumption that risk aversion increases with age.

Hypotheses Raised by These Results

The relationship between age and NDS in the absence of a significant relationship between age and behavioral LA suggests interesting hypotheses about the neural processing of LA in relation to age. First, Seidman et al. (1998) have shown that subject IQ is inversely related to brain activation levels across individuals, suggesting that the brain compensates with greater neural activity when functional capacity is lower. Given that aging is known to be associated with brain atrophy (e.g., Raz 2005) and cognitive decline (e.g., Kensinger 2009), it is inferred that the functional capacity of the brain declines with age. Thus, the findings in this study suggest the hypothesis that as an individual ages, the neural differential between losses and gains increases to achieve the same level of behavioral LA. This perspective is consistent with recent research on aging wherein preserved cognitive function in the context of age-related brain activity may be thought to represent a neurocompensation mechanism (Meunier et al. 2014), consistent with a neural efficiency hypothesis.

Alternative hypotheses must consider additional age-related asymmetries in the larger decision-making network that interact with the VS/NAc in such a way that the response to LA is either uninhibited or amplified. For example, on the other end of the age spectrum, recent imaging work has shown asynchronous developments of the VS/NAc and PFC parallels adolescents' predisposition to engage in high-risk behaviors (Barkley-Levenson and Galván 2014; Blakemore and Robbins 2012; Van Leijenhorst et al. 2010; Steinberg 2008); however, the relationship only becomes apparent when the asynchronous trajectories of PFC and VS/NAc interact within a specific window of development. The observed VS/NAc response to LA may reflect a similar interaction, however in areas that did not reach thresholds of activation that changed behavior in the current experiment, either because of the age group examined, sensitivity of the task, or sensitivity of the imaging paradigm. For example, given the limitations of imaging, relatively small and deep subcortical structures, particularly in small sample sizes, additional areas may also contribute to age-related changes in processing LA, such as functional differences between the dorsal and ventral striatum, where activations in the dorsal striatum may have been subthreshold in our data, or may only be associated with anticipation paradigms (Tom et al. 2007) related to LA. From these findings, future work will benefit from looking at larger populations within specific age categories and by increasing the number of participants to obtain a more densely packed parametric gradient of age distributions.

Both the results and limitations of this study provide a clear path for future work. Based on the disparity between neural and behavioral response, future work will benefit from examining the VS/NAc response within larger decision making networks for potential mitigating factors that may contribute to the behavioral equalization, while also examining the sensitivity of behavioral metrics. In addition, while the sample size for this study is comparable to similar such work (e.g., Tom et al. 2007), much more needs to be done to develop a better understanding of age effects. In this study, we have a sample size of 17 subjects in the age range of 20–55 years. Future studies might include a wider age range where younger and older individuals are also included in the sample to facilitate determining if there are distinct clusters of subjects who may support both of the hypotheses tested in this study. With a more comprehensive and dense parametric gradient of age, we speculate that we would see stronger correlations with VS/NAc activation; however, we may also find either nonlinear functions, or a step function based on plateaus within certain groups of ages. It is only with future work that we can have a better understanding of the neural and behavioral age effects both across different age populations and also within any specific age group.

Loss Aversion and Marketing Research

The results of this study may have implications for future marketing research. Age-related brand loyalty (Lambert-Pandraud and Laurent 2010) has been attributed to an increased aversion to risk associated with change (Erdem et al. 2006; Montgomery and Wernerfelt 1992) leading to investigations of age-related changes in decision-making and reward processing across the lifespan (Barkley-Levenson et al. 2013; Eppinger et al. 2011; Paulsen et al. 2012; Weller et al. 2011; Mata et al. 2011; Mata and Nunes 2010). In the current study, we observed no significant differences in LA behavior, but did find relatively early (i.e., range 20–55 years old) age-related increases in NDS. The parametric increase in NDS with age may indicate additional neural effort is required to obtain the same behavioral outcomes as one ages. This finding could have major influences on how marketers employ reach and frequency media models when the target market is an older population. Further, it could also have ramifications on how detailed messaging could or should be for older age groups. Previous studies support this notion; for example, aging populations show bilateral activation patterns within homologous areas of the PFC while their younger counterparts achieve the same performance with singular lateralized activations (Cabeza et al. 2002; Reuter-Lorenz et al. 1999), suggesting compensatory mechanisms in response to neural senescence (Daselaar et al. 2015; Cabeza et al. 2002; Park and Reuter-Lorenz 2009). In addition, recent imaging work on cognitive function suggests that behavioral outcomes reflect interactions between age, neural efficiency, and processing load (Turner and Spreng 2012; Vallesi et al. 2011; Cappell et al. 2010). Future marketing-based research might benefit from examining the cost of neural processing in marketing communications and how that might be mitigated for various age-related target markets.

Study Conclusions

This study provides an evidential basis for understanding the effects of age on the process of LA or the weighting of negative outcomes with a higher psychological impact than positive ones. Specifically, it found that the differential processing of negative outcomes relative to positive ones by the brain was affected by age; this effect was not clear in the LA behavior, suggesting a neural efficiency or neurocompensation hypothesis underlying the observed effects. Together, the data from this study has implications for future marketing research. For instance, the results of our study suggest that marketing communications and brands that target older adults might focus on the cost of neural processing in marketing communications. Future fMRI work might specifically target an older adult population in order to examine how brain circuits underlying decision-making may be altered in persons over the age of 65. Future fMRI work might also examine the interactions of the nature of information with other variables such as the amount of information provided (Mata and Nunes 2010) and uncertainty, and thus give us a better understanding of the subprocesses that occur when older adults make decisions.

Summary

While this study relates to only a portion of the entire concept of prospect theory, i.e., loss aversion among aging consumers, it demonstrates the potential for neural and neurological analysis to start to unlock how humans actually process and use marketing communication in various situations and activities. Thus, this moves neuromarketing beyond the simple examples of "identifying which portions of the brain 'lights up' based on external stimulation" to a more in depth and useful understanding of how and in what ways marketing concepts can be validated or found wanting and, then, adapted. Some of that work has already begun with additional papers developed by the same authors (insert various Schultz/Block/Viswanathan papers using neuro marketing).

More important, this study provides a basis for the development of neural explanations for what have commonly been taken as "marketing truisms." In this instance, the common belief in marketing is that loss aversion increases with age. In this experiment, that was found not to be the case. In our view, it is this type of more advanced analytical work which is needed to truly turn marketing communication into a science, rather than simply a "random walk" among commonly held beliefs and widely accepted but unproven, principles.

References

Abdellaoui, M., Bleichrodt, H., & Paraschiv, C. (2007). Loss aversion under prospect theory: A parameter free measurement. *Management Science, 53*, 1659–1674.

Aharon, I., Etcoff, N., Ariely, D., Chabris, C. F., O'Connor, E., & Breiter, H. C. (2001). Beautiful faces have variable reward value: fMRI and behavioral evidence. *Neuron, 32*, 537–551.

Ariely, D., Huber, J., & Wertenbroch, K. (2005). When do losses loom larger than gains? *Journal of Marketing Research, 42*, 134–138.

Avnet, T., & Higgins, E. T. (2006). How regulatory fit affects value in consumer choices and opinions. *Journal of Marketing Research, 43*, 1–10.

Barkley-Levenson, E., & Galván, A. (2014). Neural representation of expected value in the adolescent brain. *Proceedings of the National Academy of Sciences of the United States of America, 111*, 1646–1651.

Barkley-Levenson, E. E., Van Leijenhorst, L., & Galván, A. (2013). Behavioral and neural correlates of loss aversion and risk avoidance in adolescents and adults. *Developmental Cognitive Neuroscience, 3*, 72–83. doi:10.1016/j.dcn.2012.09.007.

Becerra, L., Breiter, H. C., Wise, R., Gonzalez, R. G., & Borsook, D. (2001). Reward circuitry activation by noxious thermal stimuli. *Neuron, 32*, 927–946.

Blakemore, S.-J., & Robbins, T. W. (2012). Decision-making in the adolescent brain. *Nature Neuroscience, 15*, 1184–1191. doi:10.1038/nn.3177.

Blood, A. J., Zatorre, R. J., Bermudez, P., & Evans, A. C. (1999). Emotional responses to pleasant and unpleasant music correlate with activity in paralimbic brain regions. *Nature Neuroscience, 2*, 382–387.

Botwinick, J. (1978). *Aging and behavior: A comprehensive integration of research findings* (2nd ed.). New York: Springer.

Breiter, H. C., Aharon, I., Kahneman, D., Dale, A., & Shizgal, P. (2001). Functional imaging of neural responses to expectancy and experience of monetary gains and losses. *Neuron, 30*, 619–639.

Breiter, H. C., Etcoff, N. L., Whalen, P. J., Kennedy, W. A., Rauch, S. L., Buckner, R. L., et al. (1996). Response and habituation of the human amygdala during visual processing of facial expression. *Neuron, 17*, 875–887.

Breiter, H. C., Filipek, P. A., Kennedy, D. N., Baer, L., Pitcher, D. A., Olivares, M. J., et al. (1994). Retrocallosal white matter abnormalities in patients with obsessive compulsive disorder. *Archives of General Psychiatry, 51*, 663.

Breiter, H. C., Gasic, G. P., & Makris, N. (2006). Imaging the neural systems for motivated behavior and their dysfunction in neuropsychiatric illness. In T. S. Deisboeck & J. Y. Kresh (Eds.), *Complex systems science in biomedicine* (pp. 763–810). New York: Springer.

Breiter, H. C., Gollub, R. L., Weisskoff, R. M., Kennedy, D. N., Makris, N., Berke, J. D., et al. (1997). Acute effects of cocaine on human brain activity and emotion. *Neuron, 19*, 591–611.

Breiter, H. C., & Kim, B. W. (2008). *Recurrent and robust patterns underlying human relative preference, and associations with brain circuitry plus genetics. Design principles in biology* (U Minn, Institute of Mathematics and Its Applications). Retrieved from www.ima.umn.edu/2007-2008/W4.21-25.08/abstracts.html

Breiter, H. C., & Rosen, B. R. (1999). Functional magnetic resonance imaging of brain reward circuitry in the human. *Annals of the New York Academy of Sciences, 877*, 523–547.

Cabeza, R., Anderson, N. D., Locantore, J. K., & McIntosh, A. R. (2002). Aging gracefully: Compensatory brain activity in high-performing older adults. *NeuroImage, 17*, 1394–1402. doi:10.1006/nimg.2002.1280.

Cabeza, R., Grady, C. L., Nyberg, L., McIntosh, A. R., Tulving, E., Kapur, S., et al. (1997). Age-related differences in neural activity during memory encoding and retrieval: A positron emission tomography study. *Journal of Neuroscience, 17*, 391–400.

Cappell, K. A., Gmeindl, L., & Reuter-Lorenz, P. A. (2010). Age differences in prefrontal recruitment during verbal working memory maintenance depend on memory load. *Cortex, 46*, 462–473. doi:10.1016/j.cortex.2009.11.009.

Cole, C., Laurent, G., Drolet, A., Ebert, J., Gutchess, A., Lambert-Pandraud, R., et al. (2008). Decision making and brand choice by older consumers. *Marketing Letters, 19*, 355–365.

Daselaar, S. M., Iyengar, V., Davis, S. W., Eklund, K., Hayes, S. M., & Cabeza, R. E. (2015). Less wiring, more firing: Low-performing older adults compensate for impaired white matter with greater neural activity. *Cerebral Cortex, 25*(4), 983–990. doi:10.1093/cercor/bht289.

Deichmann, R., Gottfried, J., Hutton, C., & Turner, R. (2003). Optimized EPI for fMRI studies of the orbitofrontal cortex. *NeuroImage, 19*, 430–441. doi:10.1016/S1053-8119(03)00073-9.

Ebner, N. C., Freund, A. M., & Baltes, P. B. (2006). Developmental changes in personal goal orientation from young to late adulthood: From striving for gains to maintenance and prevention of losses. *Psychology and Aging, 21*, 664–678. doi:10.1037/0882-7974.21.4.664.

Ekman, P., & Friesen, W. V. (1976). Measuring facial movement. *Environmental Psychology and Nonverbal Behavior, 1*, 56–75.

Elman, I., Ariely, D., Mazar, N., Aharon, I., Lasko, N. B., Macklin, M. L., et al. (2005). Probing reward function in post-traumatic stress disorder with beautiful facial images. *Psychiatry Research, 135*, 179–183. doi:10.1016/j.psychres.2005.04.002.

Eppinger, B., Hämmerer, D., & Li, S.-C. (2011). Neuromodulation of reward-based learning and decision making in human aging. *Annals of the New York Academy of Sciences, 1235*, 1–17. doi:10.1111/j.17496632.2011.06230.x.

Erdem, T., Swait, J., & Valenzuela, A. (2006). Brands as signals: A cross-country validation study. *Journal of Marketing, 70*, 34–49.

Gasic, G. P., Smoller, J. W., Perlis, R. H., Sun, M., Lee, S., Kim, B. W., et al. (2009). BDNF, relative preference, and reward circuitry responses to emotional communication. *American Journal of Medical Genetics Part B: Neuropsychiatric Genetics, 150B*, 762–781. doi:10.1002/ajmg.b.30944.

Good, C. D., Johnsrude, I. S., Ashburner, J., Henson, R. N., Fristen, K., & Frackowiak, R. S. (2002). A voxel based morphometric study of ageing in 465 normal adult human brains. In *Biomedical Imaging, 2002. 5th IEEE EMBS International Summer School on (IEEE), 16.*

Grady, C. L., & Craik, F. I. (2000). Changes in memory processing with age. *Current Opinion in Neurobiology, 10*, 224–231.

Grady, C. L., McIntosh, A. R., Horwitz, B., Maisog, J. M., Ungerleider, L. G., Mentis, M. J., et al. (1995). Age-related reductions in human recognition memory due to impaired encoding. *Science, 269*, 218–221.

Grady, C. L., McIntosh, A. R., Rajah, M. N., Beig, S., & Craik, F. I. (1999). The effects of age on the neural correlates of episodic encoding. *Cerebral Cortex, 9*, 805–814.

Heckhausen, J. (1997). Developmental regulation across adulthood: Primary and secondary control of age related challenges. *Developmental Psychology, 33*, 176–187.

Hedden, T., & Gabrieli, J. D. E. (2004). Insights into the ageing mind: A view from cognitive neuroscience. *Nature Reviews Neuroscience, 5*, 87–96. doi:10.1038/nrn1323.

Johnson, J. G., & Busemeyer, J. R. (2010). Decision making under risk and uncertainty. *Wiley Interdisciplinary Reviews: Cognitive Science, 1*, 736–749. doi:10.1002/wcs.76.

Kahneman, D. (2003). Maps of bounded rationality: Psychology for behavioral economics. *American Economic Review, 93*, 1449–1475.

Kahneman, D. (2011). *Thinking, fast and slow*. New York: Farrar, Strauss, Giroux.

Kahneman, D., & Tversky, A. (1979). Prospect theory: An analysis of decision under risk. *Econometrica, 47*, 263–291.

Kensinger, E. A. (2009). Cognition in aging and age related disease. In P. R. Hof & C. V. Mobbs (Eds.), *Handbook of the neuroscience of aging* (pp. 249–256). London: Elsevier.

Kim, B. W., Kennedy, D. N., Lehár, J., Lee, M. J., Blood, A. J., Lee, S., et al. (2010). Recurrent, robust and scalable patterns underlie human approach and avoidance. *PLoS One, 5*, 1–25. e10613. doi:10.1371/journal.pone.0010613.

Lambert-Pandraud, R., & Laurent, G. (2010). Impact of age on brand choice. In A. Drolet, N. Schwartz, & C. Yoon (Eds.), *The aging consumer: Perspectives from psychology and economics* (pp. 191–208). New York: Psychology Press/Routledge.

Levy, B., Ariely, D., Mazar, N., Chi, W., Lukas, S., & Elman, I. (2008). Gender differences in the motivational processing of facial beauty. *Learning and Motivation, 39*, 136–145. doi:10.1016/j.lmot.2007.09.002.

Madden, D. J., Turkington, T. G., Provenzale, J. M., Denny, L. L., Hawk, T. C., Gottlob, L. R., et al. (1999). Adult age differences in the functional neuroanatomy of verbal recognition memory. *Human Brain Mapping, 7*, 115–135.

Makris, N., Gasic, G. P., Kennedy, D. N., Hodge, S. M., Kaiser, J. R., Lee, M. J., et al. (2008). Cortical thickness abnormalities in cocaine addiction—A reflection of both drug use and a pre-existing disposition to drug abuse? *Neuron, 60*, 174–188. doi:10.1016/j.neuron.2008.08.011.

Makris, N., Gasic, G. P., Seidman, L. J., Goldstein, J. M., Gastfriend, D. R., Elman, I., et al. (2004). Decreased absolute amygdala volume in cocaine addicts. *Neuron, 44*, 729–740.

Mata, R., Josef, A. K., Samanez-Larkin, G. R., & Hertwig, R. (2011). Age differences in risky choice: A meta analysis. *Annals of the New York Academy of Sciences, 1235*, 18–29. doi:10.1111/j.1749-6632.2011.06200.x.

Mata, R., & Nunes, L. (2010). When less is enough: Cognitive aging, information search, and decision quality in consumer choice. *Psychology and Aging, 25*, 289–298. doi:10.1037/a0017927.

Meunier, D., Stamatakis, E. A., & Tyler, L. K. (2014). Age-related functional reorganization, structural changes, and preserved cognition. *Neurobiology of Aging, 35*(1), 42–544. doi:10.1016/j.neurobiolaging.2013.07.003.

Montgomery, C. A., & Wernerfelt, B. (1992). Risk reduction and umbrella branding. *Journal of Business, 65*, 31–50.

Paraschiv, C., & L'Haridon, O. (2008). Aversion aux pertes: Origine, composantes et implications marketing. *Recherche et Applications en Marketing, 23*, 67–83.

Park, D. C., & Reuter-Lorenz, P. (2009). The adaptive brain: Aging and neurocognitive scaffolding. *Annual Review of Psychology, 60*, 173–196. doi:10.1146/annurev.psych.59.103006.093656.

Paulsen, D. J., Platt, M. L., Huettel, S. A., & Brannon, E. M. (2012). From risk-seeking to risk-averse: The development of economic risk preference from childhood to adulthood. *Frontiers in Psychology, 3*, 1–17. doi:10.3389/fpsyg.2012.00313.

Perlis, R. H. (2008). Association of a polymorphism near CREB1 with differential aversion processing in the insula of healthy participants. *Archives of General Psychiatry, 65*, 882–892. doi:10.1001/archgenpsychiatry.2008.3.

Raz, N. (2000). *Aging of the brain and its impact on cognitive performance: Integration of structural and functional findings. The handbook of aging and cognition* (2nd ed.). Mahwah, NJ: Lawrence Erlbaum Associates.

Raz, N. (2005). Regional brain changes in aging healthy adults: General trends, individual differences and modifiers. *Cerebral Cortex, 15*, 1676–1689. doi:10.1093/cercor/bhi044.

Reuter-Lorenz, P. A. (2002). New visions of the aging mind and brain. *Trends in Cognitive Science, 6*, 394–400.

Reuter-Lorenz, P. A., Stanczak, L., & Miller, A. C. (1999). Neural recruitment and cognitive aging: Two hemispheres are better than one, especially as you age. *Psychological Science, 10*, 494–500.

Schindler, R. M., & Holbrook, M. B. (2003). Nostalgia for early experience as a determinant of consumer preferences. *Psychology and Marketing, 20*, 275–302. doi:10.1002/mar.10074.

Seidman, L. J., Breiter, H. C., Goodman, J. M., Goldstein, J. M., Woodruff, P. W., O'Craven, K., et al. (1998). A functional magnetic resonance imaging study of auditory vigilance with low and high information processing demands. *Neuropsychology, 12*, 505–518.

Shannon, C. E., & Weaver, W. (1949). *The mathematical theory of communication* (pp. 379–423). Urbana: University of Illinois Press.

Stebbins, G. T., Carrillo, M. C., Dorfman, J., Dirksen, C., Desmond, J. E., Turner, D. A., et al. (2002). Aging effects on memory encoding in the frontal lobes. *Psychology and Aging, 17*, 44–55.

Steinberg, L. (2008). A social neuroscience perspective on adolescent risk-taking. *Developmental Review, 28*, 78–106. doi:10.1016/j.dr.2007.08.002.

Strauss, M., Makris, N., Aharon, I., Vangel, M., Goodman, J., Kennedy, D., et al. (2005). fMRI of sensitization to angry faces. *NeuroImage, 26*, 389–413. doi:10.1016/j.neuroimage.2005.01.053.

Tom, S. M., Fox, C. R., Trepel, C., & Poldrack, R. A. (2007). The neural basis of loss aversion in decision making under risk. *Science, 315*, 515–518. doi:10.1126/science.1134239.

Turner, G. R., & Spreng, R. N. (2012). Executive functions and neurocognitive aging: Dissociable patterns of brain activity. *Neurobiology of Aging, 33*, 826.e1–826.e13. doi:10.1016/j.neurobiolaging.2011.06.005.

Tversky, A., & Kahneman, D. (1991). Loss aversion in riskless choice: A reference-dependent model. *Quarterly Journal of Economics, 106*, 1039–1061.

Tversky, A., & Kahneman, D. (1992). Advances in prospect theory: Cumulative representation of uncertainty. *Journal of Risk and Uncertainty, 5*, 297–323.

Vallesi, A., McIntosh, A. R., & Stuss, D. T. (2011). Overrecruitment in the aging brain as a function of task demands: Evidence for a compensatory view. *Journal of Cognitive Neuroscience, 23*, 801–815.

Van Leijenhorst, L., Moor, B. G., Op de Macks, Z. A., Rombouts, S. A. R. B., Westenberg, P. M., & Crone, E. A. (2010). Adolescent risky decision-making: Neurocognitive development of reward and control regions. *NeuroImage, 51*, 345–355. doi:10.1016/j.neuroimage.2010.02.038.

Weller, J. A., Levin, I. P., & Denburg, N. L. (2011). Trajectory of risky decision making for potential gains and losses from ages 5 to 85. *Journal of Behavioral Decision Making, 24*, 331–344. doi:10.1002/bdm.690.

Yamamoto, R., Ariely, D., Chi, W., Langleben, D. D., & Elman, I. (2009). Gender differences in the motivational processing of babies are determined by their facial attractiveness. *PLoS One, 4*, 1–5.e6042. doi:10.1371/journal.pone.0006042.

Don't Pester Me! Unwanted Upgrade Innovation

Yazhen Xiao and Jelena Spanjol

Abstract Consumers encounter incremental innovations that aim to improve currently owned products on a daily basis. This type of innovation, which we term upgrade innovation, can improve user experience, product security, and the overall performance of the owned product. Yet, upgrade innovation is not always appreciated by customers, at times leading customers to reject it or ignore its availability. In an extreme non-adoption condition, customers may actively seek strategies in order not to be notified the availability of upgrade innovations.

Drawing on extant innovation literature (e.g., Calantone et al. 2006; Davis 1980; Sorescue and Spanjol 2008), we explore the influence of upgrade innovation characteristics on upgrade intention, and investigate two alternative mechanisms: annoyance and anticipated regret that explain why upgrade innovation is sometimes unwanted by product owners. Customers are annoyed at upgrade innovation in that it changes the owned products. Alternatively, they could feel regretful if adopting upgrade innovation that does not bring anticipated benefit, and/or if missing the upgrade innovations that improve owned product. This research is the first to call attention to the impact of annoyance and anticipated regret in upgrade innovation adoption. When customers have strong psychological ownership on owned products, the effect of upgrade innovation on upgrade innovation adoption is expected to be enlarged.

This study contributes to marketing and innovation research in several ways. First, it raises the definition of upgrade innovation on already owned products. Second, it investigates the influence of annoyance, a frequently happening but rarely examined consumption emotion, on product decisions. Last but not least, it explores the role of anticipated regret of adopting and not adopting in innovation adoption.

References available upon request.

Y. Xiao (✉) • J. Spanjol
University of Illinois at Chicago, Chicago, IL, USA
e-mail: yxiao21@uic.edu; spanjol@uic.edu

© Academy of Marketing Science 2016   471
L. Petruzzellis, R.S. Winer (eds.), *Rediscovering the Essentiality of Marketing*,
Developments in Marketing Science: Proceedings of the Academy of Marketing
Science, DOI 10.1007/978-3-319-29877-1_96

Part XI
International Marketing

Country Reputation, Brand Reputation and Company Reputation: Their Importance in Business-to-Business Industries

Elena Cedrola, Loretta Battaglia, and Anna Grazia Quaranta

Abstract Literature and research studies on country of origin (COO) have mainly focused on its effect in business to consumer (B2C) markets. Among the few scholars who have analysed industrial sectors (B2B), some believe that COO has similar importance and the same function in B2B markets as in B2C markets. In contrast, others argue that industrial customers are less influenced by this phenomenon. To contribute to this debate, we selected a group of Italian companies in different industries operating in at least one foreign market. We administered electronic questionnaires, collecting data and information on the internationalization of these enterprises, the COO effect and its relevance, namely, the elements that most influence the COO effect. The data also enabled us to examine the importance of company and brand reputation in the internationalization of B2B industries.

Keywords Country of origin • Country reputation • Brand reputation • Company reputation • Business-to-business • Empirical study • Italy

Introduction

Literature and research studies on country of origin (COO) have largely focused on its effect in B2C markets (Nebenzahl et al. 2003). Among those that have analysed industrial sectors, some believe that COO has similar importance and the same

E. Cedrola (✉)
University of Macerata, Macerata, Italy
e-mail: elena.cedrola@unimc.it

L. Battaglia
University of the Sacred Heart of Milan, Milan, Italy
e-mail: loretta.battaglia@unicatt.it

A.G. Quaranta
University of Bologna, Bologna, Italy
e-mail: annagrazia.quaranta@unibo.it

© Academy of Marketing Science 2016
L. Petruzzellis, R.S. Winer (eds.), *Rediscovering the Essentiality of Marketing*,
Developments in Marketing Science: Proceedings of the Academy of Marketing
Science, DOI 10.1007/978-3-319-29877-1_97

475

function in B2B markets as in B2C markets. In contrast, others argue that industrial customers are less influenced by this phenomenon (Cedrola and Battaglia 2012a). Although industrial markets are well structured and complex, the diversity of customers, products and services as well as the types of enterprises makes it difficult to consider the business market as a monolithic market (Fiocca et al. 2008). Some key features of B2B markets are the higher concentration of customers and suppliers, higher sales and purchase volumes, and greater geographic concentration. It seems inconceivable that factors such as a country's culture or its tradition could influence and alter important choices in relation to the procurement of materials for semi-finished or finished products, and thus business decisions. Nevertheless, in B2B sectors, industrial buyers and their perceptions of suppliers are also affected by the COO effect (Verlegh and Steenkamp 1999).

In the same way as consumer goods markets, products made in certain countries may be subjected to the specific categorization of potential buyers in industrial markets due to stereotyping (positive or negative) in terms of the production, quality and other characteristics ascribed to those countries (Bradley 2001). In sum, the country and company image and reputation linked to the brand can affect different spheres of contact between businesses and their customers, especially in the commercial parties' approach and in the relationship-building phases (Cedrola and Battaglia 2012a, b).

Objectives and Research Questions

The proposed chapter is part of the debate on the importance of the COO effect in B2B sectors and aims to answer the following questions:

Q1. Is the COO effect also a significant phenomenon in B2B markets?
Q2. How important is the COO effect for companies operating in various industrial sectors and which aspects are most relevant to its evaluation?
Q3. How much importance is given to the country of manufacture (COM), country of design (COD) and country of brand (COB) effects?
Q4. Which elements most influence COO and how does it affect perceptions of the company's products and price?
Q5. How important is the role of brand reputation, company reputation and country reputation in B2B markets and what factors influence these?

Following the analysis of the main models for the study of the COO effect, particularly those related to B2B markets, we present a research model and methodology used in an empirical survey to which currently 94 Italian companies active in foreign markets have responded. Thereafter, we offer a summary of the first results of the survey and the main implications for management.

Literature Review: Characteristics of the Main COO Models in B2B Markets

In reviewing the main models used to study the COO effect in B2B markets (Bradley 2001; Cedrola and Battaglia 2013; Chasin and Jaffe 1987; Guerini and Uslenghi 2006; White 1979; White and Cundiff 1978), some common elements and differences emerged.

First, most authors specifically require purchasing managers, export managers or senior management to respond to the research questionnaire. This is due to the importance of the relationship between the supplier company and the client company in industrial markets.

Another common feature of the models analysed is the research tool employed, namely, the questionnaire that in the majority of cases was sent electronically followed by personal interviews aimed at expanding the information obtained in the previous step. The models for the study of industrial markets developed later than those for consumer goods and as such have always been multidimensional (multicue) (Bursi et al. 2012).

Essentially two classes of variables are used: the first concerns the direct attributes of the product such as quality, reliability and innovation, while the second concern factors relating to the marketing sphere.

In addition to the large number of variables used, the models for the study of B2B markets are characterized by a large number of countries and product categories, as shown in Table 1.

Table 1 Countries and categories used in the models

Models	Countries	Product categories
White and Cundiff (1978)	The United States, Germany, Japan and Brazil	Forklift, machinery for metal processing, transcription system
Chasin and Jaffe (1987)	The United States, Czechoslovakia, Hungary, Poland, Romania and the Soviet Union	Building materials, chemicals, electrical equipment and agricultural, machine tools, paper products, aircraft, scientific precision instruments, textiles, turbines and generators
White (1979)	Great Britain, Italy, France, Germany, the United States	Industrial products of various types
Bradley (2001)	France, Germany, Japan, Ireland, Italy, the Netherlands, Sweden, Switzerland, the United Kingdom and the United States	Electronic parts
Guerini and Uslenghi (2006)	Various	Mechanical and textile
Cedrola and Battaglia (2013)	Italy, China	Various

The first contribution chosen as the starting point for the empirical model is that of Marino and Mainolfi (2010) with the aim of assessing the dimensions at the base of the 'Made in' reputation and whether these issues are able to reinforce the symbolic, cultural and value system that endows supply systems with a comparative image advantage in consumer perceptions.

The second model, proposed by Cedrola and Battaglia (2012a), investigates the influence of the COO effect in the trade relations of Italian companies with their foreign partners to ensure greater understanding of the dynamics that contribute to defining the procurement process in industrial enterprises.

In constructing the empirical model presented in this chapter, we made recourse to the subdivision of internationalization modes and international collaboration forms proposed by Cedrola and Battaglia, while for the questions relating to COO, we made recourse to the attributes and variables proposed by Marino and Mainolfi. We also used the Cedrola and Battaglia contribution to overcome the issue of only referring to the relational dimension. A further difference with the Marino and Mainolfi model is the choice of not using the Osgood semantic differential since we considered this a method more suitable to investigating the variables that affect consumer buying behaviours.

A more complete investigation of the B2B sector therefore requires including new questions. For example, using the taxonomy of the COO effect was considered appropriate to understand which among COM, COB and COD is more influential in the purchasing decisions of industrial products. We also investigated the relevance of the reputational lever, decomposing it into three dimensions referring to the country, the brand and the company, to determine which is most influential in the industrial sector.

Research Methodology

To answer the five research questions, we selected a group of 1800 Italian companies operating in all industrial sectors and in at least one foreign market.[1] These companies were sent electronic questionnaires,[2] which enabled collecting data and information on the internationalization process of these enterprises, the importance they attach to the COO effect, and to determining which elements are

---

[1] The companies were selected from the member lists of the following associations: (Food) Federalimentare—Federation of the Italian food industry, UnionAlimentari—National Union of small and medium food companies; (Furniture-Wood) FederLegnoArredo—Federation of furniture and furnishing companies; (Chemical) Federchimica—National Federation of the chemical industry; (Electronic) ANIE—National Federation of electrotechnical and electronics companies; (Mechanical) Federmeccanica—Italian Federation of metalworking industries, AMMA—Association of mechanical and mechatronic companies; (Plastic) Federazione Gomma e Plastica—Rubber and Plastics Federation, Polimerica—Italian Institute of packaging; (Textile-clothing) ASSOMAC—National Association of Italian manufacturers of footwear, leather goods and tannery Machines and accessories, Sistema Moda Italia—textiles and fashion Federation, Uniontessile—National Union of small and medium private industrial companies.

[2] The mailings started in December 2013 and the recalls are still in progress.

Table 2 Thematic research scheme

General company information	HQ location—Type of company—Prevailing sector
	Position held by the respondent
	No. of employees—Average turnover—Foreign turnover
Business operations	Geographical areas in which it is present
	Reasons for internationalization
	Important relationships for internationalization
	Mode of presence in the markets
	National and international supply chains
	Marketing mix
Country of origin effect	Importance of the COO effect and elements that compose it
	Country of Manufacture, Country of Design, Country of Brand
	Brand reputation and elements that influence it
	Country reputation and elements that influence it
	Company reputation and elements that influence it

Table 3 Characteristics of respondent enterprises

Italian region	Companies (%)	No. of employees	Companies (%)	Turnover	Companies (%)
Campania	1.1	1–15	33.0	<2 mil. €	23.4
Emilia Romagna	14.9	16–50	24.5	2–10 mil. €	24.5
Friuli Venezia Giulia	1.1	51–100	17.0	10–50 mil. €	30.9
Lombardia	44.7	101–250	10.6	>50 mil. €	19.1
Marche	7.4	>250	13.8	ND	2.1
Piemonte	7.4	ND	1.1		
Puglia	3.2				
Toscana	7.4				
Veneto	12.8				

most influential. This has also allowed us to examine the importance of company reputation and brand reputation in the B2B internationalization process. A summary of the themes is shown in Table 2.

To date, 94 completed questionnaires have been obtained, an overall response rate of 5.2 %. Starting from the data collected with the questionnaire, the information has been decomposed, processed and stored in order to gather more detailed evidence.

The respondents hold different positions, although predominantly entrepreneurs, CEOs, marketing managers and sales manager. The characteristics of the respondent companies and their distribution in terms of location, number of employees, turnover, sector, years of international operations and weight of foreign sales are summarized in Tables 3 and 4.

Table 4 Characteristics of respondent enterprises

Industry	Companies (%)	Years of international operations	Companies (%)	Weight of foreign sales (%)	Companies (%)
Mechanical	29	0–5	12	0–25	29.9
Textile and clothing	23	6–10	13	26–50	16.1
Electronics	12	11–15	12	51–75	27.6
Furnishing	10	16–20	9	76–100	26.4
Rubber and plastics	7	21–25	7		
Food and beverage	6	26–30	12		
Chemical	6	>30	32		
Others	3	ND	4		
Metallurgy	1				
Services	1				

The data shows a substantial prevalence of joint stock (52.1 %) and limited companies (39.4), both types have limited liability and a more complex management and corporate structure than partnerships, which is necessary when wanting to operate in a sustainable way in foreign markets.

The COO Effect in Industrial Sectors: First Empirical Results

First, we asked companies to provide an evaluation of the importance of the COO effect in their sector of primary activity, obtaining overall positive responses. In fact, only 2.1 % believe this issue is not important and 11.7 % consider it not very important, while the remaining respondents expressed a positive perception: 20.2 % fairly important, important 35.1 and 30.9 % very important. Industrial enterprises are thus shown to be aware of the relevance of this effect in the strategic internationalization process. Certain in-depth interviews carried out after the administration of the questionnaires showed that the most significant effect is attributed by companies that belong to the traditional 'Made in Italy' sectors: food, furniture and textile-clothing.

Given the multidimensional nature of the construct, we considered it appropriate to investigate how country image, a component of the country effect, is influenced by variables relating to the macro- and micro-economic context. Specifically, the focus is on cultural, political and economic dimensions, the industry tradition and country system (Table 5).

Some interesting elements emerged from these results. First, the evaluation of the scarce significance of the political system in the country image evaluation, which is considered not at all or not very important by 53.2 % of the respondent group. This result is surprising since political stability is one of the elements typically considered

Table 5 Evaluation of the country image components

	Not important (%)	Not very important (%)	Fairly important (%)	Very important (%)
Cultural dimension	2	18	25	24
Political dimension	12	41	14	13
Economic dimension	3	19	22	19
Industry tradition	1	5	16	44
Country system	5	19	19	20

Table 6 Elements that influence the assessment of the COO effect

	Not important (%)	Not very important (%)	Fairly important (%)	Very important (%)	ND (%)
Competitiveness of enterprises	4.3	8.5	31.9	20.2	1.1
Innovation and scientific research	2.1	7.4	16.0	33.0	4.3
Design and aesthetics	1.1	9.6	7.4	46.8	1.1
Creativity of products	1.1	6.4	8.5	51.1	2.1
Reputation of the industry	1.1	10.6	19.1	27.7	1.1
Manufacture	0.0	5.3	12.8	40.4	–
Quality	0.0	0.0	10.6	66.0	–
Pre-/post-sales services	3.2	6.4	23.8	30.9	1.1

by companies when selecting new markets to operate in. The other items in the questionnaire were all rated as important. In particular, industry tradition is considered important or very important by 76.6 % of respondents. This is a crucial element in the industrial sector since companies often engage in specialized productions, where they try to achieve the highest levels of quality. For this to be possible, the suppliers must also have high standards, hence the tendency to choose partners from countries with a strong tradition in the manufacturing sector.

The request to evaluate the impact of a number of product and company attributes on the perception of the COO effect provided responses that generated the following results (Table 6).

Overall, the companies positively evaluated all the elements proposed, although the higher ratings relate to attributes linked to the product rather than to the reputation of the industrial sector and the company's COO. The factors relating to COO that contribute to the overall perception of the COO effect were further explored by asking respondents to evaluate the importance of sector of belonging, the maturity of the end market and stable trade relations. A top position was assigned by the majority (59.6 %) to the sector of belonging, the second position with 52.1 % to the maturity of the end market and third the stability of trade relations with 43.6 %. This third place is singular since the relational system in trade exchanges is fundamental in industrial enterprises.

To study the COO effect in greater detail, we subdivided the effect into COM, COB and COD (Table 7).

Table 7 The evaluation of COM, COD and COB

	Not important (%)	Not very important (%)	Fairly important (%)	Very important (%)	ND (%)
COM	1.1	6.4	17.0	42.6	1.1
COD	4.3	11.7	24.5	31.9	2.1
COB	2.1	9.6	25.5	34.0	2.1

All dimensions were positively evaluated: the slightly lower values of COD and COB can be justified in view of the products that industrial enterprises offer: mainly raw materials and semi-finished products that need to be further processed by another company, thus the value of the COD or brand linked to a productive component is marginal.

Finally, the companies interviewed were asked if the COO effect influences the perception of the product characteristics and the price definition, obtaining significant confirmation also in these areas (product → 67 % important and very important; price → 59.5 % important and very important). Lesser effect is attributed to the price definition, especially for those industrial sectors that are focused on the production of semi-finished products or components. These are more affected by product price comparisons.

In the last section of the study, we investigated a number of variables relating to reputation. The first question put to the companies sought to examine the role of brand reputation in defining the internationalization strategy. 72.4 % of respondents gave a positive response (important and very important). As the brand is the first point of contact between the company and the purchaser, both industrial and private, it is essential that enterprises consciously manage this element and take advantage of the ensuing benefits.

Once we ascertained the importance of brand reputation in B2B markets, we tried to understand what variables contribute to its definition. The items into which brand reputation was decomposed are sector of belonging, the corporate mission and vision, the value of products to customers, attention to design and aesthetics. All these variables were proposed in an evaluation grid and are summarized in Table 8.

Reputation tends to be studied in marketing not only in relation to the brand but also in terms of additional dimensions such as the company in its entirety. Company reputation indicates the reputation that stakeholders and consumers in general associate with a particular company.

An enterprise may have to manage numerous brand reputations when bringing their products to the market with different brands, while company reputation is, and will always be, singular and incorporates all brands. Given the complexity of this construct, we decomposed it into a number of different variables to try to understand which are most influential (Table 9).

In the case of company reputation, we found that none of the characteristics were evaluated as very important by over 40 % of respondents. This is strongly anchored in the tangible actions of the company, not only in relation to their customers but stakeholders in general, who are also interested in the social activities of the company and its overall conduct. It is apparent, therefore, that building the company's reputation is closely linked to the general characteristics of the product and the country's reputation in the manufacturing sector analysed while less linked to intangible aspects.

Table 8 Brand reputation variables

	Not important (%)	Not very important (%)	Fairly important (%)	Important (%)	Very important (%)	ND (%)
Sector of belonging	4.3	11.7	28.7	43.6	8.5	3.2
Corporate mission and vision	2.1	20.2	27.7	34.0	12.8	3.2
Value of products to customers	0.0	3.2	10.6	35.1	45.7	5.3
Attention to design and aesthetics	2.1	17.0	22.3	24.5	30.9	3.2

Table 9 The company reputation variables

	Not important (%)	Not very important (%)	Fairly important (%)	Important (%)	Very important (%)	ND (%)
Position of the company	1.1	6.4	37.2	37.2	17.0	1.1
Tradition of the company	0.0	6.4	26.6	35.1	30.9	1.1
Industry of belonging	0.0	16.0	31.9	35.1	14.9	2.1
Previous partnerships	10.6	37.2	28.7	16.0	5.3	2.1
Importance of the company in the territory	4.3	24.5	28.7	29.8	12.8	–
Corporate mission and vision	2.1	22.3	27.7	26.6	20.2	1.1
Innovation and scientific research	4.3	3.2	17.0	38.3	37.2	–

Table 10 Country, brand and company reputation evaluation

	Not important (%)	Not very important (%)	Fairly important (%)	Important (%)	Very important (%)	ND (%)
Country reputation	0.0	12.8	22.3	44.7	16.0	4.3
Brand reputation	0.0	6.4	18.1	41.5	28.7	5.3
Company reputation	0.0	3.2	12.8	30.9	48.9	4.3

In addition to company and brand reputation, there is a third dimension of reputation, namely, the country in which the company has its headquarters, or country reputation. The three proposed concepts operate at very different levels. We therefore sought to understand their scope within industrial markets and asked firms to express their evaluations on country, brand and company reputation, obtaining the following results (Table 10).

According to the interviewees, company reputation and brand reputation have greater value in the definition of international strategies of firms in industrial markets (cumulative values for important and very important above 70 % in both cases). Company size, particularly its perception by stakeholders, is the most influential element in B2B markets, by far higher than country reputation.

Research Questions and Empirical Evidences

Q1. Is the COO effect also a significant phenomenon in industrial markets (B2B)?
The findings lead us to answer this question affirmatively. Interestingly, no significant differences are attributable to sector of belonging or company size measured in terms of number of employees and turnover.

Q2. How important is the COO effect and which aspects are most relevant to its evaluation?
The available empirical values are unable to provide a clear answer to the question inasmuch as the opinions expressed by respondents in the questionnaire would seem to be equally distributed in intensity in different industrial sectors. Consequently, no evidence emerges supporting the existence of any significant level of association between the two aspects considered and, moreover, for the same reasons, between the COO effect and firm size measured in the dual sense of number of employees and turnover.[3]

With regard to the aspects that most influence the assessment of COO, the companies surveyed indicated industry tradition as the most important element, followed by similar evaluations for economic and cultural factors and country system. Decidedly not very influential is the political aspect. Also in this case, there are no differences in the evaluation associated with the sector of belonging or company size.

Q3. How much importance is given to the country of manufacture (COM), country of design (COD) and country of brand (COB) effect?
The dimensions of the construct were positively evaluated: COM was considered important and very important by the majority of respondents (74.5 %); 90 % significance was found in terms of the sector of belonging. In particular, COM is very important for the mechanical, electronic, textile, clothing and furniture sectors.

---

[3] The degree of association was evaluated by calculating the Pearson K^2 index, the Cramer's V and Phi normalized index values. The values obtained were subjected to appropriate tests to identify their actual significance.

The relatively slightly lower values of COD and COB can be justified in view of the products that many industrial companies offer: mainly raw materials and semi-finished products that need to be further processed by another company. Therefore, the value of the COD or brand associated with a production component can be unimportant or marginal.

Q4. Which elements most influence COO and how does it affect perceptions of the company's product and price?

To respond to these questions, the values of the variables in the questionnaire were used to classify the companies into homogeneous groups using a clustering procedure.[4] Two different cluster analyses were conducted in relation to question Q4. In the first (intended to respond to the first part: *Which elements most influence COO?*), we sought the most appropriate subdivision of the statistical units, assessing the following information: sector of belonging, number of employees, turnover, level of importance in the evaluation of the image of the country's cultural, political and economic aspects, industry tradition and country system, level of importance in the evaluation of country image in terms of competitiveness, innovation, design, creativity, country industry reputation, workmanship, quality of services.

In the second (intended to respond to: *How much is COO affected by perceptions of the company products and price?*), homogeneous groups were obtained based on the values assumed by the industrial sector, number of employees, turnover, evaluation of importance of COO in the connotation of the product characteristics, evaluation of the importance of COO in the price definition.

The first clustering (Table 11) yielded two groups.

The common characteristics of the two groups are:

- Fairly important: the political factor
- Important: competitiveness, innovation, reputation of the country sector, manufacture and pre-/post-sales services
- Very important: product quality, an attribute that in both groups has the greatest mean value (4.69 for cluster 1 and 4.47 for cluster 2) with respect to all the characteristics assessed.

---

[4] A preliminary analysis was conducted aimed at highlighting the eventual presence of outliers that could adversely affect the construction of groups by the software used (SPSS). The negative outcome of this analysis, suitably tested, allowed using all available information at the same time without excluding company cases that, on the contrary, would have suggested associating specific clusters to those obtained through processing the resulting subset data.

The clustering produced substantially overlapping results, both in the use of a k-means-type algorithm, which subdivides the statistical units (in our case companies) into disjoint subsets such that each cluster is associated with a centroid and each firm is assigned to the cluster whose centroid is nearest, and to one hierarchical type, which instead organizes the units on a tree diagram (dendrogram) constructed on the basis of a matrix of distances between the objects according to a chosen metric (in our case the Euclidean distance). The tests conducted on the complete matrix of information enabled verifying that all the variables included as input to the clustering were significant within the aggregation process.

Table 11 First clustering: *Which elements most influence COO?*

	Traditional	New entries
No. of companies	35	59
Size	Small	Medium to large
Turnover	Up to €10 million	€10–50 million
Industries	Textiles, clothing, furniture	Mechanical, electronic, chemical, rubber and plastic
Cultural aspect	Important	Fairly important
Economic aspect	Important	Fairly important
Country system	Important	Fairly important
Industry tradition	Very important	Important
Design	Very important	Important
Creativeness	Very important	Important

Table 12 First clustering: *How much is COO affected by perceptions of the company products and price?*

	Traditional	New entries	Commodity
No. of companies	34	41	19
Size	Small	Medium to large	Medium
Turnover	Up to €10 million	€10–50 million	€10–30 million
Industries	Textiles	Electronic	Chemical, rubber and plastic
Impact of COO on product characteristics	Very important	Important	Not very important

The second clustering (Table 12) yielded three groups.

The common characteristic of the three groups is the significance of the COO effect in the pricing of products. This means that generally for all industrial sectors, the Italian origin of products only partly justifies higher price.

Q5. How important is the role of brand reputation, company reputation and country reputation in B2B markets and what factors influence these?

In relation this question, three different cluster analyses were conducted to evaluate the three different meanings of brand, company and country reputation. In practice, the evidence on the latter aspect was exclusively obtained through a comparison since the questionnaire provided a single specific question. As the other constructs are also more complex in B2B, we simultaneously assessed the information contained in several questions.

In more detail, in the first clustering (to evaluate the role of brand reputation and the elements that affect it), we sought the most appropriate subdivision of the statistical units by analysing the following information: sector, number of employees, turnover, years of international operations, number of countries served, the importance of brand reputation in the internationalization of the company and in the choice of business partners, factors influencing brand reputation in the industrial sector (sector, mission and vision, the value of the product to the customer, design).

In the second clustering (which analyses the role of company reputation and the elements that affect it), we sought the most appropriate subdivision of the statistical units by evaluating the following information: sector, number of employees, turnover, years of international business, number of countries served, elements that affect brand reputation (corporate positioning, company tradition, sector, previous partnerships, the importance of the enterprise in the region, mission and vision, innovation).

In the third clustering (where the clusters were defined through a joint evaluation of all aspects of reputation), groups were obtained by evaluating the following information: sector, number of employees, turnover, years of international business, number of countries served, the level of importance of country, brand and company reputation.

The first clustering yielded three groups (Table 13).

The common characteristics of all three groups are that sector of belonging, company mission, vision and design are fairly important in influencing the industrial sector brand reputation. In addition, within the three groups, the value of the product to the customer is an important attribute for all.

The second clustering (Table 14) yielded three groups.

The common characteristic of all groups is that previous partnerships are unimportant in influencing industrial sector company reputation. Fairly important for members of all groups are the positioning of the company, the sector of belonging, the importance of the company in the region, the mission and vision.

The third clustering (Table 15) also yielded three groups.

The common characteristics of the three groups are internationalization activity of more than 20 years and attributing average importance to country reputation.

Table 13 First clustering *to evaluate the role of brand reputation and the elements that affect it*

	Traditional	New entries	Commodity
No. of companies	7	67	20
Size	Small and micro	ND	ND
Industries	Textiles, clothing, furniture	Mechanics, electronic, textiles, clothing	Chemical, rubber and plastic, metallurgy
International operations	<15 years	>20 years	>20 years
No. of countries served	30 %	50 %	30 %
Brand reputation	At least fairly important	At least fairly important	At least fairly important

Table 14 Second clustering *which analyses the role of company reputation and the elements that affect it*

	Traditional	New entries	Commodity
No. of companies	34	41	19
Size	Small and medium	Medium and large	Small and medium
Turnover	€10–30 million	€30–50 million	Up to €10 million
Industries	Textiles, clothing, furniture	Mechanics, electronic	Chemical, rubber and plastic
No. of countries served	30 %	50 %	ND
Brand reputation	Fairly important	Important	Fairly important
Company reputation	Very important	Very important	Important

Table 15 Third clustering: a joint evaluation of all aspects of reputation

	Traditional	New entry	Commodity
No. of companies	34	41	19
Size	Small	Medium and large	Medium
Turnover	Up to €10 million	€30–50 million	€10–30 million
Industries	Textiles, clothing, furniture	Mechanics, electronic	Chemical, rubber and plastic
No. of countries served	30 %	50 %	–
Influence of the tradition of the company on company reputation	Fairly important	Important	Fairly important
Influence of innovation on company reputation	Very important	Very important	Important
Influence of scientific research on company reputation	Very important	–	–

Conclusions and Management Implications

Although most international marketing contributions have focused on the analysis of the COO effect in the B2C sector, in examining the overall results of the survey conducted we note that this also has a significant effect in B2B markets (Q1). Nevertheless, it is important to emphasize that the COO effect assumes different significance depending on the industrial sector to which reference is made. Indeed, the sectors that aboard are more associated with the 'Made in Italy' concept benefit to a greater extent from the COO effect (Cedrola and Battaglia 2012a).

The evaluation of country image is largely influenced by all aspects highlighted in the literature on the theme and investigated in this work: industry tradition in the first place and, subsequently, the economic, cultural and economic system. In addition to these elements, an important role is also played by the competitiveness of enterprises, innovation, design, creativity, the quality of products from a given country and the industrial sector country reputation (Q2). On average, the product characteristics are considered of higher importance; therefore, in defining the country image, the industry's reputation and the quality of the products that are manufactured in the country weigh heavily. These results are also confirmed by the cluster analyses conducted to answer Q4. In view of the non-recent international-ization of the companies surveyed, we can deduce—and confirm the results of other authors who have written on the subject—that associating preferences and purchasing behaviour to the quality of products is a result of the acquired expertise of customers (Cedrola and Battaglia 2012a). It is interesting to verify this relation-ship for industrial sectors, as Schaefer (1997) and Han (1989) did for B2C sectors. In analysing COO, it is important to take into account the various dimensions that compose it. The results show that all dimensions were positively assessed, in par-ticular COM. The slightly lower values of COD and COB can be justified in view of the product that industrial firms offer.

The companies surveyed were also asked whether the COO effect could influence the perception of product characteristics and price definition, also confirming the importance in these two areas (product → 67% important and very important; price → 59.5% important and very important). A lesser effect is attributed to price definition, especially for those industrial sectors that are focused on the production of semi-finished products or components where instead a greater effect is attributed to comparisons associated to product price.

With regard to the role played by brand, company and country reputation, the analysis shows that company reputation and brand reputation have a higher value in defining international strategies. The company's COO and its reputation is in third place in the evaluation, thus, although it is a factor that companies take into account, it is not the main variable in the decision-making process.

Limitations and Future Research

The research of which these results are presented is still in progress. Thus, the first limitation is still small number of respondent firms. Moreover, some industrial sec-tors and the geographic distribution of respondents are not representative.

It would also be desirable to collect details on the internationalization experiences of enterprises, as well as information on any differences found in operating in differ-ent geographic areas. This information could be effectively collected with personal interviews and, as such, a second phase of qualitative research is being planned. Indeed, some pilot interviews with Italian companies operating in the Chinese market have already been carried out, directly involving expatriate managers in the cities of Beijing and Tianjin.

Another limitation is the composition of the group under investigation, which includes only industrial companies and not their B2B customers (one-sided research). Future research will therefore involve the managers and procurement departments of the companies surveyed to enable comparing their evaluations.

References

Bradley, F. (2001). Country-company interaction effects and supplier preferences among industrial buyers. *Industrial Marketing Management, 30*, 511–524.

Bursi, T., Grappi, S., & Martinelli, E. (2012). *Effetto country of origin. Un'analisi comparata a livello internazionale sul comportamento d'acquisto.* Bologna: Il Mulino.

Cedrola, E., & Battaglia, L. (2012a). Italian country image: The impact on business models and relations in Chinese business-to-business markets. In G. Bertoli & R. Resciniti (Eds.), *International marketing and the country of origin effect. The global impact of 'Made in Italy'* (pp. 81–107). Northampton, MA: Elgar.

Cedrola, E., & Battaglia, L. (2012b). *Storia economia, cultura, modelli di business e di marketing per operare con successo in Cina: La via verso la Terra di Mezzo.* Padua: Cedam.

Cedrola, E., & Battaglia, L. (2013). Country-of-origin effect and firm reputation influence in business-to-business markets with high cultural distance. *Journal of Global Academy of Marketing Science, 24*, 394–408.

Chasin, J. B., & Jaffe, E. D. (1987). Industrial buyer attitudes towards goods made in Eastern Europe. *European Management Journal, 5*(3), 180–189.

Fiocca, R., Snehota, I., & Tunisini, A. (2008). *Marketing business-to-business.* Milan: McGraw-Hill.

Guerini, C., & Uslenghi, A. (2006). *Valore del Made in, identità di marca e comunicazione di marketing nelle imprese distrettuali italiane.* Liuc Papers 190: Serie Economia Aziendale.

Han, C. M. (1989, May). Country image: Halo or summary construct? *Journal of Marketing Research, 26*, 222–229.

Mainolfi, G. (2010). *Il modello della country reputation: Evidenze empiriche e implicazioni strategiche per le imprese del Made in Italy nel mercato cinese.* Tourin: Giappichelli.

Nebenzahl, I. D., Jaffé, E. D., & Usunier, J. C. (2003). Personifying country-of-origin research. *Management International Review, 43*(4), 383–406.

Schaefer, A. (1997). Consumer knowledge and country of origin effects. *European Journal of Marketing, 31*(1), 56–72.

Verlegh, P. W. J., & Steenkamp, J. B. E. M. (1999). A review and meta-analysis of country of origin research. *Journal of Economic Psychology, 20*(5), 521–546.

White, P. D. (1979). Attitudes of U.S. purchasing managers toward industrial products manufactured in selected Western European nations. *Journal of International Business Studies, 10*(1), 81–90.

White, P. D., & Cundiff, E. W. (1978). Assessing the quality of industrial products. *Journal of Marketing, 42*, 80–85.

Marketing Capabilities and the "Salmon Run" Toward Adaptation

Yoel Asseraf and Aviv Shoham

Abstract Scholars agree that the longstanding standardization–adaptation debate, which is around for more than 40 years, is not solved yet. More than that, a recent systematic review by Schmid and Kotulla (2011) found that only four papers out of 330 aimed to theoretically explain why firms actually *chose* to standardize or adapt their marketing across nations in *a certain way*. Hence, the research on standardization/adaptation is characterized by nonsignificant, contradictory, and even confusing. Against this background, the authors reveal a new potential driver for the decision to adapt, namely, international marketing capabilities. In general, the authors propose that different degrees of marketing capabilities impact the strategic decision regarding whether to adapt or standardize. More specifically, the detailed knowledge acquired for a new territory (via the marketing capabilities) is posit to push toward over-adaptation of the marketing mix elements, which accounts for differences between home and host countries. This notion is in the spirit of Homburg et al. (2011) findings that there is an optimum level with regard to customer-oriented behaviors… "Thus, there are times when the customer should not be king" (p. 68). Recently, Deresiewicz (2014) noted that "The force that drives the salmon run is fear" (p. 21). The authors argue that similar phenomenon occurs in the export-marketing arena when firms are afraid to be too different from their international competitors or international customer expectations and adopt an over-adaptation strategy.

In sum, the core belief of this research is that a tradeoff approach, which seeks an *either/or* decision regarding standardization or adaptation, is not appropriate and firms should consider developing *both/and* approach (adapting some elements and standardize other elements), and avoid the "salmons run" toward the adaptation

Y. Asseraf (✉)
Emek Hefer, Ruppin Academic Center, Israel
e-mail: yoela@ruppin.ac.il

A. Shoham
University of Haifa, Haifa, Israel
e-mail: ashoham@univ.haifa.ac.il

© Academy of Marketing Science 2016
L. Petruzzellis, R.S. Winer (eds.), *Rediscovering the Essentiality of Marketing*,
Developments in Marketing Science: Proceedings of the Academy of Marketing
Science, DOI 10.1007/978-3-319-29877-1_98

491

direction that might lead to inferior performance. This research contributes to the adaptation/standardization stream of research by showing that firms' marketing capabilities may serve as driver for adaptation that ultimately affect the international marketing strategy and firm's international performance.

References available upon request.

Is Preference for Global Brands in Emerging Markets Determined by "True" Globalness or "Mere" Foreignness?

Fernando Fastoso and Nina Reynolds

Abstract The complementary literatures on perceived brand globalness and brand origin posit that consumers in emerging markets prefer nonlocal over local brands because they perceive such brands as being global and foreign, respectively. This study bridges these two literatures by disentangling the effects that perceptions of brand globalness and foreignness have on brand preference with consumers in emerging markets, i.e., consumers for whom most global brands are also foreign. Specifically, we present two alternative models of how perceived brand globalness and perceived brand foreignness interact to impact purchase likelihood. In model 1, perceived brand foreignness mediates the impact of perceived brand globalness on purchase likelihood. In model 2, perceived brand globalness and perceived brand foreignness impact purchase likelihood independently but through shared mediators. We use categorization theory to justify the expectation that consumers in emerging markets will prefer global brands because of their foreignness rather than their globalness.

F. Fastoso (✉)
University of York, York, United Kingdom
e-mail: fernando.fastoso@york.ac.uk

N. Reynolds
University of Wollongong, Wollongong, NSW, Australia
e-mail: ninar@uow.edu.au

© Academy of Marketing Science 2016
L. Petruzzellis, R.S. Winer (eds.), *Rediscovering the Essentiality of Marketing*,
Developments in Marketing Science: Proceedings of the Academy of Marketing
Science, DOI 10.1007/978-3-319-29877-1_99

493

A Cross-Cultural Analysis of Direct vs. Indirect Comparative Advertising: The Role of Consumer Motivation and Perceived Manipulative Intent

Dan Petrovici, Christian Dianoux, John Ford, Jean-Luc Herrmann, and Jeryl Whitelock

Abstract The majority of studies of the effectiveness of comparative advertising (CA) have been primarily focused on America and Asia than on European countries. The transferability of comparative advertising practices across markets is still largely unexplored notwithstanding that the effects of CA may vary according to the degree of novelty of comparative advertisements in the country (Nye et al. 2008). This observation is particularly interesting in Europe where countries such as the United Kingdom and Sweden have used CA for a longer period than France (Diannoux and Herrmann 2000). This study examines for the first time the role of opportunity, ability, and motivation to process the message on perceived manipulative intent and consumer evaluations of advertising by proposing a model of effectiveness of direct and indirect comparative advertising.

Analyses of responses from participants in France, the United Kingdom, and the United States indicate that direct comparative attacks are not equally embraced by consumers across countries. Furthermore, they tend to generate greater suspicion regarding the manipulative intent than indirect formats. The study provides for the first time evidence that perceived manipulative intent varies according to CA format and evidence of moderating effects in the relationship between motivation to

D. Petrovici (✉)
University of Kent, Kent, United Kingdom
e-mail: d.a.petrovici@kent.ac.uk

C. Dianoux • J.-L. Herrmann
Academy Nancy-Metz, Nancy, France
e-mail: christian.dianoux@univ-lorraine.fr; jean-luc.herrmann@univ-lorraine.fr

J. Ford
Old Dominion University, Norfolk, VA, USA
e-mail: jbford@odu.edu

J. Whitelock
University of Bradford, Bradford, United Kingdom
e-mail: J.Whitelock@bradford.ac.uk

© Academy of Marketing Science 2016
L. Petruzzellis, R.S. Winer (eds.), *Rediscovering the Essentiality of Marketing*,
Developments in Marketing Science: Proceedings of the Academy of Marketing
Science, DOI 10.1007/978-3-319-29877-1_100

process the message and perceived manipulative intent of Direct Comparative Advertising (DCA). The motivation to process the message reduces perceived manipulative intent only in countries with low familiarity with DCA. The ability to process the message moderates the relationship between processing motivation and perceived manipulative intent.

References available upon request.

Ethnic Minority Consumers as Brand Ambassadors: Culture, Adaptation, and Global Brand Advocacy of Chinese Migrants in Canada and France

Boris Bartikowski and Mark Cleveland

Abstract Within most developed economies, population growth comes primarily through immigration from emerging economies, rather than through natural increase. The market potential of consumers emigrating from emerging markets is obviously enormous. What is less obvious is whether well-known (primarily Western) brands will continue to reap the lion's share of their respective product-markets, given the relative ease of technology transfer, the increasingly sophisticated marketing know-how of emerging market competitors, and the proclivity for many immigrant consumers to champion their home-grown brands over host-country or foreign alternatives, a phenomenon that may be on the rise as groups reassert their identities in the face of rampant globalization. Whereas ethnic minorities have attracted much research attention, studies on how they may disseminate global brands is scarce. Immigrant consumers may fulfill a vital role as brand ambassadors, by encouraging a two-way interchange of information about brands from their home and host countries. This dynamic interchange has not yet been studied before. Brands play an important role in human life where they help consumers to express themselves or manifest their identity and place within social networks. Matters of identity may be especially salient for those consumers that migrate across international borders, as they are liable to be more conscious of their ethnic and cultural differences. This research focuses on migrant Chinese living in two countries (Canada and France), and in particular how their cultural dispositions—in terms of how Chinese ethnic identity, cosmopolitanism, and host acculturation—drive brand advocacy behaviors of Chinese home- and Canadian/French host-country brands. Global brands are defined as those brands within a given product category that are recognized as global, but also clearly associated with being from a particular nation (e.g., Apple, L'Oréal, Lenovo). We propose a research model regarding the

B. Bartikowski (✉)
Kedge Business School, Marseille, France
e-mail: boris.bartikowski@kedgebs.com

M. Cleveland
University of Western Ontario, London, ON, Canada
e-mail: mclevela@uwo.ca

© Academy of Marketing Science 2016
L. Petruzzellis, R.S. Winer (eds.), *Rediscovering the Essentiality of Marketing*,
Developments in Marketing Science: Proceedings of the Academy of Marketing
Science, DOI 10.1007/978-3-319-29877-1_101

497

direct and indirect roles played by cultural dispositions in promoting and adopting home and host-country brands, respectively. We first validate the presupposition that ethnic identity directly drives the advocacy of global brands that originate from the home-country. Scrutinizing the connection between cosmopolitanism and brand advocacy towards host-country brands, we demonstrate that this linkage is mediated by the degree of acculturation to the host culture. These relationships are contrasted for the two host countries, which differ in terms of their immigration policies on the one hand and on the relative density of fellow ethnic-group members on the other. We also considered that the duration of immigrants' stay in the host country may shape the aforementioned relationships. Hypotheses were tested with data drawn from short-term Chinese sojourners living in France/Canada, as well as from Chinese that are more permanently settled. The results reveal asymmetries in the functioning of the antecedents of brand advocacy behavior between short-term sojourners and long-term immigrants. Lastly, we explored category differences for Chinese and Canadian/French global brands from eight product categories.

The Inconsistency of Ethnocentric Bias in the Dual-Attitude Model

Ting-hsiang Tseng, George Balabanis, and T. Matthew Liu

Introduction

Empirical evidence shows that ethnocentric bias varies in its intensity from country to country (Cleveland et al. 2009) and also from product to product category (Balabanis and Diamantopoulos 2004; Cleveland et al. 2009; Verlegh 2007).

Additionally, ethnocentric attitude varies according to the way it is measured, for example, when considered explicitly or implicitly (Maison et al. 2004a).

Such variations pose problems to the generalizability of theories on consumer ethnocentric bias. Theoretically, extant research has done little beyond recognizing the existence of such variations (Roth and Romeo 1992; Manrai et al. 1998; Story 2005). To our knowledge, no study to date offers a systematic theory about the variations of ethnocentric bias across product categories assessed with available explicit or implicit measures. As such, a more refined approach is required. This study attempts to fill this gap by looking for similarity patterns across product categories that may trigger similar/inconsistent levels of ethnocentric bias between explicit and implicit measures.

T.-h. Tseng (✉)
Feng Chia University, Taichung, Taiwan
e-mail: tsength@mail.fcu.edu.tw

G. Balabanis
City University London, London, United Kingdom
e-mail: G.Balabanis@city.ac.uk

T.M. Liu
University of Macau, Macao, China
e-mail: matthewl@umac.mo

© Academy of Marketing Science 2016
L. Petruzzellis, R.S. Winer (eds.), *Rediscovering the Essentiality of Marketing*,
Developments in Marketing Science: Proceedings of the Academy of Marketing
Science, DOI 10.1007/978-3-319-29877-1_102

Background

Consumer ethnocentrism as a personality trait can predict ethnocentric bias (i.e. favourable attitudes towards domestic products and unfavourable attitudes towards foreign products). Shimp and Sharma (1987) suggest a strong positive (negative) relationship between consumer ethnocentrism and quality evaluations and buying intentions for domestic (foreign) products. Herche (1992) demonstrated similar findings in Canada that matched the findings of Supphellen and Rittenburg's (2001).

Additionally, past research has found that attitudes towards social ingroups over outgroups are more positive on explicit measures than they are on implicit measures (Cunningham et al. 2004a). This phenomenon has been explained by the dual-attitude model (Wilson et al. 2000) and the corresponding mental processes highlighted in the preceding section.

The dual-attitude model suggests the simultaneous coexistence of two attitudes towards an object or a person: one that is automatically activated (implicit) and another that is activated after conscious deliberation (explicit). Cunningham et al. (2004a) research on implicit ethnocentric attitudes in a series of possible outgroups (foreign, religious, ethnic, race and sexual orientation groups) confirmed the validity of the dual-attitude (or the dual process) model explanation. They suggested that implicit and explicit ethnocentric attitudes, while distinct, are correlated to each other. At an absolute attitude value level, Cunningham et al. (2004a) found that the inconsistency between explicit and implicit attitudes is more evident in the attitudes towards outgroups.

The dual-attitude (or dual process) model together with the concept of typicality may be able to explain ethnocentric attitude inconsistencies. Research in social psychology shows that stereotypical expectations about social groups or categories influence the views of single members of those groups or categories. In this process, typicality was found to be an important moderator. In general, Fiske and Neuberg (1990) and Fiske et al. (1999) found that the categorization of individuals takes priority in the evaluation process over their evaluation on an attribute-by-attribute basis.

According to them, once a perceiver categorizes a target, the category information prevails on their judgments and perceivers' attention is focused on the category stereotypical content. This process is more pronounced in typical members of a group or a category. When a member of a group or category is judged as typical of the category, then the attitudes towards the typical member will be more consistent to that of the category. For a member judged as atypical, a re-categorization to a different category takes place together with an attribute-by-attribute evaluation. This applies to the consumer milieu, where products are members of the country category and where we can make a similar argument.

The above arguments and consumer perceptions of products as typical or atypical of a country may be able to explain the observed inconsistencies of ethnocentric bias across product categories (Balabanis and Diamantopoulos 2004; Evanschitzky et al. 2008) and between explicit and implicit attitudes (Maison et al. 2004a). Typicality can be a key moderator of attitudes.

Methodology

The study collected data through a mall intercept survey method that is the most effective survey method in Taiwan. One hundred and ninety-eight consumers actually participated and provided usable responses. After a simple instruction about this study, participants had to fill out questionnaires measuring their explicit attitudes towards the specified products from the specified countries. Following the measurement of explicit attitudes was the SC-IAT on a desktop to gauge consumers' implicit attitudes towards each product. Measures of consumer ethnocentrism and demographics were at the end of the study.

To account for product category differences, the study included two products from durables (bicycles and cars) and two products from convenience perishable purchases (pineapple cakes and dorayaki). Dorayaki is a Japanese specialty red bean pancake.

The four products were assigned to two countries of origin: Taiwan and Japan. Japan was chosen because the country is well known to Taiwanese consumers and made experimentation easier.

The study measured consumer ethnocentrism (CE) with a five-item version of the CETSCALE (Steenkamp et al. 1999) on a seven-point scale, from 'not agree at all' to 'completely agree'.

Results and Discussion

The study uses repeated measures ANOVA to analyse the data. The within subjects factors and their levels were as follows: type of attitude (explicit vs. implicit); domesticity (domestic vs. foreign product); product category (durable vs. non-durable product) and typicality (typical vs. atypical product). Consumer ethnocentrism (CETSCALE) was used as a covariate. Demographics were found to not have a significant effect on the relationship and were omitted from the analysis. As there are only two levels for each of the within-subject factors, the sphericity and compound symmetry assumptions do not apply.

As explicit and implicit attitudes are measured on different metrics to facilitate comparison, a standard approach used by studies that compare implicit and explicit attitudes (Rydell and McConnell 2006; McConnell et al. 2008) was employed here. Attitude scores were standardized. As implicit attitude scores have been viewed as relative rather than absolute measures of attitudes (Greenwald et al. 1998; Nosek et al. 2005), standardization is in line with their relativistic nature. Standardization of both implicit and explicit attitude measures is necessary in order to treat the type of attitude (implicit vs. explicit) as a within-subjects factor, and assess differences in implicit and explicit attitudes. All the main effects and lower order interaction effects (i.e. two-way effects) need to be included in the model.

The findings confirm the inconsistency of ethnocentric bias in the type of attitudes, but only for typical products. Consumer ethnocentrism does not seem to reduce the inconsistency. Ethnocentric consumers explicitly show a clear favourability for (prejudice against) typical domestic (foreign) products, but such an effect is not evident in implicit attitudes. This may be explained by consumers' frequency of exposure to typical products which is higher than to atypical product and the generation of associations that trigger category processing (Barsalou 1985). The repeated encounters of typical products reinforce stereotypical associations at an early age and encourage automatic activation of attitudes (i.e. implicit attitudes) when a relevant cue is presented (Wilson et al. 2000).

For atypical products, there is no inconsistency of ethnocentric bias between explicit and implicit attitudes. An explanation is that consumers tend to generate weaker associations for atypical products than a typical one. In the absence of strong associations in atypical products, social norms of ethnocentrism will have a proportionately stronger influence on their evaluations. Explicit and implicit attitudes are consistent for both ethnocentric and non-ethnocentric consumers for both domestic and foreign atypical products.

References available upon request.

A Knowledge Perspective on the Uppsala and Born Global Internationalization Models

Daniel Gulanowski, Llynne Plante, and Nicolas Papadopoulos

Abstract Firms face difficult strategic dilemmas when expanding internationally to compete in today's global economy. Whether preparing to "go international" for the first time or for a subsequent expansion, a firm needs to make the international market selection (IMS) and mode of entry or expansion (MOE) decisions, determine the amount and type of resources and knowledge needed for expansion, and develop strategies to address changes in their environment. This study critically reviews and compares the seminal literature on two competing approaches to internationalization, the Uppsala and Born Global models. The study aims to contribute to our understanding of the internationalization process by integrating the theory of knowledge and learning of the firm so as to bridge the debate on rapid versus staged models of expansion.

Studies for the review were identified through a multistage iterative process, which began by identifying relevant articles between the 1970s and today through standard online databases; continued with a review of those articles' references to identify further sources that might have been missed in the previous step; considered citations to the main sources; and concluded by generating a list of the most influential sources which then formed the basis for the review.

A key finding is that proponents of the Born Global approach have mostly used Johanson and Vehlne's 1977 and 1990 models as a basis of comparison, while largely ignoring the authors' 2003 and 2006 revisions to their earlier models. More broadly, despite continued claims that born globals internationalize differently than the Uppsala model posits (Chetty and Campbell-Hunt 2004; Knight and Gavusgil 2004; Oviatt and McDougall 1994; Rennie 1993), the evidence in the literature continues to be inconclusive. In fact, many studies identify different types of born-global new international ventures following a range of incremental to rapid paths to internationalization (e.g., Barkema and Drogendijk 2007; Melén and Nordman 2009; Nordman and Melén 2008). The research reviewed provides support for continued relevance of the Uppsala model as many born globals, while taking their first steps abroad more quickly, continue to internationalize incrementally. Importantly,

D. Gulanowski (✉) • L. Plante • N. Papadopoulos
Carleton University, Ottawa, ON, Canada
e-mail: DanielGulanowski@cmail.carleton.ca; LlynnePlante@cmail.carleton.ca;
NicolasPapadopoulos@cmail.carleton.ca

© Academy of Marketing Science 2016
L. Petruzzellis, R.S. Winer (eds.), *Rediscovering the Essentiality of Marketing*,
Developments in Marketing Science: Proceedings of the Academy of Marketing
Science, DOI 10.1007/978-3-319-29877-1_103

503

both the Uppsala and Born Global theories, albeit separately from each other, increasingly emphasize the role of knowledge and learning in the internationalization process (e.g., Casillas et al. 2009; Johanson and Vahlne 2009, 2013).

Our review suggests that the Uppsala model is still well positioned to explain internationalization and that it may be more fruitful to view the two models as complementary instead of mutually exclusive. Future research should focus on further examination and integration of new influential constructs (e.g., trust, dynamic capabilities, learning, absorptive capacity). The study d etermines that it is also critical to integrate knowledge and learning theories and to investigate more efficient ways to manage tacit knowledge and other knowledge resources.

References available upon request.

Fifty Years of Empirical Research on Country-of-Origin Effects on Consumer Behavior: A Meta-Analysis

Saeed Samiee, Leonidas C. Leonidou, Bilge Aykol, Barbara Stöttinger, and Paul Christodoulides

Introduction

Country-of-origin (COO) effects, defined as the influence of foreignness of products/services on consumer choice behavior (Samiee 2011), has been one of the most frequently investigated topics in the field of international marketing. Although a significant amount of scholarly work has been published on the subject over the last five decades, there is little consensus over its nature and conceptualization, internal validity, importance to consumers, and relevance to managers, given the globalization of markets, uncertainties regarding the accuracy of consumers' knowledge of the true COO, and different regulations among countries regarding the disclosure of COO information (e.g., Harzing and Josiassen 2008; Magnusson et al. 2011; Roth and Diamantopoulos 2009; Samiee 2010, 2011; Samiee and Leonidou 2011; Samiee

S. Samiee (✉)
University of Tulsa, Tulsa, OK, USA
e-mail: saeed-samiee@utulsa.edu

L.C. Leonidou
University of Cyprus, Nicosia, Cyprus
e-mail: leonidas@ucy.ac.cy

B. Aykol
Dokuz Eylül University, Alsancak/İzmir, Turkey
e-mail: bilge.aykol@deu.edu.tr

B. Stöttinger
Vienna University of Economics and Business, Wien, Austria
e-mail: barbara.stoettinger@wu.ac.at

P. Christodoulides
Cyprus University of Technology, Limassol, Cyprus
e-mail: paul.christodoulides@cut.ac.cy

© Academy of Marketing Science 2016
L. Petruzzellis, R.S. Winer (eds.), *Rediscovering the Essentiality of Marketing*,
Developments in Marketing Science: Proceedings of the Academy of Marketing
Science, DOI 10.1007/978-3-319-29877-1_104

505

et al. 2005; Usunier 2006). This body of research has also been criticized as being too fragmented, inconsistent, and non-programmatic to yield a clear picture on the subject (Samiee 1994).

Although there have been several seminal efforts in the past to review and/or meta-analyze the findings of the extant literature and shed light on the above-mentioned controversies (e.g., Bilkey and Nes 1982; Petersen and Jolibert 1995; Verlegh and Steenkap 1999), these are outdated, cover only parts of COO research, and mainly focus on the moderating role of methodological variables. There is a need therefore to identify, synthesize, and evaluate the role of COO effects on the consumer decision-making process. Our study aims to fill this gap with a meta-analysis of extant empirical studies on the subject since the inception of this body of research in the early 1960s. Specifically, we want to address the following research questions: (a) What are the specific antecedents and outcomes of COO evaluations by consumers? (b) What influence does the COO have on the consumer decision-making process? and (c) What is the moderating role of country base, target country, product type, and time period on consumer COO perceptions?

Background Research

The issue of COO effects first made its appearance in the early 1960s with Dichter's (1962) work, while the first empirical study on the subject was conducted by Schooler (1965), who found that the national origin of a product might have an influence on consumer evaluations. Since then, we have seen more than a thousand publications coming mainly from the international business, marketing, and consumer behavior fields (Heslop et al. 2008). This research has taken various directions. For instance, some scholars focused on the information search, evaluation of alternatives, and purchase stages of the consumer decision-making process and perceived COO as an information cue—either on its own or in conjunction with other parameters. It was expected to play a role in the development of attitudes toward and intention to purchase products made in different countries (e.g., Ahmed and d'Astous 1993; Ahmed et al. 2004; Chandrasen and Paliwoda 2009; Chao 1998; Cordell 1991; Ettenson et al. 1988). Another research stream centered on the direct and/or moderating effects of demographic (e.g., age, gender, education, income) and/or psychographic (e.g., ethnocentrism, animosity, patriotism) characteristics of consumers in the evaluation of products/brands originating from different countries, attitudes toward foreign products/brands, and intention to purchase foreign products/brands, revealing that there might be COO-sensitive segments in each society (Balabanis and Diamantopoulos 2004; Brodowsky et al. 2004; Granzin and Painter 2001; Laforet and Chen 2012; Leonidou et al. 1999). A third line of research focused on the perceptions of consumers about a specific country (e.g., level of development), as well as of the general characteristics of the products produced in this country (e.g., quality) and investigated the influence of these perceptions on the attitudinal and behavioral responses of consumers, such as product preferences, willingness to buy, and actual purchase (e.g., Demirbag et al. 2010; Diamantopoulos et al. 2011; Heslop et al. 2008; Hsieh et al. 2004). Another research direction examined the direct and moderating role of product-related factors (e.g., buyer involvement) on COO evaluations of foreign products/brands and, attitude toward foreign products/brands (e.g., Ahmed et al. 2002; d'Astous et al. 2008; Erickson et al. 1984). A fifth research stream focused on the consumer behavior (e.g., evaluation) associated with foreign advertisements and foreign stores in addition to products (e.g., Chaney and Gamble 2008; Hwak et al. 2006; Moon and Jain 2002). In another stream, a group of researchers (e.g., Ahmed and d'Astous 1996; Chao 1993; Papadopoulos and Heslop 1993) draw a distinction between COO and country of manufacture, country of assembly, and country of design. Finally, more recently, some scholars investigated the role of brand origin recognition accuracy on the consumer decision-making process, as well as the personal and stimulus-related factors influencing brand origin recognition accuracy (Balabanis and Diamantopoulos 2008; Magnusson et al. 2011; Samiee et al. 2005).

Conceptual Model and Research Hypotheses

Based on a review of the COO literature and anchoring on the theories of information processing, hierarchy of effects, and of reasoned action, we have constructed an integrative model of the antecedents and outcomes of COO effects on consumer behavior. This comprises four sets of variables, namely: (a) *consumer demographic characteristics*, which include gender, age, education, and income; (b) *consumer familiarity patterns*, which include familiarity with the foreign country, product, and brand; (c) *consumer psychographic characteristics*, which includes consumer involvement and consumer ethnocentrism; (d) *COO perceptions,* country image, and brand image; and (e) *outcome dimensions,* which comprises foreign product/ brand evaluation, attitudes toward foreign product/brand, and intention to buy a foreign product/brand.

Altogether, our integrative model comprises 14 constructs and 18 hypothesized associations. Specifically, consumer demographics and consumer familiarity have an influential role on COO consumer perceptions. Buyer involvement and consumer ethnocentrism also shape COO perceptions. The COO perception subsequently influences both country image and brand image. COO perception, country image, and brand image influence foreign product/brand evaluation (e.g., Erickson et al. 1984; Hong and Wyer 1989). Foreign product/brand evaluation influences attitudes toward foreign product/brand (e.g., Auger et al. 2010), while country image and brand image are also influential on the attitude toward product/brand. Finally, attitude toward foreign products/brands has an influence on purchasing intention (e.g., Agarwal et al. 2002).

Research Method

Our investigation covers all empirical articles published from 1965 (when the first article on the subject appeared) up to 2014. To be eligible for inclusion in our meta-analysis, the articles had: (a) to examine the COO from a final consumer's perspective, rather than that of the industrial buyer; (b) to have been published in top marketing/management and international business journals; (c) to have an empirical/quantitative nature, as opposed to conceptual, qualitative, review, or commentary approach; and (d) to provide information about the relevant statistics and sample size required for carrying out the meta-analysis.

We identified the pertinent studies by conducting an electronic search of journals, based on the aforementioned criteria by using the keywords "country-of-origin," "country image," "product origin," "COO effects," "COO evaluations," "consumer perceptions," and "brand origin." We also manually reviewed the tables of contents of relevant journals and reference sections of pertinent articles. As a result, we found 213 empirical articles during the 50-year period examined, published in 23 journals. Interestingly, the bulk of the articles were published during the last decade.

All eligible articles were content analyzed using a specially designed coding protocol, which was accompanied by a coding manual, comprising definitions of constructs and description of coding procedures. The coding process was undertaken by two coders who worked independently from each other, under the supervision of a scholar with extensive experience in the field. Prior to the beginning of the coding process, both coders underwent rigorous training and coded a number of articles under the guidance of the supervisor. With the completion of the coding process, the data entries completed by the two coders were compared and contrasted, revealing a satisfactory inter-coder reliability score (ranging from 85 to 100%). In the case of inconsistencies, these were carefully discussed between the supervisor and the coders until reaching a commonly agreed code.

Data Analysis and Findings

To analyze the data, we used Mosteller and Bush's (1954) method which combines two or more studies that test essentially the same directional hypothesis (Hedges and Olkin 1985; Rosenthal 1986). This method adds the products resulting from the multiplication of sample sizes with z-values, and then divides them by the square root of the squared sample sizes. It is perhaps the most reliable among the techniques for combining probabilities (e.g., adding logs, adding probabilities, adding t's, or adding z-values) because it permits the investigator to weigh each study by its sample size (or by its degrees of freedom). In addition, this technique has three major advantages: (a) it can be used with any number of studies; (b) it takes into account the positive or negative association between dependent and independent variables; and (c) it is routinely applicable (Rosenthal 1986).

Notably, all hypotheses were supported. Specifically, the gender, age, education, and income of consumers influence were found to strongly influence their COO perceptions, and the same was also true with regard to brand, product, and country familiarity. Significant effects on COO perceptions were also observed in the case of consumer involvement with the product and consumer ethnocentrism. COO perceptions were also instrumental on the creation of country image and brand image. COO perceptions, country image, and brand image were subsequently found to have a significant impact on the evaluation of foreign product/brands. Brand image and country image were also effective in the formation of attitudes toward foreign products/brands, while the latter significantly affected intention to buy them. With regard to country base, target country, product type, and time period, with the exception of few hypotheses, these did not exhibit any serious effect on findings of the study.

Conclusions, Implications, Contributions

Our study has attempted to offer an integrative picture of the antecedents and outcomes of COO perceptions by consumers. The meta-analysis undertaken has synthesized extant knowledge on a subject that is characterized by great fragmentation, inconsistency, and controversy. The fact that all hypothesized associations examined were accepted indicates that: (a) there are COO-sensitive groups in the society which can be identified by their personal characteristics such as age, gender, education, and income; (b) increasing consumer familiarity with the country/product/brand is conducive toward the effective formation of COO perceptions; (c) consumer involvement with the product, as well as ethnocentrism are critical in COO perceptions; and (d) COO perceptions, together with country image and brand image, are influential in the consumer information processing and decision-making process, and the ultimate intention to buy the product.

This study contributes to the marketing literature by: (a) providing a comprehensive review of the COO literature from an end-user perspective over the last five decades, which can serve as an inventory of knowledge for future research; (b) synthesizing the findings of extant literature and proposing a conceptual model which identifies the role of COO within the broad consumer decision-making context; (c) evaluating the strength, sign, and causal direction of the influences of various links between constructs of this model; and (d) detecting the gaps in the literature and suggesting directions for future research.

Our findings have important implications for three major groups: (a) *business managers*, who can better understand the mechanics of how evaluations of their products are made by foreign consumers, and adjust their international marketing strategies accordingly; (b) *public policymakers*, who can better appreciate how goods exported from their country are perceived by consumers abroad and design appropriate export promotion programs to capitalize on these perceptions; and (c) *academic researchers*, who can gain an overall view of the antecedents and outcomes of COO evaluations, and identify areas that would further enhance our knowledge on the subject.

Several avenues for future research include, among others: (a) the empirical testing of our model, preferably in various contextual factors, such as product type, reference country, and consumer profile; (b) the enrichment of the model with additional antecedents, moderators, and outcomes derived from other more mature disciplines, such as consumer psychology; (c) the expansion of the analysis to cover different aspects of COO, such as design, manufacture, and assembly; and (d) the theoretical backing of the model, with such theories as categorization theory, elaboration likelihood model, theory of planned behavior, and behavioral and cognitive learning theories.

References available upon request.

International Performance: The Role of Inertia, Stability, and Multinational Flexibility

Tsipora Ehrlich, Aviv Shoham, and Yoel Asseraf

Abstract The role of relationship marketing (RM), referring to all marketing activities directed toward establishing, developing, and maintaining successful relational exchanges, as a potential driver of firm performance has been a topic of research for scholars over several decades. Successful interorganizational relationships are critical to firm performance because most firms must combine internal organizational capabilities and resources with services provided by external organizations to compete effectively. While much is known about these relationships, less is known about the roles of international distribution channels and their influence on export performance. This point will be discussed further below.

The literature has mostly neglected to consider the roles of inertia, stability, and multinational flexibility as anteceding constructs of international relationship quality. This chapter introduces a new integrative model, which includes inertia, stability, and multinational flexibility as drivers of relationship quality and, indirectly, international performance.

Second, the extant literature has focused on relationship quality using differing combinations of behavioral components. However, it has mostly neglected other potential mediators of the relationships between inertia, stability, and multinational flexibility and performance, most notably strategy-related mediators. This chapter is focused on the role of standardizations versus adaptation of the international marketing mix as a mediator. Moreover, the relationship quality literature has evolved independently of that on strategy and research integrating these theoretical domains has not emerged. This chapter includes relationship quality and international strategic thrust in an integrative model as drivers of international performance.

The model is made of 11 constructs: inertia, stability, multinational flexibility, trust, commitment, communication, conflict, standardization/adaptation, cooperation, channel flexibility, and export/international performance. It is based on the RM approach, which has recognized the roles of behavioral aspects commonly referred

T. Ehrlich (✉) • A. Shoham
University of Haifa, Haifa, Israel
e-mail: erzipi@walla.com; ashoham@univ.haifa.ac.il

Y. Asseraf
Ruppin Academic Center, Emek Hefer, Israel
e-mail: research.yoel@gmail.com

© Academy of Marketing Science 2016
L. Petruzzellis, R.S. Winer (eds.), *Rediscovering the Essentiality of Marketing*,
Developments in Marketing Science: Proceedings of the Academy of Marketing
Science, DOI 10.1007/978-3-319-29877-1_105

511

to in the literature as relationship quality (RQ hereunder). The model includes two levels of intermediary constructs. The first includes RQ indicators namely trust, commitment, communication, and conflict as well as four components of the standardization/adaptation construct. A second level of intermediary variables consists of channel cooperation and channel flexibility. The final component of the model is export/international performance.

Insights from several theories and frameworks are combined in this model. These include commitment-trust theory, the resource-based view of the firm—RBV, and the knowledge-based view of the firm—KBV. The innovative combination of these theory and views has great explanatory potential, which allow to test the relative roles of behavioral RQ and international strategies in the same study.

In sum, currently, a framework for determining export/international performance is introduced. While the proposed framework is a self-contained contribution to new marketing theories, initial results from a quantitative study being conducted are presented.

Part XII
Luxury, Fashion and Wine Marketing

Development and Validation of a Fashion Readiness Scale: A Preliminary Report

Cheng-Chieh Hsiao and Fang-Mei Liu

Abstract Recently, fashion marketers have implemented marketing strategies like fast fashion and luxury democratization. These strategies make the global fashion market more dynamic and uncertain. In order to predict a consumer's purchase decision on fashion products, prior research has proposed a number of fashion-related concepts. However, most concepts focus only on the cognitive aspect of consumers' fashion responses, and existing scales for measuring these concepts are not multidimensional. To address these issues, this study attempts to (1) propose a concept of fashion readiness which captures a consumer's propensity to embrace new fashion and (2) develop a multidimensional scale for assessing fashion readiness. After collecting data from 262 consumers, we perform a confirmatory factor analysis to evaluate scale reliability and construct validity for the fashion readiness scale. Nomological validity for our scale is also verified. Therefore, the fashion readiness scale developed in this study is psychometrically sound, and it contains 12 items belonging to four subfactors, including fashion efficacy, fashion anxiety, fashion involvement, and fashion innovativeness. We believe that the fashion readiness scale will contribute greatly to current fashion research and practice.

C.-C. Hsiao (✉)
Shih Hsin University, Taipei, Taiwan
e-mail: cchsiao@cc.shu.edu.tw

F.-M. Liu
Institute for Information Industry, Taipei, Taiwan
e-mail: julialiu@iii.org.tw

© Academy of Marketing Science 2016
L. Petruzzellis, R.S. Winer (eds.), *Rediscovering the Essentiality of Marketing*,
Developments in Marketing Science: Proceedings of the Academy of Marketing
Science, DOI 10.1007/978-3-319-29877-1_106

Terroir in a Bottle: Segmenting Consumer Choices in Generation Y

Roberta Capitello, Lara Agnoli, Steve Charters, and Diego Begalli

Abstract This study aims to understand the *terroir* effect in influencing consumer's choice and measure the utility given by the *terroir* attributes conveyed on a wine label, verifying the heterogeneity of consumer's evaluation process. It analyzes young consumers belonging to Generation Y, from Italy, applying a Discrete Choice Experiment. An online survey was carried out by a sample of 982 respondents. Latent Class Choice Models were applied and seven latent classes were identified. Findings reveal that while terroir remains important for most of the young consumers, how it is construed and the cues which denote it vary substantially. Managerial implications emerge in terms of search for luxury and fashion cues, traditional representations of terroir and reassurance attributes, and of different price sensitivity.

Keywords Terroir • Consumer heterogeneity • Discrete choice model • Wine consumer • Generation Y

Introduction

Scholars' interest in the role of product and corporate origin is still very keen because origin is one of the most important elements characterizing business strategies and is able to influence consumer choice (Magnusson et al. 2011). The origin pervades wine marketing through different meanings. It may emerge as an indication of the country-of-origin (COO) of the product (Balestrini and Gamble 2006), or more recently of the brand origin (BO) in relation to the business (Heslop et al. 2010; Spielmann 2014). Furthermore, it can concern a specific territory, its natural and human resources, and the basket of goods and services promoted through the so-called umbrella brands such as regional brands (Easingwood et al. 2011) and

R. Capitello (✉) • L. Agnoli • D. Begalli
University of Verona, Verona, Italy
e-mail: roberta.capitello@univr.it; lara.agnoli@univr.it; diego.begalli@univr.it

S. Charters
Groupe ESC Dijon Bourgogne, Dijon, France
e-mail: steve.charters@escdijon.eu

© Academy of Marketing Science 2016   517
L. Petruzzellis, R.S. Winer (eds.), *Rediscovering the Essentiality of Marketing*,
Developments in Marketing Science: Proceedings of the Academy of Marketing
Science, DOI 10.1007/978-3-319-29877-1_107

territorial brands (Charters and Spielmann 2014). The indication of the origin can finally be related to products whose qualities stem from a specific relationship with the place of origin, certified by the institutional schemes of the designation/appellation of origin (Perrouty et al. 2006).

Concerning this latter origin meaning, both scholars and practitioners have recently rekindled their interest in the concept of *terroir* (Charters 2010). The notion of *terroir* stems from the belief that certain products (especially foodstuffs and drink—but also some other natural resources) are distinctive and irreproducible as a result of the environment in which they originate. The idea started with wine, but is now widely relevant and can include cheese, fish, *salume,* and even cigars or coffee. Nowadays, *terroir* is the focus of new insights because the potential uses in wine and food marketing are expanding rapidly. It is no longer only the specific indication of the geographical origin, the topographic reference of the production place and its specific natural and human resources, but it assumes additional dimensions of an intangible nature related to the "sense of place." It transmits messages and symbols of identity, distinctiveness, authenticity, and sustainability (Beverland 2006; Charters 2010). The use of *terroir* in the business communication process has increased through packaging and the media (Mueller et al. 2010b; Spielmann et al. 2014). The market division between genuine, handcrafted wines and *terroir* wines on the one hand, and industrial wines and heavily branded wines on the other hand has intensified (Charters 2010), with the former more able to rise to be accepted as luxury products and icons than the latter (Beverland 2004; Kim et al. 2012).

This study aims to contribute to the understanding of the *terroir* effect in influencing consumer's choices. It is intended to measure the consumer utility given by the *terroir* attributes conveyed on a wine label, which are highlighted by literature as constituting the identity of the product itself (Spielmann and Charters 2013; Spielmann and Gélinas-Chebat 2012). The innovative contribution of the study lies in verifying the heterogeneity of the evaluation process of the *terroir* attributes by consumers and the resulting ability of these attributes to segment the market.

This study analyzes young consumers belonging to Generation Y, from Italy. This group is gradually entering the wine market, expressing their own cohort dynamics; furthermore, the *terroir* concept is evolving both for producers and marketers, and young consumers from a traditional producing and consuming country can give a useful insight into how it is developing.

Background

According to Hall and Mitchell (2008), wine is a complex product because of its many features (e.g., grape variety, wine making style, vintage, brand or wine region) and different meanings and symbols; consequently the consumer faces a complex decision-making process. Therefore, wine marketing requires businesses to make some adjustments to the traditional tools applied in other industries. Lockshin and

Hall (2003) stated that "automobiles are one of the few product categories that rival the complexity of the wine category, but cars are not purchased so frequently." Consumers assess many product attributes when choosing a wine, which concern its intrinsic and sensory properties, and affect the personal and social sphere of individuals at the same time.

The role of the wine cues on consumer choice has been extensively analyzed by scholars. Since the late 1990s, this topic has covered an increasing number of studies as the world of wine has faced a commercial evolution and new consumer countries have emerged (Lockshin and Corsi 2012; Lockshin and Hall 2003). The role of the many *terroir* components has not been given as much attention. They were mainly considered as an indication of origin (COO or wine region, Protected Designation/Indication of Origin, or Appellation of Origin), and few studies have taken other *terroir* components into account (e.g., local grape production or soil characteristics); for example studying the label design, the information role of the back label, or the concept of regionality (Atkin and Johnson 2010; Easingwood et al. 2011; Mueller et al. 2010b). In these cases, the *terroir* components were indirectly investigated because they did not constitute the main objective of the study, which was instead aiming to estimate the relevance of the different product attributes in providing consumers with utility. Therefore, the extrinsic components recently highlighted by literature were not considered in the experiments.

In recent times, however, scholars focused both on the viticultural/oenological and marketing spheres and have expanded the *terroir* concept (Vaudour 2002). Charters (2010) outlined the role of marketing to try to define *terroir* in a new and less ambiguous way, and he proposed a framework in which the physical dimension is strictly interlocked with the mystical and commercial ones. Additionally, a human dimension (based on local culture and techniques) is now widely accepted as an aspect of terroir (Barham 2003). Spielmann and Gélinas-Chebat (2012) have tried to shed light on the different meanings that producers, vendors, and consumers associate with *terroir*. This was the first attempt at empirical research to define the many meanings used by various people to describe *terroir*. They categorized four production- and socially based dimensions to communicate *terroir*: physical environment, *savoir faire*, historical and cultural environment and legal protection.

Spielmann and Charters (2013) were the first to empirically test the *terroir* meanings through a study of producer and consumer perceptions of *terroir* and its ability to convey product authenticity. Results supported the complex nature of terroir connected to an institutional dimension (regulation and legal protection of the appellation system), an internalized dimension (subjective perceptions and consumer experiences), and a product dimension (directly related to the product itself, to its essence and originality).

This study tests the effect of the different *terroir* dimensions highlighted by scholars on consumer's choice, when they operate as extrinsic attributes relating to product, packaging, and back label information. The different consumers' sensitivity to *terroir* and its connotations are observed, and the market segments most likely to choose wine as a luxury product are identified.

Methodology

This study applies the Discrete Choice Experiment (DCE) process to wine choice; in this process, product attributes at various levels are combined into hypothetical choice situations to analyze respondents' stated preferences (Louviere et al. 2000).

To meet the research objectives, the most relevant product characteristics in wine choice by young consumers have been analyzed by simulating the choice of a bottle of wine among different options.

Attributes and levels were chosen considering (1) previous studies applying DCE to wine choice (Jarvis et al. 2010; Mtimet and Albisu 2006; Mueller et al. 2010a, b; Perrouty et al. 2006), (2) studies analyzing the role and characteristics of different intrinsic and extrinsic cues for wine (Barber and Almanza 2007; Celhay and Passebois 2011; Capitello et al. 2012; Mueller et al. 2010b; Orth and Malkewitz 2008; Spielmann and Charters 2013; Vaudour 2002), and (3) the results of 24 in-depth interviews. Five attributes were identified as the main characteristics of a bottle of wine and the *terroir* drivers in the consumer's eyes for the experimental design: label style, collective brand, individual brand, back label information, and price.

Each attribute is characterized by levels able to include different ways in which the attribute can be included in a wine label: four levels (minimal, terroir, contrasting, and sophisticated) for label style (Celhay and Passebois 2011; Capitello et al. 2012; Orth and Malkewitz 2008; Spielmann and Charters 2013); three levels (CO_2 reduction, designation of origin, and an association of producers) for the collective brand (Spielmann and Charters 2013); four levels (winery name, product name, social media, vineyard name) for the individual brand; and four levels (soil, production process, family history, and grape variety) for back label information (Barber and Almanza 2007; Mueller et al. 2010b; Vaudour 2002). Further, the attribute price assumes four levels (8.90, 13.90, 18.90, and 23.90 euros/750 ml bottle) reflecting the Italian market of superpremium and ultrapremium quality wines.

An orthogonal design was adopted, resulting in 24 choice sets (Louviere and Hensher 1983; Louviere and Woodworth 1983); the blocking procedure identified two groups with 12 choice sets each in order to make task completion easier. Every set was composed of four bottles. Bottles have been graphically represented and attributes and levels have been included taking the results of the experimental design into account. The display of the bottles on a wineshop shelf has been simulated. Respondents were instructed to imagine that they wanted to buy a bottle of red wine to drink during a dinner with friends.

An online survey was carried out through the social media in Italy by fanpages of different Italian Universities, wine lovers, and associations of young people in November 2013. The questionnaire was posted by eight students of the University of Verona; 1021 questionnaires were collected, but 39 were excluded because respondents did not belong to the surveyed age cohort. The survey sample is therefore composed of 982 respondents (52.7 % of them are women) between 16 years (the minimum drinking age in Italy) and 37 years (those born in 1977, the upper limit of Generation Y (Alch 2000; Bakewell and Mitchell 2003; Farris et al. 2002). Most of the sample is less than 26 years old, has a high school diploma, still studies

(60.6 %), and lives with their parents. Although the sample is composed of young Italians, from a traditional wine-producing country, for a large percentage of it wine consumption occurs only sporadically.

Latent Class Choice Models (Greene and Hensher 2003; Kamakura and Mazzon 1991) have been applied to analyze the data. Following the criteria suggested Scarpa and Thiene (2005), the resolution with seven latent classes has been judged as the preferred one.

Results

The relative attribute importance has been estimated both at latent class and total sample level (Table 1). Part-worth utilities for the attribute levels have been estimated. Table 1 reports attribute levels significant at 5 % and their positive or negative effect on consumer utility.

Overall, considering the importance of the product attributes, label style is the most important attribute, highlighting the relevance of the visual impact on choice (Mueller et al. 2010a). Individual brand follows label style in importance, together influencing the 50 % of utility. Price and back label information rank third at the same importance. As pointed out by other research (Eastman and Liu 2012; Farris et al. 2002), Generation Y is not very price sensitive and looks for additional information that may help their choices. Collective brand generates the lowest interest in the total sample.

Analyzing the attribute levels, the *terroir* label style is the preferred one by the total sample. Therefore, traditional style labels, which trigger a subjective perception of *terroir*, are still preferred by young people. Considering that the experimental design included superpremium and ultrapremium wines, the purchase of which implies a certain degree of economic risk, this result is in line with the study by Celhay and Passebois (2011), which showed that when the purchase involves a certain risk level, consumers tend to choose traditional labels.

However, having a contrasting label style, with a more innovative design, also attracts young consumers and has a positive impact on utility. Tradition and innovation coexist in young people's choices. Conversely, a sophisticated label style and, even more, a minimal label style, depress the utility.

For the individual brand, the greatest utility is provided when the name of the *cru* appears on the label. Therefore, once again, the importance of a specific origin indication emerges when attached to a traditional meaning of physical *terroir*. Product and winery names have a positive impact on utility although with less intensity. Affixing the name of the winery as a social media domain gives a negative utility instead, which seems counterintuitive, given this cohort's supposed propensity to use social media.

Young people seem to promote price as a proxy for quality. Although the highest price in the experiment has a negative impact on utility, young people prefer to pay 13.90 euros for a bottle of wine than 8.90 euros, partially disregarding the law of demand.

Table 1 Attribute importance weights and level preferences for latent classes and total sample

Latent classes	LC 1	LC 2	LC 3	LC 4	LC 5	LC 6	LC 7	Total
Class size	26.2%	17.0%	14.7%	12.8%	11.2%	10.2%	8.0%	100.0%
Attributes								
Label style	25.9%	47.8%	15.6%	10.8%	6.5%	11.8%	5.3%	28.2%
	+ Contrasting	+ Terroir	+ Terroir	+ Terroir	+ Terroir	+ Terroir	+ Terroir	+ Terroir
	− Minimal	− Minimal	− Minimal	− Minimal		− Minimal		+ Contrasting
	− Sophisticated	− Sophisticated						− Sophisticated
								− Minimal
Individual brand	8.4%	24.0%	16.6%	6.0%	22.2%	22.3%	5.3%	22.9%
	+ Product name	+ Winery name	+ Vineyard name	− Social media	+Vineyard name	+ Product name	− Social media	+ Vineyard name
	+ Vineyard name	+ Product name	− Social media		+ Product name	− Social media		+ Product name
		+ Vineyard name			− Social media			+ Winery name
		− Social media						− Social media
Price	25.7%	15.1%	28.1%	16.0%	15.6%	15.3%	71.9%	19.6%
	+13.90 euros	+13.90 euros	+23.90 euros	+13.90 euros	+13.90 euros	+18.90 euros	+8.90 euros	+13.90 euros
	−18.90 euros	+8.90 euros	+18.90 euros	+18.90 euros	−23.90 euros	−23.90 euros	+13.90 euros	+8.90 euros
	−23.90 euros	−18.90 euros	−8.90 euros	−23.90 euros			−18.90 euros	−23.90 euros
		−23.90 euros					−23.90 euros	

Latent classes	LC 1	LC 2	LC 3	LC 4	LC 5	LC 6	LC 7	Total
Back label information	21.4%	4.6%	24.9%	61.6%	42.7%	11.9%	7.3%	19.5%
	+ Soil + Prod. process − Grape variety − Family history	− Soil	+ Family history − Grape variety − Soil	+ Prod. process − Grape variety − Soil	+ Grape variety − Soil	+ Prod. process	− Soil	+ Prod. process − Soil
Collective brand	18.6%	8.5%	14.8%	5.7%	13.1%	38.7%	10.2%	9.8%
	+ CO$_2$ reduction − Ass. producers	+ DOC − CO$_2$ reduction	+ DOC − CO$_2$ reduction	+ DOC	+ Ass. of producers − DOC	+ DOC − CO$_2$ reduction − Ass. producers	+ DOC − Ass. producers	+ DOC − CO$_2$ reduction − Ass. producers

Note: $R^2 = 0.256$; $LL = -14,162.1$; $BIC(LL) = 29,040.6$; classification error $= 0.145$; $n = 982$, #parameters $= 104$; $df = 878$; all reported levels are significant at $p < 0.05$. Levels with + have a positive impact on utility, levels with − have a negative impact on utility. Attribute levels are listed in descending order of provided utility

The communication of cultural *terroir* on the back label in the form of a traditional production process adopted by producers is the most attractive for young consumers. This attribute can be translated as the fusion between the physical nature and the subjective (or perhaps human) perceptions of the *terroir* product, as components of its authenticity (Spielmann and Charters 2013). This is because, from the cognitive point of view, it communicates the traditional nature of the production method, and from the emotional point of view it involves the subjective sensitivity towards the perception of the link with origin and the typicality. The properties of the soil on which the vineyards are cultivated, and therefore the purely physical nature of terroir, have a negative impact on utility.

Among collective brands, the denomination of origin, namely the legal recognition of terroir products, is the only attribute level to positively impact on the total sample utility. Environmental factors and the fact that an association of regional producers exists are therefore actually perceived to be negative; the former again contradicts Generation Y's supposed environmental commitment (Lee 2008).

Considering the results in terms of the seven latent classes (LC), consumers seem to differ considerably from one class to another.

LC1, composed of 26 % of the sample, chooses a bottle of wine mainly based on label style and price. A contrasting style label is preferred, confuting Fort and Fort (2006), who pointed out that *terroir* products refute modernism; this may well be an example of section of the cohort which rejects the perceived traditional approach of previous generations. LC1 follows the law of demand and orders its utility conversely to the magnitude of price level. However, the lower price level is not statistically significant. The back label is also considered important in choosing a bottle of wine, especially when it includes information about the soil and the production process.

About half the utility comes from the label style for LC2. Therefore, 17 % of respondents are highly attracted by the visual aspect when choosing a bottle of wine. As for the total sample, the preferences of this latent class fall on a traditional label that communicates *terroir*, associated with the presence of the winery and product brand and also (underlining the terroir) the vineyard name.

LC3 chooses a wine mainly based on price (28.1 % of attribute importance) and back label information (24.9 %). For this segment, wine is a Veblen good, which does not follow the law of demand, but for which the utility increases as price increases, therefore raising wine to a luxury and exclusive good and a status symbol. Willingness to pay for wine for this group is combined with an attention to the product characteristics on the back label. The subjective component of *terroir* prevails for this class, expressed by the family history, rather than the environmental component as communicated through grape variety and soil, which actually depress perceived utility. The choice of a product, which can be configured as a luxury good because of the willingness to pay, is supported by the business reputation, given the long production history of the producer family; the more agricultural element is perceived to undermine the more aspirational, image-based luxury focus.

LC4 is heavily guided by back label information, and the traditionalism of the production process emerges as the main driver for choice. Conversely, the physical components of *terroir*, like grape variety and soil, once again decrease utility. Perhaps for this group authenticity expressed by craftsmanship is the terroir focus.

Back label information is also important for LC5, together with individual brand. Concerning the former attribute, the physical nature of *terroir* expressed through the grape variety has a positive impact on utility, in contrast to the soil properties, reflecting a more "New World" approach to product choice. Concerning the brand, showing the vineyard name on the label has a positive effect on the choices of this class, as well as secondly the name of the product. Affixing the winery name as a domain of social media has a negative impact on choice, supporting the thesis of Fort and Fort (2006) in this case, that terroir and a more modern approach to marketing do not sit well together.

LC6 is mainly driven by collective brand, followed by individual brand. The legal certification of *terroir*, namely the denomination of origin brand, positively impacts on utility perception, conversely the social claim of CO_2 reduction and the associative brand depress utility. As far as the individual brand is concerned, the focus should be on the product name to attract this consumer segment.

LC7 is heavily driven by price in their choice (71.9 % of attribute importance), but, conversely to LC3, the utility decreases as the price increases. This small group seems entirely price driven, seeking the cheapest wine possible with little interest in background information or attention to other terroir aspects.

Discussion

The study segmented wine demand among the younger generation of consumers, using their preferences towards different product attributes, analyzed as vehicles of *terroir*.

As highlighted in other research, latent class analysis confirms the role of the visual impact of the label in determining consumer choices, and the preference towards a "French style" label by young consumers, with a clear terroir connotation. Three other product dimensions emerge: (i) the preference for specific individual brand signals (vineyard and product name more important than winery name); (ii) price as a quality cue, and; (iii) attention to additional information about the characteristics of the production process. The collective brand attracts young consumers only when certifying the designation of origin, which is the most immediate indication which distinguishes quality wines from commodity wines in Italy.

However, this overall situation is not able to reliably represent the Generation Y market in its entirety because heterogeneous preferences emerged. This heterogeneity can be explained by the different *terroir* dimensions conveyed by the attributes assessed by consumers. The latent class model highlighted the choice drivers for young consumers and useful market trends. These have clear managerial implications in terms of wine packaging and communication.

These wine marketing implications are clearly defined: (i) anchoring to *terroir* in the sense of "typicality" as a subjective perception (LC4) or physical characteristics (LC5); (ii) anchoring to "institutional" *terroir*, combined with the attention to the product (LC6) or as an additional, supporting attribute (centered on a PDO classification) when a strong price sensitiveness occurs (LC7); (iii) a propensity to perceive wine as a luxury product (LC3) and characterized by fashion elements which are indicators of social recognition (LC1); (iv) reassurance through traditional packaging, corporate brand, and price as quality cues (LC2).

Conclusion

The study underlines the value of DCEs as a means of unpicking the drivers of purchase behavior, and particularly as it operates within one cohort—as with Generation Y in this study. Thus, the research uncovers consumer preferences for *terroir* attributes embedded in a bottle of wine. As stated by many scholars (Louviere and Woodworth 1983; Mueller et al. 2010a), indirect importance measures of preferences are able to ensure more precise and informative results than direct importance measures.

Crucially, the study reveals that while terroir remains important for most young Italian consumers, how it is construed and the cues which denote it vary substantially. Specifically, there are more price focused segments, those who search for luxury, and those who expect more traditional representations of terroir, but who vary depending on whether or not it is more associated to the producer, a traditional production method, a specific vineyard site, or the soil.

The main limitation of the applied methodology comes from the hypothetical nature of the analyzed choice. Another limitation comes from the specific experiment analyzing only extrinsic cues and omitting consumption experience.

Further development of the research will be aimed at characterizing the latent classes through the socio-demographic and behavioral characteristics of consumers to understand how business can efficiently reach these segments. Another important aspect is to understand the motivations behind these choices and therefore the possibility of linking attitudes and individual value systems to choices. This will represent very important theoretical and practical developments because it would favor wine packaging design and the building of communication content consistent with young consumers' expectations.

References

Alch, M. L. (2000). The echo-boom generation: A growing force in American society. *Futurist, 34*(5), 42–51.

Atkin, T., & Johnson, R. (2010). Appellation as an indicator of quality. *International Journal of Wine Business Research, 22*(1), 42–61.

Bakewell, C., & Mitchell, V. W. (2003). Generation Y female consumer decision-making styles. *International Journal of Retail & Distribution Management, 31*(2), 95–106.

Balestrini, P., & Gamble, P. (2006). Country-of-origin effects on Chinese wine consumers. *British Food Journal, 108*(5), 396–412.

Barber, N., & Almanza, B. A. (2007). Influence of wine packaging on consumers' decision to purchase. *Journal of Food Service Business Research, 9*(4), 83–98.

Barham, E. (2003). Translating terroir: The global challenge of French AOC labeling. *Journal of Rural Studies, 19*(1), 127–138.

Beverland, M. (2004). Uncovering "theories-in-use": Building luxury wine brands. *European Journal of Marketing, 38*(3/4), 446–466.

Beverland, M. (2006). The 'real thing': Branding authenticity in the luxury wine trade. *Journal of Business Research, 59*(2), 251–258.

Capitello, R., Begalli, D., & Agnoli, L. (2012). Package styles in wine marketing: A case study of Valpolicella wines. *Scientific Papers Series Management, Economic Engineering in Agriculture and Rural Development, 12*(2), 29–34.

Celhay, F., & Passebois, J. (2011). Wine labelling: Is it time to break with tradition? A study of the moderating role of perceived risk. *International Journal of Wine Business Research, 23*(4), 318–337.

Charters, S. (2010). Marketing terroir: A conceptual approach. In *Proceedings of the 5th International Academy of Wine Business Research Conference* (pp. 8–10).

Charters, S., & Spielmann, N. (2014). Characteristics of strong territorial brands: The case of champagne. *Journal of Business Research, 67*(7), 1461–1467.

Easingwood, C., Lockshin, L., & Spawton, A. (2011). The drivers of wine regionality. *Journal of Wine Research, 22*(1), 19–33.

Eastman, J. K., & Liu, J. (2012). The impact of generational cohorts on status consumption: An exploratory look at generational cohort and demographics on status consumption. *Journal of Consumer Marketing, 29*(2), 93–102.

Farris, R., Chong, F., & Dunning, D. (2002). Generation Y: Purchasing power and implications for marketing. *Academy of Marketing Studies Journal, 6*(2), 89–101.

Fort, F., & Fort, F. (2006). Alternatives marketing pour les produits de terroir. *Revue Française de Gestion, 162*(3), 145–159.

Greene, W. H., & Hensher, D. A. (2003). A latent class model for discrete choice analysis: Contrasts with mixed logit. *Transportation Research Part B: Methodological, 37*(8), 681–698.

Hall, C. M., & Mitchell, R. (2008). *Wine marketing: A practical guide*. London: Routledge.

Heslop, L. A., Cray, D., & Armenakyan, A. (2010). Cue incongruity in wine personality formation and purchasing. *International Journal of Wine Business Research, 22*(3), 288–307.

Jarvis, W., Mueller, S., & Chiong, K. (2010). A latent analysis of images and words in wine choice. *Australasian Marketing Journal, 18*(3), 138–144.

Kamakura, W. A., & Mazzon, J. A. (1991). Value segmentation: A model for the measurement of values and value systems. *Journal of Consumer Research, 18*(2), 208–218.

Kim, K. H., Ko, E., Xu, B., & Han, Y. (2012). Increasing customer equity of luxury fashion brands through nurturing consumer attitude. *Journal of Business Research, 65*(10), 1495–1499.

Lee, K. (2008). Opportunities for green marketing: Young consumers. *Marketing Intelligence and Planning, 26*(6), 573–586.

Lockshin, L., & Corsi, A. M. (2012). Consumer behaviour for wine 2.0: A review since 2003 and future directions. *Wine Economics and Policy, 1*(1), 2–23.

Lockshin, L., & Hall, J. (2003). Consumer purchasing behaviour for wine: What we know and where we are going. In *Proceedings of the International Wine Marketing Colloquium, Adelaide*.

Louviere, J. J., & Hensher, D. A. (1983). Using discrete choice models with experimental design data to forecast consumer demand for a unique cultural event. *Journal of Consumer Research, 10*(3), 348–361.

Louviere, J. J., Hensher, D. A., & Swait, J. (2000). *Stated choice methods: Analysis and application*. Cambridge, England: Cambridge University Press.

Louviere, J. J., & Woodworth, G. (1983). Design and analysis of simulated consumer choice or allocation experiments: An approach based on aggregate data. *Journal of Marketing Research, 20*(4), 350–367.

Magnusson, P., Westjohn, S. A., & Zdravkovic, S. (2011). "What? I thought Samsung was Japanese": Accurate or not, perceived country of origin matters. *International Marketing Review, 28*(5), 454–472.

Mtimet, N., & Albisu, L. M. (2006). Spanish wine consumer behavior: A choice experiment approach. *Agribusiness, 22*(3), 343–362.

Mueller, S., Lockshin, L., & Louviere, J. J. (2010a). What you see may not be what you get: Asking consumers what matters may not reflect what they choose. *Marketing Letters, 21*(4), 335–350.

Mueller, S., Lockshin, L., Saltman, Y., & Blanford, J. (2010b). Message on a bottle: The relative influence of wine back label information on wine choice. *Food Quality and Preference, 21*(1), 22–32.

Orth, U. R., & Malkewitz, K. (2008). Holistic package design and consumer brand impressions. *Journal of Marketing, 72*(3), 64–81.

Perrouty, J. P., d'Hauteville, F., & Lockshin, L. (2006). The influence of wine attributes on region of origin equity: An analysis of the moderating effect of consumer's perceived expertise. *Agribusiness, 22*(3), 323–341.

Scarpa, R., & Thiene, M. (2005). Destination choice models for rock climbing in the Northeastern Alps: A latent-class approach based on intensity of preferences. *Land Economics, 81*(3), 426–444.

Spielmann, N. (2014). Brand equity for origin-bounded brands. *Journal of Brand Management, 21*(3), 189–201.

Spielmann, N., & Charters, S. (2013). The dimensions of authenticity in terroir products. *International Journal of Wine Business Research, 25*(4), 310–324.

Spielmann, N., & Gélinas-Chebat, C. (2012). Terroir? That's not how I would describe it. *International Journal of Wine Business Research, 24*(4), 254–270.

Spielmann, N., Jolly, S., & Parisot, F. (2014). Terroir in the media: The poetry of people, place and palate. *International Journal of Wine Business Research, 26*(3), 224–240.

Vaudour, E. (2002). The quality of grapes and wine in relation to geography: Notions of terroir at various scales. *Journal of Wine Research, 13*(2), 117–141.

How to Make Better Consumers in Luxury: The Role of Shame and Empathy

Cesare Amatulli, Matteo De Angelis, Alessandro M. Peluso, Isabella Soscia, Richard P. Bagozzi, and Gianluigi Guido

Introduction

Sustainable consumption—i.e., the use of products that minimize the use of natural resources and toxic materials as well as emissions of waste and pollutants so as not to jeopardize the needs of future generations (Oslo Roundtable 1994)—has emerged in marketing scholarship as a pressing matter. Indeed, sustainability is a key determinant of future economic growth and development. Both scientific research (e.g., Nidumolu et al. 2009) and business reports (e.g., Deloitte 2011) agree that sustainability has become a crucial driver of innovation, thus serving as a key as a critical success factor for firms. However, in some consumption contexts, such as in the luxury market, consumers are typically more reticent to consume sustainable products (Davies et al. 2011; Davies and Streit 2013). At the same time, the luxury market is also very interesting because of the influence of luxury consumption on socially valued behavior (Wilcox et al. 2014) and because of its relevance for the global economy (Bain & C. 2013). Nevertheless, despite the relevance of the relationship between sustainability and luxury, scientific research has overlooked the study of factors that might

C. Amatulli (✉) • M. De Angelis
LUISS University, Rome, Italy
e-mail: camatulli@luiss.it; mdeangelis@luiss.it

A.M. Peluso • G. Guido
University of Salento, Lecce, Italy
e-mail: alessandro.peluso@unisalento.it; gianluigi.guido@unisalento.it

I. Soscia
SKEMA Business School, Euralille, France
e-mail: isabella.soscia@skema.edu

R.P. Bagozzi
University of Michigan, Ann Arbor, MI, USA
e-mail: bagozzi@umich.edu

© Academy of Marketing Science 2016
L. Petruzzellis, R.S. Winer (eds.), *Rediscovering the Essentiality of Marketing*,
Developments in Marketing Science: Proceedings of the Academy of Marketing
Science, DOI 10.1007/978-3-319-29877-1_108

determine the effectiveness of communication strategies (e.g., advertisement scenarios or messages conveyed by salespersons) typically employed to promote sustainable luxury products. Indeed, according to Kapferer (2010), real luxury brands have already responded to the demand for sustainability, but have not adequately engaged in communicating their sustainable values. In particular, studies both from Bonini and Oppenheim (2008) and Davies et al. (2011) have underlined how one of the major barriers for sustainable luxury consumers is the lack of awareness and information. Therefore, researchers must investigate what drives consumers to become more willing to buy sustainable products.

Aiming to understand underlying mechanisms behind consumers' choice of sustainable products, in this study we consider two different and opposite types of communication about luxury products, which we label sustainability-oriented (whereby a message communicates the positive achievements related to the purchase of sustainable products) and unsustainability-oriented communication (whereby the message communicates the bad outputs related to the purchase of unsustainable products). Our goal is to detect when one versus the other type of communication is more effective in increasing consumers' preference for sustainable products. We pursue this goal by exploring the role of emotions, which might play a relevant role in luxury goods consumer behavior. Indeed, emotion seem to be a very central factor since luxury is related to social distinction, self-enhancement, dreams and high emotional values (Bernstein 1999; Vigneron and Johnson 2004; Wiedmann et al. 2007), as well as sustainability is related to the relationship between the self and others (WCED 1985). Indeed, in social psychology self-conscious emotions concern a group of emotions that are strongly connected with the self; these emotions are activated by an intentional focus on the self and have implications on the way the individual experiences and values the self. In addition, when customers are exposed to communication content, information processing occurs (Jackson 2004), and if this information is processed in a relatively automatic and intuitive way, heuristic information processing takes place (Petty and Cacioppo 2012). In this sense, communication can be either classified as "thinking" or "emotional"; the first one normally contains information requiring significant cognitive processing, the second instead is designed to trigger specific emotional reactions, at least initially (Bagozzi et al. 1999; Hansen 2005). As a consequence, in assessing the effectiveness of different types of communications related to luxury goods and sustainability, emotions may represent the underlying variables explaining specific consumption behaviors.

Background

Cognitive theories of emotions contend that the early part of the emotion processing includes the manipulation of information and so should be understood as a cognitive process (e.g., Frijda 1986; Lazarus 1991). In particular, in social psychology the appraisal theory suggests that emotions are the result of an appraisal process that has the aim to explain how events are able to trigger an emotional reaction (Kappas 2006; Moors 2009). Indeed, emotions are associated with a state of psychological arousal with cognitive aspects that depend from the specific context (Consoli 2009), and according to Leyens et al. (2001), emotions can be divided into primary or basic emotions and secondary or self-conscious emotions. In particular, self-conscious emotions include empathy and shame, among others (Ekman 1992). Interestingly, the literature concerning both luxury (Belz and Peattie 2009; Hesz and Neophytou 2010; Holbrook and Batra 1987; Hagtvedt and Patrick 2009; Silverstein and Fiske 2003; Venkatesh et al. 2010) and sustainable communication (Moons and Pelsmacker 2012; Wehrli et al. 2013) has demonstrated how emotions seem to be common features in boosting consumers' actions to buy. Nevertheless, despite the role of sustainability and ethics in the luxury market, which has been the focus of some debate among academics and managers (Ageorges 2010; Bendell and Kleanthous 2007; DeBeers 2009; La Tribune 2011), the academic literature on sustainable consumption has mainly focused on non-luxury products, such as food (Auger et al. 2003), beverages (Auger 2008), cosmetics (McGoldrick and Freestone 2008; Sriram and Forman 1993; Vermeir and Verbeke 2006), and clothing (Strong 1996). As a consequence, the literature regarding sustainable luxury is nearly nonexistent (Joergens 2006).

In this research, we propose that communication strategies, i.e., sustainability-oriented versus unsustainability-oriented, used to promote sustainable products, may elicit specific emotions, and that these emotions in turn lead consumers to behaviors that potentially benefit companies, but especially the environment and society at large (e.g., endorsing sustainable products and consumption styles through product preferences). Specifically, this study aims to show that, when exposed to unsustainability-oriented stimuli, people feel a sense of shame, thus compensating or coping with this negative emotion by increasing their preference for sustainable products. Indeed, shame refers to the negative feeling experienced by individuals as they realize they have acted inconsistently with their goals, norms, or standards they consider as important. Therefore, given that sustainability is a social concept which refers to the relationship between the self and the others (i.e., society), a relevant role for shame is expected. Moreover, shame may be conceptualized as related to empathy (Baumeister et al. 1994; Harris 2003; Hoffman 1982; Lazarus and Lazarus 1994). Thus, our study also aims to analyze the role of empathy as a moderator; in particular, by showing that the level of empathy of consumers moderates the effect of luxury communication orientation on shame and on sustainable preferences. Indeed, empathy occurs regularly and reliably in those situations involving moral judgment (Hoffman 2000); it concerns the welfare of others (Mencl and May 2009) and is not dependent on specific behaviors of others (Baumeister et al. 1994; Harris 2003; Hoffman 1982; Lazarus and Lazarus 1994).

Methodology

Ninety-seven participants were assigned to a two (narrative scenario: sustainability-oriented vs. unsustainability-oriented) × 2 (shame: high vs. low) between-participants design. Participants were randomly assigned to two different conditions: the sustainability-oriented scenario and the unsustainability-oriented scenario. Before reading the scenario, respondents were asked to complete a measure (10-items scale; Losoya and Eisenberg 2001; Tangney et al. 2007) of their level of empathy (moderator). Then, respondents were presented with the narrative scenario and were asked to indicate (7-items scale; Tangney et al. 1989) to what extent they felt a sense of shame (mediator). Finally, respondents were asked to complete a 6-items the so-called green scale (DV) which measures the tendency to express the value of environmental protection through one's purchases and consumption behaviors, predicting consumers preference for environmentally friendly products (Haws et al. 2013, 2014).

Results

Data were collected online in the USA through Mechanical Turk. We only considered American respondents who did not report missing values ($N=97$; 49 for the sustainable condition, 48 for the unsustainable condition). To establish mediation, we estimated the indirect effect of luxury communication orientation (sustainability-oriented = 1; unsustainability-oriented $=-1$) on green actions (i.e., the preference for sustainable products) using the bootstrapping technique suggested by Zhao et al. (2010) and implemented in the PROCESS macro developed by Hayes (2013). The analysis revealed an indirect effect that was negative ($b=-.20$) and significant (confidence interval $=-.43$ and $-.06$), thus showing that evoking a scenario associated with the purchase of an unsustainable (versus sustainable) luxury product increases shame in consumers, which in turn leads them to express higher preferences for sustainable products. The analysis also revealed an interaction effect between luxury communication orientation and empathy on preference for sustainable products ($b=-.26, p=.04$). In particular, simple slope analysis shows that when empathy is low (-1 SD) evoking a sustainable purchasing scenario, compared to an unsustainable one, increases individuals' preferences for more sustainable products ($b=.37, p=.04$). In contrast, when empathy is high ($+1$ SD), evoking a sustainable purchasing scenario, compared to an unsustainable one, does not increase individuals' preference for sustainable products ($b=-.15; p>.30$). Rather, our results suggest that a way to induce high-empathy individuals to increase their preferences for sustainable products is to leverage their sense of shame. Evoking an unsustainable purchasing scenario increases individuals' sense of shame, and this enhanced sense of shame, in turn, leads them prefer more sustainable products, maybe in an attempt to restore a positive view of themselves.

General Discussion

These results show that an unsustainable-oriented scenario concerning luxury products makes consumers more willing to prefer environmentally friendly products because of the sense of shame. Moreover, findings underline that priming sustainable messages directly leads to green consumption for people who are low in empathy. Counter intuitively, these findings shed light on the central role that negative emotions may have in developing sustainable consumption for luxury goods. Operationally, our research suggests that, in order to increase consumers' preferences for sustainable products, luxury brands should develop communication strategies (e.g., advertisements, sales force selling reasoning, or in-store messages) that focus on the bad potential results related to unsustainable behaviors, thus generating a sense of shame and greater desire to prefer green products. Indeed, because of the sense of shame, the preference for more environmentally friendly products seems to be an attempt to restore a positive view of themselves. Moreover, our results also suggest that luxury brands should segment their consumers on the basis of their level of empathy, thus targeting high empathic consumers through unsustainable-oriented scenarios. On the other hand, to target non-empathic consumers and make them more willing to prefer sustainable products, an aspect of manipulating the sense of shame, luxury brands can also use sustainable-oriented scenarios as primes.

Further research should focus on other emotions and on cultural differences. Indeed, given that shame is positively correlated with hubristic pride (Tracy and Robins 2007), further studies could explore whether eliciting this positive emotion may lead to similar effects as for shame. In addition, apart from shame, the potential role of guilt could also be investigated. Indeed, even though these two emotions slightly differ in terms of the focus on the self or others, respectively (Abe 2004; Glenn and Glenn 1982; Higgins 1987; Lebra 1973)—shame is defined as having a negative view of the self as a result of damage one has done to others, guilt results from the failure to meet others' expectations (Triandis et al. 1985)—they are seemingly similar. Moreover, people's reactions to the violation of norms in cross-cultural environments are related to different dominant emotions according to culture, especially according to the culture's collectivist or individualistic dimensions (i.e., individualistic cultures react with greater guilt and collectivistic cultures tend to react with more shame). Therefore, other studies may focus on the potential central role that shame and guilt may have in different cultures and countries.

References available upon request.

Customer's Higher Willingness to Pay in Accordance with Mass Customization

Saeedeh Rezaee Vessal, Pierre Valette-Florence, and Haithem Guizani

Abstract Competition among companies to attract and retain customers is increasing exponentially, thanks to the power of internet. This exacerbated competition has forced companies to find innovative ways to differentiate their marketing argumentation from those of competitors and put aside the classical tools. A company's objective of a higher profit margin and simultaneously diversified customer preferences, resulted in the decomposition of traditional mass markets into smaller niches and the emergence of a new type of production, called Mass Customization. Mass customization is discussed in literature as the ultimate solution to address challenges faced by companies to provide products highly adapted to individual customers' aesthetic and functional preferences (Dellaert and Stremersch 2005; Franke and Piller 2004; Ghosh et al. 2006; Randall et al. 2007).

Previous research illustrates customers' preferences for customized products from different points of view. They also mention that customization is correlated (associated) with added value (Piller et al. 2004). Uniqueness as one of the most important advantages of mass customization has been brought up in most of the previous studies. However, some questions still remain unanswered: is the estimation of uniqueness correct? Do others perceive their choice as unique as initially perceived? What is their internal motivation to pay more for customized products? Has mass customization the same effect on different product types (luxury vs. non-luxury)? Does customizing different product features (hedonic vs. utilitarian) have the same effect on a customer's internal motivation?

This research makes three contributions. First, it examines how people's beliefs about the degree to which they are noticed by others can affect the mass customization value. Second, the findings of this research illustrate how the product type (luxury vs. non-luxury) has a moderating role on the relation between mass customization and the spotlight effect. Third, it explains what kind of values originating from mass custom-

---

S.R. Vessal (✉) • P. Valette-Florence
Université Pierre-Mendès-France, Saint-Martin-d'Hères, France
e-mail: saeedeh.rezaee-vessal@upmf-grenoble.fr; pierre.valette-florence@iae-grenoble.fr

H. Guizani
Sciences Po Grenoble, Saint-Martin-d'Hères, France
e-mail: haithem.guizani@sciencespo-grenoble.fr

© Academy of Marketing Science 2016   535
L. Petruzzellis, R.S. Winer (eds.), *Rediscovering the Essentiality of Marketing*,
Developments in Marketing Science: Proceedings of the Academy of Marketing
Science, DOI 10.1007/978-3-319-29877-1_109

ization features has the greater impact on customer's overestimation. To test the research propositions, three experiments were designed with a total of 207 samples.

In the first experiment, we tested how spotlight effect varies with customization's possibility, and how it affects customer's willingness to pay. Consistent with our predictions, results reveal that increasing customers feeling of uniqueness through mass customization impacts their overestimation of others' attention to their possession and consequently on their willingness to pay.

In the second experiment, we studied how the product type (luxury vs. non-luxury) can impact on customer's feeling of uniqueness. To do so, the moderating role of the product type (luxury vs. non-luxury) was manipulated in interaction with product self-design possibility (mass customization vs. non-mass customization). Consistent with our theorizing, the luxurious type of the product and mass customization activity had a separate and positive effect on consumer overestimation of how people perceive their own possession.

In the third experiment, we studied the moderation effect of customizing different features (hedonic vs. utilitarian) of different product types (luxury vs. non-luxury) on spotlight effect. The results of study 3 provide evidence which proved our prediction that customizing features (hedonic vs. utilitarian) had a moderating spotlight effect.

The present research examines the interesting but largely unexamined impact of the spotlight effect on people's overestimation of others' attention to their possession. In particular, we explore how the feeling of uniqueness through mass customization impacts customer's overestimation. In other words, it demonstrates how product value can be affected by people's overestimation of their possessions' uniqueness.

Applying the results of this research would be helpful for companies to profit more from customization strategy. From a managerial point of view, customization would be effective for both luxury and non-luxury producers, although its impact would be greater for luxury companies.

References available upon request.

Part XIII
Marketing Strategy

Organizational Antecedents of External Orientation: An Empirical Analysis of Customer and Competitor Orientations

Dahan Gavriel and Shoham Aviv

Abstract Strategic orientations have attracted scholars' attention across disciplines, and their pros and cons have been studied extensively. However, research has focused more on market orientation than on other strategic orientations and has addressed outcomes of these orientations more than their antecedents. Our study aims to advance the literature on orientations by identifying drivers of customer and competitor orientations. We developed and tested a model of several antecedents of customer and competitor orientations. Based on Jaworski and Kohli (1993), the antecedents include three multifaceted sets of factors: management, departments, and the organization with five facets, namely *risk taking*, *conflicts*, *connectedness*, *formalization*, and *centralization*. We examined several hypotheses regarding the relationships between these antecedents and customer and competitor orientations.

Data were collected through a professional online panel company. The sample included 185 individuals who responded to a questionnaire which contained items in 5-point scales (1 = strongly disagree to 5 = strongly agree) and developed in previous research. All scales were reliable with Cronbach's alpha coefficient exceeding 0.70 (Nunnally 1978).

The findings show that four factors affected customer orientation, namely risk-taking, conflicts, connectedness, and centralization while two factors affected competitor orientation, namely risk-taking and conflicts. Accordingly, these findings

D. Gavriel (✉)
Western Galilee College, Acre, Israel
e-mail: gabid@wgalil.ac.il

S. Aviv
University of Haifa, Haifa, Israel
e-mail: ashoham@univ.haifa.ac.il

© Academy of Marketing Science 2016
L. Petruzzellis, R.S. Winer (eds.), *Rediscovering the Essentiality of Marketing*,
Developments in Marketing Science: Proceedings of the Academy of Marketing
Science, DOI 10.1007/978-3-319-29877-1_110

539

provide several insights that contribute to the marketing strategy literature and have implications for practicing managers. Among the two orientations, the most influential antecedent is *Risk-Taking*. Therefore, in order to be successful in improving their company on all levels, managers must be willing to take risks. Only by doing so they can capitalize on opportunities and respond to competitive threats in the marketplace.

References available upon request.

Customer Acquisition and Customer Retention in a Competitive Industry

Gerasimos Lianos and Igor Sloev

Abstract We study optimal customer acquisition and retention strategies in an infinite-horizon model of dynamic competition. We find that acquisition expenditures constitute the larger share of the marketing budget, when the customer profit margin is either low or large, but for intermediate profit margin values, firms spend more resources for customer retention. If customer profit margins rise for exogenous reasons, we find that the share of customer acquisition expenditures in the marketing budget increases in markets with high profit margins, whereas it decreases in markets with low profit margins. The impact of entry of new firms in the market on the optimal strategy depends on the effect of the entry on profit margins and absolute levels of profit margins. A similar phenomenon may also appear in a single segmented market: the impact of higher competition on the luxury and mass-consumption segments of a market would be different.

Keywords Customer acquisition • Customer retention • Competition • Customer lifetime value

Introduction

Why in some industries are firms more eager to acquire new customers, whereas in other industries firms are more eager to retain old customers? What factors determine the optimal allocation of marketing resources between customer acquisition and customer retention? How do market characteristics and competitive forces affect optimal customer acquisition (CA) and customer retention (CR) strategies? These questions have been a subject of inquiry by marketing scientists and marketing practitioners over the last 20 years (Venkatesan and Kumar 2004; Thomas et al. 2004).

G. Lianos (✉)
University of Miami, Coral Gables, FL, USA
e-mail: gerasimos.lianos@outlook.com

I. Sloev
National Research University Higher School of Economics, Moscow, Russia
e-mail: isloev@hse.ru

© Academy of Marketing Science 2016
L. Petruzzellis, R.S. Winer (eds.), *Rediscovering the Essentiality of Marketing*,
Developments in Marketing Science: Proceedings of the Academy of Marketing
Science, DOI 10.1007/978-3-319-29877-1_111

541

A fundamental concept for answering questions related to customer acquisition and customer retention has been that of Customer Lifetime Value (CLV), that is, the present value of the stream of profits accruing to a firm over the whole period of its relationship with a customer (Berger and Nasr 1998; Gupta et al. 2006). Several studies have used CLV to analyze optimal CA and CR strategies in *a single-customer/single-firm* framework. Blattberg and Deighton (1996) have presented a model of maximization of CLV giving rise to optimal allocation of marketing expenditures to CA and to CR. Berger and Nasr (1998) have further developed the model considering different customer segments and distinguishing between retention expenses and add-on selling including up-selling and cross-selling. Berger and Bechwati (2001) have used the model to examine the maximization of customer equity and optimal allocation of resources under binding condition on a promotional budget. Tsao (2013) has extended Blattberg and Deighton's model to study optimal acquisition and retention when a firm wants simultaneously to increase its market share and maximize customer equity.

Blattberg et al. (2008) summarize the findings of analytical studies. The CA and CR response curves are the key drivers of relative and absolute spending. Marginal cost (not average cost) should guide investments in CA and CR. In a single period model with an unlimited marketing budget, firms should increase their spending on CA until the marginal acquisition cost equals the lifetime value of the customer. Similarly, they should also increase spending on CR until the marginal cost of retaining another customer equals the lifetime value of the customer, adjusted for a one-period discount rate. Improvements in CA response affect CA investment but not CR investment, whereas improvements in CR response affect both CR and CA investments. Budgeting results in locally suboptimal spending. Companies with a larger installed customer base should spend more on CR, although they should possibly decrease these expenditures over time.

A few studies have analyzed the explicit effects of competition and the marketplace on a firm's optimal CA and CR strategies (see Verhoef et al. 2007; Kumar et al. 2006 for a discussion). Syam and Hess (2006) have built an analytical model to investigate the optimal CR or CA of an incumbent firm when faced with the threat of entry by a new firm. Fruchter and Zhang (2004) have analyzed the strategic use of targeted promotions for CA and CR in dynamic duopoly settings with firms of different size. They show that a firm with a larger market share should focus on CR whereas a firm with a smaller market share should focus on CA. Martin-Herran et al. (2012) have investigated the optimal spending allocation between CA and CR in a dynamic market when two firms compete for market share and they have showed that a firm's CR expenditures can either increase or decrease with its own market share depending on the parameters of the model.

A number of studies have used statistical/econometric models to address the optimal allocation of the marketing budget between CA and CR. Thomas (2001) have introduced a Tobit model to study CA and CR and applied it to data and showed that different variables drive the acquisition and lifetime in different customers segments. Reinartz et al. (2005) have extended Thomas's model by adding customer profitability into consideration and found that underspending on CR and CA is more detrimental and results in smaller returns on investment compared to overspending. Rust et al. (2004) have proposed a statistical model accounting explicitly for the relationship between a focal brand and competitors' brands. They have shown how firms can analyze drivers that have the greatest impact on profits, compared the performance of the drivers with that of the competitors' drivers, and estimated the return on investment in improvements of the drivers. Voss and Voss (2008) have given insights on the impact of market competition on optimal firm strategies in a framework of a static oligopoly model with symmetric firms and shown that firms may benefit from shifting their marketing strategy's focus from CR to CA when competition density increases.

In this chapter we present an analytical model of optimal CA and CR strategies in dynamic market interactions among many firms. We analyze how changes in the customer profit margin and the concentration of firms reshape the optimal marketing strategy (CA and CR expenditures and their shares in marketing budget) and the market outcome (size of firms, number of untapped customers, churn rate) in the long run. One of the distinguishing features of our approach is the consideration of endogenous mark-ups, which gives us a number of new insights into the optimal allocation of the budget.

The Model

Let $I \in (0, M]$ be the set of firms in the industry and let $i \in I$ be the index of an individual firm in the industry. All firms provide customers with a similar service. Examples of firms are internet providers, banks offering credit card service, and insurance companies. There is a fixed number N of identical customers. Let $l^i(t)$ be the number of customers served by firm i at time t. The number of potential (untapped) customers in the market is given by:

$$N^p(t) = N - \int_0^M l^j(t) \, \mathrm{d}j \tag{1}$$

We assume that each customer purchasing a service from a firm generates a gross-of-marketing-cost per-capita profit margin m to that firm. We assume that m is constant over time (however, we allow it to depend on M).

Following Erickson (2009) we assume that CA works through attracting untapped customers. Let $A^i(t) > 0$ be the CA expenditure made by firm i at time t. The share of potential customers that choose firm i at time t is determined by the CA expenditure the firm makes relative to all other firms in the industry according to the rule:

$$s^i(t) = A^i(t)^\theta \Big/ \int_0^M A^j(t)^\theta \, \mathrm{d}j \tag{2}$$

where $\theta \in (0, 1)$ reflects the degree of decreasing returns to the CA expenditure. That is, s^i increases at a decreasing rate in A^i and it decreases in the competitors' CA expenditures. As an example of such an acquisition effort one may think of combative advertising in markets where customers are well informed about the existence of a product/service (Bagwell 2007; Chen et al. 2009).

The number of new customers for firm i at time t is given by:

$$N_0^i(t) = s^i(t) N^p(t). \tag{3}$$

Each firm i at every period t chooses the level of retention expenditure for each customer, $e^i(t) \geq 0$. (As all customers are identical this level is the same for all customers). The CR expenditure decreases the attrition rate of customers and it determines the fraction of the time-t customers who defect at time t from the firm, $\beta(e^i(t))$. Examples of such retention actions are loyalty programs offering personalized bonuses (Blattberg et al. 2008; Kumar 2008; Dorotic et al. 2012). We assume that the shape of $\beta(\bullet)$ is the same across customers and across firms. We also assume that function $\beta(e)$ is continuously differentiable, strictly decreasing, and convex, something consistent with empirical findings (Reinartz et al. 2005). To ensure the existence and uniqueness of equilibrium, we also assume that: $-\beta'(0) \geq 2/m$, $\ln(\beta)'' > 0$. Spending $e^i(t)$ on each customer a firm's total CR expenditures at time t are as follows: $E^i = e^i(t)l^i(t)$.

Given marketing decisions by firm i at time t, the number of its customers decreases at an endogenous rate $\beta(e^i(t))$ and increases by the number of newly acquired customers $N_0^i(t)$. Thus, the law of motion of the number of customers at any moment is given by:

$$\frac{dl^i}{dt} = -\beta(e^i(t)) l^i(t) + N^p(t) s^i(t). \tag{4}$$

The instantaneous profit of firm i at time t is given by:

$$\pi^i(t) = ml^i(t) - \{e^i(t)l^i(t) + A^i(t)\}, \tag{5}$$

where $ml^i(t)$ is the gross-of-marketing-costs operations revenue and $e^i(t)\,l^i(t) + A^i(t)$ is the total marketing cost.

Let $\rho \in (0, 1)$ be the discount rate. The manager of firm i at the initial time $t = 0$ chooses the time paths of the CA expenditures, $A^i(t)$, the CR expenditures, $e^i(t)$, and the number of customers $l^i(t)$ to maximize the present discounted value of the firm's profits:

$$W^i = \int_0^\infty \exp[-\rho t] \pi^i(t) dt \tag{6}$$

subject to (4), given the initial number of customers $l^i(0)$, and taking the paths of the choices made by the other firms as given.

The Symmetric Long-Run Equilibrium

In the symmetric equilibrium of the industry, all firms make the same choices for the decision variables. Moreover, in the steady state, the optimal policy is time invariant: $e^i(t) = e^*$, $A^i(t) = A^*$, $l^i(t) = l^*$. In Appendix, we show the existence, uniqueness, and saddle-path stability of the symmetric equilibrium and derive the expressions for the optimal policy. The firm's optimal CA expenditures in the steady state are given by following condition:

$$-\beta'\left(e^*\right)\frac{m-e^*}{\beta\left(e^*\right)+\rho} = 1. \tag{7}$$

Let us denote $v^* = (m-e)/(\beta(e^*)+\rho)$. Given the discount factor ρ, v^* is equal to the net present value of the flow of constant net profit margins $m-e^*$ of a customer who is retained with the constant rate $1-\beta(e^*)$. Therefore, (7) equates the marginal cost of CR expenditure (which is unity) to its marginal benefit, which is the product of the customer value, v^*, and the increase in the retention rate $-\beta'(e^*)$. In the following, we use the notation $\beta^* = \beta(e^*)$ for the constant equilibrium attrition rate.

In the steady state, the size of the firm and the number of potential customers are given by the following expressions:

$$l^* = \frac{N}{M}\frac{1}{1+\beta^*}, \quad N^p = N\frac{\beta^*}{1+\beta^*}. \tag{8}$$

Finally, optimal CA expenditures in the steady state are given by:

$$A^* = \theta v^* N^{p^*}. \tag{9}$$

We should note that the acquisition technology has no impact on the optimal CR expenditure. However, the opposite is not true: the retention technology does have an impact on the optimal CA expenditure. Indeed, the shape of $\beta(\bullet)$, together with ρ and m, determines the customer value v^* and the number of potential customers and thus affects the optimal CA strategy. This is similar to the one obtained in single-period models; here we show that it also holds in a long-run equilibrium of dynamic interactions.

Impact of the Profit Margin

An application of the implicit function theorem to (7) immediately gives the following proposition.

Proposition 1 A higher value of the profit margin m corresponds to higher steady-state values of per-customer retention expenditures e^*, the net profit margin $(m - e^*)$, and the customer value v^*. A higher value of the profit margin m corresponds to the lower value of the effective attrition rate, β^*.

In the steady state, the number of newly acquired customers is equal to the number of customers defecting from their service providers. Thus β^* determines the churn rate (defined as the share of customers who defect). This is expressed in the following proposition.

Corollary 1 *The churn rate in steady state depends negatively on the profit margin.*

A question of interest for marketing scientists is: "why do some firms spend more on CA than on CR, while others do the opposite?" Fruchter and Zhang (2004) use the ratio of CA expenditures to CR expenditures at firm level to determine the focus of the marketing strategy; they state that a firm's strategy is *more offensive (defensive) strategy* when this ratio is larger (lower). Following Fruchter and Zhang, we introduce a similar measure defined as the share of CA expenditures in the total marketing budget in the steady state, $S_A = A^*/(A^* + E^*)$. If firms spend much more for CR than for CA, S_A is close to zero; if the situation is reversed, S_A is close to unity.

Many normative studies have considered a single-customer/single-firm relationship and so have operated with per-customer values of CA and CR expenditures. To make our results comparable with them, we introduce a measure that reflects the ratio of CA to CR expenditures in per capita terms. Spending A^*, a firm acquires N_0^* new customers. Thus, $a = A^* / N_0^*$ is the *per-new-customer* acquisition expenditure, showing how much the firm effectively spends to acquire a single customer. In all consequent periods, the firm spends e^* to retain this customer. Thus, we define $s_a = a^*/(a^* + e^*)$. Note that s_a is close to one if the firm spends much more on acquiring a single customer than on retaining this customer in each period; s_a is close to zero, if the opposite holds.

Using $N_0^* = N^{p*} / M$ and (8) and (9), s_a and S_A may be written as follows:

$$S_a = \frac{1}{1 - \beta' e / \theta}, \quad S_A = \frac{1}{1 - \beta' e / (\beta \theta)}. \tag{10}$$

The following example illustrates that the impact of changes in m on s_a and S_A is not monotone.

Example 1 Blattberg and Deighton (1996) proposed an exponential specification for the retention curve, which later has been widely used (Blattberg et al. 2001, 2008; Pfeifer 2005; Tsao 2013). Adapted to our notation, it takes the following form:

$$\beta(e) = 1 - (1 - \beta_L)(1 - \exp[-ce]), \tag{11}$$

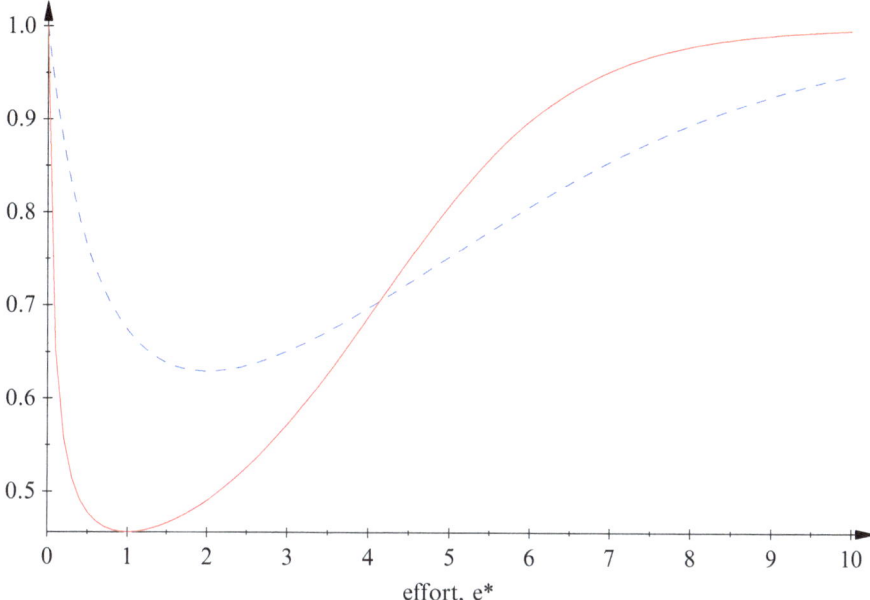

Fig. 1 S_A (*solid line*) and s_a (*dashed line*) as functions of e

where $\beta_L \in (0, 1)$ is the lower limit of the attrition rate, which may be reached at infinite cost, and the parameter $c > 0$ determines the shape of the curve. For this functional form, from (10) we obtain the following:

$$\text{sign}\left[\frac{ds_a}{de}\right] = \text{sign}\left[ce - 1\right], \quad \text{sign}\left[\frac{dS_A}{de}\right] = \text{sign}\left[\beta_L \left(ce - 1\right) - \left(1 - \beta_L\right)\exp\left[-ce\right]\right].$$

This implies that $s_a(e)$ has a unique minimum at $e = 1/c$. Because $e^*(m)$ is monotone in m, s_a has a unique minimum in m. Whenever $\beta_L > 0$, S_A also has a unique minimum in e, and therefore in m. However, if $\beta_L = 0$, then $dS_A/dA < 0$ for all e, that is, S_A monotonically decreases in m. Figure 1 displays functions $S_A(e^*)$ and $s_a(e^*)$ for $c = \frac{1}{2}$, $\beta_L = 1/5$, $\theta = \frac{1}{2}$.

The intuition of these results is the following: If m is low, then the CR expenditures (both e^* and E^*) are low. However, as the set of potential customers N^{p*} is relatively large, A^* is also relatively large. In such a case, an increase in m raises the optimal levels of the CR expenditures (both e^* and E^*) significantly. As the result both S_A and s_a decrease in m for low values of m.

Whenever the lower limit of the attrition rate is positive, the set of potential customers never vanishes. When m becomes large, the level of CR expenditures also rises and the marginal effect of a further increase in e^* on the attrition rate becomes small. Thus, a further increase in m leads to small changes in both e^* and N^{p*}. However, v^* increases almost proportionally to m, and thus both a^* and A^* do so as well. Therefore, both s_a and S_A increase.

We summarize these findings in the following proposition.

Proposition 2 Suppose $\beta(e)$ is given by (11) with $\beta_L > 0$. (*i*) A higher profit margin m results in a larger-sized firm (higher l^*), higher per-new-customer acquisition expenditures, a^*, and higher CR and CA expenditures at the firm level, E^* and A^*. (*ii*) An increase in m lowers both s_a and S_A when m is low and raises both s_a and S_A when m is large.

It follows from Example 1 that whether a firm's strategy becomes more or less oriented toward CA after a change in the profit margin depends to a great extent on the measure chosen: a decrease in S_A may be accompanied with an increase in s_a. Recall also that, by Corollary 1, the equilibrium churn rate is equal to β^* and always decreases in m. If m is low, an increase in m, according to both measures, makes firms' strategy more retention-oriented and accompanied with a lower churn rate. This is consistent with intuition. However, if m is sufficiently large, an increase in m makes firms' strategy *less retention-oriented*, whereas the *churn rate still decreases*. This is due to the fact that both s_a and S_A are based on relative expenditures, whereas β^* is determined solely by per-customer retention expenditures. Thus, an increase in both CA and CR expenditures may lead either to a decrease or an increase in their ratio, while the churn rate always decreases.

The Role of Competition

We start with the case of the profit margin independent of the number of firms, $dm/dM = 0$. Equation (7) does not include M; thus the number of firms has no impact on e^* and therefore on β^*. Together with (8)–(10), this provides the following result.

Proposition 3 Suppose $dm/dM = 0$. (*i*) An increase in competition strength (higher M) has no impact on e^* and v^*; however, a higher M leads to a lower l^*. (*ii*) Both shares S_A and s_a are independent of the number of firms.

According to both economic theory and empirical observation a lower concentration of firms (higher M) tends to raise competition strength and to have a negative impact on prices. Thus, it is reasonable to assume that a higher level of M results in a lower per-customer profit margin, $dm/dM < 0$. Combining Propositions 2 and 3, we obtain the following statement.

Proposition 4 Suppose $dm/dM < 0$ and $\beta(e)$ is given by (11) with $\beta_L > 0$. (*i*) Stronger competition (higher M) leads to lower e^*, v^*, and l^*. (*ii*) An increase in M raises both S_A and s_a when m is small, and lowers both S_A and s_a when m is large.

Note that, while m decreases in M, it does not imply that m is high when M is small, because m may be bounded from above at a level determined by properties of consumers' demand (which are orthogonal to our model). Moreover, it is not necessary that a high level of M leads to a very low level of m. As we have mentioned earlier for special consumers' preferences it even holds that m is independent of M.

Thus, in general, m may be bound from below as well as from above. The extent of indirect impact of competition is determined by the magnitude of its impact on profit margins. If the impact on profit margins is large, then the effects described in Proposition 4 are quantitatively large as well.

Conclusion

Model Limitations and Robustness

We have assumed that the shape of the attrition function does not change over time and it is the same across customers. Customer-loyalty or the cost of switching supplier, however, may be increasing over time during the period the customer stays with the firm (Gupta and Lehmann 2003; Blattberg et al. 2008). Moreover, the marketing literature (Fader and Hardie 2007, 2010) suggests that customers are heterogeneous in their attrition intentions. Capturing such heterogeneity would be an interesting extension of the present model.

We have assumed that an individual firm is inconsequential to the market. That is, whereas a joint behavior of many firms has an impact on the optimal strategy of each firm, actions of any individual firm have no impact on the market or on rivals' strategies. Clearly, this does not hold in markets with a few large firms behaving strategically.

In our model firms' acquisition activities determine the distribution of new customers across individual firms but they do not change the total number of consumers attracted by all firms. This is a good assumption for markets with a finite set of well-informed customers and combative advertising as the main acquisition channel. In other cases, however, as for instance in a market for newly introduced, innovative products, acquisition activity may increase the number of new customers, so that the whole customer base may grow over time.

Contributions and Implications

The results in Proposition 1 are in line with the results obtained in simpler models. Here, we show that these results also hold in the case of dynamic competition. The results in Propositions 2–4 give new insights and implications. Our analysis predicts that CA expenditures constitute the larger part of the marketing budget when the profit margin is either low or relatively large; however, for intermediate profit margin values, firms tend to spend more resources for CR. Moreover, if the customer profit margin rises for exogenous reasons, the effect on markets with high profit margins may be very different from the effect on markets with low profit margins. Although both CA and CR expenditures increase in both cases, the share of CA expenditures in the marketing budget increases in the former situation and decreases in the latter.

If institutional or technological changes bring new firms to the market, the impact on the optimal strategy depends on the effect on profit margins as well as on their absolute levels. This phenomenon may also appear in a single segmented market; the impact of higher competition on the luxury and mass-consumption segments would be different. This should be taken into consideration if the theoretical predictions of the model are to be tested with real data.

We have conducted the analysis in terms of two metrics: the ratios of CA and CR expenditures in the total marketing expenditure at both the firm and the per-customer level. These metrics characterize the optimal marketing budget distribution, however they should be interpreted with caution. Based on these metrics, a more retention-oriented strategy does not imply a lower customer churn rate.

The normative implications of the model may be of value to marketing and customer relations managers who, faced with the challenge to respond to perceived changes in the market environment, they often have to resort to rule-of-thumb and short-term tactics based on very simple conjectures about how short-term reactions will affect long-term outcomes.

Appendix 1: Characterization of the Equilibrium of the Firm

We write the Hamiltonian function as follows: $H^i = \exp[-\rho\ t]\{(m - e^i)l^i + \lambda^i\{-\beta\ l^i + N^p\ s^i\}$, where λ^i is a co-state variable. As $dN^p/dl^0 = 0$ and $ds^i/dA^j = 0$, the first-order conditions are as follows:

$$\lambda^i\left(-\frac{d\beta^i}{de^i}\right) = \exp[-\rho t], \tag{12}$$

$$\lambda^i N^p\left(\frac{ds^i}{dA^i}\right) = \exp[-\rho t], \tag{13}$$

$$\frac{dl^i}{dt} = -\beta^i l^i + N^p s^i, \tag{14}$$

$$\frac{d\lambda^i}{dt} = -\exp[-\rho t]\left(m - e^i\right) + \lambda^i\beta^i. \tag{15}$$

The solution paths must also satisfy the transversality condition, $\lim_{t\to\infty} \lambda^i = 0$. Equations (12) and (13) combined give the condition:

$$N^p\left(ds^i\ /\ dA^i\right) = -\left(\beta^i\right)'. \tag{16}$$

Differentiating equation (12) with respect to t and substituting the result into (15), we obtain the expression:

$$\frac{de^i}{dt} = -\left[\left(\beta^i\right)'\left(m - e^i\right) + \left(\beta^i + \rho\right)\right]\frac{\left(\beta^i\right)'}{\left(\beta^i\right)''}.$$ (17)

For the symmetric long-run equilibrium, (1), (14), (16), and (17) provide (7)–(9). It may be shown that the function H^i is quasi-concave jointly in (e^i, A^i, l^i). Hence, a path that satisfies the first-order necessary conditions gives the optimal solution.

Appendix 2: Existence and Uniqueness of the Long-Run Equilibrium

Considering the optimal path of e determined by (17), we define $G(e) \equiv \beta'(e)(m - e) + \beta(e) + \rho$. It can be seen that $G(0) < 0$, $G(e)$ monotonically increases in e on $[0, m]$, $G(m) > 0$ and $G(e)$ is positive and decreases in e for all $e > m$. Therefore, for $e \in [0, m]$, there exists the unique e^*, such that $G(e^*) = 0$. Thus, $e(t) = e^*$ is the unique stationary solution of $de/dt = 0$.

For paths that start at $e > e^*$, we have $de/dt > 0$, which implies $e(t) \rightarrow \text{const} > m$, as $t \rightarrow \infty$. These paths cannot be equilibrium, as firms get negative per-period profit in the long run. For paths starting at $e < e^*$, we have $de/dt < 0$, so they lead to $e = 0$. These paths cannot be equilibrium paths: marginal retention expenditures at unit marginal cost would bring the positive next-period gain $-\beta'(0)\, m > 1$ and would therefore increase the profit.

References

Bagwell, K. (2007). The economic analysis of advertising. In M. Armstrong & R. H. Porter (Eds.), *Handbook of industrial organization* (Vol. 3, pp. 1701–1844). Amsterdam: North-Holland.

Berger, P. D., & Bechwati, N. N. (2001). The allocation of promotion budget to maximize customer equity. *Omega, 29*, 49–61.

Berger, P. D., & Nasr, N. I. (1998). Customer lifetime value: Marketing models and applications. *Journal of Interactive Marketing, 12*, 17–30.

Blattberg, R. C., & Deighton, J. (1996). Manage marketing by the customer equity test. *Harvard Business Review, 74*, 136–144.

Blattberg, R., Getz, G., & Thomas, J. S. (2001). *Customer equity: Building and managing relationships as valuable assets*. Boston, MA: Harvard Business School Press.

Blattberg, R. C., Kim, B. D., & Neslin, S. A. (2008). Acquisition and retention management. In *Database marketing: Analyzing and managing customers* (International series in quantitative marketing, Vol. 18, pp. 675–711). New York: Springer.

Chen, Y., Joshi, Y. V., Raju, J. S., & Zhang, Z. J. (2009). A theory of combative advertising. *Marketing Science, 28*, 1–19.

Dorotic, M., Bijmolt, T. H., & Verhoef, P. C. (2012). Loyalty programmes: Current knowledge and research directions. *International Journal of Management Reviews, 14*, 217–237.

Erickson, G. M. (2009). An oligopoly model of dynamic advertising competition. *European Journal of Operational Research, 197*, 374–388.

Fader, P. S., & Hardie, B. G. (2007). How to project customer retention. *Journal of Interactive Marketing, 21*, 76–90.

Fader, P. S., & Hardie, B. G. (2010). Customer-base valuation in a contractual setting: The perils of ignoring heterogeneity. *Marketing Science, 29*, 85–93.

Fruchter, G. E., & Zhang, Z. J. (2004). Dynamic targeted promotions: A customer retention and acquisition perspective. *Journal of Service Research, 7*, 3–19.

Gupta, S., Hanssens, D., Hardie, B., Kahn, W., Kumar, V., Lin, N., et al. (2006). Modeling customer lifetime value. *Journal of Service Research, 9*, 139–155.

Gupta, S., & Lehmann, D. R. (2003). Customers as assets. *Journal of Interactive Marketing, 17*, 9–24.

Kumar, V. (2008). *Managing customers for profit: Strategies to increase profits and build loyalty.* Upper Saddle River, NJ: Prentice Hall.

Kumar, V., Lemon, K. N., & Parasuraman, A. (2006). Managing customers for value: An overview and research agenda. *Journal of Service Research, 9*, 87–94.

Martin-Herran, G., McQuitty, S., & Sigue, S. P. (2012). Offensive versus defensive marketing: What is the optimal spending allocation? *International Journal of Research in Marketing, 29*, 210–219.

Pfeifer, P. E. (2005). The optimal ratio of acquisition and retention costs. *Journal of Targeting, Measurement and Analysis for Marketing, 13*, 179–188.

Reinartz, W. J., Thomas, J. S., & Kumar, V. (2005). Balancing acquisition and retention resources to maximize customer profitability. *Journal of Marketing, 69*, 63–79.

Rust, R. T., Lemon, K., & Zeithaml, V. (2004). Return on marketing: Using customer equity to focus marketing strategy. *Journal of Marketing, 68*, 109–126.

Syam, N. B., & Hess, J. D. (2006). *Acquisition versus retention: Competitive customer relationship management.* Working paper, University of Houston.

Thomas, J. S. (2001). A methodology for linking customer acquisition to customer retention. *Journal of Marketing Research, 38*, 262–268.

Thomas, J., Reinartz, W., & Kumar, V. (2004). Getting the most out of all your customers. *Harvard Business Review, 82*, 116–123.

Tsao, H.-Y. (2013). Budget allocation for customer acquisition and retention while balancing market share growth and customer equity. *Marketing Letters, 24*, 1–11.

Venkatesan, R., & Kumar, V. (2004). A customer lifetime value framework for customer selection and resource allocation strategy. *Journal of Marketing, 68*, 106–125.

Verhoef, P. C., van Doorn, J., & Dorotic, M. (2007). Customer value management: An overview and research agenda. *Marketing ZFP – Journal of Research and Management, 3*, 105–120.

Voss, G. B., & Voss, Z. G. (2008). Competitive density and the customer acquisition-retention trade-off. *Journal of Marketing, 72*, 3–18.

Internal Marketing of Corporate Social Responsibility (CSR) Initiatives: CSR Portfolio Effects on Employee Perceptions of Corporate Hypocrisy, Attitudes, and Turnover

Sabrina Scheidler, Laura Marie Schons, and Jelena Spanjol

Abstract Firms invest significant budgets in Corporate Social Responsibility (CSR) activities. Donations to nonprofit organizations that fight poverty or protect the environment demonstrate support of a firm's external stakeholders. Customers are increasingly interested in how firms support their internal stakeholders (i.e., employees), yet many firms are lagging on such CSR activities.

Understanding employees as internal customer of firms' CSR investments is critical as they play a decisive role in extracting value from a firm's CSR activities (Korschun, Bhattacharya and Swain 2014; Rupp et al. 2013; Vlachos, Theotokis and Panagopoulos 2010) and represent an essential mediator between CSR and financial performance (Peloza 2009; Surroca, Tribo and Waddock 2010). Dissatisfied employees might negatively impact other stakeholder groups such as customers (e.g., Lings and Greenley 2005), for whom they are a highly credible source of CSR information (Dawkins 2004; Morsing, Schultz and Nielsen 2008). In other words, employees' hypocrisy perceptions evoked by an imbalanced CSR portfolio might make or break a CSR strategy.

Taking a portfolio perspective informed by stakeholder theory, our research is the first to explore the impact of CSR portfolio imbalances, i.e., larger company-external than internal CSR efforts. Two studies demonstrate the detrimental effects of such imbalances on company-internal stakeholders, i.e., employees. Study 1 utilizes a multisource secondary dataset ($n = 1902$) and shows that imbalanced CSR portfolios significantly increase objective employee turnover at the organizational

S. Scheidler (✉) • L.M. Schons
Ruhr-Universität Bochum, Bochum, Germany
e-mail: sabrina.scheidler@rub.de; laura.schons@rub.de

J. Spanjol
University of Illinois at Chicago, Chicago, IL, USA
e-mail: spanjol@uic.edu

© Academy of Marketing Science 2016
L. Petruzzellis, R.S. Winer (eds.), *Rediscovering the Essentiality of Marketing*, Developments in Marketing Science: Proceedings of the Academy of Marketing Science, DOI 10.1007/978-3-319-29877-1_112

553

level. Study 2 employs a cross-industry employee survey ($n = 3110$) to demonstrate that imbalanced CSR portfolios evoke employees' corporate hypocrisy perceptions and thereby promote emotional exhaustion and intention-to-quit. Both studies point to the crucial importance of taking a holistic approach to manage CSR portfolios, taking into account and balancing external and internal CSR customers.

References available upon request.

Part XIV
Pricing and Price-Related Issues

Effects of Price Promotions on Consumers' Reference Prices: The Role of Contextual Factors and Price Claims

Silke Bambauer-Sachse and Laura Massera

Introduction

Price-related advertising aims to create positive consumer responses such as higher purchase intentions (Ailawadi and Neslin 1998). However, consumers faced with price promotions perceive a discrepancy between their reference price (RP) and the new (lower) price information, and they tend to adjust their price beliefs (Biswas and Blair 1991) by reducing their RP related to the promoted product (Folkes and Wheat 1995; Grewal et al. 1998). This mechanism leads to higher price sensitivity (Mela et al. 1997) and lower willingness to pay (Ranyard et al. 2001). Starting from the notion that consumers' RP decrease after contact with price-related advertising, the objective of this study is to propose a regression model in order to examine the weights consumers assign to different price claims (consumers' initial RP and the reduced price displayed in the price promotion) in the context of RP adaptation after contact with a price promotion displaying the reduced price and the saving. The regression model additionally includes specific conditions: the saving format that is used to present the discount (percentage-off vs. amount-off) and the number of ad contacts consumers have. Thus, we simultaneously analyze direct and interaction effects of price claims and marketer-controlled factors that play a role in the context of consumers' RP adaptation through price promotions. There is evidence that the saving format plays a role in the context of effects of price promotions (Hardesty and Bearden 2003) because price information is processed differently depending on which saving format is displayed (DelVecchio 2005). Findings on effects on consumers' RP are inconsistent across studies (Chandrashekaran and Grewal 2006; DelVecchio et al. 2007), but there is evidence that the saving format interacts with other variables. Moreover, while previous studies were based on one ad contact,

S. Bambauer-Sachse (✉) • L. Massera
University of Fribourg, Fribourg, Switzerland
e-mail: silke.bambauer-sachse@unifr.ch; laura.massera@unifr.ch

© Academy of Marketing Science 2016
L. Petruzzellis, R.S. Winer (eds.), *Rediscovering the Essentiality of Marketing*,
Developments in Marketing Science: Proceedings of the Academy of Marketing
Science, DOI 10.1007/978-3-319-29877-1_113

consumers have more contacts with advertising in reality. Previous research provides the notion that repeated contacts with price discounts have effects on expected product prices (Chen 2011; Kalwani and Yim 1992; Lattin and Bucklin 1989), but the mechanism of consumers' RP adaptation has not been analyzed in much detail in previous studies. Given that the major goal of price-related advertising is to trigger positive consumer responses, the results of such an analysis are interesting for marketers because they get new insights into the complex mechanisms that underlie consumers' RP adaptation after contact with price-related advertising. As consumers' RP influence response variables such as willingness to pay, it is important to understand RP adaptation in order to be able to anticipate possible negative effects of price promotions. As a consequence, marketers can make appropriate strategic decisions such as choosing the most beneficial saving format.

Background

The reference price represents an internal (Cheng and Monroe 2013) and multidimensional price belief which is based on many types of price information (Lowengart 2002; Rajendran and Tellis 1994) and is the reference against which consumers compare actual prices when evaluating products and making purchase decisions (Han et al. 2001). Adaptation level theory (Helson 1964) suggests that people adjust their past beliefs by including new stimuli. Thus, the reference price is a dynamic price (Cheng and Monroe 2013) which changes over time through the inclusion of new pieces of price information (Hamelin 2000). Assumptions on the factors that cause changes of consumers' RP vary across the studies, but research agrees that consumers' RP is modified by incorporating new price information, which becomes available (Grewal et al. 1998; Kalyanaram and Winer 1995). This adaptation is based on heuristic processes on a subconscious level (Chandrashekaran and Grewal 2003). Yadav and Seiders (1998) argue that consumers consider the new price claims an anchor toward which they adjust their RP without completely replacing previous price beliefs. Lichtenstein et al. (1991) as well as Monroe (1973) argue that the adjustment of consumers' RP depends on contextual cues.

Previous studies used regression models with variables from three categories in order to analyze RP adaptation after contact with price-related advertising: type of price information (initial RP, actual/regular price, last price paid, deal price: Greenleaf 1995; Jacobson and Obermiller 1990; Kopalle and Lindsey-Mullikin 2003; Lattin and Bucklin 1989; Winer 1986), marketer-controlled factors such as deal frequency, and consumer-specific factors such as deal proneness (Briesch et al. 1997; Kalwani et al. 1990).

Going beyond previous models, we propose a model, in which consumers' initial RP (RP_{in}) and the reduced price (P_{red}) explain RP adaptation after contact with a price promotion (RP_{ad}). We include the saving format (F) used for the discount and the number of ad contacts (C) as moderator variables that affect how the two price claims are incorporated in the adapted RP instead of analyzing only direct effects as it was done in previous studies. Consumer characteristics are not included to limit complexity and to avoid bias by mixing manipulated and measured variables. The proposed model is as follows:

$$RP_{ad} = \beta_0 + \beta_1 \left(RP_{in}\right) + \beta_2 \left(P_{red}\right) + \beta_3 \left(F\right) + \beta_4 \left(C\right)$$
$$+ \beta_5 \left(RP_{in}\right)\left(F\right) + \beta_6 \left(P_{red}\right)\left(F\right)$$
$$+ \beta_7 \left(RP_{in}\right)\left(C\right) + \beta_8 \left(P_{red}\right)\left(C\right)$$
$$+ \beta_9 \left(RP_{in}\right)\left(F\right)\left(C\right) + \beta_{10} \left(P_{red}\right)\left(F\right)\left(C\right)$$

Based on this model, the hypotheses will be developed in the following. Kalwani et al. (1990) show that environmental factors such as advertising frequency are likely to affect how consumers adapt their RP. In general, repeated contacts with information have effects on consumer learning (Obermiller 1985) and lead to better message recall (Batra and Ray 1986) as well as to a reduction of the expected product price (Chen 2011; Kalwani and Yim 1992). In addition, DelVecchio and Craig (2008) argue that, with an increasing frequency of ad contacts, consumers pay more attention to the encountered price claims and they are increasingly attracted by the lowest price displayed. Therefore, the following hypothesis is formulated for an ad displaying a reduced price:

H1: With an increasing number of ad contacts, the reduced price (consumers' initial RP) has a stronger (weaker) effect on consumers' RP adaptation.

As there is evidence that consumers do not deeply assimilate the advertised information after one ad contact (Renaud 2002) and as several ad contacts represent the more realistic situation, we focus on effects of two alternative saving formats (percentage-off and amount-off) in the case of an increasing number of contacts with the price promotion. In general, repeated contacts with information provide consumers with additional opportunities to think about the information and thus lead to more precise information processing (Cacioppo and Petty 1989). With a higher number of contacts with a price promotion, the reduced price is increasingly recognized as a representative piece of price information (Kalwani and Yim 1992). The format used to present the saving is likely to affect how the different types of price claims influence consumers' RP adaptation (DelVecchio et al. 2007). The percentage-off format is more difficult to process than the amount-off format (DelVecchio 2005), communicates less clearly the price information (Chen and Rao 2007), and requires more cognitive effort. As consumers are usually not willing to spend additional effort to process abstract price cues (Krishnan et al. 2006), they are less able or willing to process the percentage-off format (Berkowitz and Walton 1980). Thus, there is a high likelihood that they blind out the saving and consider the reduced price as the fair price (Darke and Chung 2005). Furthermore, it can be argued that an increasing number of ad contacts make the reduced price salient, which leads to replacing the initial RP. The amount-off format, which shows the saving explicitly (Weisstein et al. 2013; Yin and Dubinsky 2004), can be more easily processed because it is based on the same unit as the other price claims (Chandrashekaran and Grewal

2006). Thus, consumers are more conscious that the reduced price is an exception and realize that their RP should be based on realistic prices. When consumers are repeatedly exposed to the amount-off format, they are able to easily determine the regular price based on the reduced price and the price reduction, and the so-determined piece of price information more or less confirms their initial RP. Thus, they are likely to think that their initial RP is still reasonable. Consequently:

H2: With an increasing number of ad contacts, the reduced price (consumers' initial RP) has a stronger effect on consumers' RP adaptation when the percentage-off (amount-off) format is used.

Methodology

The sample consisted of 200 respondents (48.3 % women, average age=24.3). The data collection took place in Switzerland. The study was based on 16 scenarios: 2 (saving format: percentage-off vs. amount-off)×2 (number of ad contacts: 1 vs. 5)×2 (test product: T-shirt vs. jeans)×2 (level of discount: low vs. high). The two test products and discount levels were used to generate variance in the reduced price and in the initial RP. Based on previous studies (Della Bitta and Monroe 1981; Hardesty and Bearden 2003), 10 % and 50 % were chosen as representing rather low and high discount levels. Eight test ads (2 saving format×2 products×2 levels of discount) that resulted from the experimental design were used. In order to manipulate the number of ad contacts, we used folders containing nine ads, which comprised a combination of one or five target ads and filler ads (1 contact: 1 target ad, 8 filler ads; 5 contacts: 5 target ads, 4 filler ads). The filler ads were used to guarantee that every respondent saw the same number of ads. The order of the nine ads was varied across respondents in order to counterbalance possible order effects. The data collection was based on personal interviews. First, respondents' initial RP with regard to the respective product was measured. Then, they were asked to assume that they were strolling through a shopping mall with the intention to purchase the tested product and they were shown the folder containing the stimulus material presented as the mall's brochure. Afterwards, they had to indicate their RP again. The initial and the adapted RP were measured using the same three pieces of price information (average price, price expected for the next purchase, and appropriate price) as recommended by Chandrashekaran (2004). The high α-values ($\alpha_{RPin}=.94$, $\alpha_{RPad}=.93$) show that the three items are appropriate to reliably measure consumers' RP. We calculated both overall variable values by averaging the three single pieces of price information.

Results and Discussion

Regression analysis with interaction effects was used to estimate the model parameters ($R^2=.93$). The results show basically that the adapted RP after contact with a price promotion strongly depends on consumers' initial RP ($\beta=.75$, $p<.001$).

This result confirms that past price beliefs strongly influence a recently formed RP. The reduced price has only in tendency a main effect ($\beta=.16$, $p<.10$), its influence seems to depend on specific conditions. The two-way interactions of the price claims and the number of ad contacts are at least in tendency significant. The influence of consumers' initial RP on the adapted RP is lower with a higher number of ad contacts ($\beta=-.24$, $p<.05$). After repeated contacts with the new price claims, consumers' previous price beliefs seem to loose importance, and the adapted RP is in tendency rather based on the reduced price ($\beta=.25$, $p<.10$) confirming in tendency H1. However, the two-way interactions of consumers' initial RP/reduced price and the saving format are not significant ($p>.05$) when no further conditions are considered.

The three-way interactions of consumers' initial RP (reduced price), the saving format, and the number of contacts are significant ($p<.01$, ($p<.01$)). To examine the three-way interactions in more detail, the regression model was modified in a second step in that the saving format was no longer part of the model, but was used as a split file variable. The model was estimated separately for the percentage-off ($R^2=.90$) and the amount-off ($R^2=.95$) condition. The interaction effects demonstrate that, if the percentage-off format is used, there is a significantly negative interaction of consumers' initial RP and the number of ad contacts ($\beta=-.27$, $p<.05$). Thus, the effect of consumers' initial RP on RP adaptation is attenuated with an increasing number of ad contacts and consumers replace it with the reduced price which has more weight when the number of contacts is higher ($\beta=.38$, $p<.05$). Thus, H2 is confirmed for the percentage-off format. In the case of the amount-off format, the "reduced price × number of ad contacts" interaction has a negative sign which means that the influence of the reduced price on the adapted RP gets lower with a higher number of ad contacts ($\beta=-.40$, $p<.01$). After only one ad contact consumers focus on the reduced price when adapting their RP, but with an increasing number of contacts with the reduced price and the reduction presented in the amount-off format, they are better able to process both pieces of price information. The "initial RP × number of ad contacts" interaction is not significant ($\beta=-.08$, $p>.05$). Thus, regarding the amount-off format, H2 is only partially confirmed.

Conclusion and Implications

The purpose of this study was to present a model which determines the influence of different price claims (consumers' initial RP and the reduced price displayed in the price promotion) for two saving formats (percentage-off vs. amount-off) and different numbers of ad contacts (1 vs. 5) on consumers' RP adaptation in the context of price promotions. The results show that the adapted RP depends on consumers' initial RP, and the strength of the influence decreases with a higher number of ad contacts. The influence of the reduced price depends on contextual factors. The findings show that when the percentage-off format is used, the reduced price has a stronger effect on RP adaptation after more ad contacts because the reduced price remains the only obviously available piece of price information. Such a strong influence of the reduced price on price beliefs can generate negative effects when the price promotion is over and the product is sold at the regular price again. If the amount-off format is used, the promoted price information has less impact on the adapted RP when consumers are repeatedly exposed to the discount. After repeated contacts with this piece of price information, consumers seem to focus on the regular price, which results from adding the discount to the reduced price. When consumers are exposed repeatedly to a price promotion, it can be recommended to use the amount-off format because in this case, consumers assimilate less the promoted price claims which could lead to possible negative consumer' responses in future purchase situations. As the regression model proved to well predict the effects of consumers' RP adaptation, future research could use it as a starting point to analyze additional factors such as deal proneness (Briesch et al. 1997), price confidence (Yadav and Seiders 1998), and math anxiety (Suri et al. 2013) in the context of price promotions.

References available upon request.

Consumer Preferences for Bundles and Bundle Components with Odd and Even Price Endings

Bernhard Baumgartner and Anjulie Hähnchen

Abstract Marketing literature suggests that price endings can have an impact on consumers' evaluations of the product as well as his/her intention to buy. Retailers often use odd prices, e.g. prices ending in '9'. While also bundles of products are regularly offered with odd prices, literature on the application of odd and even prices in bundles is nearly non-existent. In this research, we investigate the impact of odd and even priced bundle components as well as odd and even total prices on consumer preferences.

Choice-based conjoint analysis is applied to investigate preferences. Using a hierarchical Bayesian approach, we allow for consumer heterogeneity. Individual-specific variables (price- and quality consciousness) are included as concomitant variables. Members of a national online panel completed an online questionnaire, including 11 choice sets. In each choice set, the respondents chose between purchasing a desk chair, a trolley, a bundle of these products or none of these options. The products and the bundle were presented with varying prices ending in odd or even numbers.

We find only weak indication for direct effects of an odd component price on the choice probability of the respective component. The preference for the bundle increases if both components are labelled with even prices instead of using odd component prices. This result suggests that consumers use even prices as an indicator of quality and therefore prefer bundles consisting of even priced components. The preference for the bundle does not only depend on the price ending of the components, but also on the last digit of the bundle price. The bundle choice probability increases with an odd bundle price as compared to an even bundle price. This outcome appears plausible because we do not expect a quality image effect for the bundle price. Therefore, the odd total price causes level effects or price image effects. As a consequence, the probability of buying the bundle is highest if both components are labelled with even prices, whereas the total bundle price has an odd price ending. We did not find evidence for moderating effects of price- or quality consciousness.

B. Baumgartner (✉) • A. Hähnchen
University of Osnabrueck, Osnabrück, Germany
e-mail: bebaumga@uos.de; ahaehnch@uos.de

© Academy of Marketing Science 2016
L. Petruzzellis, R.S. Winer (eds.), *Rediscovering the Essentiality of Marketing*,
Developments in Marketing Science: Proceedings of the Academy of Marketing
Science, DOI 10.1007/978-3-319-29877-1_114

From Product Manufacturer to System Provider: Revenue Models for Product Service Systems

Marija Radic, Robert M. Liebtrau, and Dubravko Radic

Abstract Product service systems have received a lot of attention in the last decade from practitioners, politics and academia. Yet, many product service providers struggle with successfully implementing such business models. One key issue from a practitioner's standpoint is the question how to generate sustainable revenues. To date, only little research on this topic exists. The objective of this chapter is to contribute to the discussion by trying to shed light, first, on the question which types of product service systems exist. In a second step, we derive adequate revenue models for the identified types of product service systems.

Keywords Product service system • Servitization • Service innovation • Customer solution • Pricing • Revenue model • Business model • Sustainability

Introduction

Several factors such as fierce international competition, declining margins and changing customer needs lead to increased pressure for companies to continuously innovate and strive for unique selling propositions in their respective markets (Davies et al. 2006; Nordin and Kowalkowski 2010; Spencer and Cova 2012; Ulaga

M. Radic (✉) • R.M. Liebtrau
Fraunhofer MOEZ, Leipzig, Germany
e-mail: Marija.Radic@moez.fraunhofer.de; Robert.Liebtrau@moez.fraunhofer.de

D. Radic
University of Leipzig, Leipzig, Germany
e-mail: radic@wifa.uni-leipzig.de

© Academy of Marketing Science 2016
L. Petruzzellis, R.S. Winer (eds.), *Rediscovering the Essentiality of Marketing*,
Developments in Marketing Science: Proceedings of the Academy of Marketing
Science, DOI 10.1007/978-3-319-29877-1_115

565

and Reinartz 2011). In order to differentiate their own offering while at the same time creating more value for the customer, more and more companies are moving away from selling traditional products and services towards selling combinations of material goods and services. In the literature, different terms have been used to describe these bundles such as product service systems, servitization, customer solutions, integrated solutions and full services (Vandermerwe and Rada 1988; Bonnemeier et al. 2010; Ahlert and Schulze-Bentrop 2010). The benefits of offering product service systems are manifold (Neely 2009): From an economic standpoint, it offers an opportunity for differentiation and stability of revenues. Strategically, it helps to lock in customers, lock out competitors and satisfy the needs of customers. Eventually, some product service systems may have positive environmental impacts (e.g. car sharing).

Different classifications of product service systems in the literature exist and the discussion on differentiating factors is currently still going on (Van Ostaeyen et al. 2013). Tukker (2004) uses the dimension of the relation between product sales and pure service provision to categorize product service systems into the well-established trichotomy of product-oriented, use-oriented and result-oriented product service systems. Fransson and Rehme (2005) define three types of product service systems: product bundling, system selling and solution selling. These types differ along dimensions such as customer integration, customization, seller's role and success factors for the seller. All these dimensions influence the business relationship and can be used to isolate different product service systems.

The consequence is a modified allocation of risks, responsibilities and costs between provider and buyer of a product service system which differs significantly from a classical sales relationship. Customers, for example, don't purchase the property rights of photocopiers, which includes risks such as loss of function of the copier, the monitoring responsibility as well as the costs for care and maintenance. They rather acquire the ability to make copies while the responsibilities for ensuring the functioning of the copier and the resulting costs as well as the recycling costs are ceded to the provider. The producers' responsibility for the take back, recycling or refurbishment of the product is one reason why product service systems could foster sustainability (Mont 2002).

Across industries, companies have successfully introduced innovative business models to achieve competitive advantage as well as customer orientation through product service systems. Examples can be found in the office products industry where Xerox International guarantees fixed prices per copy, the manufacturing industry where DuPont Flooring Systems sells floor systems including the material, installation, take back and recycling, or the car sharing industry where customers buy mobility without owning a car.

An introduction of product service systems, however, is not a trivial exercise and different challenges arise. One elementary question is the determination of an appropriate revenue and price model. The result of a survey among 200 executives from various Fortune 1000 companies shows that only 50 % of the solution providers achieve moderate profits. Another 25 % realize losses in the area of product service systems (Stanley and Wojcik 2005). Roegner et al. (2001) show that solution providers very often fail to realize moderate prices for their offerings. Schenkl et al. (2014) also identify pricing as one of the main factors influencing the market acceptance of product service systems. Despite the relevance of this topic, only few papers deal with the design of price and revenue models for product service systems. The objective of this chapter is to close this gap and provide companies with support in determining adequate price and revenue models for different types of product service systems.

The chapter is structured as follows: We first start with a definition and discussion of the term product service system and related terms that have been used in other literature streams. In chapter 3, we analyse the literature that tries to shed light, first, on the question which types of product service systems exist and, second, papers dealing with the question of revenue models for product service systems. Based on this analysis, we develop our own classification of adequate revenue models for different types of product service systems. The chapter closes with a conclusion and outlook.

Definitions of Product Service Systems

In the literature, different terms have been used to describe bundles of products and services aiming to fulfil customer needs. Besides product service systems (PSS), these are related terms such as hybrid products, customer solutions, integrated solutions and full services. Publications in the field of 'product service systems' can be found in different research fields, especially production, ecology and sustainability (Beuren et al. 2013). In the management science literature, on the other hand, the term 'solution' and variations thereof such as 'integrated solutions', 'customer solutions' or 'hybrid products' predominate.

Beuren et al. (2013) perform a literature review analysing 149 publications dealing with product service systems. Table 1 shows the most common definitions of product service systems.

Common to all definitions is the combination of products and services that interact with each other as a system with the objective to create value and satisfy customer needs.

The major differentiating factor of the definitions in Table 1 is the focus on the environmental impact of product service systems compared to traditional business models. Several qualitative as well as quantitative studies analyse the environmental and economic benefits of product service systems (e.g. Manzini and Vezzoli 2003; Tukker 2004; Lindahl et al. 2014).

The sustainability aspect of product service systems is probably also the major differentiator compared to a business management term that is strongly related: 'customer solutions'. Tuli et al. (2007) analyse the various definitions of a customer

Table 1 Definitions of product service systems

Author(s)	Definition of product service system
(Goedkoop et al. 1999)	A product service-system is a system of products, services, networks of players and supporting infrastructure that continuously strives to be competitive, satisfy customer needs and have lower environmental impact than traditional business models
(Mont 2002)	A system of products, services, supporting networks and infrastructure that is designed to be: competitive, satisfy customer needs and have a lower environmental impact than traditional business models
(Manzini and Vezzoli 2003)	An innovation strategy, shifting the business focus from designing (and selling) physical products only, to designing (and selling) a system of products and services which are jointly capable of fulfilling specific client demands
(Brandstötter et al. 2003)	A PSS consists of tangible products and intangible services, designed and combined so that they are jointly capable of fulfilling specific customer needs. Additionally PSS tries to reach the goals of sustainable development
(Wong 2004)	Product Service Systems (PSS) may be defined as a solution offered for sale that involves both a product and a service element to deliver the required functionality
(Baines 2007)	A PSS is an integrated product and service offering that delivers value in use. A PSS offers the opportunity to decouple economic success from material consumption and hence reduce the environmental impact of economic activity

Source: Beuren et al. (2013)

solution that appear in the academic and practitioner literature and find three commonalities across the definitions:

- First, a solution involves a combination of goods and services.
- Second, the goods and services in a solution are customized, i.e. they are designed to address a customer's particular requirements.
- Third, a solution consists of an integrated set of goods and services, i.e. each good or service in a solution is compatible with other goods and services in the solution.

Several other terms in the management science literature have been used that are closely related to the term customer solution. 'Integrated customer solutions', e.g. are defined as 'a combination of goods and services designed to meet customer's specific business needs' (Bonnemeier et al. 2010: 228). 'Full services' describe 'a comprehensive bundle of products and/or services, that fully satisfies the needs and wants of a customer related to a specific problem'. (Stremersch et al. 2001: 2). Finally, the term 'servitization' 'represents business models that have evolved from a pure product orientation towards an integrated product service system (PSS)' (Gaiardelli et al. 2014: 507). For the purpose of this chapter, we prefer to stick to the wider definition of 'product service systems'. However, the derived revenue and price models can be transferred to the other concepts as well.

Which Revenue Model for Which Type of Product Service System?

Implementing a product service system requires an adaptation of the current business model if not the development of a new business model. The core of any business model is the value proposition which needs to be complemented with an adequate revenue model (Chesbrough 2010; Johnson 2010). In terms of a classification of product service systems, several approaches have been discussed in the literature and the discussion on differentiating factors is still ongoing (Van Ostaeyen et al. 2013).

A number of authors distinguish three different types of product service systems ('classical trichotomy') along the dimension of value being generated mainly with the product versus service content (e.g. Tukker 2004; Mont 2004; Baines 2007): Product-oriented product service systems, use-oriented product service systems and result-oriented product service systems.

In the case of *product-oriented product service systems*, the sale of products dominates the business model. Additional services are added by the provider, but are related to the product and aim at improving the product's functionality and durability. Examples are after sales services such as maintenance, repair, reuse, recycling, or the supply of consumables but also consulting or training services that are related to the product (Tukker 2004; Baines 2007).

The central element of the second category of product service systems is the *use-orientation* of the product. The provider stays in ownership of the product but makes it available to one or many different users. In the case of product lease, the provider is the owner of the product and often also responsible for maintenance, repair, etc. The lessee usually has unlimited and individual access to the leased product. The major difference compared to product renting or sharing is that in these models the user doesn't have unlimited access and others may use it as well in sequential order. In the case of product pooling, the same product is used by different users simultaneously (Tukker 2004).

In the case of *result-oriented product service systems*, provider and client agree on a desired result and the client pays for the result only. Tukker (2004) identifies three different subcategories of result-oriented product service systems: First, activity management or outsourcing, e.g. for office cleaning or catering services where performance indicators are included in the contracts to control for the quality of the service; second, pay-per-service unit where the client pays not for the product but for the product's output such as number of copies in the popular example of pay-per-print formulas of most copier manufacturers; and last but not least functional result where the client and provider agree on an abstract result that needs to be delivered by the client without specifying the exact way this result is obtained.

Meier and Bosslau (2012) develop a comprehensive business model concept for industrial product service systems. Within their concept, they relate the questions of types of industrial product service system and revenue streams stating that 'the issue of revenue for the provider or the payment for the customer is closely linked to the question of value and risks'. In terms of the customer value (benefit), they identify five different types of industrial product service systems in terms of the customer value which are associated with different revenue streams:

- Property of the physical product, with revenues based on order (sale of product or service: cost plus, fixed price).
- Use of the product, with revenues based on order (one-time sale of product and additional services).
- Availability of the product, with revenues not based on unit, but on availability (e.g. in percent of time).
- Result of the use of the product, with revenues not based on unit, but on utilization period.
- Consumption of the product, with revenues based on the frequency of use (e.g. produced units) and in combination with a basic fee for minimal utilization to transfer part of the risk to the client.

Compared to Tukker's (2004) classification, Meier and Bosslau (2012) divide the above called use-oriented product service systems into the subcategories use of the product, availability of the product and result of the use of the product. Tukker's (2004) result-oriented product service systems are, on the other hand, renamed into the category 'consumption of the product' and primarily aim at the specific group of result-oriented product service systems that were identified by Tukker (2004) as pay-per-service unit. Contracts where the client and provider agree on an abstract result that needs to be delivered by the client without specifying the exact way—in Tukker's classical trichotomy named functional result—are not included in Meier and Bosslau's (2012) paper.

In a recent paper, Van Ostaeyen et al. (2013) argue that the classical trichotomy does not capture the complexity of product service systems found in practice because, first, it confuses a use-oriented logic of a product service system with ownership transfer. Second, it does not distinguish between availability and usage. And, third, it does not allow differentiation between types of functional results on different levels of abstraction. They thus propose a new approach which is derived based on a theoretical framework termed Functional Hierarchy Modelling (FHM)—a new functional decomposition framework. According to the authors, a product service system can be better represented by the performance orientation of the dominant revenue mechanism and the level of integration of product and service elements (indicating how many product service elements are combined, i.e. sold in one package with a common revenue mechanism). For the purpose of our research, the question of suitable revenue mechanisms is of special interest. Van Ostaeyen et al. (2013) describe four different types of revenue mechanisms: an input-based revenue mechanism, an availability-based revenue mechanism, a usage-based revenue mechanism and a performance-based mechanism.

Input-based revenue mechanism means that 'revenue is transferred from the customer to the provider according to the inputs delivered to effectuate the function of a product or service'.(Van Ostaeyen et al. 2013). This very much resembles Meier and Bosslau's type of 'property rights of the physical product' and product-oriented product service systems in the classical trichotomy (Meier and Bosslau 2012). In terms of revenue this implies a fixed price which in reality is usually based on a cost-plus calculation for products. Services are priced per intervention and based on time and materials necessary to deliver the service.

An *availability-based revenue mechanism* implies that revenue is transferred from client to provider based on the availability of the product or service (e.g. time period). Important to note here is that revenues are independent of an actual use of the product or service. In practice, clients usually pay a fixed monthly fee for the product or service availability—no matter how extensively the service was actually used. Similar to Meier and Bosslau (2012), Van Ostaeyen et al. (2013) thus differentiate between the pure availability of a product or service and the actual use. In the classical trichotomy described above, availability falls into the category of use-oriented product service systems. As we will see in the next section on usage-based revenue mechanisms, from a pricing perspective availability and pay-per-use are treated differently.

A *usage-based revenue mechanism* means that clients pay for the actual use of the product or service. Usage could be expressed, e.g. in time units (e.g. mobile phone), number of transactions (e.g. banking services) or number of users (e.g. software) or even a combination of dimensions (e.g. taxi meters work with a combination of time and distance). Choosing the right dimension will very much depend on the product's or service's customer value proposition. In the classical trichotomy above, the usage-based revenue mechanisms proposed by Van Ostaeyen et al. (2013) fall under result-oriented product service systems in the subcategory pay-per-service unit. Meier and Bosslau (2012) also place them into the performance result category.

A *performance-based mechanism* according to Van Ostaeyen et al. (2013) means that revenue is transferred from client to provider based on the functional performance of the product or service. In the classical trichotomy, functional result product service systems were one of the subcategories within the bucket of result-oriented product service systems. According to Van Ostaeyen et al. (2013), performance-based mechanisms can be further split into solution-oriented, effect-oriented or demand fulfilment-oriented performance-based revenue mechanisms. The main difference between the three types is the underlying performance indicator. Solution-oriented performance indicators describe the performance of the solution or system itself—and not of the environment. Using the radiator example of Van Ostaeyen et al. (2013), the parameter would be the heat transfer efficiency of the radiator expressed as Equivalence of Direct Radiation. In the case of effect orientation, the underlying indicator is formulated in terms of the effect on the environment and is independent of the solution used. In the radiator example, this could be the provider's promise that the room temperature remains 99% of the time between 20 and 22 Celsius degrees. Last but not least, demand fulfilment orientation means that subjective indicators that express how well the customer demand is fulfilled are used as a pricing basis. In the radiator example, the provider's promise could be a maximum Percentage People Dissatisfied (PPD) with the current thermal comfort level of 5% at all times.

The second dimension of Van Ostaeyen et al. (2013) to classify product service systems is the level of integration between products and services. The key message is that the higher the performance orientation of the revenue mechanism, the more the company providing a product service system will benefit from an integration of products and services.

The last chapter we would like to introduce here is by Bonnemeier et al. (2010) and deals with revenue models for integrated customer solutions. Bonnemeier et al. (2010) point out that solution providers bear higher risk and costs and should thus try to compensate these effects and realize higher margins by setting the price based on customer value instead of their own cost which for a lot of companies is a fundamental change (Cornet et al. 2000; Gebauer and Friedli 2005). Bonnemeier et al. (2010) group pricing measures into traditional and innovative revenue models. In traditional revenue models, the value proposition is based on the product or service supplied by the provider. Innovative pricing models, on the other hand, focus on the actual input or output of the client according to the service-dominant logic of marketing (Vargo and Lusch 2004). This changes the mindset for pricing by shifting it from provider's cost to the value generated for the customer.

Traditional revenue models according to Bonnemeier et al. (2010) subsume in the case of products either a property rights transfer or only the transfer of possession rights to the customer. In terms of pricing, the models are a simple product sale if the contract includes a property rights transfer. If only possession rights are transferred, then the pricing model is a renting, leasing or licencing model. Transferred to the service example, according to Bonnemeier et al. (2010) the provider charges the customer either a fixed fee or uses a cost-plus approach based on time and materials. The separation of delivery and purchase of a service implies that a service that has been purchased may not be consumed (e.g. IT support services that are not consumed because the systems work well). This non-consumption is challenging for suppliers as well as customers (Shugan and Xie 2005). If the service can be specified before the contract is signed, a fixed fee model is favourable. Otherwise, a time-and-materials model should be applied. Either way, the performance parameter is usually strongly related to the provider's cost. Compared to the classifications above, the traditional models proposed by Bonnemeier et al. (2010) very much resemble the product- and availability-oriented models in the papers discussed above.

Innovative revenue models, on the other hand, use performance parameters that are no longer related to the provider's performance but to the performance of the solution to the customer's business environment. The provider's view thus changes from the so-called inside-out to an outside-in view. Besides cost, market information on competition as well as customer needs become relevant. Bonnemeier et al. (2010) differentiate innovative revenue models in terms of the provider's value proposition: If the provider's value proposition is an input for the customer's production process, a usage-based pricing model (e.g. based on time or intensity of use machines software) such as described above should be used. If the value proposition constitutes an output for the customer's production process, a performance- or value-based pricing model should be used. In the performance-based model, the provider guarantees a specific performance level to the client (e.g. response times for support services or defined quality levels). If the provider can keep this promise, the pre-negotiated price is paid. A poor performance, on the other hand, can result in penalties for the provider (Turner and Simister 2001). This model very much coincides with performance-based models we have described above. Value-based revenue models according to Bonnemeier et al. (2010) focus on optimizing the client's internal processes and thus look at parameters such as optimization or efficiency. The provider thus directly benefits from the value the solution generates for the customer. Total-cost-of-ownership (TCO) analyses could be helpful to determine the value-added for the client. Monetary figures such as increased turnover, cost savings or an increased profitability could be used as parameters. The performance parameters could, however, also be non-monetary such as customer satisfaction. Compared to the other authors above, the revenue models proposed by Bonnemeier et al. (2010) are grouped differently but indirectly use the performance orientation of the customer value proposition as the main differentiating factor.

Based on the papers discussed above, we develop a modified framework in terms of revenue streams and pricing mechanisms for different types of product service systems. Table 2 shows the result of our analysis.

At the core of any business model are customer (segments) and their specific needs. Based on these needs, a company should develop its value proposition and derive adequate revenue models. This explains why we have chosen value proposition as the fundament of our framework—in line with most authors. Based on our analysis of existing studies on product service systems, we differentiate between four different types of product service systems: product-oriented, availability-oriented, use-oriented and performance-oriented product service systems. For each of the four different value propositions, we derive the respective components of a revenue model: revenue streams and underlying pricing mechanisms. It is not unusual that companies have different models simultaneously. To reduce complexity and focus on the major differentiating factors between different types of product service systems, we look at unidimensional pricing mechanisms only at this stage. In reality, multidimensional pricing mechanisms often apply, i.e. different prices for basically the same product as well as multiple prices for multiple products (e.g. price differentiation, product line pricing, see Simon and Fassnacht 2008). They are, however, derived from the basic mechanisms described in Table 1.

Product-Oriented Product Service Systems

As has been pointed out by several authors above, companies traditionally used to be and still are often product centric. In terms of revenue generation, this implies a sale of products and additional product-related services that are needed during the use phase of the product (e.g. maintenance contracts, financing schemes) or advice and consultancy related to the product's functionality and efficiency. One example is ThyssenKrupp Elevator which manufactures elevators for all kinds of buildings. Besides, their 'capabilities are rounded out by high-quality, customer-oriented service as well as individual maintenance and modernization packages' (ThyssenKrupp Elevator 2015). Similar examples can be found across industries. Regarding the pricing structure, a fixed price for the product is usually charged to the customers. Service fees, on the other hand, are either fixed fees or calculated based on the provider's input, i.e. cost in terms of time and materials are charged to the customer. The choice of pricing mechanism depends on several factors. One important factor is the distribution of risk: In the case of a fixed fee, the risk lies with the vendor, whereas in the time and materials setup, the customer shoulders the risk. In general, if the scope can be fixed before the signing of the contract, a fixed fee may be advantageous.

In practice, prices are often determined based on a cost plus calculation. Additionally, competitor pricing or information on customers' willingness to pay should be integrated into the pricing decisions. Providers also try to increase customer orientation and margins in this setup through multidimensional pricing structures such as price bundling, product line pricing or price differentiation. As has been stated above, these advanced pricing techniques are disregarded at this stage to work out the four different core models.

Availability-Oriented Product Service Systems

Van Ostaeyen et al. (2013) point out that the classical trichotomy does not distinguish between use- and availability-oriented product service systems. We also incorporate this distinction into our framework due to its implications in terms of the revenue model: An availability-based revenue mechanism implies that revenue is transferred from client to provider based on the availability of the product or service—and not its actual use. In practice, clients usually pay a fixed monthly fee for the product or service availability, no matter how extensively the service was used. There are plenty examples for availability-oriented product service systems: In a business to business context with investment goods, customers are often not willing to purchase the products and prefer leasing or renting arrangements. There are different reasons for requiring the provider's flexibility. This could, on the one hand, be budget restrictions preventing the customer from making larger investments. On the other hand, clients often want to keep their flexibility if, e.g. the business related to the product is volatile, technological progress quickly leads to outdated products or if the customers are striving for independence from singular providers. Car leasing is another example for availability-oriented product service systems.

In terms of revenue stream types, licencing, leasing, renting, sharing or pooling models can apply. In a licencing model which is frequently found, e.g. in the software industry, revenue is generated from charging for the use of a protected intellectual property. Leasing, on the other hand, means that exclusive right is given to an asset for a particular period of time, as in the above mentioned car leasing example (Osterwalder and Pigneur 2010). The major difference of leasing concepts compared to product renting or sharing is that in these models the user doesn't have unlimited access and others may use it as well in sequential order. In the case of product pooling, the same product is used by different users simultaneously (Tukker 2004).

Use-Oriented Product Service Systems

In Table 1 above, the colour code for availability- and use-oriented product service systems is identical. The first reason is that in use-oriented models several revenue streams apply that we just discussed for availability-oriented models above: Licencing, leasing, renting, sharing and pooling models are use oriented if the pricing mechanism is tied to usage. The second reason is that in practice, multiple pricing components that combine fixed and usage-based fees are quite common, especially in the service sector (Simon and Fassnacht 2008). One example is the car rental business: The provider charges a rental fee, but additional charges apply, e.g. for fuel or usage above a predetermined miles cap. Another example is the car sharing economy where users often pay a fixed monthly fee plus additional fees based on duration or kilometres of the ride.

Table 1 additionally shows the pure pay-per-use model. In this model, revenues are tied to usage only. Compared to the other models, this imposes a larger risk on the provider because capacities have to be held available independent of their actual use by the client. Many providers shift part of this risk back to their clients by imposing an additional basic fee as we just described in the car rental and sharing examples. This emphasizes the power of pricing in terms of a redistribution of risk between client and provider. Examples for pure pay-per-use models are mobile phone contracts, laundromats, the frequently mentioned pay-per-copy models of copier manufacturers or software services where the customer is charged based on the number of searches, transactions, number of users, etc. (Bontis and Chung 2000). In general, we agree with Bonnemeier et al. (2010) who state that use-oriented product service systems make sense in setups where the provider's product or service is an input to the client's production process.

Performance-Oriented Product Service Systems

Performance-oriented models represent the highest degree of customer orientation from a provider's perspective. In this setup, a client and provider agree on a desired result of the product or service in advance and define one or multiple criteria to measure the provider's performance. Revenues are thus defined based on a performance contract. As van Ostaeyen et al. (2013) outline, the parameters can range from performance parameters of the solution itself, of a desired effect the solution has on the environment or could even be linked to demand fulfilment criteria such as subjective satisfaction levels (van Ostaeyen et al. 2013). As described by Bonnemeier et al. (2010), the performance could also focus on optimizing the client's internal processes and thus look at parameters focused on increasing optimization or efficiency. Frequently found parameters are monetary figures such as increased turnover, cost savings or an increased profitability. One of the leading providers of online shop solutions, e.g. participates in its clients' performance through a percentage per online transaction they conduct for their customers. In the consulting business, (partial) compensation based on the client's satisfaction level is also quite common. As was described in the section on use-oriented product service systems, many providers shift part of the risk associated with performance-oriented product service systems back to their clients by imposing an additional fixed fee which is why we've added the combination of pricing mechanisms.

Performance-oriented models are often found in setups where the provider's performance is related to the client's output from the production process. An important prerequisite for such a revenue model is that providers can actually influence the defined performance parameters. In many industries, it is not unusual to even charge penalties in case the desired performance hasn't been achieved by the provider.

Conclusion and Outlook

This chapter tries to contribute to the existing literature on product service systems in different respects. First, product service systems are vividly discussed in many disciplines under different 'labels'. In our chapter, we present the different terms and their variations regarding the definition, and thus try to raise awareness of important analyses performed in other disciplines. The primary objective of this chapter, however, was to determine adequate revenue models for different types of product service systems. For this purpose, we discuss the literature dealing with the classification of product service systems, on the one hand, and underlying revenue streams and pricing mechanisms on the other hand. To the best of our knowledge, there is only little literature dealing with the elementary question which revenue model to use when offering product service systems. Based on this analysis, we develop a new framework consisting of revenue streams and pricing mechanisms for different types of product service systems. We thereby contribute to the discussion on different types of product service systems as well as the elementary question for any practitioner dealing with an enhancement of its current or the development of a new business and revenue model through product service systems. Our new framework has been validated with top managers from several companies and different sectors. A valuable extension of the current work would be a systematic validation with companies from different industries which would also allow drawing conclusions regarding the state of product service systems and corresponding revenue models in different sectors. As we indicated above, future research should also include multidimensional pricing models as well as concrete recommendations for practitioners how to determine and implement a pricing scheme for their product service offer.

References

Ahlert, D., & Schulze-Bentrop, C. (2010). *Pricing of solutions*. Retrieved June 03, 2015, from http://www.marketingcenter.de/ifhm/forschung/transolve/Transolve_Projektbericht_8.pdf

Baines, T. S. (2007). State-of-the-art in product-service systems. *Proceedings of the Institution of Mechanical Engineers, Part B: Journal of Engineering Manufacture, 221*(10), 1543–1552.

Beuren, F. H., Gomes Ferreira, M. G., & Cauchick Miguel, P. (2013). Product-service systems: A literature review on integrated products and services. *Journal of Cleaner Production, 47,* 222–231.

Bonnemeier, S., Burianek, F., & Reichwald, R. (2010). Revenue models for integrated customer solutions: Concept and organizational implementation. *Journal of Revenue & Pricing Management, 9*(3), 228–238.

Bontis, N., & Chung, H. (2000). The evolution of software pricing: From box licenses to application service provider models. *Internet Research: Electronic Networking Applications and Policy, 10*(3), 246–255.

Brandstötter, M., Haberl, M., Knoth, R., Kopacek, B., & Kopacek, P. (2003). *IT on demand—towards an environmental conscious service system for Vienna (AT)*. Retrieved June 03, 2015, from http://ieeexplore.ieee.org/stamp/stamp.jsp?tp=&arnumber=1322776

Chesbrough, H. (2010). Business model innovation: Opportunities and barriers. *Long Range Planning, 43*(2–3), 354–363.

Cornet, E., Schädler, J., Katz, R., Sharma, D., Molloy, R., & Tipping, A. (2000). *Customer solutions: From pilots to profits*. Retrieved June 03, 2015, from http://www.boozallen.com/media/file/customer_solutions-pilotstoprofits.pdf

Davies, A., Brady, T., & Hobday, M. (2006). Charting a path toward integrated solutions. *MIT Sloan Management Review, 47*(3), 39–48.

Fransson, D., & Rehme, J. (2005). *From product supplier to system provider—changing role for Europe's largest wooden door manufacturer*. In IT in Business ITIB International Conference 2005, Linköping: EKI.

Gaiardelli, P., Resta, B., Martinez, V., Pinto, O., & Ablores, P. (2014). A classification model for product-service offerings. *Journal of Cleaner Production, 66,* 507–519.

Gebauer, H., & Friedli, T. (2005). Behavioral implications of the transition process from products to services. *Journal of Business & Industrial Marketing, 20*(2), 70–78.

Goedkoop, M. J., van Halen, C., te Riele, H., & Rommens, P. (1999). *Product service systems, ecological and economic basics*. Retrieved June 03, 2015, from http://teclim.ufba.br/jsf/indicadores/holan%20Product%20Service%20Systems%20main%20report.pdf

Johnson, M. W. (2010). *Seizing the white space: Business model innovation for growth and renewal*. Boston: Harvard Business Press.

Lindahl, M., Sundin, E., & Sakao, T. (2014). Environmental and economic benefits of integrated product service offerings quantified with real business cases. *Journal of Cleaner Production, 64,* 288–296.

Manzini, E., & Vezzoli, C. (2003). A strategic design approach to develop sustainable product service systems: Examples taken from the "environmentally friendly innovation" Italian prize. *Journal of Cleaner Production, 11*(8), 851–857.

Meier, H., & Bosslau, M. (2012). *Dynamic business models for industrial product-service systems*. Retrieved June 03, 2015, from http://student.systemdynamics.org/wp/wp-content/ulf/colloquia/2012-proceedings/R1465.pdf

Mont, O. K. (2002). Clarifying the concept of product–service system. *Journal of Cleaner Production, 10*(3), 237–245.

Mont, O. K. (2004). *Product-service systems: Panacea or myth*. Doctoral dissertation, IIIEE, Lund University, Lund.

Neely, A. D. (2009). Exploring the financial consequences of the servitization of manufacturing. *Operations Management Research, 2*(1), 103–118.

Nordin, F., & Kowalkowski, C. (2010). Solutions offerings: A critical review and reconceptualization. *Journal of Service Management, 21*(4), 441–459.

Roegner, E. V., Seifert, T., & Swinford, D. D. (2001). Putting a price on solutions. *The McKinsey Quarterly, 3*, 94–97.

Schenkl, S. A., Rösch, C., & Mörtl, M. (2014). Literature study on factors influencing the market acceptance of PSS. *Procedia CIRP, 16*(2014), 98–103.

Shugan, S. M., & Xie, J. (2005). Advance selling as a competitive marketing tool. *International Journal of Research in Marketing, 22*(3), 351–373.

Simon, H., & Fassnacht, M. (2008). *Preismanagement*. Wiesbaden, Germany: Gabler Verlag.

Spencer, R., & Cova, B. (2012). Market solutions: Breaking free from dyad-centric logic and broadening the scope of S-D L. *Journal of Marketing Management, 40*, 699–711.

Stanley, J. E., & Wojcik, P. J. (2005). Better B2B selling. *The McKinsey Quarterly, 38*(3), 15.

Stremersch, S., Wuyts, S., & Frambach, R. T. (2001). The purchasing of full-service contracts: Maintenance market. *Industrial Marketing Management, 30*(1), 1–12.

ThyssenKrupp Elevator. (2015). *Elevators*. Retrieved June 2, 2015, from http://www.thyssenkrupp-elevator.de/Aufzuege.55.0.html?&L=1

Tukker, A. (2004). Eight types of product-service systems: Eight ways to sustainability? Experiences from suspronet. *Business Strategy and the Environment, 13*, 246–260.

Tuli, K., Kohli, A., & Bharadwaj, S. G. (2007). Rethinking customer solutions: From product bundles to relational processes. *Journal of Marketing, 71*(3), 1–17.

Turner, J. R., & Simister, S. J. (2001). Project contract management and a theory of organization. *International Journal of Project Management, 19*(8), 457–464.

Ulaga, W., & Reinartz, W. J. (2011). Hybrid offerings: How manufacturing firms combine goods and services successfully. *Journal of Marketing, 75*(6), 5–23.

Van Ostaeyen, J., Van Horenbeek, A., Pintelon, L., & Duflou, J. R. (2013). A refined typology of product–service systems based on functional hierarchy modeling. *Journal of Cleaner Production, 51*, 261–276.

Vandermerwe, S., & Rada, J. (1988). Servitization of business: Adding value by adding services. *European Management Journal, 6*(4), 314–324.

Vargo, S. L., & Lusch, R. F. (2004). Evolving to a new dominant logic for marketing. *Journal of Marketing, 68*(1), 1–17.

Wong, M. T. N. (2004). *Implementation of innovative product service systems in the consumer goods industry*. Cambridge, MA: University of Cambridge.

Latitude of Quantity Acceptance: Conceptualization and Empirical Validation

Gurumurthy Kalyanaram, Gordhan K. Saini, and Arvind Sahay

Introduction

As a result of increasing costs, consumer packaged goods companies (i.e., fast-moving consumer goods (FMCG) companies) are facing significant pressure on operating margins. For example, the increasing cost of raw material resulted in a steep decline of almost 50 % in operating profit margins in the second quarter of 2010 for Britannia (Economic Times 2010). Firms have been using innovative strategies to adapt to increasing costs in materials. One such strategy has been to decrease the quantity (weight) of a product packet while keeping the price constant. For instance, Frito Lay has reduced the weight per pack by 10–20 %; Cadbury has reduced the pack size of Bournville chocolate by 17–18 % (DNA Syndication 2011), and ITC has substituted raw material edible oil with butter, reduced the quantity per pack, and also hiked the price of high-margin biscuit packs (Economic Times 2010).

In the quantity reduction strategy, it's the consumer who takes the hit as he is offered a lower quantity of the same product at the same price. The major argument in favor of quantity reduction is that the consumer is less likely to notice it as compared

G. Kalyanaram (✉)
International University of Japan, Niigata-ken, Japan
e-mail: kalyan@alum.mit.edu

G.K. Saini
Tata Institute of Social Sciences, Mumbai, Maharashtra, India
e-mail: gksaini@tiss.edu

A. Sahay
Indian Institute of Management, Ahmedabad, Gujarat, India
e-mail: asahay@iimahd.ernet.in

© Academy of Marketing Science 2016
L. Petruzzellis, R.S. Winer (eds.), *Rediscovering the Essentiality of Marketing*,
Developments in Marketing Science: Proceedings of the Academy of Marketing
Science, DOI 10.1007/978-3-319-29877-1_116

579

to the price increase. However, such a strategy may be successful in the short term and may be more feasible for brands with high equity as compared to low equity brands (as found in extant studies level of equity and market share are positive correlated), because the consumer is less likely to switch a brand with a higher loyalty than a brand with lower loyalty (e.g., Fournier 1998). In general, brands with higher equity generate significantly higher customer preferences and purchase intentions (Cobb-Walgren et al. 1995). However, there are several practical questions which a marketing manager would have to answer—for example, what would be the impact of quantity decrease on high equity brands vs. low equity brands? How much quantity reduction is possible for a brand under a specific product category? Can low equity brands increase their market share by offering higher product quantity at the same price? Further, in this chapter, we attempt to answer these very questions by manipulating product quantity of eight selected brands with different levels of product involvement, brand equity, and purchase frequency, asking two specific questions: First, is there a latitude of acceptance with respect to small quantity changes? Second, is there an asymmetric effect of quantity reduction (higher unit price) versus quantity increase (lower unit price)?

Hypotheses

Consistent with the extant literature, we argue that the consumer generally has a reference price for a SKU (stock keeping unit) and this reference tends to be sticky. As discussed earlier, firms consider reducing the product quantity keeping its price unchanged, as one of the options to minimize the adverse impact of higher input cost. Research has shown that consumers have a latitude of indifference around a reference point across many situations/stimuli (e.g., amount of lighting in a room, lifting weights, fluctuations in asset levels, price levels) (Luo 1998; Kardes 2013). Therefore, consumers would be indifferent to this change to an extent, as they are in the case of reference price and other assessments. Evidently, the quantity decrease scenarios are similar to price increases in the sense that they offer lower quantity of a product at the same price, leading to higher per unit price.

We postulate the following three hypotheses with regard to latitude of quantity acceptance and the quantity increase or decrease per unit price.

Hypothesis 1: There exists latitude of quantity acceptance (LQA).

Hypothesis 2: Quantity increase (lower per unit price) will increase consumer purchase intention. Similarly, quantity decrease (higher per unit price) will decrease consumer purchase intention.

Hypothesis 3: The effect of quantity reduction (higher per unit price) will be more for a large market share brand than the effect of quantity increase (lower per unit price) for a small market share brand when the market share differential is large.

Data Collection and Measurement

Selection of Product Categories

First, we selected four product categories—perfumes, fairness cream, antiseptic cream, and aerated beverages, which belonged to high/low involvement and high/low purchase frequency. In order to establish that the selected product categories truly fall in the assumed category, pretest I was done on 40 respondents using Mittal's (1989) purchase involvement scale. Purchase involvement scale showed adequate reliability and generated Cronbach Alpha from .619 to .832. The product categories of perfumes (5.53) and fairness creams (5.48) had high mean scores as compared to antiseptic cream (5.03) and beverages (4.12). *T*-tests were conducted to establish that the mean score of high involvement product categories are statistically different from the mean scores of low involvement product categories. *T*-test produced a *t*-value of 4.56 and *p*-value of less than .05 showing statistically significant difference between high involvement (i.e., perfumes and fairness cream) and low involvement (i.e., antiseptic cream and beverages) product categories. Overall, the results were as expected on the product involvement dimension while they were reverse to the expectations on the purchase frequency dimension for high involvement product category.

Identification of Brands in Product Categories

Second, we identified brands under each product category and conducted pretest II on 40 respondents to determine the brand equity of each brand under each category. Brands were identified through a combination of methods which included judgmental sampling, websites of online retailers, informal discussions with prospective respondents, and discussions with subject matter experts. In pretest II, we employed the Yoo and Donthu (2001) scale for measuring brand equity, and the scale showed sufficient reliability, measured in Cronbach Alpha. Based on pretest II results, we finally selected eight brands: Calvin Klein, Ferragamo (high involvement–high frequency), Boroline, Himalaya (low involvement–low frequency), Loreal, Chambor (high involvement–low frequency), Coke, and Mirinda (low involvement–high frequency).

Measurement of Purchase Intention and Latitude of Quantity Acceptance

Thirdly we measured purchase intention and found LQA for each brand. We therefore propose that the LQA is the level of quantity within which a brand is able to maintain 50 % of its existing market share. Specifically, we find lower LQA for a high equity brand, i.e., the volume level till which at least 50 % of the initial consumers remain with the brand when the quantity is reduced. Similarly, we find the upper LQA for a low equity brand, i.e., the volume level is stable till it attracts additional customers to the extent of at least 50 % of the initial consumers. An initial market share is calculated for both the brands by keeping both the quantity and price constant, and this market share is indicative of the difference in brand equity of the selected brands.

Using LQA, we also attempt to establish the effects of brand equity on consumer purchase intention when the product quantity is changed keeping other factors, like price, constant. To achieve this, we designed a standard questionnaire in which we varied the quantity of different brands in steps, and at each step, the purchase intention was recorded and measured using simple one-item seven-point Likert scale from "strongly disagree" to "strongly agree." A total of 88 useable responses were obtained. The respondents were pursuing their post graduate degree in business management from a business school. Average age of respondents was 22 years, and 53 of them were male. Keeping other parameters constant, purchase intention for each brand was recorded at six quantity levels, i.e., original quantity level and five quantity decrease steps for high equity brand, and original quantity level and five quantity increase steps for low equity brand.

Empirical Analysis and Discussion of Results

Empirical Support for Hypotheses

Our results support the hypotheses with which we had set off on this study, and as expected high equity brands command larger initial market share than low equity brands. Overall, the decline in market share of high equity brands is much sharper than the gain in market share of low equity brands. Under the high equity brand category, the market share declined by as much as 50 % after quantity reduction in the first two steps except for Boroline, where it happened at the third step. Contrary to this, none of the low equity brands were able to achieve even 50 % gains in market share due to the quantity increase. We find that there exists LQA in both high and low equity brands thus supporting our hypothesis 1. However, the range of the LQA is wider for low equity brands than for the high equity brands. Thus, high equity brands are more elastic to quantity reduction while consumers avoid buying low equity brands even if they are offered in higher quantity at the same price point (i.e., low unit price).

We find the positive and negative changes in the consumer purchase intention due to the quantity increase and decrease, respectively, supporting hypothesis 2. Specifically, a lower per unit price has increased the market share of low equity brands up to 47 % (i.e., Himalaya) while a higher per unit price has decreased the market share of high equity brands up to 81 % (i.e., Calvin Klein). Thus, the erosion in market share due to quantity reduction is more for a high equity brand than the gain for a low equity brand due to quantity increase, supporting hypothesis 3. The range of decline for high equity brands is from 26 to 81%, while for low equity brands, the gains range from 20 to 47%, except in the case of Mirinda.

ANOVA and ANCOVA (analysis of covariance) results show that there exists significant main effect of product involvement, brand equity, and purchase frequency with p-value <0.01. Also, there is an interaction effect between product involvement and brand equity, and three-way interaction between product involvement, purchase frequency, and brand equity with p-value <0.10. The interaction effect between product involvement and frequency, and frequency and brand equity is statistically insignificant. The interaction effect between product category involvement and brand equity suggests that the consumer may react differently to brands with different equity depending on whether the brand belongs to high or low involvement product categories. We find that for the low equity brand, purchase intention is lower for the high involvement product category than for the low involvement product category.

Summary of Research and Managerial Findings

In general, the data supports the extant findings with regard to reference price (Kalyanaram and Little 1994; Krishnamurthi et al. 1992; Mayhew and Winer 1992) but in the context of latitude of quantity acceptance. However, the exact effect depends on the brand equity, where quantity fluctuation seems to exert more influence on high equity brands than on low equity brands. The results relating to the effect of low and high unit prices on consumer purchase behavior support literature on quantity discount (i.e., Gu and Yang 2010) and quantity surcharge (i.e., Manning et al. 1998; Whitefield et al. 1995) though its captured through quantity change scenarios. We find that the effect of quantity reduction (higher per unit price) is higher for a high equity brand than the effect of quantity increase (lower per unit price) for a low equity brand. Such results are not unlikely because consumers may consider quantity discounts (i.e., quantity increase scenarios in this study) as gains received from buying larger package sizes with lower unit prices as suggested by Gu and Yang (2010) and quantity surcharges (i.e., quantity decrease scenarios in this study) as losses. Also, if consumer is able recognize the higher unit price (i.e., quantity surcharge) then it may lead to negative evaluation of brand and customers may feel exploited, consistent with Widrick (1979) and Whitfield et al. (1995), leading to lower purchase preference. Thus, lower (higher) per unit price is perceived as gains (losses). However, a consumer reacts more sharply to losses (i.e., quantity decrease in this study) than to gains (i.e., quantity increase in this study), such findings corroborate earlier literature (Hardie et al. 1993; Kalwani et al. 1990; Mayhew and Winer 1992; Putler 1992).

References available upon request.

Part XV
Product and Branding Strategies

Managing Customer-Based Brand Equity (CBBE) Through Brand Knowledge Management

Manqoosh ur Rehman and A. Rashid Kausar

Abstract Brand management literature has lately started focusing on the management of intangible sources of brand performance. This transition has also become obvious from explicit to implicit brand management practices. Customer-Based Brand Equity (CBBE) is one of the areas that are of high concern to marketers and it deals mostly with subjective perceptions about the brand. A brand knowledge management lens is proposed to effectively manage the CBBE performance of the brand. Conceptual research models are proposed to further advance the study of brand knowledge management and its link with CBBE performance.

Keywords CBBE • Brand knowledge management • Knowledge lens • Consumer learning

Introduction

Customers have number of choices in a purchase situation. One of the important factors on which their purchase decision is based is the perception about the performance of the product (Van Osselaer and Alba 2000). Customers build the perception about product performance on the basis of their prior experience and learning that they have received and felt from different cues about the product. In any purchase situation choices can be made between different products or different brands of a product. These situations are identified on the basis of the differentiation between product attribute cues and brand cues (Van Osselaer and Alba 2000). Customers distinguish between product and brand performance on the basis of the cues they receive about them.

M. ur Rehman (✉) • A.R. Kausar
University of Management and Technology, Lahore, Pakistan
e-mail: manqoosh.rehman@umt.edu.pk; ark@umt.edu.pk

© Academy of Marketing Science 2016
L. Petruzzellis, R.S. Winer (eds.), *Rediscovering the Essentiality of Marketing*,
Developments in Marketing Science: Proceedings of the Academy of Marketing
Science, DOI 10.1007/978-3-319-29877-1_117

Brands are considered to be a source of strategic competitive advantage in today's marketplace (Erdem et al. 1999). Marketers strive to build, maintain, and leverage the power of brands that they carry to gain advantage over the competition. Considered as a key marketing asset (Ambler 2003), brand equity is treated as a strong indicator of brand performance. Florek (2015) highlights that brand equity can be studied either from firm perspective (i.e., financial-based brand equity) or from customer perspective (i.e., customer-based brand equity). Firm perspective or the financial approach to brand equity measures the difference that the brand can create to a product in terms of its financial value (Farquhar 1989). Customer-based perspective of brand equity highlights the customer perceptions about a brand regarding its performance, social image, value, etc. (Lassar et al. 1995).

Customer-Based Brand Equity (CBBE) is the perceived value (physical, functional, financial, affective, or social) of a brand in the minds and hearts of the customers. These perceptions about the brand are a result of the experiential learning process about the brand that the customer has gone through. Aaker (1991) characterized CBBE as a set of brand assets and liabilities that are associated to a brand. CBBE is more precisely defined from the cognitive psychology perspective by Keller (1993) as the differential consequence of brand knowledge (explicit and tacit) on consumer responses to a particular brand.

Brand awareness and brand image are considered as the two major components of brand knowledge. Richards et al. (1998) consider brands as an archetype of knowledge and argue that knowledge is what brand represents. Consumers become aware of the brands as they learn about them. Hence, creating a better understanding of consumer learning process becomes significant to effectively manage the brand knowledge. Consumers may learn about the brand through different sources that also include their experience in any encounter with the brand.

Brand image is considered as the second major component of brand knowledge and deals with different aspects of associations that a brand possesses (Alimen and Cerit 2010). Kapferer (2012) stresses that brand image is a result of customers' decoding process of different signals given by the brand. These signals may include brand name, signs, products, events, sponsoring, advertising, etc.

The focus of this chapter is on how companies can manage CBBE of their brands through the process of brand knowledge management. The primary objective of the chapter is to propose a framework for brand knowledge management while applying the concepts of knowledge management and knowledge creation to the area of brand management. It aims to understand different aspects of customer learning and knowledge management and their role in managing CBBE performance. It is a conceptual chapter that follows an abductive strategy, and attempts to identify a new area of research by demarking the bridge between knowledge management and brand management. The study follows a constructivist approach to present a conceptual framework of knowledge-based brand management. Literature review is done to form the conceptual foundations of the framework and to highlight the core research issues.

First the concept of CBBE is explored. Then, a brand knowledge lens is employed to understand the brand knowledge management process. This second section also discusses three different components of proposed brand knowledge lens. Third section discusses the application of the proposed brand knowledge lens for managing the CBBE performance of the brands. This section also presents different models that lay the foundation for future research. Fourth and the last section concludes the discussion of managing CBBE through brand knowledge management process.

Customer-Based Brand Equity

The term brand equity has attracted both the practitioners and academicians equally since the time it was introduced in 1980s (Wang and Finn 2012) and further advanced in 1990s by Aaker (1991), Srivastava and Shocker (1991), and Keller (1993). Literature defines and measures brand equity from three different perspectives, i.e., financial perspective (Mahajan et al. 1994; Simon and Sullivan 1993), economic perspective (Kamakura and Russell 1993; Park and Srinivasan 1994), and psychological perspective (Aaker 1991; Keller 1993). Financial and economic perspectives are considered to be firm-centric whereas psychological perspective is considered to be customer-centric that addresses the decision-making process of the customer (Florek 2015). The psychological perspective of brand equity, generally referred as Customer-Based Brand Equity (CBBE), is considered to be the most complex of these three approaches to measure as it deals with the customers' perceptual evaluation of the brand (Keller 1993). CBBE is also considered as the most appropriate measure of the effectiveness of brand strategy because of its customer-centric orientation (Florek 2015).

The concept of CBBE is primarily drawn from the areas of cognitive psychology and information economics (Christodoulides and De Chernatony 2010). Aaker (1991) was the first to conceptualize CBBE and provided a conceptual link between brand equity and different customer response variables. Keller (1993) was next to elaborate the concept by approaching it from customer's perspective and highlighted the significance of brand knowledge including brand awareness and brand associations as the major determinants of CBBE. The basic premise of his CBBE model was that the customers' learning and sensing (what customer feels, sees, and hears) about the brand was a result of their longitudinal experiences with the brand. He defined CBBE as the differential effect that brand knowledge has on consumer response to the marketing of that brand which emerges from two sources: brand awareness and brand image. Erdem et al. (1999) considered CBBE as a concept that was measured in relativity and stated that it was the differentiating effect of a brand's knowledge (in relation to other brands) in the minds of the customers which created that brand's equity.

The concept entered into the twenty-first century with Faircloth et al. (2001) explaining the concept of brand equity as a behavioral construct who argued that CBBE was explained by customers' image of a brand and their attitude toward that specific brand. Temporal (2002) defined customer-based brand equity as customer's subjective and intangible opinions about a brand. Aaker and Joachimsthaler (2009) defined brand equity as brand assets linked to a brand's name and symbol that add to, or subtract from, a product or service. According to them, these assets can be grouped into four dimensions, i.e., brand awareness, perceived quality, brand associations, and brand loyalty. These dimensions have been commonly used and accepted by many researchers (Bendixen et al. 2004; Keller 1993; Kim and Kim 2004; Motameni and Shahrokhi 1998; Yoo and Donthu 2001). Christodoulides and De Chernatony (2010) stated CBBE as the customers' behavior toward a brand that could generate a strong, sustainable, and differential advantage for the brand over its competition. Florek (2015) concludes that the process of mapping CBBE of a brand involves multiple cognitive processes that lead towards a unique perception and preference about the brand, and the consumer's behavior towards that brand. These processes may include information coding, storage, recovery, and preference development about a specific brand.

The literature on CBBE seems to have consensus on different constructs of CBBE that include brand awareness, brand associations, product associations, organizational associations, social image, perceived value, trustworthiness, etc. It also puts emphasis on understanding the consumer learning process to better manage the CBBE of the brands.

Brand Knowledge Management Process

Knowledge management literature divides knowledge into direct or explicit knowledge and indirect, implicit, or tacit knowledge (Nonaka and Takeuchi 1995; Sveiby 1997). Explicit knowledge is considered as objective that relates to some object whereas, tacit knowledge is considered as subjective, practical, and personal (Sharif 2008). Alimen and Cerit (2010) suggest that brand knowledge comprehends both explicit and tacit knowledge.

In consumer research, cognitive representation of the brand is referred to as consumer brand knowledge (Peter et al. 1999). It is defined as the personal meaning about a brand stored in consumer memory (Keller 2003). Understanding more of the abstract and intangible aspects of brand knowledge has emerged as one of the important thrust in recent branding research (Keller 2003). Fournier (1998) has extended the metaphor of interpersonal relationships into the brand domain to conceptualize the relationships that consumers form with brands. An increasing trend of studying brand with abstract and intangible considerations is obviously seen in recent research on brand management (Keller 2003).

Different kinds of information can be linked to a brand. These may include (1) awareness about product category; (2) brand attributes that describe intrinsic (product performance) or extrinsic (brand personality) features; (3) benefits that relate to personal meanings given by customers to brand's product attributes; (4) images that relate to concrete or abstract visual information about the brand; (5) thoughts that are considered as the personal cognitive responses to any brand related information; (6) feelings that are considered as personal affective responses to any brand related information; (7) attitudes that summarize judgments to any brand related information; and (8) experiences that are result of purchase and consumption behaviors about the brand (Keller 2003).

Keller (2003) considers these different kinds of brand information as key dimensions of brand knowledge. He argues that these different kinds of information may become a part of consumer memory and affect consumer response to brand marketing activities. He stresses the need for developing holistic perspective towards brand knowledge that encompasses all types of information about the brand as he suggests that ultimately brand knowledge becomes the source of brand equity.

This discussion reveals that brand marketing activities affect different dimensions of brand knowledge that in turn influence consumer responses to these activities. An integration of the dimensions of brand knowledge may guide the marketers to better understand the consumer response models that may enhance the brand performance in terms of its CBBE. Next section discusses the application of brand knowledge lens in terms of managing CBBE performance.

Brand Knowledge Lens

Literature lists two broad approaches to measure CBBE performance, i.e., perceptual and behavioral. The perceptual approach uses brand awareness, brand associations, brand image, etc. to measure CBBE performance. Whereas, brand loyalty, referrals, price premiums, etc. are the methods that are used under the behavioral approach to measure CBBE performance (Florek 2015). Having identified different dimensions of brand knowledge, its relationship with CBBE performance, and different approaches to measure CBBE performance, a brand knowledge lens is proposed to manage CBBE performance. The proposed lens, presented in Fig. 1, suggests that the company should manage the consumer knowledge that, in turn, will facilitate to manage the CBBE performance. It provides a comprehensive view of managing CBBE performance as it incorporates both the perceptual and behavioral elements of measuring CBBE performance. While following the proposed lens, consumer knowledge about brand can be managed by understanding the processes through which consumers learn, images that consumers associate with the brand, and their experiences about the brand in different encounters with it.

Different customer segments are unique in their learning process. Organizations can understand the learning processes of different segments and can manage their brand communication efforts accordingly. These tuned brand communication efforts may build favorable associations about the brand and may lead to favorable brand experiences.

All the elements of brand knowledge lens are considered as important dimensions of brand knowledge as discussed above. A deeper understanding about these elements may facilitate the appropriate application of the lens in order to better manage CBBE performance.

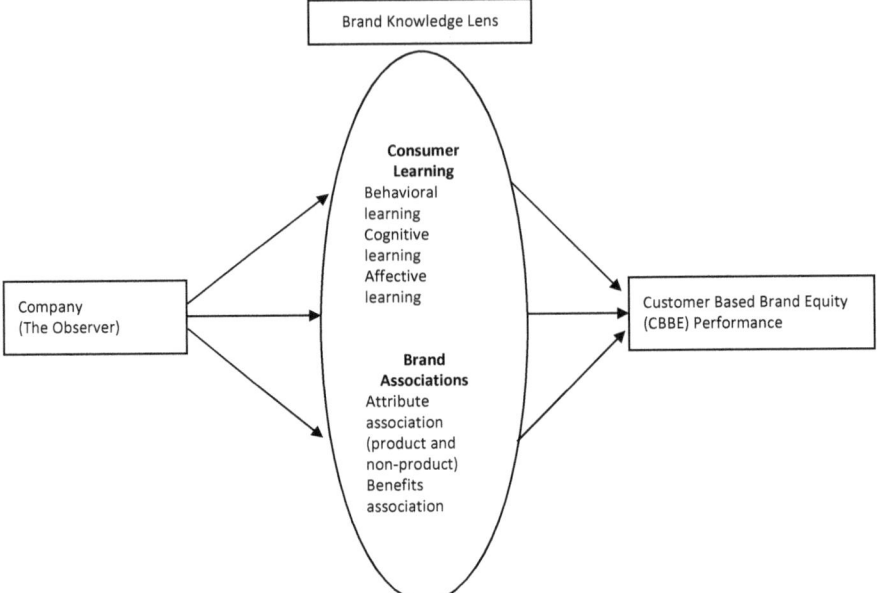

Fig. 1 Application of brand knowledge lens to manage CBBE performance

Consumer Learning

Understanding consumer brand knowledge requires the clarity about how consumers process and store different brand related stimuli (Koll et al. 2010). Consumer learning is defined as the process through which individuals obtain the knowledge about purchasing and consumption. Although some of the learning is intentional still rest of the learning is referred to as incidental. Cues, motivation, response, reinforcement, etc. are some of the elements that contribute to an individual's learning (Schiffman and Kanuk 2010).

Jonassen and Land (2012) identified three major shifts in the approach towards understanding the individual learning. They first describe learning as a meaning-making phenomenon. This approach considers learning as a process of dissonance reducing and not the knowledge transmission. The second approach considers learning as the socialization aspect of the meaning-making process where individuals process, store, retrieve, and apply the information as they compare it with others but do not share it with them. Finally, in the third phase, Jonassen and Land (2012) describe that the locus of meaning making has shifted from an individual to the communities in which individuals reside and socialize. They believe that knowledge not only resides in the individual's mind but it also exists in the discourses and dialogues among individuals and their social relationships.

Behavioral theorists consider learning as those responses to a stimulus that can be observed something view learning as observable responses to stimuli. However cognitive theorists, on the other hand, consider learning as a function of mental processing. Affective learning and mental processing give way to the final behavioral response. Cognitive theory holds that the problem solving is the type of learning that is the most characteristic of humans. The major focus of the cognitive theorists is on the way information is processed, stored, retained, and retrieved by the human mind. Cognitive theorists suggest that three different storage units exist in an individual's mind, i.e., the sensory store, short-term store (or working memory), and long-term store. They also describe that rehearsal, encoding, storage, and retrieval are major memory processes that a human mind executes (Van Osselaer and Alba 2000).

Involvement theory provides an engagement perspective of learning based on the individual's experiences. It suggests that there are situations of low importance or relevance to individuals and they involve in limited information processing in these situations. It also suggests that individuals perform an extensive information processing exercise in situations that are highly significant to them. Hemispheral lateralization (i.e., split-brain) theory gave rise to these concepts of varied involvement levels and concluded that the stronger interactivity of the communication media will result in higher cognitive information processing (Schiffman and Kanuk 2010). These findings give rise to the concept of affection with the brands, i.e., the heart share of the brand. Intrapersonal brainstorming and heartstorming lead the behavioral response of consumers towards the brands.

It is concluded that brand recall and brand recognition tests emerge as strong measures of consumer learning. Other measures of brand loyalty (both attitudinal and behavioral) are also important source of measuring consumer learning as brand loyalty consists of both attitudes and actual behaviors toward a brand. Marketers strive to understand the consumer learning process in order to communicate them the superiority of their brand to win customers' loyalty with the brand (Schiffman and Kanuk 2010).

Brand Awareness

Consumer learning results in consumers getting aware of available brands and their attributes. The ability of a potential buyer to recognize or recall a brand is known as brand awareness (Aaker 1991) and is defined as the strength of a brand's presence in the mind of the customer (Ross 2006). Ross (2006) also proposed that experience-induced antecedents do have an impact on brand awareness. Keller (2003) argues that brand awareness consists of brand recognition, the "consumer's ability to confirm prior exposure to the brand when given a brand as a cue" and brand recall, the "consumer's ability to retrieve the brand form memory when given the product category, the needs fulfilled by the category, or a purchase or usage situation as cue."

Brand Associations

Brand associations are anything that connects the customer to the brand, including user imagery, product attributes, organizational associations, brand personality, symbols, etc. Beliefs about a brand that are held by the customers are reflected in their associations about that brand (Aaker 1991; Keller 1993; Sherry 2005). These associations are not only controlled by the marketing program, but also through direct experience, brand information, word of mouth, assumptions of the brand itself, name, logo, or with the brand's identification with a certain company, country, distribution channel, person, place, or event (Keller 2003).

Consumers can create three types of brand associations that include attribute association, benefit association, and attitude association. Attributes can be product related (color, fragrance, size, etc.) or non-product related (packaging, price, user imagery, usage imagery, etc.). Benefits that can be associated to brands are functional, experiential, and symbolic. Attitudes of and about the brand along with the perceptions of attributes and benefits in turn create the brand personality image in the minds of the customers (Alimen and Cerit 2010).

Brand associations differ among customers and provide marketers an opportunity to differentiate, position, and extend their brands (Low and Lamb 2000) and consumers to process, organize, and retrieve information in making purchase decisions (Aaker 1991).

Brand Experience

Consumers also gain knowledge about the brands as they experience them. The more experience encounters customers have with the brand, the broader, stronger, and better informed their opinions about the brand become. Experiences occur when consumers search for products, shop for them, receive service, and consume them (Arnold et al. 2005; Brakus et al. 2008; Holbrook 2000).

Impression, interaction, responsiveness, and resilience are identified as four components of brand experience. Impression is the liking or disliking of a brand's offering. Interaction deals with the promises that are made by the brand and are delivered accordingly. Responsiveness deals with how well a brand responds to the needs of the customers. Resilience deals with the flexibility and adaptation level that brand offers to meet the future needs of the customers.

Brakus et al. (2009) conceptualize brand experience as sensations, feelings, cognition, and behavioral responses occurred as a result of an exposure to a brand. Marketers have started realizing that an understanding of how consumers experience brands is critical for developing the brand strategies (Brakus et al. 2009). The case of Rin Detergent Bar's launch in Pakistan (Azhar 2008) is a classic example of how consumers experience brands. Rin Detergent Bar was launched by Unilever in Pakistan as a fabric washing detergent bar but the consumers used it for dishwashing primarily because of its color and texture that were similar to that of other dishwashing bars. Unilever Pakistan had to rethink about the positioning of its Rin Detergent Bar as the brand experience of customers was much different than that of company's desires.

Managing CBBE Through Brand Knowledge Management

The brand knowledge dimensions of consumer learning, brand associations, and brand experience indicate the flow of knowledge acquisition through consumer learning, knowledge conversion by creating brand associations, and knowledge evolution caused by brand experience. Looking through the brand knowledge lens, following three questions arise.

1. How does consumer learning facilitate brand awareness which in turn affects CBBE performance?
2. How can brand associations create the image of brand that contributes to CBBE performance?
3. How can exposure to different brand cues enhance brand experience that affects CBBE performance?

Answers to these three research questions will advance the brand knowledge management debate in the area of marketing and specifically the brand management. Following three models are proposed to understand the role of brand knowledge management in managing CBBE performance based on these three research questions.

Proposed Research Models

Model 1. Role of consumer learning in managing CBBE performance: Consumer learning will enhance the brand awareness that in turn will affect the CBBE performance of the brand. There is a need to investigate the learning process of different consumer segments that will trigger the use of appropriate communication techniques and modems. This focused consumer learning may lead to enhanced brand awareness that will facilitate CBBE management (Fig. 2).

Fig. 2 Proposed research model 1

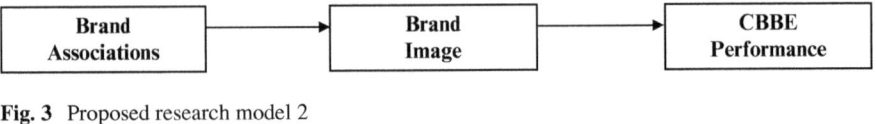

Fig. 3 Proposed research model 2

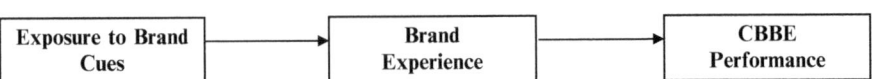

Fig. 4 Proposed research model 3

Model 2. Role of brand associations in managing CBBE performance: Based on the learning that consumers have they develop certain associations with the brand. These associations help in building an image of the brand in the minds of the customers. Positive associations will leave to a positive brand image that will ultimately contribute to enhance the CBBE performance of the brand (Fig. 3).

Model 3. Role of brand experience in managing CBBE performance: Brands communicate with the customers by variety of means. This communication enhances the awareness about the brands and thus creates an image of the brand in customers' minds. Exposure to different brand cues leads to different types of brand experience, either positive or negative, that in turn affect the CBBE performance (Fig. 4).

Conclusion

Brands being considered the most valuable marketing assets of the organizations need to be managed carefully as they provide the competitive advantage to the organizations. Customers learn about the brands that are offered by different organizations through their marketing communication programs. Organizations, in turn, also need to understand the customers' learning process through which customers build their favorable or unfavorable associations (attribute, benefit, or attitude) towards the brands. Consumers learn through their cognitive, behavioral, and affective learning processes. These learning develop the associations and create different experiences (sensational, affective, cognitive, or behavioral) about the brand. Organizations need to vigorously observe the customers' learning processes, the brand associations that they develop, and the brand experience that they go through in order to better manage the most important customer centric measure of brand performance, i.e., customer-based brand equity.

A brand knowledge lens is conceived and it is proposed to the organizations to use this brand knowledge lens through which they can observe the performance of their brand as perceived by the customers. While using this lens, organizations will have a better understanding of the customers' knowledge management process that will enable them to devise customer-centric brand management strategies that will ultimately enhance the brand performance. Three research models are also proposed to further explore the application of suggested lens to manage CBBE performance.

References

Aaker, D. A. (1991). *Managing brand equity*. New York: The Free Press.

Aaker, D. A., & Joachimsthaler, E. (2009). *Brand leadership: Building assets in an information economy*. New York: Simon and Schuster.

Alimen, N., & Cerit, A. G. (2010). Dimensions of brand knowledge: Turkish University students' consumption of international fashion brands. *Journal of Enterprise Information Management, 23*(4), 538–558.

Ambler, T. (2003). *Marketing and the bottom line: The marketing metrics to pump up cash flow*. Upper Saddle River, NJ: Pearson Education.

Arnold, M. J., Reynolds, K. E., Ponder, N., & Lueg, J. E. (2005). Customer delight in a retail context: Investigating delightful and terrible shopping experiences. *Journal of Business Research, 58*(8), 1132–1145.

Azhar, W. (2008). *Rin detergent: To position or reposition* (case studies). Stanford, CA: Stanford Graduate School of Business.

Bendixen, M., Bukasa, K. A., & Abratt, R. (2004). Brand equity in the business-to-business market. *Industrial Marketing Management, 33*(5), 371–380.

Brakus, J. J., Schmitt, B. H., & Zarantonello, L. (2009). Brand experience: What is it? How is it measured? Does it affect loyalty? *Journal of Marketing, 73*(3), 52–68.

Brakus, J. J., Schmitt, B. H., & Zhang, S. (2008). Experiential attributes and consumer judgments. In B. H. Schmitt & D. L. Rogers (Eds.), *Handbook on brand and experience management* (pp. 174–187). Northampton, MA: Edward Elgar.

Christodoulides, G., & De Chernatony, L. (2010). Consumer-based brand equity conceptualization and measurement: A literature review. *International Journal of Research in Marketing, 52*(1), 43–66.

Erdem, T., Swait, J., Broniarczyk, S., Chakravarti, D., Kapferer, J.-N., Keane, M., et al. (1999). Brand equity, consumer learning and choice. *Marketing Letters, 10*(3), 301–318.

Faircloth, J. B., Capella, L. M., & Alford, B. L. (2001). The effect of brand attitude and brand image on brand equity. *Journal of Marketing Theory and Practice, 3*, 61–75.

Farquhar, P. H. (1989). Managing brand equity. *Marketing Research, 1*(3), 24–33.

Florek, M. (2015). Rethinking brand equity—possibilities and challenges of application to places. In M. Kavaratzis, G. Warnaby, & G. J. Ashworth (Eds.), *Rethinking place branding* (pp. 225–239). Cham, Switzerland: Springer.

Fournier, S. (1998). Consumers and their brands: Developing relationship theory in consumer research. *Journal of Consumer Research, 24*(4), 343–353.

Holbrook, M. B. (2000). The millennial consumer in the texts of our times: Experience and entertainment. *Journal of Macromarketing, 20*(2), 178–192.

Jonassen, D., & Land, S. (2012). *Theoretical foundations of learning environments*. London: Routledge.

Kamakura, W. A., & Russell, G. J. (1993). Measuring brand value with scanner data. *International Journal of Research in Marketing, 10*(1), 9–22.

Kapferer, J.-N. (2012). *The new strategic brand management: Advanced insights and strategic thinking*. London: Kogan Page.

Keller, K. L. (1993). Conceptualizing, measuring, and managing customer-based brand equity. *Journal of Marketing, 57*, 1–22.

Keller, K. L. (2003). Brand synthesis: The multidimensionality of brand knowledge. *Journal of Consumer Research, 29*(4), 595–600.

Kim, W. G., & Kim, H.-B. (2004). Measuring customer-based restaurant brand equity. *Cornell Hotel and Restaurant Administration Quarterly, 45*(2), 115–131.

Koll, O., Von Wallpach, S., & Kreuzer, M. (2010). Multi-method research on consumer–brand associations: Comparing free associations, storytelling, and collages. *Psychology & Marketing, 27*(6), 584–602.

Lassar, W., Mittal, B., & Sharma, A. (1995). Measuring customer-based brand equity. *Journal of Consumer Marketing, 12*(4), 11–19.

Low, G. S., & Lamb, C. W., Jr. (2000). The measurement and dimensionality of brand associations. *Journal of Product & Brand Management, 9*(6), 350–370.

Mahajan, V., Rao, V. R., & Srivastava, R. K. (1994). An approach to assess the importance of brand equity in acquisition decisions. *Journal of Product Innovation Management, 11*(3), 221–235.

Motameni, R., & Shahrokhi, M. (1998). Brand equity valuation: A global perspective. *Journal of Product & Brand Management, 7*(4), 275–290.

Nonaka, I., & Takeuchi, H. (1995). *The knowledge-creating company: How Japanese companies create the dynamics of innovation*. New York: Oxford University Press.

Park, C. S., & Srinivasan, V. (1994). A survey-based method for measuring and understanding brand equity and its extendibility. *Journal of Marketing Research, 31*(2), 271–288.

Peter, J. P., Olson, J. C., & Grunert, K. G. (1999). *Consumer behavior and marketing strategy*. London: McGraw-Hill.

Richards, I., Foster, D., & Morgan, R. (1998). Brand knowledge management: Growing brand equity. *Journal of Knowledge Management, 2*(1), 47–54.

Ross, S. D. (2006). A conceptual framework for understanding spectator-based brand equity. *Journal of Sport Management, 20*(1), 22.

Schiffman, L., & Kanuk, L. (2010). *Consumer behavior: Global edition* (10th ed.). Upper Saddle River, NJ: Pearson Education.

Sharif, A. M. (2008). *Information, knowledge and the context of interaction*. European and Mediterranean Conference on Information Systems 2008, Dubai.

Sherry, J. F., Jr. (2005). Brand meaning. In A. M. Tybout, T. Calkins, & P. Kotler (Eds.), *Kellogg on branding* (pp. 40–69). Hoboken, NJ: Wiley.

Simon, C. J., & Sullivan, M. W. (1993). The measurement and determinants of brand equity: A financial approach. *Marketing Science, 12*(1), 28–52.

Srivastava, R. K., & Shocker, A. D. (1991). *Brand equity: A perspective on its meaning and measurement*. Cambridge, MA: Marketing Science Institute.

Sveiby, K. E. (1997). *The new organizational wealth: Managing & measuring knowledge-based assets*. San Francisco: Berrett-Koehler.

Temporal, P. (2002). *Advanced brand management: From vision to valuation*. Singapore, Singapore: Wiley.

Van Osselaer, S. M., & Alba, J. W. (2000). Consumer learning and brand equity. *Journal of Consumer Research, 27*(1), 1–16.

Wang, L., & Finn, A. (2012). Measuring CBBE across brand portfolios: Generalizability theory perspective. *Journal of Targeting, Measurement and Analysis for Marketing, 20*(2), 109–116.

Yoo, B., & Donthu, N. (2001). Developing and validating a multidimensional consumer-based brand equity scale. *Journal of Business Research, 52*(1), 1–14.

Celebrity Branding Advertising Processing: A Conceptual Model

António Azevedo

Abstract Recently, some celebrities have created their own perfume brands. This study proposes a conceptual model for the celebrity branding advertising processing which acknowledges the influence of celebrity-related factors, sociocultural trends, and the advertising copy strategy. Using a sample of 100 subjects, this study analyzes the branding advertising processing of Beyoncé/Heat and the simulation of the branding of a new celebrity brand—Lana del Rey. Focusing at the catalyst role of congruence between the celebrity brand personality and consumer self-concept, we analyze the implications of self-sexualization, scopophilia, and glamour as predictors of the willingness to pay for a bottle of perfume.

Keywords Advertising processing • Celebrity branding • Self-congruence • Scopophilia and self-sexualization

Introduction

The use of celebrity endorsement is a very popular and widely discussed research topic. The "haute couture" fashion designers often extend their clothing brand to the perfume category. However, recently some celebrities (from other areas rather than fashion design) have created and launched their own personal perfume brands[1]: top models like Kate Moss, Kate Price; singers such as Lady Gaga (Fame), Beyoncé (Heat) (see Fig. 1), Katie Perry (Purr); Madonna (Truth Dare), Christina Aguilera, Britney Spears (Curious), Justin Bieber (Someday) or Shakira (Elixir); actresses like Jennifer Lopez (Love and Glamour); sport athletes like the tennis player Maria Sharapova; TV and entertainment starts; or even socialite icons like Paris Hilton who launched a men fragrance. The departure point of this chapter was the press

---

[1]A list can be found at: http://en.wikipedia.org/wiki/List_of_celebrity_branded_fragrances http://www.mimifroufrou.com/scentedsalamander/celebrity_perfumes/

A. Azevedo (✉)
University of Minho, Braga, Portugal
e-mail: antonioa@eeg.uminho.pt

© Academy of Marketing Science 2016
L. Petruzzellis, R.S. Winer (eds.), *Rediscovering the Essentiality of Marketing*, Developments in Marketing Science: Proceedings of the Academy of Marketing Science, DOI 10.1007/978-3-319-29877-1_118

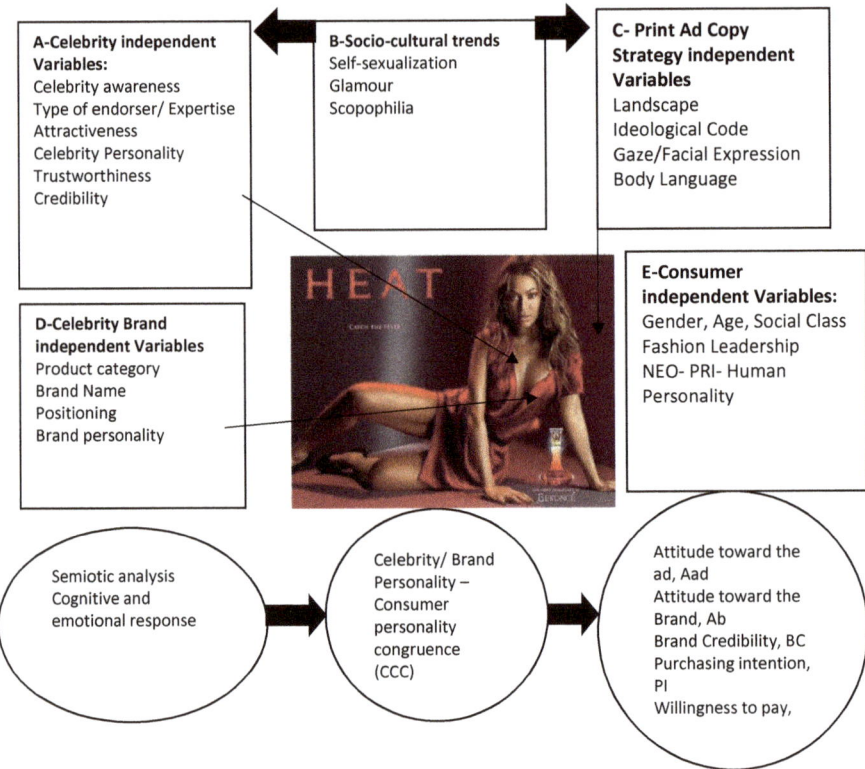

Fig. 1 Conceptual framework

release announcing that Lady Gaga would launch in 2012 a perfume called "Monster" which would have the "heady aroma of blood and semen."[2]

Therefore this chapter aims to discuss the process of branding a celebrity and the subsequent transference/extension of the celebrity's brand personality to a product with the same brand name. In this case, this study will focus in the luxury fashion sector, and in particular within the female fragrance/perfume category.

The definition of celebrity is discussed by Alexander (2010) that treats it as an iconic form of collective representation central to a meaningful construction of the contemporary society. For Alexander (2010: 324) "the celebrity-icon is structured by the interplay of surface and depth. The surface is an aesthetic structure whose sensuous qualities command attention and compel attachment; the depth projects the sacred and profane binaries that structure meaning even in postmodern societies."

Alexander (2010: 332) describes the female celebrity-icon: "is a princess, a femme fatale, or a heroine, and her stories revolve around the myth of love. She is light, delicate, erotic, and, even if she is also adventurous and clever, possesses an aura of the most conspicuous kind. There is 'something mesmerizing' about

---

[2]Read more: http://www.dailymail.co.uk/femail/article-2063262/Lady-Gagas-monstrous-fragrance-smell-like-expensive-hooker.html#ixzz20jmacpjQ

Angelina Jolie; when she appears 'everything lights up'. Gwyneth Paltrow is 'charming, elegant, beautiful, and divine'."

For Alexander (2010: 332) the male celebrity-icon is: "a hero, a villain, or an antihero; he struggles over greatness in his mythical stories. His visage communicates wisdom, strength, and courage. Female celebrity-icons are hot; males, even if 'hotties', are cool. The female-celebrity icon is appreciated for the hours devoted to surface preparation; she is highly constructed, like a paper flower. Male celebrity-icons are not constructed but soft."

Literature Review

The celebrity branding process is influenced by: (a) celebrity/endorser related factors; (b) social cultural trends; and (c) advertising copy strategy related factors.

Celebrity/Endorser Related Factors

Some aspects have been widely studied by celebrity endorsement researchers (Erdogan 1999; Erdogan and Baker 2000): celebrity attractiveness (DeBono and Telesca 1990); body shape (D'Alessandro and Chitty 2011); ideal self-image of women beauty (Bjerke and Polegato 2006); celebrity meaning transfer (Erdogan et al. 2001; Halonen-Knight and Hurmerinta 2010); celebrity credibility (Klebba and Unger 1982) which is related to celebrity expertise and category (Rossiter and Smidts 2012).

However there is a gap between the dimensions of human personality (provided by the different human personality scales) and brand personality dimensions (provided by the brand personality scales). The Big Five framework of personality traits from Costa and McCrae (1992) emerged as a robust model for understanding the relationship between personality and various academic behaviors. Several attempts to assist the endorser selection/casting process are provided by tools like the E-Score Celebrity Index developed by E-Poll Market Research described by Gergaud and Ginsburgh (2010).

The notion of brand personality, defined "as the human characteristics associated with the brand" (Aaker 1997: 347) can be designed using the identity-mix and the copy strategy elements. The Brand Personality Scale of Aaker (1997) is the most popular brand personality measurement tool comprising five dimensions: (1) sincerity; (2) excitement; (3) competence; (4) sophistication; and (5) ruggedness. However, Heine (2010) developed a new scale to measure the personality of luxury brands, comprising 52 traits which were categorized by five major personality dimensions: (1) modernity—the temporal perspective of a brand; (2) eccentricity—the level of discrepancy from social norms and expectations; (3) opulence—the level of conspicuousness of the symbols of wealth; (4) elitism—the level of status and exclusivity; and (5) strength—the level of toughness and masculinity.

Social-Cultural and Psychographic Factors

This chapter also acknowledges the influence of some sociocultural trends in modern societies that moderate the luxury branding advertising processing: the glamour magic, the self-sexualization; and the scopophilia.

The luxury brands are also often associated with "glamour." Jenifer Lopez has even launched a perfumed branded as "Glamour." Hautala (2011) argues that glamour is a myth that becomes activated through a system of signs. It depends on the use of celebrity personas, on an exclusive media treatment, and on the circulation of signs which connote luxury and feminine sexuality always with a fresh, contemporary touch. Gundle (2008: 390) defined glamour as "an image that attracts attention and arouses envy by mobilizing desirable qualities including beauty, wealth, movement, leisure, fame, and sex."

Besides the importance of glamour (Hautala 2011) and the semiotics of fashion, celebrity branding is also influenced by new sociocultural trends in fashion branding advertising such as the self-sexualization, the commodification of feminine and post-feminism (Lazar 2011) or consumers' scopophilia (Lacan 1970/2005; Soukup 2009).

Gill (2008) quoted by Coy and Garner (2010) claimed that sexual images of women in today's mainstream advertising convey the celebration and enjoyment of the sex-object status. Gill (2007: 151) describes sexualization as: "the extraordinary proliferation of discourses about sex and sexuality across all media forms ... as well the increasingly frequent erotic presentation of girls', women's and (to a lesser extent) men's bodies in public space; women can use their bodies for profit as a means to power; the importance of individual choice; makeovers as re-inventions of the self; a focus on biological differences between men and women."

The notion of woman as "object" also implies the inherent voyeurism of film spectatorship (Metz 1977, quoted by Soukup 2009) which is analogous to the Freudian notion of scopophilia defined by Naiman (1998: 334): "the pleasure of looking at the body of another" through a "keyhole."

The notion that the use of sexual content in advertisements can increase the advertising effectiveness and ultimately sell products has been confirmed by several studies (Brown and Stayman 1992; Sawang 2010). But Kilbourne (1999) quoted by Soukup (2009: 271) highlighted this focus of advertising: "...[it] fetishizes products, imbues them with an erotic charge ...."

In order to further decode the cultural and social meanings of the images, Hautala (2011) used a semiologist's checklist by Lacey (2009) and Dyer (1982) which analyzes the following points: (a) Representation of bodies—age, gender, race, hair, look; dressing code; (b) Representation of manner—gaze direction (Oswald 2010), pose, facial expression, sex-appeal and eroticism, smiling appeal, and impression management behaviors; (c) Representation of activity—touch, body movement, positional communication, body language (Sawang 2010; Oswald 2010), photographic camera angle (Meyers-Levy and Peracchio 1992); and (d) Lay out and other visual elements and symbolic cues embed in the ad "landscape" (Kilyeni 2009).

This influence of visual elements of print advertising on consumer's response has been recognized by several authors such as Rossiter and Percy (1980), Fennis et al. (2012), or Huhmann et al. (2012), amongst others. Therefore the elements of print advertising copy strategy may also be manipulated to communicate the celebrity brand.

Conceptual Framework

The model (Fig. 1) postulates that the configuration of the celebrity avatar (A), the sociocultural trends (B), and the advertising copy strategy (C) influence the advertising processing and response using a hierarchical sequence of effects expressed by the relationship Aad-Ab-PI-WTP (attitude toward the ad, attitude toward the brand, purchase intention, and willingness to pay).

This framework includes also: (D) The product related factors (product category, product brand name, brand personality, and positioning); (E) The consumer individual variables which may moderate the overall advertising processing: consumer gender, culture (Biswas et al. 2009), self-monitoring (DeBono and Telesca 1990), advertising knowledge and celebrity awareness, advertising involvement or fashion leadership.

Method

Due to the extension of the questionnaire and in order to obtain richer and deeper insights in the semiotic analysis, the researcher decided to conduct the study in a university classroom context, using a convenience sample comprising subjects that were expertise or have received some training in advertising, marketing, or semiotics. This paper and pencil procedure aimed to assure that there was a satisfactory involvement in the advertising processing tasks.

Therefore 100 undergraduate students of Marketing and Communication courses, (67 % female; 33 % male) aging from 18 to 40 years old (M=22.65; SD=5.22), with an average disposable income of 1426€ (SD=1011€), and with a monthly spending on perfumes of 12.88€ (SD=17.76€) agreed to participate in a self-administered questionnaire in order to assess the branding advertising processing of two scenarios: (a) the Beyoncé/Heat perfume (a real brand/product) and (b) the creation of the Lana del Rey brand (a fictitious brand/product).

Study N. 1: Branding Strategy Analysis of Beyoncé/Heat

First the respondents (considering the celebrity awareness) stated their cognitive response/semiotic analysis by describing with open answers (see Table 1) the Heat print ad of Fig. 1; the celebrity as endorser, the ad landscape, the body language/

Table 1 Advertising processing of Heat/Beyoncé ad

	M	SD
Willingness to pay	34.93	21.60
Endorser beauty	8.27	1.76
Credibility	7.37	2.07
Trustworthy	7.23	2.12
Endorser seduction	8.13	2.03
Consumer-endorser self-congruence	5.82	2.81
Endorser-brand fitness degree	7.95	2.34
Attitude toward ad	6.50	2.46
Attitude toward product	6.67	2.37
Attitude toward brand	4.79	2.54
Purchase intention	3.71	2.78
Brand glamour	5.93	2.60
Brand reputation	5.12	2.64
Consumer-brand self-congruence	4.04	2.73
Brand image	5.68	2.66
Modernity	4.45	.79
Eccentric	4.01	.96
Opulence	3.85	1.03
Elitism	2.89	1.20
Strength	3.97	.99

facial expression, and perceived brand image associations. In order to confirm the expected brand personality, respondents classified the brand ads according to Heine's scale dimensions using a five points bipolar scale (traditional versus modern; respectful versus eccentric; discrete versus opulent; democratic versus elitist; sensitive versus strong).

Afterwards they assessed (in a 0–10 Likert scale) the following endorser's characteristics: credibility, trustworthy, attractiveness, congruence between the celebrity and consumer self-concept and brand-endorser fitness degree. The respondents evaluated each brand in terms of: attitude toward the ad, attitude toward the package/product, attitude toward the brand, brand reputation, brand glamour, consumer-brand self-congruence, brand image, purchasing intention, and willingness to pay (as brand equity indicator). Finally, the moderating influence of glamour, self-sexualization, and scopophilia was verified using seven item (0–5 Likert scale).

Study N. 2-Branding a Celebrity: Lana del Rey

In order to simulate a creation of a celebrity branding, Lana del Rey was selected as celebrity test pilot. She is a singer/actress that has started to get awareness in the USA in 2012 when she launched in the web the hit "Video Games." Several magazines considered her "a new American icon" and she was the cover of Vogue UK in

Fig. 2 Best photo for Lana Del Rey's print ad. *Source*: Adapted from H&M advertising campaign

March 2012, which means that she was at the early stage of her life cycle and therefore she was an ideal candidate to the study in order to avoid some potential previous knowledge bias. However, 66% of respondents still recognized her (assisted awareness). The ad stimulus was adapted from an advertising campaign of H&M (see Fig. 2).

Discussion of Results

Beyoncé/Heat Advertising Response

In this study, 99% of respondents recognized Beyoncé and described her as endorser whose body language as: sensual, sexy, provocative, beautiful, attractive, and strong. The ad landscape was considered as simply, hot and neutral. The words associated to Heat image were: strong, modern, sensual, and "possessing" the Beyoncé personality. Table 1 presents the quantitative evaluation and processing of Heat ad. Considering a 10 points scale, the results showed very positive scores (above 7) for Beyoncé beauty (M = 8.27), credibility, trustworthy, seduction power, and endorser-brand fitness.

However the response was less favorable in terms of consumer-endorser self-congruence (M = 5.82), consumer brand self-congruence (M = 4.04), and purchase intention (M = 3.71). The willingness to pay for a bottle of perfume was 34.93 euros on average. The brand personality according to Heine's (2010) scale (reduced version) revealed a profile with three important dimensions: modernity, eccentricity, and strength confirming the qualitative evaluation.

A multiple regression revealed the relevant predictors of the willingness to pay for a bottle of HEAT perfume (see Table 2): monthly perfume spending, Heat's brand image, glamour as a "dreaming lifestyle" ($M=4.08$; $SD=.82$; $M_{male}=3.84$; $SD_{male}=.97$; $M_{female}=4.19$, $SD_{female}=.72$; $t_{98}=-1.999$; $p=.048$); Heat-Consumer self-congruence, self-sexualization as "woman's choice to use her body as a way to get profit" ($M=3.91$; $SD=1.24$), and Heat's perceived glamour.

Although these findings validate some influences postulated in the conceptual framework, namely: (a) the role of the social-cultural trends (glamour and self-sexualization) stressed in this chapter; (b) role of brand-consumer self-congruence. However for Heat/Beyoncé these predictors were negatively correlated with willingness to pay, which cannot be explained by the fact that particular segment with those psychographic characteristics might also have a lower purchasing power, because there were no significant correlations between those variables and income or perfume monthly spending. And there were no significant differences between male and female subjects, except for glamour as "dreaming lifestyle."

Branding a Celebrity: Lana del Rey's Case Study

At the first step of this study, respondents answered a reduced version of the Revised NEO Personality Inventory (NEO-PI-R) (see Table 3) in order to assess the perceived personality of Lana del Rey. They used as stimulus a photo selected from the set of Fig. 2. Photo G in which Lana del Rey appears in a "close-up" photo gazing directly to the viewer, was the most preferred by 25 % of respondents.

The photo H has a similar lay-out and obtained 23 % of preferences. The traits of neuroticism (vulnerability to stress and hostility) and extraversion (activity and gregariousness) got the higher scores. These results are aligned with Nettle's (2006) findings who concluded that actors of both sexes were significantly higher than comparison groups in extraversion, openness to experience, and agreeableness. There was also a trend towards higher neuroticism.

The advertising response to those ads (see Table 4) revealed some positive indicators, namely a willingness to pay of 38.13 euros (higher than the Heat/Beyoncé), which is negatively correlated with Lana's "openness to experience" trait score. On other hand, Lana's neuroticism was positively correlated with attitude toward the celebrity and attitude toward the brand, while these scores were negatively correlated with conscientiousness and agreeableness (respectively). However, again the Lana-consumer self-congruence ($M=3.95$) and purchase intention ($M=3.43$) were very low.

Finally, a multiple regression revealed the relevant predictors of the willingness to pay for a bottle of Lana del Rey perfume (see Table 2): monthly perfume spending, Lana's reputation, the A3-altruism personality trait, the scopophilia (measured by the item "I feel sexual pleasure/voyeurism when I see this perfume ad"), and the attitude toward Lana as model.

The findings confirmed the influence of scopophilia ($M=1.87$; $SD=1.04$) at the early stage of brand building pretesting as postulated in the conceptual

Table 2 Multiple regression coefficients of the predictors of perfume's willingness to pay

	Unstandardized coefficients		Standardized coefficients	t	Sig.	Correlations			Collinearity statistics	
	B	Std. error	Beta			Zero-order	Partial	Part	Tolerance	VIF
Study n° 1—Heat/Beyoncè brand analysis										
Constant	16.438	15.565		1.056	.297					
Perfume monthly spending	.712	.117	.592	6.089	.000	.557	.689	.567	.918	1.090
Heat brand image	5.850	1.211	.655	4.832	.000	.403	.602	.450	.471	2.123
Glamour as a "dreaming life style"	5.450	2.343	.228	2.326	.025	.295	.341	.217	.905	1.105
Heat-consumer self-congruence	−2.613	1.003	−.309	−2.605	.013	.188	−.377	−.242	.614	1.630
Self-sexualization: "woman body as a way to get profit"	−5.841	1.908	−.340	−3.062	.004	−.199	−.431	−.285	.701	1.427
Heat's glamour	−2.395	1.145	−.288	−2.091	.043	.090	−.310	−.195	.457	2.189
Study n° 2—Lana del Rey branding simulation										
Constant	1.041	7.709		.135	.893					
Perfume monthly spending	.508	.084	.552	6.051	.000	.608	.696	.538	.949	1.054
Lana's reputation	1.657	.703	.264	2.356	.024	.478	.353	.209	.630	1.588
NEO-PRI A3-altruism	5.619	1.581	.322	3.554	.001	.173	.495	.316	.964	1.038
Scopophilia	−3.728	1.386	−.245	−2.691	.010	−.314	−.396	−.239	.957	1.045
Lana as model	1.468	.685	.236	2.143	.038	.414	.325	.190	.653	1.532

Note: ANOVA results for the multiple regression models

Model	R	R square	Adjusted R square	Std. error of the estimate	Change statistics					Durbin-Watson	F	Sig.
					R square change	F change	df1	df2	Sig. F change			
HEAT	.803	.645	.593	12.76565	.038	4.374	1	41	.043	1.951	12.406	.000
LANA	.832	.692	.652	9.95059	.036	4.591	1	39	.038	1.829	17.512	.000

Table 3 Lana Del Rey's perceived personality using reduced version of Big Five Neo-PRI scale

	Mean	Std. deviation	Cronbach's alpha
Neuroticism	3.64	.69	.693
N1—anxiety	3.86	1.03	
N2—hostility	3.92	1.11	
N3—depression	3.13	1.14	
N4—consciousness	3.35	1.26	
N5—impulsiveness	3.62	1.06	
N6—vulnerability to stress	3.97	1.06	
Extraversion	3.55	.78	.741
E1—warmth	3.31	1.29	
E2—gregariousness	3.83	1.15	
E3—assertiveness	2.83	1.20	
E4—activity	3.96	1.12	
E5—excitement seeking	3.78	1.22	
E6—positive emotion	3.64	1.11	
Openness to experience	2.86	.69	.578
O1—fantasy	2.87	1.35	
O2—aesthetics	2.16	1.09	
O3—feelings	2.97	1.37	
O4—actions	3.02	1.18	
O5—ideas	3.17	1.27	
O6—values	2.87	121	
Agreeableness	2.86	.75	.755
A1—trust	2.66	1.25	
A2—straightforwardness	2.55	1.16	
A3—altruism	3.30	1.10	
A4—compliance	2.56	.94	
A5—modesty	2.92	1.16	
A6—tender mindedness	3.10	1.15	
Conscientiousness	2.25	.64	.679
C1—competence	2.44	1.05	
C2—order	1.84	.90	
C3—dutifulness	2.15	.93	
C4—achievement striving	2.30	1.10	
C5—self-discipline	2.20	1.02	
C6—deliberation	2.63	1.17	

framework. However in this case, the willingness to pay is negatively correlated with the scopophilia. Although there is a significant influence of respondent's gender upon scopophilia ($M_{male} = 2.45$; $SD_{male} = 1.12$ $M_{female} = 1.58$, $SD_{female} = .87$; $t_{52} = 2.92$; $p < .001$) there is no significant difference in Lana's WTP between male and female subjects.

Table 4 Response toward Lana Del Rey's Ad and Spearman[a] correlation coefficients with personality dimensions

	M	SD	Neuroticism	Extraversion	Openness	Agreeableness	Conscientiousness
Willingness to pay for a perfume	38.13	17.88			-.227*		
Lana as singer	5.43	2.88				-.267**	
Lana as model	5.71	2.37	.276**		-.316**	-.213*	
Attitude toward the celebrity	6.02	2.14	.218*				-.202*
Attitude toward the brand	482	2.52	.247*			-.267**	
Lana's brand Purchase intention	3.43	2.59				-.201*	
Lana's brand glamour	5.09	2.20					
Lana's brand reputation	4.89	2.41					
Lana-consumer self-congruence	3.95	2.70					
Lana's brand image	5.24	2.50	.233*				

Legend: $*p<.05$; $**p<.01$

[a]Spearman correlations were used because the Kolmogorov-Smirnov test confirmed that some variables don't have normal distributions

Conclusions, Limitations, and Further Research

During the traditional endorsement process, the brand managers have to undertake a celebrity casting in order to select the celebrity endorser that fits better with the brand personality. But this process is automatic when the brand is an avatar of the celebrity itself. This chapter proposes a conceptual model for the celebrity branding advertising processing which acknowledges the influence of celebrity factors, sociocultural trends, and advertising copy strategy.

The simulation of Lana del Rey's perfume brand building confirmed that some perceived celebrity's personality traits are correlated with the advertising response outputs and the perfume's brand personality dimensions. Sociocultural trends such as scopophilia, glamour, and self-sexualization may interact with advertising copy strategy and influence the advertising response even at early stage of the celebrity branding life cycle. This study have some limitations: (a) although the sample's dimension and characteristics are consequence of methodological constraints self-imposed by researcher, some sample related bias may occur; (b) there are difficulties in the generalization of findings due to the specific characteristics of the celebrities studied and the influence of previous knowledge bias; (c) the pictorial stimuli and copy strategies selected doesn't cover the full range of combinations.

Further research may provide more insights about the influence of scopophilia, self-sexualization, and glamour. The influence of individual psychographic variables that moderate the advertising processing may also be deeply analyzed.

References

Aaker, J. (1997). Dimensions of brand personality. *Journal of Marketing Research, 34*, 347–356.

Alexander, J. (2010). The celebrity-icon. *Cultural Sociology, 4*(3), 323–336.

Biswas, S., Hussain, M., & O'Donnell, K. (2009). Celebrity endorsements in advertisements and consumer perceptions: A cross-cultural study. *Journal of Global Marketing, 22*(2), 121–137.

Bjerke, R., & Polegato, R. (2006). How well do advertising images of health and beauty travel across cultures? A self-concept perspective. *Psychology & Marketing, 23*(10), 865–884.

Brown, S. P., & Stayman, D. (1992). Antecedents and consequences of attitude toward the ad: A meta-analysis. *Journal of Consumer Research, 19*(1), 34–51.

Costa, P. T., Jr., & McCrae, R. R. (1992). *Revised NEO personality inventory (NEO-PI-R) and NEO five-factor inventory (NEO-FFI) manual.* Odessa, FL: Psychological Assessment Resources.

Coy, M., & Garner, M. (2010). Glamour modelling and the marketing of self-sexualization: Critical reflections. *International Journal of Cultural Studies, 13*(6), 657–675.

D'Alessandro, S., & Chitty, B. (2011). Real or relevant beauty? Body shape and endorser effects on brand attitude and body image. *Psychology & Marketing, 28*(8), 843–878.

DeBono, K., & Telesca, C. (1990). The influence of source physical attractiveness on advertising effectiveness: A functional perspective. *Journal of Applied Social Psychology, 20*(17), 1383–1395.

Dyer, G. (1982). *Advertising as communication.* London: Methuen.

Erdogan, B. Z. (1999). Celebrity endorsement: A literature review. *Journal of Marketing Management, 15*(4), 291–314.

Erdogan, B. Z., & Baker, M. J. (2000). Towards a practitioner-based model of selecting celebrity endorsers. *International Journal of Advertising, 19*(1), 25–42.

Erdogan, B. Z., Baker, M. J., & Tagg, S. (2001). Selecting celebrity endorsers: The practitioner's perspective. *Journal of Advertising Research, 41*(3), 39–48.

Fennis, B. M., Das, E., & Fransen, M. (2012). Print advertising: Vivid content. *Journal of Business Research, 65*, 861–864.

Gergaud, O., & Ginsburgh, V. (2010). *Success: Talent, intelligence or beauty?* Discussion Paper of Center for Operations Research and Econometrics, Université Catholique de Louvain.

Gill, R. (2007). Postfeminist media culture: Elements of a sensibility. *European Journal of Cultural Studies, 10*(2), 147–166.

Gill, R. (2008). Empowerment/sexism: Figuring female sexual agency in contemporary advertising. *Feminism & Psychology, 18*, 35–60.

Gundle, S. (2008). *Glamour. A history*. Oxford, England: Oxford University Press.

Halonen-Knight, E., & Hurmerinta, L. (2010). Who endorses whom? Meanings transfer in celebrity endorsement. *Journal of Product & Brand Management, 19*(6), 452–460.

Hautala, H. (2011). *The glamorous life of chanel no. 5 –a contribution to the theory of glamour.* Thesis for the degree of Master in Media and Communication Studies. Department of Journalism, Media and Communications, Stockholm University.

Heine, K. (2010). The personality of luxury fashion brands. *Journal of Global Fashion Marketing, 1–3*, 154–163.

Huhmann, B., Franke, G., & Mothersbaugh, D. (2012). Print advertising: Executional factors and the RPB Grid. *Journal of Business Research, 65*, 849–854.

Kilbourne, J. (1999). *Deadly persuasion: Why women and girls must fight the addictive power of advertising*. New York: The Free Press.

Kilyeni, A. (2009). Nonverbal communication in print ads. *Professional Communication and Translation Studies, 2*(1–2), 17–24.

Klebba, J. M., & Unger, L. (1982). The impact of positive and negative information on source credibility in a field setting. In R. Bogazzi & A. Tybout (Eds.), *Advances in consumer research* (pp. 11–16). Provo, UT: Association for Consumer Research.

Lacan, J. (2005). *Ecrits*. New York: W.W. Norton. (Original work published 1970).

Lacey, N. (2009). *Image and representation. Key concepts in media studies*. London: Palgrave MacMillan.

Lazar, M. (2011). The right to be beautiful: Postfeminist identity and consumer beauty advertising. In R. Gill & C. Sharff (Eds.), *New femininities: Postfeminism, neoliberalism and subjectivity* (pp. 37–51). London: Palgrave MacMillan.

Metz, C. (1977). *The imaginary signifier: Psychoanalysis and the cinema*. Bloomington, IL: Indiana University Press.

Meyers-Levy, J., & Peracchio, L. (1992). Getting an angle in advertising: The effect of camera angle on product evaluations. *Journal of Marketing Research, 29*(Nov), 454–461.

Naiman, E. (1998). Shklovsky's dog and Mulvey's pleasure: The secret life of defamiliarization. *Comparative Literature, 50*, 333–352.

Nettle, D. (2006). Psychological profiles of professional actors. *Personality and Individual Differences, 40*, 375–383.

Oswald, L. (2010). Marketing hedonics: Toward a psychoanalysis of advertising response. *Journal of Marketing Communications, 16*(3), 107–131.

Rossiter, J., & Percy, L. (1980). Attitude change through visual imagery in advertising. *Journal of Advertising, 9*(2), 10–16.

Rossiter, J., & Smidts, A. (2012). Print advertising: Celebrity presenters. *Journal of Business Research, 65*, 874–879.

Sawang, S. (2010). Sex appeal in advertising: What consumers think. *Journal of Promotion Management, 16*(1–2), 167–187.

Soukup, C. (2009). Techno-scopophilia: The semiotics of technological pleasure in film. *Critical Studies in Media Communication, 26*(1), 19–35.

Origin Labelling as a Differentiation Strategy for Wood Products

Vincent Chamberland, François Robichaud, and Nancy Gélinas

Abstract The origin of a product is a critical factor in a purchasing decision. Origin can be used as a guarantee of quality, as a symbol of prestige or as a benchmark for social acceptability. The goal of this study was to determine the importance of origin for consumers of wood products in the province of Québec. An online survey of 983 consumers in Québec was carried out in 2012. The survey included two full-profile conjoint analyses dealing, respectively, with hardwood flooring (a value-added product) and softwood lumber (a commodity product). Each product was defined on the basis of four attributes: price, quality, origin and the presence or absence of an environmental certification. With respect to hardwood flooring, the most highly valued attribute was origin. In this connection, respondents expressed a strong preference for Québec products. With respect to softwood lumber, product appearance turned out to be the most important attribute whilst origin came in second on the preference scale. Product origin is therefore an important attribute for Québec consumers of wood products. It can be concluded that it would be appropriate for wood products manufacturers facing strong international competition to promote the local origin of their products, especially for value-added products.

Keywords Wood products • Origin labelling • Conjoint analysis • Commodity • Value-added

Introduction

Currently, the promotion of product origin occurs mainly in the agri-food sector. In Québec, the proliferation of labels promoting the local origin of agri-food products goes back to the mid-1990s. Origin labels promote local purchases and increase

V. Chamberland (✉) • N. Gélinas
Université Laval, Québec, QC, Canada
e-mail: vincent.chamberland@gmail.com; nancy.gelinas@sbf.ulaval.ca

F. Robichaud
FPInnovations, Pointe-Claire, QC, Canada
e-mail: francois.robichaud@fpinnovations.ca

© Academy of Marketing Science 2016   613
L. Petruzzellis, R.S. Winer (eds.), *Rediscovering the Essentiality of Marketing*,
Developments in Marketing Science: Proceedings of the Academy of Marketing
Science, DOI 10.1007/978-3-319-29877-1_119

product visibility through brand recognition. The proliferation of these labels is a sign that promotion of local products is profitable and that consumers are keenly interested in this type of information. This interest has been measured annually since 2012 by the *Observatoire de la consommation responsable*. In its 2012 report, the Observatoire ranked local purchasing as the second most important responsible behaviour among Québec consumers (Observatoire de la Consommation Responsable 2012). Nearly 70% of consumers indicated a preference for a local product when they have that option.

In the forest sector, the province of Ontario and several American states, including Massachusetts, Vermont and Minnesota, have designed and adopted labels to promote locally manufactured wood products. No such labels have been adopted in the province of Québec despite significant offerings of imported wood products on the domestic market, in particular from China and South America (Industry Canada 2013). These offerings include appearance wood products such as flooring materials, mouldings and wood furniture. In February 2011, the Québec Minister of Natural Resources expressed his government's interest in supporting the forest sector through the adoption of a label promoting Québec wood (Gouvernement du Québec 2011). Given the level of consumer interest in the consumption of local agri-food products, the government's willingness to implement a strategy to promote Québec wood and the market conditions required to justify such a strategy, several questions on the importance of the local origin of wood products for end users come to mind.

Background

Product origin is an extrinsic attribute. In other words, it is not observable (Peterson and Jolibert 1995). Its impact on consumer behaviour has been discussed at length in the scientific literature. Many studies indicate that origin plays an important role in product evaluation by consumers and thus has an impact on their behaviour (Bilkey and Nes 1982; Laroche et al. 2005; Papadopoulos and Heslop 2002). Consumers must cope with information overload. That is why they use attributes, such as a country's image, to break down information in order to lessen the perceived purchasing risk and to evaluate the social acceptability of their purchases (Papadopoulos and Heslop 2002).

Underlying Factors

A number of factors come into play in explaining the impact of origin as it relates to the evaluation of products by consumers (Pharr 2005). Consumers tend to stereotype producing countries. The resulting stereotypes can be positive or negative and reflect the range of consumer experiences associated with the consumption of products with a common origin. Stereotypes instinctively come to mind and consumers involuntarily take them into account when they evaluate a product (Liu and Johnson 2005).

Consumer animosity also affects consumer behaviour (Klein 2002). Animosity is defined as the anger of a country against another due to political, military, economic or social conflicts (Klein 2002). Animosity has a negative and direct impact on consumer purchasing decisions. It does not affect consumer evaluation of product quality (Klein 2002). Consumers may acknowledge the quality of certain products manufactured in a given country, but refuse to purchase them to protest against a conflict between their country and the country in which the products are manufactured.

Consumer ethnocentrism can also explain why the origin of a product can have an impact on purchasing decisions. Consumer ethnocentrism is defined as the conviction that it is inappropriate to purchase imported products because of the resulting impacts on local economies and on job retention regionally (Klein 2002; Shimp and Sharma 1987). Ethnocentrism differs from animosity since it affects the perception of product quality. Consumers who believe that purchasing imported products is a bad thing tend to underestimate the quality of these products whilst overestimating the quality of domestic products (Sharma et al. 1995).

Mitigators

Scientific literature also includes discussions of mitigators that can reduce the impact of product origin on consumers. These fall into two broad families: product-related and consumer-related (Pharr 2005). Product-related mitigators include price, brand, product type and product complexity. It has been demonstrated that consumers attach greater importance to price than to origin. Thus, when product prices rise, the importance of origin falls (Ahmed et al. 2004; Bilkey and Nes 1982). When consumers evaluate products, they also attach greater importance to brand than to origin (Ahmed et al. 2004). From the manufacturer's perspective, a strong brand mitigates the impact of a producing country's negative image when consumers evaluate products from that country (Jo et al. 2003). The type of product and its complexity will also mitigate the impact of product origin. The impact of a country's image will depend on the category of products under consideration (Pappu et al. 2007). There must be a coherent relation between a product and the producing country's image in order for origin to have a significant impact (Ahmed et al. 2011). Certain countries or regions are well known for their expertise in manufacturing certain products. Displaying the origin of such products should therefore have a significant impact. The type of product can also influence the impact of origin on consumer preferences. Thus, in the case of commodity products, origin plays a role in product evaluation, but its impact would likely be weak (Ahmed et al. 2004). Consumers would likely purchase this type of product out of habit.

Consumer-related mitigators include consumer familiarity with a product and involvement in the decision to purchase it. The impact of the country of origin on a consumer varies according to his level of knowledge about a product. Consumers who are very knowledgeable are less likely to use origin information, whereas consumers with less knowledge will attach greater importance to this information (Lee and Lee 2009). In the latter case, a country's image exerts a halo effect, that is, consumers judge a product on the basis of their knowledge of its country of origin (Han 1989). Consumer involvement in purchasing a product appears to have an impact on the influence of the country of origin. Research on this subject has revealed the existence of contradictory results. Liu and Johnson (2005) concluded that the greater the consumer's involvement in the purchasing decision, the lesser the influence of the country of origin. On the other hand, Hugstad and Dur (2006) in (Ahmed et al. 2011) concluded that the greater the consumer's involvement, the more he will search for information on its origin.

In the Forest Sector

A few studies have focused on the impact of wood product origin on consumer preferences. In two studies comparing consumer preferences for products made of temperate forest species on one hand and tropical forest species on the other, the majority of consumers declared their preference for temperate forest species (Aguilar and Cai 2010; Kozak et al. 2004). This preference was based on a decision to use products made of wood from sustainably managed forests. Consumers have the impression that tropical woods products come from countries in which forestry legislation does not adequately protect the forest resource (Aguilar and Cai 2010). Furthermore, some consumers have expressed a preference for locally manufactured wood products in order to foster job retention on a regional basis (Kozak et al. 2004). Alaskan consumers have shown a strong willingness to pay a premium for locally manufactured furniture (Donovan and Nicholls 2003). Oregon and Washington State architects have also expressed an interest in locally manufactured hardwood flooring (Macias and Knowles 2011) when product origin was compared to price and environmental certification.

Objective and Research Hypotheses

The literature on the impact of country of origin on consumer behaviour confirms the existence of such an impact which, however, varies according to the characteristics of both products and consumers. The few studies focusing on forest products indicate that origin can be an attractive attribute for consumers. However, findings do not permit generalization of this particular conclusion. The objective of this research project was therefore to determine whether local origin had any impact on consumer preferences with respect to wood products from the province of Québec. It was assumed that wood product origin can affect consumer purchasing behaviour and that consumers prefer products manufactured in that province (Hypothesis 1).

On the other hand, it was expected that preference for locally manufactured wood products would not be stronger than preference for other more basic attributes such as price and product quality (Hypothesis 2). Finally, whereas the impact of origin varies according to product type, it was assumed that local origin of wood products would be a more important attribute for value-added products than for commodity products (Hypothesis 3).

Method

Data Collection

Data were collected by means of an online survey of adult consumers of wood products manufactured in the province of Québec. A consumer of wood products was defined as a respondent who purchased a wood product in the past 2 years or who was planning on doing so in the coming year. Respondent recruitment was carried out by a polling firm using its own consumer panel. The selected polling company was required to have a panel where members are selected on a random basis. Especially, the firm recruited panel members by telephone using a random digit dialling technique. Overall, invitations were extended to 4385 panelists. Of these, 1481 responded to the invitation and accessed the survey questionnaire. This represents a response rate of 34 %. The number of non-eligible respondents amounted to 419. The overall response rate was therefore 72 %. Of the 1062 completed questionnaires, 983 were retained. Questionnaire with missing data were discarded.

The Survey Questionnaire

The survey questionnaire was organized into four sections. The first section was designed to develop a demographic profile. Data were used to validate panel quality by comparing the demographic characteristics of the respondents with those of the population of Québec. The second section was designed to learn about local purchasing habits in the agri-food sector. This sector was chosen because local consumption is widespread across the spectrum of agri-food products (Observatoire de la Consommation Responsable 2012). Questions were designed to achieve respondent segmentation. The third section was designed to determine the attributes taken into account by respondents when they purchase wood products. The last section of the questionnaire was designed to determine respondent attitude with respect to purchasing local wood products. The questionnaire design followed the guidelines set forth by Dillman et al. (2009) and Bradburn et al. (2004). Experts with in-depth knowledge of wood products and surveys were consulted during the question-writing process. A pretest was carried out with a dozen respondents who did not have in-depth knowledge of the wood products sector in order to determine their comprehension of the questions.

Segmentation

The questionnaire included five questions designed to allow for respondent segmentation. These questions identified respondents whose behaviour reflects a preference for purchasing local products and whose attitude towards these products is favourable. Two questions focused on purchasing habits in the agri-food sector. The three remaining questions focused on respondent behaviour and attitude when purchasing wood products. Segmentation was achieved using two different analytical methods. A hierarchic clustering using the Ward method was developed in order to determine the number of segments and a non-hierarchic clustering was developed in order to determine the segment in which each respondent belonged. Subsequently, separate conjoint analyses were carried out based on the resulting segments.

Conjoint Analysis

The conjoint analysis was the key focus of the questionnaire. This technique was used because it brings out the attributes to which consumers attach the greatest importance in a simulated purchasing situation (Orme 2006). The full-profile conjoint analysis method was selected for this study. Two analyses were carried out: one for a commodity product (softwood lumber—Table 1), the other for a value-added product (hardwood flooring—Table 2).

In each case, four attributes were selected: price, origin, certification and quality. The attribute of quality was characterized according to the product. In the case of hardwood flooring, product grade was the key; for lumber, quality was expressed in terms of overall appearance. Attribute levels were selected to reflect products offered on the domestic market.

A total of 54 combinations were possible for each product. An orthogonal design in SPSS was used to reduce the number of combinations for analysis. In an orthogonal design, each attribute level is combined at least once with each level of the other attributes. Thus, nine combinations were retained for each product. Consumers were asked to evaluate each combination individually on a scale of 1 (product to be avoided) to 9 (ideal).

Results

Segmentation

The cluster analysis revealed the existence of two distinct segments. The first included 378 respondents, that is, 38.5 % of the sample. Respondents in this segment attached less importance to local purchasing in both the agri-food and wood

Table 1 Combinations used in the lumber conjoint analysis

Combinations	Price ($) unit	Appearance	Origin	Certification
1	1	Slight crook	Québec	None
2	1	Straight, with knots or bark	United States	FSC
3	1	Straight, good visual appearance	Canada	None
4	2	Slight crook	United States	None
5	2	Straight, with knots or bark	Canada	None
6	2	Straight, good visual appearance	Québec	FSC
7	3	Slight crook	Canada	FSC
8	3	Straight, with knots or bark	Québec	None
9	3	Straight, good visual appearance	United States	None

Table 2 Combinations used in the hardwood flooring conjoint analysis

Combination	Price ($/ft²)	Grade	Origin	Certification
1	3	Low end	Québec	None
2	3	Mid-market	Canada	None
3	3	High-end	China	FSC
4	5	Low-end	China	None
5	5	Mid-market	Québec	FSC
6	5	High-end	Canada	None
7	7	Low-end	Canada	FSC
8	7	Mid-market	China	None
9	7	High-end	Québec	None

products sectors. The second segment included 605 respondents, that is, 61.5% of the sample. Members of this segment are more favourable to the purchase of local products. The two segments were compared according to the following demographic variables: region of residence, sex, age, principal occupation, level of education and household income. Respondent age and sex were the only two variables that differed significantly from one segment to the other. Segment 1 respondents (with a lesser attachment to origin) included younger individuals than segment 2 (more favourable to origin) and a higher proportion of men.

Preferences for Hardwood Flooring

Three conjoint analyses were conducted for each product: one for all the respondents and one for each identified segment. The results of the three conjoint analyses conducted with respect to hardwood flooring highlight the importance of each

Table 3 Attribute importance and utility values for hardwood flooring

Attributes	All		Segment 1		Segment 2	
	Utilities	Attribute importance	Utilities	Attribute importance	Utilities	Attribute importance
Origin		43.3%		36.9%		47.3%
Québec	1.288		.971		1.486	
Canada	.844		.668		.953	
China	−2.132		−1.639		−2.439	
Grade		2.9%		23.6%		19.2%
Low-end	−.66		−.777		−.587	
Mid-market	.07		.074		.067	
High-end	.59		.703		.52	
Certification		19.3%		19.1%		19.4%
None	−.75		−.662		−.805	
FSC	.75		.662		.805	
Price ($/ft²)		16.5%		20.3%		14.1%
3	−.289		−.516		−.148	
5	−.578		−1.033		−.295	
7	−.867		−1.549		−.443	
Constant	5.979		6.432		5.698	
Pearson's R	.994		.994		.994	
Kendall's tau	.889		.889		.944	

attribute as well as the utility values for each attribute level (Table 3). The conjoint analysis for the entire sample indicated that origin was the most important attribute for the respondents. Respondents expressed a strong preference for local products, whereas products from China were the least favourite. The second most important attribute was product grade, for which respondents expressed a preference for higher-end products. The third most important attribute was forest certification with respondents expressing a preference for FSC-certified products over non-certified products. The least important attribute was product price. Nonetheless, respondents did express a preference for less expensive flooring.

The results of the conjoint analyses conducted for the two segments of respondents differed from those of the analysis that focused on the respondents as a whole. It should be noted that origin is the most important attribute for the members of both segments. The importance of this attribute for the members of segment 1, however, was lower than for the members of segment 2. This confirms that the segmentation through which local product origin was of less interest to segment 1 respondents. The order of importance of the other attributes differed for each segment. For segment 1, product grade was the second-most important attribute, followed by price and forest certification. For segment 2, forest certification and product grade received equal consideration among respondents. Price was the least important attribute for this consumer segment.

Table 4 Attribute importance and utilities for lumber

	All		Segment 1		Segment 2	
Attributes	Utilities	Attribute importance	Utilities	Attribute importance	Utilities	Attribute importance
Appearance		41.9%		45.6%		39.5%
Slight crook	−1.215		−1.291		−1.169	
Straight, with knots or bark	−.254		−.271		−.243	
Straight, pleasing appearance	1.469		1.562		1.412	
Origin		27.9%		22.3%		31.3%
Québec	.609		.387		.746	
Canada	.277		.175		.34	
United States	−.866		−.562		−1.086	
Price ($/unit)		15.9%		18.1%		14.6%
1	−.439		−.529		−.384	
2	−.879		−1.058		−.768	
3	−1.3181		−1.588		−1.152	
Certification		14.3%		14.0%		14.6%
None	−.329		−.267		−.367	
FSC	.329		.267		.367	
Constant	3.6458		6.512		6.218	
Pearson's R	.963		.973		.971	
Kendall's tau	.889		.778		.889	

Preferences for Lumber

The results of the three conjoint analyses that focused on lumber differed significantly when compared with those of the analyses that focused on hardwood flooring (Table 4).

With softwood lumber, the most important attribute for the two segments is the visual appearance of the product. This attribute was used to express product quality. For the entire sample, the importance of this attribute was 41.9%. The importance of this attribute was greater among segment 1 consumers than among those of segment 2. Respondents expressed their preference for straight and visually attractive lumber. On the other hand, they expressed a low affinity for crooked lumber. As for the other attributes, the order of importance is the same in both segments, with product origin ranking second. On origin, respondents expressed a preference for products from Québec. Segment 1 respondents attached a lesser importance to this attribute. The two least important attributes were price and forest certification, whereas among the members of segment 2, these two attributes achieved an equal level of importance. As in the case of hardwood flooring, respondents expressed a preference for the least expensive products and FSC-certified products.

Discussion

Results indicate that consumers of wood products have a keen interest in purchasing local products, defined as coming from the province of Québec. This supports the first study Hypothesis. Specifying wood origin has a significant effect on consumer preferences (Aguilar and Cai 2010; Kozak et al. 2004) and respondents have expressed a strong preference for wood products manufactured in Québec. The impact of origin on consumer preference has been amply demonstrated in the scientific literature and for several reasons. Consumers hold stereotypes about the country of origin of the products they purchase and these stereotypes influence their evaluation of these products (Liu and Johnson 2005). Products from Asian countries are viewed as low-performing, low-quality and less original (Ahmed and D'Astous 2001). This would explain the weak desirability of flooring manufactured in China compared to flooring manufactured in Québec. Consumer ethnocentrism may also explain the favourable results for products manufactured in Québec. Balabanis and Diamantopoulos (2004) found that consumer ethnocentrism is an important predictor of consumer behaviour as it relates to information on product origin. Consumers with a preference for products originating in their region would be considered to be ethnocentric. Although the ethnocentrism of respondents was not measured here, this factor might partly explain their preference for local wood products. The desire to encourage the local economy, shared by the majority of respondents, supports this assertion. The degree ethnocentrism varies among consumers. It was noted that the group of consumers with the strongest preference for local wood products was older and included a higher proportion of women. Cleveland et al. (2009) demonstrated that older consumers show a greater propensity for ethnocentrism, but that the sex of consumers had no bearing on this factor.

Respondents showed a very low sensitivity to price, but they attach great importance to product quality. The second Hypothesis, according to which price and product quality are the most important attributes, is therefore supported by study results. Price was the least important attribute in the case of hardwood flooring, but the second most important in the case of lumber. Product quality was the most important attribute in the case of lumber and the second most important in the case of hardwood flooring. Like those of Donovan and Nicholls (2003), study results suggest that Québec consumers would also be willing to pay a premium for locally produced products. On the other hand, study results contradict those of Cameron and Elliott (1998) and those of Baker and Ballington (2002) with respect to the relative importance of price. These researchers found that Australian and Scottish consumers preferred locally manufactured products if these were equivalent, in price and quality, to imported products. With respect to product quality, our results are consistent with these two studies since this attributes ranks among the most important in terms of relative importance. It was also demonstrated that the end users of wood products attach great importance to the quality of the lumber they purchase (Forsyth et al. 1999). This was confirmed by our results.

Respondent interest with respect to local origin varied according to product function. This attribute was the most important in the case of hardwood flooring (a value-added product) compared with lumber (a commodity product). This result supports the third Hypothesis according to which local origin was more important in the case of added-value products than in the case of commodity products. The impact of origin on consumer purchasing decisions is influenced by the complexity of the product, the involvement of the consumers and their familiarity with the product (Pharr 2005). Thus, the impact of origin on product evaluation will be greater for the more complex and least frequently purchased products (Insch and McBride 2004). Origin is also important in the evaluation of commodity products like lumber, but its impact is low (Ahmed et al. 2004). Consumers attach less importance to information on the origin of such products, at least in part because their purchases are the results of past habits. This may explain the lower importance of lumber origin. Furthermore, the availability of softwood lumber from other countries is quite limited.

The interest in purchasing local wood products seems to be widely shared among the respondents. One could have expected that some respondents would attach little importance to this attribute. However, even the consumer segment least sensitized to local purchasing in the agri-food sector attached great importance to wood product origin: attribute importance was lower in the segment most sensitized to local purchasing, but origin held the same ranking in terms of attribute importance.

Limits

Respondents seem to have underrated the importance of price. This could be due to several factors. The price range used in the conjoint analysis may have had a significant impact on the relative importance of this factor. While too great a price range could lead to an overestimation of price, too narrow a price range would lead to an underestimation of the importance of price (Orme 2006). Within the framework of this study, price levels were selected on the basis of current market supply at renovation centres and specialized retailers. We believe that the price range was neither too great nor too narrow. On the other hand, the price variations provided to respondents were expressed on the basis of product units ($/ft^2 or $/unit) even though these products are seldom purchased on a per unit basis. In addition to unit price, we could have listed prices on the basis of a renovation project. For example, we could have listed the price of wood flooring on the basis of the area of a room in a house. Thus, price levels for a 200-ft^2 room would have been $600, $1000 and $1400. This might have been more realistic given the variations of expenses associated with this type of work.

Study results are similar to those obtained in the first studies which focused on consumer willingness to pay a premium for certified wood products. A sizeable proportion of consumers were willing to pay a premium of at least 5% for certified products, but some would even be willing to pay a premium of 50% or more (Forsyth et al. 1999; Ozanne and Vlosky 1997). Industrialists from the forest sector noticed that the attitudes reflected in these studies did not necessarily translate into purchasing behaviours (Anderson and Hansen 2004; Anderson et al. 2005). Our results indicate a strong consumer preference for local products, but one might wonder about their actual consumer behaviour when making real purchasing decisions. Peterson and Jolibert (1995) recommend prudence when working with the results of studies on the impact of origin on consumers. An extrinsic product attribute, such as origin, has less of an impact on consumer purchasing decisions when a greater degree of consumer involvement is required. One could expect that this attribute could be overestimated in the context of a theoretical response as opposed to a real purchasing setting. Also, the impact of origin declines as the number of product attributes increases (Verlegh and Steenkamp 1999). In this study, we limited the number of attributes to facilitate responses. Thus, its relative importance could be weaker in a real purchasing setting.

Conclusion and Managerial Implications

This study showed that Québec consumers consider product origin as an important attribute and that they are prone to favour locally manufactured products. The local origin of wood products is more important in the case of hardwood flooring (a value-added product) than in the case of lumber (a commodity product). The attribute importance of price was nonetheless lower than that of origin. Globally, price was the least important attribute for hardwood flooring and ranked second-last for lumber. The importance of product quality, expressed on the basis of product grade in the case of hardwood flooring and of lumber appearance for softwood ranged from medium to high. Even though this was not a study on the importance of product quality, these results should increase the awareness of manufacturers to the importance of this attribute in order to promote their brand.

Results indicate that Québec wood-product manufacturers should place a greater emphasis on the place of manufacture in their domestic marketing strategies since consumers have expressed an interest in this attribute. Such a marketing strategy would be more relevant for manufacturers of value-added products since respondents have expressed a greater interest in Québec products from this market. Furthermore, the domestic market for value-added products suggests that manufacturers would significantly benefit from this type of promotion in the face of significant competition from other countries. Manufacturers could expect to increase their market share in the wake of a prominent mention of the place of manufacture on their product wrapping or packaging. Consumers have nonetheless shown an interest in the local consumption of commodity products.

Should competition by imported products arise domestically in that market segment, it would be appropriate to develop a promotion strategy emphasizing the place of manufacture of the products. On the other hand, consumers have shown a strong sensitivity to product quality. They would likely show a preference for domestic products comparable in quality to imported products.

In closing, it should be noted that the results of this study only apply to Québec consumers. This consumer segment accounts for only a part of the sales of wood products on the domestic market for wood products.

References

Aguilar, F. X., & Cai, Z. (2010). Conjoint effect of environmental labeling, disclosure of forest of origin and price on consumer preferences for wood products in the US and UK. *Ecological Economics, 70*(2), 308–316.

Ahmed, S. A., & D'Astous, A. (2001). Canadian consumers perceptions of products made in newly industrializing east Asian countries. *International Journal of Commerce and Management, 11*(1), 54–81.

Ahmed, S. A., D'Astous, A., & Petersen, H. B. (2011). Product-country fit in the Canadian context. *Journal of Consumer Marketing, 28*(4), 300–309.

Ahmed, Z. U., Johnson, J. P., Yang, X., Fatt, C. K., Teng, H. S., & Boon, L. C. (2004). Does country of origin matter for low-involvement products? *International Marketing Review, 21*(1), 102–120.

Anderson, R. C., & Hansen, E. N. (2004). Determining consumer preferences for ecolabeled forest products: An experimental approach. *Journal of Forestry, 102*, 28–32.

Anderson, R. C., Laband, D. N., Hansen, E. N., & Knowles, C. D. (2005). Price premiums in the mist. *Forest Products Journal, 55*(6), 19–22.

Baker, M. J., & Ballington, L. (2002). Country of origin as a source of competitive advantage. *Journal of Strategic Marketing, 10*(2), 157–168.

Balabanis, G., & Diamantopoulos, A. (2004). Domestic country bias, country-of-origin effects, and consumer ethnocentrism: A multidimensional unfolding approach. *Journal of the Academy of Marketing Science, 32*(1), 80–95.

Bilkey, W. J., & Nes, E. (1982). Country-of-origin effects on product evaluations. *Journal of International Business Studies, 13*(1), 89–99.

Bradburn, N., Sudman, S., & Wansink, B. (2004). *Asking questions: The definitive guide to questionnaire design—for market research, political polls, and social and health questionnaires.* San Francisco: Jossey Bass.

Cameron, R. C., & Elliott, G. R. (1998). The country-of-origin effect and consumer attitudes to buy local campaigns: Australian evidence. *Australasian Marketing Journal, 6*(2), 39–50.

Cleveland, M., Laroche, M., & Papadopoulos, N. (2009). Cosmopolitanism, consumer ethnocentrism, and materialism: An eight-country study of antecedents and outcomes. *Journal of International Marketing, 17*(1), 116–146.

Dillman, D. A., Smyth, J. D., & Christian, L. M. (2009). *Internet, mail, and mixed-mode surveys—the tailored design method.* Hoboken, NJ: Wiley.

Donovan, G. H., & Nicholls, D. L. (2003). *Estimating consumer willingness to pay a price premium for Alaska secondary wood products.* US Department of Agriculture, Forest Service, Pacific Northwest Research Station research paper.

Forsyth, K., Haley, D., & Kozak, R. (1999). Will consumers pay more for certified wood products? *Journal of Forestry, 97*, 18–22.

Gouvernement du Québec. (2011). *La Ministre Normandeau propose un label propre au bois du Québec.* Press Release. Retrieved Febuary 23, 2011, from http://communiques.gouv.qc.ca/gouvqc/communiques/GPQF/Fevrier2011/18/c4278.html

Han, C. M. (1989). Country image: Halo or summary construct? *Journal of Marketing Research, 26*(2), 222–229.

Industry Canada. (2013). Trade data online. Retrieved August 4, 2013, from http://www.ic.gc.ca/eic/site/tdo-dcd.nsf/eng/home

Insch, G. S., & McBride, J. B. (2004). The impact of country-of-origin cues on consumer perceptions of product quality: A binational test of the decomposed country-of-origin construct. *Journal of Business Research, 57*(3), 256–265.

Jo, M.-S., Nakamoto, K., & Nelson, J. E. (2003). The shielding effects of brand image against lower quality countries-of-origin in global manufacturing. *Journal of Business Research, 56*(8), 637–646.

Klein, J. G. (2002). Us versus them, or us versus everyone? Delineating consumer aversion to foreign goods. *Journal of International Business Studies, 33*(2), 345–363.

Kozak, R. A., Cohen, D. H., Lerner, J., & Bull, G. Q. (2004). Western Canadian consumer attitudes towards certified value-added wood products: An exploratory assessment. *Forest Products Journal, 54*(9), 21–24.

Laroche, M., Papadopoulos, N., Heslop, L., & Mourali, M. (2005). The influence of country image structure on consumer evaluations of foreign products. *International Marketing Review, 22*(1), 96–115.

Lee, J. K., & Lee, W.-N. (2009). Country-of-origin effects on consumer product evaluation and purchase intention: The role of objective versus subjective knowledge. *Journal of International Consumer Marketing, 21*(2), 137–151.

Liu, S. S., & Johnson, K. F. (2005). The automatic country-of-origin effects on brand judgments. *Journal of Advertising, 34*(1), 87–97.

Macias, N., & Knowles, C. (2011). Examining the effect of environmental certification, wood source, and price on architects' preferences of hardwood flooring. *Silva Fennica, 45*(1), 97–109.

Observatoire de la Consommation Responsable. (2012). Le Baromètre 2012 de la consommation responsable: Université de Sherbrooke.

Orme, B. K. (2006). *Getting started with conjoint analysis—strategies for product design and pricing research*. Madison, WI: Research Publisher LLC.

Ozanne, L. K., & Vlosky, R. P. (1997). Willingness to pay for environmentally certified wood products: A consumer perspective. *Forest Products Journal, 47*(6), 39–48.

Papadopoulos, N., & Heslop, L. (2002). Country equity and country branding: Problems and prospects. *Journal of Brand Management, 9*(4/5), 294.

Pappu, R., Quester, P. G., & Cooksey, R. W. (2007). Country image and consumer-based brand equity: Relationships and implications for international marketing. *Journal of International Business Studies, 38*(5), 726–745.

Peterson, R. A., & Jolibert, A. J. P. (1995). A meta-analysis of country-of-origin effects. *Journal of International Business Studies, 26*(4), 883–900.

Pharr, J. M. (2005). Synthesizing country-of-origin research from the last decade: Is the concept still salient in an era of global brands? *Journal of Marketing Theory and Practice, 13*(4), 34–45.

Sharma, S., Shimp, T. A., & Jeongshin, S. (1995). Consumer ethnocentrism: A test of antecedents and moderators. *Journal of the Academy of Marketing Science, 23*(1), 26–37.

Shimp, T. A., & Sharma, S. (1987). Consumer ethnocentrism: Construction and validation of the CETSCALE. *Journal of Marketing Research, 24*(3), 280–289.

Verlegh, P. W. J., & Steenkamp, J.-B. E. M. (1999). A review and meta-analysis of country-of-origin research. *Journal of Economic Psychology, 20*(5), 521–546.

Virtual Brand Communities: Pathways to Brand Trust?

Sahar Mousavi, Stuart Roper, and Kathy Keeling

Abstract Little doubt exists about virtual brand communities (VBCs) strong impact on branding (e.g. Schau and Muniz 2002; Fournier and Lee 2009). Specifically, brand community identification, participation, and community commitment all empirically lead to brand loyalty and positive behavioural outcomes. However, the impact of VBC participation on customers' brand trust, which is essential to relational marketing (Albert et al. 2013), remains unclear. The mechanisms mediating and/or moderating VBC effects on customers' brand trust remain uncharted. Specifically, scholars and practitioners should understand customer pathways to brand trust through VBC participation. Furthermore, although lurkers (non-active members) make up the highest proportion of participants in virtual communities (Walker et al. 2013), little research has yet examined them (Thompson et al. 2014). Since lurkers are the majority of virtual community members, understanding how 'lurkers' build brand trust and whether this differs from 'poster' (active members) pathways in direction and/or strength would equip VBC managers in building successful communities that would lead to brand trust for all users.

This study intends to uncover such issues and proposes a model of building brand trust in VBCs by integrating elements of social identity theory with the current literature on customer–brand relationship and virtual communities. We empirically investigate the mechanism that translates VBCs into members (both posters and lurkers) brand trust. Using a sample of 734 virtual brand communities' members, the study finds that the more valuable support customers receive from a brand in its virtual community (i.e. the three constructs of recognition for contributions, encouraging interaction, and content enhancement), the stronger will be their social identity in the community which leads to their trust towards the brand. In addition,

S. Mousavi (✉) • K. Keeling
Manchester Business School, Manchester, UK
e-mail: Sahar.mousavi@mbs.ac.uk; kathy.keeling@manchester.ac.uk

S. Roper
Bradford University School of Management, Bradford, UK
e-mail: S.Roper@bradford.ac.uk

© Academy of Marketing Science 2016
L. Petruzzellis, R.S. Winer (eds.), *Rediscovering the Essentiality of Marketing*,
Developments in Marketing Science: Proceedings of the Academy of Marketing
Science, DOI 10.1007/978-3-319-29877-1_120

a brand can increase its customers' trust in its virtual community by encouraging those members to share information within the community, facilitating interaction among members, and providing accurate, complete, up-to-date information. Brand knowledge serves as such a full mediator connecting lurkers' social identity with their brand trust. Lurkers' sense of social identity in a VBC does not automatically translate into their brand trust. Without cultivating their brand knowledge, lurkers in a VBC may not necessarily trust the brand.

The study contributes to the growing research on VBCs and branding literature by articulating the key determinants of members' brand trust, as it relates to different types of participation in VBCs. Implications of this research will allow managers to know how both posters' and lurkers' participation in a VBC promote pathways to brand trust and so how to utilize a virtual community as a channel to develop and maintain strong relationships with their customers.

References available upon request.

Concurrent Sponsors' Entitativity and Purchase Intentions: An Empirical Study Within a Sporting Context

Peter Dickenson and Anne Souchon

Introduction

Enhancing consumers' purchase intentions is one of the key objectives of strategic marketing (Lukas et al. 2005). However, few studies have investigated purchase intentions within concurrent sponsorship settings. Concurrent sponsorships involve a minimum of two brands (a collective of sponsors) sponsoring the same property at the same time (Carrillat et al. 2010). In turn, social psychology tells us that collectives are characterized by the degree to which the separate entities that compose them are perceived as being groups (i.e., entitativity) (Campbell 1958; Hamilton et al. 2002). Despite not having been examined within a sponsorship context, entitativity is likely to be relevant to sponsees and associated concurrent sponsors; for example, in an entitative group, perceptions of the group as a whole are applied to the individual group members (Crawford et al. 2002), and consequently, purchase intentions towards any given sponsor will be affected by perceptions of the group as a whole. The objective of this chapter is therefore to examine the relationship between the perceived entitativity of concurrent sponsor groups and purchase intentions.

P. Dickenson (✉)
Loughborough University, Leicestershire, UK

Sheffield Hallam University, Sheffield, UK
e-mail: p.dickenson@lboro.ac.uk

A. Souchon
Loughborough University, Leicestershire, UK
e-mail: a.l.souchon@lboro.ac.uk

© Academy of Marketing Science 2016
L. Petruzzellis, R.S. Winer (eds.), *Rediscovering the Essentiality of Marketing*,
Developments in Marketing Science: Proceedings of the Academy of Marketing
Science, DOI 10.1007/978-3-319-29877-1_121

This study contributes to the brand management field in a number of ways. First, the concept of entitativity originates from social psychology and has seldom been transferred to a commercial arena. The sponsorship context provides an ideal and unusual domain within which to test entitativity's relevance to consumers' brand evaluations owing to concurrent sponsors usually originating from different product categories. Second, purchase intentions are one of the most critical outcomes of sponsorship, yet have received relatively scant attention to date in concurrent sponsorship settings (Carrillat et al. 2010; Wang et al. 2011). Given the amount of sponsorship spending combined with the need to justify such investments, an examination of antecedents to intentions to purchase sponsoring brands is topical. This study also makes a number of contributions to practice. First, the results show whether and under which conditions sponsee rights holders and marketing managers should be harnessing the perceived entitativity of sponsoring brands within concurrent sponsorship settings. Second, the results can be used as a catalyst for marketing managers to work together in innovative and collaborative ways, so that each respective company can enhance its own purchase intentions through partnering with other concurrent sponsors.

Conceptual Framework

The overall premise of this chapter is that concurrent sponsors' entitativity will ultimately drive consumer purchase intentions and this relationship acts through sponsee equity. Sponsee equity is manifested through acts of consumption such as attending the event or watching it on a TV screen (Stewart et al. 2003; Ruth and Simonin 2006; Olson 2010). Sponsee followers are generally thought to act favorably towards sponsors (Bergkvist 2012), including being more likely to purchase from them (Madrigal 2000). This occurs because sponsee followers acknowledge that the sponsees are often dependent upon sponsors to run (Witcher et al. 1991; Pracejus 2004). In turn, public goodwill perceptions towards a concurrent sponsor are created (Meenaghan 2001), which lead to reciprocity whereby the sponsee follower supports the sponsor (i.e., purchases from the sponsor) (see Madrigal 2000). Consequently:

H1: Sponsee equity is positively related to purchase intentions.

Although not firmly established in the literature, there is evidence to suggest that a positive association exists between a property being sponsored (i.e., a property being a sponsee) and sponsee equity (Olson 2010). For example, anecdotal evidence suggests that consumers perceive sponsees as being "better, more entertaining, more professional and being a higher quality product" when sponsors are involved (Marshall and Cook 1992: 158). That said, little is still known about the effects of concurrent sponsors on sponsee equity (Olson 2010; Carrillat and D'Astous 2012). In this context, social psychology informs us that collectives are characterized by the degree to which they are perceived as being groups versus loose associations of separate entities (i.e., entitativity) (Crawford et al. 2002; Hamilton et al. 2002). Consequently, people perceive concurrent sponsors as having varying degrees of entitativity (Carrillat et al.

2014). Meanwhile, entitativity is positively associated with a group's perceived collective responsibility (Denson et al. 2006). Collective responsibility refers to how "others," besides the individual directly responsible for a specific action(s), are held responsible for that action(s) as well (Lickel et al. 2003). Collective responsibility occurs because people perceive the "others" as having a social association or social influence over that individual's action(s) (Turner 1982, Johnson et al. 2006). Hence, entitativity perceptions, being associated with social association and social influence perceptions, lead to collective responsibility being assigned to the "others." Within a sponsorship context, sponsors share a social association with the sponsee (Garry et al. 2008) and are considered to have a level of responsibility towards it (Messner and Reinhard 2012). Therefore, as entitativity perceptions increase so should perceptions of the concurrent sponsors' collective responsibility towards that sponsee. Meanwhile, sponsors' increased collective responsibility towards a sponsee indicates a greater likelihood of a professionally run property. Hence:

H2: Entitativity is positively related to sponsee equity.

If people perceive a focal concurrent sponsor within an entitative sponsorship group to be sincere, this sincerity should permeate to the group as a whole, and then onto the other concurrent sponsors (Crawford et al. 2002). In turn, a strengthening of the relationship between entitativity and sponsee equity should result due to concurrent sponsors being considered sponsee-serving, relative to when all sponsors are considered sponsor-serving (i.e., insincere). Furthermore, when entitativity is at its highest, people should increasingly treat the concurrent sponsors as a single sponsor (Campbell 1958). Meanwhile, the dyadic sponsor–sponsee literature indicates that when a single sponsor is sincere, sponsee (object) equity is higher (Olson 2010). Hence:

H3: The relationship between entitativity and sponsee equity depends on sincerity. When sincerity is low, the relationship is weak. As sincerity increases the relationship becomes stronger.

Within a sponsorship context, people have varying attitudes towards sponsorship, ranging from negative to positive. A positive attitude towards sponsorship is positively associated with sponsee equity (Olson 2010). It is proposed here that people's attitudes towards the sponsorship will impact upon the relationship between entitativity and sponsee equity, due to polarization effects. That is because increased entitativity perceptions induce people to make positive evaluations more positive (Susskind et al. 1999), and negative evaluations more negative (Dasgupta et al. 1999). Consequently, if people have positive attitudes towards the sponsorship then it is likely that this will lead to a polarization whereby the relationship between entitativity and sponsee equity is stronger. Hence:

H4: The relationship between entitativity and sponsee equity depends on people's attitudes towards sponsorship. When attitude towards sponsorship is negative, the relationship is negative. As attitude towards sponsorship becomes positive, the relationship becomes positive.

Methodology

A scenario-based questionnaire (Aguinis and Bradley 2014) was used to test the hypotheses within an official provider sponsorship context. The study's measures were drawn from the literature and were all reflective in nature. Pretesting was carried out in the form of protocols, debriefs, and a pilot study. An online survey was then conducted, targeting students at a mid-sized UK university. A reasonable number of completed responses was obtained, with $N=263$. Non-response bias was tested using the time-trend method of comparing early and late respondents (Armstrong and Overton 1977), and no statistically significant results were found. Common method variance was controlled for using procedural strategies in the questionnaire design, and tested for using statistical methods (Podsakoff et al. 2003). To test H3 and H4, interaction terms were calculated using the residual-centered multiplicative approach in order to reduce potential risk of multicollinearity.

Results and Discussion

Confirmatory factor analyses (CFA) were undertaken to assess unidimensionality and validity of the measures before the structural model was examined (Gerbing and Anderson 1988). The results from the CFA suggest that the model fits the data well. Specifically, the RMSEA is below .05 and the GFI, NNFI, and CFI all approach .9 or exceed it. Each construct's composite reliability (CR) and Average Variance Extracted (AVE) are also acceptable. The lowest AVE value was higher than the largest squared correlation value, indicating good discriminant validity between constructs (Fornell and Larcker 1981). Item parceling was then performed on all but sponsee equity and purchase intentions to allow for the creation of multiplicative terms, and the path analysis was performed. All indicators for SEM also fall within the accepted thresholds.

The model explains 21.7% of sponsee equity and 25.1% of purchase intentions. Sponsee equity is positively associated with purchase intentions, in support of H1, while entitativity is positively associated with sponsee equity, in support of H2. A main effect between sponsor sincerity and sponsee equity is significant as is the interaction between sponsor sincerity and entitativity on sponsee equity. This supports H3. The interaction between attitude towards sponsorship and entitativity on sponsee equity is nonsignificant. One potential reason for this could be that there is a three-way interaction between entitativity, sincerity, and attitude towards the sponsee sponsorship.

Conclusions and Implications for Theory and Practice

The results indicate that people's perceptions of whether a sponsee's concurrent sponsors are considered as a collective of individual sponsors or as a "real" group, impacts upon their evaluations of the sponsee and subsequently their intentions to purchase from the sponsor. Furthermore, the results also suggest that the presence of (at least) one sincere sponsor positively changes the relationship between people's entitativity perceptions of the concurrent sponsors and sponsee equity.

This study makes a number of theoretical contributions. First, it adds to the scant literature on entitativity outside of the social psychology domain, and in doing so, indicates that people's perceptions of collectives can have important outcomes for businesses (sponsors and sponsees). In doing so, this study also contributes to the marketing, branding, and sponsorship literature by introducing a (relatively) new concept to these fields (e.g., Palmatier et al. 2007; Smith et al. 2013, for some exceptions). In terms of practical implications, property rights holders should encourage their (potential) consumers to perceive their sponsees' concurrent sponsors as forming a meaningful, entitative group because this should lead to an increased following of their own sponsees and also increase consumers' intentions to purchase sponsoring brands. One way to foster entitativity perceptions could be for rights holders to actively collaborate with sponsors. However, this may be easier said than done given that, presently, sponsors predominantly work independently of sponsees' rights holders, who are themselves often passive in sponsor–sponsee relationships (Farrelly and Quester 2003). It is also important that opportunities are created to communicate at least one concurrent sponsor's sincerity if sponsee equity is to be further enhanced. Concurrent sponsors should embrace "sincerity" opportunities, given that sponsorship is increasingly returning to its "original values...which were more orientated towards the betterment of society and a demonstration of corporate citizenship... there is an indication of this return to broader objectives and audiences of sponsorship, which characterized the philanthropic approach" (Ryan and Fahy 2012: 1147).

There are a number of future research directions that can result from this work. For example, an examination of the coordination, relationships, and power (a)symmetry between concurrent sponsors and a sponsee's rights holder would be an important contribution to both theory and practice. Also, future research should consider the "type" of group which is formed when concurrent sponsors are perceived to be part of an entitative group. For example, concurrent sponsors that provide their own unique resources may be perceived as being akin to a task group. Task groups are "small in size, of relatively short duration, are relatively permeable (ease of joining or leaving the group), and their members share common goals" (Hamilton et al. 2009: 181). They are also "often hierarchically structured, with a clear leader and differentiation of roles among members" (Spencer-Rodgers et al. 2007: 370). This type of group fits with "Official Provider" (Carrillat and D'Astous 2012) sponsorships because sponsors often sign product exclusivity clauses with sponsees' rights holders so that they are the sole provider of a particular product or service. Consequently, sponsors have their own unique role in a sponsee's success. Understanding the "type" of group that concurrent sponsors are perceived to be in is important because this can impact upon people's entitativity perceptions (e.g., Lickel et al. 2000) and therefore potentially any outcomes of entitativity in concurrent sponsorship contexts.

References available upon request.

The Impact of Digital Corporate Branding on Consumer-Company Identification

Jaywant Singh and Cláudia Simões

Abstract Developing a distinctive image in the marketplace is increasingly recognized as a key part of a company's marketing strategy and a route for achieving competitive advantage. Strong corporate brands (CB) can lead to a wide customer base and a distinctive image. As product and service offers become similar, companies tend to emphasize the communication of CBs to stakeholders as a way to convey distinctiveness and uniqueness. Nonetheless, although CB focuses primarily in reaching all the company's stakeholders, consumers are increasingly becoming a core target for corporate branding. Consumers are exposed to the image portrayed by a company online. The website, therefore, can be a reflection of the company's CB's characteristics and personality and a company's online atmospherics and its online stores may have an impact on consumer behaviour. In the online context, the CB dimensions of visual appeal, the way the information is communicated, and social responsibility are crucial. A well-liked corporate website could lead to favourable behavioural outcomes, such as positive word of mouth, and repatronage intentions. Despite the obvious commercial benefits and the recent research attention on online corporate branding, the impact of online dimensions of CB in consumer perceptions is overlooked. Our study investigates the impact of three online CB dimensions (visual appeal, communications, CSR) on consumer-company identification (CCI), and the behavioural outcomes (word of mouth, repatronage intention) in retail sector. We employed a scenario-based quasi-experiment in two retail settings—grocery and clothing—using two fictitiously created brands and their websites. Three scenarios for each brand were created representing high, medium, and low levels of descriptions of dimensions of CB on the websites. A questionnaire was created and the scales operationalization relied on adaptations from previous

J. Singh (✉)
Kingston University, Surrey, UK
e-mail: j.singh@kingston.ac.uk

C. Simões
Open University Business School, Milton Keynes, UK
e-mail: claudia.simoes@open.ac.uk

© Academy of Marketing Science 2016
L. Petruzzellis, R.S. Winer (eds.), *Rediscovering the Essentiality of Marketing*,
Developments in Marketing Science: Proceedings of the Academy of Marketing
Science, DOI 10.1007/978-3-319-29877-1_122

research. Following a pilot, the data were collected via web-based survey software, using a convenience sample of cross-section demographics of UK consumers, resulting in 244 valid responses. We tested the hypothesized relationships using partial least squares-based structural equation modelling (PLS SEM). The results show that the way in which a company communicates its CB online, as well as its socially responsible activities, positively influences consumers' identification with the company. Such identification also leads to the generation of positive word of mouth and repatronage intentions. The results also reveal that high degree of information placed on a website is not the most optimal tool for generating positive CCI. Further, stronger the firm's portrayed engagement in corporate giving, the more a consumer identifies with the firm. Overall, the study makes novel contributions to the domain of CB and its impact on consumer perceptions, and leads to several managerial implications and avenues for further research.

Multiple Stakeholders' Perspectives on Franchisee Brand Benefits

Nabil Ghantous and Ferry Jaolis

Abstract Several empirical studies report that the brand is one of the major factors that attract franchisees to join a network and continue in the franchise relationship. Yet little research has investigated the mechanisms through which the brand affects franchisees' intentions and behaviors. The present research addresses this gap, focusing on the franchisor's brand benefits from the franchisees' perspective through the following questions:

– What are the perceived benefits of the franchisor's brand for franchisees?
– How are these perceived benefits conveyed to the franchisees?
– To what extent are franchisee's perceptions of brand benefits well understood and anticipated by the franchisors and management consultants in franchising?

Three qualitative studies were carried out in France to address the research questions, using in-depth semi-structured interviews with 22 franchisees, 11 senior managers of franchise networks, and 6 franchising consultants.

Findings from the qualitative studies offer insights on the three research questions. The first set of results highlights six broad categories of brand benefits from franchisees' perspective. Consistent with the resource scarcity theory, the franchisor's brand is seen as a source of economic benefits for the franchisee. Through its awareness, the brand acts as a heuristic of choice for franchisees and drives consumer-based brand equity. Franchisees also perceive several functional benefits from the franchise brand, related to the brand's commercial concept, know-how and innovations. The brand also offers experiential benefits, based on the sensory elements of both the branded products and the branded outlets, as well as symbolic benefits based on franchisees' identification with the brand personality and values.

N. Ghantous (✉)
Qatar University, Doha, Qatar
e-mail: nabil.ghantous@qu.edu.qa

F. Jaolis
Aix Marseille Université, Marseille Cedex 07, France
e-mail: ferry.jaolis@univ-amu.fr

© Academy of Marketing Science 2016   637
L. Petruzzellis, R.S. Winer (eds.), *Rediscovering the Essentiality of Marketing*,
Developments in Marketing Science: Proceedings of the Academy of Marketing
Science, DOI 10.1007/978-3-319-29877-1_123

Finally, the brand is a source of relational benefits, acting as a relationship partner for franchisees and as a relationship facilitator between the franchisee and a myriad of stakeholders.

The second set of results reveals three important aspects of the process and mechanisms through which these benefits are obtained by the franchisees. First, the franchisees perceive the franchisor's brand as a source of two types of benefits: positively added benefits on the one hand, and savings on important costs on the other hand. Second, franchisees receive brand benefits both directly and indirectly, through other stakeholders. Third, the importance of each type of benefits seems to evolve differently with time and more specifically throughout the franchise relationship life cycle.

Finally, the third set of results reveals significant differences in the perceptions of the three interviewed stakeholders groups regarding the franchisee brand benefits. At the broadest level, these differences mainly point out that franchisors and consultants hold a much narrower perspective than franchisees' on the brand benefits and underlying mechanisms.

Can We See a Difference? The Influence of Consumer Characteristics on Regular and Premium Store Brand Usage

Foula Kopanidis, Linda Robinson, Mike Reid, and Cherrymae Uy

Introduction

Store brands play an integral role in shaping the supermarket industry locally and internationally. Store brands have predominantly competed on the basis of low price (Baltras 1997), which firmly delineated them from national brands. To more actively compete with national brands, retailers have moved to increase their product lines by introducing a range of premium store brands that are close to national brands in terms of quality and price (Burt and Sparks 2002). Many previous studies have considered grocery store brands to be competing on the basis of low price and low quality (Richardson 1997; Sethuraman and Cole 1999; Ailawadi et al. 2001; Garretson et al. 2002; Miranda and Joshi 2003; Mazur et al. 2009; Bao et al. 2010), however premium store brands that mimic national brands no longer compete on the basis of low price and low quality (Nenycz-Thiel and Romaniuk 2009). Thus, the aim of this study is to investigate the relationships between specific consumer characteristics and the choice and usage of both regular and premium store brands. The research adopts Ailawadi et al.'s (2001) model of shopping benefits and costs towards the usage of regular store brands, and extends the model by adding the dimensions of premium store brand usage and likelihood of future usage for both store brand levels. Implications for retailers and brand managers are also discussed.

F. Kopanidis (✉) • L. Robinson • M. Reid • C. Uy
RMIT University, Melbourne, VIC, Australia
e-mail: foula.kopanidis@rmit.edu.au; lindaj.robinson@rmit.edu.au; mike.reid@rmit.edu.au; s3274669@student.rmit.edu.au

© Academy of Marketing Science 2016
L. Petruzzellis, R.S. Winer (eds.), *Rediscovering the Essentiality of Marketing*, Developments in Marketing Science: Proceedings of the Academy of Marketing Science, DOI 10.1007/978-3-319-29877-1_124

639

Background

Whilst challenged by the perception of low quality (Richardson et al. 1994), store brands can be a threat to national brands for two main reasons. Firstly, the vast number of store brands competes directly with national brands for shelf space (Narasimhan and Wilcox 1998). Secondly, the sales of national brands may be endangered as previous national brand buyers who are price conscious switch to store brands (Davies 1992). This has prompted a number of research studies aimed at studying the different factors which influence consumer perceptions and purchase choice of store brands (Burton et al. 1998; Sethuraman and Cole 1999; Veloutsou et al. 2004; Nenycz-Thiel and Romaniuk 2009; Bao et al. 2010), and the types of buyers available (Ailawadi et al. 2001). The focus of these studies was to help both store brand and national brand managers identify the factors that work for and against their products' success in order to effectively focus their marketing on specific types of buyers and specific attitudes towards brands.

While most studies have classified store brands as generic and one-tier, some researchers have acknowledged the phenomenon of two-tier and three-tier strategies (Yang and Wang 2008; Geyskens et al. 2010). This chapter adopts the two-tier approach of "regular" and "premium" store brands as defined by Dhar and Hoch (1997). Regular store brands compete on the basis of low quality and low price, whereas premium store brands are similar to national brands in terms of price and quality. In studies that compare national brand and store brand products, it is argued that premium priced store brands are no longer viewed as store brands by default, but rather as brands with their own identity and brand image that is almost equal to that of national brands (Dunne and Narasimhan 1999; De Wulf et al. 2005). With premium store brands no longer competing with national brands on the basis of low price, it is critical to find out what drivers consumers of store brands to purchase regular versus premium store branded products.

The three main product attributes that drive purchase behavior are: economic benefits, hedonic benefits, and costs (Ailawadi et al. 2001). These consumer characteristics can then be used to profile specific types of grocery shoppers based on usage (Mittal 1994; Ailawadi et al. 2001). However, apart from income, the relationship between demographics and usage has been found to be inconsistent and conflicting, and it has been suggested that consumer characteristics are a better predictor of usage (Urbany et al. 1996; Berne et al. 1999; Ailawadi et al. 2001). This study adapts the framework used by Ailawadi et al. (2001) in linking benefits sought and shopping costs to store brand and promotion usage. Studies linking economic benefits and costs with purchase have also been conducted by Mittal (1994) and Urbany et al. (1996). The conceptual framework of this study proposes that product usage is driven by economic and hedonic benefits and inhibited by costs.

Economic benefits that can be derived from the choice and usage of store brands include price consciousness, financial constraints, and quality consciousness (Ailawadi et al. 2001). Consumers who perceive themselves as price sensitive and under budget constraint are more likely to react favorably to the low prices of regular store brands (Sethuraman 2001). In fact, Nenycz-Thiel and Romaniuk (2009) argue further that low price is the unique selling proposition of regular store brands. However, due to the price-quality differential, regular store brands are generally perceived as low in quality (Richardson et al. 1994), making the relationship between high quality consciousness and regular store brand usage negative (Dick et al. 1995; Ailawadi et al. 2001; Sethuraman 2001).

The three main hedonic benefits that can be derived from the choice and usage of store brands are entertainment, exploration, and self-expression (Ailawadi et al. 2001). For the purposes of this study, entertainment is operationalized as the consumers level of shopping enjoyment, exploration is an individual's propensity for innovativeness, impulsiveness, and variety seeking when grocery shopping, and self-expression is reflected by an individual's perception of oneself in relation to others reflected in mavenism and motivation to conform. The three types of costs incurred when choosing a grocery item are switching costs, searching costs, and thinking costs (Ailawadi et al. 2001). This chapter operationalizes switching costs as an individual's brand and store loyalty, searching costs are the amount of time and effort an individual is willing and able to spend planning for grocery shopping, and thinking costs refer to the amount of cognitive effort that an individual is willing to exert when choosing grocery items. Thus, to examine the influence of economic benefits, hedonic benefits and costs on the usage of regular and premium store brands a series of hypotheses are proposed (see Table 1).

Table 1 Summary of hypotheses

	Dependent variables	
Consumer characteristics (Cronbach's alpha)	Regular store brand usage	Premium store brand usage
Economic benefits		
Price consciousness (.831)	+	−
Financial constraints (.794)	+	−
Quality consciousness (.799)	−	+
Hedonic benefits		
Shopping enjoyment (.762)	−	+
Innovativeness (.789)	−	+
Variety seeking (.673)	+	+
Impulsiveness (.835)	−	+
Mavenism (.865)	+	−
Motivation to conform (.753)	+	+
Costs		
Store loyalty (.739)	+	−
Brand loyalty (.848)	−	+
Planning (.689)	−	−

Note: + positive influence; − negative influence

Research Method

Data was obtained using supermarket intercept surveys at four arbitrarily chosen suburban supermarkets within a large metropolitan city of Melbourne, Australia. To minimize sample bias, a quota approach was applied to ensure an even split between the two largest supermarket chains in the city. A final sample size of 208 respondents was obtained. The sample constituted of 59 % females, with most respondents living in a "3–5" person household and 20 % of the households included children under 12 years of age. Seven-point Likert scales were used to measure current usage of regular store brands, usage of premium store brands, and each of the consumer characteristics (economics benefits, hedonic benefits, search costs). Scales were adapted from Ailawadi et al. (2001) to the context of this study. Multiple regression analysis was conducted to model the relationship between the consumer variables and store brand usage. This chapter presents the results for the comparative models influence of economics benefits, hedonic benefits, and search costs on the usage of regular and premium store brands.

Results and Discussion

The results show that the consumer characteristics driving the use of regular and premium store brands are more similar than different. Results indicate both cohorts share a significant relationship with the economic benefit of price consciousness, the hedonic benefit of variety seeking, and cost benefits of brand loyalty, with the hedonic benefit of innovativeness also significant for regular store brands. No significant relationships were found between brand usage and the remaining variables in the study.

Price consciousness was positively related to usage of both regular ($\beta=.245$, $p<0.01$) and premium ($\beta=.188$, $p<0.01$) store brands. This reflects the findings of prior research which found that price consciousness to have a strong positive relationship with regular store brand usage (Richardson et al. 1996; Batra and Sinha 2000; Sethuraman 2001) because store brands compete primarily on the basis of low price (Baltras 1997). The low price image of regular store brands may have a spillover effect on the more recently introduced premium store brands. Since both levels of store brands are associated with and branded by the same retailer, they may not be completely differentiated from each other in the minds of shoppers. Customers may also associate all store brands with lower overhead costs, as a result of being labelled, distributed, and retailed by only one company, and therefore lower priced as well.

Variety seeking was also positively related to usage of both regular ($\beta=.723$, $p<.01$) and premium ($\beta=.499$, $p<.01$) store brands. It is possible that variety seekers use store brands as a change of pace (Ailawadi et al. 2001), and as suitable alternatives for national brands. This may also imply that store brands are still relatively new to consumers, and the novelty has not yet worn off.

Innovativeness was found to have a significant and negative relationship with regular store brand usage ($\beta = -.132, p < .01$). This may be due to the dependence on low costs production and that regular store brands do not characteristically take on expensive product innovations. Conversely, premium store brands may contain desirable new features that are not present in regular store brands as a result of mimicking national brands (Pauwels and Srinivasan 2007).

Brand loyalty was found to have a negative relationship with both regular ($\beta = -.161, p < .01$) and premium ($\beta = -.129, p < .1$) store brands. This result is not unexpected as national brands are more likely to be extensively promoted which leads to more familiarity and attachment than store brands (Garretson et al. 2002). The lower market share of store brands, along with the tendency of supermarket retailers to advertise their store brands generically rather than intensively for each product (Ailawadi et al. 2001), both contribute to the negative relationship between brand loyalty and usage of store brands.

Conclusion

This study investigated the relationships between specific consumer characteristics and usage of both regular and premium store brands. This research provides an important insight on the similarities and differences that the two-tiers of store brands attract. That the predictors of both regular and premium store brand usage are more similar than different provides an insight that the consumer perceives insufficient brand differentiation to make a clear choice between the different levels of store brands. It is possible that both store brand tiers are not differentiated in the minds of consumers. Having an additional premium level store brand may mean more sales, but may be at the expense of regular store brand market share. Retailers should utilize effective marketing strategies to highlight that regular and premium store brands are competing at different levels, and not just against each other. For example, as price consciousness was a significant driver for both regular and premium store brand usage retailers could capitalize on this by using external cues to highlight price savings for regular store brands. Whilst premium store brands, which compete by mimicking national brands in price and quality, should be priced just under national brands in order to persuade price sensitive shoppers.

References available upon request.

Product Complexity in Consumer Research: Literature Review and Implications for Future Research

Lisa Monika Anna Mützel and Thomas Kilian

Abstract Some consumers are overwhelmed when buying certain complicated products such as computers, mobile phones, or automobiles. Product complexity is likely to play a role in such a complex buying situation. Until now, research regarding product complexity has been scarce and fragmented. For example, no common definition of product complexity exists, as the different definitions presented by various authors reveal. We conducted a literature review to defragment the prior research on product complexity, synthesized a definition, and discussed prior measurement approaches and the role of product complexity in the consumer buying process. Thus, we provide the fundamentals for more detailed research on product complexity in the future and derive some implications for marketing practice.

Keywords Product complexity • Category complexity • Consumer buying process • Literature review

Introduction

Though consumer behavior research was established in the 1960s (Fullerton 2013) and the Internet has been promoted as a medium to finally bring transparency into markets, consumers' lives still have not become much easier. Instead, consumers' buying choices are increasingly influenced by rapid technological development, which is accompanied by frequent product innovation and an explosion of information (Bettman et al. 1998). Therefore, consumers are often overwrought by complex buying situations, and one reason for the problems that many consumers face lies in the complexity of products.

Prior research has named numerous examples of high complexity products such as used or new automobiles, computers, digital cameras, insurance policies, mobile

L.M.A. Mützel (✉) • T. Kilian
University Koblenz-Landau, Mainz, Germany
e-mail: lmuetzel@uni-koblenz.de; kilian@uni-koblenz.de

© Academy of Marketing Science 2016   645
L. Petruzzellis, R.S. Winer (eds.), *Rediscovering the Essentiality of Marketing*,
Developments in Marketing Science: Proceedings of the Academy of Marketing
Science, DOI 10.1007/978-3-319-29877-1_125

phones, and buildings (Eastman et al. 1996; Mann and Holdych 1996; Mukherjee and Hoyer 2001; Park 1976; Park et al. 2008; Wallace and Sackett 1996). These products were, in some studies, contrasted with low complexity products such as living room chairs, toothpaste, or refrigerators (e.g., Mukherjee and Hoyer 2001; Park 1976; Settle 1972).

The purchase of high complexity products is infrequent and consumers are often confronted with a large number of alternatives in different price classes that are offered by numerous brands (e.g., Kotler and Armstrong 2011; Swaminathan 2003). Much effort is needed to evaluate and compare those alternatives and the high number of attributes and functions of complex products makes evaluations and comparisons even harder (e.g., Choudhury and Karahanna 2008; Day and Deutscher 1982).

In general, though product complexity is a highly relevant phenomenon, research has put limited interest into investigating the topic in detail. The term product complexity is frequently applied in consumer research and organizational research, but especially in consumer research most authors only allude to product complexity without conceptualizing the construct. For example, Eastman et al. (1996) examine insurance policies as highly complex products but do not thoroughly characterize of high complexity products. Furthermore, although a large body of research investigates possible consequences of product complexity for consumers, for example information overload (e.g., Jacoby 1984) and consumer confusion (e.g., Mitchell and Papavassiliou 1999), only some studies examine consequences of product complexity empirically.

Thus, first of all, a detailed conceptualization of product complexity is required. Until now, there has not even been a consensus regarding the definition of product complexity. Authors' understandings of product complexity vary in depth [compare, e.g., Park (1976) with Grimes (1992)] and in the characteristics they name for complex products. A comprehensive definition is essential for developing appropriate measures and manipulations of product complexity which in turn are essential for investigating the consequences of product complexity in the consumer buying process.

Such a conceptualization of product complexity supports retailers and marketers in evaluating the complexity of the products as well as the complexity reduction strategies that they can offer to reduce complexity to their customers.

Thereby, examining product complexity also promises marketers support with the advertisement of complex products, for example, because the persuasiveness of different message types appears to differ on varying levels of product complexity (Ahearne et al. 2000).

We conducted a literature review to examine how prior studies have analyzed product complexity and set the following aims (1) to identify characteristics of different understandings of product complexity; (2) to synthesize a comprehensive definition of the phenomenon; (3) to discuss approaches to measure and to manipulate product complexity; and (4) to assign prior studies to the phases of the consumer buying process. Finally, suggestions for future research and managerial implications are given in the discussion.

Methodology

We applied the snowballing methodology in our literature review. In this process, we browsed four different databases (EmeraldInsight, JStor, ScienceDirect, SpringerLink) with the terms "product complexity," "complexity of a product," and "complex product" to identify a vast body of literature,[1] that is, approximately 50 papers. While browsing, we conducted a first selection based on the impact factor of the journal, the article's name, its context, and its abstract. Our main interest focused on consumer research articles and articles from similar research streams such as organizational research. In the next step, articles that only mentioned product complexity were scanned for relevant information, and the remaining articles were reviewed in detail. Additionally, we reviewed further articles from the references of some articles, and we excluded articles of poor quality. Eventually, this process lead to 27 articles in consumer research and similar research streams. Of these 27 papers, only nine investigated product complexity empirically. Furthermore, two articles developed measurements for preferences for complex products (Park et al. 2008; Scholz et al. 2010).

We categorized the 27 papers in Table 1 based on how detailed they investigated the product complexity phenomenon. We found that product complexity serves as the central construct only in Sitzia and Zizzo's (2011) study. Other authors such as Settle (1972) investigated consequences of perceived complexity, such as the preference for certain information sources when buying high complexity products. Still other authors employed product complexity as a moderator, for example, of the influence of message type on persuasion (Ahearne et al. 2000). Further authors such as Burnham et al. (2003) investigated product complexity as a determinant of the major construct of their research, for example., of consumer switching costs. Although complex products are at the center of the research of Scholz et al. (2010) and Park et al. (2008), these authors did not conceptualize the phenomenon in detail. However, they developed measurement approaches for consumer preferences for complex products, though that topic is not the focus of this literature review. Finally, some authors (e.g., Day and Deutscher 1982; Lambert 1972) only mentioned product complexity during their explanations while investigating other phenomena.

These findings emphasize the need for more detailed research on the conceptualization and measurement of product complexity. The high amount of studies that only mention product complexity leads to a very fragmented understanding. Therefore, it is necessary to defragment and combine existing knowledge as a basis for future research to systematically investigate the possible consumer consequences of product complexity.

---

[1] We did not explicitly include research on choice complexity and choice experiment-based models and choice complexity (e.g., Dellaert et al. 2012) in this literature review due to the page constraint and because these studies do not aim at conceptualizing product or category complexity. Instead, they aim at investigating consumer choice behavior.

Table 1 Relevance of product complexity in consumer research

Only mentioned → Only of minor interest	As a determinant	As a moderator	As central construct Consequences of complexity	Consequences of complexity
1. Lambert (1972)	12. Choudhury and Karahanna (2008)	19. Holak and Lehman (1990)	22. Ahearne et al. (2000)	25. Settle (1972)	27. Sitzia and Zizzo (2011)
2. Bernardo and Blin (1977)	13. Rogers (1983)	20. Burnham et al. (2003)	23. Mukherjee and Hoyer (2001)	26. Park (1976)	
3. Day and Deutscher (1982)	14. Mick and Fournier (1998)	21. Creusen et al. (2010)	24. Swaminathan (2003)		
4. Grimes (1992)	15. Martin et al. (2003)				
5. Kempf and Smith (1998)	16. Herstein and Tifferet (2007)				
6. Nayyar (1993)	*Developing measurements of preferences for high complexity products*				
7. Bloch (1995)	17. Park et al. (2008)				
8. Eastman et al. (1996)	18. Scholz et al. (2010)				
9. Mann and Holdych (1996)					
10. Rao (1998)					
11. Thompson et al. (2005)					

Findings of the Literature Review

Characteristics of Product Complexity

The literature review revealed various characteristics of product complexity. To defragment existing knowledge about product complexity, these characteristics have been assigned to four categories (1) product characteristics, (2) market characteristics, (3) consumer characteristics, and (4) buyer–seller characteristics.

1. *Product characteristics*: Several papers found that high complexity products, such as computers, digital cameras, or automobiles, incorporate a large number of attributes and functions (e.g., Park et al. 2008; Scholz et al. 2010) and often, consumers must make choices concerning numerous configurable attributes (e.g., Choudhury and Karahanna 2008). Furthermore, high complexity products are often high-priced products and therefore bear a high financial risk (e.g., Herstein and Tifferet 2007; Mann and Holdych 1996; Park et al. 2008). Additionally, the design of a product can be complex, such as a video recorder that has many buttons with different forms and sizes (Bloch 1995; Creusen et al. 2010).

2. *Market characteristics*: In most markets for high complexity products, a large number of alternatives with large brand differences is offered (e.g., Herstein and Tifferet 2007; Park et al. 2008; Swaminathan 2003), even in the same price class (Rao 1998) and even though the products serve the same function (Grimes 1992). For example, in the market for mobile phones is characterized by a large number of competitors (e.g., Alcatel, Apple, Samsung) that sell various models (e.g., Samsung Galaxy Avant™, Samsung Galaxy S®5 Sport) in different price classes that typically span a large price range.

Furthermore, most markets in which high complexity products such as insurance policies and (used) cars are traded are characterized by high information asymmetry (e.g., Akerlof 1970; Mann and Holdych 1996). Though consumers are often exposed to a fairly large amount of product information (Scholz et al. 2010), the amount of information that buyers can obtain in the market is low compared with the amount of information that sellers or manufacturers have (Grimes 1992; Mann and Holdych 1996; see, e.g., Akerlof 1970).

3. *Consumer characteristics*: Consumers' difficulty in evaluating high complexity products can result from consumers' low levels of expertise, knowledge, and familiarity with the product or product category (Bernardo and Blin 1977; Mann and Holdych 1996; Rao 1998). Furthermore, consumers are often highly involved with high complexity products (e.g., Herstein and Tifferet 2007). Thus, if consumers score high on variables such as expertise and knowledge, their difficulty of evaluating high complexity products appears to decrease (e.g., Mukherjee and Hoyer 2001; Raju et al. 1995).

Table 2 Definitions of product complexity

Author and context	Definition
Product characteristics	
1. Park (1976) *Consumer's judgmental models*	"A product which requires a relatively large number of attributes to be examined for evaluation" (p. 145) demonstrates high product complexity
2. Grimes (1992) *Vertical price restraints*	"More complex products that serve the same function vary substantially in construction, quality, features, and price" (p. 823)
3. Griffin (1997)	Product complexity refers to "the number of functions of a product" (p. 24)
Product development	*Application of this definition*:
	Martin et al. (2003) applied this definition to consumer research
4. Choudhury and Karahanna (2008) *Product adoption*	A high complexity product consists of "a bundle of options, types and levels of coverage, and deductibles" (p. 186)
5. Park et al. (2008) *Formation of preferences for high complexity products*	A high complexity product is "characterized by a large number of attributes and/or levels, and reasonably expensive" (p. 566)
6. Scholz et al. (2010) *Formation of preferences for high complexity products*	A high complexity product is "characterized by a comparatively large number of attributes and attribute levels that are relevant in purchase decisions" (p. 685)
Difficulty in understanding and using complex products	
7. Settle (1972) *Acceptance of information sources*	"Some products are so complex that the consumer is unable to evaluate them from casual inspection or use. This condition correspondents to the internalization mode because the consumer desires 'objectively' correct information" (p. 85)
8. Rogers (1983)	"Complexity is the degree to which an innovation is perceived as relatively difficult to understand and use. Any new idea may be classified on the complexity-simplicity continuum" (p. 230 f.)
Innovations	*Application of this definition*:
	Holak and Lehman (1990) and Mukherjee and Hoyer (2001) applied the definition for innovations. Thereby, the latter do not name a source for their applied definition, but in addition, they highlight the difficulty of the usage of high complexity products
	Burnham et al. (2003) applied the definition generally for all types of products and not only innovations

4. *Buyer–seller relationship characteristics*: In consumer markets, Eastman et al. (1996) and Sitzia and Zizzo (2011) emphasize consumers' danger of being exploited or of being confronted with unethical behavior of a salesperson (e.g., by consciously withholding information) when buying high complexity products. Furthermore, salespersons of high complexity products seem to need high levels of expertise to support consumers in their decisions (Burnham et al. 2003).

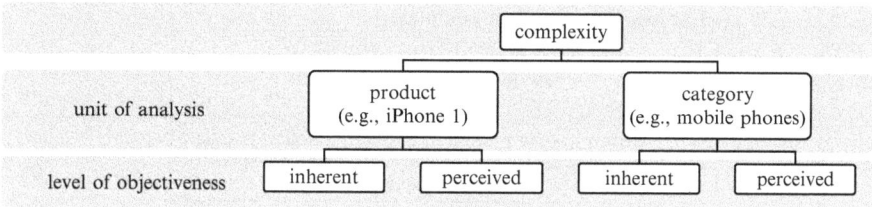

Fig. 1 Types of complexity

Defining Complexity

Of the 27 papers that addressed product complexity from a consumer's perspective, we extracted eight explicit definitions (Table 2).

Comparison of definitions. The definitions can be divided into six definitions that refer to product characteristics (e.g., Park et al. 2008) and two definitions that refer to the consumers' difficulty in understanding and/or utilizing complex products (e.g., Settle 1972). Griffin's (1997) study had a product development background, but nevertheless, Martin et al. (2003) applied his definition in their consumer research study. Similarly, Rogers (1983) originally defined the complexity of an innovation, but Burnham et al. (2003) adopted his definition as a general definition of product complexity. In all definitions, the unit of analysis is a product and not a product category. However, in contrast to their definitions, some authors (e.g., Park 1976; Settle 1972) employed product categories as stimuli in their studies. This finding indicates some inconsistencies in the prior research.

Proposed definitions of product and category complexity and inherent and perceived complexity. Until now, research has not distinguished between product and category complexity. Authors such as Settle (1972), Park (1976), and Sitzia and Zizzo (2011) applied the term "product complexity," independent of whether they used specific products of product categories as stimuli in their studies (see above). A distinction between these two types of complexity is highly relevant because they are conceptually different phenomena.

Based on the definitions and the prior characteristics, we propose four types of complexity that vary based on the unit of analysis and the level of objectiveness (1) product complexity, (2) category complexity, (3) inherent complexity, and (4) perceived complexity (Fig. 1).

We propose the following definitions:

Category complexity and product complexity. If the unit of analysis is a product category (e.g., mobile phones), the corresponding complexity is termed "category complexity," but if the unit of analysis is a specific product (e.g., iPhone 1), it is termed "product complexity." Specific products inherit most product attributes from their corresponding product category. Therefore, we propose decomposing product complexity into (1) product-specific complexity, which stems from the attributes of a particular product (e.g., the design of a specific smartphone) and (2) category complexity. Additionally, we propose decomposing category complexity into (1)

Component	Product complexity
1.	Product-specific complexity
2.	Category complexity
	1. Market complexity
	2. Category-specific complexity

Fig. 2 Decomposition of product complexity

market complexity, which stems from market characteristics (e.g., high number of alternatives) and (2) category-specific complexity, which stems from the characteristics of a product category independent of the market (see Fig. 2). Consequently, differences in the product complexity of two products from the same product category can be explained through differences in product-specific complexity because category complexity is equal.

The following example illustrates category and product complexity: approximately 10 years ago, most consumers perceived the complexity of mobile phones to be rather low. They were familiar with the product category because mobile phones had been around for several years. However, in 2007, Apple's iPhone 1 entered the market—a product that Apple described at that time as a "revolutionary mobile phone" that offered numerous new features (Apple 2007). Although most consumers still perceived the category complexity of mobile phones as low, they perceived the product complexity of the iPhone 1 as high because they were unfamiliar with its features and usage, such as the use of the touch screen or the e-mail client.

Products and categories can be further described by the objectiveness in the attribution of complexity. Thus, we distinguish between inherent and perceived complexity. For clarity, only "inherent" and "perceived" product complexity is defined here because the terms are easily transferable to category complexity.

Inherent product complexity.[2] Inherent complexity is objective and therefore independent of consumer perceptions and therefore, of consumer characteristics such as prior knowledge. It results from immanent characteristics of a specific product (e.g., the total number of attributes of the iPhone 1) or of a product category (e.g., the average number of attributes in the category mobile phones and the amount of alternatives on the mobile phone market).

A product with a high inherent product complexity is characterized by (1) an objectively large number of attributes and functions that are often described in technical terms, (2) a high price, (3) high product risk, (4) multiple configurable attributes, and (5) high design complexity, but it does not need to incorporate all of these characteristics. Furthermore, a market on which inherently high complexity products are traded is often characterized by a large number of alternatives with high brand differences, asymmetric, incomplete, and inaccurate information and the

---

[2] The term "inherent" is taken from Prasad (1998), who describes inherent product complexity as a source of "the complexity of product development efforts" (Prasad 1998: 208).

offers in the product category cover a large price range. Additionally, salespersons need to have high levels of expertise.[3]

Perceived product complexity.[4] Perceived product complexity is a subjective phenomenon that results from consumer's evaluation of a product and that depends on consumer traits such as product knowledge, familiarity, or expertise or on the number of the consumer's evaluation criteria.[5] It describes how high or low consumers perceive the inherent complexity of a specific product.

For example, the product category "laptops" shows high inherent category complexity because it is characterized by a large number of attributes and functions. A consumer with little knowledge about laptops might perceive category complexity as high, but a consumer with high product knowledge might perceive it as low, for example, because he/she has more information about important product attributes and about the offers on the market.

Prior Operationalization and Measurements of Product and Category Complexity

The prior operationalization of complexity can be distinguished into measurements or manipulations of inherent or perceived complexity. Although such operationalizations match the definitions of complexity of their authors, these operationalizations match our proposed definition of complexity only to a small degree (Table 3). Furthermore, some authors such as Swaminathan (2003), Creusen et al. (2010), and Sitzia and Zizzo (2011) compared specific products of the same product category to each other, whereas, for example, Park (1976) compared different product categories to each other and Ahearne et al. (2000) employed two specific products from two different product categories as stimuli for their research.

Operationalization of inherent product complexity. As given in Table 3, three studies manipulated complexity by choosing products with low and high complexity for their experimental studies. Swaminathan (2003) manipulated the number of product attributes. By manipulating the number of possible outcomes, Sitzia and Zizzo (2011) address high risk as a characteristic of high complexity products and Creusen et al. (2010) manipulated design complexity. Scholz et al. (2010) did not have a high and a low complexity condition in their study but employed only a high complexity stimulus. Thus, they did not manipulate inherent complexity, but their approach for assuring the high complexity of their units of analysis was similar to that of Swaminathan (2003). Their units of analysis were vacation packages and cell phones, and they presented product descriptions with a deliberately large number of

---

[3] These characteristics were revealed by the literature review (see product characteristics and market characteristics).

[4] The term "perceived complexity" is taken from Park (1976), who states explicitly that he investigates "perceived product complexity" in his study.

[5] These characteristics were revealed by the literature review (see consumer characteristics).

Table 3 Comparison between prior measurement approaches and the proposed definition of complexity

Author	Choice of a high complexity product/ manipulation of product complexity	Criteria that match the proposed definitions
Inherent complexity		
1. Swaminathan (2003) **Manipulation**	Variation of product complexity based on: 1. High/low number of product attribute 2. High/low number of alternatives	• Large number of attributes and functions
Park et al. (2008) **Direct measurement**	1. Online shops (e.g., http://www.bestbuy.com) were used as data sources for counting the number of major attributes in product descriptions	• Large number of attributes and functions
2. Creusen et al. (2010) **Manipulation**	Complexity of the product design: 1. Development of different stimuli based on the design principles	• Design complexity
3. Scholz et al. (2010) **High complexity condition**	Summer vacation packages and cell phones selected for the study. They presented product descriptions with a large number of attributes and attribute levels to the consumers for evaluating measurement approaches for preferences. Thus, only the high complexity condition was investigated	• Large number of attributes and functions
4. Sitzia and Zizzo (2011) **Manipulation**	A high complexity product (lottery) has 27 possible outcomes, whereas a simple product (lottery) has only three different outcomes	• Large number of attributes and functions • High product risk
Perceived complexity		
5. Park (1976)	Pretest: one-item measurement	• Number of product attributes

(continued)

Table 3 (continued)

Author	Choice of a high complexity product/ manipulation of product complexity	Criteria that match the proposed definitions
Indirect measurement + single item rating	"When I buy (a product name) I evaluate it on the basis of (a) a relatively large number of characteristics, (b) a relatively small number of characteristics"	• Number of evaluation criteria
	Main study:	
	Number of evaluation criteria of consumers	
	1. Products divided based on number of attributes	
	2. Development of a list of evaluation criteria for the products	
	3. Rating of these evaluation criteria according to their importance for the respondents	
	4. Attribute of high importance a evaluation criterion	
	5. Products with number of evaluation criteria >5 as high complexity products	
	6. One Item: "How complex is this product for you to evaluate?"	
6. Holak and Lehman (1990) **Single-item rating**	Consumers rated complexity with a single item on a six-point scale. The wording of the item is not given in the paper	• Difficulty of product usage
7. Mukherjee and Hoyer (2001)	Use of a two item, seven-point scale (p. 465):	• How complex a consumer perceives a product in general
Study 1	1. "Difficulty/easy to use"	• Difficulty of product usage
Scale	2. "High/low complexity"	
Mukherjee and Hoyer (2001)	Use of a four item, seven-point scale (p. 469):	• How complex a consumer perceives a product in general
Study 2	1. "Difficulty/easy to use"	• Difficulty of product usage
Scale	2. "High/low complexity"	
	3. "Lot/little new knowledge required for effective use"	
	4. "Many/few new procedures needed to be mastered for effective use"	

(continued)

Table 3 (continued)

Author	Choice of a high complexity product/ manipulation of product complexity	Criteria that match the proposed definitions
8. Burnham et al. (2003)	Scale development: Complexity of the service	• How complex a consumer perceives a product in general
Scale	Items (p. 123):	
	1. "I would have to know a lot to take advantage of the options/programs offered by service providers"	
	2. "The offerings in this industry are difficult to understand"	
	3. "A salesperson selling this kind of service needs to know a lot to do a good job"	
	4. "This service is complicated in nature"	
Studies not assignable to perceived or inherent complexity		
10. Settle (1972)	5 Judges' agreement	–
Indirect measurement		
11. Ahearne et al. (2000)	1. Pretest: generation of a list of interesting products	–
Measurement not specified	2. Pretest: three of the most frequently mentioned products in the same general price range chosen for the second pretest. Product with the highest complexity rating in the second pretest was chosen for the main study (rating of complexity not specified)	

attributes (e.g., brand) and attribute levels (e.g., Nokia, Sony) to their respondents. Regarding these manipulation approaches, the approach of Swaminathan (2003) seems to be most suitable for manipulating inherent product complexity because the number of attributes and functions, which is the main criterion of our proposed definition, is manipulated.

Measurement approaches for inherent product complexity. The literature review revealed one direct measurement approach for inherent product complexity. Park et al. (2008) counted the number of major attributes in product descriptions in online shops after they had identified products for their analysis through interviews with university students. Our definition includes the number of product attributes and functions, too. Counting these characteristics seems to be an obvious measurement approach for inherent product complexity. However, though this approach can be easily applied for low complexity products such as pens, it is much more difficult to realize for high complexity products such as computers.

Measurement approaches for perceived product complexity. To measure perceived product complexity, three scales (Burnham et al. 2003; Mukherjee and Hoyer 2001), two items (Holak and Lehman 1990; Park 1976) and one indirect measurement approach (Park 1976) could be identified. However, none of these approaches matches the definition sufficiently. Not a single measurement approach refers to how large a consumer perceives the general number of product attributes and functions. For example, Mukherjee and Hoyer (2001) used their scale to assess an overall level of complexity by asking their respondents how complex they perceived a product to be and of our proposed criteria, they only addressed the difficulty of product usage. Park's (1976) procedure revealed the consumers' number of evaluation criteria [contrary to Park et al. (2008), who counted the number of major product attributes] but reduced the perceived product complexity to this single criterion. Holak and Lehman (1990) only stated that participants rated complexity with a single item on a six-point scale but did not provide the item in their paper. Furthermore, the scale development processes of Burnham et al. (2003) and Mukherjee and Hoyer (2001) were not documented sufficiently transparently, and the authors did not apply a detailed scale development process. Thus, an important research gap is to develop an appropriate scale to measure perceived complexity.

Studies not assignable to perceived or inherent complexity. Neither the studies by Settle (1972) nor by Ahearne et al. (2000) can be assigned to perceived or inherent product complexity. Settle (1972) selected product categories based on the agreement of five judges without specifying their selection criteria. Ahearne et al. (2000) generated in a first pretest a list of products that were rated as interesting for the respondents. From this list, they selected three of the most frequently mentioned products in the same general price range for a second pretest. Based on the results of the second pretest, they selected the compact disc player as the unit of analysis. One reason was that it had the highest complexity rating, but they did not specify this complexity rating in their paper.

Discussion and Implications

Complexity as research focus. The findings of the literature review show that future research is required that treats complexity as the focal construct. Therefore, in the course of this discussion, some suggestions and starting points for future research are given.

Characteristics of complex products and definitions of product complexity. The literature review revealed not only product but also market, consumer, and buyer–seller characteristics of high complexity products and summarized different but rather short definitions of product complexity. However, further qualitative studies could reveal more characteristics that contribute to our understanding of product complexity from a consumer's perspective and the role of the characteristics of complexity in different phases of the buying process. Conceptual and empirical studies are needed to evaluate the definitions of complexity (e.g., inherent vs. perceived complexity and product vs. category complexity).

Thereby, future research could evaluate the relationship between inherent complexity (that has been measured directly) and perceived complexity (e.g., that has been measured using scales), for example, to further clarify moderators and mediators.

Developing research designs. In this context, future research should specify more precisely their research designs. A further comparison of the measurement and manipulation approaches revealed three different ways of comparing complexity based on the units of analysis, but previous authors did not consider these differences (1) comparing product categories (e.g., Park 1976), (2) intraproduct category comparisons (e.g., Swaminathan 2003), and (3) interproduct category comparisons (Ahearne et al. 2000). In the last case, Ahearne et al. (2000) utilized advertisements of a specific razor and of a specific compact disc player as stimuli associated with low and high levels of complexity.

The comparison of two or more products from one category allows for a more focused view of the effects of product characteristics (e.g., number of attributes, features, and functions), that is, product-specific complexity, because differences in perceived product complexity (and in turn the consequences of perceived complexity) cannot result from different market characteristics (market complexity) or general characteristics of the product category (category-specific complexity).

Contrarily, when investigating two or more products from different product categories (e.g., Ahearne et al. 2000), the difference in complexity is more likely to result from different market characteristics, different characteristics of the product categories, and differences in the specific products. Thus, when the aim of the research is to evaluate the consequences of different levels of perceived complexity, this approach is more relevant because larger differences in perceived complexity can be reached.

Measuring perceived complexity. A parsimonious but comprehensive scale is needed to measure perceived complexity.

Toward a model of product complexity. The literature review did not reveal a model that sufficiently illustrates the consumer consequences of product and or category complexity, though a great deal of research on constructs such as consumer confusion or information overload exists. Only some authors have identified a few consequences of high level of complexity. For example, Settle (1972) found that for complex products, consumers tend to rely on expert opinions, and Burnham et al. (2003) found that higher product complexity leads to higher perceptions of switching costs. Sitzia and Zizzo (2011) found that when buying high complexity products, consumers take more time to make their decision compared with buying low complexity products. Holak and Lehman (1990) found empirically that high levels of complexity lead to high levels of perceived risk, which in turn lead to a decrease in purchase intention. This finding could be a starting point for evaluating risk reduction strategies as consequences of perceived complexity. Literature offers numerous risk reduction strategies such as searching for more information, applying decision heuristics such as selecting a product as a result of brand loyalty and seeking reassurance through, for example, money-back guarantees, test results or word of mouth (e.g., Roselius 1971; Schiffman et al. 2008). For marketers, it is furthermore highly important to identify whether high levels of perceived complexity lead to preacquisition avoidance strategies, such as ignoring

Table 4 Organizing empirical studies that address product complexity around the buyer decision process

1. **Need recognition**	2. **Information search**	3. **Evaluation of alternatives**
• Ahearne et al. (2000)	• Settle (1972)	• Park (1976)
• Burnham et al. (2003)	**Information search + evaluation of alternatives**	• Holak and Lehman (1990)
	• Mukherjee and Hoyer (2001)	• Park et al. (2008)
	• Swaminathan (2003)	• Creusen et al. (2010)
		• Scholz et al. (2010)
4. **Purchase decision**		5. **Postpurchase behavior**
• Sitzia and Zizzo (2011)		–

certain information or postponing the purchase decision, as well as to consumption avoidance strategies, such as decreasing the usage of a high complexity product or leaving it unrepaired in the case of a malfunction (Mick and Fournier 1998).

Role of product and category complexity in the consumer buying process. Product and category complexity can have different effects during each of the five phases of the consumer buying process (need recognition, information search, evaluation of alternatives, purchase decision, and postpurchase behavior, e.g., Assael 1995). We organized the nine empirical studies plus two studies that developed measurements for consumer preferences around the consumer buying process based on their research design (Table 4). For example, Ahearne et al. (2000) investigated the influence of different message types in advertisements of complex products on consumers, so their study describes a possible situation in the need recognition phase.

This categorization revealed that until now, no study has evaluated the role of product or category complexity in postpurchase behavior. We could even only assign one study to the purchase decision phase (Sitzia and Zizzo 2011).

The possibly different effects of perceived complexity during the consumer buying process are illustrated by the following example. Consumers might perceive category complexity of automobiles as high in the need recognition phase, but after having searched for information and after having evaluated alternatives, their perceived product complexity and category complexity decreased through an increase of knowledge (Brucks 1985).

Implications for practice: Firms must decrease their products' perceived complexity during the consumer buying process to prevent negative consequences of perceived complexity that result, for example, from higher levels of perceived risk (Holak and Lehman 1990). Additionally, consumer protection organizations aim at decreasing perceived complexity because perceived complexity can hinder consumers from making informed choices and makes them prone to exploitation (e.g., Sitzia and Zizzo 2011). In both cases, the effectiveness of certain marketing and communication actions of firms or education strategies of consumer protection organizations and consumer consequences of perceived complexity might depend on the phase of the buying process.

Future research should try to develop a matrix that allocates these complexity reduction strategies to different levels of perceived complexity and to the phases of the consumer buying process. These strategies should aim at influencing certain consumer characteristics, for example, at increasing consumer knowledge, expertise, or familiarity with the product and the product category, because high levels of these variables seem to decrease the levels of perceived complexity (e.g., Mann and Holdych 1996). A starting point could be investigating "risk relievers" such as brand image, retailer's reputation, money-back guarantees, free trials, and reference group appeal (Tan 1999) because perceived complexity appears to increase perceived risk (Holak and Lehman 1990).

References

Ahearne, M., Gruen, T., & Saxton, M. K. (2000). When the product is complex, does the advertisement's conclusion matter? *Journal of Business Research, 48*(1), 55–62.

Akerlof, G. A. (1970). The market for "Lemons": Quality uncertainty and the market mechanism. *The Quarterly Journal of Economics, 84*(3), 488–500.

Apple. (2007). Apple reinvents the phone with iPhone. Retrieved September 21, from https://www.apple.com/pr/library/2007/01/09Apple-Reinvents-the-Phone-with-iPhone.html.

Assael, H. (1995). *Consumer behavior and marketing action* (5th ed.). Cincinnati, OH: South-Western College.

Bernardo, J. J., & Blin, J. M. (1977). A programming model of consumer choice among multi-attributed brands. *Journal of Consumer Research, 4*(2), 111–118.

Bettman, J. R., Luce, M. F., & Payne, J. W. (1998). Constructive consumer choice processes. *Journal of Consumer Research, 25*(3), 187–217.

Bloch, P. H. (1995). Seeking the ideal form: Product design and consumer response. *Journal of Marketing, 59*(3), 16–29.

Brucks, M. (1985). The effects of product class knowledge on information search behavior. *Journal of Consumer Research, 12*(1), 1–16.

Burnham, T. A., Frels, J. K., & Mahajan, V. (2003). Consumer switching costs: A typology, antecedents, and consequences. *Journal of the Academy of Marketing Science, 31*(2), 109–126.

Choudhury, V., & Karahanna, E. (2008). The relative advantage of electronic channels: A multidimensional view. *MIS Quarterly, 32*(1), 179–200.

Creusen, M. E., Veryzer, R. W., & Schoormans, J. P. (2010). Product value importance and consumer preference for visual complexity and symmetry. *European Journal of Marketing, 49*(9/10), 1437–1452.

Day, G. S., & Deutscher, T. (1982). Attitudinal predictions of choices of major appliance brands. *Journal of Marketing Research, 19*(2), 192–198.

Dellaert, B. G., Donkers, B., & van Soest, A. (2012). Complexity effects in choice experiment–based models. *Journal of Marketing Research, 49*(3), 424–434.

Eastman, K. L., Eastman, J. K., & Eastman, A. D. (1996). The ethics of insurance professionals: Comparison of personal versus professional ethics. *Journal of Business Ethics, 15*(9), 951–962.

Fullerton, R. A. (2013). The birth of consumer behavior: Motivation research in the 1940s and 1950s. *Journal of Historical Research in Marketing, 5*(2), 212–222.

Griffin, A. (1997). The effect of project and process characteristics on product development cycle time. *Journal of Marketing Research, 34*(1), 24–35.

Grimes, W. S. (1992). Spiff, polish, and consumer demand quality: Vertical price restraints revisited. *California Law Review, 80*(4), 815–855.

Herstein, R., & Tifferet, S. (2007). An investigation of the new generic consumer. *Journal of Consumer Marketing, 24*(3), 133–141.

Holak, S. L., & Lehman, D. R. (1990). Purchase intentions and the dimensions of innovation: An exploratory model. *Journal of Product Innovation Management, 7*(1), 59–73.

Jacoby, J. (1984). Perspectives on Information Overload. *Journal of Consumer Research, 10*(4), 432–436.

Kempf, D. S., & Smith, R. E. (1998). Consumer processing of product trial and the influence of prior advertising: A structural modeling approach. *Journal of Marketing Research, 35*(3), 325–338.

Kotler, P., & Armstrong, G. (2011). *Principles of marketing* (14th ed.). Boston: Pearson.

Lambert, Z. V. (1972). Price and choice behavior. *Journal of Marketing Research, 9*(1), 35–40.

Mann, B., & Holdych, T. J. (1996). When lemons are better than lemonade: The case against mandatory used car warranties. *Yale Law & Policy Review, 15*(1), 1–48.

Martin, B. A., Lang, B., & Wong, S. (2003). Conclusion explicitness in advertising: The moderating role of need for cognition (NFC) and argument quality (AQ) on persuasion. *Journal of Advertising, 32*(4), 57–65.

Mick, G. D., & Fournier, S. (1998). Paradoxes of technology: Consumer cognizance, emotions, and coping strategies. *Journal of Consumer Research, 25*(2), 123–143.

Mitchell, V., & Papavassiliou, V. (1999). Marketing causes and implications of consumer confusion. *Journal of Product & Brand Management, 8*(4), 319–342.

Mukherjee, A., & Hoyer, W. D. (2001). The effect of novel attributes on product evaluation. *Journal of Consumer Research, 28*(3), 462–472.

Nayyar, P. R. (1993). Stock market reactions to related diversification moves by service firms seeking benefits from information asymmetry and economies of scope. *Strategic Management Journal, 14*(8), 569–591.

Park, C. W. (1976). The effect of individual and situation-related factors on consumer selection of judgmental models. *Journal of Marketing Research, 13*(2), 144–151.

Park, Y.-H., Ding, M., & Rao, V. R. (2008). Eliciting preference for complex products: A web-based upgrading method. *Journal of Marketing Research, 45*(5), 562–574.

Prasad, B. (1998). Designing products for variety and how to manage complexity. *Journal of Product & Brand Management, 7*(3), 208–222.

Raju, P. S., Lonial, S. C., & Mangold, W. G. (1995). Differential effects of subjective knowledge, objective knowledge, and usage experience on decision making: An exploratory investigation. *Journal of Consumer Psychology, 4*(2), 153–180.

Rao, H. (1998). Caveat emptor: The construction of nonprofit consumer watchdog organizations. *American Journal of Sociology, 103*(4), 912–961.

Rogers, E. M. (1983). *Diffusion of innovations* (3rd ed.). New York: The Free Press.

Roselius, T. (1971). Consumer rankings of risk reduction methods. *Journal of Marketing, 35*(1), 56–61.

Schiffman, L. G., Kanuk, L. L., & Hansen, H. (2008). *Consumer behavior—a European outlook.* Upper Saddle River, NJ: Pearson.

Scholz, S. W., Meissner, M., & Decker, R. (2010). Measuring consumer preferences for complex products: A compositional approach based on paired comparisons. *Journal of Marketing Research, 47*(4), 685–698.

Settle, R. B. (1972). Attribution theory and acceptance of information. *Journal of Marketing Research, 9*(1), 85–88.

Sitzia, S., & Zizzo, D. J. (2011). Does product complexity matter for competition in experimental retail markets? *Theory and Decision, 70*(1), 65–82.

Swaminathan, V. (2003). The impact of recommendation agents on consumer evaluation and choice: The moderating role of category risk, product complexity, and consumer knowledge. *Journal of Consumer Psychology, 13*(1/2), 93–101.

Tan, S. J. (1999). Strategies for reducing consumers' risk aversion in Internet shopping. *Journal of Consumer Marketing, 16*(2), 163–180.

Thompson, D. V., Hamilton, R. W., & Rust, R. T. (2005). Feature fatigue: When product capabilities become too much of a good thing. *Journal of Marketing Research, 42*(4), 31–442.

Wallace, G., & Sackett, P. (1996). Integrated design for low production volume, large, complex products. *Integrated Manufacturing Systems, 7*(3), 5–16.

My Brand? Your Brand? Or Our Brand? Integrating Front-Line Employees Post an Acquisition

Keith Glanfield, Leslie de Chernatony, and Yannis Suvatjis

Abstract Organisations are continually searching for their next source of growth. One potential option is growth by acquisition. Acquisitions are not risk free, many fail to achieve their potential. One reason for failure is employees from the acquired firm not developing sufficiently strong bonds with the acquiring organisation, leading to poor integration and subsequent negative effects upon firm performance. This chapter presents an empirical study of UK front-line employees, 3 years post acquisition, finding a role for the acquiring organisation's corporate brand to positively influence this integration. Establishing that aspects of the acquiring organisation's corporate brand equally influences the organisational identification of both acquired and non-acquired employees, integrating both groups into the acquiring organisation. In addition the study establishes that employees from the acquired organisation use the corporate brand to integrate further by more strongly participating in the new organisation's brand community to deploy their identification with the acquiring organisation and integrate. Determining corporate branding as a means of positively integrating all front-line employees post an acquisition and consequently reducing the attendant acquisition risks associated with poor employee integration.

Keywords Corporate branding • Organisational identification • Acquisition • Front-line employees • Retailing

K. Glanfield (✉) • L. de Chernatony
Aston Business School, Birmingham, UK
e-mail: k.glanfield2@aston.ac.uk; dechernatony@aston.ac.uk

Y. Suvatjis
Swiss Alpine Centre, Glyfada, Greece
e-mail: jean58@otenet.gr

© Academy of Marketing Science 2016   663
L. Petruzzellis, R.S. Winer (eds.), *Rediscovering the Essentiality of Marketing*,
Developments in Marketing Science: Proceedings of the Academy of Marketing
Science, DOI 10.1007/978-3-319-29877-1_126

Introduction

Retailers are continually challenged with identifying their next source of growth and face a choice between a number of options including organic growth or growth by merger and acquisition (M&A) on a national and international basis (Reinartz et al. 2012). Growth by M&A is a popular option. During 2013 alone there were more than 35,000 transactions globally, worth a total of US$3.9 trillion (Institute of Mergers and Acquisitions 2014). Despite their popularity M&As do not come without risk. Frequently many fail to reach their potential and often lead to poor performance (Haleblian et al. 2009).

A specific and important reason for failure is the poor integration into the acquiring organisation of employees from the acquired organisation (Edwards and Edwards 2012). They fail to form a psychological bond with the acquiring organisation, termed organisational identification (Teerikangas and Very 2006). This is a troublesome issue for the acquirer. Especially as strong, not weak, organisational identification is a pre-requisite to positive employee outcomes such as extra-role behaviours, organisational citizenship behaviours, employee satisfaction and employee performance (He and Brown 2013). Indeed, in a retail environment strong employee organisational identification is positively related to the level of customers' identification with the retailer, which results in increased levels of store financial performance (Lichtenstein et al. 2010).

Therefore, the challenge for retailers, in an M&A environment, is to find post-acquisition a means of influencing and reinforcing the organisational identification of the acquirer's employees whilst also strongly influencing the organisational identification of employees from the acquired organisation. In doing so it will be increasing the likelihood of integrating both groups of employees into the acquiring organisation.

One potential source of influence is the acquiring organisation's corporate brand. All employees are exposed to it and, to a greater or lesser degree associate with it (de Chernatony et al. 2006). In their day-to-day environment front-line employees (FLEs), those who interact directly with customers during service encounters are surrounded by their organisation's corporate brand and its cues, directly referring to the organisation of which they are members (Simões et al. 2005). These cues are present in a post-acquisition operating environment for both acquired and non-acquired FLEs. Their membership of the acquiring organisation's brand community brings FLEs together with various organisational stakeholder groups integrating them into the organisation through regular interaction (Brodie et al. 2009).

This quantitative study researches both acquired and non-acquired retail front-line employees, 3 years post an acquisition, across nine UK retail stores of a UK national retailer. In deploying structural equation modelling to this empirical study, this chapter makes three contributions.

First, it establishes that the central, enduring and distinctive elements of the acquiring organisation's corporate brand equally influence the post-acquisition integration of both acquired and non-acquired employees given their equal influence on the organisational identification held by both groups.

Second, it determines that both groups deploy their organisational identification differently. Importantly, acquired employees organisational identification is deployed more to socialise and integrate within an organisation's corporate brand community in the form of its influence upon their relatedness to the corporate brand community and corporate brand community word of mouth.

Third, it demonstrates an acquiring organisation's corporate brand appeals to the acquired FLEs need to be members of a high status and prestigious organisation. Acting as a means of increasing the likelihood of acquired FLE integration into the acquiring organisation and reducing the likelihood of acquisition failure.

Conceptual Background

Organisational Identification Post-Acquisition

Prior to an acquisition, acquired and non-acquired employees hold an organisational identity for their respective organisation. Organisational identity, a form of social identity, contends that individuals do not just hold a sense of their self in terms of the unique, individualising characteristics that distinguish them from others, but that their self-definition is extended and considered in terms of their membership of social groups (Taijfel and Turner 1979). Organisational identity is held by individuals for the organisation they are members of and is defined as "*the extent to which individuals define the self in terms of membership of the organisation and where identification with an organisation partly answers the question of who am I?*"(Mael and Ashforth 1992: 104). It is a sense of perceived oneness with the organisation, reflecting the merging of the self and the organisation. Individual's sense of self is considered in terms of "we", organisational identity, not "I", personal identity (van Knippenberg 2000).

During mergers and acquisitions, employee's identification processes are threatened (Edwards and Edwards 2012). In the case of acquisitions, employees from the acquired organisation neither quickly, nor automatically, form new psychological bonds with the new entity they now work for, leading to poor integration (Jetten et al. 2002). To do so requires them to dis-identify with their previous organisation and form a new identity with the new organisation (Guerrero 2008). Such identity formation is threatened by dis-continuity in the new working environment (Edwards and Edwards 2012). Dis-continuity takes the form of changing location, changes of management, changes in culture and so on, that represent threats (Teerikangas and Very 2006) and generate feelings of uncertainty (Jetten et al. 2002). Dis-continuity makes it less likely for acquired employees to integrate into the acquiring organisation.

The characteristics of dis-continuity form a series of negative cues that inform an individual's organisational identity (Guerrero 2008). Those who form an organisational identity receive signals and cues about the organisation making them aware of their group membership and informing their identity formation process, termed social categorisation (Turner et al. 1994). Increasing the sense of continuity for this group increases the likelihood of their integration into the new organisation in the sharing of a common organisational identification for the acquired organisation with employees who worked for the organisation prior to acquisition. However, given the high degree of change that is often required in an acquisition, it is not often possible to provide the requisite level of continuity (Edwards and Edwards 2012).

However, social categorisation theory presents an alternative to increasing FLE organisational identification and integration by reducing continuity. Individuals seek to enhance their self-esteem by joining groups perceived as attractive, distinctive or prestigious (Turner et al. 1994). Inevitably, post-acquisition, the group of non-acquired employees hold a much higher level of identification with the acquiring organisation than those in the acquired group, due to the esteem they hold and status they attach to the organisation (Van Knippenberg and Van Leeuwen 2001). If individuals from the acquired organisation consider the acquiring organisation to be of high status and prestigious, it is more likely they will adopt the organisational identity of the acquiring firm (Terry et al. 2001). It is possible to influence the integration of acquired and non-acquired groups of employees if they share an organisational identity containing the central, enduring and distinctive characteristics of the organisation, providing *"a 'bedrock quality' to the individual—organisational relationships"* (Ashforth and Mael 1996: 26). What is required, post-acquisition, is to identify a phenomena that communicates the central, enduring and distinctive characteristics of the acquiring organisation that influence the organisational identification of both acquired and non-acquired employees.

A corporate brand communicates to all employees what is central, enduring and distinctive about an organisation (Brown et al. 2006).

Hypothesis Development

Corporate Branding and the Saliency of Organisational Identification Post-Acquisition

In order for social identities to form, in this case, organisational identification, the foci group requires saliency. For example those who form organisational identification receive signals and cues about the organisation, making them aware of their group membership and informing their identity formation process. This is termed social categorisation (Turner et al. 1994). Individuals mentally hold and store information about specific foci in the form of associations, termed associative network memory. These associations when combined comprise an individual's knowledge of a particular foci e.g. an organisation, and are formed when associative pathways link individual and discrete elements of memory termed nodes (Sirsi et al. 1996). Corporate brands present these cues to an organisation's stakeholders, including FLEs, developing their association with and knowledge of the organisation (de Chernatony et al. 2006).

FLEs hold associations about the organisation, i.e. corporate associations, representing all the information about a company that a person holds (Brown and Dacin 1997). Conveyed through the organisation's presentation of itself to its constituent stakeholder groups, they serve as the reality of the organisation for the individual members of the organisation holding them. A number of central and enduring associations, once internalised, form a basis for self referential meaning, constituting an organisationally relevant but individually held identity for the organisation member. Specifically those corporate associations held by members of the organisation are termed member organisational associations, the mental associations held by organisational members about the organisation (Brown et al. 2006).

These internal signals and internal aspects of the corporate brand require managing the time when to communicate the mission and vision of the organisation, presenting a consistent internal image of the organisation and inconsistent implementation of the corporate brands visual identity (Simões et al. 2005). It is proposed that such internal branding phenomena add to the information held about the company by retail FLEs, informing their organisational associations and contributing to the saliency of their organisational identification.

The organisation's mission and vision is a recognised component of an organisation's presentation to stakeholder groups (Melewar 2003; Melewar and Karaosmanoglu 2006). Communicated via the internal management of the organisation's corporate brand, front-line employees are an important stakeholder audience (Suvatjis and de Chernatony 2005). As a consequence of the literature review, it is proposed that:

Hypothesis 1: The dissemination of the organisation's mission and vision directly affects retail front-line employee organisational identification.

Corporate image is also a recognised component of an organisation's presentation of itself, as communicated by the organisation's corporate brand, contributing *to "the totality of stakeholders' perceptions of the way an organisation presents itself, either deliberately or accidentally"* (Melewar 2003: 209). In order to be effective the organisation's corporate image requires internal management to co-ordinate its internal operations so that the corporate image is consistent across all stakeholder groups, including front-line employees (Simões et al. 2005). Therefore it is contended that:

Hypothesis 2: The organisation's consistent implementation of its corporate image directly affects retail front-line employee organisational identification.

The components of an organisation's corporate visual identity consist of corporate symbols such as corporate name, a symbol or logo type, typography, colour and slogan and as such are recognised components of an organisation's presentation of itself to its stakeholder groups (Melewar and Karaosmanoglu 2006). Therefore it is proposed that:

Hypothesis 3: The organisation's implementation of its corporate visual identity directly affects retail front-line employee organisational identification.

It is proposed that the dissemination of the organisation's mission and vision, the consistent implementation of its corporate image and the implementation of its corporate visual identity are signals and cues that, in the form of organisational associations, influence and make salient retail front-line employee organisational identification. It is also proposed that these cues and symbols do not contribute to reducing dis-continuity for acquired employees but rather appeal to individuals seeking to enhance their self-esteem by joining groups perceived as attractive, distinctive or prestigious. Equally communicating the central and enduring characteristics of the organisation to both acquired and non-acquired employee groups and equally influencing both groups organisational identification by reinforcing the status and prestige attached to their membership of the organisation. It is therefore proposed that:

Hypothesis 4: There is no significant difference between the acquired and non-acquired retail front-line employee groups in the influence of dissemination of the organisation's mission and vision, the consistent implementation of its corporate image and the implementation of its corporate visual identity upon organisational identification.

Post-Acquisition Deployment of Retail Front-Line Employee Organisational Identification in the Corporate Brand Community

Once salient the deployment of organisational identification is not uniform between individuals (van Dick et al. 2006). Although organisational identification is a prerequisite to positive employee outcomes such as extra-role behaviours, organisational citizenship behaviours, employee satisfaction and employee performance, the extent and significance of these relationships vary between groups (He and Brown 2013). Individual's social identities vary in strength. Some are temporary and are a response to a given social situation, and others are more enduring and deep structured highly influencing individuals' sense of their self. However, it is established that irrespective of the nature of the social identities held they are deployed more in the context of inter-group relationships and their socialisation rather than in binding individuals to an organisation's specific projects, goals and targets (Meyer et al. 2006).

Post-acquisition both the acquired and non-acquired groups of retail front-line employees are members of another cross-organisational group, the corporate brand community. A corporate brand community is a means of integrating an organisation's stakeholder groups as it is centred around a structured set of social relations among admirers of a brand and brand communities are strengthened by its members shared branding experiences (McAlexander et al. 2002). Social interaction leads to social influence between the community members (Algesheimer et al. 2005). In a front-line employee context, Thurston et al. (2009) propose and verify that such social interaction, in the form of employee interaction, results from employee membership of a brand community (Miles and Mangold 2004). Therefore, post-acquisition, it is proposed that retail front-line employee organisational identification, which is influenced and made salient by corporate branding phenomena, is deployed by retail front-line employees in their participation of the corporate brand community. Morhart et al. (2009) contend that the effectiveness of this participation is to be found in the strength of the perceived relatedness between individual members of a corporate brand community, termed relatedness-to-brand community. It is therefore proposed that:

Hypothesis 5: Retail front-line employee organisational identification directly affects their relatedness to a corporate brand community.

As members of a brand community retail FLEs exercise their advocacy of the organisation, and in particular its brand, during the continuous social process of interacting with other stakeholders (Brodie et al. 2009). Such interaction is not restricted to just customers but wider internal and external stakeholder groups, formally, with the job role and, informally, outside of the job role (Gregory 2007). Morhart et al. (2009) consider word-of-mouth advocacy to be stronger if delivered outside the job context. Such advocacy is considered to be another indication of individuals integrating with the organisation as such interaction and negotiation with all stakeholders is discretionary, termed word of mouth.

Hypothesis 6: Retail front-line employee organisational identification directly affects front-line employee corporate brand community positive word of mouth.

It is proposed, in the context of a corporate brand community, acquired retail front-line employees deploy their organisational identification differently to their non-acquisition colleagues. Acquired retail front-line employees are under pressure to dis-identify with the previous organisation and form a new identity and a re-identification with the new entity. This requires them to find ways of deploying their organisational identification to socialise and integrate into the new organisation when becoming members of a number of organisational groups. By contrast, those who do not originate from the acquired organisation are likely integrated into the organisation and are relatively less inclined to deploy their organisational identification for the purpose of socialising and integrating into the organisations brand community. It is therefore proposed:

Hypothesis 7: There is a significant difference between the acquired and non-acquired retail front-line employee groups in the influence of organisational identification upon relatedness to the corporate brand community and corporate brand community positive word of mouth.

Research Methodology

Data Collection and Sample

To test the theoretical model, a quantitative survey was conducted with operational retail front-line employees over nine retail stores, within a national UK retailer that had 3 years previously acquired a number of stores from a UK competitor. From a total population of 1600 front-line employees, 599 usable questionnaires were returned, a response rate of 37.4%.

Measure Development and Assessment

The six-item Mael and Ashforth (1992) scale for organisational identification was adopted to measure organisational identification. The measures developed by Simões et al. (2005) were adapted for use at the front-line employee level to measure dissemination of the organisation's mission and vision, consistent corporate image implementation and corporate visual identity implementation. The three item measures developed by Morhart et al. (2009) were deployed to measure relatedness to corporate brand community and corporate brand community and corporate brand community word of mouth.

The constructs were measured with reflective measurement models, suggesting that the latent constructs cause the measurement variables (Hair et al. 2010). All items are measured on 7-point Likert scales with a range of "strongly disagree" to "strongly agree". Prior to conducting a confirmatory factor analysis, the sample was successfully tested for non-response bias (Armstrong and Overton 1977) and common method variance (Podsakoff et al. 2003). The former was tested by deploying a surrogate measure, continuance commitment, in a confirmatory factor analysis. The factor loadings for the measurement models constructs remain the same with or without the surrogate measure (Lindell and Whitney 2001).

The confirmatory factor analysis conducted to assess the validity of the scales led to some item deletions and generated more than satisfactory goodness-of-fit indices (Hair et al. 2010): χ^2 (155)=374.17, p=.00; CFI=.99; GFI=.941; AGFI=.920; RMSEA=.049. Overall reliability and validity of the measurement model is good: composite reliability (CR) ranges from .62 to .89; average variance extracted (AVE) from .58 to .83; none of the squared correlations between pairs of constructs exceeded the AVE, therefore discriminant validity was satisfied (Table 1) (Fornell and Larcker 1981).

In order to compare structural equation model results across groups, in this case between acquired and non-acquired groups of retail front line employees, two forms of invariance are considered. Configural and metric invariance (Steenkamp and Baumgartner 1998). In the presence of metric-invariance it is possible to compare relationships between the studied constructs across groups (Table 2).

In this case, as there is no substantial deterioration in the goodness-of-fit indices between the configural invariance and metric invariance models, the comparison of structural model paths for both the acquired and non-acquired groups is therefore permitted. LISREL version 8.80, using maximum-likelihood estimation, was used to test the theoretical model and its hypotheses. The goodness-of-fit measures indicate that the hypothesised model is a good representation of the empirical data (Hair et al. 2010): χ^2 (162)=545.444, p=.00; CFI=.984; GFI=.917; AGFI=.892; RMSEA=.063.

As hypothesised in H1 the relationship between MVD and OI is statistically significant (p>.001) and strong (Υ=.20) as is that between CII and OI, as proposed in H2, which is also statistically significant (p>.001) and strong (Υ=.40). The hypothesised relationship between VII and OI, postulated through H3, is relatively less statistically significant (p>.05) and strong (Υ=.13). As hypothesised in H4,

Table 1 CR, AVE inter-correlations and squared correlations

	CR	1.	2.	3.	4.	5.	6.
MVD	.86	**.61**	.39	.41	.25	.27	.25
CII	.62	.62	**.62**	.40	.34	.22	.28
VII	.81	.64	.63	**.58**	.24	.20	.21
OID	.88	.50	.59	.49	**.66**	.25	.64
RBC	.89	.52	.47	.45	.50	**.81**	.41
WOM	.83	.50	.53	.46	.80	.64	**.83**

MVD Mission and Vision Dissemination, *CII* Corporate Image Implementation, *VII* Visual Identity Implementation, *OID* Organisational identification department, *RBC* Relatedness to brand community, *WOM* Word of Mouth; AVE on the diagonal in bold; inter-correlations below the diagonal and squared correlations above the diagonal

Table 2 Invariance test results

Invariance level	χ^2	d.f.	$\Delta\chi^2$/d.f.	RMSEA	CAIC	NNFI	CFI	GFI
Configural	613.35	328	1.86997	.055	1616.739	.983	.985	.936
Metric	638.29	339	1.882861	.054	1533.117	.983	.985	.936

when tested, there were no significant differences in the paths for H1, H2, H3 between the structural models for the acquired and non-acquired groups. The increase in χ^2 for one degree of freedom for each path did not meet or exceed the stated threshold.

H5 the link between OI and RBC ($\beta=.549$) is statistically significant ($p>.001$), as it that for H6 between OI and WOM ($\beta=.822$; $p>.001$). When tested there was a statistically significant difference in the paths of two models for both H5 and H6. For H5, χ^2 increased by 22.28 for an increase in one degree of freedom, with respective differences in the Beta coefficients for the acquired group ($\beta=.940$) and the non-acquired group ($\beta=.51$) at a similar significance level ($p>.001$). For H6, χ^2 increased by 5.75 for an increase in one degree of freedom, with respective differences in the Beta coefficients for the acquired group ($\beta=092$) and the non-acquired group ($\beta=.81$) at a similar significance level ($p>.001$). As hypothesised in H7, when tested, there were significant differences in the paths for H5 and H6 between the structural models for the acquired and non-acquired groups.

Discussion

The Findings

The study's results indicate that, both for the acquired and non-acquired groups, corporate branding cues, post-acquisition, influence the saliency of retail front-line employee organisational identification. It is therefore evident that branding phenomena influence the transitioning of acquired employees' organisational identification from their previous organisation onto building an identification with the acquiring organisation. It is interesting to find that there is no difference in the influence of mission and vision dissemination, corporate image implementation and implementation of corporate visual identity upon the organisational identification of both groups. If the acquired group of employees apply the influence of these branding signals, in a dis-continuity context, it would be expected that the relative influence of these phenomena on organisational identification would vary between the groups. As this is not the case, this similarity indicates these signals likely influence the inter-group comparative nature of social identity, in using them to inform what is central, enduring and distinctive about the organisation to reinforce the prestige and esteem attached to group membership. Therefore, in this case, branding phenomena, through their influence upon organisational identification, equally influence, post-acquisition, in the medium term, the integration of both groups into the organisation.

Theoretical Implications

The study's results also indicate that the organisational identification held by both groups influences their relatedness to the corporate brand community and brand community positive word of mouth. This indicates that both groups, post-acquisition, to an extent, direct their organisational identification towards corporate brand community activity. The differences shown between both groups, where the influence of organisational identity on both brand community constructs is much stronger for the acquired group, indicate that, post-acquisition, in the medium term, acquired employees use the brand community as a means of integrating into the organisation more than non-acquired employees.

Theoretically, the study indicates that the corporate brand of an organisation and its resulting corporate brand community are a means of integrating acquired retail front-line employees, post-acquisition, into the acquiring organisation. Moreover, the branding phenomena equally influencing both groups' organisational identification imply that these phenomena reinforce the similarity of both groups in communicating what makes the organisation central enduring and distinctive. In a retailing context, it is notable, that the brand community is accessed more by non-acquired front-line employees, as a form of integrating into the organisation. This indicates the importance of corporate branding in the integration of acquired front-line employees into the acquiring organisation.

Practical Implications

The study also has several important implications for retailers considering growth by acquisition. First, the distinctiveness of the acquiring organisation's brand, in its ability to strongly communicate what is central, enduring and distinctive about the organisation, should be a consideration when assessing the feasibility of potential acquisitions. Second, the acquiring organisation's corporate brand likely has a positive influence upon acquired employees' psychological bonds with the organisation, representing one means of encouraging front-line employee integration. As such, the internal influence of the acquiring organisation's corporate brand requires managing post acquisition. Finally, in this context, although it might be considered that the acquiring organisation's corporate brand communicates differences between the acquired and acquiring organisation, this study indicates that instead it reinforces the organisational identification of both acquired and non-acquired groups by communicating what is prestigious and distinctive about the organisation. It is therefore important that marketing, post-acquisition, takes not just an external role, but also an internal role, in brand management and the communication of the implications of the acquisition.

Study Limitations and Further Research

One of the limitations of this study is that it is not longitudinal. Although the study does not show how the theoretical relationships in the study develop over time, it is evident that in this case corporate branding phenomena, 3 years into a retail acquisition, influence the integration of acquired retail front-line employees into the acquiring organisation. Indeed, in terms of future research, there are opportunities to research both how the relationships contained within the study change over time, how the branding of both organisations pre-acquisition influences the organisational identification of both groups post-acquisition and finally how other branding phenomena, from a customer perspective, influence the organisational identification and subsequent employee integration post- acquisition.

References

Algesheimer, R., Dholakia, U. M., & Herrmann, A. (2005). The social influence of brand community: Evidence from European car clubs. *Journal of Marketing, 69*(3), 19–34.
Armstrong, J. S., & Overton, T. S. (1977). Estimating nonresponse bias in mail surveys. *Journal of Marketing Research, 14*(3), 396–402.
Ashforth, B. E., & Mael, F. A. (1996). The social identity theory and the organisation. In B. E. Baam & J. E. Dutton (Eds.), *Advances in strategic management* (pp. 61–76). Greenwich. CT: JAI Press.
Brodie, R. J., Whittome, J. R. M., & Brush, G. J. (2009). Investigating the service brand: A customer value perspective. *Journal of Business Research, 62*(3), 345–355.
Brown, T. J., & Dacin, P. A. (1997). The company and the product: Corporate associations and consumer product responses. *Journal of Marketing, 61*(1), 68–84.
Brown, T. J., Dacin, P. A., Pratt, M. G., & Whetten, D. A. (2006). Identity, intended image, construed image, and reputation: An interdisciplinary framework and suggested terminology. *Journal of the Academy of Marketing Science, 34*(2), 99–106.

de Chernatony, L., Cottam, S., & Segal-Horn, S. (2006). Communicating services brands' values internally and externally. *Service Industries Journal, 26*(8), 819–836.

Edwards, M. R., & Edwards, T. (2012). Procedural justice and identification with the acquirer: The moderating effects of job continuity, organisational identity strength and organisational similarity. *Human Resource Management Journal, 22*(2), 109–128.

Fornell, C., & Larcker, D. F. (1981). Structural equation models with unobservable variables and measurement error: Algebra and statistics. *Journal of Marketing Research, 18*(3), 382–388.

Gregory, A. (2007). Involving stakeholders in developing corporate brands: The communication dimension. *Journal of Marketing Management, 23*(1/2), 59–73.

Guerrero, S. (2008). Changes in employees' attitudes at work following an acquisition: a comparative study by acquisition type. *Human Resource Management Journal, 18*(3), 216–236.

Hair, J. F., Jr., Black, W. C., Babin, B. J., & Anderson, R. E. (2010). *Multivariate data analysis: A global perspective*. Upper Saddle River, NJ: Pearson.

Haleblian, J., Devers, C. E., McNamara, G., Carpenter, M. A., & Davison, R. B. (2009). Taking stock of what we know about mergers and acquisitions: A review and research agenda. *Journal of Management, 35*(3), 469–502.

He, H., & Brown, A. D. (2013). Organizational identity and organizational identification: A review of the literature and suggestions for future research. *Group & Organization Management, 38*(1), 3–35.

Jetten, J., O'Brien, A., & Trindall, N. (2002). Changing identity: Predicting adjustment to organisational restructure as a function of subgroup superordinate identification. *British Journal of Social Psychology, 41*(3), 281–298.

Lichtenstein, D. R., Netemeyer, R. G., & Maxham, J. G. (2010). The relationships among manager-, employee-, and customer-company identification: Implications for retail store financial performance. *Journal of Retailing, 86*(1), 85–93.

Lindell, M. K., & Whitney, D. J. (2001). Accounting for common method variance in cross-selectional research designs. *Journal of Applied Psychology, 86*(1), 114–121.

Mael, F., & Ashforth, B. E. (1992). Alumni and their alma mater: A partial test of the reformulated model of organizational identification. *Journal of Organizational Behavior, 13*(2), 103–123.

McAlexander, J. H., Schouten, J. W., & Koenig, H. F. (2002). Building brand community. *Journal of Marketing, 66*(1), 38–54.

Melewar, T. C. (2003). Determinants of the corporate identity construct: A review of the literature. *Journal of Marketing Communications, 9*(4), 195–220.

Melewar, T. C., & Karaosmanoglu, E. (2006). Corporate branding, identity and communications: A contemporary perspective. *Journal of Brand Management, 14*(1/2), 1–4.

Meyer, J. P., Becker, T. E., & van Dick, R. (2006). Social identities and commitments at work: Toward an integrative model. *Journal of Organizational Behavior, 27*(5), 665–683.

Miles, S. J., & Mangold, G. (2004). A conceptualisation of the employee branding process. *Journal of Relationship Marketing, 3*(2–3), 65–87.

Morhart, F. M., Herzog, W., & Tomczak, T. (2009). Brand-specific leadership: Turning employees into brand champions. *Journal of Marketing, 73*(5), 122–142.

Podsakoff, P. M., MacKenzie, S. B., Jeong-Yeon, L., & Podsakoff, N. P. (2003). Common method biases in behavioral research: A critical review of the literature and recommended remedies. *Journal of Applied Psychology, 88*(5), 879.

Reinartz, W., Dellaert, B., Krafft, M., Kumar, V., & Varadarajan, R. (2012). Retailing innovations in a globalizing retail market environment. *Journal of Retailing, 87*, S53–S66.

Simões, C., Dibb, S., & Fisk, R. P. (2005). Managing corporate identity: An internal perspective. *Journal of the Academy of Marketing Science, 33*(2), 153–168.

Sirsi, A. K., Ward, J. C., & Reingen, P. H. (1996). Microcultural analysis of variation in sharing of causal reasoning about behavior. *Journal of Consumer Research, 22*(4), 345–372.

Steenkamp, J.-B. E. M., & Baumgartner, H. (1998). Assessing measurement invariance in cross-national consumer research. *Journal of Consumer Research, 25*(1), 78–90.

Suvatjis, J. Y., de Chernatony, L. (2005). Corporate Identity Modelling: A Review and Presentation of a New Multi-dimensional Model, Journal of Marketing Management vol. 21 Issue 7-8, 809–834.

Taijfel, H., & Turner, J. C. (1979). An integrative theory of intergroup conflict. In S. Worchel & W. G. Austin (Eds.), *The social psychology of intergroup relations* (pp. 7–24). Monterey, CA: Brooks/Cole.

Terry, D.J., Carey, C.J., & Callan, V.J. (2001). Employee adjustment to an organizational merger: An intergroup perspective. *Personality and Social Psychology Bulletin, 27*, 267–280.

Teerikangas, S., & Very, P. (2006). The culture–performance relationship in M&A: From yes/no to how. *British Journal of Management, 17*, S31–S48.

Turner, J. C., Oakes, P. J., Haslam, S. A., & McGarty, C. A. (1994). Self and collective: Cognition and social context. *Personality and Social Psychology Bulletin, 20*, 454–463.

van Dick, R., Grojean, M. W., Christ, O., & Wieseke, J. (2006). Identity and the extra mile: Relationships between organizational identification and organizational citizenship behaviour. *British Journal of Management, 17*(4), 283–301.

van Knippenberg, D. (2000). Work motivation and performance: A social identity perspective. *Applied Psychology, 49*(3), 357.

van Knippenberg, D., & van Leeuwen, E. (2002). Organizational identity after a merger: Sense of continuity as the key to postmerger identification. In M.A. Hogg, & D.J. Terry (Eds.), Social identity processes in organizational contexts (pp. 249–264). Philadelphia, PA: Psychology Press.

Growing Without Getting Bigger: A Structured Abstract

Adrian Peretz and Lars Erling Olsen

Introduction

One of the key goals for brand organizations is to make brands grow (Samuelsen and Olsen 2012)—and one of the most attractive ways of achieving brand growth is through brand extensions: extending an existing brand into a new product category (Keller 2012). The epic growth of the Apple brand illustrates that the rewards from even a small number of truly successful brand extensions are significant. The Apple brand also suggests another key issue that may be important for brand growth strategies—while Apple may loom large in the mind of most consumers, it does not seem to require much mental effort to maintain this image.

Brands may follow different patterns of growth. Some brands, such as H&M, Kellogg's, and Gillette, have stayed relatively close to their core categories—they have moderate brand variance (Boush and Loken 1991), while other equally successful brands, e.g., Nike, Louis Vuitton, and Samsung have over time been extended a long way from their original categories, have relatively large brand variance, and have become broad brands. Conversely, there are brands that have been stretched in many directions, but which in doing so seem to have weakened their core brand associations—e.g., Hewlett Packard.

These different growth patterns, and the levels of success associated with them, raise the interesting question of how some brands achieve successful growth in categories that seem distant from the brands' core category and become broad brands—while others fail. Previous research has shown that broad brands—brands with core brand benefits that are relevant and valuable over a range of somewhat dissimilar categories—achieve greater levels of overall brand strength (Meyvis and Janiszewski 2004). However, the current research on brand extensions is primarily concerned

A. Peretz (✉) • L.E. Olsen
Oslo School of Management, Oslo, Norway
e-mail: adrian.peretz@mh.no; lars.olsen@mh.no

© Academy of Marketing Science 2016   677
L. Petruzzellis, R.S. Winer (eds.), *Rediscovering the Essentiality of Marketing*,
Developments in Marketing Science: Proceedings of the Academy of Marketing
Science, DOI 10.1007/978-3-319-29877-1_127

with the immediate success of each brand extension, and there has been little focus on what it takes to create a broad brand. The ultimate goal of the current research is to identify factors that allow brands to achieve brand growth through extensions that broaden the parent brand—but do not weaken the core of the brand.

Theoretical Background

Previous research has shown that a brand's strategic concept (Park et al. 1986) may influence the potential breadth of the brand. Brands that provide symbolic value to the consumer tend to have more abstract brand benefits—and the abstraction level of these associations allows symbolic brands to be more easily extended into categories that, from a purely functional perspective, may seem quite distant (Park et al. 1991). Louis Vuitton was able to expand greatly in the 1990s, from luxurious luggage to all-round luxury brand, including such functionally dissimilar categories as clothing and jewelry—as the LV brand had developed into a symbolic brand concept. However, although research has shown that functional brand concepts, which tend to have more specific and concrete brand benefits, have more limited stretch capability, there are many examples of broad, functionally based brands, e.g., Nike and Samsung, that have achieved growth and success in categories that may seem distant from the core. These two brands have followed somewhat different growth strategies: Nike has followed an evolutionary growth strategy (each category extension has been close to existing categories), while Samsung has followed a more discontinuous growth strategy—extending its brand franchise from that of domestic appliance brand to the world's number one TV brand, and more recently to global leader in mobile phones. However, these two brands do have one thing in common: the functional benefits they provide are expressed at a very abstract level. The success of these two functional brands suggests that it is possible to increase the potential breadth of functional brands by increasing the level of abstraction of the brand's key benefit associations.

In terms of brand associations, brand extensions involve learning on the part of the consumer (Janiszewski and Van Osselaer 2000). When a brand name is extended into a new category, the consumer must update the number of category associations linked to the brand. And similarly, extending or increasing the number of benefits a brand provides also requires learning on the part of the consumer. In both cases, the associative network linked to the brand increases in size, and over time it requires increased effort to maintain a coherent model of the brand in memory—and further update the model for each successive brand extension. This is in fact the basis for the claim that broader brands may be stronger brands (Meyvis and Janiszewski 2008). If however, a brand extension merely served to increase the abstraction level of the brand benefit(s)—essentially storing more global brand beliefs than brand exemplars (Ng and Houston 2006) this would require less effort to learn and maintain, as there would not be an increase in the number of associations in the network—but merely a moderate redefinition of existing associations. Increased levels of abstraction could even make it easier to maintain a coherent model of the brand in memory, as a smaller number of associations would be required to recall the solutions to a greater number of consumer goals. The current research proposes that one important factor for creating broad, yet strong, functional brands is by carefully selecting brand extensions that increase the abstraction level of parent brand benefits such that this improves the likelihood of success for each brand extension while minimizing the amount of learning required by the customer.

Methodology

Two studies have been carried out. The objective of first study was to demonstrate how an initial brand extension with a moderate degree of stretch from a parent brand could be used to increase the likelihood of acceptance for a more distant target extension by using the intermediate brand extension to broaden the associations linked to the parent brand. The parent brand selected was a fictitious brand of suits and dress suits, and the intermediate and target extensions (levels of consistency to parent brand on ten-point scale) were dress shoes (8.35) and running shoes (2.21)—consistency score between intermediate and target brand extensions was 5.81. Over a period of 3 weeks, 152 students participated in a single factor (extension sequence) between-subjects design. At each exposure, participants were provided with a brief description of brand/brand extension and asked to rate purchase intention and attitude toward the parent brand (week 1) or both parent brand and brand extension (weeks 2 and 3).

As hypothesized, attitudes toward the target extension in week 3 were more favorable for participants that had been exposed to an intermediate extension in week 2 (4.12 versus 2.85; $t=25.11$, $p<.001$). Interestingly, the results also revealed a significant difference in attitudes toward the parent brand between the two conditions at week 3. Participants that were only exposed to the parent brand and the dissimilar target brand showed a much larger drop in favorability ratings of the parent brand (4.93–3.99; $t=4.89$, $p<.001$) after exposure to the target brand than participants that were exposed to an intermediate brand extension (4.86–4.58; ns.), and the difference between mean scores at week 3 showed a significant effect of the sequential extension strategy (Ms $=4.58$ versus 3.99; $t=29.23$, $p<.001$). Experiment 1 demonstrates that brand extensions provide new information about the parent brand to the consumer, and that this information may be used to broaden the parent brand. This feedback effect has also been found in other stu dies, and it raises the interesting question of how brand managers can create brand extensions that strengthen or enhance the parent brand—without adding new associations to the brand image?

The objectives for study 2 were to provide some initial evidence of how respondents update the parent brand image through multiple extensions, and to identify which type of sequential extension strategy is more likely to generate extension success through multiple extensions. Prior research indicates that brand extensions based on category similarity are easy for consumers to understand and are thus favorable when extending a parent brand into a similar and consistent category, but that consumers prefer extensions where the brand benefit is diagnostic when extending into a more dissimilar category (Broniarczyk and Alba 1994). There is however evidence that extending a brand into dissimilar categories may dilute the brand by making the image of the brand less clear in memory. These two different extension strategies were used to explore the ease with which parent brand associations are updated.

The design was a single factor (extension strategy: category-based versus brand benefit-based) between-subjects design. Participants received product and positioning information in three stages: first the parent brand (fictitious), then the intermediate brand extension, and finally the target brand extension. At each stage participants were asked to rate their attitude towards both the parent brand and the brand extension (intermediate extension at stage two and target extension at stage three). Immediately after having been presented with product and positioning information at each stage—but before being asked to complete attitude measures, participants were instructed to do three things: (1) write down their associations to the brand; (2) write down what type of customer segment they thought would be most interested in purchasing the brand (extension); (3) rate the brand (extension) in terms of perceived relevance to what they had previously learned about the brand (seven-point scale, "highly relevant/highly irrelevant").

Pretesting identified three suitable product categories: cookware (pots & pans etc.) as a parent brand category from which a relatively consistent intermediate extension—food processor (5.94), and more distant target extension—espresso machine (2.98), could be extended (perceived distance between brands—rated in pretests, $N=41$, using two ten-point scales anchored by *extremely representative/ extremely unrepresentative* and *extremely consistent/extremely inconsistent*). In order to test the ease with which parent brand associations could be updated, one group of respondents was presented with a brand-benefit (user-friendly) based extension strategy from parent brand to both extensions, while the other group was presented with a category-based extension strategy. The product categories and extension strategies were selected such that under the brand-benefit based extension strategy, the parent brand and both extensions could easily be grouped under the abstract term "user-friendly," while under the category extension strategy the three categories involved: cookware, food processor, and espresso machine—could not be easily stored into a single abstract category definition—and would thus require more effort to process and store.

Results and Discussion

A one-way Anova on the attitudes toward target extension at stage 3 revealed a significant effect of extension strategy. As expected the brand-benefit extension strategy resulted in a more favorable attitude towards the target extension than the product category extension strategy $F(1, 101)=33.10$, $p<.001$. Planned contrasts showed that attitude towards the target extension was significantly more favorable for participants that had been exposed to a brand-benefit extension strategy than participants that had been exposed to a product-category extension strategy ($M_{Benefit-Ex}=4.49$ versus $M_{Category-Ex}=3.12$; $t_{101}=5.75$, $p<.001$).

Planned contrasts of attitude to the parent brand at stage three also revealed that participants that had been exposed to a brand-benefit extension strategy had a more favorable attitude towards the parent brand than participants that had been exposed to a product-category extension strategy ($M_{Benefit-P}=4.72$ versus $M_{Category-P}=3.61$; $t_{101}=5.18$, $p<.001$). Note that participants exposed to a category extension strategy showed a significant drop in attitude towards parent brand from stage two to stage three ($M_{Category-P2}=4.68$ to $M_{Category-P3}=3.61$; $t_{50}=7.36$, $p<.001$). By comparison, participants exposed to a brand-benefit extension strategy showed a slight improvement in attitude towards parent brand actually from stage 2 (4.55) to stage 3 (4.72), although this increase was not significant.

To further reveal the thought process underlying the attitude scores towards parent brand and target brand extension at stage three, mediation analysis using the data collected on participants' evaluations of the perceived relevance of the brand extension in terms of what they previously learned about the brand was used as a mediator between brand extension strategy (brand benefit versus product category) and attitude towards parent brand/target extension. There was a significant indirect effect of extension strategy on attitude towards parent brand through perceived relevance of the extension, $b=.345$, BCa CI [.094, .722]. This represents a medium-sized effect, $k^2=.145$, 95% BCa CI [.043, .272]. There was also a significant indirect effect of extension strategy on attitude towards target extension through perceived relevance of brand extension, $b=.474$, BCa CI [.209, .927], and this effect was relatively large $k^2=.178$, 95% BCa CI [.078, .317]. This evidence suggests that evaluations of both brand extensions and parent brand are at least partially based on the ease with which the relevance of extension-relevant associations can be recalled.

The results of experiments 1 and 2 provide initial evidence that the associations linked to a parent brand are updated each time the brand is extended. These experiments also provide initial evidence that using an extension strategy that allows consumers to store and maintain information about the brand with minimal effort is advantageous. Next research steps involve confirming the learning advantage for abstract versus concrete benefit associations.

References available upon request.

Does a Short Brand Story on the Package Affect Consumers' Brand Responses?

Eeva Solja, Veronica Liljander, and Magnus Söderlund

Abstract The persuasiveness of stories and their influence on consumers have been acknowledged within the fields of advertising, tourism, and services. Despite these findings, stories have not caught the attention that they deserve in the product and brand literature. Nothing indicates that stories would have less of an effect when applied to brands. It is especially intriguing that stories—of various kinds—have become ubiquitous on product packaging in practice. Yet there are no studies on the effect of such stories on the consumer's response to the brand. Can it be taken for given that consumers will react more positively to a package when some of the brand information is presented in story form? Packages have limited space and are filled with information required by law, which is not the case for advertisements. Thus, findings from advertising cannot be directly applied to packing. Currently, there is scant empirical research that directly investigates the impact of short brand stories on consumer responses, and such research is particularly lacking on packaging, where stories are ubiquitously used in practice.

This study uses a between-subjects experiment to test hypotheses pertaining to the impact of a short brand story communicated on a packaging on consumers' brand responses. The chapter shows that a company originated short brand story, which is added to the marketing communication of an existing, fast-moving consumer brand packaging produces a higher level of on brand attitude, perceived value, and behavioral intentions as opposed to when no story is present.

The study contributes to the product and brand literature in three ways. First, it provides empirical evidence of the effects of brand stories on packaging. Second, it shows that even a short story—within the limited space available on packaging—is capable of influencing consumers' brand responses. Third, it widens the application context of previous findings by examining a FMCG. The major practical implication is that managers may consider packaging as a channel to communicate short brand stories.

E. Solja (✉) • V. Liljander
Hanken School of Economics, CERS, Helsinki, Finland
e-mail: eeva.solja@hanken.fi; veronica.liljander@hanken.fi

M. Söderlund
Stockholm School Economics, Stockholm, Sweden
e-mail: magnus.soderlund@hhs.se

© Academy of Marketing Science 2016
L. Petruzzellis, R.S. Winer (eds.), *Rediscovering the Essentiality of Marketing*,
Developments in Marketing Science: Proceedings of the Academy of Marketing
Science, DOI 10.1007/978-3-319-29877-1_128

683

Saving the Planet or Saving the Brand? How Brand Strength Influences Consumers' Perceptions of Brand Sustainability

Patricia Rossi, Diego Costa Pinto, Marcia Herter, and Dilney Gonçalves

Abstract Sustainability actions, such as ecolabels, are increasingly prevalent among companies. However, relatively little is known about consumer response to these actions for brands. The authors propose that the degree to which ecolabels enhance consumers' perceptions of brand sustainability depends on brand strength (i.e., the differential effect of brand knowledge on consumer response to the brand). Two studies demonstrate that brand strength changes the impact of ecolabels on consumers' perceptions of brand sustainability and purchase intentions. The findings suggest that consumers use ecolabels as cue for brand sustainability for weak brands (i.e., brands without significant positive brand equity), but not for strong brands (i.e., brands with significant positive brand equity). In addition, results suggest that sustainability mediates purchase intentions, but these effects are stronger for weak brands than for strong brands.

P. Rossi (✉)
Grenoble Ecole de Management, Grenoble, France
e-mail: patricia.rossi@grenoble-em.com

D.C. Pinto
ESPM Business School, São Paulo, Brazil
e-mail: diego.pinto@espm.br

M. Herter
FADERGS, Porto Alegre, Brazil
e-mail: marcia.herter@fadergs.edu.br

D. Gonçalves
IE Business School, Madrid, Spain
e-mail: dilney.goncalves@ie.edu

© Academy of Marketing Science 2016
L. Petruzzellis, R.S. Winer (eds.), *Rediscovering the Essentiality of Marketing*,
Developments in Marketing Science: Proceedings of the Academy of Marketing
Science, DOI 10.1007/978-3-319-29877-1_129

The Impact of Corporate Brand Transgression on Punishing Corporate Transgressor: Moderating Role of Religious Orientation

Elif Karaosmanoglu and Didem Gamze Isiksal

Introduction

Since branding is a social construct as much as an economic construct (Fan 2005), brands are considered as a part of modern-day social customer's life. Therefore, corporate brands and their unethical behavior are scrutinized more closely. The examples such as Apple's labor violations while producing iPhone in China or Samsung's infringing on several patents and design of Apple products had significant effects on the brand–consumer relationships (Aaker et al. 2004; Paulssen and Bagozzi 2009) regardless of loss types and severity of transgressions.

Therefore, this study builds on consumers' judgment of corporate brand transgressions and its effect on their punishing behavior. It claims that corporate brand transgression, in other words, intentional unethical behavior, leads to punishing behavior of consumers and such negative consequence gets strengthened when the ethical abuse is more severe. It also asserts that ethical judgments are culturally embedded. Accordingly, it is argued that cultural aspects, such as religious orientation in this study, will accentuate the punishing behavior towards corporate brand especially for intrinsically religious consumers.

In the next sections, first the theoretical background, which clarifies concepts and relationships among them, is presented. Following that, the research design and the results of the study are explained. In the last section, the implications for corporate brand management and contributions to this body of knowledge are asserted.

E. Karaosmanoglu (✉) • D.G. Isiksal
Istanbul Technical University, Istanbul, Turkey
e-mail: karaosman5@itu.edu.tr; isiksal@itu.edu.tr

© Academy of Marketing Science 2016   687
L. Petruzzellis, R.S. Winer (eds.), *Rediscovering the Essentiality of Marketing*,
Developments in Marketing Science: Proceedings of the Academy of Marketing
Science, DOI 10.1007/978-3-319-29877-1_130

Theoretical Background

In today's consumption-oriented world, companies and their brands are increasingly eager to make more profit, which drives them to engage in some unethical behaviors. Although the research by Ethisphere Institute proves that there is a direct relationship between strong ethical principles and higher profit margins (Ethisphere Institute 2012), there are still brands that show unethical behavior. It is known that negative information always receives more attention than positive information and information about negative behavior has a stronger impact on customers (Amine 1996; Herr et al. 1991; Klein and Dawar 2004; Vélez-Garcìa and Ostrosky-Solìs 2006). Therefore, companies should expect that if they violate ethical rules, customers will be more likely to punish unethical behavior than rewarding it (Carrigan and Attalla 2001).

Despite all these assertions, there are still recent examples of brand transgressions in the marketplace. For example, Apple has got negative reaction due to working conditions abuse, which led to worker suicides in China (The Guardian 2011). Similarly, Nestle, producer of Kit Kat, was protested all around the world against the usage of palm oil, which results in deforestation and hence, endangers Orangutans' lives (Greenpeace International 2010). Samsung was also accused of copying Apple's iconic designs and intuitive user interface (Los Angeles Times 2012).

As the literature implies (e.g., Ahluwalia et al. 2000), unintentional unethical behavior may be excused by consumers more easily than intentional ones. However, the examples above demonstrate that intentional cases (brand transgressions) still exist and are tolerated by some consumers to some degree. It still remains unanswered what makes individuals to overlook certain intentional ethical abuses. Although, some earlier studies showed the negative impacts of brand transgressions at product level (e.g., Aaker et al. 2004; Steinman 2012), to our knowledge, there is a lack of interest in studying it at corporate brand level.

According to Metts (1994), brand transgressions refer to the violation of the implicit or explicit rules in the relationship between the consumer and the brand. While explicit rules are relationship specific rules between both sides such as bad habits of a partner, implicit rules are much widely counted as cultural standards that are accepted for a proper relationship (Metts and Cupach 2007) such as being honest, monogamy. This explanation suggests us perception of a transgression's severity may change from one culture to another. Therefore, in this study, religious orientation as a cultural aspect is taken into account to study the impact of corporate brand transgression on punishing behavior for different religious orientations.

Religiosity has an influence on individual's values, ethical judgments (Hunt and Vitell 1993), attitudes, and also on the prevention of deviant behaviors (Stack and Kposowa 2006). Several studies (e.g., Giorgi and Marsh 1990; Kennedy and Lawton 1998; McCabe and Trevino 1993; Muhamad 2009) indicated that religiousness has positive/negative impact on ethical/unethical behavior. Religious beliefs and activities stem from intrinsic or/and extrinsic motivational factors (Allport 1950; Allport and Ross 1967). While intrinsic religiosity comes from self-satisfaction about religion, extrinsic religiosity is motivated by external benefits such as material gains. It would be expected that intrinsically motivated believer reads the profane world and its values more conservatively, whereas the extrinsically motivated believer may bend some values of life to suit his/her benefits. Hereby, it could be argued that an intrinsically religious person, who follows and practices religious rules without any profane expectation might be expected to criticize a corporate brand's intentional unethical behavior (corporate brand transgression) more harshly than an extrinsically religious individual who identifies himself/herself with a religion for the externalities it breeds.

Drawing on the arguments above, a consumer's religion orientation as well as different levels of corporate brand transgression may influence punishing behavior towards a corporate brand in the form of reduced purchase intention and online and off-line negative word-of-mouth. Accordingly, we hypothesize that:

H1: When low-level corporate brand transgression is performed by the corporate brand, consumers, who have extrinsic level of religiosity, will judge corporate brand behavior as less unethical and will be less willing to punish corporate transgressor than consumers, who have intrinsic level of religiosity.

H2: When high-level corporate brand transgression is performed by the corporate brand, ethical judgments will not vary between extrinsically and intrinsically religious consumers.

Methodology

This study adopts a 2×2 experimental design where different levels of the corporate brand transgression (mild versus severe) are manipulated against different types of religiosity (intrinsic versus extrinsic) to examine how consumers' punishing behavior change towards an unethical corporate behavior. Participants were randomly assigned to one of four different scenarios. A questionnaire that illustrated a scenario in which hypothetical smartphone brand described as a corporate brand transgressor, that violates ethical rules at two different severity levels, i.e., low (withholding overtime payment) and extreme (uninsured child employment). Participants were asked to evaluate the case in the name of a hypothetical consumer, who is described in two different ways such as extrinsically religious (seeking for business network) and intrinsically religious (being a good follower of a religion). Following the scenario, we seek to examine the effect of religious orientation (extrinsically religious vs. intrinsically religious) of consumer on the punishing behavior in the case of corporate brand transgression at different severity levels (low vs. high).

Measures used in the study were adapted from previous studies as follows: corporate brand transgression perception (Hyman 1996), religious orientation (Vitell et al. 2006), and punishing behavior of consumer (Creyer and Ross 1997). It should be noted that religious orientation did not indicate a specific religion but rather motivation to follow religious rules. Furthermore, third person technique is used in the scenario due to the subject's sensitivity. Responses to the items measured with a five-point scale form (1) *strongly agree* to (5) *strongly disagree*. Scenario believability and attention checks were done at the end as well.

Results and Discussion

Item refinement, scale validation, and model testing stages of data analysis were done on the basis of 134 participants' answers. The sample composition was as 56% female, 76.9% 26–35 years old and 11.2% unemployed students. Exploratory factor analysis (EFA) indicated expected construct structures and all constructs demonstrated high reliabilities (all $\alpha > .70$) (Nunnally 1978) as follows: corporate brand transgression ($\alpha_{trans} = 0.88$), religious orientation ($\alpha_{relorient} = .88$), and punishing behavior ($\alpha_{punish} = .93$). Manipulation check confirmed that corporate brand transgression ($M_H = 4.39$ vs. $M_M = 2.36$), ($F = 11.85$, $p < .05$) and religious orientation ($M_E = 4.27$ vs. $M_I = 2.62$), ($F = 16.12$, $p < .05$) were successfully manipulated in the scenarios. Furthermore, scenario believability across conditions was significantly below the critical value of 3 ($M = 2.10$, $p < .05$).

Following the manipulation check, a 2×2 factorial design was used to analyze the effect of brand transgression and religious orientation on consumer's punishing behavior. ANOVA results indicated that religious orientation had main effect on consumer punishing behavior ($F = 35.95$, $p < .05$), whereas brand transgression had no main effect on consumer punishing behavior ($F = 1.49$, $p > .05$). Brand transgression $\times$ religious orientation interaction was also not significant ($F = 2.10$, $p > .05$).

Experimental study results highlight the importance of consumer religious orientation rather than severity level of brand transgression, as an indicator of consumer punishing behavior. Interestingly, the results also indicate that intrinsically religious individuals were less willing to punish the corporate transgressor rather than extrinsically oriented, regardless of the severity level of brand transgression. More specifically, punishing behavior diminishes under conditions of low transgression vs. intrinsic religious orientation ($M_{PLI} = 2.87$) and high transgression vs. intrinsic religious orientation ($M_{PHI} = 2.37$), and accelerates under conditions of low transgression vs. extrinsic religious orientation ($M_{PLE} = 3.73$) and high transgression vs. extrinsic religious orientation ($M_{PHE} = 3.78$).

Theoretically, strong reaction was expected from intrinsically religious oriented consumers in terms of punishing behavior since ethical values would be more embedded in their value systems due to their religious orientation. Contrary to this expectation and Muhamad's study (2009), the findings indicate that extrinsically religious individuals overreact to corporate brand transgressions more than intrinsically religious ones. This result may imply that intrinsically religious consumers are mild-mannered and more forgiving, whereas extrinsically religious consumers are more though minded and less tolerant in any case of brand transgression. The extrinsically religious consumer may perceive brand transgressions as a sign of increasing possibility of explicit rules' violations, hence consider that his/her material gain from the relationship with a company will be directly influenced in the future. Moreover, since extrinsically religious individuals are concerned with instrumental gains, they may consider a brand transgression situation as another opportunity to show off their religiousness. However, since intrinsically religious people are not focused on any profane expectations when exercising religion, this underlying value may spill over external world relationships and hence manifest itself as more tolerance towards the faults of companies.

Results also show that while the transgression severity increases, intrinsically religious consumers' punishing behavior decreases. As in the Fear Appeal Theory, there is a curvilinear relationship between transgression intensity and change in consumer behavior (Williams 2012). If it reaches a sensitive threshold that is too high for that person, the consumer may engage in denial or avoidance.

Conclusion

Based on our study's findings, the following could be recommended to brands those got involved in transgressions in countries like Turkey in which an increasing conservative population exits. Although, all brands should abide with the universal principle of avoiding intentional unethical violations, when they do so, they should not only recover the unwanted consequence but also find a way of ensuring less tolerant parties' (extrinsic religious individuals) forgiveness as to prevent further damage on their brands. As the findings imply that since extrinsic religious people are looking for an excuse to punish unethical brands and tend not to forget about the issue, rather than overstating the recovery about the specific incident, they should act beyond the expectations and invest in another immediate good cause that would trigger appreciation of both groups. Especially, if the favorable interest of intrinsically religious people is ensured, it would be expected to be followed by extrinsically religious ones.

References available upon request.

A Distinct Impact of the Brand Management System on Brand Performance Across Service and Product Business Sectors

Mathieu Dunes

Introduction

Brand management efficiency is a key issue for CEOs and the need to better understand how marketing capabilities and organizational structure influence business performance is among the 2014–2016 MSI research priorities.[1] Even if brand managers are essential for strategic decisions and are expected to play an increasing role within the organization in the coming years,[2] CEOs do not have a clear view of brand management actions and activities, and of their contribution to shareholder value (Madden et al. 2006). Verhoef and Leeflang (2009) indicate that the status of the marketing department within the firm depends upon its ability to demonstrate how it contributes to the firms' return on investment. Brand management is both valued and criticized and there is a need to better understand the brand management system and assess its impact on performance.

Our purpose with this chapter is to determine through a BMS grounded-in-practice scale, brand management practices impact on subjective and objective measures of brand performance, considering business sectors specificities (product vs. service sectors). It can be informative for brand and top managers in decision taking and brand management legitimacy.

---

[1] For instance, we address a response concerning the following issue : « *How should ROI of internal marketing activities be measured* »

[2] A TNS-Sofres survey predicts an increasing role of marketing and communication directors in the following years; *Les Nouveaux métiers du Marketing et de la Communication* (TNS Sofres, oct 2011)

M. Dunes (✉)
University Paris Dauphine, Paris, France
e-mail: mathieudunes@gmail.com

© Academy of Marketing Science 2016
L. Petruzzellis, R.S. Winer (eds.), *Rediscovering the Essentiality of Marketing*,
Developments in Marketing Science: Proceedings of the Academy of Marketing
Science, DOI 10.1007/978-3-319-29877-1_131

Literature Review: BMS, Brand Performance, Consideration for Business Sectors

Performance is associated to the brand manager role (Low and Fullerton 1994). Measures of performance are generally focused on subjective measures. In most studies, subjective measures are chosen to overcome difficulties associated with obtaining, what could be described as, competitively sensitive information (Caruana et al. 1998). Furthermore, measuring an organization's performance using objective financial data can be difficult, as the information may either be unavailable, unreliable or difficult to validate with external sources (Sapienza et al. 1998). However, it can be interesting to integrate objective associated with subjective measures. For instance, Mizik and Jacobson (2008) assert a positive impact between subjective measures of brand equity using the Brand Asset Valuator model of Young and Rubicam, and return on asset (ROA). In the brand management literature, no studies introduce relationships between subjective and objective financial measures, while it can be an advantage to confront brand managers assertions to accountant results.

H1: the subjective brand performance has a positive impact on objective financial performance

The definition of the Brand Management System (BMS) has evolved during the last decades. A first conception restricted the BMS to the definition of the brand manager's responsibilities in an organizational structure: "*a type of organizational structure in which brands or products are assigned to managers who are responsible for their performance*" (Low and Fullerton 1994). Later on, the understanding of the brand manager interface role (Luck 1969) with the environment, leads to a new definition, focused on the brand management information system (Katsanis 1999). The last step is the cultural approach introduced with Lee et al. (2008). The BMS can be defined "*as a set of any systems, organizational structure, or culture of a firm supporting brand building activities*" (p. 849). It can be conceptualized "*as the degree of infrastructure building activities with respect to brand-related (1) organization and culture, (2) knowledge and education, and (3) implementation and performance evaluation systems*" (p. 851). With this cultural approach, they find a positive impact of the BMS on subjective measures of brand performance (customer and financial performance). Following this result, we consider that:

H2: The Brand Management System has a positive impact on subjective brand performance

Recently, in a study based on a Spanish sample of knowledge-intensive service firms, Santos-Vijande et al. (2013) confirm the previous analysis of Lee et al. (2008) using subjective measures of brand performance (sales, market share, profit growth). While no research focused on the BMS integrate objective measures of brand performance, one could imagine that this impact could be positive on objective measures of performance.

H3: The Brand Management system has a positive impact on objective financial performance

Business sectors shall definitely be taken into account while studying the impact of the BMS on brand performance. Environmental variables are said to have an effect on brand manager's activities (Katsanis 1999). Historically, studies show brand managers practices differences comparing consumer and industrial goods sectors (Hise and Kelly 1979; Murphy and Gorchels 1996). Santos-Vijande et al. (2013) determine a positive impact of the BMS on the subjective brand performance focusing on service activities (knowledge intensive business service firms). Besides, Singh Mann and Kaur (2013) comparing branding strategies across service and FMCG insist on the lack of comparison between fast-moving consumer goods (FMCG), services and activities. This comparison is particularly interesting to understand why Santos-Vijande et al. (2013) eliminate the implementation dimension of their BMS scale while the brand management literature asserts its importance (Lee et al. 2008).

H4: Type of business activities (product vs. service) has a moderating effect on the relationship between the BMS and subjective brand performance.

Methodology

To collect data, a quantitative survey was administered during 3 months (from April to June 2013). Brand managers were prospected via social networks (LinkedIn, Viadeo) in addition to professional contacts (former students associations, Marketing Directors association of ADETEM). Pursuing a qualitative work (Dunes and Pras 2013), we prospected respondents on a quota selection with five business sectors. We obtain a good distribution between business sectors (61 brand managers for the Cosmetics sector; 61 for the convenience goods sector; 58 for the industrial sector; 59 for the media sector; 61 for the bank/insurance) and responsibilities levels (CEO and Marketing directors 48 %, product managers 52 %). To sum up, 300 brand managers have completed the survey (response rate of 24.42 %), with 120 brand managers from service activities (bank/insurance; media sectors) and 180 brand managers from product sectors (convenience goods, cosmetics, industrial sectors).

To operationalize *the BMS scale*, a qualitative research phase went before this study. In-depth semi-structured interviews were conducted with 15 marketing directors following the *"strategy as practice"* theory. It leads to a quantitative survey administered in a pretest phase with 50 brand managers to reduce the survey length. The final survey administered to 300 brand managers indicates the relevance of the three-dimensional scale emerged from the qualitative survey. On the confirmatory factor analysis on AMOS, the Jöreskog's rho value is equal to .876 for the global scale. For the components, the rhos are also acceptable for brand management implementation (rho BM IMPLEM = .65) and brand management role in the hierarchy (rho BM HR = .71), and slightly below .6 for brand identity and values use in the

organizational culture (rho BM CULTURE = .55), but the reliability of this component is noticeably improved when we focus on the brand identity protection items for
this dimension (rho = .73). Since the reliability varies between business sectors (for
example, cosmetics vs. industry) and that "sharing brand values" (VAP items) makes
sense conceptually on this BM CULTURE dimension, we shall keep all the items to
assess the model fit. Using the maximum likelihood method, the three-dimensional
measurement model demonstrates satisfactory level of fits (GFI = .90; AGFI = .86;
RMSEA = .076; Chi-square = 2.76, $p < .001$). Convergent validity is assumed when
all standardized factor loadings are greater than .5 (McCallum 1995), which is
asserted here (ρvc = .81; .86; .84, respectively, for BMIMPLEM, BMHR, and
BMCULTURE). Discriminant validity was also obtained. For each couple of constructs, the square of the correlation between these two constructs was smaller than
their variance extracted. Finally, the variance extracted estimates were greater than
the square of the correlations for each pair of dimensions (the correlations between
BMIMPLEM and BMCULTURE = .458; between BMIMPLEM and BMHR = .458;
between BMHR and BM CULTURE = .521). Compared to Santos-Vijande et al.
(2013) study, we can notice that the brand management implementation (BM
IMPLEM) is introduced.

For the conceptualization of the *subjective brand performance scale*, we used and
adapted the organizational performance scale of Homburg and Plfesser (2000). They
distinguish the subjective market and financial performance. To reduce response
bias, we added assertions on financial measures of performance. Items were only
related to the average business sectors performance, to face with respondent inexpe-
rience on financial results. Moreover, reputation items were added to integrate service sector specificities (Harris et al. 2004). We proceed to an exploratory and
confirmatory factorial analysis on AMOS with the 300 brand managers and obtain
four components of the subjective brand performance: customer performance
(PERFCLIENT); market performance (PERFCCIALE); profitability (PROFIT); and
productivity (RDMT). On the confirmatory factor analysis on AMOS, the Jöreskog's
rho value is equal to .840 for the global scale. For each components, the rhos are also
acceptable (rho PERF CLIENT = .812; rho PERF CCIALE = .826; rho RDMT = .666;
rho PERF PROFIT = .780). Using the maximum likelihood method, the four-dimen-
sional measurement model demonstrates satisfactory level of fits (GFI = .933;
AGFI = .89; RMSEA = .076; Chi-square = 2.71, $p < .001$). Convergent validity, under
the strict condition of McCallum is assumed (ρvc = .673; .806; .660, respectively, for
PERF CLIENT, PERFCCIALE, and PROFIT). Only the RDMT component has a
value below the condition (ρvc = .332). This result shall be due to the lack of items
for this dimension (2 items). However, we keep this dimension. Discriminant
validity is also obtained. For each couple of constructs, the square of the correlation
between these two constructs was smaller than their variance extracted. The variance
of extracted estimates were greater than the square of the correlations for each
pair of dimensions (for example, the correlation between PERFCLIENT and
RDMT = .057 is smaller than the ρvc for RDMT = .332).

Objective measures of performance completed this research using the financial
database of DIANE. This database was chosen due to information availability and

representation for the sample. Among the accountant criteria, we have used the objective data of ROI, ROA, ROS, and ROE (return on investment, asset, share, equity). Measures were normally distributed with the Z-score. We replaced 37 missing and/or excessive values among the data by an average value on the dataset. Then, we computed a factorial score (ROAEIS). After a descriptive analysis, two outliers were finally withdrawn, due to a statistical scattering with the global trend. For the following results, all the hypotheses are tested with a final sample of 298 brand managers.

Results and Discussion

To test the relationship between constructs, we adopted the *path analysis* on AMOS. This choice is due to the comparison of subjective and objective measures. Subjective measures of the constructs are reflexive whereas objective measures of financial performance are formative. Factorial scores were computed on SPSS using the constructs from the confirmatory analysis. To test relationships and to assure us that data were normally distributed, we used the bootstrap procedure (2000 bootstrap computation). We obtained a good fit for the construct model (GFI = .998; AGFI = .989; NFI = .993; RMR = .013; RMSEA = .000; Chi-square = 1.27, $p = .53 > .05$).

An interesting aspect is to analyze the mediator effect of the subjective brand performance. We use Baron and Keny procedure (1986). Following the first condition, a positive and significant relationship between the BMS and the subjective brand performance ($\beta_1 = .361$, $t = 6.679$ with *bootstrap*, $p < .001$). The more, brand management practices are developed in the organization (brand management implementation, brand organizational culture, brand management role in the hierarchical relationships), better is the subjective brand performance considering measures based on customer, market, and financial components. Hence, *H2 is supported*. The second condition compares the relationship between subjective brand performance and objective financial performance. The relationship is significant; subjective performance is related to objective performance ($\beta_3 = .243$, $t = 4.316$ with *bootstrap*, $p < .001$). *H1 is confirmed*. The last condition is not supported. There is no significant relationship between the BMS and objective financial performance ($\beta_2 = -.029$, $t = -.503$ with *bootstrap*, $p = .615 > .001$). Practices of brand managers have no effect on objective financial performance. *H3 is not supported*. Thus, according to Baron and Keny (1986), the subjective brand performance is a complete mediator effect since the last condition is not granted. It means that the direct impact of the BMS on financial objective performance disappears when is introduced subjective brand performance (Chumpitaz-Caceres and Vanhamme 2003). This result is a new theoretical contribution. Moreover, we can notice that the structural model explains 13 % of the variance for the subjective brand performance, 6 % for the objective financial performance. This last result is low, but must not be neglected since we compare different kind of measures.

Considering business sectors specificities, we use the structural path model with the chain effect BMS-pmarque-ROAEIS. We followed the Dabholkar and Bagozzi (2002) procedure to compare groups, replacing low/high value of a moderating effect with modalities of the nominal variable called "business activities type." We distinguish two groups: the first group gathers product-oriented activities ($N_1 = 180$) and the second group brand managers from the bank/insurance and media sectors ($N_2 = 118$). The multigroup analysis was conduct with 2000 bootstraps.

The Chi-square difference is significant at 5 % level if we focus on model C versus model D ($\Delta\chi^2 = 6.518$; $p = .038 < .05$) following the Dabholkar and Bagozzi (2002) procedure to analyze the presence of moderating effect. The difference is caused by factor loadings across groups. There is a moderating effect of the "business activities type" on the relationship in the structural model. The free model used for groups comparison (Model C) presents a very good fit (GFI = .999; AGFI = .996; RMR = .010; RMSEA = .000; Chi-square = .322, $p = .851 > .05$). Comparing groups, we observe a significant and positive relationship between the BMS and subjective brand performance for brand managers belonging to product sectors ($\beta = .246$, $p < .001$), whereas there is no relationship in the case of brand managers from the service sectors ($\beta = .106$, $t = 6.679$, $p = .289 > .05$). We conclude that the impact of the BMS on subjective brand performance is stronger for product-oriented sectors compared to service-oriented sectors. Moreover, the square multiple correlation is higher for product activities with the subjective brand performance than service activities. *Hypothesis H4 is supported.*

To sum up these results, the BMS has an indirect impact on objective financial performance through the mediator effect of the subjective brand performance. This new result is interesting since no survey introduce objective measures to study the impact of brand management practices. Besides, the BMS scale includes the brand management implementation dimension while Santos Vijande et al. (2013) reject this aspect considering service sector specificities. This leads us to a business sector comparison. The moderating effect of "business activities type" is confirmed, which suggests that the use and impact of brand management practices is contingent to environmental variables. It could be interesting to deepen this relationship considering "sector by sector" effects and subdimensions of BMS valued in each sector.

References available upon request.

The Effect of Negative Electronic Word of Mouth on Switching Intentions: A Social Interaction Utility Approach

Carla Ruiz-Mafé, Joaquin Aldas-Manzano, and Cleopatra Veloutsou

Abstract The aim of this chapter is to gain insight on negative eWom about brands from a sender perspective, taking into account individual and social factors. We develop and test a conceptual model using a sample of 302 Spanish active users of social networks who have complained online in 2013. This study provides several theoretical implications. Firstly, using the Social Interaction Utility framework, we analyse the influence of social motivations on negative eWom. Our results show that social motivations are the primary antecedents leading consumers to communicate their negative experiences to other consumers. Successful network sites should identify the effect of social motivations and manage the needs of community members. Secondly, we extend academic literature on the influence of eWom on the behaviour of its receivers by focusing on the sender perspective. This study confirms that negative eWom derives value to the brands by directly impacting on consumer's switching intentions.

Keywords Electronic word of mouth • Social motivations • Switching intentions

C. Ruiz-Mafé (✉) • J. Aldas-Manzano
University of Valencia, Valencia, Spain
e-mail: Carla.ruiz@uv.es; joaquin.aldas@uv.es

C. Veloutsou
University of Glasgow, Glasgow, UK
e-mail: Cleopatra.veloutsou@glasgow.ac.uk

© Academy of Marketing Science 2016
L. Petruzzellis, R.S. Winer (eds.), *Rediscovering the Essentiality of Marketing*,
Developments in Marketing Science: Proceedings of the Academy of Marketing
Science, DOI 10.1007/978-3-319-29877-1_132

Introduction

Most of the existing research in electronic word of mouth (eWOM) is focusing in the exchange of positive comments about products and brands (Casalo et al. 2010; Jeong and Jang 2011; Tsao and Hsie 2012). However, next to sharing positive experiences, more and more consumers use the online medium to distribute unfavourable experiences. The *negative electronic word of mouth (negative eWOM)* can be defined as any negative statement made by actual, or former consumers about a brand, which is available to a multitude of people and institutions via social network sites (Hennig-Thurau et al. 2004).

The aim of this chapter is to gain insight on negative eWom about brands from a sender perspective, taking into account individual and social factors. This chapter intends to make three specific contributions. Firstly, we focus on the sender perspective. Most of previous research analyses the impact of negative eWOM on the receiver, leaving negative e-Wom behaviour of the sender unaddressed (Lee et al. 2012; Sparks et al. 2012). Secondly, it analyses the impact of the negative eWom on switching intentions. eWom is often the major reason for brand non-choice and can decrease the revenues of firms, therefore, more research on how negative eWom contributes to this influence is openly called for (Verhagen et al. 2013; To and Ho 2014). Thirdly, we analyse the influence of social motivations on negative eWom. We try to overcome a limitation of previous research on social media that have only focused on individuals' employment of the technology (i.e., using Technology Acceptance Model), overlooking other factors inherent to eWom that can be related to the individual's behaviour such as social motivations.

Literature Review and Research Hypotheses

Negative e-WOM and Switching Behaviour

Prior research shows the impact of eWOM generated in different platforms on purchase intention (Chan and Ngai 2011; Verhagen et al. 2013). The rationale for this behaviour can be found in cognitive dissonance theory. This suggests that consumers will avoid situations in which beliefs about a behaviour (complaining online) are inconsistent with other (repatronage intentions) as this will lead to uncomfortable feelings and inner tension. In eWOM settings, consumers openly express their negative feelings. Therefore, we propose that a consumer who has distributed negative eWOM about a brand will stick to this position and most likely will interrupt his/her relationship with this brand.

H1. Negative eWOM positively influences switching intentions.

Social Motivations

According to the Social Interaction Utility framework (Balasubramanian and Mahajan 2001), different kinds of utilities are derived by consumers from their communicative behaviour in an online community, resulting in a total social interaction utility (p. 126). We propose that social motivations represent the individual's perception of how his/her actions are viewed by others and the effects of his/her behaviour on general welfare. They capture the individual's desire to exchange information, maintain ongoing relationships with others, and establish relational bonds (Bock et al. 2005). Based on the relevant literature (e.g., Algesheimer et al. 2005; Hennig-Thurau 2004), we identify three major social motivations to negative eWom: (1) venting negative feelings, (2) concern by other consumers and (3) community identification.

Venting negative feelings is defined as the desire to share with other members of the community negative emotions that are experienced as a part of an unsatisfactory consumption experience. Balance theory suggests individuals will strive to restore equilibrium after their originally balanced state has become unbalanced (Heider 1946, 1958; Newcomb 1953). Therefore, if the source of imbalance comes from a strong negative consumption experience, balance can be restored by writing a comment on an opinion platform. Sharing a negative consumption experience through the publication of online comments can serve to lessen the frustration and reduce the anxiety associated with the brand experience (Sundaram et al. 1998). Therefore,

H2. Consumers' desire of venting negative feelings positively influences negative eWom

Concern for other consumers. According to Engel et al. (1993, p. 158), engaging in negative Ewom is not something people do only for themselves, it may also be initiated by the motivation to inform others, a desire to help others in their purchase decisions or to save them from negative experiences. This concern for other consumers motive is closely related to the concept of altruism (or prosocial behaviour) (e.g., Carman 1992; Price, et. al. 1995). Consumers who are concerned about community members try to add value, providing reviews and commentaries on products of interest to other consumers (Balasubramanian and Mahajan 2001). Research has found that individuals' altruistic motivation to help other consumers influences their engagement in eWom communication (Kwon and Wen 2010; Hsu and Lin 2008). Hence, we propose that,

H3. Consumers' concern for other consumers positively influences negative eWom

Community identification. According to Social Identity Theory, a sense of community refers to a person's belief that he or she is an integral part of a community or social group (Algesheimer et al. 2005 and Koh and Kim 2004). It reflects a perception of similarity and interdependency with others, which results in a higher willingness to maintain a relationship with other members of the community (Sarason 1974). Previous research found that individuals with higher community identification perceive more affiliation to the group and greater social utilities from their interactions, so that they feel greater emotional connections and are more motivated to share their experiences (Qu and Lee 2011; Kim et al. 2009; Hsu and Lin 2008). Consequently,

H4. Community identification motivation positively influences negative eWom

Methodology

Data was collected in May–June 2014 using a sample of 302 Spanish active users of social networks who have complained online in the past year. A questionnaire was drafted using existing scales and pilot tested with 25 individuals with previous experience writing negative reviews online and certain revisions were made. In the final instrument, Community identification was measured with four items adapted from Lee et al. (2011), Venting negative feelings with three items adapted from Henning-Thurau et al. (2004), Concern by other consumers with four items adapted from Henning-Thurau et al. (2004), Negative eWOM with three items adapted from Bougie et al. (2003) and Switching intentions with three items adapted from Putrevu and Lord (1994). All the variables were measured using 7-point Likert scales ("strongly agree-strongly disagree"). We collected data in a University campus located in an eastern Spanish city. We randomly selected five classes and delivered 320 questionnaires. We asked the students to fill in the questionnaires based on a brand with which they have had a bad experience, obtaining 302 valid questionnaires. Out of the total sample, 45.3% were men and 54.7%, women. A large percentage of respondents were 20–24 years old (40.1%) followed by users younger than 20 years old (23.1%), and by users of 24–30 (18%), some of them being postgraduate students (23%) and an average or higher than average income (34.4% and 39.4%, respectively). All of them are social media active users with 90% of them being online at least between 1 and 2 h every day. 56% have complained online several times in the last year (2013). The brands the respondents have complained of are mainly tourist accommodation services (33%).

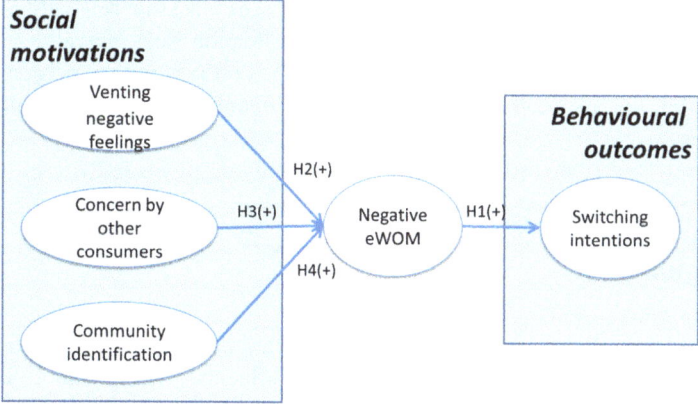

Fig. 1 Conceptual model

Results

Measurement model was evaluated in terms of reliability, convergent and discriminant validity obtaining satisfactory results. The proposed conceptual model was tested (Fig. 1) using structural equation modelling with EQS 6.2 software (Bentler 1995). The results indicate a good fit of the data to our conceptual model (S-Bχ2 = 278.04, df = 12, $p < .01$; RMSEA (90% CI) = .07 (.06;0.08); NFI = .92; TLI = .94; CFI = .95). Our model confirms that negative eWom has a direct and positive effect on consumer's switching intentions (H1; $\beta = .77$; $p < .01$). This result is consistent with previous research (Godes and Mayzlin 2004; Gruen et al. 2006). We demonstrate that this relationship also holds in an online context when we focus on the sender's perspective.

Regarding negative eWom antecedents, although community identification has not a significant effect on negative eWom (H4; $\beta = .11$; $p > .05$), concern by other consumers (H3; $\beta = .26$; $p < .01$) and venting negative feelings (H2; $\beta = .32$; $p < .01$) are clear drivers of negative eWom. Therefore, when consumers are confronted with negative consumption experiences with a brand, this elicits their desire of venting negative feelings towards the brand, which drives them to share openly their negative experiences online. Research has shown that social motivations are substantial to enhance consumer participation on SNS (Chang and Zhu 2011; Xiang and Gretzel 2010). Our results are also consistent with findings by Zeelenberg and Pieters (2004) and Nyer (1997) that consumers use eWom as a venting mechanism. Thus, when dissatisfied consumers participate online with the objective to help other community members, they will be more inclined to express negatively about a brand than if they do it just for themselves (i.e., seeking self-enhancement). Contrary to our expectations, community identification does not affect negative Ewom. This result can be explained because some consumers may perceive online communities not to be the right medium for openly distributing feed-back to companies.

Conclusion

This study provides several theoretical implications. Firstly, using the Social Interaction Utility framework, we analyse the influence of social motivations on negative eWom. Our findings underline the relevance of social motivations as recognized by Henning-Thurau et al. (2004). Social network sites allow consumers to exchange information peer-to-peer and provide important social utilities. These utilities motivate consumers' engagement on e-Wom and can be considered as fundamental factors to study their behaviour. Our results show that social motivations are the primary antecedents leading consumers to communicate their negative experiences to other consumers. Successful network sites should identify the effect of social motivations and manage the needs of community members. Secondly, we extend academic literature on the influence of eWom on the behaviour of its receivers by focusing on the sender perspective. The proposed model rooted in self-perception and dissonance theory demonstrates that negative eWom is indicative for the intended switching behaviour of the sender of these messages. Therefore, this study confirms that negative eWom derives value to the brands by directly impacting on consumer's switching intentions.

We recommend companies use customer centred teams to resolve problems. This would result in fewer negative messages online. Companies also should try to engage in communication with consumers who recently expressed themselves negatively in order to help them to restore their balance. Moreover, companies should try to detect altruistic consumers and to focus their efforts on solving the problems that triggered the disclosure of negative responses among this group.

This study has been subject to a few limitations. Despite students are heavy-users of online platforms, where to engage in complaining behaviour, alternative sample groups might be used to further test the robustness of our findings. We examined a limited set of variables as predictors of negative eWom communication. Following the consumer–brand relationship literature (Veloutsou 2007; Oliver 1980; Zeithlam et al. 1996) other relevant variables such as brand reputation and satisfaction may have influenced sender's complaining behaviour. Adding such variables could represent another step in the exploration of this research area.

References are available upon request.

Acknowledgment This work was supported by the Ministry of Economy (Spain) under Grant ECO2014-53837R.

Towards an Enhanced Model for Customer Patronage: A Structured Abstract

Irini Rigopoulou and John Kehagias

Introduction

Understanding brand equity dimensions and antecedents enables managers to build strategies that strengthen brand–customer relationships. However, prior research has dealt with the effect of brand equity on purchase intention and patronage in such a manner that allows for further contributions (Cobb-Walgren et al. 1995; Veloutsou et al. 2013).

The objective of this study is to develop an enhanced model of customer patronage centered on Keller's customer-based brand equity building blocks by incorporating personal traits like self-construal, as well as other individual consciousness-related drivers. The chapter evaluates the model proposed by Keller in the context of the gap between intention and actual behavior, and thus sheds light on the complex customer–brand relationships. Using Keller's brand resonance pyramid model as its basis, the study contributes to the existing literature by answering three research questions. These questions refer to the impact of each of the customer-based brand equity blocks on patronage, the moderating role of self-schema, and the leverage of other individual factors like customer-consciousness, citizen-consciousness, and crisis-management consciousness on the customer–brand relationship. The study was designed as part of a multilevel study that will take the findings further in terms of reliability and applicability.

I. Rigopoulou (✉)
Athens University of Economics and Business, Athens, Greece
e-mail: Erigop@Aueb.Gr

J. Kehagias
Hellenic Open University, Patras, Greece
e-mail: Jkehagias@Eap.Gr

© Academy of Marketing Science 2016
L. Petruzzellis, R.S. Winer (eds.), *Rediscovering the Essentiality of Marketing*,
Developments in Marketing Science: Proceedings of the Academy of Marketing
Science, DOI 10.1007/978-3-319-29877-1_133

Background

Brand equity as a market-based indicator of brands as company assets (Davis 2000; Ambler 2003) provides a reliable reading of marketing performance (Ambler 2003). The customer-based brand equity pyramid, proposed by Keller (2001) and by now established by 738 citations (400 in the last 4 years), is based on the premise that the concept of customer-based brand equity (CBBE) is the "differential effect of brand knowledge on customer response to the marketing of the brand" (Keller 1993, p. 2).

As Keller argues in order to build strong brands, marketers should give emphasis on four steps: identity establishment, brand meaning creation, positive response elicitation, and brand relationship forge. These four strategic steps can be implemented by establishing six brand equity blocks, namely salience, performance, imagery, judgments, feelings, and resonance, and it is by enhancing these blocks that customers' intentions are transformed to patronage.

Apart from the brand equity blocks, the distinct self views were found to activate variations in customers' beliefs and perceptions. As Escalas and Bettman (2005, p. 387) argue, "...consumers use brands to create or communicate their Self-concept...." Similarly, Millan and Reynolds, (2011, p. 164) clarified Self-concept as "a distinctive configuration of traits, thoughts, feelings that regulate individual behaviour...."

Along this line, Schmitt (2011, p. 8) states that "... consumers have different levels of psychological engagement with brands because of different needs, motives, and goals...." These needs, motives and goals, being a central component of a person's identity, differ according to one's Self-construal, that is according to the way people perceive themselves to be linked (or not) with other people (Markus and Kitayama 1991). Self-construal has also been defined as a "constellation of thoughts, feelings, and actions concerning the relationship of the self to others and the self as distinct from others" (Singelis and Sharkey 1995, p. 624). The interaction of individuals' self-view (interdependent-independent) in the customer decision-making process has attracted research attention particularly by examining the moderating role of self-construal on a person's relationships (Kim and Johnson 2014).

In this domain, the research question that remains partly unanswered refers to whether one's self-construal as well as other personal traits have a mediating and moderating effect on the consumer's relationship with the brand, as it is reflected in the perceived value-indicator of brand equity. Since Broyles et al. 2009 recognize that the lack of the employment of potential moderators affects negatively the consistency, and thus the accuracy, of brand equity models, the need for empirically testing a model incorporating moderators and mediators becomes inescapable.

Last, self-consciousness, as a personal trait which refers to the propensity to direct one's attention to the self, is recognized as an additional self-concept parameter which has a crucial impact on making decisions or plans involving one's self, (Scheier and Carver 1985). The notion that consciousness of the self will exert a strong impact on a variety of behaviors, including the acquisition and consumption of products, has very early received further support (Fenigstein et al. 1975; Duval and Wicklund 1972). Along the same line, Escalas and Bettman (2005) claim that consumers' loyalty towards a brand increases as self-brand connection grows, which then helps to boost brand equity, whereas the self-brand connection is being affected mostly by the level of self-consciousness.

Again, the inclusion of the self-consciousness notion into strategic brand-related aspects remains mostly unexplored, thus calling for empirical investigation.

Methodology

In order to investigate the gap between intentions and actual behavior, the proposed model that was developed and empirically tested incorporates Behavioral intention as the Independent Variable (IV) and Actual behavior as the Dependent one (DV). Self-construal factors and the Self-consciousness parameter are included as moderating parameters and the Brand equity building blocks as the mediating factor.

The methodological procedure followed involved first asking respondents to recall a top-of-mind brand, irrespective of product category, and to fill the brand in the (self-reported) questionnaire. Capturing the brand awareness of the respondents was deemed necessary since, as Christodoulides and de Chernatony (2010, p. 47) claim: "…awareness and associations are important components of consumer-based brand equity."

In relation to Behavioral intention, respondents were asked how likely they considered to use the chosen brand, whereas Patronage was measured by asking three questions about loyalty, intensity of usage, and frequency of buying.

Coming to brand equity measurement, the relevant literature contains a plurality of direct and indirect measurement scales. Since indirect approaches allow for a more holistic view of the brand (Christodoulides and de Chernatony 2010), the widely used measure of Brand-building blocks, borrowed from the customer-based Brand Equity Pyramid (Keller 2001), was chosen, as it utilizes both associations and behavioral components.

The Independence–Interdependence factors of Self-construal were measured using Singelis's (1994) 24-item scale.

For Self-consciousness, we used one-item measures, covering three aspects of consciousness, customer, citizen, and crisis-handling consciousness (Fenigstein et al. 1975).

Since the particular empirical study is planned to be part of a broader multilevel study, the initial sample chosen comprised of young consumers/buying decision makers as verified by a filter question. A total of 172 reliable questionnaires were put for statistical analysis. Participants indicated their agreement with each statement/item, using 7-point scales ranging from 1=strongly disagree to 7=strongly agree. (The means, standard deviations are available if needed).

For the statistical analysis, Macro command (INDIRECT), proposed by Preacher and Hayes (2008), as well as linear regression analysis were utilized. Reliability analysis and confirmatory factor analysis (CFA) were performed before testing the research questions. Refinements have been made in order Cronbach's alpha coefficients to exceed the threshold of .70, and the CFA coefficients to have sufficient loadings. The structure of the measure was further examined by means of principal components analysis. Four Brand Equity Factors were extracted, explaining 69.49 % of the data variance (with min factor loadings .70). Similarly for Self-construal, four factors were extracted by the screen plot.

Results and Discussion

The four brand equity factors that have been finally included in the model are in line with the four brand equity categories that are proposed by Veloutsou et al. (2013) to be used when defining brand equity, namely consumers' understanding of brand characteristics, consumers' brand evaluation, consumers' affective response towards the brand, and consumers' behavior towards the brand.

More specifically, as the statistical analysis has shown the effect of behavioral intention is transmitted to actual patronage through customer-based Brand Equity blocks (herewith Factors), particularly through FACTOR 2: "Uniqueness, Salience," while Cronbach alpha scores for FACTOR1: "Community, engagement, attachment" a= .899 (nine items), for FACTOR2: "Uniqueness, salience", a= .906 (seven items), for FACTOR3: "functionality, quality judgment", a= .827 (five items) and for FACTOR4: "feelings (sense of..)," a= .829 (four items), thus quite satisfactorily.

As regard to the Independent Variable to Mediators (a paths) Coeff scored (.1727) for FAC1 (with p=.1723 (>.5)), (.3935) for FAC2 (p=.0014, (< .005)), (.5548) for FAC3 (p=.0000, (<.05)) and (.0664) for FAC4 (p=.6061 (> .5)).

Similarly, as regard the Direct Effects of Mediators on DV (b paths), Coeff scored (.1871) for FAC1 (p=.0138, <.5), at (.7179) for FAC2 (p=.0000), (.2098) for FAC3 (p=.0162, <.5), and (.1247) for FAC4 (p=.0877, <.5).

So, the Total Effect of IV on DV (c path) is Coeff (.4918); se (.1201); t (4.0961) and p=.0001

while the Direct Effect of IV on DV (c' path) is Coeff (.0522); se (.1059), t (.4936) and p=.6230.

The Model Summary for the DV Model is described below:

R-sq	Adj R-sq	F	df1	df2	p
.6109	.5863	24.8085	5.0000	79.0000	.0000

Regarding the interaction effects that the personal related constructs have on customer–brand relationship, the model is proven valid (F [9.371], p .003<.01). The Adj. $R2$ value was .407 and Self-consciousness is shown to have a significant moderation effect (β=.184, p=.005). However all Self-construal factors appeared to have no effect (all four p values were higher than the expected level).

Conclusion and Implications for Theory and Practice

Summarizing the conclusions, it is suggested that, in their effort to minimize the gap between customers' intentions and actual behavior, Marketing Managers should bear in mind that the Brand equity resonance pyramid can be used as an effective strategic tool. Functional aspects of brand equity, like "functionality," "quality judgments," as well as other, more "symbolic" aspects, like "feelings," the sense of "uniqueness," the sense of "attachment" and "engagement," emerge as parameters that a brand management team can utilize for leveraging their brands. This is in line with empirical studies from several fields (Anselmsson and Anders 2013), recommending that managers should have a more balanced view, as they put more effort into measuring the emotional components of their brands. On the other hand, it seems that product quality perceptions can only partly explain consumers' preferences and willingness to pay premium prices and this does not apply for food brands only (Anselmsson et al. 2007; Sethuraman 2003; Tikkanen and Vääriskoski 2010). Moreover, quality judgments are strongly influenced by non-quality related perceptions (Méndez et al. 2011; Vranešević and Stancec 2003). This more holistic perspective is in line with the brand equity resonance pyramid and the factors that the particular study brings out. Moreover, managers should also keep in mind that the Self-construal element does not leverage the intention-behavior gap, and this can be partly explained by the fact that product primary features become more important when the psychological distance is greater, and secondary features become more important when the psychological distance is more proximate (Trope and Liberman 2000). Therefore, a strategic priority could be first, to eliminate the psychological distance and then to leverage self-construal aspects, keeping in mind that Self-consciousness appears to do so. In conclusion, this particular study, although it is part of a broader multilevel investigation, contributes to the area of consumers' attention to self, in various loyalty conditions.

References available upon request.

Animosity, Affinity, and Purchase Intentions Among Ethnic Consumers

Alia El Banna, Nicolas Papadopoulos, Steven A. Murphy,
José Rojas-Méndez, and Michel Rod

Abstract This research examines the purchase intention effects of ethnic consumers' views toward "animosity" and "affinity" target countries against a "neutral" benchmark country. The findings show that "old country" views persist in ethnic consumers' new country, with very negative views of the animosity target and positive views of the affinity target, with views of the benchmark country being slightly positive. Implications and future research suggestions are discussed.

Keywords Affinity • Animosity • Product-country images • Ethnic consumers

Introduction

The role of country images in shaping consumer attitudes and behaviour toward products from various origins has been the subject of much research in international business, comprising well over 1000 publications since the 1960s (e.g., Bilkey and Nes 1982; Han 1989; Papadopoulos 2004; Schooler 1965). A product's "country image" may refer to where it is actually made ("made-in" or "country of origin") or, more broadly, to its Product-Country Image (PCI)—the term to be used here, which refers to any country with which a product is associated regardless of where it was made (e.g., a car made in Mexico but advertised as "engineered in Germany").

Research contributions in PCI have investigated various place-related correlates and predictors of consumer behaviour such as ethnocentric or nationalistic tendencies (Balabanis and Diamantopoulos 2004; Klein et al. 2006; Shimp and Sharma 1987), animosity toward a specific country(ies) (Heslop et al. 1998; Klein et al. 1998; Leong et al. 2008), cosmopolitanism and world-mindedness (Cleveland et al. 2009; Rawwas

A. El Banna (✉) • N. Papadopoulos • J. Rojas-Méndez • M. Rod
Carleton University, Ottawa, ON, Canada
e-mail: AliaElBanna@cmail.carleton.ca; nicolas.papadopoulos@carleton.ca; Jose.
RojasMendez@carleton.ca; Michel.Rod@carleton.ca

S.A. Murphy
Ryerson University, Toronto, ON, Canada
e-mail: murphy@ryerson.ca

© Academy of Marketing Science 2016
L. Petruzzellis, R.S. Winer (eds.), *Rediscovering the Essentiality of Marketing*,
Developments in Marketing Science: Proceedings of the Academy of Marketing
Science, DOI 10.1007/978-3-319-29877-1_134

et al. 1996), and affinity (Laroche et al. 2003; Oberecker et al. 2008; Papadopoulos et al. 2008; Oberecker and Diamantopoulos 2011). Some of these constructs denote positive feelings about places and their offerings, such as consumer affinity, cosmopolitanism, and world-mindedness, while negative feelings about places and their offerings are explained in terms of ethnocentrism and animosity.

Swift (1999) has noted that the more similar an individual's culture is to a specific country (cultural closeness), the more individuals tend to like this country (cultural affinity). Research further shows that consumers' attachment and affinity toward a certain country can directly impact their willingness to purchase products from the affinity country without much cognitive judgement involved (Papadopoulos et al. 2008; Vida and Reardon 2008). Studies show that consumers are willing to buy from an affinity country only because they share a positive affect toward it and emphasize the need to further investigate consumer's willingness to buy from affinity countries; for instance, Oberecker and Diamantopoulos (2011: 6) state that the ethnic background of consumers "might affect the choice of the affinity country because members of immigrant groups might harbour affinity for their country of origin." Even though "the purchase of ethnic products by emigrants is often motivated by feelings of affinity with the country from which they have emigrated" (Jaffe and Nebenzahl 2001: 79), a study of ethnic consumers and their ratings of products from ethnically linked countries found that French Canadians did not favour French over British products, suggesting that affinity with a parent country might have faded or been reshaped over time (Heslop et al. 1998). The same study showed that another construct, sub-cultural affinity, seemed to show significant influence on product evaluations to products originating from the home region.

Conversely to affinity, long-lasting negative feelings toward a specific country, i.e., animosity, can arise for many reasons, such as territorial and economic disputes, political disagreements, religious conflicts, and inter-ethnic factors (Riefler and Diamantopoulos 2007; Wood et al. 2008). Consumer animosity has been found to have a direct negative impact on willingness to buy (Klein et al. 1998; Leong et al. 2008; Papadopoulos et al. 2011). Research shows, however, that consumer animosity is not a driver of product judgements, and so anger toward a country does not necessarily imply negative judgements of its products (Klein 2002).

Notwithstanding advances in this area of research, several gaps remain. One is that the vast majority of studies in animosity has dealt with old instead of current enmities (e.g., China vs. Japan (Klein et al. 1998) and Holland vs. Germany (Nijssen and Douglas 2004), in which cases consumer views may differ substantively from those referring to contemporary conflicts. Furthermore, both animosity and affinity-focused research have not differentiated between the types of consumers who have formed the studies' samples—even though a strong case can be made that views may differ not only along traditional demographic factors, but also, and more importantly, across other characteristics such as consumer ethnicity. For instance, it may be assumed that native and long-time resident Dutch consumers may hold entirely different views of Germany compared to more recent immigrants to Holland from, for example, Indonesia, to whom the relevant theatre of the Second World War was entirely different.

Given the above, this study was designed to investigate potential long-lasting affinity and animosity directed at specific countries, and their possible effects on buyer behaviour, by ethnic consumers—specifically, those who live in a particular country but have either migrated there from their home country or were born there to immigrant parents. The fact that ethnic consumers may harbour feelings toward countries that are positively or negatively associated with their ethnic origin country, which will be referred to for facility as the "home" country, provides an opportunity to study the nature and strength of animosity and affinity in the PCI context.

Following this introduction, the paper reviews the theoretical underpinnings of consumer animosity and affinity, outlines the research methodology, presents the main results, and concludes with a discussion of implications, limitations, and directions for future research.

Literature Review and Hypotheses

Consumer Animosity

Some of the recent contributions to PCI research have become more focused on the study of the impacts of negative emotions toward countries on product evaluations (Ettenson and Klein 2005; Klein 2002; Klein et al. 1998; Nijssen and Douglas 2004; Papadopoulos et al. 2011; Phau and Chao 2008), as well as consumer reactions to "incidents that generate animosity" (Heslop et al. 2008: 355). Animosity, defined as the "remnants of antipathy related to previous or ongoing military, political or economic events" (Klein et al. 1998: 90), may arise for many reasons, such as territory and economic disputes, diplomatic disagreements, religious conflicts, and inter-ethnic factors (e.g., Wood et al. 2008). The construct differs from ethnocentrism, in that the latter refers to general beliefs about the superiority of one's own country's products, whereas animosity is country-specific (Wang 2005). Ethnocentric consumers may "… avoid buying products from any foreign country, [while] consumers possessing feelings of animosity may … refuse to purchase products coming from one specific foreign country" (Riefler and Diamantopoulos 2007: 88). Country-specific animosity may vary as a function of the country and may thus be of a more transient, situational nature as compared to consumer ethnocentrism (Lwin et al. 2010).

In addition, animosity comes in different forms. Research has examined the construct between sub-cultures (Hinck 2005; Rose et al. 2009; Shoham et al. 2006), as well as between nations (Klein et al. 1998; Leong et al. 2008) and nation dyads (Papadopoulos et al. 2011). Of particular interest to the present study, Jung et al. (2002) and Leong et al. (2008: 997) distinguished between "situational" animosity, which is "sparked by a particular episode" and "stable" animosity, which "tends to accumulate over time, evolving into a long-lasting hostility." Situational animosities are temporary and may be incident-specific, but over time may evolve into stable animosities, which are deeply rooted and based on historical perspectives (Wood et al. 2008; Leong et al. 2008).

As noted earlier, animosity has a negative influence on purchase behaviour, but not necessarily on product evaluations. On the other hand, over the longer term strong feelings of animosity may influence product judgements as well (e.g., Rose et al. 2009). Such country-specific feelings can last for long periods of time; examples include holocaust effects on Jewish consumers' willingness to buy German products (Podoshen 2009), Chinese consumers' refusal to buy Japanese products in spite of positive quality product perceptions (Klein 2002; Klein et al. 1998), and South Korea's ban on Japanese products that lasted more than 50 years after the end of WWII and was just removed in 2002 (Leong et al. 2008). Conversely, some studies show that animosity feelings can also be very, or somewhat, transient and situational (Amine et al. 2005; Lwin et al. 2010); examples include the changing public opinion of the British towards the Germans (Lwin et al. 2010) and the improvement of Australian consumers' view of France and French products after that country's nuclear testing in the South Pacific (Heslop et al. 2009). Moreover, Maher and Mady's (2010) longitudinal study noted that the intensity of animosity may decrease with time and even be replaced by positive feelings.

Consumer Affinity

Unlike research on consumer animosity, which, though not as extensive as that on ethnocentrism, does have a 15-year history and more than 35 publications to date, the subfield of consumer affinity is newer and studies in it are scarce. According to Oberecker et al. (2008: 26), consumer affinity is defined as "a feeling of liking, sympathy, and even attachment toward a specific foreign country … as a result of the consumer's direct personal experience and/or normative exposure that positively affects the consumer's decision making associated with products and services originating from the affinity country." In the study that first coined the term "affinity" in the international marketing context, Papadopoulos et al. (2008) studied affect towards culturally linked countries and concluded that the relationship between affect, on the one hand, and countries and their offerings, on the other, seems to be of higher importance and complexity than previously known. Oberecker and Diamantopoulos (2011) note that, due to the recency of the affinity construct to international marketing, its theoretical composition and dimensionality are yet to be explored.

The term "consumer affinity" in the international marketing literature is used to examine country-specific favourable attitudes towards foreign countries, unlike general positive attitudes arising from world-mindedness and xenophilia (Papadopoulos et al. 2012). Wood et al. (2008: 423) state that individuals may experience affinity towards nations "based on their perception (built on their direct and indirect experience) of those nation's companies and organizations, their citizen's lifestyle and well-being, the physical landscape and scenery of a country itself, its political and economic climate, its historical realities, its affiliation with higher causes and other attributes considered important." As indicated above in the definition of the construct (Oberecker et al. 2008), and similarly to the effects of animosity, affinity towards a country affects consumers' purchase intentions and is considered an important predictor of their buying behaviour regardless of the product's quality. Moreover, Heslop et al. (1998) found that immigrants' affinity with their home country can be reshaped into another form of affinity, namely sub-cultural affinity with the host country, which seemed to show a significant influence on product evaluations to products that originate from the home region.

Oberecker and Diamantopoulos (2011) further conceptualize affinity as a two-dimensional construct that consists of soft and strong emotions, which correspond to lower (i.e., sympathy) and higher (i.e., attachment) positive affect; strong positive emotions are then accompanied with arousal that leads to increased sensitivity and responsiveness to incoming information about the affinity country. When faced with product choices, consumers tend to rely on extrinsic cues such as price, brand, as well as product familiarity, which may lead them toward products from affinity countries that may help to reduce risk and maximize utility (Oberecker et al. 2008). In practice, the main goal of affinity-based marketing is to link products to an affinity group, organization, or cause, for the purpose of enabling consumers to "express their identity through the use of the affinity product" as well as providing "a tangible representation of the consumer's affiliation with… [the] affinity group" (Mekonnen et al. 2008: 137).

On the whole, the previous review highlights the importance of consumer animosity and affinity, both of which are directed to specific countries which are perceived as being negatively or positively affiliated with their country—which in the case of ethnic consumers may be the original "home" country. Based on this review, a set of testable hypotheses for the empirical investigation of the effects of consumer animosity and consumer affinity on purchase intentions is proposed. The following four hypotheses examine ethnic consumers' potential "attachment" toward and/or "affinity" with countries that share several cultural similarities to home; their "animosity," if any, toward an animosity country; and the potential effects of affinity and/or animosity on the respondents' purchase intentions from both types of countries.

H1:   Consumers are expected to show unfavourable feelings toward the animosity country.

H2:   Consumers are expected to show favourable feelings toward the affinity country.

H3:   Consumers with higher levels of animosity toward a target country will have lesser Likelihood to Purchase (LTP) affiliated with that country.

H4:   Consumers with higher levels of Affinity toward a target country will have higher LTP products affiliated with that country.

While the first two of the above hypotheses may appear intuitively obvious, they are particularly important in the context of this study which focuses, for the first time in international marketing research on animosity and affinity, on ethnic consumers. The study was conceptualized so as to (a) use a distinct ethnic group, (b) within a country that can be considered neutral or objective toward the consumers' potential animosity and affinity targets, (c) in order to test the ethnic group members' potential strong or weak feelings of animosity and/or affinity, (d) toward target countries viewed from the perspective of the respondents' original "home" country, as opposed to their present country of residence.

Methodology

Sampling Frame

The research was part of a larger study carried out in Canada, which is one of the most culturally diverse countries in the world and welcomes hundreds of thousands of immigrants annually of virtually every nationality. To enable a robust application, it was decided to focus on the Middle East where both enmities and friendships across nations are among the strongest in the world. First- or second-generation Egyptian-Canadians were selected as the sample group, rather than a larger community such as Middle Eastern or Arab Canadians. This avoids the frequently mentioned error (e.g., Pires et al. 2003) of aggregating ethnic communities from many countries to achieve larger sample sizes, on the mistaken assumption that linguistic or religious similarity means similarity in overall views and consumption behaviour.

The sample choice presented the opportunity to study the target relationships in the context of clearly distinct country associations, specifically Israel and Tunisia, selected respectively as the animosity and affinity countries. Although the rationale for these choices is fairly obvious, it may be noted that: (a) Israel's selection lies in its deeply rooted negative relationship with Egypt; despite the 1979 bilateral peace treaty, enmities go back to the 1967 and 1973 wars, disputes over the Sinai Peninsula at various times, and historical cultural, religious, and ethnic differences (Eilam 2012; Lea and Rowe 2002); and (b) Tunisia is the obverse of Israel in its cultural, religious, and ethnic similarities with Egypt; the relationship goes back to the "Fatimid era" in 909–1171 (Lev 1991); recently Tunisia and Egypt have signed a number of agreements to cooperate in trade, tourism, and sports events (e.g., Fiorentino et al. 2007); and the Egyptian "Arab Spring" was inspired by its Tunisian predecessor.

A key weakness of past research on animosity and affinity has been that studies focused on a single target country each time, which may result in substantive research confounds; for instance, a view of animosity/affinity toward Israel/Tunisia would mean little if respondents held similar feelings toward "all" countries except those that are perceived as, respectively, hostile or friendly to their ethnic origin country. The best way to tell whether such feelings are unique to a country(ies) or universal is to include a benchmark country for comparison, and for this reason, for the first time in animosity/affinity research, a third, benchmark country was included. Brazil was selected for this purpose, since a review of political and other relationships indicated that it is neutral in the Arab-Israeli context.

Operationalization of Key Constructs

Our review of the literature provided the basis for the items selected in the questionnaire to measure the study concepts, which are summarized below.

Animosity (ANI). In their research of Chinese consumers concerning Japan, Klein et al. (1998) conceptualized animosity as having economic and war components, in addition to general animosity that was measured using a single item. That animosity model has been validated in several studies (e.g., Huang et al. 2010; Nijssen and Douglas 2004; Shoham et al. 2006) and the present study includes items from that model. Seven items were used for the "affinity" and "benchmark" countries, and certain additional questions were used only for Israel, as they would not make sense to the respondent if asked for the other two countries (e.g., typical animosity items refer to "anger" or "forgiveness"—and while such items need to be included for the target animosity country, there is no reason why an Egyptian–Canadian might feel "angry" toward Brazil or have anything to "forgive" in the case of Tunisia; the total number of items for Israel was 11).

Affinity (AFF). In their study, Oberecker et al. (2008) identified seven categories of underlying sources of consumer affinity toward a specific foreign country: lifestyle, culture, scenery, politics and economics, length of stay in the country, travel, and contact. As noted above, in a more recent study Oberecker and Diamantopoulos (2011) further conceptualized affinity into a two-dimensional construct comprising two types of emotions, sympathy and attachment, using a 20-item scale. Drawing on this research, the current study developed a seven-item affinity scale that was applied equally to the affinity, animosity, and benchmark countries. (Note: One reason for not using a more extended affinity scale was that, since this was part of a larger study, the total number of questions had to be contained in order to prevent respondent fatigue.)

Likelihood to Purchase (LTP). Scale items for assessing purchase intentions toward products based on the places with which they are associated are among the most standard measures in PCI studies, resulting in various sets of items that share both similarities and differences. For this study, two measures that have been developed and tested in a large number of studies were selected (e.g., Heslop et al. 2004; Knight and Calantone 2000; Nadeau et al. 2008; Papadopoulos et al. 2008; Papadopoulos et al. 2000, 2008; Parameswaran and Pisharodi 1994): Willingness to try and willingness to buy.

Research Instrument and Sampling Outcomes

The data for the study was collected through a self-administered questionnaire, using 7-point Likert-type scales ranging from Strongly Disagree (1) to Strongly Agree (7), in line with the vast majority of past studies in the areas of interest to the present research.

Data collection was completed within a 40-day period. Considering the difficulties in accessing a "pure" ethnic sample, and in line with suggestions in the literature on ethnicity and acculturation, the questionnaire was distributed both online and in hard copy format with help from centrally positioned key informants and facilitators such as community leaders (e.g., Peñaloza 1994; Pires et al. 2003).

A total of 300 questionnaires were distributed systematically in hard copy and 147 were returned, yielding a highly acceptable response rate of 49 % (Baruch 1999). Although tracking "forwards" makes the calculation of online response rates difficult, based on the available information in this case, including follow-up reports from the facilitators, approximately 800 potential respondents were accessed and asked to complete the online questionnaire. This sample yielded 174 usable responses, i.e., a response rate of 22 %, which is higher than in other online surveys and in line, comparatively, with the hard copy sample.

All but 13 of the 321 respondents identified themselves as Muslims, and so, to prevent religion-based confounds, the 13 "other" responses were excluded resulting in a final sample of 308 respondents; this sample size is considerably larger than those used in similar consumer ethnic studies (see Pires et al. 2003; Rajagopalan and Heitmeyer 2005; Rosenbaum and Montoya 2007; Xu et al. 2004).

Results and Discussion

Animosity: Old Country Enmities Die Hard

As anticipated, the participants' mean scores on the animosity variables for Brazil and Tunisia are all below the scale's midpoint (range = 1.8–3.3), while those for Israel are well above that point (range = 4.5–6.2). Compared to Brazil, Tunisia scored lower on two items related to dislike of the country and the people (mean = 1.8). On the other hand, Israel, the animosity country, had considerably higher means on all animosity items. In particular, the highest means were reflected in four items, where the scores approximate the maximum point on the scale: "I dislike Israel" (mean = 6.0), "I feel guilty if I buy Israeli products" (6.0), "I don't like owning Israeli products" (6.2), and "I feel angry toward Israel for its actions in Palestine" (6.4). The animosity means are shown in Table 1. While they are in line with the study's expectations, it is worth noting (a) the very high animosity scores for Israel, reflecting, perhaps, the recency and currency of differences between the respondent's "home" and the target country; and (b) the fact that, even though the scores for Tunisia and Brazil are significantly lower, in some instances they approach the scale mid-point—which validates the usefulness of assessing more than one country on the animosity scale. Overall, H1 is supported and shows strongly unfavourable views of the animosity country.

Affinity: Old Country Friendships Stay Strong

Overall, as expected, Tunisia achieved the highest mean scores compared to Brazil and Israel. The results are in line with H2, which states that consumers are expected to show favourable feelings toward the affinity country. For both Tunisia and Brazil, there were slight differences in the mean scores of two items, "very interesting

Table 1 Descriptives: Animosity toward Brazil, Israel, and Tunisia
Question wording slightly abbreviated to fit; Highest/lowest mean in a row is in bold/underscore; Vacant cells (greyed-out) show questions not relevant to a country, not asked; Cross-country differences of .3 or more are significant at .001 (MANOVA)
*Reversed animosity item

Animosity variables	BR		IL		TU	
	mean	sd	mean	sd	mean	sd
Angry for (country) lack of support of Canada in intl affairs	**2.6**	1.50			2.3	1.43
Angry for (country) lack of support of Egypt in intl affairs	**2.6**	1.42			2.4	1.43
Don't like owning products of (country)	2.6	1.47	**6.2**	1.55	2.3	1.54
Dislike (country)	2.0	1.29	**6.0**	1.68	1.8	1.14
Dislike (people)	1.9	1.24	**5.3**	1.92	1.8	1.19
(Country) not a reliable trading partner	3.0	1.32	**5.1**	2.00	2.9	1.31
Need to be careful when doing business with (people)	3.3	1.39	**5.6**	1.74	3.1	1.39
In spite of past actions, would not forgive Israel*			4.5	2.05		
Angry toward Israel for its actions in Palestine			6.4	1.43		
Israel wants to gain military power over Egypt			5.9	1.59		
Angry toward Israel over 1967 war			5.6	1.73		
Feel guilty if I buy Israeli products			6.0	1.61		
Would never buy an Israeli products			5.7	1.86		

culture," and "like to travel." The similar mean values on these variables could possibly indicate that, to be interested in a country's culture and have a desire to visit it, both of which have been suggested in the literature as affinity measures, does not necessarily have to be based on affinity feelings toward that specific country. One could simply feel the desire to explore a new culture without having any affective connections with the travel destination. On the other hand, as shown in Table 2 below, the mean values for Israel were consistently below the 7-point scale's midpoint (mean range = 1.5–3), indicating negative feelings toward the animosity country. Participants strongly experienced an unpleasant feeling (mean = 1.6) and a low sense of attachment (mean = 1.5) toward Israel. On the other hand, one might say that the findings for Brazil are "uncomfortably close" to those for Tunisia: As with animosity, it appears that having a benchmark country may help to cast doubt on what "affinity" for a friendly or similar nation may actually mean.

Likelihood to Purchase: Likes, Dislikes, and Buyer Behaviour

The LTP items for each of the three countries in the study is presented in Table 3 below. The findings reveal that respondents tend to give similar ratings to Brazil, the benchmark country, and Tunisia, the affinity country, when it comes to both "willingness to try" and "willingness to buy" items. This casts further doubt on the traditional measurement of affinity and supports the decision to use a benchmark country. On the other hand, the item means show that there is a difference between Israel and both Brazil and Tunisia when asking respondents about their willingness to try or buy

Table 2 Descriptives: Affinity toward Brazil, Israel, and Tunisia

	BR		IL		TU	
Affinity variables	Mean	SD	Mean	SD	Mean	SD
Friendly	4.8	1.27	3.0	1.76	**5.3**	1.36
Heard good things	4.9	1.31	2.5	1.77	**5.4**	1.30
Like to travel	5.2	1.55	2.0	1.72	**5.5**	1.45
Very interesting culture	5.0	1.41	2.3	1.75	**5.3**	1.36
Similar to EG culture	3.6	1.38	2.4	1.74	**4.9**	1.36
Pleasant feeling	4.7	1.32	1.6	1.25	**5.1**	1.35
Sense of attachment	3.5	1.58	1.5	1.22	**4.7**	1.57

Highest/lowest mean in a row is in bold/underscore; Cross-country differences of 0.3 or more are significant at .001 (MANOVA)

Table 3 Descriptives: Likelihood to purchase from Brazil, Israel, and Tunisia

	BR		IL		TU	
Purchase intention variables	Mean	SD	Mean	SD	Mean	SD
Willing to try	4.8	1.43	2.0	1.51	4.8	1.36
Willing to buy	4.8	1.38	1.9	1.45	4.7	1.32

Highest/lowest mean in a row is in bold/underscore; Cross-country differences of 0.3 or more are significant at 0.001 (MANOVA)

Israeli products (means, respectively, of 2.0 and 1.9). These findings are consistent with PCI research that assumes consumers' purchase intentions can be based on image projections of specific countries (Ahmed et al. 2002; Bilkey and Nes 1982; Han 1989). As mentioned earlier, Israel has been perceived negatively by the sample due to its deeply rooted negative historical relationship with Egypt and generally the cultural, religious, and ethnic differences between the two people.

Old Country Views Transfer to New Country Behaviour

A series of multiple linear regression analyses were undertaken to test H3 and H4, which represent the relationships among study variables as they were presented earlier. As can be seen in Table 4, the effect of Animosity on LTP (H3) was pronounced for Israel ($\beta = -.52$, $p < .05$)—i.e., the more negative feelings about a country, the less the LTP from this specific country.

As expected, there were no animosity effects related to Brazil and Tunisia, since, respectively, these were the "benchmark" and "affinity" countries and therefore there was no particular reason to expect noteworthy negative feelings toward them. In fact, the animosity questions were asked about Brazil and Tunisia specifically to make it possible to contrast the results against those for Israel—otherwise there it would not be possible to judge whether any animosity toward the latter was unique to it or was part of a general feeling addressed to other countries as well.

Table 4 Regression coefficients summary—The effect of Animosity and Affinity on LTP

Countries	BR	IL	TU
Predictors	Unstandardized βs		
ANI	n.s.	−.52	n.s.
AFF	.49	n.s.	.46
R^2	.19	.23	.20
F	37.33	44.70	38.15

βs and F (2, 307) values are significant at $p < 0.05$; n.s.: not significant

The Affinity construct showed a positive and significant impact on LTP from Brazil ($\beta = .49$, $p < .05$), the benchmark country, and Tunisia ($\beta = .46$, $p < .05$), the affinity country. This provides support for H4: The general positive feelings about a country and its people (i.e., friendly people, interesting culture, like to travel, sense of attachment, etc.) contribute positively to LTP in relation to products from both the affinity and benchmark countries.

Conclusion

The findings of this study contribute to the current conceptual and empirical under-standing of the animosity and affinity constructs by exposing their relationships with consumers' likelihood to buy products from countries that are negatively or positively affiliated with their ethnic origin.

The effect of animosity, which represents negative feelings associated with buy-ing products from the animosity country, as well as feelings of resentment and anger due to military conflicts, returned a significant positive coefficient pertaining to the respondent's LTP for Israeli products. As anticipated, the effect of animosity on LTP was pronounced only in relation to Israel, the animosity country. On the other hand, affinity appeared to be an important predictor of LTP for both Tunisia and Brazil.

In line with the conceptualization of affinity, it was expected that it would be country-specific toward Tunisia, the study's choice of a country which is friendly to Egypt and culturally, religiously, and ethnically linked to it. Indeed, while affinity ratings were high for both Brazil and Tunisia, ethnic consumers rated them differently on all affinity items and with clearly higher means for Tunisia, the country chosen as the affinity target for this study. Nevertheless, affinity appeared to play a significant role for the benchmark country as well, and this is, perhaps, one of the most important findings of this study. LTP products was partially explained by ethnic consumers' positive feelings toward both Tunisia and Brazil. In this study, the ethnic and cultural connections toward Tunisia are already established, and the openness to build a posi-tive relationship with Brazil was not hindered by any animosity feelings.

Affinity toward Brazil cannot be explained easily by reference to notions of "cultural affinity" and "cultural closeness" (Swift 1999), since that country is quite unlike the respondents' "home" country in all respects. Findings show that there are other possible types of affinity, such as "sports affinity," which can explain positive feelings toward a specific country—and so it is conceivable that the positive view of Brazil may also be nurtured, at least partly, by the ethnic consumers' passion about Brazilian soccer, which can create a positive image that ultimately contributes to positive feelings toward the country (Houlihan 1994; Hough 2008). Another view of affinity might be explained as reflecting a sort of cosmopolitanism. As put forth by Cannon and Yaprak (2002: 45–46), "a common pattern of cosmopolitanism might be an affinity for the best of everything." These thoughts suggest that the conceptualization of affinity and animosity may need to be reconsidered, and that the presence of a benchmark country(ies) in future study designs may help to uncover relationships that have not been attended to.

While lack of space does not permit elaboration of certain observations that arose from the sampling and fieldwork, it should be noted that, as became evident during implementation of the study, reaching out to a minority ethnic group can be a demanding, time-consuming, and challenging process. Quite aside from the difficult task of "finding" respondents who meet the sampling criteria, the reaction of potential participants to a request to provide information about their ethnic behaviours as consumers can be unpredictable and often negative—not to mention the complications, of requesting information a) on such sensitive topics as the respondents' views of a clear and current "animosity" country, in this case Israel, and b) in the midst of political upheaval in the home country, in this case Egypt.

Overall, the study shows that "old views die hard": Even though they live in a country whose mainstream consumers, other things being equal, would have no particular reason to show a particularly strong or weak preference for the products of Israel or Tunisia further to general product quality and overall country image considerations, Egyptian–Canadians appear to carry with them strong views emanating more from their original than their current "home" country's situation. This, coupled with the somewhat perplexing findings concerning the effects of affinity and animosity in the case of Brazil, the benchmark country, points to rich possibilities for future research that will help us understand the relevant phenomena more fully.

References

Ahmed, Z. U., Johnson, J. P., Ling, C. P., Fang, T. W., & Hui, A. K. (2002). Country-of-origin and brand effects on consumers' evaluations of cruise lines. *International Marketing Review, 19*(3), 279–302.

Amine, L. S., Chao, M. C., & Arnold, M. J. (2005). Exploring the practical effects of country of origin, animosity, and price-quality issues: two case studies of Taiwan and Acer in China. *Journal of International Marketing, 13*(2), 114–150.

Balabanis, G., & Diamantopoulos, A. (2004). Domestic country bias, country-of-origin effects, and consumer ethnocentrism: A multidimensional unfolding approach. *Journal of the Academy of Marketing Science, 32*(1), 80–95.

Baruch, Y. (1999). Response rate in academic studies-A comparative analysis. *Human relations, 52*(4), 421–438.

Bilkey, W. J., & Nes, E. (1982). Country of origin effect on product evaluations. *Journal of International Business Studies, 13*(1), 89–99.

Cannon, H. M., & Yaprak, A. (2002). Will the real-world citizen please stand up! The many faces of cosmopolitan consumer behavior. *Journal of International Marketing, 10*(4), 30–52.

Cleveland, M., Laroche, M., & Papadopoulos, N. (2009). Cosmopolitanism, consumer ethnocentrism, and materialism: An eight-country study of antecedents and outcomes. *Journal of International Marketing, 17*(1), 116–146.

Eilam, E. (2012). Operational aspects of a future war between Egypt and Israel. *Defense and Security Analysis, 28*(3), 260–267.

Ettenson, R., & Klein, J. G. (2005). The fallout from French nuclear testing in the south pacific: A longitudinal study of consumer boycott. *International Marketing Review, 22*(2), 199–224.

Fiorentino, R. V., Verdeja, L., & Toqueboeuf, C. (2007). *The changing landscape of regional trade agreements: 2006 update*. Geneva: World Trade Organization.

Han, C. (1989). Country image: Halo or summary construct? *Journal of Marketing Research, 26*(2), 222–229.

Heslop, L. A., Lu, I. R., & Cray, D. (2008). Modeling country image effects through an international crisis. *International Marketing Review, 25*(4), 354–378.

Heslop, L. A., Lu, I. R., & Cray, D. (2009). Australian consumers' attitudes toward France a decade after nuclear testing: Evidence of forgiveness. *Journal of Consumer Behaviour, 8*(4), 192–210.

Heslop, L. A., Papadopoulos, N., Dowdles, M., Wall, M., & Compeau, D. (2004). Who controls the purse strings: A study of consumers' and retail buyers' reactions in an America's FTA environment. *Journal of Business Research, 57*(10), 1177–1188.

Heslop, L. A., Papadopoulos, N., & Bourk, M. (1998). An interregional and intercultural perspective on subcultural differences in product evaluations. *Canadian Journal of Administrative Sciences, 15*(2), 113–126.

Hinck, W. (2005). The role of domestic animosity in consumer choice: Empirical evidence from Germany. *Journal of Euromarketing, 14*(1/2), 87–104.

Hough, P. (2008). 'Make Goals Not War': The Contribution of International Football to World Peace. *The International Journal of the History of Sport, 25*(10), 1287–1305.

Houlihan, B. (1994). *Sport and international politics* (p. 110). New York: Harvester Wheatsheaf.

Huang, Y. A., Phau, I., & Lin, C. (2010). Effects of animosity and allocentrism on consumer ethnocentrism: Social identity on consumer willingness to purchase. *Asia Pacific Management Review, 15*(3), 359–376.

Jaffe, E. D., & Nebenzahl, I. D. (2001). *National image and competitive advantage : The theory and practice of country-of-origin effect* (1st ed.). Copenhagen: Copehagen Business School Press.

Jung, K., Ang, S. H., Leong, S. M., Tan, S. J., Pornpitakpan, C., & Kau, A. K. (2002). A typology of animosity and its cross-national validation. *Journal of Cross-Cultural Psychology, 33*(6), 525–539.

Klein, J. G. (2002). Us versus them, or us versus everyone? Delineating consumer aversion to foreign goods. *Journal of International Business Studies, 32*(2), 345–363.

Klein, J. G., Ettenson, R., & Krishnan, B. C. (2006). Extending the construct of consumer ethnocentrism: when foreign products are preferred. *International Marketing Review, 23*(3), 304–321.

Klein, J. G., Ettenson, R., & Morris, M. D. (1998). The animosity model of foreign product purchase: An empirical test in the People's Republic of China. *The Journal of Marketing, 62*(1), 89–100.

Knight, G. A., & Calantone, R. J. (2000). A flexible model of consumer country-of-origin perceptions. *International Marketing Review, 17*(2), 127–145.

Laroche, M., Papadopoulos, N., Heslop, L. A., & Bergeron, J. (2003). Effects of Subcultural Differences on Country and Product Evaluations. *Journal of Consumer Behaviour, 2*(3), 232–247.

Lea, D., & Rowe, A. (2002). *Survey of Arab-Israeli Relations 1947–2001*. London: Europa.

Leong, S. M., Cote, J. A., Ang, S. H., Tan, S. J., Jung, K., Kau, A. K., et al. (2008). Understanding consumer animosity in an international crisis: nature, antecedents, and consequences. *Journal of International Business Studies, 39*(6), 996–1009.

Lev, Y. (1991). *State and society in Fatimid Egypt* (Vol. 1). Leiden: Brill Academic.

Lwin, M. O., Stanaland, A. J. S., & Williams, J. D. (2010). Exporting America. *International Journal of Advertising, 29*(2), 245–278.

Maher, A. A., & Mady, S. (2010). Animosity, subjective norms, and anticipated emotions during an international crisis. *International Marketing Review, 27*(6), 630–651.

Mekonnen, A., Harris, F., & Laing, A. (2008). Linking products to a cause or affinity group: Does this really make them more attractive to consumers? *European Journal of Marketing, 42*(1/2), 135–153.

Nadeau, J., Heslop, L. A., O'Reilly, N., & Luk, P. (2008). Destination image in a country context. *Annals of Tourism Research, 35*(1), 84–106.

Nijssen, E. J., & Douglas, S. P. (2004). Examining the animosity model in a country with a high level of foreign trade. *International Journal of Research in Marketing, 21*(1), 23–38.

Oberecker, E. M., & Diamantopoulos, A. (2011). Consumers' emotional bonds with foreign countries: Does consumer affinity affect behavioural intentions? *Journal of International Marketing, 19*(2), 45–72.

Oberecker, E. M., Riefler, P., & Diamantopoulos, A. (2008). The consumer affinity construct: Conceptualization, qualitative investigation, and research agenda. *Journal of International Marketing, 16*(3), 23–56.

Papadopoulos, N. (2004). Place branding: Evolution, meaning and implications. *Place Branding, 1*(1), 36–49.

Papadopoulos, N., el Banna, A., Murphy, Steven A., & Rojas-Méndez, J. I. (2012). Place brands and brand-place associations: The role of 'place' in international marketing. In S. Jain & D. A. Griffith (Eds.), *Handbook of research in international marketing* (2nd ed., pp. 88–113). Northampton, MA: Edward Elgar.

Papadopoulos, N., Hamzaoui-Essoussi, L., & Rojas-Méndez, J. I. (2011). Consumer animosity: A comparative perspective. In *Developments in marketing science, academy of marketing science: Vol. XXXIV, Coral Gables, FL, May 24–27.*

Papadopoulos, N., Heslop, L. A., & The IKON Research Group (2000). A cross-national and longitudinal study of product-country images with a focus on the U.S. and Japan. *Marketing Science Institute Reports*, 00–106, 67 pp.

Papadopoulos, N., Laroche, M., Elliot, S., & Rojas-Méndez, J. I. (2008). Subcultural effects of product origins: consumer ethnicity and product nationality. In *Proceedings, 37th Annual Conference, European Marketing Academy, Brighton, England, May 27–30.*

Parameswaran, R., & Pisharodi, R. M. (1994). Facets of country of origin image: An empirical assessment. *Journal of Advertising, 23*(1), 43–56.

Peñaloza, L. (1994). Atravesando fronteras/border crossings: A critical ethnographic exploration of the consumer acculturation of Mexican immigrants. *Journal of Consumer Research, 21*(1), 32–54.

Phau, I., & Chao, P. (2008). Country-of-origin: State of the art review for international marketing strategy and practice. *International Marketing Review, 25*(4), 349–353.

Pires, G. D., Stanton, P. J., & Cheek, B. (2003). Identifying and reaching an ethnic market: Methodological issues. *Qualitative Market Research: An International Journal, 6*(4), 224–235.

Podoshen, J. (2009). Distressing events and future purchase decisions: Jewish consumers and the holocaust. *Journal of Consumer Marketing, 26*(4), 263–276.

Rajagopalan, R., & Heitmeyer, J. (2005). Ethnicity and consumer choice: A study of consumer levels of involvement in Indian ethnic apparel and contemporary American clothing. *Journal of Fashion Marketing and Management, 9*(1), 83–105.

Rawwas, M. Y. A., Rajendran, K. N., & Wuehrer, G. A. (1996). The influence of worldmindedness and nationalism on consumer evaluation of domestic and foreign products. *International Marketing Review, 13*(2), 20–38.

Riefler, P., & Diamantopoulos, A. (2007). Consumer animosity: A literature review and a reconsideration of its measurement. *International Marketing Review, 24*(1), 87–119.

Rose, M., Rose, G. M., & Shoham, A. (2009). The impact of consumer animosity on attitudes towards foreign goods: A study of Jewish and Arab Israelis. *Journal of Consumer Marketing, 26*(5), 330–339.

Rosenbaum, M. S., & Montoya, D. Y. (2007). Am I welcome here? Exploring how ethnic consumers assess their place identity. *Journal of Business Research, 60*(3), 206–214.

Schooler, R. D. (1965). Product bias in the Central American Common Market. *Journal of Marketing Research, 2*(4), 394–397.

Shimp, T., & Sharma, S. (1987). Consumer ethnocentrism: Construction and validation of the CETSCALE. *Journal of Marketing Research, 24*(8), 280–289.

Shoham, A., Davidow, M., Klein, J. G., & Ruvio, A. (2006). Animosity on the home front: The intifada in Israel and its impact on consumer behavior. *Journal of International Marketing, 14*(3), 92–114.

Swift, J. S. (1999). Cultural closeness as a facet of cultural affinity: A contribution to the theory of psychic distance. *International Marketing Review, 16*(3), 182–201.

Vida, I., & Reardon, J. (2008). Domestic consumption: Rational, affective or normative choice? *Journal of Consumer Marketing, 25*(1), 34–44.

Wang, J. (2005). Consumer nationalism and corporate reputation management in the global era. *Corporate Communications: An International Journal, 10*(3), 223–239.

Wood, V. R., Pitta, D. A., & Franzak, F. J. (2008). Successful marketing by multinational firms to the bottom of the pyramid: Connecting share of heart, global "umbrella brands", and responsible marketing. *Journal of Consumer Marketing, 25*(7), 419–429.

Xu, J., Shim, S., Lotz, S., & Almeida, D. (2004). Ethnic identity, socialization factors, and culture-specific consumption behavior. *Psychology and Marketing, 21*(2), 93–112.

Part XVI
Relationship Marketing

The Linkages Between Customer Satisfaction and Four Loyalty Behaviors in the Presence of Moderators

Birgit Leisen Pollack

Abstract This study investigates the effects of moderators on the relationship between customer satisfaction and four common loyalty behaviors: (1) repurchase intentions, (2) positive word-of-mouth, (3) negative word-of-mouth, and (4) share-of-wallet. This evaluation is performed across three service industries and for two moderators—switching costs and variety seeking. The former is thought to be most relevant at low satisfaction levels whereas the latter is thought to be most relevant at high satisfaction levels. Eight hypotheses are formulated and tested.

The data were collected from about 150 customers of cell phone services, restaurant services, and banking services, each. The three services differ in their potential to invite switching costs and variety seeking behavior. The survey consisted of questions assessing overall satisfaction, repurchase intentions, positive word-of-mouth, negative word-of-mouth, variety seeking, and switching cost. One questions assessed the share-of-wallet loyalty behavior. Published scales were used. An inspection of the Cronbach coefficients revealed very good scale reliabilities with alpha score mostly well above 0.85 (Nunnally 1978).

Following Hayes (2013), the hypotheses were tested using regression-based moderator analysis. The analysis produced mixed results at $\alpha < .05$. For switching costs as a moderator, the effects seem to be service and loyalty behavior dependent. For the phone services, switching costs significantly moderate the satisfaction–repurchase intention relationship, the satisfaction–negative word-of-mouth relationship, and the satisfaction–share-of-wallet relationship. Switching costs do not moderate the relationship between satisfaction and positive word-of-mouth for any of the services. Switching costs do not moderate any of the relationships for banking and restaurant services.

For variety seeking as a moderator, the effects are also service and loyalty behavior dependent. Variety seeking significantly moderates the satisfaction–repurchase intention relationship only for the restaurant service. The findings further suggest that variety seeking does not moderate the relationship between satisfaction and word-of-mouth. For banking services variety seeking significantly moderates the satisfaction–

B.L. Pollack (✉)
University of Wisconsin Oshkosh, Oshkosh, WI, USA
e-mail: leisen@uwosh.edu

© Academy of Marketing Science 2016
L. Petruzzellis, R.S. Winer (eds.), *Rediscovering the Essentiality of Marketing*,
Developments in Marketing Science: Proceedings of the Academy of Marketing
Science, DOI 10.1007/978-3-319-29877-1_135

731

negative word-of-mouth relationship. The results suggest that variety seeking does not moderate the relationship between satisfaction and share-of-wallet.

The findings yield two general implications. First, with respect to future investigations into moderators of the satisfaction–loyalty relationship, loyalty should not be operationalized as a single behavior construct. Different loyalty related behaviors exhibit different moderators. The second key conclusion is that moderators are service dependent. Therefore, future studies into moderators should refrain from analyzing and reporting on pooled industry results.

References available upon request.

Consumers' Willingness to Pay for Privacy Services

Frauke Mattison Thompson and Kirk Plangger

Abstract To alleviate consumer privacy concerns, governments have introduced privacy regulations to manage excessive consumer privacy intrusion by organizations (Solove 2008; Bennett 2008). Yet research shows that these regulations are not sufficient in reducing consumer privacy fears as privacy concerns vary in magnitude from consumer to consumer (Mattison Thompson 2007) and the law can only protect against privacy intrusion on a uniform level. Despite the extensive body of research investigating the variance in consumer privacy concerns within the context of legislative boundaries (e.g., Milne et al. 2004; Milne et al. 2006; Shilton 2009; King and Raja 2012; King and Jessen 2010), little has been done to understand whether consumers would be willing to pay for additional privacy services offered by organizations to protect their privacy above and beyond the protection the law provides. Since consumers vary in their privacy needs, one solution that firms could adopt to reduce their customers' privacy concern is to offer privacy as an individualized, personalized service or "Privacy Services" that cater to the higher privacy needs of some customers. Privacy services involve a customer paying an additional fee to receive privacy protection above what is offered to other customers, thus potentially mitigating the customers' privacy concern for transactions they have with that firm.

In this study, we explore how consumer privacy concern impacts consumers' willingness to pay for "Privacy Services," as well as the moderating effect of consumer trust on this relationship. We present empirical evidence from over 16,000 consumers in 20 countries. We contribute to the consumer privacy literature by showing that consumer privacy concern influences consumers' willingness to pay for "Privacy Services," and that consumer trust moderates this relationship.

References available upon request.

F.M. Thompson (✉) • K. Plangger
King's College London, London, UK
e-mail: frauke.mattison_thompson@kcl.ac.uk; kirk.plangger@kcl.ac.uk

© Academy of Marketing Science 2016
L. Petruzzellis, R.S. Winer (eds.), *Rediscovering the Essentiality of Marketing*, Developments in Marketing Science: Proceedings of the Academy of Marketing Science, DOI 10.1007/978-3-319-29877-1_136

733

Achieving Relationship Termination Quality: A Conceptual Model

Ting Yu and Christopher White

Introduction

Business strategies often demand refinements, such that core or supplementary offerings change frequently and possibly create imbalances that lead to dissatisfaction among some target customers. Therefore, relationship termination is an inevitable phase that arises when relationships between a firm and a particular group of customers are no longer mutually beneficial. With the existing resources and prices charged, the highest service quality the firm can provide no longer satisfies these customers. For example, the Australian Internet service provider Exetel recently terminated a group of unprofitable accounts, asking customers to switch to other providers (Cheng 2010). Reynolds and Harris (2009) challenge the assumption that customers act functionally and with good manners during service encounters; some customers routinely behave destructively. Retaining such customers may cause more harm than good and impose heavy financial burdens on both firms and other customers (McColl-Kennedy et al. 2009). Accordingly, it seems more appropriate and effective to terminate customers, before they reach the point of destruction. Effective management of the termination of unhealthy relationships thus is a crucial tactic that can reduce the service costs accrued by trying to satisfy misfit customers, as well as increase profit margins with remaining customers. This important strategic move can improve returns on resource allocations (Alajoutsijärvi et al. 2000).

T. Yu (✉)
University of New South Wales, Sydney, NSW, Australia
e-mail: ting.yu@unsw.edu.au

C. White
RMIT University, Melbourne, VIC, Australia
e-mail: christopher.white@rmit.edu.au

© Academy of Marketing Science 2016
L. Petruzzellis, R.S. Winer (eds.), *Rediscovering the Essentiality of Marketing*,
Developments in Marketing Science: Proceedings of the Academy of Marketing
Science, DOI 10.1007/978-3-319-29877-1_137

Although necessary, relationship termination also can backfire. Hogan et al. (2003) outline the direct and indirect costs of losing a customer, including the obvious financial loss when the customer no longer purchases the firm's service or product, as well as negative word of mouth by terminated customers that could damage the firm's reputation or retaliations (Mittal and Sarkees 2006). Thus a relationship termination decision cannot be taken lightly, and its implementation requires careful planning (Alajoutsijärvi et al. 2000). For firms in various service industries though (e.g. information technology, healthcare, finance, professional; Mittal et al. 2008), a dearth of relationship termination studies means that managers lack guidelines for undertaking this important strategic move. It is important that firms achieve quality relationship termination to minimise the negative effect for such strategic move. This chapter seeks to further our understanding of relationship termination quality by proposing relationship termination typology. Drawn from attitude theory, this study identifies potential antecedents, consequences, and moderators of relationship termination.

Relationship Termination: Typology

Relationship termination refers to an intentional strategic move and is initiated by the service provider with the purpose of ending the buyer–seller relationship, either completely or partially. Based on the level of relationship termination, there are three types of customer termination strategies: passive, active, and partial.

Passive Termination

Passive termination strategies use implicit mechanisms to encourage customers to leave the relationship by not providing the exchange benefits customers expect, such as paying less attention to customers' needs (Mittal et al. 2008). In the mobile phone industry, a telecommunication provider might not offer a new phone at the end of the acquisition contract to customers who have not provided sufficient revenue during that contract period. This passive approach encourages the customers to leave the relationship. Such strategies are common when a firm has decided to terminate and hopes that the customers will switch, such as to another telecommunication provider (Haenlein et al. 2006).

Firms that employ a passive termination strategy do not actively attempt to sell any new products to existing customers; thus, the telecom service provider would not seek to extend or renew the existing contract after it expires. However, a passive termination strategy can look like poor service, so it needs to be implemented with caution to avoid creating a bad reputation that might spread among other, more profitable customers (Mittal et al. 2008).

Active Termination

With an active termination strategy, the firm explicitly asks customers to leave the relationship, either directly or indirectly (Baxter 1985). With a direct, active approach, the firm explicitly expresses its desire to leave the relationship, which effectively ensures termination but also may cause hurt feelings or disappointment. Zeithaml et al. (2001) suggest using price and cost tactics to actively encourage customers to leave the relationship. By increasing the price and reducing operating costs (e.g. by offering poorer quality service), the firm renegotiates the value exchange, which represents an active, indirect approach.

Partial Termination

The buyer–seller relationship includes the category level, such that a customer may purchase various service and product offerings; a retail bank customer might hold multiple bank accounts, for example. Even if this customer is less profitable in one product category, she or he could be very profitable in another. Rather than completely terminate the relationship at all levels, the service firm may decide to partially terminate the relationship at one product level, using either a passive or an active termination strategy, and thus push the customer out of one product category but retain him or her in others.

Relationship Termination Quality: Antecedents, Consequences, and Moderators

Relationship termination scholars note the importance of a high quality termination, though the notion has not been fully conceptualized in business-to-consumer studies. Limited discussions of a related concept in business-to-business contexts suggests that relationship termination quality is multidimensional, consisting of both process and outcome quality. Process quality refers to interactions in each stage during the termination process; outcome quality reflects the results of each stage during the process (Alajoutsijärvi et al. 2000).

In line with these extant notions, the working definition of relationship termination quality for this project refers to customers' attitudes toward the process and outcomes of a firm-initiated relationship termination. This attitudinal construct comprises cognitive, affective, and behavioural processes, expressed when customers evaluate the relationship termination process and outcome as favourable or unfavourable (Eagly and Chaiken 1993). In addition, functional approaches indicate that attitudes reflect important social and personal needs, with four main functions:

utilitarian, knowledge, ego-defensive, and value-expressive. These functions provide a motivational basis for attitudes toward an attitude object. Understanding why people hold and express certain attitudes is fundamental to understanding their attitude formation and changes. These functions also activate certain behaviours, consistent with the relevant attitudes, so they become crucial for understanding attitude consequences (Eagly and Chaiken 1993). To understand the formation and changes of people's attitudes toward relationship termination processes and outcomes, it is essential to understand the functional meaning of their attitudes about relationship termination quality.

Attitude scholars take into consideration of three types of variation, object, person, and situation when studying the formation and change of attitudes, i.e. attitude is object specific and are formed or changed based on personal and situation characteristics (Tesser and Shaffer 1990). The formation and change of attitudes are influenced by both social and psychological process (Eagly and Chaiken 1993). In conjunction with previous studies on relationship termination, potential antecedents and moderators are identified and discussed.

Antecedents

Both organizational input and customers characteristics influence customers' attitudes toward relationship termination. The organizational inputs include the firm's efforts to avoid termination, and the communication strategy and implementation. With appropriate communication strategies, the firm can minimize the harm to customers and improve the quality of the termination process. Such communication might be written, verbal, or active (e.g. sudden, significant price increase, no communication for an unexpected period; Alajoutsijärvi et al. 2000). If the business relationship is bound by legal contracts, the firm finalizes its official termination arrangement. Without sufficient investigations of appropriate communication strategies though, it is impossible to identify which specific strategies are most suitable in different termination circumstances. A direct approach may be the most efficient, but it also creates challenges if the firm hopes to avoid hurting its customer (Alajoutsijärvi et al. 2000). Kalaignanam and Varadarajan (2012) also question whether customer relationship management activities, including communication, should be performed in-house or outsourced to reduce costs, though this question also raises quality control issues. In addition, customer characteristics have direct impacts on perceptions of relationship termination, including the importance they assign to the service, the resources they have at their disposal to pursue alternatives, their attitudes toward the firm prior to the termination, and their service experiences (Alajoutsijärvi et al. 2000; Mittal and Sarkees 2006).

Moderators

Contextual factors are highly pertinent in relationship marketing literature (e.g. Homburg et al. 2011). Kalaignanam and Varadarajan (2012) identify the macro-business environment, together with industry, firm, product, and task characteristics, as the main contextual factors to consider when undertaking relationship management activities. For example, environmental uncertainty and the partners' interdependence strongly influence relationship strength (Frazier and Antia 1995). Contextual influences might act as moderators at various levels, such as the individual (e.g. customer communication styles), relationship (e.g. between terminated customers and the brand), and external environment (e.g. competitive environment, competitor offering) levels. Consider the environment, for example. Consumers view their relationship with the firm as an instrument for goal achievement (Bagozzi 1995). In this case, their goal is to acquire a service, and the relationship facilitates the fulfilment of that goal. Termination instead hinders consumers from achieving these goals, so it represents an undesirable option. However, if the surrounding market offers multiple, alternative, desirable options, it may influence (i.e. strengthen or weaken) the link between the organizational input or customer characteristics and relationship termination quality. Furthermore, even if firms make relationship termination decisions using a rational process (e.g. based on profitability or costs), customers' responses might be less rational and largely influenced by their social surroundings. For some customers, the desire to retain the relationship reflects the influence of their family and friends (i.e. joint desire; Bagozzi 1995). Therefore, understanding customers' reactions to relationship termination, and thus the outcomes of the process, requires a determination of the social influences and goal pursuits that surrounded the relationship in the first place.

Conclusion

The recognition that "service investments across all customer groups will not yield similar returns and are not equally advantageous to the firm" (Zeithaml et al. 2001, p. 120) provides a strong rationale for terminating business relationships with specific customers that offer poor returns on the firm's service investment. However, it is rarely easy to establish customer relationships, and even if the current value exchange is not optimal for the firm, the service provider cannot undertake relationship termination lightly or without careful consideration. Companies should take relationship termination as a final resort as a strategic move and try to achieve quality relationship termination.

References available upon request.

The Emotional and Professional Costs of Pleasing Customers

Hana Medler-Liraz and Dana Yagil

Abstract The goal of this study was to explore the emotional and the professional costs incurred by service providers with a strong need to belong (i.e., craving for social acceptance, Baumeister and Leary 1995; Lavigne et al. 2011). The research model predicts that service providers with a strong need to belong will develop emotional labor strategies to please their customers, which will subsequently lead to emotional exhaustion, failing to provide high quality service, and low customer loyalty intentions.

The sample consisted of 170 restaurant servers and customer dyads. Both parties were asked to relate to their latest service interaction. The results suggest that the service providers' need to belong is positively related to emotional labor strategies, which are positively related to emotional exhaustion. Emotional exhaustion is negatively related to customers' loyalty intentions. Furthermore, emotional labor strategies mediate the relationship of the need to belong with emotional exhaustion.

The study sheds light on the complexity of service providers' motivation to please customers. On the one hand, recruiting service providers who are internally motivated to please the customers appear to be desirable in the service context. On the other hand, such service providers are at a higher risk of burnout which might ultimately undermine business profitability.

References available upon request.

H. Medler-Liraz (✉)
Academic College of Tel-Aviv-Yaffo, Tel Aviv, Israel
e-mail: hanamedl@mta.ac.il

D. Yagil
University of Haifa, Haifa, Israel
e-mail: dyagil@research.haifa.ac.il

© Academy of Marketing Science 2016   741
L. Petruzzellis, R.S. Winer (eds.), *Rediscovering the Essentiality of Marketing*,
Developments in Marketing Science: Proceedings of the Academy of Marketing
Science, DOI 10.1007/978-3-319-29877-1_138

Forgiveness in Buyer–Seller Relationships Gone Bad

Nina Stuebiger, Jasmin Baumann, Alexander Haas, and Kenneth Le Meunier-FitzHugh

Abstract Getting out of a buyer–seller relationship gone bad can be even worse than an ugly divorce, with a multitude of examples for transgressions in business-to-business (B2B) relationships making headlines every year. But what happens to the relationship after a transgression has occurred? For example, Karachi Electric Supply Corporation (KESC) threatened to terminate its collaboration with Siemens after accusing the latter of causing substantial losses to the power utility and sabotaging the SAP software used in managerial operations. In the end, however, the two firms decided to put the past behind them and KESC agreed to withdraw all court claims and instead continue the cooperation, thereby reestablishing an atmosphere of understanding and trust between the partners (Dawn 2007; Tribune 2013). Here, the customer decided to forgive the supplier after the transgression and to restore the relationship to its original state. Transgressions are violations of the relationship between at least two partners, e.g., customers and manufacturers or service providers (Tsarenko and Tojib 2011; Beverland et al. 2009), which can lead to dissatisfaction on both sides, and reactions such as negative word of mouth and relationship termination (Bendapudi and Berry 1997). While past research has especially focused on service failure and recovery (e.g., Maxham and Netemeyer 2002) and reinvigorations after transgressions in customer–brand relationships (e.g., Aaker et al. 2004), the impact of forgiveness as a complex social behavioral pattern in interorganizational buyer–seller relationships has not yet been empirically examined. We address this gap by investigating how forgiveness affects the performance and management of a buyer–seller relationship after a transgression.

To this end, this qualitative study is first in advancing theory construction for the concept of forgiveness in interorganizational buyer–seller relationships. In doing so, it offers a number of theoretical and managerial contributions. From a theoretical perspective, our study (1) examines the potential effect of forgiveness as a moderator on the management and performance of the buyer–seller relationship, and

N. Stuebiger (✉) • A. Haas
University of Giessen, Giessen, Germany
e-mail: nina.stuebiger@wirtschaft.uni-giessen.de; alexander.haas@wirtschaft.uni-giessen.de

J. Baumann • K. Le Meunier-FitzHugh
University of East Anglia, Norwich, UK
e-mail: j.baumann@uea.ac.uk; K.Le-Meunier-Fitzhugh@uea.ac.uk

© Academy of Marketing Science 2016   743
L. Petruzzellis, R.S. Winer (eds.), *Rediscovering the Essentiality of Marketing*,
Developments in Marketing Science: Proceedings of the Academy of Marketing
Science, DOI 10.1007/978-3-319-29877-1_139

thereby on the organizational success of both partner firms. Further, conclusions are drawn as to how full forgiveness (i.e., comprising both the cognitive and affective dimension) can be achieved in interorganizational contexts involving different groups of actors, in order to avoid the presumably negative effects of partial forgiveness on relationship quality and performance. (2) The construct is examined from an investment-expectancy perspective, thus allowing for the development of explicit indicators of when it is appropriate for firms to either restore or terminate the business relationship. (3) Finally, it integrates prior findings from diverse disciplines such as psychology and management and thereby introduces the forgiveness construct into the relationship marketing research stream.

From a managerial perspective, this research provides (1) key insights which allow examination of the conditions under which it is either appropriate to successfully restore or otherwise end the collaboration between buyer and seller, thereby facilitating effective relationship performance management. To this end, our study (2) enhances managers understanding of the transformation of the buyer–seller relationship after a transgression occurred, which may affect the satisfaction, trust, loyalty, and closeness of involved actors. (3) It identifies decisive influencing factors, which advise firms on what way to forgive is most effective in order to avoid longlasting discontent between partner firms (e.g., whether to display and/or communicate forgiveness openly, apologize, or compensate the victim).

Our study is unique in its examination of the effect of forgiveness on buyer and supplier performance leading to a new way of thinking about transgressions in buyer–supplier relationships and highlighting the importance of appropriate reactions. In line with these first insights, this research provides a conceptual basis for future—qualitative and quantitative—examination of the implementation of forgiveness by both organizational actors (buyer and seller) and identifies forgiveness as a driver for future firm profits.

References available upon request.

Relationship Communication and Relationship Quality as Predictors of Relationship Continuity

Walfried M. Lassar, Sanjit Roy, and Sathyaprakash Balaji Makam

Abstract Communication is considered as one of the important factors in fostering relationship development and maintenance (Finne and Grönroos 2009; Dagger et al. 2011). It provides an understanding of the exchange partners' intentions, and fosters trust and information exchange needed to promote long-term customer relationships. It is considered as a "necessary process" for developing and maintaining enduring and mutually beneficial relationships between the firm and its customers (Berry 1995). Despite its significance, communication has attracted limited attention in the relationship marketing and services marketing domain. In response to the recent calls for empirical inquiries into the role of communication (Finne and Grönroos 2009), this study contributes to literature by examining the strategic role of relationship communication in the B2C service relationships. More specifically, based on the intercultural and interpersonal communication and relationship marketing literature we propose and examine the role of relationship communication in enhancing the relationship quality and improving relationship continuity with the service provider.

We conceptualize relationship communication as a multidimensional construct consisting of cognitive, affective, and behavioral components. Based on the extant literature, relationship communication is determined by the customers' assessment of firm communication in terms of the clarity, pleasantness, responsiveness, and language (Coviello et al. 2002). Further, prior researchers suggest that relationship quality is a multidimensional construct consisting of trust, satisfaction, and commitment (Balaji 2015). Based on the review of literature, we propose that the relationship communication dimensions directly and indirectly influence relationship continuity through relationship quality dimensions. To test the proposed relation-

W.M. Lassar (✉)
Florida International University, Miami, FL, USA
e-mail: lassarw@fiu.edu

S. Roy
University of Western Australia Business School, Crawley, WA, Australia
e-mail: Sajit.roy@uwa.edu.au

S.B. Makam
Nottingham University Business School, Ningbo, China
e-mail: Sathyaprakashbalaji.makam@nottingham.edu.cn

© Academy of Marketing Science 2016
L. Petruzzellis, R.S. Winer (eds.), *Rediscovering the Essentiality of Marketing*,
Developments in Marketing Science: Proceedings of the Academy of Marketing
Science, DOI 10.1007/978-3-319-29877-1_140

745

ships, two studies are conducted. In the first study, 148 participants provided responses on their assessment of the firm communication. Following the exploratory factor analysis four factors representing the relationship communication dimensions of clarity, pleasantness, reciprocity, and language were extracted. In the second study, 200 actual banking customers in Malaysia provided response on the 18-item relationship communication scale identified in study 1, relationship quality dimensions of trust, satisfaction and commitment, and relationship continuity. Results of the structural equation modeling using SmartPLS revealed that relationship quality dimensions mediate the relationship between relationship communication dimensions and relationship continuity. In other words, the results suggest that customers' perception of firm communication plays a key role in developing, maintaining, and enhancing customer relationships. Since the success of relationship marketing strategies largely depends on the effectiveness of marketing communications (Herington et al. 2009), our study extends previous research by empirically examining how communication affects relationship quality and relationship continuity in the B2C service relationships.

References available upon request.

Predicting Customer Churn in the Insurance Industry: A Data Mining Case Study

Francesco Schena

Introduction

In markets with fierce competition and low switching costs customer attrition (or churn) is a key concern. In the past marketers addressed the problem primarily by making the customer loyal to the brand. More recently, roles are reverting and brands are being committed to demonstrate loyalty to the customer, through virtuous customer relationship management (CRM) that pre-empts churn before it occurs. As the business know-how is becoming increasingly data-literate and technology breaking down the barriers for IT infrastructure costs, analytics is proved effective in anticipating churn behaviour, enabling targeted, cost-effective retention campaigns towards customers at risk of defection.

The purpose of this research is to develop an effective and easy-to-interpret model for predicting churn in commercial line insurance, an industry that, particularly in mature markets, strongly relies on customers' lifetime.

Methodology

The research methodology followed one of the most popular frameworks for data mining projects: CRISP-DM (*Cross Industry Standard Process for Data Mining*) framework (Chapman et al. 2000; Shearer 2000). It consists of the following six phases: (1) Business Understanding; (2) Data Understanding; (3) Data Preparation; (4) Modelling; (5) Evaluation and (6) Deployment.

F. Schena (✉)
Etihad Airways, Khalifa City, United Arab Emirates
e-mail: francesco.schena@gmail.com

© Academy of Marketing Science 2016
L. Petruzzellis, R.S. Winer (eds.), *Rediscovering the Essentiality of Marketing*,
Developments in Marketing Science: Proceedings of the Academy of Marketing
Science, DOI 10.1007/978-3-319-29877-1_141

747

Business Understanding

In conjunction with business experts, it has been defined that the data mining project should answer the question: 'which policies will be cancelled within the next 12 months?' through binary classifiers that output 1 if the contract will be cancelled, 0 otherwise.

Giving a definition to the word "cancelled" is non-trivial. According to Hadden (2007), deliberate churn (i.e. churn due to voluntary and explicit decision of the customer) is the only case of attrition that companies can avoid. In our case, we modelled any cancellation event, irrespective of whether it was deliberate or not, because the quality of the data was not good enough to infer a reliable classification of deliberate churners. Unsurprisingly, any attempts of modelling deliberate churn had no success.

Data Understanding and Preparation

The data set was made up of over 600 k records, which were randomly split among training, validation and test sets. Each record had 410 attributes. These can be grouped into the following six categories (Schena 2014): (a) product specifications; (b) premium, (c) customer demographics, (d) customer behaviour, (e) claims history and (f) customer relationship.

The main challenge at this phase was to deal with the rarity of the positive class, as cancelled policies were less than 10 % of the data set. This is a recurring issue in churn modelling (Burez and Van den Poel 2009) that biases the model in favour of the majority class (Longadge and Dongre 2013; Weiss 2004), since there would be more chances to classify correctly a non-churner than a churner. To address this limitation we evaluated three approaches: undersampling, which means removing instances from the majority class at random until obtaining a 50:50 balanced data set; cost-sensitive learning, which would weigh the accuracy of churn classification more than the one of non-churn classification; rule induction tree pruning, a tree ensemble algorithm that removes the purest splits recursively to minimise class imbalance bias.

Another problem at this stage was to reduce the number of features, being the data too wide. The disadvantages of handling too many features are (Yu and Liu 2004): (a) high computational time, (b) difficulties in model interpretation and, above all, (c) overfitting. To work around this problem, we combined expert judgement with the following methods: R^2-based selection and decision tree-based selection.

Modelling

As the literature confirms, the most widespread models in churn prediction are decision tree and logistic regression. These were the preferred choice also on this study because of the ease of understanding and interpretation for decision-makers.

Rule Induction Pruning (RIP) Ensemble

This algorithm builds rule classifiers in a tree-based fashion (de Ville 2007; SAS-Institute 2014) with the aim of improving learning from the rare class. The mechanism is the following: leaves purer than a certain threshold are removed from the training set and a new tree is built on the remaining instances. This step is reiterated until no more leaves reach the given purity threshold. Finally, residuals are cleared through an artificial neural network.

Model Evaluation

After discarding invalid or poor performing models, the choice for the final model was drawn among eight competing options. The models were assessed against (1) predictive performance, (2) robustness and (3) interpretability criteria, as shown below.

Predictive performance. We used the following metrics: *accuracy*, the percentage of correct predictions, *sensitivity,* the percentage of positive instances classified as such and *specificity,* the percentage of negative instances classified as such. From a managers' view, accuracy, sensitivity and specificity were found extremely intuitive and thus preferred to other performance indicators. Nonetheless, the champion model was tested against other metrics as well: AUC/ROC and cumulative lift.

The *ROC chart* plots sensitivity in the vertical axis versus false positive rate (i.e. 1—specificity) in the horizontal axis, at each percentile of the population. The broader the underlying area (called AUC or ROC index), the more accurate the predictions.

The *cumulative captured response* is the percentage of positive instances captured up to a given percentile of the population. The *cumulative captured response* chart draws the cumulative response captured for each percentile. The *cumulative lift chart* is a variant that benchmarks the cumulative response to the random classification.

Robustness. The robustness is the ability of the model to resist external disturbances. Clemente et al. (2010) suggest the difference in absolute values between the AUC for the validation set and the AUC for the training set as a measure of the model's resistance to noise.

Interpretability. There is often trade-off between predictive accuracy and ease of interpretation, and the challenge for the modeller is to determine how to weight both factors so that the model chosen is the best suited for the problem at hand (Feelders, Daniels and Holsheimer 2000). Overly sophisticated models make the models less understandable, therefore less successfully deployable by the business. Generally, classifiers based on 'if-then' rules like decision trees are the most intuitive, whereas models like artificial neural networks require more abstraction. In this study, the firm was very concerned about the deployability of the model, to such an extent that comprehensible classifiers were always preferred to *black box* models, irrespective of their accuracy.

Findings

The choice of the model to deploy was drawn among four decision trees, three logistic regression and one ensemble model. All models were trained by cost-sensitive algorithms that penalise the misclassification of positives. Plus, some models were fitted to an undersampled data set.

Overall, logistic regression models consistently outperformed in estimating the correct churn probability. Nonetheless, the model chosen was a decision tree because of its great simplicity and comprehensibility, having only 21 leaves derived from nine variables. What is more, this model had acceptable accuracy and the highest robustness (lowest $|AUC_{valid} - AUC_{train}|$) among the options available.

Undersampling the training data little improved decision tree models, whereas no benefits were seen on logistic regression models.

Testing the champion model it was found, as expected, very small I-type error and considerable type-II error: almost every non-churner (98.8%) was predicted as such, versus 11.5% of churners correctly classified. This is due to the strong imbalance between the two classes.

The cumulative lift chart demonstrated reasonably good performance at the top percentiles. At the 5th percentile, it was 3.88. This result was judged satisfactory from both managers and business experts, being it an improvement over previous in-house attempts. The most important attribute by far was the difference between the premium at the current year and the premium at the previous year. Businesswise, this variable can be translated into the amount of upsells/downsells year-to-date: the more often the customer withdraws its insurance coverages from its portfolio, the more likely it will churn. Other important variables are: the time since the last record mutation, interpreted as the number of months since the last time the contract has been changed; and a Boolean variable that gives information on whether the contract is about to expire or not.

Conclusion

In saturated markets such as the commercial line insurance, predictive analytics tools for churn behaviour are important support for marketing decision-making. In order to predict which contracts will be cancelled within the next 12 months in an insurance company, there have been built decision trees and logistic regression models. The key challenges that arose for the problem at hand were the following:

1. **Giving a definition of "churn" that is consistent with the project objectives**. There is not a universal definition of churn: the definition depends on company-specific business objectives, but also technical constraints. In this study we mapped all possible churn events, distinguishing between deliberate and non-deliberate churn. However, this theoretical distinction did not find practical application due to the poor quality of the data stored in the database.

2. **Dealing with class imbalance**. Churn is a rare—yet not negligible—event. From a modelling perspective this entails working with data sets biased towards the non-churn event. This is considered a problem because the cost of misclassifying a churner (false negative) is much higher than the cost of misclassifying a non-churner (false positive). For this reason, three approaches have been explored: cost-sensitive learning, undersampling, ensemble learning algorithms. It is worth mentioning that undersampling improved decision tree models, but not logistic regression models, which are by their nature more resistant to these biases.

3. **Selecting relevant variables**. The insurance business is characterised by large volumes of data, spanning from customer demographics to their behaviour and claims history. Appropriate algorithms for dimensions reduction were forward selection methods and tree-based approaches.

4. **Coping with trade-off decisions between ease of interpretation and accuracy**. In business contexts, the most accurate model is not necessarily the best suited to the problem at hand. Rather, predictive performance and deployability of the model should be considered together and weighted each according to the client needs and expertise. Indeed, the model chosen in this study was very simple and intuitive, as it learned from only nine variables. Since final users, i.e. underwriters and salespersons, are not expected to have a statistical modelling background, an easy-to-interpret model increases dramatically the chances of success of the retention strategy.

The model constructed was a cost-sensitive tree based on a CS-C4.5 algorithm. It fulfilled both requirements of performance and deployability. On the one hand, its performance was better than any previous model developed in the past by the company. On the other, it was pruned in such a way that the structure was simple and intuitive.

References available upon request.

Part XVII
Retailing

Examining Reactive Customer Engagement Strategies in Online Shopping Cart Abandonment: A Regulatory Fit Perspective

Jessica Ogilvie, Kris Lindsey, Kristy Reynolds, and William Magnus Northington

Abstract Online retailing is thriving as consumers become more comfortable shopping online (Cho 2004). In the USA alone, online retailing total revenue topped $280 billion by the end of 2013 (Sehgal 2014), an increase of greater than 20 % from just 2 years ago. Electronic commerce (e-commerce) has been identified as an increasingly important component of marketing strategy and customer relations (Close and Kukar-Kinney 2010). Consequently, marketing scholars have acknowledged the need for new models and theories which contribute to a more comprehensive understanding of online consumer behavior (Kukar-Kinney and Close 2010).

According to industry reports, continued growth in the e-commerce industry will result largely from existing web shoppers spending increased time and money online (Forrester 2013). With this in mind, firms must consider marketing strategies aimed at increasing purchases of existing online shoppers as opposed to a focus aimed only at acquiring new customers. A promising avenue to better understand the behavior of current online shoppers involves addressing an issue of considerable importance in today's online retailing environment (Close and Kukar-Kinney 2010)—understanding why consumers take the time to make purchase decisions (browsing for and placing items into an online shopping cart) only to abandon that shopping cart without making a purchase. As the importance and relevance of e-commerce continues to grow, it is imperative that scholars gain a deeper understanding of "non-buyer behavior" (Kukar-Kinney and Close 2010, p. 250), an important but understudied segment of online consumer behavior (Close et al. 2012).

Formally defined, online shopping cart abandonment occurs when a consumer places an item or items into their online shopping cart and then leaves the retail website without purchasing the item(s) during that online shopping session (Kukar-Kinney and Close 2010, p. 240). This "epidemic" is costing online retailers $18 billion of revenue a year in the USA alone (Kramer 2011). While the ability to

J. Ogilvie (✉) • K. Lindsey • K. Reynolds
University of Alabama, Tuscaloosa, AL, USA
e-mail: jlogilvie@crimson.ua.edu; kklindsey@crimson.ua.edu; kreynold@cba.ua.edu

W.M. Northington
Idaho State University, Pocatello, ID, USA
e-mail: nortwill@isu.edu

© Academy of Marketing Science 2016
L. Petruzzellis, R.S. Winer (eds.), *Rediscovering the Essentiality of Marketing*,
Developments in Marketing Science: Proceedings of the Academy of Marketing
Science, DOI 10.1007/978-3-319-29877-1_142

755

effectively recapture abandoned carts would clearly boost revenues, it is imperative to note that, in the eyes of the consumers, these virtual shopping carts have multiple uses that are not always tied to procurement (Kukar-Kinney and Close 2010).

Additionally, the varying effects of risk and benefit perceptions on consumers' likelihood to abort online transactions shown in previous research (Cho 2004) suggest relevance in examining this issue through a regulatory focus framework (Higgins 1998). Regulatory focus theory suggests that individuals assign different importance to the same decision based on their promotion-focused (i.e., individuals are concerned with maximizing gains) or prevention-focused (i.e., individuals attempt to minimize losses) regulatory orientation. With billions of dollars at stake (Close et al. 2012), this opportunity presents a compelling case for research that expands the knowledge of regulatory focus theory in the online retailing environment.

Based upon these pressing calls to research and the limited online shopping cart abandonment research, this study addresses two main questions: (1) How does consumer shopping motivation (specifically hedonic shopping motivation and utilitarian shopping motivation) influence consumer online shopping cart abandonment? and (2) How does regulatory focus theory apply within this context? That is, how do promotion and prevention framed messages aid in the recapture of abandoned shopping carts? Specifically, this research proposes that a retailer is more likely to recapture sales through initiated contact with the customer when the strategic focus of their message fits the regulatory focus of the customer's end-goal.

References available upon request.

Antecedents of Peripheral Services Cross-Buying Behavior

Heiner Evanschitzky, Neeru Malhotra, Florian v. Wangenheim, and Katherine N. Lemon

Abstract In order to improve customer lifetime value, retailers are increasingly trying to extend relationships with their customers. The "breadth" of a buyer–seller relationship is defined as the number of additional (different) products or services purchased from a company over time. It is commonly viewed as customer cross-buying or add-on buying behavior. Cross-buying has been associated with customer retention, revenue generation, switching costs, and loyalty and is vital for a company's stable financial development. Despite its obvious relevance, the breadth dimension of a buyer–seller relationship is a relatively unexplored issue and only little research has attempted to identify the drivers of cross-buying. Furthermore, there is no research so far that has investigated an arguable even more important type of cross-buying: cross-buying of peripheral services. This study is the first attempt to empirically investigate the determinants of that type of relationship breadth extension strategy. Findings demonstrate that factors stimulating customers to cross-buy additional peripheral services from the focal retailer are not be the same as previously found by studies in the financial services context. Some factors like commitment, which are considered crucial for stimulating cross-buying behavior in financial services, do not seem to be important for peripheral services purchase behavior in the retailing context. On the other hand, convenience and social benefits seem to be quite crucial in the retailing sector. We discuss implications for academic research as well as retail management.

H. Evanschitzky (✉) • N. Malhotra
Aston Business School, Birmingham, UK
e-mail: h.evanschitzky@aston.ac.uk; n.malhotra@aston.ac.uk

F.v. Wangenheim
D-MTEC, ETH Zürich, Zürich, Switzerland
e-mail: fwangenheim@ethz.ch

K.N. Lemon
Boston College, Chestnut Hill, MA, USA
e-mail: kay.lemon@bc.edu

© Academy of Marketing Science 2016
L. Petruzzellis, R.S. Winer (eds.), *Rediscovering the Essentiality of Marketing*,
Developments in Marketing Science: Proceedings of the Academy of Marketing
Science, DOI 10.1007/978-3-319-29877-1_143

757

Emotional and Behavioral Consequences of Cross-Border Shopping

Liane Nagengast, Marc Linzmajer, Tim Boettger, and Thomas Rudolph

Motivated by potential savings, an increasing number of consumers travel to neighboring countries for the main purpose of shopping (e.g., Canadians to the USA, Swiss to Germany). This cross-border shopping might seriously harm local economies, for example in terms of revenue, unemployment, and social well-being.

In a quasi-field experiment with 301 Swiss consumers, we show that cross-border shoppers are consciously aware that their behavior might harm their local economy. They feel inner conflicts which affect their shopping emotions and their intended future cross-border purchases. Moreover, referring to Attribution Theory, we show that consumers' inner conflicts depend on who they blame for the price differences between the countries. Consumers who attribute price differences to internal causes (i.e., national retailers) feel less conflicted than consumers who attribute the price differences to external causes (i.e., the foreign economy).

These results have important implications for local retailers and public policy makers. Cross-border shopping behavior can be influenced by actively communicating the reasons for price differences between neighboring countries.

L. Nagengast (✉) • M. Linzmajer • T. Boettger • T. Rudolph
University of St. Gallen, St. Gallen, Switzerland
e-mail: liane.nagengast@unisg.ch; marc.linzmajer@unisg.ch; tim.boettger@unisg.ch; thomas.rudolph@unisg.ch

© Academy of Marketing Science 2016
L. Petruzzellis, R.S. Winer (eds.), *Rediscovering the Essentiality of Marketing*,
Developments in Marketing Science: Proceedings of the Academy of Marketing
Science, DOI 10.1007/978-3-319-29877-1_144

Linking Initial Beliefs, Trust, Perceived Value and Purchase Intentions in the Context of Second-Hand Goods Sold by Unknown Online Retailers

Laura Salciuviene and Ahmad Daryanto

Abstract Online shopping is significantly increasing worldwide and is showing a continuous potential in terms of growth, security, price and shopping convenience. A constant 11 % increase in online retail revenues suggests that online orders are increasing and will grow steadily to $370 billion in 2017 (Abramovich 2014). This growing trend might be also advantageous for second-hand online retailers as it has been reported that one third of consumers buy more second-hand goods compared to previous years (Chahai 2013).

Second-hand online shopping is one of the industries that everlastingly remain unaffected even if it undergoes any economic circumstances (Heller 2011) as recession might even have a positive effect on sales growth of second-hand goods. Currently, at least seven out of ten customers have purchased second-hand goods, such as DVDs, CDs, books or adult clothing (Chahai 2013). Since the second-hand industry has been predicted to grow steadily, second-hand retailers need to have a better understanding of their target market's initial beliefs and their purchase intentions of second-hand goods. Thus, our study investigates how initial beliefs, trust and perceived value influence intentions to purchase second-hand goods from unknown online retailers.

To achieve the objective of the study, we conducted an online survey with 251 respondents who purchase second-hand goods from online retailers. Respondents were recruited using online social communities (i.e., *Myspace* and *Facebook*). Our findings suggest that information on safety and reliability that second-hand good

L. Salciuviene (✉) • A. Daryanto
Lancaster University Management School, Lancaster, UK
e-mail: l.salciuviene@lancaster.ac.uk; a.daryanto@lancaster.ac.uk

© Academy of Marketing Science 2016
L. Petruzzellis, R.S. Winer (eds.), *Rediscovering the Essentiality of Marketing*,
Developments in Marketing Science: Proceedings of the Academy of Marketing
Science, DOI 10.1007/978-3-319-29877-1_145

online retailers present on their websites affects customer intentions to purchase second-hand goods from those retailers. The perceived safety of the website translates into positive perceptions about second-hand goods and contributes to customer purchase intentions from that online retailer. This research offers implications with a practical focus on maximising purchases of second-hand goods sold online.

References available upon request.

Modeling and Measuring Home Brands Ability to Capture Customer Loyalty to Nonfood Retailers

Gonzalo Moreno Warleta, María Puelles Gallo, and Mónica Díaz-Bustamante Ventisca

Introduction

Retailers, more specifically nonfood vendors, struggle to reduce consumer churn when shopping for consumer goods. From simple coupons to sophisticated big-data-based loyalty systems, modern merchants undertake all sorts of initiatives to maintain customers' loyalty to their stores (Grönroos 1991; Iniesta and Agustín 2003; Knox and Walker 2003; Lohr 2012; Uncles et al. 2003).

At the same time, there is a general consensus in literature that retail brands have the ability to generate store loyalty (Dick and Basu 1994). Nevertheless, this particular fact has seldom been empirically corroborated. Probably due to this lack of certainty, many nonfood retailers carry out "private label" (PL) product strategies as a way to preserve healthy business ratios, as revenue, contribution margin, operating profit, etc.; though more often than not, these strategies are short-term oriented: Aiming to improve those "general business metrics"—better negotiating with National Brands manufacturers which leads to lower costs; or pocketing the sometimes scarce PL products margins, for instance—vendors tend to forget the PL's potential contribution to their power to "stand out from the crowd" when consumers select where to shop.

G.M. Warleta (✉)
Saint Louis University, St. Louis, MO, USA

Universidad Complutense de Madrid, Madrid, Spain
e-mail: gmoreno@slu.edu

M.P. Gallo • M.D.-B. Ventisca
Universidad Complutense de Madrid, Madrid, Spain
e-mail: mpuelles@ccee.ucm.es; monica.diazbustamante@gmail.com

© Academy of Marketing Science 2016
L. Petruzzellis, R.S. Winer (eds.), *Rediscovering the Essentiality of Marketing*,
Developments in Marketing Science: Proceedings of the Academy of Marketing
Science, DOI 10.1007/978-3-319-29877-1_146

It is unusual, still today, to see Retail Brand strategies in nonfood specialty markets that are as sophisticated as they have become in packaged consumer goods distribution, throughout the last 40 years (Puelles and Manzano 2009).

Background

Literature on Private Labels has become plentiful in the last decade, usually focused on the first stages of consumers' brand valuation (Brand Equity), leading to purchase decision and behavior. In general terms, these models pretty much make Retail Brands comparable to any "regular" National Brand (Jara and Cliquet 2012).

On the other hand, while analyzing consumer behavior towards Brands, Loyalty researchers have pushed different versions of the Ajzen and Fishbein's Theory of Reasoned Action (T.R.A.) further ahead (Ajzen and Fishbein 1980), into (purchase) behavior repetition, which would generate informational feedback, thus becoming a source of newer and stronger Brand Associations: A newer and stronger Brand Image would shape and reinforce consumer's attitude, thus generating a more persistent future purchase intention (Jacoby and Chestnut 1978). Initially created around National Brands, as one would expect, these postulates have been later applied to Retail Brands as well.

To end with, modeling of customer loyalty to retail distribution has followed similar patterns, starting from T.R.A. as a general model for human behavior analysis and prediction, combining it with different service quality and customer value models (Ruiz-Molina 2009; Swait and Sweeney 2000; Sweeney and Soutar 2001) from the 1990s of the past century.

Brand Loyalty and Store Loyalty research trends have evolved concurrently, since, as two parallel lines never crossing each other. Our work aims to generate a meaningful contribution to PL strategizing, and Big-Box retailers efforts towards increasing customer store loyalty, by jointly approaching these two research trends.

Research Methods

A comprehensive model was created, representing the full "Loyalty chains" for Brands and Stores: Brand Image (Associations) and Store Perceived Value as their starting points; and Attitude, Intention, Behavior and, finally, Loyalty following in both cases.

Product and Store attributes and benefits were firstly approached through a set of interviews with expert DIY practitioners, afterwards validated through a second qualitative research stage that consisted in focus groups. Attitudes towards the DIY activity, the products used, and the stores where these were purchased were explored in order to create the best possible survey questionnaire.

Quantitative phase included more than 700 interviews, of which 320 finally constituted a subsample of private brand knowledgeable consumers that were DYI practitioners of all performance levels, at the same time.

The variables used in the analysis were the following:

1. On the Private Brand side: For Private Labels A (DIY tools) and B (paint):

   (a) Brand Awareness and Knowledge
   (b) Actual past purchase
   (c) General A and B Brand Assessments, composed variable that included:

   • Brand Associations (*Image*)
   • Attitudes towards Brand
   • Intention to repurchase
   • Declared self-perceived Loyalty to the Brands

2. On the Store Side: For Retailer X (owner of both PLs)

   (a) Store Brand Name Awareness and Knowledge
   (b) Actual past purchase
   (c) Store Brand Name Associations (*Image*)
   (d) Attitudes towards Store Brand Name
   (e) Intention to repurchase
   (f) Declared self-perceived Loyalty to the Store Brand Name

As it can be inferred by this description, the initial comprehensive model was simplified, by not questioning the general Consumer Readiness Stages and Loyalty models for Brands, as they are both generally accepted in doctrine. The store-loyalty model, though, was indeed put to the test.

Results and Discussion

The statistic analysis proved the existence of a strong correlation between the different constructs of consumer store-loyalty, reinforcing the idea of mental processes towards attitudinal loyalty to behave as a chain reaction. This can be considered to validate the parallel "double chain" framework.

Further on, when analyzing relationship between Brand Loyalty and Store Loyalty, data proved different levels of correlation between "Brand indicators" and "Store Indicators." This correlation could not be proven for all analyzed brands, nor for all the different constructs, though. This was until a signified attitude (positive or negative) towards the Retail Brand was declared by the consumer. Once this signified attitude towards the PL becomes apparent, a clear and statistically significant correlation shows in all cases, between the general Brand Valuation and all the different components of Store Loyalty, as shown in Table 1.

Finally, a cluster analysis based on individual variables proved the existing correlation to vary depending on the consumer's expected shopping benefits (price,

Table 1 Retail brand valuation (DEXTER) vs. Components of store loyalty (Leroy Merlin): Spearman rank correlation analysis

Variables	Attitude towards Leroy	Intention towards Leroy	Behavior towards Leroy	General valuation DEXTER
Attitude towards Leroy	1.0000			
N. cases	67			
$p=$	.0000			
Intention towards Leroy	.9799	1.0000		
N. cases	67	67		
$p=$	.0000	.0000		
Behavior towards Leroy	.9247	.9691	1.0000	
N. cases	67	67	67	
$p=$	.0000	.0000	.0000	
General valuation DEXTER	**.9695**	**.9611**	**.8880**	1.0000
N. cases	**67**	**67**	**67**	68
$p=$	**.0000**	**.0000**	**.0000**	.0000

Sample: $n=67$ ("*declare a signified positive or negative attitude towards DEXTER*")

promotion and quality sensitivity, intrinsic loyalty, and the enjoyment provided by the purchase experience), her general perception of Retail Brands (likes PLs/purchases PLs), and her relationship with the product category (DIY enjoyment and performance).

According to these variables, consumers were clustered into "Big Savers," "Brand Loyal," and "Rational Shoppers." These last ones proved to be keener on PLs, and also to be the group where PL Valuation and Attitude towards the Store showed the highest codependent relationship.

References available upon request.

Part XVIII
Selling and Sales Management

Industrial Lifestyles from the Perspective of B2B Sales

Ann-Kathrin Bossler, Kristina Kovac, Marc Kuhn, and Vanessa Reit

Abstract Intensive competition in B2B markets is leading to a sustained change in customer behavior. The altered conditions lead to aggressive price negotiations and abuse of power, while making negotiation situations in sales more difficult. Bearing these facts in mind, we can see that for a sales employee, the ultimate indicator of success lies in the final result of negotiation. This is clearly determined by the price. Surveys among sales executives in the B2B sector show that other negotiation elements, such as the duration of the business relationship, are ascribed virtually to importance in the negotiation situation itself. Despite these tendencies, the question remains as to whether other elements, including the character of the negotiation partners, can either consciously or unconsciously influence the negotiation situation in a positive or negative way in everyday negotiations. This paper examines the role extreme typologies from the purchasing company have on sales and the importance of long-term business relationships in comparison to the type of negotiation partner and immediate pricing.

An adaptive choice-based conjoint analysis (ACBC), based on Kuhn and Zajontz's "Industrial Lifestyle" model, was conducted with a total of 102 sales employees from various sectors.

Keywords Buying Center • Conjoint Analysis • B2B Marketing; Industrial Lifestyles • Sales

A.-K. Bossler (✉) • K. Kovac • M. Kuhn • V. Reit
Baden-Wuerttemberg Cooperative State University, Stuttgart, Germany
e-mail: ann-katrin.bossler@web.de; kristina.kovac@gmx.de; marc.kuhn@dhbw-stuttgart.de; vanessa.reit@dhbw-stuttgart.de

© Academy of Marketing Science 2016
L. Petruzzellis, R.S. Winer (eds.), *Rediscovering the Essentiality of Marketing*, Developments in Marketing Science: Proceedings of the Academy of Marketing Science, DOI 10.1007/978-3-319-29877-1_147

Theoretical Background

In the analysis of industrial business relationships, the concepts of the buying center and buying network are still stubbornly cited, even after several decades (Webster and Wind 1972; Hutt and Speh 2004; Backhaus and Voeth 2010). The notional grouping of business representatives who participate in a purchasing decision is still linked to functions and organizational allocation when it comes to practical implementation (Kennedy 1982). Decision-makers are role players who are allocated certain behavioral expectations (role sending) in the purchasing process and who must meet these expectations in more or less strong behavioral models (role behavior) (Backhaus and Voeth 2010). Typical examples are "the cost-focused purchaser" or the "tech-loving development project manager." In a dynamically and internationally influenced industrial environment however, this classical role concept is defined too narrowly. Organizational representatives participating in a purchasing process should of course be allocated organizational functions, but in an industrial environment, they often behave contrary to the way their role is commonly understood. The traditional buying center approach does not take important institutional and individual influencing factors into account (Homburg 2012).

In addition to the partial approaches, which include the buying center concept, there are also so-called total models that are used to try to better understand organizational purchasing behavior (Johnston and Lewin 1996). Here, the factors that influence purchasing behavior are analyzed and viewed simultaneously (Backhaus and Voeth 2010). Although multiple empirical analyses have found correlations in the total models, they are more complex and are still highly abstract due to their limited practical applicability (Skarmeas et al. 2008).

Furthermore, there are approaches to industrial market segmentation that are essentially multi-stage approaches and involve sequential segmentation criteria relevant to B2B. These take the complexity of organizational purchasing behavior into account (Kohrmann 2003). While the three-stage segmentation models of Scheuch (1975) and Groene (1977) characterized industrial goods companies according to environmental, organizational and individual characteristics, Robertson and Barich (1992) divided industrial firms into three categories according to buyer types, potential customers, first-time purchasers, and regular customers.

Five-stage shell models (such as the "nested approach" of Bonoma and Shapiro 1983) or nine-stage phase concepts (Hlavacek and Reddy 1986) consider performance characteristics, customer purchasing characteristics, and situational factors in addition to organizational criteria. These models attempt to take into account the complexity of industrial markets using increasing granularity. The approaches not only consider external characteristics of purchasing companies, but also internal aspects, therefore making them suitable to the peculiarities of the industrial goods market. Due to the multi-stage approach however, a tree structure is created that means that a business allocated to a certain segment can no longer be allocated to another segment in the next stage. In addition, many segmentation criteria fail to sufficiently take into account the behavior of industrial decision-makers (Kuhn and

Zajontz 2011). Multi-stage segmentation approaches have one thing in common: The first step is always a macro-segmentation based on the characteristics of the industrial company or relevant market (Backhaus and Voeth 2010). The subsequent micro-segmentation applies a further disaggregation to the criteria of the buying center relevant to behavior. It therefore forms the basis for analyzing organizational purchasing behavior and enables deductions to be made for price negotiations and other operative marketing decisions. In this regard, the transfer of lifestyle typologies from the consumer goods sector to the industrial environment is new (Kuhn and Zajontz 2011).

Lifestyles describe the personal self-projection, which comprises the economic and social status, role, life orientation, and the values of an individual (Koschnick 2006). Based on the results of research in this area, groups or so-called lifestyle typologies can be defined that can be used to implement target group strategies or characterize purchasing behavior. There are a total of five relevant lifestyle typologies used around the world. In Germany, Austria, and Switzerland, the Sinus-Milieu-System®, developed by the market research institute Sinus Sociovision in Heidelberg, is most common and offers an outstanding opportunity within consumer research (Kalka and Allgayer 2006). In this system, the target groups are categorized according to a detailed analysis of social worlds. The fundamental consideration is that people who share identical characteristics such as age, gender, job, or income, known as socio-demographic twins, can be allocated to different target groups. Formal commonalities or an identical social status can go hand in hand with completely different views and values. The expectations and purchasing behavior of these consumers can only be methodically compiled through a holistic examination of their lifestyles and views (Kalka and Allgayer 2006). Toward the end of the 1970s, Sinus Sociovision first provided results through qualitative interviews related to the everyday life of the consumers. The Sinus-Milieu® indicators now classify people according to sociocultural aspects, such as the "established" or "modern performer," with the Sinus-Milieus® positioned correspondingly to lifestyles, i.e., to the values system and social status. The limited behavioral relevance in the orientation toward "socio-demographic twins" in the consumer goods sector can be transferred to the presumably identical roles of a single buying center function in the industrial goods environment. No two purchasing managers are the same just as no two production planners are the same. This means that "buying center twins" can vary greatly in their purchasing behavior. Therefore, Kuhn conducted a micro-segmentation to characterize various individuals involved in purchasing that went beyond the purely structural and functional orientation of the buying center. Kuhn separated these so-called industrial lifestyle types (Kuhn and Zajontz 2011) using group workshops, in which young professionals or trainees from over 50 industrial companies were asked to share their experiences of sales and purchasing roles to determine industrial lifestyle types. Aside from the functional and hierarchical aspects, the lifestyle-typical value principles and characteristics influencing personality were used as segmentation characteristics. This resulted in 8 different industrial lifestyle types (see Fig. 1).

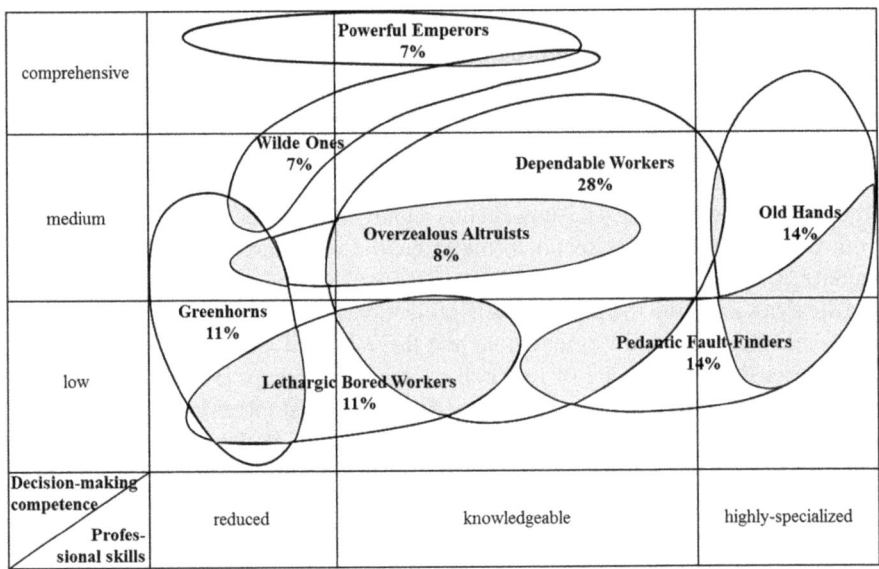

Fig. 1 Industrial lifestyle types (Kuhn 2009)

In addition to different industrial lifestyle types on the purchasing side, other aspects such as quality and the price of the service are important in industrial purchasing decisions (Homburg 2012). The duration of the business relationship also has an influence on purchasing behavior, as it is assumed that the advantage of a negotiation result diminishes as the length of the negotiation increases (Roth 2006).

Research Question and Hypotheses

The following core hypotheses were derived for testing, based on the central questions asked at the start, which focus both on the role of extreme typologies from the purchasing business and the importance of long-term business relationships compared to the type of negotiation partner and pricing:

H1: Sellers ascribe the greatest importance to price in negotiations.

Strategic sales goals are formulated based on the business objectives and the strategic marketing goals derived from these. In this regard, increasing revenue represents an important success goal for the sales staff. This forms the basis for hypothesis H1 (Hofbauer and Hellwig 2012).

H2: Long-term business relationships are an important influencing factor in the negotiation situation.

Longer business relationships lead to an improved flow of information and increased trust between the interacting partners. Therefore, the duration of the business relationship has a significant influence on the course of negotiations (Stock-Homburg 2009).

H3: The utility values of different negotiation partners (different industrial lifestyle types) deviate from each other from the seller's perspective.

The interaction between customer (purchaser) and sales employee represents an important deciding factor for the success of a sale. Based on active relationship management, it is possible to retain the loyalty of the customer to the business and increase value creation. The success of the personal interaction here has heavily influenced the abilities and behavior of those involved (Belz and Bieger 2006). As a result, we can presume that different purchaser types are preferred in negotiations according to their abilities and behavior.

Research Methodology

In order to generate realistic statements about the actual importance of the individual negotiation elements from the perspective of B2B sales, an adaptive choice-based conjoint analysis (ACBC) was used. The population is comprised of sales employees in the German B2B sector. The test subjects were selected consciously through a snowball sampling procedure. A total of 102 test subjects ($n = 102$) from a range of sectors took part in the study.

In order to verify the hypotheses, the conjoint analysis procedure was used as a multivariate method to evaluate preference and benefit (Baier and Brusch 2009; Teichert et al. 2008; Völckner et al. 2008). The term "conjoint analysis" (synonymous use in specialist literature: "conjoint measurement") refers to a method of illustrating and evaluating a variety of objects by a single person. This means that, in the first instance, conjoint analyses are individual analyses that enable the evaluation behavior of the test person to be understood. The objects concerned are defined by certain product attributes or features, although an integrated approach is taken to the consideration or evaluation of the individual objects (see http://www.sawtooth-software.com/-products/acbc/ (as at: 31/08/2012)). This decompositional approach is a specific advantage of the conjoint analysis. Taking this approach allows us to determine the contribution of individual product attributes to the benefit of a product empirically. Combination and further development of the classical conjoint analysis leads to ACBC. This form of analysis is a new approach that takes the best aspects of choice-based conjoint analysis (CBC) and adaptive conjoint analysis and combines them into a single procedure (see http://www.sawtoothsoftware.com/products/acbc/ (as at: 31/08/2012)).

ACBC was launched as marketable software by Sawtooth Software at the beginning of 2009. The basic concept behind the new approach is to improve the efficiency of interviews by allowing the integration of a variety of attributes and considering information relating to the purpose underlying the choice (Pelz 2012). In this approach, characteristics judged to be of no importance for the test subjects are excluded in the questioning stage (Schmaus 2010), in order to gain as much information as possible from the test subjects' decisions. The individual data sets are then assessed and aggregated for metric utility values for each characteristic, based on a mathematical statistical process (hierarchical bayes). We can assume here that the total utility of the object can be determined from the additive partial utility values (Dietz 2007). According to data provided by Sawtooth Software, ACBC is currently the most advanced method of its kind. It helps to provide information on how people make decisions concerning complex products and services.

In order to test the hypotheses set out above, the following characteristics were defined with different manifestations: price, duration of the business relationship, and the various purchaser personalities. In order to increase the validity of the results however, the characteristic "price" was not surveyed directly, but rather integrated as "price reduction" together with the duration of the negotiation discussion. This resulted in the following characteristics: "after a short period" or "after multi-stage negotiation," each in combination with "without price reduction," "with low price reduction," and "with high price reduction." For duration of the business relationship, the dimensions "one-time purchase," "occasional, irregular business," and "long-term and close business relationship" were defined and surveyed. To survey purchaser personality, the characteristics of the eight industrial lifestyle types were each transferred to an actual sales situation.

Results

In regard to hypothesis H1 "Sellers ascribe the greatest importance to price in negotiations," we can see that the negotiation result has the highest weighting of importance at 46.3 % (Table 1).

When we consider the individual utility values within the negotiation result, however, we can see that the manifestation "after a short period with low price reduction" is ascribed a greater importance with 39.7 utility points than "after multi-stage negotiations without price reduction" at 31.9 utility points. This means that price does not represent the most important element in negotiation. Nevertheless, the results show that a high price reduction is ascribed negative values, therefore always leading to a decrease in utility. Hypothesis H1 can be falsified based on these results.

In the test of the hypothesis H2: "Long-term business relationships are an important influencing factor in the negotiation situation," we see that the duration of the business relationship appears to play a role with 20.5 % importance weighting. Compared to the other two variables (negotiation result and industrial lifestyle types) however, we can see that it is only a secondary factor. When we consider the manifestations of the business relationship duration, we can see that the "long-term business," with 35.6 utility points, is given the greatest utility by some distance, compared to "occasional business" (−11.3) and "one-time purchase" (−24.3). This

Table 1 Results ACBC analysis

Average utilities (zero-centered diffs)	Average utilities	Standard deviation
Dependable workers	43.47153	20.16951
Overzealous altruists	41.82404	19.55714
Powerful emperors	6.17914	14.48696
Old hands	2.77595	11.21890
Pedantic fault-finders	−8.65821	16.74529
Greenhorns	−13.65418	21.11744
Wild ones	−28.56362	18.18538
lethargic bored-workers	−43.37464	17.99773
Long-term	35.63341	10.19007
Occasional purchases	−11.30714	7.95381
One-off purchase	−24.32627	11.20400
Your offer is accepted after a short period without price reduction	49.99113	23.35042
Your offer is accepted after a short period with a small price reduction	39.79160	16.19560
Your offer is accepted after multi-stage negotiation phases without price reduction	31.91885	20.45084
Your offer is accepted after multi-stage negotiation phases with a small price reduction	15.08158	16.47154
Your offer is accepted after a short period with a high price reduction	−58.45636	29.44150
Your offer is accepted after multi-stage negotiation phases with a high price reduction	−78.32681	27.14695
None	10.27340	21.28781
Average importances	Average importances	Standard deviation
Purchaser types	33.13858	9.96447
Duration of business relationship	20.55840	5.96664
Result of negotiations	46.30302	9.80269

means that both the duration of the business relationship and the long-term nature of the business in general are ascribed a positive value. Hypothesis H2 can therefore not be falsified.

To test hypothesis H3: "The utility values of different negotiation partners (different industrial lifestyle types) deviate from each other from the seller's perspective," the average utility values of the industrial lifestyle types are compared in the upper region of the table. The utilities of the different types vary greatly from a sales perspective. The "dependable worker" and "overzealous altruistics" are ascribed very high utility values (43.4 and 41.8 points respectively). In contrast, the "wild ones," "greenhorns," and "lethargic bored-workers" were given universally negative values of up to −43.3 utility points. This means that hypothesis H3 can be verified.

In this context, further analyses (ANOVA) indicate an interesting correlation ($p = .015$) between the duration of the role (the duration that the subject has been performing this task in sales) and the importance of the various types. We can see

Table 2 ANOVA results

	Importance of types (%)
Less than 2 years	35.5
2–5 years	30.9
5–10 years	29.9
More than 10 years	37.9

that the type of negotiation partner is important above all for sales staff with low experience (less than 2 years) and for sales staff with high experience (over 10 years) (Table 2).

Conclusion

In summary, the fact remains that as suspected, sales experts in negotiation situations place the greatest importance on the result of the negotiation and therefore on price. Surprisingly however, the importance of extreme typologies from the purchasing business cannot be dismissed. Depending on the purchaser type, clear differences can be seen between very negative and very positive utility values. Furthermore, the long-term nature of a business relationship is also of clearly recognizable importance to negotiations.

To conclude, the limitations of the present study should be explained for purposes of completeness and to aid continued investigations. The targeted scattering of the survey among different sales experts, for example, meant that the sample for the survey was selected consciously and not at random. This means that no conclusions can be drawn on the population. The number of investigated variables is also limited due to the complexity of a more comprehensive study. In addition to the elements studied here (negotiation result, industrial lifestyle type, and duration of business relationship), other factors also influence the utility of a negotiation situation from a sales perspective. A further study could, for example, examine the importance of profit margins, customer value, prestige customers, or strategic business goals. Furthermore, the test subjects assessed the different industrial lifestyle types based on the supplied information. The allocation of utility is therefore based on the subjective descriptions of the various types. If the type descriptions were formulated too positively or negatively, this could affect the judgment of the test subjects.

References

Backhaus, K., & Voeth, M. (2010). *Industriegütermarketing*. Munich: Vahlen.

Baier, D., & Brusch, M. (2009). *Conjointanalyse: Methoden—Anwendungen—Praxisbeispiele*. Berlin: Springer.

Belz, C., & Bieger, T. (2006). *Customer-Value: Kundenvorteile schaffen Unternehmensvorteile*. Heidelberg: Thexis.

Bonoma, T., & Shapiro, B. (1983). *Segmenting the industrial market*. Lexington: Lexington Books.

Dietz, W. (2007). *Grundlagen der Conjoint-Analyse: Varianten, Vorgehensweise, Anwendungen*. Saarbrücken: VDM Publishing.

Gröne, A. (1977). *Marktsegmentierung bei Investitionsgütern*. Wiesbaden: Gabler.

Hlavacek, J. D., & Reddy, N. M. (1986). Identifying and qualifying industrial market segments. *European Journal of Marketing, 20*, 8–22.

Hofbauer, G., & Hellwig, C. (2012). *Professionelles Vertriebsmanagement*. Erlangen: Publicis Publishing.

Homburg, C. (2012). *Marketingmanagement: Strategie—Instrumente—Umsetzung— Unternehmensführung*. Heidelberg: Gabler.

Hutt, M. D., & Speh, T. W. (2004). *Business marketing management: A strategic view of industrial and organizational markets*. London: Thomson.

Johnston, W. J., & Lewin, J. E. (1996). Organizational buying behaviour: Towards an integrative framework. *Journal of Business Research, 35*, 1–16.

Kalka, J., & Allgayer, F. (2006). *Zielgruppen—wie sie leben, was sie kaufen, woran sie glauben*. Moderne Industrie: Landsberg am Lech.

Kennedy, A. (1982). Industrial buying behaviour: A review of literature and research needs. *Management Decision, 20*, 38–51.

Kohrmann, O. (2003). *Mehrstufige Marktsegmentierung zur Neukundenakquisition*. Wiesbaden: Gabler.

Koschnick, W. J. (2006). *Von der Poesie der schönen Namensgebung—Glanz und Elend von Lifestyle-Typologien*. Munich: Focus Jahrbuch.

Kuhn, M. (2009). Beyond the Buying Center—Industrial Lifestyles and their implications on price negotiations, *Proceedings AMS World Marketing Congress Oslo*, 419–427.

Kuhn, M., & Zajontz, Y. (2011). *Industrielles Marketing*. Munich: Oldenbourg.

Pelz, J. (2012). *Aussagefähigkeit und Aussagewilligkeit von Probanden bei der Conjoint-Analyse*. Wiesbaden: Gabler.

Roth, S. (2006). *Preismanagement für Leistungsbündel*. Wiesbaden: Deutscher Universitätsverlag.

Scheuch, F. (1975). *Investitionsgüter-Marketing*. Opladen: Westdeutscher Verlag.

Schmaus, P. (2010). *Conjoint-Analysen im Target Costing: Grundlagen, Vorgehensweise und Methoden zur Target-Price-Bestimmung*. Saarbrücken: VDM Verlag Dr. Müller.

Skarmeas, D., Katsikeas, C. S., Spyropoulou, S., & Saleh-Sangari, E. (2008). Market and supplier characteristics driving distributor relationship quality in international marketing channels of industrial products. *Industrial Marketing Management, 37*, 23–36.

Stock-Homburg, R. (2009). *Der Zusammenhang zwischen Mitarbeiter- und Kundenzufriedenheit: Direkte, indirekte und moderierende Effekte*. Wiesbaden: Gabler.

Teichert, T., Sattler, H., & Völckner, F. (2008). Traditionelle Verfahren der Conjoint Analyse. In A. Herrmann, C. Homburg, & M. Klarmann (Eds.), *Handbuch Marktforschung: Methoden— Anwendungen—Praxisbeispiele* (pp. 651–685). Wiesbaden: Gabler.

Völckner, F., Sattler, H., & Teichert, T. (2008). Wahlbasierte Verfahren der Conjoint-Analyse. In A. Herrmann, C. Homburg, & M. Klarmann (Eds.), *Handbuch Marktforschung: Methoden— Anwendungen—Praxisbeispiele* (pp. 687–711). Wiesbaden: Gabler.

Webster, F. E. J., & Wind, Y. (1972). *Organizational buying behavior*. Englewood Cliffs, NJ: Prentice Hall.

Sales and Marketing, and Customer Relationships: A Structured Abstract

Kenneth Le Meunier-FitzHugh and Leslie Caroline Le Meunier-FitzHugh

Abstract This research investigates the impact of sales and marketing collaboration on the customer's propensity to purchase and customer value, thereby extending the current research into the sales and marketing interface. Prior research has established that sales departments may fail to support marketing initiatives and that marketing been known to fail to communicate marketing objectives effectively and to exclude sales from decision-making. This lack of coordination may become visible to the customer and consequently influence their relationship with the supplier. We suggest that internal sales and marketing relationships can impact on relationship quality and consequently the customers' propensity to purchase.

Customers demand greater value from their suppliers and consequently a relationship-building approach to marketing has been more widely adopted by many organizations (Harker and Egan 2006; Biggemann and Buttle 2012). Further, sustainable long-term relationships benefit the supplier by reducing costs and increasing sales (e.g., Hennig-Thurau et al. 2002). It has been suggested that relationship quality encompasses the concepts of satisfaction, trust and commitment related to the selling organization (Crosby et al. 1990; Palmatier et al. 2006).

The study was conducted through a series of semi-structured, hour-long interviews within the sales and marketing personnel from four B2B organizations in the UK, and with a selection of their customers. This approach produces rich qualitative

K. Le Meunier-FitzHugh (✉) • L.C. Le Meunier-FitzHugh
University of East Anglia, Norwich, UK
e-mail: k.le-meunier-fitzhugh@uea.ac.uk; l.le-meunier-fitzhugh@uea.ac.uk

© Academy of Marketing Science 2016
L. Petruzzellis, R.S. Winer (eds.), *Rediscovering the Essentiality of Marketing*,
Developments in Marketing Science: Proceedings of the Academy of Marketing
Science, DOI 10.1007/978-3-319-29877-1_148

data on the participants' attitudes and experiences of the interface between buyer and seller. The customer respondents were selected randomly from the organizations' databases.

The study highlights that conflict or collaboration between sales and marketing is visible to the customer and affects the different dimensions of relationship quality. Collaboration creates customer satisfaction and operating through the dimensions of trust to improve customer commitment, and creates customer value in the relationship and leads to an increased propensity to purchase.

References available upon request.

Changes to Sales Force Control Systems in Times of Crisis: What Do Salespeople Feel? How Do They Respond? A Structured Abstract

Laure Lavorata and Madeleine Besson

Introduction

The succession of events referred to in the media as the financial crisis (2008), the economic crisis (2009), and the sovereign debt crisis (2011) has produced an environment which is manifestly uncertain. Characterized by periods of economic recession, this uncertain environment has in recent times presented management with new challenges, with the potential to cause major organizational problems. In the light of this, we thought it would be of interest to analyze the management of an operational unit at a time when "the organization has to deal with a new situation" (Weick 2001, p. 27). Our research relates more specifically to the way in which companies modify their control systems in response to a crisis, and to the strategies that salespeople adopt in response to any changes. As a result, it aims to answer the following questions about what happens during a crisis: Do firms or their management modify existing sales force control systems? What is the effect of any changes on the salespeople? In the front line with clients, what do salespeople feel, and how do they respond? Is there any sign of a fall in ethical standards?

L. Lavorata (✉)
University East of Paris—IRG, Paris, France
e-mail: lavorata@u-pec.fr

M. Besson
Telecom School of Management/LITEM, Evry, France
e-mail: madeleine.besson@telecom-em.eu

© Academy of Marketing Science 2016
L. Petruzzellis, R.S. Winer (eds.), *Rediscovering the Essentiality of Marketing*,
Developments in Marketing Science: Proceedings of the Academy of Marketing
Science, DOI 10.1007/978-3-319-29877-1_149

Background

Darmon (2001) proposes a systemic model of a two-level sales force control system. Strategic sales force management is about "defining goals and structuring the sales organization"; operational sales force management is about "managing the sales effort in such a way that these goals are achieved." While it is unlikely that changes in the economic environment could lead an organization to make radical changes to its sales goals or organization within the space of a few months, it is nonetheless reasonable to expect it to try to make changes at the operational level. The literature relating to corporate crisis management has given rise to recommendations for firms' internal use. These emphasize the importance of communication, both internally and with other stakeholders (Coombs 2007). There are two main schools of thought. The first stresses the importance of giving clear, consistent information, which can be interpreted unambiguously by all involved. The second suggests that in a crisis it is essential that the stakeholders should have a common vision which will then allow them to adapt and develop coherent strategies (Roux-Dufort and Vidaillet 2003). For our part, we think that the economic crisis which has gripped Europe since 2009 is both objective (as shown by indicators like periods of economic recession or redundancies) and experienced subjectively, and in potentially different ways, by stakeholders in different sectors. As a result, we focus in our research on the external nature of a crisis, and the implications that a crisis has, in particular, for internal control systems.

In a paper which heralds a whole series of studies of sales force control systems, Anderson and Oliver propose the following definition of a control system: "an organization's set of procedures for monitoring, directing, evaluating, and compensating its employees" (1987, p. 76). A few years later, Jaworski et al. suggest defining control as "attempts by managers (…) to influence the behavior and activities of marketing personnel to achieve desired outcomes" (1993, p. 58). Building on the theoretical framework developed in 1988, Jaworski et al. (1993) suggest distinguishing between four types of control system (high control, clan system, bureaucratic system, or low control) and analyze the antecedents and consequences of each. They find that a strong control system characterized by tight formal and informal controls seems to lead to better performance, a result confirmed by Cravens et al. (1993). Darmon and Martin (2011) propose a new integrated framework within which to examine sales force control systems. This theoretical framework takes account of the dynamic nature of control systems and introduces the concepts of how much use is made of the various control tools, and of the "rigor of enforcement" of management control. To summarize, a sales force control system can be defined as "an influence process that management uses in order to induce salespeople to work toward the achievement of the firm's short and/or long-run objectives" (Darmon and Martin 2011, p. 301). By increasing or decreasing the amount of control, and by providing or withholding support to the sales force, local line management can alleviate the dysfunctional effects of formal control systems put in place by the firm. So if the crisis means that the sales force has to share a "common vision," what are the implications for the formal control system and for day-to-day management?

In a study of the role of economic cycle peaks and troughs in the USA, Cravens et al. (1993) find that "during unfavorable economic cycles (...) the importance of enhancing overall motivation levels by increasing salespeople's (*sic*) intrinsic motivation levels (...) could become more critical" (p. 56). Few other empirical studies have been made of the impact of environmental factors on sales force control systems. This is no doubt because it is difficult for researchers to make quantitative measures of the various components of a firm's external environment. In our research, we attempted to overcome this difficulty by adopting a qualitative approach which was able to take account of the context, and which did allow it to be analyzed in more detail.

Research Methods

We undertook two qualitative studies, one after the other. Both involved the conduct of semi-structured interviews. The first study was undertaken in March 2009, six months after the bankruptcy of Lehman Brothers in the USA. We chose to focus on the banking sector because it had been badly hit by the subprime crisis of 2008–2009. Twelve representatives of two firms were interviewed—five men and seven women. With an average age of 33, they had been working in sales for an average of 5 years each. The study was extended to additional sectors in 2010 in order to investigate how firms had reacted as the economic crisis of 2009 took hold, and to determine if there had been any variation by sector in the response of the sales force. The firms that agreed to take part were drawn from a variety of sectors, including the property business, the automobile industry, and the home equipment sector. Second phase interviews were conducted in April 2010 with 46 salespeople (32 men and 14 women). With an average age of 37, they had been working in sales for an average of 13 years. Two-thirds of them were working in business-to-consumer (B2C) roles. The same interview guide was used, in order to facilitate identification of similarities or differences between sectors.

Semi-structured interviews were thus conducted with a total of 58 salespeople. Thematic content analysis followed, based on full transcripts of the interviews. Given that our aim was to identify similarities and differences in salespeople's opinions, not to define a sales force classification system, we decided to take an interpretative approach and use horizontal content analysis rather than a text analysis software providing word frequency counts which may be of use at identifying similarities, but is not always suitable when the aim is to identify differences.

Results and Discussion

Irrespective of sector, the salespeople reported that significant changes were made to the way in which they were managed as soon as the crisis started, and that these changes then remained in place. Pressure from management increased everywhere and management controls were tightened everywhere, but the extra effort that managers invested in accompanying salespeople to meetings and to keeping them motivated was much less widespread. The increased pressure on sales people during the crisis was universal. It was clear from our interviews with sales advisers in the banking sector, for example, that they felt under daily pressure from branch management: "(Over the years) objectives relating to giving advice have been replaced by sales objectives." They also felt that there was a growing emphasis on quotas and on "micromanagement." "These days it is all about the numbers, and nothing but the numbers (…) our numbers are scrutinized, checked and analyzed endlessly." It seemed, on the other hand, that some firms saw the need to support and motivate their sales force in a difficult period. So some firms reduced quotas, despite falling revenues, in order to "make sure salespeople did not get demotivated."

When interviewing sales advisers in the banking sector about the effects of the crisis, all the respondents, without prompting, mentioned a change in client behavior before anything else. The B2C team spoke of the need to reassure clients and to provide them with explanations in 2009. The bankruptcy of Lehman Brothers in October 2008 prompted lots of questions from clients and provoked a real panic in some of them: "In October the clients were panic-stricken; I was getting in the region of 15 calls a day about it"; "There was a panic, but things have calmed down again now." The financial and economic crisis also had to be explained: "(I have to use) more theory (to explain) what is happening in economic terms." Salespeople were more on the defensive. In the second study, salespeople again reported that their clients were worried by the crisis, and by the uncertainty it was causing. But their response, from a commercial point of view, was to be more proactive: "We have to reassure the clients." Despite these efforts, in 2010, by which time the crisis had set in, they reported more profound changes: "Our relationships with clients have become more strained"; "Client relationships have got tougher." The response of clients to the crisis was to demand more of their suppliers. Professional and private buyers alike were "pushing for more discounts" and "negotiating harder on price." There was thus an increase in what Porter calls the negotiating power of clients (1980); falling demand was giving clients the ability to apply pressure to their suppliers.

Confronted head-on by this new client behavior, salespeople faced growing tension and uncertainty. In 2010, the crisis having taken hold, salespeople complained of stress related to "the impossibility of planning for the future." Many emphasized: "We are more stressed"; "The uncertainty in the market creates a lot of tension." Teams reacted to the tension in one of the two ways: in some teams, there was more cooperation: "We help one another"; "We stick together"; "The team is stronger; these days we have to present a united front in order to cope better with the crisis." In other teams, rivalry increased: "The atmosphere is more tense"; "The atmosphere has got worse"; "There is more competition between salespeople". Salespeople showed that they could adapt to changes in client behavior. In 2009, we were already seeing evidence of a more aggressive approach to selling: "I use a more aggressive sales technique, telling my clients that they need to hurry up and buy a car while prices are lower"; "I am out on the road all the time"; etc. In 2010, this aggressive sales approach was combined with what Weitz et al. (1986) call adaptive selling: "I tailor my approach to the needs of the client, not of the crisis"; "I listen more, and spend more time on follow-up"; "I try to build client loyalty by creating a climate of confidence."

Our study shows that the factors which result in changes in sales force behavior during a crisis are both internal (salespeople adapt) and external (client behavior changes; changes are made to sales force control systems). We set out to answer the question of whether sales force control systems change in times of crisis. Our study complete, we can now confirm that the elements of a sales force control system, which are most fundamental to its structure, like the compensation plan, do not change. Many other elements, which local line management can modify more easily, do change. This greater involvement of local line management can be considered to be empirical confirmation of the dynamic of control systems proposed by Darmon and Martin (2011). To combat the market uncertainty caused by a crisis, local line managers play a more active role in directing the activities of the sales force, specifying sales objectives and exercising tighter control over the salespeople.

Conclusion

In the light of these findings, we are able to offer the following advice to sales force management: "out of adversity create loyalty." In order to build client loyalty, it is important in the early stages of a crisis, when uncertainty suddenly appears, for a sales force to tailor its response to the needs of its clients. In times of uncertainty, clients are trying to get their bearings and welcome clear guidance from a financial firm, or the offer of an optimal solution from a supplier. Once the initial uncertainty dies away a little, clients form their own views; where applicable, they know they have more negotiating power, and play their hands accordingly. Our study shows that many salespeople, of their own initiative, go back to sales basics by refocusing on what is important to their clients: listening to them, understanding their requirements, and tailoring solutions to their needs. While this observation may appear self-evident, it is nonetheless clear from our study that some firms manage to lose sight of the basics and are happy simply to manage objectives and performance indicators. To make it easier for salespeople to tailor their approach, and to support them in a crisis, it is important for firms to provide support in the form of information, of help in dealing with clients, and of extra staff resources. The literature relating to corporate crisis management has emphasized the importance of communication, both internally and with other stakeholders (Coombs 2007). In a crisis, salespeople, like colleagues in other functions, need information; they need to know what is happening, and where their employer stands. When dealing with clients, it is useful for salespeople to have access to dedicated resources; the "crisis kit" which one bank put together for its salespeople is a particularly good example.

Moreover, crises are likely to occur again, be it economic crises due to increased competition and technological transformation or consumer confidence crisis. In so far, the firms should train their sales force and sales management on a regular basis. Sales managers have to be aware must be trained in order to react to a crisis by playing a more active role in directing the activities of the sales force, specifying sales objectives, and exercising tighter control over the salespeople. Conversely, sales people have to be trained in order to react to the crisis by going back to adaptive selling (Weitz et al. 1986), tailoring their sales approach, and listening more to the client. Among other variables that can affect the sales functions during a crisis future research can focus on ethical behavior. We cannot say for sure that a crisis leads to unethical behavior. But the fact remains that if a firm responds to a crisis by implementing a control system that focuses exclusively on results then there is a risk that the sales force will respond with unethical behavior (Lavorata 2012). For Ingrams et al. (2007), the way to guarantee that a sales force behaves ethically is to put in place a "Sales Management Control Strategy" which is integrated, incorporating multiple control elements. It is no longer enough simply to control results in one way and sales force behavior in another.

References available upon request.

How Do Firms Value Their Sales Organizations?

Alireza Keshavarz and Dominique Rouziès

Abstract The wide disparities of sales compensation plans observed across firms and industries imply that firms do not value their sales organizations similarly. More to the point, sales compensation research does not take directly into account the compensation of other functions, as if sales compensation policy decisions were isolated from other compensation decisions. Needless to say decisions regarding salesforces are included in wider strategic plans. Curiously, literature on the relative value firms attribute to various functions does not include the sales function. This chapter investigates organizational (e.g., innovativeness, marketing resource endowment) and environmental (e.g., market uncertainty) factors that can affect the pay level and structure of sales jobs as compared to jobs in other functions. We test our theory with a unique data set of all large firms (i.e., with more than 100 salespeople) in France. Our results shed new light on pay practices of sales organizations.

A. Keshavarz (✉) • D. Rouziès
HEC Paris, Paris, France
e-mail: alireza.keshavarz@hec.edu; rouzies@hec.fr

© Academy of Marketing Science 2016
L. Petruzzellis, R.S. Winer (eds.), *Rediscovering the Essentiality of Marketing*,
Developments in Marketing Science: Proceedings of the Academy of Marketing
Science, DOI 10.1007/978-3-319-29877-1_150

Toward a Global Perspective of Sales Strategy Components

Xavier C. Martin

Abstract There is a global consensus today on the relevance to consider the strategic role of sales departments, at least in BtoB. Nevertheless, to our knowledge and recently, only two empirical research studies have proposed what could be the components of a sales strategy (SS). The choices of these components are based only on salespeople's interviews in one case, and on convenience choices in the second one. The authors conclude that their measures of sales strategy need to be further validated and established.

The contribution of the present research is to broaden the perspective of SS to consider more congruent components, by considering some conceptual contributions from the strategic literature.

SS can be associated with the concepts of operational strategy, the Balanced Score Card, the questioning approach of strategy, and the customer approach of strategy. These approaches confirm the pertinence of considering these three dimensions of SS (clustering, organization structure and relational objectives/ selling models), even though they suggest some sub-dimensions of the three main components considered by the sales strategy literature. Moreover, a fourth dimension is proposed to foster a holistic view of a SS.

Empirically, 22 in-depth interviews were conducted with Sales Managers in France. Even though great discrepancy was noticed in the responses, these dimensions were mentioned frequently. Our next step will be to quantitatively validate these components.

X.C. Martin (✉)
Novancia Business School, Paris, France
e-mail: xmartin@novancia.fr

© Academy of Marketing Science 2016
L. Petruzzellis, R.S. Winer (eds.), *Rediscovering the Essentiality of Marketing*,
Developments in Marketing Science: Proceedings of the Academy of Marketing
Science, DOI 10.1007/978-3-319-29877-1_151

Part XIX
Sensory Marketing

The Halo Effect in Fragrance Perception: The Relevance of the "Natural Ingredients" Claim

Vanessa Apaolaza, Patrick Hartmann, Cristina M. López, Carmen Echebarria, and Jose M. Barrutia

Abstract Can consumer knowledge that a scent is 100 % composed of natural ingredients influence sensory perception of the fragrance? In the present study, 112 participants were asked to test and evaluate a floral fragrance. Prior to the test and the evaluation of the scent, half of the consumers were informed of the 100 % natural origin of its components, while the other half were not provided with that information, even though the individuals were exposed to exactly the same perfume made from totally natural essential vegetable oils. Results found that participants gave a higher mark to the scent when they had been informed that it was completely natural in origin. This study demonstrates that information proclaiming the natural origin of substances comprising a scent may change consumers' sensory perception of the fragrance. This finding is of great relevance for scent manufacturers and cosmetics companies, enabling them to manage such claims as tools to market their products.

Keywords Halo effect • Sensory perception • Natural ingredients claims • Fragrances

Introduction

The cosmetic market includes, among others, the segments of perfumes and fragrances. According to Weber and De Villebonne (2002), when purchasing cosmetics, there are important competitive factors that affect consumer's choice. Factors that intervene in the purchase behavior process are the following: price, quality, packaging, advertising, promotion, local recognition, opinion toward

V. Apaolaza (✉) • P. Hartmann • C.M. López • C. Echebarria • J.M. Barrutia
University of the Basque Country UPV/EHU, Bizkaia, Spain
e-mail: vanessa.apaolaza@ehu.es; patrick.hartmann@ehu.es; cristinamaria.lopez@ehu.es; carmen.etxebarria@ehu.es; josemaria.barrutia@ehu.es

© Academy of Marketing Science 2016
L. Petruzzellis, R.S. Winer (eds.), *Rediscovering the Essentiality of Marketing*, Developments in Marketing Science: Proceedings of the Academy of Marketing Science, DOI 10.1007/978-3-319-29877-1_152

particular firms or products, and the knowledgeable salesperson. Nowadays, the "natural" selling point takes on great importance for consumers too, who are increasingly particular about not using chemical substances on the skin (Dickson-Spillmann et al. 2011). Product and brand managers of personal care, perfumery, and cosmetic products are faced with decisions such as to diversify towards the natural cosmetics to speed the diffusion and increase the usage of their products, given that society is increasingly more aware and informed of the benefits of natural products. This becomes more important when it has been suggested that fragrances are one of the major causes of allergic contact dermatitis from the use of cosmetics in adults and children (Rastogi et al. 1999). So industry needs to responsibly address concerns and ensure that scented products are safe for users, those inadvertently exposed, and the environment (Bridges 2002). According to Dimitrova et al. (2009), during the nineteenth century, chemicals were used to replace more expensive natural ingredients making the cosmetics more widely used. At present, the health aspect is changing this trend involving an increased interest in natural ingredients, with consumers worried about treating their bodies with care and respect. Thus, natural and organic products today constitute the major growth segment in the cosmetics industry; their sales registering an annual increase of 20% against 2% for cosmetics as a whole. France's rates of between 30 and 40% over the last 2 years make it the third major growth market in Europe, after Germany and the United Kingdom. In the cosmetics industry, a natural product is understood to be one that is made up of natural substances of botanical, animal, or mineral origin, including their mixtures. They must be safe for human health and can only be obtained and processed following physical, microbiological, or enzymatic methods. In the case of perfumery products, no studies to date have analyzed the possible halo effect of the "natural" selling point in fragrance evaluation. The present investigation's objective is to analyze, by means of real tests, whether consumer knowledge to the effect that a scent is made up of 100% natural substances can influence individuals' sensory perception.

Conceptual Framework

Research has indicated that, when buying scent, consumer purchase decision processes generally occur in low-involvement situations (Laurent and Kapferer 1985). With this product type, the risk that is customarily associated with purchase is low, and there is a strong drive of affective or hedonic activation (Hirschman and Holbrook 1982). In perfumery, buying often takes place through impulse or through inertia. Limited cognitive involvement leads people to choose a perfume because of brand, price, advertising, attraction aroused by the celebrity it is associated with, information provided at the time by sales point staff, etc., but very often a lack of background knowledge about perfumes means that there is no deliberate process of evaluation and decision on the part of the consumer. Scarcely any information search takes place and little time is given over to choosing brand and product

(Silayoi and Speece 2004). Accordingly, consumers are liable to be affected by a phenomenon termed the halo effect. This happens when an individual's assessment of one particular characteristic of an item powerfully affects or slants their impressions of other attributes of the same item (Lee et al. 2013). An illustration of this is provided when acquaintance with the positive and negative qualities of an individual affects, in an unconscious manner, whether or not this person is seen to be attractive in the eye of the beholder (e.g., Kniffin and Wilson 2004). Following the original definition of Thorndike (1920), Leuthesser et al. (1995) considered the halo effect as a rater's failure to discriminate among conceptually distinct and potentially independent attributes, with the result that individual attribute ratings co-vary more than they otherwise would. The investigation of the halo effect has also received attention in marketing within the context of attitude theory. Bagozzi (1996) conducted a laboratory experiment to induce physiological arousal as a mechanism for influencing halo. The context for the study was attitudes toward blood donation. Using a spreading activation model of semantic memory to frame predictions, it was hypothesized and found that arousal produced a halo effect for positive beliefs, tended to reduce halo for negative beliefs, and eliminated halo (marginally) for all beliefs treated as an aggregate.

In the case of food products, some researches have shown the existence of a halo effect on several behavior variables of the "natural" and "organic" eye-catcher on food packages, including consumer perception of product quality, evaluation of a product as being more healthy, with lower risk for the organism, a feel good sensation, more positive attitude toward the product, or a stronger intention to buy (Abrams et al. 2010; Dickson-Spillmann et al. 2011; Lockie et al. 2004). Also, Roe et al.'s (1999) study showed that a health label (e.g., high in calcium for yogurt) led consumers to consider a product to be better for their health and, therefore, to be more inclined to buy it. Further, the recent study carried out by researchers Lee et al. (2013) found that participants estimated foods with organic labels to be lower in calories than those without the organic label. And foods with the organic label elicited a higher willingness to pay and yielded better nutritional evaluations (e.g., tastes lower in fat, higher in fiber) than foods without the organic label.

In the specific case of perfumery products, though, no studies to date have analyzed the possible halo effect of the natural ingredients' claim on consumers' sensory perception of fragrances. In the literature, sensory perception is defined as a mental process that involves the interpretation of a series of sensations (capacity to capture modifications in the external and internal environment) (Worch et al. 2010). Researchers De la Fuente and Romo (2005), in a study published in *Nature Neuroscience* and carried out with macaques, show that sensory perceptions do not always correspond with reality, but are the result of our expectations of something. Perceptions, according to this research, arise from the combination, in different brain areas, of sensation, attention, and expectation and can be manipulated in line with the information presented to an individual. In the same regard, Raghubir (2010) finds that sensory perception of a cosmetic product can be easily distorted through stimuli presented by marketing experts that alter consumer expectations, since consumers very often "feel or experience what they *expect* to feel or experience."

Accordingly, sensory perception of a scent can be expected to become distorted by what consumers "expect" of the fragrance in line with the information they have been given as to whether the substances it is comprised of are or are not natural. Similarly, sensory perception of fragrance, through its effect on the consumer's mood (Rétiveau et al. 2004), will have the capacity to impact an individual's cognitive assessments of a product (Bone and Jantrania 1992).

As previously mentioned, the aim of this study is to analyze whether knowledge possessed by the consumer to the effect that a scent is 100% natural, in the sense that it comes from nature and has been transformed through environmentally respectful procedures, exercises a halo effect on the evaluation of a fragrance. Specifically, we hypothesize that this information will positively influence sensory perception of the perfume and induce a more favorable attitude towards it, accompanied by greater willingness to buy.

We thus establish the following hypotheses for our research:

H1: Consumer knowledge that the components of a perfume are 100% natural increases sensory perception of the fragrance.

H2: Consumer knowledge that the components of a perfume are 100% natural increases attitude toward the fragrance.

H3: Consumer knowledge that the components of a perfume are 100% natural increases willingness to buy the fragrance.

Method

The data for the present study come from an experiment performed with 112 students (53 male, 59 female). The participants' ages ranged from 18 to 47 years old ($M=22.45$, $SD=4.35$). For the data collection, a floral fragrance was used. Half of the total number of individuals in the sample were informed that the scent components were 100% natural, while the other half were not provided with this information, even when all the individuals were exposed to exactly the same kind of scent, which was made from essential vegetable oils of 100% natural origin. Participants used paper strips to evaluate the different perfumes. After smelling the scent, participants were instructed to answer a series of questions in the form of a paper questionnaire. The questionnaire asked participants to evaluate their sensory perception of the fragrance, their attitude toward the perfume, and their willingness to buy it.

Development of the measurement scales for the variables studied is based on the review of the relevant literature, in order to ensure the validity of content. In first place, for measurement of sensory perception of fragrance, we found different measurement scales in the literature (e.g., Ferdenzi et al. 2013). For this study, a multi-item scale of 12 items was used, through which the different sensations evoked by the fragrance are captured. Response categories ranged from 1, not at all, to 10, very much. In second place, the attitude toward the fragrance was measured by means of

Table 1 Mean and standard deviation in sensory perception of perfume, attitude, and purchase intention when information is provided concerning the 100 % natural origin of the components of the scent, and when there is no information (control condition)

Dependent variable	Experimental Factor				
	Information 100 % natural origin		Control		
	M	SD	M	SD	F-value
Natural	6.02	2.01	4.46	2.40	13.74***
Agreeable	6.07	1.94	4.91	2.56	7.27**
Feel-good	5.80	1.97	4.68	2.41	7.31**
Good-mood inducing	5.93	1.92	4.43	2.27	14.21***
Attractive	5.43	1.87	3.73	2.15	19.84***
Sensual	4.98	2.07	3.02	2.07	25.18***
Comfortable	5.77	1.95	4.16	2.34	15.61***
Pleasant	5.55	1.96	3.68	2.27	21.83***
Harmonious	5.64	2.19	4.55	2.29	6.58*
Healthy	5.71	2.09	4.39	2.52	9.10**
Relaxing	5.66	2.09	4.18	2.69	10.59**
Sense-stimulating	5.89	1.87	4.77	2.19	8.48**
Attitude toward the perfume	5.50	2.04	4.21	2.42	9.20**
Purchase intention	4.63	2.34	3.20	2.35	10.37**

Notes: All items were measured on 10-point scales ranging from 1 (*not at all*) to 10 (*very much*); *p < .05; **p < .01; ***p < .001

a semantic differential scale, with scores ranging from 1 to 10, using the pair of bipolar items: I didn't like it at all/I liked it a lot (Kempf and Smith 1998). Thirdly, consumer willingness to buy the fragrance was also measured via a semantic differential scale, with scores ranging from 1 to 10, using the pair of bipolar items: "I would be very unlikely to buy it"/"I would be very likely to buy it" (Homer 1990).

Results

As predicted, a series of within-participants ANOVAs revealed that information revealing the totally natural origin of the components of the fragrance did influence participants' evaluations of their sensory perception of the scent (Table 1). The fact that participants possessed knowledge regarding the 100 % natural origin of the components of the fragrance caused them to have a better sensory perception of it, over the 12 dimensions evaluated. So, in the group in which participants were informed that the scent components were of natural origin, the fragrance was evaluated as significantly more natural, healthful (produces well-being), agreeable, attractive, sensual, comfortable, pleasant, harmonious, relaxing, good mood inducing, as having more feel-good appeal and being more sense-stimulating, than in the group where participants were not provided with that information (control condition). In consequence, information to the effect that the components of a fragrance are of a 100 % natural origin is demonstrated to have a consistent halo effect on the evaluation of sensory perception of that fragrance. Therefore, the first hypothesis is corroborated.

Meanwhile, information imparted proclaiming the 100 % natural origin of the perfume components likewise showed a consistent halo effect in the evaluation of the scent in reference to the attitude demonstrated by participants toward the perfume. For the floral aroma tested in the experiment, the participants who had been exposed to the information concerning the totally natural origin of the scent showed a significantly more favorable attitude toward the product than did their counterparts under the control condition. Thus, hypothesis 2 is corroborated.

Finally, the results of the ANOVA analysis also indicate that the information announcing the 100 % natural origin of the perfume components, imparted to only half of the sample group, exerted a consistent halo effect on the evaluation of the perfume, when it came to the willingness shown by participants to buy the product. Therefore, hypothesis 3 is confirmed.

Conclusion and Future Research

The aim of the present study was to provide concrete and specific findings regarding the influence of information imparted announcing the completely natural origin of the components of a fragrance on consumer perceptions of the product, which has not to date been tested in the scientific literature. While the literature includes various works that have analyzed the halo effect of the organic label or the 100 % natural origin of ingredients where food products are concerned (Abrams et al. 2010; Dickson-Spillmann et al. 2011; Lockie et al. 2004), until now no studies have analyzed this circumstance in relation to perfumery products. The results indicated that information announcing the 100 % natural origin of perfume components exercises a halo effect on evaluations of the product. The study shows that this information influences consumers' sensory perception of the scent, as well as attitude toward it, and willingness to buy. This corroborates the findings of other studies with regard to food products, which indicated that the sensory perception and evaluation of a product can be manipulated by the information provided to consumers (Lee et al. 2006; Wansink et al. 2005). Future research should also analyze the halo effect of the "natural origin" claim for other odor categories in the market and for other cosmetic products. Likewise, it would be of interest to study whether there are differences in the consistency of the halo effect of "natural" claim on consumer evaluations between countries with different cultures.

References

Abrams, K. M., Meyers, C. A., & Irani, T. A. (2010). Naturally confused: Consumers' perceptions of all-natural and organic pork products. *Agriculture and Human Values, 27*, 365–374.
Bagozzi, R. P. (1996). The role of arousal in the creation and control of the halo effect in attitude models. *Psychology and Marketing, 13*(3), 235–264.

Bone, P. F., & Jantrania, S. (1992). Olfaction as a Cue for Product Quality. *Marketing Letters, 3*(July), 289–296.

Bridges, B. (2002). Fragrance: Emerging health and environmental concerns. *Flavour and Fragrance Journal, 17*, 361–371.

De Lafuente, V., & Romo, R. (2005). Neuronal correlates of subjective sensory experience. *Nature Neuroscience, 8*, 1698–1703.

Dickson-Spillmann, M., Siegrist, M., & Keller, C. (2011). Attitudes toward chemicals are associated with preference for natural food. *Food Quality and Preference, 22*, 149–156.

Dimitrova, V., Kaneva, M., & Galluci, T. (2009). Customer knowledge management in the natural cosmetics industry. *Industrial Management and Data Systems, 109*(9), 1155–1165.

Ferdenzi, C., Delplanque, S., Barbosa, P., Court, K., Guinard, J. X., Guo, T., et al. (2013). Affective semantic space of scents. Toward a universal scale to measure self-reported odor-related feelings. *Food Quality and Preference, 30*, 128–138.

Hirschman, E. C., & Holbrook, M. B. (1982). Hedonic consumption: Emerging concepts, methods and propositions. *Journal of Marketing, 46*(3), 92–101.

Homer, P. M. (1990). The mediating role of attitude toward the ad: Some additional evidence. *Journal of Marketing Research, 27*(February), 78–86.

Kempf, D. S., & Smith, R. E. (1998). Consumer processing of product trial and the influence of prior advertising: A structural modelling approach. *Journal of Marketing Research, 35*(August), 325–338.

Kniffin, K. M., & Wilson, D. S. (2004). The effect of nonphysical traits on the perception of physical attractiveness: Three naturalistic studies. *Evolution and Human Behavior, 25*, 88–101.

Laurent, G., & Kapferer, J. N. (1985). Measuring consumer involvement profiles. *Journal of Marketing Research, 22*(February), 41–53.

Lee, L., Frederick, S., & Ariely, D. (2006). Try it, you'll like it. *Psychological Science, 17*, 1054–1058.

Lee, W. J., Shimizu, M., Kniffin, K. M., & Wansink, B. (2013). You taste what you see: Do organic labels bias taste perceptions? *Food Quality and Preference, 29*, 33–39.

Leuthesser, L., Kohli, C. S., & Harich, K. R. (1995). Brand equity: The halo effect measure. *European Journal of Marketing, 29*(4), 57–66.

Lockie, S., Lyons, K., Lawrence, G., & Grice, J. (2004). Choosing organics: A path analysis of factors underlying the selection of organic food among Australian consumers. *Appetite, 43*, 135–146.

Raghubir, P. (2010). Visual Perception. In A. Krishna (Ed.), *Sensory marketing: Research on the sensuality of products* (pp. 201–215). New York: Taylor & Francis Group.

Rastogi, S. C., Johansen, J. D., Menné, T., Frosch, P., Bruze, M., Andersen, K. E., et al. (1999). Contents of fragrance allergens in children's cosmetics and cosmetic-toys. *Contact Dermatitis, 41*, 84–88.

Rétiveau, A. N., Chambers, E., IV, & Milliken, G. A. (2004). Common and specific effects of fine fragrances on the mood of women. *Journal of Sensory Studies, 19*(5), 373–394.

Roe, B., Levy, A. S., & Derby, B. M. (1999). The impact of health claims on consumer search and product evaluation outcomes: Results from FDA experimental data. *Journal of Public Policy and Marketing, 18*(1), 89–105.

Silayoi, P., & Speece, M. (2004). Packaging and purchase decisions: An exploratory study on the impact of involvement level and time pressure. *British Food Journal, 106*(8), 607–628.

Thorndike, E. L. (1920). A constant error in psychological rating. *Journal of Applied Psychology, 4*, 25–29.

Wansink, B., van Ittersum, K., & Painter, J. E. (2005). How descriptive food names bias sensory perceptions in restaurants. *Food Quality and Preference, 16*, 393–400.

Weber, J. M., & De Villebonne, J. C. (2002). Differences in purchase behavior between France and the USA: The cosmetic industry. *Journal of Fashion Marketing and Management, 6*(4), 396–407.

Worch, T., Le, S., & Punter, P. (2010). How reliable are the consumers? Comparison of sensory profiles from consumers and experts. *Food Quality and Preference, 21*, 309–318.

Assessing the Role of Haptic Imagery in Print Advertising: An Empirical Investigation

Giovanni Pino, Gianluigi Guido, Carla Tomacelli, and Mauro Capestro

Abstract Previous research showed that imagining touching an object—the so-called *haptic imagery*—may engender sensations that closely resemble those aroused by tactile perceptions (Peck et al. 2013). Little is still known, however, about the exact nature of such cues as well as the mechanisms through which they affect individuals' perceptions and behavioral intentions. To fill this gap, the present research aimed to empirically assess the extent to which an advertisement incorporating a haptic cue is able to shape consumers' dispositions and behavioral intentions, thus attempting to throw light on the mechanisms through which such a phenomenon occurs. We argued that a visual representation of the physical contact between human hands (which are the most important means to acquire haptic information) and a product may act as a cue capable of activating haptic imagery and have positive effects on consumer purchase intentions. The study concentrated on technology-based products, which are increasingly sold through online commerce and hence without a previous physical evaluation by consumers.

We created two versions of an advertisement featuring a technology-based product: one featuring only the advertised product (*haptic version*), the other featuring the advertised product held in a person's hands (*non-haptic version*). Then, we administered a short online survey to a total of 80 subjects. They were asked to fill in Peck and Childers' (2003) NFT scale. Next, they were randomly assigned to our two experimental conditions, and hence saw one of the two pretested advertisements. All of them were subsequently asked to rate the perceived ease of use comfort of the advertised product (Davis 1989), their intention to purchase the advertised product, and the extent to which the advertisement made them imagine themselves touching the advertised product.

G. Pino (✉) • G. Guido • C. Tomacelli • M. Capestro
University of Salento, Lecce, Italy
e-mail: giovanni.pino@unisalento.it; gianluigi.guido@unisalento.it; carla.tomacelli@unisalento.it; mauro.capestro@unisalento.it

© Academy of Marketing Science 2016
L. Petruzzellis, R.S. Winer (eds.), *Rediscovering the Essentiality of Marketing*, Developments in Marketing Science: Proceedings of the Academy of Marketing Science, DOI 10.1007/978-3-319-29877-1_153

A moderated mediation model allowed to establish that the presence of a haptic cue raises the perceived ease of use of the advertised product, which, in turn, favorably affects the related purchase intention. Such an effect resulted stronger for highly *autotelic* individuals, i.e., individuals who tend to touch products to experience a sense of enjoyment. From a theoretical perspective, this result suggests that the presence of a haptic cue in a print advertisement may compensate highly autotelic individuals' need for instrumental haptic information. While, from an operational point of view, this result could be taken into account by marketing practitioners interested in fostering confidence in technology-based products through advertising messages.

References available upon request.

Communication in Relief: Should We Embosse the Brand or the Product?

Sonia Capelli, Bruno Ferreira, and Fanny Thomas

Introduction

During a sunny summer afternoon on the beach, who has never been attracted by a relief picture of an ice cream on a poster? This type of poster highlights some products and invites the consumer in order to touch them. Our communication focuses on this advertising tactic consisting in adding relief to some elements presented in a printed medium. Past research in advertising has scarcely considered the question of the sense of touch when the target contacts the medium. Those studies have considered the influences of an external tactile stimulation (Peck and Wiggins 2006; Peck and Johnson 2011) or the influences of the smell and the touch of a paper on its evaluation (Krishna et al. 2010). Both underline the opportunity of considering the role of touch as an interesting lever for enhancing persuasion.

On the contrary, in the field of packaging, the texture retains a special attention from researchers, it provides information about the product by attracting the attention of the consumers (Peck and Childers 2006; Peck and Wiggins 2006; Peck and Johnson 2011). When exposed to a textured packaging, the senses of vision and touch interact to improve awareness and purchase intent toward food products (Authors 2012, 2013; Krishna 2010). In particular, the texture of the packaging influences perceptions of the product (Authors 2012; Krishna and Morrin 2008). The handling of products also plays a role in evaluation and decision making (Peck and Childers 2003a). Following those results, we propose that adding a texture to an advertising medium should enhance its efficacy. In fact, on a «flat» advertising

S. Capelli (✉) • F. Thomas
IAE Lyon School of Management, Lyon, France
e-mail: Sonia.capelli@univ-lyon3.fr; fanny.thomas@univ-lyon3.fr

B. Ferreira
Clermont School of Management—CRCGM, Clermont-Ferrand, France
e-mail: bruno.ferreira@udamail.fr

© Academy of Marketing Science 2016
L. Petruzzellis, R.S. Winer (eds.), *Rediscovering the Essentiality of Marketing*,
Developments in Marketing Science: Proceedings of the Academy of Marketing
Science, DOI 10.1007/978-3-319-29877-1_154

medium such as displays, brochures or leaflets, relief may be added on textual cues as brand name or on iconic cues as the product picture. Our communication focuses on the impact of relief vs. smooth advertising poster by manipulating the relief element: the brand and/or product picture. Adding relief on an advertising medium should lead to more haptic contacts with the medium and increase persuasion its impact. Moreover, a food product picture in relief should increase the desire to eat while the relief brand should enhance brand recall.

Research Model

Hypothesis About the Number of Tactile Contacts

Sight is the sense that enables a first texture approach (Marlow and Jansson-Boyd 2011). The invitation to touch a textured product encourages consumers to take the product in hand and then to purchase it (Peck and Childers 2006). Previous research has shown that touching a persuasive appeal can increase persuasion (Peck and Wiggins 2006). We therefore propose that, similarly, texturing an advertisement medium will incite consumers to touch it, whatever the relief element (the product picture or the brand name).

H1: Adding relief on the depicted product induces more tactile contacts with the given advertising medium.

H2: Adding relief on the promoted brand name induces more tactile contacts with the given advertising medium.

Even when the product itself is not textured, other tactile stimulations present in the environment influence product evaluation (Ackerman et al. 2010; Authors 2012). So, as tactile priming, the textured elements increase tactile contacts of the other non-textured elements. Adapted to advertising, we propose that the presence of relief on a medium plays the role of tactile priming influences the attraction of other smooth media.

H3: Adding relief on the depicted product induces more tactile contacts with all the other un-relief printed presented advertising media.

H4: Adding relief on the promoted brand name induces more tactile contacts with all the other un-relief printed presented advertising media.

Hypothesis About Consumed Quantity of Product

By viewing the salience of elements on an advertising medium, the product mental representation increases and prepares consumers for the evaluation and appreciation of a food product (Rogers and Hill 1989). Moreover, craving eating increases with the exhibition signals such as visualization of the product, (Cornell et al. 1989). The promotion of food, such as snacking and attractive, automatically triggers the consumption of such type of food, non-consciously in individuals (Harris et al. 2009; Fedoroff et al. 1997). The relief added to the advertising support improves the product realism and reinforces the mental imagery of flavor, enhancing the intent to eat the promoted product (Authors 2013). Consequently, relief product picture should attract attention and then induce craving eating.

H5: Adding relief on the depicted product induces a higher consumption of the product.

Opposite to food product picture, when relief is added to the brand name, it catches attention to the textual cues and it diverts attention from the product. Therefore we should have less mental imagery associated with the product, so less desire to eat the product, inducing less consumption.

H6: Adding relief on the promoted brand name induces a weaker consumption of product.

Hypothesis About Brand Recall

When the brand is in relief, the information is given to both sight and touch. This sensorial intermodality has been shown to be more efficient for lecturing learning (Fredembach et al. 2009). In the field of products, the sensorial reinforcement between sight and touch leads to a better memorization in the brain (Authors 2014). Adapted to persuasive appeal, we hypothesize reinforcement between sight and touch as follow.

H7: Adding relief on the promoted brand name enhances brand recall.

Hypothesis About Brand Preference

Previous research has shown that haptic elements attached to a persuasive appeal can increase attitude toward the appeal and persuasion (Peck and Wiggins 2006; Peck and Johnson 2011). Adapted to food product persuasive appeal, we propose that the addition of a haptic element in the message should enhance brand preference as follow.

H8: Adding relief on the depicted product enhances the preference for the given brand.

H9: Adding relief on the promoted brand name enhances the preference for the given brand.

Method

We conducted a between subject experiment 2 (relief of the depicted product: relief /
smooth) * 2 (relief on the promoted brand name: relief/smooth).

Stimuli

We used A6 leaflet format on coated paper of 0.8 lb as advertising medium (card)
because it allows an easy handling. We focused on confectionary market, and in
particular chocolate candy, as a research field since it allows considering craving eating
after exposition to a message (Harris et al. 2009) and since this kind of products is
usually advertised via promotional cards. We selected five unknown brand names
(*Chococo, Ovay, Goni, Pifoo, Ycao*) associated with five candy pictures. All the five
cards were black and white printed to avoid influences of color variation. Relief
printing of the depicted product and promoted brand name were manipulated with a
domed label. This technique consists in adding 2–3 mm of thickness by a resin on the
product image and or on the brand. The manipulating card was the one of *Chococo*
brand, the four other cards were smooth for all the experimental conditions. Four
Chococo cards were designed: one without relief elements, one with only the product
picture in relief, one with brand name in relief and, one with both product picture and
brand name in relief.

Sample

We chose a homogeneous sample in order to study consumer behaviors toward
the hedonic product retained. Participants were students of a west European
University and had subscribed to a lottery in order to win presents. We obtained
193 participants (average age 21.2, 125 women). The experiment was conducted
in laboratory conditions and was composed of three steps. Firstly, the participants were randomly assigned to one of the four conditions and exposed during
2 min to a set of five cards. They were asked to observe and manipulate as much
as they want the cards. The hands of each respondent were filmed during this
sequence. Secondly, the participants played on a test on a computer that requires
a high concentration level without connection with our experiment, as a ploy to
distract the participant for a duration of 10 min. In this time, 0.54 lb of M&M's
were offered to consume and claimed to be an incentive for the test. After
10 min, the remaining candies were weighted for each respondent. To finish,
participants had to fill a questionnaire about brand recall and individual
characteristics.

Measures

Brand recall is assessed with the following item *"What are the names of the brands you have saved."* Preference is evaluated with the item *"What is the card you prefer? Can you describe it?"* The answers were binary recoded ("1" if value equal Chococo, "0" if not). We coded the filmed observation of number contact with the leaflets and also, the weight of M&M's consumption. We measured the need for touch with its original scale (Peck and Childers 2003b, Authors 2014). Brand and product picture attitudes were controlled with the use of Bergkvist and Rossiter scale (2007) of three items. All those items were associated with a seven point Likert scale. The last meal intake was requested with *"At what time do you ended your last meal?"* and compared with the experiment hour. Gender and age were also requested.

Results

Results Concerning the Haptic Contacts Number

In order to test our hypothesis concerning contact number with the manipulated promotional card, we lead an ANCOVA with the contact number as dependent variable, the two relief conditions (on the product and/or on the brand) as fixed factors and all the controlled variables described below as covariables. Our results show that the mean number of tactile contacts with the targeted card differs significantly from a product picture endowed of relief compared to smooth cards ($M_{relief}=6.43$, $M_{smooth}=4.17$, $p=.14$) and that the instrumental need for touch level moderates this relationship positively ($p=.029$). In other words, the higher the instrumental need for touch is the more the relief printed product picture induces tactile contacts with the advertising medium. H1 is then validated. At the opposite, the relief brand name has no significant effect on the tactile contact number with the manipulated card ($p>.10$). Consequently, H2 is not validated.

In order to test our hypothesis concerning the contact numbers with the other smooth cards, in competition with the manipulated card, we lead the same ANCOVA but we change the dependent variable, namely the number of tactile contacts with the other cards. In this case, both relief of the product picture and the brand name have a significant simple effect on the number of tactile contacts with no interaction effects. The relief product on the manipulated card induces a higher mean number of tactile contacts with the other competitor smooth cards ($M_{relief}=16.92$ and $M_{smooth}=13.05$; $p=.051$). The relief product induces a higher mean number of tactile contacts compared to the smooth cards ($M_{relief}=16.92$ and $M_{smooth}=13.05$; $p=.051$). The relief brand name also induces a higher mean number of tactile contacts with the smooth cards ($M_{relief}=16.79$ and $M_{smooth}=13.15$; $p=.033$). These results validate H3 and H4 concerning the positive effect of adding relief to product picture and brand name on the contact with the brand in competition with the brand of the manipulated card.

Results Concerning Quantity of Product Consumed

We proceed again with an ANCOVA for assessing the impact of relief conditions (on the product and on the brand)—fixed factors—on the quantity of candies consumed by the respondent during the experience—dependent variable, introducing all the potentially moderating variables described below. If the product picture in relief presents no significant effect on the consumed quantity ($p > .10$), the brand in relief has a negative impact on the mean on the quantity of candies eaten ($M_{relief} = 0.07$ lb and $M_{smooth} = 0.1$ lb; $p = .05$). Consequently, we fail to validate H5 concerning the positive impact of relief printing product picture, and we validate H6 highlighting a negative impact of relief printing brand name on the consumed quantity of candies after exposure to the promotional cards. Moreover, our findings show a direct positive impact of the respondent hunger to explain the eaten candy quantity ($p = 0.00$).

Results Concerning Brand Recall and Brand Preference

In our study, both brand recall and brand preferences are binary variables. Consequently we lead a logit analysis in order to test H7, H8 and H9. On the one hand, the results concerning the impact of the brand name in relief—variable entered at step 1—on brand recall—choice variable explained in the model—conclude to no significant effect. Consequently, H7 is no validated. The relief printed brand name doesn't enhance its memorization. On the other hand, we find a significant relationship between the product picture in relief and the preference for the brand. The quote report predicting the decision of preferring the brand is 5.53 times higher when the product picture appears in relief. This result validates H8 concerning the positive impact of relief of product picture on brand preference. However, the effect of relief of brand name is not significant ($p > .10$) and consequently we fail to validate H9. Our results emphasize the positive effect of instrumental need for touch level on the relationship between relief product and preference for the brand.

Discussion

In this study, we study the effects of adding relief on the product image and on the brand name of an advertising medium. The presence of relief on a product causes more haptic contacts with the advertising medium but this is not the case when the brand is in relief. Adding relief on the product or the brand leads to more haptic contacts with smooth advertising media competitors. Our results support the packaging literature by showing that the adding of relief conducts the consumers to touch by attracting their attention. However, they also show that in a competitive world this haptic baiting also works in favor of a touch contact with the advertising medium competitors. Finally this is something to explore in the packaging field. Adding relief to the product image seems to be the best choice. Indeed, it enhances brand preference. At the opposite, the relief brand decreases the consumed quantity of product and incites touching competitive smooth media without enhancing brand preference or recall. Moreover our results do not conclude to a reinforcement effect between relief product picture and relief brand name, inviting to relief only one of them. So the managers must take this fact into account. Thus, our results show that the reliefs of some elements of an advertising media don't have the same impact on the consumer. In this way, we suggested to highlight the product picture rather than the brand name in order to reinforce the brand preference and not to divert the consumer attention from the product image inducing craving eating.

References available upon request.

The Conceptual Chain From Event Activities to Emotions to Atmosphere, and Sponsor Awareness and Patronage

T. Bettina Cornwell, Steffen Jahn, and Wang Suk Suh

Abstract Sport, arts, and cause events are a service product in their own right and also often a platform for the marketing of other products. Emotions are recognized as important both in marketing of the event (attendance and future attendance) and marketing of products via the event. When positive emotions prevail, this can influence both future attendance as well as responses to sponsorship. This study examines the role of emotions and atmosphere at an international track and field event. Mediated regression results show that event activities support positive emotions and in turn the development of a good atmosphere; the resulting atmosphere influences both sponsor awareness and future patronage in a positive way. As well, event activities hold a direct positive influence on sponsor awareness.

T.B. Cornwell (✉) • W.S. Suh
University of Oregon, Eugene, OR, USA
e-mail: tbc@uoregon.edu; wsuh@uoregon.edu

S. Jahn
University of Goettingen, Goettingen, Germany
e-mail: steffen.jahn@wiwi.uni-goettingen.de

© Academy of Marketing Science 2016   811
L. Petruzzellis, R.S. Winer (eds.), *Rediscovering the Essentiality of Marketing*,
Developments in Marketing Science: Proceedings of the Academy of Marketing
Science, DOI 10.1007/978-3-319-29877-1_155

Part XX
Services Marketing

The Impact of Didactic Resources' Quality and the Instructor's Attitude: E-Learning Continuance Explained by Flow and Presence Experiences

Inma Rodríguez-Ardura, Antoni Meseguer-Artola, and Gisela Ammetller

Abstract The perceived quality of online didactic resources and the instructor's attitude are conceived as pillars of e-learning environments (Edwards et al. 2011; Udo et al. 2011). However, research has not delivered evidence about the connections of these two important elements with the e-learners' post-adoption decision, throughout which they reconsider the e-learning environment and determine whether they will continue using e-learning or not.

To analyse the potential effects of the perceived quality of online didactic resources and the instructor's attitude on e-learner's post-adoption decisions, TAM (Davis 1985, 1989) can be a valid model (King and He 2006). First because, in e-learning, didactic resources—which include content and tools of all kind of origins and formats—become one of the main sources of information and knowledge (Rodríguez-Ardura et al. 2009), so they can activate e-learner's favourable perceptions about the ease of use and the usefulness of the learning environment (Cheng 2012). And second, because the positive instructor's approach in conducting teaching activities and providing guidance helps e-learners to construct knowledge, and leads them to perceive the e-learning environment as easy to use (Lin 2011) and useful (Lee et al. 2009). Yet, on the basis of literature in consumer behaviour that suggests that individuals interpret incoming information online through both affective and cognitive mechanisms (Rose et al. 2012), we further propose to capture a range of psychological phenomena that go beyond TAM's utilitarian beliefs of ease of use and usefulness. Consistent with this, we build an integrative model that considers the mediating role of flow episodes and presence feelings in the perceived quality of online didactic resources and the instructor's attitude.

To test the integrative model, we used data from a web-based survey and merged them with registrar's office data on e-learners' academic records. A database of 2530 records was built. The substantial predicting power of the structural equation modelling robustly supports the hypothesized causal paths. The findings confirm the crucial link of perceived didactic resource quality, and instructor attitude, with

I. Rodríguez-Ardura (✉) • A. Meseguer-Artola • G. Ammetller
Internet Interdisciplinary Institute, Universitat Oberta de Catalunya, Barcelona, Spain
e-mail: irodriguez@uoc.edu; ameseguer@uoc.edu; gammetller@uoc.edu

© Academy of Marketing Science 2016   815
L. Petruzzellis, R.S. Winer (eds.), *Rediscovering the Essentiality of Marketing*,
Developments in Marketing Science: Proceedings of the Academy of Marketing
Science, DOI 10.1007/978-3-319-29877-1_156

TAM's beliefs; and also that these two pillars of e-learning environments elicit both flow episodes and presence feelings. Indeed, it shows a causal connection between perceived ease of use and flow, in line with Self-Efficacy Theory (Bandura 1982) and Tao et al. findings (2009), and that flow episodes and presence feelings trigger e-learning continuance.

References available upon request.

The Antecedents of Service Innovation: The Roles of Explorative and Exploitative Marketing Capabilities

Hui-Ling Huang and Yue-Yang Chen

Abstract With the growing significant development of economics, the industry has changed from physical property-driven machines and facilities to services-driven knowledge. In this knowledge-based economy, innovation capability is the key factor to attain the competitive advantages. Therefore, for facing the trend of service industry, service innovation is regarded as a value-creating activity which derived from customers' needs. It is also a critical strategic weapon for firms achieving competitive advantages. Evidences showed for acquiring superior business performance, the link from marketing capability to service innovation is important and necessary for firms introducing new products into market. Thus, drawing on the previous studies, this present research tried to examine the relationships between two types of marketing capabilities, i.e. explorative marketing capability and exploitative marketing capability on service innovation. According to the empirical data collected from service sector companies in Taiwan, meaningful findings and conclusions will be proposed and discussed.

Keywords Marketing capability • Explorative marketing capability • Exploitative marketing capability • Service innovation

H.-L. Huang (✉)
Chang Jung Christian University, Tainan, Taiwan
e-mail: ling@mail.cjcu.edu.tw

Y.-Y. Chen
I-Shou University, Kaohsiung, Taiwan
e-mail: ray@isu.edu.tw

© Academy of Marketing Science 2016
L. Petruzzellis, R.S. Winer (eds.), *Rediscovering the Essentiality of Marketing*,
Developments in Marketing Science: Proceedings of the Academy of Marketing
Science, DOI 10.1007/978-3-319-29877-1_157

Introduction

Service innovation is a sort of value-creating activity. The creation of value must be determined by customers. However, the complexity of customers and the advancement of technology result in more complicated operation of service industry and higher environmental uncertainty (Smith et al. 2007). In such a trend, the service innovation becomes the core of competitiveness of enterprises.

In the knowledge-based perspective, the enterprises are the carrier of knowledge, the gains derived from knowledge application, and creation can be regarded as the income from innovation, as for the quality of business operation, different abilities of enterprises to integrate knowledge result in different results of value creation. It is indicated that the marketing capabilities of enterprises are not only the important sources of performance, but also the important sources of differences in new products (Lisboa et al. 2011). Therefore, this study takes service industry as the research subject; the specific research purposes are: (1) Examining the correlations between marketing capability (i.e., explorative and exploitative capabilities) and service innovation; (2) Testing the role of the two types of marketing capabilities on service innovation.

Literature Review

Marketing Capability

The marketing capability is a sort of capability of enterprise to use its knowledge, technology, and resources to meet customer requirements (Day 1994). Vorhies and Morgan (2005) defined the marketing capability on marketing mix activity as the capability of enterprises to perform routine marketing affairs and convert resources into valuable output. In the resource-based view (RBV) on marketing capability, the source of business performance is attributed to the difference in the resources owned by the enterprises. The enterprise has competitive advantage when it has scarce, distinct, valuable, and nonreplaceable resources. In comparison to this, the knowledge-based perspective is based on the assumption of RBV, and it emphasizes the role of knowledge; it regards knowledge as the most important asset of organizations.

Slater and Narver (1995) indicated that an enterprise with marketing capability used its marketing knowledge and skills repeatedly to support its marketing decisions and activities, to solve marketing problems, and learned in the process. In terms of research on marketing capability based on the activity process, Atuahene-Gima (1993) used customer service, sales promotion, skills of sales force, marketing network extension, advertising, marketing research, capability for product diversification, and the new product introduction speed to measure the marketing capability. In addition, in terms of marketing policy, the effective implementation of marketing policy is the driving force for enterprise performance (Olsen et al. 2005).

It is observed that owning resources does not determine absolute advantage, but the capability to allocate resources and this capability is the accumulation of a set of complex skills and knowledge. Both the convention and process of the organization can assist the organization in coordinating activities and using resources, as specific presentation of knowledge body operation.

In terms of the type of marketing capability, based on knowledge, the enterprise is a knowledge body; the marketing capability shall not only integrate the existing and new market knowledge, but also evolve gradually. Therefore, the enterprise can use marketing exploration and marketing exploitation to increase market knowledge (March 1991; Atuahene-Gima 2005). The former one escapes the existing products, markets, technologies, and skills and develops new knowledge; the latter one emphasizes the development of the existing product, market, technology, and skill knowledge. The two capabilities can be regarded as the core value-creating capabilities; they are the source of main competitive advantages (Yalcinkaya et al. 2007).

Service Innovation

The service innovation is offerings which may be from the variation of service combination or the variation of service delivery process. There are several forms of service innovation: brand-new innovation, new to enterprises, improvement on the existing service, new delivery process, or amendment of service. The service innovation can be classified into product innovation and process innovation. Kivisaari et al. (2004) indicated that the innovation model of service system defined by EU had six dimensions, including technical and product innovations, service innovation, mechanism of network value, organizational innovation, customer interface, and service delivery system innovation. The meanings of these innovation degrees to the market include competition and variation of consumer behavior, brand-new service, the consumers' need to change use behavior. In a general way, the market acceptance is challenged considerably, which is rarely seen.

For the concept of service innovation, many studies laid emphasis on the type and degree of service innovation (Kivisaari et al. 2004; Edvardsson and Olsson 1996). Some scholars defined the service innovation as how much the enterprise integrated new knowledge to provide the customers with new service offerings, creating the values of enterprise and customers directly or indirectly. In the view of knowledge management, the service innovation centers on the customers in demand, emphasizing the acquisition of customer knowledge to develop new service based on the knowledge. Therefore, the service innovation can be conceptualized as service concept, process, and service system (Edvardsson and Olsson 1996).

The service innovation can be defined as new service offerings or new process to market a company. It aims to promote the value obtained by the service-correlated stakeholders (Thakur and Hale 2012). In order to develop high-performance service, the service enterprise must be in accordance with many different critical activities (Johne and Storey 1998). It is indicated that senior executives are the driving force for service innovation (Cooper et al. 1994; Drew 1995). When the enterprise has explicit visions, the manager is the important source of shaping innovative organizational culture, so as to push service innovation successfully (Johne and Storey 1998).

Hypotheses Development and the Research Design

The service innovation can be regarded as the information result obtained by integrating the internal and external network relationships of enterprise. The knowledge resources of previous experience, competitors' actions, customer feedback, and the interaction between enterprises and social network resources provide the information of service process innovation. Such dependence between knowledge acquisition and innovation is more apparent in service industry than in manufacturing industry (Eisingerich et al. 2009). The demand of customers and competition are the force driving service innovation. The knowledge network also promotes service innovation (Kandampully 2002).

The success of innovation depends on the diversity of management and job skills (Hipp and Grupp 2005). In the view of knowledge management, the exchange of market information between departments or partners can promote information processing and learning of organization effectively (Gulati 1999), contributive to innovation. The internal and external connections of enterprises reduce the transaction cost, increasing the speed and effectiveness of new knowledge development and information transfer (Lee et al. 2001; Sherif et al. 2006).

The better performance of enterprises is resulted from the increase of market knowledge stock (Kohli and Jaworski 1990; Narver and Slater 1990) and the ability to allocate the knowledge stock by the marketing capability of enterprises (Barney 1991; Day 1994). The marketing exploitation type of marketing capability is highly correlated with the present knowledge base of enterprises, contributing to progressive innovation, e.g. product improvement and line stretching (Atuahene-Gima 2005). Valuable market information can be obtained by successful interaction with external customers; continuous exchange of information and generating knowledge can further concrete a better service delivery process (Berthon and John 2006; Ramani and Kumar 2008).

The marketing capability of enterprises has key effect for their operations; it helps the enterprises sell products and services successfully (Day 1994). The market demand is the driving force in the service innovation process. The marketing exploitation type of marketing capability emphasizes obtaining and using the information of experienced customers and competitors the enterprises are familiar with. The emphasis is to strengthen and improve the existing services, so as to guarantee the operational efficiency of enterprises, so that the advice and feedback of customers become important driver elements of service innovation. In addition, in the process of enterprise service innovation, the application and integration of resources depend on the exertion of enterprise's marketing capability. The marketing exploration type of marketing capability emphasizes obtaining and using the knowledge beyond the existing knowledge of enterprises, using brand new skills to explore new markets, and to look for potential customers.

The marketing exploration capability emphasizes the spirit of research and development, and as the enterprise introduces the participation of customers actively in information sharing, relationship exchange, and co-production, the combinations of product and service offerings can be changed dynamically (Chen et al. 2012). The marketing exploration capability enables the enterprises to grasp new concepts and technologies actively, attempting to master market opportunities. For general product innovation domain, it has been proved that the marketing exploration capability has positive effect on innovation (He and Wong 2004; Smith and Tushman 2005). Therefore, the following hypotheses are proposed and the research model is shown as Fig. 1.

H1: The marketing exploitation type of marketing capability of organization has positive influence on service innovation.
H2: The marketing exploration type of marketing capability of organization has positive influence on service innovation.

Measurement and Sampling

According to the discussions about marketing capability of Vorhies et al. (2011), this study defines the exploration marketing capability as the marketing capability of using new market knowledge when the enterprise lays emphasis on developing new techniques and process. Furthermore, exploitation marketing capability is defined as emphasizing improving and revising the existing skills and process, laying emphasis on the value that can be created for customers by marketing capability in current market. The measurement items are also derived from Vorhies et al. (2011).

Drawing on Chen and Tsou (2007), this study defines service innovation as proceedings of organization for changing products or services by product innovation or process innovation. The measurement items are also derived from those of Chen and Tsou's (2007) research.

The respondents of this present study are the managers of the companies, because of their more familiar corporate strategy making, overall business operations, and company's capability than general employees. The service industry was investi-

Fig. 1 The research model

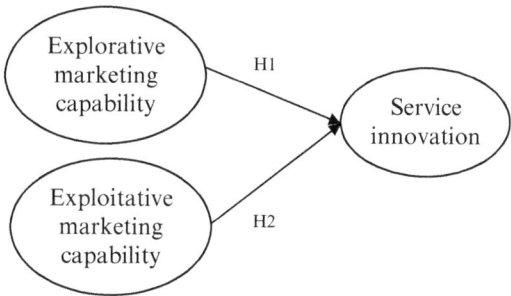

gated, the enterprises were contacted via telephone and E-mail, 17 rejected, the questionnaires were sent out by post and E-mail, there were 483 questionnaires sent out, then 132 returned, yielding the response rate of 27.33 %. When the questionnaires were collected, the effective questionnaires were analyzed by statistical packages of SPSS19.0, which include descriptive statistics, correlation analysis, and regression analysis.

Research Results and Findings

Descriptive Statistics

Demographic data of the respondents' firms are summarized as follows. The largest number of respondents came from the department store, representing 20 % of the responding companies. The largest share of the companies had 251–500 employees (20 %). The job titles of the respondents include top managers (50.8 %) and middle managers (49.2 %). This suggests that the respondents had enough experience and knowledge to complete the questionnaire. Approximately 88 % of the companies have been built up more than 9 years.

Reliability and Validity Analysis

The questionnaires were presented to several experts to improve face and content validity. Reliability was examined using Cronbach's α values for each variable. As presented in Table 1, most of these, except for Internet quality, were above to 0.77 which is a commonly acceptable level.

Pearson Correlation Analysis

Table 1 also presents the means, standard deviations, and correlations between variables. The explorative marketing capability variable ($r = .43$, $p < .001$) has the highest correlation to the dependent variable. Exploitative marketing capability is also

Table 1 Descriptive statistics, correlations[a], and reliabilities[b]

Variables	Means	S.D.	(1)	(2)	(3)
(1) Explorative marketing capability	5.65	.64	(.83)		
(2) Exploitative marketing capability	4.93	.87	.65	(.77)	
(3) Service innovation	5.56	.66	.43	.48	(.88)

[a]Absolute values of Correlations above .12 are significant at $p < .05$ level

[b]Reliabilities (Cronbach's α) are shown in parentheses

showed significantly correlated with the dependent variable ($r = .48$, $p < .001$). The findings showed that the two types of marketing capabilities have positive correlation with service innovation, demonstrating the higher marketing capabilities of the firms and the more service innovation opportunities to initiative.

Hypothesis Testing

To test the hypotheses, an enter regression analysis was conducted. Two antecedents were applied as independent variables, while service innovation was used as the dependent variable. Table 2 presents the results of this analysis. As we can see in the table, the two independent variables showed to have impacts on service innovation. Thus, the test supports hypothesis 1 and 2, demonstrating that explorative marketing capability has a positive impact on service innovation ($\beta = .35$, t-value $= 3.522$, $p < .001$), and exploitative marketing capability also has a positive impact on service innovation ($\beta = .19$, t-value $= 1.996$, $p < .05$). According to the findings, explorative marketing capability showed more influence on service innovation than that of exploitative. Totally, the two antecedents share 24 % of the variance of service innovation. The result of the path analysis is summarized in Fig. 2.

In order to avoid violating the basic assumptions underlying the method of least squares used by the classical linear regression model, we conducted a P-P Plot for assessing the assumption of normality. The plot showed that the quantile pairs fell nearly on a straight line. It is, therefore, reasonable to conclude that the data used in this research are approximately normal. Secondly, this research used the condition index (CI) to assess the multicollinearity among independent variables in the model. The value of 25.10 indicated no severe multicollinearity problem among the regressors. Finally, we used the Durbin-Watson d statistic for detecting serial correlation. The value of 1.84 (less than 2) indicated the autocorrelation problem does not exist (Gujarati 2003).

Table 2 Results of regression analysis ($n = 132$)

	Dependent variable: service innovation	
Independent variable	β	t-value
Explorative marketing capability	.35***	3.522
Exploitative marketing capability	.19*	1.996
F	21.79***	
R^2	.25	
Adjusted R^2	.24	
C.I.	25.10	
Durbin-Watson	1.84	

Note: *$p < .05$; **$p < .01$; ***$p < .001$

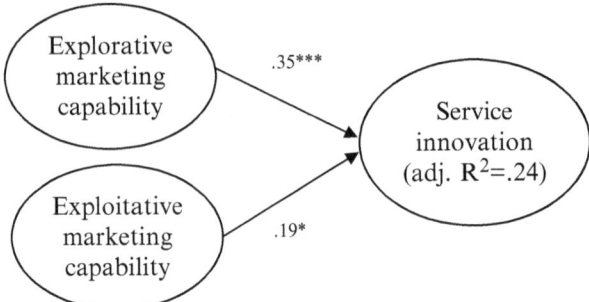

Fig. 2 The result of the research model

Conclusion

According to the correlation coefficient table, the marketing capability is significantly positive correlation with service innovation, that is to say, the better the marketing capability, the better the service innovation of a firm. Second, the exploitative marketing capability is significantly positive correlation with the explorative marketing capability, meaning that the marketing capabilities of enterprises are actually inter-correlation to some extent. Additionally, exploitation marketing capability also showed to have a great significantly positive influence on service innovation than that of exploration marketing capability, demonstrating that the explorative is an important factor to explain service innovation.

The purposes of enterprise developing new services include providing the original customers with new services, increasing added value, and attracting new customers and developing new markets, as well as enhancing the enterprise performance. However, while developing new services, the enterprises shall respond to the market fluctuations and trends to enhance market competitiveness, so it is very important for the enterprises to master the market. The empirical research findings showed that implementing obvious service innovation results from improving the marketing capabilities of enterprises, thus the higher performance achieved.

Innovation is always regarded as the core capability of an enterprise which can keep competitiveness only by continuous change and innovation. This study discusses and combines service innovation from the angles of discovery and application, enlarging the layers of research on marketing capability; this is the main theoretical implication of marketing capability. Calantone et al. (1994) mentioned that the enterprises must have appropriate marketing resources and techniques in order to develop new products successfully. Javalgi et al. (2005) and Kirca et al. (2005) also indicated that the old concept of better strategy better effect was not a guarantee anymore; the strategy must be "converted (intermediary factor)" effectively in order to generate the expected performance. Therefore, the enterprises shall plan the direction of innovation clearly, keeping flexible responsiveness. At ordinary times, the marketing knowledge management capability shall be implemented completely; the knowledge of the existing and potential customers, competitors, and market environment shall be collected systematically and analyzed objectively, so as to further create new market knowledge as the basis of diffusing and accumulating knowledge inside organization.

Acknowledgment This study was funded by the Taiwan Ministry of Science and Technology under project number MOST104-2914-I-309-002-A1 and NSC102-2410-H-309-010.

References

Atuahene-Gima, K. (1993). The determinants of inward technology licensing intentions: an empirical analysis of Australian engineering firms. *The Journal of Product Innovation Management, 10*(3), 230–240.

Atuahene-Gima, K. (2005). Resolving the capability-rigidity paradox in new product innovation. *Journal of Marketing, 69*(4), 61–68.

Barney, J. (1991). Firm resources and sustained competitive advantage. *Journal of Management, 17*(1), 99–120.

Berthon, P., & John, J. (2006). From entities to interfaces: Delineating value in customer-firm interactions. In R. F. Lusch & S. L. Vargo (Eds.), *The service-dominant logic of marketing* (pp. 196–207). Armonk, NY: M.E. Sharpe.

Calantone, R. C., Benedetto, A. D., & Bhoovaraghava, S. (1994). Examining the relationship between degree of innovation and new product success. *Journal of Business Research, 30*, 143–148.

Chen, Y. C., Li, P. C., & Evans, K. R. (2012). Effects of interaction and entrepreneurial orientation on organizational performance: Insights into market devein and market driving. *Industrial Marketing Management, 31*, 1019–1034.

Chen, J. S., & Tsou, T. H. (2007). Information technology adoption for service innovation practices and competitive advantage: The case of financial firms. *Information Research, 12*(3), 1–23.

Cooper, R. G., Easingwood, C. J., Edgett, S., Kleinschmidt, E. J., & Story, C. (1994). What distinguishes the top performing new products in financial services? *Journal of Product Innovation Management, 11*, 281–299.

Day, G. S. (1994). The capabilities of market-driven organizations. *Journal of Marketing, 58*(4), 37–52.

Drew, S. A. W. (1995). Accelerating innovation in financial services. *Long Range Planning, 28*(4), 11–21.

Edvardsson, B., & Olsson, J. (1996). Key concepts for new service development. *The Service Industries Journal, 16*(2), 140–164.

Eisingerich, A. B., Rubera, G., & Seifert, M. (2009). Managing service innovation and interorganizational relationships for firm performance: To commit or diversity? *Journal of Service Research, 11*(4), 344–356.

Gujarati, D. N. (2003). *Basic econometrics*. New York: McGraw-Hill.

Gulati, R. (1999). Network location and learning: The influence of network resources and firm capabilities on alliance formation. *Strategic Management Journal, 20*(5), 397–420.

He, Z. L., & Wong, O. K. (2004). Exploration vs. Exploitation: A empirical test of the ambidexterity hypothesis. *Organization Science, 15*(4), 481–494.

Hipp, C., & Grupp, H. (2005). Innovation in the service sector, the demand for service-specific innovation measurement concepts and typologies. *Research Policy, 34*, 517–535.

Javalgi, R. G., Whipple, T. W., Ghosh, A. K., & Young, R. (2005). Market orientation, strategic flexibility, and performance: Implications for services providers. *Journal of Services Marketing, 19*(4), 212–231.

Johne, A., & Storey, C. (1998). New service development: A review of the literature and annotated bibliography. *European Journal of Marketing, 32*(3/4), 184–251.

Kandampully, J. (2002). Innovation as the core competency of a service organization: The role of technology, knowledge and network. *European Journal of Innovation Management, 5*(1), 18–26.

Kirca, A. H., Jayachandran, S., & Bearden, W. O. (2005). Market orientation: A meta-analytic review and assessment of its antecedents and impact on performance. *Journal of Marketing, 69*(2), 24–41.

Kivisaari, S., Lovio, R., & Väyrynen, E. (2004). Managing experiments for transition: Examples of societal embedding in energy and health care sectors. In B. Elzen, F. Geels, & K. Green (Eds.), *System innovation and the transition to sustainability: Theory, evidence and policy*. Cheltenham, England: Edward Elgar.

Kohli, A. K., & Jaworski, B. J. (1990). Market orientation: The construct, research propositions and management implications. *Journal of Marketing, 54*(2), 1–18.

Lee, C., Lee, K., & Pennings, J. M. (2001). Internal capabilities, external networks, and performance: A study on technology-based ventures. *Strategic Management Journal, 22*(6-7), 615–640.

Lisboa, A., Skarmeas, D., & Lages, C. (2011). Entrepreneurial orientation, exploitative and explorative capabilities, and performance outcomes in export markets: A resource-based approach. *Industrial Marketing Management, 40*, 1274–1284.

March, J. G. (1991). Exploration and exploitation in organization learning. *Organization Science, 2*(1), 71–87.

Narver, J. C., & Slater, S. F. (1990). The effect of a market orientation on business profitability. *Journal of Marketing, 54*(4), 20–35.

Olsen, E. M., Slater, S. F., & Hult, G. T. M. (2005). The importance of structure and process to strategy implementation. *Business Horizon, 48*(1), 47–54.

Ramani, G., & Kumar, V. (2008). Interaction orientation and firm performance. *Journal of Marketing, 72*(1), 27–45.

Sherif, K., Hoffman, J., & Thomas, B. (2006). Can technology build organizational social capital? The case of a global IT consulting firm. *Information Management, 43*, 795–804.

Slater, S. F., & Narver, J. C. (1995). Market orientation and the learning organization. *Journal of Marketing, 59*, 63–74.

Smith, A. M., Fischbacher, M., & Wilson, F. A. (2007). New service development: From panoramas to precision. *European Management Journal, 25*(5), 370–383.

Smith, W., & Tushman, M. (2005). Managing strategic contradictions: A top management model for managing innovation streams. *Organization Science, 16*(5), 522–536.

Thakur, R., & Hale, D. (2012). Service innovation: A comparative study of U.S. and Indian service firms. *Journal of Business Research, 66*(8), 1108–1123.

Vorhies, D. W., & Morgan, N. A. (2005). Benchmarking marketing capabilities for sustainable competitive advantage. *Journal of Marketing, 69*, 80–94.

Vorhies, D. W., Orr, L. M., & Bush, V. D. (2011). Improving customer-focused marketing capabilities and firm financial performance via marketing exploration and exploitation. *Journal of the Academy Marketing Science, 39*, 736–756.

Yalcinkaya, G., Calantone, R. J., & Griffith, D. A. (2007). An examination of exploration and exploitation capabilities: Implications for product innovation and market performance. *Journal of International Marketing, 15*(4), 63–93.

Why B2B Firms Measure Service Productivity

Gianfranco Walsh, Heiner Evanschitzky, Mario Schaarschmidt,
Peter Walgenbach, and Sharon E. Beatty

Introduction

Increasingly competitive service markets force firms to look for ways to increase the operational efficiency of service delivery (e.g., Ostrom et al. 2010; Ulaga and Reinartz 2011). At both conceptual (e.g., Sahay 2005; Parasuraman 2002, 2010) and empirical (e.g., Lääts et al. 2011; Rust and Huang 2012) levels, growing management and marketing literature centers on service productivity, generally defined as units of output (e.g., processed customers, sales) divided by units of input (e.g., labor hours) (e.g., López and Sune 2012). However, productivity measurement continues to pose a challenge for service firms, primarily because of the difficulty of accurately quantifying service inputs and outputs. One reason for this relative lack of measurement especially in people-processing services may be the complexity involved in measuring service productivity, particularly the difficulty of modeling the trade-off between changes in productivity (e.g., increasing customer throughput) and key service outcomes such as satisfaction (e.g., Brady et al. 2002; Wirtz et al. 2012), as well as the difficulty of aligning productivity measures with varying levels of customer integration. Beyond the trade-off, little is known about the antecedents of service firms' decisions to measure productivity. This is surprising given

G. Walsh (✉) • M. Schaarschmidt • P. Walgenbach
Friedrich-Schiller-University of Jena, Jena, Germany
e-mail: walsh@uni-jena.de; mario.schaarschmidt@uni-koblenz.de; Peter.Walgenbach@
uni-jena.de

H. Evanschitzky
Aston University, Birmingham, UK
e-mail: h.evanschitzky@aston.ac.uk

S.E. Beatty
University of Alabama, Tuscaloosa, AL, USA
e-mail: sbeatty@cba.ua.edu

© Academy of Marketing Science 2016
L. Petruzzellis, R.S. Winer (eds.), *Rediscovering the Essentiality of Marketing*,
Developments in Marketing Science: Proceedings of the Academy of Marketing
Science, DOI 10.1007/978-3-319-29877-1_158

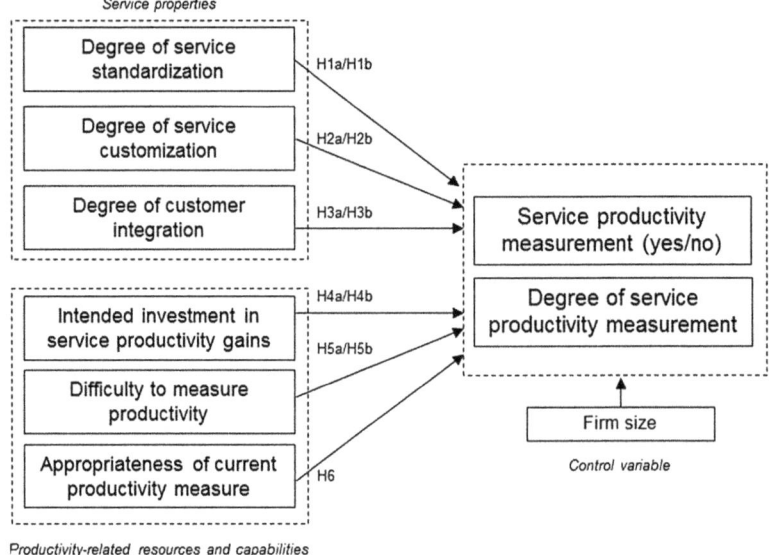

Fig. 1 Conceptual model

that performance measurement continues to be an important topic in management practice and research (e.g., Lai et al. 2012; O'Cass and Ngo 2011). Also, in many industries, efficient service delivery processes are built into business models (Meuter et al. 2005). Against this background, the authors explore why few service firms have adequate service productivity measurement (SPM) systems in place.

Background and Method

By combining field interviews and literature-based insights, the authors develop a conceptual model of multiple antecedents of SPM in business-to-business service firms (see Fig. 1).

To develop a conceptualization that reflects the interactional nature (between customer and firm) of service delivery and narrow the focus onto the key factors required for a model, the authors used an inductive–deductive approach (Gooner et al. 2011; Swamidass 1991). Inductive reasoning is more exploratory in nature (i.e., open-ended), which is why the authors commenced with qualitative fieldwork. Consistent with deductive reasoning, which is narrower in nature, the authors synthesized practitioner and academic literature relevant to SPM. Based on inductive-deductive insights, testable hypotheses are developed. The authors developed an interview protocol based on in-depth discussions with a sample of 15 senior service managers involved in assessing performance in their respective firms (see Table 1).

Table 1 Description of informants

	Name/gender	Position/industry	Age	Education
1	Alexander/m	Managing director/point of sale software	42	Master's degree
2	David/m	Area manager/telecommunications	43	Secondary school graduation
3	Ralph/m	Division manager/insurances	42	Master's degree
4	Axel/m	Managing director/logistics	43	Bachelor's degree
5	Hugh/m	President/Estate agent	48	High school graduate
6	Leonard/m	Senior manager/IT consulting	40	Master's degree
7	Jacob/m	Director/hotel	52	Bachelor's degree
8	Herbert/m	Director/auditing	68	Ph.D.
9	Lucas/m	Managing director/wholesaling	36	Master's degree
10	Stephan/m	Branch manager/restaurant chain	54	Secondary school graduation
11	Tanja/f	Manager/hotel	38	Bachelor's degree
13	Owen/m	Manager/bank	42	Bachelor's degree
14	Rita/f	Director/network equipment and services	38	Master's degree
15	Vincent/m	Managing director/electrical engineering	46	Bachelor's degree

Note: *m* male, *f* female. The real names of informants have been replaced to ensure confidentiality

These firms come from different B2B service industries. Amongst others, managers were asked whether their firm employed SPM and, where applicable, about their experience with the measures used.

The authors test the hypotheses that result from this conceptual model using data from 276 service firms. The results indicate that one antecedent affects the choice to use SPM, namely, the degree of service standardization. In addition, results reveal that all five hypothesized antecedents and one additional antecedent (perceived appropriateness of the current SPM) predict the degree of SPM. Thus, the degree of service standardization and service customization positively, and customer integration negatively, affects SPM. Investments in service productivity gains and the appropriateness of current service productivity measures positively, and the perceived difficulty of measuring service productivity negatively affect SPM. The authors conclude with implications for service firms and directions for research.

References available upon request.

The Role of Marketing in Achieving and Maintaining Financial Health of Nonprofit Arts Organizations: The Case of the Symphony Orchestra Sector

Theresa A. Kirchner, Edward P. Markowski, and John B. Ford

Abstract Nonprofit arts organizations historically have struggled to survive and thrive, since their business models, including their marketing and fund development efforts, often develop reactively rather than being strategically planned and tactically managed to successfully target key stakeholder groups and individuals. In addition, both program ticket sales and contributions from all sources are often affected by changes in economic environments at all levels, which are not directly controllable by arts organizations. The challenges for arts organizations of achieving and maintaining sustainable financial health are serious ones, particularly in many countries which are moving towards government support models which require organizations to become more self-sufficient by improving their fund development and marketing programs.

This study builds on the authors' prior research (Kirchner et al. 2007) which assessed potential correlational and causal relationships of Levels of Nonprofit Organization Government Support and Marketing Investment on Organizational Financial Health. It presents an expanded conceptual model which utilizes a more detailed breakout of the previous study's summary variables in order to assess, at a finer level, factors which are proposed to contribute to, and/or be affected by, Organizational Financial Health. The current longitudinal research project analyzes, over a period of 10 arts organization seasons (fiscal years), financial ratios which are used to assess financial health of the symphony orchestra sector. Those ratios capture empirical interrelationships among key revenue variables (government support, foundation support, business support, individual support, and concert revenue) and expense variables (marketing expense, fund development expense, artistic expense, and administrative expense), and a variable which measures organizational financial health. The model also incorporates demographic variables (e.g., organization age, budget size, and number of concerts) which are proposed to moderate those relationships. The study also assesses differences between pre-2008 (pre-recession) data, 2008–2009 (recession) and post-2009 (post-recession) data to

T.A. Kirchner (✉) • E.P. Markowski • J.B. Ford
Old Dominion University, Norfolk, VA, USA
e-mail: tkirchne@odu.edu; emarkows@odu.edu; jbford@odu.edu

© Academy of Marketing Science 2016   831
L. Petruzzellis, R.S. Winer (eds.), *Rediscovering the Essentiality of Marketing*,
Developments in Marketing Science: Proceedings of the Academy of Marketing
Science, DOI 10.1007/978-3-319-29877-1_159

discern implications of significant changes in the macroeconomic environment for the symphony orchestra sector and its marketing-related efforts and results.

From a methodological standpoint, this research utilizes a combination of correlational analysis and Granger causality analysis, proposing that organizational financial health can be predicted by projecting future values of time series data based on measurement of past values of time series data variables which have been shown to be empirically correlated with financial health. It uses secondary data from the League of American Orchestras' annual Orchestra Statistical Report financial and operational survey data.

References available upon request.

Customer Coping Behaviour During Service Failures: The Role of Self-Efficacy and Failure Severity

Jaywant Singh, Benedetta Crisafulli, and Sanjit Kumar Roy

Abstract Due to the complexity of services, service failures are inevitable events for service organisations and can make customers dissatisfied and willing to switch. When these events occur, organisations often attempt service recovery. Notwithstanding, recovery efforts do not always reduce customer discontentment and restore repatronage intentions. This is attributed to other factors outside the firm's control, including how customers cope with service failures. Some customers cope with equanimity, whilst others vent their frustration and anger by complaining and generating negative word-of-mouth. Service failures are stressful and emotion-laden events, which trigger coping processes; thus, understanding these processes is vital for service organisations. However, evidence in this research area is rather sparse. This study investigates the role of individual characteristics and situational factors in shaping customer coping with service failures. In particular, the study examines how self-efficacy and failure severity, and their interaction, influence customer coping mechanisms in the context of failed health services. In the healthcare sector, patient safety is a priority for health service providers. Yet, ensuring patient safety is challenging. Medical errors occur frequently, with serious consequences for patient health and the finances of health service providers. The healthcare sector, therefore, provides a timely and relevant context for examining customer coping. The study employed a scenario-based experiment. For data collection, a self-administered questionnaire was designed embedding a scenario of a customer experience of service failure with a private US healthcare service provider. Two versions of the same questionnaire were designed based on the manipulation of failure severity set at two levels, high and low. Prior to the main study, a pilot test was conducted ($n=30$) in order to establish the ecological and internal validity of findings. In the main study, respondents included a convenience sample of US consumers using a private healthcare service provider ($n=113$). For data analysis, linear and moderated regression analyses were conducted. The study's findings reveal that individuals high in

J. Singh (✉) • B. Crisafulli
Kingston University London, Surrey, UK
e-mail: J.Singh@kingston.ac.uk; B.Crisafulli@kingston.ac.uk

S.K. Roy
University of Western Australia, Crawley, WA, Australia
e-mail: Sanjit.roy@uwa.edu.au

© Academy of Marketing Science 2016   833
L. Petruzzellis, R.S. Winer (eds.), *Rediscovering the Essentiality of Marketing*,
Developments in Marketing Science: Proceedings of the Academy of Marketing
Science, DOI 10.1007/978-3-319-29877-1_160

self-efficacy are inclined to use their individual capabilities to actively attempt to find a solution, especially when health service failures are low in severity. When failures are severe, on the other hand, customers foresee the lack of capability to resolve the failure, thereby engaging less in active coping. Further, results show that customers high in self-efficacy rarely engage in denial coping, thereby avoiding that the service failure even happened. The study makes two important theoretical contributions. First, it investigates customer coping in the private healthcare service context, which has been largely overlooked in past research. Second, it demonstrates how self-efficacy differentially impacts customer coping strategies depending on the level of failure severity. From a managerial perspective, the study's findings indicate that some customers are keen to be actively involved in the recovery process, especially in the context of high involvement health services. Service providers could identify efficacious customers and engage them in co-created service recovery. Further, employees could be trained to deal with different types of customer coping behaviour.

How Does Frontline Employees' Perceived External Reputation Affect Service Innovation Implementation? A Dual-Path Model

Mario Schaarschmidt and Gianfranco Walsh

Abstract Service firms typically focus on increasing their operational proficiency and generating service innovations to stay competitive (Wilder et al. 2014). Researchers as well as practitioners widely acknowledge that service innovation especially is crucial for service organizations' financial performance (e.g., Ordanini and Parasuraman 2011). However, in contrast to research that centers on firm-level data, research that is devoted to employees' roles in generating and delivering service innovations remains rare (Cadwallader et al. 2010). Customer contact personnel especially are important to execute service offerings. Or, as Zeithaml et al. (2009, p. 352) state, "employees *are* the service" in many people-processing services. Frontline service employees are also important to successfully introduce and explain services to customers. Thus, through their motivation to recommend newly designed service offerings to customers (or not), service employees are in a position to either promote or impede service innovation implementation (McKnight and Hawkrigg 2005).

The authors draw on two theoretical perspectives in the innovation literature, that is, the efficiency-oriented perspective and the social–political perspective, in conjunction with social identity theory to predict how employees' perceived external reputation affect service innovation implementation. We test resulting hypotheses with two data sets from German ($N=150$) and the USA ($N=208$)-based frontline service employees. Results imply that the path from perceived external reputation to employees' willingness to recommend service innovations is significant across both studies. In addition, the path is fully mediated by expected positive performance outcomes and expected reputational gains. The authors discuss implications for practice and for innovation and marketing theory.

References available upon request.

M. Schaarschmidt (✉)
University of Koblenz-Landau, Mainz, Germany
e-mail: mario.schaarschmidt@uni-koblenz.de

G. Walsh
Friedrich-Schiller-University of Jena, Jena, Germany
e-mail: walsh@uni-jena.de

© Academy of Marketing Science 2016
L. Petruzzellis, R.S. Winer (eds.), *Rediscovering the Essentiality of Marketing*,
Developments in Marketing Science: Proceedings of the Academy of Marketing
Science, DOI 10.1007/978-3-319-29877-1_161

Insights from Coworking Spaces as Unique Service Organizations: The Role of Physical and Social Elements

Bamini K.P.D. Balakrishnan, Siva Muthaly, and Mark Leenders

Abstract This chapter puts forward the elements of service environment termed as 'servicescape' that will influence the behavioural intentions (loyalty, word of mouth, and recommendation) in service organizations, which provides service environment as their predominant offering. Interestingly, there is a growing group of service firms where consumers pay to consume the environment rather treating the environment as a facilitator of their purchase of merchandise or services. One such service environment focused business is the coworking spaces. They are business that offers the physical and social environment for consumption. It is an environment where creative, entrepreneurs and knowledge workers work in a commercial space, work on flexible work stations with a host of facilities at their disposal. These coworking spaces are designed to create a productive physical and social atmosphere. We propose an enriched servicescape framework specific to this industry and label it as 'Coworkingscape'. The conceptual focus of this chapter enables contribution in the field of service environment marketing and management. The practical implication of this chapter will be of help to coworking space providers/managers to further plan, design and manage the coworking spaces.

Keywords Servicescape • Coworking space • Coworkingscape • Social interaction • Behavioural intentions

Introduction

Service-oriented organizations are always exploring and developing new and improved ways to differentiate their market in order to attract customers, achieve a competitive advantage and maximize profit (Prahalad and Ramaswamy 2004). One of such attempt is to create and offer attractive prerequisites through the design of service environment offering service value (Edvardsson et al. 2005; Pareigis et al.

B.K.P.D. Balakrishnan (✉) • S. Muthaly • M. Leenders
RMIT University, Melbourne, VIC, Australia
e-mail: bamini.balakrishnan@rmit.edu.au; siva.muthaly@rmit.edu.au; mark.leenders@rmit.edu.au

© Academy of Marketing Science 2016   837
L. Petruzzellis, R.S. Winer (eds.), *Rediscovering the Essentiality of Marketing*,
Developments in Marketing Science: Proceedings of the Academy of Marketing
Science, DOI 10.1007/978-3-319-29877-1_162

2011). The importance of the service environment in creating favourable experiences is unquestioned (Högström et al. 2010; Lovelock 2011; Reimer and Kuehn 2005). Thus, the imperative role of service environment in influencing consumers' behaviour is an area of interest both in academia and among service marketing practitioners (Högström et al. 2010; Lovelock 2011; Reimer and Kuehn 2005).

Service environments are often studied in the context of shopping trips and consumer behaviour. The servicescape at large facilitates and enriches the service experience and influence behavioural responses that create value for the service provider. Interestingly, there is a growing group of service firms where consumers more or less consume the environment rather than the merchandize or services inside the service environment. For instance coworking spaces are business that offers environment for consumption. It is an environment where creative, entrepreneurs and knowledge workers work in a commercial space, work on flexible work stations with a host of facilities at their disposal. These coworking spaces are designed to create a productive physical and social atmosphere. We propose an enriched servicescape framework specific to this industry and label it as 'Coworkingscape'.

Literatures shows the effectiveness of service environment is an orientation that being barely attempted by many service marketers (Harris and Ezeh 2008; Pareigis et al. 2011). Therefore, there is a call for further research in the field of service environment. We further extend this research gap to understand service business that offers their service environment not to facilitate purchase but as predominant consumption itself. Interestingly, there is a growing group of service firms where consumers more or less consume the environment rather than the merchandize or services inside the service environment. Therefore, in order to extend this research specific to industry that provide environment as their main offering, we chose the growing coworking business settings as our research focus.

Theoretical Rationale

Servicescape is a concept introduced by Bitner (1992) to emphasize the influence of the physical environment in which a service process takes place. Booms and Bitner (1981: 36) defined a servicescape as 'the environment in which the service is assembled and in which the seller and customer interact, combined with tangible commodities that facilitate performance or communication of the service'. Servicescape refers to the physical facility in which a service is delivered and in which the service provider and the customer interact, and to any material or tangible elements that facilitate the service (Bitner 1992; Tombs and McColl-Kennedy 2003). The servicescape concept builds upon well-established research traditions in design, environmental psychology and marketing, that the design of the physical environment can be an extremely important element in influencing consumption patterns and practices (Booms and Bitner 1992; Kotler 1973). The servicescape framework includes interior design and deco, ambience, equipment, signage, layout, air quality and temperature.

Literature on servicescape for the past three decades (1983–2013) makes a strong case for improved servicescape elements (physical, functional, ambience and artefacts) and contributes to improved customer responses (Bitner 1992; Kotler 1973; Ryu and Han 2011), but it is not clear whether this relationship would be constant across all service provider business setting or even across all firms within a particular type of service industry. It is found the marginal benefit of servicescape is assumed to be higher for firms who promote and emphasize servicescape as a part of their competitive approach (Miles et al. 2012). For example, the service environment design might be more important in a restaurant premise compared to a laundry services premise.

The important role of the service environment or 'servicescape' (Bitner 1992) and 'social servicescape' (Tombs and McColl-Kennedy 2003) is gaining greater attention in the service marketing literature. Even though there are numerous literatures highlights the effectiveness of the physical environment of a service provider, yet there are lack of studies which takes into account the relative effect of social domain of the service environment. Therefore, researchers and practitioners calls for further research to include the humanistic cues within the social environment to be considered as important components. In this chapter we aim to response to these gaps in the literature.

This research builds on the inspirational works of Bitner (1992) and Tombs and McColl-Kennedy (2003), contributing to work in, management of service environment and consumer behaviour. The framework extends from the basic 'stimulus-organism-response' (SOR) theory from Meharabian and Russell's Model (M–R Model) (1974). This explains 'Stimulus' represented by physical elements and 'organism' the customers' experiences. The experiences then results in customer and employees 'response' in changed or unchanged behaviour depending on their reactions to the physical evidence. On the other hand the social psychologist through the Social Facilitation theory emphasizes presence of others will elicit monitoring of other social behaviours (Zajonc 1965) in other words presence of one person affects another person (Guerin and Innes 2009).

Servicescape has evolved based on the idea that a given setting or environment cannot be explained only by evaluating its elements separately from each other, instead should be studied as a whole (Harris and Ezeh 2008). Bitner's model has been integrated with Gestalt theory approach to provide a holistic perspective and approach. Researchers are focusing the impact of multiple servicescape elements on quality perception and loyalty (Baker et al. 2002; Harris and Ezeh 2008). In the consideration of holistic perspective, Tombs and McColl-Kennedy (2003) argue that the humanistic cues (e.g. customer to customer interactions, customer to staff interactions) play a key role in influencing the emotions of others either positively or negatively, and calls for social element to be added to the servicescape study.

The evolving nature of servicescape model in research have demonstrated understudied research area concerns how physical and social environments can influence customers in service industries, especially the sport encounter ('sportscape') (Wakefield and Sloan 1995), restaurant encounter ('dinescape') (Ryu and Jang 2008) and hospital experience ('healthscape') (Yogesh and Satyanarayana 2013).

Reviews once again identifies the distinctive features and the newness of this service cluster lie in the introduction and inclusion of industry specific stimuli in further investigation, thus extending the servicescape and M–R model (Mari and Pogessi 2013; Rosenbaum and Massiah 2011).

The purpose of this study was to explore the physical and social qualities that influence consumer's behavioural intentions specifically in coworking spaces, reflected by loyalty, spread word of mouth, intentions to stay longer and affiliate more in the space. Several supporting research questions are:

1. What characteristics and design features attract people and cause them to have favourable behavioural intentions to the coworking spaces?
2. What social interactions or human contacts attract people and cause them to behave favourably towards the coworking spaces?

Therefore, one of the objectives of this research is to identify servicescape elements specific to coworking space which contributes to the term 'Coworkingscape'. We argue that in atmospheric dominant service environment (Brocato et al. 2014) such as the coworking spaces, it is imperative to test the relative effect of both the physical elements and the social elements. We are proposing to identify the characteristics of both the physical and social environment that influence the behavioural intentions of the coworking members (customers) and extend the model to better account for the integration of social elements that develop within the coworking space firms. Therefore, in this chapter we will present a servicescape framework by including both the physical and social dimension specific to coworking space and conceptualize a specific term 'Coworkingscape' to explain the service environment specific to coworking spaces. In doing so, we provide useful insights for the ongoing scholarly work, refining, enriching and developing the framework of enriched servicescape for coworking space.

The remainder of the chapter is organized as follows. The theoretical framework for the study is presented in the following sections: (1) Coworking space as the service setting, (2) physical environment, (3) social environment and (4) behavioural intentions. The study then describes how the physical and social environment influence the behavioural intentions of the members by suggesting two major propositions, and how these relate to possible avenues for future research. The chapter concludes with a summary of the main contributions and limitations of the study, and directions for future research.

Coworking Space as the Research Setting

Coworking space services have taken off as a global phenomenon over the past few years and continue to grow (Butcher 2013). Coworking spaces are designed to be regarded as a 'serendipity accelerator' (Moriset 2014) which hosts freelancers, creative people and entrepreneurs. Coworking offers a self-employed business person, nomadic employees, and entrepreneurs to be well linked in an ergonomic environment, away from nuisance of huge, buzzy open spaces and without suffering the loneliness that is reflected from working at home (Kwiatkowski and Buczynski 2011). Coworking members pay for membership in order to work and achieve their objectives by being in the space. It is worth noting that, to date there is very limited research to actually determine the appropriate mix of physical and social environmental design that may create a better value for the coworking consumers whom are addressed as the members. Little is known about effectiveness of service environment factors and their influence the way members behave towards the coworking space either by being loyal to the space, spreading positive comments (word of mouth) about the space and inviting others to join the space (recommendation).

The distinct in characters of these coworking spaces with physical resources and social community is becoming a way to attract prospective small business entrepreneurs, professionals and creative designers to occupy a space in these coworking spaces (Spinuzzi 2012). Data from Deskmag Global Survey (2013b) outline the important value why people join in a space are to be part of community (94 %), followed by interaction with others, flexible work styles, serendipitous encounters and discoveries and opportunities. Linking it to the industrial relevance, we argue that effective design and management of service environment offered by coworking space providers will foster valuable experience and benefit for the members consequently influence their behavioural intentions towards the coworking space.

The proprietors of these coworking spaces are spending substantial amount of dollars in designing, renovating, refurbishing and building (Deskmag 2013a). In order to practically explain the social environment of the coworking spaces, the content analysis from websites of major coworking spaces across the region shows the use of certain vocabularies repetitively to explain the nature and benefit of becoming part of the coworking space. Those terms are such as 'collaborative', 'community', 'co-creation', 'creativity' and 'innovative'. However, little is known about what and why are these service environment factors promoted and their effect on the members. We would like to take these elements into consideration within the enriched framework.

By extending the servicescape framework and further enriching the social domain of the service environment we coined the 'Coworkingscape'. This term has similarity with the inspirational work of 'servicescape' by Bitner (1992) and social servicescape by Tombs and McColl-Kennedy (2003). Notwithstanding that, the 'Coworkingscape' is conceptualized as the design and management of physical and social elements in a coworking space environment where the members occupy, work, interact and experience in achieving their desired goals.

Conceptual Framework and Literature Review

Therefore, we put forth an enriched servicescape framework that illustrates two environmental dimensions of the coworkingscape. Figure 1 depicts the physical stimulus (Bitner 1992; Ryu and Jang 2008) and social stimulus (Berry et al. 2002;

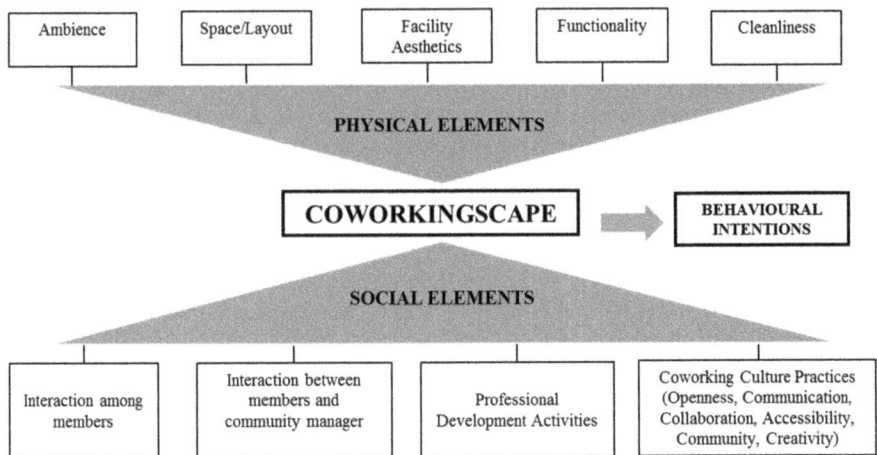

Fig. 1 'Coworkingscape' framework

Rosenbaum and Montoya 2007; Tombs and McColl-Kennedy 2003; Wall and Berry 2007; Fliegner et al. 2012).

To enrich further the social environment stimulus we enriched it by including some elements which is related specifically to the coworking spaces which has not been tested before. These elements are practical social element discussed in the book *Coworking: Building Community as a Space Catalyst* by Kwiatkowski and Buczynski (2011) which are assumed to effect the behaviour of the members. At this point, we are focused in highlighting these servicescape elements in order to develop the term 'coworkingscape'. The enrichment of the framework will need a further exploratory research in understanding relevance of these elements.

Physical Environment

Ambience

Ambient conditions mainly include temperature, lighting, music, aroma and air quality. Weise (2008) documented the effect of temperature in both meeting and event spaces. There are also extensive documentation in servicescape studies on the effect of music on customers' mood (Mattila and Wirtz 2001), purchase intentions (Areni and Kim 1993), as well as on service outcomes (Morin et al. 2007). Pleasant aroma is emphasized to generate heightened psychological arousal of consumer in a service setting (Lorig and Scwartz 1988) therefore encourage customers to spend more time in the servicescape (Morrin and Ratneshwar 2003). Research shows customer will feel more fascinated if venue managers could ensure a good ambience for guests including temperature, lighting, music, aroma and air quality (Yee et al. 2012; Ryu and Jang 2008). Relating past findings to the coworking space, we argue that it is important to create a desirable ambience for the coworking members who are spending extended amount of time in the space which could to facilitate their performance. Dube et al. (1994) and Soriano (2002) highlighted that atmosphere/ambience significantly influence the intention on return patronage. It can be assumed that the service atmosphere directly stimulates behaviour.

Facility Aesthetics

Aesthetic appeal of the facility architecture and decor are identified as the one of the primary determinant of perceived servicescape in service settings (Wakefield and Blodgett 1996). Often a first impression is formed about a service provider based on the appearance of the facilities. In the case of coworking spaces provider promoting their environment to be different, the servicescape should be constantly observed and evaluated in order to intensify the effect. Even when major decision on architectural design is important, yet other small changes in enhancing the aesthetic quality should not be compromised (Wakefield and Blodgett 1996). Simple efforts as repainting the facility, renewing the carpets, adding decorative fixtures such as pictures or other interesting props, or completely changing the interior decor may contribute in enhancing the attractiveness of the coworking space, which may influence the time spent by members in the service environment.

Space and Spatial Layout

Spatial layout reflects the way furnishing and equipment, service areas and passageway are arranged as well as spatial relationships among these elements (Bitner 1992). A well planned and designed layout of a space will provide convenient entry, exit and access to various kinds of facilities within an environment (Yee et al. 2012; Siu et al. 2012). Spinuzzi (2012) highlighted that coworkers across few coworking sites in Texas discussed specifically the importance of furniture and space design with varying criteria, facilitating comfort and relationship within the coworking site.

Functionality

It is of vital importance for the coworking space provider to create a functional physical environment, as members are observing and experiencing the environment's facilities intensively. Bitner (1992: 66) defined functionality as '...the ability of the same items to facilitate performance and the accomplishment of goals'. Quoting an interview response from the work of Spinuzzi (2012: 24) on the importance of design and space in coworking space '*if you are going to be sitting somewhere for three or four hours, the chair better be comfortable*'. Functionality is also identified as an important servicescape facet influencing customers' satisfaction and behavioural intention (Siu et al. 2012). Adequate ventilation, state-of-the-art audio-visual equipment, comfortable seating, adequate restrooms possibly contribute to the influence of functionality (Siu et al. 2012; Wu and Weber 2005). Good interior design in terms of furniture, plants and flowers and other kinds of decoration can heighten perceptions of functional quality in a service environment (Kim and Moon 2009).

Signs and Symbols

Signs and symbols are inclusive of explicit and implicit elements (Bitner 1992; Rosenbaum 2009). These elements are intended to communicate the environment and offerings. Signs and ambient conditions are important. Clear signage helps people find sections of interest without the need to wander around the whole floor. Suitable signs and symbols also assist customers to form their first impressions of the overall servicescape and represent a firm's aptitude to offer high-quality service (Bitner 1992). Signs and symbols could also communicate the non-verbally the service organization's value and culture to the consumers (Stumpf et al. 2013).

Cleanliness

It is crucial for service managers to ensure the cleanliness of a service venue. For example, in a coworking space the members usually spend several hours working and they will definitely expect high levels of cleanliness and comfort, as Wakefield and Blodgett (1996) and more recently Siu et al. (2012) argued the importance of cleanliness in a servicescape. Evidence shows that improving a service facility's ambient condition; functionality, signs symbols and cleanliness can enhance customers' perceptions, assessment of and behaviours within the service environment utilization experience (Siu et al. 2012).

Social Environment

Customer approach/avoidance decisions are influenced not only by physical stimuli but also by social, humanistic stimuli. 'Social servicescape' is a term introduced by Tombs and McColl-Kennedy (2003) and further conceptualized by Rosenbaum and Montoya (2007) as an environment comprising customer and employee elements that are encapsulated in a consumption setting. Tombs and McColl-Kennedy (2003) and Rosenbaum and Massiah (2011) pointed out the importance of customer to customer interactions, customer to employee interaction, displayed emotions of others and social densities as part of the social servicescape elements. Yet to date, the role of these social elements are mostly discussed conceptually (Tombs and McColl-Kennedy 2003). There are very limited research discusses the influence of social and spatial elements in service marketing literature (Tombs and McColl Kennedy 2010).

Groat and Stern (2002) argued 'The social architecture in a given setting is assumed to be more important than the physical architecture'. In the context of coworking, we argue that the design of social environment provides opportunity for members to engage themselves in establishing networking while the physical environment drives the dynamics of it. Fliegner et al. (2012), through BYO consulting team's research on 'Improving Coworking Experience' outlined few social indicators of the space that are adaptable for empirical testing. The social indicators *are interactions, professional development activities* and *collaborations.* As there were no prior academic empirical researches carried out on the social environment aspect of a coworking setting, the practical indicators from the research are essential to be adopted and explored. The indicators outline the social elements of the coworking-scape. Moreover, research in the commercial (Rosenbaum 2008) and not-for-profit (Glover and Parry 2009) domains reveals that patrons often patronize certain establishments because they can obtain social supportive resources from other customers. For example, in a coworking space the coworking members may gain comfort and relief by talking to other members.

We propose to include coworking culture as part of the social environment. Coworking culture is explained through shared value and vision, beliefs and attitudes towards social interaction and collaboration (Kwiatkowsly 2011). 'Coworking is a self-directed, collaborative and flexible work style that is based on mutual trust and the sharing of common core objectives and values between members' (Deskwanted 2012). The six values of coworking culture are *openness, accessibility, community, communication, collaboration* and *creativity* (Deskwanted 2012; Kwiatkowsly 2011). Sense of community that provides sense of belonging is seen as the central success factor of a coworking space (Kwiatkowsky 2011: 21). People benefit each other within the community and contribute back to the community, which creates a reciprocal effect (Kwiatkowsly 2011). The discussion above leads to the second proposition of this study.

Behavioural Intentions

Zeithaml et al. (1996) suggest that favourable behavioural intentions associate with a service provider's ability to get its customers to (1) say positive things about them, (2) recommend them to other consumers, (3) remain loyal to them (i.e., repurchase from them), (4) spend more with the company and (5) pay price premiums.

Behavioural intentions are defined as the disposition of customers to either repurchase a product/service from a providing organization by staying loyal, fostering a positive word of mouth and referrals thus extending their purchase or use of product or services (Baker et al. 2002; Hwa et al. 2011). Bitner (1992) emphasized that human behaviour is influenced by the physical design of the organization as well the social elements (Tombs and McColl-Kennedy 2003). Since the service environment consists of both the tangible and intangible elements (Namasivayam and Lin 2008), it is consumed simultaneously by the consumer. Both the physical and social element of the service environment is consumed and experienced by the consumer therefore they respond to these surrounding elements.

Numerous robust publications provided empirical evidence of the influence of servicescape elements on customer's loyalty intentions (Dijkstra et al. 2008; Foxall and Greenley 1999; Grayson and McNeill 2009; Kearney et al. 2013; Mattila and Wirtz 2001; Morin et al. 2007; Oakes and North 2008; Turley and Milliman 2000), but surprisingly little research has investigated the relative importance of multiple servicescape dimensions to bring forth the dynamics of physical and social environmental influence on behavioural intentions.

Conclusion, Limitation and Future Research

Through this chapter we have introduced the term 'Coworkingscape' to explain the service environment specific to coworking space service business. The physical elements suggested in the framework were adapted from previous researches. Nevertheless, the contribution lies in the enrichment of the framework by introducing some practical and social elements specific to coworking spaces notwithstanding those highlighted in previous research. Theoretically this chapter provides a conceptual framework to demonstrate how servicescape can be extended to coworking space based on industry specific stimuli. The enriched coworkingscape framework established will be further tested to show the influence on coworking member's behavioural intentions. At level of managerial contribution this framework will provide managers of coworking space with important constructs for consideration during the strategic design of the service environment. Service managers can understand how servicescape management affects the customer experience and the relationship between the various environmental cues. Therefore, strategic and systematic design of appealing and efficient service environment will enable service organizations realize their differentiation and competitive advantage (Yee et al. 2012).

This research contributes to a better conceptualization of the servicescape elements outlining the effect of both the physical and social elements that facilitates the behavioural intentions. It has the limitations inherent to a conceptualized framework which requires an in-depth qualitative study to explore the constructs of physical and social elements based on coworking context. The important goal for coworking space service management is to create and maintain a satisfying environment to influence members to stay for extended period of time, work and affiliate better while being in the space. We expect the same that the 'coworkingscape' to hold such relationship effect on behavioural intentions.

References

Baker, J., Parasuraman, A., Grewal, D., & Voss, G. B. (2002). The influence of multiple store environment cues on perceived merchandise value and patronage intentions. *Journal of Marketing, 66*(2), 120–141.

Bitner, M. J. (1992). Servicescapes: The impact of physical surroundings on customers and employees. *Journal of Marketing, 56*(April), 57–71.

Butcher, T. (2013). *Coworking: Locating community at work.* Paper presented at the Australia New Zealand Academy of Management 2013.

Deskmag. (2013a). *Coworking challenge: 16 ideas for the future of coworking spaces.* Retrieved January 20, 2014, from http://www.deskmag.com/en/design-architecture-furniture-coworking-challenge-17-ideas-for-the-future-of-coworking-spaces

Deskmag. (2013b). *The coworking forecast 2013.*

Deskwanted. (2012). *What is coworking?* Retrieved September 12, 2013, from https://www.deskwanted.com/about/what-is-coworking.html

Dijkstra, K., Pieterse, M., & Pruyn, A. (2008). Stress-reducing effects of indoor plants in the built healthcare environment: The mediating role of perceived attractiveness. *Preventive Medicine, 47*(3), 279–283.

Edvardsson, B., Enquist, B., & Johnston, R. (2005). Co-creating customer value through hyperreality in the prepurchase service experience. *Journal of Service Research, 8*(2), 149–161.

Fliegner, C., Baier, L., & Fidil, Y. (2012). *Improving the co-working experience.* New York: BYO Consulting.

Foxall, G. R., & Greenley, G. E. (1999). Consumers' emotional responses to service environments. *Journal of Business Research, 46*(2), 149–158.

Glover, T. D., & Parry, D. C. (2009). A third place in the everyday lives of people living with cancer: Functions of Gilda's Club of Greater Toronto. *Health and Place, 15*(1), 97–106.

Grayson, R. A., & McNeill, L. S. (2009). Using atmospheric elements in service retailing: Understanding the bar environment. *Journal of Services Marketing, 23*(7), 517–527.

Groat, L., & Stern, L. (2002). Cultivating organizational values: A new model for workplace planning. *Journal for Quality and Participation, 25*(4).

Guerin, B., & Innes, J. (2009). *Social facilitation.* Cambridge, England: Cambridge University Press.

Harris, L. C., & Ezeh, C. (2008). Servicescape and loyalty intentions: An empirical investigation. *European Journal of Marketing, 42*(3–4), 390–422.

Högström, C., Rosner, M., & Gustafsson, A. (2010). How to create attractive and unique customer experiences: An application of Kano's theory of attractive quality to recreational tourism. *Marketing Intelligence and Planning, 28*(4), 385–402.

Kearney, T., Coughlan, J., & Kennedy, A. (2013). An exploration of the effects of the servicescape on customer and employee responses in a grocery retail context. *Irish Journal of Management, 32*(2), 71–91.

Kim, W. G., & Moon, Y. J. (2009). Customers' cognitive, emotional, and actionable response to the servicescape: A test of the moderating effect of the restaurant type. *International Journal of Hospitality Management, 28*(1), 144–156.

Kotler, P. (1973). Atmospherics as a marketing tool. *Journal of Retailing, 49*(4), 48–64.

Lovelock, C. (2011). *Services marketing* (7th ed.). New Delhi, India: Pearson Education India.

Mari, N., & Pogessi, S. (2013). Servicescape cues and customer behavior: A systematic literature and research agenda. *The Service Industries Journal, 33*(2), 171–179.

Mattila, A. S., & Wirtz, J. (2001). Congruency of scent and music as a driver of in-store evaluations and behavior. *Journal of Retailing, 77*(2), 273.

Mehrabian, A., & Russell, J. A. (1974). *An approach to environmental psychology.* Cambridge, England: The MIT Press.

Miles, P., Miles, G., & Cannon, A. (2012). Linking servicescape to customer satisfaction: Exploring the role of competitive strategy. *International Journal of Operations and Production Management, 32*(7), 772–795.

Morin, S., Dubé, L., & Chebat, J.-C. (2007). The role of pleasant music in servicescapes: A test of the dual model of environmental perception. *Journal of Retailing, 83*(1), 115–130.

Moriset, B. (2014). Building new places of the creative economy. The rise of coworking spaces. In *2nd Geography of Innovation International Conference 2014,* Utrecht University, Utrecht (The Netherlands), January 23–25.

Oakes, S., & North, A. C. (2008). Reviewing congruity effects in the service environment musics-cape. *International Journal of Service Industry Management, 19*(1), 63–82.

Pareigis, J., Edvardsson, B., & Enquist, B. (2011). Exploring the role of the service environment in forming customer's service experience. *International Journal of Quality and Service Sciences, 3*(1), 110–124.

Prahalad, C. K., & Ramaswamy, V. (2004). Co-creation experiences: The next practice in value creation. *Journal of Interactive Marketing, 18*(3), 5–14.

Reimer, A., & Kuehn, R. (2005). The impact of servicescape on quality perception. *European Journal of Marketing, 39*(7/8), 785–808.

Rosenbaum, M. S. (2008). Return on community for consumers and service establishments. *Journal of Service Research, 11*(2), 179–196.

Rosenbaum, M. S., & Massiah, C. (2011). An expanded servicescape perspective. *Journal of Service Management, 22*(4), 471–490.

Ryu, K., & Han, H. (2011). New or repeat customers: How does physical environment influence their restaurant experience? *International Journal of Hospitality Management, 30*(3), 599–611.

Ryu, K., & Jang, S. (2008). DINESCAPE: A scale for customers' perception of dining environments. *Journal of Foodservice Business Research, 11*(1), 2–22.

Siu, N. Y.-M., Wan, P. Y. K., & Dong, P. (2012). The impact of the servicescape on the desire to stay in convention and exhibition centers: The case of Macao. *International Journal of Hospitality Management, 31*(1), 236–246.

Spinuzzi, C. (2012). Working alone together coworking as emergent collaborative activity. *Journal of Business and Technical Communication, 26*(4), 399–441.

Stumpf, D.-I. C., Opitz, C., & Gunkel, J. (2013). *The power of Ba in coworking spaces. The rise of coworking spaces.* Paper presented at the 2nd Geography of Innovation International Conference 2014, Utrecht (The Netherlands), January 23–25.

Tombs, A., & McColl-Kennedy, J. R. (2003). Social-Servicescape conceptual model. *Marketing Theory, 3*(4), 447–475.

Turley, L. W., & Milliman, R. E. (2000). Atmospheric effects on shopping behavior: A review of the experimental evidence. *Journal of Business Research, 49*(2), 193–211.

Wakefield, K. L., & Sloan, H. J. (1995). The effects of team loyalty and selected stadium factors on spectator attendance. *Journal of Sport Management, 9*(2).

Wu, A., & Weber, K. (2005). Convention centre facilities, attributes and services: The delegates' perspective. *Asia Pacific Journal of Tourism Research, 10*(4), 399–410.

Yogesh, P. P., & Satyanarayana, C. T. (2013). Assessing Healthscapes—A comparison among inpatients and outpatients. *Review Integrative Business and Economic Research, 2*(1), 521–527.

The Role of Online Reviews in Services Sector and Implications for Services Firms

Nitin Sanghavi, Claudio De Mattos, Mary McGuffog, Jain Kumar, and Laura Salciuviene

Abstract Today, consumers share their positive and negative experiences about products and services using social media sites and online platforms provided by companies. Electronic word-of-mouth (e-WOM) usually spreads through social networking sites (e.g., *Facebook*), and it affects how consumers make their decisions on what to buy or recommend within their network (Simonson and Rosen 2014). In particular, online reviews have been noted as providing useful information (Yin and Zhang 2014) not only for other customers but also for companies searching for new ways to attract their customers to visit their websites. This chapter aims to investigate the role of online reviews in social media in the services sector and offers implications for services firms.

Two independent studies in a large emerging market of India were conducted to achieve the aim of this research. The first study consisted of two phases: in phase I, advantages and disadvantages of online reviews along with judgement criteria about online reviews were identified using data from a focus group with nine participants. In phase II, various factors that consumers consider before making their final decisions to book a hotel were identified through an online survey with 110 responses. The second study also utilized an online survey to collect the data from 223 respondents about the use of social media sites and online interviews on various travel aspects when planning and booking travel.

The results of the first study suggest the increasing role of online reviews in India, in particular among young adults. The main advantages sought from online reviews were to search for up-to-date information and comparisons of previous customer experiences. Negative reviews did contribute to discouraging potential travelers using those sites to book their trips. The results of the second study indicate that females use social media more often than males when traveling (e.g., they might look for "things to do" while at their destination). Our study

N. Sanghavi (✉) • C. De Mattos • M. McGuffog • J. Kumar
Manchester Business School, Manchester, UK
e-mail: nitin.sanghavi@mbs.ac.uk; claudio.de-mattos@mbs.ac.uk; mary.mcguffog@postgrad.mbs.ac.uk; sonujain.jitendrakumar@postgrad.mbs.ac.uk

L. Salciuviene
Lancaster University Management School, Lancaster, UK
e-mail: l.salciuviene@lancaster.ac.uk

© Academy of Marketing Science 2016

849

L. Petruzzellis, R.S. Winer (eds.), *Rediscovering the Essentiality of Marketing*, Developments in Marketing Science: Proceedings of the Academy of Marketing Science, DOI 10.1007/978-3-319-29877-1_163

offers managerial guidelines for services companies. For instance, companies should tailor their websites to fulfill the needs of specific customer segments (e.g., female travelers). Future studies might investigate how companies can strategically respond to negative reviews and minimize their impact on consumer decision-making.

References available upon request.

Interactive Effects of Service Attributes on Customer Satisfaction

Yan Li (Eliane), Matthew Tingchi Liu, and James L. Brock

Introduction

It is widely acknowledged that service quality is profoundly affected by the service providers with the frontline employees playing a critical role in providing customer satisfaction (e.g., Bacon 2012; Dagger et al. 2013). Achieving customer satisfaction through superior service is a strategy that service providers such as retail banks strive to pursue (Frey et al. 2013). Prior literature showed that the intangible nature of services is critical determinants in creating customer satisfaction (Dagger et al. 2013). More recently, Keh et al. (2013) concluded that the simultaneous and interactive effects of different employee attributes collectively drive customer satisfaction. However, what is lacking in the literature is the relative importance of different attributes and interaction effects among them in different physical and cultural service settings (Dagger et al. 2013). This study builds on this stream of research to investigate the relative and interactive effects of three employee attributes, namely friendliness, helpfulness, and respectfulness on customer satisfaction with the employee in the Chinese banking industry.

Y. Li (✉) • M.T. Liu
University of Macau, Taipa, Macau
e-mail: yb47003@umac.mo; MatthewL@umac.mo

J.L. Brock
Pacific Lutheran University, Tacoma, WA, USA
e-mail: brockjl@plu.edu

© Academy of Marketing Science 2016
L. Petruzzellis, R.S. Winer (eds.), *Rediscovering the Essentiality of Marketing*,
Developments in Marketing Science: Proceedings of the Academy of Marketing
Science, DOI 10.1007/978-3-319-29877-1_164

Hypotheses Development

Friendliness is one of the most common exemplifications of positive display emotion in the service industry. *Employee friendliness* refers to the warmth and personal approachability (rather than physical approachability) of the contact staff, including a cheerful attitude and making the customer feel welcome. A friendly service employee can result in positive customer reactions (Hennig-Thurau et al. 2006). *Employee helpfulness* refers to the extent to which frontline staff either provide help to the customer or give the impression of being interested in the customer, and show a willingness to serve (Anderson et al. 2008). It reflects the motivational aspect of employee behavior and is linked to his/her intrinsic motivation (Thomas et al. 1981). Frontline employees' helpfulness or willingness to spend extra time and effort helping the customer are positively influences customer satisfaction (Brady and Cronin 2001).

Employee respectfulness refers to the politeness, respect, and propriety shown by frontline staff towards customers and is a dimension most often mentioned as an important criterion for evaluating personal services (Brown and Swartz 1989). Research shows that courtesy/politeness is considered as one of the critical success factors in service industries influencing customer satisfaction (e.g., Kaura 2013). While in Chinese culture, courtesy or politeness means *Keqi* or *Limao* which is derived from the old Chinese character *Li* (禮).The core concept of courtesy in Chinese culture is to show respect towards others through polite behavior. Showing respect is considered as the propriety of good manner. The importance of respect or social regard has been extensively researched in various contexts. The genuine respect and interest shown to the customer by the service provider make customers feel valued (Danaher et al. 2008).

Though employee friendliness, helpfulness and respectfulness are all positively related to customer satisfaction, the effect of these attributes are not treated equally in the Chinese culture. When it comes to the friendliness and helpfulness, one is considered as noncore service delivery while the other is core service delivery. Friendliness only serves as "icing on the cake." It may enhance the customer satisfaction but not fundamental to the functional consequence (i.e., outcome) which was the most concern of customer expectation (Pieter et al. 1998). The warmth and approachability generated by friendliness will help build rapport between employee and customer but not as efficient as helpfulness which will be directly linked to the outcome. As such it can be hypothesized that:

H1a: Employee helpfulness will have a stronger effect on customer satisfaction than employee friendliness.

However, considering the increasing importance of respect in business world, respectfulness will exert the strongest effect compared with friendliness and helpfulness. Some researchers equate respect or lack of respect for customers with service-quality evaluations (Bitran and Hoech 1990). In the Chinese culture, *Jing* (Respect) relates to the perc*eived worth* of the person and it draws parallels with words like honor and esteem. Being polite to others or showing respect is still considered as a basic norm of Chinese conduct in social interaction and is closely related to many indigenous Chinese terms such as keeping "*Mianzi*" (face) and "*Keqi*" (being humble and respect others). Failing to treat others with respect is sinful from the Chinese view in that the lack of respect may be interpreted as threatening (Chan 2006). Thus we have:

H1b: Employee respectfulness has a stronger effect on customer satisfaction than either employee helpfulness or friendliness.

In reality, employee demonstrates these attributes simultaneously or demonstrates more than one attribute at the same time. Therefore, investigating the interaction effects of three attributes would be more meaningful. Employees' friendliness enhances the service experience, but is not fundamental to the core service outcome (Keh et al. 2013). As such, customer satisfaction is not dependent on positive emotion through friendliness, but rather, the level of the service personnel's expertise and their competency to deliver an outcome. However, if respectfulness is present, such interaction effect is more salient in the low respectfulness condition rather than high respectfulness condition. Because in the high respectfulness condition, customer will have higher expectation of service quality from the employee and the predominant effect of respectfulness will make the interaction effect not salient. Conversely, customer will have lower expectation from the employee demonstrating low respectfulness. Consequently, the interaction effect of friendliness and helpfulness will be more prominent in the low respectfulness condition compared with high condition.

With regard to the interaction between helpfulness and respectfulness, recall that showing respect to others is instrumental to achieving *Li* (politeness) in Chinese Society, customers are expected to be treated as "superior" through the frontline employees' respectful behavior. Showing respect not only indicates the customers' importance, but is also a moral expectation in Chinese culture. Employee respectfulness demonstrated through polite behaviors is something beyond the core service (Butcher et al. 2003). Therefore, the effect of helpfulness will be stronger when respectfulness is high rather than low since customer will be easy to catch the interpersonal clue in their interaction with the employee.

Meanwhile, we have indicated that friendliness influences customer emotion through the primitive emotional contagion effect and further influence the service evaluation, thus we would expect that the effect of friendliness would also influence the interaction effect between helpfulness and respectfulness. As Lin et al. (2001) pointed out that for credence-based services, such as medical treatments and bank industry, interaction quality, or relational quality has a significant impact on perception of service quality. Hence, employee friendliness will impact the interaction effect of helpfulness and respectfulness in a positive way. Thus, based on above rationales, we have:

H2a: Employee friendliness exerts a stronger effect on customer satisfaction when employee helpfulness is high rather than low.

H2b: Employee helpfulness exerts a stronger effect on customer satisfaction when employee respectfulness is high rather than low.

H2c: The interaction effect of H2a would be salient when respectfulness is low rather than high while the interaction effect of H2b would be salient when friendliness is high rather than low.

Methodology and Results

Experimental Design

The experiment was 2 (friendliness: high/low) × 2 (helpfulness: high/low) × 2 (respectfulness: high/low) between-subjects factorial design. Totally, eight scenarios were developed. For each scenario, the participant took the role of a customer in the bank applying for a credit card. The employee displayed emotions were manipulated by four aspects of behaviors as proposed by Sutton and Rafaeli (1988): greetings, thanks, smiling, and establishing eye contact. The employee's helpfulness is manipulated by the willingness to help and capability to help. Employee respectfulness is manipulated by four elements: (1) being taken seriously and politely; (2) face saving behavior; (3) being involved in the decision through being *Keqi* (courteous), such as asking for the customer's opinion on options; and (4) not wasting the customer's time.

Sample and Experimental Procedure

The experiment was conducted in a large company in Beijing, China. All the employees are active customers of at least one of the four major banks in China. 200 Participants (50.5% female) were recruited as experimental samples on a voluntary basis. The sample was generally young (88% age ranging from 21 to 40), highly educated working professionals (96.5% with bachelor's degree or above). The data were collected during the 1-h lunch break of working days in January and February, 2014.

Manipulation Check

Analysis of variance (ANOVA) results showed that participants rated the high friendly employees ($n = 101$, $M = 5.99$, SD = 1.12) significantly higher than the low friendly employees ($n = 99$, $M = 2.31$, SD = 1.54), $F(1, 198) = 370.13$, $p < .001$). They were able to distinguish the high helpfulness condition ($n = 100$, $M = 5.35$, SD = 1.47) and low helpfulness condition ($n = 100$, $M = 3.09$, SD = 1.58), $F(1, 240) = 109.68$, $p < .001$). Similarly, participants found highly significant differences between the high respectful employees ($n=123$, $M=5.30$, SD$=1.36$) and low respectful employees ($n=119$, $M=2.60$, SD$=1.16$, $F(1, 240)=227.43$, $p<.001$). There were no other interaction effects (all $p>.05$).

Relative Effects

The analysis of importance (ANIMP) methodology, proposed by Soofi et al. (2000), was conducted to test the relative importance of the three attributes on customer satisfaction with the employee. All three attributes contributed a net mean response of 4.51 on customer satisfaction across all different conditions and a joint contribution of 4.32 to customer satisfaction within each ordering. The overall share of each attribute in its joint contribution by averaging the partial importance over all six possible orderings. The ratio of the overall importance of respectfulness to friendliness was 3.13 (2.53/0.81), the ratio of helpfulness to friendliness was 1.45 (1.17/0.81), and the ratio of respectfulness to helpfulness was 2.15 (2.53/1.17), thus supporting H1a–H1b.

Interactive Effects

The main effect of each attribute on customer satisfaction is significant while the interaction effect between each other is different. The interaction effect of employee friendliness and helpfulness is surprisingly not significant ($F=1.18$, $p>.05$). As expected, the interaction of employee helpfulness and respectfulness *is significant* ($F=2.18$, $p<.05$), so does the interactive of respectfulness and friendliness ($F=2.65$, $p<.001$). Thus, H2a is not supported while H2b is supported. The means of customer satisfaction were further analyzed. As predicted, the customer satisfaction generated by friendliness is higher when the helpfulness is high rather than low. But we notice that even though the interaction effect of helpfulness and friendliness is not significant overall ($F=1.18$, $p>.05$), when considering the respectfulness, such interactive effect is more salient ($F=3.34$, $p<.05$) in low respectfulness condition rather than in high condition ($F=.49$, $p>.05$). Likewise, customer satisfaction generated by helpfulness is higher when the employee respectfulness is high rather than low. The interaction effect between helpfulness and respectfulness is significant ($F=7.18$, $p<.05$) in high friendliness condition than in low condition ($F=.00$, $p>.05$). Hence, H2c is fully supported.

Conclusion

This study revealed that employee friendliness, helpfulness, and respectfulness were all positively related to customer satisfaction, while what is new is that their relative strength of the effect on customer satisfaction as well as interaction effects are different. The importance of respectfulness demonstrated by the service provider implies that communication of respectfulness may override the effects of employees' friendliness and helpfulness. The relative strength of three attributes confirms and extends many previous studies (e.g., Butcher et al. 2003; Goodwin and Smith 1990; Hocutt et al. 2006). The predominant effect of respectfulness has a stronger influence on service encounter satisfaction than on either perceived core service quality. It is also found that the interaction effect of helpfulness and respectfulness is significantly higher when friendliness is high than when it is low. This indicates that service firms should thus prioritize employee training to serve the customers with politeness to enhance customer satisfaction, along with employees' competence and positive emotional display such as friendliness. Though the relative effects and interactive effects of employee attributes on customer satisfaction are supported, additional research is recommended to verify the findings in different fields. Future studies should expand the service categories to validate the generalization of this model.

References

Anderson, S., Pearo, L. K., & Widener, S. K. (2008). Drivers of service satisfaction: Linking customer satisfaction to the service concept and customer characteristics. *Journal of Service Research, 10*(4), 365–381.

Bacon, D. R. (2012). Understanding priorities for service attribute improvement. *Journal of Service Research, 15*(2), 199–214.

Bitran, G. R., & Hoech, J. (1990). The humanization of service: Respect at the moment of truth. *Sloan Management Review, 31*(2), 89–96.

Brady, M. K., & Cronin, J. J. (2001). Some new thoughts on conceptualizing perceived service quality: A hierarchical approach. *Journal of Marketing, 65*(3), 34–49.

Brown, S., & Swartz, T. (1989). A gap analysis of professional service quality. *Journal of Marketing, 53*(2), 92–98.

Butcher, K., Sparks, B., & O'Callaghan, F. (2003). Beyond core service. *Psychology and Marketing, 20*(3), 187–208.

Chan, S. Y. (2006). The Confucian notion of Jing 敬 (respect). *Philosophy East and West, 56*(2), 229–252.

Dagger, T. S., Danaher, P. J., Sweeney, J. C., & McColl-Kennedy, J. R. (2013). Selective halo effect arising from improving the interpersonal skills of frontline employees. *Journal of Service Research, 16*(4), 488–502.

Danaher, P. J., Conroy, D. M., & McColl-Kennedy, J. R. (2008). Who wants a relationship anyway?: Conditions when consumers expect a relationship with their service provider. *Journal of Service Research, 11*(1), 43–62.

Frey, R., Bayon, T., & Totzek, D. (2013). How customer satisfaction affects employee satisfaction and retention in a professional services context. *Journal of Service Research, 16*(4), 503–517.

Goodwin, C., & Smith, K. (1990). Courtesy and friendliness: Conflicting goals for the service provider? *Journal of Services Marketing, 4*(1), 5–20.

Hennig-Thurau, T., Groth, M., Paul, M., & Gremler, D. D. (2006). Are all smiles created equal? How emotional contagion and emotional labor affect service relationships. *Journal of Marketing, 70*(3), 58–73.

Hocutt, M. A., Bowers, M. R., & Donavan, D. T. (2006). The art of service recovery: Fact or fiction? *Journal of Services Marketing, 20*(3), 199–207.

Kaura, V. (2013). Antecedents of customer satisfaction: A study of Indian public and private sector banks. *International Journal of Bank Marketing, 31*(3), 167–186.

Keh, H. T., Ren, R., Hill, S. R., & Li, X. (2013). The beautiful, the cheerful, and the helpful: The effects of service employee attributes on customer satisfaction. *Psychology and Marketing, 30*(3), 211–226.

Soofi, E. S., Retzer, J. J., & Yasai-Ardekani, M. (2000). A framework for measuring the importance of variables with applications to management research and decision models. *Decision Sciences, 31*(3), 595–625.

Sutton, R. I., & Rafaeli, A. (1988). Untangling the relationship between displayed emotions and organizational sales: The case of convenience stores. *Academy of Management Journal, 31*(3), 461–487.

Thomas, G. C., Batson, C. D., & Coke, J. S. (1981). Do good Samaritans discourage helpfulness? Self-perceived altruism after exposure to highly helpful others. *Journal of Personality and Social Psychology, 40*(1), 194–200.

Participation Behaviour Among International Students: The Role of Satisfaction with Service Augmentation and Brand Choice Attainment

Tamer H. Elsharnouby

Abstract Interest in understanding and managing the student experience has been growing in order to develop and offer high-quality, satisfaction-creating service experiences (Bowden and D'Alessandro 2011; Fagerstrøm and Ghinea 2013). This interest appears to be driven by a range of changes in the higher education sector. Students are becoming more demanding and active information seekers and prefer informal and personal forms of information to formal information (Fagerstrøm and Ghinea 2013). With technology-literate and highly diverse students, universities are increasingly facing pressure to manage students' expectations and offer a high-quality learning experience. This pressure is coupled with the introduction of higher tuition fees and constraints on public funding in some countries, such as the UK.

These changes reinforce the perspective in which students are viewed not only as customers who seek personalized services and high-quality outcomes, but also as active players in shaping the university experience. Therefore, the challenge remains for universities to determine how to respond to these changes and engage students as active co-producers of the university experience (Bowden and D'Alessandro 2011). In view of this orientation, this study examines the role of students' satisfaction with university augmentation services (financial, maintenance, campus life, and health augmenters) in generating their overall satisfaction with the university and explores the influence of brand choice attainment and satisfaction on student participation behaviour.

Drawing on an empirical survey of 238 international students in UK universities, the model was tested using structural equation modeling. The findings reveal that not all service augmenters are equally important in creating satisfaction. Campus life and maintenance augmenters are found to be the crucial elements in generating satisfaction for current international students. The results also suggest that satisfied students are more likely to participate actively in co-producing the university services compared to dissatisfied students. The effect of brand choice attainment on participation behaviour is mediated by satisfaction. This implies that it is not sufficient for a university to be students' first choice of brand to get them to participate

T.H. Elsharnouby (✉)
Qatar University, Doha, Qatar

Cairo University, Cairo, Egypt
e-mail: sharnouby@qu.edu.qa

© Academy of Marketing Science 2016   859
L. Petruzzellis, R.S. Winer (eds.), *Rediscovering the Essentiality of Marketing*,
Developments in Marketing Science: Proceedings of the Academy of Marketing
Science, DOI 10.1007/978-3-319-29877-1_165

actively in co-producing the services. Whether they enrol in their preferred university or an alternate university, students should be satisfied to participate actively in co-producing non-academic services.

University administrations should prioritize their efforts to put more emphasis on some elements especially crucial for international students and could embellish or deplete the core of education services. There is also a pressing need for universities to segment their international students based on the brand choice and give more emphasis to those students not accepted by their preferred university. A superior university experience should be created, particularly for ensuring this type of students can overcome the disappointment of not enrolling in the preferred university.

References available upon request.

Do We Click at the First Sight? Exploring the Customer–Employee Instant Rapport in the First Service Encounter

Jiun-Sheng Chris Lin, Chih-Ying Chu, and Haw-Yi Liang

Introduction

Interactions between service employees and customers have long been suggested to have a tremendous impact on customer assessment of service delivery. Among a variety of constructs in the studies of employee–customer relationships, rapport is an important issue for service organizations. Researchers have found customer–employee rapport is influential in the creation of customer satisfaction and loyalty (Yim et al. 2008). Increased customer perception of rapport also positively influences customers' judgments about the service and commitment toward a service relationship (Gremler and Gwinner 2000, 2008). Customer–employee rapport could be achieved in the very first service interaction (Gremler and Gwinner 2000). In building a customer relationship, a service employee's interaction with a customer in the initial encounter is critically important in creating the customer's impression of the firm and thereby his/her desire to have future interactions with the firm (Bitner 1995).

While researchers have addressed the significant consequence of rapport in the service settings, seldom do we know the emergence of instant rapport between customers and service providers. Concerning the rapid assessment of rapport and the important outcome of the construct, this study attempts to develop and test a model that describes the building of instant rapport and customers' perception of rapport in the first service interaction. Dyadic survey data collected from 257 customer–employee pairs in various service industries was examined through structural equation modeling (SEM).

J.-S. C. Lin (✉) • C.-Y. Chu • H.-Y. Liang
National Taiwan University, Taipei City, Taiwan
e-mail: chrislin@ntu.edu.tw; d03724013@ntu.edu.tw; crystalhy.liang@gmail.com

© Academy of Marketing Science 2016
L. Petruzzellis, R.S. Winer (eds.), *Rediscovering the Essentiality of Marketing*,
Developments in Marketing Science: Proceedings of the Academy of Marketing
Science, DOI 10.1007/978-3-319-29877-1_166

Background

Tickle-Degnen and Rosenthal (1990) propose that individuals initiate the assessment of rapport in their very first interactions with one another. A "thin slice" perspective also suggests people could use limited information to make quick impressions about someone's behavior, deposition, and internal states. Such rapid-building impressions could be maintained over time owing to confirmation and belief perseverance biases (Fiske and Taylor 1991). Past research even found that participants made their judgments of rapport between two target interactants in merely 10 s; their judgments also attended a significant degree of agreement with target's self-assessments (Grahe and Bernieri 1999).

Based on the nature of initial rapport proposed by Tickle-Degnen and Rosenthal (1990) and literature on the connection between rapport and (non)verbal behaviors, we propose two important initial-rapport-building behaviors: employee affective delivery and connecting behaviors. These behaviors are found to directly influence the level of initial rapport, which leads to service outcome; the relationships are also partially mediated by customer emotions. The objective of this study is twofold. First, the authors attempt to contribute to the service literature by shedding more light on the understanding of employee–customer instant rapport. Second, we hope to help service marketers identify and verify useful service employees' behaviors that facilitate the development of rapport in the early stage of service interactions.

Methodology

Service employees and customers of 168 apparel retailers participated in this research, resulting in three data sources: (1) data on employee affective delivery behaviors collected by trained observers, (2) customer data collected in exit interviews, and (3) survey data from service employee. The procedures for data collection followed Pugh (2001), Rafaeli and Sutton (1990) and Tasi and Huang (2002). Twenty research assistants were recruited and trained as observers, collecting information on employee affective delivery behaviors as well as soliciting opinions from customers and employees. To reduce error variance caused by observer heterogeneity, a training session included practicing rating employee affective delivery behaviors. Additionally, all observers were required to practice rating skills at several service sites, familiarizing themselves with the data collection process.

A team of two field observers visited each store during regular business hours, randomly selecting customers and time frames based on a sampling schedule. Sample schedules were generated based on peak/off peak hours during weekdays and weekends. The observers first observed the interaction between a service employee and customer, rating affective delivery by the service provider throughout the entire interaction. The observers did not record the data until after leaving the store. Upon the customer exiting the store, one observer invited him or her to fill out a questionnaire concerning connecting behaviors, customer emotions, perceived customer–employee instant rapport and outcomes. Simultaneously, the remaining observer invited the specific service employee to rate the average transaction amount during the preceding service encounter. The total sample included 257 pairs of employees and customers.

Multi-item scales from previous research were employed to empirically test the hypotheses. A questionnaire was constructed and pretested four times to ensure that question meaning aligned with research intentions as well as to assess feasibility of the survey approach. Each construct was measured using a 7-point scale anchored from "strongly agree" (7) to 'strongly disagree" (1).

Results

We estimated a CFA model using LISREL XIII. The CFA resulted in GFI, CFI, NFI, IFI, and RMSEA values of 0.90, 0.99, 0.97, 0.99, and 0.039, respectively, indicating acceptable fit. Reliability of the construct indicators was high, indicating strong internal consistency. Examining construct validity, all factor loadings in the CFA for the total measurement model were significant (with all t-values at $p < 0.01$ level), demonstrating convergent validity. In addition, all cross-construct correlations were significantly less than 1.0, tested via the confidence interval for each pairwise correlation estimate (± 2 standard errors) not including the value of one, providing further evidence of discriminant validity. The above results demonstrated adequate construct validity and reliability for the measures employed.

The proposed structural model was estimated. The estimation produced the following statistics: $\chi^2 = 322.62$ ($p < .01$), $\chi^2/\text{df} = 1.60$, NFI $= .97$, NNFI $= .99$, CFI $= .99$, IFI $= .99$, GFI $= .90$, RMSEA $= .048$. The model's fit as indicated by these indexes was deemed satisfactory. The construct of employee affective delivery is statistically significantly related to customer–employee initial rapport ($\gamma 21 = .08$, $t = 2.03$, p-value $< .05$). Results employee's connecting behavior is positively related to customer–employee initial rapport ($\gamma 22 = .77$, $t = 11.13$, p-value $< .01$). Results also support a relationship between employee affective delivery and customer positive emotions ($\gamma 11 = .11$, $t = 1.97$, p-value $< .05$) as well as between employee's connecting behavior and customer positive emotions ($\gamma 12 = .55$, $t = 8.61$, p-value $< .01$). Customer positive emotions was also positively related to customer–employee initial rapport ($\beta 21 = 0.11$, $t = 2.07$, p-value $< .01$). Results also found that customer–employee initial rapport is positively related to customer satisfaction ($\beta 32 = .80$, $t = 14.10$, p-value $< .01$), positive word of mouth ($\beta 42 = .70$, $t = 12.31$, p-value $< .01$) and actual purchasing behavior ($\beta 52 = .22$, $t = 3.55$, p-value $< .01$).

Discussion

Although services marketing research discusses customer–employee relationships at great length, there is a lack of empirical investigations on how service providers establish rapport in the first service encounter. This study fills this important research gap, proposing and testing a model of how service providers build initial rapport with customers. Using structural equation modeling, we found that 257 pairs of employees and consumers in service settings exhibited strong correlations between two service employees' behaviors, employee affective delivery as well as connecting behaviors, and initial rapport. The current research showed that customer emotions also mediated the relationships between employees' behaviors and instant rapport.

Results of the current study entail several managerial implications for service firms. First, service firms should hence emphasize initial-rapport-building mechanisms, such as employee affective delivery and connecting behaviors, training, motivating, and rewarding employees to exert, develop, and strengthen interpersonal bonds in receiving unacquainted customers. Second, Managers of frontline service staff should identify and hire frontline employees who exhibit strong positive affective delivery. Service organizations might include friendly, cheerful, and extroverted personalities as a criterion in the employee selection process. In addition, service firms should provide appropriate training for employees to enhance their emotional displays, such as greeting, smiling, and eye contact. Third, Training should encourage employees to engage in connecting skills such as pleasant conversation, friendly interaction, giving advice, and using humor when interacting with customers. Finally, Firms can educate service employees to be aware of customer emotional states responses. Service firms can develop a portfolio of diagnostic cues that customers typically display in various situations, creating templates of customer facial expressions, such as different degrees of joy, surprise, excitement, anger, or sadness, to help employees determine a customer's emotional state.

References available upon request.

Satisfying Customers Through Satisfied Employees: Exploring the Emotional Mechanism Linking Employee Satisfaction and Customer Satisfaction

Jiun-Sheng Chris Lin, Haw-Yi Liang, and Chih-Ying Chu

Introduction

Creating superior customer satisfaction has been the primary objective for service firms. The importance of service employee satisfaction in enhancing customer satisfaction has been emphasized in past research, yet there is limited research exploring the mechanism linking them. As service employees are mainly responsible for service delivery, the interpersonal interaction between customers and service employees has been found to substantially affect customer perceptions of services and considered as the key to customer satisfaction (Brown and Lam 2008). Past research also indicated that employee satisfaction can enhance customer–employee interactions, which, in turn, increases customer satisfaction (Homburg et al. 2009). Thus, there has been particular academic call for exploring the mechanisms linking employee and customer satisfaction. Integrating emotional labor and emotional contagion theories, this study attempts to bridge this research gap by developing and testing a framework that includes the mediating emotional mechanism through which employee satisfaction affects customer satisfaction in service context.

A theoretical framework was developed to explore the employee–customer satisfaction linkage mediated by emotional labor and contagion. Dyadic survey data collected from 388 customer–employee pairs in fashion apparel industry was examined through structural equation modeling. Results demonstrated that employee's satisfaction affects the employees' emotional labor strategies (i.e., deep acting and surface acting). Emotional labor, in turn, influences the emotional contagion between the employs and customers (i.e., employee affective delivery and customer emotion), which affects customer satisfaction.

J.-S.C. Lin (✉) • H.-Y. Liang • C.-Y. Chu
National Taiwan University, Taipei City, Taiwan
e-mail: chrislin@ntu.edu.tw; crystalhy.liang@gmail.com; d03724013@ntu.edu.tw

© Academy of Marketing Science 2016
L. Petruzzellis, R.S. Winer (eds.), *Rediscovering the Essentiality of Marketing*,
Developments in Marketing Science: Proceedings of the Academy of Marketing
Science, DOI 10.1007/978-3-319-29877-1_167

Background

Extant studies suggested that firms can enjoy superior service performance when service employees convey positive emotions to enhance customer satisfaction (Brown and Lam 2008; Hennig-Thurau et al. 2006; Keh et al. 2013), indicating that emotion plays an important role in elevating customer satisfaction. Consequently, understanding such emotional mechanism linking employee and customer satisfaction will furnish effective guidance for service managers (Brown and Lam 2008).

In spite of the emphasis on customer satisfaction being critical to service effectiveness, little research has been done to investigate the emotional mechanisms through which employee satisfaction influences customer satisfaction (Brown and Lam 2008). Therefore, understanding such a mechanism linking employee and customer satisfaction relationship will furnish effective guidance for service managers (Brown and Lam 2008). Two major research streams that address the role of emotions in service encounters include emotional labor (Hochschild 1983) and emotional contagion (Hatfield et al. 1994). Emotional labor refers to service employees' display of expected emotions as a self-regulatory process (Groth et al. 2009), while emotional contagion is defined as the flow of emotions from one person to another, with the receiver catching the emotions that the sender displays (Hennig-Thurau et al. 2006). Research indicated that employee satisfaction will influence service employee's emotional labor (Groth et al. 2009). In turn, emotional labor can affect the emotional contagion between service employees and customers (Gosserand and Diefendorff 2005; Grandey 2003), which eventually influences customer satisfaction (Pugh 2001; Tsai and Huang 2002). In other words, the relationship between employee and customer satisfaction can be mediated by both emotional labor and contagion, yet such an emotional mechanism still remains to be explored. Therefore, current study aims to fill this research gap by developing and testing an empirical framework that examines the emotional mechanism through which satisfied employees satisfy customers.

Methodology

Service employees and customers of 388 apparel retailers participated in this research, resulting in three data sources: (1) survey data from service employees, (2) data on service interactions collected by trained observers, and (3) customer data collected from exit interviews. A random sample of fashion apparel retailers were selected for this study. Sample schedules were generated based on peak/off-peak time intervals (morning, afternoon, and evening) during weekdays and weekends. Twenty research assistants were recruited for this study and grouped into ten teams. Each team consisted of two research assistants acting as field observers, collecting information on employee displayed emotions and soliciting opinions from customers and employees (Tsai and Huang 2002). They first observed the interaction between a service employee and a customer, and rated the employee affective delivery by the service provider throughout the entire interaction. One observer then followed the customer outside the retail location asking for ratings of customer positive emotions and customer satisfaction. Another observer would ask the service provider to fill out a questionnaire concerning employee job satisfaction, employee deep acting, and employee surface acting. To empirically test the hypotheses, multi-item scales from previous studies were adopted for this study. A questionnaire was constructed and pretested in four rounds to ensure questions were understood as intended and to assess the feasibility of the survey approach. Each item related to the studied constructs was rated on a 7-point Likert scale, ranging from "strongly disagree" (1) to "strongly agree" (7).

Results

A 21-item confirmatory factor analysis (CFA), including employee's job satisfaction, employee surface acting, employee deep acting, employee affective delivery, customer positive emotions, and customer satisfaction, was employed as the primary data analysis tool. Results suggested a good fit overall ($\chi^2 = 330.13$, df $= 174$, RMSEA $= .048$, CFI $= .98$, GFI $= .92$, NFI $= .96$, NNFI $= .97$, IFI $= .98$). For internal consistency, we evaluated reliability by means of composite scale reliability (CR). For all measures, the CR is well above the cut-off value of .60, exhibiting satisfactory reliability. Furthermore, all factor loadings in the CFA for the total measurement model were significant (with all t values at $p < .01$ level), demonstrating convergent validity. Discriminant validity is exhibited when the unconstrained model fits significantly better than the constrained model. Pairwise chi-square difference tests indicated that in each case, the chi-square difference statistic is significant at the 0.01 level, providing evidence of discriminant validity. Next, all cross-construct correlations were significantly less than 1.0, tested via the confidence interval for each pairwise correlation estimate (±2 standard errors) not including the value of one, providing further evidence of discriminant validity.

After confirming the total measurement model, the structural model was estimated, producing the following statistics: $\chi^2 = 329.59$, $\chi^2/df = 1.83$, RMSEA $= .046$, CFI $= .98$, GFI $= .93$, NFI $= .95$, NNFI $= .97$, IFI $= .98$. Results indicated an acceptable level of fit between the hypothesized model and the data. Estimated structural coefficients were next examined to evaluate individual hypotheses. As predicted, there is a positive relationship between employee job satisfaction and employee deep acting ($\gamma 11 = .39$, $p < .01$). Employee job satisfaction is significantly negatively related to employee surface acting ($\gamma 21 = -.18$, $p < .05$). The construct of employee' deep acting is statistically significantly related to employee affective delivery ($\beta 31 = .23$, $p < .01$) and customer positive emotion ($\beta 41 = .16$, $p < .01$). Employee's surface acting has a significant, negative impact on employee affective delivery ($\beta 32 = -.15$, $p < .01$) and customer positive emotions H6 ($\beta 42 = -.11$, $p < .05$). Employee's affective delivery was positively related to customer positive emotion

($\beta 43 = .40$, $p < .01$) and customer satisfaction ($\beta 53 = .29$, $p < .01$). In addition, customer positive emotion has a positive relationship with customer satisfaction ($\beta 54 = .49$, $p < .01$).

Discussion

This study developed and empirically examined a conceptual model that explores the emotional mechanism in the employee–customer satisfaction linkage. Results demonstrated that employee's satisfaction affects the employees' emotional labor strategies (deep acting and surface acting). Emotional labor, in turn, influences the emotional contagion between the employs and customers (employee affective delivery and customer emotion), which affects customer satisfaction. It is empirically verified that there is such an important emotional mechanism linking employee and customer satisfaction, filling the research gap called by Brown and Lam (2008).

   Current results provide important practical implications for customer-service representatives and for service organizations. The results suggest employee satisfaction is the key to customer satisfaction through the mediation of emotional mechanisms. Specifically, customers often interpret a service employee's emotional display as part of service itself. Thus, managers should always take managerial actions that can potentially enhance employee satisfaction. For example, managerial policies and actions that clarify role expectations and provide material and psychological support for employees are of primary importance. In addition, empowering employees to do what is necessary to satisfy customers without fear of sanction also enhances employee satisfaction. Employee affective delivery has received increasing attention in an effort to satisfy customers (Groth et al. 2009). Present study illustrates that the affective delivery by service employees is an important driver of the relationships between service employees and customers. Our findings suggest that the received view in many service firms regarding the importance of positive affective delivery in service encounters appears to be valid (Groth et al. 2009). Employees are subject to variation in how happy they are, and the way in which they express emotions, and those who are relatively more positively charged are of course, the best candidates for a firm who seriously wishes to exploit the emotional display-satisfaction link (Söderlund and Rosengren 2008). Given the impact of the employee affective delivery on customer emotions and customer satisfaction, such element requires increased managerial emphasis on hiring talented and qualified frontline employees with lively, courteous, cheerful, and extroverted personalities, which should be included as a criterion within the employee selection process.

References available upon request.

Projecting the Outcomes of Consumer–Brand Value Congruence: The Mediating Role of Relationship Quality

Tamer H. Elsharnouby, Mohamed Elsharnouby, Chanaka Jayawardhena, and Alaa M. Elbedweihy

Abstract How does consumer–brand relationship quality (CBRQ) influence behaviors attributed to personal values? We answer this question by proposing a model that links customer voluntary performance and propensity to leave with CBRQ that stems from customer–brand value congruence. We collected data from an online survey of 371 consumers of restaurants and hospitals in Egypt. Irrespective of the service context, we find that, (1) value congruence is positively related to CBRQ, (2) there is a negative relationship between CBRQ and propensity to leave, and (3) a positive relationship with customer voluntary performance. However, the positive relationship between value congruence and customer voluntary performance was only observed in the hospital context. Furthermore, CBRQ partially mediates the effects of value congruence on customer voluntary performance and fully mediates the effects of value congruence on propensity to leave.

Our findings suggest that, by focusing on the notion that brands have similar values to those of consumers, brand managers could achieve some important and desired consequences, most notably consumers voluntary behaviors such as cooperation, participation, and loyalty. In addition, invest in building customers relationships pays

T.H. Elsharnouby (✉)
Qatar University, Doha, Qatar

Cairo University, Cairo, Egypt
e-mail: sharnouby@qu.edu.qa

M. Elsharnouby
Cairo University, Cairo, Egypt

University of Hull, East Riding of Yorkshire, UK
e-mail: m.h.elsharnouby@2011.hull.ac.uk

C. Jayawardhena
University of Hull, East Riding of Yorkshire, UK
e-mail: c.jayawardhena@hull.ac.uk

A.M. Elbedweihy
Cairo University, Cairo, Egypt
e-mail: a.m.elbedweihy@2011.hull.ac.uk

© Academy of Marketing Science 2016
L. Petruzzellis, R.S. Winer (eds.), *Rediscovering the Essentiality of Marketing*,
Developments in Marketing Science: Proceedings of the Academy of Marketing
Science, DOI 10.1007/978-3-319-29877-1_168

dividends as high quality customer–brand relationship acts as a deterrent to customers' willingness to leave.

By synthesizing the literature from relationship marketing and branding research streams, the current study represents a new endeavor to specify the direct association between value congruence and propensity to leave and customer voluntary performance and the indirect associations through CBRQ in the services context. This opens the door for future conceptual and empirical evaluations. Given that a considerable bulk of research on value congruence and CBRQ has been developed in Western contexts, our contribution is salient in that we test hypothesized associations in an emerging market. Overall, our study takes relationship marketing and branding literature one step further by identifying the role of value congruence might play in enhancing the relationship quality with the service brand as well as projecting the outcomes of both constructs in a new research setting.

"I'm Not Old Enough!" Why Older Single Women Are Not Engaging in Retirement Planning Services

Foula Kopanidis, Linda Robinson, and Michael Shaw

Introduction

Retirement is often perceived to be an important life stage or event that requires significant planning and preparation. Demographic shifts in the retirement population across the globe have driven the need for proactive planning and financial preparedness for retirement. As the composition of consumers in this traditionally aging, male-oriented product category alters, an increased understanding of female behavior towards consumption of retirement planning products and services is critical. With marital status as one of the most significant predictors (Glass Jnr and Kilpatrick 1998) of retirement wealth, planning for retirement income outside a married or partnered context is a determinant of wealth differences between single and married women (Butrica and Iams 2003). As a consequence, this research focuses on this cohort of single women who are at a significantly higher risk of a reduced standard of living post-retirement to illuminate the concepts under study. With the women of the baby boomer generation, born between 1945 and 1964, the largest cohort of women to reach retirement age in history (Lusardi and Mitchell 2007), they present a good unit of analysis to study the retirement preparedness by single women. Building on a very small body of research, this study provides exploratory insights into how older single women plan and prepare for retirement. Through examining the psychological drivers and barriers to accessing retirement planning services this study identifies factors critical to the development, delivery, and management of products within the financial services industry.

F. Kopanidis (✉) • L. Robinson • M. Shaw
RMIT University, Melbourne, VIC, Australia
e-mail: foula.kopanidis@rmit.edu.au; lindaj.robinson@rmit.edu.au; michael.shaw@rmit.edu.au

© Academy of Marketing Science 2016   871
L. Petruzzellis, R.S. Winer (eds.), *Rediscovering the Essentiality of Marketing*,
Developments in Marketing Science: Proceedings of the Academy of Marketing
Science, DOI 10.1007/978-3-319-29877-1_169

Background

Retirement planning is crucial to a happy retirement, with the preparation put into retirement and the satisfaction enjoyed in retirement significantly aligned (Lee 2003; Topa et al. 2009; Noone et al. 2010). While there has been substantial research into the post-retirement economic well-being of retirees (Sanders and Porterfield 2010), it has been noted that individuals also need to prepare psychologically for this change and the transition from employment to retirement (Lee 2003). During the planning of the financial component of retirement consumers often become disinterested and confused about retirement planning services and how to best manage the multitude of service offerings (Grace et al. 2010), especially when they are unwilling to acknowledge their impending retirement. Thus, engaging in psychological preparation for retirement can raise confidence, self-empowerment, and acceptance of this transition in their life, as well as better understand and engage financial planning services.

With the vast majority of research on retirement conducted within the married or partnered context, limited emphasis has been placed on examining planning and preparation of women and in particular single older women. Thus, it is imperative for the financial services industry to recognize and address the specific needs and psychological barriers faced by single older women in order to better develop and communicate service offerings targeted to this specific cohort.

Research Method

Data were collected through long in-home interviews with seven single women born between 1945 and 1964 and were living in both urban and rural regions of Australia. The sampling procedure was purposive (Strauss and Corbin 1998). Informants were aged between 49 and 67, with only one informant retired, two working part-time and the remaining four informants working full time. Depth interviews were selected as the data collection method as they allow the researcher to focus the discussion, yet provide space and time to allow the participants opinions and insights to emerge (Charmaz 2014). The interviews involved guided discussion designed to collect data on feelings towards and expectations of retirement as well as retirement planning. Grand tour questions and prompts were used such as "How do you feel about retirement in general"; "what are you looking forward to in retirement"; and "what are some of your concerns about retiring." Interviews averaged between 1 and 2 h were recorded electronically and professionally transcribed. The data collected in this study was analyzed using a Grounded Theory approach (Strauss and Corbin 1990). Through a process of open and axial coding, the analysis identified patterns in the women's preparedness towards retirement, and also revealed several underlying themes that give insight to their interaction, or lack thereof, with retirement planning services.

Results and Discussion

The analysis revealed two broad themes that reflect the retirement planning and preparation of older single women—living for the moment and lost in transition.

Living for the Moment

The concept of "living for the moment," which was explicitly expressed by a number of informants, reflected the use of delay tactics to rationalize the lack of engagement in retirement planning services. This was complemented by a treadmill approach to life, where the informants felt that they were living within a comfort zone created by self-imposed boundaries that would then prevent them from transitioning into the retirement phase of their life. The idea that informants were "living for the moment" as a delay tactic to retirement preparation was driven by their perceived cognitive age, the importance of social capital, and an anxiety about the impact of poor health on their lifestyle as they age.

Cognitive age is a measure of one's self-perceived age rather than their chronological age (Barak and Schiffman 1981) in our study reflects the four dimensions of the age a woman feels, the age she thinks she looks, the age she perceives herself to act, and the age she perceives to be reflective of her interests (Wilkes 1992). For example, "I still feel like I am in my 40s… Life's good" (Jen). The women in this study strongly identified themselves to be younger than they are, and this idea allowed them the belief that they will be able to continue working as long as they like, thus delay the concept of retirement indefinitely. This idea was reinforced by those around them, such as in the case of Jackie (aged 55):

> Late 40s or 50. Most people are surprised when I tell them how old I am. In the community groups a lot of people are retired and have been retired a long time. Most of them say to me "You are too young to retire."

Being able to continue to work, even in a limited or part-time capacity, appears to afford some women the opportunity to delay making decisions about retirement. Part-time work was seen as valuable and desirable for a number of reasons. It allows the woman to remain active, engaged, and "useful," while also providing income to supplement the pension or other income sources. Several were considering volunteering once they had fully retired to ensure they remain active and connected socially. Maintaining some level of work life was seen to effectively delay full retirement.

> Whether I go and do volunteer work or something else I would always be working … It keeps you connected working, it keeps you interested, it keeps you young, it keeps your mind active, all of those things. (Helen)

Working also allows decisions to be made about retirement and financial planning to be put off. Long-service leave provided some women with the opportunity to test the appeal and their ability to reduce their workload or cease working alto-gether. For example, Jackie saw long service leave as "a trial run" for retirement.

Living for the moment was also rationalized in terms of the potential to be restricted by illness that could incapacitate their ability to enjoy life once retired. This perceived correlation between retirement and ill health encouraged a prevailing view that they may as well live for the moment because they might suddenly get sick. Margaret expressed this as her greatest concern about retirement, "There is no point having all this wealth and you retire and you can't do anything." There was also the view that to fund their personal goals, such as travel, they would need to delay retirement in order to "work to travel while I am healthy enough" (Tara). These concerns were summated in the overall fear and anxiety for entering the "next phase" of their life which was exemplified by Jen:

> I feel this transition to retirement is one of the biggest things I have ever had to handle in my life. It is bigger than getting married, bigger than having babies. This is huge.

These significant life events that Jen refers to have had a negative impact on the finances and retirement preparedness of the women in our study. The women in our study are single, including those that are divorced, widowed, and never married, and they don't expect to be "rescued" by future relationships. While relationships are not regarded as a negative, it is discussed that past relationships have left then some-what poorer, financially speaking.

Many of the women interviewed still had adult children living with them and several still support or contribute to their adult children financially. Having children meant that many had, at least got some period of time, not worked, worked part-time or intermittently, thus limiting their assets and superannuation. Acknowledging this financial situation leading into retirement inheritance was identified as one method for financing retirement. Significantly while the probability of inheriting assets from their own aged parents was discussed, none of the informants spoke of leaving anything for their children.

Effectively, these women are snookered by family obligations, past and present, allowing them to create and maintain a comfort zone built around their identity as a mother and provider. Thus while they feel they are living for the moment, their for-ward towards retirement is boundary drove by their perceived and actual family obligations, as if to be stuck on a treadmill.

Lost in Transition

A lack of funds for retirement was commonly expressed as a barrier to accessing retirement planning services. There was a tendency towards the deliberate avoidance of seeking professional above which was rationalized in two ways: no immediate need for such advice ("No. I'm not old enough. See I'm in denial!"—Margaret) or the anticipation of being told they did not have enough funds for retirement ("All I wanted to know was do I have enough money to see me through to pension age?"—Jackie). This also raised the issue of trust with retirement and financial planning services. Informants did not feel that they would be able to understand the advice they are given or that thinking they would not like the advice they would shy away from it. To seek formal above would mean they would have to face the facts of their position. Engaging a service provider would mean they would have to form a plan for retirement, but by avoiding planning they do not have to acknowledge the situation. There is also the belief that financial advice received from seminars would be generic, not easily understood or tailored to their personal situation.

> I would go on websites and use those calculators for how much you need to fund retirement and I would think no, they are for people with partners and 2 cars and overseas trips. I could never relate to any of those, I just thought that my lifestyle doesn't fit with that they are saying there. (Jackie)

This was compounded by concern over not having someone close (a partner or husband) to "talk things through with" (Kerry). However, informal above and the first-hand experiences of friends and family was actively sought and considered valuable.

Conclusion

The journey towards retirement is a transitional path very much influenced by the expectations, desires, and circumstance of those involved. The older single women in this study perceived the process of retirement planning and preparation as an inevitable life stage; however, most women in the sample did not make methodical plans for retirement nor was this a priority to do so. Instead choosing to "live for the moment" within self-imposed boundaries, they inadvertently created barriers that potentially impacted on their financial readiness in retirement years.

The financial services sector has a critical role to play in the development, delivery, and communication of retirement planning services they offer to older single women. In order to do this, financial services should recognize the distinctive characteristics of this cohort of single older women and avoid a one-size-fits-all approach to retirement. This study highlighted insights into single older women's expectations of retirement relating to their perceived cognitive age, importance of social capital and anxieties surrounding the future, as well as the accessing and understanding the plethora of retirement planning services available. Thus, financial product and service offerings should be customized to reflect an understanding of what is important, and what is relevant, in order to facilitate a pathway for to reach the retirement goals they have constructed for themselves. This includes professional services and advice to assist in prompting their financial preparedness for retirement and overcoming barriers confronting single women as they age.

References available upon request.

Does Incivility Cost? Examining the Effects of Incivility in Service Settings

Mehmet Okan, A. Banu Elmadağ Baş, and Selime Sezgin

Abstract Uncivil behaviors, which include rude, humiliating, and disrespectful behaviors, generally create unmanageable and uncontrollable conditions in service settings. Incivility is one of the most experienced interpersonal misbehaviors in organizations (Cortina et al. 2001; Pearson and Porath 2005) but organizational studies have dealt with incivility as a latent intra-organizational problem, disregarding the effects on customers. However, incivility is a human conduct that can occur not only among employees but also among all social actors. By drawing on Appraisal Theory (Lazarus 1991), this chapter encompasses three experimental studies to understand the effects of uncivil interactions (among employees and among other customers) on customers' emotional appraisals of the service context and behavioral intentions. Incivility and its role in the appraisal process will be evaluated in Study 1 by comparing high incivility, low incivility, civil, and no messages conditions. We hypothesized that high incivility will result in higher degree of regret and disappointment than low incivility. Furthermore, all incivility conditions will result in higher degree of regret and disappointment than civil and control conditions. We also hypothesized that regret and disappointment mediates the effect of the level of incivility on customer's overall satisfaction from their service experience and generalized judgments from service provider. Moreover, the incivility source (employee vs. other customer) moderates the effect of incivility level on these emotions (moderated mediation). To have a profound understanding of the influence of incivility with further studies, service expectancy (Study 2—high vs. low value proposition) and the agency role (Study 3—customer is the decider for the service provider vs.

M. Okan (✉) • A.B.E. Baş
Istanbul Technical University, Istanbul, Turkey
e-mail: mokan@itu.edu.tr; elmadaga@itu.edu.tr

S. Sezgin
Bilgi University, Istanbul, Turkey
e-mail: selime.sezgin@bilgi.edu.tr

© Academy of Marketing Science 2016
L. Petruzzellis, R.S. Winer (eds.), *Rediscovering the Essentiality of Marketing*,
Developments in Marketing Science: Proceedings of the Academy of Marketing
Science, DOI 10.1007/978-3-319-29877-1_170

not) will be examined with between group scenario-based experiments. In these studies, we expect that appraisals of these factors influence customers' attitudes and intentions via the mediation of certain emotions (regret and disappointment). In study 3, by drawing on the literature on regret and disappointment (Zeelenberg et al. 1998, 2000) we also hypothesized that regret is significantly higher than disappointment only for incivility among employees condition when the customer is the decision-maker (self-agency). Appraisal theory indicates that emotional states of individuals vary by self-agency level, due to the perceived responsibility of what is experienced (Dijk and Zeelenberg 2002). In all of the studies customer's empathy tendencies (McBane 1995), proximity to emotional contagion (Doherty 1997) and tolerance to negativity levels will be measured and integrated to the model as covariates because in social contexts, personality traits that are prone to emotional contagion may introduce bias. After pretests for manipulation and credibility checks, scenario-based experiments will be conducted using online data collection methods (MTurk). MANOVA, Hayes and Preacher's (2014) moderation analyses, and bootstrapping methods for testing moderated serial mediation will be used for testing group differences.

References available upon request.

Knocking Opportunities: The Impact of Damage Values on Opportunistic Customer Claiming Behavior After Service Failure

Sören Köcher, Sarah Küsgen, and Hartmut H. Holzmüller

Abstract Many firms feel obliged to reply to customer complaints and even knowingly unjustified high claims after service failures with generous compensations in order to keep customer satisfaction on a maximum level. An expanding body of literature has focused on opportunistic customer behavior reflected in customers who intentionally engage in cheating or fraudulent actions to take monetary advantages after a company's service failure during service recovery (e.g., Wirtz and Kum 2004; Berry and Seiders 2008). However, the majority of this work is related to knowingly and incorrect reported failures which did not occur such that customers' cheating on firms is not necessarily triggered by dissatisfaction or service failures at all (Ro and Wong 2012). Although several factors driving opportunistic customer claiming behavior have been identified (see also Baker et al. 2012)—i.e., customer-centric (e.g., customer financial greed, customer personality traits, and customer oppositional cultural model; Reynolds and Harris 2005; Andreasen 1988; Ringberg et al. 2007), firm-centric (e.g., generous redress practices and firm size; Harris and Reynolds 2003; Wirtz and McColl-Kennedy 2010), and relationship-centric drivers (e.g., low justice perceptions and one-time transactions; Wirtz and McColl-Kennedy 2010)—the impact of damage values on opportunistic claims still remains unexplored. Thus, the purpose of this research is to improve our knowledge of the underlying mechanisms of customer claiming behavior triggered by the value of damage caused by service failures.

The results of three experiments detect a seemingly paradoxical behavior: The likelihood of engaging in opportunistic claiming declines with increasing damage values, whereas the magnitude of opportunistic claims rises. Further analysis reveals that these opposing effects can be ascribed to perceived risk of opportunistic claiming.

S. Köcher (✉) • H.H. Holzmüller
TU Dortmund University, Dortmund, Germany
e-mail: soeren.koecher@tu-dortmund.de; hartmut.holzmueller@tu-dortmund.de

S. Küsgen
RWTH Aachen University, Aachen, Germany
e-mail: kuesgen@time.rwth-aachen.de

© Academy of Marketing Science 2016
L. Petruzzellis, R.S. Winer (eds.), *Rediscovering the Essentiality of Marketing*,
Developments in Marketing Science: Proceedings of the Academy of Marketing
Science, DOI 10.1007/978-3-319-29877-1_171

This research provides important implications for a more efficient complaint management in business practices. For instance, firms could develop a classification scheme of damage values tailored to their specific businesses. For each respective type of failure value, strategies referring to different levels of generosity should be developed. For high value level situations, stricter checking routines for the assessment of claims have to be put in place. Thereby, companies should generate a sense of thinking in trade-offs between high-frequency complaints associated with relatively low amounts of fraud and, in contrast, opportunistic claims of high magnitudes which occur less frequently.

References available upon request.

Nostalgic Consumption: Does It Also Work for Services?

Tali Seger-Guttmann and Iris Vilnai-Yavetz

Introduction

Nostalgic cues can be identified in many areas of consumption (Cui 2015) such as nostalgic brands of toys and cars (Barnes 2008), as well as in advertising (Reisenwitz et al. 2004; Muehling and Sprott 2004). The decision to use nostalgic cues relies on the assumption that nostalgic symbols induce nostalgic memories, which in turn evoke positive (sometimes negative) emotions in consumers (Wildschut et al. 2006). These responses are expected to influence consumer behavior in the marketplace (Chebat and Michon 2003; Cui 2015). Most of the studies on nostalgia have been conducted in the context of marketing, and specifically product advertising (Muehling and Sprott 2004). The issue of whether and how nostalgic cues actually work in the context of services remains largely unknown. In this work, we present a set of five experiments aimed at studying differences between goods and services in terms of the impact of nostalgic cues on customers.

Background

Holbrook and Schindler (1991) defined nostalgia as: "a preference … toward objects (people, places, or things) that were more common … when one was younger…." (p. 330). Thus, individuals attempt to bring aspects of the past into their present lives

T. Seger-Guttmann (✉) • I. Vilnai-Yavetz
Ruppin Academic Center, Hamerkaz, Israel
e-mail: talis@ruppin.ac.il; yavetzir@ruppin.ac.il

© Academy of Marketing Science 2016   881
L. Petruzzellis, R.S. Winer (eds.), *Rediscovering the Essentiality of Marketing*,
Developments in Marketing Science: Proceedings of the Academy of Marketing
Science, DOI 10.1007/978-3-319-29877-1_172

by repeating past activities and focusing on things that ring a bell from their past (Sierra and McQuitty 2007). Consumers cannot return to the past, but they can try to preserve it through nostalgic consumption activities and that can renew their ties with their past (Sierra and McQuitty 2007). Meyers-Levy (2005) showed that the positive feelings that emerge from nostalgic cues are context dependent. In his brief review, Cochoy (2005) described a huge positive shift in customer importance and experience over the years. Services have significantly improved and customers' perceived service quality has become key factors in increasing satisfaction with service. This change may imply that memories of past services are less attractive to customers than memories of past goods. Previous works have used stimuli including music and scents to trigger nostalgic thoughts (Holak and Havlena 1992; Ehrlichman and Halpern 1988). The influence of physical artifacts is well known. Bitner's (1992) Servicescape model focused on how inanimate environmental factors influence customers and employees, and the interactions between them. In the current work, we used physical artifacts as nostalgic cues to trigger customer responses. Hence, the main purpose of this work was to examine whether the known impact of nostalgic cues in the promotion and sales of goods (e.g., Cui 2015) is also relevant and efficient in the service context.

Methodology

This project integrates five experimental studies designed to examine differences between service and goods contexts in the relationship between nostalgic cues and customers' perceptions and behavioral intentions.

All five studies used a between-subject design. In four of the studies, participants were shown photos which showed service providers wearing shirts with logos (Study II) or service providers sitting in their office with a picture on the wall (Studies III and IV) or a restaurant menu (Study V). The only difference between the photos was the presence or absence of a nostalgic cue. In the fifth study (Study I), a real product was presented in packing designed to explore the same research question. The independent variable (IDV)—the existence of a nostalgic cue—was manipulated as explained below. In Study I, the IDV was an actual product: a chocolate bar in a nostalgic/non-nostalgic wrapper. Study II tested the impact of the service provider by placing a nostalgic/non-nostalgic logo on the service provider's shirt. Study III manipulated a picture of a landscape on the wall of the service provider's office to be nostalgic vs. prestige or plain. Study IV used the same experimental design as in Study III but with a picture of a service interaction on the wall. Study V showed a picture of nostalgic/non-nostalgic restaurant menu. This was a service manipulated IDV with no product or service provider as a stimulus. The nostalgic cues were defined as *"nostalgic"* by at least 70 % of the pretest participants.

Study I: A Wrapped Chocolate Bar

Data were collected from 90 randomly sampled adults. The participants were roughly 51 % male and 49 % female, and ranged in age from 18 to 75, with a median in the age category of 36–45. IDV: Three types of packaging were tested nostalgic, plain, and prestige. DV: Purchase intentions, perceived product quality. Description: Research assistants in a mall, presented a bowl of individually wrapped mini-chocolates to mall visitors and asked them to choose one and taste it. One wrapped chocolate bar (designed in accordance with the experimental condition) was placed next to the bowl. After tasting, the visitors were asked to report how much they would like to purchase this bar if they found it in a grocery store and evaluate the quality of the product. Prediction: Purchase intentions and perceived product quality should be higher for the nostalgic and the prestige packaging than for the plain one (H1a and H1b, respectively).

Study II: Logo on the Service Provider's Shirt

Data were collected from 575 randomly sampled adults. The participants were roughly 42 % male and 58 % female, and ranged in age from 18 to 67, with a median in the age category of 26–35. IDV: A nostalgic/non-nostalgic logo on the service provider's shirt. DV: Intention to be served by the service provider. Moderators/mediators: Nostalgic prominence, dispositional affect style (PANAS), consumer involvement. Description: Participants were told they would be taking part in a study on customer expectations from services. Following brief instructions, participants viewed a randomly selected photo (which manipulated the independent variable). They were then invited by the research assistants to complete the study questionnaire, which included a set of structured questions designed to measure the dependent variables as well as demographic information. Prediction: Intention to be served by the service provider should be higher for the nostalgic condition (H2).

Study III: Picture of a Landscape on the Service Provider's Office Wall

Data were collected from 105 randomly sampled adults. The participants were roughly 45 % male and 55 % female, and ranged in age from 18 to 67, with a median in the age category of 36–45. IDV: The same photo was used but framed and designed in accordance with one of the conditions: Nostalgic/prestige/plain. DV: Intention to be served by the service provider, perceived service quality (five dimensions of SEVQUAL). Description: The same as in Study II. Prediction: Perceived service quality and intentions to be served should be higher in an office with a picture designed in a nostalgic manner (H3a and H3b, respectively).

Study IV: Picture of a Service Interaction on the Service Provider's Office Wall

Data were collected from 320 randomly sampled adults. The participants were roughly 49 % male and 51 % female, and ranged in age from 18 to 70, with a median in the age category of 36–45. IDV: The same as in Study III but with a picture of a service interaction. DV: Description, and prediction: same as in study III (H4a and H4b, respectively).

Study V: A Restaurant Menu

Data were collected from 100 randomly sampled adults. The participants were roughly 47 % male and 53 % female, and ranged in age from 18 to 68, with a median in the age category of 36–45. IDV: A restaurant menu designed in a nostalgic/non-nostalgic manner. DV: Type of dishes on the menu, expected atmosphere of the restaurant (appearance of waiters, food, and tables), expected service quality (five dimensions of SEVQUAL). Description: The same as in Study II. Prediction: For the nostalgic condition, the chosen type of dish and the preferred restaurant atmosphere should be more farm-style and less urban. Expected service quality should be higher when the menu is designed in a nostalgic manner (H5a, H5b, and H5c, respectively).

Results and Discussion

The impact of nostalgic cues on consumers' reactions to products, H1a, predicting that the chocolate purchase intentions would be higher in response to a nostalgic packaging as well as to prestige packaging than to a plain packaging in Study 1, was confirmed ($F(2,87) = 10.33$, $p < 0.001$). Post hoc tests revealed significant differences between the plain packaging and the other two types of packaging, but no differences were found between the nostalgic and prestige condition. H1b, predicting that the perceived quality of the chocolate would be higher in response to a nostalgic packaging as well as to prestige packaging than to a plain packaging, was also supported ($F(2,87) = 18.86$, $p < 0.001$). Post hoc tests revealed the same differences as for H1a.

However, the impact of nostalgic cues in the service context, H2 to H4b, predicting higher perceived service quality and purchase intentions for nostalgic cues were not supported ($p > 0.05$). No differences were found between the nostalgic and non-nostalgic conditions in any of the service-context experimental studies (II–IV).

Finally, Study V had mixed results. It was found that nostalgic menu increased the request of farm-style dishes (H5a; χ^2 (1100) = 33.75; $p < 0.001$) and increased expectations for a farm-style atmosphere. By contrast (but consistent with the results of Studies II–IV), H5c was not confirmed and no differences were found between the experimental conditions.

This set of studies aimed to explore whether nostalgic cues, found to be relevant in the consumptions of goods, would be also relevant in services. The findings indicate that nostalgic cues do not have an impact on customers in the service context; no differences were found between the nostalgic and non-nostalgic conditions in almost all the service-context studies (Studies II–IV). By contrast and in line with previous studies (Reisenwitz et al. 2004; Muehling and Sprott 2004), nostalgic cues attached to a product (chocolate bar package) affected customers' intentions to purchase, and their perception of product quality (Study I). There was also a significant impact of a nostalgic restaurant menu on increased request of farm-style dishes (product; H5a) and on increased expectations for a farm-style atmosphere in the restaurant (service; H5b) in Study V. However, the nostalgic menu design did not have a significant impact on perceived service quality (H5c).

Conclusions

We suggest that nostalgic cues may not have an effect in technically sophisticated services when customers expect quick and efficient responses to their requests by professional, expert service providers. The type of services that were tested in each experiment can partially account for the results reported here. In Studies II–IV, different levels of customer involvement and service situations were tested. High involvement included expertise services such as "seeing a physician at a hospital emergency room," "consulting an investment adviser for a serious investment," and "hiring a child minder to take care of an infant." Low involvement services included for instance "dealing with clerk at city hall" or "getting a service from a carpenter (firewood)." Although different customer involvement levels and different services were examined, nostalgic cues did not have the expected effect in all of these experiments. What may explain these results is a different conceptualization; rather than high and low involvement, the difference may have resided in high and low technical skills (using up-to-date technology and equipment). Thus, when the services presented are physician, carpenter, city hall clerk, etc. nostalgic cues (representing emotional longing and idealization of the past) have no effect on the customer. It is reasonable to assume that customers in these situations expect efficient and professional responses. By contrast when the participants were presented with a nostalgic menu in a restaurant (service) setting, the nostalgic cues were relevant and had an effect on customers' preference for a farm-style atmosphere in the restaurant, since in this type of setting (i.e., leisure) the emotional component of nostalgia is triggered and the service require low technical skills.

Implications for Theory and Practice

Using nostalgic cues for emotion-oriented goods (Claeys et al. 1995) that have no technical components (i.e., problem solution), when time and progress have no relevance, seem to have a high impact on customers' perceptions of quality and intention to purchase (chocolate in Study I and preferring farm-style atmosphere in a restaurant (Study V; H5a and H5b)).

It should be mentioned that advertisements use nostalgic cues also for rational-oriented (Claeys et al. 1995) highly technical products, such as cars, but the car's cutting-edge technological devices are presented separately from the outer nostalgic elements. In this way, the customer is prompted to enjoy the emotion evoking nostalgic look ("retro" design) but at the same time can trust the prestige technology as well. Future research should investigate the role of nostalgia in services that require high technical sophisticated skills and expertise compared to services that do not (i.e., hospitality). Further studies could also generalize to the purchasing of products.

References available upon request.

Does CSR Mean Performance for Consumers? An Implicit Study in the Field of Banking

Charlotte Lécuyer, Sonia Capelli, and William Sabadie

Introduction

In real situations, ethical buying intention does not correlate with ethical buying behaviour (Madar et al. 2013). This is because when consumers have to make their purchasing choices, even if they are informed from the ethical cues of the products, they do not automatically give it priority. Buying a socially responsible product or service often implies arbitration between a socially responsible cue and a utilitarian cue. In this communication, we propose to investigate the compatibility between solidarity and performance in consumer's perceptions of brands.

Corporate social responsibility (CSR) represents the deliberate engagement of the company to allocate resources to social or ethical actions beyond the financial and shareholders obligations (Brown and Dacin 1997). Numerous researches have already studied the association between perceived CSR and traditional financial performance (Margolis and Walsh 2003; Brown and Dacin 1997; Ehrich and Irwin 2005; Luo and Battacharya 2006; Sen and Bhattacharya 2001). In line with Friedman (1970), many theories have pointed to the fact that social activities are costly to the firm, so one would expect a negative relationship between CSR and financial performance at the individual firm level (Pava and Krausz 1996; Waddock and Graves 1997; Gond et al. 2009). According to Friedman, the aim of business should only be to increase profits and there are no "values", no social responsibilities, other than the shared values and responsibilities of individuals formed voluntarily in society. Consequently, actors can no longer be considered as external to the CSR-Performance

C. Lécuyer (✉) • S. Capelli • W. Sabadie
University of Lyon 3, Lyon, France
e-mail: charlotte.lecuyer@univ-lyon3.fr; sonia.capelli@univ-lyon3.fr; william.sabadie@univ-lyon3.fr

© Academy of Marketing Science 2016   887
L. Petruzzellis, R.S. Winer (eds.), *Rediscovering the Essentiality of Marketing*,
Developments in Marketing Science: Proceedings of the Academy of Marketing
Science, DOI 10.1007/978-3-319-29877-1_173

debate, but should be integrated as an endogenous variable. It offers the opportunity to reframe theoretically the classical and over-studied debate around "the CSR-Performance link" by studying the point of view of an external stakeholder: the consumer. From this point of view, performance is related to perceived quality and value and can be defined as consumer's judgments or overall assessments about a product or service's overall utility or superiority (Zeithaml 1988).

Contrary to what Friedman pointed to in the 1970s, companies are today encouraged to spend significant resources on CSR actions to increase their profits (Brown and Dacin 1997). Existing studies have investigated consumers reactions to corporate ethics and CSR (Berens et al. 2005; Mohr and Webb 2005; Sen and Bhattacharya 2001), such as attitudes or purchase intents. However, most of the studies considering consumers' perceptions of CSR suffer from a social desirability bias (Randall and Fernandes 1991). We propose in this communication to go further than this limitation by assessing implicit attitudes.

To investigate this question of solidarity versus performance perception, the banking sector has been selected. Indeed, two kinds of governance are represented in this market: commercial and cooperative banking. Cooperative banking is by essence socially responsible and involved in all the fields of CSR whereas commercial banking grounded its profitability on the delivery of very competitive products and services. Democratically controlled firms, such as cooperatives, may be more efficient—from the internal shareholder point of view—than the traditional corporate form of organization (Bowles and Gintis 1987). The research question then is to know if cooperative organizations may be more effective—from the external shareholder point of view—in the market place in conciliating performance and social responsibility, in harmony with their values of durability, democracy and solidarity. Our study aims at understanding the consumers' implicit attitudes toward banking brands, in particular in testing if consumers oppose CSR and performance when considering those brands, depending on their kind of governance.

Methodology

The main objective of this study was to examine if performance and solidarity are compatible in the mind of consumers. Therefore, two different kinds of governances were compared (cooperative and capitalistic) to understand the influence of the cooperative status on perceived solidarity and performance. Indeed, cooperative value is a derived version of corporate value and has been examined under various headings such as ethics and social responsibility (Carroll 1999) or citizenship (Bolino 1999).

The banking sector has been selected because it allows consideration of a variety of perceived CSR and performance levels with very famous brands adapted for an implicit measurement protocol. Moreover, cooperative and capitalistic banks coexist in the marketplace. Since the 1980s, the pressure of competition has increased the temptation to win business and has progressively decreased the distinction which previously exists between commercial banks and cooperative banks (Harvey 1995). That is why we propose to consider whether there is still a difference between those banks in terms of perceived CSR and performance.

We conducted two experiments with implicit measures because they assess beliefs and attitudes by measuring the underlying automatic activation of the cognitive process (Aidman and Carroll 2003). The first experiment aims at positioning cooperative and commercial banks in terms of perceived solidarity—term selected for labelling "CSR" in consumer words— and the second study in terms of perceived performance—term selected for labelling "costumer value" in consumer words. Experiment 1 and 2 implemented the implicit association test— IAT(Greenwald et al. 1998) to assess implicit attitudes toward two pairs of target attitude concepts. Subjects in Experiment 1 responded to two target-concept discriminations: (a) solidarity names (represented by logos of cooperative banks) versus (b) non-solidarity names (represented by logos of commercial banks). Subjects in experiment 2 responded to two target-concept discriminations: (a) performance names (represented by logos of commercial banks) versus (b) non-performance names (represented by logos of cooperative banks). The target concepts were selected via a pre-test conducted on 69 students. Each target-concept discrimination was used in combination with discrimination of good meaning words (e.g. wonderful, seducing, best, magnificent, excellent) and from bad meaning words (e.g. terrible, worst, horrible, unpleasant, disagreeable).

One hundred and twenty six students (81 females, $M_{age} = 22$) in experiment 1 and one hundred and six students (65 females, $M_{age} = 23$) in experiment 2 from a West European university took part in the study in exchange for the participation in a random draw to win an electronic gift. The standard IAT consisted in five phases. Positive and negative words (wonderful, seducing, best, terrible, ugly, worst, horrible) had to be categorized on the basis of their valence, between *Good* and *Bad* attributes. After the IAT computer tasks, subjects filled in a short questionnaire. Respondents were asked to classify each bank logo presented in the IAT between "cooperative" and "commercial".

Results and Discussion

Consistent with data reduction procedures described by Greenwald et al. (1998), data from participants for each trial block were analysed. We conserve latencies between 300 and 3000 ms which suggest automatic responses only. Consequently, 5185 lines were conserved for experiment 1 and 4406 for experiment 2.

Relationship between perceived performance and perceived CSR. First of all, we analysed the number of occurrences concerning the respondent's implicit associations either for *solidarity* versus *non-solidarity* choices, and for *performant* versus *non-performant* choices. Firstly, we analyse the percentage of occurrences for the concept of performance and solidarity. When exposed them to bank logos, respondents associate 58.3 % of banks with the notion of performance (and 41.6 % with non-performance, $p = .05$). Then, respondents associate 55.2% of banks with the notion of solidarity, compared to 44.8% which associated them with the notion of non-solidarity. These results suggest that, in terms of occurrences, banks are perceived to be performant but also to be socially responsible. Secondly, when we analyse the mean time (latencies in milliseconds) of experiment 1, we find significant differences between the notion of solidarity versus non-solidarity considering banks. It appears that banks are much more quickly associated with the notion of solidarity than with the notion of non-solidarity ($M_{solidarity} = 1046$ ms and $M_{non\text{-}solidarity} = 1125$ ms, $F(3,683) = 5183$; $p < .05$). Then, when we analyse the mean time of experiment 2, we find significant differences between the notion of performance versus non-performance considering banks. It appears that banks are much more quickly associated with the notion of performance than with the notion of non-performance ($M_{performance} = 993$ ms and $M_{non\text{-}performance} = 1022$ ms, $F(0,125) = 4404$; $p < .077$). These results illustrate that, even in terms of latency, banks are associated both with the notion of performance and with the notion of solidarity.

Results according to the kind of governance. On the one hand, when exposed to bank logos, respondents classified 71.1% of cooperative banks as being associated with solidarity, whereas only 39.5% commercial banks are associated with the solidarity notion ($p < .05$). These results suggest that, when we compared the percentage of occurrences, cooperative banks are more associated with the notion of solidarity than commercial banks.

On the other hand, our results suggest that cooperative banks are perceived as commercial banks in terms of performance. Indeed, when exposed to stimuli, respondents classified 54.6% of cooperative banks as being associated with performance, whereas the percentage for commercial banks is 55.5% ($p = .2$). Banks are not well positioned in terms of perceived performance according to the fact that half of respondents consider banks perform poorly. Unlike the conclusions derived about perceived solidarity, our findings failed to support a significant difference in terms of performance according to the kind of governance.

Finally, when we analyse the mean time (latencies in milliseconds) of experiment 1, we find no significant differences between cooperative and commercial banks in terms of solidarity. However; we find significant differences between cooperative and commercial banks in experiment 2. It appears that commercial banks are associated significantly faster with performance than cooperative banks ($M_{cooperative} = 1024$ ms and $M_{commercial} = 971$ ms, $F(2,177) = 5.325$; $p < .01$). These results illustrate that, whereas in terms of percentage associated to performance cooperative and commercial banks are close, automatic associations significantly differ between these two kinds of banks. Indeed, it appears that consumers implicitly associated much more quickly commercial banks with the notion of performance compared to cooperative banks. These findings provide supports that significant differences exist in terms of perceived solidarity and perceived performance between cooperative banks and commercial banks.

To summarize, this study illustrates the fact that banks are associated with the notions of performance and of solidarity. Indeed, from the consumer's point of view, banks which are perceived to be socially responsible are also perceived to be less efficient in the commercial area. However, the two experiments support the notion that cooperative governance manages to conciliate these two notions of solidarity and performance more effectively. More research is underway to study different types of arguments used by banks for grounding those perceptions in consumer' minds, either in terms of CSR and solidarity or in terms of quality of services and prices. At the same time, this work is open to develop causal relationships between performance and CSR.

References

Aidman, E. V., & Carroll, S. M. (2003). Implicit individual differences: Relationships between implicit self-esteem, gender identity, and gender attitudes. *European Journal of Personality, 17*, 19–37.

Bolino, M. C. (1999). Citizenship and impression management: Good soldiers or good actors? *Academy of Management Review, 24*, 82–98.

Bowles, S., & Gintis, H. (1987). Contested exchange: Political economy and modern economic theory. *The American Economic Review, 78*, 145–150.

Brown, J., & Dacin, P. (1997). The company and the product: Corporate associations and consumer product responses. *Journal of Marketing, 61*, 68–84.

Carroll, A. B. (1999). Corporate social responsibility: Evolution of a definitional construct. *Business and Society, 38*, 268–295.

Ehrich, K. R., & Irwin, J. R. (2005). Wilful ignorance in the request for product attributes information. *Journal of Marketing Research, 42*, 266–277.

Friedman, M. (1970). *The social responsibility of business is to increase its profits.* New York: The New York Times Company.

Gond, J. P., Palazzo, G., & Basu, K. (2009). Reconsidering instrumental corporate social responsibility through the Mafia metaphor. *Business Ethics Quarterly, 19*, 57–85.

Greenwald, A. G., McGhee, D. E., & Schwartz, J. L. (1998). Measuring individual differences in implicit cognition: The implicit association test. *Journal of Personality and Social Psychology, 74*, 14–64.

Luo, X., & Battacharya, C. B. (2006). Corporate social responsibility, customer satisfaction, and market value. *Journal of Marketing, 70*, 1–18.

Margolis, J. D., & Walsh, J. P. (2003). Misery loves companies: Rethinking social initiatives by business. *Administrative Science Quarterly, 48*, 268–305.

Mohr, L. A., & Webb, D. J. (2005). The effects of corporate social responsibility and price on consumer responses. *The Journal of Consumer Affairs, 39*, 121–147.

Pava, M. L., & Krausz, J. (1996). The association between corporate social-responsibility and financial performance: The paradox of social cost. *Journal of Business Ethics, 15*, 321–357.

Randall, D. M., & Fernandes, M. F. (1991). The social desirability response bias in ethics research. *Journal of Business Ethics, 10*, 805–817.

Sen, S., & Bhattacharya, C. B. (2001). Does doing good always lead to doing better? Consumer reactions to corporate social responsibility. *Journal of Marketing Research, 38*, 225–243.

Waddock, S. A., & Graves, S. B. (1997). The corporate social performance—Financial performance link. *Strategic Management Journal, 18*, 303–319.

Zeithaml, V. A. (1988). Consumer perceptions of price, quality and value: A means-end model and synthesis of evidence. *Journal of Marketing, 52*, 2–22.

Examining Customer Referral Reward Programs: Does Reward Fairness Matter?

David Dose and Gianfranco Walsh

Abstract Customer referral reward programs (CRPs) are an important and widespread marketing tool in various service industries. However, the effectiveness of CRPs is contingent on the success of the recommender–receiver interaction. This research focuses on reward schemes, that is, systems that involve payments from service providers to customers that help the provider acquire new customers. Specifically, the authors investigate situations in which the referral reward is split between recommender and referral receiver, whereby both parties negotiate how much of the referral reward each party receives. In studying referral-reward allocations the present research investigates an important issue regarding the effectiveness of CRPs in general and the recommender–receiver interaction in particular. Building on equity aversion models, the authors show that rewarding only the recommender brings about perceptions of unfairness on part of the referral receiver, resulting in disruptive behavior and inefficient referral processes. The results expand the existing theoretical assumption that CRPs are continuously controlled by firms and indicate that due to biases in fairness perceptions the interaction between recommender and referral receiver remains unpredictable and difficult to control for referring firms. However, results also reveal that tie strength cushions the effect of biased fairness perceptions on successful referral processes.

D. Dose (✉) • G. Walsh
University of Jena, Jena, Germany
e-mail: david.dose@uni-jena.de; walsh@uni-jena.de

© Academy of Marketing Science 2016   893
L. Petruzzellis, R.S. Winer (eds.), *Rediscovering the Essentiality of Marketing*,
Developments in Marketing Science: Proceedings of the Academy of Marketing
Science, DOI 10.1007/978-3-319-29877-1_174

An Empirical Examination of Antecedent and Consequence of Service-Intensive Quality Evaluation Within Bridal Retail Setting

Sasikarn Chatvijit Cook and Kittichai Watchravesringkan

Abstract Given the difficulties in assessing and delivering acceptable service due to the varying degree of consumer service expectations, scholars have introduced the zone-of-tolerance (ZOT) concept to represent the range of expectation (desired-to-adequate) as an acceptable level of service quality (Zeithaml et al. 1993). The major objective of this research was to propose and empirically examine a theoretical model of BRIDAL-ZOT. Specifically, a number of antecedents of service expectations were expected to influence ZOT, which in turn, affected perceived service quality, satisfaction, and word of mouth (WOM). ZOT is the range of service performance a customer would consider satisfactory because it is bounded by the customer's desired and adequate expectations of service quality (Zeithaml et al. 1993). According to Zeithaml et al. (1993), changes in the adequate expectations of service level may have caused ZOT to be either wider or narrower, given the relative stability of desired service level. That is, the customers with a wider ZOT tend to tolerate acceptable levels of service as compared to the customers with a narrower ZOT because they are likely to pay more attention to detect any errors that might occur in service performance. The 38-item scale measuring the antecedents of expectation levels based on Zeithaml et al.'s (1993) model of consumer expectations was pretested with 30 soon-to-be brides. Data were collected from 192 soon-to-be brides who had been to, at least, one bridal shopping retailer within the past 6 months. A series of multiple regressions, a paired-sample t-test, and a structural equation modeling technique were employed to test the hypothesized relationships. All measures, adopted from previous research, displayed acceptable reliability (≥ 0.70). Results revealed that customers' past bridal shopping experience positively influenced both desired and adequate service expectations ($\beta = .28^{**}$ and $\beta = .32^{**}$, respectively), whereas the explicit service promises given by bridal retailer only positively influenced desired service expectation ($\beta = .19^{*}$). As expected, desired service quality expectation was significantly higher than adequate service quality expectation (t-value $= 2.95^{**}$). Results also revealed that the BRIDAL-ZOT model explains that the differences between desired and adequate service expectations (ZOT) negatively influenced customers' overall perceived service quality

S.C. Cook (✉) • K. Watchravesringkan
University of North Carolina at Greensboro, Greensboro, NC, USA
e-mail: s_chatvi@uncg.edu; k_watchr@uncg.edu

© Academy of Marketing Science 2016
L. Petruzzellis, R.S. Winer (eds.), *Rediscovering the Essentiality of Marketing*,
Developments in Marketing Science: Proceedings of the Academy of Marketing
Science, DOI 10.1007/978-3-319-29877-1_175

($\gamma=-0.25^{**}$, t-value$=-2.88$), which in turn, positively influenced satisfaction ($\beta=0.81^{***}$, t-value$=13.30$). The results also were also in line with previous studies in that perceived service quality positively influenced satisfaction, which in turn, influenced word of mouth (Anderson 1998). Based on our findings, it is suggested that bridal retailers must provide positive shopping experiences to these customers because such experiences can create the carryover effects on the different levels of service expectations (desired versus adequate) when visiting a store in the future. As such, the soon-to-be brides can become demanding customers as their ZOT are narrower due to a high involvement nature of bridal products and their prior experiences. To gain a competitive advantage, the bridal stores should provide a superior service quality as this level of service will satisfy most customers and create positive marketing outcomes for a future business (e.g., positive WOM). A future study needs to replicate this BRIDAL-ZOT model with other retail industries (e.g., personalized services).

References available upon request.

Prosumption and Value-in-Use: The Complementary Role of Transaction Cost in S-D Logic

J. Joseph Cronin, Duane M. Nagel, and Brian L. Bourdeau

Introduction

The recent economic downturn is causing consumers to examine their personal budgets with a critical eye as they endeavor to become more efficient in their spending. One means of increasing the efficiency of expenditures is for consumers to participate in the creation of the products they consume. Popularly depicted as do-it-yourself, academics are using the term prosumption to describe this trend. Its popularity is evident in the highly rated HGTV and DIY (do-it-yourself) networks and shows such as Income Property, Renovation Realities, and I Hate My Kitchen. The movement to prosumption is not insignificant as the global do-it-yourself market is expected to reach $716.2 billion by 2015 (Global Industry Analysts 2012). Because SDL suggests that all value is co-created, research that investigates the effect of prosumption on value creation. Specifically, firms are relying on consumers to "do-it-themselves" rather than to co-create.

Background

Prosumption is not a new idea as it was first defined by Tofler (1980) more than three decades ago as the production of goods or services by an individual for one's own consumption rather than purchasing a finished product from a supplier. Unfortunately,

J.J. Cronin (✉) • D.M. Nagel
Florida State University, Tallahassee, FL, USA
e-mail: jcronin@fsu.edu; dmn11c@my.fsu.edu

B.L. Bourdeau
Auburn University, Auburn, AL, USA
e-mail: bourdl@auburn.edu

© Academy of Marketing Science 2016
L. Petruzzellis, R.S. Winer (eds.), *Rediscovering the Essentiality of Marketing*, Developments in Marketing Science: Proceedings of the Academy of Marketing Science, DOI 10.1007/978-3-319-29877-1_176

research examining why consumers decide to engage in prosumption is limited. Prosumption differs from more commonly studied processes such as co-production and co-creation in that during prosumption the firm is not involved in any phase of the production or consumption process. Currently, within the marketing literature, little is known as to why people choose to prosume. However, the recent focus on Service Dominant Logic (SDL) (Vargo and Lusch 2004, 2008) is spurring research interest in the creation of value by consumers through their co-creation activities (Edvardsson et al. 2011; Grönroos and Ravald 2011; Grönroos and Vioma 2013; Vargo and Lusch 2004, 2008). One notable research effort suggests a further expansion of SDL into the area of prosumption where higher levels of customer involvement are required.

Specifically, Xie et al. (2008) examine prosumption within the context of SDL (Vargo and Lusch 2004, 2008) and define prosumption as "value creation activities undertaken by the consumer that results in the production of products they eventually consume and that become their consumption experience" (p. 110). This definition of prosumption is based on a core principle of SDL, which is that all value is co-created and can only be determined by use (Vargo and Lusch 2004, 2008). The current research argues SDL is limiting given its suggestion that all value is created in-use. By focusing on value-in-use, the SDL lacks the ability to provide insights into how the decision to prosume is made *prior* to usage of the product. By focusing on value-in-use, SDL lacks the ability to provide insights into how the decision to prosume is made *prior* to usage of the product. For example, if value is only determined during the use of a good or service, as proposed by SDL, how does a consumer evaluate the sacrifice (i.e., money, time, effort, and other resources appropriate to an exchange, see Zeithaml 1988) required to obtain or self-produce a product?

The current study argues that value-in-use alone is not a sufficient basis on which to evaluate and predict an individual's make-or-buy decision. That is, the incongruity of restricting the conceptualization of the prosumption/consumption, or make or buy, decision to value-in-use is fundamentally obvious. It lies in the fact that one cannot "use" a product before making or buying it. As a result, we argue that very little is currently known as to how and why consumers actually make the decision to make or buy, prosume or consume. This represents a significant theoretical gap in the marketing literature (Wolf and McQuitty 2013).

The current research turns to the organizational literature, specifically to transaction cost analysis (TCA) to assist in explaining the theory on which the research is based. Originally proposed by Coase (1937), expanded upon by Williamson (1975), and brought into a marketing context by Anderson (1985), TCA is considered by many to be the primary basis for theory development in the make-or-buy area of research. The importance of transaction cost analysis theory is underscored by the fact that TCA research has resulted in two Nobel Prizes in Economics (i.e., Coase 1991; Williamson 2009). Williamson also suggests that the contribution of TCA lies not as a standalone theory, but as a means to enrich complementary theory. It is this vane that TCA theory is used in the current research.

The use of TCA in the context of consumer decision-making is supported within the literature as previous studies apply transaction cost in the analysis of consumers'

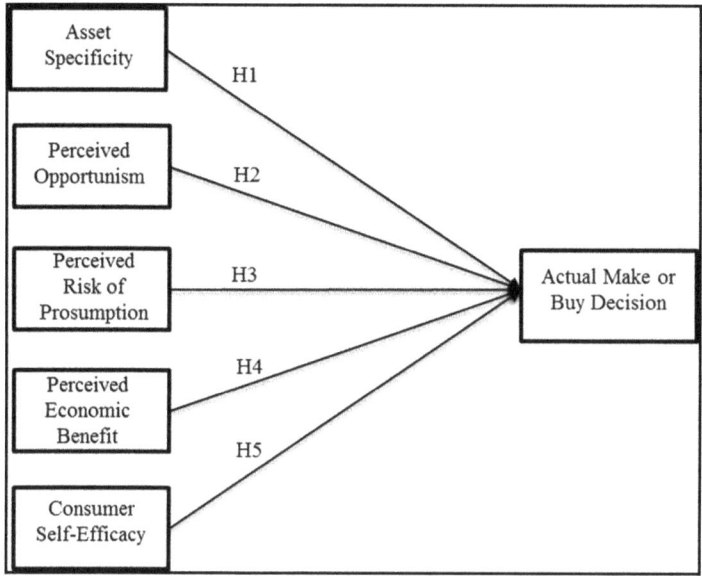

Fig. 1 Prosumption decision model

store choice (Bell et al. 1998; Chintagunta et al. 2012). The current research extends the use of TCA, specifically as a means to assess consumer decision-making in the context of consumption versus prosumption, or the make-or-buy decision. The conceptual model presented in Fig. 1 identifies five decision drivers consumers consider when deciding whether to engage in prosumption or a market transaction. The identification of these drivers is accomplished through a review of the relevant literature and insights gathered from an exploratory study. The drivers identified include asset specificity, perceived opportunism, perceived risk of prosumption, perceived economic benefit, and consumer self-efficacy.

Using Fig. 1 as a foundation, the current research has three primary objectives. First, with an exploratory case study is used to identify the five decision drivers noted in the last sentence. Second, the current research answers the call of previous research (Wolf and McQuitty 2013) for a theoretical explanation as to why individuals choose to engage in prosumption (i.e., the "make" decision). Finally, we empirically test the conceptual model and identify implications for both theory and practice. By accomplishing these objectives, the current research addresses the gap in the literature relative to what consumer decision factors drive prosumption and answers the call of previous research for a theoretical explanation of consumer prosumption decisions (Wolf and McQuitty 2013). Additionally, the study contributes to practitioners by providing managers a better understanding of how customers make the decision whether to purchase an organization's product offerings or self-produce. The managerial implications for this research are unique in that two distinct and competing relationships are identified and discussed. Specifically, we identify those factors for organizations that encourage individuals to prosume.

Research Method

Because of the lack of prior research related to why a consumer decides to self-produce a product, an exploratory study designed to identify what drives such a decision was undertaken as an initial step in the research process. Specifically, to gain insight as to what consumers evaluate when facing a make-or-buy decision, an open-ended questionnaire was employed (Eisenhardt and Graebner 2007). The open-ended questionnaire consisted of nine questions to identify decision drivers evaluated by respondents when facing an actual make-or-buy opportunity. Students in an online MBA class offered by a major US university were used to gather the qualitative data. In addition to filling out the questionnaire, respondents were asked to recruit an additional volunteer not within their household. Thirty-one responses were generated and used to generate the following hypotheses.

H1: The level of asset specificity associated with prosumption has a direct effect on an individual's decision to make of buy.
H2: The level of perceived opportunism associated with a supplier has a direct effect on an individual's decision to prosume.
H3: The perceived risk of prosumption has a negative effect on an individual's decision to engage in prosumption.
H4: The level of perceived economic benefit expected by a consumer directly affects the decision to make or buy.
H5: The level of customer self-efficacy directly and positively affects the decision to engage in prosumption.

To test the research model, a total of 396 nonstudent participants were recruited using Amazon.com's Mechanical Turk online panel. Thirteen responses were excluded for abandoned surveys or failed quality checks. All respondents were from the USA. The respondents were randomly assigned to one of two scenarios (landscaping or installing tile) that represented the make-or-buy decisions. After reading the supplied passage, respondents completed a series of questions that indicated the extent to which each construct of interest applied to their personal circumstance along with built in quality checks and potential control variable. The measures used are available upon request. A confirmatory factor analysis utilizing STATA 13 confirmed the reliability and validity of the research measures.

A main effects binary logistic regression model (Hosmer et al. 2013) was fitted to the full data set ($N=383$). The results are summarized in Table 1. We also included gender, household income, project type (landscaping or installing tile), and if the respondents self-identified as a do-it-yourselfer, as control variables. Of the 383 respondents, 172 (45 %) chose to engage in a market transaction and hire someone to do the job, while 211 (55 %) opted to engage in prosumption and do the job themselves. The results of the regression analysis indicated that four of the five predictor variables exhibited a significant effect on consumers' prosumption decisions. Specifically, the results suggest that asset specificity (H1) has a negative effect on an individual's decision to engage in prosumption activities ($\beta=-.426$, Wald$=4.40$, $p=.04$). The level of consumer perceived opportunism (H2) was found not to have a

Table 1 Logistic regression analysis of make-or-buy decision

Hypothesis	Predictor variable	α	Mean	SD	β	Wald	P
H1	Asset specificity	.87	4.32	1.45	−.426	4.40	.04
H2	Perceived opportunism	.89	3.93	1.26	.237	1.58	.02
H3	Perceived risk of prosumption	.86	4.33	1.34	−1.797	29.31	<.000
H4	Perceived economic benefit	.91	5.62	1.10	1.71	24.62	<.000
H5	Consumer self-efficacy	.96	4.10	1.67	.654	11.24	.001

significant effect on the make-or-buy decision ($\beta=.237$, Wald$=1.58$, *n.s.*). Next, we examined perceived risk of prosumption (H3) and found it also had a negative effect on the decision to engage in prosumption as hypothesized ($\beta=-1.797$, Wald$=29.31$, $p=.000$). The main effect of perceived economic benefit (H4) on a make-or-buy decision was also significant as hypothesized ($\beta=1.706$, Wald$=24.62$, $p=.000$). Finally, the relationship between self-efficacy (H5) and an individual's decision to engage in prosumption was examined. The main effect was significant and positive as predicted ($\beta=.654$, Wald$=11.24$, $p=.001$).

Discussion

The current study argues that value-in-use is not a sufficient basis on which to evaluate and predict an individual's prosumption decision. The current study does not seek to disavow previous research, but to suggest that economic factors (e.g., cost reductions) must be considered when examining an individual's decision to prosume. Importantly, the current study also demonstrates TCA's effectiveness and applicability in consumer purchase contexts. Specifically, TCA suggest individuals choose the transaction mode (make or buy) that possesses the lowest transaction cost. Examining prosumption under the perspective of SDL, one would predict that an individual would choose the transaction mode that maximizes benefits. This is unrealistic because individuals do not have unlimited resources and therefore the transaction mode that offers the greatest benefits may not be feasible. In contrast, the application of TCA posits an individual selects the transaction mode that minimizes transaction costs, which also leads to greater value assessments, but is more realistic when the resources constraints of individual consumers is considered. Moreover, the results clearly indicate that, in contrast to SDL's direct implication that the focus of value creation is on benefits, the costs inherent in a transaction also drive consumers' decision-making. In addition to the current research's contribution to marketing theory, the findings presented here also have significant relevance for practitioners. Specifically, they renew the notion that managing costs can be as important as providing benefits.

References available upon request.

Consumer Co-production in Prolonged and Complex Services: The Case of Medication Adherence in Chronically Ill Individuals

Jelena Spanjol, Anna S. Cui, Cheryl Nakata, Lisa Sharp, Stephanie Y. Crawford, Yazhen Xiao, and Mary Beth Watson-Manheim

Abstract This study examines customer co-production in a prolonged, complex, and negative service context—medication adherence in chronically ill individuals. We integrate services and medical perspectives to develop a novel theoretical framework of adherence as a nested system of co-production behaviors, characterized by temporal and scope dimensions. Utilizing a qualitative approach, our findings point to two key insights about co-production in the customer sphere. First, the enactment and form of regular-restricted, intermittent-intermediate, and irregular-expansive co-production behaviors are determined by the characteristics of the customer sphere—that is, co-production is contextualized. Second, the co-production system in the customer sphere is complex, and the different levels are interdependent. Our research contributes to the emerging literature on service co-production by elucidating the behaviors through which customers strive towards adherence. The identified co-production framework holds important implications for providers of prolonged and complex services and future research directions.

J. Spanjol (✉) • A.S. Cui • C. Nakata • L. Sharp • S.Y. Crawford • Y. Xiao
M.B. Watson-Manheim
University of Illinois at Chicago, Chicago, IL, USA
e-mail: spanjol@uic.edu; ascui@uic.edu; cnakat1@uic.edu; sharpl@uic.edu;
crawford@uic.edu; yxiao21@uic.edu; mbwm@uic.edu

© Academy of Marketing Science 2016   903
L. Petruzzellis, R.S. Winer (eds.), *Rediscovering the Essentiality of Marketing*,
Developments in Marketing Science: Proceedings of the Academy of Marketing
Science, DOI 10.1007/978-3-319-29877-1_177

Customers' Attribution of Blame When Other Customers Enhance or Destroy the Service Offering

Alastair Tombs and Jörg Finsterwalder

Abstract Imagine you are in a restaurant and your experience is either enhanced or diminished by the behavior of other customers within the same environment. To whom do you attribute your experience? When things go well the enjoyment of other customers creates or enhances a positive atmosphere within environment (Grayson and McNiell 2009; Yoshida and James 2010) and may increase the value a customer places on the service experience. The positive atmosphere and enhanced value the customer experiences is likely to be reflected in positive attitudes and feelings toward the firm and result in positive repurchase intentions (Tombs and McColl-Kennedy 2013) and positive word-of-mouth (Hooper et al. 2013). However, if other customers' behavior is incompatible with the particular service or creates any sort of negative event, then the value the customer attaches to the service experience decreases (Tombs and McColl-Kennedy 2013) and often results in customers not wanting to go back to that establishment. Even worse than that they are likely to indulge in negative word-of-mouth (Huang et al. 2010) therefore dissuading others from going. These approach or avoidance behaviors are often the result of customers perceiving that the atmosphere of the service environment and subsequent enjoyable or dissatisfactory experiences are reflective of the overall service experience provided by the organization. This chapter examines the responses of customers when exposed the positive or negative behavior of other customers. Specifically it applies Attribution Theory (Weiner 1980, 1986) to explain how customers allocate blame for having their experience within a service environment disturbed (either positively or negatively) and what this blame does to service evaluations and repurchase intentions. We report

A. Tombs (✉)
University of Queensland, St Lucia, QLD, Australia
e-mail: a.tombs@business.uq.edu.au

J. Finsterwalder
University of Canterbury, Christchurch, New Zealand
e-mail: joerg.finsterwalder@canterbury.ac.nz

© Academy of Marketing Science 2016   905
L. Petruzzellis, R.S. Winer (eds.), *Rediscovering the Essentiality of Marketing*,
Developments in Marketing Science: Proceedings of the Academy of Marketing
Science, DOI 10.1007/978-3-319-29877-1_178

on a qualitative study of regular restaurant patrons. The findings revealed that the attribution of blame for a disrupted service experience will vary, i.e., to the perpetrators (other customers), the organization and its staff, or even to the affected customer, depending on such factors as controllability, and perceived stability. These factors may be more stable and better predictors of customers' reactions to disruption than the apparently shifting locus of causality. Conversely positive behavior of other customers appeared to be attributed not to the other customers but to the firm itself. This may be because when a customer is in a positive mood they perceive the elements of the servicescape are in harmony and as such look at the service environment more holistically. Whereas the disturbance caused by other customers may produce conflicting signals from the servicescape (positive things the firm does to attract the customer in the first place and the negative actions of others within that same environment) thus causing customers to be more analytical in an effort to resolve these apparent conflicts.

References available upon request.

Financial Services for the Poor: The Case for a Catholic Bank

P. Sergius Koku

Introduction

"Poverty is the worst kind of disease to have" is a literal translation of an African proverb. However, the ravages of poverty are not limited to Africa. Poverty is a world-wide problem that is being fought with tools such as economic aids to developing countries (Daud and Nor Azam Abdul 2012; Ekanayake and Dasha 2010), programs against world hunger (Mowbray 2007), and several other micro-finance programs (Halvorson-Quevedo 1991/1992). In this chapter, I argue for yet another tool in fighting poverty, using the principles of services marketing, religion, and an established church—the Catholic Church.

People's faith and beliefs do significantly shape their lives and how they behave. Thus, it is not surprising that several studies in marketing have examined the role of religion in people's consumption behavior or wealth (Hirschman 1983; Haq and Wong 2010). However, to the best of my knowledge, none has yet explicitly examined the role of religion in fighting poverty in spite of the current popularity of *Sha'riah*-compliant banks and *Sha'riah* investment portfolios. Given the disproportionately large number of lives affected by poverty and equally large number of lives touched by religion, I think it is worthwhile that a bridge between wealth, religion, and poverty be examined.

This chapter explores an alternative banking modality for the poor. It examines the issue of fighting poverty with a Catholic Bank within the institutional framework of the Catholic Church. Drawing on the tenets of the Catholic Social Teachings (CST), the Bible and the principles of marketing, and the results of my interview, the chapter argues that there is space for a Catholic Bank that is similar to Islamic Banks, but devoted to fighting poverty.

P.S. Koku (✉)
Florida Atlantic University, Boca Raton, FL, USA
e-mail: Koku@fau.edu

© Academy of Marketing Science 2016   907
L. Petruzzellis, R.S. Winer (eds.), *Rediscovering the Essentiality of Marketing*,
Developments in Marketing Science: Proceedings of the Academy of Marketing
Science, DOI 10.1007/978-3-319-29877-1_179

Who Are the Poor?

The poor are those who fall on or below the level of poverty; however, what constitutes the level of poverty has not been rigidly defined. The US government, for example, uses the definition to shape its policies that are intended to help the poor relies on the definition provided by the Bureau of Census.

Microcredit Summit which uses a different definition distinguishes the "very poor" from the "poor." It defines the "very poor" as households living on less than $1 per person, per day at international prices, and the "poor" as those living on incomes that put them in the lower half of the poor population (Delay-Harris 2007). The World Bank, on the other hand, defines the "poor" in terms of "extreme poverty" and "moderate poverty." According to the World Bank, "extreme poverty" is living on less than US $1.25 per day, and "moderate poverty" is living on less than $2.00 per day (Ravallion et al. 2009).

Because developing countries have a larger percentage of the world's poor, the world's attention on tackling poverty has focused on them. Hence, the establishment of debt forgiveness programs such as the HIPC (Highly Indebted Poor Country) by the International Monetary Fund and World Bank, and the Millennium Development Initiative which was intended to reduce the world's extreme poverty by 2015 (United Nations Development Program 2002; IMF Factsheets 2010).

The efforts of non-governmental organizations (NGOs) have also been similarly focused on developing countries where governments fight poverty through programs that fight diseases and illiteracy, and develop better sanitation facilities. All these efforts have enjoyed varying degrees of success (Morduch and Haley 2001; Masud and Yontcheva 2005).

However, several studies have found that access to finance is a major stumbling block to the poor in fighting poverty (Beck and Demirguc-Kent 2008; Rank et al. 2001. Without collateral and a steady stream of income, the poor are considered too high a credit risk for the traditional financial institutions (Koku 2009; Lee 2002). Thus, I argue that programs that are intended to improve conditions of the poor must have not only strategies, but also mechanisms to achieve this end.

The success of MFIs, particularly the Grameen bank of Bangladesh, in improving the economic circumstances of the poor (Ahmed 2009), has encouraged similar efforts in other places. While Islamic banks that operate according to the *Sha'riah* laws also fill a need, there seems to be a space for other religious establishments to help poor entrepreneurs who need small capitals. The Bible, the foundation of Christianity, in several instances teaches Christians to help the poor. For example, in the Old Testament, God through Moses encouraged the Israelites to let the land lie unplowed for the 7th year so the poor among them may get food (Exodus 23:11; Leviticus 19:10) and be generous towards the poor (Deuteronomy 15:7–8). In the New Testament, Jesus urged his followers to help the poor (Matthew 26:11; Mark 14:7; John 12:8) and in Matthew (6:2–3). These and several other examples constitute the basis of Christian charity.

The Catholic Church

The Catholic Church helps the poor in several ways. It has built hospitals in several parts of the world to take care of the sick, skills and vocational training centers to train people, and homes for orphans and refugees (Bruce 2006). The efforts of Mother Theresa and her order in helping the poor in India are well known around the world. Efforts such as Mother Theresa's have in many ways supplemented the efforts of governments in helping the poor. However, access to capital remains problematic for the poor. As expressed by one graduate of these skills training centers in Ghana, West Africa, "of what help are vocational skills, if no one will employ you and if you do not have money to start your own shop?" (Koku and Acquaye 2011). Similar sentiments have been expressed by graduates of vocational training programs run by charity organizations in other countries in Africa and elsewhere. I focus on the Catholic Church in this chapter because of its long tradition in helping the poor and because of The Catholic Social Teachings.

The Catholic Social Teachings

The Theory of Distributive Justice forms the underpinnings of The Catholic Social Teachings (CST) was formulated by Pope Leo XIII (Leo XIII 1892). Distributive justice "deals with the inequalities of wealth under the free-enterprise system of economics," (Kilchrist and Block 2006), and "Catholic Social Teachings" is part of a larger philosophy known as social justice which involves the church's self-imposed duty toward all mankind" (Kilchrist and Block 2006). The CST has seven main themes (Hoverstad 2008; United States Catholic Bishops 1998). These are:

1. Life and dignity of the human person
2. A call to family, community, and participation in society
3. The right to life and its basic necessities and the responsibility to ensure others have those rights
4. A preferential option for the poor and vulnerable
5. The dignity of work and protecting the rights of workers
6. Solidarity among all people
7. Care of God's creation

The CST emphasizes respect for life and human dignity as well as compassion for the poor. Given the results of studies that have shown that access to capital is one of the biggest stumbling blocks in the way of the poor to getting out of poverty (Koku 2009; Beck and Demirguc-Kent 2008; Rank et al. 2001), one of the better ways to break the cycle of poverty is to enable the poor access to capital. The framework that I propose is based on the 8Ps of services marketing (Lovelock and Wright 2002), the results of my interview, the CST, and the Bible.

Interview with the Poor

To understand the problems of the poor I interviewed 25 poor individuals between the ages of 24 and 50 in Accra, Ghana. They consisted of 15 men and ten women. These individuals were recruited by an acquaintance through a church. Twelve of these individuals all men, by their local standards, have some skills. None of the women had any meaningful skills even though four or five of them claimed they could braid hair for money, and one said she had started learning dress making before she quit due to lack of money. Five of the men claimed they were licensed drivers. One of them was a cobbler; two were wood carvers, one of them was an auto mechanic; two of them were carpenters, and one a bricklayer. The question is can the church have a viable role in financially rehabilitating these people?

One of the five drivers a mam 30 said "All that I need is someone to buy a vehicle on work-and-pay basis and I can take care of myself." This statement seemed to resonate with the rest of the drivers. One of the carpenters, 24 who had graduated from a job training program said "What is the point is having a employable skill and still be hungry and homeless? I can open my own shop and make furniture—chairs and the like, if I had some money. I was very good at carpentry during my training." What was clear to me from out of the interview is that all of them had expressed the willingness to work. It was also clear that most of them did not quite understand the role of competition in driving out inefficiency.

The 8Ps of a Catholic Bank

Here, I discuss the 8Ps of such a bank. What are the Product Elements? These are the first issues that must be addressed. The product elements should seamlessly connect with the target market. The product elements deal with the core offering and the supplementary services. Here, the core offering is a small capital, the target market is the poor; therefore, the supplementary services should be such that they make it possible for the poor to be serviced.

Place, cyberspace, and time in services marketing generally deal with "where and how to deliver services" to the target market. At first blush, it seems incongruent that cyberspace is relevant to servicing the poor or useful in the delivery of small capital to the poor. However, a closer examination shows that the poor, particularly in developing countries do not have access to landline telephones, but in most cases do have access to affordable or inexpensive cell/mobile phones. Thus, cyberspace here means using cell/mobile phones to service the loans.

Process deals with the sequence of activities involved in the service delivery, and Productivity deals with the efficiency as well as the effectiveness with which the service is delivered. Process and Productivity are the two sides of the same coin. A bank that services the poor must operate in such a way that its operations are flexible to carter to its target market (the poor). Productivity in this sphere will deal with minimizing the default rate by educating loan recipients.

People as captured in the 8Ps paradigm deals with the workers who are employed by the service organization. These individuals constitute the heart of the organization. Because of their importance to the success of the bank's mission—that is to provide a financial bridge to the poor, I suggest that they (potential employees of the bank) are carefully screened to ensure that they share the vision of the organization.

Promotion and education of the clientele of the bank will also, for several reasons, be essential for success. First, because of the nature of the client base, often not very educated, and may not have access to "mainstream" news media and current information, special effort must be made to reach them. This may mean using mobile means such as vehicles to broadcast news on the bank and its programs. It may also mean mobile classrooms to teach clients and potential clients how to save, manage cash flows from their businesses, and manage inventory.

Physical evidence in 8Ps speaks to the servicescape. It is important that the ambience in which these banks be low keyed so as not to intimidate the clientele. Similarly, the workers must be trained to be able to communicate in nonthreatening manner in which they can be clearly understood by their clients who are less sophisticated or not very educated.

Price and other User Outlays are particularly important. Here, they address the interest rate as well as the other conditions of the micro loans. Because the products are especially packaged to help the poor, the interest rate must be low. Interest rates must nonetheless be charged for two reasons. First, it has been shown that people appreciate things more when they pay for them (Eisenhauer 2006). Second, even the small interests that are paid may over time be large enough to constitute a loan for someone else or cover the operating cost of the bank.

The most overarching question is where will the Catholic Church get the money from to start a Catholic bank, even if it were interested in such an operation? The church does have a long experience in doing charity work. This experience could be offered as the Church's contribution in a partnership with other social entrepreneurs who have the financial capital and wish to help the poor.

Conclusion

Drawing on the Bible and the CSTs, and an insight from interviews with the poor, this chapter makes the argument that there is a space for a Catholic bank that helps the poor who are entrepreneurial to gain access to small loans. Arguing that such a service could complement the efforts of governments and other NGOs, the chapter proceeds to outline the operational framework for such a bank using the 8Ps.

References available upon request.

Part XXI
Tourism and Hospitality

Political Tourism/Tourist Revisited: Extending the Concept in a Developing Country's Point of View: A Thought-Provoking Case from Turkey

Nihat Kamil Anil, Gregor Pfajfar, and E. Tugba Kocabiyik

Abstract The main goal of this chapter is to broaden the extent of political tourism phenomenon in order to explain recent practices in Turkish political life theoretically. Very few researchers dealt with the non-monetary outputs of tourism which falls beyond the conventional economical value of it. Thus firstly, the political tourism and political tourist concepts were reviewed by introducing *daily election meetings* as a new type of political tourism and *election meeting tourists* as a new political tourist classification. Secondly, the pull factors for election tourism were indicated as solidarity, support (emotional and/or financial), nostalgic/patriotic/nationalistic reasons following the motivation list of Simone-Charteris and Boyd (2010). The other motivators such as the thrill of political violence or none of the attractions defined by Simone-Charteris and Boyd (2010) were found relevant with the Turkish phenomena. Besides meeting areas can be introduced as attractions.

References available upon request.

N.K. Anil (✉)
Kirklareli University, Kirklareli, Turkey
e-mail: nihatanil@yahoo.com

G. Pfajfar
University of Ljubljana, Ljubljana, Slovenia
e-mail: gregor.pfajfar@ef.uni-lj.si

E.T. Kocabiyik
Gediz University, Izmir, Turkey
e-mail: tugba.kocabiyik@gediz.edu.tr

© Academy of Marketing Science 2016
L. Petruzzellis, R.S. Winer (eds.), *Rediscovering the Essentiality of Marketing*,
Developments in Marketing Science: Proceedings of the Academy of Marketing
Science, DOI 10.1007/978-3-319-29877-1_180

Happiness, Willingness-to-Share and Materialism in the Experiential Purchase

I-Ling Ling, Yi-Fen Liu, and Edwin Rajah

Abstract This research investigates how people experience happiness via experiential purchases and explains the mechanisms of how willingness-to-share, materialism and life satisfaction affect happiness. Interpersonal communication is important. As consumers often tell others about their travel experiences (e.g. hotels, attractions or restaurants), do the "talkable" characteristics of tourism make a difference in advancing happiness? Prior research has shown that higher well-being is associated with spending less time alone and more time talking to others. By using naturalistic observation, this research shows that happy and unhappy people differ in the amount of small talk and substantive conversations they participate in. By measuring the extent to which consumers are willing to share their purchase information with others, we provide insight into why tourism provides more happiness through experiential rather than material purchases.

Two studies which asked people to recall or imagine happy tourism experiences revealed a meaningful distinction between experiential and material purchases. The results of Study 1 show that people's higher willingness-to-share share their experiences explains why experiential purchases elicit greater happiness than material purchases. That experiential purchases elicit greater happiness than material purchases is demonstrated by people's higher willingness to share their experiences (Study 1). For individuals who are high in materialism, the effect of experiential purchases on greater happiness is reduced. The results of Study 2 reveal that consumers gain more happiness by participating in non-commission-based package tours than in commission-based package tours. For individuals who have high life satisfaction, the effect is reduced. Together, these findings help better understand the interplay across experiential (vs. material) purchases, materialism, and life satisfaction in advancing tourism happiness.

I.-L. Ling (✉)
National Chiayi University, Chiayi City, Taiwan
e-mail: yiling@mail.ncyu.edu.tw

Y.-F. Liu
National Kaohsiung First University of Science and Technology, Kaohsiung City, Taiwan
e-mail: yifenliu@nkfust.edu.tw

E. Rajah
Auckland University of Technology, Auckland, New Zealand
e-mail: erajah@aut.ac.nz

© Academy of Marketing Science 2016
L. Petruzzellis, R.S. Winer (eds.), *Rediscovering the Essentiality of Marketing*,
Developments in Marketing Science: Proceedings of the Academy of Marketing
Science, DOI 10.1007/978-3-319-29877-1_181

Do Customers Prefer Casinos with CSR? An Empirical Study

Matthew Tingchi Liu, Guicheng Shi, and Ting-Hsiang Tseng

Introduction

Corporate social responsibility (CSR) has been an important research area for more than three decades, and has evolved from executives' idiosyncratic philanthropic activities to widespread acceptance as a valuable component of stakeholder management and incorporation into strategic performance models (Liu et al. 2014). As such, this study refers to CSR performance as customer perceptions of a firm's efforts in fulfilling its obligations toward a society and its stakeholders, rather than the actual CSR activities that a firm implements.

Literature Review and Hypotheses

Keeping in mind all the CSR related factors thus far, Mohr et al. (2001) have clearly divided CSR into two general classifications. The first category discusses CSR in relation to the various stakeholders of the organization (e.g., owners, customers, and employees). The second classification is based on Kotler and Lee's (2008) societal marketing concept. The current study also applies the two major types of CSR as the

M.T. Liu (✉)
University of Macau, Taipa, Macau
e-mail: MatthewL@umac.mo

G. Shi
Macau University of Science and Technology, Taipa, Macau
e-mail: gcshi@must.edu.mo

T.-H. Tseng
Feng Chia University, Taichung City, Taiwan
e-mail: tsength@fcu.edu.tw

© Academy of Marketing Science 2016   919
L. Petruzzellis, R.S. Winer (eds.), *Rediscovering the Essentiality of Marketing*,
Developments in Marketing Science: Proceedings of the Academy of Marketing
Science, DOI 10.1007/978-3-319-29877-1_182

components of CSR performance perception and tries to find out how the two CSR performance items influence customers' loyalty intention.

CSR with respect to society generally refers to an activity that contributes to society's well-being (Turker 2009). Pedersen (2010) indicated that a large number of managers believe that the firm has responsibilities to local communities and society in general. Yet, despite much research on CSR, the influence of CSR on actual customer behavior is still unclear. If we are to understand the influence of CSR on society and towards consumers' purchase and repurchase intention, an understanding of the relationship between companies' socially responsible behavior and consumers' purchase decision becomes increasingly relevant, as consumers are looking for more information about their rights and about the responsibility of the companies towards society (Titus and Bradford 1996). Empirical findings from Homburg et al. (2009) further warrant a direct linkage between customer-company identification and loyalty. Accordingly, we argue that if a casino engages in CSR and publicizes its CSR efforts, it is more likely to be perceived as socially responsible (Vong and Wong 2013). The resulting brand image from CSR efforts encourages players to be more inclined to identify themselves as customers with such a casino than those that are perceived as less socially responsible, thus resulting in higher customer loyalty. In this sense, we introduced:

H1: Customers' perceptions that CSR performance is directed toward society are positively related to their loyalty intention.

CSR to stakeholders CSR activities have the potential to create stronger relationships between firms and stakeholders (Turker 2009). Communication of CSR concerns and activities not only creates awareness for CSR and support for an image or a brand, it is also a way of creating a bond between the company and its stakeholders (Maignan and Ferrell 2004; Liu et al. 2014). Sen et al. (2006) indicated that stakeholders aware of a company's CSR activities reacted positively to the focal company by purchasing their products, and also had more positive perceptions about the company's employment practices and investment behaviors. Accordingly, we propose:

H2: Customers' perceptions that CSR performance is being directed toward stakeholders are positively related to their loyalty intention.

Brand preference is understood as an antecedent of brand loyalty and is defined as the relative preference for choosing and using a specific brand (Cobb-Walgren et al. 1995). It follows that brand preference has a direct influence on a customer's purchase and loyalty intention. The fact that brand preference enhances customers' purchase and loyalty intention is confirmed by many studies (e.g., Cobb-Walgren et al. 1995). Constructive progress also appears in the structural models of customer preference and repurchase. This chapter put forwards that there is a causal link between the disposition of the customer to favor the service of a specific provider (brand preference) and the customer's willingness to purchase that service again (loyalty intention) from the same provider.

H3: Customers' brand preference is positively related to their loyalty intention.

Although the mediating effect of brand related attributes has been extensively studied in the marketing literature, its role as a mediator on the link between perceived CSR and customer behaviors has received far less attention in the hospitality literature. Given that brand preference is a key antecedent to customer loyalty, it follows that perceived CSR performance of a firm would eventually lead to higher level of customer loyalty through the mediating role of brand preference. A review of the literature also shows support for our contention. For example, Lai et al. (2010) found the relationship between CSR and brand performance to be partially mediated by corporate reputation. Accordingly, we propose:

H4a: Brand preference plays a significant mediating role between perceived CSR toward society and loyalty intention.
H4b: Brand preference plays a significant mediating role between perceived CSR toward stakeholders and loyalty intention.

Method

Measurements

The measures used in this study were adopted from well-established scales. With regard to *CSR performance*, the literature acknowledges that the construct commonly pertains to aspects relating to the society and stakeholders (Kotler and Lee 2008; Mohr et al. 2001; Turker 2009). The two major domains of CSR play significant roles in the gambling industry operation (Lee and Park 2009). We adopted a 4-item measure of societal CSR concerns from Clarkson (1995). We also generated a 5-item measure of CSR to stakeholders concerns from Tuker (2009) and Clarkson (1995). As to *Loyalty intention*, it refers to the individual's inclination for revisiting a casino, taking into account their current situation and likely circumstances (Hellier et al. 2003). The 3-item measure is adapted from the study by Hellier et al. (2003). *Brand preference* was adapted from Sirgy et al. (1997). In above, each item of all was assessed on a seven-point Likert-type scale ranging from 1 (strongly disagree) to 7 (strongly agree). To guarantee face validity, a pilot study was conducted using a Macau sample before the formal survey.

Scale Assessment

In Table 1, the reliability assessment and confirmatory factor analysis (CFA) were significant. Two factors (i.e., CSR to society and CSR to stakeholders) were extracted from all the 9 items of CSR performance perception. Cronbach's α for

Table 1 Squared correlation and average variance extracted

	1	2	3	4
1. CSR to society	.80			
2. CSR to stakeholders	.51	.62		
3. Brand preference	.32	.39	.58	
4. Loyalty intention	.16	.31	.34	.81

two factors are satisfactory (.91 and .92, respectively) and related to those reported by Turker (2009). Brand preference ($\alpha = .83$, total variance $= 68.141\%$) and Loyalty intention ($\alpha = .91$, total variance $= 63.468\%$) were also satisfactory and all items were kept. Factor loadings of all items were acceptable ($> .7$) based on Hair et al. (2006)'s work. Bartlett's test of sphericity was conducted for each variable. The result shows significance ($p < .001$) and indicates the presence of nonzero correlation among the items. The overall measure of sampling adequacy was above the cutoff value of .5. These results satisfied the fundamental requirements for factor analysis (Hair et al. 2006). Furthermore, all the estimates for the average variance extracted (AVE) were greater than .50, in support of convergent validity. Moreover, the AVE for each construct was larger than the squared correlations between constructs, thereby satisfying the discriminant validity criterion.

Samples and Procedures

This study focuses on the gaming industry in Macau, the world gambling capital which expected to generate 45 billion USD in gaming revenue (sevenfold than Las Vegas) in 2014. To rule out possible response bias due to differences in casino gambler type, the current study focused on high stake customers (high-rollers) who play in a high amount betting limit area in one of major six casinos in Macau. This study regards high-rollers in the high limit area as the most suitable sample to represent premium customers with high customer profitability and high future relationship value (Watson and Kale 2003). Data were collected from major casinos in middle 2014. The survey was conducted with assistance from well-trained casino personnel before the respondents started playing. Furthermore, we asked the respondents to fill another well-developed simplified pathological gamblers diagnosis scale from the *American Psychiatric Association* after the main research questionnaire. This was done to ensure that the respondents were not self-perceived as addicted pathological gamblers, which may lead to compulsive gambling behaviors. Based on research ethics, the respondents were free to reject our interview anytime if they had any concerns. Eventually, 520 questionnaires (out of 600 ones delivered) were identified as eligible for further analysis. Among all the subjects, about 72% were male, 75% were between 30 and 50 years old, and 35% reported being college educated. Most of the participants were from mainland China (58%) and Hong Kong (25%).

Results

The results indicate that the overall model for each regressed equation has a good fit with a highly significant F value and satisfactory R^2 (between 0.310 and 0.510) and adjusted R^2 (between 0.308 and 0.490). All variance inflationary factor (VIF) values of independent variables in this model are less than 3.0; therefore no significant multicollinearity problem exists. Regression analyses were used to test the impact of perceptions associated with perceived CSR performance and brand preference on loyalty intention. The two perceived CSR variables and brand preference produce significant effects on loyalty intention. Between the two perceived CSR factors, CSR to stakeholders displayed a stronger influence on loyalty intention ($\beta = .486$, $p < .001$) than CSR to society ($\beta = .377$, $p < .001$). The results indicated that H1, H2, and H3 are all supported.

The mediating effect of brand preference between CSR performance perception and loyalty intention was tested based on the method by Baron and Kenny (1986). The results show that the beta values all decreased when brand preference was introduced in each regression equation. That is, the parameter estimate for CSR to society decreased from .621 to .461, while the parameter estimate for CSR to stakeholders decreased from .830 to .698. R-square values increased by including brand preference as a mediator in the model. Furthermore, the Sobel test proved the significant mediation effects (Sobel value = 5.436 for CSR to society; Sobel value = 6.653 for CSR to stakeholders). Partial mediating effect of brand preference between perceived CSR performance and loyalty intention was supported by the results from H4a and H4b.

Discussion

This study examined whether and to what extent perceived CSR performance influence casino players' loyalty intention through the mediating role of brand preference. It addressed an important research question on which aspect of a casino's perceived CSR efforts could become valuable and important to its brand and in attracting loyal customers. This study shows that perceived CSR to stakeholders plays a more salient role in both customer brand preference and loyalty intention than perceived CSR to society. These findings help in addressing the research question and also extend the research stream on consumer CSR-induced attributions. This study also contributes to the literature by highlighting the partial mediating role of brand preference on the relationship between perceived CSR and customer loyalty base on the study by Lai et al. (2010). That is, this research identifies brand preference as an additional step or process regulating the impact of perceived CSR performance on customer's behavioral intentions. By examining both the effects of perceived CSR and brand preference on customer loyalty, this study offers a more complete understanding of the CSR—customer preference—behavior process. More importantly, this study provides insights into the literature on casino gambling by showing a chain of relationships leading from perceived CSR to customer loyalty. It further shows how casinos could mitigate a negative brand image by leveraging CSR, especially CSR programs devoted to a company's stakeholders and the society.

References available upon request.

Innovativeness and Market Orientation as Forerunners of the New Service Added Value and Performance in the Hotel Industry

Primitiva Pascual-Fernández, José Ángel López-Sánchez, Javier Reynoso, and María Leticia Santos-Vijande

Abstract The tourism industry is widely recognized for its prominent role to foster economic development, wealth creation, and employment opportunities in modern economies (Lee and Chang 2008; WTTC 2013; OMT 2014). In this sense, during the last 5 years the tourism sector has experienced a higher growth than other economic sectors (OMT 2014; sectors (OMT 2014; sectors (OMT 2014; sectors (OMT 2014; WTTC 2013). The cross-sectorial nature of tourism-related activities enhances this effect and reinforces the vision of tourism industry as an engine for global economic recovery (Vellas 2011).

In order to guarantee its future competitiveness, tourism firms experiment an increasing pressure to innovate (Edvardsson et al. 2013; Ernst and Young 2013; Ordanini et al. 2014; Salunke et al. 2013; Thomas and Wood 2014). Several studies have analyzed the determinants of successful service innovation although empirical evidence in the tourism industry is still scarce (Kuester et al. 2013; Ottenbacher et al. 2006, 2010; Papastathopoulou and Hultink 2012). Similarly, there is a lack of research about the potential impact of organization-level characteristics in the presence of project-level determinants for new service success (Edvardsson et al. 2013; Melton and Hartline 2010; Ordanini et al. 2014).

Accordingly, using a sample of Spanish hotels, this study analyzes the impact of the hotel's innovativeness and market orientation (Papastathopoulou and Hultink 2012) on a key driver of service innovation performance, the new service added value (Kuester et al. 2013; Ordanini et al. 2014); as well as how these effects translate to the new service performance. In this way, this research seeks to contribute to our understanding of how organizational factors and project-level factors favor new service success.

P. Pascual-Fernández (✉) • M.L. Santos-Vijande
University of Oviedo, Asturias, Spain
e-mail: pascualprimitiva@uniovi.es; lsantos@uniovi.es

J.Á. López-Sánchez
University of Extremadura, Cáceres, Spain
e-mail: jangel@unex.es

J. Reynoso
EGADE Business School, Ciudad de México, D.F., Mexico
e-mail: jreynoso@itesm.mx

© Academy of Marketing Science 2016   925
L. Petruzzellis, R.S. Winer (eds.), *Rediscovering the Essentiality of Marketing*,
Developments in Marketing Science: Proceedings of the Academy of Marketing
Science, DOI 10.1007/978-3-319-29877-1_183

Results indicate that the hotel's market orientation exerts a direct, positive effect on the new service added value, and that fully mediates the relationship between the hotel's innovativeness and the new service added value. This finding suggests that in the hotel industry an innovative culture is not enough to provide added value from the customers' perspective and that, therefore, hotels need to incorporate the market insights provided by a market-oriented behavior. The research also confirms that the new service added value favors its performance at a customer level (satisfaction, improved hotel's image, and leadership among customers) and a market level (sales, market assessment, profitability).

References available upon request.

Technology and Cultural Heritage Management: Can Technology Have an Impact on Word-of-Mouth and Territorial Attractiveness?

Laura Di Pietro, Roberta Guglielmetti Mugion, Maria Francesca Renzi, and Martina Toni

Introduction

The main aim of this chapter is to explore the existence of a bond that tied together the satisfaction of a cultural heritage' visitors (after the experience of the technological visits), their propensity towards the word-of-mouth and their intention to discover the local territory in which the cultural attraction is located. To achieve this purpose, a theoretical review was carried out, in order to analyze the existing literature on cultural tourism and relative flows, visitors' satisfaction, word-of-mouth, and destination management. Nowadays, the cultural visit is changing and a wide number of sites provide to their customers the possibility to experiment a "technological visit." Starting from the results of the literature analysis, a theoretical model was developed with the following objectives: (a) detecting the main aspects that impact on the visitors' satisfaction; (b) understanding the relation between the visitors' satisfaction and the word-of-mouth (WOM) inherent to a cultural site; (c) identifying the existence of positive relation between the WOM and the willingness to come back to discover the local territory. Many authors studied the factors that affect visitors' satisfaction, but only few researches have been oriented to deep analyze the specific role played by the technological applications along the cultural path. In addition, the literature on cultural tourism shows a lack in the analysis of the tourists' satisfaction ability to generate a positive WOM, in turn able to increase the attractiveness of the territory in an important way. To verify the developed model, a survey on the visitors of the Etruscan Necropolises of Cerveteri was carried out. The presented cultural site is part of the Cultural and Technology District (CTD) of

L. Di Pietro (✉) • R.G. Mugion • M.F. Renzi • M. Toni
University of Roma Tre, Rome, Italy
e-mail: laura.dipietro@uniroma3.it; roberta.guglielmettimugion@uniroma3.it; mariafrancesca.renzi@uniroma3.it; martina.toni@uniroma3.it

© Academy of Marketing Science 2016   927
L. Petruzzellis, R.S. Winer (eds.), *Rediscovering the Essentiality of Marketing*,
Developments in Marketing Science: Proceedings of the Academy of Marketing
Science, DOI 10.1007/978-3-319-29877-1_184

Lazio region and providing the possibility to experiment a technological visit, allows the study of this new feature on visitors' satisfaction. The model was test by using a structural equations modeling (SEM).

Background

Cultural heritage represents an attractions from tourists' perspective, and as posit by Copley and Robson (1996) the consequence of the heritage assets aptitude to encompass the main features of a place and, at the same time, of their ability to promote and share local traditions and ethnic backgrounds (Mckercher and Ho 2006). As recognized by Di Pietro et al. (2013) the tourist traffic due to the presence of cultural heritage resources, contributes to stimulate the surrounding activities generating an economic impact (e.g. restaurants, crafts, and transportation). This type of development enhances the attractiveness of local areas (Bowitz and Ibenholt 2009). Ritchie and Crouch (2010) formulated a model which asserts that the success of a tourist destination depends on some components, including "core resources and attractors" that represents the primary elements of destination appeal and the key motivators that prospective visitors choose one destination over another. Within this component a key role is played by the "culture and history" of a destination that, as the authors state is a basic and powerful attracting force.

In Italy a specific district model, namely the Cultural and Technological District (CTD) has been introduced in order to stimulate the local tourism and the relative local economy through the implementation of technology. The first definition of CTD is provided by Di Pietro et al. (2013), who combining Ghafele and Santagata's (2006) description of cultural districts and the meaning of technological district in order to define the Cultural and Technological District as "*an interdependent system of entities situated within a limited geographical area with the purpose of achieving sustained value creation through two drivers: culture and technology.*" From this perspective emerges that this innovative district model provides a strong link among cultural sites, technological application and local attractively. At the same time, this bond can be generated only in consequence to the occurrence of a double effect: (1) the positive influence of technology installations on visitors' satisfaction (together with other traditional elements related to the visit, such as tangible aspects and personnel); (2) the impact of visitors' satisfaction on WOM addressed to the cultural site. In fact, the technological application in cultural heritage context can contribute to improve the visitors' satisfaction, to attract new target, and to increase the tourist flows. The cultural heritage users are seeking new modalities to experience and live the visit in a much more interactive and creative way (Di Pietro et al. forthcoming; Arcese et al. 2012; Kalay et al. 2008). However, only few studies deal and measure the direct impact of technology on the visitors' satisfaction.

As asserted by a wide number of authors (e.g., Smith and Vogt 1995; Chevalier and Mayzlin 2006; Sen and Lerman 2007; Xia and Bechwati 2008; Jalilvand and Samiei 2012a, b; Reza Jalilvand et al. 2012), the WOM is useful in order to influence and form the consumer attitudes and behavioral intentions. In the cultural heritage tourism, one of the most widely used source of information is found to be word-of-mouth (Alvarez and Korzay 2011).

Research Methods

On the basis of the literature review, a model composed of five hypotheses was identified. Here following the research hypothesis of the model are presented:

H1: The Technological application implemented within the visit path positively affects the level of visitors' satisfaction.

H2: The Personnel of the cultural site positively affects the level of visitors' satisfaction.

H3: The Tangible Aspects of the cultural site positively affects the level of visitors' satisfaction.

H4: The level of Visitors' Satisfaction positively affects the propensity towards the Word-of-Mouth of the visitors.

H5: The propensity towards the Word-of-Mouth of the visitor positively affects the Intention to come back visit the territory

An empirical survey was carried out in order to collect data and test the presented model. The data collection was realized by using of a specific questionnaire structured into five sections. All of the questions related to the constructs of the hypothesized model (Fig. 1) were measured using a 6-point Likert scale (1 = disagree; 6 = agree) and are reported in Table 1. The questionnaire was tested through a pilot survey to improve its structure. The final version of the questionnaire was administered at the end of the visit at the cultural site of the Cerveteri's Etruscan Necropolises. In the study, a non-probabilistic sample was considered appropriate considering the preliminary stage of the research (Grewal et al. 2000; O'Cass 2000). The number of questionnaires completely filled out was 219, but for the purposes of the present analysis, only the questionnaires of respondents that experienced the technological visits it has been considered, that are 169 questionnaires. Regarding the methodology, firstly, a descriptive analysis of the data were conducted, and secondly structural equation modeling (SEM) to test the proposed theoretical model.

Results and Discussion

An EFA was carried out in order to provide initial insight into the scale's validity. The Kaiser-Meyer-Olkin (KMO) statistic is .838 and Bartlett's test $p = .000$. The number of factors was chosen on the basis of an eigenvalues greater than 1 and with a cumulative variance of 63.357%. Three factors that characterize a cultural visit (Table 1) were detected: *Technological application* (F1), *Personnel* (F2) and *Tangible aspects* (F3).

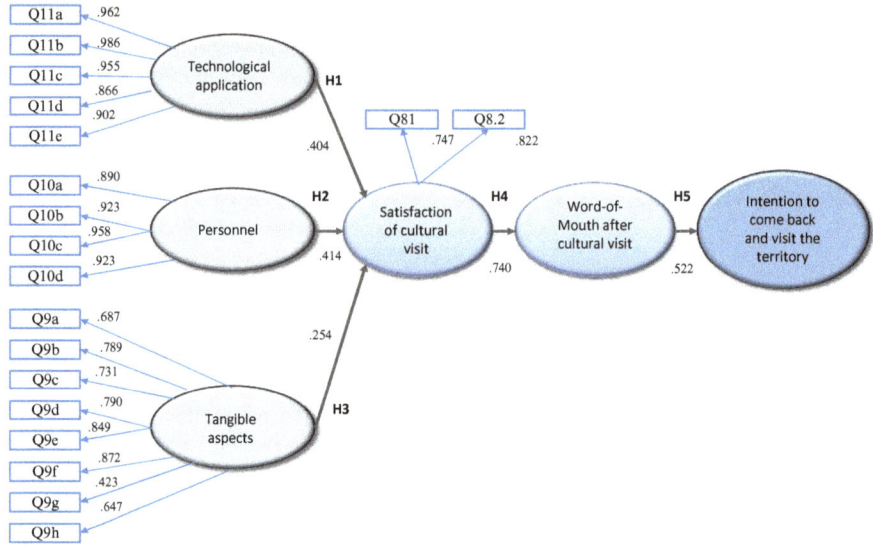

Fig. 1 The graphical representation of the tested model (all the *p*-value are significant)

Table 1 Status of research hypothesis

Hypothesis	Predictor/latent	Dependent	Estimate	S.E.	*P*-value	Status
H1	Technological application	Satisfaction of cultural visit	.404	.094	.000	Supported
H2	Personnel	Satisfaction of cultural visit	.414	.102	.000	Supported
H3	Tangible aspects	Satisfaction of cultural visit	.254	.096	.008	Supported
H4	Satisfaction of cultural visit	Word-of-mouth after cultural visit	.740	.058	.000	Supported
H5	Word-of-mouth after cultural visit	Intention to come back and visit the territory	.522	.045	.000	Supported

Afterwards also a confirmatory factor analysis (CFA), for validating the significant variables of the theoretical model, was carried out. CFA provided a good fit for the original dimensional structure that we supposed (CFI = .986.; TLI = .983; RMSEA = .064; WRMR = .909; Chi-Square = 245.707 with 146 degrees of freedom and a *p*-value = .000).

After the CFA, the hypothesis have been tested through a Structural Equation Modeling (SEM) to verify the hypothesized theoretical model with the collected data and answer to the two research questions. In particular, the data were treated as categorical data and a robust method for estimating the parameters was applied (WLSMV).

The indicators of goodness of fit are located within the acceptable thresholds suggested by the literature. This finding can be considered proof that the model is an acceptable fit for the data collected in this study.

All the five hypothesis formulated at the theoretical level are supported (Table 1). In particular, three latent factors ("*technological application*"—H1, "*personnel*"— H2, and "*Tangible aspects*"—H3) directly influence the "visitors' satisfaction"), highlighting the important role played by the technology in the transformation of the cultural experience. At the same time, the "visitors' satisfaction" shows a positive impact on "*WOM addressed to the cultural visit*" (H4). Finally, also the hypotheses relations among the positive "*WOM*" and the "intention to come back and visit the territory" are confirmed (H5).

Summarizing the research questions are confirmed through the test of the model on the collected data in the Etruscan Necropolises of Cerveteri. The integration of technological application along the cultural path represents an important part of visitors' satisfaction, as well as the more traditional aspects such as personnel and tangible aspects. At the same time, the application of SEM demonstrates a direct impact of positive WOM addressed to the cultural visit on the intention to discover and acquire knowledge about the local territory in which the cultural site is located.

This work represents a first exploratory study finalized to verify the formulated model, but its replications in other cultural heritage sites need to be tested. Thus, future researches should be carried out in order to check on a larger scale the validity of the presented five hypotheses to confirm the discussed findings.

References available upon request.

A Holistic Approach to the Effects of Fandom: An Application of Self-Expansion Theory

Lanlung Chiang, Aikaterini Manthiou, and Cindy Yunhsin Chou

Abstract Research on the effect of fans' psychological response to pop-culture destination is arguably limited (Lee et al. 2008). To develop a better understanding of fans' psychological response to pop-culture destination and its relation to their post behaviors, this study expanded self-expansion theory to the existing place attachment framework to examine the relationships between self-expansion, fandom, recollection, place attachment, and post-behavioral intentions. Furthermore, this study argues that place attachment as a key mediates the relationship between fandom and recollection. The survey population were international tourists who are interested in or favor Chinese pop-culture. To represent Chinese pop-culture, particular Chinese pop-stars and their fans were sampled. One-to-one interview method was used to investigate more detailed information from the fans. Nine hundred copies of the questionnaires were used in the survey, and a total of 768 questionnaires were collected during on-site data collection. This study empirically demonstrated that fans and tourists respond to pop-culture tourism emotionally and thus develop further behavioral intentions. This study also examined the bridge created by place attachment and memory recall as it occurs in the cognitive process. The relationship between fandom and post-behavioral intentions is shown.

L. Chiang (✉) • C.Y. Chou
Yuan Ze University, Taoyuan City, Taiwan
e-mail: lukech@saturn.yzu.edu.tw; cindy.chou@saturn.yzu.edu.tw

A. Manthiou
NEOMA Business School—Rouen Campus, Mont-Saint-Aignan, France
e-mail: aikaterini.manthiou@neoma-bs.fr

© Academy of Marketing Science 2016   933
L. Petruzzellis, R.S. Winer (eds.), *Rediscovering the Essentiality of Marketing*,
Developments in Marketing Science: Proceedings of the Academy of Marketing
Science, DOI 10.1007/978-3-319-29877-1_185

The Role of Wine Tourism in Italian SMEs' Internationalization: Eight Cases

Barbara Francioni, Tiia Vissak, and Fabio Musso

Introduction

Although several scholars have examined a possible relation between international tourism flow and international trade and confirmed that wine tourism creates marketing opportunities to sell products, most have carried out quantitative research. Therefore, there is a lack of exploratory and qualitative research. Moreover, it is also necessary to study why some wine producers internationalize suddenly after being local-market oriented for decades (become born-again globals/-internationals) and why they experience difficulties in internationalization as such firms have received less attention in internationalization literature. This study contributes toward closing these gaps and aims to examine the influence of international tourism on the internationalization process of Italian SMEs producing Bianchello del Metauro wine.

Literature Review

Researchers have identified several factors affecting/leading to wine producers' internationalization: declining profits, high local competition, or following local competitors (Duarte Alonso et al. 2014), but also being well connected and interested in internationalization (Maurel 2009). Still, for many wineries, the decision to start

B. Francioni (✉) • F. Musso
University of Urbino, Urbino, Italy
e-mail: Barbara.Francioni@uniurb.it; Fabio.Musso@uniurb.it

T. Vissak
University of Tartu, Tartu, Estonia
e-mail: Tiia.Vissak@ut.ee

© Academy of Marketing Science 2016
L. Petruzzellis, R.S. Winer (eds.), *Rediscovering the Essentiality of Marketing*,
Developments in Marketing Science: Proceedings of the Academy of Marketing
Science, DOI 10.1007/978-3-319-29877-1_186

exporting is unplanned (Duarte Alonso et al. 2014). Some authors have also empha-sized the link between wine tourism and wine exports. For instance, Beames (2003, p. 212) stated: "If the winery provides a good experience and image, visitors return-ing home from their holidays will then seek to buy that wine." In addition, some authors have concluded that wine tourism offers wineries opportunities to improve their image (Williams and Kelly 2001), acquire foreign market knowledge (Szivas 1999), sell directly to foreign customers (Getz and Brown 2006), and promote themselves (Sevil and Yüncü 2009).

In internationalization literature, most research has focused on slow or fast internationalizers, but we will focus on born-again globals and -internationals defined as "…firms that have been well established in their domestic markets, with apparently no great motivation to internationalise, but which have suddenly embraced rapid and dedicated internationalisation" (Bell et al. 2001, p. 173) as most of our case firms belong to this category. These firms' suppliers, customers, and competitors are often already international but they themselves have still remained domestic (Johanson and Mattsson 1988) because of lacking network relationships, knowledge or other resources (Chetty and Blankenburg Holm 2000), attractive domestic growth opportunities, low awareness of international opportunities, or low international competitiveness (Wilkinson et al. 2000). They may suddenly interna-tionalize because of a critical incident (e.g., ownership or management change), getting an order from a customer that already has international operations (Bell et al. 2003) or participating in international trade fairs/exhibitions (Kontinen and Ojala 2012). Innovative products, network ties (some formed during internationalization), readiness to adapt to market changes and perceiving only a small difference between the home and host country can also affect these firms' sudden internationalization (Kontinen and Ojala 2012; Schueffel et al. 2014). Still, compared to already interna-tional companies, these firms may be disadvantaged because their competitors have more foreign market knowledge and because it is hard for newcomers to enter existing networks (Chetty and Blankenburg Holm 2000). On the other hand, increasing domestic competition may push them abroad (Schueffel et al. 2014).

Methodology

This chapter is based on eight cases. To study different aspects of the phenomenon, the selected firms belonged to different owners and were oriented at different mar-kets. Still, they all (a) had their headquarters in Marche region, Italy, (b) produced Bianchello del Metauro wine, (c) owned a wine store or a farm or organized events for attracting tourists, (d) had less than 250 employees, and (e) were engaged in some international activities. Six were local market oriented for a long time, then internationalized fast, thus they could be regarded as born-again globals or -internationals. For comparison, a fast internationalizer and a non-exporter were also studied. Italy was chosen as the country of origin due to long wine production tradition. The Bianchello del Metauro production area was selected due to its tourism potential. A single area was selected to avoid the influence of location-related factors.

To select suitable firms, the database of the Istituto Marchigiano di Tutela Vini was used. From 49 Italian firms producing Bianchello del Metauro wine only 26 were located in the Marche region. From these, we selected internationalized firms and from those, in turn, focused on born-again globals/internationals. In-depth 1–2 h interviews with owners were conducted in July–October 2014, and we also collected additional data via short follow-up telephone interviews in December 2014. All interviews were conducted in Italian and digitally recorded.

We followed the critical analyst perspective (Chapelle et al. 2003) and post-positivist paradigm (Guba and Lincoln 1994). For data triangulation and verification of the initial conclusions (Leonard-Barton 1990), we compared the interview results with other sources: the firms' homepages, annual reports, and other documents. Following the suggestions by Miles and Huberman (1994), we reduced and organized the mass of data through writing summaries and discarding irrelevant data.

Results and Discussion

Although 6 firms can be categorized as born-again globals or -internationals, they represent different internationalization paths: some are passive/sporadic exporters, while others are more active. We can conclude that for some wineries, the decision to start exporting is unplanned (Duarte Alonso et al. 2014) as Firms 3, 4, and 7 internationalized due to a sudden order. On the other hand, some owners—for instance, of Firms 6 and 8—actively pursued internationalization. Some internationalization attempts have not succeeded: five firms have partially or fully exited one or more markets and three have made unsuccessful entry attempts, but two firms have also managed to reenter the exited markets.

Reasons for internationalizing but also factors affecting internationalization differed. Some firms—for instance, Firms 6 and 8—started exporting due to declining profits or high local competition (Duarte Alonso et al. 2014; Schueffel et al. 2014) but none did it due to following local competitors. Also, due to lacking network relationships, knowledge, or other resources (Chetty and Blankenburg Holm 2000), Firm 5 has still not started exporting and several owners admitted that due to the firm's smallness and lack of contacts, they internationalized later. Low awareness of international opportunities, low international competitiveness, or attractive domestic growth opportunities (Wilkinson et al. 2000) also resulted in internationalizing late as these firms were small and did not need to internationalize soon after establishment.

In addition to getting sudden foreign orders in cases of Firms 3, 4, and 7, the firms' sudden internationalization was caused by management change or changes in the owners' mindsets (1, 2 and 8). Thus, critical incidents like ownership/

management changes or getting foreign orders may cause internationalization (Bell et al. 2003). In addition, participating in international trade fairs/exhibitions may result in internationalization (Kontinen and Ojala 2012) but some owners—for instance, of Firms 1, 2, 3, and 5—also did not manage to create useful contacts at some of them as it is hard for newcomers to enter existing networks (Chetty and Blankenburg Holm 2000).

Due to language barriers, some owners had to rely mainly on their friends/ acquaintances during internationalization, while some used such connections as an additional exporting opportunity. Thus, networking—although it is not always easy—can help firms to internationalize (Carneiro Zenbet al. 2013; Dalmoro 2007; Kontinen and Ojala 2012; Maurel 2009; Schueffel et al. 2014).

In addition to being affected by different factors, the owners have not shared the same attitude toward internationalization; some (owners of Firms 2, 4, 6 and 7) are interested and optimistic while some (Firm 3) are somewhat disappointed or lack time/resources to export more (1 and 8); for instance, according to the owner of Firm 8, exporting "is difficult, as I am the only person working on everything." Consequently, for internationalization, it is important that the manager perceives benefit from it (Maurel 2009; Suarez-Ortega and Alamo-Vera 2005) as firms with most interested owners have internationalized faster and entered more distant markets.

All firms have been, to some extent, tourist oriented: they have organized wine tastings and/or other events for local/foreign tourists, cooperated with tourist agencies, other producers, hotels, or other partners; moreover, they have websites and road signs. All have benefited from tourists in their internationalization: for instance, sold wine directly to tourists. Thus, we can conclude that wine tourism can create opportunities to sell directly to foreign customers (Beames 2003; Charters and Ali-Knight 2002; Getz et al. 1999; Getz and Brown 2006; Mancino and Lo Presti 2012; Marzo-Navarro and Pedraja-Iglesias 2009, 2012). Also, we can state that international tourists may (help to) identify business opportunities and, as a result, wineries can start exporting (Beames 2003; Fischer and Gil-Alana 2009; Kulendran and Wilson 2000) as in six cases, tourists either started importing wine themselves or contacted an importer in their home country.

Despite the above positive effects, for several firms, tourists were not the main priority. The owners of Firms 1, 4, and 8 evaluated the share of tourist-related income to be 20 % or less, and the owner of Firm 6 complained that attracting tourists did not result in sufficient increase in revenue and turnover. Moreover, the owner of Firm 1 admitted: "In several occasions, tourists have told me that they know a friend or relative or have a contact for importing our wine to their country, but they have never contacted us again. We have never contacted them, either, because we lack time and we do not have an export manager." Thus, we can conclude that for many wine-makers, the main focus is on growing grapes/ producing wine: tourism is perceived as a secondary activity, a distraction or a cause of additional costs (Beames 2003; Mancino and Lo Presti 2012; Sevil and Yüncü 2009).

Conclusion and Implications for Theory and Practice

This chapter contributed to the literature on international business, international entrepreneurship, and wine tourism/wine business by explaining why several Italian wine producers internationalized like born-again globals or -internationals and how international tourism affected their internationalization. Based on eight cases, we can conclude that international tourism permitted Italian wine SMEs to create relationships/networks in tourists' foreign markets and to expand internationally. In several cases, both wine SMEs and international visitors identified business opportunities, and this led to collaboration for selling wine to the visitors' home countries. In other cases, international tourists suggested the firm to contact an importer or decided to contact an importer themselves for getting access to Bianchello del Metauro wine in their country of origin. Despite the above positive effects, tourism was not the main activity for some owners/managers, and not all of them fully understood its importance for internationalization. Also, we have to note that in addition to tourism, these firms' internationalization was also affected by management/ownership changes, personal relationships/networks, increased local competition, receiving sudden foreign orders or other factors.

Although most of these firms were relatively successful in internationalization, they seemed to suffer from a lack of strategy: for instance, the owners/managers attended trade fairs and conducted other activities without a clear plan/objective. Consequently, they could consider following a more strategic approach: develop an internationalization strategy, analyze foreign markets' potential, and determine a minimum level of investments. Also, to overcome the lack of time and financial resources, they could cooperate with other local producers.

In the future, more firms from this and other regions should be studied. For example, it would be interesting to find out if (wine) tourists contribute to souvenir or food producers' exports or to increasing foreign investment flows. Collecting survey data would increase the generalizability of the results. Finally, firms that have exited and reentered markets once or, especially, several times due to mainly relying on tourists' assistance need more attention as they are still under-researched.

Acknowledgements The research was financed by the Estonian Science Foundation's Grant No. 8546 and institutional research grant of the Estonian Research Council No. IUT20-49.

References available upon request.

Community Destination Branding: Potential and Paradox

Samantha Murdy and Matthew Alexander

Abstract For destinations to compete in a context of global competition, they rely on their destination image as a way to position themselves and resonate with prospective visitors. The image of the destination is created in part through the identity of the community. Despite longstanding efforts to move community-based initiatives more to the centre of tourism planning (Hall 2008; Jamal and Getz 1995; Murphy 1985), research on community involvement in tourism activities can often result in pessimistic conclusions. Concerns are usually centred on efforts to involve communities which are driven by multinational corporations and, as such, are largely top-down processes. In these cases, only lip service is paid to involving local residents in planning and as such community involvement may suffer from tokenism. Alternatively, doubt is also placed on the ability of communities to make a valuable contribution (Aas et al. 2005; Campbell 1999; Simmons 1994) or the lack of cohesion within communities (Burns 2004; Simpson 2008). Hamilton and Alexander (2013) suggest that success can be achieved through a more organic co-created approach, where communities are given the freedom to develop their own identities.

This study focuses on a case study of a town in the highlands of Scotland — Pitlochry. Pitlochry is a small town located on the River Tummel within the Perth and Kinross county, and with a population of approximately 2500 the town remains reliant on the income generated by tourism. In line with well-established case study methods and procedures (Yin 2003), multiple methods of data collection were utilised including interviews, observation, and documentary analysis. In-depth interviews were undertaken with residents of the community. Interview participants were selected on the basis of their involvement in a wide range of tourism activities with varying degrees of community involvement. Participant and non-participant observation at various tourist attractions and sites and documentary analysis (including analysis of photographs) were also conducted. Four overall themes were identified within the data collection: the Pitlochry brand, community engagement, motivations,

S. Murdy (✉) • M. Alexander
University of Strathclyde, Glasgow, UK
e-mail: samantha.murdy@strath.ac.uk; matthew.j.alexander@strath.ac.uk

© Academy of Marketing Science 2016
L. Petruzzellis, R.S. Winer (eds.), *Rediscovering the Essentiality of Marketing*,
Developments in Marketing Science: Proceedings of the Academy of Marketing
Science, DOI 10.1007/978-3-319-29877-1_187

941

and funding. The Pitlochry brand explored the community-driven promotion of the destination. Community engagement consisted of four sub-themes: taking owner-ship, free riders, surrogate council, and succession planning. Motivations consisted of two sub-themes: satisfaction and business success. Funding revolved around the need to compete for grants and fundraise to ensure the projects could continue. All of these themes revolved around the need to enhance the beauty and liveability of the town, and a benefit of this is the increased visitation. Community involvement in destination branding presents a paradox. Our case suggests that on the one hand community involvement can create many benefits for a community including increased tourism visits; increased satisfaction of residents and visitors and; a more focussed branding effort created through a bottom-up process. However, community involvement is not without sacrifices particularly, in our case, considerable time and effort by a few committed individuals. There is also evidence here of both free rider, funding and sustainability problems which may dissuade other communities from embarking on similar programmes. Our study suggests that value can be gained by empowering smaller communities to take increased ownership of destination branding but handing over complete control may lead to sustainability problems and lead to a lack of continuity.

References available upon request.

Tempest in a Tea-Pot or a Crisis on the Sea: An Analysis of the Effect of Spectacular Cruise Failures

P. Sergius Koku

Introduction

This study assesses the financial effects of spectacular "cruise failures" and will, on the basis of this assessment, make macro and micro policy recommendations. The macro policies will involve public policy in general while the micro policies involve the individual companies.

Because the term "cruise failure" is new to the literature, I will begin the paper by explaining its meaning. By "cruise failure," I mean the failure of the cruise line to deliver fun, relaxation, and safety that the passengers had anticipated and have been promised by cruise line. Cruise failures could be attributed to several causes some of which are man-made while others are not. Cruise failures include but are not limited to outbreak of diseases on board such as the gastrointestinal problems that attacked passengers on a Crown Princess' ship in February 2012, engine failure which plagued Carnival's Triumph in February 2013 during which the engine caught fire, hurricanes, death or drowning while on the high seas, and fatal accidents such as the boat running aground as in the case of Costa Concordia off the coast of Italy.

Cruise failures lead to early termination of the cruise. Passengers who feel cheated out of their much anticipated fun vacations are left with a range of emotions (see (http://www.cnn.com/2013/03/14/travel/cruise-ship-trouble). While some passengers may feel relieved to be back on dry land safely, others feel may extreme anger. Because of the anticlimactic nature of cruise failures and the human stories involved, they often attract heavy media attention (see U.S. News and World Report, November 17, 2014).

P.S. Koku (✉)
Florida Atlantic University, Boca Raton, FL, USA
e-mail: Koku@fau.edu

© Academy of Marketing Science 2016   943
L. Petruzzellis, R.S. Winer (eds.), *Rediscovering the Essentiality of Marketing*,
Developments in Marketing Science: Proceedings of the Academy of Marketing
Science, DOI 10.1007/978-3-319-29877-1_188

Because passengers who feel cheated out of their vacation and are angry may likely file lawsuits for breach of contract and the fact that the negative news coverage may scare away future passengers as well as potential investors, I hypothesize that cruise failures cost cruise lines significant sums of money both out-of-pocket and loss in equity.

Previous Studies

Vacation cruises are not new. In fact, an argument could be made that even the *Titanic* was partly a cruise liner in addition to serving as a means of transportation on its disastrous maiden voyage in 1912. Unfortunately, the legendary *Titanic* also represents a quintessential "cruise failure" as I have defined it above. The popularity of vacation cruises has increased over the years and so is the number of consumers who patronize the industry. According to Satistica (2014), the worldwide expenditure of the industry increased from 17.59 billion dollars in 2011 to 18.72 billion dollars in 2013 notwithstanding the recession. The Cruise Lines International also reported a 77 % increase in worldwide demand for cruising from 12 million in 2003 to 21.3 million in 2013.

It is not surprising that the popularity of cruise vacations has attracted the interest of scholars as well. These scholars are interested in such issues as the motivation of cruise vacationers (Hung and Petrick 2011), their perception of the value of a cruise (Duman and Mattila 2005), and the perceived image of cruise travel (Park 2006). However, only a few studies such as the current study examined the financial dimension to the cruise industry. Li and Petrick (2008) who were interested in the role of loyalty programs in cruising intentions as well as their financial implications used an investment model to analyze cruise loyalty programs. The authors found that loyalty is a function of cruise passengers' satisfaction with the quality of the cruise. In examining the financial value of first-time cruise vacationers and repeat cruise vacationers, Petrick (2004) concluded that whereas first-time passengers are less price-sensitive and spend more than loyal passengers, the latter are more likely than the former to spread positive word of mouth.

While these studies are interesting, none, to the best of my knowledge has investigated the actual financial cost of cruise failures even though news of cruise failures have been spectacularly stunning. Could it be that these failures were cost-less? Even if they were costless, could they not have triggered any policy changes? The fact that cruise failures, at the minimum, put people's lives at risk should lead inquiry along the policy lines. Secondly, the fact the cruise failures were not limited to only the United Sates as evidenced in the Costa Concordia episode in Italy (http://www.cnn.com/2015/02/11/world/costa-concordia-trial) furthers the argument for a global policy solution. Thirdly, analysis of the actual cost of these failures could push investors to demand more accountability from the company officers, that is, if the financial costs are significant.

The true cost of a cruise failure is a sum of several costs. For example, as indicated above, cruise failures have cost the cruise liners in negative publicity. Secondly, there is the cost that is associated with possible litigation. Furthermore, there are costs due to lost customers, and possibly due to lost investors. I assess these costs through the use of the event study technique which I briefly discuss under methodology.

Hypotheses

Based on the above discussions, I developed the following hypotheses:

H_1: Cruise failures are costly to the cruise industry in general.

This hypothesis is based on the fact that many people will be scared away from taking a cruise as a result of a particular failure.

H_2: Cruise failures are not costly to the cruise industry.

The second hypothesis is a rival hypothesis to H_1 and is based on the fact that in order to blunt the effect of a failure, the cruise industry in general goes into "high gear" with publicity and advertising campaign whenever a failure occurs. If these advertisements are effective and achieve their goals which are to paint the picture that everything is rosy and that the failure is only an isolated incident, then the financial effect of the failure will be negligible.

H_3: A cruise failure is costly to the company that experiences the failure.

The third hypothesis is based on the fact that the company that experienced the failure will be the direct target of lawsuits, negative word-of-mouth advertisements, and the (direct) negative media.

Data

I obtained data on cruise failures that occurred between January 1, 2000 and December 31, 2013 using such databases as Lexis Nexis, indices to newspapers such as the *New York Times, Washington Post, Christian Monitor, London Times,* and the *Wall Street Journal*. I obtained a total of 21 events. Because the event study methodology works only for publicly traded firms, I obtained information on only publicly traded firms and extracted the daily market returns data from CRSP tapes (Center for Research in Security Prices, University of Chicago). Five of the events were dropped because of confounding information, events, or gaps in the trading the period over which I estimated the parameters.

Methodology

Because cruise failures are unanticipated events, I argue that the event study technique is appropriate for measuring the market's reaction to their occurrence. This reaction will then be used to estimate the financial cost of the failure to both the firm and industry. I therefore analyzed the effects of news of cruise failures on the market value of the firms using the event study methodology (Brown and Warner 1985; Fama et al. 1969). I used the market model which is based on the argument that the expected return on any asset i in the market is linearly related to the contemporaneous return on the market portfolio such that

$$R_{i,t} = \alpha_i + \beta_i R_{m,t} + \varepsilon_{i,t} \tag{1}$$

where

$R_{i,t}$ = random return on asset i
α_i and β_i are parameters,
$R_{m,t}$ = return on the market portfolio, and
$\varepsilon_{i,t}$ = residuals, and

$$\varepsilon_{i,t} = R_{i,t} - \alpha_i - \beta_i R_{m,t} \tag{2}$$

The event-study methodology is based on the efficient market hypothesis and the rational expectations theory which in simple language could be said to posit that the asset prices in the market quickly adjust to incorporate information available in the market in order to establish market prices (Fama et al. 1969). After incorporating the expected information in the market, the market quickly reestablishes equilibrium. The residuals ($\varepsilon_{i,t}$), as indicated in Eq. (2) above, under such a condition, are not significantly different from zero. Thus, a positively significant residual deviation from zero is indicative of positive unexpected news in the market. Vice versa, a significantly negative deviation from zero is indicative of negative unexpected news. In case of cruise failures, I expect negative abnormal returns.

I estimated the parameters of Eq. (1) using a linear regression over a period starting from 220 trading days to 15 trading days before t0, the day that news of the cruise failure was made public. I used the parameters to forecast expected returns for a period of 15 days prior to the day that the news was made public (t0) to 5 days after the news became public (t+5), and measured the impact of the event by subtracting the actual returns from the forecasted returns. I divided each firm's excess returns by the estimated standard deviation to correct for variance.

The presence of significantly positive abnormal returns is indicative of the presence of new unanticipated good news, and the presence of significantly negative abnormal returns is indicative of new unanticipated bad news (Brown and Warner 1985). I computed the z-statistics of the abnormal returns following Mikkelson and Partch (1988). Because news of cruise failures are nationally and internally covered, the negative publicity is similar to that of a product recall (Jarrel and Peltzman 1985).

Table 1 Cumulative abnormal returns

Days (t)	Mean cumulative abnormal returns (%)	Generalized sign z
−30, −2	−5.6	.256 not significant
−1, 0	−0.64	−1.376 significant at 10 %
0	−0.64	−1.3677 significant at 10 %
+1, +30	−1.84	.278 not significant

Results

The results of my analyses are interesting and insightful and reported in Table 1.

The abnormal return for the industry's shares was −1.366 at $t0$ the day that the event occurred and was marginally negatively significant at 10 % one-tail t-test. This result marginally supports H_1. Because H_1 is supported, H_2 is rejected. Firm level analysis shows that only three of the 16 events have significant abnormal returns on day $t0$. Two of them were significant at the 10 % level while one was significant at 1 % level. These results fail to support H_3 which is counterintuitive. It suggests that even though the market reacts (generally) negatively to the industry when news of a cruise failure "hits" the "wires" or reaches the market, investors do not react significantly negatively to the individual cruise line.

While different interpretations can be assigned to this result, it could also be interpreted as a win for the public relations campaign for the company that suffers the cruise failure. On the basis of this result, perhaps a micro-level policy change by the board of directors of the company that suffers from cruise failure might be unnecessary. However, the public policy issues remain relevant. For example, how could cruise lines be held to the sanitation or health standards in the country from which they draw their primary passengers? How could the different countries around the world from which the cruise line draw passengers regulate the safety of the passengers? How could forum shopping in which the cruise lines limit the venues/jurisdictions in which they can be sued be eliminated? Perhaps, a good start is to eliminate the policy that makes it possible for a liner to be registered under a foreign flag where it does not operate. Making the liners operate under the flag of the country in which they conduct their primary business/activity could make it possible to properly hold them accountable.

References available upon request.

Exploring Resident Versus Visiting Nationalities' Perceptions on Airport Service Quality

Angelos Pantouvakis, Maria Karakasnaki, and Maria Francesca Renzi

Introduction

In order to survive in the current customer-driven market economy, companies should continuously strive for enhancing customer satisfaction through offering high-quality services. The airport industry constitutes no exception. Due to the specific, multicultural nature of this industry, in which hundreds of passengers coming from different nations interact and experience the same airport services, managers should dedicate considerable effort towards improving the service quality provided to them. In the tourism literature, the important role that different cultures play when exploring service quality or satisfaction issues has gained increased support. Specifically, it has been proven that customers from different countries of origin tend to evaluate differently the service quality they receive. However, these issues are rather unexplored in the international airport environment. The purpose of this chapter is to address this gap in the literature. Drawing data from 911 passengers departing from Fiumicino Airport in Rome, Italy (Aeroporti di Roma), the aims of this study are (1) to explore the underlying dimensions of airport service quality and (2) to identify potential differences in perceptions of Italian passengers and those of other nationalities. Results indicate that Italian air travelers tend to under-value the service quality provided to them by their homeland's airport compared to their foreign counterparts.

A. Pantouvakis (✉) • M. Karakasnaki
University of Piraeus, Piraeus, Greece
e-mail: angelos@pantouvakis.eu; mariakar@webmail.unipi.gr

M.F. Renzi
University of Roma Tre, Rome, Italy
e-mail: mariafrancesca.renzi@uniroma3.it

© Academy of Marketing Science 2016
L. Petruzzellis, R.S. Winer (eds.), *Rediscovering the Essentiality of Marketing*,
Developments in Marketing Science: Proceedings of the Academy of Marketing
Science, DOI 10.1007/978-3-319-29877-1_189

Background

Cultures/Nationalities

It is widely acknowledged in the literature that different national or cultural characteristics can strongly affect customers' perceptions of the satisfaction from the service offered (Keillor et al. 2007; Woodside et al. 2011). In the academic world, one of the most widely accepted national cultural frameworks is that of Hofstede (1980, 2001). In fact, the framework that he designed has been adopted by many authors in their effort to explore a variety of marketing issues. For instance, Van Birgelen et al. (2002) indicated that national culture moderates the relationship between perceived service quality and customer satisfaction in the case of an after-sales service contact mode mediated by technology.

So far, various studies have been undertaken to emphasize the role that culture plays when examining service quality or satisfaction issues. Specifically, in the fields of tourism and hospitality, it has been demonstrated that individual preferences and expectations (Yuksel 2004) as well as level of satisfaction (Bowen and Clarke 2002) can vary significantly between travelers from different countries. Specifically, Kozak (2001) found that British travelers to Turkey and Mallorca were more satisfied in terms of accommodation, cleanliness, and hygiene than Germans. Moreover, Pantouvakis (2013) confirmed that national culture differences affect perceived satisfaction when he examined a number of hotel tourists from ten different countries visiting the island of Crete.

Airport Service Quality

Considering the rapidly changing nature of airport industry, airports should place a great emphasis on improving the service quality offered to their passengers. In order to attain a sustainable competitive advantage, airport managers should continuously concentrate their efforts towards meeting or exceeding airport users' demands (Fodness and Murray 2007). As Yeh and Kuo (2003) point out, the increasing urgency of adopting passenger-oriented management practices is also dictated by the fact that airport users' perceptions of their experience in an international airport can have a determinant influence on the future tourist flow of that country.

Recognizing the importance of enhancing passenger satisfaction through the provision of high-quality services, many studies have been conducted so far stressing that issue. In fact, various authors have attempted to highlight the complicated nature of airport services through the development of solid conceptual models that reflect the different dimensions of airport service quality (e.g., Fodness and Murray 2007). In recent studies, Liou et al. (2011), using a large sample of customers from an international airport in Taiwan, investigated passengers' perceptions of the overall landside level of service, whereas De Nicola et al. (2013) analyzed 20 Italian airports management companies in order to determine the impact of airport service quality on its productive performance. Moreover, Lubbe et al. (2011) drawing data from an international airport in South Africa, concluded that differences in airport service quality perceptions are exhibited between business and leisure travelers or between frequent and infrequent passengers.

Cultures/Nationalities and Airport Service Quality

Although airport service quality considerations have received increased academic attention, the investigation of how different national cultures perceive and assess the various services offered in an airport setting is rather limited. In fact, only a few studies have been found exploring that issue. Crotts and Erdmann (2000), using a sample of overseas visitors to the USA and adopting Hofstede's national culture framework, concluded, among other things, that the respondents' ratings of airport facilities varied significantly between the different masculinity national cultures groups. Also, in his study, Kozak (2001) noted that British tourists were slightly more satisfied than German tourists in terms of availability of facilities and services at the destination airport in Mallorca.

Generally, from the above discussion it can be surmised that given the complexity and variety of airport services, a closer identification of passengers' perceptions and expectations of what constitutes high airport service quality would contribute towards boosting their airport experience. On the other hand, airports constitute an industry where numerous multinational encounters take place on a daily basis. Since it has been generally proven that the different national or cultural characteristics influence the way customers perceive service quality and accordingly their satisfaction level, a need emerges to examine national differences of service quality perceptions in international airports, a field in which this issue is rather under researched. Accordingly, two research questions are formulated:

Research question 1: Which are the underlying dimensions of airport service quality?

Research question 2: Do passengers from one country evaluate differently the service quality offered by their homeland's airport industry compared to other visiting foreign nationalities?

Methodology

A structured questionnaire was administered to a randomly selected sample of air passengers of different nationalities departing from Fiumicino Airport in Rome, Italy, one of the emerging most important EU airports. Nine hundred and eleven usable responses were obtained in 25 not consecutive days at different times. The scale items used to measure airport service quality were derived from previous literature in the relevant topics and were organized in four categories, namely servicescape/physical environment (e.g., Tsai et al. 2011; Bogicevic et al. 2013), image (e.g., Ariffin and Yahaya 2013), signage (Liou et al. 2011; Bogicevic et al. 2013; Yeh and Kuo 2003), and speed of control (e.g., De Nicola et al. 2013; Lubbe et al. 2011; Fodness and Murray 2007). All items were measured on a 6-point Likert type scale (1 = strongly disagree, 6 = strongly agree). Exploratory Factor Analysis was performed to extract the underlying factors of airport service quality. The perceptions' differences among respondents of different nationalities were analyzed through ANOVA.

Results and Discussion

Exploratory factor analysis resulted in three factors with an eigenvalue greater than 1. The KMO Measure of Sampling Adequacy is .932 and the total variance explained is 59.54 %. Specifically, factor 1 represents different aspects of the airport's physical environment (such as the cleanliness, availability of seats, lighting and level of noise), as well as passengers' impressions of the various facilities. Factor 2 includes statements about the level of information available at the airport, regarding external and internal signs, screens, and video information displays). Factor 3 consists of items referring to the control procedures (security or check in), for example, the speed of control execution and staff competence. It becomes obvious that the two dimensions of servicescape and image collapse in one single factor. Subsequently, the resulting factors are labeled as follows: Factor 1: "Servicescape and Image," Factor 2: "Signage," Factor 3: "Speed of control."

Although the EFA results revealed three distinct underlying factors of airport service quality, however perceptions' differences were analyzed based on the initial four dimensions. In order to detect different perceptions of airport service quality among the respondents of various nationalities, two groups were developed. Group 1 of respondents includes the Italian passengers. Group 2 consists of other travelers from foreign, visiting nationalities (from the USA, Canada, Southern America, Australia, Europe, Africa, and Asia). ANOVA results revealed significant differences among the two groups of respondents in all dimensions except for "Image" (research question 2).

The analysis results confirm that passengers' perceptions of provided quality can vary significantly when their different national characteristics are taken into account. In an international airport, all travelers, irrespective of their country of origin, experience the same service at the same time; however, they tend to value the wide range of services offered and evaluate airport facilities in a diverse way. The current study demonstrates that Italian passengers tend to be more conservative and stricter than their counterparts from different countries of the world, when they are requested to evaluate the service quality offered by their homeland's airport industry. This becomes strongly evident by the fact that Italian air travelers displayed significant lower rating scores in all dimensions of airport service quality, except for one, compared to visiting passengers from foreign countries. Moreover, a rather interesting conclusion emerges when examining the nonsignificant difference regarding the "Image" dimension. Specifically, it is revealed that although Italians and passengers from other nationalities appear to have different perceptions of airport service quality, nevertheless their expectations, as they are reflected in the "Image" dimension, tend to coincide.

To sum up, increasing customer satisfaction should become an important priority for airport managers. The current study can provide useful insights regarding the way passengers evaluate airport service quality. Moreover, it highlights the importance of taking into consideration national differences when assessing passengers' evaluation of airport services.

References available upon request.

Hedonic Ethics: Understanding Tourists' Self-Defined Ethical Experiences

Sheila Malone

Introduction

not he who abstains, but he who enjoys without being carried away, is the master of his pleasures
   (Ueberweg 1891, p. 97)

This chapter explores the ways in which individuals seek out consumption experiences that are driven by pleasure and which connect with a sense of self-identity. We theorize the experience of pleasure stemming from ethical consumption practices as "hedonic ethics"; a particular type of hedonic experience inspired by ethically driven consumption practices. Building on Soper's theory of Alternative Hedonism, we investigate the notion of hedonic ethics in a participant-defined "ethical" tourism context. We employ a qualitative, hermeneutic phenomenological approach, which concentrates on individuals' subjective experiences as part of their lifeword, their meaning, and how they make sense of them. The findings provide detailed insight into the role emotion plays in the process of self-verification. The self-conscious emotions of pride, both positive and negative (i.e., hubris), and disgust are highlighted as significant. Implications for marketing research and practice are outlined.

S. Malone (✉)
Lancaster University, Lancaster, UK
e-mail: sheila.malone@lancaster.ac.uk

© Academy of Marketing Science 2016
L. Petruzzellis, R.S. Winer (eds.), *Rediscovering the Essentiality of Marketing*,
Developments in Marketing Science: Proceedings of the Academy of Marketing
Science, DOI 10.1007/978-3-319-29877-1_190

The Role of Emotion in Ethical Choice

How individuals think, feel and act is often representative of their sense of self. The emotional dimensions of self-identity, especially those felt in the practice of identity-consistent behavior, are important as they can lead to a deeper level of personal fulfillment. This chapter aims to address the need for detailed analyses of consumers' experiences of emotions in the context of their identities. That is, our behavior is not only guided by who we are, our sense of self, but also by how these experiences makes us feel. Thus, we investigate how emotions are linked to the self-concept. In doing so, we consider an alternative view of hedonic consumption as motivated by a sense of self; an ethically driven self. The need to embrace new modes of thinking about human pleasure and self-realization is highlighted by Soper (2008) in her conceptualization of the pleasure principle, which she terms: "alternative hedonism" (p. 572). Here, Soper argues that to consume differently from others, "in line" with one's ethical beliefs and values is intrinsically a hedonic experience. She suggests that a hedonistic aspect is derived from an oppositional sense of self, as the consumer positions oneself against the "mainstream." In this case, the oppositional sense of self may be motivated by two goals: an ideal social self, to be perceived by others as an "ethical consumer" or by one's interpersonal goals based on self-expression and feelings of pleasure and belonging. Although Soper does not comprehensively link alternative hedonism to the self-concept, she positions pleasure within the realm of alternative, more rewarding consumption practices. According to Wattanasuwan (2005) such practices are often based on an individual's sense of self as a more rewarding way of experiencing. They are the foundation of one's sense of self, based on the consumption choices a person makes. That is, we "make choices to enhance their experience of identity-consistent emotions" (Coleman and Williams 2013, p. 203). To date, Soper's (2007, 2008) work remains at the conceptual level and has yet to be explored via empirical research.

The context for this research is ethical tourism. Tourism is self-evidently an emotionally rich, hedonically charged consumption experience (Pearce 2009) that often acts as a platform from which the consumer can construct a sense of self-identity (Cohen 1984; Rojek 1995). Self-defined ethical consumers reflect their identities through their behaviors (e.g., Shaw and Newholm 2002). Such choices are often strongly linked to identity constructions (Oyserman 2009), as identity is "the motivational impetus for identity-oriented beliefs and behavior" (Reed et al. 2012, p. 315). Thus, ethical actions can serve both intrapersonal (self-verification) and interpersonal (self-expression or belonging) goals and can thus influence future behavior. Although the self-concept has received considerable attention in the marketing and consumer behavior literature (Reed et al. 2012), the need for a better understanding of the role emotion plays in the identity-formation process is necessary, not only in relation to how we feel about our possessions and their symbolic representations or as a means for identity-conflict resolution (Ahuvia 2005), but how such experiences make us feel, how they impact our sense of self and how they help guide our behavior. The role of emotion in linking consumption to self-identity is ambiguous despite the fact that consumption encounters are often regarded as emotion rich (Richins 1997) or even emotionally driven experiences (Elliott 1998).

Methods

Given the malleable nature of emotional experience, a qualitative research approach was applied. Specifically, a hermeneutic phenomenology approach (Heidegger 1962), which focused on the exploration and understanding of participants' lived experiences and perceptions as part of their "lifeworld" was adopted. Based on the theory of hermeneutic phenomenology, we focus on three theoretical roots: phenomenology, hermeneutics, and the study that is idiographic in nature. It differs from other qualitative research methods such as grounded theory and content analysis, although some similarities are evident. An idiographic focus concentrates on the particular, that is, a particular phenomenon in a "particular context" interpreted by a "particular" participant group, hence offering "a deeper, more personal, individualised analysis" (Brocki and Wearden 2006, p. 99). Thus, a relatively homogenous participant group was required. On the basis of self-identified ethical beliefs in tourism choices, participants were accessed through ethical tourism networks and social networking sites. Using a semi-structured interview style with the aid of an interview schedule to complement phenomenological protocols to allow the lifeworld of the participant to emerge through depth probing, a total of 13 interviews were carried out (six males and seven females) with participants ranging between 29 and 48 years. It is considered to be a solid study that ensures depth of analysis over breadth (Brocki and Wearden 2006). Once the data was collected and transcribed, the analytic stages commenced according to the guidelines of Braun and Clarke's (2006) thematic analysis.

Findings and Discussion

The following section presents and discusses the themes emerging from the data using *illustrative* examples from the data. Due to the phenomenological perspective, it is important to note that this study concentrates on the subjective representation of an individual's emotional experiences (i.e., pleasure) often expressed through feeling states. We discuss how identity-consistent emotions enable individuals to verify their ethical sense of self. We highlight how such emotions are experienced in a positive and negative manner, with both having an important role to play in the self-verification process.

Hedonic Ethics: Verifying an Ethical Sense of Self—Feelings of Pride and Disgust

The primary self-conscious emotion of pride was evident in the participants' descriptions of their ethical tourism encounters. For instance, negative pride is conveyed through implied feelings of superiority as participants tended to describe their tourism experiences as very different from conventional mass-market holidays, which was interpreted as a means of establishing and maintaining an ethical sense of self. Hart and Matsuba (2007) and Lewis (2007) refer to negative pride as expressed through feelings of arrogance or superiority often resulting in narcissistic characteristics. In general, the experience of negative or hubristic pride in this study was action–other related, aimed at mass package tourists and their associated behaviors. For instance, Joanna talked about her ethical tourism experience by contrasting it with a mainstream tourism encounter as she claimed: *"When I think of mainstream tourism, it seems like a nightmare, no real immersion or experience to be had, just the same old thing wherever you go. No responsibility. I love my tourism choice and I'm sure mainstream tourists love their choice but for me, the trips I do, I am happy. I wouldn't want to do mass tourism; it wouldn't give me any pleasure. Whereas for some people, to sit on the sand that is all they want. ....This is what I do, this is where I feel I belong, it gives me the most pleasure, and I am relaxed and happy. It's a pity that there isn't more engagement, but you cannot make people engage themselves if they don't want to. It's a pity that there isn't more curiosity, but for me, I'd have no pleasure in it. I want to engage with people. My pleasure is in the simple things."* Expressed through a sense of pity, Joanna's negative pride leads to inferred feelings of superiority over mainstream tourism experiences, which lack engagement and curiosity. Epitomized in her attempt to differentiate and provide a rationale for her choice, here Joanna is suggesting that mainstream tourism encounters are incongruent with her sense of self as there is *"no responsibility"* consequently she claims such practices are: *"like a nightmare, no real immersion or experiences to be had."* In making such claims, connects her ethical choice and identity construction with phrases such as *"This is what I do"* (see Coleman and Williams 2013; Oyserman 2009). In this case, her perceived ethical actions serve two purposes: (1) verification of her sense of self as an ethical person, reflected in her beliefs and actions which she contrasts with the experiences of others, and (2) valediction of her self-identity, expressed through contrasting emotions of mainstream tourists, which are perceived to lack pleasure and her own sense of what is pleasurable: *"I'd have no pleasure in it...I want to engage with people...my pleasure is in the simple things."* In this case, Joanna acts in a way that is consonant with her ethical self-identity, reinforcing it, and which is qualified by emotional outcomes.

Negative pride can have an inverse effect that results in a highly positive and rewarding experience (Lewis 1992). Pride is often constructed through feelings of joy over an action, thought, or feeling well done (Lewis 1993, 2007). Therefore, it is possible to infer that Joanna feel pride in her actions in relation to what other people do because these offer a more positive and rewarding way of experiencing travel. In this case, Joanna's identity is reflected in hedonic experiences. Joanna's sense of pleasure is constructed as a more rewarding way of experiencing, which is defined by her consumption choice. These feelings emanate from a particular type of consumption experience, which is validated on an emotional level. Although this highlights a more righteous form of hedonism, as expressed through feelings of superiority and a sense of belonging, Joanna's sense of self is verified as she claims: *"This is what I do (ethical tourism), this is where I feel I belong, it gives me the most pleasure, and I am relaxed and happy."* Her feelings of pride enable her to self-verify and as such Joanna could be construed as constructing an ideal self as she does not appear to be motivated by altruistic issues or the negative practices of mainstream tourists per se, but by self-interested motives for pleasure as she claims: "*I wouldn't want to do mass tourism; it wouldn't give me any pleasure.* Nonetheless, Joanna demonstrates not only a desire to consume differently, but also one that offers a more pleasurable experience. In a similar vein, Maureen talks about the efforts she exerts to source out more ethical options while on holiday. While contrasting such holidays to mainstream offerings, Maureen states: "*It's the thoughtlessness* (referring to mainstream tourist's behavior*), it's the waste of money and the impact that thoughtlessness is having. It is very hard to say actually because that means that I making a judgment on these people and I'm not, it just seems to be the right thing to do. […] I love camping in the UK. If I do other holidays they tend to be self-catered. I stay in hotels, and in the last six months I stayed in a hotel that had a very ethical stance on things and this makes me feel better. […] If you believe in it, you will source it out.*" Maureen proclaims a higher moral self as she states that choosing an ethical option is "*the right thing to do*," which "*makes me feel better.*" Redolent of Kant's normative ethics based on duty, Maureen appears to evaluate mainstream practices in a negative manner. In doing so, she expresses an ethical identity through her beliefs and actions: "*If you believe in it, you will source it out*," and her use of self-catered accommodation and UK camping holidays. Likewise, Sara demonstrates the pleasure derived from an ethical choice, not only as a holiday but also because it provides her with a sense of great pleasure, which is comforting. This provides a further example of the valedictory nature of hedonic pleasure in ethical consumption is provided as Sara states: "*I also think there is great pleasure in the choosing, I prefer to choose my own holiday and that is how I like it. To me, that's more pleasurable, I relax more and it is more comfortable with that choice because I made that choice. I enjoy it more.*" However, variations existed across the interviews with regard to the intensity of negative emotions experienced (i.e., pride) that were associated with the displeasure of others and their actions. For instance, Maureen expressed disgust towards mainstream tourists' behavior thus causing her to shun such places. She stated: "*I remember not going to Koh Penang because I heard about the filth of the place and the full moon parties where people were openly going to the toilet in the middle of the sea because there was nowhere else, and rubbish all over the place and drugs (.) that's disgusting! I avoided it, boycotted it […] it's not for me.*" Maureen actively sought to avoid perceived unethical behaviors and destinations, whereby boycotting connotes an active stance, linking the emotional response, implied feelings of disgust that are attached to particular actions of mass tourists, which in turn contributes to her own ethical identity. According to Haidt (2003, p. 857), "disgust helps to draw lines that separate a group from groups or individuals that are thought to be below one's own group." Such experiences echo Soper's (2008) notion of an alternative hedonism as individuals strive for their conceptualization of the "good life." The "good life," according to Soper, refers to ones dissatisfaction with materialism and consumerism, resulting in a tendency to opt for alternative forms of consumption practices and more rewarding ways of experiencing. For the participants in this study, they do not deny their desire for consumption per se; they refine such practices to complement their ethical beliefs and choose alternatives that are congruent with their sense of self. Soper argues that to consume differently in line with one's moral beliefs and values is, in itself, a hedonic experience: it is an "alternative hedonism" (Soper 2008, p. 572). It is evident in this study that negative feelings emanating from incongruent behaviors often led to more positive, albeit righteous, ways of consumption leading to positive feelings which enables a process of self-verification and valediction.

Conclusion and Implications for Practice and Theory

The findings of this study build on previous research in the fields of consumer ethics and tourism marketing by providing initial insight into the role of emotion in consumers' ethical consumption practices and how emotions play a pivotal role in self-verification process. As our knowledge of ethics in tourism is modest, understanding the role of emotions in consumers' self-defined ethical practices can facilitate the production of a more customized ethical tourism offering and promote and sustain future ethical behavior. From this study, it is apparent that ethical consumption behavior is grounded in a sense of self and is bound by emotion experience. It appears that emotions can have a direct impact on an individual's creation and maintenance of an ethical sense of self. As positive emotions tend to promote ethical action, it appears that negative emotions have an important role to play in discouraging unethical behavior, and in turn, reaffirming one's ethical self-concept. Such experiences often act as a catalyst for eliciting other emotions in the consumption experience. Thus, emotions have an integral role to play in ethical consumption experiences. We contribute to the literature by providing empirical support for the role of pleasure as central to sustaining and maintaining an individual's self-concept. In particular, we demonstrate how identity formation is reflected in the ways in which a subject feels about their actions and behavior (similar to the work of Passyn and Sujan 2012). However, we extend such studies by highlighting the interplay between pleasure, identity, and consumption. Specifically, we illustrate when, how and why individuals experience pleasure, as called for by Alba and Williams (2013), in a self-defining, ethical consumption context. It is evident from the findings that self-proclaimed ethical tourists experience pleasure not only in their choice formation, actions or behavior (when) but also experientially in the consumption encounter (how). This is because (why) an individual's self-identity, behavior and actions are considered fitting as reflected through their positive emotional state, i.e., pleasure. These emotional experiences occur during the consumption experience and are an important part of the consumption encounter.

From a supplier's perspective, understanding the alternative hedonism concept and its role in choosing an ethical tourism alternative facilitates a more customized offering therefore enabling suppliers to modify their marketing communications, to potentially gain customers or leverage any existing loyal customers. Malär et al. (2011) highlighted the significance of consumers' strong emotional attachment with products or services as enhancing their sense of self, which in turn generates greater consumer loyalty. From a marketing point of view, such knowledge enables an enhanced consumer segmentation process aimed at long-term commitment for existing ethical consumers, and the development of new targeting strategies through customizing marketing communications, branding of ethical products and services and by enhancing product/service design to elicit the relevant emotions required.

References available upon request.

A Proposed Benchmark Analysis of the Connection Between Wine Production and Destination Perception

Alessandro Bigi and Michelle Bonera

Introduction

Internet presents a special channel in the personal process of finding the touristic information, the formation of an individual opinion, and the communication of it to others. The tourists can find the information necessary for their travel needs, using a wide range of Internet tools like search engines (mainly Google), destination management systems (such as visitbritain.com), social networks and Web 2.0 portals (such as Tripadvisor, Facebook, Twitter, Ebookers, HolydayCheck, Orkut), price comparison websites (such as Expedia, Kelkoo, and also Trivago), photo sharing sites (like Flickr), software applications for tourist mobile phones, gps, Iphone app (like Foursquare), interactive guides (as Tripwolf), Q&A sites (i.e., Traveller and Mygola). In particular the world of social networks provides essential tools in the information and feedbacks exchange. Web 2.0 is, therefore, the place where it is now possible to interchange travel opinions and experiences and travel portals promote the formation of consumers communities with a relevant amount of user-generated contents (sharing of information). The social networking tools have been joined (canceling partially their effectiveness) by intermediaries tools, such as travel agencies, tour operators, and hotels social networks channels.

A. Bigi (✉)
KTH Royal Institute of Technology, Stockholm, Sweden
e-mail: abigi@marketingconcept.it

M. Bonera
Università degli Studi di Brescia, Brescia, Italy
e-mail: mbonera@eco.unibs.it

© Academy of Marketing Science 2016   963
L. Petruzzellis, R.S. Winer (eds.), *Rediscovering the Essentiality of Marketing*,
Developments in Marketing Science: Proceedings of the Academy of Marketing
Science, DOI 10.1007/978-3-319-29877-1_191

The relevance of consumer reviews has been acknowledged broadly, and tourism marketing managers are aware of the necessity for companies to monitor and manage their online reputation (e.g., O'Connor 2010; Ye et al. 2009; Zhang et al. 2010). The social networks influence deeply also the image of the touristic destinations, through them it is possible to know the general opinion and the perceived overall image of each destination. According to the recent studies on the image of the destinations, the flow of information that the tourist acquires allows the formation of the image of the destination, as Reynolds said (Echtner and Ritchie 2003), this process may consist of several steps that the model of Gunn (1072) fixed at seven: organic image that is the accumulation of mental images on travel experiences; induced image, as amended by additional information acquired from commercial sources; decision to make a journey; route to a destination; participate in the destination; return home; organic and induced image editing, based on the travel experience.

The purpose of this chapter is to determine what are the best user generated information and world of mouse feedbacks on the selected wine destinations perceived features and therefore perceived images and how the product image and the destination image are connected. It was conducted by comparing the French district of Reims in Champagne-Ardenne, known throughout the world for the production of Champagne and some emerging districts of Australia, Brazil, Chile, and South Africa. Especially for Australia, it was decided to consider the wine region of the Barossa Valley, for Brazil the Serra Gaucha in Rio Grande do Soul, for Chile, the Central Valley and finally to South Africa's Cape Winelands.

Background

Existent literature (Chang and Chen 1998) indicates that service quality is an important antecedent to business profitability. It is strongly linked with word-of-mouth and customer satisfaction, and indirectly with purchase intention and customer loyalty (Cronin and Taylor 1992; Harrison-Walker 2001; Sureshchandar et al. 2002). Most of the research conducted regarding service quality was conducted in the 1990s and early 2000s, and resulted in a large number of conceptual models and measurement tools (Seth et al. 2005). Although service quality no longer gets as much consideration from scholars as a decade ago, its importance cannot be overstated.

Customer satisfaction relies on the perceived difference (or gap) between service quality expectation and performance (Parasuraman et al. 1985; Seth et al. 2005). Its popular measurement scale is SERVQUAL (Parasuraman et al. 1988, 1991), which is based on the premise that service quality consists of five dimensions: tangibles, reliability, responsiveness, assurance, and empathy. The scale has been extensively used in a range of different industries and research settings, but not without criticism because of both conceptual and methodological concerns (Carman 1990; Babakus and Boller 1992; Buttle 1996).

SERVQUAL has, as well, been used in research that focused on the hospitality industry, with varying results. Saleh and Ryan (1991) applied SERQUAL effectively in a study of consumers' perception of service quality in hotels, and Akbaba (2006) confirmed that there were five dimensions but found a different factor structure. Over the time many authors developed revised measurement scales, including HOLSERV (Mei et al. 1999) and LODGSERV (Knutson et al. 1990) for hotels, and DINESERV (Stevens et al. 1995) for restaurants.

The research project takes off from the identification of the main perceived features of the tourist districts of wine taken into consideration, as they are identified by those who have had direct experience of the bid. For the analysis we use the HOLSERV plus scale that makes a distinction between "Employees" (personal service), "Tangibles" (tangible elements), and "Reliability" (reliability). Within the category of "tangibles" there is a distinction between "Tangible-Room," "Tangible-Hotel," and "Tangible-Outside," useful to our work because it allows us to understand if for tourists are more important the rooms, the Hotel or, on the other side, the location landscape and the environment and the destination.

Research Methods

The present research aims to determine what are the tourists perceptions of the wine districts features and hotels by comparing the French district of Reims in Champagne-Ardenne, known throughout the world for the production of Champagne and some emerging districts of Australia, Brazil, Chile, and South Africa. The analysis was conducted by processing the content of ratings obtained from the site www. tripadvisor.com, using the software Leximancer. Inspired by these considerations, the purpose of the research is to evaluate the different perceptions that consumers have with respect to the different areas.

The content analysis is a social science that is based on an understanding of human communication, including both the written communication, both graphical representations and the context (Kripprndorff 2004). This analysis involves understanding the meaning of the texts, phrases used, the keywords, and the authenticity of the same. It's a scientific and quantitative method, which has as its foundation concepts such as objectivity, intersubjectivity, the validity, and replicability of a specific document (Neuendorf 2002).

The information is represented by a conceptual map that provides the overall vision of the material, representing the main concepts in the text, as well as information on the ways in which they are connected. Essentially, the map allows the user to view the conceptual structure of a body text, and perform a direct search of documents. The interactive nature of the map allows to explore examples of concepts, the connections between them, as well as links to the original text.

The goal of concept learning is to find clusters of words that, when taken together as a concept, maximize the relevance of all the other words in the document. Once Leximancer ran the learning process, has developed a list of concepts in the text and identified their relationship with each other, the information is shown through a concept map. The concepts are grouped together at a higher level in "themes" when the map is generated. The concepts that frequently appear together in the same parts of the text are attracted to one another with force, and thus tend to settle near one another in the space of the map.

The themes help the interpretation of grouping concepts into clusters that are shown as colored circles on the map. The themes are "heat-mapped" to indicate its importance. This means that the most important topics are shown in red, the next in order of importance in orange and so on according to the chromatic scale. Therefore it is possible to identify a number of key issues relating to each wine-growing district. The identification of these issues considers a degree of connectivity equal to or greater than 2 % between the different concepts expressed in the reviews, and the importance attached to the issues themselves. The connectivity is the count of the concomitant presence of added each concept within the theme, with all concepts available. It provides an estimate of the coverage of a subject through the data.

The relevance is a representation of a percentage of the count value of each concept divided by the single count higher value. Consequently the concept more frequent will always have 100 % of relevance, regardless of the fact that it is necessary in all blocks of context.

Results and Discussion

To facilitate the description and comparison of the different destinations, it was decided to incorporate the themes that emerged from processing with Leximancer into five main categories: elements of the accommodation, personal, beverage, elements of attractiveness of the destination, brand or territorial.

The first category includes inside the hotel rooms and their related concepts such as comfort, cleanliness, the presence of Internet connection, parking, the view, the service of reception and ancillary services such as spa and sports facilities and food service inside. The second category concerns the performance of the staff, the courtesy, kindness, empathy, the ability to empathize with customers, and professionalism. The third category refers to both the atmosphere and the furnishings of the restaurants, and the food service itself, which includes the performance of the staff and the quality of food and wine. The fourth category includes a diverse set of factors ranging from the presence of the typical attractions and the beauty of its landscapes, its proximity to most popular places to accessibility of means of transport.

The category represented by the territorial brand encloses all those elements relating distinctiveness, exclusivity and recognition in the eyes of the tourist, can provide the destination, and the local wine image that boast of that mark, a clear and specific identity and at the same time to increase the perception of the value contained in the offer, in such a way as to generate and maintain a competitive advantage sustainable and lasting. At this point a comparison of each emerging destination with the well-established wine district of Reims can represent an interesting benchmark analysis in order to understand which are the main features that the emerging districts should invest on in order to reach a good positioning.

Barossa Valley and Reims

The comparison between concept maps on the Australian region of the Barossa Valley and those relating to the wine-growing district of Reims allows us to highlight a few minor differences. In particular, if the main theme in the reviews that refer to the Barossa Valley regards the performance of the staff, as far as Reims is instead the characteristics of which have elements of accommodation, such as comfort, cleanliness, modernity of and furnishings of the rooms, and the location of these facilities. The second element in the Barossa Valley wine tourism offering that has attracted the positive reactions of the visitors is represented by the components of accommodation, while Reims for the item you came in at a lower level of significance is made up of staff performance. In both cases, the reviews that contain descriptions on the attractiveness of the destination have a relatively lower frequency, although quite high in percentage terms.

Among the elements of attractiveness of the Barossa Valley wine bars are counted, while the French champagne and the houses of the Champagne producing contribute to the appeal exercised by Reims. The difference that can be detected between the two destinations is essentially due to the different degree of knowledge that they possess. While Reims and the Champagne region have a distinctive and evocative local brand in the world, the reputation of the Barossa Valley as a tourist destination wine does not have that character instead of exclusivity that characterizes the Champagne and its wine production.

Serra Gaucha in Rio Grande do Sul and Reims

The comparison between concept maps can highlight some similarities and some differences at the same time in what are the elements of tourism that have had the greatest impact on the perceptions of visitors to the two destinations. As regards the Serra Gaucha, the most influential element is constituted by the components of accommodation facilities and in particular by their characteristics and the same can be said for Reims. The restaurant service and food are the second component in order of impact on the perception of tourism in Serra Gaucha, in contrast to Reims consists of the performance of the staff. At a lower level stands for both wine districts, the influence of the elements of attractiveness of destinations. In particular, the Serra Gaucha is related to the appreciation of wine, while French champagne and champagne production houses contribute to the allure of Reims. Even in this case, despite the identification of the Serra Gaucha as wine production area, as opposed to what happens in Reims, the comments of tourists refer to the goals distinctly less wine and more generally to the attractiveness of the landscape of the region. Therefore we can say that there is ample scope to increase the reputation of the region and characterize the tourist offer in terms more closely connected with the development of a destination image wine.

Central Valley and Reims

A comparative analysis of graphs ball for the two destinations can identify as both the Central Valley and for the characteristics of Reims accommodation represent the most important theme in reviews of tourists. Assessments relate in both cases the location of the hotel and the comfort, cleanliness, and furnishing of the bedrooms. To a lesser degree of importance of the subject stands the city of Santiago with regard to the Central Valley, while Reims this theme is represented by its position, the French champagne and the "case of champagne." The relevance of the theme restaurant and food is lower than other sectors for the two districts. Furthermore in relation to the Central Valley is to note the lack of reference to the theme of wine that has a significance of 5 %, so as to elements able to connote the destination as a tourism destination wine.

Cape Winelands and Reims

Through the observation of concept maps, you can detect differences in relation to the components of the tourist who most influenced visitors to the two destinations confronted. The element that has the most significance in the comments of visitors to the Cape Winelands is the food and wine, atmosphere and service, while catering for tourists to Reims are the facilities the theme most influential on their perceptions. The performance of the staff is the second in order of importance in the comments regarding the Cape Winelands, as well as those that relate to Reims.

At a lower level we find the comments about the attractive factor of Cape Winelands and Reims. In particular, the first destination appreciation refers to restaurants and to the people, for the second concern as well as restaurants, French champagne and champagne. Therefore we can say that, despite the general appreciation addressed to the destination and its wine production, these do not appear relevant references can be found in the perceptions of tourists characterization distinctive type of wine in the tourist and Cape Winelands.

References available upon request.

Exploring the Importance of Basic Hotel Attributes: A Focus on Senior Wellness Tourists

Vania Vigolo and Angelo Bonfanti

Abstract Senior tourists represent an attractive target for the wellness industry. Despite the diversifying needs in the senior market, the tourism and hospitality literature has only recently started to investigate the importance of hotel attributes for this specific target. In particular, very few studies have explored the importance of hotel attributes for senior tourists involved in wellness tourism activities. Hence, the aim of this study is twofold. First, it intends to explore the importance of basic hotel attributes according to senior tourists. Second, it aims to identify the underlying dimensions of those hotel attributes.

A quantitative study was conducted on a sample of 200 senior tourists at hot spring hotels located in Italy, a European country with a high proportion of senior residents. The findings reveal that the most important attributes are the personnel's friendliness and kindness, efficiency, reactivity, and the presence of a doctor at the hotel. In addition, four dimensions of hotel attributes emerged: senior-friendly facilities; customer care; spa facilities; servicescape. The results allow interesting theoretical and marketing contributions.

Keywords Senior tourists • Wellness tourism • Hot-spring hotels • Service quality • Hotel attributes

Introduction

Population aging is a demographic phenomenon affecting the whole world. In particular, it is more evident in the developed countries, where the proportion of people aged 60 years and senior is larger than the population aged 0–19 years (United Nations 2013). Further, senior people are projected to outnumber the 40

V. Vigolo (✉) • A. Bonfanti
University of Verona, Verona, Italy
e-mail: vania.vigolo@univr.it; angelo.bonfanti@univr.it

© Academy of Marketing Science 2016   969
L. Petruzzellis, R.S. Winer (eds.), *Rediscovering the Essentiality of Marketing*,
Developments in Marketing Science: Proceedings of the Academy of Marketing
Science, DOI 10.1007/978-3-319-29877-1_192

year old and younger groups in the next 20 years (United Nations 2013). This tendency is the result of advances in healthcare, nutrition, sanitation, education, and economic prosperity, which have led to lower infant mortality, and increased life expectancy (HelpAge International 2014). As a consequence, in recent years scholars and practitioners in the tourism industry have devoted increasing attention to the senior adult group, which represent one of the most attractive targets for wellness tourism (Smith and Kelly 2006).

Wellness tourism activities are pursued by individuals who want to maintain and enhance their personal health and well-being (Smith and Puczkó 2014). In this sense, wellness tourism does not focus on medical treatment, which is the core of medical tourism, but rather on promoting health though tourism activities (Mueller and Kaufmann 2001). Extant studies emphasized that health is a crucial travel motivation among senior tourists (Guinn 1980; Horneman et al. 2002), who travel to health resorts and spas seeking the benefits of natural resources combined with recreational facilities (Erfurt-Cooper and Cooper 2009). The concept of wellness can thus be extended to include the "harmony between the body, mind, and spirit" (Mueller and Kaufmann 2001). In addition, Mueller and Kaufmann (2001, p. 7) emphasized the role of hospitality in wellness tourism, intended as "the sum of all the relationships and phenomena resulting from a journey or residence by people whose main motive is to preserve or promote their health. They stay in specialized hotels that provide appropriate professional knowledge and individual care."

Hence, for wellness tourists hotels represent not only an accommodation, but also the place where wellness activities are provided. Despite the relevance of senior people for the wellness tourism, and the importance of hotels in this type of tourism, very few studies have investigated the importance of hotel attributes for senior tourists in this specific industry (Caber and Albayrak 2014). Scholars agree that there is a gap between the services provided by operators and the services considered important by customers (Chen et al. 2013a, b; Nysveen et al. 2003). Particularly, there is a need to further investigate hot spring hotel service from the perspective of senior tourists. Considered these premises, the aim of this study is twofold. First, it intends to explore the importance of basic hotel attributes for service quality according to senior tourists. Second, it aims to identify the underlying dimensions of those hotel attributes.

The context of the study is Italy, a European country with a high proportion of aging residents. According to the European Commission, people aged 65 and senior will comprise more than 28 % of the population in Germany and 25 % in Italy by 2030 (European Commission 2012). In addition, Italy has a long tradition of thermal/hot spring activities. In ancient times, around 2000 years ago and longer, the Romans established thermal baths which had natural thermal waters for recreational purposes as well as for the prevention and the treatment of chronic diseases (Erfurt-Cooper and Cooper 2009). Hence, wellness tourism offers relevant opportunities for the Italian tourism and hospitality industry.

A quantitative study was conducted on a sample of 200 senior tourists at hot spring hotels located in the North of Italy. The rest of the chapter is organized as follows. First, a theoretical background for wellness tourism and hotel attributes for the senior market is provided. After that, the methodology is outlined and the results are presented. Finally, discussion and managerial implications are presented, along with conclusions, limitations, and directions for future research.

Wellness Tourism and Spa

Wellness tourism is one of the most ancient forms of travel, dating back to the Ancient Greece and the Roman Empire. Those civilizations enjoyed the spas and baths of the time not only for their healing properties, but also for their social and recreational dimensions (Smith and Kelly 2006). Dunn (1959) first introduced the concept of wellness by combining the words "well-being" and "fitness." According to Dunn (1959, p. 447), wellness is "an integrated method of functioning which is oriented toward maximizing the potential of which the individual is capable." In this sense, wellness is a dynamic concept, a "condition of change in which the individual moves forward" (Dunn 1959, p. 447). From this perspective, wellness tourism is a subcategory of health tourism (Mueller and Kaufmann 2001; Chen et al. 2013a). However, while medical tourism is illness-oriented and emphasizes a curative approach, wellness tourism is wellness-oriented and emphasized health-promotion and disease prevention (Voigt 2014). Even though there is no exhaustive definition of wellness tourism, according to Medina-Muñoz and Medina-Muñoz (2014, p. 3) it could be described as "the sum of all the relationships and phenomena that occur as a result of travelling" by "individuals interested in promoting, stabilizing and, when necessary, restoring physical, mental and/or social well-being by means of the use of services that favor health."

Some scholars provided wider concepts of wellness. For example, the extended wellness model developed by Mueller and Kaufmann (2001) involves "elements of lifestyle; physical, mental, and spiritual well-being; and one's relationship with oneself, others, and environment." Similarly, Konu et al. (2010) supported that wellness includes various related concepts, such as well-being, happiness, quality of life, holistic practice, and spiritual beliefs. The variety of definitions lead to argue that wellness is a relative, subjective, and perceptual concept (Adams 2003).

Nevertheless, there is a general agreement that the senior-adult segment offers great opportunities for the wellness industry (Szmigin and Carrigan 2001). Various authors adopted different age groups classifications of senior consumers in their study. However the age of 50 is commonly used as a criterion to define senior people (e.g., Chen et al. 2013b; Le Serre and Chevalier 2012; Littrell et al. 2004; Sellick 2004; Sudbury and Simcock 2009; Vigolo and Confente 2013). Although there is a large variety in income and wealth among seniors, in developed countries they have a purchasing power that is above average (Thébault et al. 2013). In addition, various studies suggest that senior tourists tend to spend more and travel more frequently with respect to other tourists (Huang and Tsai 2003; Jang et al. 2009). In particular, senior tourists also regard wellness tourism as a lifestyle (Smith and Puckzo 2009). With a focus on Italy, a study conducted among 1422 customers of eight wellness destinations showed that seniors, and particularly retired people, are the main category of visitors (Gregori 2005).

Many types of wellness tourism focus on water-based healing, with an emphasis on relaxation and cures. Examples are hot springs, saunas, and steam rooms (Cohen 2008). In particular, the motivation to look for wellness benefits from natural hot spring waters has led to a revival of many hot and mineral spring resorts and spas (Erfurt-Cooper and Cooper 2009) to a degree that the term "spa tourism" is often interchangeable with wellness tourism (Smith and Puckzo 2009). Spas have been described as a business offering water-based therapies which are practiced by quali-fied personnel in a professional and relaxing context (Garrow 2008). Italy is abundant with hot spring resources and there are about 380 thermal centers (Federterme 2014).

Hotel Attributes for Senior Tourists

Several scholar identified the diversifying needs in the senior market (Sedgley et al. 2011; Sudbury and Simcock 2009; Thompson and Thompson 2009). Nevertheless, despite some early studies (e.g., Callan and Bowman 2000; Gustin and Weaver 1993), the tourism and hospitality literature has only recently started to investigate the importance of hotel attributes for this specific target.

Callan and Bowman (2000) investigated the salient attributes of hotels for British travelers aged 50 and senior. The respondents had high expectations of hotel service quality, placing great emphasis on value for money, on service staff attitude and behavior. Juwaheer (2004) found that a basic factor attribute as "room attractiveness and decor" was an important predictor of hotel recommendation among senior travelers. Similarly, Zhang et al. (2011) found that "room quality" was the most relevant factor on senior customers' intention to stay in an economy hotel. More recently, Ladhari (2012) found that "tangibility" (i.e., the physical attributes of hotels such as facilities in the room) was an important attribute for senior tourists. Further, Caber and Albayrak (2014) adopted Callan and Bowman's (2000) scale to explore the importance of hotel attributes among three market segments of senior tourists (German, Dutch, and British). Besides slight differences among the segments, the findings showed that basic attributes such as cleanliness and staff attitude had the highest importance ratings.

With regard to wellness tourism in particular, Mueller and Kaufmann (2001) emphasized that wellness tourists choose an accommodation specialized in wellness, such as a hotel with a wellness center on or near its premises and/or an offer of well-ness services and treatments. In a recent study, Chen et al. (2013b) explored the ser-vice factors for senior visitors within wellness tourism based on hot springs hotels in Taiwan. The results identified seven factors: health promotion treatments, mental learning, experience of unique tourism resources, complementary therapies, relax-ation, healthy diet, and social activities.

In general, when customers choose a hotel, they consider not only functional attri-butes (e.g., room furnishings), but also hedonic attributes (e.g., entertainment) and sensory attributes (e.g., atmosphere) (Palazon and Delgado-Ballester 2013). Nevertheless, when evaluating alternative offers, functional attributes are easier to compare than hedonic or sensory attributes. As such, this study will focus mainly on the functional attributes of hotels because of their key role in tourists' decision-making process. Functional attributes include basic (i.e., must-be or expected) attributes, which often go unnoticed by most customers because customers expect these requirements to be met in the product or service (Lim et al. 1999). However, their absence is very dissatisfying. Basic attributes include also relational aspects such as staff friendliness and efficiency (Grougiou and Pettigrew 2011; Ladhari 2012). Hence, basic factors should not be taken for granted by hotel managers, or regarded as easy to satisfy. Further, some attributes perceived as basic by customers may even be exceptionally difficult to identify. Therefore, there is a need to further investigate the basic attributes of hot-spring hotels from the perspective of senior tourists.

Methodology

Participants

Purposive sampling was conducted for senior adults staying in seven hot-spring hotels in two wellness destinations in the north of Italy. Prospective respondents were informed about the aims of the study and were invited to participate in the survey. The questionnaires were administered by some research assistants during August and September 2014 and 200 valid questionnaires were collected.

Measures

A structured questionnaire was developed for the purpose of this study. The questionnaire was originally prepared in English and then translated into Italian using the back translation method (McGorry 2000). A pretest was conducted on a convenience sample of 30 senior tourists and no particular critical aspects emerged. The attributes used in the questionnaire were adapted from previous studies on senior tourists (Caber and Albayrak 2014; Callan and Bowman 2000) and wellness tourism in particular (Chen et al. 2013a, b). Since we wanted to explore the importance of basic hotel attributes for service quality, each item was rated on a 7-point Likert-type scale from 1 (not at all important) to 7 (extremely important). Additional questions referred to demographic information (gender, age, education, occupation).

Data Analyses

Descriptive statistics (mean and frequency) were used to identify the importance of hotel attributes, while Principal component factor analysis was used to identify the underlying dimensions. The IBM Statistical Package for the Social Sciences 17.0 (2008) was employed for analyses of results.

Findings

The majority of respondents were female (65 %). Respondents' age ranged from 50 to 87 years (the average age was 67.5 years). The majority (63 %) was retired, while 25 % were still working and 12 % were homemakers. As regards self-perception of income, the majority of respondents (61 %) stated that it was average, 28 % below average and 10 % above average.

Since participants tended to rate as highly important (mean above 6.0) almost all attributes, slight differences in responses were considered relevant to identify the most important attributes. The top-five attributes, based on mean of responses, were personnel's friendliness and kindness (mean = 6.8 each), followed by personnel's efficiency (6.7), the presence of a swimming pool (6.6), personnel's reactivity (6.5), and the presence of a doctor at the hotel (6.4).

Table 1 shows means in responses but gives little information about any structure in responses by individuals. Following Rittichainuwat and Chakraborty (2012), exploratory factor analysis can be used to determine dimension in ratings of hotel attributes (Table 2). Principal component analysis with Varimax rotation was conducted on the 16 items to identify the underlying dimensions of hotel attributes. To test the appropriateness of factor analysis, the Kaiser-Meyer-Olkin (KMO) overall measure of sampling adequacy and the Bartlett's test of sphericity were used. The KMO value (0.719) was comfortably above the recommended value of 0.60 (Kaiser 1974), and Barlett's test reached statistical significance

Table 1 Importance of hotel attributes

Hotel attributes	Mean	Std. deviation
Personnel's friendliness	6.88	.408
Personnel's kindness	6.83	.427
Personnel's efficiency	6.74	.542
Personnel's reactivity	6.52	.879
Doctor availability at the hotel	6.45	1.146
Personnel's physical appearance	6.41	1.108
Grab-bars in the bathroom	6.36	1.256
Room furnishings	6.17	1.052
Common areas furnishings	6.12	1.015
Large corridors and doors	6.03	1.686
Ramps	6.010	1.745
Relaxing lounge or bar	6.01	1.504
Special dietary menus	5.73	2.116
No-smoking bedrooms	5.36	2.421
Steam bath	5.06	2.163
Gym	4.53	2.374

Table 2 Underlying dimensions of hotel attributes

	Dimensions			
	Senior-friendly facilities	Customer care	Spa facilities	Servicescape
Ramps	.891			
Large corridors and doors	.882			
Grab-bars in bathrooms	.835			
Special dietary menus	.774			
Doctor availability at the hotel	.662			
Personnel's reactivity	.510			
Personnel's kindness		.860		
Personnel's efficiency		.826		
Personnel's friendliness		.788		
Steam bath			.832	
Gym			.761	
No smoking rooms			.743	
Relaxing lounge or bar			.600	
Common areas furnishings				.846
Room furnishings				.828
Personnel's physical appearance				.612
Cronbach's alpha	*.860*	*.809*	*.736*	*.754*
Variance explained	*22.9*	*15.9*	*14.3*	*13.7*

($p < .000$), thus supporting the factorability of the correlation matrix. As suggested by Hair et al. (2006), the latent root criterion of 1.0 was used for factor extraction. Following Stevens (2009), items that were highly loaded on more than one factor were excluded from the analysis. As recommended by Hair et al. (2006), factor loadings greater than .50 were considered necessary for practical significance. The final solution yielded a four-factor model with 16 attributes that explained 66.9 % of the total variance. Based on the factor loadings, the factor were labeled: (1) senior-friendly facilities; (2) customer care; (3) spa facilities; (4) servicescape.

The factor analysis is presented in Table 2. The dimension senior-friendly facilities accounted for 22.9 % of the variance and included attributes such as wider corridors, handlings, and the presence of a physician at the hotel. The customer-care dimension accounted for 15.9 % of the variance and included personnel's friendliness, kindness, and efficiency. The third dimension accounted for 14.3 % of the variance and encompassed typical spa facilities which characterize hot spring hotels, whereas the servicescape dimension accounted for 13.7 % of the variance and included the general appearance of the hotel and staff. Additionally, the reliability test was used to assess the internal consistency for the extracted factors. All values were satisfactory, ranging from .736 to .860 (Table 2).

Discussion

This study explored the importance of basic hotel attributes for senior travelers when evaluating hot spring hotels. In addition, it identified four underlying dimensions of such attributes, thus contributing to the literature on wellness hospitality for senior tourists. In general, respondents tended to rate as highly important almost all attributes, hence only a limited number of attributes (five) were identified as being perceived as more important: staff's friendliness, kindness, efficiency and responsiveness, as well as the presence of a physician and staff's physical appearance. In other words, the first four attributes out of 16 regard hotel personnel. This is also the second dimension in terms of variance explained that emerged from factor analysis. Hence, we can argue that staff attitude was the most important attribute in terms of perceived service quality. This finding is consistent with the results of previous studies. For example, Caber and Albayrak (2014) highlighted that "politeness of staff" and "friendliness of staff" were positioned among the five most important hotel attributes in all nationality and age-groups. Conversely, in a previous study Wei et al. (1999) reported that "staff attitude" received low importance ratings from respondents. With this regard, Grougiou and Pettigrew (2011) emphasized that service providers should appreciate the personalities of staff members who can provide satisfactory service experience for senior adults. In general, interacting with customers and satisfying customer needs is vitally important (Sigala 2005).

Besides customer care, three other dimensions emerged: Senior-friendly facilities, Spa facilities, and Servicescape. Senior-friendly facilities explain most of the variance in responses. It includes elements such as ramps, large corridors and doors, grab-bars in bathrooms, special dietary menus, availability of a doctor at the hotel, and personnel's reactivity (promptness). It is interesting to note that the presence of a doctor at the hotel was considered extremely important by senior tourists. This is an original contribution of this study. In our study, senior tourists seem to be more concerned about the possibility of having medication consultation than in Chen et al. (2013b) study, who also excluded barrier-free facilities from factor analysis.

Spa facilities constitute the core offer of hot spring hotels. In this sense, this study is in line with previous studies about wellness tourism and senior tourists (e.g., Chen et al. 2013a, b; Medina-Muñoz and Medina-Muñoz 2014). Finally, servicescape attributes include both environment and personnel physical aspects. This result confirms previous studies that emphasized the importance of tangible attributes such as room décor (Juwaheer 2004) or room facilities (Ladhari 2012) for senior tourists.

Managerial Implications

This study offers a number of practical implications for service managers willing to target senior tourists to hot spring hotels. In the first place, the most important attributes emerged from this study provide a helpful benchmark and should not be ignored because their lack will contribute to generate customers dissatisfaction. In particular, the findings highlight that senior tourists perceive personnel's friendliness and kindness, efficiency, and reactivity as very important attributes. These hotel attributes essentially are related to relational component of service quality (Grönroos 2000; Baccarani et al. 2010) which is source of competitive advantage: the skill of interaction with customers is difficult to imitate because of the relational element involved, which, unlike the impersonal aspects of service, is very personal in nature. To improve it, service managers may ensure to senior tourists the presence of skilled and motivated in their roles front-line staff in hot spring hotel. In this regard, they can both invest in continuous training and implement incentive programs for employees who more are able to develop relational skills during the service encounters. It is important in these strategies to determine the award to be given: if the reward is too small, the program will not work; if it is too large, the strategy may be too expensive. Employees who are content in their job are more motivated to satisfy their customers than ones who are not (Yoon et al. 2007). It is possible to monitor the service quality and productivity levels by using both the mystery client method and key performance indicators (KPI). From a strategic perspective, service organizations may develop a service orientation (Homburg et al. 2002; Teng and Barrows 2009) at an individual level in relation to the personal traits of the service provider (Cran 1994; Hogan et al. 1984), and from the organizational point of view (e.g., Lytle and Timmerman 2006) in relation to the characteristics of both the external and internal service environment (Wu et al. 2008), and corporate structure, climate, and culture (Bowen et al. 1989). Unlike the concept of customer orientation, service orientation not only focuses on satisfying customer needs during service delivery, but also requires personnel and organizations to take the initiative in providing services (Charles and Schwepker 2003) in such a way as to meet the needs and expectations of senior tourists in terms of service experience.

In the second place, the exploratory factor analysis revealed four dimensions of hotel attributes that could be addressed by hotel managers to guarantee service quality and satisfy guests' basic needs. Investing in these four dimensions means providing senior tourists with services and facilities aimed at satisfying more utilitarian (functional) than hedonic (experiential) needs. The presence of ramps, wide corridors and doors, handles support, special dietary menus, physician and promptness of service (senior-friendly facilities), availability of sauna, gym, non-smoking bedrooms, and relaxing lounges or bars (spa facilities), the decor of common areas and bedrooms (servicescape care) and efficiency of service provide a functional utility to seniors tourists and, thus, meet their physical needs. Because of their functional utility, such attributes are easier to identify and to monitor.

As customers' expectations are fueled by the progressive effect of their perceptions (Boulding et al. 1999; O'Neill and Palmer 2004; Rust et al. 1999), hot spring hotel service managers may leverage the senior tourists' responses emerged by this analysis in order to improve service quality from the external communication point of view. They can design a communication plan specifically oriented to seniors' needs: for example, brochures and flyers developed in clubs for elderly or in travel agencies, as well as hot spring hotel websites may emphasize the presence in hotel of the four dimensions of hotel attributes here proposed in such a way as highlight their services offered and attract senior tourists in these hotels.

Conclusion and Limitations

This chapter explored the importance of basic hotel attributes in terms of perceived service quality. The findings revealed that the most important attributes are personnel's friendliness and kindness, efficiency, and reactivity, as well as the presence of a doctor at the hotel. In addition, from the factor analysis four dimensions of hotel attributes emerged: senior-friendly facilities; customer care; spa facilities; servicescape. These findings contribute in theoretical terms to highlight the importance of hotel attributes for senior travelers involved in wellness tourism. In addition, this study identifies the underlying dimensions of hotel attributes, by contributing to expand the literature on wellness hospitality for senior tourists. The attributes and dimensions emerged in this study serve as a starting point for future research aimed at measuring senior guests' satisfaction.

This study is not without limitations. The choice of the sampling, the selection of respondents and the exclusive consideration of senior tourists of hot spring hotels located in the North of Italy means further study is required. Future research should extend the analysis by considering the perspective of a larger sample and highlighting possible differences between the needs and expectations of male versus female senior tourists. In addition, it would be interesting to conduct a longitudinal research by investigating respondents from diverse countries and areas, as any country is different in terms of unique regulations and cultural norms in spa and wellness tourism (Chen et al. 2013a).

Another limitation is that this chapter particularly focused on must-be quality by investigating mainly utilitarian hotel attributes. It did not examine expected vs. unexpected quality, i.e., what senior tourists desire or not expect to find in a hotel during their stay. This analysis may highlight the necessity for service managers to balance utilitarian and hedonic factors for improving service quality in hot spring hotel service.

Acknowledgement The authors wish to acknowledge, with appreciation, the support of Arianna Donegatti, M.Sc. in Languages for Tourism, in the data collection phase.

References

Adams, T. B. (2003). The power of perceptions: Measuring wellness in a globally acceptable, philosophically consistent way. *Wellness Management*. Retrieved August 28, 2014, from http://www.hedir.org

Baccarani, C., Ugolini, M., & Bonfanti, A. (2010). A conceptual service quality map: The value of a wide opened perspective. In *Organizational Excellence in Service, 13th Toulon-Verona Conference Proceedings* (pp. 1–20), 2–4 September 2010, University of Coimbra, Portugal.

Boulding, W., Kalra, A., & Staelin, R. (1999). The quality double whammy. *Marketing Science, 18*, 463–484.

Bowen, D. E., Siehl, C., & Schneider, B. (1989). A framework for analyzing customer service orientations in manufacturing. *Academy of Management Review, 14*, 75–95.

Caber, M., & Albayrak, T. (2014). Does the importance of hotel attribute differ for senior tourists? A comparison of three markets. *International Journal of Contemporary Hospitality Management, 26*, 610–628.

Callan, R. J., & Bowman, L. (2000). Selecting a hotel and determining salient quality attributes: A preliminary study of mature British travellers. *International Journal of Tourism Research, 2*, 97–118.

Charles, H., & Schwepker, C. H., Jr. (2003). Customer-orientated selling: A review, extension, and directions for future research. *Journal of Personal Selling and Sales Management, 23*, 151–171.

Chen, K.-H., Chang, F.-H., & Wu, C. (2013a). Investigating the wellness tourism factors in hot spring hotel customer service. *International Journal of Contemporary Hospitality Management, 25*, 1092–1114.

Chen, K.-H., Liu, H.-H., & Chang, F.-H. (2013b). Essential customer service factors and the segmentation of senior visitors within wellness tourism based on hot spring hotels. *International Journal of Hospitality Management, 35*, 122–132.

Cohen, M. (2008). Spa introduction. In M. Cohen & G. Bodeker (Eds.), *Understanding the global spa industry: Spa management*. Cambridge, MA: Elsevier.

Cran, D. J. (1994). Towards validation of the service orientation construct. *Service Industries Journal, 14*, 34–44.

Dunn, H. L. (1959). What high-level wellness means. *Canadian Journal of Public Health/Revue Canadienne de Sante'e Publique, 50*, 447–457.

Erfurt-Cooper, P., & Cooper, M. (2009). *Health and wellness tourism: Spas and hot springs*. Bristol: Channel View Publications.

European Commission. (2012). *Population projection. Population by sex and 5-year age groups*. Retrieved August 28, 2014, from http://epp.eurostat.ec.europa.eu/statistics_explained/index. php/Population_structure_and_ageing

Federterme. (2014). *Rapporto sul settore termale 2013–2014*.

Garrow, J. (2008). Spa industry benchmarking. In M. Cohen & G. Bodeker (Eds.), *Understanding the global spa industry: Spa management*. Cambridge, MA: Elsevier.

Gregori, G. (2005). *Le Strategie di Sviluppo delle Imprese nel Mercato del Benessere*. Torino: Giappichelli.

Grönroos, C. (2000). *Service management and marketing. A consumer relationship management approach*. Chichester: Wiley.

Grougiou, V., & Pettigrew, S. (2011). Senior customers' service encounter preferences. *Journal of Service Research, 14*, 475–488.

Guinn, R. (1980). Elderly recreational vehicle tourists: Motivations for leisure. *Journal of Travel Research, 19*, 9–12.

Gustin, M. E., & Weaver, P. A. (1993). The mature market: Underlying dimensions and group differences of a potential market for the hotel industry. *FIU Hospitality Review, 11*, 45–59.

Hair, J. F., Black, W. C., Babin, B. J., Anderson, R. E., & Tatham, R. L. (2006). *Multivariate data analysis*. Upper Saddle River: Pearson Prentice Hall.

HelpAge International. (2014). *Global age watch index*. Retrieved August 28, 2014, from http:// www.helpage.org/global-agewatch/

Hogan, J., Hogan, R., & Busch, C. M. (1984). How to measure service orientation. *Journal of Applied Psychology, 69*, 167–173.

Homburg, C., Hoyer, W. D., & Fassnacht, M. (2002). Service orientation of a retailer's business strategy: Dimensions, antecedents, and performance outcomes. *Journal of Marketing, 66*, 86–101.

Horneman, L., Carter, R. W., Wei, S., & Ruys, H. (2002). Profiling the senior traveler: An Australian perspective. *Journal of Travel Research, 41*, 23–37.

Huang, L., & Tsai, H. T. (2003). The study of senior traveler behavior in Taiwan. *Tourism Management, 24*, 561–574.

Jang, S. S., Bai, B., Hu, C., & Wu, C. M. E. (2009). Affect, travel motivation, and travel intention: A senior market. *Journal of Hospitality and Tourism Research, 33*, 51–73.

Juwaheer, T. D. (2004). Exploring international tourists' perceptions of hotel operations by using a modified SERVQUAL approach—A case study of Mauritius. *Managing Service Quality, 14,* 350–364.

Kaiser, H. F. (1974). An index of factorial simplicity. *Psychometrika, 39,* 31–36.

Konu, H., Tuohino, A., & Komppula, R. (2010). Lake wellness—A practical example of a new service development (NSD) concept in tourism industries. *Journal of Vacation Marketing, 16,* 125–139.

Ladhari, R. (2012). The lodging quality index: An independent assessment of validity and dimensions. *International Journal of Contemporary Hospitality Management, 24,* 628–652.

Le Serre, D., & Chevalier, C. (2012). Marketing travel services to senior consumers. *Journal of Consumer Marketing, 29,* 262–270.

Lim, P. C., Tang, N. K., & Jackson, P. M. (1999). An innovative framework for health care performance measurement. *Managing Service Quality, 9,* 423–433.

Littrell, M. A., Paige, R. C., & Song, K. (2004). Senior travellers: Tourism activities and shopping behaviors. *Journal of Vacation Marketing, 10,* 348–362.

Lytle, R. S., & Timmerman, J. E. (2006). Service orientation and performance: An organizational perspective. *Journal of Services Marketing, 20,* 136–147.

McGorry, S. Y. (2000). Measurement in a cross-cultural environment: Survey translation issues. *Qualitative Market Research: An International Journal, 3,* 74–81.

Medina-Muñoz, D. R., & Medina-Muñoz, R. D. (2014). The attractiveness of wellness destinations: An importance-performance-satisfaction approach. *International Journal of Tourism Research, 16*(6), 521–533.

Mueller, H., & Kaufmann, E. L. (2001). Wellness tourism: Market Analysis of a special health tourism segment and implications for the hotel industry. *Journal of Vacation Marketing, 7,* 5–17.

Nysveen, H., Methlie, L. B., & Pedersen, P. E. (2003). Tourism web sites and value-added services: The gap between customer preferences and web site's offerings. *Information Technology and Tourism, 5,* 165–174.

O'Neill, M., & Palmer, A. (2004). Cognitive dissonance and the stability of service quality perceptions. *Journal of Services Marketing, 18,* 433–449.

Palazon, M., & Delgado-Ballester, E. (2013). Hedonic or utilitarian premiums: Does it matter? *European Journal of Marketing, 47,* 1256–1275.

Rittichainuwat, B. N., & Chakraborty, G. (2012). Perceptions of importance and what safety is enough. *Journal of Business Research, 65,* 42–50.

Rust, R. T., Inman, J. J., Jia, J., & Zahorik, A. (1999). What you don't know about customer perceived quality: The role of customer expectation distributions. *Marketing Science, 18,* 77–92.

Sedgley, D., Pritchard, A., & Morgan, N. (2011). Tourism and ageing: A transformative research agenda. *Annals of Tourism Research, 38,* 422–436.

Sellick, M. C. (2004). Discovery, connection, nostalgia: Key travel motives within the senior market. *Journal of Travel and Tourism Marketing, 17,* 55–71.

Sigala, M. (2005). Integrating customer relationship management in hotel operations: Managerial and operational implications. *International Journal of Hospitality Management, 24,* 391–413.

Smith, M., & Kelly, C. (2006). Holistic tourism: Journeys of the self? *Tourism Recreation Research, 31,* 15–25.

Smith, M., & Puckzo, L. (Eds.). (2009). *Health and wellness tourism.* Oxford, England: Butterworth-Heinemann.

Smith, M., & Puczkó, L. (2014). *Health tourism and hospitality: Spas, wellness and medical travel.* London: Routledge.

Stevens, J. (2009). *Applied multivariate statistics for the social sciences.* Boca Raton: Taylor & Francis.

Sudbury, L., & Simcock, P. (2009). A multivariate segmentation model of senior consumers. *Journal of Consumer Marketing, 26,* 251–262.

Szmigin, I., & Carrigan, M. (2001). Leisure and tourism services and the senior innovator. *The Service Industries Journal, 21,* 113–129.

Teng, C.-C., & Barrows, C. W. (2009). Service orientation: Antecedents, outcomes, and implications for hospitality research and practice. *Service Industries Journal, 29*, 1413–1435.

Thébault, M., Picard, P., & Ouedraogo, A. (2013). Seniors and tourism: An international exploratory study on the use of the internet for researching recreational information. *International Business Research, 6*, 22–28.

Thompson, N. J., & Thompson, K. E. (2009). Can marketing practice keep up with Europe's ageing population? *European Journal of Marketing, 43*, 1281–1288.

United Nations. (2013). *World population ageing 2013*. Retrieved November 4, 2014, from http://www.un.org/en/development/desa/population/publications/pdf/ageing/WorldPopulationAgeing2013.pdf

Vigolo, V., & Confente, I. (2013). Older tourists: An exploratory study on online behaviour. In Z. Xiang & I. Tussyadiah (Eds.), *Information and communication technologies in tourism 2014* (pp. 439–452). Cham: Springer International Publishing.

Voigt, C. (2014). Towards a conceptualization of wellness tourism. In C. Voigt & C. Pforr (Eds.), *Wellness tourism. A destination perspective*. New York: Routledge.

Wei, S., Ruys, H., & Muller, T. E. (1999). A gap analysis of perceptions of hotel attributes by marketing managers and older people in Australia. *Journal of Marketing Practice: Applied Marketing Science, 5*, 200–212.

Wu, C. H.-J., Liang, R.-D., Tung, W., & Chang, C.-S. (2008). Structural relationships among organisation service orientation, employee service performance, and consumer identification. *The Service Industries Journal, 28*, 1247–1263.

Yoon, S.-J., Choi, D.-C., & Park, J.-W. (2007). Service orientation: Its impact on business performance in the medical service industry. *The Service Industries Journal, 27*, 371–388.

Zhang, Z., Ye, Q., & Law, R. (2011). Determinants of hotel room price: An exploration of travelers' hierarchy of accommodation needs. *International Journal of Contemporary Hospitality Management, 23*, 972–981.

The Moderating Role of Attention on Country-of-Origin (COO) Effects: A Structured Abstract

Renaud Frazer

Introduction

Research on the influence of a product's country-of-origin (COO) on consumers has been a very active field for many years (Usunier 2006), and many studies have claimed the existence of such effects (Pharr 2005). Nevertheless, some academics more recently suggested a decreasing interest in products' COO by consumers, and raised questions on the actual strength of this influence (Samiee 2011; Samiee et al. 2005; Usunier 2002).

In a world where commercial communication is so intense, people are unable to pay the same level of attention to the different pieces of information they are exposed to (Sauerland et al. 2012). The impact of those elements—brand names, logos, product attributes, etc.—, that consumers cannot even recall having seen, can then become rather uncertain. Several works however, seem to consider that full attention to a stimulus is not a requirement for an influence to be observed on consumers' attitudes (Ferraro et al. 2009; Sauerland et al. 2012 for example).

The main purpose of this Ph.D. research is therefore to understand whether COO can have effects on consumers' attitudes towards the product, even when attention to this stimulus is very limited. After a first year of thesis focusing on the literature review and on defining the scope of the research question, experimental work is now expected to start in this second year. The aim of this chapter is to present the conceptual framework and preliminary research proposal.

R. Frazer (✉)
Université de Lorraine, Nancy, France
e-mail: renaud.frazer@univ-lorraine.fr

© Academy of Marketing Science 2016
L. Petruzzellis, R.S. Winer (eds.), *Rediscovering the Essentiality of Marketing*,
Developments in Marketing Science: Proceedings of the Academy of Marketing
Science, DOI 10.1007/978-3-319-29877-1_193

Background

While first articles mentioned the "made in" effect (Nagashima 1970), the expression remains common although its meaning is much more complex in a globalized world where productions are delocalized or shared between partners. COO needs to be understood as a multi-dimensional construct, which can refer to the country of manufacture of a product, the country of its main parts, the country of design, or the country of the brand, for example (Insch and McBride 1998; Usunier 2011). Encompassing these different facets, Jaffé and Nebenzahl (2006, p. 29) proposed to define the COO as the "country which a consumer associates with a certain product or brand as being its source, regardless of where the product is actually produced."

Over the past 50 years, hundreds of articles (Usunier 2006) have been published in this field, showing the emergence of a consensus whereby a product's COO could influence consumers' attitudes towards this product, following the activation of a number of antecedents (Pharr 2005)—in particular country stereotypes (Liu and Johnson 2005). It is worth noting though, that most works followed a cognitive learning approach, where focused attention is required for COO information to be perceived, memorized, and to influence consumers. However such conditions may not be so frequent in our natural consumption environment, and concerns appeared in the literature on the actual size of these effects, which may have been amplified by artificially increasing attention to the origin during the experiments, and might be biased by research designs and the nature of the measurement procedures (direct self-report in most cases) (Peterson and Jolibert 1995; Samiee 2010; Trendel and Warlop 2005; Verlegh and Steenkamp 1999).

Flowing from these observations, the focus of this research is to understand if people exposed to COO information at low levels of attention can register and integrate it in their judgments—and if so, whether this influence is any different at higher levels of attention.

Theoretical Development

In order to approach the question of potential effects of the level of attention to COO on a consumer's attitude toward the product, it is important to understand in the first place what "country images" can refer to.

Exposure to a COO can trigger associations linked to several different levels of country image, which may contribute to the formation of product images (Jaffé and Nebenzahl 2006). Roth and Diamantopoulos (2009) more specifically distinguish "country images," which consist of "generalized images" about the country, from "product-country images" which relate to "the image of countries in their role as origins of products" (2009, p. 727). The literature highlights that these country associations can also vary in terms of nature, and contain either affective or cognitive components (Janda and Rao 1997; Verlegh and Steenkamp 1999) such as, for instance, stereotypes, personal beliefs, or emotions. While this variability depends on people and context (Pharr 2005), product and country perception can also be involved, hedonic (utilitarian) perception being more likely to activate affective (cognitive) elements (Herz and Diamantopoulos 2013; Melnyk et al. 2012).

Among these associations, country stereotypes seem to play a major role (Janda and Rao 1997; Maheswaran 1994). They can be defined as "beliefs about characteristics of a specific country which are socially shared" (Herz and Diamantopoulos 2013, p. 402). Identical sources of variability can apply here again: stereotypes can contain either affective or cognitive components (Leyens et al. 1996), and relate to the country in general or to the country as a manufacturer of products—it is important to note that in the latter case, a distinction can also be made between *products in general*, or *specific product categories* (Liu and Johnson 2005). This may imply that activated country stereotypes could differ in terms of level of image, and possibly in terms of nature (cognitive/affective) depending on the types of components linked to this particular stereotype. Any variation in the observed COO influence on consumers' attitudes toward products, should therefore take into account possible differences in the type of country association activated. Considering the potential importance of country stereotypes in COO effects, works relating to the study of social stereotypes and how they can be activated, may be helpful in understanding the possible role of attention on this relationship.

Exposure to a stimulus at a low level of attention is often referred to as "incidental exposure." In such situations, a number of authors in the fields of consumer behavior and social psychology consider that perception, processing, and influence of the stimulus could be possible (Bargh 1994; Chartrand 2005; Fazio et al. 1986; Ferraro et al. 2009; Sauerland et al. 2012). Upon incidental exposure to COO information in particular, activation of the categorical label (country name) may increase memorial accessibility of related concepts (such as stereotypical content), hence increasing chances these stereotypes will be activated automatically and influence consumers (Bargh 1994, 2002; Fazio et al. 1986; Leyens et al. 1996; Macrae et al. 1994).

At higher levels of attention, however, some differences may be observed. Indeed, several authors (Devine 1989; Janda and Rao 1997) suggest that personal beliefs and stereotypes are distinct cognitive structures. Beliefs may be developed later, be less accessible than stereotypes, and require more time to be retrieved. Could incidental exposure to a stimulus then favor the activation and use of stereotypes, while a high level of attention to the COO would facilitate the retrieval and integration in judgment of (potentially non stereotypical, and less shared) personal beliefs?

We thus propose to formulate the following hypotheses:

H1: Incidental exposure to COO information and its subsequent stereotype activation leads to the automatic integration of country-stereotypes in consumers' judgments of products.

H2: As the level of attention to COO information increases, COO influence becomes less stereotypical.

Preliminary Research Proposal Considerations

Specific countries are believed to be more closely related to specific product categories (Roth and Romeo 1992). Such "product-country matches" (be it favorable ones or not) may appear plausible to consumers, are hence less likely to create surprise or suspicion, and may be linked to potentially easily accessible stereotypical associations. These elements should be taken into account during product and country selection. Besides, both favorable and unfavorable origins could be selected to study a potential interaction between stereotype valence and attention level (exploratory approach). However, country stereotype valence may vary depending on the level of image activated (country in general, country as a manufacturer of products in general, country as a manufacturer of a specific product category). Selecting countries with extreme average values of these three stereotype levels (procedure followed by Liu and Johnson 2005, p. 91) could help us avoid different observations caused by different levels of image activated by respondents.

High involvement can be expected to negatively moderate the influence of elements processed through the peripheral route (Petty et al. 1983), which could concern attributes such as the COO (Gürhan-Canli and Maheswaran 2000). Choosing rather low involvement products may therefore make it easier to observe COO effects. In addition, both "hedonic" and "utilitarian" products should be used, so as not to let our variables selection reduce the possibility of either affective or emotional associations being activated (which may have unexpected effects and should be controlled). Finally, participants will be students, and should therefore belong to these products' target market for external validity reasons. Considering the various prerequisites presented here, products from the electronic appliances category with Asian COOs seem interesting and will be pretested.

A mixed factorial design is envisaged, with attention (high, low, control) as a between-subjects variable, and country (favorable stereotypes, unfavorable stereotypes) and products (three similar products, in order to avoid repeated exposures to perfectly identical product-country pairs) as within-subjects variables. Studies could be duplicated to focus on "utilitarian" products and "hedonic" products separately.

Although work is still in progress at this stage, the expected stimulus is likely to be a product presentation (product picture + key attributes including COO, fictitious brand) on a fictitious retailer's webpage (screenshot). At all levels of attention, respondents could be exposed to the stimulus during a limited amount of time and then asked to express their judgment before moving on to the next stimulus (different product-country pair). Instructions in the different groups would differ however, with "high attention" respondents requested to form an impression of the product, while "low attention" respondents would be requested to complete a concurring task preventing them from allocating their attention to COO information. In order to better control attention allocation, the use of an eye tracker could be appropriate. After this first phase, respondents would then be invited to complete a thought-listing task—in order to detect potential country-stereotypical thoughts—, as well as other direct measures related to control variables (pretested items, country image, perceived importance of COO, familiarity with COO, product category involvement, knowledge of the product class, age, sex, and education).

Conclusion

This doctoral work aims at addressing some of the concerns raised in the literature, concerning the relevance of research on COO effects (Samiee 2011; Usunier 2002, 2006), by positioning its approach at the crossroads of this field and of research on incidental exposure effects. From a theoretical standpoint, we hope to help achieve a better understanding of the influence of COO when attention to this stimulus is very limited. Additionally, the methodological approach—uncommon in COO research—could bring new contributions by helping simulate a natural exposure situation (online shopping) while offering a rather good control of attention levels. Furthermore, clarifying if COO is able to influence consumers' evaluations of products during an online shopping experience, and understanding if this influence can differ depending on the level of attention to this specific attribute, appears managerially relevant. Finally, should the exploratory analysis reveal a [stereotype valence] × [attention level] interaction, further options could be considered in terms of communication, in order to inhibit or enhance the influence of COO information.

References available upon request.

Lightning Source UK Ltd.
Milton Keynes UK
UKHW05f2332020718
325138UK00002B/3/P